THE OXFORD HANI

SOCIAL RELATIONS IN THE ROMAN WORLD

THE OXFORD HANDBOOK OF

SOCIAL RELATIONS IN THE ROMAN WORLD

Edited by

MICHAEL PEACHIN

OXFORD

UNIVERSITY PRESS

OXFORD
UNIVERSITY PRESS

Oxford University Press is a department of the University of Oxford.
It furthers the University's objective of excellence in research, scholarship,
and education by publishing worldwide.

Oxford   New York
Auckland   Cape Town   Dar es Salaam   Hong Kong   Karachi
Kuala Lumpur   Madrid   Melbourne   Mexico City   Nairobi
New Delhi   Shanghai   Taipei   Toronto

With offices in
Argentina   Austria   Brazil   Chile   Czech Republic   France   Greece
Guatemala   Hungary   Italy   Japan   Poland   Portugal   Singapore
South Korea   Switzerland   Thailand   Turkey   Ukraine   Vietnam

Oxford is a registered trade mark of Oxford University Press
in the UK and certain other countries.

Published in the United States of America by
Oxford University Press
198 Madison Avenue, New York, NY 10016

© Oxford University Press 2011

First issued as an Oxford University Press paperback, 2014.

Library of Congress Cataloging-in-Publication Data
The Oxford handbook of social relations in the Roman world / edited by Michael Peachin.
p. cm.
ISBN 978-0-19-518800-4 (hardcover); 978-0-19-937600-1 (paperback)
1. Rome—Social conditions.   2. Rome—Social life and customs.   3. Social structure—Rome.
I. Peachin, Michael, 1954–
HN10.R7O94 2011
306.0937—dc22   2010003812

Acknowledgments

THE gestation period of this volume has been significant, and during that time I have incurred a number of debts. Three members of the Oxford University Press team—Stefan Vranka, Deirdre Brady, and Liz Smith—did a wonderful job of shepherding this project through the various stages of production. The NYU Humanities Initiative was generous enough to provide a grant for translating several of the articles. That funding supported the work of three people, who deserve great credit for producing splendid English versions of those essays: Dan Childers (Jördens and Scheid); William Rauscher (Stahl); and Beate Witzler (Hahn, Krause, and Riess). Two of the graduate students in Classics at NYU also graciously offered assistance. Kyle Johnson shared with me bibliography and thoughts on strategies of communication in antiquity, and Danielle La Londe read, helped to edit, and made extremely useful suggestions about one of the articles. Paul Cartledge, during a fall-term visit to NYU, caused me to start thinking much harder about the difficult business of defining social history. Cliff Ando, Kathleen Coleman, Leonhard Schumacher, and Seth Schwartz made various constructive suggestions regarding my introductory chapter. So, too, did Clemens Zimmermann, whose advice regarding the history of social history was extremely helpful. Professor Coleman was also incredibly generous, offering editorial help of all kinds as the volume approached its completion. Most of all, though, I owe a great debt of thanks to Ted Lendon, who read and commented upon the introduction not once, but twice. His careful remarks have very greatly improved the final product—though, given my stubbornness, not as much as he would have liked. I want also to thank the contributors. It has been both a great honor and a real pleasure to work with them all. And finally, a heartfelt debt of gratitude is due to the three people—Beate, Antonia, and Nora—who tolerated my repeated absence, in more ways than one, because of this volume.

CONTENTS

....

Contributors

Clifford Ando (University of Chicago)
Leanne Bablitz (University of British Columbia)
Adam H. Becker (New York University)
Kathleen M. Coleman (Harvard University)
Joy Connolly (New York University)
Katherine M. D. Dunbabin (McMaster University)
Garrett G. Fagan (Penn State University)
Harriet I. Flower (Princeton University)
Johannes Hahn (Universität Münster)
Charles W. Hedrick, Jr. (University of California, Santa Cruz)
Marietta Horster (Universität Mainz)
Andrea Jördens (Universität Heidelberg)
Dennis P. Kehoe (Tulane University)
Jens-Uwe Krause (Universität München)
Hartmut Leppin (Universität Frankfurt)
J. E. Lendon (University of Virginia)
Thomas A. J. McGinn (Vanderbilt University)
Elizabeth A. Meyer (University of Virginia)
Kristina Milnor (Barnard College)
John Nicols (University of Oregon)
Carlos F. Noreña (University of California, Berkeley)
Josiah Osgood (Georgetown University)
Michael Peachin (New York University)
Jonathan S. Perry (University of South Florida)
Francisco Pina Polo (Universidad de Zaragoza)
David Potter (University of Michigan)
Werner Riess (University of North Carolina at Chapel Hill)
J. B. Rives (University of North Carolina at Chapel Hill)
John Scheid (Collège de France)
Thomas A. Schmitz (Universität Bonn)
Leonhard Schumacher (Universität Mainz)
Seth Schwartz (Columbia University)
William J. Slater (McMaster University)
Johannes Stahl (Scheffold-Gymnasium, Schwäbisch Gmünd)
Koenraad Verboven (Ghent University)

Abbreviations

....

THE abbreviations of ancient literary sources, with only a few exceptions, are those employed by the standard English-language dictionaries of ancient Greek and Latin: H. G. Liddell, R. Scott, and H. S. Jones (eds.), *A Greek-English Lexicon*. 9th ed. Oxford: Oxford University Press 1968; P. G. W. Glare (ed.), *Oxford Latin Dictionary*. Oxford: Oxford University Press 1982.

Greek and Latin inscriptions are cited according to the short forms provided by F. Bérard et al., *Guide de l'épigraphiste. Bibliographie choisie des épigraphies antiques et médiévales.* 3rd ed. Paris: Éditions Rue d'Ulm 1986 (esp. pp. 17–18). Several supplements to this volume can be downloaded from the Internet: www.antiquite.ens.fr/txt/dsa-publications-guidepigraphiste-en.htm.

For the abbreviations of volumes publishing papyrus texts, see J. F. Oates et al., *Checklist of Editions of Greek, Latin, Demotic and Coptic Papyri, Ostraca and Tablets,* which is now best consulted on the Internet at this address: http://scriptorium.lib.duke.edu/papyrus/texts/clist.html.

In cases where these tools do not include an abbreviation, one has been created for this volume, and is listed below. Also, in one or two instances, an abbreviation suggested by one of the volumes above has been replaced by the generally more recognizable form of citation. This is the case, for example, with Cassius Dio, and his *Roman History*—we have replaced the 'D.C.' of Liddell, Scott, and Jones with the more recognizable 'Dio.'

Note lastly that wherever editions with English translations of the texts in question are reasonably easily available, these, rather than the standard scholarly editions in the original languages, are referred to. Also, for translations of many Latin texts, one may consult http://www.forumromanum.org.

Amm. Marc.	J. C. Rolfe (ed.), *Ammianus Marcellinus. With an English Translation*. 3 vols. Cambridge, Mass.: Harvard University Press 1956.
Augustine, *Ordine*	W. M. Green and K.-D. Daur (eds.), *Augustinus, Contra academicos. De beata vita. De ordine. De magistro. De libero arbitrio.* CCSL 29. Turnhout: Brepols 1970.
BMCRE	H. Mattingly (ed.), *Coins of the Roman Empire in the British Museum.* 6 vols. London: British Museum 1923–62.
CCSL	*Corpus Christianorum: Series Latina.* Turnhout: Brepols 1953–.

CJ	P. Krueger (ed.), *Corpus Iuris Civilis. Volumen Secundum. Codex Justinianus.* Berlin: Weidmann 1877.
Coll. Leg. Mos.	*Mosaicarum et Romanarum legum collatio.* In P. Krueger, Th. Mommsen, and G. Studemund (eds.), *Collectio Librorum Iuris Anteiustiniani*, vol. I. Berlin: Weidmann 1890.
CTh	Th. Mommsen and P. Meyer (eds.), *Codex Theodosianus cum Constitutionibus Sirmondianis et Leges Novellae ad Theodosianum pertinentes.* Berlin: Weidmann 1905. For a translation, see C. Pharr, *The Theodosian Code and Novels and the Sirmondian Constitutions. A Translation with Commentary, Glossary and Bibliography.* Princeton: Princeton University Press 1952.
Dig.	Th. Mommsen (ed.), *Corpus Iuris Civilis. Volumen Primum. Institutiones, Digesta.* Berlin: Weidmann 1872. For a translation see A. Watson (ed.), *The Digest of Justinian.* Rev. ed. Philadelphia: University of Pennsylvania Press 1998.
Dio	E. Cary (ed.), *Dio's Roman History.* 9 vols. Cambridge, Mass.: Harvard University Press 1914–27.
FGrHist	F. Jacoby et al., *Die Fragmente der griechischen Historiker.* Leiden: E. J. Brill 1926–.
FIRA	S. Riccobono, et al. (eds.), *Fontes Iuris Romani Anteiustiani.* 2nd ed. 3 vols. Florence: Barbera 1940–43.
HA	D. Magie (ed.), *The Scriptores Historiae Augustae.* 3 vols. Cambridge, Mass.: Harvard University Press 1921.
Jerome *Ep.*	I. Hilberg (ed.), *Sancti Eusebii Hieronymi Epistulae. Corpus Scriptorum Ecclesiasticorum Latinorum*, vols. 54–56. Vienna: Österreichische Akademie der Wissenschaften 1996. Some of these letters are available in English translation in F. A. Wright (ed.), *Jerome, Select Letters.* Cambridge, Mass.: Harvard University Press 1933.
Just. *Epit.*	O. Seel (ed.), *Iustini epitoma historiae Philippicae Pompeii Trogi.* Stuttgart: B. G. Teubner 1935.
Lact. *Epit.*	E. Heck and A. Wlosok (ed.), *Lactantius: Epitome divinarum institutionum.* Leipzig: B. G. Teubner. 1994.
Max. Tyr. *Or.*	M. B. Trapp, *Maximus of Tyre. The Philosophical Orations.* Oxford: Clarendon Press 1997.
Nov.	R. Schöll and G. Kroll (eds.), *Corpus Iuris Civilis. Volumen Tertium. Novellae.* Berlin: Weidmann 1928.
NTh	See *CTh.*

Oros. *Hist.*	R. J. Deferrari (ed.), *Paulus Orosius. The Seven Books of History against the Pagans.* Washington, D.C.: Catholic University of America Press 1964.
Pan. Lat.	C. E. V. Nixon and B. Saylor Rodgers, *In Praise of Later Roman Emperors. The Panegyrici Latini. Introduction, Translation, and Historical Commentary.* Berkeley: University of California Press 1994.
Pass. Perpet.	*Passio Perpetuae et Felicitatis.* In: H. Musurillo, *The Acts of the Christian Martyrs.* Oxford: Clarendon Press 1972.
*PIR*²	E. Groag et al., *Prosopographia Imperii Romani.* 2nd ed. Berlin: Walter de Gruyter 1933–.
Proc. *Build.*	H. B. Dewing and G. Downey (eds.), *Procopius, VII, On Buildings.* Cambridge, Mass.: Harvard University Press 1940.
PS	D. Liebs, "Die pseudopaulinischen Sentenzen II. Versuch einer neuen Palingenesie, Ausführung." *Zeitschrift der Savigny-Stiftung für Rechtsgeschichte. Romanistische Abteilung* 113 (1996): 132–242.
RE	*Realencyclopädie der classischen Altertumswissenschaften.* Stuttgart: J. B. Metzler 1894–1980.
RIC	H. Mattingly et al. (eds.), *The Roman Imperial Coinage.* 9 vols. London: Spink 1923–68.
*RIC*²	C. H. V. Sutherland and R. A. G. Carson (eds.), *The Roman Imperial Coinage.* Rev. ed. London: Spink 1984–.
RPC	A. M. Burnett et al., *Roman Provincial Coinage.* London: British Museum Press 1992–. See also http://rpc.ashmus.ox.ac.uk/project/
RRC	M. Crawford, *Roman Republican Coinage.* 2 vols. Cambridge: Cambridge University Press 1974.
Sidonius	W. B. Anderson (ed.), *Sidonius Apollinaris. Poems and Letters. With an English Translation, Introduction, and Notes.* 2 vols. Cambridge, Mass.: Harvard University Press 1936–65.
Socrates, *HE*	Socrates, *The Ecclesiastical History of Socrates, Surnamed Scholasticus: or the Advocate; Comprising a History of the Church, in Seven Books, from the Accession of Constantine, A.D. 305, to the 38th Year of Theodosius II, Including a Period of 140 Years.* London: G. Bell 1884.
Suet. *Vit. Hor.*	Suetonius, *Vita Horatii poetae.* In A. Reifferscheid (ed.), *C. Suetoni Tranquilli praeter 'Caesarum' libros reliquiae.* Leipzig: B. G. Teubner 1860.
Tert. *Fuga*	A. Gerlo, E. Evans, and A. Harnack (eds.), *Tertullianus, Opera II. Opera montanistica. CCSL 2.* Turnhout: Brepols 1954.

Tit. Ulp.   F. Schulz (ed.), *Die Epitome Ulpiani des Codex Vaticanus Reginae 1128*. Bonn: A. Marcus und E. Weber's Verlag 1926.

Ulp. *Reg.*   Ulpian, *Liber singularis regularum*. In P. Krueger, Th. Mommsen, and G. Studemund (eds.), *Collectio Librorum Iuris Anteiustiniani*, vol. II. Berlin: Weidmann 1878.

Zos.   R. T. Ridley (ed.), *Zosimus. New History. A Translation with Commentary*. Canberra: Australian National University 1982 (repr. 1984).

PART I

PREFATORY MATERIAL

CHAPTER 1

INTRODUCTION

MICHAEL PEACHIN

THE STUDY OF ANCIENT ROMAN SOCIETY

IN prefacing the first edition of his monumental *Social and Economic History of the Roman Empire*, M. Rostovtzeff lamented, "We have not, however, a single book or monograph treating of the social and economic life of the Roman Empire as a whole and tracing the main lines of its evolution" (Rostovtzeff 1926: vii). The volume thus introduced served precisely to launch the study of ancient Roman society.[1] Two premises underlay Rostovtzeff's approach: (a) that Roman society was necessarily to be understood as an historical phenomenon, in other words, was to be investigated over the course of time, as it passed through a series of wrenching evolutions; and (b) that society and economy were intimately woven together, so that neither could individually be grasped without meticulous attention to the other. Rostovtzeff's story, then, was the following.

The mighty landlords and businessmen who had long dominated Republican Rome were swept from their perches of power by Augustus. The first emperor thereupon initiated a policy of nurturing his realm's urban centers, which led to an era of great prosperity for the metropolitan populations. Neglected, however, were the peasants, who languished miserably in the countryside. Thus, come the third century AD, the armies, which had always sought their recruits precisely among the rural folk, revolted against those who had for so long oppressed them, and the Roman world was tumbled into crisis. Fifty-odd years of social and economic uproar could lead, in the end, only to an absolutist military monarchy. Soon thereafter, collapse.

---

1. One piece of scholarship that might perhaps be considered a proper forerunner to Rostovtzeff—and it is still an invaluable mine of information, well worth consulting—is Friedlaender 1922. Cf. also Marquardt 1886, or Warde Fowler 1926.

While Rostovtzeff's overarching exposition was immediately controversial, and was in fact neither then nor now generally accepted in its main outlines, the book was yet so prodigious in its learning that it has long exerted a justified influence.[2] Indeed, the *Social and Economic History* arguably worked in a sort of dual fashion: on the one hand, it spurred scholarly curiosity about Roman society; at the same time, though, by virtue of its very monumentality, it may well have forestalled subsequent development of the enterprise. The real blooming of Roman social history would not get underway until about the 1970s.

Just as Rostovtzeff wrote, however, another avenue of scholarship concerned with the Roman world was also being opened up—one important to keep in mind when considering the manner in which research on the social history of Rome progressed. Two German academics, in roughly the decade just prior to publication of Rostovtzeff's *Social and Economic History*, had begun to apply a type of historical inquiry known as prosopography to the study of ancient Rome (Gelzer 1912; Münzer 1920). This vein of scholarship held, to put the matter in blunt terms, that among Rome's ruling elite, personal relationships of various kinds very largely determined the functioning of government, hence, of the empire altogether.[3] Thus, in order to understand Roman history—especially political, governmental, or administrative, for these were the areas in which prosopography was usually applied—one would

2. There was quickly a German (1931), and then an Italian (1933) edition. These were followed by a second English-language edition (1957). There has also appeared a French edition (1988), which offers much information about Rostovtzeff himself, and now a new Italian rendering (2003). Indeed, this last is only the latest Italian version of the book; there was a 1965 edition, and another in 1976. As to scholarly acceptance (or not) of Rostovtzeff's picture of Roman social history, note Shaw 1992: 219–20: "…one could still hold that the theoretical frameworks of his great works were neither convincing nor very important.…But he himself recognized the problems with the theory, and gradually came to abandon it of his own accord." Cf. also the critical, though sympathetic, judgment of Momigliano 1994 (orig. 1954): 40–43, and the similar assessment by Horden and Purcell 2000: 31–32. The initial reviews of, e.g., Hugh Last (1926) and Tenney Frank (1926) tell the tale. Nonetheless, for an intriguing tour of the life of one Egyptian town, done precisely in Rostovtzeff's terms, see MacLennan 1968.

3. Throughout this introduction (and beyond), there will be much talk of the 'elite,' or of the 'haves,' or the 'upper classes'—and of those who did not belong to this stratum. It is thus desirable to have some sense of the people intended. That is not at all a simple matter; nor, for the purposes of the discussion that follows, can there be one simple group that is always intended. That said, one way of getting at this dilemma is to consider levels of income, and the proportion of the total population disposing of a given income level. Scheidel and Friesen (2009: 75–91) calculate with an elite (the senatorial, equestrian, and decurional orders, along with other particularly wealthy persons) comprising about 3% of the total population (mid-second century AD). One might also profitably think in the terms suggested by Harris (1988: 603): "Those people who drew most of their livelihood from the work done by the strictly controlled labour of others, as was true of practically all members of the Roman elite, may be thought of as having for that reason a common identity and as forming a social class, even if within that class there were steep gradations of snobbery." If we combine Harris' suggestion with the calculations made by Scheidel and Friesen, then we

have to understand certain aspects of what were effectively the social interactions of the elite. This approach was becoming influential in the study of ancient Rome just at the moment Rostovtzeff wrote, and it would hold sway over historians of Rome for some time thereafter.

Now, while the kind of investigation that marks this scholarship is most properly classified as political history, it must be said that there was always, nonetheless, a very strong social element at least implicitly involved in the prosopographic approach. Indeed, among the significant results of all the efforts in and around prosopography was the demonstration that Roman political history must be understood as being intimately entangled with the social history of that civilization—or in any case, of its elites.[4] Nevertheless, this social element remained to a great extent under-argued, and was never the prime interest of those who used the prosopographic method.[5] And so it was that Roman history was in the main pursued with an eye to its (most strictly speaking) political aspects into the 1970s.[6]

But as scholarship on ancient Rome was taking this singular path, social history was growing to be a dominant force in the world of historical studies overall.[7] One might argue that the seeds are to be detected in the German periodical *Vierteljahresschrift für Sozial- und Wirtschaftsgeschichte*, which began to appear in

---

ought probably to envisage a slightly larger economic upper class. But as will be noticed in the pages to follow, factors beyond wealth, such as cultural or intellectual attainments, must be added to the mix that made the haves. For another recent attempt, depending much on the work of Pierre Bourdieu, to define the elite (in Roman Macedonia), cf. Bartels 2008. Also, regarding use of the term 'class,' see n. 45 below.

4. Some of the most important work informed by the prosopographic method was: Syme 1939; Pflaum 1950, 1960; Broughton 1951–86; Nicolet 1966–74; Bowersock 1969; Eck 1970; Wiseman 1971; Alföldy 1977. Also worth mention here is Syme 1999 (originally completed in 1935 or 1936, but then laid aside). Cf. now Cameron 2003.

5. Syme (1964: 17 n. 3), for example, talks of the "social basis of Roman political life," referring his readers to Gelzer and Münzer. Still, what he was interested in, ultimately, was that political life. The connection between the prosopographic method and social history is put explicitly by Eck 1993: v–vi (and see various articles in the volume). For a sense of the way in which the workings of elite society itself can indeed be got at via prosopography, see Jones 1971: 39–64.

6. There were exceptions. An important book, published well before what is generally perceived as the heyday of Roman social history, and which is perhaps most often viewed as tackling problems of a more political nature, was nonetheless in many ways a treatment of what now would surely be considered social-historical (or perhaps cultural-historical) questions: Sherwin-White 1939. In particular, Sherwin-White's chapters on the attitude of the provincials to the empire (pp. 397–468) already confronted head-on various problems of identity, allegiance, and loyalty that have quite recently ignited much scholarly interest. Two other pioneering works that might be mentioned here involve urban history: Jones 1940 provided a wide-ranging study of the Hellenic city-state in the ancient world; and, though it came much closer to the 'beginning' of Roman social history, Downey 1961 offered a panoramic study of the urban texture of Antioch, one of the Roman world's most important metropolises.

7. For a convenient overview, see Burke 2005: 13–20.

1903, along with the French *Revue d'Histoire des Doctrines économiques et sociales*, whose inception dates to 1908. The real push came, though, when the French scholars Marc Bloch and Lucien Febvre began a journal, and an entire school of historical work, at Strasbourg in 1929. The journal was the *Annales d'histoire économique et sociale*, and the school of historical study that quickly arose was the Annales School. Scholars working in this intellectual vein sought to bring the advances made in other disciplines (e.g., sociology, or geography, or anthropology) directly to bear upon the understanding of historical processes, and they wanted especially to investigate particular societal, or historical, or cultural phenomena over large periods of time, thinking and writing in terms of the so-called *longue durée*.[8] Moreover, the upper echelons of a given society, and that group's political activities, were of considerably less interest and importance to historians working in this mode than were the undertakings of the lower sectors of the community. History, for the adherents of this school, was often history from below. These directions fixed by the Annales School have proved to be some of the most essential and enduring tenets of social history altogether, and eventually came to exert significant and sustained influence in Roman studies.[9]

Right on the heels of this development came publication of a compendious overview of the social sciences (Seligman 1930–35), which provided impetus and support for those who desired to engage such scholarship in any historical project.[10] And while the havoc of the Second World War slowed the progress of scholarship, by the 1950s a move toward social history had taken off in earnest. In Germany another school of social historical work and thought was founded in the mid-1950s, and various journals devoted to the field of social history began to be published in both Europe and the United States.[11] And, by the 1960s, path-breaking works of social history were appearing in English (just two examples, the latter quite important for

8. Two monuments of this school were Braudel 1966 and Ariès 1977. Braudel's model of Mediterranean history must now be read against that of Horden and Purcell 2000. On this book, see the important review article by Brent Shaw (2001), as well as what is effectively a companion volume overseen by William Harris (2005).

9. It is perhaps worth noting that, in the field of American history, the work of Frederick Turner (e.g., Turner 1920) or Charles and Mary Beard (e.g., Beard and Beard 1927) had begun to bring socioeconomic concerns to the forefront of the historical project just when the Annales School was forming. But such efforts in the sphere of American history seem never to have influenced Roman historians in quite the way that the Annales School—or indeed, European social history generally—has. The split between the old world and the new, in its full ensemble (both historical and historiographic), is surely at work here. Cf. Potter 2006: 3, concerning Beard's lack of reception in Europe.

10. A successor to this encyclopedia appeared in 1968 (Sills 1968), and there have been further such projects since. Note also Brunner, Conze, and Koselleck 1972–97.

11. The 'Arbeitskreis für moderne Sozialgeschichte' (Working Group for Modern Social History) was created in 1957 by Werner Conze (Heidelberg University) and Otto Brunner (Hamburg University); see the preceding footnote for one result of that group's efforts. Furthermore, when the University of Bielefeld was opened (roughly a decade later, in 1969), another highly influential German movement in social history was brought to life by two of the professors newly appointed there: Hans-Ulrich Wehler and Jürgen Kocka. In the United

Roman history: Thompson 1963; Hobsbawm 1969). In any case, the ultimate point is that, by the late 1960s, social history had come to be an established and influential movement in the world of historical scholarship altogether.[12]

Historians of Rome had not much participated in this development. They were delayed, as has been suggested above, perhaps by Rostovtzeff's colossal and intimidating *Social and Economic History*; perhaps, too, by the great influence of political history and the authoritative practitioners of prosopography. In any case, as historians of ancient Rome did begin to think and write earnestly about social issues, they initially built mainly upon the work of Rostovtzeff, or other traditionally minded historians of Rome.[13] Perhaps, then, it was the social ferment of the 1960s and early 1970s, more than scholarly trends in the wider field of history, that caused Roman historians to turn toward society as an object of study. Be that as it may, the 1970s witnessed an explosion of interest in social-historical issues concerning the Roman world, and ever since, Roman society has been a focal point for vibrant research. So as to provide at least a rough sketch of the way the social history of ancient Rome grew, we might first consider several books that aimed, in one sense or another, to produce some kind of synthetic picture of Roman society, and then move on to a selection of more specialized, though nonetheless particularly influential works.

In 1974, Moses Finley brought out a collection of essays by a variety of authors, all previously published in the journal *Past and Present*. While the book, *Studies in Ancient Society*, had no overarching theme, its editor averred that his contributors would each pretty certainly accept "…the view that neither institutions nor their transformations (past or present) can be understood except in their role within the social structure of their day, in the network of interrelationships that make up any complex society—and it is sometimes necessary to insist that these societies *were* complex" (Finley 1974: ix).[14] Such a vision of Roman history was now beginning

---

Kingdom, the Social History Society was created somewhat later, in 1976. As for periodicals, an extremely influential journal, *Past and Present*, began to be issued in 1952. Its mission was (and continues to be) to publish articles detailing historical, social, and cultural change. Eric Hobsbawm (1997: 73) nonetheless suggests that the first English-language journal to specialize in social history might be considered to have been the *Comparative Studies in Society and History*, founded in 1958. In any case, various other major journals for social history would soon appear in both the United Kingdom and the United States; to name but one example, *The Journal of Social History* (founded in 1967).

12. For thought-provoking comments on the nature of social history, see Hobsbawm 1997 (the text of a lecture originally delivered in 1970, and first published in 1972), or more recently Cartledge 2002.

13. One example is an important article on the living conditions of Rome's urban *plebs*, published by Zvi Yavetz in 1958. He did not locate his arguments in the context of (say) Annales-style social history. Rather, the scholarly forerunners Yavetz mentions are (e.g.) Beloch, Rice Holmes, Friedlaender, or Carcopino.

14. Some of the (Roman) topics covered in the volume were elite mobility (Keith Hopkins); the Roman mob (P. A. Brunt); freedmen and social mobility (P. R. C. Weaver); legal privilege (Peter Garnsey); persecution of Christians (G. E. M. de Ste. Croix and A. N. Sherwin-White); and peasant revolts in later antiquity (E. A. Thompson).

to gain sway; indeed, the year before, Finley had put theory into practice with his monograph, *The Ancient Economy* (Finley 1973).[15] For present purposes, the point is that Finley there argued ancient economic activity to have been very largely conditioned by social realities. Thus, for example, he asks about the Romans of Cicero's day, "…whether, by law or convention, men were still being pressed towards certain sources of wealth according to status"; and his answer would be that "…a model of economic choices, an investment model, in antiquity would give considerable weight to this factor of status" (Finley 1973: 52 and 60, respectively). In short, whereas Rostovtzeff had preferred to conceive of society and economy dancing intimately and pretty well coterminously through time, Finley suggested that we see the former as having preponderantly determined the steps: on his model, certain dictates of a social nature very largely shaped what was, at best, a rudimentary economy (on Finley's approach, cf. Scheidel, Morris, and Saller 2007: 2–4).

Just as Finley was delivering the Sather Lectures at Berkeley (winter 1972)—for these are what is published in his *The Ancient Economy*—Ramsay MacMullen was finalizing a book-length essay, *Roman Social Relations*, that aimed "…to get at the feelings that governed the behavior of broad social groups or conditions" (MacMullen 1974a: vii).[16] He discovered a miserably destitute rural population (not, n.b., unlike Rostovtzeff's), who squinted at the world through lenses fogged by superstition, suspicion, and, most characteristically, acute conservatism (MacMullen 1974a: 27). In conjunction with this reigned the "almost incredible snobbery" of the urban gentleman (MacMullen 1974a: 58). Ultimately, MacMullen's Roman world was utterly dominated by an extreme social verticality, this reinforced over and over again by numerous varieties of abusive—or at the very least, blatantly class-conscious—behavior.[17]

Meanwhile, Géza Alföldy was likewise putting the finishing touches to his *Römische Sozialgeschichte*. This was a different creature altogether. The idea of the book was to provide, insofar as this was possible, a comprehensive structural and historical account

15. Note also, most recently, the updated edition published by the University of California Press in 1999, with a foreword by Ian Morris.

16. It is worth remarking that MacMullen's view of the Roman economy was quite similar to Finley's (MacMullen 1974a: 126): "What could have induced the Romans to be so blind? Surely they saw that, in their gathering of wealth by conquest, they gathered a giant market. Surely *someone* realized that the great swelling of cities in later Republican Italy offered perfectly extraordinary economic opportunities, especially in luxury goods, services, trades, and crafts. But no; with unteachable conservatism, rich Romans turned to the land, and even those of relatively modest means could not lower themselves to the running of an arms factory or a fuller's mill." Interpretation of the ancient economy generally, however, has in the meanwhile shifted significantly. See Scheidel, Morris, and Saller 2007: 1–7 and passim.

17. Appendix B in the book comprises, for example, a three-page "lexicon of snobbery," a list of words and phrases that "indicate the range of prejudice felt by the literate upper classes for the lower" (MacMullen 1974a: 138–41). Note also the various expressions of disgust applied by the haves to Rome's less-well-off urban population (Yavetz 1969: 141–42), or the nasty vocabulary used to refer to slaves (Hopkins 1993: 23 n. 37).

of Roman society.[18] In order to achieve that goal, Alföldy divided his subject matter into seven different epochs, and then examined the structures of Roman society during each of these periods, looking for what had changed, how the transformations came about, and seeking the causes of those mutations. Aside from this diachronic structural approach, which itself provided a useful framework for subsequent work on Roman society, one particular aspect of the book has tended to stick in the minds of many: the pyramid-like model of high-imperial society that Alföldy proposed (Alföldy 1988: 146).[19] All in all, Alföldy's depiction served forcefully to press home the innate, potent, and widely institutionalized hierarchic character of Roman society.[20]

Aside from these attempts at comprehensive or synthetic views of Roman society, the same period witnessed the appearance of more specialized studies. A pressing question, right from the start, involved the relationships between elite and non-elite members of the community. Thus, as student revolts and social unrest shook Europe, the United States, and beyond, Zvi Yavetz asked about the potential power of ancient Rome's impoverished urban crowd (Yavetz 1969, quote at p. viii): "Could the shouts of the populace really shake the throne, or were the various outbursts in circuses and theatres initiated, controlled, or perhaps even organized from above?" His answer (Yavetz 1969: 132, 134; and cf. Horsfall 2003: 41):

> While the political influence of the individual Roman citizen was not great, when crowds gathered together in the circuses or at the theatres they expressed their feelings as a collective body; and to such manifestations no ruler dared to remain indifferent.... Thus, in brief, the emperors took account of the opinion of the masses and took great pains to organize it.

The core of Yavetz's research was, of course, more political than strictly social; nonetheless, the view was from below, and the repercussions for an understanding of Roman society were significant (cf. Coleman and Pina Polo in this volume). Relations between those in power and those not were again on display a year later, when Peter Garnsey demonstrated that "[i]n law, as in other aspects of Roman society, the principal benefits and rewards were available to those groups most

---

18. The book was published in a first German edition in 1975, which was superseded by a second (1979) and then a third (1984) edition in that language. It is best to consult this work, however, in its most recent English version, which made yet further emendations to the second and third German editions: Alföldy 1988.

19. Regarding the influence of Alföldy's model, see Winterling 2001: 101. Cf. also Shaw 2001b: 389, who uses a diagram of seating arrangements in the theater (which were regulated by law; see below, n. 43) to map Rome's ideal social world.

20. See what is said, for example, at Alföldy 1988: 106–15. Though it was never so influential a book as Alföldy's (which has been translated into eight different languages), another synthetic overview of Roman society was that of Henry Boren (1977). Furthermore, Helmuth Schneider produced, at roughly the same time, two important volumes: Schneider 1976; Schneider 1981. Though it is not a book of primarily social history, for the Roman Republic one should also be aware of Nicolet 1976. And for the late imperial period, Jones 1964, though again, not merely a social history, is still fundamental.

advantageously placed in the stratification system by reason of their greater property, power, and prestige" (Garnsey 1970: 280). Garnsey had been anticipated in some basic ways by John Crook, who pointed out that, "…Roman society was very oligarchical. It perpetuated enormous differences in wealth and social power, and the upper class which determined its legal rules enshrined in them a code of values relevant to itself which cannot automatically be assumed to have been equally relevant to the lives and habits of the mass of people" (1967: 10). The repercussions of findings such as those reached by Crook and Garnsey traveled well beyond the confines of the law and legal history (cf. Kehoe in this volume). The elite was again front and center just a few years later in a book by Paul Veyne (1976). This was an extremely wide-ranging demonstration of how members of both the Greek and the Roman upper crust thought themselves so vastly superior to their lesser contemporaries as to be obligated to undertake numerous works of public benefaction, for which they were accordingly (in multifarious ways) praised and honored.

All of this raises the obvious question as to how non-elite persons were classified as such to begin with. And that, given especially the modern experience, causes the matter of race relations to become compelling. In another important book, Frank Snowden came to the conclusion (Snowden 1970, quote at p. 216) that for the Greeks and Romans, "…race is of no consequence in judging man's worth." Instead, factors that we would broadly classify as cultural made the ancient individual. Recently, however, Benjamin Isaac has argued that we must allow for at least a "proto-racism" in the ancient Roman world.[21] As things presently stand, we probably would do best to factor in both Isaac's proto-racist tendencies, as well as (in line with Snowden) various social, cultural, and legal elements in our understanding of how personal social status could be calculated in the Roman world.

Also in the mid-1970s, the topic of women in the Roman world—indeed, in the classical world altogether—was treated by Sarah Pomeroy.[22] This book largely animated the study of women in antiquity; furthermore, it would be influential in giving rise to a keen interest in family history among the Romans, which has meanwhile become one of the central aspects of Roman social history altogether. The work of

21. See Isaac 2004. The book has been somewhat controversial; but, for a balanced view of it, principally accepting Isaac's arguments, see Shaw 2005. For some comments on tensions between soldiers and local populations apparently brought on by racist (or, let us say, ethnically driven) attitudes, see Potter in this volume.

22. Pomeroy 1975. She notes in her introduction (p. xii) that Rostovtzeff, for example, had paid effectively no attention to women whatsoever. Pomeroy had been preceded in the study of Roman women by Balsdon 1962, though his was a more antiquarian examination of the topic, and had nothing like the impact of Pomeroy's book. One might note also Hobsbawm 1997: 71, talking of the initial publication (in 1972) of his article "From Social History to the History of Society": "The author cannot but note with embarrassed astonishment that it contained no reference at all to women's history. Admittedly this field had scarcely begun to develop before the end of the 1960s, but neither I nor any of the other contributors to the volume, among the most distinguished in the profession—all males— appears to have been aware of the gap."

Christopher Jones on several individual Roman authors, studying their perspectives on Roman society, was likewise of great interest.[23] Extremely influential also was the work of Keith Hopkins. He explicitly set out "... to experiment with methods borrowed from sociology in order to gain new insights into changes in Roman society" (Hopkins 1978: x). Under this lens was placed, in his book *Conquerors and Slaves*, an arguably odd mix of topics, namely, the various historical consequences of a world that depended utterly on the availability of slaves, that eventually would allow court eunuchs astonishing levels of power, and that chose to worship its emperors as deities. But regardless of the topics chosen for investigation, most important here, as in his scholarship that would follow, was Hopkins' insistence on looking at the ancient world with the aid of modern scholarly (and preponderantly sociological) tools.

Lastly, two books published in the early 1980s deserve, I think, particular mention. John D'Arms asked about the juncture of economics and society by examining the ways in which social attitudes affected commerce. In particular, he was able to demonstrate that, despite the blatant contempt habitually professed by the Roman senatorial elite for moneymaking in any guise, these men simply conducted their business dealings at second hand, so as not to sully themselves palpably with such a vulgar occupation (D'Arms 1981).[24] Once again, economic and social concerns marched in tandem; and also, again, it was possible to conceive of the social as taking a certain precedence. Then, in 1982, Richard Saller's book on personal patronage during the early imperial period was published. What he managed to demonstrate was that this fundamentally social relationship was vital to the workings of many aspects of Roman life, though most important, for his study, to the functioning of the government. This book forged the explicit social link, so to speak, between prosopography and political history.

From this point on, Roman social history fairly exploded. Indeed, it ramified so extensively from the late 1970s to the early 1990s that a very large proportion of the scholarly effort of Roman historians altogether came to be concentrated upon matters that could be labeled social: women, the family, slaves and freedmen, patronage, law and society, urbanism, leisure and entertainment, and so forth. The tale of this scholarship cannot be traced here even in outline. However, there are excellent bibliographies (though we now want updates) that can guide anyone interested in gaining an acquaintance with the range of work in this field (Krause 1992; Krause, Mylonopoulos, and Cengia 1998); and a fairly recent book by Susan Treggiari provides a very nice introduction to the field (Treggiari 2002).[25]

---

23. See Jones 1971 (Plutarch), Jones 1978 (Dio Chrysostom), and Jones 1986 (Lucian). A most revealing article, in a roughly similar vein, but on Apuleius, is Millar 1981.

24. Shaw (2001a: 442 n. 86) argues that D'Arms was not aggressive enough in staking out this position.

25. For an interesting sense of the slightly differing ways in which Roman social history can be conceived, note the content headings from two sourcebooks on this field. Also reflected here are some of the developments of the field in recent years. Shelton 1998 includes chapters on: the structure of Roman society; families; marriage; housing and city life; domestic and personal concerns; education; occupations; slaves; freedmen and freedwomen;

Most recently, during the 1990s and over the course of the present decade, there has occurred a broad shift in the interests of historians dealing with the society of ancient Rome, a shift toward what is called cultural history.[26] In particular, a great deal of concern has arisen about two far-reaching issues: identity and collective memory. With regard to the first, scholars have been engaged in a lot of hard thinking about the rather astonishing cohesive capacity of an empire that was so thoroughly multi-ethnic, or multicultural, and that remained so over the long course of its political survival. It has therefore seemed urgent to ask: What did being Roman actually mean? How did one become a Roman? Why was it so attractive to be Roman? How did one display one's standing as a Roman? What happened to the many local cultures as they were subsumed by Roman (at least political) hegemony? In short, the matter of identity formation and its wide implications for the harmony of an extremely far-flung realm have recently been issues of paramount interest to historians working on what is, ultimately, the fabric of Roman society.[27] Second, the related matter of collective memory has been of very great interest. For it has become clear that an essential component of Roman culture (and hence, society) involved a continual engagement with the project of forming the present on the basis of a past which was persistently reconfigured in accord with the experiences of that evolving present. In short, the shape of the Roman community at any given moment in time depended very heavily upon the ways in which that community chose to construct remembrances of its past, and then to communicate those memories.[28]

Finally, the past two decades have also witnessed a significant revival of interest in two other areas intimately related to the social history of Rome: economics and

---

government and politics; the army; the provinces; women; leisure and entertainment; religion and philosophy. Parkin and Pomeroy 2007 is divided thus: social classes; demography; family; education; slavery; poverty; economy; legal system and courts; games.

26. For an account of cultural history, see Burke 2008. While a precise definition of this type of history is quite difficult, Burke's suggestion (2008: 3) is useful: "The common ground of cultural historians might be described as a concern with the symbolic and its interpretation."

27. To begin to get a sense of the range of complexities involved in this whole matter of Roman identity formation (rather less in favor now is the term 'Romanization'—e.g., Mattingly 2002: 537–38), see Millett 1990; Gruen 1992; Laurence and Berry 1998; Woolf 1998; MacMullen 2000; Mattingly 2004; Alföldy 2005; Dench 2005; Hingley 2005; Farney 2007; Roth 2007; van Dommelen and Terrenato 2007; Wallace-Hadrill 2008: esp. 3–37; Revell 2009.

28. The most substantial treatment of collective memory in the Roman world is now Stein-Hölkeskamp and Hölkeskamp 2006 (with earlier bibliography). See also, however, Hölkeskamp 2006a. Other important contributions are: Flower 1996; Hedrick 2000; Gowing 2005; Flower 2006. Cf. also Meyer in this volume. Lobur 2008: 170 talks of the Romans' "indigenous sense of the past *in* the present" (he offers, in this chapter of this book, a nice overview of the force of exemplarity, an absolutely crucial factor in the matter of Roman memory, both collective and individual). Furthermore, Karl Galinsky is presently embarking on a major effort to investigate this aspect of the Roman world; see the website http://www.utexas.edu/research/memoria/. The essays in Bell and Hansen 2008 nicely draw together the issues of exemplarity, identity, and memory.

demography. Both of these fields have recently been conveniently and thoroughly surveyed (Scheidel, Morris, and Saller 2007).[29]

THE PRESENT VOLUME

We now have a sketch of the evolving scholarly engagement with Roman society; and the book in your hands tackles an essential component of that Roman social history—perhaps *the* essential component.When an editor at the Oxford University Press first approached me with the idea for an 'Oxford Handbook of Roman Social Relations,' I took the last word in the projected title very seriously, and set out to design a book with it in mind—that is to say, to assemble a volume about the various ways people in the ancient Roman world related to each other.[30] What we want to impart here is a sense of the arguably most basic or characteristic sorts of interpersonal interaction engaged in by the Romans. We want something like the primary colors, from which all the other shades of Roman social relations were mixed—an emblematic picture, as it were. The matter of the choice of topics for this volume, such as would create this kind of portrait, will be taken up momentarily.

But first, what does it mean to be Roman?[31] How, that is, are we to recognize *Roman* social relations? What we are dealing with here, it must be realized, is a culturally determined phenomenon; being 'Roman' in a thoroughgoing sense—and thus, interacting with others in a 'Roman' way—is not a simple matter of, for example, possessing Roman

---

29. For a sense of the ways in which demography (here, of death) might be "of considerable relevance to appraisals of family formation, social structure, political activity and the preservation of civic memory in the capital (Rome)," see Scheidel 2003. Scheidel, Morris, and Saller (2007: 7) also make the crucially important point that "[t]he cultural achievements of classical Mediterranean civilization rested on a remarkable economic efflorescence."

30. Note, for example, Scupin and DeCorse 1992: 46: "Society refers to a particular group of people within a specific territory. In particular it refers to *the patterns of relationships among people* within a definite territory." Or Calhoun 2000: 453 ('society'): "Used to describe both the general phenomenon of social life and the specific units into which social life is organized. Thus, all human beings live in society—*their lives are social and involve relationships to others.*" See also the "second idea of 'society'" described by Morley 2004: 72: "...the arena of social relationships and the institutions that govern them....This then offers a way of understanding human behaviour, or at least of those aspects of human behaviour with a 'social character,' *above all those involving interaction between individuals.*" (The emphasis in each of the preceding quotations is mine.) Or, on the absolute centrality to social history of "social roles," i.e., "patterns or norms of behaviour expected from the occupant of a particular position in the social structure," see Burke 2005: 47–50. In short, social *relations*, in the sense of interactions between members of the community in question, can be argued to be the very basis of society. More fully on all of this: Mayhew 1968.

31. See the literature cited above, n. 27. John Crook was long ago similarly troubled (1967: 10–11): "One more question arises: what are we going to mean by 'Roman' law and

citizenship, or of speaking Latin, or of living within the boundaries of the Roman Empire. It is, rather, a matter of self-identity, of feeling Roman, of being able to make a strong claim to such status among those who likewise feel themselves to be Roman; and it is very much a question of being treated as a Roman by those others.

Now, members of the senatorial or equestrian orders will obviously have been able to stake the most powerful claim in this regard; hence, what they have transmitted regarding Roman social relations (which represents, of course, the lion's share of what we now have) will deserve our full attention. The minute we go beyond these two categories of people, however, the situation becomes murkier—and in more ways than one. The members of the multifarious governing elites in the empire's many urban centers will likewise gradually have come to possess some discernable title to a position as cultural insider, and thus to varying degrees of 'Romanness.'[32] And, of course, once we drop below the level of the urban upper classes and enter the realm of the common citizens of such places, or if we move beyond the more urbanized settlements and out to the villages and the countryside, then we truly enter less well known territory (indeed, both in terms of the available source materials and as to the business of interpreting the evidence we do possess).

In the end, we are largely constrained by the situation that has always prevailed. We possess many discrete pieces of evidence that were created by many different ancient individuals, though preponderantly by various members of various sectors of the upper classes. We can do little more than to take that evidence, examine it with sensitivity for the complexities involved in the formation of identities, and hope thereby to come away with the sociocultural attitudes of 'the Romans.' The picture we extract, whether we like it or not, is unavoidably going to be heavily upper crust (and almost entirely urban) in its outlook and preferences. That notwithstanding, it is always essential to peer further down the social scale, and when

---

'Roman' society? The dominions of Rome embraced many culturally very un-Roman people: Greeks, Egyptians, Semites, Celts and so on. Rome did not (or only in a sense that will be briefly discussed at the very end of this book) impose a unitary system of legal institutions like a giant dishcover upon all these diverse sets of people....Can one, then, obtain only so vague, partial and distorted a reflection of Rome in its heyday, by looking through the eyes of the law, as to make the entire undertaking worthless? One or two considerations, at least, can be set on the other side of the scale, and how far they help to tip it the reader will judge by results." See also the recent comments of Richard Brilliant (2007) on the great difficulty of delimiting a body of art that could confidently be called Roman.

32. There were, n.b., local varieties of Roman identity: cf. Hingley 2005: 49–71; also Revell 2009. One might think here about the problems conjured by a figure such as Apuleius, the second-century AD African-born author of several works in Latin that are considered central to Roman literature (cf. von Albrecht 1997: 1449–50). For a lucid treatment of the question "Is Apuleius a Roman?" by Carlos Noreña, see http://www9.georgetown.edu/faculty/jod/apuleius/norena.apulrome.html. Noreña's conclusion is this: "Apuleius was, to be sure, a Roman citizen, and he also admitted to being half Numidian, half Gaetulian, but if he were asked to define himself, he probably would have answered, simply, 'I am a disciple of Plato.'"

possible, beyond the city walls, and to try, there too, to isolate attitudes about social conditions. We should be hunting, ultimately, for consistencies of attitude—up and down the social scale, and across the wide geographical expanses of the empire. From all of this, for better or for worse, we can then construct a vision of 'Roman' social relations.[33]

The contributors to this volume have not been asked to adopt any particular methodological stance. Each has worked on his or her own, guided by his or her own view of how to establish what 'Roman social relations' were. Nonetheless, I think most of the authors here would consider themselves to have been engaging in an approach to 'Roman social relations' not far afield from that just laid out. So, let us turn to what actually resides in the following pages.

Under the emperor Augustus, the Roman world was thoroughly transformed. Given that, and given also that the chronological boundaries of this book are such as to encompass, albeit rather loosely, large periods on both sides of this pivotal epoch (i.e., from roughly the middle republic down to about the time of Constantine the Great, or somewhat later), it seemed best to provide a sense of the complexities brought on by the institutional shift from republic to empire. To that end, a second introductory essay on that topic follows the present one.

The book proper begins (section II: Mechanisms of Socialization) with the proposition that little Romans did not spring to life, ready-made to consort in all the appropriate ways with their peers. So as to be capable of Roman social relations, would-be Romans wanted education and socialization—they had to be shaped as properly functioning members of their community. The initial section, then, attempts to show some of the principal ways in which self-avowed (and mainly elite) Romans set out to ensure that they would be reproduced as social beings. The underlying thought is that the processes of *how* incipient Romans were brought to comprehend the matter of being Roman will reveal much about the actual nature of that particular state of being. And this, of course, will in turn betray very much about the complexion of interacting with others in a Roman way.

Another assumption follows (section III: Mechanisms of Communication and Interaction), namely, that if there are to be relations and interactions, social or otherwise, there must be communication—and, again, that such communication will exert pressure on social relations. Study of Rome, though, takes us to a pre-industrial world, where the available tools for communication were, relatively speaking, limited in both their variety and their capabilities. This means that the technologies to hand will have determined the parameters of the possible, and will thus have had an effect on the shape of Roman social relations. This section of this

---

33. It is, of course, both possible and often highly desirable to adduce the results of work in (say) sociology, or anthropology, or to make historical comparisons with other pre-modern societies, in our attempts to take the measure of the Roman social world. Cf. the comments of Morley 2004: 74–76, arguing for the necessity of a more theoretical approach. In the context of the present volume, this is done in an ad hoc fashion. See, as one example, the essay by Riess.

book, then, attempts to portray some of the more prominent media a Roman might have employed to connect with another Roman (or, potentially, a non-Roman), and to see how communication via these media functioned.[34]

We next tackle communal contexts for communication and interaction (section IV: Communal Contexts for Social Interaction). Three such contexts are set out first; in all three (elite self-representation, public speaking at Rome, the Second Sophistic) those who belonged to the *crème de la crème* strove to preen before their compatriots, one result of which was that their own primacy in the community was cemented. We can observe here some of the ways in which the social hierarchies referred to above were actually woven into the society's collective fabric by (and principally for) the gentry—though, of course, with the intimate participation of the rest. We then turn to three venues where the entire society, including slaves, might actually commingle, sometimes with even some vague aura of equality. To observe the Romans together in the law courts, in the theaters and arenas, and at the baths is to get a fairly immediate and a most revealing glimpse of the whole community with its social hair let down—yet, simultaneously done up to perfection. Here too, the members of the elite hardly forgot to express their ascendency, and to demand the prerogatives that ascendency conveyed.

From the communal, we take a turn in the direction of the private, and consider several modes of (often) more intimate interpersonal relations (section V: Modes of Interpersonal Relations). Honor (and dishonor) and friendship lay at the very core of the Romans' efforts to relate with one another on a personal basis. These two modes of interaction are crucial for understanding pretty well any other kind of social interaction; and, in particular, it was via these two types of intercourse that the Romans could most effectively set about constructing the hierarchic grids to which they were so devoted. The stage upon which individuals might most intimately put these (as well as other mechanisms of socializing) into play was the home. Welcoming guests into one's household altogether, but especially at dinner parties, provides us with a revealing vista of the ways a Roman might forge his or her more cherished contacts. But, despite all the politesse enveloping friendship, honor, dinners, guest friendship, and beyond, there yet was another side of the coin. The Romans often enough gravitated to distressingly violent behavior. Here is their darker side.

Another aspect of the ways in which Romans fraternized entails their predilection for joining together in smaller organizations—micro-communities, as it

34. One must be aware that there has appeared, especially in the last decade or two, much literature (very largely from continental Europe) on communications just generally in the ancient world. Although matters other than those of direct concern here are often the subjects dealt with (e.g., military, administrative, or religious communications, the communicative practices of ancient civilizations other than Rome's), nonetheless it seems worth at least indicating what this literature is. See, for example, Achard 1991; Kolb 2000; Andreau and Virlouvet 2002; Donati 2002; Capdetrey and Nelis-Clément 2006; Peter and Seidlmayer 2006; Angeli Bertinelli and Donati 2008; Schörner and Sterbenc Erker 2008; Osgood 2009. See also Ando 2000: 73–130.

were (section VI: Societies within the Roman Community). These took a variety of forms, and served a variety of purposes (professional, military, religious, drinking, etc.). To observe Romans in these more intimate social constellations is revealing. The ways in which they quite consciously and formally structured these purpose-oriented mini-societies, and then related to one another in such contexts, can tell us very much about the influences of society at large over the perceptions held by the members of these smaller communities as to how a human conglomerate could or should function. In particular, we here are often treated to a quite revealing vista of the social proclivities of the non-elite members of that world. We have also included essays on two rather idiosyncratic societies that functioned within the larger community—one Jewish, the other Christian. The historical importance of these two communities is patent; and how they did or did not integrate with the rest of Roman society casts an interesting light on the matter of group interactions. Also, the status of the members of these groups as at once insider and outsider moves us in the direction of the last section of this book.

Finally, the outsiders (section VII: Marginalized Persons). Any society will have its pariahs. We have attempted to gather the most obvious types of person marginalized in the Roman world (Jews and Christians having already been considered). The point is to try to assess how and why such individuals were pushed away from the community's notional core; but we also want to know how, why, and to what extent these figures remained, nonetheless, crucial to the society. In short, to grasp the outsider is very often to grasp some quite essential things about the insider—who she or he is, how she or he perceives her or himself, and then, how such individuals will be likely to relate to others.

Now, there are three areas of research that are relevant to many of the essays in this volume, and that are raised repeatedly over the course of the volume. Given the prevalence of these matters in this book, I have thought it best to draw the reader's attention to these topics at this point. In question are: non-verbal communicative strategies; the difficulties of knowing much about the social lives of the non-elite; and the history of emotions.

The present volume concentrates heavily upon verbal and/or literate communications, and how these served to shape social relations.[35] That notwithstanding, the Romans disposed of a large and potent repertoire of non-verbal communicative

---

35. Given this concentration, something should be said at this point, if only very briefly, about the matter of literacy. There is now a sophisticated literature on the subject, with Harris 1989 being the seminal examination. That book generated a very wide-ranging discussion, especially because Harris was quite pessimistic about the overall levels of literacy. On the whole, Harris' arguments stand firm, though we must always keep in mind that various mechanisms (e.g., reading out loud to those who could not read themselves—which was not, n.b., at all ignored by Harris) could mitigate the effects of widespread illiteracy. The discussion regarding ancient literacy can be followed up in (e.g.): Humphrey 1991; Cooley 2002; Johnson and Parker 2009. Cf. also Thomas 1992. With regard to the cultural pursuits of non-elite persons, and the matter of literacy among such persons, see Horsfall 2003: 30, 72–74. He puts the matter succinctly (p. 72): "It was not a text-based culture, and rested

strategies. Therefore, it is important to keep in mind the fact that many a Roman social interaction did not depend upon either the spoken or the written word.

First of all, there existed for the Roman a copious and powerful semantic world that involved the body—its innate appearance, how it was clothed, how it was positioned and moved, and so forth. The point is that a Roman, by effecting a presence with (say) a particular hairstyle, outfit, stance, movements, or non-verbal exclamations, could establish many things about his or her relationship to those with whom he or she was interacting. We now have a fair amount of literature on all of this.[36]

There also existed an entire cosmos of artistic and architectural representations (or, one might say, of representations in material culture), which spoke volumes to the ancient Roman—and, again, did so without the intervention of a single artic-ulated word. A statue, a painting, a piece of pottery, a building, a physical space (for example, the composite impression generated by an imperial forum): all these things and many more were designed so as to converse with the person contemplat-ing them. Again here, there is now a rich literature.[37]

---

upon memory rather than active literacy." For cautionary observations regarding the extent of non-elite textually based engagement with literature, see also Hedrick in this volume. Cf. also Jördens in this volume, though, on the wide use of written communications of all sorts by individuals from all walks of life.

36. There existed an entire category of ancient literature treating physiognomy, i.e., personal physical appearance and its meaning. Access to this realm may be found via Barton 1994: 95–131 and Swain and Boys-Stones 2007. On dress and personal styling, Sebesta and Bonfante 1994 was pioneering. That book has now been complemented by (esp.): Cleland, Davies, and Llewellyn-Jones 2007; Colburn and Heyn 2008; Edmondson and Keith 2008; Olson 2008; Wallace-Hadrill 2008: 38–57. There is also much good material on dress and society/culture/communication in (e.g.): Gleason 1995; Dench 2005; Sumi 2005. For an exploration of the affinities between Julius Caesar's style of personal grooming, on the one hand, and his manner of literary composition, on the other, see Kraus 2005. Her arguments are particularly interesting in the present context, since she demonstrates how Caesar's liter-ary style and manner of bodily adornment could be discussed in precisely the same terms, and could likewise be perceived to communicate, each in its own right, exactly the same picture of the man. Cf. also Fagan in this volume on dress, and nudity, at the baths. As for gesture, and the positioning of the body generally, one may consult the pioneering work of Brilliant (1963), and more recently: Bremmer and Roodenburg 1991; Aldrete 1999; Gunderson 2000; Newbold 2000; Corbeill 2003; Flaig 2003; Cairns 2005; Roller 2006. See also the remarks of Connolly in this volume. For gestures replacing words in pantomime performances, see Jory 2008: 162–67. Then, there were various types of non-verbal communication that involved sounds of all kinds. See, for example, Klauser 1950: 221 (clapping, whistling, hissing); Purcell 1995: 17–18 (snorting). Further on acclamations (many involving just a few ritualized words): Roueché 1984; Potter 1996; and cf. Horsfall 2003: 37–42.

37. What is listed can be only very broadly indicative: Brilliant 1984; Hölscher 1984; Hölscher 1987; Zanker 1990; Wallace-Hadrill 1994; Elsner 1996; Hales 2003; Stewart 2003; Leach 2004; Clarke 2007; Diefenbach 2007; Elsner 2007; Roth 2007; Thomas 2007; Wallace-Hadrill 2008: 73–210. For an interesting debate on the potential for a social interpretation of

A plaint that at times feels nearly like the theme song of Roman social history, which is sounded repeatedly in this volume, and which must be squarely faced, concerns the difficulty of getting at the society of Roman-era have-nots—and especially those who resided beyond the large urban centers.[38] The matter is nicely put by Lin Foxhall in a dictionary article on peasants in the ancient world: "Peasants are like postholes: it is much easier to see where they ought to have been in the classical world than where they actually were" (Foxhall 2003: 1130). This is important—if for no other reason than that a significantly large proportion of the population of the Roman world lived out life beyond the confines of urban centers.[39] But despite all the difficulties, we are now beginning to have a decent literature that examines life—and to some degree, even social life, as opposed to economic conditions—in the ancient countryside. One particularly interesting aspect of the recent work involves the periodic markets and fairs, where the lesser folk, on a regular basis, shopped, socialized, and were entertained. So, although we will never know well the quotidian lifestyle of the rural populations, the state of our knowledge has lately improved.[40]

Finally, an area of research that has become quite fruitful in recent years, and is closely linked to the whole matter of social relations, involves the history of emotions. Emotions come into play in various of the essays that follow. However, the reader may find it convenient to have some of the important bibliography on this topic drawn together in one place.[41]

---

domestic wall painting, see Tybout 2001, with the attendant comments of Bettina Bergmann and Christopher Hallett. Pina Polo, in this volume, draws attention to the ways in which the spaces of public meetings were able to communicate meaning. Note also Dunbabin and Slater, in this volume, on the semantics of the architecture of dining spaces. And Bablitz's essay on the law courts moves in this direction as well.

38. We must be very careful, let it be said, about making too sharp a divide between the rural and urban spheres—for it is increasingly clear that there was a great deal of interplay (of every conceivable kind) between town and countryside. See Witcher 2005, with earlier literature on this matter.

39. Cf. the comments of Harris 2005: 29–34, concerning the importance of rural areas to the history of the Mediterranean. Scheidel (in Scheidel, Morris, and Saller 2007: 79) suggests that perhaps one-eighth or one-ninth of the total population under the early Roman Empire lived in urban centers; though as he notes, there will certainly have been regional variation.

40. As for the markets and fairs, it should be noted that the chief focus of the scholarship has still been economic. Again, this is largely a function of the available evidence. Nonetheless, see MacMullen 1970; Shaw 1981; de Ligt 1993; Frayn 1993; Morley 1996: 166–74. Generally on rural social (as opposed to, again especially, economic) conditions, see MacMullen 1974a: 1–27. For a lucid sense of the rhythms of rural life in one area of the Roman Empire (Anatolia), see Mitchell 1993: 165–97. A glimpse into the rural society of central Anatolia is also offered by Gordon 2004. Or for Egypt, cf. Lewis 1983: 65–83. Generally on the rural folk in the Roman world: MacMullen 1974b; Evans 1980; Garnsey 1988: 44–48. Note also the useful bibliographic essay in Horden and Purcell 2000: 590–92, and cf. Dyson 2003.

41. See now: Kneppe 1994; Konstan 1997; Harris 2001; Konstan 2001; Braund and Most 2003; MacMullen 2003; Marincola 2003; Kaster 2005.

A View of Roman Social Relations

From all of the scholarship on Roman society to date there have emerged several overarching points that individually will make repeated appearances in the following essays. It is important, on the one hand, to isolate and draw attention to these matters right from the start, for each, in its own way, corresponds to an absolutely vital element of the composite that was Roman society. But even more important is the realization that these individual aspects of the Roman social cosmos were in fact interrelated, that they operated sympathetically, and that together they stand behind any and every examination of Roman society.

First, social concerns among the Romans exerted significant influence upon economic affairs, politics, law, religion, and more—and indeed, did so in a manner that can appear quite extreme as compared with many another society.[42] Second, the structural elements of Roman society, which were many and highly valued, as well as the roles they played in the community, tended to be meticulously formalized, or insitutionalized.[43] Third, when social conditions were not explicitly arranged by formal regulations of some kind, they could quite effectively be reined in by a wide assortment of conventional, or traditional, or ritualized actions and modes of behavior—and of course, when and where there were statutory acts constraining social matters, such tacit conventions presumably stood behind the laws.[44] In short:

42. To provide but one example, Brent Shaw (2001a: 430) argues that if we want to investigate economic rationalism in Roman agriculture, then we must correlate this to "the nature of the social system of which the cycles of production, distribution, and consumption were part." He then says, regarding the Roman agricultural economy, "At its leading edges, the extremes of surplus wealth seem to be invested in efforts 'to trump nature' that were 'artistic' or 'architectural' in type: qualitative in form, quantitative in effect. In this sense, compared to the leading sectors of 17th-c. capitalism, this earlier social order appears to be an exotic *Fabergé Welt.*"

43. A few salient examples of this would be that: the elite was largely grouped into so-called orders, senators and equestrians at Rome, decurions in the provincial municipalities, and each of these estates had formal requirements for membership and various attendant marks of privilege (Alföldy 1988); the legal position of the so-called *honestiores* (the better people) was, by the second century AD, statutorily mandated as superior to that of the rest in several ways (Garnsey 1970); legislation of the emperor Augustus fixed theater seating according to the principles of social rank (Rawson 1987; also Coleman in this volume).

44. Seating arrangements, in various contexts, make for a nice example here. Again, in the theater, one's seat was fixed by (an Augustan) law according to social rank (see the preceding note). At banquets put on by *collegia* (private associations), the club's rules might work similarly. Yet at dinner parties in private homes—which were likewise occasions of great social moment, which might not have an all-so-private atmosphere to them, and where seating arrangements therefore mattered hugely—tacit social conventions, along with the finesse of the host, regulated things (cf. Peachin 2001: 138; also Dunbabin and Slater in this volume). Seating at publicly sponsored banquets was again tightly controlled, though not specifically by law (cf. Donahue 2004: 22–23). And for the spectrum of intricate conventions about the *way* one sat at dinners, see Roller 2006. In short, how and where one sat, in various contexts,

(a) nearly every aspect of life was, for a Roman, somehow social; (b) there was a very strong impulse among the Romans to structure their society fastidiously; and (c) the social structures thus created tended toward a notably rigid formalization.

Now, in the present volume the influence of social considerations upon other areas of life (say, economics or politics), along with the structural aspects of Roman society (that is, the groupings of people into social orders, the legal definitions of various persons' rights, matters of social class, and so forth) are issues that will fade largely into the background.[45] We will be more interested in the mechanics, as it were, of Roman society—the matrix of interpersonal relationships and behaviors that characterized daily existence for a Roman. This book seeks to provide an emblematic picture of these interactions; in other words, something approaching an etiquette of Roman social behavior. We are engaged in what might be labeled a cultural approach to Roman social relations. As we shall see, the workings of social interaction, just like the basic structures of Roman society, tended to a high degree of formalization. That said, we are still left with two important questions, which must be confronted before progressing to our narrative.

First, can we suggest what it is that makes the social relations we are about to portray peculiarly or particularly Roman? Can we, in other words, isolate something like a defining characteristic of *Roman* social relations? Such an undertaking will entail an obvious hazard of reductionism, but the suggestions that follow may be useful enough to think with that they justify the risk of oversimplification.

Second, if we can plausibly single out such a characteristic, then how universally accepted and applied was it? Given that the great majority of our evidence was produced by and about the elite, we must ask to what extent that evidence represents life as it was lived and perceived by the have-nots. Can we, in other words, safely use the evidence we have to move back and forth between elite and non-elite realms of social interaction? In short, ought we to be thinking of distinct realms of social relations, or was this a world fairly united in its social dispositions?[46]

---

was meticulously arranged—perhaps by law, perhaps 'only' by insistent social conventions. But the rules, in either case, were powerful, and were always carefully calculated to display and to reinforce accepted social hierarchies.

45. It should be noted that the use of 'class,' as an interpretative device in the study of Roman society, has often been rejected. Harris 1988, though, makes a very strong case for its applicability and usefulness in certain ways, while pointing out that a Marxist sense of the word is not at all binding upon us, and can simply be ignored. Uses of 'class' in this introduction, then, follow the guidelines laid out by Harris. On the whole problem of establishing a model for Roman imperial society that could gain universal consent, see Winterling 2001: 99–106. He relates the paradoxes of the Roman imperial social structure to the paradoxical political situation—i.e., an absolute monarchy parading as a democratic republic—that so influenced everything in the Roman world during the early imperial period.

46. Morely 2004: 75, for example, seems generally quite pessimistic about the ability of our source tradition, precisely because of its largely elite bias, to reveal much about social conditions toward the bottom of Roman society. As will be argued here, though, there may well be reason for a bit more optimism.

Let us tackle the first matter first. I think an argument can indeed be made that one particular mode of behavior, or thinking, underlies pretty well all of what will follow in this volume—and hence, Roman social relations overall—that there is a particular something that makes the Roman world of social relations coherent. This something emerges clearly from the survey of scholarship offered above, and has always been plain to Roman historians: it is effectively a truism (cf. Harris 1988: 598). But the very fact that we are dealing with a truism serves to indicate that we are confronting a matter possessed of great explanatory force. One of the more doggedly salient results of all the work on Roman society to date is that the Roman community, in all of its vastness and variety, was fundamentally characterized by a striking predilection for establishing acute social hierarchies. One simply sees this everywhere in ancient Rome and, hence, everywhere in this volume.

What much of the scholarship in recent years has attempted to do, however— and precisely this is also reflected in the present volume—is to examine the ways in which various culturally ingrained ideas and attitudes molded behavior, social and otherwise. This approach has tended to move us away from looking at the structural modes of stratification so characteristic of Roman society (again, for example, the establishment of legally defined social orders), and toward the insistent, quotidian mechanisms of creating or reinforcing individualized pecking orders via particular modes of personal interaction. In other words, to know how to relate in a proper Roman way, one had to know what to do and say at dinner, at the baths, in the courtroom, and so forth. Each and every daily scenario had its protocol. But in all of these situations, there occurred, in an utterly fundamental fashion, a continual ranking and re-ranking of people. Pretty well everything one said and did in any given Roman social interaction, served ultimately to position one in a hierarchy with respect to one's interlocutor.[47] Thus, knowing how to negotiate this punctiliously graded universe with aplomb made you, at some very essential level, Roman, and simultaneously served to establish your proper place in the stratified maze that was ancient Roman society.

This brings us to our second question. If we grant what has just been suggested about hierarchic thinking and acting, then can it also be supposed that *everyone* functioned like this? It is perfectly clear that the senatorial elite operated just exactly this way—both with regard to those below them socially and with respect to members of their own social group. To provide but one example of the latter (for all senators were not equal): senator A could establish his social position relative to senator B by deciding whether to write a letter to B in his own handwriting, or to have the missive set to paper by a slave scribe. The first choice would communicate A's social parity with B; the second option would announce the social superiority of A to his senatorial colleague (McDonnell 1996: 474–75). If we next think of such a Roman, now either senator A or senator B, peering down at the classes of people beneath him, then we can rely on Pliny the Younger to put things succinctly: nothing could

---

47. On this matter of a continual ranking and re-ranking of people in nearly any and every situation, see Rillinger 1985, with the comments of Winterling 2001: 104–6.

possibly be more distressingly inequitable than unflinching equality for all (Plin. *Ep.* 9. 5. 3). Moreover, we can be confident that attitudes of this sort were common not just among senators, but also elsewhere among the upper class. But is this kind of attitude confined to the elite, or did people of lesser social caliber also grapple among themselves for social position? Did the relatively comfortable shoemaker, like the grandees of Rome's senate, incline to loathe and revile those beneath him who could not claw their way higher—and to display those feelings whenever it suited him?

Before going any farther, one thing needs to be stressed. What must have worked very largely to shape all of this type of thinking and doing, at least at the society's top, was another salient characteristic of the Roman elite world, namely, an unabated drive to compete—socially, politically, and otherwise—with a level of ferocity that is nearly incredible. This dog-eat-dog condition of life among the haves is mentioned repeatedly below (see, e.g., Connolly, Lendon, Leppin, Meyer, Milnor, or Schmitz in this volume), and has gained significant attention from scholars in recent years.[48] But again, what we want to know right now is whether the have-nots tussled with each other in a similar fashion. In short, did those of the lower class believe in and value that disposition for establishing social rank—something that often strikes the modern observer as an incredible snobbery—to which we so plainly see the elite clinging?

Various things point generally toward an affirmative answer to this question. First, one might expect significant displeasure with the existing social order, if there was such, to have resulted in some notable outward manifestation of a desire for change. We encounter really nothing of the sort. There was, especially during the Hellenistic period, a vogue of writing on utopian societies, which were often imagined as being egalitarian in their social structures; this (n.b.) elite-produced literature may even have been popular among the less well-to-do segments of the society. However, this kind of writing appears largely to have faded away by the later Roman republican period, and seems never to have occasioned, at least so far as we can tell, any pragmatic results.[49] There were slave revolts, serious ones, yet these did not mean to alter society; the goals were much more immediate.[50] Nor does it seem at all likely

---

48. Harris 1979: 17–34 (esp.) some time ago dealt with the drive of Roman aristocrats of the middle republic to distinguish themselves in warfare, showing how this very largely served to determine the shape of Rome's imperial project. Aristocratic competition, not merely social (n.b.), but also political, in the military, and altogether is handled by (e.g.): Rosenstein 1990; Flaig 1995; Flower 1996; Bleckmann 2002; Hölkeskamp 2006b; Farney 2007. The writing of literature, too, was an arena for aristocratic competition: cf. Scholz 2003: 186–90. On competitive behavior in the Roman military, affecting elite and non-elite soldiers alike, see Lendon 2005: 163–315. Ultimately, the whole matter of elite self-representation, which Harriet Flower describes in this volume, was determined by, and is arguably one of our best reflections of, this deep-seated drive to compete.

49. See Ferguson 1975: 122–29 and Gabba 1981: (esp.) 58–59. On unrealistically egalitarian utopias in the writings of Lucian, see Carsana 2008.

50. See Bradley 1989. As Harris 1988: 605 points out, class antagonism is not needed to make sense of these slave wars. Also now Urbainczyk 2008: 75–80.

that we can point to something like class struggle at any point in the period here under consideration.[51] Nor would we be soundly advised to envision a welling up of popular unrest in the form of social banditry.[52] And while there was serious opposition to Roman rule at several points in time, this involved groups that desired to be rid of an outside hegemony, either for political or ethnic or religious reasons, not people who sought some socially oriented reform of the world.[53] In short, it is all but impossible to isolate any significant hope on the part of the non-elites of the Roman world to change society such as they knew it. The corollary would be, of course, that they ultimately held (even if with a large dose of cynicism) attitudes regarding society that resembled those known to us from elite-produced source materials.

Indeed, Géza Alföldy has proposed specifically that the masses moved generally in lockstep with the aristocrats (Alföldy 1991: 315–16; Alföldy 2004: 144). Several extended studies of some aspects of non-elite culture have likewise tended to reflect an overall conformity with elite attitudes.[54] J. E. Lendon has revealed various lower-class "communities of honor," which closely mimicked the social institutions of those from above (Lendon 1997: 95–103; also his essay in this volume). And again, this is a theme that surfaces repeatedly in the pages that will follow here.[55] Not only, then, did the non-elites decline to revolt against any possibly perceived oppression,

51. Alföldy 1988: 152–56 argues that there were no serious outbreaks of any such thing. Harris 1988: 602 is not persuaded by De Ste. Croix 1981 and the idea of class struggle in the Graeco-Roman world. E. A. Thompson indeed saw in the turmoil caused by the so-called Bagaudae, during the late third century AD and beyond, a persistent manifestation of class warfare (Thompson 1952), and this was argued more extensively by León 1996. See, however, the cautionary remarks of Drinkwater 1999.

52. Shaw 1984: 51: "As for the bandits themselves, the argument tends to indicate that they could not have been social rebels and, more important, that the phenomenon of banditry per se is not a type of social protest. Rather, it is a form of political *anachoresis*, leading from its smallest beginnings, over an unbroken trajectory, to its final form: *the formation of another state patterned on an existing type*." (I have added the emphasis.) In any case, no desire here for a substantively different order of things. Cf. also Riess in this volume.

53. Cf. Schwartz, in this volume, on the Jewish revolts. Generally on resistance to Roman rule, see Fuchs 1938; Bowersock 1965: 101–11; Bowersock 1987; Gutsfeld 1989; Elsner 2007: 225–88; and cf. Riess in this volume for characterizations of violent malcontents as 'bandits' (*latrones*). Cf. also Daube 1972.

54. See, e.g., Horsfall 2003; Clarke 2003; Petersen 2006; Roller 2006: 22–80; Morgan 2007. Cf. also Rawson 2003: 3–4, Laes 2007: 36, or Noreña forthcoming: chpt. 6. On the contributions to this area made by finds of papyri and other written documents from sub-elite contexts, see Jördens in this volume; and with regard to the non-elites as audience for the messages on coins, cf. Noreña in this volume. Note also Meyer in this volume (n. 61). For a fascinating picture of the way in which elites and non-elites could come together socioculturally (albeit in an often grudging manner) via dicing, see Purcell 1995: esp. 28–37.

55. See, in this volume, the chapters by Ando; Fagan (Baths); Fagan (Violence); Flower; Hahn; Horster; Kehoe; Leppin; Meyer; Noreña; Perry; Schmitz. And on the hierarchy of slave society imitating quite closely that of the larger community, see the concluding remarks by Schumacher in this volume.

but they also appear generally to have internalized societal forms that are known to us principally from above.

Even so, we still want to know (with as much precision as our evidence will allow), whether persons of lower social levels actually competed with one another on a daily basis for social distinction. In other words, we can frequently observe intra-class struggles among (say) the members of the senatorial order over relative social rank. But did the same kind of thing go on in the taverns of Pompeii, or out in country villages? While one might incline to suppose that such things must have occurred there too, all of this has yet to be studied properly. And of course, it could well be that we would find slightly differing versions of the same basic phenomenon as we look for its manifestations within different social classes. Be that as it may, the essays in this volume will push us toward assuming a very widespread taste within any given social class for a quotidian wrangling over social preeminence. In short, it would seem that pretty well everyone in the Roman world felt a need constantly to jostle for social position, and did so via a complicated, wide-ranging, and highly formalized or ritualized series of mechanisms. For now, though, let me provide merely two epigraphic texts, to illustrate at least roughly this phenomenon, and in particular, to show the kinds of evidence we have (they are meager), and how that evidence might be squeezed for information (with a large measure of conjecture).

In 7 BC, four assistants (*ministri*) in the administration of a country district (*pagus*) just outside Pompeii set up a dedicatory inscription (*CIL* X 924 = *ILS* 6381). All four were slaves. But one of these men, his name was Dama (thus, he was of Greek origins), was listed first. Why? Apparently because he belonged to the emperor Augustus' grandson, Agrippa Postumus. That will have brought Dama significant social cachet among his fellow slaves. Next, we read in the rules and regulations of a club (*collegium*) that operated at Lanuvium that if anyone were to insult another club member at one of the association's dinner parties, the offender would have to pay a fine of twelve *sestertii*. If the person offended, however, happened to be the *quinquennalis* (the club's chief official), then the fine would be twenty *sestertii* (*CIL* XIV 2112 = *ILS* 7212, lines 26–28).

Obviously, this kind of evidence offers us nothing like the detail that (say) Pliny's correspondence does. However, with Pliny and his kind in the background, perhaps material such as these two stones can indeed reveal something about the social attitudes of their creators. The points to be made might then go like this. These more humble individuals, when functioning among themselves, rather than inventing and implementing a world where equality would reign, apparently preferred to arrange themselves into socially determined hierarchies. Their mini-communities, in other words, were constructed socially in a fashion quite similar to the larger universe in which they revolved. A group of slaves does not seek parity within its little circle; rather, its members gravitate to a hierarchical ordering of themselves. Or, in an aggregation such as a *collegium*, the established mini-hierarchy might function in determining, for example, the punishment of misdeeds—and not at all dissimilarly to the way in which such things were done in the broader commonwealth. That is to say, some members of the *collegium* were obviously better than others, despite the fact that they all will have belonged to roughly the same social class. Further, there was clearly a competitive streak to the social interactions of these lesser persons. That emerges in the kind of one-upmanship indicated by the Lanuvian association's attempt to regulate insulting behavior at its dinner parties. It was precisely such abusive behavior that often served to establish the pecking order at an elite banquet (see D'Arms 1990, followed by Peachin 2001). So, this club apparently hoped to establish a less combative tone at its dinner parties. Was the intent also to create a more egalitarian atmosphere? And did that succeed? We cannot know (cf. Dunbabin and Slater in this volume; also Perry). However, we can be confident that the kind of competitive and abusive behavior we are familiar with from elite dinner parties was not foreign to the soirees of these lesser individuals. And finally, the evidence from the countryside beyond the walls of Pompeii shows that we should not be surprised to find what we know from many an urban context cropping up in more rustic settings.

In short, once we begin carefully to observe the world of the Roman have-nots, we find not only that these people lapped up some portion of (say) the elite's literary and/or artistic confections, but that they also apparently had internalized the kind of social mores to which the haves were so plainly devoted. When left to themselves, the Roman underdogs seemingly opted for something along the lines of the dog-eat-dog communal ethos celebrated by Pliny. Thus, it would begin to appear that where the operational principles of social relations are concerned, the Roman world was, from social top to social bottom, and in both town and country, fairly unified in its preferences. Indeed, it might be argued that to internalize the sundry nuances of this taste for an eternal ranking of people was a chief hallmark of being Roman.

One last suggestion is perhaps worth making. It may well be that we should avoid the temptation to presume—despite an understandable inclination to do so, given the preponderance, the intellectual and aesthetic allure, and the unflinchingly assertive tone of our extant elite-produced source materials—that this manner of structuring interpersonal relations was inevitably and entirely devised at the top and imposed from above. It is probably better to accept that the societal dispositions that we suspect colored the entire Roman cosmos may well have been generated in a roughly discursive manner that involved degrees of creativity at both the top and the bottom of the social scale.[56] In short, the formation of the preferences for interpersonal relations that would characterize Roman society is perhaps not to be imagined as an inexorably one-way, top-to-bottom process.[57]

56. I borrow from Keith Hopkins (1993: 138 n. 40), describing the basic thesis of Giddens 1984: "...actors are not simply the passive victims of external pressures, but themselves repeatedly reinterpret conventional social values and mores, and so by their actions reproduce the social order." Cf. also Wallace-Hadrill 2008: 12–13.

57. For a fascinating parallel from the world of literature, where there is exchange back and forth between elite and non-elite realms (and where, n.b., non-elite participants can indeed express some displeasure about their betters), see Ruffell 2003, arguing that (quote at p. 61) "...the tradition of popular verse is a promiscuous, public, uncontrolled, and anti-hierarchical literary form, which both feeds into and draws on contemporary elite poetry."

Let us sum up. We have seen that attempts to define 'society' often suggest that the element most basic to the formation of any such grouping can be understood as involving primarily the interpersonal relations among those who belong to the community. In this book, we examine a variety of interactions that occurred in the ancient these Roman community. It is to be hoped that the interactions we have chosen will be broadly representative of Roman social relations writ large. It has now also been argued in this introduction that the most basic driving force in the world of these Roman social relations involved an intense appetite for ranking people socially, for constantly establishing finely tuned hierarchies. It has furthermore been proposed that this habit infected all the social levels of the Roman community. To the extent that this all holds, then we ought to be very close to the bottom line of Roman society altogether. In other words, to be socially a Roman, and to relate to others in the Roman social fashion, should have involved most essentially a perpetual attempt to establish, as it were, one's social *auctoritas* (influence, authority, prestige, ascendancy, esteem); and for doing that there were particular mechanisms, which could ultimately be comprehended as Roman. Let us now proceed to observe a social world thoroughly informed by this kind of thinking and doing.

BIBLIOGRAPHY

Achard, G. 1991. *La communication à Rome*. Paris: Les Belles Lettres.

Aldrete, G. 1999. *Gestures and Acclamations in Ancient Rome*. Baltimore: Johns Hopkins University Press.

Alföldy, G. 1977. *Konsulat und Senatorenstand unter den Antoninen*. Bonn: Rudolf Habelt Verlag.

———. 1984. *Römische Sozialgeschichte*. 3rd ed. Wiesbaden: Franz Steiner Verlag.

———. 1988. *The Social History of Rome*. Trans. David Braund and Frank Pollock. Baltimore: Johns Hopkins University Press.

———. 1991. "Augustus und die Inschriften: Tradition und Innovation. Die Geburt der imperialen Epigraphik." *Gymnasium. Zeitschrift für Kultur der Antike und humanistische Bildung* 98: 289–324.

———. 2004. "La Cultura epigráfica de los Romanos: la difusión de un medio de comunicación y su papel en la integración cultural." In F. Marco Simón, F. Pina Polo, and J. Remesal Rodríguez (eds.), *Vivir en tierra extraña: emigración e integración cultural en el mundo antiguo. Actas de la reunión realizada en Zaragoza los días 2 y 3 de junio de 2003*. Barcelona: Publicacions Universitat de Barcelona. 137–49.

———. 2005. "Romanisation—Grundbegriff oder Fehlgriff? Überlegungen zum gegenwärtigen Stand der Erforschung von Integrationsprozessen im römischen Weltreich." In Z. Visy (ed.), *Limes XIX. Proceedings of the XIXth International Congress of Roman Frontier Studies held in Pécs, Hungary, September 2003*. Pécs: University of Pécs. 25–56.

Ando, C. 2000. *Imperial Ideology and Provincial Loyalty in the Roman Empire*. Berkeley: University of California Press.

Andreau, J., and C. Virlouvet (eds.). 2002. *L'Information et la mer dans le monde antique*. Rome: Ecole française de Rome.

Angeli Bertinelli, M. G., and A. Donati (eds.). 2008. *La comunicazione nella storia antica. Fantasie e realità. Atti del III incontro internazionale di sotria antica (Genova 23–24 novembre 2006)*. Rome: Bretschneider.

Ariès, P. 1977. *L'Homme devant la mort*. Paris: Éditions du Seuil. English: *The Hour of Our Death*. Trans. H. Weaver. Oxford: Oxford University Press 1991.

Balsdon, J. P. V. D. 1962. *Roman Women. Their History and Habits*. London: Bodley Head.

Bartels, J. 2008. *Städtische Eliten im römischen Madedonien. Untersuchungen zur Formierung und Struktur*. Berlin: Walter de Gruyter.

Barton, T. 1994. *Power and Knowledge. Astrology, Physiognomics, and Medicine under the Roman Empire*. Ann Arbor: University of Michigan Press.

Beard, C., and M. Beard. 1927. *The Rise of American Civilization*. New York: MacMillan Company.

Bell, S., and I. L. Hansen (eds.). 2008. *Role Models in the Roman World. Identity and Assimilation*. Ann Arbor: University of Michigan Press.

Birley, A. R. 2005. *The Roman Government of Britain*. Oxford: Oxford University Press.

Bleckmann, B. 2002. *Die römische Nobilität im Ersten Punischen Krieg. Untersuchungen zur aristokratischen Konkurrenz in der römischen Republik*. Berlin: Akademie Verlag.

Boren, H. C. 1977. *Roman Society. A Social, Economic, and Cultural History*. Lexington, Mass.: D. C. Heath. [A second edition was published in 1992.]

Bowersock, G. 1965. *Augustus and the Greek World*. Oxford: Clarendon Press.

———. 1969. *Greek Sophists in the Roman Empire*. Oxford: Clarendon Press.

———. 1987. "The Mechanics of Subversion in the Roman Provinces." In K. Raaflaub (ed.), *Opposition et résistances à l'Empire d'Auguste à Trajan*. Entretiens sur l'Antiquité classique 33. Geneva: Fondation Hardt. 291–320.

Bradley, K. R. 1989. *Slavery and Rebellion in the Roman World 140–70 BC*. Bloomington: Indiana University Press.

Braudel, F. 1966 [orig. 1949]. *La Méditerranée et le Monde Méditerranéan à l'Epoque de Philippe II*. 2nd ed. Paris: Librairie Armand Colin. English: *The Mediterranean and the Mediterranean World in the Age of Philip II*. Trans. S. Reynolds. New York: Harper & Row. 1972.

Braund, S., and G. Most (eds.). 2003. *Ancient Anger. Perspectives from Homer to Galen*. New York: Cambridge University Press.

Bremmer, J. N., and H. Roodenburg (eds.). 1991. *A Cultural History of Gesture. From Antiquity to the Present Day*. Cambridge: Polity Press.

Brilliant, R. 1963. *Gesture and Rank in Roman Art. The Use of Gestures to Denote Status in Roman Sculpture and Coinage*. New Haven: The Academy.

———. 1984. *Visual Narratives. Storytelling in Etruscan and Roman Art*. Ithaca: Cornell University Press.

———. 2007. "Forwards and Backwards in the Historiography of Roman Art." *Journal of Roman Archaeology*. 20: 7–24.

Broughton, T. R. S. 1951–86. *The Magistrates of the Roman Republic*. Cleveland: The American Philological Association.

Brunner, O., W. Conze, and R. Koselleck. 1972–97. *Geschichtliche Grundbegriffe— Historisches Lexikon zur politisch sozialen Sprache*. Stuttgart: Klett-Cotta.

Burke, P. 2005. *History and Social Theory*. 2nd ed. Ithaca: Cornell University Press.

———. 2008. *What Is Cultural History?* 2nd ed. Cambridge: Polity.

Cairns, D. (ed.). 2005. *Body Language in the Greek and Roman Worlds*. Swansea: Classical Press of Wales.

Calhoun, C. (ed.). 2000. *Dictionary of the Social Sciences*. Oxford: Oxford University Press.

Cameron, A. (ed.). 2003. *Fifty Years of Prosopography. The Later Roman Empire, Byzantium and Beyond*. Oxford: Oxford University Press.

Capdetrey, L., and J. Nelis-Clément (eds.). 2006. *La circulation de l'information dans les états antiques*. Paris: De Boccard.

Carsana, C. 2008. "Gli *altri mondi* nella satira di Luciano." In C. Carsana and M. T. Schettino (eds.), *Utopia e utopie nel pensiero storico antico*. Rome: "L'Erma" di Bretschneider. 177–84.

Cartledge, P. 2002. "What Is Social History Now?" In D. Cannadine (ed.), *What Is History Now?* Houndmills: Palgrave Macmillan. 19–35.

Chastagnol, A. 1975. "*Latus clavus et adlectio*. L'accès des hommes nouveaux au sénat romain sous le Haut-Empire." *Revue historique de droit français et étranger* 53: 375–94.

Clarke, J. R. 2003. *Art in the Lives of Ordinary Romans. Visual Representation and Non-Elite Viewers in Italy, 100 B.C.–A.D. 315*. Berkeley: University of California Press.

––––––. 2007. *Looking at Laughter. Humor, Power, and Transgression in Roman Visual Culture*. Berkeley: University of California Press.

Cleland, L., G. Davies, and L. Llewellyn-Jones. 2007. *Greek and Roman Dress from A to Z*. London: Routledge.

Colburn, C., and M. Heyn (eds.). 2008. *Reading a Dynamic Canvas. Adornment in the Ancient Mediterranean World*. Newcastle: Cambridge Scholars.

Cooley, A. (ed.). 2002. *Becoming Roman, Writing Latin? Literacy and Epigraphy in the Roman West*. Portsmouth, R.I.: Journal of Roman Archaeology.

Corbeill, A. 2003. *Nature Embodied. Gesture in Ancient Rome*. Princeton: Princeton University Press.

Crook, J. A. 1967. *Law and Life of Rome, 90 B.C.–A.D. 212*. Ithaca: Cornell University Press.

D'Arms, J. H. 1981. *Commerce and Social Standing in Ancient Rome*. Cambridge, Mass.: Harvard University Press.

––––––. 1990. "The Roman *convivium* and the Idea of Equality." In O. Murray (ed.), *Sympotica. A Symposium on the Symposion*. Oxford: Clarendon Press. 308–20.

Daube, D. 1972. *Civil Disobedience in Antiquity*. Edinburgh: Edinburgh University Press.

de Ligt, L. 1993. *Fairs and Markets in the Roman Empire. Economic and Social Aspects of Periodic Trade in a Pre-Industrial Society*. Amsterdam: J.C. Gieben.

Dench, E. 2005. *Romulus' Asylum. Roman Identities from the Age of Alexander to the Age of Hadrian*. Oxford: Oxford University Press.

De Ste. Croix, G. E. M. 1981. *The Class Struggle in the Ancient Greek World from the Archaic Age to the Arab Conquests*. London: Duckworth.

Diefenbach, S. 2007. *Römische Erinnerungsräume. Heiligenmemoria und kollektive Identitäten in Rom des 3. bis 5. Jahrhunderts n. Chr*. Berlin: Walter De Gruyter.

Donahue, J. F. 2004. *The Roman Community at Table during the Principate*. Ann Arbor: University of Michigan Press.

Donati, A. 2002. *Epigrafia romana. La communicazione nell'antichità*. Bologne: Il Mulino.

Downey, G. 1961. *A History of Antioch in Syria from Seleucus to the Arab Conquest*. Princeton: Princeton University Press.

Drinkwater, J. F. 1999. Review of León 1996. *Classical Review* 49: 287–88.

Dyson, S. L. 2003. *The Roman Countryside*. London: Duckworth.

Eck, W. 1970. *Senatoren von Vespasian bis Hadrian*. Munich: Verlag C. H. Beck.

–––––– (ed.). 1993. *Prosopographie und Sozialgeschichte. Studien zur Methodik und Erkenntnismöglichkeit der kaiserzeitlichen Prosopographie. Kolloquium Köln 24.–26. November 1991*. Cologne: Böhlau Verlag.

Edmondson, J., and A. Keith (eds.). 2008. *Roman Dress and the Fabrics of Roman Culture.* Toronto: University of Toronto Press.

Elsner, J. 1996. *Art and Text in Roman Culture.* Cambridge: Cambridge University Press.

———. 2007. *Roman Eyes. Visuality and Subjectivity in Art and Text.* Princeton: Princeton University Press.

Evans, J. K. 1980. "*Plebs rustica.* The Peasantry of Classical Italy I." *American Journal of Ancient History* 5: 19–47.

Farney, G. 2007. *Ethnic Identity and Aristocratic Competition in Republican Rome.* Cambridge: Cambridge University Press.

Ferguson, J. 1975. *Utopias of the Classical World.* London: Thames and Hudson.

Finley, M. 1973. *The Ancient Economy.* Berkeley: University of California Press.

———. (ed.). 1974. *Studies in Ancient Society.* London and Boston: Routledge and Kegan Paul.

Flaig, E. 1995. "Die Pompa funebris. Adlige Konkurrenz und annalistische Erinnerung in der Römischen Republik." In O. G. Oexle (ed.), *Memoria als Kultur.* Göttingen: Vandenhoeck & Ruprecht. 115–48.

———. 2003. *Ritualisierte Politik. Zeichen, Gesten und Herrschaft im Alten Rom.* Göttingen: Vandenhoeck & Ruprecht.

Flower, H. I. 1996. *Ancestor Masks and Aristocratic Power in Roman Culture.* Oxford: Clarendon Press.

———. 2006. *The Art of Forgetting. Disgrace and Oblivion in Roman Political Culture.* Chapel Hill: University of North Carolina Press.

Foxhall, L. 2003. "Peasants." In S. Hornblower and A. Spawforth (eds.), *The Oxford Classical Dictionary.* 3rd rev. ed. Oxford: Oxford University Press. 1130.

Frank, T. 1926. Review of Rostovtzeff 1926. *American Journal of Philology* 47: 290–92.

Frayn, J. M. 1993. *Markets and Fairs in Roman Italy. Their Social and Economic Importance from the Second Century BC to the Third Century AD.* Oxford: Clarendon Press.

Friedlaender, L. 1922. *Darstellungen aus der Sittengeschichte Roms in der Zeit von Augustus bis zum Ausgang der Antonine.* 10th ed. Ed. G. Wissowa. Leipzig: S. Hirzel. English: *Roman Life and Manners under the Early Empire.* New York: Barnes & Noble 1965.

Fuchs, H. 1938. *Der geistige Widerstand gegen Rom in der antiken Welt.* Berlin: Walter de Gruyter.

Gabba, E. 1981. "True History and False History in Classical Antiquity." *Journal of Roman Studies* 71: 50–62.

Garnsey, P. 1970. *Social Status and Legal Privilege in the Roman Empire.* Oxford: Clarendon Press.

———. 1988. *Famine and Food Supply in the Graeco-Roman World. Responses to Risk and Crisis.* Cambridge: Cambridge University Press.

Garnsey, P., and R. Saller. 1987. *The Roman Empire. Economy, Society and Culture.* Berkeley: University of California Press.

Gelzer, M. 1912. *Die Nobilität der römischen Republik.* Leipzig: B. G. Teubner. (2nd ed. Stuttgart: B. G. Teubner 1983. English: *The Roman Nobility.* Trans. R. Seager. Oxford: Basil Blackwell 1969.)

Giddens, A. 1984. *The Constitution of Society. Outline of the Theory of Structuration.* Berkeley: University of California Press.

Gleason, M. 1995. *Making Men. Sophists and Self-Presentation in Ancient Rome.* Princeton: Princeton University Press.

Gordon, R. 2004. "Raising a Sceptre: Confession-Narratives from Lydia and Phrygia." *Journal of Roman Archaeology* 17: 177–96.

Gowing, A. 2005. *Empire and Memory. The Representation of the Roman Republic in Imperial Culture.* Cambridge: Cambridge University Press.

Gruen, E. 1992. *Culture and National Identity in Republican Rome*. Ithaca: Cornell University Press.

Gunderson, E. 2000. *Staging Masculinity. The Rhetoric of Performance in the Roman World*. Ann Arbor: University of Michigan Press.

Gutsfeld, A. 1989. *Römische Herrschaft und einheimischer Widerstand in Nordafrika. Militärische Auseinandersetzungen Roms mit den Nomaden*. Stuttgart: Franz Steiner Verlag.

Hales, S. 2003. *The Roman House and Social Identity*. Cambridge: Cambridge University Press.

Harris, W. V. 1979. *War and Imperialism in Republican Rome 327–70 B.C.* Oxford: Clarendon Press.

———. 1988. "On the Applicability of the Concept of Class in Roman History." In T. Yuge and M. Doi (eds.), *Forms of Subordination and Control in Antiquity*. Leiden: E. J. Brill. 598–610.

———. 1989. *Ancient Literacy*. Cambridge, Mass.: Harvard University Press.

———. 2001. *Restraining Rage. The Ideology of Anger Control in Classical Antiquity*. Cambridge, Mass.: Harvard University Press.

——— (ed.). 2005. *Rethinking the Mediterranean*. Oxford: Oxford University Press.

Hedrick, C. W., Jr. 2000. *History and Silence. Purge and Rehabilitation of Memory in Late Antiquity*. Austin: University of Texas Press.

Hingley, R. 2005. *Globalizing Roman Culture. Unity, Diversity and Empire*. London: Routledge.

Hobsbawm, E. J. 1969. *Bandits*. London: Weidenfeld & Nicolson.

———. 1997. *On History*. London: Weidenfeld & Nicolson.

Hölkeskamp, K.-J. 2006a. "History and Collective Memory in the Middle Republic." In N. Rosenstein and R. Morstein-Marx (eds.), *A Companion to the Roman Republic*. Oxford: Oxford University Press. 478–95.

———. 2006b. "Konsens und Konkurrenz. Die politische Kultur der römischen Republik in neuer Sicht." *Klio* 88: 360–96.

Hölscher, T. 1984. *Staatsdenkmal und Publikum. Vom Untergang der Republik bis zur Festigung des Kaisertums in Rom*. Konstanz: Universitätsverlag Konstanz.

———. 1987. *Römische Bildsprache als semantisches System*. Heidelberg: C. Winter. English: *The Language of Images in Roman Art*. Trans. A. Snodgrass and A. Künzl-Snodgrass. Cambridge: Cambridge University Press 2004.

Hopkins, K. 1965. "Élite Mobility in the Roman Empire." *Past & Present* 32: 12–26 = Finley 1974: 103–20.

———. 1978. *Conquerors and Slaves. Sociological Studies in Roman History 1*. Cambridge: Cambridge University Press.

———. 1993. "Novel Evidence for Roman Slavery." *Past & Present* 138: 3–27.

Horden, P., and N. Purcell. 2000. *The Corrupting Sea. A Study of Mediterranean History*. Malden: Blackwell.

Horsfall, N. 2003. *The Culture of the Roman Plebs*. London: Duckworth. Originally: *La cultura della plebs Romana*. Barcelona: Departament Filologia Llatina UB 1996.

Humphrey, J. (ed.). 1991. *Literacy in the Roman World*. Ann Arbor: Journal of Roman Archaeology.

Isaac, B. 2004. *The Invention of Racism in Classical Antiquity*. Princeton: Princeton University Press.

Johnson, W. A., and H. N. Parker (eds.). 2009. *Ancient Literacies. The Culture of Reading in Greece and Rome*. Oxford: Oxford University Press.

Jones, A. H. M. 1940. *The Greek City from Alexander to Justinian*. Oxford: Clarendon Press.

———. 1964. *The Later Roman Empire 284–602. A Social, Economic, and Administrative Survey*. Norman: University of Oklahoma Press.

Jones, C. P. 1971. *Plutarch and Rome*. Oxford: Clarendon Press.

———. 1978. *The Roman World of Dio Chrysostom*. Cambridge, Mass.: Harvard University Press.

———. 1986. *Culture and Society in Lucian*. Cambridge, Mass.: Harvard University Press.

Jory, J. 2008. "The Pantomime Dancer and his Libretto." In E. Hall and R. Wyles (eds.), *New Directions in Ancient Pantomime*. Oxford: Oxford University Press. 157–68.

Kaster, R. 2005. *Emotion, Restraint, and Community in Ancient Rome*. Oxford: Oxford University Press.

Klauser, Th. 1950. "Akklamation." *Reallexikon für Antike und Christentum*. Stuttgart: Verlag Anton Hiersemann. Vol. I, 216–33.

Kneppe, A. 1994. Metus temporum. *Zur Bedeutung von Angst in Politik und Gesellschaft der römischen Kaiserzeit des 1. und 2. Jhdts. n. Chr.* Stuttgart: Franz Steiner Verlag.

Kolb, A. 2000. *Transport und Nachrichtentransfer im Römischen Reich*. Berlin: Akademie Verlag.

Konstan, D. 1997. *Friendship in the Classical World*. Cambridge: Cambridge University Press.

———. 2001. *Pity Transformed*. London: Duckworth.

Kraus, C. S. 2005. "Hair, Hegemony, and Historiography: Caesar's Style and Its Earliest Critics." In T. Reinhardt, M. Lapidge, and J. N. Adams (eds.), *Aspects of the Language of Latin Prose*. Oxford: Oxford University Press. 97–115.

Krause, J.-U. 1992. *Bibliographie zur römischen Sozialgeschichte 1. Die Familie und weitere anthropologische Grundlagen*. Stuttgart: Franz Steiner Verlag.

Krause, J.-U., J. Mylonopoulos, and R. Cengia. 1998. *Bibliographie zur römischen Sozialgeschichte 2. Schichten—Konflikte—religiöse Gruppen—materielle Kultur*. Stuttgart: Franz Steiner Verlag.

Laes, C. 2007. "Inscriptions from Rome and the History of Childhood." In M. Harlow and R. Laurence (eds.), *Age and Ageing in the Roman Empire*. Portsmouth, R.I.: Journal of Roman Archaeology. 25–37.

Last, H. 1926. Review of Rostovtzeff 1926. *Journal of Roman Studies* 16: 120–28.

Laurence, R., and J. Berry (eds.). 1998. *Cultural Identity in the Roman Empire*. London: Routledge.

Leach, E. W. 2004. *The Social Life of Painting in Ancient Rome and on the Bay of Naples*. Cambridge: Cambridge University Press.

Lendon, J. E. 1997. *Empire of Honour. The Art of Government in the Roman World*. Oxford: Clarendon Press.

———. 2005. *Soldiers and Ghosts. A History of Battle in Classical Antiquity*. New Haven: Yale University Press.

León, J. C. S. 1996. *Los Bagaudas: rebeldes, demonios, mártires. Revueltas campesinas en Galia e Hispania durante el Bajo Imperio*. Jaén: Universidad de Jaén.

Lewis, N. 1983. *Life in Egypt under Roman Rule*. Oxford: Clarendon Press.

Lobur, J. A. 2008. Consensus, Concordia, *and the Formation of Roman Imperial Ideology*. London: Routledge.

MacLennan, H. 1968. *Oxyrhynchus. An Economic and Social Study*. Amsterdam: Adolf M. Hakkert.

MacMullen, R. 1970. "Market Days in the Roman Empire." *Phoenix* 24: 331–41.

———. 1974a. *Roman Social Relations 50 B.C. to A.D. 284*. New Haven: Yale University Press.

———. 1974b. "Peasants during the Principate." In *Aufstieg und Niedergang der römischen Welt*. Berlin: Walter de Gruyter. II,1: 253–61.

————. 2000. *Romanization in the Time of Augustus*. New Haven: Yale University Press.

————. 2003. *Feelings in History, Ancient and Modern*. Claremont: Regina Books.

Marincola, J. 2003. "Beyond Pity and Fear: The Emotions of History." *Ancient Society* 33: 285–315.

Marquardt, J. 1886. *Das Privatleben der Römer*. 2nd ed. Leipzig: S. Hirzel. (Reprint, Darmstadt: Wissenschaftliche Buchgesellschaft 1975.)

Mattingly, D. 2002. "Vulgar and weak 'Romanization', or a time for a paradigm shift?" *Journal of Roman Archaeology* 15: 536–40.

————. 2004. "Being Roman: Expressing Identity in a Provincial Setting." *Journal of Roman Archaeology* 17: 5–25.

Mayhew, L. H. 1968. "Society." In Sills 1968: 14, 577–86.

McDonnell, M. 1996. "Writing, Copying, and Autograph Manuscripts in Ancient Rome." *The Classical Quarterly* 2: 469–91.

Millar, F. 1981. "The World of the *Golden Ass*." *Journal of Roman Studies* 71: 63–75 = Millar, F., *Rome, the Greek World, and the East. Volume 2. Government, Society, and Culture in the Roman Empire*. Eds. H. Cotton and G. M. Rogers. Chapel Hill: University of North Carolina Press 2004. 313–35.

Millett, M. 1990. *The Romanization of Britain. An Essay in Archaeological Interpretation*. Cambridge: Cambridge University Press.

Mitchell, S. 1993. *Anatolia. Land, Men, and Gods in Asia Minor*. Oxford: Clarendon Press.

Momigliano, A. 1994. *Studies on Modern Scholarship*. Eds. G. W. Bowersock and T. J. Cornell. Berkeley: University of California Press. Originally: "M.I. Rostovtzeff," *The Cambridge Journal* 7 (1954) 334–46.

Morgan, T. 2007. *Popular Morality in the Early Roman Empire*. Cambridge: Cambridge University Press.

Morley, N. 1996. *Metropolis and Hinterland. The City of Rome and the Italian Economy 200 B.C.–A.D. 200*. Cambridge: Cambridge University Press.

————. 2004. *Theories, Models and Concepts in Ancient History*. London: Routledge.

Morstein-Marx, R. 2004. *Mass Oratory and Political Power in the Late Roman Republic*. Cambridge: Cambridge University Press.

Münzer, F. 1920. *Römische Adelsparteien und Adelsfamilien*. Stuttgart: J. B. Metzler. English: *Roman Aristocratic Parties and Families*. Trans. T. Ridley. Baltimore: Johns Hopkins University Press 1999.

Newbold, R. 2000. "Non-verbal Communication in Suetonius and the *Historia Augusta*. Power, Posture, and Proxemics." *Acta Classica* 43: 101–18.

Nicolet, C. 1966–74. *L'Ordre équestre à l'époque républicaine (312–43 av. J.-C.)*. 2 vols. Paris: E. de Boccard.

————. 1976. *Le métier de citoyen dans la Rome républicaine*. Paris: Editions Gallimard. English: *The World of the Citizen in Republican Rome*. Trans. P. S. Falla. Berkeley: University of California Press 1980.

Noreña, C. Forthcoming. *Imperial Ideals in the Roman West. Representation, Circulation, Power*. Cambridge: Cambridge University Press.

Olson, K. 2008. *Dress and the Roman Woman. Self-Presentation and Society*. London: Routledge.

Osgood, J. 2009. "The Pen and the Sword: Writing and Conquest in Caesar's Gaul." *Classical Antiquity* 28: 328–58.

Parkin, T. G., and A.J. Pomeroy. 2007. *Roman Social History. A Sourcebook*. London: Routledge.

Peachin, M. 2001. "Friendship and Abuse at the Dinner Table." In Peachin, M. (ed.), *Aspects of Friendship in the Graeco-Roman World. Proceedings of a conference held at the Seminar für Alte Geschichte, Heidelberg, on 10–11 June, 2000*. Portsmouth, R.I.: Journal of Roman Archaeology. 137–46.

Peter, U., and S. J. Seidlmayer (eds.). 2006. *Mediengesellschaft Antike? Information und Kommunikation von Alten Ägypten bis Byzanz*. Berlin: Akademie Verlag.

Petersen, L. H. 2006. *The Freedman in Roman Art and Art History*. Cambridge: Cambridge University Press.

Pflaum, H-G. 1950. *Les procurateurs équestres sous le Haut-Empire romain*. Paris: Librairie d'Amérique et d'Orient.

———. 1960. *Les carrières procuratoriennes équestres sous le Haut-Empire romain*. Paris: Imprimerie National.

Pomeroy, S. 1975. *Goddesses, Whores, Wives, and Slaves*. New York: Schocken Books.

Potter, D. S. 1996. "Performance, Power, and Justice in the High Empire." In W. J. Slater (ed.), *Roman Theater and Society*. Ann Arbor: University of Michigan Press. 129–59.

———. (ed.). 2006. *A Companion to the Roman Empire*. Malden: Blackwell.

Purcell, N. 1995. "Literate Games: Roman Urban Society and the Game of *Alea*." *Past & Present* 147: 3–37.

Rawson, B. 2003. *Children and Childhood in Roman Italy*. Oxford: Oxford University Press.

Rawson, E. 1987. "Discrimina Ordinum: the Lex Julia Theatralis." *Papers of the British School at Rome* 55: 83–114.

Revell, L. 2009. *Roman Imperialism and Local Identities*. Cambridge: Cambridge University Press.

Rillinger, R. 1985. "Moderne und zeitgenössische Vorstellungen von der Gesellschaftsordnung der römischen Kaiserzeit." *Saeculum* 36: 299–325.

Roller, M. B. 2006. *Dining Posture in Ancient Rome. Bodies, Values, and Status*. Princeton: Princeton University Press.

Rosenstein, N. 1990. *Imperatores Victi: Military Defeat and Aristocratic Competition in the Middle and Late Republic*. Berkeley: University of California Press.

Rostovtzeff, M. 1926. *The Social and Economic History of the Roman Empire*. Oxford: Clarendon Press.

———. 1931. *Gesellschaft und Wirtschaft im römischen Kaiserreich*. Leipzig: Quelle & Meyer. Repr. Aalen: Scientia-Verlag 1985.

———. 1933. *Storia economica e sociale dell'impero romano*. Trans. G. Sanna. Florence: La Nuova Italia.

———. 1965. *Storia economica e sociale dell'impero romano*. Trans. G. Sanna, and rev. ed. G. De Sanctis. Florence: La Nuova Italia.

———. 1976. *Storia economica e sociale dell'impero romano*. Ed. G. De Sanctis. Florence: La Nuova Italia.

———. 1988. *Histoire économique et sociale de l'Empire Romain*. Trans. O. Demange. Introduction, etc. J. Andreau. Paris: Laffont.

———. 2003. *Storia economica e sociale dell'Impero romano*. Ed. A. Marcone. Milan: Sansoni.

Roth, R. 2007. *Styling Romanisation. Pottery and Society in Central Italy*. Cambridge: Cambridge University Press.

Roueché, C. 1984. "Acclamations in the Later Roman Empire: New Evidence from Aphrodisias." *Journal of Roman Studies* 74: 181–99.

Ruffell, I. A. 2003. "Beyond Satire: Horace, Popular Invective and the Segregation of Literature." *Journal of Roman Studies* 93: 35–65.

Saller, R. P. 1982. *Personal Patronage under the Early Empire*. Cambridge: Cambridge University Press.

Scheidel, W. 2003. "Germs for Rome." In C. Edwards and G. Woolf (eds.), *Rome the Cosmopolis*. Cambridge: Cambridge University Press. 158–76.

Scheidel, W., I. Morris, and R. Saller (eds.). 2007. *The Cambridge Economic History of the Greco-Roman World*. Cambridge: Cambridge University Press.

Scheidel, W., and S. J. Friesen. 2009. "The Size of the Economy and the Distribution of Income in the Roman Empire." *Journal of Roman Studies* 99: 61–91.

Schneider, H. 1976. *Zur Sozial- und Wirtschaftsgeschichte der späten römischen Republik*. Darmstadt: Wissenschaftliche Buchgesellschaft.

———. 1981. *Sozial- und Wirtschaftsgeschichte der römischen Kaiserzeit*. Darmstadt: Wissenschaftliche Buchgesellschaft.

Scholz, P. 2003. "Sullas *commentarii*—eine literarische Rechtfertigung. Zu Wesen und Funktion der autobiographischen Schriften in der späten Römischen Republik." In U. Eigler, U. Gotter, N. Luraghi, and U. Walter (eds.), *Formen römischer Geschichtsschreibung von den Anfängen bis Livius. Gattungen, Autoren, Kontexte*. Darmstadt: Wissenschaftliche Buchgesellschaft. 172–95.

Schörner, G., and D. Sterbenc Erker (eds.). 2008. *Medien religiöser Kommunikation im Imperium Romanum*. Stuttgart: Franz Steiner Verlag.

Scupin, R., and C. R. DeCorse. 1992. *Cultural Anthropology. A Global Perspective*. 6th ed. Englewood Cliffs: Prentice Hall.

Sebesta, J. L., and L. Bonfante (eds.). 1994. *The World of Roman Costume*. Madison: University of Wisconsin Press.

Seligman, E. (ed.). 1930–35. *Encyclopaedia of the Social Sciences*. 15 vols. New York: Macmillan and Free Press.

Shaw, B. D. 1981. "Rural Markets in North Africa and the Political Economy of the Roman Empire." *Antiquités Africaines* 17: 37–83.

———. 1984. "Bandits in the Roman Empire." *Past & Present* 105: 3–52.

———. 1992. "Under Russian Eyes." *Journal of Roman Studies* 82: 216–28.

———. 2001a. "Challenging Braudel: A New Vision of the Mediterranean." *Journal of Roman Archaeology* 14: 419–53.

———. 2001b. "Rebels and Outsiders." In A. K. Bowman, P. Garnsey, and D. Rathbone (eds.), *The Cambridge Ancient History. Vol. XI. The High Empire, A.D. 70–192*. 2nd ed. Cambridge: Cambridge University Press. 361–403.

———. 2005. Review of Isaac 2004 in *Journal of World History* 16: 227–32.

Shelton, J. 1998. *As the Romans Did. A Sourcebook in Roman Social History*. 2nd ed. Oxford: Oxford University Press.

Sherwin-White, A. N. 1939. *The Roman Citizenship*. Oxford: Clarendon Press. (2nd ed. Oxford: Clarendon Press 1973.)

Sills, D. L. (ed.). 1968. *International Encyclopedia of the Social Sciences*. 17 vols. New York: Macmillan and Free Press.

Snowden, F., Jr. 1970. *Blacks in Antiquity*. Cambridge, Mass.: Belknap Press of Harvard University Press.

Stein-Hölkeskamp, E. and K.-J. Hölkeskamp (eds.). 2006. *Erinnerungsorte der Antike. Die römische Welt*. Munich: Verlag C. H. Beck.

Stewart, P. 2003. *Statues in Roman Society. Representation and Response*. Oxford: Oxford University Press.

Sumi, G. S. 2005. *Ceremony and Power. Performing Politics in Rome between Republic and Empire*. Ann Arbor: University of Michigan Press.

Swain, S., and G. R. Boys-Stones (eds.). 2007. *Seeing the Face, Seeing the Soul. Polemon's Physiognomy from Classical Antiquity to Medieval Islam*. Oxford: Oxford University Press.

Syme, R. 1939. *The Roman Revolution*. Oxford: Clarendon Press.

————. 1964. *Sallust*. Berkeley: University of California Press.

————. 1999. *The Provincial at Rome and Rome and the Balkans 80 BC–AD 14*. Ed. A. R. Birley. Exeter: University of Exeter Press.

Thomas, E. 2007. *Monumentality and the Roman Empire. Architecture in the Antonine Age*. Oxford: Oxford University Press.

Thomas, R. 1992. *Literacy and Orality in Ancient Greece*. Cambridge: Cambridge University Press.

Thompson, E. A. 1952. "Peasant Revolts in Late Roman Gaul and Spain." *Past & Present* 2: 11–23. Reprinted in Finley 1974: 304–20.

Thompson, E. P. 1963. *The Making of the English Working Class*. London: Victor Gollancz.

Treggiari, S. 2002. *Roman Social History*. London: Routledge.

Turner, F. 1920. *The Frontier in American History*. New York: H. Holt.

Tybout, R. A. 2001. "Roman Wall Painting and Social Significance." *Journal of Roman Archaeology* 14: 33–56.

Urbainczyk, T. 2008. *Slave Revolts in Antiquity*. Berkeley: University of California Press.

van Dommelen, P., and N. Terrenato (eds.). 2007. *Articulating Local Cultures. Power and Identity under the Expanding Roman Republic*. Portsmouth, R.I.: Journal of Roman Archaeology.

Veyne, P. 1976. *Le pain et le cirque. Sociologie historique d'un pluralisme politique*. Paris: Éditions Seuil. English (abridged): *Bread and Circuses. Historical Sociology and Political Pluralism*. Trans. B. Pearce. London: Penguin 1990.

von Albrecht, M. 1997. *A History of Roman Literature. From Livius Andronicus to Boethius*. Leiden: E. J. Brill.

Wallace-Hadrill, A. 1994. *Houses and Society in Pompeii and Herculaneum*. Princeton: Princeton University Press.

————. 2008. *Rome's Cultural Revolution*. Cambridge: Cambridge University Press.

Warde Fowler, W. 1926. *Social Life at Rome in the Age of Cicero*. New York: MacMillan.

Weaver, P. R. C. 1967. "Social Mobility in the Early Roman Empire. The Evidence of the Imperial Freedmen and Slaves." *Past & Present* 37: 3–20 = Finley 1974: 121–40.

Winterling, A. 2001. "Staat, Gesellschaft und politische Integration in der römischen Kaiserzeit." *Klio* 83: 93–112. English: Winterling, A., *Politics and Society in Imperial Rome*. Malden: Blackwell 2009. 9–33.

Wiseman, T. P. 1971. *New Men in the Roman Senate 139 BC–AD 14*. Oxford: Oxford University Press.

————. 2009. *Remembering the Roman People. Essays on Late-Republican Politics and Literature*. Oxford: Oxford University Press.

Witcher, R. 2005. "The Extended Metropolis: *Urbs, Suburbium* and Population." *Journal of Roman Archaeology* 18: 120–38.

Woolf, G. 1998. *Becoming Roman. The Origins of Provincial Civilization in Gaul*. Cambridge: Cambridge University Press.

Yavetz, Z. 1958. "The Living Conditions of the Urban Plebs in Republican Rome." *Latomus* 17: 500–17.

————. 1969. *Plebs and Princeps*. Oxford: Clarendon Press.

Zanker, P. 1990. *Augustus und die Macht der Bilder*. 2nd ed. Munich: Verlag C. H. Beck. English: *The Power of Images in the Age of Augustus*. Trans. A. Shapiro. Ann Arbor: University of Michigan Press 1988.

CHAPTER 2

....

FROM REPUBLIC TO EMPIRE

....

CLIFFORD ANDO

INTRODUCTION

....

AT meetings of the Roman Senate on January 13 and 16, 27 BC, the grandnephew, later adoptive son of Julius Caesar, laid down the complex of extraordinary political, military, and legal powers he had accrued since Caesar's death. This act brought to an end something like a century of crisis, a sequence of civil wars, whose nature I shall attempt shortly to unpack. In place of the prerogatives he had just relinquished the young Caesar accepted a new name heavy with religious import, Augustus, as well as an agglomeration of powers and offices that could each on its own be described in constitutional language, and in particular as respecting traditional limits on magisterial power and principles of collegiality among office-holders (Dio 53. 17–18, esp. 18. 2). In his *Res Gestae* Augustus described this transaction as follows:

> In my sixth and seventh consulships, after I had extinguished the civil wars,
> having through universal consent mastery in all things, I transferred the
> commonwealth from my power to the discretion of the Senate and People of
> Rome. For this good deed I was named Augustus by decree of the Senate.... After
> this time I excelled all in authority, but I had no more power than the others who
> were my colleagues in office. (Aug. *Anc.* 34)

This settlement was not, of course, final (Badian 1982; Ferrary 2001). As we shall see, it marked rather a first attempt to craft an ideological and legal framework to describe and to justify what rapidly became known as the *statio*, the position of the *princeps* within the persistent anachronism of republican government that Augustus sought at once to preserve, exploit, and transform.[1]

Tacitus made the contrast between the monarchical power of the princeps and the persistence of republican offices a major theme of his *Annals*—under the title of *princeps*, Augustus took unto himself *munia senatus magistratuum legum* (the separate powers of the Senate, magistrates, and laws), even as *eadem magistratuum vocabula* (the titles of magistracies remained the same) (*Ann.* 1. 1. 1, 2. 1 and 3. 7)—and it is thanks in large measure to him that scholarly attention has focused so often on the legal, political, and psychological tensions that issued from individual and collective accommodation to this façade (Gibbon 1994: 1. 388–89). That said, in the perspective of later authors, as well as contemporaneous Greeks, who for various reasons did not share the Romans' need to mask this transformation, the settlement of 27 in itself, and the reign of Augustus more generally, marked the end of the republic and commencement of the principate—a form of government led by a *princeps*, which Greeks did not shy to call monarchy (App. *Praef.* 14. 60 and *Civ.* 1. 24; Dio 53. 17. 1–2, 53. 18. 2; Béranger 1953: 31–40, 55–61).

Described in these terms, the change from republic to principate appears chimerical, at once a vast concentration of power, a momentous shift in sovereignty from the people to a monarch, and yet also a return to an idealized constitutionalism so successful that "the titles of magistracies remained the same." In the light of that contrast between the perception and presentation of merely constitutional realities, the magnitude of the Augustan achievement, whatever it was and whomever it affected, no doubt appears the greater, in response to contemporaries' varied suffering and despair at what went before. Indeed, in a fascinating reading of the *Georgics*, Llewelyn Morgan suggests that precisely such a model of trauma and recovery is thematized by Vergil himself, such that the brilliance and vigor of rebirth in nature corresponds in due measure to the violence it has suffered (Morgan 1999: 105–211). Not that it was easy for contemporaries so to forgive and forget (Gabba 1984; cf. Millar 2002 [1973]: 241–70). One important hurdle that Augustus himself had to overcome was precisely his own role in the savagery worked by the triumvirs in the early 30s BC: the mass slaughter that followed the young Caesar's victory over the republican and Antonian forces at Perusia, for example, was widely described in early imperial literature as encompassing a sacrifice of 300 senators and *equites*

---

1. The first use of *statio* (station) to designate Augustus' position as not an office, but heritable, nonetheless, traces to Augustus himself. Aulus Gellius (15. 7. 3) quotes a letter from Augustus to his grandson Gaius, in the aftermath of the former's sixty-fourth birthday, in which he "beseeches the gods that whatever time is left to me might pass with us all well, the *status* of the *res publica* most fortunate, and you playing the man and succeeding to my *statio.*" On this passage see Béranger 1975: 153–63. *Statio* was no doubt discovered in part because of the quiet identification it achieved between the state and the person of the *princeps*, for *status rei publicae* (the condition of the state) had been a catchphrase of republican politics. See also the *Senatus Consultum de Cn. Pisone patre* l. 129, with Eck, Caballos, and Fernández 1996: 240.

at an altar to Julius Caesar on the Ides of March, nor can there be many documents from antiquity so arrogant or chilling as the triumviral edict that prefaced the list of those proscribed.[2]

Tacitus himself suggests Augustus' contemporaries felt upon his death that there had been "no other remedy for their strife-torn state than that it should be ruled by one; and so, the *res publica* was established as neither a kingship nor dictatorship, but under the title of *princeps*" (*Ann*. 1. 9. 4–5).[3] In his argument, quiescence in the face of this revolution had appealed to, or was purchased from, the soldiery, the people, and the nobility, each of which had its price; nor did the provinces object, the rulership of the Senate and People having become suspect because of the strife of dynasts and greed of magistrates (*Ann*. 1. 2). The assessment of Velleius Paterculus, writing under Tiberius and hence closer to the time than Tacitus, reflects a more profound sense of relief at the return not of constitutional normalcy, but social order writ large:

> The civil wars were ended after twenty years, foreign wars were buried; peace restored; the madness of arms everywhere put to rest. Strength was returned to the laws; authority to the law courts; dignity to the Senate. The power of magistracies was constrained to its ancient limits, excepting only that two more praetors were added to the former eight. The hallowed and ancient form of the Republic was restored. Cultivation came back to the fields; honor to religious rites; and safety and security to all people in their persons and their property. (Vell. 2. 89. 3–4)

And yet, momentous as were the events they describe, enduring as are their themes, little about these assessments can in itself justify the significance accorded the Augustan settlement in histories of the ancient world. It would seem to require a profound and unwise fetishization of constitutional arrangements to name it a revolution, or to hang upon it any such periodization as might suggest that a new world came into being with the passage of Rome from republic to principate, or empire.

In framing a set of questions about the meaning and social-historical import of that passage, it helps to remember that 'republic' and 'empire' are terms of art in quite distinct registers of political thought, and that Rome embarked upon the systematic subjugation of its neighbors already in the fifth century BC. Rome thus had, rather than was, an empire some centuries before the arrival of Augustus on the

2. Suetonius (*Aug*. 15) explicitly declines to credit the report (*scribunt quidam*—certain people write). See also Vell. 2. 74. 4 (assigning blame to Caesar's soldiers rather than to Caesar himself); Sen. *Clem*. 1. 11. 1 (speaking of *Perusinae arae*—the Perusine altars); Dio 48. 14. 4, who also declines to credit or refute the transformation of the slaughter into a sacrifice. The triumviral edict: App. *Civ*. 4. 31–44, with Henderson 1998: 11–36.

3. 'Principate' is a fine example of the delay between political invention (in this case, a new office, together with a new use for the term 'princeps'), on the one hand, and the psychological accommodation and conceptual work needed to derive an abstraction from it and thereby to naturalize it, on the other.

throne.[4] In narrating the history of Rome and its empire, particularly in Italy and the west, we necessarily rely heavily on Roman sources, but we should beware following the Romans in privileging events at Rome, narrated by Romans, in charting broader patterns of social-historical study in the ancient Mediterranean. As social historians, our interpretive position exists in a continual tension between the information we wish to discover and the stories that our literary sources in particular overtly tell.

For example, when identifying turning points in history the Romans' own practice not surprisingly often privileged events and experiences that victims of Roman violence would have deemed negligible. Hence, Cicero claimed that Rome's imperial expansion commenced only with the annexation of Sicily as a province in 241 BC, and not with the colonization or appropriation of land in peninsular Italy: "for Sicily was the first of all foreign nations to place itself in the friendship and trust of the Roman people; Sicily was the first province to be so named, an ornament, as it were, of empire; Sicily it was who taught our ancestors how outstanding a thing it is to exercise imperial power over a foreign race" (2 *Verr.* 2. 2). The question whether we should follow Cicero in so privileging public-law arrangements, and more particularly those imposed by a conquering power, is at the very least an open one. It may be that the municipalities of Italy, forced into a notionally defensive alliance with Rome and robbed of their autonomy in foreign affairs, did not chafe under the yoke earlier as they would later, and no doubt their experiences as allies were qualitatively different than those of the subject cities of Sicily. This is so regardless of whether we credit service by allied Italians alongside Roman citizens on military campaigns as having contributed in any way to political and cultural integration (Jehne 2006), and likewise credible even apart from the interested glosses placed on the history of Italian-Roman relations already in the principate (on which see Mouritsen 2006). We should nevertheless be cautious of writing colonial histories in the language and perspective of the metropole. The Etruscans or the Samnites, say, might have answered differently than did the Romans, had they been asked whether Rome began its pursuit of dominion only with Sicily.

The division of Roman history into periods denominated 'republic' and 'empire' thus cuts across multiple systems of analysis, and demands sustained interrogation. On the one hand, it effaces the history of the victims of Roman imperialism even as the Romans understood it: it would not be false to say that outside of specialist literature, the story of Roman conquest is told as a Roman story, and belongs to narratives of the republic, while the history of the conquered lands and peoples—which is to say, histories that embrace provincials—belong to narratives of the empire or, rather, the principate. Such a division likewise collaborates with a certain modern

---

4. I follow here a distinction that Charles Maier (2006: 5–6) adopts from Geoffrey Hosking: states that *are* empires rule all or much of their territory according to a single authoritarian regime; states that *have* empires rule subject territories by such a regime, but are internally organized according to democratic, republican, or representative systems.

reluctance to associate democracy and imperial ambition, as though only emperors might have empires.

To do the converse—to study the Roman Republic as an imperial state—is to invite inter alia the question whether the end of the republic was not an effect of empire, rather than the birth of one. This was, as we shall see, a traditional question. Adopting a different perspective, we might ask, "What sort of revolution was the Roman revolution?" What changed, and whom did those changes affect?[5] Addressing those questions requires reflection on several problems of theory and method. Most particularly, we shall have to ask what kinds of history it is possible to write in the evidentiary regime obtaining in ancient history, and how far warfare writ small, and the history of government writ large, affected broader micro- and macro-regional patterns in social and economic conduct—affected life—across the vast and vastly variegated landscapes of the Mediterranean world.[6]

It is, of course, one object of this volume as a whole to frame and to answer precisely these and many other questions. The aim of this chapter is therefore rather more narrow. Using a variety of models for politics and political subjectivity, I seek to provide a framework within which to ask in what sense the change from republic to principate constituted a social-historical event, in Rome, Italy, and the Mediterranean at large. The answer even to that narrower question depends, of course, in part on how widely one casts one's net, both perspectively and chronologically. My own story, for reasons I hope in due course to clarify, begins in the late second century BC and terminates in AD 212, when the emperor Caracalla granted Roman citizenship to virtually all free-born residents of the empire. By the stroke of his pen, the history of social relations in the Roman world, as they are mediated by the institutions of public and private law, changed once again, but that history lies outside the scope of this work.[7]

In what follows, I turn first to perhaps the most robust and capacious ancient attempt to diagnose the ills of the Roman Republic, namely that associated by the imperial Greek historian Appian with the cause of Tiberius and Gaius Gracchus ("Ancient Perspectives"). I then examine understandings of the crisis of the late republic developed under the principate, with two aims pursued in counterpoint: to set these understandings against modern social-theoretical perspectives on the distribution of power in Roman society, the better to understand the crisis itself; and to see what light those understandings shed on the foundation of the principate itself ("Looking Forward"). Even as they wrestled with evidence and reduced it to narrative or deployed it in argument, scholars in the early principate also worked to make sense of their own society, and the stories they told of even the remote past were necessarily interested ones, and they should be read in that light, too. I turn last to the early principate, when, I argue, the histories of politics and power, and

5. For a helpful formulation of a similar set of questions see Wallace-Hadrill 1997.

6. Millar 2002 (1984): 215–37; Shaw 2000; Horden and Purcell 2000; Shaw 2001.

7. For two distinct perspectives on the background and effects of the Antonine constitution, see Ando Forthcoming a, chapter 5.

particularly of the institutions through which these were articulated in Rome and the provinces, converged, and new forms of subjectivity and new expressions of political engagement came into being ("Empire as Political Form"). I argue, too, that these can, up to a point, be understood as effects of the solution wrought at Rome to the failure of the republic, as it was by them perceived and withal addressed.

Overall my argument runs as follows. A number of factors converged in the late republic to produce crises on multiple levels. Many were effects of empire, which is to say, they were created or exacerbated by the rapid distortion of prior understandings of the appropriate distribution of wealth in society and the role of wealth in politics brought about by the vast conquests undertaken across the last century of the republic. Relations between Rome and its Italian allies were deeply implicated in these processes. Many of these difficulties were, in fact, diagnosed in antiquity, but the solutions then crafted were either insufficient or themselves produced further strain.[8] In particular, the extension of citizenship to all Italy threatened the legitimacy of the political system itself, if only because of a patent unwillingness on the part of Romans at Rome to devise mechanisms to permit the meaningful exercise of the franchise by those new citizens. What did it solve to grant the Italians citizenship, if one crafted no mechanism to permit them to vote? At the same time, no gloss of cultural homogeneity or unarticulated convergence of class interest between municipal and Roman elites, such as undoubtedly existed by the late first century BC (Galsterer 2006), could overcome the economic and pragmatic difficulties that prevented local Italian elites from entering the world of Roman aristocratic competition in meaningful numbers.[9] A discrepancy thus yawned, waiting to be perceived, between the varied outcomes of the Social War in law and their realization in politics. This threat was ultimately defused only through the evacuation of meaning from the institutions of republican government in the early principate.

At the same time, we should beware indicting the Romans, or the republican system itself, for insufficient adherence to constitutional propriety, as though the republic might have survived, if the Romans had only hewed more closely to the letter and spirit of their own laws. Such laws, frankly, did not exist. Institutional fluidity, rather, was the true hallmark of Roman republican government, and it was this aspect that was widely theorized in the final decades of the republic, and which in many respects paved the way for the virtuoso institutional and legislative improvisations that created the principate.

In part because the civil wars had distracted Rome from the work of pacification and acculturation in newly conquered territories, the Augustan age had

---

8. This incapacity in itself is a major subject of Meier 1966.

9. One route to understanding the nature and magnitude of these difficulties lies in comparing the economic and demographic situation of Rome with those of other cities: pressures of demand so corrupted the local real estate market (itself already peculiar: Frier 1980) as to produce in the environs of Rome a quite distinct mode of production, concentrating, e.g., on luxury vegetables, and relying on economic and political power to bring staples to the city: Purcell 1987b; Morley 1996.

scope—and, as it happens, ambition and ability—to accomplish an extraordinary systematization of practice in matters of law and administration throughout the empire. This required a proportionately deeper penetration into provincial life by institutions of Roman government than had theretofore occurred, and awareness and appreciation of forms of Roman cultural production rapidly followed.

Two controversial indices of social change in the provinces are the spread of citizenship and the cooptation of provincials into the imperial governing class (Shaw 2000: 362–73). Another important aspect of imperial social history, one less often discussed, describes the gradual reduction of Italy to the form of a province. How far we credit these indices depends in part, of course, on the role we assign to institutions of government in antiquity in the formation of subjectivity. This is very precisely a problem of social theory. The cogency of these indices in social-historical analysis appears the greater when their stories are told together, and in particular when regarded in light the crises of the late republic. Even as Roman citizenship was used more and more broadly as both inducement to and reward for allegiance and acculturation, its embeddedness in an increasingly anachronistic public-law framework of republican constitutionalism gradually evacuated it of meaning. That is to say, in both formal status and actual rights before the law, Italians and provincials were converging. At the same time, as it had failed to extend the institutions of republican government to the residents of Italy so as to render their citizenship meaningful, so the Roman state of the early principate could conceive the vitality of local communities only through the paradigmatic framework of Roman public law itself. It therefore encouraged the development of institutional frameworks to guide political, social, and economic conduct at the local level through the de facto and, up to a point, de jure creation of purely local *res publicae*. Whatever hope the increasingly attenuated Roman citizenship might have had for uniting the empire was thus counter-balanced by the simultaneous tessalation of the emergent state into multiple republics. This was a problem for which the Romans developed no answer (cf. Ando 2009).

THE CRISIS OF THE REPUBLIC:
ANCIENT PERSPECTIVES

The language deployed by Tacitus, that monarchy was felt by Romans to be the only "remedy for their strife-torn state," reflects a perception that the social and political ills of the late republic were systemic, and that their solution had, in fact, lain in the censorious power of the state. That is to say, the post eventum critiques of the republic mounted under the principate were largely immanent rather than rejectionist in orientation. On this view, excessive competition and corruption in the political elite, as well as failures of allegiance among citizen-soldiers, were found to be sufficient causes of the crises of the late republic, and their restraint under the early principate, in ways I shall explore below, held likewise adequate, if not ideal (Syme 1986: 439–54, a simply remarkable essay; see also Syme 1979: 205–17; Brunt 1988: 2–12; Gowing 2005). What was not generally imagined was any need for a thorough-going revision of either the interrelated systems for distributing political, economic, or cultural capital at a domestic level, or, more spectacularly, the project of empire as a whole. These were in fact canvassed, often in rather limited conceptualizations, but only in one significant respect undertaken, namely, the extension of citizenship to Italy in the aftermath of the Social War. But this was done ultimately at the point of a gun, as it were, and itself contributed to further crises in the nature of citizenship and conduct of politics as a whole, which were themselves resolved only in and through the principate.

In so assessing Roman understandings of late republic, I do not mean to imply that their diagnoses were either sufficient or full or, conversely, that they were wrong. I want rather to raise three problems, to each of which I shall ultimately return. First, the Romans had specific understandings of the relationship between politics, economics, and social order, of political subjectivity, and of the distinct roles played by public and private structures in the socialization of citizens— understandings that are not ours—and these underlie not simply Roman analyses of their society, but also their perception and accounts of the world. Second, these understandings condition at every turn the information that ancient historical narrative provides (Pocock 1996: 3–8), and it is an enduring challenge of ancient history more generally, and of social history in particular, to devise hermeneutic strategies or locate non-textual sources that might enable ancient evidence to answer our questions. This is not to say, of course, that complex and far-reaching political actions were not taken in the ancient world on the basis of partial or even incorrect apprehensions of socio-economic realities, or that such actions did not bring new realities into existence. Nor am I urging only that we practice social history and they did not, a simple enough statement and perhaps in a narrow formulation even a true one. I urge, rather, that Roman intellectuals, too, developed forms of social theory, and that these informed both political and historiographic practice (Moatti 1997; cf. Ando 2008b: chapter 4; Ando, forthcoming a). They therefore impinge upon our projects of historical understanding at several junctures.

Third, most simply but at this juncture most crucially, such social-theoretical awareness was itself hard-won, and alongside it survive multiple forms of testimony from the late republic that view specific incidents of violence, corruption, or even evidence of profound economic difficulty as both narrowly contingent and causally isolable. These leave us with the task of reconciling sources, both those of the late republic, one with another, and them with those of the principate. The last named also understandably display very considerable investment in shoring up the structural solutions to the late republican crisis enacted by the principate. The stories Romans told, and the diagnoses they gave, of the failure of their state and culture are thus multiply interested and difficult to disentangle.

So, for example, in an *elogium* inscribed below a portrait of Marius at Arretium, he is described as having delivered the state, the *rem publicam*, when it was distressed by sedition and the Capitol had been seized by armed men (in his sixth consulship, in 100 BC), and likewise as having been expelled *per arma civilia* (through the violence of citizens) and later restored, likewise by arms, in his seventh consulship (86 BC) (*ILS* 59). The matter-of-fact account is symptomatic of the naturalization of violence in the landscape of late republican politics, but that naturalization took place against a background in which violence was understood as a part of politics and not as an expression of a wider, deeper social ill. On another level, some years after what we call the "Social War," it remained possible for the Romans, following their practice, to name that struggle after one of their opponents in it—as the *Bellum Marsicum*, the War against the Marsi, for example (Hor. *Carm.* 3. 14. 14–20; Strabo 5. 4. 2)—and in so doing, to avoid naming it after its type, namely, a *bellum cum sociis*, a war against one's allies. The emergence of the term *bellum sociale* (social war) to denominate *the* Allied War of 90–88 BC (Plin. *Nat.* 3. 70; Flor. *Epit.* 2. 6. 1) then required a renaming of the general category from *sociale* to *internum* (domestic), to sit alongside *gentile, servile,* and *civile* (wars with foreign races, slaves, and civil wars, respectively; Amp. 41. 1). The refusal to confront the moral and political grievances at the heart of the Social War—a refusal enabled by the scapegoating implicit in the act of naming—did ultimately yield to social-historical reflection on the causes of that war, but it was the work of generations (Ando 2002b).

Where the civil wars are concerned, it remained possible for Romans of later generations to enumerate them individually. According to Servius, for example, Augustus alone fought five: against Antony at Mutina; against Lucius Antonius at Perusia; against Sextus Pompey; against Brutus and Cassius; and against Antony and Cleopatra (Serv. *ad Georg.* 4. 13, but cf. *ad Aen.* 6. 832, on *adsuescite bella,* where he names seven, three fought by Caesar and four by Augustus, omitting Mutina). But Servius also recognizes Vergil's anxiety that the Romans were growing "accustomed" and so inured to civil strife, and for his part Servius understands Vergil to have shied from Horace's pessimism of the 30s and early 20s that the civil wars were not simply continuous, one with another, but also grown endemic (Serv. *ad Ecl.* 4.31; Hor. *Epod.* 7, *Carm.* 1. 2). It was a kindred despair, of both situation and solution, that provoked from Gaius Matius his famous lament following the death of Caesar, "If Caesar, for all his genius, could not find an *exitum* (a way out), who will find one now?" (Cic. *Att.* 355. 1, Shackleton Bailey). It was the work of later generations, operating through hindsight, to assimilate the allied and civil wars, assign them an order and hence a beginning, and grant them a cause (App. *Civ.* 1. 1–25, esp. 4; Flor. *Epit.* 1. 47, esp. 7ff., drawing on moralizing themes already visible in Sall. *Cat.* 10–11 and Liv. *praef.* 9).

Contemporaries of the late republic faced another obstacle in the perception of their society's ills as systemic rather than contingent, and it was largely of their own devising: constant change. I refer not simply to changes the Romans set in motion through traditional forms of political action, nor of indirect effects of actions that were themselves deliberate, such as the conquest of new territories or the influx of goods and people that occurred as Rome became more and more central to an increasingly sophisticated command economy. The Romans also themselves undertook complex and far-reaching adjustments to the public practices and normative codes that structured social and political conduct as they understood it. In other words, they proposed, debated, and enacted solutions to a wide range of contemporary problems, variously diagnosed. What is more, and archetypally Roman, even this activity could be described as thoroughly traditional. As Cicero said in his speech urging the passage of the Manilian law, granting an extraordinary command to Pompey in 66 BC: "I am also urged that nothing new should be done contrary to the precedents and practices of our ancestors. I will not bother to point out here that our ancestors obeyed custom in times of peace, but necessity in times of war, always developing new plans and policies to meet the new crises of the day" (Cic. *Man.* 60). In other words, according to Cicero, nothing was so in keeping with the "precedents and practices of our ancestors" as constant innovation. Nor was Cicero alone in so manipulating the data of history. Faced with constant change in culture and politics, Romans generally domesticated novelty by retrojecting the new into the past and so couched innovation as the recuperation of some ancient practice long in abeyance. One important result was the loss to Romans of any capacity to imagine the archaic Roman community as anything other than a classical city; this was so, despite the Romans' deep interest in understanding historical change as incremental and the production of their own state institutions as accomplished through human experimentation.

Perhaps the most perceptive, and certainly the most robust, analyses of the ills of the middle and late republic are those embedded in narratives of the Gracchan land reforms, of which that by Appian is far the fullest extant. For Appian, those reforms, and the political upheaval they impelled, marked the beginning of the civil wars, the problem being that the wealth acquired by empire so distorted the economic basis of political and social relations in Italy as to upend the fragile social consensus that had sustained its acquisition. Appian therefore opens his narrative of the civil wars by reflecting on the multiple purposes of colonization, which process he understood to lie at the heart of Roman-Italian relations:

> As they gained control over Italy through warfare, bit by bit, the Romans either seized part of the land and founded cities or chose settlers from among their own people to send into preexisting ones. They devised these alternatives instead of garrisons. Of the land that became theirs by conquest on each occasion, they distributed the cultivated area immediately to settlers, or sold or leased it. The land that lay fallow because of war, which was very abundant and which they did not have the leisure to distribute, they announced could be worked by whosoever wished for a share of the annual harvest, being one tenth of sown crops or one fifth of orchard-grown fruits. Rents were also established for those pasturing larger and smaller animals. They did these things with an eye toward the propagation of the peoples of Italy, believing them to possess exceptional endurance, so that they might have them as kin and allies in war. (App. *Civ.* 1. 26–28)

At a fundamental level, Appian represents colonization and urbanization in the sec-ond century BC as producing three things: security, wealth, and manpower. This understanding developed from arguments elaborated in the Gracchan period, and it is to an analysis derived from partisans of the tribune that Appian turns next, delivered first through indirect speech and attributed to the Roman people, and next in an oration of Tiberius Gracchus himself. This analysis consists in a dou-ble insight: first, conquest acquires land, upon which the stock of Italy settles and expands; the legions thus replenished engage in further conquests; and the end must be either the subjugation of the world through sheer fertility, or the loss of all they had theretofore acquired, through weakness (App. *Civ.* 1. 45); second, the wealthy made disproportionate use of undistributed land—what Appian above calls "land that lay fallow"—and devised for their estates systems of exploitation that relied increasingly on slave labor; buttressed by the fruits of empire, the wealthy drove the poor from the land, while their slaves filled the demand for labor by which the poor might otherwise have been sustained; thus did the pursuit of empire turn inward upon its agents and its seat.

This understanding of Roman travails in the late second century BC has been remarkably influential (Pocock 2003). Indeed, two of the finest works of Roman history of the twentieth century sought in quite different ways to substantiate it (Toynbee 1965; Brunt 1987 [1971]; see also Tibiletti 1950). In its articulation by Livy, who transposes many of its themes in anachronistic form into his history of the early Republic, it also provoked searching reflection among early modern repub-licans, especially Leonardo Bruni and Niccolò Machiavelli, who added to ancient analyses one crucial component. Roman historians largely understood the actions of individual republican politicians that they deemed harmful to the republic as expressions of moral corruption, lodged necessarily in individuals but brought home to the citizenry at large through twin psychological pressures generated by success, namely, the removal of an enemy that Rome might fear, on the one hand, and the corrosive effects of luxury on the other. For Bruni, and particularly for Machiavelli, the problem was thus aristocratic competition itself: service and lead-ership in war were, after all, preeminent expressions of virtue for the republican citizen and aristocrat, respectively. But the success in war that republics demand of their leaders generated at Rome wealth that ultimately worked to dispossess the populations who carried their arms.

Bruni and Machiavelli thus help us to see beneath the Gracchan analysis three social-theoretical postulates that widely informed Roman diagnoses of the later republic and its troubles. First, citizens were both soldiers and heads of household. In the latter capacity they were both economic agents and producers of children, and for both those activities it was widely felt that citizens ideally should be owners of land. The connection between land and citizen identity was both ancient and long-lived, nor was it, in the prevailing economic regime, a merely political fan-tasy. And though Roman law envisaged other routes to citizenship—some tied, like manumission, to households as instruments of socialization—the full realization of citizenship by individuals relied ultimately on their intimate relation to the Roman soil (see, e.g., [Sallust], *Ep. AD Caes.* 2. 5; Ando 2008b). Second, wealth was an index that helped the community to distinguish the appropriate kinds and quantities of service that might be assessed upon individuals; it likewise determined, up to a point, the voice that individuals had in the political arena. However, as economic misfortune was ruled out as a basis for depriving citizens of freedom, so it was felt, however inchoately, that wealth could be so distributed as to corrupt the political process, whether by effectively disenfranchising the poor or rendering meaningful competition impossible. This was, as much as anything, a theoretical elaboration of late republican theories of popular sovereignty, which held the citizen body sovereign within the state. But should not then all citizens, qua holders of citizenship, be at least in some respects equal? (The question became moot before ever it was resolved.) Third, the practice of politics, meaning in particular both elections and legislation, involved deliberation, persuasion, and voting. Their conduct had unavoidable practical components whose resolution was the more difficult, the more far-flung the Roman community became. Nor were the practical obstacles the only ones. But for republican citizenship meaningfully to endure as something more than a vessel of civil law rights and civic obligations, those difficulties would have to be surmounted.

Looking Forward to Look Back, and Vice Versa: Constitutionalism, Sovereignty, and Elite Power from Republic to Principate

The Romans faced one very considerable hurdle in analyzing the structural woes of their state and, to the extent that modern historians rely on ancient textual evidence and the percipience that informs it, that hurdle stands for us, too. This was, and is, sheer human mobility: the massive and ever increasing circulation of Romans to Italy and the provinces, and of provincials and Italians to Rome, that was perhaps the principal effect of empire (Scheidel 2004, 2005, 2006). This had important and interconnected effects in the labor market, in political culture, and political life. The movement of some million or more Italians from the countryside to cities, and many of those to Rome, was itself partly motivated by the importation to Italy of some two to four million slaves over the last two centuries of the republic. The destabilization of the political process that this movement occasioned found expression above all in the demand that the revenues of empire should be used to restore some measure of economic and demographic stability, of whatever form (Millar 2002 [1986]: 143–61). The result of these pressures on social life was thus not an understanding, let alone a critique, of the causal role played by empire in producing instability and upheaval, as they were perceived, but the demand that empire be made to assuage them. Within the parameters of Roman aristocratic competition, this proved fatal to the republic.

In point of fact, Romans had an embryonic awareness of some of these factors—of changes to the labor market, to fertility, and to the contribution to the aggregate population made by slaves and free, immigrants and citizen—but they did not develop the institutional means or statistical tools to assess those changes in a meaningful fashion until precisely the last decades of the late republic, if not a bit later (see for now Ando 2006: 183–88; cf. Ando, forthcoming a: chapter 3), by which time the context could no longer sustain reasoned debate on problems so complex, and it is in any event unclear whether the Romans could have devised a program to address them.

Nor did this sophistication, largely developed and deployed within branches of government, ever penetrate the models of state formation deployed in ancient historiography. There, one finds instead a staggering uninterest in the aggregate effects of migrations, which are presented in narrative as atomized, contingent events, combined with wholly unrealistic assumptions of demographic stasis at the level of the household. This emerges with particular relevance to my own story in ancient accounts of the creation and consolidation of the Roman political elite. The story the Romans came to tell about this process concentrated in no way on the horizontal migration of political elites across communities in the archaic period, say, nor on the difficulty of a patrician elite in the proto-classical city to reproduce itself across generations, or that of a plebeian family similarly to sustain its wealth and privilege. Rather, the tale they came to tell by the age of Cicero, which is firmly entrenched in Livy, has two axes: on the one hand, the opening up of offices to plebeians (the existence of two separate orders, patrician and plebeian, being taken for granted), and the elaboration of a legal superstructure ranking those offices and articulating their powers on the other.[10]

The body of material attesting this narrative is, of course, interesting for what it does not say—that the cooptation of plebeians into what had been an aristocracy of birth attests the growing influence of class interest in the fifth century BC, but this cooptation must have been expressed in daily life and political speech not as a convergence of interests, but through competition for symbolic capital, itself increasingly a function of wealth rather than inherited prestige. Notional competition, however narrow its terms, more easily hegemonizes debate than does mere harmony. At Rome, this competition so dominated public life that the narrow interests of the socio-economic elite, and above all the publicly articulated values that guided competition within it, came to be civic values, to be exercised by the mere citizen only in derivative form, as soldier, say, rather than leader. On this understanding the function of Roman voters might be said to have been the granting of honor, power, and opportunity for further self-aggrandizement to successful competitors among

---

10. Hölkeskamp 1987; Beck 2005: 9–113; Cornell 2005; and Develin 2005 provide quite different perspectives on the quality and interpretation of our sources on the consolidation (such as it was) of an aristocracy at Rome in the fourth and third centuries.

the elite, who fought on terms set by themselves in their own self-interest, but which had been successfully universalized and naturalized over generations (Meier 1966: 45–63; Gordon 1990; Hölkeskamp 2004: 73–105). The result was a fundamental incapacity of the Roman political imagination, or of Roman political language, to conceive and then to articulate meaningful reform. The differing crises of the late republic—under the Gracchi, Saturninus, Marius, Sulla, Pompey, and Caesar (and it is significant that we associate them with individuals; as Cicero remarked to Atticus, the dynasts contended not over policy, but "each for his own power, to the peril of the state" [*Att.* 126. 4, Shackleton Bailey])[11]—which we might diagnose as reflecting the inability of Roman civic institutions, still largely those of an ancient city-state, to contain the distortionate effects of magnitude and wealth—were thus addressed by the Romans through merely incremental reform: the reduplication of magistracies, the institution of momentary checks on career advancement, the institution and adaptation of courts as a further venue for competition, or the settlement of people on the land (but the land must come from somewhere). In other words, more (or less) of the same.[12]

Accounts from the late republic and early principate of the consolidation of Rome's socio-economic elite and its monopolization of political power are also interesting for what they do say, and in particular for how they understand that process of consolidation to have occurred. For the story they chose above all to tell, and which therefore emerges most clearly from our sources, situates this history within a framework of constitutional or public law, what the Romans would call *ius publicum*. It might therefore be rehearsed as a history of laws, whether normative like the *lex Villia annalis* of 180 BC, which established age qualifications for individual magistracies (Liv. 40. 44. 1), or contingent, like the comitial and curiate enactments that endowed particular individuals, however selected, with *imperium*, the power to command Roman citizens (Kunkel 1995: 21–28, 96–103).

Within that framework two issues were very broadly understood to be at stake. On the one hand, the interest of the people in subordinating aristocratic ambition to the common good, and the interest of the elite in restraining class-destructive competition and constraining particular individuals, occasionally converged, and laws were produced and norms articulated on topics so diverse as the placing of geographic limits on the exercise of magisterial power, or the right of generals to hold triumphs, or the distinguishing between a magistrate's acting in his public or private capacity in the founding of a cult. But these laws were also understood even then as staking out positions on the situation of sovereignty within the state, and within that framework the movement of both legislative action and popular constitutionalism from the mid-second century BC on was firmly in the direction of a radical popular sovereignty. This is expressed in at least two quite distinct fashions, through the insistence that in general and in particular no actions could be binding

---

11. Ungern-Sternberg 2004 provides a brief history.

12. Brunt 1988: 68–81, perhaps agreeing more closely with Meier 1966 than Brunt did in his review in 1968 (*Journal of Roman Studies* 58: 229–32).

on the *populus* (the state figured as citizen body) that were taken *iniussu populi* (without the people's command), or through the elaboration of legal language that described election as the transfer by the people *ei et in eum omne suum imperium et potestatem*, "to and into [the magistrate] of all its power of command and control of force" (Ulp. *Inst.* bk. 1 frag. 1916 = *Dig.* 1. 4. 1 *pr.*).[13]

This mode of understanding the history and the failure of the republic has many flaws, and I shall shortly discuss some of the most salient of those. But it had one very great virtue for the Romans, and that is that it enabled them to understand the history of their community from the early second century BC, if not before, straight through to the principate within a single interpretive framework. This is not to say that they understood that history as continuous, for while the doctrine of popular sovereignty might stand as explanation for certain forms of structural change, not least by domesticating them to a Roman story rather than casting them as responses to foreign contingency, it clearly could also stand as an indictment of the *populus* itself.

Take, for example, the language used by Ulpian to describe the transfer of power effected by *leges de imperio* (legislative grants of magisterial power).[14] On the understanding to which he gives final articulation there was no such thing as an "extraordinary" command; the term (or phrase: Latin *extra ordinem*[15]) has meaning only by reference to custom. For as it lay within the discretion of the people to restrict grants of *imperium* to some particular sphere of responsibility, so surely it lay within the people's discretion *not* so to restrict them. Hence, Augustus could (correctly) describe the triumvirate as the result of the *populus* having "created" him as *triumvir rei publicae constituendae* (one of the board of three for organizing the state), an action we know from Appian to have occurred *stricto sensu* not by election as such, but through plebiscite, a *lex* proposed by the tribune Publius Titius; and it is from the contemporaneous *Fasti Colotiani* that we know the *lex Titia* to have been

13. On the sovereignty of the people at Rome see Millar 2002 [1988]: 352–54; idem 2002 [1995]: 162–82; and Ando 2008a.

14. In the *Digest* the language attributed to Ulpian speaks of a *lex regia*, but this seems overwhelmingly likely to be a six-century interpolation for *lex de imperio, vel sim.* On the extant clauses of the so-called *lex de imperio Vespasiani*, see Brunt 1977 and the important corrective in Mantovani 2005.

15. Mommsen 1887: 2.1.645–674, on "ausserordentliche Aushülfsbeamte"; cf. Kunkel 1995: 314–15. In the last decades of the republic the description *extra ordinem* has not surprisingly both technical legal and polemical orientations, being applied to electoral campaigns conducted, or magistracies bestowed, in violation of legislation on the *cursus honorum* (Cic. *Brut.* 226: *consulatus petitionem extraordinariam* (an extraordinary campaign for the consulate); Caes. *Civ.* 1. 32. 2: Caesar seemed to himself *nullum extraordinarium honorem adpetisse, sed exspectato legitimo tempore consulatus eo fuisse contentum*—not to have attempted any extraordinary position, but to have been content with the consulate at its eagerly awaited proper moment), as well as to military commands of unprecedented scope, duration, or context (Cic. *Phil.* 11. 20 on the *imperium extraordinarium* granted to Octavian). Further evidence cited at Mommsen 1887: 1. 20–21.

carried on November 27, 43 BC, and that the powers were to expire in five years, on December 31, 38.[16] Among our sources it is largely left to the later Greeks, Appian and Dio, to voice outrage at the legitimation "the people" thereby granted to the use of extrajudicial executions against itself. That said, it is no radical extension of ancient doctrines of popular sovereignty to say that the people might one day act in contravention of its will the day before. On such an understanding, the *lex Titia*, like the *leges de imperio* by which emperors well into the third century AD were endowed with their agglomeration of powers, was a true exercise of popular power and a genuine product of a purely republican politics, and self-abrogation only the most radical of republican acts.

The republicanism of the early principate has functioned since antiquity as the principal heuristic device by which its *Roman* political culture might be understood (it was widely felt in antiquity that the diplomatic forms by which communication between center and periphery were conducted still in the Augustan period were better suited, in several respects, to monarchy[17]). For Tacitus, the notional persistence of republican institutions, albeit in the absence of republican liberties, engendered among the aristocracy a culture of *dissimulatio*, of role-playing, that penetrated so deeply into household and individual psychology as to induce a radical dissociation of self and speech. Renaissance and early modern readers of Tacitus—Machiavelli, Bruni, and Lipsius among them—who had different interpretive agendas than Tacitus himself, not least because they did not see their worlds as continuous with the Roman Republic, but also because unlike Tacitus they understood the reality that polities and states could fail, saw in the principate the end of politics, by which they meant the foreclosure for aristocrats of opportunities for the free exercise of republican virtue. Such virtue at Rome had consisted almost exclusively in the furtherance of its imperial project (however much that project changed), and both de jure and de facto military glory were under the principate monopolized by the imperial house. That narrower conception of politics and virtue was, of course, thematized by Tacitus himself, and is widely read from his work back into the early principate with much sentiment and some anachronism by moderns, not least by Tacitus' and the Roman revolution's greatest modern student:

> The theme of history remains, as before, 'clarorum virorum facta moresque.'
> Therein lay the tragedy—the Empire gave no scope for the display of civic virtue at
> home and abroad, for it sought to abolish war and politics. There could be no great
> men anymore: the aristocracy was degraded and persecuted. The record of their
> ruin might be instructive—it was not a happy task for an historian. The author of
> the *Annals* was moved to despair of his work. 'Nobis in arto et inglorius labor.'[18]

---

16. Aug. *Anc.* 1. 4; App. *Civ.* 4. 7. 27; *Fasti Colotiani: Inscr. Ital.* XIII, 1: 273–274; see also Liv. *Per.* 120 and Dio 46. 55. The relevant texts are generously quoted at Scheid 2007: 29–30. See also Millar 2002 [1973]: 243–44.

17. Tac. *Ann.* 1. 2. 2; Millar 2002 [1984]: 292–313.

18. Syme 1939: 508. The first quotation is Tac. *Ann.* 1. 1, "the deeds and characters of famous men." The second is *Ann.* 4. 32, "to me is left a constricted and inglorious theme."

It is Syme's most Machiavellian moment.

Of course, far more serious changes were afoot in the establishment of the principate than the imposition of constraints on rapine and theft by the Roman elite, as Tacitus (and Syme) knew well. For the disappearance of some of the old Roman aristocracy created space at Rome, rapidly filled by elites first from Italy, then Gaul, and eventually all the provinces, while the diffusion of Roman institutions to the municipalities of the empire provoked the development within provincial societies of something like a multi-tiered governing class. These changes themselves rested upon, and likewise provoked, on-going changes in political culture and local and regional political economies, and to these I shall shortly turn. But I want first to draw forth another significant ancient mode of understanding late republican Roman history, one that cast a far more critical eye upon the state of affairs than was apparently possible within political thought and public speech.

As city, community of citizens, and empire, Rome of the first century BC surpassed in magnitude and economic and social connectivity all other political formations the Mediterranean world then knew, in history or lived experience, and the pace and scope of the empire's integration would vastly increase across the first century of the principate. That said, the scale of these worlds, for each of which Rome might stand as name or metonym, presented wholly unprecedented challenges to political theory and political practice, which the pace of political life scarcely permitted the Romans to address—despite what can only be called quite remarkable sophistication in the task Cicero described as "knowing the state" (Nicolet 1996). A single generation, between 91 and 62 BC, embraced the Social War (91–87 BC, with most fighting confined to 90–89), whose outcome (regardless of aims on either side at the outset) was the promise to integrate the Italian peninsula as a community of full and equal citizens; the massacre of Romans in Asia that opened the Mithridatic wars and spurred revolts in peninsular Greece and around the Aegean, which led almost without cease to three wars and ultimately to Pompey's annexation of nearly the whole of Asia Minor and Near East down to Egypt (88–85, 83–81, 74–65 BC, with Pompey's tour concluding 62); the coups d'état of Marius and Sulla, the latter's constitutional reforms, and the further reforms and repeals those provoked; and popular agitation over debt and land reform that may have provoked the Catilinarian conspiracy and certainly sharpened the Senate's fear of its appeal (63 BC). These events were of course connected at the level of pragmatic politics—where possible, Mithridates timed his aggression in response to Roman distraction elsewhere—but they were also connected structurally. What response did all this provoke?

As it happens, of course, the massive successes of Pompey in the east were instrumental in exacerbating the republican aristocracy's race to self-destruction, and thorough-going absorption of the new realities of empire, in both administration and conceptualization, awaited the return of peace. (That said, Asia and the East *do* have a history between Pompey and Actium, one too little told by Roman historians.) But Romans in the age of Pompey and later regularly construed the experience of assimilating his conquests, and of integrating Italy, by reference to the challenges posed and the solutions crafted in an earlier age of expansion, namely, the long century that began with the settlement of Latium and ended with the annexation of transpadane Gaul—the century that witnessed, on Cicero's understanding, the genesis of the province as an administrative unit and with it, the birth of empire (Cic. 2 *Verr.* 2. 2). These were complex events, whose history I will rehearse with the aim only of demonstrating how late republican and early Augustan understandings of this period help us to see, as it helped them retroactively to understand, the structural consequences for Rome and Italy of late republican imperialism.

First, the settlement between Rome and the Latins in 338 BC involved inter alia attributing definitively and universally to citizens of the Latin cities a body of rights and obligations vis-à-vis the Roman state and Roman citizens. These were at their origin assigned strictly to members of polities conceived of as Latin, tied to each other not simply by membership in particular communities but also by language and race. This body of rights was subsequently conceptualized apart from its original political context, and its name, *ius Latii*, was likewise abstracted from its specific reference with simply astonishing speed; it was then attached to persons, interpellating them in relation to Rome and creating them as subjects of (Roman) law (Humbert 1978; Kremer 2006).

Second, Romans of the late republic and early Augustan period believed that early Roman foreign policy, and in particular rituals connected with the start and end of wars, had been conducted through a body of priests known as the fetials. Famously, the final stage of fetial ritual in declaring war was the hurling of a ceremonial spear into the enemy's territory. Equally famously, we are told by the fourth-century commentator on Vergil, Servius, drawing as it seems on Augustan sources, that the Romans were forced by the practical realities of "transmarine" warfare to change fetial ritual in the early third century BC. Because they "could not find a place where they could perform through the *fetiales* this ritual of declaring war," they forced a captured soldier to buy a plot in the Circus Flaminius adjacent to the temple of Bellona, outside the *pomerium* (the sacred boundary of Rome), and satisfied the law of declaring war *quasi in hostili loco*, "as if in hostile territory" (Serv. *ad Aen.* 9. 52). Here, too, we witness among other things an abstraction of the category "hostile territory" from the particular; we see also an awareness that institutions developed or adopted in treating with similarly ordered city-states of central Italy had to adapt, and sometimes could not adapt, to the realities created by empire (Ando 2008a).

And third, in another vast oversimplification, the Roman law of persons had long organized voters and territory into tribes; and with the annexation of significant new territory, Rome had intermittently created new voting tribes to organize the land and peoples thus embraced (Taylor 1960). The last new tribes were created in 241 BC. Through intermittent action and occasional warfare over the next two decades, the Romans gradually seized control of Italy north of the Po, then considered by them not part of Italy at all, but rather Gaul. Here they settled, in the 220s, an enormous number of colonists, many *viritim* (man by man or, rather, household by household). But the decision was made *not* to create new tribes to account for this land or any new citizens then settled or later born there. Citizen colonists were rather assigned to one of the pre-existing thirty-one rural tribes, and so the once native and essential connection between citizenship and territoriality, between person and place, was radically ruptured.[19]

Two conclusions emerge from this history, and from the language and reckoning given them in literature of the late republic and early principate. First, the Romans themselves had a nascent understanding that in some significant respects—the language here eluded them—they were no longer a city-state, of the sort that contemporaneous philosophy theorized or contemporaneous law might govern, and hence they came to doubt whether the institutions and practices that had brought them to power, and the ethical and cultural commitments that these expressed, could adapt to the world they had brought into being. Second, the principal adaptation they did make consisted in the development of a law of persons and, indeed, a conceptualization of legal personhood that proved essential to the articulation of the empire as a community—not simply of provinces, cities, and other administrative units, but of people. The polity that developed out of this revolution was deeply flawed, of course, but the revolution itself was and remains a remarkable achievement (Ando, forthcoming b).

EMPIRE AS POLITICAL FORM: ROME AND ROMANS IN PROVINCIAL LANDSCAPES

The story of the Roman Revolution is at some level a Roman story, and it can validly (if limitedly) be understood as political in character. That is so, however much the contest for power at Rome was played out in the provinces (Millar 2002 [1984]: 215–37): it was from Rome that the principals were understood to derive their authority and control of force, and was in Rome that they sought legitimation for their status in government and society. In contrast, the story of the principate is imperial in scope, and it is largely one of acculturation and consolidation—forms of historical change neither easily narrated nor on ancient evidence readily periodized (Ando 1999: 5–9; Ando 2000: 1–3). This is not to say that the institution of monarchy did in fact bring about an end to politics. Rather, the structures of political economics became geographically more diffuse, and the channels of legitimation less susceptible to strict constitutional analysis (Ando 2007b). Tacitus' famous observation, that the upheaval following the death of Nero revealed that an emperor might be made somewhere other than Rome, gestures in the first instance to the agency exercised by the army, to be sure, but armies not only campaigned, but were recruited, stationed, and fed and, indeed, retired outside of Rome. Even on this very narrow

19. By far the most sophisticated inquiry into the body of law and thought that came into being in the aftermath is Thomas 1996.

understanding—and I would in fact advocate a far more capacious one—regional interests now found a voice in Roman politics, such as they had not found in the middle and late republic.

That said, all histories of the principate must first take into account the truly fundamental role played at its inception by murder, warfare, and the movement of populations, and those on a number of levels. For example, in various stages between the dictatorship of Julius Caesar in 46 (who raised the membership from perhaps 600 to 900) and two grants to Augustus of the power to review the rolls, in 29/28 and 18 BC, radical changes were made in the membership of the Senate, sometimes through the expansion of its size and simple addition of new members, at others through wholesale murder and replacement. This was, in fact, the second such massive turnover in the Senate's composition in half a century—the first having occurred under Sulla, who between replacing his victims and mere expansion contributed some 400 new members to that body (Badian 1990: 26). One result of the Julian and Augustan revisions in particular was vastly expanded representation from the municipalities of Italy, men who may well have lacked the sharp personal ambition of old Roman *nobiles* and whose allegiance to republican constitutionalism, such as it was, will have been tempered by memories of senatorial intransigence in the face of Italian demands for a seat at the table in the run-up to the Social War. This theme was given definitive articulation by Ronald Syme (1939), who also produced (actually even before the book on Rome's revolution) an evocative analysis of the recruitment and cooptation of provincials into the imperial governing class (Syme 1999).

Dramatic as those changes at Rome were, death, displacement, and resettlement occurred on a far greater scale, and to greater long-term historical effect, in Italy outside Rome and in the provinces. These were principally of two kinds. First, cash and land had been the price of loyalty in the late republican civil wars; hence each abortive peace and every demobilization of veterans required a staggering amount of land. While the tensions lasted, veterans generally had the leverage to demand plots in Italy, and they were therefore injected as colonists into pre-existing towns, often enough onto plots from which earlier residents and owners were forcibly removed, themselves to wander, impoverished, disenfranchised, and desperate. In the aftermath of Actium, as sole dynast Augustus had the upper hand and, like Pompey in Asia Minor before the civil wars had ever commenced, he planted veterans in colonies in the provinces. The numbers are vast. In Italy alone, veterans claimed perhaps 150,000 farmsteads, and they filled dozens of towns throughout the provinces of the empire (Keppie 1983; Brunt 1987: 589–601, 608–10).

The second major form of displacement and resettlement worked in this period was the forcible transfer of towns from one location to another, or gathering of multiple populations into a single site, which processes Greek geographers of the period named metoecism and synoecism, respectively (Ando, forthcoming a, chapter 3). These were effected not least to remove indigenous populations from defensible hilltop locations into plains, where they were often encouraged to practice cereal-based agriculture. Such moves were also understood as integrating local communities more easily into regional trade networks, or as making the articulation of communal identity through Roman-style institutions economically and materially feasible. Despite the existence of fine case studies and several regional surveys, no synthetic study of such resettlements has been attempted, and therefore no estimate has been made of the aggregate population affected (Purcell 1987a; Mitchell 1993: 1. 36–37, 72–77, 86–91; Reddé et al. 2003; Abad Casal, Keay, and Ramallo Asensio 2006). It cannot have been small. In the end, counting both colonies and resettlements, between one million and one and a half million people were moved across two generations, perhaps 3% of the population of the entire Mediterranean world.

In all this Gaul must be treated separately, as the largest victim of Rome's most savage war of conquest. The war itself was conducted with brutality that leaves one speechless: some few Romans were sufficiently appalled at Caesar's behavior to propose his prosecution. Caesar himself boasted that he had killed 1,192,000 in his foreign wars alone, of which the majority were surely Gauls (Plin. *Nat.* 7. 92). To the dead must be added perhaps another million enslaved (Plut. *Caes.* 15. 5)—many of whom were sold or granted as gifts en masse to the towns of Italy. Combined, these constituted a vast percentage, surely a majority, of the adult male population of all of Gaul. Caesar's personal profit, from rapine, murder, and slaves amounted to several billion sesterces, a figure estimated from the amount he gave away (Badian 1990: 30–31). This was the human cost of Caesar's monstrous ambition, soon to be exercised on Rome itself.

Naturally the effect on individuals and communities actually displaced will have been enormous; that on neighboring communities, through alterations to regional patterns of trade, transhumance and mobility, as also to access to natural resources, somewhat smaller and different in kind. For directly affected communities, the disruption must have produced substantial loss of collective memory, especially in populations torn from the landscapes wherein their memories were invested, as well as profound rupture in communal and individual self-understanding. They are likely also to have suffered substantial delegitimation of earlier conceptions of social order, or at the very least, of the contingent realization of those conceptions in offices, institutions, and individuals. Over the long term, these ruptures provided ground in which new communities—new Roman communities—came into being; in the short term, there was no doubt great suffering, to which the material record is now often the only witness.

In so concentrating on structural analysis I do not wish to discount the role of personality in history. To ask the contrafactual, what if Pompey or Antony had triumphed rather than Caesar or Augustus, is to glimpse, however evanescently, the force of personal intellect in the social history of the empire at large. One need only correlate patterns in the urbanization and governance of Gaul and Spain against the physical presence of Augustus in those regions to sense this. The same is likewise true of the arts, whereby the public spaces in particular of those cities were adorned.[20] This is so however much we credit the conceptual and artistic

20. Ward-Perkins 1970; *Enceintes* 1987; Zanker 1988; Boschung 1993; Woolf 1998: 37–40; Edmondson 2006: 253–55, 260–72.

achievements of the late republic with having developed ways of understanding and representing empire: the consolidation of public discourse in the empire at large around one particular conceptualization of what we might call an imperial project reflects not simply homogenization impelled by monarchy but also, one senses, the force of personality at the top.[21]

In that perspective, the reign of Vespasian (AD 69–79) emerges as another such moment when politics and personality converged so as to impel long-term changes in the fabric of social order. This was so for at least two reasons. First, at that time a military and political crisis focused on Rome once again produced, through varied forms of amplification, large-scale disruption in the provinces, itself to be corrected (and the resultant budget shortfalls to be addressed) through deeper and more intense penetration by Roman government and Roman cultural forms into provincial life. Second, the succession of someone outside the Julio-Claudian house—and, indeed, the difficult process by which it came to fruition—worked powerfully to naturalize the constitutional innovations by which the Romans described the principate to themselves and others. This was so above all because the varied constituencies at the table—among which were the army, Senate, and voters at Rome, and ultimately Italian and provincial towns—persisted in crafting and ultimately honoring the use of republican mechanisms of election to magistracy and priesthood, followed by curiate law on *imperium,* that had been used already in the 20s BC for Augustus himself (Ando 2000: 33–36, 152–57, building on Brunt 1977). We might deplore, as the Romans occasionally deplored, the tension this produced, not least between republican form and hereditary substance of the imperial office, but it produced an order of surprising durability, in which the non-recurrence of proscriptions or civil wars to rival those of the late republic seemed to contemporaries a huge victory, and no doubt it was.

We might plot this intensification in the penetration of Roman government along several axes. It was above all inscribed upon the land, and through that action cemented the relationship between individuals and the land as a function of their status as Roman subjects. This happened through a dramatic extension in the land surveyed according to Roman methods, which not only insisted upon orthogonal plots, but also marked the boundaries of those plots with ditches and stones that remain visible from the air today. This went hand in hand with a demand that land previously surveyed remain under cultivation—expressed, naturally enough, in the language of central governments: land was to be taxed as though it were under cultivation, and it was assumed that communities would respond to that pressure by making the land productive (regional studies of the Flavian land survey include Piganiol 1962, Salviat 1977, and Romano 2003).

21. On the influence of late republican modes of thought in Augustan administration, see Nicolet 1991; Ando 2002a: 524. On the development of an imperial project see Woolf 1998: 48–76.

But this intensification took place most famously in the extension to select cities throughout the west, and most notably to many towns in Spain, of the status of *municipium*, incorporated, independent town. Where Spain is concerned, this act took place through the delivery into communities of a town charter, written and approved by statutory process at Rome, by which the structures of communal life in all their variety were brought into alignment with Roman norms.[22] Social history cannot be written from normative documents like town charters alone, and I will not attempt here to do so. But I do wish to emphasize two distinct features of these documents, one of which highlights their drive to assimilate provincial to Roman, the other of which responds, however obliquely, to structural concerns regarding the division of political and religious authority raised at Rome in the late republic.

One function of Roman towns within the landscape was the provision of institutions for dispute resolution, between villages, villagers, and residents of the town (Ando, forthcoming a, chapter 6). The Flavian municipal charters envision this taking place before the provincial governor, or before local magistrates holding jurisdiction, and rules are laid out on significant matters of procedure in many cases. The section on jurisdiction closes with an astonishing umbrella clause:

> <Ch. 93.> Rubric. Concerning the law of the *municipes*. On whatever matters there is no explicit provision or rule in this statute, concerning the law under which the *municipes*...should deal with each other, they are to deal with each other in all these matters under the civil law under which Roman citizens deal or will deal with each other. (*lex Flavia municipalis* ch. 93 = González 1986: 198–199, trans. Crawford)

It is remarkably not specified how residents of municipalities in Spain might learn the requirements of Roman civil law on any given topic (on which problem see Galsterer 1986; Crawford 1988; and Ando 2009), but this problem pales beside the quite remarkable work this requirement performs, in assimilating aliens to citizens before the law, even in relations with other non-citizens (Gardner 2001; Ando, forthcoming a, chapter 5).

Where religion is concerned, the municipal charters follow the practice already visible in very late republican colonial charters, by which significant areas of religious activity that remained at Rome either loosely regulated or in the hands of priests, rather than magistrates or civic bodies, were in these new foundations subordinated to civic authority, and above all to the collective authority of the town council.[23] In this way the agency of individuals, and even of magistrates, was subordinated to collective control.

22. See González 1986, and Galsterer 1988. The process used in Spain had antecedents—Galsterer 1987; Crawford 1998—but it is from Spain that copies survive.

23. On *municipia* see Scheid 1999; on colonies see Rüpke 2006; on the transfer of Roman cults to the provinces in general see Ando 2007a.

CONCLUSION

This chapter has attempted to chart the passage of Rome from republic to empire along several axes, some ancient, some modern. My principal argument has been that the Romans shaped the institutional structures of the principate, as well as their understandings of its form, in light of complex systems of analysis visible already in the late second century BC and under continuous development thereafter. Indeed, many of the reforms and innovations in Roman law and politics of the late republic should be understood as designed in light of such percipience as they possessed, and naturally constrained by long-standing ideological and motivated commitments to empire, for example, and against monarchy. And while I have urged that we not underestimate the sophistication of the Romans' social-theoretical awareness, I have likewise observed the tendency of contemporaries in the late republic to discover problems and propose solutions of an ad hoc rather than systemic nature: most of the time, Roman etiologies identified aberrant ambition on the part of an individual, or the unreliability of an ethnic group, as the source of difficulty, rather than broad-scale inequities in the distribution of wealth or a mismatch between institutional structures and magnitude of empire.

The establishment of the principate issued in social-historical changes of complex kinds, many of which cannot have been intended by the agents in that action. But those changes are visible to us, and indeed explicable by us, not least because we can assess the reforms undertaken by Augustus and his successors in light very precisely of a modern perception of systemic difficulties in the political economy of late republican Italy. Efforts under Augustus to (re)establish a demographically stable governing class at Rome, for example, should thus be understood in light of the forms of understanding of both politics and demography visible in Augustan sources, in which the establishment of a ruling class in early and mid-republic not surprisingly figures as a dominant theme. But they should also be assessed against our admittedly partial but still quite potent understanding of the demographic effects of civil war on the upper class at Rome on the one hand, and vast migration to Rome by municipal Italians on the other.

The conjoined use by Rome of citizenship and municipalization, to bring order to provincial landscapes and populations and promote the growth of Romanizing elites within them, should likewise be understood as a complex response by Rome to a profound problem of governance, a response crafted after centuries of experience—often enough of failure—in the unification of Italy. Indeed, one might well say that true understanding of both what they had achieved and where they had failed in Italy came to Romans only after the Social War, when unification emerged as a joint need of both the Romans themselves and their Italian fellow citizens. That said, I have argued that no small part of the social-historical importance of the Roman revolution lies in the unintended consequences of precisely the extension of Roman citizenship and public law to the urbanized communities of the Roman West. The Romans sought to organize them as Roman communities, run and ultimately peopled by Roman citizens; but they did so without a robust understanding in law or politics of how individuals or cities could be Roman, let alone republican, away from Rome. In what consisted virtue, in what consisted politics, in communities so organized?

These questions are important, I have urged, because, despite their Roman form, and despite the existence within them of Roman citizens—shareholders in the *res publica* and in their corporate capacity still sovereign in the state—the cities of the empire did not encourage the continuance of republican politics. Ambition and debate in the public sphere were as much capped as were local militias. But this did not portend an end to politics altogether.

What emerged, rather, throughout the empire was an astonishing efflorescence of public-mindedness, of attention to the place of the self and of private corporate bodies in the public sphere. At some level, of course, this movement reflected the success achieved by economic elites at the local level in inducing the worse-off into playing the game by their rules, as it were: by accepting as honors derivative versions of status markers among the elite, those excluded from power colluded with the powerful in naturalizing a political and cultural economy that worked to their disadvantage. What is more, in both local life and between localities, a primary object of public aspiration became the voicing, at least, of loyalty to emperor and empire. These cultures of euergetism and loyalism are two sides of a single imperial coin.[24]

That said, neither of those frameworks can explain the astonishing politicization of the previously silent—the enormous contribution made by freedmen, for example, to the epigraphic habit, or the vast role played by freedmen in public priesthoods (Nock 1972 [1934]: 348–56), or the rush of women, freedmen, and sometimes slaves and children to courts of law (Huchthausen 1974a, 1974b, 1975, 1976). The principate is, on these terms, an explosion of voices. Part of the explanation here must rest with empire itself as a political form, and with the distinct cast given to local politics and individual identity by the extension throughout the empire of an essentially anachronistic and deeply attenuated republicanism. For in ways both specific and general, individuals were invited to understand themselves not only as residents or citizens in local communities, but as citizens in the superordinate polity of Rome (Ando 1999, 2000). This was something in ancient experience altogether new.

The imposition of this framework, however theorized, at the level of law, ritual, and political practice had the unintended and perhaps imperceptible effect of atomizing individuals and disembedding social practices and institutions that had theretofore worked in harmony with purely local norms. In the light of imperial power, these latter were gradually reconstituted in a fractal relationship to the structures of the metropole, while the individual subjects-cum-citizens of empire were encouraged, many for the first time, to speak to history (Ando, 2010). This was the end of the Roman Revolution.

24. Veyne 1976; Gordon 1990, "Civic Compromise," and idem 1990, "Veil"; Lendon 1997; Rowe 2002.

BIBLIOGRAPHY

Abad Casal, L., S. Keay, and S. Ramallo Asensio (eds.). 2006. *Early Roman Towns in Hispania Tarraconensis*. Portsmouth, R.I.: Journal of Roman Archaeology.

Ando, C. 1999. "Was Rome a *polis?*" *Classical Antiquity* 18: 5–34.

————. 2000. *Imperial Ideology and Provincial Loyalty in the Roman Empire*. Berkeley: University of California Press.

————. 2002a. "The Impact of Administration in the Empire." A review of de Blois 2001. *Journal of Roman Archaeology* 15: 516–24.

————. 2002b. "Vergil's Italy: Ethnography and Politics in First-Century Rome." In D. S. Levene and D. Nelis (eds.), *Clio and the Poets: Augustan Poetry and the Traditions of Ancient Historiography*. Leiden: E. J. Brill. 123–42.

————. 2006. "The Administration of the Provinces." In Potter 2006. 177–92.

————. 2007a. "Exporting Roman Religion." In J. Rüpke (ed.), *A Companion to Roman Religion*. Malden: Blackwell. 429–45.

————. 2007b. "The Army and the Urban Elite: A Competition for Power." In P. Erdkamp (ed.), *A Companion to the Roman Army*. Malden: Blackwell. 359–78.

————. 2008a. "Aliens, Ambassadors and the Integrity of the Empire." *Law and History Review* 26(3): 491–519.

————. 2008b. *The Matter of the Gods*. Berkeley: University of California Press.

————. 2009. "Diana on the Aventine." In J. Rüpke (ed.), *Die Religion des Imperium Romanum*. Tübingen: Mohr Siebeck. 99–113.

————. 2010. "Imperial Identities." In T. Whitmarsh (ed.), *Local Knowledge and Microidentities in the Imperial Greek World*. Cambridge: Cambridge University Press.

————. Forthcoming a. *The Ambitions of Government*.

————. Forthcoming b. "Sovereignty and Solipsism in Democratic Empires."

Badian, E. 1982. "'Crisis Theories' and the Beginning of the Principate." In G. Wirth (ed.), *Romanitas-Christianitas: Untersuchungen zur Geschichte und Literatur der römischen Kaiserzeit, Johannes Straub zum 70. Geburtstag gewidmet*. Berlin: Walter de Gruyter. 18–41.

————. 1990. Review of C. Meier, *Caesar* (Berlin: Severin und Siedler 1982). *Gnomon* 62: 22–39.

Beck, H. 2005. *Karriere und Hierarchie: die römische Aristokratie und die Anfänge des cursus honorum in der mittleren Republik*. Berlin: Akademie Verlag.

Béranger, J. 1953. *Recherches sur l'aspect idéologique du principat*. Basel: Verlag Friedrich Reinhardt AG.

————. 1975. *Principatus*. Geneva: Droz.

Boschung, D. 1993. *Die Bildnisse des Augustus*. Berlin: Gebr. Mann.

Brunt, P. A. 1977. "Lex de imperio Vespasiani." *Journal of Roman Studies* 67: 95–116.

————. 1987. *Italian Manpower 225 B.C.—A.D. 14*. 2nd ed. Oxford: Clarendon Press.

————. 1988. *The Fall of the Roman Republic and Related Essays*. Oxford: Clarendon Press.

Cornell, T. J. 2005. "The Value of the Literary Tradition Concerning Archaic Rome." In Raaflaub 2005: 47–74.

Crawford, M. H. 1988. "The Laws of the Romans: Knowledge and Diffusion." In J. González and J. Arce (eds.), *Estudios sobre la Tabula Siarensis*. Madrid: CSIC. 127–39.

de Blois, L. (ed.). 2001. *Administration, Prosopography and Appointment Policies in the Roman Empire*. Amsterdam: J. C. Gieben.

Develin, R. 2005. "The Integration of the Plebeians into the Political Order after 366 B.C." In Raaflaub 2005: 293–311.

Eck, W., A. Caballos, and F. Fernández. 1996. *Das senatus consultum de Cn. Pisone patre.* Munich: Verlag C. H. Beck.

Edmondson, J. 2006. "Cities and Urban Life in the Western Provinces of the Roman Empire 30 B.C.E.—250 C.E." In Potter 2006: 250–80.

Enceintes augustéennes. 1987. *Les enceintes augustéennes dans l'occident romain (France, Italie, Espagne, Afrique du Nord). Bulletin annuel de l'école antique de Nimes 18.* Nimes: École Antique de Nimes.

Ferrary, J.-L. 2001. "À propos des pouvoirs d'Auguste." *Cahiers Glotz* 12: 101–54.

Frier, B. 1980. *Landlords and Tenants in Imperial Rome.* Princeton: Princeton University Press.

Gabba, E. 1984. "The Historians and Augustus." In Millar and Segal 1984: 61–88.

Galsterer, H. 1986. "Roman Law in the Provinces: Some Problems of Transmission." In M. H. Crawford (ed.), *L'Impero romano e le struture economiche e sociali delle province.* Como: New Press. 13–27.

———. 1987. "La loi municipale des Romains: chimère ou réalité?" *Revue historique de droit français et étranger* 65: 181–203.

———. 1988. "Municipium Flavium Irnitanum: A Latin town in Spain." *Journal of Roman Studies* 78: 78–90.

———. 2006. "Rom und Italien vom Bendesgenossenkrieg bis zu Augustus." In Jehne und Pfeilschifter 2006: 293–308.

Gardner, J. F. 2001. "Making Citizens: The Operation of the *Lex Irnitana.*" In de Blois 2001: 215–29.

Gibbon, E. 1994. *History of the Decline and Fall of the Roman Empire.* Ed. D. Womersley. London: Allen Lane.

González, J. 1986. "The *Lex Irnitana*: A New Flavian Municipal Law." *Journal of Roman Studies* 76: 147–243.

Gordon, R. 1990. "From Republic to Principate: Priesthood, Religion and Ideology"; "The Veil of Power: Emperors, Sacrificers and Benefactors"; "Religion in the Roman Empire: The Civic Compromise and Its Limits." In M. Beard and J. North (eds.), *Pagan Priests.* Ithaca: Cornell University Press. 179–98, 201–31, 235–55.

Gowing, A. 2005. *Empire and Memory: The Representation of the Roman Republic in Imperial Culture.* Cambridge: Cambridge University Press.

Henderson, J. 1998. *Fighting for Rome. Poets and Caesars, History and Civil War.* Cambridge: Cambridge University Press.

Hölkeskamp, K.-J. 1987. *Die Entstehung der Nobilität: Studien zur sozialen und politischen Geschichte der römischen Republik um 4. Jhdt. v. Chr.* Stuttgart: Franz Steiner Verlag.

———. 2004. *Rekonstruktionen einer Republik: die politische Kultur des antiken Rom und die Forschung der letzten Jahrzehnte.* Munich: R. Oldenbourg Verlag.

Horden, P., and N. Purcell. 2000. *The Corrupting Sea: A Study of Mediterranean History.* Malden: Blackwell.

Huchthausen, L. 1974a. "Herkunft und ökonomische Stellung weiblicher Adressaten von Reskripten des *Codex Iustinianus* (2. und 3. Jh. u. Z.)." *Klio* 56: 199–228.

———. 1974b. "Kaiserliche Rechtsauskünfte an Sklaven und in ihrer Freiheit angefochtene Personen aus dem Codex Iustinianus." *Wissenschaftliche Zeitschrift der Wilhelm-Pieck-Universität Rostock. Gesellschaftliche & sprachwissenschaftliche Reihe* 23: 251–57.

———. 1975. "Kaiserliche Reskripte an Frauen aus den Jahren 117 bis 217 u. Z." In *Actes de la XIIe conférence internationale d'études classiques 'Eirene.'* Bucharest: Editura Academiei. 479–88.

———. 1976. "Zu kaiserlichen Reskripten an weibliche Adressaten aus der Zeit Diokletians (284–305 u. Z.)." *Klio* 58: 55–85.

Humbert, M. 1978. *Municipium et civitas sine suffragio. L'Organisation de la conquête jusqu'à la guerre sociale.* Rome: École Française de Rome.

Jehne, M. 2006. "Römer, Latiner und Bundesgenossen im Krieg. Zu Formen und Ausmaß der Integration in der republikanischen Armee." In Jehne and Pfeilschifter 2006: 243–67.

Jehne, M., and R. Pfeilschifter (eds.). 2006. *Herrschaft ohne Integration? Rom und Italien in republikanischer Zeit.* Frankfurt: Verlag Antike.

Keppie, L. J. F. 1983. *Colonisation and Veteran Settlement in Italy, 47–14 B.C.* London: British School at Rome.

Kremer, D. 2006. *Ius Latinum: le concept de droit latin sous la république et l'empire.* Paris: de Boccard.

Kunkel, W. 1995. *Staatsordnung und Staatspraxis der römischen Republik.* Part 2: *Die Magistratur.* Munich: Verlag C. H. Beck.

Lendon, J. E. 1997. *Empire of Honour. The Art of Government in the Roman World.* Oxford: Clarendon Press.

Maier, C. S. 2006. *Among Empires. American Ascendancy and Its Predecessors.* Cambridge, Mass.: Harvard University Press.

Mantovani, D. 2005. "Les clauses 'sans précédents' de la *Lex de imperio Vespasiani.* Une interprétation juridique." *Cahiers Glotz* 16: 25–43.

Meier, C. 1966. *Res publica amissa. Eine Studie zu Verfassung und Geschichte der späten römischen Republik.* Wiesbaden: Franz Steiner Verlag.

Millar, F. 2002. *Rome, the Greek World, and the East. Vol. 1: The Roman Republic and the Augustan Revolution.* Ed. H. M. Cotton and G. M. Rogers. Chapel Hill: University of North Carolina Press.

Millar, F., and E. Segal (eds.). 1984. *Caesar Augustus. Seven Aspects.* Oxford: Clarendon Press.

Mitchell, S. 1993. *Anatolia: Land, Men, and Gods in Asia Minor.* Oxford: Clarendon Press.

Moatti, C. 1997. *La raison de Rome: naissance de l'esprit critique à la fin de la République.* Paris: Seuil.

Mommsen, T. 1887. *Römisches Staatsrecht.* 3rd ed. Leipzig: S. Hirzel.

Morgan, L. 1999. *Patterns of Redemption in Virgil's* Georgics. Cambridge: Cambridge University Press.

Morley, N. 1996. *Metropolis and Hinterland. The City of Rome and the Italian Economy 200 B.C.—A.D. 200.* Cambridge: Cambridge University Press.

Mouritsen, H. 2006. "Hindsight and Historiography: Writing the History of Pre-Roman Italy." In Jehne and Pfeilschifter 2006: 23–37.

Nicolet, C. 1991. *Space, Geography and Politics in the Early Roman Empire.* Ann Arbor: University of Michigan Press.

———. 1996. *Financial Documents and Geographical Knowledge in the Roman World.* Oxford: Leopard's Head Press.

Nock, A. D. 1972. *Essays on Religion and the Ancient World.* Ed. Z. Stewart. Oxford: Clarendon Press.

Piganiol, A. 1962. *Les documents cadastraux de la colonie romaine d'Orange.* Paris: CNRS.

Pocock, J. G. A. 1996. "Classical and Civil History: The Transformation of Humanism." *Cromohs* 1: 1–34. http://www.cromohs.unifi.it/

———. 2003. *Barbarism and Religion. Volume 3: The First Decline and Fall.* Cambridge: Cambridge University Press.

Potter, D. S. (ed.). 2006. *A Companion to the Roman Empire.* Malden: Blackwell.

Purcell, N. 1987a. "The Nicopolitan Synoecism and Roman Urban Policy." In E. Chrysos (ed.), *Nicopolis I. Proceedings of the First International Symposium on Nicopolis (23–29 September 1984)*. Preveza: Demos Prevezas. 71–90.

———. 1987b. "Town in Country and Country in Town." In E. B. MacDougall (ed.), *Ancient Roman Villa Gardens*. Washington, D.C.: Dumbarton Oaks. 187–203.

Raaflaub, K. A. (ed.). 2005. *Social Struggles in Archaic Rome. New Perspectives on the Conflict of the Orders*. 2nd ed. Oxford: Blackwell.

Reddé, M., et al. (eds.). 2003. *La naissance de la ville dans l'antiquité*. Paris: de Boccard.

Romano, D. G. 2003. "City Planning, Centuriation, and Land Division in Roman Corinth." In. C. K. Williams II and N. Bookidis (eds.), *Corinth. Results of Excavations Conducted by the American School of Classical Studies at Athens*, vol. XX. Athens: American School of Classical Studies at Athens. 279–301.

Rowe, G. 2002. *Princes and Political Cultures*. Ann Arbor: University of Michigan Press.

Rüpke, J. 2006. "Religion in the lex Ursonensis." In C. Ando and J. Rüpke (eds.), *Religion and Law in Classical and Christian Rome*. Stuttgart: Franz Steiner Verlag. 34–46.

Salviat, F. 1977. "Orientation, extension et chronologie des plans cadastraux d'Orange." *Revue archéologique de Narbonnaise* 10: 107–18.

Scheid, J. 1999. "Aspects religieux de la municipalisation. Quelques réflexions générales." In M. Dondin-Payre and M.-T. Raepsaet-Charlier (eds.), *Cités, Municipes, Colonies. Les processus de municipalisation en Gaule et en Germanie sous le Haut Empire romain*. Paris: Publications de la Sorbonne. 381–423.

———. (ed.). 2007. *Res Gestae Divi Augusti. Hauts faits du divin Auguste*. Paris: Les Belles Lettres.

Scheidel, W. 2004. "Human Mobility in Roman Italy, I: The Free Population." *Journal of Roman Studies* 94: 1–26.

———. 2005. "Human Mobility in Roman Italy, II: The Slave Population." *Journal of Roman Studies* 95: 64–79.

———. 2006. "The Demography of Roman State Formation in Italy." In Jehne and Pfeilschifter 2006: 207–26.

Shaw, B. 2000. "Rebels and Outsiders." In A. K. Bowman, P. Garnsey, and D. Rathbone (eds.), *The Cambridge Ancient History, Vol. XI: The High Empire AD 70–192*. 2nd ed. Cambridge: Cambridge University Press. 361–403.

———. 2001. "Challenging Braudel: A New Vision of the Mediterranean." *Journal of Roman Archaeology* 14: 419–53.

Syme, R. 1939. *The Roman Revolution*. Oxford: Clarendon Press.

———. 1979. *Roman Papers*. Ed. E. Badian. Oxford: Clarendon Press.

———. 1986. *The Augustan Aristocracy*. Oxford: Clarendon Press.

———. 1999. *The Provincial at Rome*. Exeter: University of Exeter Press.

Taylor, L. R. 1960. *The Voting Districts of the Roman Republic: The Thirty-Five Urban and Rural Tribes*. Rome: American Academy in Rome.

Thomas, Y. 1996. *"Origine" et "commune patrie." Étude de droit public romain (89 av. J.-C.—212 ap. J.C.)*. Rome: École Française de Rome.

Tibiletti, G. 1950. "Ricerche di storia agraria romana." *Athenaeum* 28: 183–266.

Toynbee, A. J. 1965. *Hannibal's Legacy*. Oxford: Oxford University Press.

Ungern-Sternberg, J. von. 2004. "The Crisis of the Republic." In H. Flower (ed.), *The Cambridge Companion to the Roman Republic*. Cambridge: Cambridge University Press. 89–109.

Veyne, P. 1976. *Le pain et le circque*. Paris: Seuil.

Wallace-Hadrill, A. 1997. "*Mutatio morum*: The Idea of a Cultural Revolution." In
     T. N. Habinek and A. Schiesaro (eds.), *The Roman Cultural Revolution*. Cambridge:
     Cambridge University Press. 3–22.
Ward-Perkins, J. B. 1970. "From Republic to Empire: Reflections on the Early Provincial
     Architecture of the Roman West." *Journal of Roman Studies* 60: 1–19.
Woolf, G. 1998. *Becoming Roman: the Origins of Provincial Civilization in Gaul*. Cambridge:
     Cambridge University Press.
Zanker, P. 1988. *The Power of Images in the Age of Augustus*. Ann Arbor: University of
     Michigan Press.

PART II

MECHANISMS OF SOCIALIZATION

CHAPTER 3

MAKING ROMANS IN THE FAMILY

JOSIAH OSGOOD

INTRODUCTION

THE family was the basic social and economic unit of Roman society, and so of fundamental importance in all areas of life. To a large degree it made individuals into who they were; for many it was the chief 'school' they knew. Families—urban and rural, in Italy and the provinces, of high status and low—trained the young for the place they would have in society, largely as a result of birth. Yet only in the last generation or so has the Roman family really been discovered, in an astonishingly original body of scholarship. Influenced by the rise of family history (a field that emerged in the 1960s), while also contributing to it, researchers have brought in a wide range of sometimes unlikely evidence, as well as comparisons with other, better documented periods, to describe how Roman families, in all their variety, really functioned. In doing so, they have shattered some cherished myths, of ancients as well as moderns—an unveiling that parallels efforts to show how much misplaced nostalgia can surround the idea of the family today. Yet much work remains to be done. Scholars are turning to neglected evidence; they are starting to look at just how 'Roman' the family was in different parts of a sprawling empire stretching from Syria to Spain, and how it shaped other aspects of individual identity (for instance, gender roles); and they will debate how discoveries about the family relate to major episodes of political and cultural change, such as the fall of the Roman Republic or the rise of Christianity. The focus here is on the family's socializing force, but first some questions of definition and evidence must be reviewed.

Family and *Familia*—Practice and Theory

One of the key questions of scholarship has been: how was the Roman family constituted? Or, to put it better, what *was* the Roman family, or what *were* Roman families? The jurist Ulpian, writing in the early third century AD, offered a series of explicit definitions of the Latin word *familia* that has attracted great attention (*Dig.* 50. 16. 195). *Familia*, he says, can refer to an estate or a group of household slaves; in the "strict legal sense" it means all those under the authority of the head of household, called the *paterfamilias*, "even if he has no children." (This authority, the infamous *patria potestas* that extended over all descendants through the male line, e.g., sons of sons, and prohibited them from owning property in their own right, seemed almost as peculiar to the Romans as it does to us, and legal writers discuss its ramifications at length—see Kehoe in this volume.) *Familia*, then, in Ulpian's conception—and indeed as other sources confirm—is usually more what we could call 'house' (in a metaphoric sense) or 'household' than 'family.' In fact, there was no explicit word for what we often mean by 'family' today, in other words, those individuals related by blood and marriage who live together under one roof (Saller 1984).

Yet legal definitions, even words more generally, hardly tell the whole truth about how people actually live. While studies of the family in the early modern era might draw on detailed records of (say) parish churches, scholars of the Roman period set out on a heroic quest to discover just who was living with whom, and what sort of affective ties they might have had. A landmark study by Saller and Shaw (1984), two pioneers in this field, assembled over ten thousand epitaphs that survive on stone from the western half of the Roman Empire, to show that among civilians it tended to be parents and children, husbands and wives, who commemorated one another. This, in turn, suggested that "the nuclear family was the primary focus of certain types of familial obligation" (Saller and Shaw 1984: 124). Apparently, then, a model well known today can be found after all. The inscriptions do not directly attest the actual composition of households, but they point to the possibility that in some segment of the (predominantly urban) population, so-called extended and multiple families (e.g., a married couple living together with two sons and grandchildren) were less common, or at least that within an extended family, nuclear ties were the strongest. This crucial discovery has guided much subsequent research and has not itself been refuted (Rawson 1997).

Still, recent scholarship has suggested that there was great diversity in household composition: Saller and Shaw's evidence cannot speak for *all* of the Roman Empire. Most significant has been the gathering of 300 census declarations from the province of Egypt, in which householders declared the names and ages of themselves and all other residents (Bagnall and Frier 1994). Over a third of the households recorded are extended or multiple, rather than nuclear, and other patterns emerge, for example, a number of younger widows (Hanson 2000). In Judea, in the Roman period, compound families (i.e., those where a male head of household had several wives) were known (Williams 2005). A preliminary study of Greek inscriptions of the eastern half of the empire highlights patterns different from those from the west and suggests an area where more study is needed (Martin 1996). The 'Roman' family studied, in other words, is no longer just that of Italy or the western provinces.

Other research, including some notable papers of Keith Bradley, has pointed to the range of individuals (often slaves) who might reside in a household of means and provide much of the day-to-day care, including wet-nursing, of young children (Bradley 1991; Dixon 1988: 141–67). Study of houses (including physical remains) complements such work, revealing that modern notions of 'public' and 'private' should not be imposed on Roman society (e.g., Wallace-Hadrill 1994; Riggsby 1997; George 1997a; George 1997b). The frequency of divorce and remarriage, and all its consequences, has also received attention—though this material has proved far harder to quantify (Bradley 1991: 156–76). Real families were very much in flux, it is important always to remember.

Closely linked to the questions of household structure and affective ties is research into other aspects of demography, where again the Egyptian census returns, thoroughly studied by Bagnall and Frier (1994), shed light. They are hardly equivalent to a full database; scholars supplement them with epitaphs (again), where patterns of commemoration seem to point, for instance, to the age at first marriage, and also with comparative evidence from other pre-industrial populations (Saller 1987; Shaw 1987a). Though avowedly speculative, this research has been nothing short of eye-opening, and helps to solve other problems in the history of the family (Saller 1994; Krause 1994–95; Scheidel 2001). It paints a picture of a society in which death was ubiquitous, among children as well as the old. Infant mortality was very high, and perhaps only half of all those born made it into adulthood. In urban populations, at least, girls could marry with the onset of puberty, but probably waited until their later teenage years, while men in general seem to have been older and remarried more frequently. The age gap, along with high mortality, meant that widowhood at a young age was a familiar experience; children growing up without a father is the necessary corollary. Demography, closer to the sciences than any other area of family studies, has allowed scholars to transcend their data and grapple with biological realities. *Patria potestas* might seem to point to an almighty father, exercising control ruthlessly over several generations of his family in an extended household; but the demographic reality, it is postulated, was that only one in fifty teenagers had a paternal grandfather alive (Saller 1994: 52).

Epitaphs and census returns, our equivalent to the parish records, along with demographic analysis, allow us to see patterns, but do not give much sense of the emotional side of family life. They cannot answer even such basic questions as: how did courtship work? What expectations did parents place on their young children? Here scholars must rely on evidence that will supply only partial answers, especially works of literature and also documents, including further papyri preserved in the sands of Egypt and elsewhere in the east. Two examples show the value, and limits, of such sources.

Quintilian, an advocate in the courts of Rome and an authority on rhetoric, tells us something of his own family in an emotive passage of his book *Training of the Orator* (6 *praef.*). There he reveals that his wife, having given birth to two sons, died before her nineteenth year had passed, resulting in "incurable" grief. In her absence a grandmother helped the nurses in bringing up the children, though the younger son, we are told, favored his father. He died at just five years old, though he already showed great promise—a "lofty mind" even. The other son died in childhood too, aged nine or ten; he had all the makings of an orator, "charm and clarity in his voice, a sweetness of speech." For eight months he faced his illness bravely, even (it is said) comforting his father in his final hours. This account vividly personalizes demographic realities, while also illustrating ideals, for instance, that a son would follow in his father's footsteps. The passage adduces emotions that we might expect Quintilian's well-educated (and therefore well-off) readers to share. But it does not speak to the concerns of the great majority of Roman families, and its rhetorical purpose (as with all literary sources) likely results in much being concealed, if not distorted: Quintilian himself is very much 'on display' here.[1]

Papyri sometimes give a seamier look at the real problems that more ordinary families faced, not least when many documents pertaining to one household survive. Several dozen texts illuminate the family of Tryphon, a weaver born in 8 or 9 AD, in the Egyptian village of Oxyrhynchus, where he spent the rest of his life (Biscottini 1966; Rowlandson 1998: 112–18). Several years after Tryphon's birth, his grandfather, also a weaver, reported during the census that he was living with his three sons (weavers too), as well as the little grandson. As with Quintilian's family, the children followed in the father's footsteps: Tryphon himself taught one of his sons (perhaps ten years old) to weave, but apprenticed another in the trade, perhaps because of his own failing eyesight. How the children spent their early years we do not know, but it was almost certainly not in school: Tryphon remained illiterate his whole life. We do know that he married twice, and that his second wife, Seraeus, complained that her predecessor had attacked her and made her miscarry. Several years later, after a son was born to her, Seraeus undertook the wet-nursing of another child, a foundling taken up to become a slave. Tryphon's family was probably short of money, and Seraeus' nursing a way that, as a woman, she could contribute financially (indeed, wet-nursing was often a professional activity for women). When one of these two infants died, Seraeus and the foundling's father quarreled over whose child was the survivor. The struggle that ensued, culminating in an appeal to the prefect of Egypt, is known through copies of official records.

Such documents, as one expert has well put it, allow scholars to "mind other people's business" (Hanson 2001). They are sometimes joined by letters, which may furnish a more intimate glimpse of families. A key problem, though, is that our records are very incomplete—we have a few snapshots, as it were, instead of a full album. Crucial questions will go unanswered, and comparisons can be difficult to make. And as with literary sources, the unevenness of what survives frustrates

---

1. For an overview of elite self-representation, see Flower in this volume.

efforts to trace change over time. Still, documents from Egypt and elsewhere, which continue to be discovered and published, should earn more of a role in family studies in years to come.

A further, and unique, source worth mentioning here is the collection of nearly a thousand letters to and from the orator Cicero. Published only after Cicero's death, and not intended for wide circulation, these offer some immediate reflections on family life among those of high status in Rome, and are priceless for showing such families in action—the raising of children, negotiation of dowries, dissolution of marriages, and so forth. Through the hopes and fears they express, they offer a (partial) control on literary sources that stem from the same milieu. A number of exemplary studies draw on them (e.g., Dixon 1986; Bradley 1991: 171–204; Treggiari 2007).

A third category of evidence, legal sources, reveals, at the minimum, regulations that in principle constrained but also enabled Roman citizens (and, to some degree, provincials). Moreover, changes in these rules over time may reflect changing attitudes in the society more broadly to the family. The emperor Antoninus Pius, for instance, held that a *paterfamilias* could not break up a harmonious marriage of those in his *potestas*; Marcus Aurelius then confirmed the decision (*PS* 5. 6. 15; *CJ* 5. 17. 5). Yet, how much the concerns of legal writers truly represented the concerns of various segments of society is, as with literary texts, open to question. One exceptional source is the series of several thousand responses (preserved in later compilations) that emperors issued to various citizens concerning their legal problems, usually called 'rescripts.' Difficult to interpret, since the original petitions do not survive, they still highlight what role law played in the families of more ordinary Romans—how, for instance, law could be invoked in a family feud—and so deserve more analysis: a fine paper has shown the way (Evans Grubbs 2005). Also of great value are the wax tablets discovered in Herculaneum, which document the legal struggles of Petronia Justa, daughter of a freedwoman (Weaver 1991). Though it remains uncertain how the dispute between Petronia and her mother's former mistress was resolved, the records do reveal the difficulties a former slave could face in starting her own family.

Valuable studies can focus on just one type of evidence. These are ultimately best combined to produce as complete a picture as possible. Treggiari's study of Roman marriage (1991) uses legal and literary sources to show that the making and breaking of unions could at times be messy, but also at times remarkably easy, and she also powerfully shows how, even in a society where many marriages were arranged, a companionate love could arise between spouses. Rawson's study of children and childhood in Roman Italy uses not just written sources, but also insights from demography and—importantly—visual evidence (2003). Dixon's excellent synthesis on the family, published in 1992, exploits visual, as well as much textual evidence, too, but the field is moving so fast; there is already much to add. In what follows, a view of how families socialized their members emerges from a rich array of sources.

THE SOCIALIZING FORCE OF THE FAMILY: PRODUCTIVE FUNCTIONS AND AFFECTIVE TIES

The *familia*, in the Roman world, was everywhere the main unit of consumption, and also of production (Saller 2003). As a slave force, it might number into the hundreds (or more) and operate a large estate (or estates); as a small group of biologically related individuals, it might farm a tiny plot of land. But however different these undertakings, it was generally true that one's livelihood was determined by the *familia* in which one was born, or lived, rather than personal choice as such. Thus, families (even in our more modern sense of the term), of whatever background socially, devoted great attention to the practical training of their young. Children were to be equipped to survive in the world into which they were born. What their parents did, they often would, too—and for the majority of those in the ancient world this was some type of agricultural activity, often in a countryside without much other economic opportunity (Erdkamp 2005: 55–105). For these individuals, mere survival could be the goal in the grim match they played—often with remarkable agility—against (variously) nature, the landlord, tax collectors, and so on.

Documentation of such families is wretched, making it difficult to answer key questions. Further comparative work would thus be welcome here. Was there a large role for extended or multiple households? We might expect so, since it would allow, for instance, increased access to land (Erdkamp 2005: 64–71). And what of women: did they do the same work as men? It seems likely that at times they did perform agricultural labor—during the harvest, for instance, when all hands were needed. But apparently they were above all associated with a necessary, though underappreciated, housework, which included raising children and the production of textiles (Erdkamp 2005: 87–94; Saller 2003). Long hours were spent weaving—and telling stories to make the time go by: this is a whole culture now lost to us. Women, we must imagine, passed their skills, along with the stories, on to the girls, while men prepared the boys for agricultural labor, both transmitting along the way distinct gender roles. Children were, without a doubt, put to work as soon as they were able to do anything of use and contribute to the family's survival. The accounts, preserved on papyrus, of a large Egyptian estate functioning during the reign of Vespasian record payments of 3–4 obols for men, 2–2½ for boys in the flood season; during pruning season, men received 3–6 obols for pruning, 6–7 for pumping water, 4–6 for manuring fields, while boys earned 2–2½ for weeding or gathering leaves, 3–4 for pruning (*P. Lond.* 131).

Even in larger towns and cities, where a greater diversity of occupations persisted, families—including those of ex-slaves—often, though by no means always, planned for their young to follow in their footsteps. We saw, in Tryphon's family, three generations of weavers, apparently operating independently: in AD 54, Tryphon bought a new loom and he also trained his elder son in the family's craft. Families might produce pottery together, or operate a bank, or run an export business—'families' here often included slaves: it proves tellingly difficult to sort out one-time slaves from biological kin in our records (Dixon 2001b; Weaver 2001). Children of those who worked in the imperial palace in Rome also frequently went on to do the same kinds of work as their parents had (Weaver 1972). Artemidorus, the author of a book on the interpretation of dreams, wrote that he expected his son to adopt the same profession (4 *praef.*). Camillus Polynices, a goldsmith, had a son Paulus who was also a goldsmith (*ILS* 7687). Ti. Claudius Vitalis and his son were both builders (*CIL* VI 9151–52). Certainly there was mobility, too—instances of children doing better (or worse) than their parents, of moving into new walks of life—but to quantify here seems impossible.

The notion that children should replicate the economic roles of their parents was especially true among those of the highest status. A famous passage of Cicero's *On Duties* (1. 150–51)—yet another book addressed by father to son—advises the Roman gentleman to segregate himself from many types of money-making. The sons of Senatorial aristocrats, instead, were to be trained in warfare, oratory, and the law, which were the 'professions' of their fathers. Cicero's correspondence sheds light on his own role in the upbringing of young Marcus, born in 65 BC (Bradley 1991: 103–6). Not only did he make sure to get the best teachers for his son (and also his nephew), he conferred with those teachers regularly and offered his own encouragement (in learning Greek, for instance): such training would provide the boy with the polish that men of his station were expected to have. Further, Cicero brought the teenage Marcus with him when he served as governor of the province of Cilicia; and father and son again left Italy together in 49 BC to join the forces of Pompey, where Marcus' formal military service began. Though civil war and the intellectual attainments of his father made this aristocrat's youth somewhat unusual, overall he was typical of his class. Marcus' sister, Tullia, though we learn less of her girlhood, was also raised to be a reflection of her parents; Cicero once calls her "the image of my face and speech and mind" (*Q. fr.* 1. 3. 3). But it must be remembered that she had personal qualities that shaped the dynamics of Cicero's family, and his personal life, too: parents socialize children, but children, in a sense, socialize parents, too.

Boys like Marcus had, besides politics and warfare, other practical skills to learn—as did their sisters—from their parents, nurses, and tutors, not the least of which was how to manage a household and give orders to the many slaves who would, or did, work for them. School texts by which young children learned Latin and Greek (Dionisotti 1982) tellingly include, among items of vocabulary, commands that we can imagine children themselves being trained to utter, for instance: "Day. The sun has risen. Sunrise. Daylight. Light. It is now light. Dawn. Daybreak. In the morning I get up. He got up from bed. He was up a long time yesterday. Dress me. Give me shoes and slippers and trousers." It is, according to this and other texts, virtually always the slaves who get the child through the rest of day: "Boy! Get up, see if it is light. Open the door and window." We also see the child playing the role of head of household: "Bring the cups and a dish, a candelabrum, decorate the table, sprinkle flowers in the dining room, set out charcoal and the incense burners, have everything prepared. Tell your fellow slave to make the food tasty, as I have important men as guests." Girls of means, by contrast, must have been taught how to give orders to those slaves who would tend to their physical appearance, a topic we will return to later.

Children being put to work, slaves getting them through the day, parents obsessed with propriety: these, and other scenarios (for instance, the undoubtedly frequent deaths of the very young and the regular exposure of new-born children) have suggested to some researchers that parents, regardless of background, may have distanced themselves from their children, or taken an unduly harsh attitude to them, treating them more as 'little adults' than a differentiated group. While exceptions always can be found to any kind of generalization, more recent work has successfully shown that throughout our period childhood was represented as a distinctive period of life, one patently fragile, and that children were often treated with fondness by parents, as well as other relatives and caretakers (Dixon 1991; Dixon 1992: 98–108; Saller 1994: 102–53; Rawson 2003). Those caretakers, in turn, could be remembered years afterward. As Bradley (2001) suggests, examining the evidence of Artemidorus' book on interpreting dreams (which purports to include the experiences of a wide cross-section of the population across the empire), children were precious, not because they were sentimentalized as such, but because families placed high hopes in these vulnerable creatures.

And what of relations between husband and wife: how did the family model those for their young? A key development must first be noted, which has generated much discussion. In the last two centuries of the republic, an older form of marriage, the so-called marriage with *manus*, in which the wife passed out of the control of her *paterfamilias* and into that of her husband, became nearly obsolete. Instead, wives tended to stay legally in the *familia* of their birth; they still brought a dowry to the marriage, but that dowry (along with any other property they owned) was recoverable if they divorced (Treggiari 1991: 13–36). This legal segregation of property facilitated the breaking of unions, and the making of new ones. Yet rigid rules did govern who was eligible for a marriage recognized in law, because it was of great concern to determine the legal status of any children born: Romans guarded citizenship rights jealously. A whole range of practices known in other cultures (including those that came under Rome's sway) was forbidden, or at least not recognized: polygamy, for instance, or certain types of close-kin marriage (Evans Grubbs 2002: 136–86). Marriage and the formation of families, as we will see further in a moment, played a key role in the creation of the Romans' identity as Romans.

The law aside, scholarship has emphasized that a variety of sources (e.g., comedies of Plautus, marriage contracts, the Greek physician Soranus' work on gynecology) proclaim the purpose of marriage to be the creation of children (rather than, say, personal satisfaction); there is little sign, among those who have left traces of their existences, that love was a prerequisite, though there is abundant evidence that it did develop, and that it was an ideal (Treggiari 1991: 229–61; Dixon 1991; Dixon

1992: 83–90). Spouses counted on each other to get through thick and thin, and might contribute to each other's emotional growth. That said, the relationship was hardly always symmetrical.

Among the top levels of society, which we know better, a clear double standard existed, allowing men to enjoy sex with certain other categories of women (e.g., slaves, and free concubines), while for citizen women sex outside marriage was, after legislation of Augustus, a criminal offense (Treggiari 1991: 262–319). Also, a potentially large age difference meant that older husbands might complete the 'education' of their teenage wives (Cohen and Saller 1994). A famous example is the marriage of Pliny the Younger, who, when he was over forty years old, took a bride in her mid-teenage years; with suitable deference she modeled her own behavior, Pliny tells us, after his. Pliny does not indicate whether he educated his wife sexually as well, but it seems very probable that husbands did give wives a sense of the role they were to play in that regard. This, too, brings us to the question of identity.

THE SOCIALIZING FORCE OF THE FAMILY: IDENTITY

In revealing all the rich varieties of the 'Roman family,' scholars have started to realize that the family was itself crucial in shaping the varied identities of its members. Families did not just impart economic roles and models of affective ties: they also gave individuals a sense of themselves as Romans, as Greeks, as Jews, or something else yet, or several of these at once (George 2005). Thus, because there was great diversity across the empire, the laws and customs of the traditional Roman (i.e., Italian) family did distinguish it from other types of families. *Patria potestas* we have mentioned, and also the recognition of monogamy only (and only certain types of monogamy at that). Soranus claims that in Rome mothers were less devoted to their children than was the case among the Greeks (2. 44). Ease of divorce was another trait seen as distinctive of the Romans. The Jewish historian Josephus, perfectly illustrating how individuals could see their identity in terms of family life, explains how a bill of divorce was issued among his own people: "It is only the husband who is permitted by us to do this, and not even a divorced woman may marry again on her own initiative unless her former husband consents" (*AJ* 15. 259). A contrast with Rome is clearly implied (Williams 2005).

Thus, for provincials becoming Roman citizens (and so subject to Roman civil law), family life proved an excellent way to witness, and take on, something of a Roman identity. Yet as recent discussions of 'Romanization' have stressed, old identities need not be, and were not, forgotten. The result was that in the cosmopolitan world of the high empire, traditional boundaries between Roman (i.e., Italian) and provincial families could break down (Arjava 1998; Osgood 2006). To give just one example: in some provincial societies there was a custom of rewarding a bride with a substantial gift for her virginity. This had not been the practice in Rome, and indeed gifts between brides and grooms were in principle illegal, since husband and wife, outside of a marriage with *manus*, were to segregate their property. Yet the gifts became a part of 'Roman' marriage, to the extent that Juvenal could refer to them in his notorious satire on the subject (6. 200–205), and law finally was created to deal with them (Evans Grubbs 1995: 156–83; Osgood 2006: 417–19). Families, then, could pass on a distinctive mixture of cultural practices to their young, which served to define their individual identities.

Economic aspects of family life were discussed above, but it is worth elaborating how families prepared their members for their role in the social hierarchy that characterized Roman society. For those of means, formal education was essential, but instruction in dress, deportment, and the display of emotion was no less crucial (Wiedemann 1989: 143–75). The Stoic Seneca, worried about how it is that a man comes to be crippled by anger, tellingly points to influences in childhood. A whole range of individuals in the *familia*, he argues, shapes the child's behavior: "'This is the way to walk. This is the way to eat. This behavior is appropriate for a man, this for a woman, this for a married man, this for a bachelor'... These are the instructions of a tutor to a boy, a grandmother to a grandson" (*Ep.* 94. 8–9). It is important to regulate how the very youngest children walk, according to Soranus, and even how newborns are swaddled, for otherwise (he thinks) their bodies will not develop suitably (Sor. 2. 14–15, 43–45). Clearly the most prominent Romans worried about the training of their young, not only for the sake of these young people, but also because it reflected on themselves. Augustus, for instance, according to his biographer, taught his grandsons such skills as swimming and writing (making sure they copied his own penmanship), while his daughter and granddaughters had to practice spinning wool (Suet. *Aug.* 64). The spastic disorder of Livia's grandson Claudius so concerned the couple, that they kept the child out of public life as much as possible: he would be an embarrassment to the family (Suet. *Cl.* 4). Evidence for the lower orders of society is scarcer, but parallel training can be deduced: fathers introducing their sons to a family patron or the landlord, for instance, or shopkeepers training their children in how to speak to their lofty customers.

Dress, deportment, and the display of emotion marked not just social standing but also gender. Though scholars have profitably considered gender as a sort of performance that society cues (rather than simply a consequence of biology), the role of the family in shaping the 'performance' has not yet been fully elucidated, important as it must have been. One tantalizing piece of evidence is a series of dolls, often jointed, made of a variety of materials (ranging from rags and bone to ivory), and found in a variety of archeological contexts (Wiedemann 1989: 149–50; Battaglia 1983). These are not 'baby dolls,' but depict adult women, sometimes sporting—in the most elaborate examples—hairstyles familiar from portraits of the empresses.

A well-known example (found outside Rome in the sarcophagus of a girl, Creperia Tryphaena, who was buried with her father) exhibits an elaborate tower coiffure, has traces of red paint on her cheek, and enjoys pierced ears. The doll was found with her other jewelry (e.g., a ring with a key on it), as well as toy mirrors, and larger combs—which perhaps belonged to her owner. Another instance is the ivory doll discovered in 1964 during construction on the Via Cassia in Rome, along with cosmetic containers and—amazingly—the embalmed body of a girl about eight years old.

Toys help children to internalize a picture of the world their families might wish them to have; in discussing playthings, anthropologists often see them as a model or metaphor of the culture from which they come, while psychologists emphasize their role as an actual mechanism of cultural transmission. Our dolls, then, illustrate the desired gender roles of Romans with at least some property, and how families tried to pass on their own notions of these roles. Girls at this level of society were apparently expected to grow up not as child-minders (hence, no baby dolls), but as attractive wives. They would distinguish themselves from their male counterparts, and showed off their high status in a variety of ways, including the use of clothing, jewelry, and cosmetics—distinctions beautifully illustrated on the mummy portraits of the prosperous denizens of Roman Egypt. A fascinating selection of lawyer's opinions on the subject of wills (preserved in Justinian's *Digest* 34. 2) usefully itemizes what was involved. Women's jewelry, for instance, included "earrings, bracelets, small bangles, rings with the exception of signet rings, and everything acquired for no other purpose than adorning the body" (Ulpian *Dig.* 34. 2. 25. 10). Their clothes were those "which a man cannot easily use without incurring censure" (Ulpian *Dig.* 34. 2. 23. 2). Women often passed these objects on to each other, the lawyers make clear, friend to friend, but also mother to daughter.

From the archeological evidence, then, and the legal texts, a picture emerges of Roman families making women of their young girls, in ways appropriate to their status. We glimpse this socialization, too, precisely as Jerome, writing at the start of the fifth century AD to a Christian mother, Laeta, tried to undermine it: "Do not pierce her ears," he advises, "do not paint cheeks consecrated to Christ with white lead or rouge; do not weigh down her neck with pearls and gold; do not burden her head with gems; do not dye her hair red and presage for her the fires of hell" (*Ep.* 107. 5). The letter illumines something of traditional practice (albeit in caricatured form), while also pointing to a momentous change that was to take place in the ideology of the family, with which we shall end. The point here is to recognize that parents and other members of the household undoubtedly encouraged a variety of activities, including types of play, as a way to suggest appropriate roles in life. And of course, these activities pertained not just to gender. The rhetorician Fronto, who functioned as Marcus Aurelius' tutor, writes that he gave his own grandson toy writing tablets and little pieces of paper—obviously in the hope that the boy would become an enthusiastic writer (*Amic.* 1. 12).

THE FAMILY AS METAPHOR: "I AM GLAD YOU HAVE COME CHILD"

The letter to Laeta quoted just above goes on to mention the story of Praetextata, aunt of a Christian girl who had been consecrated to God. When, on orders of her husband (who was hostile to the new faith), she had her teenage niece's hair waved and gave her new clothes, Jerome claims that an angel came to Praetextata in her sleep and said, "Have you dared to put your husband's power before Christ's?" The tale well exemplifies the claim made by Christian writers that faith could generate conflict with respect to traditional family practices (Pagels 1988: 3–31; Bradley 2003). An even more dramatic example is to be found in the case of the martyr Vibia Perpetua, who in her early twenties was turned over to the beasts in Carthage (in AD 203). Her story survives in an account that includes her very own words, a sort of 'prison diary' (Salisbury 1997; Bradley 2003: 166–72). By virtue of this text, we see how a young mother breaks with her own family members, especially her (non-Christian) father, but also, ultimately, deserts her infant son, and in a series of dreams imagines a different family for herself, including a father who resembles Christ far more than her own. For some early Christians, when parents or the other members of their worldly families did not embrace the new faith, a new, metaphorical, family substituted for the kin of birth: Christians had each other as brothers and sisters, and God was their Father. The hostility to the (non-Christian) household in Christian rhetoric suggests just how powerful a force that group traditionally was. And yet, once all members of a family were Christian, it could pass on identities to its young members precisely as it had before.

It thus has been questioned how much Christianity, as it became the dominant religion, changed the way Roman families actually worked (Evans Grubbs 1995; Arjava 1996; Nathan 2000; Cooper 2007). The answer may be not so much as one might guess—though as always, tracing changes in real practice (as opposed to ideology) is difficult, and change may have occurred for reasons other than those involving religion: above all, the disintegration of the empire, and the countless dislocations it caused. But without a doubt, there was at least a real transformation in the moral climate of the late antique period. We might offer one example of this kind of shift. Augustine, who thought that, since all men were sinners, all needed correction, recommended in his sermons beating miscreant members of the household, including wives and children: this kind of advice had never been given in classical texts before; such methods were supposed to be reserved for slaves (Saller 1994: 145–56; Shaw 1987b). Augustine now openly suggests what appears to be a new manner of using familial relations to generate a new kind of citizen for a new kind of community (on the new Christian community, see Becker in this volume). In short, we have here one Christian prescription for socialization via the family, and it differs from what had gone before. It is representative, though, of a much broader level of innovation in this realm brought about by the new religious situation. Ideas about the family, like those about the rest of the world around it, are now moving into the medieval period.

In years to come, historians of the Roman family may choose to scrutinize the large body of Christian writings more fully, to continue grappling with the problem of change, and in doing so, to illumine further how families of earlier times shaped their member's identities.

SUGGESTED READING

Developments in the study of the Roman family are best traced through a series of conference proceedings: Rawson 1986, Rawson 1991, Rawson and Weaver 1997, and George 2005. Note also the papers in Moxnes 1997, Corbier 1999, Dixon 2001a, and Balch and Osiek 2003. Valuable studies (often synchronic) of specific aspects of family relations include Dixon 1988, Bradley 1991, Treggiari 1991, Dixon 1992, Phang 2001, and Rawson 2003. For the family at key moments in Rome's history see Rosenstein 2004, Severy 2003, Milnor 2005, Nathan 2000, and Cooper 2007. Demographic aspects, always to be kept in mind, are powerfully revealed by Saller 1994. On how Roman law affected the family, see the recent studies of Evans Grubbs 1995, Arjava 1996, and Gardner 1998.

BIBLIOGRAPHY

Arjava, A. 1996. *Women and Law in Late Antiquity*. Oxford: Clarendon Press.
———. 1998. "Paternal Power in Late Antiquity." *Journal of Roman Studies* 88: 147–65.
Bagnall, R. S., and B. W. Frier. 1994. *The Demography of Roman Egypt*. Cambridge: Cambridge University Press.
Balch, D. L., and C. Osiek. 2003. *Early Christian Families in Context: An Interdisciplinary Dialogue*. Grand Rapids, Mich.: Eerdmans.
Battaglia, G. B. 1983. *Corredi funerari di età imperiale e barbarica nel Museo nazionale romano*. Rome: Edizioni Quasar.
Biscottini, M. V. 1966. "L'archivio di Tryphon, tessitore di Oxyrhynchos." *Aegyptus* 46: 60–90; 186–292.
Bradley, K. R. 1991. *Discovering the Roman Family*. Oxford: Oxford University Press.
———. 2001. "Children and Dreams." In Dixon 2001a: 43–51.
———. 2003. "Sacrificing the Family: Christian Martyrs and Their Kin." *Ancient Narrative* 3: 1–32.
Cohen, D., and R. Saller. 1994. 'Foucault on Sexuality in Greco-Roman Antiquity.' In J. Goldstein (ed.), *Foucault and the Writing of History*. Oxford: Blackwell. 35–59.
Cooper, K. 2007. *The Fall of the Roman Household*. Cambridge: Cambridge University Press.
Corbier, M. 1999. *Adoption et fosterage*. Paris: De Boccard.
Dionisotti, A. C. 1982. "From Ausonius' Schooldays? A Schoolbook and Its Relatives." *Journal of Roman Studies* 72: 83–125.
Dixon, S. 1986. "Family Finances: Terentia and Tullia." In B. Rawson (ed.), *The Family in Ancient Rome: New Perspectives*. Ithaca: Cornell University Press. 93–120.
———. 1988. *The Roman Mother*. Norman: University of Oklahoma Press.

———. 1991. "The Sentimental Ideal of the Roman Family." In B. Rawson (ed.), *Marriage, Divorce, and Children in Ancient Rome*. Oxford: Oxford University Press. 99–113.

———. 1992. *The Roman Family*. Baltimore: Johns Hopkins University Press.

———. 2001a. *Chilhood, Class and Kin in the Roman World*. 43–51. London: Routledge.

———. 2001b. "*Familia Veturia*: towards a Lower-class Economic Prosopography." In Dixon 2001a: 115–27.

Erdkamp, P. 2005. *The Grain Market in the Roman Empire: A Social, Political, and Economic Study*. Cambridge: Cambridge University Press.

Evans Grubbs, J. 1995. *Law and Family in Late Antiquity: The Emperor Constantine's Marriage Legislation*. Oxford: Clarendon Press.

———. 2002. *Women and the Law in the Roman Empire: A Sourcebook on Marriage, Divorce, and Widowhood*. London: Routledge.

———. 2005. "Parent-Child Conflict in the Roman Family: The Evidence of the Code of Justininian." In George 2005: 93–128.

Gardner, J. F. 1998. *Family and Familia in Roman Law and Life*. Oxford: Clarendon Press.

George, M. 1997a. "Repopulating the Roman House." In B. Rawson and P. Weaver (eds.), *The Roman Family in Italy: Status, Sentiment, and Space*. Oxford: Oxford University Press. 297–319.

———. 1997b. "*Servus* and *Domus*: The Slave in the Roman House." In R. Laurence and A. Wallace-Hadrill (eds.), *Domestic Space in the Roman World: Pompeii and Beyond*. Portsmouth, R.I.: Journal of Roman Archaeology. 15–24.

———. 2005. *The Roman Family in the Empire: Rome, Italy, and Beyond*. Oxford: Oxford University Press.

Hanson, A. E. 2000. "Widows Too Young in Their Widowhood." In D. E. E. Kleiner and S. B. Matheson (eds.), *I Claudia II: Women in Roman Art and Society*. Austin: University of Texas Press. 149–65.

———. 2001. "Papyrology: Minding Other People's Business." *Transactions of the American Philological Association* 131: 297–313.

Krause, J.-U. 1994–95. *Witwen und Waisen im römischen Reich*. 4 vols. Stuttgart: Franz Steiner Verlag.

Martin, D. B. 1996. "The Construction of the Ancient Family: Methodological Considerations." *Journal of Roman Studies* 86: 40–60.

Milnor, K. 2005. *Gender, Domesticity, and the Age of Augustus: Inventing Private Life*. Oxford: Oxford University Press.

Moxnes, H. 1997. *Constructing Early Christian Families: Family as Social Reality and Metaphor*. London: Routledge.

Nathan, G. 2000. *The Family in Late Antiquity: The Rise of Christianity and the Endurance of Tradition*. London: Routledge.

Osgood, J. 2006. "*Nuptiae iure civili congruae*: Apuleius's Story of Cupid and Psyche and the Roman Law of Marriage." *Transactions of the American Philological Association* 136: 415–41.

Pagels, E. 1988. *Adam, Eve, and the Serpent*. New York: Random House.

Phang, S. E. 2001. *The Marriage of Roman Soldiers (13 B.C.—A.D. 235): Law and Family in the Imperial Army*. Leiden: E. J. Brill.

Rawson, B. 1986. *The Family in Ancient Rome: New Perspectives*. Ithaca: Cornell University Press.

———. 1991. *Marriage, Divorce and Children in Ancient Rome*. Oxford: Clarendon Press.

———. 1997. "'The Family' in the Ancient Mediterranean: Past, Present, Future." *Zeitschrift für Papyrologie und Epigraphik* 117: 294–96.

————. 2003. *Children and Childhood in Roman Italy*. Oxford: Clarendon Press.

Rawson, B., and P. Weaver. 1997. *The Roman Family in Italy: Status, Sentiment, Space*. Oxford: Clarendon Press.

Riggsby, A. 1997. "'Private' and 'Public' in Roman Culture: The Case of the *Cubiculum*." *Journal of Roman Archaeology* 10: 36–56.

Rosenstein, N. 2004. *Rome at War: Farms, Families, and Death in the Middle Republic*. Chapel Hill: University of North Carolina Press.

Rowlandson, J. 1998. *Women and Society in Greek and Roman Egypt*. Cambridge: Cambridge University Press.

Salisbury, J. 1997. *Perpetua's Passion: The Death and Memory of a Young Roman Woman*. London: Routledge.

Saller, R. P. 1984. "*Familia, domus*, and the Roman Conception of the Family." *Phoenix* 38: 336–55.

————. 1987. "Men's Age at Marriage and Its Consequences in the Roman Family." *Classical Philology* 82: 20–35.

————. 1994. *Patriarchy, Property, and Death in the Roman Family*. Cambridge: Cambridge University Press.

————. 2003. "Women, Slaves, and the Economy of the Roman Household." In Balch and Osiek 2003: 185–204.

Saller, R. P., and B. D. Shaw. 1984. "Tombstones and Roman Family Relations in the Principate: Civilians, Soldiers, and Slaves." *Journal of Roman Studies* 74: 124–56.

Scheidel, W. 2001. *Debating Roman Demography*. Leiden: E. J. Brill.

Severy, B. 2003. *Augustus and the Family at the Birth of the Roman Empire*. London: Routledge.

Shaw, B. D. 1987a. "The Age of Roman Girls at Marriage: Some Reconsiderations." *Journal of Roman Studies* 77: 30–46.

————. 1987b. "The Family of Late Antiquity: The Experience of Augustine." *Past and Present* 115: 3–51.

Treggiari, S. M. 1991. *Roman Marriage: Iusti Coniuges from the Time of Cicero to the Time of Ulpian*. Oxford: Clarendon Press.

————. 2007. *Terentia, Tullia and Publilia: The Women of Cicero's Family*. London: Routledge.

Wallace-Hadrill, A. 1994. *Houses and Society in Pompeii and Herculaneum*. Princeton: Princeton University Press.

Weaver, P. R. C. 1972. *Familia Caesaris: A Social Study of the Emperor's Freedmen and Slaves*. Cambridge: Cambridge University Press.

————. 1991. "Children of Freedmen (and Freedwomen)." In Rawson 1991: 166–90.

————. 2001. "Reconstructing Lower-Class Roman Families." In Dixon 2001a: 101–14.

Wiedemann, T. 1989. *Adults and Children in the Roman Empire*. New Haven: Yale University Press.

Williams, M. 2005. "The Jewish Family from Pompey to Hadrian—the Limits of Romanization." In George 2005: 159–82.

CHAPTER 4

PRIMARY EDUCATION

MARIETTA HORSTER

INTRODUCTION: EDUCATIONAL CONCEPTS, NARRATIVE STRATEGIES

THE Roman literary discourse upon Roman education conceptualized its distinctiveness in values and institutions: Roman education was narrowly linked to the history of Rome, to the greatness of the early Romans, and it was especially characterized as being distinct from Greek education. The literary topos of a dichotomy between the 'theoretical' Greeks and the 'utilitarian' Romans was thus repeated in this context. This distinctiveness was heavily based on Roman predilection for the *exemplum* (example, precedent) and the *mos maiorum* (customary way of the elders). Even in imperial times, when it was common to use private teachers and to send children to school, the praised ideal continued to be the republican senator M. Porcius Cato (cos. 195 BC), who had educated his sons by his personal example, thus preparing them for their offices, and integrating them into the world of the *exempla* of Roman heroes and traditions of the past.

As compared to the Greeks, a Roman might claim that "our customs (*mores*) and ways of life (*instituta vitae*), our family and domestic affairs are much better and nobler. Beyond doubt, our ancestors have established our Republic with better institutions and laws (*instituta et leges*). What shall I say of military affairs, in which our (ancestors) were outstanding because of their manly virtues (*virtus*), and still even more because of their discipline (*disciplina*)? As to those things which are attained by nature (*natura*) and not by intellectual education (*non litterae*), neither the Greeks nor any other people may be compared to us. Is there any other nation in which such dignity (*gravitas*), steadiness (*constantia*), magnanimity (*magnitudo animi*), propriety (*probitas*), faith (*fides*), and such distinguished virtue (*virtus*) exists, as to be compared to our ancestors? In erudition (*doctrina*) and all kinds of writing (*genus literarum*), indeed, the Greeks excelled us, and this was easy because we accepted our inferiority (in this very domain)." Cicero (*Tusc.* 1. 2) presents this praise of Roman institutions, Roman virtues, and Roman history at the very beginning of a long and learned discussion of Greek philosophy in Latin language. The context makes quite clear that, according to Cicero's protagonist, the Romans used to be superior in every respect except in learning, literature, and philosophy—but, even in the intellectual sphere, Greek predominance belongs to the past, because the Romans now (in the first century BC) compete successfully with and rival them in, for example, oratory.

The Roman elite's concept of education by examples, then, leads to the notion that Roman virtue could not simply be learned from books or in school, and could not be appropriately taught by a non-Roman teacher. The city, with its monuments, institutions, rituals, and its people, incorporated the collective memory about individual exploits and Rome's rise to imperial greatness (cf. Hölkeskamp 2006). Accordingly, moral courage, discipline, and virtues like *pietas* (piety, respect) and *constantia* (resolution, constancy) had to be passed on to the next generation by *exemplum*. A child's most important examples, according to this model of education, were the family members: father, mother—and mothers served as examples not only for girls (Dixon 1988: 109)—elder brothers, and the ancestors. In short, the family, especially the parents, were personally responsible for their children's education (cf. Osgood in this volume). In the elaborated biographies of the great men of the second century BC, we are told that, accordingly, only public affairs could restrain a good Roman senator from being engaged in his boys' education (Plut. *Cato* 20. 4; *Aem. Paul.* 6. 4). Now, while Cato as well as Aemilius Paulus guided and supervised their respective children's moral education, the latter decided in addition to use teachers—in accordance with the Greek model—at least for knowledge transfer, for literary education.

During the second century BC, public and private booty, the extensive use of Greek slaves, personal contacts of senators and wealthy knights with Greek culture and learning, the presence of Greek philosophers and physicians, Egyptian astronomers, and other learned men from the East in the city of Rome and some Italian cities all made alternatives of life-style and values, as well as differences in cultural attitudes, more visible and present than they had been previously, when access to other such cultural models had been limited to contacts with the inhabitants of Magna Graecia in southern Italy and Sicily. More and more, especially as the Romans expanded their empire in the East, Rome became a melting pot, a multicultural city (Q. Cic. *Pet.* 14. 54; Sen. *Dial.* 12. 6. 2–4, cf. Juvenal's satire on Rome 3. 60–74).[1] However, it is rather difficult to discern the direct and indirect influences of Greek educational concepts on Roman primary education, because our knowledge of the Roman republican educational concepts are influenced and distorted by the

---

1. Cf. the various essays in Edwards and Woolf 2003.

long-propagated image of the stern, just, and unaffected Roman nobles, exemplified by the life and maxims of a Cato.

That said, despite the portrait of Cato so fastidiously drawn by Roman authors, Cato was neither a Hellenophobe, nor in general did he resist writings, habits, objects, and so forth alien to Roman culture—nor did he object to learning Greek, if learned properly (Gruen 1992: 56–61). He nonetheless admonished the Roman senators in his speeches and writings to keep to the Roman *mores* (traditions—see Kienast 1954: 101–16; Astin 1978: 157–81, Gruen 1992: 52–83). But Cato's fears were wrong, to the extent that the Roman *exemplum*-model for learning was not replaced by the Greek model. Instead, the Roman elite "selectively fashioned Greek educational principles into a uniquely Roman form of citizen training" (Corbeill 2001: 261). This adaptation facilitated the continuity both of the elite's educational practices and objectives under changing social and political conditions, as well as of the *exemplum*-discourse, with its focus on the elite family's role in transmitting senatorial traditions and republican values into imperial times.

The nature of teaching in schools is known from Athens, and a very few other places in mainland Greece, already in the second half of the fifth century BC (cf. Marrou 1965: 74–86; Harris 1989: 98–102; Morgan 1998: 9–24). In Hellenistic times, intellectual and physical instruction by teachers for boys (sometimes girls) and teenagers became widespread in Greek-speaking cities in the east, and gradually spread to the west. Thus, it would appear that schools and teachers, outside of Roman households, may have begun to occur at Rome in the third century BC; earlier examples, however, surely belong to the realm of mythography (e.g., that Romulus and Remus went to school in Gabii, where they were taught Greek learning: Dion. Hal. 1. 84. 5).

Connected to the *exemplum*-discourse is the use of words like kneading, molding, and shaping both a child's body and mind. The forming of a child's body is meant quite literally: wrapping the baby in swaddling clothes so as to perfect the child's physical shape (cf. Krause in this volume), and later, physically training the body of a young boy.[2] Many Roman texts of different genres communicate the idea that every (free-born) child has an inborn natural intellect and character (e.g., Plut. *TG* 1. 4). Consequently, the child was thought to be a kind of initial raw material, from which the Roman citizen was to be fashioned; and herein lay the purpose of education.

The result of this all was that such ideals caused much of an education, at least insofar as it concerned one's place and function in society, to be got from one's family members. However, there were basics that had to be learned first. Here, family members were generally not considered to be the best teachers. Thus, professionals

---

2. The corporal aspect, however, is often neglected in Roman intellectuals' discourses on rearing and educating. Modern appraisals of sports in Roman times focus on the aspect of athletic contests, sometimes integrating even gladiatorial games as part of the subject. On physical education, which involved sports and athletics, see Fortuin 1996; Cagniart 2000; Corbeill 2001: 277–81; Newby 2005.

could well be engaged for much of a child's primary education. In what follows, we will be interested to observe just who taught what to children, and also to see just how these various lessons were imparted.

Differences in Social Classes and Gender

As already stated, the *exemplum*, the commemoration of ancestors, the high standards of moral education were the fundaments of education in senatorial families and for those equestrians who were closely connected to senatorial families. The middle and lower classes' ideals and educational concepts in republican times remain blurry (though, cf. Horsfall 2003: 48–63). We may be sure that usually children of low social contexts did not learn reading and writing at all. However, some low-born adults may have later learned some second language—for example, in the army, with business partners, or by other personal contacts (cf. Horsfall 2003: 48–50). A little and very specific 'reading' knowledge (e.g., to recognize a firm's trademark like a picture on some pottery) and some calculating may have been another effect of a young man's occupational needs. The many immigrants, the integrative power of the auxiliary units of the army, the mobility of business people and craftsmen, as well as the use and presence of slaves with other mother tongues may have added to the integration of some other language elements into Latin and Greek even on a quite vulgar level. This was not the effect of an 'education' of children from the lower strata, but the practical and unspectacular consequence of low-class acculturation to the needs of very specific living conditions. In any case, sources like the second-century BC Terentian comedy *Adelphoi*, which deal with notions of education in a seemingly middle-class setting, emulated Greek models; in any case, here and in other such plays, the plot was set in Athens and Attica. The validity of the embedded information on Roman middle-class concerns is therefore debatable.

When, in the late republic, and increasingly in imperial times, primary schools became more common in Rome, Italy, and cities in the West of the Roman Empire, the probability of learning the basics of reading, writing, and arithmetic increased for non-upper-class persons. We may only guess that the moral ideals transmitted in primary schools for middle-class boys (and some girls) were orientated toward the upper-class education and, in general outlines, did not differ much from what a senator's son might have learned from his private teachers and his father (cf. also Hor. *Sat.* 1. 4. 76–79).

The collections of letters that we have from several senators (Cicero, Pliny, Fronto), and many other writings, demonstrate that learning and education constituted an essential part of the elite's perception of social status (see Hedrick and Hahn in this volume). However, the elite ideal, that only politics, public affairs and office-holding, military matters, and the practice of law constituted serious and noble activities, deferred all intellectual ambitions and pursuits to *otium*, leisure time. It was here that the aristocrat might put much of his education on display, and thus cut for himself a place of distinction in Roman social circles.

Such *otium*, defined by the temporary absence of public duties, did not, however, exist for women. Rather, women's life was organized in accordance with male social and public life and obligations. Married upper-class women and widows in the cities all over the empire could at least make public use of their wealth; they participated in their husbands' and families' social life, and obviously needed a particular education to fulfill such obligations like taking part in the social and religious life inside and outside the house, taking over some responsibilities in the household and the city, behaving properly in any public situation, raising their children according to the accepted standards (cf. Hemelrijk 1999: 7–16). Traditional female virtues like chastity (*pudicita, castitas*) and modesty (*modestia*) (cf. von Hesberg-Tonn 1983) were transmitted by examples and role models, and we can expect that all members, both male and female, of an elite family will have helped to pass such information on to their young girls.

In Rome, Italy, and the western provinces, then, the primary education mainly consisted of learning to read and write, with the addition of some arithmetic that enabled one to count, weigh, and measure. In the eastern provinces, the Hellenistic tradition of instruction in reading, writing, mathematics, music, and physical training, which started with teachers for smaller children and continued in the gymnasium for teenagers, continued under Roman domination (cf. Scholz 2004). Thus, in the huge Roman Empire, the educational ideas, methods, and subject matters differed between the Latin-speaking West and the Greek-speaking East.

Yet, despite these differences, the elementary level of education in elite families was generally thought best to take place at home, under the father's supervision, or in imperial times in the West, and from Hellenistic times onward in the East, might be realized by a private teacher at home. Parents who could not afford a private teacher but were wealthy enough to pay for a primary education sent their children to school. In any case, early education, in late republican and imperial times, was followed by instruction in literature and language under the supervision of a grammarian (lat. *grammaticus*, gr. *grammatikos*).

The exposition and discussion of literary texts, in both prose and verse, was the fundament and background to acquiring additional knowledge in the fields of mythology, geography, history, astronomy, and so forth. This secondary education in language and literature continued until about the age of fourteen, but it should be noted that the school organization, the stages of education and age brackets, were flexible. A senator's son who had reached the age of fourteen replaced his *toga praetexta* (the youth's clothes) with the *toga virilis* (the adult's vesture), and was then supposed to start a period of apprenticeship in politics, law, and rhetoric. For this purpose he accompanied a male member of the family, or a close friend of his father, into the senate, the forum, and the courts. This practical instruction, which was the basis of republican senatorial education in politics and public actions, rituals, and procedures, continued into imperial times, but was combined with the higher education by professional teachers. This combined style of education started in the late second century

BC, when senators' sons increasingly received additional formation with rhetors and philosophers (cf. Connolly and Hahn in this volume; and on the law, Kehoe).

Ambitious parents from the Roman upper classes had their children educated from the very beginning in both languages, namely, Latin and Greek. The learning of Latin in the eastern part of the empire seems to have been of no less interest for the member of the elites than was Greek for the westerners, but obviously for different reasons. Greek for the non-Greeks was the language of education, the language of civilization, the language of Homer, the language of philosophy, the language of a high percentage of Roman subjects and citizens born and educated in the East—whereas Latin for the Greeks (and other non-native-Latin speakers) was the language of administration and the law, the language of the army, the language of careers in international administration, politics, and business (Adams 2003: 9–14; Eck 2000; Eck 2004).

The numbers of schools at all levels of education increased during the principate, and a primary education outside the home became easier to obtain all over the empire. As a rule, in Rome and the western part of the empire, primary education was paid for by the parents. In difference to exclusively private education, several parents would pay for one teacher, which made him, or the school (if there existed more than one teacher), a 'public' one. The wealthy senator Pliny, for example, was willing to contribute one-third of a (grammar) teacher's remuneration as a special kind of benefaction to the fellow citizens of his hometown Como (Plin. *Ep.* 4. 13). In the Greek East, with its tradition of gymnasia, private donations, and liturgical contributions to the gymnasia, primary and secondary education was perhaps often less expensive, or sometimes even free.

In spite of the facilitation of access to primary education by the spread of schools and teachers, at no time and in no place was there established a public educational system with free access to all children. Children of the senatorial class, as well as of wealthy and ambitious other families, did not attend primary schools, but continued to study with private teachers (i.e., their families' own slaves or paid instructors) (Booth 1979b). Thus, Pliny the Elder designates a boy attending a (public) school as poor (Plin. *Nat.* 9. 8. 25). The style of one's education, then, was socially determined. A thorough (private) education on the primary level continued to be connected to wealth and social status. The consequences of such practices, that is to say, the quality (literacy, semi-literacy) and quantification of literacy in the late republic and the principate are still matters of debate. Apart from the social strata concerned, modern estimates of the overall population's literacy quota vary between 5% and 20%, with great differences regarding periods, cities, regions, and individual provinces.[3]

Most often, texts speak about the education of boys in general, or of individual male children: boys became soldiers, citizens, senators; young men participated

3. Harris 1989: 3–42, 175–284, 328–30. Harris is still a standard work and an invaluable survey on the subject of literacy, but some of his definitions, methods, and conclusions have been criticized. For different approaches regarding the differences in writing and reading skills, the uses and functions of literacy, as well as the challenge and complexity of an approach to literacy in bi- and multi-lingual societies, see the papers of M. Beard, J. L. Franklin, N. Horsfall, M. Corbier, A. K. Bowman, K. Hopkins, and A. E. Hanson in Humphrey 1991: 35–198. See also Woolf 2000, Adams 2003, and Johnson and Parker 2009.

in politics, earned money, defended Roman soil with arms and Roman values and morals with words and deeds. Accordingly, the ancient sources barely speak of the upbringing and education of girls. A few remarks about exceptionally well educated (in literature, philosophy, music, etc.) upper-class women, however, imply that a basic intellectual education had been a standard at least for senatorial daughters during the republic, and for many girls of the senatorial and equestrian orders and the municipal elites in imperial times (Hemelrijk 1999: 17–28). High moral standards and specific Roman values, as well as a sense of propriety, were the objectives in the education of both boys and girls. Girls of well-to-do parents, who could afford private teachers, probably received private instruction, whereas most of the other girls presumably did not have such a chance. Few authors mention girls in (primary) schools, though the following seem to: Horace (*Sat.* 1. 10. 91), Martial (*Ep.* 3. 69. 8; 8. 3. 15–16; 9. 68. 2), and Apuleius (*Met.* 9. 17. 2). More evidence for girls' public education is known from Asia Minor and Egypt (Cribiore 2001: 74–101), but much of the extant documentation dates to Hellenistic times; only one inscribed text reveals an endowment, which explicitly mentions free education for both boys and girls.[4]

But what of the children who were not even free-born? The rearing of slaves was likewise based on the concept of forming a particular kind of individual, but had significantly other aims in this, and thus a significantly different educational concept: not to bring out the best, to anchor virtues and values in the mind by education and the teaching of letters, literature, and the cultural memory of the Romans, but rather, 'training.' Young slaves were manipulated, trained, and taught like whelps or colts (Plut. *Cato* 21. 1). The fostering of 'homeborn' slave children (*vernae*) was useful for the master's own requirements in the household (e.g., Nep. *Atticus* 13. 3; Plut. *Cato* 21. 7; Plut. *Crassus* 2. 6), and it was quite literally an economic investment, since trained slaves—for example, as singers, hairdressers, financial administrators, private secretaries, or teachers of Greek language and literature—could be sold at a higher price than they had been worth before such training. Accordingly, some slave children received a primary education either at home, if they were owned by wealthy families in which private education was common, or with teachers in the local community (Booth 1979a).

The Parent's Role

The personal involvement of a good father in the moral and intellectual education of his young sons may have been a reality, but it was also a literary topos in (esp.) Roman biography. Literature of the late first and second century AD presents the noble Roman as someone who supervised his wife's caring for the children (the *exemplum* here might be Cato), and who controlled the teachers of his adolescent

---

4. The inscription is from Xanthus, in Lycia, and dates to the second century AD: *SEG* 30 (1980) 1535.

sons (for this, Aemilius Paulus could be isolated as the exemplar)—that is to say, if he had decided not personally to teach the boys (sons or grandsons) in all (as did Cato) or at least some (as did Augustus) subjects (Plut. *Cato* 20. 2, 4; *Aem. Paul.* 6. 10; Suet. *Aug.* 64. 3; cf. Tac. *Dial.* 34).

The father's responsibility and important engagement in his sons' moral education is attested as well for some middle-class literati. Horace, for example, praises his father, a freedman and money collector, to whom he owed all his good features and virtues. He says explicitly that his own essence derived from his father's personal qualities, as well as from his father's financial and personal sacrifices, which provided Horace with a good school education (Hor. *Sat.* 1. 6. 65–92). Or there is Juvenal, who ridicules a father's bad, even monstrous, example, which made his son worse and less scrupulous than even the father (Juv. *Sat.* 5. 14). Both poets attest the widespread view that it was the father's example and influence that most of all formed a boy's character, for good or for bad. In such late republican and early imperial (potentially) middle-class contexts, however, the attendant literary and intellectual education is typically not dependent upon the father, but left to teachers.

A mother's commitment in her children's upbringing and education is in general mentioned only in the context of few extraordinary women (cf. Tac. *Dial.* 28. 4–6). Here, the topic of noble widows like Cornelia, the mother of the Gracchi, or Julia Procilla, mother of Agricola, who were praised for the moral guidance and the forming of their children into morally excellent young men (Plut. *TG* 1. 4; Tac. *Agr.* 4. 2–4; cf. Sen. *Cons. AD Marciam* 24. 1–4), was more common than that of women's engagement in the intellectual education of their children (but see Quint. *Inst.* 1. 1. 6–8 on Cornelia). Admittedly, mothers and their educational influence are rarely mentioned in Roman literature (Dixon 1988).[5]

Teachers and 'Schools': The First Years

Not later than the mid-first century BC, the cherished ideal of the Roman father as his son's moral and intellectual teacher was a well-established part in the literary discourse about Rome's grandeur and superiority. The employment and use of teachers was thus often characterized as un-Roman. One of the anecdotes that manifested the Roman ideal was incorporated into the heroic picture of M. Furius Camillus, the incarnation of Roman *mores* (traditional values).[6] Livy (5. 27) demonstrates what it could mean to make use of a professional teacher (in the Greek manner) because one would entrust the education of the youth to a non-Roman and thus potentially un-reliable man. When Camillus waged war against

---

5. Again, see also Osgood in this volume on the educative role of the family.

6. It seems likely that Camillus was one of the famous Roman nobles who were praised at banquets, for example, at Cato's house (Plut. *Cato* 25. 3; cf. Cic. *Brutus* 75).

the Faliscans and laid siege to their city Falerii in 395 BC, he was able to end the siege because of the young Faliscans' treacherous professional teacher (*magister et comes*, teacher and companion), who attempted to give his students as hostages to the Romans besieging the town. In any case, Livy's remark in this context, namely, that the use of one teacher for several boys is still a common feature of the Greek education of his own time, insinuates that at the end of the first century BC it was not, by contrast, a common practice in Rome and Italy.

In Greece, *paedagogoi*, generally slaves who supervised the children of the richer people, are attested from the late fifth century BC. The earliest attestations of such persons in the Roman world—apart from unhistorical 'heroic' accounts (Liv. 3. 44. 6; Dion. Hal. *Ant.* 11. 28. 3)—are supplied by Cicero in the mid-first century BC. As soon as schools and public teaching had become more common, though, boys (and few girls) went to their classes often accompanied by a slave or freedman (the *paedagogus*). In addition, these pedagogues tutored the children and supervised their lessons and school exercises. Most of the pedagogues, who are typically known from their own epitaphs, are male; only four females are attested in the city of Rome.[7]

Public primary teaching in Rome, and the Roman Empire, was not always organized in schools with several teachers; actually, one teacher per school seems to have been the prevalent model. When taught by one teacher in one room, groups with children of different levels might be separated in different corners, and assistant teachers or elder pupils might be asked to help with the education of the beginners. A third century AD school handbook (*Hermeneumata*) from Gaul gives an example of an elder pupil's day at school:

> I go to school. I enter and I say, "Good morning, teacher." (...) My slave gives me the tablets, the case; I take out the stylus and sit down at my place: I erase and copy according to the model. Afterwards, I show my writing to the teacher, who makes every kind of correction. (...) "Give me a dictation," I ask. Another student dictates to me. (...) When the teacher bids them, the little ones engage in letters and syllables, and one of the older students pronounces them aloud for them. Others recite in order the words to the assistant teacher and write verses. Being in the first group, I take a dictation.[8]

In this example, children of the elementary level were taught together with students of the secondary level. It should be noted that there did not always exist distinct successive stages in education (primary education, grammar and literature, rhetoric) with different schools or different teachers (Booth 1979b; Vössing 2003: 475–78).

The teaching of children outside the private household could take place in diverse settings: in especially separated rooms of some private or public buildings as well as in the street, in a corner of the forum or under a portico, not always even

---

7. Some pedagogues might also have been teachers to the children entrusted to their care, on which cf. Bonner 1977: 37–46; Booth 1979b. For female *paedagogae* from Rome, see: *CIL* VI 4459, 6331, 9754, 9758. Only one female pedagogue is attested in the papyri, *P. Oxy.* L 3555, cf. Cribiore 2001: 47.

8. Translation by Cribiore 2001: 15.

separated by a curtain from the passers-by.[9] The schools were called *ludus, schola* (Latin), or *didaskaleia* (Greek), but most often were referred to by one of the miscellaneous designations for primary teacher: *litterator, magister, institutor, praeceptor* (Latin), *grammatistes, didaskalos* (Greek), or the like. *Calculatores* (elementary teachers of mathematics) are attested as well. The teachers of the advanced education in either Greek or Latin (or both) were most often named grammarians (*grammaticus, grammatikos*); they focused on their pupils' refinement in speaking abilities, in reading and writing skills. By reading and memorizing poems and larger parts of various works of literature, the boys (and few girls) gained wider and deeper knowledge, learning, and cultivation, and were thus prepared for a continuing formation in rhetoric, which, at least by the mid-first century AD, was viewed as a necessary prerequisite to take over public duties and offices (cf. Connolly in this volume).

Primary teachers had a low social status. The monthly, or periodical, remuneration was minimal. They were usually paid directly by the children's parents, of whom not all were entirely trustworthy. Grammarians (i.e., secondary teachers) enjoyed a much better income. Those who instructed pupils of wealthy and famous families had quite a high social standing and were able to attain real prosperity. Apart from origin and family background, a teacher's social standing depended very much on his learning, the level of his teaching, and on the socio-economic contexts of his pupil's family. But, as with many other professionals, there were significant differences concerning qualifications, competence, and, thus, income.[10] It should also be noted that some teachers of the higher levels of education (grammarians, rhetors, and philosophers) might receive an exemption from taxes and civic duties (see Hahn in this volume), whereas teachers of the elementary level were explicitly excluded from any such privileges by a late second-/early third-century imperial decree (*Dig.* 50. 4. 11. 4). We know of only one exception to that rule: in a remote Portuguese village, with a state-run mine, the difficulty in obtaining elementary teachers (*ludi magistri*), as it would appear, was counter-balanced via a grant from the overseer of the mine (the *procurator metallorum*) of such exemptions to teachers who would volunteer to go there (*ILS* 6891 line 57).

A specific pedagogical training for teachers did not exist, and 'pedagogical accomplishments' seem to have been of little importance. With the exception of few critical voices (Quint. *Inst.* 1. 1. 20; 1. 3. 13–17; Ps.-Plut. *Lib. educ.* 12), coercive education and corporal punishment—liberally applied blows with a cane (*ferula*) or a birch—were entirely accepted and often used to correct and direct the pupils who were unwilling, lazy, slow, or who misbehaved. The few authors, from whom we have commentaries on their school days, and who reflect on their teachers' behavior, represent school as

9. On teaching in the streets, or at street corners, see, e.g., Hor. *Ep.* 1. 20. 17–18, D. Chr. *Or.* 20. 9. For an overview of the various attested localities (excluding Greek gymnasia), see Bonner 1977: 115–125.

10. On the social status of both, teachers of the elementary level and grammarians, in the city of Rome, see Christes 1979; Riess 2001. On payment and social status of teachers in late antiquity, see Kaster 1983.

a severe and painful experience.[11] Quintilian's arguments against beatings and other corporal punishments in school have to do with the awkward consequences of too much pressure on the young: the child might come to hate and dread learning. Thus, Quintilian recommends strongly that one should not force young children to learn, but ought to make them like the subjects by incentives (*Inst.* 1. 1. 20; 1. 3. 8–12). During the lessons, young children should have pleasure, volunteer answers, be praised, and be rewarded with prizes attractive for their age group. In addition, he recommends that children be taught in groups, so that they might learn by competition.[12] The ideal teacher should behave like an ideal father-teacher, and would thereby gain respect and veneration similar to that of the pupil for his father (*Inst.* 2. 2. 4–5; 2. 9. 1–2).

As already demonstrated by Quintilian's educational theories, and the above-mentioned coercive education, the teachers' pedagogic leeway was significant—and their intellectual qualifications might likewise range fairly widely. Thus, Horace praises his father for having spared him from receiving his early schooling in Venusia, his small hometown; in Horace's witty account, the boys attending this one-room schoolhouse were the sturdy sons of Roman military sergeants, who paid a paltry tuition fee of eight asses, and got precisely their money's worth (Hor. *Sat.* 1. 6. 69–75). Horace's ambitious father, however, enabled him to attend school in Rome, so that he might receive a truly intellectual education (*docendum artis*), one comparable to that had by the sons of Roman knights and senators who were taught by their fathers and then private teachers (Hor. *Sat.* 1. 6. 76–80). School fees and the cost of living were much higher in Rome than at Venusia—and decent clothes for the schoolboy, and the company of one or more slaves to escort him on his way, were part of the capital's lifestyle. In short, the options, organization, quality, and costs of primary education differed greatly in the Roman world.

A Pupil's Day

From the late first century BC, teaching—both with a private tutor at home, and with a teacher in a public school—started early in the morning.[13] The children who went to school were most often accompanied by an adult pedagogue. The pupils

11. Thus, e.g.: Hor. *Ep.* 2. 1. 70; Juv. *Sat.* 1. 15; cf. Mart. 9. 68. 1–4; 10. 62. 10. Augustine was less than happy about his school days and the teachers' brutality (*Conf.* 1. 9. 4; *Civ. Dei* 21. 14. 26); yet, he acknowledges the efficiency of this kind of pedagogy (*Conf.* 1. 12. 19). For more references to physical punishments by teachers, see Bonner 1977: 143–45; Cribiore 2001: 65–73; Christes 2003. On the general background of a coercive and violent education, see Krause in this volume.

12. Competition and awards, as pedagogical means, are better attested on the advanced levels of education; see Bonner 1977: 134–35.

13. Bonner 1977: 126–45 gives an overview of the schools' equipment and organization. Some corrections to his presentation, with additions especially concerning the evidence from Roman Egypt, are offered by Cribiore 2001: 127–59.

had a writing kit (*loculus*; see Hor. *Sat.* 1. 6. 74), a small case with pens, possibly an ink pot, and a sponge. Awaited by their teacher, they would take a seat on the floor, on benches, or sometimes chairs. The lessons lasted until noon. There was a lunch break, after which the lessons re-started for a short period in the early afternoon. It is unknown whether the pupils usually had homework, or weather that depended entirely on their parents' and pedagogues' ambition to force or encourage the children to rehearse and deepen what they had learned during the day. A pupil might go home in tears—this topos in Graeco-Roman literature (e.g., Lucian *Par.* 13) reflects the severe and harsh methods of instruction (see above), but it is not likely that this was the typical end of a boy's or girl's day of school. Apart from Roman holidays like the Saturnalia in December, the children had a day off every eight days, and long vacations in summer.

The main skills worked on during the lessons were careful listening, memorizing and repeating, and copying and writing. Depending on the material available, exercises were written on wooden tablets (generally coated with wax), on papyri (often recycled or of low quality), or on potsherds (*ostraca*). The pupils used a sharpened stick (*stilus*) to write in the wax; the non-sharpened end of the sticks was flat, and used for erasure of letters and texts and smoothing the wax. The ink-writing on papyri could be washed out with a sponge, or the blank back of a papyrus could be used. Small pieces cut out from larger papyri were sufficient for school exercises. Ostraca fulfilled the same needs for the children, and were easily available.

Elementary training began with an introduction to the alphabet. The letters' shapes had to be learned and recognized, and there were exercises to train the children to reproduce the letters skillfully. Gradually, combinations of letters, short syllables, and then larger syllables and monosyllabic words were introduced. This picture of a linear movement, from simple letters to words and finally sentences, is presented (e.g.) by Quintilian's description of the ideal technique for mastering reading and writing (*Inst.* 24–33). The pupils formed their letters according to alphabetic tables used as models, or they were given ivory or wooden letters to play with, or were asked to trace letters in carved templates (*Inst.* 1. 1. 26–27). However, Cribiore (2001: 169–72) has now demonstrated that, at least in exercises from Graeco-Roman Egypt, this rectilinear kind of training was not always observed. Some teachers preferred that their students copy sentences and brief passages to improve their letter-writing, even before they were able to read and understand what they had written.

Private teachers had more options to motivate and stimulate children who were not learning properly. Sometimes, imaginative and attentive parents might support them in their difficult task, as an anecdote concerning the "foolish" son of the rich and erudite Herodes Atticus (second century AD) exhibits: twenty-four slaves, who were each named with one letter of the alphabet, were supposed to accompany the boy and help him learn the letters by heart (Philostr. *VS* 558). Without such extraordinary help, though, a good memory and much concentration were needed for most of the alphabet exercises, in which the pupils had to write down letters in all imaginable sequences and combinations (Quint. *Inst.* 1. 1. 30–37; cf. Cribiore 1996: 40–42). Apart from the knowledge of letters, a very important effect of this kind of "mental gymnastics" (Cribiore 2001: 166) was the improvement and training of the memory.

After the pupils had obtained sufficient knowledge in the writing and reading of letters and syllables, they started writing words, first their personal names, and then other words, often in the order of the alphabet. Some such word lists (which are preserved on Greek papyri in both teachers' and pupils' handwritings) were grouped by subjects: proper names of gods, months of the year, animals, rivers, and so forth (Cribiore 1996: 42–43; Morgan 1998: 77, 101–3, 314–15). Frequently, such words were split up into syllables, which made reading, writing, and memorizing much easier for these pupils who had earlier been thoroughly drilled in these syllables. This training in recognizing and recollecting syllables enabled the pupil to read—very slowly—sentences and longer texts. Improvement of writing skills was simultaneously furthered by copying and dictation. However, reading and writing skills were not necessarily equally well acquired, and, as already noted, the ideal linear order of teaching and training these skills was not always maintained. The texts almost universally used at the elementary level were maxims and sayings (Quint. *Inst.* 1. 1. 36; Sen. *Ep.* 33. 6, 94. 9; cf. Morgan 1998: 120–51) and some short quotes from a few well-established authors like Homer, Euripides, and Isocrates (Cribiore 2001: 178–79) for Greek, Vergil and few other authors for Latin education.

Apart from literacy, and a rudimentary literary/cultural knowledge, primary education also provided a training in basic mathematical operations. As there is very little written evidence of this, it seems likely that most of these simple numerical operations were practiced orally. Following the teacher's models, pupils will have memorized and made use of their fingers to exercise. An *abacus* (reckoning board), or small objects like beans, were also helpful to learn how to calculate. The ability to calculate (including basic knowledge of multiplication and fractions) was useful and necessary: whatever the social context, mostly everyone was confronted at least with weights, measures, prices, and money.[14]

After these first years of training, in which the children learned to write, read, and calculate, came the 'secondary' education, with an extended focus on reading and writing, but now beginning to concentrate on discussing longer and more complex texts. In the Latin West, boys, and some girls, of the upper classes would continue to be instructed at home by a private teacher (a slave or a paid grammarian); the sons of the less fortunate families, but wealthy enough to afford the financial burden of further years of intellectual education, were sent to school and paid tuition fees to their teacher, a grammarian. In the Greek East, the gymnasium might have had a more integrative function than Roman and western grammar schools,

---

14. Marrou 1965: 396–97, Bonner 1977: 180–88, and others are convinced that arithmetic was an important standard subject in primary education, and that pupils practiced calculating by writing down exercises. Their vivid picture of complicated operations dependent on the intensive use of specific finger exercises and the abacus is adjusted by Cribiore 2001: 180–82.

since even the wealthiest sons took part at least in the gymnasium's offer of physical training and competition.

CONCLUSION: THE AIMS OF A PRIMARY EDUCATION

Private teachers for the elementary level were most probably the standard in wealthy families all over the empire, and over the centuries. Accordingly, primary schools will mainly have been attended by pupils of the sub-elite—or even by slaves whenever their masters desired, for whatever reason, to have them educated. There existed no school system supported by the state. And so, education remained entirely the responsibility of the parents. Apart from few exceptions, when rich benefactors supported the installment and financing of teachers for their communities, it was up to the parents to pay the fees for the lessons. Teachers depended on these payments, and needed as many pupils as were possible and manageable. In small cities and in the countryside, there might have been problems in attracting and keeping good teachers. Differences in education thus depended not only on a parent's income and wealth, but also on other circumstances.

The functions and aims of an elementary education were, in a similar fashion, by no means the same for all children. Of course, the obvious goal to instruct children in reading, writing, and some basic knowledge of arithmetic was common to all—so it was for the sons and daughters of senators, of equestrian families, for members of the municipal elites, as well as for the many children whose parents could not afford to have a specialized teacher-slave or pay for private teaching, but had to send their children to school. However, even more children than belonged to the latter group never received any such primary education at all. There were surely very many children of less well-to-do backgrounds, who were simply shuffled into the workforce at an early age, and who never had the benefit of an education as described above.

Nevertheless, some skill with writing and reading was necessary, to one degree or another, for many purposes and probably at all levels of society—for politics, law, administration, military communications, commercial activities, and many private matters—and many public communications depended upon some level of literacy. Literature, documents, records, and masses of inscriptions (from monumental-scale dedications on buildings to tiny votives) demonstrate that nearly everyone was confronted constantly with written texts. The different functions and uses of writing corresponded to the different levels of literary education needed.

It seems likely that very many of the pupils who went to a public primary school enjoyed no opportunity to receive a higher education. Depending on their individual capabilities, they will thus have finished their school education as semi-literates, or perhaps as, in some sense, fully literate, but the majority will most likely not have

gone further than this. Some such students, though, may even have acquired rudimentary knowledge in a second language, namely, Greek; they probably will not
have become anything like fluent.

What of the maxims and sayings—clearly designed to impart a distinct set
of ideals, values, and virtues—that all students learned at school? While it is clear
that these exercises were intended to do so, we cannot be absolutely sure that
they ultimately produced a deep influence on students' moral and civic behavior.
Nonetheless, we can be fairly sure that the schooling did indeed serve to socialize
the children, to some degree: it trained them in memorization and social skills, like
obedience and subordination, conscientiousness, and modesty. Whatever the educational and social value of the primary education by public teachers was, the basic
reading and writing skills obtained were sufficient for the demands of the children's
future private and professional lives, and made them superior to the mass of the
altogether uneducated.

A minority of pupils proceeded to higher education (grammar, rhetoric, philosophy). For these boys and girls, basic literacy was only a first step into the world of
cultural patrimony, literate communication, and professional and political careers.
But just as in the case of children who attended a public school, the conditions of
primary education for the offspring of wealthy families differed, and the exact style
and extent of these children's educations depended on the cultural milieu and social
world (status, wealth, profession, geography) the individual child was born into.
For example, the boy or girl in the Latin West who had a Greek-speaking nurse and
Greek-speaking pedagogues had quite an easy path into a bilingual education.

The primary education imparted by private teachers was surely also focused on
the technical and social skills mentioned above, but it will almost certainly also have
involved the deeply rooted republican tradition of learning from *exempla*. That is
to say, aside from the formal teaching supplied by professionals, family members,
too, will have been intimately involved in the intellectual, moral, and personal
development of their children. Under these circumstances, the maxims and sayings
universally employed for reading and writing exercises are likely to have fallen on
well-prepared ground (at least on an intellectual level); but this was not so much
the result of their formal primary education, which was in most ways similar to the
publicly offered education. The combination, then, of a more formal training by
hired teachers and a broader social inculcation by family members will have produced elite children of a particular type. In short, children of wealthy families with
private teachers were prepared for quite another social life than were those who had
only a public schooling.

However, even though the style of education was socially determined—private
teachers, 'public' schools, or no education at all—and the requirements and needs
connected to the respective socially determined purpose of education (the preparation for life as an Roman adult) differed heavily depending on the families' standing
in society, the overall concept of the ideal Roman, poor or rich, soldier or general,
fishmonger or senator, seems to have been shaped by some general ideas developed
in the late Roman Republic. Although the top of the Roman elites and the non-elite

members at the bottom of society lived in worlds that seem completely incommensurable and far apart, the ideas and concepts of what was supposed to make up a proper little Roman boy or girl were somewhat universally accepted. Or at least this is what Roman literature of the late Roman Republic and of imperial times insinuates.

SUGGESTED READING

Only selected topics of the complex subject are brought up in this chapter. Rawson 2003 and Krause (this volume) give introductions into the various conceptualizations of children and childhood. Bonner 1977 gives a good overview of the Roman curriculum and the settings of education. Cribiore 2001 corrects some of his views, and gives insight into the material from Roman Egypt. On grammarians and the grammatical curriculum, which were left out in this chapter because they are better conceived as being a part of the 'higher' education, see Bonner 1977: 47–64, 189–249; Christes 1979; and Rawson 1985: 117–31, 267–81.

BIBLIOGRAPHY

Adams, J. N. 2003. *Bilingualism and the Latin Language*. Cambridge: Cambridge University Press.

Astin, A. E. 1978. *Cato the Censor*. Oxford: Clarendon Press.

Bonner, S. F. 1977. *Education in Ancient Rome. From the Elder Cato to the Younger Pliny*. Berkeley: University of California Press.

Booth, A. D. 1979a. "The Schooling of Slaves in First-Century Rome." *Transactions of the American Philological Association* 109: 11–19.

————. 1979b. "Elementary and Secondary Education in the Roman Empire." *Florilegium* 1: 1–14.

Cagniart, P. F. 2000. "Seneca's Attitude towards Sports and Athletics." *Ancient History Bulletin* 14: 162–70.

Christes, J. 1979. *Sklaven und Freigelassene als Grammatiker und Philologen in Rom*. Wiesbaden: Franz Steiner Verlag.

————. 2003. "Et nos ergo manum ferulae subduximus. Von brutaler Pädagogik bei Griechen und Römern." In U. Krebs (ed.), *Vom Opfer zum Täter? Gewalt in Schule und Erziehung von den Sumerern bis zur Gegenwart*. Bad Heilbrunn: Klinkhardt Verlag. 51–70.

Corbeill, A. 2001. "Education in the Roman Republic: Creating Traditions." In Y. L. Too (ed.), *Education in Greek and Roman Antiquity*. Leiden: E. J. Brill. 261–87.

Cribiore, R. 1996. *Writing, Teachers, and Students in Greco-Roman Egypt*. Atlanta: Scholars Press.

————. 2001. *Gymnastics of the Mind. Greek Education in Hellenistic and Roman Egypt*. Princeton: Princeton University Press.

Dixon, S. 1988. *The Roman Mother*. London: Croom Helm.

Eck, W. 2000. "Latein als Sprache politischer Kommunikation in Städten der östlichen Provinzen." *Chiron* 30: 641–60.

———. 2004. "Lateinisch, Griechisch, Germanisch…? Wie sprach Rom mit seinen Untertanen." In L. De Ligt, E. A. Hemelrijk, and H. W. Singor (eds.), *Roman Rule and Civic Life: Local and Regional Perspectives*. Amsterdam: J. C. Gieben. 3–19.

Edwards, C., and G. Woolf (eds.). 2003. *Rome the Cosmopolis*. Cambridge: Cambridge University Press.

Fortuin, R. W. 1996. *Der Sport im augusteischen Rom: philologische und sporthistorische Untersuchungen*. Stuttgart: Franz Steiner Verlag.

Gruen, E. S. 1992. *Culture and National Identity in Republican Rome*. Ithaca: Cornell University Press.

Harris, W. V. 1989. *Ancient Literacy*. Cambridge, Mass.: Harvard University Press.

Hemelrijk, E. A. 1999. Matrona docta. *Educated Women in the Roman Élite from Cornelia to Julia Domna*. London: Routledge.

Hesberg-Tonn, B. von. 1983. *Coniunx Carissima: Untersuchungen zum Normcharakter im Erscheinungsbild der römischen Frau*. PhD Thesis, Universität Stuttgart.

Hölkeskamp, K.-J. 2006. "History and Collective Memory in the Middle Republic." In N. Rosenstein and R. Morstein-Marx (eds.), *A Companion to the Roman Republic*. Malden: Blackwell.

Horsfall, N. 2003. *The Culture of the Roman Plebs*. London: Duckworth.

Humphrey, J. H. (ed.). 1991. *Literacy in the Roman World*. Ann Arbor: Journal of Roman Archaeology.

Johnson, W. H., and H. N. Parker (eds.). 2009. *Ancient Literacies. The Culture of Reading in Greece and Rome*. Oxford: Oxford University Press.

Kaster, R. A. 1983. "Notes on 'Primary' and 'Secondary' Schools in Late Antiquity." *Transactions of the American Philological Association* 113: 323–46.

Kienast, D. 1954. *Cato der Zensor*. Heidelberg: Quelle & Meyer.

Marrou, H. 1965. *Histoire de l'éducation de l'antiquité*. 6th ed. Paris: Seuil. English: *A History of Education in Antiquity*. New York: Sheed and Ward 1956.

Morgan, T. 1998. *Literate Education in the Hellenistic and Roman Worlds*. Cambridge: Cambridge University Press.

Newby, Z. 2005. *Greek Athletics in the Roman World. Victory and Virtue*. Oxford: Oxford University Press.

Rawson, B. 2003. *Children and Childhood in Roman Italy*. Oxford: Oxford University Press.

Rawson, E. 1985. *Intellectual Life in the Later Roman Republic*. Baltimore: Johns Hopkins University Press.

Riess, W. 2001. "Stadtrömische Lehrer zwischen Anpassung und Nonkonformismus." In G. Alföldy and S. Panciera (eds.), *Inschriftliche Denkmäler als Medien der Selbstdarstellung*. Stuttgart: Franz Steiner Verlag. 163–207.

Scholz, P. 2004. "Elementarunterricht und intellektuelle Bildung im hellenistischen Gymnasion." In D. Kah and P. Scholz (eds.), *Das hellenistische Gymnasion*. Berlin: Akademie Verlag. 103–28.

Vössing, K. 2003. "Die Geschichte der römischen Schule—ein Abriß vor dem Hintergrund der neueren Forschung." *Gymnasium* 110: 455–97.

Woolf, G. 2000. "Literacy." In A. K. Bowman, P. Garnsey, and D. Rathbone (eds.), *Cambridge Ancient History, Vol. XI: The High Empire, A.D. 70–192*. 2nd ed. Cambridge: Cambridge University Press. 875–97.

CHAPTER 5

RHETORICAL EDUCATION

JOY CONNOLLY

INTRODUCTION

SCANT weeks after being shipwrecked on a desert island, Daniel Defoe's Robinson Crusoe begins to keep a journal. Writing the text freshens his memory, provides a calendar, and delivers him from despair by reminding him of his achievements and his evolving relationship with God. It also creates a sense of order: the journal's repetitive, almost ritualistic record of meals, prayers, foraging, and building projects gives structure and meaning to Crusoe's solitary experiences. It sharpens his judgment: "I began...to set the good against the evil, that I might have something to distinguish my case from worse," he writes in an early entry, constructing a list of pros and cons that he uses to assess his lot. Finally, and perhaps most important, the journal forms another self for Crusoe to talk to, a self that is no less important for all its imaginary nature. To survive, the journal implies, Crusoe must do more than eat, drink, find shelter, and clothe himself. To preserve himself as a self, he must simulate social relations using the verbal conventions that make those relations possible. In form and matter, Defoe's novel suggests that the essence of humanity is the capacity to communicate—and the civilized man communicates not just through simple utterances of fact, but in an ornamented style that conveys his self's complexities.

Roman teachers of rhetoric agreed. Influential treatises—notably Cicero's *De Inventione* and *De Oratore* and Quintilian's *Institutio Oratoria*—represent *eloquentia* as the catalyst of communal life. This notion was a commonplace of Greek rhetoricians like the fourth-century Athenian teacher Isocrates, but it assumed a new and distinctive flavor in the strongly hierarchical, class-conscious context of Roman society.[1] Rhetorical pedagogy gave a political edge to the inculcation of the dispositions assumed to be 'proper' to the well-off governing class—proper both in the sense of 'naturally appropriate' and 'the property of.' The *ars dicendi* (art of speaking) taught men how to channel the psychological forces necessary for the aristocratic competition that was the bedrock of Roman society into habits of self-restraint and civility, bringing the inevitable conflicts that arose among them out of the arena of physical combat into the controlled, institutionalized context of the law court or public assembly. "Among every free people, but especially in peaceful and tranquil communities, this one thing has always flourished...the restraint and wisdom of the ideal orator sustains his dignity and that of the multitude of private individuals, and the security of the republic as a whole" (Cic. *de Orat.* 1. 30, 34).

Throughout much of the history of the Roman Empire under the Caesars, rhetoricians instilled this principle in the sons of the propertied classes in cities and towns from Italica near modern Seville to Samosata in eastern Turkey, from Autun in central France to North African Hippo. Grown up, these men served as the governors, magistrates, lawyers, priests, merchants, and poets of the empire where, like Crusoe, they put words to practical use. They cultivated collective memory in occasional speeches such as the funeral oration, the most common example of the *genus demonstrativum* or epideictic type of oratory. To keep their towns and cities in order, they resolved legal disputes with forensic pleading and made public policy and law with deliberative oratory. Armed with the rhetorician's habits of division and evaluation, they refined their judgments about the world. Even Augustine, who sought to rewrite classical rhetoric for Christian audiences, paid tribute to the way the tradition had systematized the presentation of facts and convictions (*Doct. Christ.* 4. 10. 25). The training they received in constructing narrative, ornamenting simple words with elaborate figures, and arousing emotion shaped Roman poetry and fiction in far-reaching ways.[2] Because social relations are greatly influenced by expectations and tastes formed through the experience of literature, we may say without exaggeration that rhetoric constitutes the ABCs of the cultural imagination of literate Romans across the empire.

Just as Crusoe's journal helps him articulate his understanding of the inter-dependencies of the small society he establishes—himself, a dog, cats, goats, and ultimately another human being who becomes his servant—so by learning the styl-ized expression of persuasive speech, Roman students gained insight into, and some measure of control over, the relationships that structured Roman public and private life: the unequal hierarchies of emperor and elite, wealthy and poor, patron and cli-

1. Two well-known examples: Cicero's *De Inventione* 1. 5 and *De Oratore* 1. 32 rework the topos from Isocrates' *Antidosis* 253.

2. The focus of this essay is on Latin texts and Roman culture of the late republican to the middle imperial period, but Swain 1998 explores similar issues in the case of Greek sources from the second to fourth centuries AD. On the interpenetration of rhetoric and Latin literature, see the essays in part 3 of Dominik 1997, especially Farrell.

ent, father and son, owner and slave, man and woman, native and immigrant; and the contests among equals that took place in the senate, town council, forum, marketplace, gymnasia, baths, and villas. Rhetorical training gave students the tools to negotiate social relations, and our evidence suggests that they used these tools both to renew and subtly to resist inequalities of wealth and power.

LEARNING TO BE ROMAN

Rhetorical training, as Robert Kaster observed in his landmark study of grammarians in the Roman Empire, offered little by way of systematic knowledge or habits of critical or innovative thinking (Kaster 1988: 12). On the contrary, it created a learnable language of word and gesture that remained remarkably consistent and predictable over time and space. "I too have winced under the rod, I too have composed 'advice to Sulla': 'the tyrant should now retire into private life,'" Juvenal says in the opening lines of his first satire, referring to the themes set for students' practice arguments in the rhetorical schools (Juv. 1. 15–16). Cicero would have recognized the exercises that the Spanish-born satirist's readers practiced under the Flavians in the first century, which three centuries later Libanius assigned to his students in Antioch (Bonner 1949; Cribiore 2007).

Cicero and Quintilian describe the goal of rhetorical education as teaching boys to become manly men, quoting the elder Cato's definition of the orator as the good man skilled in speaking (*vir bonus dicendi peritus*), but their ideal orator is not a private individual. He is an entity defined by his relations with others, "that man who is really a man: a man involved in civic life" (*vir ille vere civilis*, Quint. *Inst.* 1 pref. 10).[3] Learning how to be *civilis*, that is, how to engage in social relations in the proper way, began with refining the basics of language that the grammarian would have already instilled: proper pronunciation, correct grammar, and diction conforming to the style of the time (Quint. *Inst.* 1. 1. 3, 8. 1. 3). Failure to follow the rules invited ridicule. Catullus, mocking a certain Arrius' habit of hyper-aspiration, jokes that "the Ionian waves, ever since Arrius went there / are now not 'Ionian' but 'Hionian'" (Catul. 84. 11–12). By saying that Arrius' accent imitates his mother's, and by calling Arrius' uncle *liber* (free), the poet hints that Arrius' mother comes from a family of freedpeople—a cruel twist on Cicero's claim that women make excellent models for pure accent and diction because, living serenely shut away from the fast, slang-ridden exchange of everyday talk, they preserve the speech of their ancestors (Cic. *Brut.* 211, *de Orat.* 3. 45).

In the preface to his stylish novel *Metamorphoses*, written in the second century AD, Apuleius begs ironic pardon in advance for any mistakes in his "rustic" Latin, a

---

3. On the history of the Aristotelian idea that only life in the polis permits men to live life according to their nature and to acquire virtue (*Pol.* 1.2), see Pocock 1974: 50–76.

joke whose point is enhanced by another of his works, a (probably fictional) oration of self-defense where Apuleius repeatedly appeals to his judge, Maximus Claudius, as a fellow intellectual and arbiter of proper Graeco-Roman taste. The accusations against him, Apuleius claims, amount to this: "that 'he is a philosopher, handsome and as fluent in Greek as in Latin.' What a crime it is to be a very learned man (*disertissimum*)," he comments sardonically, "and unless I'm mistaken, with these very words my accuser opened his charge—Tannonius Pudens, really not a very learned man" (*homo vere ille quidem non disertissimus, Apol.* 4). Sprinkling his speech with quotations of Homer, Plato, and Cicero, Apuleius suggests that the literary taste he and his judge share distinguishes them both from his boorish opponent, and stands as part of his defense (27).

The range of Apuleius' quotations in the *Apology* testifies to the staying power of the literary canon that was more or less finalized by the early first century AD. Exemplified by Quintilian's list of authors in the tenth book of his *Institutio Oratoria*, this canon composed, if not quite a 'national' literature (see Hedrick in this volume), at least a common pool of reference that permitted educated men to exhibit themselves as such in the public eye. To know the authors in Quintilian's list is to participate and advertise one's membership in the shared culture of the well-off.[4] The literary canon provided a standard by which educated men like Apuleius could appeal when justifying the exclusion of those whose natural capacities might otherwise make an argument for inclusion in the charmed circle of the educated. In other words, the 'civilizing' power claimed by Roman rhetorical discourse usually involves the 'savaging' of the Other (Cheyfitz 1991: 21): hence, the tendency for the Roman treatise to refer dismissively to the garrulousness of women and non-Romans (especially Greeks), the jerky movements of slaves, and the facile attractions of low-class actors (Atherton 1998; Connolly 1998). Rhetorical pedagogy is shaped by and in turn authorizes habits of thought about who rules and who is ruled: if the eloquent word is a powerful civilizing technology, it is also conceived as cultural property that allows its owners to claim superiority over those holding lower places in the social or human order. Tacitus' Germans use eloquent persuasion, for instance, but he notes that its efficacy among them is strictly limited: the Germans "conduct no business, public or private, without being armed" (*Germ.* 11, 13).

Not all rhetoricians and orators were learned men, of course, and not all learned men were rhetoricians or orators. The anecdotes that cluster around rhetoricians and orators, however, offer insight into the impact of rhetorical education on social relations. Competition is a major theme. Many authors attest to the role that knowledge of literature played in competing for status among the Latin *disertissimi* and

---

4. Gruen 1992 discusses middle and late republican expressions of anxiety about the influence of Greece on Roman culture, complicated (as he notes) by eager assimilation of Greek literature and learning; Feeney 1998: 8, 25–27 adroitly phrases the conventional Roman attitude to Greece as a studied, self-conscious construction of difference and distance. On the invention of 'classical' Greek culture in the second century AD and its role in the consolidation of a 'global' imperial culture, see Porter 2005, Connolly 2007a.

Greek *pepaideumenoi* (learned, cultured individuals), but the elder Seneca, Aulus Gellius, and Philostratus provide a cross-section of the most memorable scenes. In their texts, not only Romans and Greeks but Italians, Spaniards, Gauls, and Egyptians elegantly skewer one another's mastery of the imperial canon, on occasion resorting to cruder means of persuasion. Maud Gleason vividly recounts the Gallic sophist Favorinus' barbed exchanges with a pretentious grammarian over the gender of a Latin word (Gleason 1995: 136–39). For men who made their livelihood from the *ars dicendi* (art of speaking), clearly a great deal was at stake in such a dispute, but the pressure to display familiarity with the tradition affected non-professionals too. Petronius' rich freedman Trimalchio boasts about his knowledge of Homer, and Juvenal represents rhetoricians as key players in the culture of social climbing he abhors, helping the nouveau riche, immigrants, and freedmen learn to talk the talk and walk the walk of the upper class.

Literature's role in the civilizing power of rhetorical education, however, was not solely a punitive litmus test of class and ethnic belonging. To Cicero, Quintilian, Pliny, Apuleius, and the Gallic rhetorician Eumenius, whose speech of AD 287 is included in the canonical late antique collection of twelve panegyrics, literature is an important instrument in the orator's toolbox of *eloquentia* because it is the glue of the community, the substance of the common imagination.[5] "Literature is the foundation of all the virtues," Eumenius tells the Caesar who had given financial support to his school, "because it is the mistress of self-restraint, modesty, vigilance, and endurance which, taken together, once they have turned into habit in tender youth, lend strength for every duty of life in turn, and to those functions of military life in the field and in the camps which appear most remote from them (*Pan. Lat.* 9(4). 8. 2). The literary canon offered readers a diverse but coherent view of the world past and present: Cicero, Pliny, pseudo-Quintilian, Dio Chrysostom, and Lucian employ history, poetry, geography, ethnography, and natural science in their speeches and declamations, sometimes sincerely, sometimes with irony, and Apuleius surely parodies this habit in his learned description of parrots (Apul. *Fl.* 12).

Also linking the linguistically and culturally diverse imperial elites was the image of the ideal orator. Where modern education speaks of its respect for the uniqueness and individual potential of every child, ancient education looked to the model, the exemplum. Cicero made an ideal exemplum for the empire partly because he viewed Rome in a global context. Profoundly invested in defining the Roman *res-publica* (polity) as a regime of virtue, Cicero rewrites the parochial role traditionally played by Roman literature and oratory in strengthening local ties of memory and shared practice into a universal script of eternal empire. His speech *Pro Archia*, which defends the Greek poet Archias' contested possession of Roman citizenship, begins by appealing to the Roman judges' cultivated sense of civil fellowship, their *humanitas* (*Arch.* 3). With its references to the preservation of individual glory in the communal memory (*Arch.* 14–15, 20–22), the *pro Archia* meta-textually performs the function it praises, leaving a literary monument that will serve as the common

---

5. On the Attic background of this association, see Ford 1999.

knowledge binding future generations (*Arch.* 30). So Quintilian casts Cicero as the common object of desire for generations of Roman students perusing his speeches and Quintilian's own *Institutio*, seeking to revive in their own *corpora* (bodies— both physical and textual) the republican model. Aulus Gellius and Fronto, the two authors to whom we can trace back the earliest uses of the word *classicus*, treat Cicero as the exemplary 'classical' orator (Citroni 2005: 226–27).

A 'high-culture' literary education was one way to inculcate the student in the values and manners of the dominant order; the *tirocinium fori* or 'apprenticeship of the forum' was another. The phrase refers to the intergenerational network of close male relatives and their friends, active in the forum in politics and related business, who brought the youth on their daily rounds to witness their greetings, meet their wider circle of friends, and listen to cases they argued in the courts. Ever anxious about the alienating effects of professionalism on relations and developments that were supposed to be natural—that were justified and valorized by their own claim to being natural—Roman writers reserve their highest praise for the instruction carried out in the bosom of the family (Stroup 2007: 30; cf. Osgood in this volume).

Rhetorical pedagogy went beyond the intellectual work involved in the preparation of arguments to shape the student's oral delivery and appearance, from the wrap of his toga to his posture, haircut, and choice of jewelry. In lectures on the relations between emperor and elite in late antiquity that were prepared in the late 1980s, Peter Brown quoted Pierre Bourdieu's *Outline of a Theory of Practice*, where the sociologist spoke of a "structural apprenticeship" of deportment and manners that compelled the body to perform the rules of the world, to embody the taxonomic principles of male and female, sacred and profane, wealthy and poor, noble and common, that underlay and sustained the distribution of social power (Brown 1992: 49; Bourdieu 1977: 89). "The whole trick of pedagogic reason," Bourdieu argued (1977: 94), "lies precisely in the way it extorts the essential while seeming to demand the insignificant...the concessions of politeness always contain political concessions." Since the appearance of Brown's study, several scholars have pursued Bourdieu's approach to posture, gesture, and verbal expression; they have shed light on the rhetorical handbook's role in sustaining relations of dominance and subordination in Roman literature and society with its generic prescriptions for the elite Roman body. A leading example is Maud Gleason's path-breaking work on *paideia* (culture, education) and Greek sophists in the second and third centuries AD (Gleason 1995).[6]

As this scholarship shows, rhetorical training left recognizable traces on its students' step and gestures. Rhetoric thus provided visible and audible evidence of the reach of Roman *imperium* (command) in a culturally and linguistically diverse world where travel grew increasingly easier and more secure, where a man might make seventy-two boat crossings between Asia Minor and Italy in the course of his adult life, as the artisan/businessman (*ergastes*) Flavius Zeuxis claims on his funerary inscription (*IGRR* IV 841). As this kind of training enabled intra-elite recognition,

---

6. A selection: Connolly 1998; Gunderson 2000; Newbold 2000; Roller 2006.

it helped standardize their relations, providing a script for greeting, introduction, autobiographical stories, expressions of goodwill, and anecdotal commonplaces. So durable were Roman rhetoricians' set themes and prescriptions for posture and gesture in the post-imperial curriculum that they were still taught in the standard curricula in Europe and North America well into the eighteenth-century age of revolutions, and appear in modified form in handbooks of manners and composition manuals even today. This is proof that rhetorical education is among the most spectacularly enduring of Rome's legacies in the cultural practice of Western modernity.[7]

Fashions change over time, but the statue of Aulus Metellus, colloquially known as 'L'Arringatore,' provides most of the elements of the standard model: a dynamic but well-balanced posture, the arm energetically jutted forward, hair combed forward in springy short curls, the torso straight, the gaze attentive but restrained—the very picture of the orators commemorated in Cicero's *Orator* (*Orat.* 59; and see Roller 2006; also fig. 13.1 in this volume). As with accent, grammar, and knowledge of literature, habituation to an upright posture and controlled gestures signaled the orator's membership in a privileged class: "It is considered a vice (*vitiosum*) for the hand to be lifted above the head or lowered beneath the belly," advises Quintilian, bidding the student beware of "the lightning-quick movements common among slaves, maidservants, parasites and fishermen" on the Roman comic stage (Quint. *Inst.* 11. 3. 112).

CULTIVATING SYMPATHIES, MASTERING THE CROWD

Learning to be eloquent meant more than looking and speaking the right way and peppering one's talk with the proper literary tags. From Aristotle onward, the rhetorician incorporated into his teaching what we would call individual and social psychology. Most treatises divided the field of rhetoric in several different ways: into the three types or *genera* of oratory by venue, described above; into the five tasks of the orator, namely 'invention' or the gathering up of material, arrangement, style, memorization, and delivery; and the parts of speech, also variously defined by different writers, but usually including the exordium, narration, division and partition, confirmation, refutation, and conclusion or peroration (Quint. *Inst.* 3. 3. 1–4). To teach these components—especially invention, arrangement, and style—meant encouraging the student to make educated guesses about the psychological make-up of his audience and their grasp of the material. A successful speaker

---

7. The evidence is also suggestive for research seeking universal tendencies in human behaviors and connections between human and nonhuman primate behaviors.

grasped the beliefs and expectations typically associated with particular classes, ages, and ethnic identities and political tendencies, which he might seek either to shift or reinforce. "For giving counsel about the republic, the key is to know the republic," Cicero advises, "but for speaking persuasively the key is to know the customs of the community (*mores civitatis*), and as this changes frequently, the type of speech must also change frequently" (*de Orat.* 2. 337). Students learned to match their capacities and character with the tone of their audiences, meeting anger with sarcasm, rebuke, or apology (*de Orat.* 2. 339).

Each of the parts of speech similarly required the student to reflect upon himself as an object of the audience's gaze, to think about how best to control the interaction between himself and them in order to gain trust, credibility, and authority. "There is no reason for the exordium," says Quintilian, "other than to prepare the listener so that he will be the readier to listen to the rest of the speech" (Quint. *Inst.* 4. 1. 5). His account of the *exordium* offers one compelling perspective on the criteria by which Romans judged one another and the tricks that they used to gain favor. Displays of patriotism, loyalty to friends and relatives, serious moral purpose, and dignified poise were obvious tactics, but given the right conditions, Quintilian also encourages representing oneself as surrounded and overtopped by powerful men, "for there is a natural tendency to favor men who are struggling," and "the scrupulous judge" (*religiosus iudex*) prefers men whose apparent weakness suggests that they cannot manipulate him for their own interests (Quint. *Inst.* 4. 1. 8–11).

It is critical to understand that the rhetoricians' interest in psychology is neither dispassionate nor altruistic. On the contrary, knowledge is power. As Cicero put it, "Only the man who has examined deeply the natures of men, the whole capacity of humanity, and the reasons for which minds are either aroused or changed will by saying these things be able to accomplish his desires" (*de Orat.* 1. 12. 53). When Quintilian claims that gesture "seems to me the common language of all humans amid the vast diversity across all peoples and polities" (Quint. *Inst.* 11. 3. 87), his authority rests on his ability to teach those who had the means to pay how to master the putatively universal language of gesture in order to manipulate others. This is a pedagogy perfectly suited to prepare the socially prominent student for the lifelong casual give-and-take of informal occasions, from gossiping at dinner parties to canvassing for votes. We might say that the cultural fabric of the Roman Empire was woven through the techniques and dispositions Dale Carnegie sketched in his 1936 bestselling book *How to Win Friends and Influence People*, with all Carnegie's insistence on authenticity.

No doubt, Cicero's and Quintilian's injunctions against faking amiability and interest in the plight of others were difficult to enforce in the course of the mechanical exercises in case-argument and status theory practiced in the schools. Notwithstanding the inevitability of artifice, given that pedagogy tends to form itself to serve elite interests, the usefulness of these texts for understanding Roman social relations is their exposure of chronic fractures in the system. These authors represent themselves as expressing conventional wisdom about the subtleties of social interaction. As they examine the points where sensibilities might be offended, they reveal the stress points where certain stylizations of interaction among people were necessary to balance or conceal relations of power. The republican forum was one important site where these stress points clustered.

When Carnegie exhorts the would-be leader to give friends and employees encouragement, praise, and a steady smile, he discloses the massive importance of civil amiability in the industrial and service economies of mid-twentieth-century American democratic capitalism, which finds its source in the hail-fellow-well-met courtesies that surprised and pleased Tocqueville a century earlier (Tocqueville 1969: 536). Carnegie aims to create the appearance of social equality in the presence of substantial economic inequality, to cultivate a workplace culture where cut-throat competition for limited resources may be rewritten as healthy, friendly rivalry, to conceal the anxiety and boredom involved in most work with a mask of personal fulfillment and commitment to the system.

The late republican treatise that most closely resembles Carnegie's work, the *Commentariolum Petitionis* or "handbook of electioneering" supposedly written by Cicero's brother Quintus for 'new men' seeking a magistracy, reminds its reader at the start of the importance of eloquence in the politician's quest (Q. Cic. *Pet.* 3). Offering Carnegie-esque advice about affability and ingratiation, the treatise encourages readers to speak in language appropriate to the economic and social standing of the crowd (Q. Cic. *Pet.* 31)—the choice of which, as we have seen, he would have learned by practicing the psychological speculation and self-stylization encouraged by the rhetorical treatise. Concern for *dignitas*, standing, is not the exclusive property of a Caesar (Caes. *Civ.* 1 .7. 5); the job of the rhetorically trained Roman politician seeking votes (and virtually all of them were so trained) was to create the appearance of cross-class-equality with verbal and gestural expressions of greeting and respect.

Republican Rome was not a democracy, but *libertas* (freedom) and *aequitas* (fairness) played a powerful and prominent role in the social and political self-understanding of the citizenry (Wirszubski 1960: 3–12). The significance of the orator's performance in the law court and the public assembly in renewing (and sometimes reconfiguring) the conventional balance of power between senate and people is difficult to exaggerate. In the *contio*, the public gathering where debate, but no votes, took place, political debates were acted out as dramatic moral contests won or lost on the good character of the politician, that is, his ability convincingly to project decency and honorableness (Morstein-Marx 2004; also Pina Polo in this volume). Flattering the crowd who was listening in on a legal argument or attending a public assembly did not affect the material inequities of Roman society, or give power to the people. On the contrary, every time the orator addressed the Quirites with reverent respect, his speech reinforced the role of senatorial elite as the voice and leader of policy, law, and ritual and the people's role as witness and follower.[8] This does not mean that the rhetorician taught the would-be magistrate and senator to dupe the people. The realities are more complex. Scenes in Sallust or Livy where tribunes

8. See Flaig 2003, Horsfall 2003, Connolly 2007b.

or generals inflame the people with contional speeches suggest that the loud public rehearsal of rights and liberties itself exerted political force: it reminded the senatorial elite of the limits circumscribing their authority and (temporarily) consolidated the people as a self-conscious legislative and electoral power.

Even 'conservative' politicians supported by noble and well-off senatorial families at times found it useful to speak the 'popular' language of the tribunes, precisely because it renewed the politically crucial notion that senate and people were linked in a common purpose expressed through shared moral and cultural values. The *Rhetorica ad Herennium*, a treatise that bears all the signs of a conventional standard, includes several examples of commonplaces useful for speeches in this context (*Rhet. Her.* 4. 52. 66–54. 67). "If the great Brutus should come to life again and appear here at your feet, would he not employ this language? 'I threw out the kings; you bring in tyrants. I created liberty when it did not exist; you refuse to preserve what I made'" (*Rhet. Her.* 4. 53. 66). As Robert Morstein-Marx argues of the rhetorical strategies in Cicero's consular speech against a populist proposal for agrarian reform, these are "expressions of allegiance to the People's cause [which] attempt to assure the audience that despite superficial appearances no ideological gap in fact separates them from the speaker" (2004: 215). Closely studied and imitated in imperial education, Cicero's rhetorical tactics continued to teach elites how to smooth relations strained by differences of class and interest even after the contestatory politics of the republic gave way to the imperial scene.

Rhetorical education also shaped the interaction of the senatorial elites with one another. The attention paid in rhetorical treatises to humor and wit prepared the student for the intense competition of senatorial politics, which regularly manifested itself in speeches of invective (Corbeill 1996; Fantham 2004; Dugan 2005). The stylized abuse of speeches like Cicero's *Philippics*, which probably mirrors pamphlets and circulars like Caesar's lost *Anti-Cato*, obeyed conventions as rigorous as the unspoken rules structuring the polite civil encounters memorialized in Cicero's dialogues. These latter texts, especially *De Oratore*, *De Republica*, and the topically relevant *De Amicitia*, furnished enduring models of civility. Social and political equals, the participants yet recognize small differences of age and achievement that emerge in carefully calibrated exchanges of politeness and precedence (Hall 1996). Cicero is an unparalleled technician of manners.

Roman rhetoricians stress the necessity of restraint, coolness under pressure, modesty, and good humor—a behavioral code of decorum that, when widely adhered to, ideally restrained men of immense, even unlimited power from exercising it indiscriminately and violently (see both Lendon and Fagan, on violence, in this volume). The function of decorum so important for intra-elite relations in the republic gains special importance in the context of imperial autocracy. When the emperor grew angry, the presence of calm, self-controlled courtiers could act as a powerful disincentive to immoderation (Brown 1992: 56–57). This dynamic emerges in the immediate pre-history of the principate, in Cicero's 'Caesarian' speeches, especially the speech begging Caesar to recall Marcellus from exile. Whether or not, as R. R. Dyer forcefully argues, the *Pro Marcello* should be interpreted as a subtly indignant critique of Caesar's policy of clemency (Dyer 1990: 20), it unquestionably praises his dignified restraint. Pliny pursues a similar strategy in the *Panegyricus* of the emperor Trajan (Braund 1998). On the other side of the coin, rhetoricians trained students to color their performances with powerful emotion in a channeled release of passion that ostensibly put right the injustice or offense that created the conditions for the speech in the first place (Quint. *Inst.* 6. 1. 14–6. 2. 7). The *paterfamilias* dominated his wife, children, and slaves; the patron, his client; the emperor, his subjects and his courtiers: the emphasis rhetorical education placed on the control of passion encouraged, though it could and would never enforce, restraint from abusing the dominated.

What happened, literally, when Caesar came to town? The imperial progression or *adventus* was an important moment in civic life, where local notables gave speeches normalizing political relations and confirming their own status in the eyes of their contemporaries. Orations like Pliny's *Panegyricus* of Trajan and Aelius Aristides' *Eis Basilea* ("Regarding the emperor") about Antoninus Pius reveal how rhetorical tropes and strategies helped elites negotiate what were sometimes troubled relations with the emperor. When the emperor was not present in person, his written edicts summoned the attention and obedience of his subjects. Seneca speaks of the enormous pile of petitions "collected from every part of the world" (*Ad Polybium* 6. 5). Claudia Moatti notes that at the beginning of the principate, the emperor communicated with the people in a "republican" style, brief and clear, but over time, as the emperor's written documents became a source of law, they became verbose and perceptibly "rhetorical" (Moatti 2006: 134): here, the emperor draws on the rhetorical tradition to lend a distinctive and repeatable style to his expressions of power. Back at Rome, the senate used the *acta senatus* (records of senatorial proceedings) to communicate with the emperor and the public: the descriptions of the senators' daily doings were concise and plain, but extant *acclamationes* (formal expressions of praise) point to the creation of a highly formalized vocabulary and syntax that through repetition reinforced, even ritualized, relations of loyalty and allegiance between emperor and senate (*HA, Gord.* 11, *Tac.* 4). This 'bureaucratic' language was indirectly shaped by rhetorical training, which taught students to pay close attention to moments of salutation and farewell, thanks and praise.

DECLAIMING SOCIAL RELATIONS

"I hand over my little son to you so that you may make a man out of a beast," wrote the sixteenth-century humanist Juan Luis Vives in the *Deductio ad Ludum*, a fictional dialogue set in ancient times between a Roman father and a schoolmaster. What does it take to make a man? Once the student learned the basics of composing a speech, he began to prepare and perform set themes of two types: the *controversia*, whose fictional situations mimicked law court cases, and the *suasoria*, which imitated the deliberative speech with its arguments for or against ethical problems ("Antonius threatens to kill Cicero unless he burns his work; should Cicero do so?" Sen. *Suas.* 7; Quint. *Inst.* 3. 8. 46). The resulting 'declamations' have attracted close attention in recent scholarship as a source of insight into social relations in the *domus* (household), especially between spouses, parents and children, and free and slave members of the household, between rich and poor, and between tyrants and those who resisted them (Gunderson 2003).

Consider the following *controversia* from the pseudo-Quintilianic *Major Declamations*, the *Apes Pauperis* or "The Poor Man's Bees" (13):

> A poor man and a rich man were neighbors in the countryside and had adjacent garden plots. The rich man had flowers on his plot, the poor man had bees. The rich man complained that the bees were feeding on his flowers (to their detriment) and gave notice that the poor man should change their location. When he did not do so, the rich man sprinkled his flowers with poison. All the poor man's bees then died. The rich man is charged with unlawful damage to property.

The sample speech that follows the theme (a typical arrangement in extant collections of declamation) is delivered in the voice of the poor man. He begins, logically enough, with the claim that the damage to his property is proportionally worse than the damage done to his neighbor's ([Quint.] *Decl.* 1. 1). His next theme, a *narratio* of his own life and experience on his property, reveals the power of declamation to inculcate a rich array of social values. The poor man cultivates a small acreage whose pastoral qualities (it is not sufficiently fertile for wheat, nor grassy enough for intensive pasturage) recall the appealing scrublands of Latin pastoral and georgic poetry: secluded, fragrant with thyme, and ornamented with a sodroof cottage ([Quint.] *Decl.* 13. 2–4). Like a hero from Livy's history of early Rome, the poor man works with his own hands, but he loses his neighbors when the rich man buys up the surrounding land to create a *latifundium*, an extensive holding worked by slaves (13. 2). The elder Pliny provides the context for the speaker's passionate lament: "Men in ancient times believed that above all moderation should be observed in landholding, for it was their judgment that it was better to sow less and plow more intensively. Virgil, too, I see, agreed with this view. In truth, the *latifundia* have ruined Italy, and soon will ruin the provinces as well" (*Nat.* 18. 7. 35). The speech continues to develop themes familiar from Sallust and the younger Seneca: the moral corruption caused by luxury, the unnaturalness of massive building projects, and the arrogance of the wealthy. Halfway through the speech, the emotional climax describes the pathetic death of the bees in mid-flight, hanging from flowers, and creeping along the ground ([Quint.] *Decl.* 13. 6).

What were such melodramatic displays supposed to teach? Declamation is certainly a rich example of how pedagogy reinforces and helps to justify the social order, by using mythic (some would say 'fairy-tale') elements to make arbitrary hierarchies of power seem the natural stuff of the world, beyond criticism or question. In cases involving evil stepmothers and adulterous wives, the declaimer usually underlines the vices that these groups 'naturally' tend toward, simultaneously distancing himself and his audience from their acts. In a sense, as several scholars have recently argued, declamation engages in justificatory mythmaking about humans and their proper roles from an elite perspective (Beard 1993: 55; Connolly 1998). Declamation provided the student with a chance to enrich his ideological repertoire with icons from popular culture and high literature that defined some types as natural inferiors, and to pair that knowledge with a trained bodily *hexis* (disposition) that literally put free men's sense of natural superiority into social practice. Conditions distorted by crime throw into relief social frictions that everyday relations cannot resolve, but that oratory, properly applied in the appropriate legal context, can. Seeking to account for the prominence of rape as a theme in declamation, Robert Kaster argues that the final message of the exercise is that eloquent speech can cure all ills, even the crime of rape, with its profound consequences for the victim, her or his family, and the community (Kaster 2001). Like New Comedy, declamation acknowledges and partly resolves the wounds commonly suffered in social life, especially within the family.

The cases and the arguments in extant collections of declamations suggest that the exercise simultaneously relied on and reinforced stereotypes about gender, class, and ethnicity. This corresponds with the rhetoricians' habit of complaining about the corrupting power—and the seductive pleasures—of effeminate, slavish, and Greekish habits. Yet the inadequacy of social stereotypes is also an important theme in rhetorical exercises, and the major extant rhetorical treatises exhibit acute if discomfited awareness of the crucial importance of the most 'dangerous' elements of rhetoric to the project of persuasion itself. The student of oratory was not supposed to behave like a woman, but he still had to learn the arts of charm and the verbal ornaments the imperial rhetorician Quintilian compares to cosmetics (Quint. *Inst.* 8 pref. 19–20, 8. 3. 6–11). Though the teacher could well be a slave or a freedman, the student was to consider him "the parent of his mind" (Quint. *Inst.* 2. 9. 1–2). Ideally, boys should grow up speaking Greek, because "Latin learning was born from the Greeks," but they must not permit Greek to corrupt the purity and clarity of their Latin (Quint. *Inst.* 1. 1. 12). Though the student is everywhere enjoined to avoid faking emotion and high-flown language unfamiliar to the common man, the dramatic talent of the actor and the argumentative skills of the philosopher are everywhere acknowledged as important elements of the orator's repertoire.[9]

In [Quint.] *Decl.* 13, the case of the poor farmer who has lost his bees, the declaimer exploits moral stereotypes in order to summon resentment and anger against the arrogant rich man who appears to value human livelihood more lightly than the health of his flowers. Nowhere does the declaimer scrutinize the system of economic inequality and exploitation that produced the farmer's woeful condition;

---

9. On the capacity of declamation to take on big questions of ethics, and especially its power to configure ethical dilemmas and conflicts of power in unexpected ways, see Morales 1996 (on Sen. *Suas.* 10. 5. 2), Gunderson 2003: 90–115, Connolly 2009.

his speech's trade in familiar moralism eschews analysis of motives. But these commonplaces preserved a space for a more critically grounded sympathetic sensibility. Woven into Sallust's histories, Paul's letters, Seneca's praise of philosophy, or Plutarch's biographies, the moralistic commonplaces of the rhetorical tradition became tools of critique and analysis of imperial structures of power.[10]

IMAGINING THE EMPIRE

Recent work in anthropology, political theory, and cultural studies has shown the importance of imagination in sustaining social relations in the context of the organized community. The elements of imagination's psychic potential are legion: the imagination of home and family peculiar to nostalgia, the erotic imagination that often colors a community's vision of its leaders, the utopian imagination that thinks past and beyond existing inequalities and injustices, and many other types. All communities, in a sense, derive their meaning, and their meaningfulness, from imagination. Benedict Anderson's influential *Imagined Communities* treats national identity as a product of modern technologies of communication in the age of mechanical reproduction, technologies that brought the communal imagination to life in startling new ways and with novel consequences. Anderson distinguishes the peculiar technical means by which newspapers and novels represent the imagined community of the modern nation-state from earlier media, on the grounds that print culture produces unified fields where capital, consumption, and communication merge, creating the conditions for the growth of national consciousness as we currently understand it (cf. also Hedrick in this volume). In conclusion, I want to discuss the peculiar way rhetorical training and treatises construed social relations in ethical and aesthetic terms, and the consequences of that for our understanding of how, to use Benedict Anderson's oft-quoted phrase, the Romans "imagined" their imperial community (Anderson 1983).

The limited communication technology of Mediterranean antiquity did not permit the instant replication and consequent multiplicity of re-inscriptions of national values, the stuff of Anderson's communal imagination. But the broad and deep reach of rhetoric as a discursive system, borne out by its endurance over time, suggests that its replication of a civic ideal played a major role in making sense of what it meant to be Roman when Rome had long since lost its identity as a small homogeneous Italic town.

The Roman rhetorician sought to form students whose skills at communication were perfectly matched by their sense of civic commitment, affective attachments,

---

10. Batstone 1988 is a good example of the way a historian uses a rhetorical figure (here, Sallust using syncrisis or comparison) complicates the reader's interpretation of the moral problems at the heart of Roman politics.

and moral virtue. As Matthew Arnold saw the state, Cicero and Quintilian saw the orator as representing the community's "best self" to itself (Arnold 1993: 99). Rhetorical training thus assumed an ethical aura that the rhetoricians tend to express in aesthetic language. Rhetoric homogenized time and space, as Marc Redfield has said in a different context, representing itself "as the continuous arc of an unfolding identity" (Redfield 1999: 66). It promised to create men who would be masters of communication, and in doing so it created networks of communication linked by more than a common tongue or manners.

The depth and intensity of the associations Cicero, Quintilian, Tacitus, and others make between rhetoric and the civilized order should be understood in terms of rhetoric's claim to bind the self together with itself, and to other selves, through the medium of emotional identification, the kind of identification that the properly cultivated imagination best encourages. This explanation accounts for the common thread of interest in emotion and the imagination running through rhetorical theory and practice: the melodramatic tone of many extant declamations; the treatises' intent focus on the emotions and the means of their arousal; the autopsy of close relationships in the *controversia*. Philippe Lacoue-Labarthe's analysis of the notion of the political captures the interaction of ethics, emotion, political identification, and corporeality in rhetorical pedagogy: "The political…belongs to a form of plastic art, formation and information, fiction in the strict sense. This is a deep theme that…reappears in the guise of such concepts as Gestaltung (configuration, fashioning) or Bildung, a term with a revealingly polysemic character (formation, constitution, organization, education, culture, etc.)" (Lacoue-Labarthe 1990: 66).

The Roman Empire was a violent, diverse, sprawling area, where the abuse of slaves and the disempowered was endemic, and where failure to establish reliable networks of *philia* or *amicitia* (friendship) could literally be deadly. It is not surprising, then, that the empire's lasting pedagogical system promises to provide a 'whole package' of support for the cultivation of meaningful relations: familiarity not only with the law and political constitutions, of logic, of the rules of deportment, but with the intangible language of emotion, and the psychology of the other.

SUGGESTED READING

Clarke 1996 provides a useful overview of rhetorical education from the republic through the high empire. The ground-breaking works of Peter Brown and Maud Gleason, which brought rhetorical education to the attention of classical scholars interested in Roman social practice, remain excellent resources. More recently, Richlin 1997, Habinek 2005, and Corbeill 2007 offer insights into rhetoric's role in sustaining the social order and ideas about it: Richlin focuses on the impact of prejudices about gender and class on the structure of pedagogy, while Habinek and Corbeill are concerned with class and national identity. Hall 1996 and Fantham 2004 explore rhetoric's central role in modulating the highly nuanced sphere of late republican social relations. Anyone interested in pedagogy as an instrument of social and political authority will benefit from the collection of Too and Livingstone 1998 and the theoretically sophisticated work on rhetoric as an imperializing discourse in modern European and American studies, such as Cmiel 1990 and Cheyfitz 1991.

BIBLIOGRAPHY

Anderson, B. 1983. *Imagined Communities*. London: Verso.

Arnold, M. 1993. *Culture and Anarchy and Other Writings*. Ed. S. Collini. Cambridge: Cambridge University Press.

Atherton, C. 1998. "Children, Animals, Slaves, and Grammar." In Y. L. Too (ed.), *Pedagogy and Power*. Cambridge: Cambridge University Press. 214–44.

Batstone, W. 1988. "The Antithesis of Virtue: Sallust's Synkrisis and the Crisis of the Late Republic." *Classical Antiquity* 7: 1–29.

Beard, M. 1993. "Looking (Harder) for Roman Myth: Dumézil, Declamation, and the Problems of Definition." In F. Graf (ed.), *Colloquium Rauricum 3: Mythos in mythenloser Gesellschaft*. Stuttgart: B. G. Teubner. 44–64.

Bonner, S. F. 1949. *Roman Declamation in the Late Republic and Early Empire*. Liverpool: University Press of Liverpool.

Bourdieu, P. 1977. *Outline of a Theory of Practice*. Stanford: Stanford University Press.

Braund, S. M. 1998. "Praise and Protreptic in Early Imperial Panegyric." In M. Whitby (ed.), *The Propaganda of Power: The Role of Panegyric in Late Antiquity*. Leiden: E. J. Brill. 53–76.

Brown, P. 1992. *Power and Persuasion in Late Antiquity*. Madison: University of Wisconsin Press.

Carnegie, D. 1982. *How to Win Friends and Influence People*. New York: Pocket Books. (1st ed. 1936.)

Cheyfitz. E. 1991. *The Poetics of Imperialism: Translation and Colonization from* The Tempest *to* Tarzan. Oxford: Oxford University Press.

Citroni, M. 2005. "The Concept of the Classical and the Canons of Model Authors in Roman Literature." In J. Porter (ed.), *Classical Pasts: The Classical Traditions of Greece and Rome*. Princeton: Princeton University Press. 204–34.

Clarke, M. L. 1996. *Rhetoric at Rome*. 2nd ed. London: Routledge.

Cmiel, K. 1990. *Democratic Eloquence: The Fight over Popular Speech in Nineteenth-Century America*. Berkeley: University of California Press.

Connolly, J. 1998. "Mastering Eloquence." In S. Joshel and S. Murnaghan (eds.), *Women and Slaves in Greco-Roman Antiquity: Differential Equations*. London: Routledge. 131–51.

———. 2007a. "Being Greek/Being Roman: Hellenism and Assimilation in the Roman Empire." *Millennium Jahrbuch zu Kultur und Geschichte* 4: 21–42.

———. 2007b. *The State of Speech: Rhetoric and Political Thought in Ancient Rome*. Princeton: Princeton University Press.

———. 2009. "The Strange Art of the Augustan Declaimer." In P. Hardie (ed.), *Paradox and the Marvellous in Augustan Culture*. Oxford: Oxford University Press. 330–49.

Corbeill, A. 1996. *Controlling Laughter*. Princeton: Princeton University Press.

———. 2007. "Rhetorical Education and Social Reproduction in the Republic and Early Empire." In W. Dominik and J. Hall (eds.), *A Companion to Roman Rhetoric*. London: Routledge.

Cribiore, R. 2007. *The School of Libanius in Late Antique Antioch*. Princeton: Princeton University Press.

Dominik, W. J., and J. C. Hall (eds.). 2007. *A Companion to Roman Rhetoric*. Malden: Blackwell.

Dugan, J. 2005. *Making a New Man*. Oxford: Oxford University Press.

Dyer, R. 1990. "Rhetoric and Intention in Cicero's *Pro Marcello*." *Journal of Roman Studies* 80: 17–30.

Fantham, E. 2004. *The Roman World of Cicero's* De Oratore. Oxford: Oxford University Press.

Farrell, J. 2007. "Toward a Rhetoric of (Roman?) Epic." In W. Dominik (ed.), *Roman Eloquence*. London: Routledge. 131–46.

Feeney, D. 1998. *Literature and Religion at Rome*. Cambridge: Cambridge University Press.

Flaig, E. 2003. *Ritualisierte Politik*. Stuttgart: Franz Steiner Verlag.

Ford, A. 1999. "Reading Homer from the Rostrum: Poems and Laws in Aeschines' *Against Timarchus*." In S. Goldhill (ed.), *Performance Culture and Athenian Democracy*. Cambridge: Cambridge University Press. 231–56.

Gleason, M. 1995. *Making Men: Greek Sophists in the Roman Empire*. Princeton: Princeton University Press.

Gruen, E. 1992. *Culture and National Identity in Republican Rome*. Ithaca: Cornell University Press.

Gunderson, E. 2000. *Staging Masculinity*. Ann Arbor: University of Michigan Press.

———. 2003. *Declamation, Paternity, and Identity*. Cambridge: Cambridge University Press.

Habinek, T. 2005. *Ancient Rhetoric and Oratory*. Oxford: Blackwell.

Hall, J. 1996. "Social Evasion and Aristocratic Manners in Cicero's *De Oratore*." *American Journal of Philology* 117: 95–120.

Horsfall, N. 2003. *The Culture of the Roman Plebs*. London: Duckworth.

Kaster, R. 1988. *Guardians of Language: The Grammarian and Society in Late Antiquity*. Berkeley: University of California Press.

———. 2001. "Controlling Reason: Declamation in Rhetorical Education at Rome." In Y. L. Too (ed.), *Education in Greek and Roman Antiquity*. Leiden: E. J. Brill.

Lacoue-Labarthe, P. 1990. *Heidegger, Art, and Politics: The Fiction of the Political*. Oxford: Blackwell.

Moatti, C. 2006. "Translation, Migration, and Communication in the Roman Empire: Three Aspects of Movement in History." *Classical Antiquity* 25: 109–40.

Morales, H. 1996. "The Torturer's Apprentice: Parrhasius and the Limits of Art." In J. Elsner (ed.), *Art and Text in Roman Culture*. Cambridge: Cambridge University Press. 182–209.

Morstein-Marx, R. 2004. *Mass Oratory and Political Power in the Late Roman Republic*. Cambridge: Cambridge University Press.

Newbold, R. F. 2000. "Non-Verbal Communication in Suetonius and the *Historia Augusta*: Power, Posture, and Proxemics." *Acta Classica* 43: 101–18.

Pocock, J. G. A. 1974. *The Machiavellian Moment: Florentine Political Thought and the Atlantic Republican Tradition*. Princeton: Princeton University Press.

Porter, J. (ed.). 2005. *Classical Pasts: The Classical Traditions of Greece and Rome*. Princeton: Princeton University Press.

Redfield, M. 1999. "Imagi-nation: The Imagined Community and the Aesthetics of Mourning." *Diacritics* 29: 58–83.

Richlin, A. 1997. "Gender and Rhetoric: Producing Manhood in the Schools." In W. Dominik (ed.), *Roman Eloquence*. London: Routledge. 90–110.

Roller, M. 2006. *Dining Posture in Ancient Rome: Bodies, Values, and Status.* Princeton: Princeton University Press.

Stroup, S. C. 2007. "Greek Rhetoric Meets Rome." In W. Dominik and J. Hall (eds.), *Companion to Roman Rhetoric.* Malden: Blackwell. 23–37.

Swain, S. 1998. *Hellenism and Empire.* Oxford: Oxford University Press.

Tocqueville, A. de. 1969. *Democracy in America.* New York: Vintage.

Too, Y. L., and N. Livingstone. 1998. *Pedagogy and Power: Rhetorics of Classical Learning.* Cambridge: Cambridge University Press.

Wirszubski, C. 1960. Libertas *as a Political Idea at Rome.* Cambridge: Cambridge University Press.

CHAPTER 6

PHILOSOPHY AS SOCIO-POLITICAL UPBRINGING

JOHANNES HAHN

INTRODUCTION

THE young Marcus Aurelius, when he was already presumptive heir to the throne, would daily quit the imperial palace to visit his various philosophical teachers—a habit he would later, as emperor, seek to maintain.[1] It is no wonder that Marcus should have developed this interest, given that philosophy had, by the mid-second century AD, been a recognized academic discipline for more than half a millennium. In any case, during Marcus' reign, this intellectual pursuit achieved a level of reputation and popularity that it was not to regain at any other time in Western history, not even during the Enlightenment; and Marcus Aurelius himself would ever after be chronicled as the philosopher emperor. In a very real sense, it may be averred that with the dominion of this man, philosophy had come to rule the Roman world.

Yet, despite the high esteem enjoyed by the representatives of the discipline in the Roman Empire's cities, philosophers—and this, actually, is an astonishing thing—never numbered, on quite an equal basis, among the beneficiaries of the various governmental regulations that, beginning in the late republic, and intensifying with the Flavian emperors and thenceforth, promoted the liberal arts, their

---

1. *HA Ant. P.* 10. 4; and *HA M. Aur.* 3.1; Philostr. *VS* 2. 1. 9 (p. 557).

teaching, and their teachers. Thus, doctors, elementary teachers, grammarians, and professors of rhetoric all basked in privileges that could, insofar as these individuals practiced their professions publicly, bring them (e.g.) immunity from municipal offices and obligations. Philosophers, however, did not gain admittance to this fortunate circle until the time of Vespasian (and even this dating is controversial).[2] The underlying causes of the resistance by the Roman authorities to favoring philosophers are most likely complex.[3] However, such disinclination pretty certainly reflects the circumstance that philosophy, as part of the curriculum of higher education, held a particular status, at least under the conditions prevailing during the high imperial period.

Marcus Aurelius would, in AD 176, endow four professorships of philosophy at Athens; there was one person appointed from, respectively, the Academy, the Peripatos, the Stoa, and the Kepos—and it should be noted that four chairs in rhetoric were established there simultaneously. This benefaction must not obscure the fact, however, that these *thronoi* (chairs) were the only publicly financed teaching positions for philosophy in the entire empire. Thus, this innovation is probably better perceived as a sign of reverence toward Greece and Hellenic culture—and most especially Athens, since that city was the 'school of the world'—rather than as an indication of imperial policy with respect to philosophical education itself.[4] On the other hand, government-funded teaching positions in rhetoric, for example, had already been arranged at Rome by Vespasian; and elsewhere in the empire, publicly financed teachers of rhetoric enjoyed a long-standing tradition.[5] In contrast, while it was possible to study philosophy in many places beyond significant cultural centers like Athens, Alexandria, and Rome, and indeed, in the Greek East even in comparatively small towns, such studies had to be conducted on a private basis, and were not in any way directly promoted by the empire's central government or by local communities.[6] In short, then, whereas teachers of rhetoric, for example,

---

2. Hübner 1996: 1108–11; Fein 1994: 282–98. The limits of imperial educational policies are correctly stressed by Vössing 2003: 487–91. Regarding the earliest grants of *immunitas* (relief from taxes or public duties) to philosophers, see Hahn 1989: 101–18.

3. Antoninus Pius formulated his resentments in a remarkable statement: "The number of philosophers (who could be granted *immunitas*) was not fixed, since those who study philosophy are few. I suppose the very wealthy (among them) will voluntarily give the benefits of their studies to their countries, but if they direct their arguments to their own ends, they will immediately be revealed not to be philosophers." (*Dig.* 27. 1. 6. 7). Cf. *Dig.* 50. 13. 1. 4, as well as Hahn 1989: 102–6.

4. Dio 72. 31. 3; Philostr., *VS* 2. 2 (p. 566). See Oliver 1981: 213–25; Hahn 1989: 119–28; Walden 1912: 93–94, 134–38; Lynch 1972: 169–77; Liebeschuetz 1991: 867–71; Dörrie and Baltes 1993: 135–39.

5. On rhetorical training generally, see Connolly in this volume.

6. Regarding the centers of philosophical education during the principate see Hahn 1989: 119–36 (Athens), 137–41 (Alexandria), 141–47 (further cities), 148–55 (Rome); also Liebeschuetz 1991: 867–71. Even the modest Cilician town Aigai supposedly offered the possibility of philosophical instruction by representatives of the four classical and, additionally, the Pythagorean schools. See Philostr., *VA* 1. 7; Long 2002: 44.

received certain immunities and were also fairly commonly supported with public funding—Vespasian had created chairs of rhetoric in Rome, as did Marcus Aurelius for Athens—philosophers did not generally experience such backing. What surely lies behind this is a kind of special status awarded to philosophy and philosophers—in other words, they were highly regarded, yet not considered worthy of (much) public support. This special status of philosophy and philosophers will concern us throughout the rest of the present essay. And that, of course, will raise the question as to the exact place occupied by philosophy, and its practitioners, in the making of community under the Roman Empire.

PHILOSOPHY AS TRAINING FOR PUBLIC SERVICE

In the East, the area of genuinely Greek culture, the pursuit of philosophy, even in the form of intensive study (as opposed to a moderate 'tasting' of the discipline, which was generally considered most appropriate), had been highly regarded since the classical period, and had been deemed an integral component, if not the very core, of higher education (*paideia*). To name but one example, a pamphlet entitled *On the Education of Free Children*, which was attributed to Plutarch, merely recommends a cursory study of the *enkyklia paideumata* (roughly, the liberal arts), but considers a thorough education in philosophy as indispensible.[7] On the other hand, wide circles of the Roman aristocracy found this imported philosophy, and its pedagogical-cultural connotations, hard to swallow—and this (again) quite in contrast to Greek rhetorical techniques, which were accepted quickly and found widespread use in the political life of the late Roman Republic.

Even after the spectacular appearance of the so-called philosophers' embassy in 133 BC, when three of the most important contemporary Greek philosophers had utilized their politically motivated stay in Rome to demonstrate their ethical and political doctrines publicly (merely to be removed from the city by senatorial decree), philosophy initially found just individual sympathizers among the Roman elite.[8] Only the habit of Roman aristocrats to pay educational visits to Athens, which emerged somewhat later (Cicero, in 79/78 BC, being an early and the most famous example),[9] prepared the ground for the esteem and diffusion of this Greek discipline

---

7. Plu. *De lib. educ.* 9 (*Moralia* 7 C). See Bonner 1977: 109–10 ("no better summary of philosophical education at its best could be found…"). On the concept of the *enkyklia paideumata*, see Kühnert 1961, Visky 1977, and especially Hadot 1984.

8. Plu., *Cat. Ma.* 22; cf. Cic., *Luc.* 137; Gell. 6. 14. 8–10; Plin., *Nat.* 7. 112 on the appearance of the Stoic Diogenes, the Peripatetic Critolaus, and the Sceptic Carneades in Rome. According to Sen. *Helv.* 10. 8, philosophers were driven out of Rome as *corruptores iuventutis* (corrupters of the youth). On Rome's first encounter with Greek philosophy, see Garbarino 1973; Jocelyn 1976; Rawson 1985: 282–97; Griffin 1989: 2–5.

9. Bonner 1977: 90–96.

in the capital of the empire. Almost two centuries later, Tacitus would note that an orator, in the days of the waning republic, could ignite a sensation by firing off a few philosophical commonplaces: "They were novel and unknown, and only a small minority of the orators themselves knew the principles of rhetoric and the tenets of philosophy; but now it is all common knowledge, and there is scarcely anyone in the crowd who is not familiar with, if not actually instructed in, the rudiments of both."[10] Ennius' slogan from the early second century BC, which asserted that it was fine to take a sip of philosophy, but not a good thing to become inebriated on it, was frequently repeated in the imperial period, and characterizes the enduring Roman uneasiness toward any all-too-intensive preoccupation with philosophy.[11]

Philosophical instruction, as well as rhetorical training, entailed not only the transfer of theoretical knowledge, but at the same time also an intensive confrontation with the matrix of Roman society's rules and expectations, indeed, an initial pregnant engagement with the practical aspects of social and political life altogether. During the imperial period, established rhetoricians and philosophers who taught young members of the upper class were themselves regularly members of the upper class (quite unlike the grammarians, who, at least in Rome, tended to be of un-free origin).[12] Thus, these individuals moved comfortably in those lofty circles, held (as did the sophists of the Greek East) high positions in political life, or at least entertained close relationships with important persons, and therefore found a ready and willing audience for the opinions they voiced.[13]

The teaching of rhetoric was not confined to a merely technical transfer of speaking skills; rather, the topics dealt with—as bizarre as they might partially seem today—served the purpose of conveying crucially important social norms.[14] Equally, participation in a well-regarded philosopher's class meant, especially during the time of the Principate, much more than the abstract pursuit of a traditional education, or the acquisition of some abstract wisdom that could be considered useless only in the 'real' world. In fact, numerous aspects of a training in philosophy

10. Tac. *Dial.* 19. Regarding these developments generally, see Kennedy 1972 and Bonner 1977.

11. Fr. *Scen.* 376 Vahlen. See Behrends 1983. On the reception of Greek philosophy by the Roman elites during the late republic, cf. Rawson 1985: 282–97 and Griffin 1989. Later quotes: Apul. *Apol.* 13; Gell. 5. 15. 9 and 5. 16. 5.

12. On the remarkable exception of the (freedman) Stoic Epictetus, see Millar 1965; Brunt 1977. Regarding the provenience of imperial philosophers, Hahn 1989: 80. On grammarians, see Christes 1979, Kaster 1988 (for the third and fourth centuries AD), and Horster in this volume.

13. Galen's Platonic teacher in Pergamon was so heavily involved in public affairs that his pupil hardly ever enjoyed the opportunity of meeting with him: Gal. *Anim. Pass.* 8 (V 41 Kühn = Scripta Minora I p. 32, Marquardt). Plutarch's teacher Ammonios, though an Egyptian Greek, was at least three times named *strategos* (general, or chief executive) at Athens, and was also entrusted with the education of the city's ephebes (the still under-age young men): Jones 1966.

14. On this, and as representative of a significant literature by now, see Kaster 2001.

can be discerned, which indicate a distinctively educational and eminently social-izing function of that instruction. In short, a grounding in philosophy could well serve to form personality, and to do so precisely in line with the aristocratic norms and realities of Roman life.

On the basis of some still-extant notes and pupils' reports, we possess rela-tively decent access to the teachings and circles of a few philosophers during the Principate—namely, of Musonius Rufus, Epictetus, and Calvenus Taurus, who operated respectively in Rome, Nicopolis, and Athens.[15] It is impressive to see the frequently informal approach to the lessons, which tends to suggest a cultivated social environment, rather than the atmosphere of a lecture hall. Now, although there was some lecturing and some formal instruction, the teaching of a philoso-pher was largely characterized by his personal engagement with his students, espe-cially via open conversations and spontaneous discussions. Musonius, for example, who is exclusively represented by the preserved fragments as engaged in conver-sations with pupils or listeners, and who always uses their questions as a starting point for his deliberations, even demands a lasting, personal relationship between a philosopher and his pupils as the pedagogical ideal.[16] In the same way, Epictetus or Calvenus Taurus seem less to be professors transferring abstract knowledge than, through their personalized instruction and exemplary conduct, educators who, by the standards they set, guide their disciples both morally and socially.

Informal conversations within a circle of pupils, as well individual tutoring, serve, then, as the more practically oriented components of a training in philoso-phy. In this context, the personal situation of the students is of crucial importance, indeed, is decisive with regard to the pedagogic and didactic constellation. Students of philosophy are those who have just entered adulthood, are no longer under the supervision of a teacher or their *paedagogus*, and who, for the first time, find them-selves confronted with the freedoms and possibilities of a self-determined life—a life, though, that would soon be regimented by strict social constraints.

Now, philosophers' lectures routinely focused on one particular area of elite self-definition, which was of the highest importance for an aristocrat's public appear-ances, and, furthermore, which very largely determined his reputation among his peers: emotional self-control. By the early imperial period, the Greek concept of *sophrosyne* (soundness of mind, moderation) had come to be one of four virtues held cardinal by Graeco-Roman society (n.b., the Roman ideal of *gravitas*—dignity, authority—offers only a partial equivalent of *sophrosyne*). That society, which showed distinct features of a shame culture, proceeded to construct a standard of behavior intimately reliant upon this virtue—and the resultant behavioral norms, in turn, formed a most basic part of the aristocratic self-image.[17] Philosophical

15. We know very little about the financial and administrative circumstances of philosoph-ical schools (which always were private), and even less about procedures of enrollment, etc.

16. See esp. Muson. *Fr.* XI.

17. Regarding the place of *sophrosyne* in the aristocratic system of norms, see Lendon 1997: 41–42, comprehensively North 1966, and more recently Harris 2001.

training thus fostered a particular standard of behavior, which had wide-ranging results. In particular, this aspect of that education caused the extreme competition over access to honor, which so obsessively worried Roman aristocrats, to run up against a decisive barrier.[18] The importance accorded *sophrosyne* prevented rampant urges to prestige and power from escalating into violent feuds, while it also reconciled individual aristocratic aspirations for eminence with the functioning of society as a whole.[19]

Thus, the acquisition of emotional self-control played an important part in the education of a young aristocrat, beginning in childhood.[20] Philosophical monographs on the topic of anger control—which was from the time of Plato, at the latest, part of the teaching about the soul, itself a classical subject of philosophical reflection—are especially well documented for the imperial period. While this might be a quirk in the preservation of our sources, it still reflects the contemporary need for such tracts.[21]

In this context it might be even more relevant to consider the great attention paid to emotional self-control as part of the philosophical education during the imperial period. Plutarch's work *De audiendo* ("On Listening"), aimed at the target group of exactly these young adults (*neoi*, in Greek) who formed the audiences for teaching philosophers, systematically develops rules that were to be obeyed when attending and listening to a philosophical lecture. Behind the facade of giving practical rules for behavior, Plutarch, proceeding on the assumption of the audience's co-responsibility, outlines a psychology of appropriate listening and correct behavior in public. All essential emotions and character traits are mentioned and are, at times pragmatically, discussed. Envy and benevolence, ambition and thirst for glory, love and hate, masculinity and shamelessness, excitability and unaffectedness, pretense, and others. The terminology used reflects the basic values and categories of the agonistic world, as well as the overall social thinking of the Greeks and Romans.

Plutarch's addressees—young men about to enter a public life of high social and political responsibility—are thus subjected in the lecture hall, and with clearly socializing intentions, to a codex of behavior that the listeners will need to follow if they ultimately hope to succeed in an agonistic society where, at the same time, they will have to cooperate and find consensus with their peers. Under this perspective, philosophical instruction seems a prep course to aristocratic existence in public life. It teaches poise and appropriate behavior in any imaginable situation of conflict. At

18. On honor, see Lendon in this volume.

19. On the lack of feuding in Roman society, see both Fagan (on violence) and Lendon in this volume.

20. Plu. *Lib. Educ.* 8C, 10B–E.

21. Sen. *Ira*; Plu. *Cohib. Ira* (Mor. 453D); Muson. *Fr.* XXXVI. Also see Gal. *De An. Aff. Dign. Et Cur.* (V 1–57 Kühn = CMG V 4,1,1). For an overview of philosophies of restraining rage see Harris 2001: 88–121 (with a catalogue of treatises on the emotions and on anger on 127–28); see also Nussbaum 1994 (here 402–38 "Seneca on Anger in Public Life").

the same time, it supports the canon of values inherent to this socio-political and cultural elite, and indirectly stresses that elite's exclusiveness.

Many of the topics discussed in Musonius Rufus' or Epictetus' lectures and conversations hint at the concrete living situation of their young students, who were on the verge of founding their own households, or starting political careers. Musonius deals in detail with the ideal goals of marriage, and with the philosophical education of unmarried and married women; he devotes time to the right measure of, and the conditions for, sexual encounters, the adequate education of daughters, and economic moderation with regard to housekeeping.[22] The moral-educational aspect of Musonius' teaching is further stressed by the fact that he clearly does not focus on an all-too-detailed, strictly methodical argumentation, but instead appeals to his listeners' common sense, and prefers to model the desired forms of behavior.[23]

It is furthermore essential to realize that the intellectual atmosphere of the named philosophers' schools is also broadly influenced by social and public life from outside the classroom. Frequently, visitors, relatives, or people looking for advice join the lessons. Thus, the coming together of high-ranking personalities with important philosophers could influence the course and choice of topic during a given moment of philosophical instruction; this convergence of persons might, for instance, present an occasion to discuss a ruler's virtues.[24]

Arrian's report on Epictetus is especially fertile and conclusive with regard to the casual and continuous presence of the broader social and political environment in philosophical teaching. In Nikopolis, not only did various individuals from elite circles in other towns visit the philosopher and his circle of pupils, but the Stoic also corresponded with the Roman procurator (governor) of Epirus. On their way to Rome, for example, to attend trials before the emperor, distinguished people paid visits to Epictetus. Various other notable personages are known to have called upon him: an exile on his way back to the capital, who would later be advanced to the position of *praefectus annonae* (overseer of the grain supply at Rome); an influential equestrian, or perhaps senator, named Naso, who was accompanied by his son; a consul, who was *amicus Augusti* (friend of the emperor—a quasi-titular label).[25] Epictetus was a virtual magnate, attracting any elite person who happened to find himself anywhere in the vicinity of Nikopolis.

The integration of such a constant stream of visitors into the quotidian teaching schedule lent a philosopher's school the appearance of an intellectually and socially open—and always practically oriented—forum, and in its character reminds us of the philosophical salon of modern times. This habit offered pupils an opportunity

---

22. *Frg.* XIIIa and b; III; XII; IV; XVIII–XX (Hense 1905; trans. Lutz 1947).

23. *Frg.* I. In the fragments questions of physics, metaphysics, or logic are not dealt with anywhere. Fundamental on Musonius' works and teachings see van Geytenbeck 1962.

24. *Frg.* VIII: Visit of a Syrian ruler to Musonius' classroom. See van Geytenbeck 1976: 124–29.

25. Millar 1965 with evidence and prosopographic discussion. See also Brunt 1977, and Long 2002: 12–16.

to participate in their teacher's social interactions, in individual cases even in his consultations with influential clients. The engagement with basic questions of political order, the discussion of social and political questions, and the dealing with, or implicit adoption of, aristocratic norms of behavior happens here in the context of a real-world constellation of problems and interactions; and so, by attending upon the lessons of a man like Epictetus, the student came directly into contact with many of the empire's most important figures, and thereby learned not only philosophy, but likewise how to comport himself in such circles. Thus, we might remember the governor of the province Crete and Cyrene, who had arrived with his father towards the end of a lesson by Calvenus Taurus. He became involved in an exchange about the rules of conduct between father and son, when the latter is holding an office—a topic that doubtlessly appealed immensely to Taurus' Roman pupils (such as Gellius).[26] On that day, philosophy and provincial administration were on full display, and were thoroughly integrated with one another in Taurus' classroom. The lesson will not have been lost on the students.

Conversational situations like these—among persons of distinguished social lineage, yet who were clearly distinct with regard to rank, honor, experience, and age—are reminiscent not only of the informal circles of friends and advisors typical for the public life of Roman aristocrats altogether (and one thinks here of the apprentice-like education of young nobles according to their social rank via their attendance upon quotidian political affairs—*in foro*). For the *cohors amicorum* (circle of friends) of a republican high magistrate, the semi-official *consilium* (board of advisors) of an imperial provincial governor (or of the emperor himself), and equally the *contubernium* (staff) of a consul in the capital (which served the purposes of both cultural and political exchange and networking),[27] followed the same rank-determined set of rules for social, intellectual, and political interactions. Therefore, in the *schola* (classroom) of a well-regarded philosopher, a young aristocrat, be he of curial or senatorial provenance, might receive his first opportunity to taste the ambience that would determine his future existence as a social, political, and cultural leader of his community.

The 'Curriculum' of a Training in Philosophy

This does not at all mean that a philosopher's teachings did not, or could not, also include systematic philosophical training of a more advanced sort. Still, we have to imagine, of course, that such a training's breadth and depth could vary greatly. The

---

26. Gell. 2. 2. On this, see Lakman 1995: 46–57.

27. Regarding Fronto's *contubernium*—"of exceptional importance"—in Rome, see Champlin 1980: 45–46.

different expectations of a paying clientele and the distinct financial situations of the teachers will both have played a role in this.

There is no evidence that higher philosophical instruction in imperial times followed some strictly defined curriculum—hardly a surprise, given the widely differing personalities of the instructors, along with the lack of any centralized authority that might have regulated such an education. Still, this kind of training seems generally to have followed some basic traditions, and as a rule appears most usually to have included the teaching of logic, physics, and ethics. Depending on the school, the content and respective weighting of these elements could vary. The dominance of ethics during the imperial period, and this not only in the teaching of the Stoic philosophers, is, for example, obvious.[28] On the other hand, it is hardly coincidence that we seldom hear from the Aristotelian school, which, all but untouched by popular trends, held on to an intensive logical and mathematical education, and preferred to deal with ethical questions only minimally. Despite the indisputable importance of its founder and his teachings, this school barely registered in the public perception of imperial times; and the reason for that would seem clearly to be that the Aristotelian school did not offer 'competitive' practically oriented philosophical lessons.[29] In short, a philosophical education that gave the impression of being divorced from 'real-world' concerns might easily find itself doomed to isolation and obscurity.

In Epictetus' circle, which, as has already been adumbrated, was more in tune with the public's needs and desires, a lesson would begin with the reading by a student of a classic Stoic text, for example, a passage from Chrysippus (an early and particularly influential Stoic philosopher). The student could either paraphrase the text or offer a comment. Next, Epictetus himself usually took the lead, offering a free lecture, wherein he would use the text and the questions raised by it as a starting point for deeper insights.[30] Such discourses are preserved for us by Arrian's lecture notes (which also contain his detailed additions). At least in these notes, Epictetus' arguments do not seem to resemble a formal lecture; rather, they are improvised, and allow for the sort of dialogue and discussion mentioned above.

Thus, the lessons taught by Epictetus in the second century AD did not cover the school founder's writings in a systematic fashion, but loosely dealt with individual texts or passages, partially also with the aid of existing commentaries. Of considerable—probably the greatest—importance was the communication of the philosopher-teacher's opinions and comments with respect to any given subject; and his subject on any given day was chosen depending upon the immediate

28. The programmatic article by Hadot 2003 offers interesting materials on theoretical philosophical teachings on the basis of, in particular, contemporary Platonic and Aristotelian commentaries (for instance on the value of mathematics), but, basically, leaves out the issue here of interest, namely, practical teachings; the popular Stoic school and her representatives are not considered either.

29. Sharples 2002. See Gottschalk 1987.

30. Clarke 1971: 87ff. Long 2002: 44–46 offers thoughts on Epictetus' structure, reading materials, and lecturing. See also Lakmann 1995: 166–78 on Taurus' teachings.

composition of the circle of pupils (and potentially visitors), their expectations, and current events. The philosophical teaching of the early imperial period, then, was not at all divorced from the world of everyday affairs. And indeed, this training was perfectly embedded in the broader socio-political context, even at the expense of a formalized curriculum for teaching the stuff. Thus, the establishment of a strict Platonic curriculum, which included close study of a hierarchical sequence of twelve dialogues by the master, these scrupulously ordered by subject matter, cannot be documented before Iamblichus (ca. AD 245–325), and reflects the much stricter doctrine and organization of the Neoplatonic school, which arose in late antiquity.[31] In other words, with Iamblichus and the Neoplatonists, we come up against a more purely academic school atmosphere than had prevailed earlier.

Now, a philosopher who hoped to assemble a devoted circle of pupils successfully did not necessarily have to be an original thinker or a productive author. Longinus offers the interesting differentiation that, among the teachers of his youth, there were those who did not write at all, but focused solely on verbal teaching. Others wrote, but only as parergon with regard to their classroom offerings. Further, there were those who wrote, but merely repeated previously published insights. And, finally, there were some exceptional thinkers who taught, but whose texts also contributed enormously to the development of the philosophical discipline.[32]

This perception reflects the preferences of an important thinker of the third century, but obscures the remarkable fact that we can still discern quite a series of eisagogic texts—in other words, tracts introducing or leading to the study of philosophy—dating from the second century.[33] Such texts could themselves form an important medium for philosophical instruction—as well as the marketing of philosophical teachers—and doubtlessly met a demand. Public lectures served as another widely used means for philosophical teaching, hence the dissemination of the doctrines there put forward.

Now, a young person's turn toward philosophy, and a particular philosophical teacher, could lead to a long-term relationship, and thus required adequate funding. Galen studied philosophy and medicine for ten years with various teachers of different schools before he accepted his first position as a doctor in the gladiatorial arena.[34] Plotinus studied with the philosopher Ammonios for eleven years, and

31. See Goulet-Cazé 1982: 277–82; Lamberton 2001.

32. According to Porph. *Plot.* 104ff. Regarding this, see Männlein-Robert 2001: 169–78.

33. Steinmetz 1982: 116–17. To be mentioned are, for instance, Alcinous' *Didaskalos*, a systematic description of Platonic philosophy (Dillon 1993, with introduction), but also a Latin equivalent of Apuleius, written for a more general readership, *De Platone et eius dogmate*. Or, in his text *De mundo*, Apuleius offers an overview of Peripatetic natural philosophy (based on a translation from the Greek); see Sandy 1997: 190–96. The genre is not limited to philosophy, however, but at that time flourished with regard to other subjects (Steinmetz 1982). Especially pronounced we find this in the physician (and philosopher) Galen's works; see Oser-Grote 1998.

34. Gal. *Meth. Med.* 8. 3 (X 560 Kühn); cf. Schlange-Schöningen 2003: 64–99 with further evidence. Apuleius could have studied literature and philosophy for an equally long period: Vössing 1997: 436–37; Sandy 1997: 9–12.

some of his own pupils exceeded this time span considerably.[35] It is also evident that serious students of philosophy tended to hear several teachers in different educational centers, such as Athens or Alexandria, and that they might travel widely even beyond such intellectual Meccas, to satisfy their appetite for philosophical sophistication.[36] Pricey philosophical instruction was also a matter of social prestige, and indeed there are many indications that the joining of a philosophical school was not inspired entirely by a genuine or deep interest in the matters taught there. Nonetheless, we can hardly come to the conclusion that a large majority of these young men (or their families) truly favored such an intensive study.

But even if most parents (including the very wealthy ones) would have been less than amused to discover their offspring skipping about the world in search of philosophical enlightenment, still it must be said that imperial society did indeed very largely consider philosophy to be an *ars vitae*, which could offer very real practical benefits. For example, as we have seen above, such a training provided moral teachings and character education, whose goal it was to internalize self-restraint and self-discipline. However, under such a practical perspective, the engagement with philosophical texts, methods, and topics seemed to offer yet other benefits, and to have awakened further expectations of a visit to a philosopher. It must also be said that the traditional competition with rhetorical training (which has been adumbrated above) became more acute in high imperial times because of an enormous boom of a public entertainment culture and the phenomenon of the Second Sophistic, with its wide-ranging sociocultural aspirations.[37] All of this had far-reaching effects on the self-image and teachings of philosophy.

The Function and Perception of Philosophy in the High Empire

One result of what we have thus far seen is that, over the course of the second century AD, we find increasing complaints by teachers of philosophy about the fact that their high-ranking pupils showed interest solely in discussion of rhetorical stylistic devices—for instance, as these were used in the Platonic dialogues—but ignored real philosophical problems, and thus read Plato not in order to perfect their lives, but to adorn their oratorical skills. Yet, even these teachers could not refrain from advertising themselves on the basis of the linguistic and stylistic elegance to be

35. Plot. 16. 21ff.

36. Of such 'traveling scholars,' searching for the true philosophy, there were enough that they came to serve as a topos in Christian apologetics: Justin. *Trypho* praef.; Clem. Al. *Strom.* 1. 1. 11. An example is also Plotinus' development in Porhyrius' report: Plot. 13.

37. On the Second Sophistic, see Schmitz in this volume.

gleaned from the classics of their discipline.[38] A personality like Apuleius, adherent of Plato and the Sophists at once, and committed to the zeitgeist, programmatically explained that the 'queen of all disciplines' had its task in cultivating well-developed speech (*ad bene dicendum*) as well as in fostering the appropriate way of living (*ad bene vivendum*).[39] Even a conservative Roman—Tacitus, for example—who was normally not inclined toward philosophy, could recommend a discriminating dabbling, though with the ultimate aim of improving one's rhetorical skills. When undertaking the psychological analysis of different types of listeners, he elaborates thus:[40]

> There are some with whom a concise, succinct style carries most conviction, one that makes the several lines of proof yield a rapid conclusion: with such it will be an advantage to have paid attention to dialectic. Others are more taken with a smooth and steady flow of speech, drawn from the fountain-head of universal experience: in order to make an impression upon these we shall borrow from the Peripatetics their stock arguments, suited and ready in advance for either side of any discussion. Combativeness will be the contribution of the Academics, sublimity that of Plato, and charm that of Xenophon; nay, there will be nothing amiss in a speaker taking over some of the excellent aphorisms of Epicurus and Metrodorus, and applying them as the case may demand.

Philosophy, as a quarry for oratorical building materials, or as a bauble that could adorn the skilled speaker's cultivation, thus becomes a decisive leitmotif, at least of the Roman relationship with the discipline.[41] But even beyond this, philosophy and its areas of concern, at least as these were publicly perceived, were greatly popularized over the course of the second century. Hence, the discipline and its representatives profited from the general advancement of education at the time, from the remarkable ascent of Greek as the language of the educated elites (even in the West during the second century), and finally, from

38. Gell. 1. 9. 10. Cf. also the equally humorous and critical addressing of his pupil, Gellius, as *rhetorisce* ("well, my young rhetorician") by the Platonist Taurus—Gell. 17. 20. See further Lakmann 1995: 168–69.

39. Apul. *Fl.* 7. 9.

40. Tac. *Dial.* 31: *sunt apud quos adstrictum et collectum et singula statim argumenta concludens dicendi genus plus fidei meretur: apud hos dedisse operam dialecticae proficiet. Alios fusa et aequalis et ex communibus ducta sensibus oratio magis delectat: ad hos permovendos mutuabimur a Peripateticis aptos et in omnem disputationem paratos iam locos. dabunt Academici pugnacitatem, Plato altitudinem, Xenophon iucunditatem; ne Epicuri quidem et Metrodori honestas quasdam exclamationes adsumere iisque, prout res poscit, uti alienum erit oratori.* For stances more critical of philosophy, see Tac. *Ag.* 4 and Tac. *Dial.* 30.

41. Fronto, Marcus Aurelius' teacher, quite similarly promoted rhetoric as being practical philosophy, and argued for its indispensability for a philosopher with his hesitant pupil: Fro. *de eloqu.* 1. 18 (2. 70 Haines = p. 141 van den Hout). See further Champlin 1980: 29–30, and—though less convincing—Kasulke 2005.

the 'rhetorization' of public life and culture in imperial society just generally.[42] Philosophy's inexhaustible treasure of ethical positions and arguments, and of intellectual topics and materials for rhetorical exercises and showpiece speeches, allowed this pursuit to gain a central role in both the educational and cultural affairs of the day.

The *Dialexeis* of Maximus of Tyre, who successfully lectured in Rome toward the end of the second century AD, perhaps reflects these processes most clearly. These brief texts—they were intellectual tidbits of maximally twenty-five minutes in length, when recited—deal with issues such as whether Homer should be considered the founder of a philosophical school; or they examine Socrates' 'erotics'; or they tackle the question as to how that philosopher might have defended himself more successfully in his trial. The pieces are reminiscent of the *suasoriae*, exercises used in rhetorical schools to teach persuasion. Explicitly, Maximus welcomes lovers of rhetoric, of poetry, and of statesmanship among his listeners, and he promises them rich profits.[43] Platonic, Stoic, Peripatetic, Cynic philosophy—all can be found in his literarily outfitted and artfully manufactured lectures: as a true leader of a salon, or better, as a 'concert' philosopher, he plays skillfully to the tastes of his audience.[44]

Maximus' lectures addressed young men, and in particular, the rising generation of the Roman (though Greek-speaking) aristocracy.[45] These lectures also reflect the fact that philosophical teachings—which were not imparted, please note, behind the high walls of a schoolroom, but rather, under the open porticos of public buildings—increasingly found their way to a very wide public. In the second century, this accessible form of teaching—along with further public appearances by philosophers, which frequently involved competition with other intellectuals or artists[46]—served to catapult philosophers into the spotlight of cultural affairs altogether, and brought them likewise into the fold of educational practices generally.

Indeed, the study of philosophy, aside from the fact that it was an integral part of higher education altogether, was specifically geared toward molding an individual's native personality, to produce a future public figure. But this kind of learning

42. Marcus Aurelius' *Meditations*, written in Greek, are just one expression of the fact that, in his time, Greek had finally triumphed as the language for philosophical reflection. The philosopher and sophist Apuleius, who came from North Africa, was the last to write his treatises in Latin (he was, though, fluent in both Greek and Latin); after him, we hear nothing of Latin as the language of philosophers.

43. Max. Tyr. *Or.* 1. 7e. Regarding this author and his works Szarmach 1985; Trapp 1997: xi–lv; as well as Hahn 1989: 92–98.

44. Max. Tyr. *Or.* 26. 1 offers the following definition of philosophy: "And how are we to understand philosophy, if not as detailed knowledge of matters divine and human, the source of virtue and noble thoughts and a harmonious style of life and sophisticated habits?"

45. Max. Tyr. *Or.* 1. 7; see also Trapp 1997: xxi.

46. Apul. *Fl.* 18. 2–3.

went, in fact, even further, for philosophy was, ultimately, a highly effective and much valued medium for aristocratic self-representation (on which, see Flower in this volume). Put simply, proper study of philosophy, and indeed, any occupation with it altogether, functioned as a particular technique for the construction of one's own socio-cultural position, especially within elite circles.

First, with respect to the society at large, a demonstrable expertise in philosophy brought prominence, and could be understood effectively as proof of membership in the elite. But the demonstration of personal philosophical ambition within the circle of one's peers, in other words, in the context of a local upper class that clearly considered itself to stand above and to function beyond the limits of its community, was a powerful tool in the contest for visibility, prestige, and eminence. And so, a philosophical training taken in a prestigious educational center, such as Athens or Alexandria, led to considerable respect at home—even if only because of the cosmopolitan experience and the surely lofty contacts gained abroad.[47]

In the context of the social interactions among provincial urban elites, however, such philosophical study assumed yet another meaning. Only a very small minority, even in those circles, dealt with philosophical topics in a truly serious and intense fashion. Those few who did exert themselves this way attended formal (always private) lessons offered by philosophers, and these individuals gained a level of insight that reached well beyond the rough outline of philosophical ideas they (or others) might acquire en passant via basic grammatical and rhetorical educations. But beyond even this, we must realize that only a very few individuals, even within the circles of the elites, could afford the significant travel and lengthy absence from home that a truly extensive study of this field would demand. Therefore, those who could manage such luxury would be adorned both by the highest conceivable level of sophistication and by the mere fact of their ability to attain this kind of worldly wisdom. Such a man quickly found himself placed a notch above the other grandees of his hometown.[48]

Of course, every educated person was well aware that philosophy, with its universal claim to method, knowledge, and prestige, had to be regarded as the crown jewel of an aristocratic education, if only because all other relevant disciplines—be they architecture, law, medicine, or even rhetoric—aligned themselves, at least in the culture of the high empire, with philosophy in their intellectual endeavors, and

---

47. Social and political 'networks' based on common studies or philosophical views can clearly be identified, especially in the environment of the Epicurean school in the second century (Clay 1989; Gordon 1996: 40–41, 56; Scholz 2003; van Bremen 2005), and in late antiquity in those of the Neoplatonists of Athens and Alexandria (Fowden 1977 and 1982; Athanassiadi 1993), but even beyond those.

48. Apuleius, for example, when addressing fellow citizens of high social standing, is careful to emphasize his lengthy travel (*longa peregrinatio*) to Athens for a protracted period of study (*diutinis studiis*) of philosophy; *Apol.* 23. 2; *Flor.* 18. 5; Sandy 1997: 27–36. Regarding his education and curriculum, see Vössing 1997: 436–67.

even sometimes attempted to be considered as philosophy.[49] Thus, to undertake a philosophical training that occurred in the public eye, or otherwise publicly to demonstrate some familiarity with this field, was often an integral part of a broader strategy of self-representation. Now, this matter of elite self-representation was generally accomplished by means of one's bearing in public, by one's gestures, by one's visual presentation altogether. Philosophical sophistication could be tailored to become a part of this outfit.

Apuleius, for example, utilized this socio-rhetorical complex in his—unfortunately only partially preserved—show speeches. These orations were addressed to distinguished audiences at the provincial capital Carthage on numerous occasions. In this context, he was interested not only to accentuate his exceptional and diversified literary education and productivity, but even more to underscore his claim—based on intensive study at Athens and elsewhere—to be a *philosophus Platonicus*, a Platonic philosopher. This, in particular, would ensure his membership in the highest circles of provincial society, and would thereby provide a foundation for public honors: Apuleius was especially interested in statues of himself wearing philosophical garb.[50]

At one point in his life, Apuleius found himself facing the governor of Africa Proconsularis in court, charged with having committed a capital offense, namely, the practice of magic (on which, cf. Rives in this volume). The defense that Apuleius launched consisted very largely of allusions to his intensive philosophical education: frequent quotations of Plato (not to mention Aristotle and other venerable philosophers), and the implicit reference to Athens as the place of his studies.[51] To the typical Roman aristocrat, mention of Athens must have carried the tone that Oxford or Princeton does nowadays. In other words, the chief thrust of Apuleius' defense was to attempt to cast himself as belonging to the same social (and intellectual) circles as did the proconsul who was sitting in judgment of him. This was accomplished by establishing their common expertise in and devotion to philosophy. Let us not forget that, as we have seen above, only a very small group in the Roman Empire possessed the wherewithal that could support entry into this club. Moreover, that small group was reduced yet further by virtue of its members' varied interests. Those who both could and did become 'Platonic philosophers' constituted a tiny and tight-knit community. Thus, in view of Apuleius' obvious rhetorical strategy, we can reasonably assume that the Roman patrician who was to decide his case by the end of the

49. With regard to rhetoric, cf. footnote 42 above. Ulpian (*Dig.* 1. 1. 1. 2) envisioned law as being the *ars boni at aequi* (the practice of that which is good and just) and even considered it as *veram (nisi fallor) philosophiam* (a true, unless I am mistaken, way of philosophy). The inseparable connection between medicine and philosophy was expressed by Galen in his treatise "That the best physician has to be a philosopher" (cf. also Celsus, Prooem. 8). Regarding architecture see Vitr. 1. 2–3, esp. 7. For mathematics and geography in the second century, see Taub 1993 and Mansfeld 1998; also Hadot 2003: 56–62.

50. See esp. *Flor.* 9. 4 and 20. 4–6; cf. also 18. 3. Statues: *Flor.* 16. 36ff. For inscriptions honoring Apuleius preserved at his hometown, Madaurus, see the evidence in *PIR*² A 958.

51. *Apol.* 25. 10; 36. 5; 38. 1; 41. 4; 48. 13; 51. 1; 64. 4; 65. 8; 91. 3; cf. 19. 2.

day, namely, Claudius Maximus, must have studied philosophy in Athens himself.[52] By harping on his philosophical credentials, then, Apuleius was demonstrating to Claudius that here was a defendant of almost equal social status, and of identical intellectual tastes—hence, a man who should be found innocent. In the case of Apuleius, a serious involvement with philosophy ultimately turned out to be not mere intellectual fluff, but, in a very literal sense, a life-saver.

Be that as it may, the same kind of phenomenon, in other words, the cultural self-staging of the educated urban and provincial elites in the high empire, has recently been examined intensively for the fields of language and rhetoric, especially with respect to the Greek East.[53] The obsession of the Greco-Roman elites with language, their ideal of absolutely mastering both Greek (pursued via the Atticism of the Second Sophistic) and Latin (manifest in the archaism of Fronto and others), represents an attempt to isolate themselves as an exclusive and stable fraternity, and to display their cultural (hence, social as well as moral) superiority to the rest of society. Paideia as multi-faceted cultural education and activity—this expressed by physical appearance, literary activity, moral and political thought—thus helped to distinguish these elites (as *pepaideuómenoi* or *litterati*—i.e., highly educated and cultivated individuals) from *hoi polloi*. Philosophy functioned as part of a shining badge of elite identity; it served to strengthen the members' collective identity; and, at the same time, it allowed them to develop and practice a special communicative code within their own circles.

CONCLUSIONS

The kind of education we have been discussing, one that involved, at its acme, a thorough-going training in philosophy, had long functioned as a self-evident sign of the urban elites (especially in the Hellenophone areas of the empire), who traditionally monopolized wealth and power in their local societies. However, higher education now, under the particular conditions of the high empire—in other words, a prospering, increasingly open, and geographically mobile society, living in the shadow of the utterly dominant figure of an autocratic monarch—achieved a markedly increased importance. An elite education became, and this applies to philosophy even more than to rhetoric, a highly exclusive social mark. This was because such education could not—in contrast to mere wealth, and partially to power—be

---

52. The philosophical education and effect of Claudius Maximus (on whom, *PIR*² C 933)—his tutor in Stoic philosophy—is gratefully mentioned by Marcus Aurelius: *Med.* 1. 15 (cf. 1. 16 and 1. 17); Dio 71. 35. 1.

53. There is now a relatively large literature here. See, e.g., Anderson 1993; Gleason 1995; Swain 1996; Sandy 1997; Schmitz 1997; Korenjak 2000; Borg 2004. Also, see Schmitz in this volume.

easily acquired or imparted. Beginning in early youth, this form of breeding had to be experienced and internalized over many years via a complex process of intertwined learning and socialization. Only in that way could it develop its intended effect, namely, to elicit the respect of its possessor's peers. As social capital, this kind of training could—again, as opposed to money and power—actually be mobilized only over the course of generations, and thus could not at all easily be claimed by social climbers.

The testamentary declaration and self-stylization of the upstart (and freedman) Trimalchio, who claimed not even once in his life to have heard a philosopher,[54] in its defiant negation signaled nothing so much as the unassailable strength of the norm. For even enormous wealth, while socially beneficial, could become truly effective only when it was accompanied by the proper social provenance and an exclusive education. In the framework of cultural self-insinuation by the imperial elites, philosophy held, then, a distinguished, indeed, a symbolic meaning. Therefore, it was defended vehemently as a truly exclusive aristocratic form of educational experience. Individuals who did not belong to the upper class (or whose affiliation with it was disputed) could be challenged with respect to their mastery of acceptable language. Proof of lacking position—an ill-educated choice of words, for instance—was easily brought to public attention.[55] Philosophical education, however, as a socially exclusive discipline, was a priori, from the elites' perspective, beyond the reach of social inferiors. Those thus excluded—among these, it must be noted, the Cynic philosophers—were routinely and categorically denied any claim to wisdom or philosophical standing; and an extensive and engaged aristocratic discourse, during the imperial period, about pseudo-philosophers is witness to this. Anecdotes regarding the exposure of 'false' philosophers thus were quite popular conversation pieces in educated circles.[56] Apuleius could assume that his stirring plea against the Cynics would be met with unrestricted approval from his educated audience in Carthage: "I wish that a similar kind of edict concerning philosophy were in force: that no one should attempt its likeness without reason..., and that the rude, vulgar, unskilled people who are only philosophers because they wear cloaks should not imitate them, nor should they debase the royal discipline...by speaking badly and living in the same way."[57] *Sordidi*, unclean and miserable ones, in other words, persons of lower social rank, have no claim to the 'royal discipline,' for it is the exclusive privilege of the educated elite to attain the philosopher's cloak.

54. Petr. *Sat.* 71: *nec umquam philosophum audivi* (I have never had lessons from a philosopher).

55. This was the bludgeon chiefly wielded by Apuleius against his opponents when he was on trial before Claudius Maximus. See Apul. *Apol.* 4. 2; 5. 6; 7. 5; 8. 2; 9. 1; 10. 6, etc.

56. Sen. *Ben.* 7. 11. 1–2; Gell. 9. 2. 8; Lucian *Fug.* 3. Compare Plu. *Apophth. Reg.* (*Mor.* 179F. 181E. 182E) and *Alex.* 8. For a rather different technique of radically denouncing false philosophers, see Bartsch 2006: 164–82.

57. Apul. *Fl.* 7.9–10: *Quod utinam...philosophiae edictum valeret, ne qui imaginem eius temere adsimularet...neu rudes, sordidi, imperiti pallio tenus philosophos imitarentur et disciplinam regalem...male dicendo et similiter vivendo contaminarent.*

At the same time, one thing becomes obvious. A quest for the high esteem accorded to philosophers and their art of living was not limited to aristocratic circles. The Cynic movement, which had nearly been extinguished in late Hellenistic times, experienced an unprecedented revival during the high imperial period. Cynic traveling preachers appealed to wide strata of the population with their message of asceticism and stimulating moral exempla.[58] In the East, this was a crucial factor in lending clout to philosophy as a part of the public self-representation engaged in by the urban elites.[59] The adoption of ethical popular-philosophical terms by large sectors of the society, the singular success of philosophy as a universally respected teacher and transmitter of ethical living, the sense that this was the highest form of intellectual pursuit, all this was now clearly on display. To name but one example of this, deserving persons could actually be granted the honorific title 'philosopher.' The combined attributes *philósophos kaì philópatris* (philosopher and patriot), which occur with some regularity in inscriptions honoring elite members of the Hellenophone communities in the East, signal clearly the intimate bond between outstanding political activities, stellar education, and high moral standards.[60]

Thus, it will be no surprise that the incessant self-stylization by aristocrats of themselves as *pepaideuómenoi* (thoroughly cultured individuals), with a bent to philosophy—all of this often framed by an attitude of polymathy[61]—became, in some circles of the urban elites in the East, but soon among the Hellenized imperial elite at Rome also, and in particular under Marcus Aurelius, effectively the benchmark of intellectual life altogether. To retain a Greek philosopher in one's home on a permanent basis was one method, though a costly one, of advertising such cultural sophistication. For those whose financial means were less extensive, the exhibition of philosophers' busts, the decoration of a country villa with an impressive gallery of philosophers' statues, or a library equipped with a collection of exquisite philosophical texts could likewise signify an owner's considerable intellectual ambition.[62] This increasingly intensifying cult of learning under the high empire is, last but

58. It is also worth noting that, in the early imperial period, Cynic philosophy exercised not a small influence on the otherwise dominant Stoic philosophy, and especially in the area of ethics. See Billerbeck 1979; Manning 1994: 5012–15.

59. Dudley 1937: 143–83; Döring 1979; Hahn 1989: 172–81.

60. On this in detail, see Hahn 1989: 161–64.

61. See, e.g., Suid. 4 (on Favorinus): "a polymath in all areas of learning…full of philosophy, who applied himself more to rhetoric." Bowersock 2002: 160 speaks of, "a vast and complex cultural fabric" and a "commerce in Hellenic traditions," in which members of the elites were embedded.

62. To serve as a house philosopher, as one of the 'friends' of the master of the house—potentially a last-chance occupation for impoverished Greek aristocrats, and one that might be vaguely suitable to their social station—was often judged rather scathingly: Lucian *Nigr.* 24; Lucian *Merc. Cond.* passim; Juv. *Sat.* 3 and passim. On portrait galleries displaying philosophers, see: Wölfel 1995; Zanker 1995: 206–12 (with Smith 1990 on the late antique finds from Aphrodisias); ibid. on portraits. Cf. also Smith 1999 and 1998.

not least, reflected by extant portraits of elite Romans; the philosopher's beard is omnipresent in the likenesses of Antonine aristocrats. Moreover, an overall intellectual character—and one that bears distinctly the marks of philosophy—becomes a dominating motif in the iconography of Roman sarcophagi in the second and third centuries AD.[63]

Does, then, the Roman aristocratic desire to be linked with philosophy, given the overall prominence of Greek culture in the second century AD, primarily reflect what was actually a superficial interest in this discipline and a tribute to some form of zeitgeist? Did the real attraction lie in the moral, social, and political dividends that might attach to such a sheen of philosophy?[64] That will surely have been the case sometimes. Nonetheless, Rome offers a few very impressive cases of intensive participation by the imperial elite in philosophical debates. For example, Galen, the great Greek doctor, was able to welcome a truly prominent audience for a public anatomical demonstration intended to solve the highly disputed philosophical question about the origin of language. The event's host was one of the consuls of the year. Beyond that, Marcus Aurelius' father-in-law was present at that affair, as were three other highly regarded ex-consuls. These important men observed the demonstration and the ensuing philosophical and medical discussions over the course of several days, and later asked for transcripts.[65] Such cultural events were frequent occurrences in Rome's aristocratic social life of the time, and reflected the value of philosophical education to the imperial elite. Displays like this will also further have promoted the demand for philosophical instruction.

But even more impressive in their implicit message are the expectations put into words by the very same Galen—who, for long years, let us remember, was a physician at the court of Marcus Aurelius and his successors. In a treatise extant only in an Arabic translation ("On the examinations by which the best physicians are recognized"), Galen addresses just such an elite audience, and offers the following advice. A senator who wished to decide on the professional competence of doctors seeking employment in his household had to possess extraordinary knowledge. Not only must he know the different opinions of great doctors of the past with regard to concrete physical ailments, but he also would have to be able to identify the philosophical underpinnings of their medical diagnoses and cures.[66] Roman senators—whose ancestors had from time to time caused the expulsion of Greek philosophers from Rome and Italy—as philosophical experts during the high imperial period? Indeed, only two generations after Galen, sarcophagi begin regularly to show members of this elite in philosophical garb. One such piece from

---

63. Zanker 1995: 271–72, 279ff.; Borg 2004b; and especially Ewald 1999, with complete documentation.

64. Regarding the opportunistic turn of Roman aristocrats toward philosophy under Marcus Aurelius, see Dio 72. 35. 2.

65. Gal. *Praecogn.* 5. 17ff. (CMG V 8. 1; p. 99, 12–13); cf. Gal. *Praecogn.* 2. 24 (p. 81, 15ff.), with an excellent commentary by Nutton 1979: ad loc.

66. Iskandar 1988.

the mid-third century plainly displays its senatorial occupant in a dual role: he appears as both magistrate and philosopher.[67] And so, philosophical education as the badge of elite status had finally won its place in the social and political world of the Latin-speaking West. The city of Rome itself was now, one could believe, in the hands of the philosophers.

SUGGESTED READING

Clarke 1971, Bonner 1977, and Marrou 1982 are classics on education, giving due place to philosophy; Too 2001 offers a more recent overview, with updated bibliography; and Goulet 1989ff. is an enormously rich philosophers' encyclopedia, with further bibliography. The collections edited by Griffin and Barnes (1989), Barnes and Griffin (1999), and Borg (2004a) comprise many excellent articles. On the cultural developments from the first to the third centuries AD Swain 1996 is most important. Hahn 1989 focuses on the social and public role of philosophers. From the archaeological point of view Zanker 1995 [with Smith (1999)] and Smith 1998 are superb and stimulating introductions.

BIBLIOGRAPHY

Anderson, G. 1993. *The Second Sophistic. A Cultural Phenomenon in the Roman Empire.* London: Routledge.
Athanassiadi, P. 1993. "Persecution and Response in Late Paganism: The Evidence of Damascius." *Journal of Hellenic Studies* 113: 1–29.
Banham, R. B., and M.-O. Goulet-Cazé (eds.). 1996. *The Cynics. The Cynic Movement in Antiquity and Its Legacy.* Berkeley: University of California Press.
Barnes, J., and M. Griffin (eds.). 1999. *Philosophia Togata II. Plato and Aristotle at Rome.* Oxford: Oxford University Press.
Bartsch, S. 2006. *The Mirror of the Self: Sexuality, Self-Knowledge, and the Gaze in the Early Roman Empire.* Chicago: University of Chicago Press.
Behrends, O. 1983. "Staatsrecht und Philosophie in der ausgehenden Republik—oder zur Bedeutung des Mottos *philosophari se velle, sed paucis.*" *Zeitschrift der Savigny-Stiftung für Rechtsgeschichte, Romanistische Abteilung* 100: 458–84.

67. Himmelmann 1962 (with tables 32; 39.1 and 39.2); Ewald 1999: 54–62, 200–201; Wrede 2001: 70–75 (with table 17ff.); Borg 2004b: 168–69. Also on the muses' sarcophagus as related group of monuments, see Wrede 2001: 70–75, and Borg 2004b: 166–67. Cf. also Ewald 1999 (but with the reservations of Borg 2004b: 167 with n. 48 and n. 53). Also consider the sarcophagus of L. Pullius Peregrinus and his wife, the couple there surrounded by philosophers and muses (Rome, in the Museo Torlonia), also the so-called 'Plotinus-sarcophagus' (Musei Vaticani); Ewald 1999: 93–94, 167–69, with tables 42, 1–2, and 43, 1–4.

Billerbeck, M. 1979. *Der Kyniker Demetrius: ein Beitrag zur Geschichte der frühkaiserzeitlichen Popularphilosophie.* Leiden: E. J. Brill.

Bonner, S. F. 1977. *Education in Ancient Rome: From the Elder Cato to the Younger Pliny.* Berkeley: University of California Press.

Borg, B. E. (ed.). 2004a. *Paideia: The World of the Second Sophistic.* Berlin: Walter de Gruyter.

———. 2004b. "Glamorous Intellectuals: Portraits of Pedaideumenoi in the Second and Third Centuries." In B. Borg (ed.), *Paideia: The World of the Second Sophistic.* Berlin: Walter de Gruyter. 157–78.

Bowersock, G. W. 1969. *Greek Sophists in the Roman Empire.* Oxford: Clarendon Press.

———. 2002. "Philosophy in the Second Sophistic." In Clark and Rajak 2002: 157–70.

Bowie, E.L. 1982. "The Importance of Sophists." *Yale Classical Studies* 27: 29–59.

Brisson, J.-L. 1992. "Plotin, une biographie." In L. Brisson et al. (eds.), *Porphyre, La vie des Plotin,* II. Paris: Vrin.

Brown, P. 1978. *The Philosopher and Society in Late Antiquity.* Berkeley: University of California Press.

Brunt, P. A. 1973. "Aspects of the Social Thought of Dio Chrysostom and of the Stoics." *Proceedings of the Cambridge Philological Society* 19: 9–34.

———. 1974. "Marcus Aurelius in His *Meditations.*" *Journal of Roman Studies* 64: 1–20.

———. 1977. "From Epictetus to Arrian." *Athenaeum* 55: 19–48.

Champlin, E. 1980. *Fronto and Antonine Rome.* Cambridge, Mass.: Harvard University Press.

Christes, J. 1975. *Bildung und Gesellschaft: Die Einschätzung der Bildung und ihrer Vermittler in der Antike.* Darmstadt: Wissenschaftliche Buchgesellschaft.

———. 1979. *Sklaven und Freigelassene als Grammatiker und Philologen im antiken Rom.* Wiesbaden: Franz Steiner Verlag.

Christes, J., R. Klein, and C. Lüth (eds.). 2006. *Handbuch der Erziehung und Bildung in der Antike.* Darmstadt: Wissenschaftliche Buchgesellschaft.

Clark, G., and T. Rajak (eds.). 2002. *Philosophy and Power in the Graeco-Roman World. Essays in Honour of Miriam Griffin.* Oxford: Oxford University Press.

Clarke, M. L. 1971. *Higher Education in the Ancient World.* London: Routledge.

Clay, D. 1989. "A Lost Epicurean Community." *Greek, Roman & Byzantine Studies* 30: 313–35.

Desideri, P. 1978. *Dione di Prusa: Un intellettuale greco nell'impero romano.* Florence: Casa Editrice G. d'Anna.

Dihle, A. 1986. "Philosophie—Fachwissenschaft—Allgemeinbildung." In H. Flashar, O. Gigon, and I. Kidd (eds.), *Aspects de la philosophie hellénistique* (Entretiens sur l'antiquité classique 32). Geneva: Fondation Hardt. 185–223.

Dillon, J. 1977. *The Middle Platonists.* London: Duckworth.

———. 1993. *Alcinous: The Handbook of Platonism.* Oxford: Clarendon Press.

———. 2003. "The Social Role of the Philosopher in Athens in the Second Century C.E.: Some Remarks." In P. A. Stadter and L. van der Stockt (eds.), *Sage and Emperor: Plutarch, Greek Intellectuals and Roman Power in the Time of Trajan, 98–117 A.D.* Leuven: Leuven University Press. 29–40.

Döring, K. 1979. *Exemplum Socratis. Studien zur Sokratesnachwirkung in der kynisch-stoischen Popularphilosophie der frühen Kaiserzeit und im frühen Christentum.* Wiesbaden: Franz Steiner Verlag.

Dörrie, H. 1973. "L. Kalbenos Tauros. Das Persönlichkeitsbild eines platonischen Philosophen um die Mitte des 2. Jahrh. n. Chr." *Kairos* 15: 24–35.

Dörrie, H., and M. Baltes. 1993. *Der Platonismus in der Antike III.* Stuttgart–Bad Cannstadt: Frommann-Holzboog.

Dudley, D. 1937. *A History of Cynicism. From Diogenes to the 6th Century A.D.* London: Methuen.

Erler, M. (ed.). 2000. *Epikureismus in der späten Republik und der Kaiserzeit.* Stuttgart—Leipzig: B. G. Teubner.

Ewald, B. C. 1999. *Der Philosoph als Leitbild: Ikonographische Untersuchungen an römischen Sarkophagreliefs.* Mainz: von Zabern.

Fein, S. 1994. Die Beziehungen der Kaiser Trajan und Hadrian zu den *litterati.* Stuttgart—Leipzig: B. G. Teubner.

Flinterman, J. J. 1995. *Power, Paideia and Pythagoreanism. Greek Identity, Conceptions of the Relationship between Philosophers and Monarchs and Political Ideas in Philostratus' "Life of Apollonius."* Amsterdam: J. C. Gieben.

Fowden, G. 1977. "The Platonist Philosopher and his Circle in Late Antiquity." *Philosophia* 7: 359–83.

———. 1982. "The Pagan Holy Man in Late Antique Society." *Journal of Hellenic Studies* 102: 33–59.

Garbarino, G. 1973. *Roma e la filosofia greca dalle origini alle fine del II secolo a.C., I-II.* Torino: G. B. Paravia.

Gleason, M. W. 1995. *Making Men. Sophists and Self-Presentation in Ancient Rome.* Princeton: Princeton University Press.

Glucker, J. 1978. *Antiochus and the Late Academy.* Göttingen: Vandenhoeck & Ruprecht.

Gordon, P. 1996. *Epicurus in Lycia. The Second Century World of Diogenes of Oenoanda.* Ann Arbor: University of Michigan Press.

Gottschalk, H. B. 1987. "Aristotelian Philosophy in the Roman World from the Time of Cicero to the End of the Second Century AD." In *Aufstieg und Niedergang der Römischen Welt* II 36.2. Berlin: Walter de Gruyter. 1079–1174.

Goulet, R. (ed.). 1989–. *Dictionnaire des philosophes antiques I–IV.* Paris: CNRS Editions.

Goulet-Cazé, M.-O. 1982. "L'arrière-plan scolaire de la Vie de Plotin." In L. Brisson et al. (eds.), *Porphyre "La Vie de Plotin."* Paris: Librairie Philosophique J. Vrin.

Griffin, M. 1989. "Philosophy, Politics, and Politicians at Rome." In Griffin and Barnes 1989: 1–37.

Griffin, M., and J. Barnes (eds.). 1989. *Philosophia Togata. Essays on Philosophy and Roman Society.* Oxford: Clarendon Press.

Hadot, I. 1984. *Arts libéraux et philosophie dans la pensée antique.* Paris: Etudes Augustiniennes.

———. 1997. "Geschichte der Bildung: *artes liberales.*" In F. Graf (ed.), *Einleitung in die lateinische Philologie.* Stuttgart–Leipzig: B. G. Teubner. 17–34.

———. 2003. "Der philosophische Unterrichtsbetrieb in der römischen Kaiserzeit." *Rheinisches Museum* 146: 49–72.

Hahn, J. 1989. *Der Philosoph und die Gesellschaft. Selbstverständnis, öffentliches Auftreten und populäre Erwartungen in der hohen Kaiserzeit.* Stuttgart: Franz Steiner Verlag.

———. 2007. "Philosophen zwischen Kaiserzeit und Spätantike. Das 3. Jahrhundert n. Chr." In O. Hekster, G. de Kleijn, and D. Slootjes (eds.), *The Impact of Crises on the Roman Empire. Proceedings of the Seventh Workshop of the International Network Impact of Empire (Roman Empire, c. 200 B.C.–A.D. 476).* Leiden: E. J. Brill. 397–412.

Harris, W. V. 2001. *Restraining Rage. The Ideology of Anger Control in Classical Antiquity.* Cambridge, Mass.: Harvard University Press.

Heath, M. 2004. *Menander. A Rhetor in Context.* Oxford: Oxford University Press.

Herzog, R. 1935. *Urkunden zur Hochschulpolitik der römischen Kaiser.* Berlin: Verlag der Preussischen Akademie der Wissenschaften.

Himmelmann, N. 1962. "Der Sarkophag eines gallienischen Konsuln." In N. Himmelmann,
H. Wildschütz, and H. Biesantz (eds.), *Festschrift für Friedrich Matz*. Mainz: von
Zabern. 111–24.

Hübner, A. 1996. "Immunitas." *Reallexikon für Antike und Christentum* 17: 1092–1121.

Inwood, B. (ed.). 2003. *The Cambridge Companion to the Stoics*. Cambridge: Cambridge
University Press.

Iskandar, A. Z. (ed.). 1988. *Galen, De optimo medico cognoscendo: On Examinations by
which the Best Physicians Are Recognized. Edition of the Arabic Version with English
Translation and Commentary*. Berlin: Akademie Verlag.

Jocelyn, P. H. 1976. "The Ruling Class of the Roman Republic and Greek Philosophers."
Bulletin of the Rylands Library 59: 323–66.

Johnson, W. A. 2010. *Readers and Reading Culture in the High Roman Empire: A Study of
Elite Communities*. New York: Oxford University Press.

Johnson, W. A., and H. N. Parker. (eds.). 2009. *Ancient Literacies: The Culture of Reading in
Greece and Rome*. Oxford: Oxford University Press.

Jones, C. P. 1966. "The Teacher of Plutarch." *Harvard Studies in Classical Philology* 71:
205–13.

———. 1978. *The Roman World of Dio Chrysostom*. Cambridge, Mass.: Harvard University
Press.

Kaster, R. A. 1988. *Guardians of Language. The Grammarian and Society in Late Antiquity*.
Berkeley: University of California Press.

———. 2001. "Controlling Reason: Declamation in Rhetorical Education at Rome." In Too
2001: 317–37.

Kasulke, C. T. 2005. *Fronto, Marc Aurel und kein Konflikt zwischen Rhetorik und Philosophie
im 2. Jh. n. Chr*. München: K. G. Saur.

Kennedy, G. 1972. *A History of Rhetoric II: the Art of Rhetoric in the Roman World 300
B.C.—A.D. 300*. Princeton: Princeton University Press.

Korenjak, M. 2000. *Publikum und Redner: ihre Interaktion in der sophistischen Rhetorik der
Kaiserzeit*. Munich: Verlag C. H. Beck.

Kühnert, F. 1961. *Allgemeinbildung und Fachbildung in der Antike*. Berlin: Akademie Verlag.

Lakmann, M.-L. 1995. *Der Platoniker Tauros in der Darstellung des Aulus Gellius*. Leiden: E.
J. Brill.

Lamberton, R. 2001. "The Schools of Platonic Philosophy of the Roman Empire: The
Evidence of the Biographies." In Too 2001: 433–85.

La Rocca, A. 2005. *Il filosofo e la citta. Commento storico ai Florida di Apuleio*. Roma:
"L'Erma" di Bretschneider.

Lendon, J. E. 1997. *Empire of Honour. The Art of Government in the Roman World*. Oxford:
Clarendon Press.

Liebeschuetz, W. 1991. "Hochschule." *Reallexikon für Antike & Christentum* 15: 858–911.

Long, A. A. 2002. *Epictetus. A Stoic and Socratic Guide to Life*. Oxford: Oxford University
Press.

Lorenz, T. 1997. "Bildnisse griechischer Philosophen. Ihre Funktion und Interpretabilität."
Perspektiven der Philosophie 23: 401–24.

Lumpe, A. 1994. "Honorarium." *Reallexikon für Antike & Christentum* 16: 473–90.

Lutz, C. E. 1947. "Musonius Rufus, the 'Roman Socrates.'" *Yale Classical Studies* 10: 3–147.

Lynch, J. P. 1972. *Aristotle's School. A Study of a Greek Educational Institution*. Berkeley:
University of California Press.

MacMullen, R. 1967. *Enemies of the Roman Order. Treason, Unrest, and Alienation in the
Empire*. Cambridge, Mass.: Harvard University Press.

Manning, C. E. 1994. "School Philosophy and Popular Philosophy in the Roman Empire." *Aufstieg und Niedergang der römischen Welt* II 36.7. Berlin: Walter de Gruyter. 4995–5026.

Männlein-Robert, I. 2001. *Longin, Philologe und Philosoph. Eine Interpretation der erhaltenen Zeugnisse.* Munich: K. G. Saur.

Mansfeld, J. 1998. *Prolegomena mathematica. From Apollonius of Perga to the Late Neoplatonists.* Leiden: E. J. Brill.

Marrou, H.-I. 1982. *A History of Education in Antiquity.* Madison: University of Wisconsin Press.

Millar, F. 1965. "Epictetus and the Imperial Court." *Journal of Roman Studies* 55: 141–48.

Nock, A. D. 1933. *Conversion. The Old and the New in Religion from Alexander the Great to Augustine of Hippo.* Oxford: Clarendon Press.

North, H. 1966. *Sophrosyne: Self-Knowledge and Self-Restraint in Greek Literature.* Ithaca: Cornell University Press.

Nussbaum, M. C. 1994. *The Therapy of Desire: Theory and Practice in Hellenistic Ethics.* Princeton: Princeton University Press.

Nutton, V. 1971. "Two Notes on Immunities: Digest 27,1,6,10 and 11." *Journal of Roman Studies* 61: 52–63.

———. 1979. *Galen, On prognosis = De praecognitione.* Berlin: Akademie Verlag.

Oliver, J. H. 1970. *Marcus Aurelius: Aspects of Civic and Cultural Policy in the East.* Princeton: Princeton University Press.

———. 1977. "The *Diadochê* at Athens under the Humanistic Emperors." *American Journal of Philology* 98: 160–78.

———. 1981. "Marcus Aurelius and the Philosophical Schools at Athens." *American Journal of Philology* 102: 213–25.

O'Meara, D. J. 2003. *Platonopolis. Platonic Political Philosophy in Late Antiquity.* Cambridge: Cambridge University Press.

Oser-Grote, C. 1998. "Einführung in das Studium der Medizin. Eisagogische Schriften des Galen in ihrem Verhältnis zum Corpus Hippocraticum." In W. Kullmann, et al. (eds.), *Gattungen wissenschaftlicher Literatur in der Antike.* Tübingen: Gunter Narr. 95–117.

Pohlenz, M. 1980. *Die Stoa. Geschichte einer geistigen Bewegung, I–II.* Göttingen: Vandenhoeck & Ruprecht.

Rawson, E. 1985. *Intellectual Life in the Late Roman Republic.* London: Duckworth.

———. 1989. "Roman Rulers and the Philosophical Adviser." In Griffin and Barnes 1989: 233–57.

Sandy, G. N. 1997. *The Greek World of Apuleius. Apuleius and the Second Sophistic.* Leiden: E. J. Brill.

Schlange-Schöningen, H. 2003. *Die römische Gesellschaft bei Galen. Biographie und Sozialgeschichte.* Berlin: Walter de Gruyter.

Schmitz, T. 1997. *Bildung und Macht. Zur sozialen und politischen Funktion der zweiten Sophistik in der griechischen Welt der Kaiserzeit.* Munich: C. H. Beck.

Scholz, P. 2003. "Ein römischer Epikureer in der Provinz: Der Adressatenkreis der Inschrift des Diogenes von Oinoanda—Bemerkungen zur Verbreitung von Literalität und Bildung im kaiserzeitlichen Kleinasien." In K. Piepenbrink (ed.), *Philosophie und Lebenswelt in der Antike.* Darmstadt: Wissenschaftliche Buchgesellschaft. 208–28.

Sharples, R. W. 2002. "Alexander of Aphrodisias and the End of Aristotelian Philosophy." In T. Kobusch and M. Erler (eds.), *Metaphysik und Religion. Zur Signatur des spätantiken Denkens.* Munich: K. G. Saur. 1–22.

Smith, R. R. R. 1990. "Late Roman Philosopher Portraits from Aphrodisias." *Journal of Roman Studies* 80: 127–55.

————. 1998. "Cultural Choice and Political Identity in Honorific Portrait Statues in the Greek East in the Second Century AD." *Journal of Roman Studies* 88: 56–93.

————. 1999. "Review P. Zanker, *Die Maske des Sokrates*. Munich 1995." *Gnomon* 71: 448–57.

Steinmetz, P. 1982. *Untersuchungen zur römischen Literatur des 2. Jahrhunderts nach Christi Geburt*. Wiesbaden: Franz Steiner Verlag.

Swain, S. 1996. *Hellenism and Empire: Language, Classicism, and Power in the Greek World, AD 50–250*. Oxford: Clarendon Press.

————. (ed.). 2000. *Dio Chrysostom: Politics, Letters, and Philosophy*. Oxford: Oxford University Press.

Szarmach, M. 1985. *Maximos von Tyros. Eine literarische Monographie*. Torún: Uniwersytet M. Kopernika.

Taub, L. C. 1993. *Ptolemy's Universe. The Natural, Philosophical and Ethical Foundations of Ptolemy's Astronomy*. Chicago: La Salle.

Thielemann, A. and H. Wrede. 1989. "Bildnisstatuen stoischer Philosophen." *Mitteilungen des Deutschen Archäologischen Instituts (Athen)* 104: 109–55.

Too, Y. Lee (ed.). 2001. *Education in Greek and Roman Antiquity*. Cambridge: Cambridge University Press.

Trapp, M. B. 1997. *Maximus of Tyre: the Philosophical Orations*. Oxford: Clarendon Press.

van Bremen, R. 2005. "'Plotina to All Her Friends.' The Letter(s) of the Empress Plotina to the Epicureans of Athens." *Chiron* 35: 499–532.

van Geytenbeck, A. C. 1976. *Musonius Rufus and Greek Diatribe*. 2nd ed. Assen: Van Gorcum.

Visky, K. 1977. *Geistige Arbeit und die "Artes Liberales" in den Quellen des römischen Rechts*. Budapest: Akadémiai Kiadó.

Vössing, K. 1997. *Schule und Bildung im Nordafrika der Römischen Kaiserzeit*. Brussels: Latomus.

————. 2003. "Die Geschichte der römischen Schule—ein Abriss vor dem Hintergrund der neueren Forschung." *Gymnasium* 110: 455–97.

Walden, J. H. W. 1912. *The Universities of Ancient Greece*. London: Routledge.

Wölfel, C. 1995. "Porträts griechischer Dichter, Redner und Denker in römischen Villen." In K. Stemmer (ed.), *Standorte. Kontext und Funktion antiker Skulptur. Ausstellungskatalog Abgußsammlung Berlin*. Berlin: Freunde und Förderer der Abguss-Sammlung Antiker Plastik e.V. 441–45.

Wrede, H. 2001. *Senatorische Sarkophage Roms. Der Beitrag des Senatorenstandes zur römischen Kunst der hohen und späten Kaiserzeit*. Mainz: von Zabern.

Zanker, P. 1995. *The Mask of Socrates. The Image of the Intellectual in Antiquity*. Berkeley: University of California Press.

CHAPTER 7

LAW AND SOCIAL FORMATION IN THE ROMAN EMPIRE

DENNIS P. KEHOE

INTRODUCTION

ROMAN law's potential to play a significant role in shaping the lives of ordinary people depended on the degree to which the Roman government was able to foster a consistent legal order in an empire with diverse legal traditions. Such a legal order would have been the result not simply of a policy from the center, but also of a willingness of the empire's population to adopt Roman legal conventions and procedures (cf. Meyer 2004). In the west, the adoption of Roman private law was a natural by-product of the imperial government's policy of developing an urban culture based on Roman models of governance. The east, with its own legal traditions, offered a more complicated situation. In Egypt, for example, which had its own centuries-old tradition of Graeco-Egyptian law, Roman legal norms were gradually combined with local practices. The result, in the third century, after the promulgation in 212 of the *Constitutio Antoniniana* (an imperial decree conferring Roman citizenship on virtually all free inhabitants of the empire), was a legal system that was an amalgam of these two traditions.

Thus, if jurisprudence is one of the most significant legacies of the Roman Empire, it is still a question to what extent this jurisprudence affected people in their daily lives. A number of scholars have argued persuasively that the Roman jurists, who played the most important role in shaping Roman law during the principate, were careful to consider the social implications of the legal doctrines they were developing. This can be seen in the jurists' treatment of diverse areas of the law such as lease (Frier 1979), prostitution and adultery (McGinn 1998), and land transportation (Martin 2002). But did the Roman legal authorities' concern for the social implications of the law translate into the law's shaping the lives of everyday Romans? For this to have happened, the categories that defined status in the Roman law had to play a meaningful role in the lives of people across the empire. In addition, ordinary citizens and subjects would have used Roman law as the basis for conducting their most important business, such as marriage and inheritance, sales of property, or even land tenure. Finally, no legal order based on Roman law could have been successful without the development of legal institutions that were responsive to the needs of ordinary people. Put simply, if the Romans did not succeed in developing courts of law and other legal avenues to resolve disputes, then any effort to develop a legal culture revolving around Roman law would have been likely to fail, with people forced to turn to other means to resolve disputes, and, ultimately, to conduct the most important business of their lives. In what follows, we shall attempt to gain a sense of how these issues played themselves out on a daily basis during the early Roman imperial period.

Patria Potestas and the Economy

Perhaps the most basic institution to Roman legal relationships, and one that the Romans saw as distinguishing them from other societies, was *patria potestas*, the power that the father exercised over his agnatic descendants, even the right of life and death over children in his power, the *ius vitae necisque* (Saller 1994: 102–32; see also Krause in this volume).

In terms of the law, the institution of *patria potestas* is most significant for defining property relations. The *pater familias* had formal control over all legal relationships entered into by children in his power; one obvious example was that the agreement of the *pater familias* was required for a son or daughter to enter into a legal marriage. Formally, children in power did not own property in their own right. Any property that they might hold, termed the *peculium*, ultimately belonged to the *pater familias*. In this respect, the relationship between a *pater familias* and a child in power was much like that between a slave owner and a slave; the master might grant the slave a *peculium* as an award or as an endowment to manage a business, but formally, all property in the slave's hands belonged to the slave owner.

This hierarchical property structure had far-reaching implications for both social and economic life in the Roman Empire. That is the case because the *familia* structure, obviously a fundamental building block of Roman society, also provided the basis for organizing large-scale enterprises, from the business interests of an upper-class Roman to the bureaucracy of the Roman government, which depended to a large extent on the slaves and freedmen in the *familia Caesaris* (the household of the emperor).

We might first consider briefly the formal institutions surrounding Roman business organization, and how these were influenced by notions related to the family and the powers of the father in that context. Now, it has often been suggested that economic development in the Roman world was hampered by certain shortcomings in Roman law. One of these was in the law of partnership (*societas*). In the Roman law of *societas*, partnerships never achieved a juristic personality that allowed them to function as a legal entity distinct from the individuals comprising the partnership. Indeed, in Roman law, a partnership would generally dissolve at the death or withdrawal of one of the partners. In addition, the Roman law of agency, at least from a modern perspective, was also incomplete, since it lacked the legal category of an agent who could have full power to act on behalf of a principal, or property owner (Plescia 1984). Such agency law as did exist consisted of six legal remedies, introduced in the third or second century BC, and later jointly called the *actiones adiecticiae qualitatis* (Aubert 1994; de Ligt 1999). Through these actions, the praetor granted people who were owed money by agents or who had otherwise entered into contractual relationships a way to recover their losses by suing the principal, often a *pater familias* or a slave owner.

The limitation of the legal liability of the principal in these remedies—in most cases, it was limited to the *peculium* granted the agent—had important consequences for the Roman economy. These rules reduced the property owners' exposure in potentially lucrative but also risky business ventures. To some extent the law codified a very cautious orientation toward risk on the part of upper-class Romans, one that is traceable in other areas of the economy, particularly agriculture (Kehoe 1997). At times, certainly, upper-class Romans showed an entrepreneurial spirit in investing in commerce (Verboven 2002; Wilson 2002), but the possibilities for this were limited by the overall constraints on an economy based largely on agriculture (Zelener 2003). In sum, then, the institution of the *peculium*, together with the principal's limited liability, provided property owners with the legal tools to establish business relationships, but it also gave them a great deal of legal protection against risk.

The *familia* structure also provided a way for property owners to monitor and profit from the activities of people managing their business affairs. Reliance on agents who were under their personal control, such as sons-in-power, slaves, and freedmen, provided property owners with a great deal of leverage that they might not have been able to exercise against an independent employee. Firing an independent employee would provide some deterrent against poor performance, but it would hardly enable a property owner to recoup losses. Suing an employee or agent would also not be of much help overall, since this drastic step would only sever irreparably damaged business relationships. It created little positive incentive for the agent to work on behalf of the property owner's interest. The *peculium*, however, helped to align the incentives of agents managing businesses with those of property owners. A slave business manager using a *peculium* became a kind of residual claimant in the business, since his profit was directly tied to the business (Furubotn and Richter 2005: 162–70). The successful slave manager could use his earnings to purchase his freedom from his owner, or, at the very least, he could expect greater privileges and perhaps eventually be awarded his freedom. If property owners sacrificed potential profits they might have achieved from a more centralized control over their business interests, they gained by reaping a portion of the profits from agents acting autonomously, and so they lowered their costs of monitoring. From the perspective of economic institutions, the *peculium* as an economic category represented a self-reinforcing institution (Hodgson 1999: 199–219).

We might summarize the foregoing as follows. The *peculium* had real economic consequences, and shaped in significant ways the law produced by the Romans with respect to economic matters, as well as the actual economic behavior of the Romans. It also represented, however, a social institution that, as a product of the hierarchical structure of Roman society, reinforced the status of upper-class Romans (Andreau 2004). In other words, the functioning of law and of society were here closely intertwined.

LEGAL DEFINITIONS OF STATUS

To move beyond the realm of the family and its wide reach, Roman law shaped the lives of the empire's subjects by defining them juridically, and people's rights and privileges derived from this legal definition of their status. The most obvious distinction was between slaves and the free, as emphasized by the jurist Gaius (*Dig.* 1. 5. 3 = *Inst.* 1. 9; Frier and McGinn 2004: 14), and, among free people, between citizens and non-citizens. As the jurist Florentinus recognized, slavery was a universal institution (it was part of the 'law of nations') that, as a result of force or legal definition, countered the natural capacity to act freely (*Dig.* 1. 5. 4 pr.-1 = *Inst.* 1. 9; Frier and McGinn 2004: 14). If the distinction between slave and free defined people juridically, it did not necessarily represent a complete yardstick to measure a person's status or influence, let alone his or her material wealth in Roman society. There were certainly slaves who were able to amass considerable wealth and achieve their freedom. In the private sphere, Roman aristocratic families depended on slaves to perform a wide variety of skilled functions; wealthy people often owned, for example, slaves who functioned as their private doctors. Some slaves could use the opportunities offered by such service to achieve remarkable social mobility. Although a fictional character, the figure of Trimalchio in Petronius' *Satyricon* suggests, at least at the extreme, the possibilities for social and economic advancement for a slave— as a slave he worked as an accountant, eventually being manumitted in his master's will and gaining a large inheritance. Still, the tension that existed between freedmen like Trimalchio or the economically more humble fellow freedmen who were guests at his fictional dinner party and those of free status may have been keenly felt. Thus, the character Hermeros, who purchased his own freedom and that of his wife and was defiantly proud of the status that he had gained as a man of business, reacts with great anger against the mocking that he perceived from Encolpius and Ascyltus, whom he assumes to be members of the upper class (*Sat.* 57).

Perhaps the clearest indication of the dissonance that might exist between juridical status and wealth and influence in Roman society can be seen in the *familia Caesaris*, the slaves and freedmen and freedwomen of the emperor, who performed a wide range of duties in the limited bureaucracy of the Roman government (Weaver 1972). Some imperial slaves and freedmen achieved levels of wealth unimaginable for the average Roman; the most spectacular examples are the imperial freedmen prominent under Claudius, Pallas, and Narcissus, who reportedly amassed fortunes measured in the hundreds of millions of sesterces (Scheidel 1996: 228). But the contradiction between social status as defined juridically and wealth was probably most obvious in the realm of marriage. Wealthy imperial freedmen, or even slaves, might make attractive marriage partners for some aristocratic women (McGinn 2002: 63–66); however, marriages between senatorial women and freedmen were proscribed by the Augustan marriage legislation. Indeed, marriages between any freeborn women and slaves had no legal standing whatsoever. But apparently this type of 'marriage' was perceived as enough of a problem that the Roman government intervened to establish penalties for women who tried to marry slaves. According to the *Senatus Consultum Claudianum*, promulgated in AD 53, women who married slaves without the knowledge of the slave's owner would themselves be reduced to the status of slaves, while women who married slaves with the owner's knowledge would become freedwomen of the slave's owner. This measure, at least in part, served to maintain the distinction between the classes so stringently defined in the Augustan marriage legislation (see below); but at the same time, the problem is likely to have arisen because of the occasional contradiction between wealth and juridical status. Whether it was successful or not, the *senatus consultum* was designed to restrict social practice by imposing a legal definition on people, in accordance with which their marriage rights would be defined.

Defining a social hierarchy was a major component of the Augustan social legislation, in particular, in the *lex Iulia de maritandis ordinibus*, originally promulgated in 18 BC, and then amended in AD 9 by the *lex Papia et Poppaea*. The statute, as interpreted by the classical Roman jurists and by modern legal historians, is commonly referred to as the *lex Iulia et Papia*. One aspect of this law was to define marriage and the procreation of legitimate children as a basic duty of Roman citizens (Frier and McGinn 2004: 39). And so, people who did not marry or produce children were subject to various civil penalties, especially restrictions on their rights to inherit. The law also offered incentives for people who did produce children. For example, senators who gained the 'right of children' (the *ius liberorum*, a right that conferred full civic privileges on a person—such as, for a woman, the right to make significant financial transactions without the approval of a tutor), in addition to having full inheritance rights, enjoyed advantages in running for senatorial offices. At a local level, the recipients of this privilege might be exempt from some liturgies or compulsory public services. Women who produced three children on that basis obtained the *ius liberorum*, and therefore no longer required the services of a tutor to transact business, including making their wills. So, ultimately, one's enjoyment of full legal rights as a Roman citizen (at least from the Augustan period on) depended on being married and producing children. The fact that emperors often awarded the *ius liberorum* without requiring children (for example, the childless Pliny the Younger enjoyed this right) does not undercut this principle; emperors were free to bestow any and all favors, as they saw fit.

The Augustan legislation established marriage as a basic duty of Roman citizens, but in doing so it formally divided Roman citizens into a hierarchy of classes. One purpose of this was to maintain the distinction of the upper classes in Roman society. Accordingly, no senator or his male descendants could marry a freedwoman or a woman whose mother or father had been an actor or actress. In addition, no daughter, granddaughter, or great-granddaughter of a senator could marry a husband from the same classes (*Dig.* 22. 3. 44 pr.; Frier and McGinn 2004: 34). The notion of a social hierarchy, though, extended beyond the elite. Other freeborn people (not freedmen or freedwomen) were barred by the Augustan laws from marrying anyone who had made a living by being a prostitute, procurer, or procuress, anyone who had been condemned for adultery, anyone condemned in a public trial, and anyone who had been an actor (*Tit. Ulp.* 13. 2; Frier and McGinn 2004: 34). The aristocracy took the social hierarchy that formed the basis of this law very seriously. Thus, the Roman senator Pliny the Younger, writing in the early second century AD, vented his rage in a series of letters to a fellow senator at the accolades, including an honorary praetorship and an award of 15 million sesterces, that the senate under the emperor Claudius offered the powerful imperial freedman Pallas (*Ep.* 7. 29, 8. 6). In short, status, for the Roman aristocrat, was all-important; and the law was created so as to establish, teach, and uphold the status distinctions conceived of and believed in by the Roman elites.

LAW AND HONOR

The state was concerned not simply to maintain a social hierarchy based on class, but to define a 'community of honor,' or a 'meritocracy of virtue,' as Thomas McGinn expresses it (McGinn 1998: 21–69, 213), that unambiguously distinguished between respectable members of society and those whose profession or past or present behavior were considered disgraceful.[1] Membership in the ruling classes of the cities and towns of the empire was, at least in theory, a function of a legally defined honor, as well as plain wealth. Thus, municipal laws of the late republic and

---

1. Various of the types of person driven to the margins of Roman society are discussed below, in section VII of this volume. And on the workings of honor in Roman society, see Lendon in this volume.

principate excluded from the civic duties expected of responsible persons, such as holding local office or serving on juries, men who had engaged (or would do so) in such dishonorable professions as fighting as gladiators, or acting on the stage, not to mention pandering (McGinn 1998: 21–69).

But the effort to define a community of honor can most clearly be seen in another Augustan law, this one on adultery (the *Lex Iulia de adulteriis coercendis*), both as it originally was promulgated by the emperor and then in its interpretation by the classical Roman jurists (McGinn 1998). Adultery was defined as sexual relationships outside of marriage with a married woman. The offended party was either the husband, or the adulterous woman's father. The husband's sexual relations outside of marriage were not of interest to the law, as long as they did not involve properly married women (or unmarried women of respectable status). Women convicted of adultery were subject to severe penalties, including relegation (a mild form of exile) and the loss of inheritance rights. Likewise, husbands who were complicit in their wives' adultery, either by profiting from it, failing to divorce a wife caught in adultery, offering a house for adulterous purposes, or, at least in later juristic interpretation, marrying a woman convicted of adultery (McGinn 1998: 171–94), were also subject to criminal penalties; in the definition of the law, they were guilty of pandering, *lenocinium*.

The purpose behind this law is likely to have been complex. In one interpretation, the statute responded to upper-class male concerns about control over their families. A wife involved in adultery compromised the control that society expected the husband to exercise. Adultery, then, represented a threat to the very foundations of society (Edwards 1993: 34–62). Thus, Juvenal, in his early second-century satire on women (*Sat.* 6), complains that upper-class women seemingly engage in affairs with impunity. The Augustan law responded to this perceived threat by making adultery, which previously had been a private matter, into a public crime. Since adultery severely compromised the husband's honor, he was expected to seek some kind of lawful vengeance against his wife and the adulterer to restore it. Thus, a husband aware of his wife's adultery was legally required to divorce her, and was also expected to prosecute her. A wife, upon conviction, would lose the most important privileges of status. She might be relegated, and she would lose many of her inheritance rights. She would not be able to contract a legal marriage. More broadly, she would be a *femina probrosa* (a blameworthy or disgraced woman), a person formally excluded from respectable society.

But the social reality was often quite different from the community of honor envisioned in the Augustan legislation. This is apparent in Cicero's efforts, in 56 BC, to defend Marcus Caelius Rufus against insinuations of serial philandering. Cicero's strategy involved depicting Rufus' jilted lover, Clodia, as a prostitute since, as an unmarried widow, she had opened her house to men (Cic. *Cael.* 48–50). In Cicero's portrayal, it was hardly admirable for Caelius to have sown his wild oats with a 'prostitute'; but, by usual Roman standards, there was nothing criminal, or even seriously dishonorable, in this type of behavior. For Clodia, a very different standard applied. On the face of it, Cicero's characterization of Clodia was absurd, since she obviously did not fit the juristic definition of a prostitute, namely, one who openly and regularly received money for sex (McGinn 1998: 70–104), but it seems likely that these charges found some resonance with the jurors hearing the case.

Still, Clodia continued to lead her life undeterred, and many other women must have followed her example. Showing official disapproval to lifestyles like that of Clodia thus remained a continuing concern of the Roman government. For example, under the emperor Tiberius, in AD 19, a woman named Vistilia attempted to avoid liability for criminal charges under the adultery statute by registering as a prostitute (Tac. *Ann.* 2. 85. 1–3; McGinn 1998: 197; McGinn 1992). Prostitution was legal in the Roman Empire; the prostitutes themselves had to register with the aediles (at least until AD 19; McGinn 1998: 201), were subject to taxation, and of course endured social disgrace— but they were exempt from the penalties of the Augustan adultery law. The senate took action to close this loophole by passing the *senatus consultum Larinum*; henceforth, upper-class women engaged in illicit sexual relations could not escape their criminal liability. Among the lower classes, it is not clear to what extent the Augustan legislation made a real difference in people's lives. Certainly many prostitutes were slaves and were horribly exploited. This is surely a motivation for the restrictive covenants, in sales of slave women, against employing them as prostitutes (McGinn 1990). But there is also reason to believe that for many women, prostitution represented one of the few economic opportunities available, and there may have been less of a social stigma outside of the elite classes attached to prostitution (Flemming 1999). Despite being debarred from a legal Roman marriage, it seems likely that some women who had worked as prostitutes were able to form stable and lasting unions.

The Augustan law on adultery also classified men in accordance with their respectability. The husband who discovered his wife in adultery was to pursue his vengeance through law courts by divorcing his wife and prosecuting her and her lover. He was not permitted to kill the lover, but the law offered him an affirmative defense against a murder charge if he caught his wife and her lover in his own house and the lover were a member of the despised classes, defined as a panderer, actor, someone condemned in a public trial, a freedman of his or his wife's family, or a slave (*Dig.* 48. 5. 25 pr.-1; Frier and McGinn 2004: 112). How often enraged husbands could use this defense is difficult to determine, but this does indicate the basic assumptions underlying the law about the social construction of status in Roman society. Overall, the Augustan legislation demonstrates a significant willingness on the part of the Roman state to guide citizens (especially members of the elite orders) in their sexual relationships.

CITIZENSHIP

In the early principate, Roman citizenship conferred a bundle of privileges not available to people of foreign or peregrine status. Roman citizens could make contracts, including marriage, enforceable under Roman law, serve in the legions, and be exempt from poll taxes (at least in Egypt, along with the people who enjoyed 'Greek' citizenship). Some Roman citizens could hope to be recruited into the equestrian order and enjoy careers in public service. The Roman state also provided a regular path toward citizenship for many of the provincial elite. In cities with the rank of *municipium* with Latin rights, office holders would attain Roman citizenship, while in cities with 'greater Latin rights,' all the members of the town councils would receive Roman citizenship.

Practically speaking, the conferment of Roman citizenship on people in the provinces seems to have affected their social networks in fundamental ways. It shaped their choice of marriage partners, heirs, and guardians for their children. This can be seen especially in the archives of documents of Roman citizens that are preserved on papyri from Roman Egypt. One good example is the archive of Marcus Lucretius Diogenes, a citizen from Antinoopolis in the early third century (Schubert 1990). His social network, to judge by the documents preserved in the archive, include primarily Roman citizens, who, like him, were also citizens of the Greek city Antinoopolis. Though hardly members of the elite of the Roman Empire, these individuals represented a relatively small class of citizens in a province in which most people were of native Egyptian status. Their status as Roman citizens, in other words, allowed them to cohere as a particular social group within the context of the larger provincial society. Veterans from the legions and the auxiliary forces, who were often citizens or received citizenship upon retirement, also tended to cohere as yet another group of citizens within the larger surrounding society (Cherry 1998).

The types of relationship (both personal and more broadly social) fostered by rules over citizenship can also be seen in the will of Gaius Longinus Kastor, a veteran from the fleet at Misenum, who lived in the Egyptian village of Karanis in the late second century AD (*Sel. Pap.* I 85, AD 189–94). As a member of the military, Kastor could not enter into a legal marriage (this privilege was granted to soldiers by Septimius Severus, early in the third century; Phang 2001: 17–19, 86–114), and so, Kastor seems to have had an unconventional family. He named as his heirs two slave women, Marcella and Kleopatra, whom he also manumitted. In addition, he manumitted the daughter of Kleopatra, named Sarapias, and provided her with a legacy of land. In all likelihood, Sarapias was the testator's own daughter, and any 'marriage' that he had, involved a slave; hence, the union will not have been recognized in Roman law (Keenan 1994). But whereas Kastor's family apparently consisted of slaves, the witnesses to his Roman will all had to be Roman citizens. It seems likely that the seven witnesses named in the will were recruited from the circle of veterans, or their relatives, in and around Karanis; one of the witnesses is explicitly designated as a veteran. Thus, Kastor's familial situation, his circle of friends and acquaintances, and his testamentary dispensations were all thoroughly informed by the dictates of Roman law.

It is not clear, though, what portion of free people in the Roman Empire were citizens before the promulgation of the *constitutio Antoniniana* (the nearly universal grant of citizenship to the residents of the empire) by Caracalla in 212. One purpose of this enactment was to rationalize the distribution of taxes and liturgical obligations, so that people could no longer gain exemption from these charges by virtue of their citizen status. Whatever the case, before the *constitutio Antoniniana*, citizenship carried with it privileges that were jealously guarded. For example, in a petition to the emperor Commodus in 182 concerning their rights to land tenure, tenants on an imperial estate in Africa complained about the violent treatment accorded them by their adversaries, the procurator who administered the estate and the middleman who was collecting the rent. What was especially outrageous for these imperial tenants was that their adversaries had connived to send soldiers onto the estate to beat the tenants, some of whom were Roman citizens (Kehoe 1988). Certainly citizens in the provinces were supposed to be exempt from this type of treatment.

HONESTIORES AND HUMILIORES

As the privilege of Roman citizenship spread throughout the empire (over the course of the first and second centuries AD), it gradually lost its role as the key factor in defining status and privilege. In the second century, and then increasingly in the third, class distinctions based on citizenship gave way to one based on a hierarchy within the ranks of citizens. Society was divided into two distinct groups of people, the *honestiores*, the 'more honorable,' and the *humiliores*, the 'more modest' (Garnsey 1970). The first group included senators, equestrians, members of town councils, and some military officers, thus leaving the vast majority of the population to comprise the *humiliores*. The (ultimately legal) distinction between a well-defined 'elite' class and the rest of the population affected both the duties imposed on people and the types of penalties that could be visited upon malefactors for their criminal behavior. In terms of duties, members of local town councils, *curiales*, who were classified as *honestiores*, played a key role in the governance of the empire. They not only held local offices, but were also responsible to perform liturgies, or compulsory services (*munera*), involving substantial financial liability, especially the collection of taxes. People classified as *humiliores* might also perform liturgies involving financial liability—for instance, in Egypt, landowners at the village level would be required to take their turn at collecting local taxes, including the most important tax on agriculture, the grain tax, collected by the *sitologoi* (Bagnall 1993: 22–23, 133–38). But the *humiliores* were also liable to perform liturgies involving physical labor, such as the days of construction and road maintenance labor required from townspeople in Spain (*lex Ursonensis*), or the five days of labor each year required of villagers in Egypt to work on the dykes and canals to maintain the local irrigation systems (Bagnall 1993: ibid.). In terms of punishment, *honestiores* were generally exempt from humiliating physical abuse. For capital offenses, they faced exile, or other forms of deportation, and for less serious offenses, the most common punishment was a fine. *Humiliores* could be scourged for less serious offenses, and faced execution for capital crimes (Aubert 2002). For very serious crimes, such as conviction for persisting in the Christian faith and refusing to acknowledge the Roman gods, a person of high status might be reduced in rank and so be subject to the most brutal physical punishments (Clarke 2005: 642, quoting Cyprian, *Ep.* 80. 1. 2, on the edict of Valerian).

In some circumstances the law created an ideology that defined people as excluded from the community of the Roman Empire. This can be seen especially in the case of brigands, or *latrones*, who were juridically defined as enemies of the Roman order, and so not protected by any of the laws that preserved the rights of ordinary citizens or subjects (Riess 2001, and his chapter in this volume). This definition could be extended to other groups, such as senators found guilty of treason, rebels, or groups, such as certain mountain dwellers, whose violent way of life was deemed incompatible with the expectations of orderly Roman society (Riess 2001: 49–62).

ACCESS TO LEGAL PROTECTIONS

A key factor affecting the role that Roman law played in shaping the society of the empire was the capacity of the government to maintain broad access to the protection of legal institutions. The degree to which the Roman government responded to the needs of ordinary people is much debated, and many scholars see the Roman government as seeking primarily to serve the interests of the elite classes in the cities across the empire. According to this view, the elite were granted many social and political privileges, and in exchange they were expected to shoulder many of the tasks and costs associated with local government. In this circumstance, the possibility that ordinary people might be able to use the courts to protect their interests can seem remote. Indeed, one very pessimistic assessment of this issue is that of Fergus Millar, who, in an analysis of the Apuleius' *Golden Ass*, a novel whose action takes place against a basically realistic portrayal of provincial life, argues that the law and legal institutions are depicted as far removed from the lives of ordinary subjects (Millar 1981; Riess 2001). Certainly the lack of legal expertise of many judges limited the degree to which the law of the jurists could be applied in the Roman Empire, since provincial governors and other officials who might judge cases were often not appointed on the basis of their expertise, but rather as a result of patronage (Peachin 1996; Saller 1982 on patronage). It is hard to avoid the sense that the courts chiefly served the interests of the elite, who otherwise dominated the government. The dominance of the elite in the courts would be a product of the hierarchical structure so fundamental to Roman society, which would have made it more difficult for a humble litigant to challenge a socially more prominent foe in court. In addition, one has to factor the expense and time involved in pursuing a case in court, which would have deterred many a humble litigant.

However, this conception of the law as being of limited utility to the vast majority of the empire's population seems overstated. For one, there is ample evidence that ordinary people in the Roman Empire, both citizens and non-citizens, looked to the law and legal institutions, whether at the local level, the level of the provincial governor, or even that of the emperor himself, to protect their interests. To begin at the top, the emperor represented the highest legal authority, and the numerous rescripts, or written responses to petitions, preserved in the Code of Justinian suggest that people of a broad range of statuses regularly petitioned the emperor to seek authoritative legal rulings that they could use in local courts (Nörr 1981; Turpin 1991; Peachin 1996; Corcoran 1996; Connolly 2010). The emperor, or the official in charge of responding to petitions, the *a libellis*, was in no position to rule on the facts of a case, but instead, would offer a definitive opinion on the legal rule that might apply. The successful petitioner, then, would take the rescript from the emperor to a local court, where the judge would be bound to follow the emperor's instructions. It must have involved a great deal of expense to bring a petition to the emperor, but many people took the trouble to do so. They must have been confident that a written response from the emperor would be respected in a local court, and that the local court would have the authority to enforce the law. To be sure, the petitioning process required a great deal of individual initiative, and no litigant could count on the local court's being aware of the imperial rescripts or other enactments that might apply to his or her case. For this reason, litigants often collected past petitions and rescripts to support their position in judicial proceedings.

People outside the elite viewed the petitioning process as effective in settling issues in family law, as Judith Evans Grubbs demonstrates in her analysis of third-century petitions (Evans Grubbs 2005). People petitioned lower ranking officials as well, including, in Egypt, the *strategos*, that is, the local governor of the nome, or administrative division, as well as the provincial governor, who would regularly travel around the province to hear cases in various administrative centers. One famous document records that an early third-century prefect of Egypt, Subatianus Aquila, received 1,804 petitions during a three-day stop to hear cases in the capital of the Arsinoite nome (*P. Yale* I 61, ca. AD 208–10). Clearly, answering petitions and judging legal cases was a basic and time-consuming responsibility of the provincial governor, and the numerous surviving petitions from Roman Egypt indicate that the ranks of the petitioners extended far beyond the province's wealthier classes. On a broader level, the emperor's role in answering petitions has been identified as part of a continuing effort to manage communications between the emperor and the empire's subjects to promote and maintain Roman authority (Ando 2000). This principle also applied on the local level as well; the petition process indicates what people in the empire expected of their government, namely, that it would serve to defend the rights of the oppressed and dispense justice.

If the Roman legal institutions, from the emperor down to the provincial level, provided a means for people in the empire to resolve disputes, it still remains to be examined how the possibility of going to court shaped people's lives, in other words, their interactions with one another. Certainly, very few disputes that potentially could go to court—over such issues as property rights, leases, sales or other contracts, and inheritance—ever actually did so, and most were resolved informally.

Still, even under this circumstance, it seems likely that people conducted their affairs "in the shadow of the law" (Mnookin and Kornhauser 1979). This is a concept that has been introduced into the contemporary debate about the relationship between law and the economy, specifically, to assess to what extent the existence of potential legal remedies influences how people bargain in disputes. The formal legal rules surrounding a contract provide a sort of default as to what will happen should negotiations break down and the dispute go to court, and so they offer the parties bargaining chips that affect negotiations in cases that do not wind up in court.

This principle seems applicable to the Roman world, for example, in such an important relationship to the ancient world as land tenure. In Egypt, documentary papyri preserve numerous leases, with the obligations of both the landowner and tenant spelled out in considerable detail. The point is that, even if only a tiny portion of such leases ever resulted in a dispute requiring the intervention of legal authorities, the possibility of petitioning the governor or the local *strategos* provided both parties with a degree of leverage; the written terms of the lease established default rules, and affected how any disputes might be resolved if the lease relationship dissolved (cf. Rowlandson 1994). The possibility of court proceedings surely influenced people's behavior in other important areas of their lives in which the law might be involved, such as marriage or bequeathing property through wills.

In fact, the government did take some steps to make sure that the courts were available to a broad class of litigants. The jurist Ulpian, writing in the early third century, considered it to be a basic duty of the proconsul, or governor of a province, to assure that litigants be able to find advocates to take up their cases, especially people who might otherwise have trouble availing themselves of the courts, such as widows, children in guardianship, the mentally incompetent, and people involved in litigation with powerful adversaries (*Dig.* 1. 16. 9. 4–5). In more general terms, the jurists took pains to make the process of going to court predictable and understandable by establishing clear rules of civil procedure (Bürge 1995). Later, the Roman government sought to suppress the practice of legal patronage, *patrocinium*, by which powerful people took up in their own name cases originally raised by people of more modest resources. The point was to prevent the courts from being dominated by the rich and powerful, and so anyone who turned over his case to a powerful patron was sanctioned with automatic forfeiture (*CJ* 2. 13. 1, AD 293; Kehoe 2007: 19).

These efforts of the Roman government and the jurists met some success, since we have evidence that Roman legal norms were widely adopted in the provinces of the empire, even by people who did not enjoy the privilege of Roman citizenship. For example, in Dacia, in the second century, slave sales recorded on tablets were carried out in accordance with the Roman law of sale, even though the parties to the contracts were not Roman citizens (Meyer 2004: 56–57, 177–79; Weßel 2003: 67–68). Another example of the importance of Roman law for people in the provinces comes from the so-called Babatha archive, a collection of documents recording the financial affairs of a Jewish family, and hid in a cave for safe-keeping at the time of the Bar Kochba War, never to be recovered. The family used Nabataean law to protect its interests when it lived under Nabataean rule, but upon the annexation of the Nabataean kingdom by Rome in 106, the family ordered its business in accordance with Roman legal conventions, including those involving the tutorship of minors (Cotton 1993, as well as Nörr 1998, and Meyer 2004: 191–93). For this family, the availability of Roman legal institutions provided a means to seek redress, and, more significantly, shaped the way it defined its own legal rights and obligations. In the mid-third century, a group of farmers from an imperial estate at Beth Phouraia in the middle Euphrates region in Syria traveled all the way to Antioch to petition the governor in a dispute over cultivation rights. This group of farmers formulated its petition in terms of the Roman law of possession, and cited constitutions by the emperors on this issue (*P. Euphrates* 1, AD 245 = Feissel and Gascou 1995; Ando 2000: 73–80).

The example of Babatha and the farmers from Beth Phouraia provide more concrete examples of the reality that must have shaped many of the petitions standing behind the rescripts preserved in the *Code of Justinian*; the protection of Roman legal institutions was available to people of a broad range of social backgrounds, and they had enough confidence in the effectiveness of those institutions to use them to resolve disputes. Based on this, it seems likely that the possibility of seeking justice in a Roman court affected the informal resolution of many more legal disputes, and, in broader terms, affected the way in which legal relationships were formulated to begin with. This does not mean that the Roman government was ever completely successful in establishing the authority of its courts and, say, countering the excessive influence that locally powerful people might exercise. But it does suggest that Roman law and legal institutions shaped the way that a broad spectrum of the population in the Roman Empire managed their most important affairs.

What could play a crucial role in the Roman Empire was the social relationship between the parties to a dispute; a landowner in a dispute with a tenant, for example, might be able to use his social influence to force on his adversary a much less favorable settlement than the latter would theoretically be entitled to in a court of law; but, the possibility of foisting a legally unfair settlement on another party would be much reduced when the parties were of more or less equal social standing.

Self-Help and Its Limitations

Certainly, the Roman imperial authorities were concerned to assert the authority of their courts. It has nevertheless long been recognized that Roman law accorded a wide scope for self-help in enforcing contracts, and here, certainly, the social relationship of the parties to a contract could play a decisive role in how a dispute might be resolved (Bürge 1980). For example, a creditor enjoying a superior social standing could exercise a great deal of latitude in enforcing a debt; he might take unilateral action against the debtor, say by confiscating property belonging to the debtor or even by imprisoning him to compel repayment. A debtor with few resources would have little capacity to use a legal remedy to make sure that his or her rights were fully protected in such a proceeding. Still, the Roman government seems to have been nervous about the possible abuses that might arise from self-help. It discouraged the private use of prisons, even if these continued to be maintained throughout antiquity (Krause 1996). By the second century, the government began to insist on the exclusive authority of its courts to enforce debts and other legal obligations. For example, the emperor Marcus Aurelius, in a constitution quoted by the jurist Callistratus, regarded any means that a creditor might use to enforce a debt outside the authority of the courts as force, or *vis* (*Dig.* 48. 7. 7). The creditor's actions in using self-help would have no legal standing, and resorting to actions that could be classified as force made the creditor liable to prosecution. In subsequent rescripts, the emperors upheld this principle, insisting that any settlement of debt that involved the confiscation of property pledged as security for the debt be carried out under the watchful eye of the courts (Kehoe 2007: 148–55). In fact, the Roman government's opposition to the unilateral exercise of force became a basic part of the ideology of the empire. This can be seen in many petitions from people seeking legal relief in Roman Egypt. In these petitions, it was common for the petitioner to lend urgency to his or her cause by alleging that the adversary has used force. In the enforcement of criminal law, self-help is likely to have been more sanctioned by the Roman government, which had only limited resources to maintain any kind of a standing police force and formal institutions to prosecute crime, outside the provincial governor's general responsibility to maintain order (Riess 2001: 190–216).

Perhaps the best evidence for the state's efforts to reduce the role of self-help and to bring important disputes under the authority of the courts is the Augustan legislation on adultery, which dealt with life-or-death situations. One aspect of this law was to allow, under certain circumstances, the husband or the father to kill. It is not that the law specifically authorized either party to commit murder, but it rather provided an affirmative defense against a charge of murder that could be used in certain carefully defined situations. The husband could kill his wife's lover with impunity as long as he caught the couple in the act, and as long as the lover belonged to certain despised classes. Even though this permission to kill has been interpreted as providing a deterrent to would-be adulterers, it seems more likely that the Augustan law was intended to restrict, without condoning, a practice of honor-killing that may have been fairly widespread, even if upper-class oriented sources from the late republic do not offer much evidence for this (McGinn 1998: 146–47, 202–7; Edwards 1993: 47–62). Under the Augustan law, the husband had no right to kill his wife; instead, he was required by law to instigate legal proceedings against her, and he could be subject to legal sanctions himself if he failed to do so. He was preferred over all other accusers because, in the interpretation of the jurists, he was expected to feel the pain, or *dolor*, over a dishonored marriage most keenly (*Dig.* 48. 5. 2. 8; Frier and McGinn 2004: 110). Only her father, who exercised *patria potestas*, could kill an adulterous woman, and again, the legal justification for such killing was tightly restricted. In the interpretation of the jurists, it was expected that the father's natural affection for his daughter would cause him to hesitate to take such a drastic measure (*Dig.* 48. 5. 23. 4; Frier and McGinn 2004: 206). In addition, the father in power had to catch his daughter in the act, in his own house, or in that of his son-in-law, and he had to kill both the daughter and the lover, as if with one blow. If he killed the lover and not the daughter, he could be charged with murder. The jurists interpreted catching the errant lovers in the act quite strictly. This phrase was interpreted to mean that the father had to catch the lovers in the very act of copulation; otherwise, any killing would result in murder charges (*Dig.* 48. 5. 24 pr.).

It seems plausible that, both in the Augustan legislation and in its subsequent interpretation by the jurists, the legal authorities sought to make state-sanctioned killing as a solution to a social outrage exceedingly rare by carefully restricting the circumstances in which it might be allowed. However, it is also apparent that the state had time and again to confront social attitudes that saw husbands as somehow entitled to restore their honor by taking lethal vengeance against lovers who compromised their marriages. Thus, Antoninus Pius (138–161) and Marcus Aurelius (161–180) were willing to reduce the penalties for husbands who had killed their wives (*Dig.* 48. 5. 39. 8). Later, Alexander Severus (222–235) authorized the same reduction in penalty for a cuckolded husband who killed his wife's lover (*CJ* 9. 9. 4. 1; Frier and McGinn 2004: 112). The Roman state was willing to modify the penalty for such murders, but only to a certain extent, and its approach to this problem is to be contrasted with the indulgence toward husbands granted by later Italian states in the medieval and early modern period (Cantarella 1991).

Written Documents

One important aspect of the Roman government's efforts to foster a legal order in the empire was its policy of promoting the use of written documents as authoritative legal instruments. In her recent book, Elizabeth Meyer has carefully traced the development of *tabulae*, documents written on wood, as legal instruments (Meyer 2004). Under the republic, these documents, including both legal documents as wills and even curse tablets, were written in a formulaic language that gave them a solemnity and authority not associated with written legal documents in most other cultures. In the realm of private law, written tablets came to be used in contracts and transactions that were originally oral, public acts, such as the mancipation of property, which was necessary to transfer full quiritary rights of ownership of land and the movable property connected with the cultivation of land, such as livestock and slaves. Tablets might also be used to record a stipulation, a formal promise in response to a question that bound the promisor to perform some action. In private law, the writing of a tablet provided the strongest proof possible of a person's *fides*. And so, the process that originally had wills written in wax on wooden tablets and sealed was extended to other types of transactions, such as the sales of slaves and promises to pay debts, as attested in the wax tablets preserved from Herculaneum. Gradually, the use of tablets as authoritative documents spread to the provinces, at least in part as the result of practices favored by the Roman government. The result of this, eventually, was an increasing imitation in the provinces of Roman ways of composing legal documents, whether they were written on papyrus or other media, in addition to wood. This phenomenon is likely to have differed from province to province, depending on the strength and persistence of local legal traditions. In Egypt, for example, with its own tradition of Graeco-Egyptian law, the adoption of Roman forms was slower than in newly assimilated provinces, such as Arabia, the former Nabataean kingdom, which passed into Roman rule in AD 106.

In its quintessential form, the tablet represented an authoritative written version of what was also in essence an oral act before witnesses. But as subjects in the Roman Empire came to rely on such documents more and more, the Roman legal authorities were careful to maintain that written instruments were not necessary to establish contracts, such as marriage, or other legal obligations. However, the effect of relying on written documents can be seen in the Roman government's moving away (particularly under Constantine) from insisting on precise legal formulaic language in such acts as stipulations and wills, as long as the intentions of the parties were clear and sufficient safeguards were taken to prevent fraud. So, one influence of the Roman rule in the provinces was to promote a greater reliance on Roman legal forms through the use of written documents. The use of such documents, in turn, helped Roman law to accommodate a large and diverse population with differing customs under the broad authority of Roman law, a Roman law that was now more flexible and less formalistic than it had been at the beginning of the principate.

Conclusion

The Roman government faced many challenges in establishing and maintaining the rule of law in the empire. But this survey of the evidence suggests strongly the profound role that Roman law played in the daily lives of people across the empire. Roman legal categories were meaningful to the conditions under which people lived. Roman categories of status and privilege materially affected how people went about their daily lives, and the possibilities they had for social mobility. The Roman concept of *patria potestas* played a significant role in shaping the organization of economic activity at every social level in the empire, from that of the elite down to the stratum of the very humble. The Romans made it a basic principle of their approach to ruling the empire to try as much as possible to make the protection of legal institutions available to ordinary people, and to keep the playing field in the courts as level as possible. Partly, this was a result of the natural tendency of people to turn to the Roman government for protection against locally powerful individuals, and the state responded to this by fostering a petitions process. The result was a mutually reinforcing system—as people looked more toward the central government for protection, the central government attempted to be more responsive. The result was, by the end of our period (i.e., the reign of Diocletian), that the adjudication of petitions became one of the primary functions not just of provincial governors or other local officials, but of the emperor himself. To be sure, there were overlapping jurisdictions, while corruption, the influence of the well-connected, and the expense of bringing cases continued to undermine the system. But by the third century, virtually all free people in the Roman Empire were citizens. Nominally bound by the same law, they were able, to a surprising extent, to organize their lives around Roman legal conventions and, when necessary, to avail themselves of the protection of Roman legal institutions. The continuing strength of these legal institutions was surely a major factor that helped the Roman Empire to survive the crisis of the third century.

SUGGESTED READING

Johnston (1999) offers a concise introduction to Roman private law. Frier and McGinn (2004) provide a very illuminating introduction to the law of the family through discussion of hundreds of individual cases or hypothetical problems considered by the jurists. Garnsey (1970) discusses the role that social rank played in the application of the law. For the role of the emperor in answering petitions, see especially Peachin (1996), Corcoran (1996), and Connolly (2010).

BIBLIOGRAPHY

Ando, C. 2000. *Imperial Ideology and Provincial Loyalty in the Roman Empire*. Berkeley: University of California Press.

Andreau, J. 2004. "Sur les choix économiques des notables romains." In J. Andreau, J. France, and S. Pittia (eds.), *Mentalités et choix économiques des Romains*. Paris: Ausonius Éditions. 71–85.

Aubert, J.-J. 1994. *Business Managers in Ancient Rome: A Social and Economic Study of Institores, 200 B.C.–A.D. 250*. Leiden: E. J. Brill.

———. 2002. "A Double Standard in Roman Criminal Law? The Death Penalty and Social Structure in Late Republican and Early Imperial Rome." In J.-J. Aubert and B. Sirks (eds.), *Speculum Iuris: Roman Law as a Reflection of Social and Economic Life in Antiquity*. Ann Arbor: University of Michigan Press. 94–133.

Bagnall, R. S. 1993. *Egypt in Late Antiquity*. Princeton: Princeton University Press.

Bürge, A. 1980. "Vertrag und personale Abhängigkeiten im Rom der späten Republik und der frühen Kaiserzeit." *Zeitschrift der Savigny-Stiftung für Rechtsgeschichte. Romanistiche Abteilung* 97: 105–56.

———. 1995. "Zum Edikt de edendo: Ein Beitrag zur Struktur des römischen Zivilprozesses." *Zeitschrift der Savigny-Stiftung für Rechtsgeschichte. Romanistiche Abteilung* 112: 1–50.

Cantarella, E. 1991. "Homicide of Honor: The Development of Italian Adultery Law over Two Millennia." In D. L. Kertzer and R. P. Saller (eds.), *The Family in Italy: from Antiquity to the Present*. New Haven: Yale University Press. 229–44.

Cherry, D. 1998. *Frontier and Society in Roman North Africa*. Oxford: Clarendon Press.

Clarke, G. 2005. "Third-Century Christianity." In A. Bowman, P. Garnsey, and A. Cameron (eds.), *The Cambridge Ancient History. Vol. XII. The Crisis of Empire, A.D. 193–337*. 2nd ed. Cambridge: Cambridge University Press. 589–671.

Connolly, S. 2010. *Lives behind the Laws: The World of the Codex Hermogenianus*. Bloomington: Indiana University Press.

Corcoran, S. 1996. *The Empire of the Tetrarchs: Imperial Pronouncements and Government A.D. 284–324*. Oxford: Oxford University Press.

Cotton, H. 1993. "The Guardianship of Jesus Son of Babatha: Roman and Local Law in the Province of Arabia." *Journal of Roman Studies* 83: 94–108.

de Ligt, L. 1999. "Legal History and Economic History: The Case of the *actiones adiecticiae qualitatis*." *Tijdschrift voor Rechtsgeschiedenis* 47: 205–26.

Edwards, C. 1993. *The Politics of Immorality in Ancient Rome*. Cambridge: Cambridge University Press.

Evans Grubbs, J. 2005. "Parent-Child Conflict in the Roman Family: The Evidence of the Code of Justinian." in M. George (ed.), *The Roman Family in the Empire: Rome, Italy, and Beyond*. Oxford: Oxford University Press. 93–128.

Feissel, D., and J. Gascou. 1995. "Documents d'archives romains inédits du moyen Euphrate (IIIᵉ s. après J.-C.)." *Journal des savants*: 65–119.

Flemming, R. 1999. "Quae Corpore Quaestum Facit: The Sexual Economy of Female Prostitution in the Roman Empire." *Journal of Roman Studies* 89: 38–61.

Frier, B. W. 1979. *Landlords and Tenants in Imperial Rome*. Princeton: Princeton University Press.

Frier, B. W., and T. A. J. McGinn. 2004. *A Casebook on Roman Family Law*. Oxford: Oxford University Press.

Furubotn, E. G., and R. Richter. 2005. *Institutions and Economic Theory: The Contribution of New Institutional Economics*. 2nd ed. Ann Arbor: University of Michigan Press.

Garnsey, P. 1970. *Social Status and Legal Privilege in the Roman Empire*. Oxford: Oxford University Press.

Hodgson, G. 1999. *Evolution and Institutions: On Evolutionary Economics and the Evolution of Economics*. Cheltenham: Edward Elgar.

Johnston, D. 1999. *Roman Law in Context*. Cambridge: Cambridge University Press.

Keenan, J. G. 1994. "The Will of Gaius Longinus Castor." *Bulletin of the American Society of Papyrologists* 94: 101–7.

Kehoe, D. P. 1988. *The Economics of Agriculture on Roman Imperial Estates in North Africa*. Göttingen: Vandenhoeck & Ruprecht.

———. 1997. *Investment, Profit, and Tenancy: The Jurists and the Roman Agrarian Economy*. Ann Arbor: University of Michigan Press.

———. 2007. *Law and the Rural Economy in the Roman Empire*. Ann Arbor: University of Michigan Press.

Krause, J.-U. 1996. *Gefängnisse im römischen Reich*. Stuttgart: Franz Steiner Verlag.

Martin, S. D. 2002. "Roman Law and the Study of Land Transportation." In J.-J. Aubert and B. Sirks (eds.), *Speculum Iuris: Roman Law as a Reflection of Social and Economic Life in Antiquity*. Ann Arbor: University of Michigan Press. 151–68.

McGinn, T. A. J. 1990. "Ne Serva Prostituatur: Restrictive Covenants in the Sale of Slaves." *Zeitschrift der Savigny-Stiftung für Rechtsgeschichte. Romanistische Abteilung* 107: 315–53.

———. 1992. "The SC from Larinum and the Suppression of Adultery at Rome." *Zeitschrift für Papyrologie und Epigraphik* 93: 273–95.

———. 1998. *Prostitution, Sexuality, and the Law in Ancient Rome.* Oxford: Oxford University Press.

———. 2002. "The Augustan Marriage Legislation and Social Practice: Elite Endogamy versus Male 'Marrying Down.'" In J.-J. Aubert, B. Sirks (eds.), *Speculum Iuris: Roman Law as a Reflection of Social and Economic Life in Antiquity.* Ann Arbor: University of Michigan Press. 46–93.

Meyer, E. A. 2004. *Legitimacy and Law in the Roman World: Tabulae in Roman Belief and Practice.* Cambridge: Cambridge University Press.

Millar, F. 1981. "The World of the *Golden Ass.*" *Journal of Roman Studies* 71: 63–75.

Mnookin, R. H., and L. Kornhauser. 1979. "Bargaining in the Shadow of the Law: The Case of Divorce." *Yale Law Journal* 88: 950–97.

Nörr, D. 1981. "Zur Reskriptenpraxis in der hohen Prinzipatszeit." *Zeitschrift der Savigny-Stiftung für Rechtsgeschichte. Romanistiche Abteilung* 98: 1–46.

———. 1998. "Römisches Zivilprozeßrecht nach Max Kaser: Prozeßrecht und Prozeßpraxis in der Provinz Arabia." *Zeitschrift der Savigny-Stiftung für Rechtsgeschichte. Romanistiche Abteilung* 115: 80–98.

Peachin, M. 1996. *Iudex vice Caesaris: Deputy Emperors and the Administration of Justice during the Principate.* Stuttgart: Franz Steiner Verlag.

Phang, S. E. 2001. *The Marriage of Roman Soldiers (13 B.C.–A.D. 235): Law and Family in the Imperial Army.* Leiden: E. J. Brill.

Plescia, J. 1984. "The Development of Agency in Roman Law." *Labeo* 30: 171–90.

Riess, W. 2001. *Apuleius und die Räuber.* Stuttgart: Franz Steiner Verlag.

Rowlandson, J. 1994. "Crop Rotation and Rent Payment in Oxyrhynchite Land Leases: Social and Economic Interpretations." In A. Bülow-Jacobsen (ed.), *Proceedings of the 20th International Congress of Papyrologists.* Copenhagen: Museum Tusculanum Press. 495–99.

Saller, R. P. 1982. *Personal Patronage under the Early Empire.* Cambridge: Cambridge University Press.

———. 1994. *Patriarchy, Property and Death in the Roman Family.* Cambridge: Cambridge University Press.

Scheidel, W. 1996. "Finances, Figures and Fiction." *Classical Quarterly* 46.1: 222–38.

Schubert, P. 1990. *Les archives de Marcus Lucretius Diogenes et textes apparentés.* Bonn: Rudolf Habelt Verlag.

Turpin, W. 1991. "Imperial Subscriptions and the Administration of Justice." *Journal of Roman Studies* 81: 101–18.

Verboven, K. 2002. *The Economy of Friends: Economic Aspects of Amicitia and Patronage in the Late Republic.* Brussels: Latomus.

Weaver, P. R. C. 1972. *Familia Caesaris: A Social Study of the Emperor's Freedmen and Slaves.* Cambridge: Cambridge University Press.

Weßel, H. 2003. *Das Recht der Tablettes Albertini.* Berlin: Duncker & Humblot.

Wilson, A. 2002. "Machines, Power and the Ancient Economy." *Journal of Roman Studies* 92: 1–32.

Zelener, Y. 2003. *Smallpox and the Disintegration of the Roman Economy after 165 AD.* PhD Thesis, Columbia University.

PART III

MECHANISMS OF COMMUNICATION AND INTERACTION

CHAPTER 8

LITERATURE AND COMMUNICATION

CHARLES W. HEDRICK, JR.

Introduction

In the military camp at Vindolanda, at the northwestern limit of the Roman Empire, someone—an officer? a studious army brat?—picked up a discarded strip of bark that had previously been used to draft a letter. He flipped it over and began to copy out a line from Vergil's *Aeneid*: "meanwhile feathered it flew through the trembling town" (*interea pavidam volitans pinnata per urbem*, Verg. A. 9. 473: *Tab. Vindol.* II 118).[1] A little earlier, about AD 75, at the other end of the empire, a Roman gazed at the siege-ramp sloping up from the desert floor to the fortified hill of Masada and was moved to write a line from the fourth book of Vergil's epic. The lovelorn Carthaginian queen, Dido, there confides: "Sister Anna, what nightmares terrify me in my anxiety" (*Anna soror quae me suspensam insomnia terrent*, Verg. A. 4. 9: *P. Masada* 721). Meanwhile in Italy, in the shadow of Vesuvius, some townsman of Pompeii—perhaps, as I like to imagine, a disgruntled poet whose inspiration had been stymied by the hurly-burly of his neighborhood—daubed a graffito on a house wall alluding to the first line of the *Aeneid*: "Launderers and wailing I sing, not arms and the man" (*fullones ululamque cano, non arma virumque, CIL* IV 9131).[2] Some sixty graffiti quoting the *Aeneid* and the *Georgics* have so far come to light in

1. Cf. *Tab. Vindol.* II 453. The tablets are available online, at http://vindolanda.csad.ox. ac.uk; the text from Vergil is also conveniently illustrated and discussed in Bowman 1998: 88–89, 95 n. 24 with plate 3.

2. On the Pompeian graffiti, see recently Franklin 1991.

Pompeii, some in such incongruous places as a whorehouse and the gladiatorial barracks.

By the end of the first century AD Vergil's poetry can be found from England to Judaea; but then, his works were renowned in literary circles practically from the moment they were conceived. Before the *Aeneid* was available to be read, Propertius announces its imminent arrival (Prop. 2. 34b. 61–66), and Vergil's poetry speedily became staple fare in the literary coteries of Augustus' Rome. In his own lifetime, his poems were taught in schools: the grammarian Caecilius Epirota lectured on him (Suet. *Gram.* 16). By the first century AD elementary instruction typically began with the memorization and reading of Homer and Vergil (Quint. *Inst.* 1. 8. 5). In the eastern empire students translated the *Aeneid* into prosaic Greek as part of their lessons. In the fourth century AD St. Augustine recalls that in his school days he won prizes for declamations on themes from the *Aeneid* (*Confessions* 1. 13). Snippets of Vergil's poetry have been recovered from the walls of classrooms, as at the Basilica Argentaria in the Forum Julium at Rome and the Great Palaestra at Pompeii. Roman soldiers brought his poetry with them to their far-flung military postings: there are some half a dozen examples of lines of Vergil written in military contexts. Inscriptions and other documents from throughout the Roman Empire attest a familiarity with his writing.

Vergil has been regarded since antiquity as the chief poet of Rome; indeed, in the devastated aftermath of the Second World War, T. S. Eliot described him as "the Classic of all Europe" (Eliot 1945: 70; cf. Martindale 1997). And from the nineteenth century he has often been described as "the national poet of Rome." The implications of this idea are spelled out in books like R. S. Conway's *Vergilian Age* (1928), which presumes that the Roman tradition was comprised of splendid stories that were "to every Roman the greatest part of the records of his own country," and that were important elements of "the national consciousness."[3] The association of Vergil, and especially the *Aeneid*, with 'Roman nationalism' remains vigorous: so Nicholas Horsfall remarks that before Vergil "the Aeneas legend…was a political plaything of the Iulii Caesares. It was the *Aeneid* which transformed it into a truly national story" (Horsfall 1995: 249). The evidence for the extent of the ancient dissemination Vergil's writing seems to suggest that he had a prompt and dominating influence in the Roman world, that knowledge of his poetry was historically enduring, geographically widespread, and socially saturating. Were it so, the characterization of the Aeneid as a 'national epic' might be accurate or persuasive: the circulation of the text might have contributed to the establishment of a common base of knowledge and culture shared by every Roman, drawing together the disparate population of the empire and helping to create a sense of community, as

---

3. Conway 1928: 75, speaking of the account of the Hannibalic war; for the national purpose of the *Aeneid*, see Conway 1928: 137. Unsurprisingly, many of the outstanding statements about Vergil's 'nationalist purposes' date to the late nineteenth and early twentieth century, which in many respects marked the high tide of the ideals of modern European and American nationalism: for another example, cf. Glover 1912: 105.

Horsfall repeatedly asserts, basing his position particularly on allusions to the poet in the Pompeian graffiti and inscriptions: "there are signs that Virgil was known at all levels of society…that Virgil is diffused rapidly and widely among all classes could also have been demonstrated with massive and certain documentation from Virgilian citations and echoes in the *Carmina Epigraphica Latina* and in later collections of metrical inscriptions…I repeat that the taste for Virgil penetrates all social classes" (Horsfall 1984: 50).

No one doubts that Vergil's poetry played a part in defining *elite* culture and community: he was certainly read—by those who could read—throughout the Roman Empire. The extent to which his poetry, or any literature, somehow influenced directly or even distantly the great majority of the populace, however, is questionable. Pessimists have especially stressed the presumably low rate of literacy among the Roman populace and the relatively high cost of books. If, comparing available statistics for other premodern societies, we estimate the literacy rate in the Roman world in the region of 10% to 20% (see Harris 1989: 3–24 and 323–32), then Vergil's writing cannot have been directly accessible to more than a small minority of the population. Furthermore, few Romans had income sufficient to indulge their supposed literary enthusiasms. Martial famously remarks that a book of his epigrams cost five *denarii* from a bookseller (Mart. 1. 117. 15–17).[4] For most Romans this would have been a considerable sum, considering that under Domitian Roman legionaries, who were (in contrast with many Romans) compensated lavishly and in cash, received 300 *denarii* a year (Watson 1969: 89–102). Optimists have countered that, even admitting the limited literacy and financial resources of the 'typical Roman,' the gist of Vergil's stories and even the precise words of his poetry can have been transmitted in other ways: through their association with the pictorial representations of paintings, mosaics, and public sculpture, through public recitations and intimate oral readings, and through conversation. Horsfall has particularly emphasized the role of drama in promoting a popular awareness of the *Georgics* and the *Aeneid* (Horsfall 1984: 47–48; 1995: 249–52).[5] As St. Augustine wrote several centuries later, literary works were better known to the multitude through drama than through the written word (August. *C.D.* 1. 3; cf. Jerome *Ep.* 21. 13. 9)—and doubtless the substance of some literary works circulated in such ways. Nevertheless, access to drama and art would have been restricted to those who frequented cities. In the Roman world, as in all pre-modern societies, the vast majority of the population lived and worked in the countryside (see, e.g., Finley 1999, especially chapter 5).

4. This would be a relatively though not inordinately expensive book, as the emphasis on its fine paper and purple ornament suggests; Martial elsewhere mentions books that cost about a fifth this amount—still a substantial price. On this view, the epigram's conclusion, that Martial is "not worth the price," should be understood as a repetition of the theme of the insignificance of his poetic frippery, which would jar were his pieces incongruously enshrined in the pages of so lavish a book.

5. Horsfall 1991 gives a fuller statement of his more general ideas about the extent of ancient literacy and the relevance of alternate means of communication to the circulation of literature.

Roman aristocrats may have read their books in their urban dwellings and country retreats; city-dwellers may have watched dramatizations of episodes from literature and told one another stories about the monumental sculptures and mosaics they encountered; but how many hardscrabble farmers ever had even a glancing encounter with Vergil's *Aeneid*?

Still, Vergil came to have extraordinary prestige: among certain Romans, anyway, his writing was regarded as something like what we today call a 'classic.' But what precisely would it mean to say that any work was a 'classic' for the Romans, and how might it have acquired such a status? How was it possible for knowledge of the *Aeneid* to spread throughout the empire? The common and persuasive explanation attributes its prestige to its early use in elementary education, and it is unmistakably true that the *Aeneid* was promoted by schools. But this explanation only defers the problem. Why did schools everywhere come to adopt the *Aeneid* for the purposes of instruction in reading? There was no central educational authority, no imposed or standardized curriculum. Perhaps Vergil was simply a more elegant writer than others? Or the story of Aeneas was more accessible to students? Perhaps the values epitomized in the *Aeneid* tapped into some Mediterranean Zeitgeist? The ultimate cause for the quick and wide dissemination of the *Aeneid* is likely its association with the ideals and images of the Julio-Claudian house.

Understood as a form of communication, literature has a social function: as commonly held knowledge, it contributes to community formation and coherence. A literary work may, for example, embody a standard of language, codify appropriate manners and customs, and justify ethical presumptions. I have begun this essay on 'literature and communication' by considering the example of Vergil's writing because of its prestige and the extraordinary evidence for its circulation in antiquity. The works of other ancient authors, however, were also widely read in the ancient world: Homer, to take only the most obvious case, had canonical stature (cf., e.g., Cribiore 2001: 194–97). And, as is evident from the many allusions of ancient authors to one another, works of literature circulated among the literate elite and were expected to be familiar to a wide audience of (at least) such readers. The example of any ancient author, Greek or Latin, would in principle have served as well as Vergil. But despite the optimism of some modern scholars and some apparent indications to the contrary, there are substantial reasons to be pessimistic about the degree to which literature suffused the consciousness of the Roman masses or of any pre-modern population. Given the limitations of Graeco-Roman scribal production, ancient literature cannot have been widely disseminated—at least not in comparison with any period subsequent to the invention of the printing press.

When modern scholars describe Vergil as a 'national poet' and his *Aeneid* as a 'national epic,' they subtly impute a peculiarly modern social function to ancient literary activity. Most academics can name the 'national poets' of the modern European states: among the English, Shakespeare; for the Germans, Goethe; and the French have Molière. Such authors qualify as 'national poets' because they are thought to manifest the essential and idiosyncratic character, values, and aspirations of the nation's people, and through the familiarity and broad national dissemination of their writing, they reflect these values back to the people, mold and perpetuate the 'national spirit.' Such an association of literature and nationalism is an anachronistic projection of the conditions of modern literature into the ancient world. Nations are characterized by centralized political exploitation of industrialized media to create and disseminate a unified and coherent mass culture among the entire population of the state. The archetypal technology of mass culture was the printing press, and the first artifact of mass culture was print literature. The rulers of Rome never evinced an ambition to create and disseminate a mass culture; even had they contrived such a plan, they lacked the technology to implement it. The modern, industrialized media are centralized, but ancient communication was diffused; modern books are manufactured, but ancient manuscripts were copied; modern publishers sell their books to a market, but ancient readers very frequently acquired their books through gift exchange. Vergil may indeed have been the great poet of ancient Rome, but he was not a 'national poet'; Rome was not a nation.[6]

In evaluating the social significance of a text, the question of distribution is clearly central, though notoriously difficult to document. Vergil's *Aeneid* circulated throughout the Roman Empire; still, the evidence, though comparatively ample, is anecdotal. We might quite reasonably ask: Who, precisely, were Vergil's readers? The evidence allows for little refinement of assessment. Everyone will grant that many of the literate elite of the empire imbibed the *Aeneid* along with their elementary education in letters, though no one can estimate how many of even this select group were exposed to the poem: what percentage of elite women, for example, were familiar with Vergil's story of Dido, and how do we know? Should we presume that the humbler population, the farmers and peasants and shepherds and slaves, had a comparable familiarity with the poem? The Pompeian graffiti have been taken to show that Vergil's writing influenced 'all levels of society,' but we do not know who wrote them or why: must we imagine that graffiti are always and everywhere written by the poor and uneducated, for the consumption of the poor and uneducated?[7] How does the readership of Vergil break down in terms of gender? age? ethnicity? In the absence of statistical evidence—and we have none; every indication from antiquity is anecdotal—we must rely on general considerations, that is, plausibility. In this essay I will concentrate on the general circumstances of literary production and circulation and the relevance of this situation for the question of the social significance of ancient literature.

Given the focus of this essay, it is unfortunately incumbent on me to define what I mean by 'literature.' For the purposes of my argument I will adopt a

---

6. It is now generally agreed that the concept of the nation is modern and so absent from the ancient world, pace, e.g., Gruen 1992 (Rome) or Cohen 2000 (Athens). Of course, evaluation of the question whether or not there was such a thing as 'Roman nationalism' depends on the definition of 'nationalism.' For informed arguments against the current academic consensus, see, e.g., Smith 2002.

7. For an interesting general essay, sensitive to the historical variety of contexts and purposes of graffiti, cf. Petrucii 1993: chapter 13.

material criterion and regard as literature any written materials that are circulated through reproduction—in the ancient world, through scribal copying, in the modern through printing and other media. To put the point another way, literature will here be defined as any text that is susceptible to the techniques of stemmatic textual criticism. Other 'documentary' texts, such as contracts or bills of lading or honorific inscriptions, are by this standard excluded, for though they may exhibit formulaic language that is to be found in other comparable texts, each is by its nature to be regarded as an 'autograph,' which can play its social role only if it is treated as an original. It would be absurd to construct a stemma of a document, correcting errors of spelling and grammar, because every document is already an archetype, and errors in it are 'original.' Like a signed check, they take their validity from their supposed uniqueness (cf. also Meyer and Jördens, this volume; further, Hedrick 2006: chapters 4 and 5). I recognize that by my definition certain texts typically described as 'sub-literary,' such as mathematical treatises, copies of law codes, government circulars addressed to soldiers or others, or recipes, may be exalted to the status of literature, while texts that many regard as literary will be relegated to the status of documents—Emily Dickinson's poetry, for example, would not be counted as literature until it is circulated. But any definition will provoke argument around the edges.

I have structured the argument of the essay in order to contrast the social functions of literature in antiquity with its functions in our own modern, nationalist environment. It will become clear that the two situations are mutually illuminating. I begin with some preliminary remarks about the differences between modern nations and pre-modern states. I proceed to consider the role of modern literary production in the constitution of modern nations; against these familiar circumstances I then contrast the scribal techniques of manuscript production that prevailed in Europe until the fifteenth century and the kinds of contributions they make to the constitution of community in the pre-modern world. I conclude with a summary appraisal of the social context of the consumption of literature in the ancient Roman world.

COMMUNITY AND COMMUNICATION: THE NATION

The boundaries of a community may be defined with reference to the limits of communication. The group is created and maintained by shared knowledge; when communication fails, the group ends. The nature of group interaction, however, is not always and everywhere the same; the onset of modernity, in particular, constitutes a watershed in practices of communication. The change is linked to the development of the characteristic political entity of the contemporary world, the nation.

The nation is first of all defined by the size of its territory and population. I would hesitate to name any particular number that defines the threshold of a nation; the boundary is established with reference to the nature of community formation. A contemporary nation such as the United States or China has a population and territory of a size that precludes the possibility of the development of a sense of social solidarity through concrete, spontaneous, and diffuse popular interactions. "Members of even the smallest nation will never know most of their fellow-members, meet them, or even hear of them" (Anderson 1991: 15); and in a geographically expansive state with a large and ethnically diverse population running to the hundreds of millions, schism, regional and demographic, is an ever-present danger. The preeminent challenge for the modern nation is thus how to create community on a vast scale, among people who have no personal contact with one another. Nationalism is conventionally defined in terms of this problem: it is "a political principle, which holds that the political and national unit should be congruent....In brief, nationalism is a theory of political legitimacy, which requires that ethnic boundaries should not cut across political ones, and, in particular, that ethnic boundaries within a given state—a contingency already formally excluded by the principle in its general formulation—should not separate power-holders from the rest" (Gellner 2005: 1). Because of the size of the nation-state, the sense of community cannot emerge from the bottom up, from the myriad personal interactions of purposeful or chance encounters; it must somehow be imposed politically, from the top down. As a consequence, nationalism becomes possible only with the development of the methods that permit such an arrangement: an industrialized media. For this reason, it can rightly be said that nationalism precedes the nation. Before the group can be said to exist, the sense of belonging must be created in the mind of every citizen, "the image of their communion" (Anderson 1991: 15). The nation is an 'imagined community.' The sense of belonging to a group does not spring from physical contact, but from an unobtrusive yet omnipresent media.

Traditional communities can also be defined with reference to communication, but in such cases communication is manifested in disaggregated, particular interactions. Members of the group must come into contact for a sense of community to emerge. Traditional communities are generated from the bottom up; they are "face-to-face societies," as M. I. Finley famously described ancient Athens (in, e.g., Finley 1985: 17–18). The size and geographical dimensions of these states are sufficiently intimate that it is possible for a degree of social and cultural homogeneity to develop spontaneously, without central political orchestration.

The development of nationalism was made possible by the technologies of mass production and the mass culture they spawned (cf., e.g., Hobsbawm and Ranger 1992). Of these, the printing press is the archetype, and it appears in Europe as late as the fifteenth century. Long familiarity and powerful new technologies have obscured the novelty and effectiveness of print literature for the creation and maintenance of our vast political communities. With printing it became possible for the first time to create and disseminate a common culture effectively over great territories to an immense population. The printed text made it possible to transcend regional differences and to produce a much greater sense of a unified population.

Large states existed before the modern period. Ancient Athens, for example, had a substantial population, something on the order of 100,000 in total, including non-citizens (cf., e.g., Cohen 2000: 11–15). Not every Athenian would or could have had direct knowledge of every other inhabitant of the state, but it would not be reasonable for that reason to criticize Finley's characterization of Athens as a "face-to-face" society: it was not necessary for every Athenian citizen to know every other Athenian citizen, but that the population be sufficiently small and geographically concentrated that information might be spread through a network of personal interactions, whether through first- or fifth-hand encounters. Even so, to Greek tastes, Athens was excessively large: Aristotle suggests that a city should be small and intimate enough that citizens should know one another and that a crier can address the population assembled (see generally Arist. *Pol.* 7. 4–5; cf. *EN* 9. 10. 3).

The Athenian state was tiny by the standards of a modern nation, with a population comparable to that of a small American city, and a territory considerably smaller than that of the smallest American state. States the size of modern nations, of course, did exist before the modern period. Japan, for example, possessed an extensive and politically unified territory for centuries before its modern period began in 1868. Yet pre-modern Japan was not a nation. Although there was a common elite culture throughout the islands, the general population remained culturally diverse: custom and dialect varied from region to region and even from village to village (Burns 2003). As for the definition of community, the common Japanese did not identify themselves in terms of nationality, but according to ethnic, and village or family affiliation. No national Japanese community existed in pre-modern times, because the state had no interest in imposing a homogeneous culture among the humble majority of their population; indeed, such a mass culture could not have been created without the means to do so, that is, without a mass media. The beginnings of Japanese mass culture can be traced to the promulgation of a print media. Woodblock printing came to Japan from China in connection with the diffusion of Buddhism as early as the eighth century, but the printing press did not come into widespread use for secular literature until the seventeenth century, under the influence of Korea and, to a smaller extent, the Jesuits. In the course of the seventeenth and eighteenth centuries a "library of public information" was gradually created, which informed the development of an incipient sense of national identity, which was then rapidly developed in the wake of the modernization of the Meiji period (Berry 2007). With the Meiji period the state, following explicitly European models, 'modernized' and self-consciously cultivated a mass culture identified as 'Japanese.'

The Roman Empire, too, was a large state, in extent larger than many modern nations. The elite of the empire certainly possessed to some degree a common culture—one of its remarkable characteristics was precisely the shared knowledge of a literary canon, resulting, for example, in certain common values and accepted standards of elegance in written expression. But the state made no significant or sustained effort to create a comparable mass culture among the general

population.[8] The government did care about the political allegiance of the population, and promoted it in various ways: through military and religious institutions,
oaths of allegiance, and imperial cult (cf. Potter and Scheid in this volume), for
example, or by public artistic representations, painting, and sculpture. Even such
efforts, limited as they were, however, will have chiefly reached the urban inhabitants of the empire. The vast majority of the population, who remained in the
countryside, will have had only brief and sporadic contacts with such political
programs. The Roman state, like other pre-modern states, had neither the means
nor the desire to create a universal national culture among the entire population
of the state.

To sum up: a nation is not to be defined merely in terms of the size of the political
entity; nationalism aims not only at political coherence, but at the cultural unification
of the state's population; in nationalism, the body politic should also be a cultural
community. Large pre-modern states have a common elite culture, but at the level
of the general population they are unified only politically, not culturally. Cultivation
of a national community becomes possible with the development of the technology
for producing and disseminating mass culture, and the original and exemplary form
of mass culture is print literature. With the printing press, literary works can be produced in great numbers and can be translated across vast expanses of space and time
to effectively unlimited numbers of people. For this reason literature quickly became
indispensable to the national project of constructing a large and dispersed, yet unified,
community. The function and social value of modern literature has been to reveal and
spread the spirit of the nation. The nation is a modern phenomenon; nationalism is
marked by the emergence of a mass culture, and this mass culture is characteristic of,
perhaps even the definition of, modern political communities.

Modern Literature: Production and Dissemination

The introduction of the printing press affected every aspect of book production,
dissemination and consumption. Mass production of anything requires an extraordinary initial investment of time, labor, and money, and this commitment is a wager,

---

8. I do not mean to suggest that Roman culture did not spread to a greater or lesser
extent among the various populations of the empire, only that this spread was not a consequence of organized state policy. The state governed through local elites and implemented
policies through cities, and not surprisingly it is in such contexts that the spread of an 'imperial culture' can most readily be seen. Interest in the nature and techniques of 'Romanization'
has given rise to a proliferating bibliography in recent years, and archaeologists have been
especially concerned to find signs of it in rural contexts: cf. Millett 1990; Woolf 1998; Mattingly
2006. For recent essays and a review of bibliography, see Roth and Keller 2007.

calculated against the prospect of the reimbursement and profit to be reaped from sales. In the case of print literature, the press itself must be purchased, the literature produced and edited, the galleys assembled, proofs read, paper and ink acquired, finished pages distributed, and all in advance of any income from the project.[9] It would be unthinkable to employ such a process to produce a single copy of a book: the cost of such a text would be prohibitive; if the object is to produce one book, it would be far less costly and risky to copy it out by hand, in the traditional way. The use of the printing press becomes practicable only when the goal is to mass-produce texts: the initial costs of print production can then be recovered through the savings generated by producing and selling a number of texts. The technology of the printing press, in other words, does not give rise to the idea of mass production; it is the idea of mass production that makes the printing press conceivable.[10] In this case, at least, technology is a part of the history of ideas; it does not drive history.

Nevertheless, the use of the printing press imposes a new 'logic of production,' which will come to characterize all forms of mass production, and this calculation has immediate and extraordinary consequences for printers. Labor savings accumulate with the fabrication of multiple copies; every copy printed generates progressively larger savings. Almost all labor costs come in advance, with the design and fabrication of the prototype—in the case of the printing press, the galleys. Once the prototype has been made, many copies can be made at the cost of little additional labor. Thus, the work devoted to complete even the first book off the press is substantial, and if only that book were to be produced, it would be enormously expensive. With the production of the second book, labor costs per book are roughly halved; with the third book they are cut to a third; with the fourth, to a fourth; and so on. At the same time, however, the material costs of production remain constant. However, although labor costs decline the more copies that are made, the cost of the materials used to make the object—in the case of books, paper and ink—do not change, but accumulate. This material must be purchased in advance, and the more copies of the book that are printed, the greater the financial risk represented by investment in materials.

So, a publisher must balance two competing pressures. On the one hand, there is the incentive of the savings in labor reaped from producing multiple copies: the more copies produced, the greater the potential profit, and the closer the labor costs per book approach zero. Still, there is a point of diminishing returns: though labor costs may approach zero, they never decline to absolutely nothing. On the other hand, there is risk incurred by investment in materials: the greater the number of copies produced, the larger the necessary investment in materials, and the more potentially ruinous the losses from this outlay if the books cannot be sold. Thus, from a business perspective, publishers must simultaneously try to profit as much

9. For detailed description of the various aspects of the modern business of printing, see Gaskell 1974.

10. In fact, many formal features of the printed book are anticipated in the scribal culture of the high Middle Ages in Europe; see Saenger 1982 and 1997: ix–x, 256–76.

as possible from savings in labor costs by printing as many books as possible, and to keep the risk of investment in materials to a minimum by producing as few books as possible.

Early printers understood the dilemma. Print runs of early books tend to be small, on the order of 200 to 300 copies, sufficient to enjoy the profit from labor savings, but not so large as to ruin the publisher if the book does not sell (Gaskell 1974: 160–63). For the same reason, academic publishers today tend to produce texts in small numbers, unless there is some reason to hope that the book may sell to others besides the handful of academic libraries around the world—for example, if the text is likely to be adopted for classroom use. The nature of print production may be clarified by means of a crude graph (see fig. 8.1).

Given the nature of print production, then, publishers needed to take steps to guarantee and expand the market for the sales of their books. With the growth of the potential audience for books, the material risks of publishing could be cushioned, the profit from labor savings maximized. For publishers, dissemination was an urgent problem from the outset.

This complex of problems led to changes in the materials and format of books. Publishers, to increase potential sales, made their books of cheaper materials and in smaller format; their books so became more affordable and conveniently useful for a broader public. Early printed books tended to imitate earlier scribal productions. They might, for example, be printed on expensive materials, such as parchment, and adorned with hand-painted illuminations. They also tended, like manuscript books, to be large in format: unwieldy objects requiring dedicated places for reading and storage. Many of the early fonts imitated medieval scribal hands. The use of cheaper

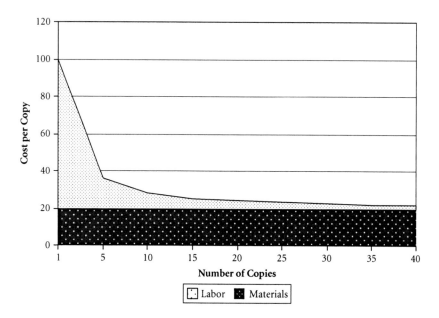

Figure 8.1. Print production.

materials, paper for parchment, and smaller, pocket-size formats[11] reduced the cost of materials and diminished the necessary advance investment of publishers. At the same time, books became more affordable and more portable, thus expanding the number of potential buyers. Such developments also lead to changes in the subjects favored by publishers.

Distribution and publicity were obvious and immediate concerns for printers, but not so easy for them to control. Little is known about the character of the early trade in printed books; as a rule we are far better informed about publishing houses than about booksellers. The early presses as a rule seem to have sold directly to readers. By the seventeenth century, when more is known about the shipment and sales of texts, a broadly dispersed network of independent local booksellers has emerged in Europe, many with ties to particular publishing houses.[12]

The most intractable problem for publishing houses was the cultivation of widespread literacy and the establishment of a broadly based reading public. Here their interests coincided with those of the state. Printers wished to see the expansion of the reading public in order to develop the market for their books; the state supported the requirement of literacy for its citizens because reading made possible the formation of popular tastes and ideals.[13] In the world of the nation-state, the citizen must be first of all a reader; without reading there can be no citizens. Ultimately literacy would be imposed by state-mandated education. Once more the commercial interests of the presses corresponded with the political ambitions of the nation: the state assigned the reading lists and publishers printed and sold the books.

The implication of nation and press can perhaps be most clearly seen in the history of copyright law.[14] Every publisher had to worry about competition from other presses. Once a book was published, what was to stop some unscrupulous competitor from rushing it into print as well, destroying prospects of future sales and voiding the original investment of labor and materials? The problem was resolved by collaboration between the press and the political authority, and the introduction of copyright law, which protected presses from literary piracy (at least within the territory controlled by the state). The state offered its protection not because of any altruistic appreciation of the intrinsic sanctity of intellectual property, but because it was in the interest of the nation that publishing houses, as essential agents of nationalism, prosper. In exchange for the protection of the state, presses

11. It should be noted that scribes produced smaller books too; Mart. 1. 2 and 14. 188, already speaks of portable "travelers books," and certain medieval scribal texts—missals, for example—were often of approximately pocket size; yet, Aldus Manutius is generally and rightly credited with the invention and general promotion of the 'pocket book.'

12. Much of the pioneering work on this subject has been done by Robert Darnton: see Darnton 1979 and the essays collected in Darnton 1990; cf. more generally Gaskell 1974: 179–83.

13. The connection of nationalism and public education is most overtly avowed in essays dating earlier than the 1960s in America: see, e.g., Reisner 1922.

14. For the development of state protections for printers in the early modern period, see generally Gaskell 1974: 183–85; in more detail, Armstrong 1990.

submitted to government censorship. Willy-nilly publishing houses became associated with nationalism. By the nineteenth century, the association of state and press is approved by ideology and confirmed by the state's presumption in approving the political and moral content of print books. Carlyle's remarks on the 'fourth estate' in his 1841 essay on *Heroes and Hero-Worship* exemplify the attitude:

> Literature is our Parliament too. Printing, which comes necessarily out of Writing, I say often, is equivalent to Democracy: invent Writing, Democracy is inevitable. Writing brings Printing; brings universal everyday extempore Printing, as we see at present. Whoever can speak, speaking now to the whole nation, becomes a power, a branch of government, with inalienable weight in lawmaking, in all acts of authority.[15]

Inevitably, the development of mass-produced texts, the association of the press and the state, and the cultivation of a mass-reading public had an effect on the status and aims of authors. Copyright protections were developed to protect the interests of the presses, not of authors. Still, in this new environment it gradually became possible for writers to earn their livelihood by writing. Initially authors sold their works for a flat fee to publishers, who were then free to dispose of the work as they saw fit. Clever and unscrupulous authors sometimes supplemented this income by immediately producing 'revised' editions, so they could repeatedly sell the same manuscript to different publishers or double their income by cooperating in the issue of pirated editions by presses outside of the country. Ideas of intellectual property are relatively late developments: only in the nineteenth century did authors begin to receive a percentage of the profits from distribution of the book rather than a simple fee (e.g., Darnton 1990: 107–90).

The nature of print production spurred publishers to cultivate a market for their books: these both reflect and shape the attitudes of their readership.[16] At the same time national governments were attempting to create national citizenries. The two projects dovetailed. The publisher had an interest in supporting the nation because of the legal protections the state afforded him. And the state quickly realized that it had a vested interest in the publisher, because the new print media were producing the mass culture necessary for the maintenance of a broadly based and dispersed national community. Modern literary canons and academic disciplinary divisions of the study of literature according to nation of origin (departments of English literature, American literature, French literature, and so on) are products of this partnership; the contemporary academic study of literature developed in tandem with nationalist movements of the nineteenth century (e.g., Jusdanis

---

15. The essay has been many times reprinted. The quote is to be found in lecture 5, "Hero as Man of Letters," in Carlyle 1901: 164.

16. The point is nicely articulated by Berry 2007: 21–22. My argument here should not be construed as an assertion that printing of itself created mass literacy and culture. Eisenstein 1984: 30–34, lists a number of contributing causes; Clanchy 1993: 1 and passim, argues that the beginnings of the phenomenon of mass literacy date from twelfth century. Nevertheless, the development of print books makes a decisive contribution. Cf. McKeon 2002: 35, 51–52.

1991). The dissemination of printed literature is the business of printers, conducted under the aegis of the nation. Against this background, let us now consider the ancient situation.

Ancient Literature: Production and Dissemination

Ancient books were fabricated by a process of scribal copying. The significance of the point becomes clear by the contrast with the production of modern print books. In scribal culture every book was copied individually. Material and labor were constants; each book cost the same amount to produce. Production of multiple copies would have brought little or no savings of labor; to the contrary, producing books without a guaranteed buyer entailed risk of both labor and materials. As a consequence, there was no reason to produce any book that had not been commissioned, nor was there any incentive to develop or enlarge a 'market' of readers. Expansion of the reading public would not increase anyone's (monetary) profits, though it would admittedly have created work for more scribes. A comparison of fig. 8.2 with fig. 8.1 illustrates the point.

Modern printers were necessarily attentive to the prospect of sales for their books, which led to the conception of the potential reading audience as a 'market'—an idea lacking before print. Scribes paid no attention to the potential buyers

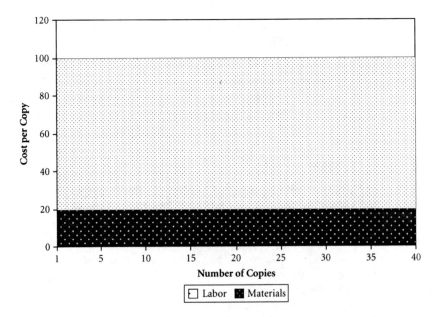

Figure 8.2. Scribal production.

for their wares; to the contrary, because they made books one by one, they had a practical disincentive to the speculative production of books with a view to sales. For scribes, such production entails unnecessary risk, with no offsetting potential of reward or even any conveniences of production.

Techniques of larger scale (re)production were not entirely alien to Graeco-Roman antiquity. Certain objects, notably ceramics such as bricks, vases and lamps, were produced in quantities, sometimes by using molds,[17] and of course coinage was produced in mass quantities by stamping (cf. Noreña in this volume). Yet, even should we suppose that such operations were not carried out in large, traditional workshops, but in establishments approximating modern industrial manufacturing in their management, scale, and specialized internal organization—an implausible and unsubstantiated idea, in my view—they had no effect on general Roman attitudes about the 'market,' nor did they spur widespread innovation in methods of production. The Roman state never distributed mass produced objects to produce a broadly based, unifying popular culture.

That said, even in the context of the scribal production of books, on occasion multiple copies might be produced, and some economies of production might occasionally be achieved (cf., e.g., Skeat 1957). Political figures, such as Cicero, might have political screeds churned out for distribution to friends and enemies, using teams of scribes of their own or of their friends (e.g., Cic. *Att.* 12. 40 and 44). Pliny tells us that Aquilius Regulus had a thousand copies of his eulogy for his son produced (*Ep.* 4. 7. 2).[18] Multiple copies might have been produced a bit more speedily and economically by having an individual read the text aloud to a group of scribes, who copied it out simultaneously, or again, a number of scribes might divvy up a book, each working at once on a page or two. Such efforts would have been extraordinary—and even if they were not, they do not change the fundamental character of scribal book production. When multiple copies were produced they were not made with a view to selling them to the wider public, but with the idea of distributing them to appropriate people as gifts. Political 'pamphlets' and mortuary eulogies were produced more in the way a person now might commission business cards, or funeral programs. Production of multiple copies in such cases occasioned no financial risk, because it was absolutely guaranteed that there would be no return on the outlay: these texts were made to be gifts, and were commissioned with no expectation of sales on something like an open market. The benefit anticipated from their production was not financial profit.

Absent a concern or even a concept of a 'market for literature,' neither the authors nor the fabricators of books felt any incentive or pressure to make sweeping

---

17. See generally Greene 1986: 158–59. On the famous 'terra sigillata' ceramic, see Fülle 1997; on lamps, see, e.g., Harris 1980. Indeed, agriculture seems to have remained the preferred method of enrichment throughout Roman antiquity: Kehoe 2007.

18. As Michael Peachin remarks to me, in Pliny's eyes, everything Regulus did was bad, so the comment here is probably meant as reproof, suggesting that the making of so many copies was a bad thing—self-indulgent, or the like. For Pliny's attitude toward Regulus, see, e.g., *Ep.* 1. 5 with Sherwin-White 1966: comm. ad loc.

innovations in materials and format, to make literature into something like 'mass culture.' Because scribes produced every book to order, they were able to accommodate any specifications of particular buyers. Book prices thus varied enormously in antiquity. We hear of cheap pocket-sized travelers' books and expensive, deluxe, table-sized copies. Rare or autographed manuscripts might, as today, command practically any price. Still, the attested variety should not distract from the essential constancy of materials and format. In Roman antiquity, literary texts were written on papyrus, which was imported from Egypt and, though it was produced in abundance, was relatively expensive: various grades were sold, the best and priciest of which was described as 'Augustan.' The standard format was the scroll, which was unwieldy and fragile, unsuitable for use except by those who could afford to dedicate space in their houses for reading and storage. And the characterization of certain ancient books as 'cheap' is entirely relative to the possible range in the price of books. From the perspective of the income of the general population, reading materials were neither easily available nor well affordable. Most people in the Roman world were agricultural workers, many of whom were isolated from the monetary economy; even a salaried Roman legionary would have winced at the cost of a book. The flexibility of scribal production would not have put literary texts within financial reach of 'the common man,' no matter how generously we define this person.

Broadly based social literacy is a characteristic of the modern world. Such literacy does not occur naturally, but must be created. Within modern nations, as I have suggested, the technology to mass-produce literary texts provides publishers with an incentive to encourage literacy, thus expanding the market for their wares, making possible the fusion of their commercial interests with the political interests of the national state. This is one important factor leading to the political and commercial cultivation of mass literacy. For many reasons it is implausible that the Romans attempted to produce a literate population in their empire; not least, because the mass media are entirely absent from their culture. There is no indication that the Romans ever attempted to create universal literacy. There was, notably, no publicly mandated or subsidized educational system (e.g., Marrou 1956: 299–313); those who wished to have an education had to seek it out and pay for it themselves. Of course there were schools, and these surely played their part in disseminating the works of Vergil and others among those who attended. But instruction was voluntary, not required, as in modern nations; costly, not free or even subsidized. And there was nothing like a standard curriculum. If Vergil and Homer were widely read, it was because some people—the minority who could afford to educate their children— chose to have it so, not because the state required it.

In view of the differences in the production of literature in the ancient and modern worlds, the extent and nature of circulation and consumption cannot have been comparable to what we are accustomed to. "We know a great deal about book circulation [in ancient Rome], even though we know little about the book trade" (Starr 1987: 213), because the 'book trade' did not exist in ancient Rome. As a rule, copies of books were commissioned from individual craftsmen, not purchased ready-made:

for example, if a wealthy individual wished to acquire a book, he might borrow it from a friend and have a scribe, whether a slave of his own or a hired man, copy it out. I do not mean to suggest, of course, that books could not be bought from merchants, but ancient bookstores operated in much the same way as individuals. Martial describes the stalls of booksellers in ancient Rome, which were festooned with copies of books for sale (Mart. 1. 117. 11). These booksellers were in effect copy shops, and if an individual wanted to buy a copy of the book displayed, or have a friend's book copied, the bookseller could have such texts produced by his corps of copyists. Some of the best evidence for the circulation of ancient literary texts comes from the great letter writers of the late antiquity, notably Jerome, Augustine and Paulinus (Rebenich 1992: 132–33 and passim; Conybeare 2000: 30–33). The works of these authors were copied at the expense of patrons, who also promoted their dissemination. The serendipity of the process is well illustrated by the way the letters of Jerome and Augustine were carried across the Mediterranean, and along the way were read, copied, and shared by friends.

Ancient literature was not marketed to potential readers, but distributed freely or acquired voluntarily by interested parties. Nor, despite occasional outbursts of censorship and book burning, was there ever the kind of collaboration between the state and book producers that we see in the modern world. There were no copyright protections, and censorship was directed at readers and authors, not at scribal book producers.[19] Because book production was the province of craftsmen who had been engaged by the authors or patrons of the literature being transcribed and/or by the persons who desired to own copies of those works, there was no reason or possibility for the state to attend to the physical fabrication of books, any more than a modern state could now effectively regulate the use of particular Xerox machines. Without mass production, it was unimaginable that the state should become in any significant fashion involved in the production and dissemination of books; and had the Roman state ever done so, this would have proved more difficult to regulate than a Xerox machine, or contemporary blogging. The example of samizdat, or desktop publishing, in the former Soviet Union provides an instructive example of the difficulties for even a highly organized state of regulating decentralized book production and informal distribution (e.g., Feldbrugge 1975: 1–6). When Romans banned books, penalties were imposed for possession or writing of the text, not fabrication of it—in part, doubtless because the possessor and writers were uniformly also responsible for its fabrication. Scribes worked in isolation, like butchers, or cobblers, carpenters, or any other craftsmen. To describe this activity as a 'publishing industry,' or as a general 'book trade,' is anachronistic.

In one of his epigrams, Martial tells how a certain Quintus has asked for a copy of his book (Mart. 4. 72). He claims that he has not got one, but that the bookseller Tryphon does. Quintus responds by asking rhetorically whether he should spend money on such fluff and buy Martial's poetry; he will not act so foolishly.

19. The evidence for Roman book burning has been collected in Cramer 1945 and also Speyer 1981.

"Nor will I," is Martial's punch line. In Rome, books circulated in the first place as gifts and trades. Authors sent copies of their books—made at their own expense, whether by scribes belonging to them or their patrons, or by hiring third parties— to friends, or allowed friends to borrow them and have them copied. Older books circulated in much the same way: if a person desired a copy of work that was not in his possession, he would canvas friends and acquaintances for it, borrow it, and then have a copy made; it might be difficult to find certain books. From the late republic on, it was also possible to have copies made from books deposited in public libraries. Those so unfortunate as to have no other access to books might also acquire texts from a bookseller, who, in Rome, provided services more like those of a Xeroxing center than of a modern bookstore. Booksellers kept single copies of some books—presumably popular ones—on hand; if someone wished to buy a copy, the bookseller would have it transcribed from this 'master' on receipt of the order. It is unlikely that booksellers often made multiple copies in advance of commissions. They were doubtless also willing to make copies of texts that were furnished to them.

So the point of Martial's epigram: Quintus asks him, the author, for a copy of his book. Martial sends him to a bookseller, who has a copy on file that he can reproduce, but Quintus does not want to pay a copyist; he wants a gift, which will be free, as such fluff should be. To give him a copy, however, Martial will have to pay a copyist himself, and Quintus does not rate the expense, any more than does (according to Quintus or—and this is the joke—Martial) the book of epigrams. Books were not written or circulated for profit; there was no systematic 'book trade,' in the larger sense of a 'publishing business.' The only ones in a position to make money from books were individual copyists, independent craftsmen who made each book to order.

In this environment the status of the author was necessarily different than in the modern world. Because production of texts was in the hands of readers and writers, not publishers, there very often was no money to be made from 'publication.' The common Latin and Greek words for 'publication' mean something closer to 'release' or even 'abandonment;' for once an author allowed a written copy of the text out of his hands he lost control of it (van Groningen 1963). Authors in the ancient world made their money in other ways. They might be independently wealthy, like the Roman senators Cicero and Cato; such authors typically wrote to further their social and/or political ambitions. Others supported themselves through performances or teaching (so famous rhetoricians); these profited from the reputation that the circulation of their writings conferred on them. Others got their livelihood from wealthy patrons; in such cases the motivation of the patron matters as much as, and perhaps more than, that of the author (Gold 1982; White 1993). In the case of Vergil, his last poem was linked to the family lore of the ruling house, the Julio-Claudians; the story of Aeneas became associated with the prestige of the emperor and his family and that fact surely accounts to no small degree for the speedy and wide circulation of the *Aeneid* among the elite of the empire. But (and this is the important point) no ancient author derived income from the circulation of his writing; to the contrary, texts were frequently circulated at the expense of the author, as we have just seen with Martial. The *Aeneid* doubtless circulated (at least initially) largely at the expense of the emperor Augustus. And it was precisely because Augustus and his family came to embody the state that the *Aeneid* has come to be associated with the Roman political order.

CONCLUSION: LITERARY CIRCULATION AND COMMUNICATION IN CONTEXT

"Why do I not send you my books, Pontilianus? So you won't send me yours" (Mart. 7. 3). The epigram implies, of course, that Pontilianus' writing is not worth reading; but the joke is enriched by some knowledge about the nature of the circulation of books in the Roman world. Roman books were ideally disseminated by gift, and the kind of exchange repudiated by Martial not only would have served to spread information, but to reinforce a personal relationship. By preempting the book exchange, Martial slaps away the proffered friendship of Pontilianus.

Modern print books are distributed for sale to a market. The purchase of such publications is an economic transaction: obviously information is communicated, and this shared content can contribute to the creation of community. The purchase of a mass-market paperback, however, creates no obligation or personal relationship between the reader and author, or for that matter anyone else. By contrast, in the Roman world, circulation of texts as a rule involves both a sharing of content and the reinforcement of a personal relationship, and this association subtly changes the nature and social function of reading.

Traditional gift exchange has not been entirely abolished from the circulation of modern, commercially distributed literature. I often give books to my wife, for example, as she gives books to me. I take some care in choosing something appropriate, for it would be unpleasant to give her a book that matters to me and have her despise it, find it poorly written, or offensive, or boring; her opinion of a book that I value enough to recommend to her reflects on me too. Reciprocally, when she gives me a book I am disposed to read and appreciate it—and if I cannot, to try to understand and sympathize with what she sees in it. In the context of gift giving, reading becomes an ethical activity, by which I mean that it is implicated in the values that govern social interactions among friends and equals, superiors and subordinates, and the evaluation of the text has an impact on the giver's and recipient's status and interaction. People today—employers and employees, teachers and students, friends and lovers—still may on occasion define their relationships by exchanges of books. How might one read, though, a book given by the ruler of the known world? By contrast, and as a rule, mass-produced books are circulated by impersonal purchase, not by gift exchange, and they create community of content only. If many of us have read a particular Stephen King novel, we all share the information contained in it. In general that is the only way that printed books can create community. The 'verdict of the market' is manifested in the quantity of sales, not in personal interactions.

Because of the nature of the circulation of literature in ancient Rome, the social function of literature needs to be understood with reference to the institutions and ideals that governed relationships between individuals: the environments within which literary works were read or performed, practices of gift giving, ideals of egalitarian friendship (*amicitia*), or the hierarchical patron-client relationship (cf., e.g., Verboven and Lendon in this volume). In its circulation, ancient literature established or confirmed relationships among individuals. The content of books helps to establish a common set of values and expectations; the giving of gifts establishes more particular and concrete relationships; and those involved in all of these are limited, at least initially, to the givers and receivers of the texts in question.

The evidence for the circulation of Vergil's writings in the Roman Empire is remarkable. The *Aeneid* is doubtless an extraordinary case; even so, the evidence for its dissemination should be judged in light of our general knowledge about the production and circulation of Roman literary texts. Certainly it would have been impossible, or highly unlikely, that army personnel stationed in England and Judaea obtained copies of Vergil's writings locally from a 'bookseller.' It is far more likely that they obtained their books in the usual way, by gift exchange with friends. So Martial mentions that he sent copies of his writings to Appius Norbanus, who was campaigning on the Danube (Mart. 4. 84; cf. 10. 78, 14. 188); and Pliny tells how the consul of AD 91, Maecilius Nepos, asks him to correct copies of his speeches, which Nepos intends to take with him when he leaves to take up the governorship of a province (Plin. *Ep.* 4. 26). The writings of Vergil spread to Vindolanda and Masada not because Romans found 'bookstores' everywhere they went (though doubtless scribes accompanied the Roman army in its billets and bivouacs), but because elite obligations and expectations, the network of Roman friendship, extended so far.

As in the modern world, shared literature contributed to the formation of community in the ancient Roman world. Moderns tend to think of the social effects of literature exclusively in terms of the content of books, in large part because that is how we are predisposed to regard print books because of the nature of their production and dissemination. We know Roman literature through later copies; we experience it through printed editions, as we experience most literature (cf. Hedrick 2006: chapter 4). Of course ancient books were texts, and it is legitimate to take as an object of research 'what Vergil wrote.' But it is necessary too to attempt to imagine how the books themselves functioned in Vergil's society. Books are not only texts; they are objects as well. Modern books are mass-produced, market goods. In the ancient world they were individually crafted artifacts: they circulated by personal exchange among a small, elite group, so helping to define, as gifts and personal loans and inheritances will, the relationships among the givers and getters of these objects. The Roman elite was characterized not merely by the shared knowledge of literary texts, but by the concrete nature of the circulation of texts; and the circulation affected the way that the texts were understood, which depended upon the experience and social implications of reading. The community produced by ancient literature was small and intimate, personal, and defined by mutual obligation and regard for status.

Texts such as the *Aeneid* did of course quickly circulate beyond the confines of the uppermost strata of Roman society, to reach humbler parvenus who had to resort to bookstores for their reading material.[20] We cannot plausibly presume that Roman literature communicated to such people as it did to the elite—nor would we be well advised in thinking that it was ever intended to do so. A few may have had no conception of the richness of the social context that fostered these texts, and, like moderns, they may have regarded literature merely in terms of its content; but I suspect that most will have had some sense of what they were missing. For these, unrolling a scroll must have triggered emulative feelings of longing and envy, like those of Dickensian waifs, standing with their noses smudging the window of a candy store—a glimpse of the sweets, a whiff of chocolate, and the shopkeeper bustles out the door to sweep them off the sidewalk.

SUGGESTED READING

The most important essays on the evidence for the social influence of Vergil in antiquity are Hoogma 1959 with Horsfall 1984 and 1995. For the literary transmission of Vergil in antiquity, see, for example, Geymonat 1995. On Roman education, see Marrou 1956, Bonner 1977, and Cribiore 2001 along with Horster, Connolly, and Hahn in this volume. Orientation in the vast bibliography on nationalism may begin with Anderson 1991 and Gellner 2005. The bibliography on the effects on European politics and society and culture of the introduction of printing is vast: see generally Eisenstein 1984, Gaskell 1974 and, for a specific case study vividly describing the intellectual and industrial and business activities of early publishers, Lowry 1979. A standard introduction to ancient and medieval book production is Reynolds and Wilson 1991; in the extensive scholarship since, I will cite only a recent essay, Johnson 2004, for further bibliography and a consideration of surviving ancient book-rolls. For the circulation of literary texts in ancient Rome, see the excellent essays, Starr 1987 and 1990.

20. Starr 1987: 221–23, noting that bookstores seem to become more important in the first century AD, suggests that increasing resort to such sources of literary texts reflects, among other causes, "a weakening of the hold of the traditional aristocracy to control of access to social status" in the early empire.

BIBLIOGRAPHY

Anderson, B. 1991. *Imagined Communities: Reflections on the Origin and Spread of Nationalism*. London: Verso.

Armstrong, E. 1990. *Before Copyright: The French Book-Privilege System 1498–1526*. Cambridge: Cambridge University Press.

Bagnall, R. S. 1995. *Reading Papyri, Writing Ancient History*. London: Routledge.

Berry, M. E. 2007. *Japan in Print: Information in the Early Modern Period*. Berkeley: University of California Press.

Bonner, S. F. 1977. *Education in Ancient Rome: From the Elder Cato to the Younger Pliny*. Berkeley: University of California Press.

Bowman, A. K. 1998. *Life and Letters on the Roman Frontier: Vindolanda and Its People*. London: Routledge.

Burns, S. L. 2003. *Before the Nation: Kokugaku and the Imagining of Community in Early Modern Japan*. Durham: Duke University Press.

Carlyle, T. 1901. *On Heroes and Hero-Worship and the Heroic in History* (Carlyle's Collected Works). New York: Scribners.

Clanchy, M. T. 1993. *From Memory to Written Record, England 1066–1307*. Oxford: Blackwell.

Cohen, E. 2000. *The Athenian Nation*. Princeton: Princeton University Press.

Conway, R. S. 1928. *Harvard Lectures on the Vergilian Age*. Cambridge, Mass.: Harvard University Press.

Conybeare, C. 2000. *Paulinus Noster: Self and Symbols in the Letters of Paulinus of Nola*. Oxford: Oxford University Press.

Cramer, F. H. 1945. "Bookburning and Censorship in Ancient Rome." *Journal of the History of Ideas* 6: 157–96.

Cribiore, R. 2001. *Gymnastics of the Mind: Greek Education in Hellenistic and Roman Egypt*. Princeton: Princeton University Press.

Darnton, R. 1979. *The Business of Enlightenment: a Publishing History of the Encyclopédie, 1775–1800*. Cambridge, Mass.: Harvard University Press.

———. 1990. *The Kiss of Lamourette: Reflections in Cultural History*. New York: Norton.

Eisenstein, E. 1984. *The Printing Revolution in Early Modern Europe*. Cambridge: Cambridge University Press.

Eliot, T. S. 1945. *What Is a Classic? An Address Delivered before the Vergil Society on the 16th of October, 1944*. London: Faber.

Feldbrugge, F. J. M. 1975. *Samizdat and Political Dissent in the Soviet Union*. Leiden: E. J. Brill.

Finley, M. I. 1985. *Democracy Ancient and Modern* (rev. ed.). New Brunswick: Rutgers University Press.

———. 1999. *The Ancient Economy*. Berkeley: University of California Press.

Franklin, J. L., Jr. 1991. "Literacy and the Parietal Inscriptions of Pompeii." in M. Beard et al., *Literacy in the Roman World*. Ann Arbor: Journal of Roman Archaeology. 77–98.

Fülle, G. 1997. "The Internal Organization of the Arretine Terra Sigillata Industry: Problems of Evidence and Interpretation." *Journal of Roman Studies* 87: 111–55.

Gaskell, P. 1974. *A New Introduction to Bibliography*. Oxford: Clarendon Press.

Gellner, E. 2005. *Nations and Nationalism*. 2nd ed. Oxford: Blackwell.

Geymonat, M. 1995. "The Transmission of Virgil's Works in Antiquity and the Middle Ages." In N. Horsfall (ed.), *A Companion to the Study of Virgil*. Leiden: E. J. Brill. 249–55.

Glover, T. R. 1912. *Vergil*. 2nd ed. New York: MacMillan.

Gold, B. 1982. *Literary and Artistic Patronage in Ancient Rome*. Austin: University of Texas Press.

Greene, K. 1986. *The Archaeology of the Roman Economy*. Berkeley: University of California Press.

van Groningen, B. 1963. "EKDOSIS." *Mnemosyne* 16: 1–17.

Gruen, E. S. 1992. *Culture and National Identity in Republican Rome*. Ithaca: Cornell University Press.

Harris, W. V. 1980. "Roman Terracotta Lamps: The Organization of an Industry." *The Journal of Roman Studies* 70: 126–145.

———. 1989. *Ancient Literacy*. Cambridge, Mass.: Harvard University Press.

Hedrick, C. W., Jr. 2006. *Ancient History: Monuments and Documents*. Oxford: Blackwell.

Hobsbawm, E., and T. Ranger. 1992. *The Invention of Tradition*. Cambridge: Cambridge University Press.

Hoogma, R. P. 1959. *Der Einfluss Vergils auf die Carmina Latina Epigraphica: eine Studie mit besonderer Berücksichtigung der metrisch-technischen Grundsätze der Entlehnung*. Amsterdam: North-Holland.

Horsfall, N. 1984. "Aspects of Virgilian influence in Roman Life." In *Accademia nazionale virgiliana, Atti del Convegno mondiale scientifico di studi su Virgilio, Mantova, Roma, Napoli, 19–24 settembre 1981*. Milano: A. Mondadori. 47–63.

———. 1991. "Statistics or States of Mind?" In Mary Beard et al., *Literacy in the Roman World*. Ann Arbor: Journal of Roman Archaeology. 59–76.

———. 1995. "Virgil's Impact at Rome: The Non-literary Evidence." In N. Horsfall (ed.), *A Companion to the Study of Virgil*. Leiden: E. J. Brill. 249–55.

Johnson, W. A. 2004. *Bookrolls and Scribes in Oxyrhynchus*. Toronto: University of Toronto Press.

———. 2010. *Readers and Reading Culture in the High Roman Empire: A Study of Elite Communities*. New York: Oxford University Press.

Johnson, W. A., and H. N. Parker. (eds.). 2009. *Ancient Literacies: The Culture of Reading in Greece and Rome*. New York: Oxford University Press.

Jusdanis, G. 1991. *Belated Modernity and Aesthetic Culture: Inventing National Literature*. Minneapolis: University of Minnesota Press.

Kehoe, D. 2007. "The Early Roman Empire: Production." In W. Scheidel, I. Morris, and R. Saller (eds.), *The Cambridge Economic History of the Greco-Roman World*. Cambridge: Cambridge University Press. 543–69.

Lowry, M. 1979. *The World of Aldus Manutius. Business and Scholarship in Renaissance Venice*. Ithaca: Cornell University Press.

Marrou, H. -I. 1956. *A History of Education in Antiquity*. Trans. George Lamb. New York: Sheed and Ward.

Martindale, C. 1997. "Introduction: The Classic of All Europe." In C. Martindale (ed.), *The Cambridge Companion to Vergil*. Cambridge: Cambridge University Press. 1–18.

Mattingly, D. J. 2006. *Britannia: An Imperial Possession*. London: Allen Lane.

McKeon, M. 2002. *The Origins of the English Novel, 1600–1740*. Baltimore: Johns Hopkins University Press.

Millett, M. 1990. *The Romanization of Britain: An Essay in Archaeological Interpretation*. Cambridge: Cambridge University Press.

Petrucci, A. 1993. *Public Lettering: Script, Culture, and Power*. Chicago: University of Chicago Press.

Rebenich, S. 1992. *Hieronymus und sein Kreis: Prosopographische und sozialgeschichtliche Untersuchungen*. Stuttgart: Franz Steiner Verlag.

Reisner, E. H. 1922. *Nationalism and Education since 1789: A Social and Political History of Modern Education*. New York: Macmillan.

Reynolds, L. D., and N. G. Wilson. 1991. *Scribes and Scholars: A Guide to the Transmission of Greek and Latin Literature*. 3rd ed. Oxford: Oxford University Press.

Roth, R., and J. Keller (eds.). 2007. *Roman by Integration: Dimensions of Group Identity in Material Culture and Text*. Portsmouth, R.I.: Journal of Roman Archaeology.

Saenger, P. 1982. "Silent Reading: Its Impact on Late Medieval Script and Society." *Viator* 13: 366–414.

———. 1997. *The Space between Words: The Origins of Silent Reading*. Palo Alto: Stanford University Press.

Sherwin-White, A. N. 1966. *The Letters of Pliny: A Historical and Social Commentary*. Oxford: Clarendon Press.

Skeat, T. C. 1957. *The Use of Dictation in Ancient Book Production*. Oxford: Oxford University Press.

Smith, A. D. 2002. "When Is a Nation." *Geopolitics* 7: 5–32.

Speyer, W. 1981. *Büchervernichtung und Zensur des Geistes bei Heiden, Juden und Christen*. Stuttgart: Anton Hiersmann Verlag.

Starr, R. J. 1987. "The Circulation of Literary Texts in the Roman World." *The Classical Quarterly* n.s. 37: 213–23.

———. 1990. "The Used-Book Trade in the Roman World." *Phoenix* 44: 148–57.

Watson, G. R. 1969. *The Roman Soldier*. London: Thames and Hudson.

White, P. 1993. *Promised Verse: Poets in the Society of Augustan Rome*. Cambridge, Mass.: Harvard University Press.

Woolf, G. 1998. *Becoming Roman: The Origins of Provincial Civilization in Gaul*. Cambridge: Cambridge University Press.

CHAPTER 9

EPIGRAPHY AND COMMUNICATION

ELIZABETH A. MEYER

Introduction

WITH Augustus, what had been intermittent or impermanent acts of inscribing in Latin became widespread and durable: "Rome and the cities of the empire filled with inscriptions."[1] Latin stone inscriptions survive in vast numbers, perhaps more than 300,000, from all parts of the ancient Roman world.[2] Such durable inscriptions (and bronze letters or plaques posted on stone) could appear on walls and buildings, for example, as well as pavements, statue bases, free-standing stelae, and altars. Very different kinds of inscriptions were scratched into other metals, clay, and plaster—and on amphorae, tiles, mirrors, sling bullets, and other portable objects.[3] All of these types of writing are loosely grouped as 'epigraphy,'

My thanks to J. E. Lendon, M. Peachin, and A. J. Woodman.

1. Alföldy 1991: 321.

2. Alföldy 1991: 292, not counting inscribed 'household objects' (*instrumenta domestica*)—defined as "most kinds of portable objects" (Harris 1993: 7); total numbers confirmed, Eck 1997a: 98 and Alföldy 1999: 90, who also (88–89) estimated about 1,500 new Latin inscriptions found each year. Alföldy (2004a: 148) speculated that there may have originally been between 20 and 40 *million* inscriptions total.

3. On varieties of inscribing and materials, see Lassère 2005: 1, 4–10. Legends on coins (cf. Noreña in this volume), engravings on gems, and writing on wood (cf. Jördens in this volume) are now classified as their own sub-specialties and no longer considered within the realm of 'epigraphy,' see Bodel 2001: 2.

and all were part of the visual and cognitive experience of most in the Roman Empire. But it is likely that a person's experience of the two types of epigraphy was not the same, since the writing on portable objects was smaller and usually more directly functional (signaling—often by a stamp—ownership, content, or origin of a product),[4] or occasional (a list of names on a broken piece of pottery),[5] or performative ("Strike Pompeius!" on a sling bullet)[6] than that on objects intended to stay in place. By contrast, fixed stone (and bronze) epigraphy, sometimes called "monumental,"[7] was intended to last, and assumed communication with a wide audience.

This epigraphy therefore constituted, and takes its rightful place at the center of, a complex Roman communicative system that included many sub-genres of monumental inscription and had its own idiosyncratic characteristics (see "Monumental Inscriptions as a Communicative System," below). This system is, in particular, distinguished by an over-emphasis on monuments that assert belonging and connection; that report (only) positive achievements; that are socially appropriate, that is, they endorse or embody harmonious, elite-dominated social relationships; and that intentionally create not just personal but also political and communal memories. These four qualities also characterize the emperor's monumental inscriptions, and this correspondence reflects the emperor's involvement in this communicative system and reinforces his position at the top of its hierarchies (see "The Emperor as Epigraphical Audience and Actor," below). Precisely because of the emperor's involvement, this Roman communicative system—only inchoately in existence under the republic— also has its own history, beginning with Augustus (see "The Epigraphic Habit," below). This history was one in which the production of monumental inscriptions varied from place to place but also demonstrated a notable pattern of rise and fall over time, between the early first and the mid-third centuries AD. These thousands of Roman monumental inscriptions, once valued chiefly as historical documents, are now studied also as elements of an historical process: monumental inscriptions are now valued for how, to whom, and under what circumstances they communicated; how discernable patterns of epigraphic communication could lock together into a system; what the emperor's place in this system was; and how all these patterns changed over time.

---

4. Lassère 2005: 1, 218–20, 440–49, 450–55; Pucci 2001.

5. Mayer 2003.

6. Sling bullet, *CIL* I² 857 = IX 6086.ix, in Bodel 2001: 21–23; or a sword inscribed "I strike well!" cited in Corbier 2006: 48; or curse tablets, see (e.g.) Meyer 2004: 103–7.

7. Woolf 1996: 22–30, "monumental" stone and bronze inscriptions are defined by "expense and durability" and establish "presence" (identity, deeds, qualities) and memory.

Monumental Inscriptions as a
Communicative System

Monumental inscriptions of the Roman Empire are, typically and traditionally, classified and categorized by language, place of origin, and type. The languages are primarily Latin and Greek. Origins (when known) are predominantly cities, villages, and sanctuaries, but also roadsides, country estates, and army camps—places where people lived or gathered, and where they could be expected to notice and read, or be read to.[8] The most numerous surviving type of inscription in Greek and Latin is, by far, the epitaph.[9] Next most common were votive dedications, then honorific inscriptions, then (probably) edicts, municipal decrees, and laws.[10] The inscribing entities could vary, from cities to associations (*collegia*), priestly groups, army units, individuals, and families. In this mix of group and individual no one wished to be alone, ignored, or unadmired,[11] but there are deducible presumptions that inscriptions (and therefore their makers) made about audience that allow us to postulate qualitative differences—gradations—in intent and impact.

First, if monumental inscriptions are associated with immovable objects, where were these objects? Laws, edicts, and honorific decrees were all inscribed or nailed up, usually in crowded Roman city centers (e.g., on walls and statue bases). Their placement thus presumes an audience not unlike a modern one, an audience likely to congregate in such an urban space, thus perhaps the politically active classes, or those who had business there, or those who liked to walk in the most central, and probably most famous, area of the city. The placement of epitaphs suggests similar presumptions about audience. Ancient Roman cemeteries, oriented in strips along the sides of frequented roads right outside city gates,[12] were from their very location more visible than modern ones, and many of their monuments faced the road and clamored for the attention of passers-by. Moreover, Romans visited their cemeteries

8. Urban and military, emphasized by Woolf 1996: 37; in contrast to Greek (pre-Roman) inscriptions, which are found almost exclusively in cities and sanctuaries, Rowe 2009: 28. Where people gathered: the *celeberrimus locus*, "most frequented place," was noted as a place in which Roman inscriptions were erected, see (e.g.) Plin. *Ep.* 8. 6. 14 and examples and discussion in Eck 2004: 26–39, who rightly notes that a street was a prime *celeberrimus locus*.

9. McLean 2002: 260 (Greek); Saller and Shaw 1984: 124 (three-quarters of surviving Latin inscriptions); Woolf 1996: 23 n. 3 (noting regional variations in the breakdown of inscriptions by type).

10. No handbook is willing to commit itself on this breakdown, but see general remarks by, e.g., Woolf 1996: 27.

11. Giorcelli Bersani 2004: 13 (but a point often made).

12. See von Hesberg and Zanker 1987 (overview); tomb fronts oriented toward street, Eck 1987: 64; Zanker 1992: 340; Eck 2004: 28 (quoting the *agrimensores* [land surveyors], a *monumentum* or *sepulchrum* erected *ad itinera publica propter testimonium perennitatis*— "beside public ways so as to create a record in perpetuity").

at least four times a year.[13] The placement of a Latin epitaph on a Roman stone grave monument and in a Roman cemetery therefore presumes for most of them a significantly wider audience, a more generic public, than its equivalent modern one generally does, even if modern habits can be quite various.[14]

Another way to deduce intended audience comes from the content of the inscription itself. "Stop, traveller!" or "...so that all might read": although perhaps optimistic appeals in epitaphs or laws, these references clearly attest the intent of the inscriber.[15] But do (for example) dedications to the gods, set up in temples and sanctuaries, have an intended human audience? One might think that the dedicator intended to communicate only with the divinity. Yet the contents of inscribed dedications, with human names and reasons for dedication, imply an audience wider than that of just the god, who might be expected to know these facts already. This is not a universal audience, like the "traveller" or the "all" in "that all might read," but a moderately sized group, limited by its interest in god and sanctuary, and deducible from the fact and content of the inscription itself.

Epitaphs and dedications are the two major categories in which individuals were the chief inscribers; honors, laws, and edicts are usually the consequence of group decisions. All, by their placement and content, presume an audience of significant if varying size. They also usually shared four further characteristics that suggest audiences interested in these same characteristics. These characteristics (and the implication of interest in them) help to set monumental inscriptions off from other types of Latin inscriptions, and may also, eventually, suggest why (despite local variations) the production of these inscriptions rose and fell together: why so many Latin epigraphical cultures on stone could form, together, a system and an identifiably Roman epigraphic 'habit.'

Belonging and Connection

The first quality that monumental inscription writers wished to record, make, or assert was that they belonged: to city or army, for example; among fellow freed or fellow slaves; or among Roman citizens or learned Hellenes. One way this belonging was communicated was through extremely stereotyped expression: although

13. Champlin 1991: 163–64.

14. Davies 2000: 120–23. That such 'monumental' inscribing of epitaphs was a significant choice (Eck 1987 and 1988) is reinforced by the fact that many dead were not commemorated (Eck 1988), including infants (Nielsen 1997: 174) and those who died in battle (Hope 2003); graves could be marked, but the marker not inscribed (Woolf 1996: 27); and many dead could be commemorated only by name, but under the auspices of the man whose epitaph did face the street, like family members within a large built tomb (Feraudi-Gruénais 2003: 25–42), or a slave-*familia* within the master's *columbarium* (communal burial site).

15. *Viator resiste et lege*...("Traveler, stop and read..."), e.g., *CIL* III 6155, or *quisque viator*...("each and every traveler..."), *AE* 1982, 356 (Caecina); and see examples in Lattimore 1962: 118–26 and 232–37. "So that...," see (mostly republican) examples collected by Crawford 1996: 1, 19–20.

the voices are often individual, the language is usually familiar, even repetitively common. Indeed, most Latin inscriptions (unlike most Greek) are very formulaic, as is shown by the widespread use of abbreviations, which could be brief (e.g.: "d.d." either *dono dedit*, "he gave as a gift," or *decreto decurionum*, "by decree of the decurions"), or more complex (e.g.: "h.m.d.m.a." *hoc monumento dolus malus abesto*, "let malicious evil be absent from this monument").[16] These Latin abbreviations are all shorthand ways of conveying a concept or an action to an audience that already knows what the shorthand means, as well as what to expect in the context where the inscription can be seen.[17] Moreover, by writing in formulae and abbreviations, the authors of the inscription also wanted to be, or show themselves to be, just like everyone else who gave a benefaction or set up a monument in accordance with a will, and thus to belong among those, and in the tradition of those, who saw these specific actions, expressions, and emotions as appropriate.

So a bronze plaque, found at the summit of the Great St. Bernard Pass in the Alps, was simply inscribed but nonetheless conveyed much of exactly this sort:

> To Poeninus, for the going and the coming back, G(aius) Julius Primus w(illingly)
> and d(uly) p(aid back) (his) v(ow) (*ILS* 4850a: letters in parentheses expand
> abbreviations and supply words necessary for translation).

This inscription was in Latin, so for a Latin-reading god (Jupiter Poeninus), and other Latin readers tending the sanctuary, or hazarding life and fortune on a crossing of the Alps. As the inscription notes, Primus "paid back his vow willingly and duly," a statement (*votum solvit libens merito*) entirely abbreviated (*v.s.l.m.*). Romans knew that vows, once made, had to be "paid back" or one would remain burdened by debt,[18] and that one approached the gods with a free heart and a sense of appropriate—merited—balancing of favors given and received. This is indeed Roman, for the Hellenistic Greek formula for dedicating after an implied vow, when used, was only "he dedicated...having prayed" (εὐξάμενος) or "...as promised" (καθὼς ὑπέσχετο),[19] with none of the technical implications of a debt cleared (*solvere*), and without the participle and adverb reflecting state of heart and mind. On this small bronze plaque a legalistic, specifically Roman view of a man's relationship to the gods is conveyed, all in an abbreviated formula. To inscribe, especially formulaically like this, was then to signal one's membership in a club characterized by mutual comprehensibility and cultural agreement.

Gaius Julius Primus was, in his inscription, gratefully repaying a debt in a way its recipient (the god Poeninus) and a certain audience (Latin readers who understood the way the Romans thought about vowing and their gods) would

16. Greek abbreviations: see Guarducci 1967: 398–406; Avi-Yonah 1940: 10 ("the use of abbreviation is...as foreign to the Greeks as it is congenial to the Romans") and 13 (most known Greek abbreviations arise after contact with the Romans); Meyer 2004: 65–66.

17. See, e.g., Giorcelli Bersani 2004: 15.

18. Meyer 2004: 101–3.

19. McLean 2002: 254.

fully comprehend and appreciate. In that sense his direct or intended audience was twofold: he communicated outward, to this group, and upward, to the divinity. Epigraphical communication in the Roman Empire was often of this sort, a way of connecting *out*, to the group(s) in which one claimed membership, but also *up*, to a more powerful entity to whom one had been, was, would like to be, or would like to be seen as, connected.[20]

A range of inscription types, from simple tombstones to complex honorific inscriptions, can demonstrate this desire to connect and be connected. So, first, a tombstone:

> M(arcus) Favoni(us) Facilis, s(on of) M(arcus), of the Pol(lia) tribe, centurion of leg(ion) XX. The freed(men) Verecundus and Novicius put (it) up. H(e) l(ies) h(ere) (*RIB* I 200; Colchester, England, AD 40–70).

This tombstone uses a common abbreviation and, as in over 80% of Latin epitaphs of the imperial period, but as is only rarely seen in Greek epitaphs, the commemorators name themselves as well as the man (in this case, their former master) who has died.[21] One can therefore see, here and elsewhere, relationships in (and behind) Latin epitaphs that one cannot see in Greek ones. In an honorific inscription the nature of the connection is made very clear:

> To the best citizen, the man most deferential (*obsequentissimo*) to his home-city (*patria*) and fellow-citizens, Titius Faebius Saeverus, patron of the colony, by whose care and solicitude all public works (*opera publica*) were restored. To him, the most splendid *ordo* and the most honorable Telesinian populace ordered a statue erected (*CIL* IX 2238 = *ILS* 5507; Telesinus, late third century).

Here too a relationship is celebrated, that of the *ordo* of decurions (the town council) and the populace of a city with their patron;[22] and an inscribed gift is given upward, to the man who has been so generous to his fellow townsmen. Here substantives, as well as adjectives that characterize both giver and recipient, associate them with others who possess these same abstract public and moral qualities—public-spirited, deferential, most splendid, most honorable. In fact, even *opera publica* must here be an abstraction, subsuming Saeverus' gift into a larger but vaguer category of prestigious achievement, since the archaeological record of his town shows no restorations of its major buildings in Saeverus' time.[23] This, then, is a different, or

20. Woolf 1996: 29.

21. Latin epitaphs are highly formulaic, although there are personal variants, Lattimore 1962; an abusive epitaph in Kajanto (1968) proves that freedom of expression is very much possible, which makes the adherence to standard formulae that much more striking. Eighty percent, see refs. in Meyer 1990: 75 nn. 6–8 (in the republican period only 58%, Saller and Shaw 1984: 147 col. 1), also (e.g.) de Brestian 2008: 269 (75% in northern Iberia); rarely Greek, Meyer 1990: 75 and McLean 2002: 262.

22. Also a phenomenon of the developed epigraphy of the empire: the first honorific inscription in Latin with the honoree in the dative is from 91 BC (*ILS* 7172), and many from the republican period omit the name of the dedicator, Salomies 1994: 70.

23. Restoration a metaphor, Thomas and Witschel 1992: 171.

additional, way of conceiving those to whom a connection is being asserted: again a group characterized by their understanding of a code, like the audience for Julius Primus' dedication, but this time the code is conveyed not by formulaic abbreviation, but by the expressive (albeit stereotyped) language of virtues.[24]

Dedicator to a god, freedmen for a former master, *ordo* and people to a patron delightfully outstanding in his liberality: these inscriptions convey relationships, situate parties in groups to which they belong, and establish a connection with a more powerful man (or god). Belonging and connections—both outward and upward, both human and supra-human—were important, and were a matter of triumphant advertisement.[25]

Success

This triumphant advertising is a universal characteristic. The agents in these inscriptions were successful in completing or achieving what they had wanted. These inscriptions—and this is a second quality that all such monumental inscriptions have in common—therefore make manifest not just the fact of belonging and connection, but the completion of the desired action. These three inscriptions, standing in for thousands of others, report on positive achievements; no hint that others had frozen to death in the Great St. Bernard Pass, for example, or that municipal euergetism was an iron or even legal obligation for the rich[26]—because no matter the actual situation, no inscription actually ever conveyed that sort of truth. Roman monumental epigraphy is not an accurate or even-handed reflection of both the good and the bad: if the bad cannot be made positive, it is not inscribed. Roman monumental epigraphy was about achievements, obligations fulfilled, and successful lives.[27]

---

24. Forbis 1996: 97, on language of virtues; high levels of standardized praise (the most frequently used was *bene merens* ("well deserving"), which primarily characterized "relationships based on obligation") also used in epitaphs, Zanker 1992: 340 and Nielsen 1997: 175–203, showing that here too "self-fashioning" was "under powerful collective control."

25. "The predominance of Latin epigraphy lies in its association with Roman power structures…the extension of inscriptions…strongly correlated with the extension of patronage bonds and hierarchical links that reached most of the Roman empire," Häussler 2002: 73–74, and see also Häussler 1998; Eck (1994) notes that naming the inscriber records both sides of a relationship and brings the inscriber (also) epigraphic immortality.

26. That municipal euergetism in the late republic was "stimulated by legislation…authorizing or requiring magistrates of colonies and *municipia* to expend public monies" (Gordon and Reynolds 2003: 227–28) is suggested by Crawford 1998: 38–39 and Pobjoy 2000.

27. Noted also by (e.g.) Millar 1983: 129; Eck 1997a: 109–10; Eck 1997b; Pobjoy 2000 (obligations fulfilled); Alföldy 2005 (for the relentless praise of only positive qualities in epitaphs).

Social Appropriateness: The Roman View of the World

These three inscriptions not only report on positive achievements and successful actions, but do so with the proper emotion: a vow "freely and duly" fulfilled, obligations responsibly fulfilled, a town patron suitably, indeed fulsomely, flattered. These inscriptions therefore—their third common quality—also embody social appropriateness, showing social relationships, attitudes, and correct emotions as a Roman, indeed an elite Roman, would say they should be: deferential, supportive, admiring, and predictable. This was Roman society viewed from its best and most flattering angle, society as a harmonious and interconnected hierarchy of status groups whose tendons and tendrils were given lasting epigraphic expression.[28] This positive outlook, this social appropriateness, was above all an elite view of social relations, but one that non-elites imitated and in which non-elites clearly had a part to play. This is why monumental inscriptions in general, and inscriptions put up to elites by others in particular, especially convey what this elite would most want to hear: Saeverus wants to be acknowledged as "most deferential" and as the best citizen.[29] It was in return for such display and acknowledgment, or the expectation thereof, that such men were the source of a flowing stream of benefaction: inscriptions therefore anticipate such a man's view of himself, and reflect his wishes. The formulaic, if gradually inflating, qualities of praise and honor suggest the same—that honoring bodies wished to please, and were therefore taking care not to be wrong by praising an unusual characteristic or action that might raise a supercilious eyebrow.[30]

This channeling of the public expression of appropriate praise for appropriate elite behavior and achievements through other bodies was very common, but not always necessary. For outstanding men also performed their own status and acted out society's vision of appropriate behavior, and saw to it themselves that these performances were inscribed on stone. Such men (and even those below the uppermost rungs in rank) were, above all, good *patresfamiliae* ("heads of family") and good patrons. So, for example, from the tomb of two freedmen, we find:

> C. Caecilius Felix and C. Caecilius Urbicus consecrated this place just as it is,
> vaulted over and with its walls and monument included, in length six paces, in
> width seven-and-a-half paces, for themselves and for C. Caecilius Rufinus and for
> C. Caecilius Maternus and for their freedmen and freedwomen and their
> offspring, with the exception of the freedwoman Secundina, undutiful (*impia*)
> towards her patron, Caecilius Felix. T(his) m(onument) is n(ot) t(o follow the)
> h(eirs) (*ILS* 8115 = *CIL* VI 13732; Rome).

28. See Van Nijf 1997: 247 on the creation of Roman society in the East: "epigraphy was instrumental in this process... in this way, hierarchy was not only accepted; it was internalized and reproduced across the entire social spectrum."

29. The use of superlatives in honorific inscriptions seems to become more common starting with the late Antonines, Salomies 1994: 74–78.

30. Eck (1995) and Forbis (1996: 4–5 and n. 14) argue convincingly that great men were consulted even about the wording of inscriptions honoring them.

The good man makes sure that he is seen to take care of his *familia* and dependents (while simultaneously showing his good judgment in excluding the unworthy), but does so in a way that also performs one of his privileges, his right as a Roman citizen to employ Roman law (here, that of testation). This kind of self-fashioning self-advertisement communicated *out* (to those who came to cemeteries and could decipher abbreviated Latin formulae) and *down* (to those included or remembered with appropriate affection, like wives, children, and the freed), and that downward direction was as much an appropriate expression of standing as upward communication from others could be.

Just as heads of families could state quite directly their requirements in their tomb inscriptions, and indeed plan their own monuments (like Petronius' Trimalchio, *Sat.* 71), so too could benefactors simply announce their benefactions themselves, either in life or through a posthumous endowment in a will. "Tib(erius) Cl(audius) Ianuarius, *Aug(ustalis)* of the col(ony), patr(on) of the first dec(ury), (contributed) the wall-painting and the porticus and the bench; similarly Cl(audius) Verus his son, on account of the doubled honor, the fore-portico, the kitchen, and the retaining wall: they made these from their own money" (*CIL* III 7960); and this very Roman gift, in very Roman language, is found inscribed in Sarmizegetusa, in distant, half-barbarian Dacia. It was also common that direct gifts like this, inscribed by the donors themselves, were bestowed after death, and not at all unusual that the terms of the donor's will (or the specifically relevant provisions thereof) would be inscribed by grateful recipients or family.[31] Very explicit, for example, were the testamentary instructions inscribed on the monuments of Manlius Megonius Leo, in the south Italian city of Petelium. This man left endowments (amounts carefully enumerated) to various groups in his city—*Augustales*, decurions, and others—on the condition that they set up statues to him and inscribe the relevant chapter(s) of his will on his statue bases. As one inscribed quotation from his will then enjoined:

> From you, best of municipal citizens, I seek and ask—by the health of the most sacred *princeps* Antoninus Augustus Pius and his children—that you consider my will and disposition thought-through and perpetual, and that you undertake to inscribe this chapter of my will in its entirety on the base of my pedestrian (i.e. non-equestrian) statue, which, above, I sought that you erect to me; so that it might be more noteworthy to those who come after as well as to contemporaries, and might prompt also those who would be munificent to their own hometown (*ILS* 6468; mid-second century AD).

The endowments were accepted, the statues were erected, and the chapters of the will were inscribed: it was accepted that the rich could script, and publish in permanent form, the terms even of their posthumous generosity, expressed in their own words. The fundamental Roman social compact, that the important and wealthy take care of their own and are honored for it in return, is attested by socially appropriate epigraphic expression, which records, publicly, the specifics: names, quantities,

---

31. Champlin 1991: 155–68; Eck 1997b: 326 (very common).

magistracies and achievements, obligations fulfilled, the very terms of their own memory. Even after death, Megonius Leo could control and dictate the terms in which he would be honored and remembered; and contemporaries, no doubt especially those with whom Megonius competed, were to take note.

Memory

To take note also were, in Megonius Leo's case, potential donors and posterity. In all sorts of 'monumental' inscriptions, claims to memory like these can be seen, a fourth quality these inscriptions have in common. Reputation was shaped, and functioned actively, not just among contemporaries but in the future, and epigraphical monuments of all sorts would help to forge this future memory of a person. So monumental inscriptions intentionally communicate not just in three directions, but in another dimension as well: out, up, and down, but also backward and forward in time, 'rewriting history' by presenting a sanitized retrospective view of a (now) exemplary person, and propelling (only) that view forward into future generations.

Memory was, however, shaped in different ways and to different ends. There are differences between attempts to memorialize thousands of names by inscribing them (and their virtues) on funerary monuments; attempts to reach across time to effect specific political ends; and attempts to create a communal historical memory for a city. The distinction between the first two types is the difference between Varro's observation that "monuments (*monimenta*) on tombs and indeed along the road…admonish (*admoneant*) the passers-by that both they themselves (*se*) were, and others (*illos*) as well are, mortal" (*Ling. Lat.* 6. 49), and Megonius Leo using his inscribed will to "prompt" or "admonish" (*admoniat*) others, present and future, to give gifts to their shared town. The memory created by epitaphs was, often as not, individual, for family and friends, while simultaneously universal, inspiring recollection and self-examination in any passer-by: whoever you are, "read this and be either more or less fortunate in your lifetime…Live honorably while your star grants you time for life," as the tombstone of Titus Flaminius from Wroxeter (*RIB* I 292, lines 4–7) instructs. The memory of Titus Flaminius (and thousands like him) was a specific contribution to the universal human confrontation with mortality and forgetting.[32] The memory of Megonius Leo, by contrast, was political—designed to produce admiration and emulation of the man, and action benefiting the city.

For Megonius Leo expressed a desire to serve as, and be seen as, an example to others. Exemplarity in the great was important, for just as aristocratic funerals had "inflamed" the young to deeds of glory in the Roman republic of Polybius' day (παρορμῶνται, Polyb. 6. 54), so an exemplary person could, and would wish to,

---

32. Hope 2001: 2, "memory is both individual and collective; the dead are both forgotten and ever present." For *memoria* in Latin epitaphs, see (e.g.) Häusle 1980. Cf. Peachin in this volume (n. 28).

reach out to future generations ("those who come after") with a specific purpose beyond mere human memory itself in mind.[33] "This monument was erected to render his memory eternal" (*ad memoriae aeternitatem*), reads an honorific inscription to a generous local notable in Arles in the first century AD (*CIL* XII 670)—so that, as is made explicit in Megonius Leo's case, others will follow in his well-heeled and munificent footsteps.[34]

Inscribed political memory of this sort, aimed at inspiring action, is an intentional contribution to the historical and communal memory of the community. Over time, dedications and restorations of buildings, municipal laws, lists of magistrates, decrees of small-town senates and decurions, and imperial edicts, letters, and gifts, all inscribed in prominent places,[35] would also become part of the cumulative and visible historical memory of a town. Or instant 'history' could be created, by the side-by-side inscribing of a series of related documents not too separated in time, like a statue base inscribed with documents in Lavinium (Italy) in AD 227, put up to an equestrian by his wife. In addition to the dedication, this base also had inscribed on it a letter from the honorand to a senator; an exchange of letters between the senator and two officials; an official vote of the *collegium* involved in this correspondence; and a letter in which the equestrian accepts the honor of this monument (*AE* 1998, 282). Thus, an instant 'archive' that gave an instant history of a process, all on display.

After the fact—and especially in the Greek East—older documents and acts, or excerpts from them, could be inscribed all at one (later) time, often in the form of an 'archive wall,' an act of inscribing that determined and created the important highlights of the collective, indeed the communal, memory of the city.[36] One of the most famous was that at Aphrodisias, where the city in the early third century AD inscribed sixteen documents: a *senatusconsultum*, a triumviral decree, eight imperial letters, a letter from a man thought to be an agent of the triumvir Mark Antony, two imperial subscripts, and paragraphs from a treaty and from grants of privileges made by the emperors, the senate, and people of Rome.[37] This act of selecting from

33. Monuments of 'exemplarity' also implicate all levels of society in the same ideological structure, see Hölkeskamp 1996: 303–12, and would provoke imitation and "social reproduction," Roller 2004: 7 (and see 32 on "temporal dislocation," a concept also stressed by Barrett 1993).

34. See also Pliny *HN* 34. 17. Such inscriptions also transform *collective* memory (what everyone in the city has experienced) into *cultural* memory (what everyone, present and future, in the city knows or will know): Chaniotis 2009: 255–59. But the inscription's more directly instrumental purpose *in* the city also makes its inscribing an act of intentional *political* memory.

35. Eck 1992: 359 (forum above all; also theaters, porticos, gardens, temple porticos); Corbier 2006: 35–37.

36. For a list, Ando 2000: 94–95; for an overview, Potter 1994: 117–20.

37. Reynolds 1982: 33–140 (nos. 6–19); more were added in the reign of Gordian III. Chaniotis (2003: 251–52) notes that 'archive wall' is a misleading name, since all the documents are selected (or selections), rather than a full archive.

the city's past to display both *in* the present and *for* the future was a way of deciding at one moment in time what was worthy of being remembered. This constructed memory was intended to prompt certain actions—in this case, that Romans and others should allow the city to continue to bask in the warm embrace of Roman favor by proving the privileges granted to the city by the Romans and "proclaim[ing] them as a warning to the other cities of Asia."[38] This inscribed wall was a communication *out* (to citizens and the other cities of Asia Minor) and *up* (to the Romans); it conveyed only the best of news (260 years of Roman favor), itself the consequence of helpful actions and proper, deferential relations between Aphrodisias and Rome; and it shaped the historical and communal memory of the city toward a purpose in both present and future (the protection of Aphrodisias' honored and favored status). This is the way, it implies, social and political relations in the Roman Empire worked for those who understood both power and the established proprieties.

Aphrodisians inscribed for themselves, their neighbors, and for distant Romans, like the emperor, who might never see their archive wall. Gaius Julius Primus inscribed for himself, for sanctuary visitors, and for a god. Megonius Leo decreed inscriptions for himself and his own memory, for various groups within his own city, and for others present and future who might give benefactions, invoking as he did so the emperor by means of an oath. For all, in other words, there was a distant or imagined audience as well as more immediate and easily identifiable groups, and all audiences were imagined as interested in seeing and hearing about the four shared qualities of belonging and connection, success, social appropriateness—embodying a happily elite view of social relations—and the intentional creation of various sorts of memory. Indeed, the perception that one imagined audience in particular cared about the epigraphical manifestations of these actions, states, and values was important for the generation of these monuments, and also for their eventual disappearance. For this most important imagined audience—and one of the most active participants in the system—was the emperor, and the first emperor, Augustus, was the man most important in shaping and launching this Roman "epigraphical habit."

THE EMPEROR AS EPIGRAPHICAL AUDIENCE AND ACTOR

The emperor himself was the quintessential imagined or symbolic audience in the Roman Empire, receiving toasts and libations as well as other acts of cult, dedications, oaths in his name, and sworn professions of loyalty.[39] The emperor

38. Reynolds 1982: 36–37.
39. Toasts, Hopkins 1978: 202; imperial cult, e.g., Lendon 1997: 166–72 (on the offering of cult to one who might never know); see also Ando 2000: 134–38 and 168–74, on the

came to be thought of as watching events through the eyes of his statues,[40] and of him it might be believed, no matter how implausibly, that he cared about each and every person in the Roman Empire.[41] If inscriptions communicated not only out but very often up, the inscriber's eye could well be imagined to swivel, hopefully, all the way up, to the approving presence at the top of society.[42] The emperor was not only an imagined endorser of the qualities conveyed by monumental epigraphy, he was the participant in the system of monumental epigraphy whose participation most affected what others did. The emperor's virtues overlapped with those praised in others, the emperor's patronage of cities sparked imitation by senators and equestrians as well as prospective honors to the emperor from city elites, and the emperor's ideology of unqualified success and benevolent (while steeply hierarchical) social relations was displayed in his monuments and repeated through the mass of individual monuments throughout the Roman Empire.[43] Emperors bestrode and anchored this epigraphical system, their public image and their Roman world to a great extent entwined in, and created by, it.

As befitted their rank at the very top, emperors received and they gave. Each received innumerable forms of inscribed dedications and honors throughout the Roman world, from individuals and from groups.[44] Each gave, for like good fathers and good patrons, most planned funerary monuments for their families and dependents,[45] and all saw to it that others were honored in turn, or granted benefactions and buildings to cities and individuals in need, benefactions that they announced themselves, or that were ecstatically received and memorialized by the

---

significance of (real and imagined) "dialogues" between emperor and people. Oaths, Herrmann 1968: 90–129 and Ando 2000: 359–62.

40. Statues, Hopkins 1978: 223–24 and Liertz 1998: 203–4; and their ubiquity, Ando 2000: 232–45.

41. Caring for each, Hopkins 1978: 221–23; Millar 1977: 7–12, 465–516; Corbier 2006: 32–33.

42. As Beard (1998: 98–99), for example, suggests for inscribed religious records.

43. Virtues overlapping, Forbis 1996: 93 (*munificentia, liberalitas, fides, pietas, honos, aequitas, iustitia, providentia, virtus*, among others—and the virtues of generous abundance in particular), and cf. Noreña 2001 (esp. *liberalitas*). City patronage, all but one case outside Italy by emperor and his family date to the Augustan period, but thereafter senators and equestrians (esp. in Italy and Africa) accept this honorable role, Eilers 2002: 170–71, 284–86 (emperors), 287–92 (senators); city elites give statues "in appreciation and anticipation of imperial benefaction," Høtje 2005: 187. Ideology, e.g., Alföldy 2003 (monuments of emperors), Zimmer 1992: 313 (on individual and public reflections of this ideology); Devijver 1996: 152 (epigraphical responses to the emperor that make clear his omnipresence and his role as "realizer of the Roman social order"); Revell 2009: 80–109. Styles in honoring individuals, like having laudatory epithets that precede the name, begin with emperors (Caracalla) and are picked up in honors to individuals fifty years later (Gordian and Philip), Salomies 1994: 80–81.

44. Revell 2009: 95–96 (with further references).

45. See Davies 2000; von Hesberg and Panciera 1994 (the mausoleum of Augustus).

recipient.[46] Imperial letters, a courteous form of address that could (quite spuriously) imply equality,[47] were particularly treasured and inscribed. Here content was less important than the fact of the letter itself, as the mausoleum of Opramoas of Rhodiapolis, in Lycia (on the south coast of Turkey), shows. This monument, in the theater area of this hilltop town, was covered with documents: thirty-two decrees of the provincial council of Lycia honoring Opramoas for his benefactions, twenty-five letters of the governor of Lycia honoring him for the same, one letter of a procurator, and twelve imperial letters, all of them brief acknowledgments of the 'duly noted' type.[48] The mere fact that the emperor 'noticed' Opramoas and his philanthropy was something to be proud of, and remembered.[49]

As this example demonstrates, although emperors do often enjoin that their edicts (and at times also *senatusconsulta*) be widely published and can (somewhat more rarely) specifically require their inscription, most of the inscribed versions of imperial communications we have are the result of civic or personal initiatives taken to prove connection, privilege, and honor.[50] So, although an imperial communication was a written gift handed *down*, its stone acknowledgment was the response to it, inscribed *out* and *up*. The emperors in this and many similar ways became the most connected of any party in this empire-wide communicative system, tethered to their subjects by innumerable hopeful and grateful inscriptions reaching up to them, and in turn reaching down to grant benefactions, even the simplest ones of a letter. The emperors' inscribed actions are always successful, and their participation in the system an endorsement of its stable and elite nature that invited others to join in.

The memories the epigraphy of emperors creates are political and communal, the history of an empire preserved and publicized for present and future. Imperial relationships and imperial achievements were even embedded in imperial names themselves, with their multiple *nomina* and filiations, and their triumphal *cognomina*.[51] Specific achievements could be retrospectively shaped and inscribed, most famously under the first emperor, who not only summarized his own achievements in his inscribed *Res Gestae*, but also inscribed, or re-inscribed, the list of Roman consuls and *triumphatores* from the beginning of the republic and filled his own

---

46. On imperial building-inscriptions (and imperial self-representation through them), see Horster 2001 (the actions of the empire's greatest patron and richest man, 12 and 250), with Alföldy 2002a and 2002b.

47. Millar 1977: 215–28.

48. *TAM* II 905, best read in Kokkinia (2000). The imperial titulature in the letters (of Antoninus Pius), Kokkinia nos. 39–43, 45, 47–52, takes up more space than the contents of the letter itself.

49. Devijver (1996: 123–28), *euergesia* in *poleis* of Asia (like Rhodiapolis; or, in his case, Sagalassos) is local but also focused on loyalty to the emperor, to the Roman social order, and to the connections of patronage that linked locals to Rome and the reward of Roman citizenship.

50. Eck 1997c; Eck 2000: 269–71.

51. See, e.g., Schmidt 2004: 91–95; Lassère 2005: 2, 591–98.

forum in Rome with statues and inscriptions to heroes of the republic chosen specifically by him.[52] History, honor, and inscribed monuments were to inspire future
generations—not to imperial power, but to greatness within an imperial world. So
Augustus' *Res Gestae* stated that he himself "left behind for those who come after me
examples of many things, which should be imitated"; so Tiberius' inscribed honors to Germanicus also specifically insisted that they were to be "useful," to inspire
imitation of the great prince; so Claudius' honors for his freedman Pallas similarly insisted that they were to inspire other imperial servants to follow Pallas' loyal
path.[53] Appropriate imitation by appropriate persons was intended; the empire's
hierarchical social relations were reinforced even through inscribed memory, and
announced and buttressed by the power of imperial name and voice. The god Mars
was impressed by Augustus' forum, wrote Ovid, but thought the achievement even
greater after he read the inscription on the temple with Augustus' name on it:[54] the
name 'powered up' the magnificent complex, as it must have every place it appeared.
In the complex communicative system that was the Roman epigraphy of the early
and high empire, the emperor was naturally its powerful center, its foundation and
its pinnacle, an animating participant and a sensed, or hoped-for, audience; and this
system, this epigraphic habit, began with Augustus, the first of them.

THE EPIGRAPHIC HABIT

Many components of this communicative system were in place before the first
emperor, yet the habit of inscribing does not really begin to become widespread
in the West—marked by its use either at many different levels of society or in significant numbers—until the time of Augustus.[55] This is not a coincidence. The first
princeps used, and drew attention to, inscriptions (as well as many other cultural
forms) in interlocking ways that no famous or powerful predecessor had: Géza

52. A hugely examined topic; see (e.g.) Lassère 2005: 2, 848–52 (*fasti*), Niquet 2003: 159–
60; Spannagel 1999 (Augustan forum); on the revision of history and the theme of Augustan
victory across media, Roddaz 2005: 36–42.

53. Augustus, *RG* 8.5 (*ipse multarum rerum exempla imitanda posteris tradidi*), and
Yavetz (1984: 16–20) argued that the *RG* was indeed directed at the young; Germanicus,
Crawford 1996: 1, 517–18, lines 16–17 ([529]); Pallas, Plin. *Ep.* 8. 6. 13 (quoting the inscribed
decree). The Roman senate also inscribed for the sake of *memoria*, e.g., the *senatusconsultum*
and other edicts about the Secular Games of 17 BC, *CIL* VI 32323 line 59, *ad conservandam
memoriam* ("in order to preserve the memory").

54. Ov. *Fast.* 5. 567–68: *Spectat et Augusto praetextum nomine templum,* | *et visum lecto
Caesare maius opus.*

55. Gordon and Reynolds (2003: 219–20) argue that "an epigraphic culture...was firmly
established in Italy well before the Principate": from the second and first centuries BC, 1456
inscriptions survive from Republican Rome, Latium, and Campania, 1525 from the rest of

Alföldy therefore characterized Augustus as "not just father of the fatherland [*pater patriae*], but father of Roman epigraphy, at least the most important creator of the 'epigraphic culture' of the Roman imperial period."[56] Alföldy highlighted the changes Augustus effected in a variety of different types of inscription (like gilded letters in building inscriptions), as well as the new ubiquity of the imperial name.[57] Particularly significant were the many honorific statues, arches, and (with them) inscriptions Augustus had indicated that he wished to receive, which he then also received from a far wider circle of people than any previous recipient of honors had enjoyed—from, among others, sitting Roman magistrates and, for the first time, decurions of cities.[58] The consequence was, as Andrew Wallace-Hadrill has noted, that Augustus symbolically "associate[d] aristocratic power with the social structure. Civility"—*civilitas*, the word for acting as if one were a citizen among fellow citizens—"both reinforced the social hierarchy by demonstrating imperial respect for it, and strengthened the autocracy by linking it with the social structure...to be honored in the same coin as his subjects ensured that the currency retained its value."[59] He also built for himself a magnificent mausoleum, in front of which stood his *Res Gestae* inscribed on bronze, and in which were found inscriptions identifying the many members of his family buried there, as well as an inscription noting that the senate had in his eighth consulship voted him the shield inscribed with his four virtues.[60] By shaping his own image in these and other ways, Augustus not only decreed a consistent (and positive) memory of himself and his stupendous achievements, but also made others active agents in its creation and perpetuation, and

---

Italy. Yet a crude average of seven inscriptions per year is qualitatively not the same as a crude average of 1200 inscriptions per year throughout an expanded empire; and republican inscriptions do not consistently show the patterns and qualities explored in "Monumental Inscriptions as a Communicative System," above.

56. Alföldy 1991: 322.

57. Alföldy 1991: 293–99; Niquet 2003: 150 n. 41 (on the *princeps bonus* and building inscriptions), 156–62; Alföldy 2003 (showing the impact of Augustan innovations on the epigraphy of later emperors).

58. Because a law of 44 BC (the *lex Rufrena*, "doubtless expressing the future Augustus' wish") required all Italian cities to honor the deified Julius Caesar with a statue (and an inscription), Alföldy (1991: 305–7) argued that this marks the moment when it became clear that Augustus himself also wished to be honored; a flood of honorific inscriptions for Augustus and his family followed, couched in terms calculated to please him. Wider group, Alföldy 1991: 310–12; arches, Wallace-Hadrill 1990: 146 (emphasizing that now, senate and people start dedicating arches to emperors, whereas republican aristocrats had done this for themselves).

59. Wallace-Hadrill 1982: 47; he later argued (1990: 157–69) that Augustus introduced not the fact of honorific inscriptions, but the (Greek) 'system' of honorific inscriptions to Rome, which was a restriction on the republican tradition of *self*-assertion; in (2003: 194–206) he traced the consequences of imperial *civilitas* ("a social pact of mutual respect," 199) in imperial actions toward and in the city of Rome. See also Peachin 2006: 149–52.

60. For the inscriptions in the Augustan mausoleum, von Hesberg and Panciera 1994: 88–175; a copy of the *clupeum*-inscription was also found at Arles, *AE* 1952, 165 = 1955, 82.

strengthened his own position and the elite-dominated vision of social relations. The inhabitants of the Roman Empire were to honor, and remember, Augustus and his achievements as *he* wished; he desired, and they then constructed, the backbone of the socially appropriate 'system' that would constitute the 'monumental' epigraphic habit of the Roman Empire.

Thus, as noted at the beginning of this essay, "Rome and the cities of the empire filled with inscriptions, either those the emperor had erected or those that were erected in his honor"—and other inscriptions, too, multiplied in imitation during and after Augustus' time.[61] That this change so clearly begins with Augustus shows that inscribing, both in its details and in its totality, was an historical as well as cultural phenomenon; and the historical course of this imperial "epigraphic habit," as Ramsay MacMullen first characterized it in 1982, was to grow exponentially and then fall dramatically, peaking in the late second and early third centuries AD.[62]

No one explanation of this overall historical pattern of inscribing has been able to win widespread acceptance. That the explosion of inscribing was driven, for example, by "the expansion of society"—as a reaction to the spread of a "new Roman order" that was "a dynamic system in which the places of individuals were less fixed than before," encouraging them to *fix* their place in stone—is a speculation that has won adherents, although a reversing change in the third century AD that would account for the dramatic fall-off in inscriptions is harder to identify within the parameters of this explanation, especially given that *anxiety* over fixing place and position is identified as the key motivation for inscribing, and there is no reason why anxiety would be any lower in the third century.[63] A second suggestion has been to index epigraphical production to the rise and fall of cities, and especially to attribute the fall-off to the declining political and economic health of many cities in the third century AD (and with it, or causing it, their apparent inability to attract

---

61. Alföldy 1991: 321; in (1997: 301–2), Alföldy argued for the imitation of imperial largesse by provincials; in (2004a: 144) he argued that formulaic epitaphs and dedications show direct imitation of elite practice by the "inferior classes," and the internalization of appropriate elite values and emotions like *pietas* and *sanctitas*; Corbier (2006: 29–32) notes imitation of other imperial forms, like *fasti* and calendars; cf. Gordon and Reynolds (2003: 229), "the asymmetry thus established [by imperial benefaction], and continually re-affirmed, serves as a model for the dependent asymmetries lower down the socio-political hierarchy." Outside Italy, the agents of imitation and the spread of Roman epigraphy were Roman colonists (Edmondson 2002: 46, Lusitania in the Julio-Claudian period) and local rulers, senators, and equestrians with patronage ties to Rome (Häussler 2002: 73, Cisalpine Gaul).

62. MacMullen 1982, depending in part on the chart of Mrozek 1973 (which may overcount Severan inscriptions, Eilers 2002: 167–68, but not so dramatically as to undercut the overall observation).

63. Woolf 1996 (quotation at 34); at (38–39) he himself notes some problems explaining what happens in the third century; warnings about misdiagnosing "anxiety" and the way its timing does not correspond to the drop in the epigraphic habit in Pleket 1999: 83–84.

as many patrons as they once had).[64] Attention has, however, necessarily focused most on epitaphs in understanding the epigraphic habit,[65] no doubt because they constitute, along with votives, the bulk of all inscriptions. Since epitaphs cannot *in principle* stand in for all inscriptions, however, it is probably best to think of the curve, the epigraphical distribution of all different types of monumental inscriptions over time, as the aggregate of the rise and fall of a number of different but related 'habits,'[66] the flicker of separate flames along a log that roar into a single great pennant of fire at the end of the second century AD.

Regarding epitaphs, though: I argued in 1990 that pride in newly acquired Roman status and in the exercise of the rights of testation and of the obligations of inheritance under Roman law by new Roman citizens drove the sharp rise in the production of epitaphs in the western provinces in the second half of the second century. This pride (and the high number of inscriptions) dissipated in the generation after the *Constitutio Antoniniana* of AD 212, for once almost everyone had citizenship it was no longer as exciting or necessary to display its privileges.[67] This argument, despite some complaint,[68] has at its core a durable observation, since a similar dynamic of announced status improvement and self-fashioning display can be seen motivating other (non-provincial) 'epigraphic habits.' For example: one group strongly over-represented in the funerary epigraphy of Rome, Italy, and indeed the Roman West is freedmen.[69] Why? In first-century AD Pompeii a contrast is helpful. There, first-generation freedmen and the first generation of their free children were competitive monument-builders and commemorators, while elites were withdrawing from ostentatious tomb building.[70] These freed were much more

64. Mrozek (1973: 117) had first pointed out the possible connection to the social and economic life of cities; Millar (1983: 124) noted the spread of public inscriptions with urbanization; and the relationship between cities and dedications of statues to the emperors is particularly marked, Høtje 2005: 103–8. Liebeschuetz (2001: 29–43 and 74–95) looked at the decline of cities, and (at 11–19) the decline of the epigraphic habit; Witschel (2006: 368–70) doubts that civic decline caused decline in civic inscriptions.

65. See Niquet 2003: 146–47 nn. 12–14, 156–57 nn. 89–84, and Alföldy 2004b: 238–39 n. 79 for lengthy footnotes listing work on the 'epigraphic habit' to 2003.

66. Bodel 2001: 7; Eilers 2002: 167; Mouritsen 2005: 62–63.

67. Meyer 1990.

68. Cherry 1995: 149–50, complaining especially that epitaphs cannot be exactly dated. Edmondson (2002: 47) notes the increase in numbers of funerary inscriptions by new citizens in Emerita after that city was granted municipal status in the Flavian period, exactly the phenomenon I note but a century or so earlier.

69. Taylor 1961; Eck 1988. Note also a preponderance of freedmen (two-thirds of all inscribers) in Narbonne, in Gaul (Woolf 1998: 98–100)—"and all over the Latin West" (100).

70. Elite burials between AD 36 and AD 79 become less visible, perhaps because family members were buried in group tombs already constructed, perhaps because families were burying on their country estates, or perhaps because the elite espoused an "ideal of funerary restraint" and concentrated epigraphic monuments to their own distinction, and competition, in Pompeii's forum, see Eck 1992: 371–72; Mouritsen 2005: 45–54.

aware of their (new) status, much more determined to advertise their worth and contribution, and much more likely to build functional tomb enclosures for family members as well. Their monuments convey both a sense of where they think they belong—among the worthy citizens of their city—and a clear sense of what their new Roman citizen rights are—to testation and inheritance, property ownership, and, above all, to family, which in slavery they could neither legally acknowledge, nor enjoy without fear, nor always mourn. Yet when the transition is made away from the memory of slavery, the epigraphy vanishes as well: after one generation of epigraphic visibility, the freeborn descendants disappear.[71] As with second-century provincials who came new into Roman citizenship but not by the hard and degrading path of slavery, once the memory of the past and the novelty of the present wear off, the 'epitaphic' habit drops off.

Studies of epitaphs still *in situ* in the great extramural cemeteries of the city of Rome, mostly (also) of freed and some free, show a variation on this theme: communal 'family' tombs with more buried than memorialized, yes; close family members memorialized and mourned, yes; but strong ties that reach beyond the biological and involve patrons instead are also frequently asserted in epitaphs.[72] In contrast to Pompeii, the ruling elite of Rome—the senators—never cede pride of place in the city's cemeteries to freedmen, although their funerary monuments also become self-consciously modest and functional over the first and second centuries.[73] Control of the forum, the center of the city, and the Field of Mars senators had by necessity relinquished to the emperors, for whom these areas were the prime locations for imperial self-representation and imperial versions of the historical, communal memory of Rome—and for the imperial gift of honorific commemoration to a select and favored few. Perhaps that is why the epigraphic honors paid to imperial senators in Rome are more often found in houses, gardens, and suburban villas than in the city's public spaces,[74] and why senatorial families never abandoned the city's cemeteries entirely.

Within these variations there are some important common themes. Although different groups had their own experiences that would affect "how...individual[s] related to the surrounding community," as well as their own "sense of audience," and

---

71. Mouritsen 2005: 55–63; freedmen are similarly prominent (numerically; but also with large or eye-catching monuments and sculpture) in Aquileia, Mainz, and Nîmes, Hope 2001: 29–36, 91.

72. More buried than commemorated, Eck 1987 and 1988 (second century AD); more communal (with individual niches or graves inside), noted by Eck 1997a: 106; patronage ties, Nielsen 1996 and 1997: 173 (the fourth most common relationship mentioned).

73. Eck 1984: 148 (smaller size at first attributed to imperial restrictions); 1987: 80 n. 111 (some *cursus* inscriptions even on insides of mausolea); 1997a; 1998 (size of altars correlates with status and, presumably, income); and 2001: 200 (despite decline in grave-plot size, senatorial funerary *tituli* are larger than those of other social ranks); see also Mouritsen 2005: 59 n. 105.

74. Eck 1992: 363–66, 375; Alföldy 2001 (noting that emperors rewarded specific senators with honorific statues in public spaces—but this space was the emperor's to control).

thus groups to which they wished, especially, to assert a connection,[75] the freed were prominent in most cemeteries studied. Moreover, many of the same factors seem to have been in play. In the funerary epigraphy of the cities of the Roman Empire, status (and rights), honors (and distinction), connections (and appropriate emotions), as well as a sense that others cared about these qualities, combined in various ways to create multiple patterns that nonetheless belong in what is recognizably the same mental universe: funerary epigraphy that proclaimed "social differentiation" and "cultural integration" at the same time.[76]

A study of epitaphs in Roman Britain, where the epigraphy derives more from army encampments than cities and where votive altars actually outnumber epitaphs,[77] has found that, here too, the municipal elite evinced no particular interest in commemorative display. Rather, it was legionary soldiers, auxiliaries, and their women who favored epitaphs as a form of self-representation: the legionaries who claimed "initial superiority" in the new province, the foreign auxiliaries who claimed the Roman citizenship they wished they had had, and the women who claimed the status of legal wife they wished they had enjoyed—all those who had earned themselves a place in Britannia and their new Roman community, and wished to assert what they had achieved and more.[78] 'Fringe' groups elsewhere, making claims of belonging, are also prominent in epitaphs.[79] Those whose families had long ago crossed the most difficult social divides—freedom and citizenship—will (over the generations) advertise these aspects of their standing with less assiduousness, but will emphasize, if they inscribe, different types of belonging instead. Among legionary rather than auxiliary soldiers in Mainz, for example, commemorations stress citizenship (through the Roman name), but especially career distinctions—placing a man within the military community in very standardized language[80]—and connections, whether with heirs, patrons, or

75. Relating to surrounding community, Hope 2001: 91; "sense of audience," MacMullen 1982: 246.

76. Van Nijf 1997: 38; he adds that funerary monuments in general "speak a language of belonging," and when undertaken by the *plebs media* "us[e] or emulat[e] the symbolic language of the élite."

77. Biró 1975: 42.

78. See Mann 1985: 206 (the first to observe that "the epigraphic record from the military zone reflects incomers rather than the local population"); developed by Hope 1997, who also argues that monuments became less necessary as the army became known in British life, as the social distance between legionary and auxiliary narrowed, and when soldiers were allowed lawfully to marry (255, 258). For soldiers' epigraphy preceding that of locals and then becoming less common, see also Häussler 1993: 63 (northern Gaul). Hope also emphasized (2000a: 179–81 and 2001: 43) that at Mainz too, "symbols and attributes of status seem to have been particularly significant to members of the auxiliary units."

79. Hope 2000b (gladiators); Hope 2001 (Aquileia, Mainz, Nimes); Edmondson et al. 2001: 77–94 (Emerita: freedmen, immigrants, slaves, alumni); Woolf (1996: 32–33) and Häussler (1998: 45) emphasize a more literal sense of "having arrived," associating Latin funerary epigraphy with "a very Roman phenomenon, namely mobility" (45).

80. Hope 2001: 39.

friends.[81] So whether provincial, freed, auxiliary, or female, in certain contexts (especially cities and army camps) an improvement in standing, or a desire to assert it, or a claim to belong—inflected in different ways depending on group history and audience—was worth commemorating. For others, already free or citizen or with notable accomplishments to their credit, associations with other groups and achievements can be stressed instead. Social prestige and identity are what epigraphy, especially funerary epigraphy, conveyed: the epigraphy of individuals is a *personal* response to the world they live in and the ways they wish to be seen.[82] And, as everywhere, it was always good news—achievement, belonging, community, connection—that was inscribed.

Epitaphs were numerically the most important inscriptions, but votives were significant too. Contributing also to the rise in sheer numbers of inscriptions in the second part of the second century AD and the first decades of the third is the increasing propensity of individuals to erect not just tombstones, but also dedications (like altars) to gods and emperors, as cities and villages also did.[83] Sanctuaries were "a new social arena in which, for the first time, large groups from the lower social classes seize[d] upon the votive ritual to advertise their *pietas* by means of a lasting votive monument, and thus preserve for posterity the memory of their personal achievements and the merits of the god," concludes an assessment of an explosion of votive inscriptions between AD 180 and 230.[84] In the provinces, votives are also heavily associated with imperial cult, whose dedicators seem to see vowing as a conscious act of loyalty "to the maintenance of a political system in which

81. In the Greek East epigraphically attested membership in *collegia* becomes visible in the second century AD, a new element of self-identification conveyed by "imitat[ing] the epigraphic forms of the élite," Van Nijf 1997: 27–28, 247.

82. Quotation, Alföldy 1995: 130 (on Augustan Spain, but as a general principle); also Eck 1997c: 380.

83. Epitaphs and votives conforming to the curve in Gaul, Woolf 1998: 96–97; in Africa, Duncan-Jones 1982: 351–52 (votives to the emperors); in Moesia, Mrozewicz 1999: 464–69 (those from individuals disappear mid-third century, and when they re-appear, are from imperial officials and soldiers); focus on individual altars, Spickermann 2003: 14 and 16–17 (1034 of 1774 dedicated objects from Upper Germany), with a boom AD 180–230 (Spickermann 2003: 365), and see Haensch 2007: 183–85 for other sites as well; in Spain, dedications associated with imperial cult are put up by many individuals in the first and second centuries, but the proportion of individuals as dedicators decreases in the third, when only 13% are erected by individuals, Étienne 1974: 503. Dedications of the more expensive imperial statues, on the other hand, peak under Hadrian and then again under Commodus and Severus, because of the number of statues erected by communities, Høtje 2005: 187, 193–94.

84. Derks 1998: 90, examining 2000 votives (1400 from Lower Germany, 83); other cult sites with a contemporary explosion of inscribed stone objects listed by Haensch 2007: 183; see also Alföldy 1989: 81–84 (fall-off after AD 240); Spickermann 2003: 365 (shift from funerary epigraphy *to* votives by non-elite provincials in the second century); and Witschel 1999: 76–77 n. 90.

they have their proper place."[85] These votives, too, are assertions of self-fashioning connection, as the details given about the individual dedicators also suggest.[86] In the second and early third centuries, individuals participated in individual acts of inscribed reverence as never before—and in Roman (and Latin) terms, again expressing social prestige and identity, and reaching upward within a clearly Roman, and imperial, hierarchy.

All this is, at one level, "the expansion of Roman society." But rather than emphasizing an unsettling degree of disguised anxiety over "insecurities engendered by the pace and nature of social upheavals" in Roman society,[87] this epigraphy, by its use of Latin, by the many social distinctions drawn and advertised,[88] by the verbal and chronological patterns it settles into, by the "ethical continuity" assumed by its trumpeting of standard and exemplary virtues,[89] and by its astounding longevity, emphasizes the stability, the mental conformity, and the normative weight of the world so many of these people were so proud of joining. Those who inscribed, whether commemorating or commemorated, honoring or honored, chose in their epigraphy to endorse a vision of social relations that *was* deferential, tranquil, predictable, and supportive; by them, status and belonging *were* highly valued; and for them, legal proprieties *were* a privilege to be exercised, just as emotions were acceptable when they were appropriately expressed, often through abbreviated formulae. The emperors' own epigraphy anchored their system, a system whose values and dynamic Augustus himself had enunciated. *Civilitas*, the supremely imperial quality that included concern and interest for fellow citizens of all social ranks, came to be even more important and stressed in the second century,[90] and the results may well be epigraphical as well as metaphorical, as more and more responded to the proffered lure of belonging and mattering, of respect and connection. The joiners (and their actions were voluntary) came to the epigraphy of empire at different times and by different paths through thickets of different experiences, communities, and identities, but come to it, and embrace it, they did. Connection—of whatever sort—to Roman society and the Roman order was what was most desirable, and was demonstrated by assertions of membership in an epigraphical community, or even communities, whose audiences, expressions, and values were admired, and perceived not to change.

The dramatic drop-off in inscribing in the third century was more marked in the municipal (building, philanthropic foundations, administration) and private

85. Gordon and Reynolds 2003: 262, summarizing Liertz 1998, who deduces standardized loyalty-declarations not least from an abbreviation *in h.d.d.* (*in honorem domus divinae*, 112–13).

86. Eck 1989: 34–39.

87. Woolf 1996: 33–34.

88. Woolf 1996: 29 (only words were "precise enough to convey the complex names and relationships that defined the identity of the individual Roman"); Giorcelli Bersani 2004: 17.

89. Roller 2004: 32–34.

90. Noreña 2001: 156 (a "larger, discursive shift that took place around the beginning of the second century"); Potter 2004: 60–62 (on Marcus Aurelius); Peachin 2006: 149–52.

(votives, epitaphs, freedmen) realms than it was in the realm of the army and the emperors' own epigraphy, and indeed Stanislaw Mrozek concluded in 1973 that it was in the third century that the habit of inscribing disappeared among the lower and middle levels of society.[91] If so, then this decline in the third century—geographically uneven, chronologically marked, but not quite the same, in nature or timing, everywhere[92]—should be a response to a number of different changes that were felt or perceived in towns and, especially, at the lower and middle levels of society. That is, circumstances changed, but the perception of, and response to, circumstances also changed, and for many towns and individuals, inscribing on stone was no longer seen as an appropriate method of communication. The third-century decline of cities as political entities and as the focus of euergetism is therefore an important historical change, but important too must be a concomitant change in the ways in which cities perceived that (remaining) benefactors wished to be honored, and whether cities (therefore) thought it appropriate to honor benefactors and construct a town's identity and history through epigraphy.[93]

For individuals erecting epitaphs and votives, the dramatic drop-off must reflect the same types of change: circumstantial—what actually happened to individuals, and their resources, in the unsettled third century—and how individuals perceived those changes. Perhaps the solid and unchanging Roman world of achievements and values to which one had wished to assert that one belonged was now, in the chaos

91. Municipal and private compared to army and emperor, Mrozek 1973: 117; also Mrozek 1998: 16–20, and Roueché 1989: xx. MacMullen (1982) broadened the database to include epitaphs, where the same dramatic third-century fall-off was visible, thus strengthening his claim that this was a *Roman* "epigraphic habit" because it comprised both public and private inscriptions. Lower- and middle-level disappearance, Mrozek 1973: 118.

92. Overall, Witschel 1999: 70–73; Borg and Witschel 2001: 50–78. For example: Africa produces more dated inscriptions than elsewhere in the third century, Mrozek 1988: 64, and civic inscriptions continue in Africa until the early fifth century, Lepelley 1979: 72–120 (building inscriptions, but with a sizable dip AD 235–276); a downturn in inscriptions in fora starts after Marcus Aurelius in Spain (Rodà 1999), and, overall (but in Latin inscriptions only), in Sicily (Prag 2002: 23); in the third quarter of the third century in Gallia Belgica, Wightman 1985: 163, and in the two provinces of Moesia, Mrozewicz 1999: 462–64, 472; inscriptions with a man's *cursus* (whether honorific or funerary) for the most part survive only in Italy after AD 284 (90/99), 64 of them from Rome, Delmaire 2005 (and Horster 1998: 51); epigraphical language grows more abstract, Mrozek 1994 (perhaps following a trend for the language of emperor's virtues to become more abstract, which begins in the second century, Wallace-Hadrill 1981: 312).

93. Although cities continue to honor provincial governors in late antiquity (Horster 1998: 51–54); Roueché (1989: xix) notes that even in Aphrodisias, a city with a continuous epigraphy across the third century, "the nature and function" of inscribing changed in mid-century. Economic decline itself not a sufficient answer, Witschel 1999: 65–66; Witschel (2006: 370–77) argues instead for a shift in the usage and meaning of city centers, a change in self-understanding on the part of civic elites, and a growth of specifically Christian euergetism, memorialized through mosaic inscriptions in the interiors of buildings.

of third-century events, changing too much, too dangerously, and too fast.[94] But at the same time individual monumental epigraphy of the imperial age should be not only about uniquely individual experiences and perceptions: the dramatic decline in monumental epigraphy must suggest some shared experience and some shared perception. In the first and second centuries, self-perceptions and self-fashioning had had an objective core, some successful Roman action or prestigious Roman achievement to convey, even while these various (but not limitless) definitions of Roman success also inspired a penumbra of imitating self-fashioning 'wannabees.'[95] Freedom and citizenship were especially prestigious accomplishments in the high empire. The *Constitutio Antoniniana* took much of the prestige out of the achievement of Roman citizenship after AD 212 for millions of people: this had to have a sizeable and numerically significant impact on the desire to inscribe and the perceived worth of inscribing, although examples of two generations' announcement of it in the East continue to appear after 212.[96] A fall in the monumental epigraphy of individuals, epitaphs and votives, should say something about what they experience, what they see, *and* what they have achieved, and it is when it is perceived that age-old, prideful achievements are no longer as valued as they were, just as when it is perceived that individuals may no longer have achieved, or can assert, belonging to a solid, stable, connected, hierarchical world, that some—many—may choose to invest their money elsewhere.[97] Because the erection of monuments is a voluntary action, perception of reception will always be important, but the qualities to be asserted have a basis in the realities of society and even in particular political events. There is probably no specific factor that can explain the decline of civic inscriptions

94. Suggested by MacMullen 1982: 246; Mrozek (1998: 18) argued for "the destruction of confidence in the state" in the mid-third century; Witschel (1999: 79) envisioned a longer-term shift of emphasis from stone inscription to "more temporary forms of representation" and a one-generation-long "feeling of insecurity" that created the gap in epigraphical production in the third quarter of the third century AD.

95. Khanoussi and Maurin 2002: 84 (from epitaphs at Dougga, deduce "l'adhésion presque totale des pérégrins à la culture romaine," but in psychological and cultural—not juridical—forms only); Häussler 1993: 65–67 (attempts of a "less Romanised stratum...to copy Latin names," purely Celtic names, and poor quality inscriptions correlate); Woolf 1998: 103 (adoption of Roman tombstone form without Roman names, although he suggests that this could be imitation of the local elite without "asserting or claiming a Roman identity").

96. Meyer 1990: 94 (on Thessalonica and Nicomedia), although the epigraphic curves in the eastern half of the empire are less clearly part of the Latin, Western phenomenon of rise and fall (see MacMullen 1986 and the observations of Pleket in *SEG* XL, 1654); Buraselis (2007: 94–120) tracks the number of new Aurelii, esp. in the East, after AD 212; Ratté and Smith (2004: 180–82) suggested a connection between the "arrival into Roman citizenship of large numbers of middle-level propertied families" (181) and an explosion of Aphrodisian sarcophagi after AD 212.

97. Even late-antique provincial governors received very few honorific inscriptions from members of their own staffs (who had contributed significantly to honorific inscriptions to such officials in the high empire), Horster 1998: 49–51.

as well as the *Constitutio Antoniniana* can explain the decline of epitaphs—even if that imperial action cannot explain everything, and even if it is (and always will be) difficult to prove correlations between general (and inexactly dated) cultural phenomena and specific, exactly dated events.

The stone monuments of individuals did not, however, start their march to numerical superiority on a whim. Augustus' interventions in the world of epigraphy involved his subjects in the world of stone honors, stone dedications, and stone imitations of imperial examples, giving each individual a role in a hierarchical Roman universe of which the emperor himself was a connected part, and reinforcing the idea that inscribing in certain socially appropriate ways was itself Roman and the correct way to behave. What was good enough for the emperor was good enough for his humblest subject. So perhaps imperial actions and attitudes in the crucial third century could also have had important effects on the emperor's audiences and their perceptions of the value of individual monumental inscriptions and the system they constituted, and help to explain the observable "paradigm change" away from inscribing in general.[98]

Changes in imperial attitudes are not, however, easy to document precisely. Nor are their consequences easy to prove, although attempts to read the imperial mind show close attention given to imperial actions.[99] The reign of Caracalla might provide a first turning point, however, a moment of blending of old attitudes and epigraphical system, and new. In announcing his gift of universal citizenship, Caracalla depicted himself as leading old and new citizens to the sanctuaries of the gods, thereby making a "suitable response" to the gods' greatness (τῇ μεγαλειότητι αὐτῶν τὸ ἱκανόν) and expanding the greatness of the Roman people; he also linked new citizens to himself in the most obvious of ways, by changing their names to include his own.[100] Thus, perhaps, the crowning moment of a series of actions that reinforced *civilitas* and the interconnections of a hierarchical society with the emperor its zenith—its supremely pious leader, and greatest patron, leading a majestic empire, many of whose inhabitants now received a gift that was not merely rhetorical. At the same time, however, Caracalla continued some of the centralizing trends initiated by his father—tightening the bonds between emperor and army, and increasingly leaving the administration of empire in the hands of an equestrian military leadership and 'bureaucracy'—that effectively buffered the emperor from his own (non-military) citizens, trends that only strengthened under the two young cousins, Elagabulus and Severus Alexander, who succeeded him.[101] The roots of the developed late-antique bureaucracy are to be found here, a bureaucracy that kept citizens away from the emperor.

98. Spickermann 2008: 317.

99. E.g., people tore down many statues of the praetorian prefect Plautianus after Severus ordered some statues of him melted down, for people assumed that Plautianus had fallen from imperial favor, Dio 75. 16. 2.

100. *P.Giss.* 40 col. 1 (*M.Chrest.* no. 377); see Potter 2004: 138–39 (with notes on the controversies) and Buraselis 2007: 1–13.

101. See Carrié and Rousselle 1999: 660–8; Potter 2004: 239–40, 258; Eich 2005: 352–90.

Deliberately undertaken changes in the emperor's self-presentation also kept citizens away from the emperor. Thus, although the overall number of statue bases honoring emperors declines with all other inscriptions, when their numbers revive in the reign of Diocletian,[102] the gap these honors announce, between honoring body and honoree, has widened. Emperors who had been *invictus* ("undefeated") or *invictissimus* ("most undefeated"), Commodus and Caracalla, become *ubique vincens* ("altogether and everywhere victorious"), Arcadius and Honorius, and other claims to ever-greater world domination become even more inflated in the fourth century.[103] In late-antique epigraphy the emperor's god-like qualities are emphasized, indeed triumphant; the last emperor called *civilis* was the atypical Julian, but before him the last so named was Severus Alexander. The apparent give-and-take of the earlier empire, the presentation of the citizen-emperor's power as embedded in the existing social structure, eroded over the third century, and a more absolute, and distant, relationship of ruler to subject, with officials standing between emperor and subject, eventually takes its place.[104]

Perhaps, therefore, it was as a result of a perception of this change too that individuals inscribed less: perhaps it became impossible to imagine the emperor as part of an epigraphic system that included small people, and with that failure it also became, or was perceived to become, less appropriate to participate in an epigraphic system at all. Without the emperor as its greatest imagined audience and actor, widespread faith in any system, and any imagined audience, collapsed, and the epigraphical realm became appreciably smaller. Emperors and members of the imperial family become more prominent in inscriptions in the later third and fourth centuries—proportionally more prominent overall, but they were also more often the recipients or agents of inscription.[105] This reflects other actions

102. Højte 2005: 17 (2300 inscribed statue bases to Augusti between Augustus and Commodus) and Alföldy 2003: 16 (2800 more thereafter [although many were no doubt Severan], including Caesares and Augusti); but Højte (2005: 194 n. 453) notes that in the third century there was radical change: "the system governing the erection of statues seems to have broken down in many places."

103. Alföldy 2003: 8–9.

104. Severus Alexander and Julian, Wallace-Hadrill 1982: 48; on the reworking of the *civilis* theme in late antiquity, Kelly 1998: 139–50 (and Julian's "often idiosyncratic" views on the nature and presentation of imperial power noted, 148); Potter 2004: 294–98. See also MacMullen 1976: 33: "...in the third century...the emperor's own image swells to fill the field of vision."

105. Witschel (1999: 71) characterizes late-antique (non-Christian) epigraphic culture as consisting of emperors' inscriptions, milestones (which he argues [Witschel 2002: 367–72] become honorific monuments to emperors in the fourth century), and a few honorific inscriptions for officials and building inscriptions; note that these honorific inscriptions are, starting in the third century, no longer formulaic, as they had been in the high empire, but rhetorical "and leave the impression of being unique in their expressions," Salomies 1994: 90 (and also Rouché 1989: xxii: "uniformity no longer seemed particularly desirable"). See Mrozek 1998: 13–15, 19 (emperors and members of imperial family increasingly receive lion's share of dedications in third century); Witschel (2006: 364, 383–85) notes only five honorific statue bases for non-imperial people from the province of Venetia and Histria after the mid-third century.

the emperors have taken, with consequences for cities and their epigraphy. So as the emperor asserts his more direct involvement in governance and benefaction, city patrons are no longer as useful as mediators and as honored by their appointment, and fewer of them are chosen (or accept) the honor and are epigraphically attested as having done so; municipal autonomy itself is undermined by Diocletian "in favor of central imperial control... so representatives of the emperor usurped the public spotlight;" inscriptions that praise and honor the emperors are mostly generated by a narrower circle of people, chiefly the emperor himself, imperial officials, and soldiers; and emperors decree the inscribing of their own edicts.[106] In the third century, in short, "the virtuous circle of direct and indirect honour broke down."[107] The patience to wait to be praised and honored and vowed to by others wore thin in a world in crisis, and the emperor and those close to him took up the job themselves.

The way in which the emperor was perceived, and the way in which the emperor participated in the epigraphical system that had situated and strengthened both him and the empire's social relations, changed over the third century. The emperor and his court then took up the direct projection of dazzling power through procession and court ritual rather than disguising imperial power's dangerous radiation behind the shield of others' apparently voluntary acts, and his elites followed suit.[108] He is so apparently powerful that little people are no longer fellow citizens, but merely subjects, and this attitude, while awe-inspiring, is not inscription-inspiring. The great epigraphic habit of the high empire was, in retrospect, a testament to the emperor's imagined accessibility within his timelessly powerful empire, both now gone. Those who had "gaped in stupefaction" at inscriptions and ancestral images in Augustus' triumviral days now gaped at glittering public performances of rich imperial grandeur, immobility, and inaccessibility.[109]

In the end, however, self-fashioning was a fashion and the 'epigraphic habit' was a habit: something that could go in and out of style, something that people got used to doing but to which they could also become unaccustomed. When interrupted,

106. City patrons, Eilers 2002: 172–81 ("the benefactor did not vanish but benefactors became less numerous," reflecting the "changing self-perception of the ruling class" as well, Pleket 1999: 85); municipal autonomy undermined, Forbis 1996: 7. Narrower circle: Horster 1998: 58 and Mrozewicz 1999: 468–72 (Moesia, where *miliaria* come to be especially well attested). Alföldy (1989: 84–92) argues that this narrower circle of dedicators is also responsible for a robust and continuous series of dedications to Jupiter, Mars, and Hercules in the Danube provinces over the third century, cult encouraged by the emperors through the themes of their coinage. Own edicts, Millar 1977: 257–58.

107. Gordon and Reynolds 2003: 238, summarizing Le Roux 2001: 51–52 on Baetica; Horster (1998: 51) notes that honorific inscriptions for late-antique provincial governors record chiefly ranks or magistracies that position the governor in relationship to the emperor.

108. Borg and Witschel 2001: 93–116.

109. The *stultus* (idiotic) populace *stupet in titulis et imaginibus*, Hor. Sat. 1. 6. 15–17 (37–36 BC); awestruck gaping at display in the late-antique period, Kelly 1998: 139–45.

habits do not necessarily return, even if some of the factors and conditions for them do, as seems to have been true in the fourth century. That century produced a numerically reduced, participant-constricted, rhetorically inflected, emperor-oriented version of the magnificent epigraphic habit of the high empire: grander but contracted and brittle, with no deep roots in the wider population, a locked rooftop garden rather than a great national park. In that century, one kind of monumental inscription, the Christian epitaph, became prevalent—but mentioned neither family nor commemorators nor achievements nor social status.[110] Christian epigraphy was a new habit, growing up amid the ancient and abandoned monuments of the past, and one that deliberately avoided the qualities of the old. It communicates, but to Christians and the Christian God—and not of social relations, or of the emperor who ruled those social relations, or of Rome.

SUGGESTED READING

Descriptive handbooks of epigraphy, like Schmidt 2004 and Lassère 2005, are the best places to start; there is no existing discussion of the 'system' of the epigraphy of the imperial age or a good up-to-date summary of opinions on the epigraphic habit.

BIBLIOGRAPHY

Alföldy, G. 1989. "Die Krise des Imperium Romanum und die Religion Roms." In W. Eck (ed.), *Religion und Gesellschaft in der römischen Kaiserzeit. Kolloqium zu Ehren von Friedrich Vittinghoff.* Cologne: Böhlau Verlag. 53–102.

———. 1991. "Augustus und die Inschriften: Tradition und Innovation. Die Geburt der imperialen Epigraphik." *Gymnasium. Zeitschrift für Kultur der Antike und humanistische Bildung* 98: 289–324.

———. 1995. "Die Entstehung der epigraphischen Kultur der Römer an der Levanteküste." In F. Beltrán Lloris (ed.), *Roma y el nacimento de la cultura epigráfica en occidente. Actas del Coloquio Roma y las primeras culturas epigráficas del occidente mediterráneo (siglos II a.E.–I d.E.) (Zaragoza, 4 a 6 de noviembre de 1992).* Zaragoza: Institución 'Fernando el Católico.' 121–37.

———. 1997. "Euergetismus und Epigraphik in der Augusteischen Zeit." In M. Christol and O. Masson (eds.), *Actes du Xᵉ Congrès international d'épigraphie grecque et latine, Nîmes, 4–9 octobre 1992.* Paris: Publications de la Sorbonne. 293–304.

110. Eck 1997a, 106; names in late-antique Aphrodisian epigraphy also rarely mention patronymics or other family members, Roueché 1989: xx; Witschel (2006: 377–79) notes the appearance of new 'Christian' virtues also.

————. 1999. "Il futuro dell'epigrafia." In S. Panciera (ed.), *XI Congresso Internazionale di Epigrafia Greca e Latina (Roma 18–24 settembre 1997), Atti I*. Rome: Edizioni Quasar. 87–102.

————. 2001. "Pietas immobilis erga principem und ihr Lohn: Öffentliche Ehrenmonumenta von Senatoren in Rom während der Frühen und Hohen Kaiserzeit." In G. Alföldy and S. Panciera (eds.), *Inschriftliche Denkmäler als Medien der Selbstdarstellung in der römischen Welt*. Stuttgart: Franz Steiner Verlag. 11–46.

————. 2002a. "Roms Kaiser als Bauherren." *Journal of Roman Archaeology* 15: 489–98.

————. 2002b. "Zu kaiserlichen Bauinschriften aus Italien." *Epigraphica* 64: 113–45.

————. 2003. "Die Repräsentation der kaiserlichen Macht in den Inschriften Roms und des Imperium Romanum." In L. de Blois, P. Erdkamp, O. Hekster, G. de Kleijn, and S. Mols (eds.), *The Representation and Perception of Roman Imperial Power. Proceedings of the Third Workshop of the International Network Impact of Empire (Roman Empire, c. 200 B.C.–A.D. 476), Netherlands Institute in Rome, March 20–23, 2002*. Amsterdam: J. C. Gieben. 3–19.

————. 2004a. "La Cultura epigráfica de los Romanos: la difusión de un medio de comunicación y su papel en la integración cultural." In F. Marco Simón, F. Pina Polo, J. Remesal Rodríguez (eds.), *Vivir en tierra extraña: emigración e integración cultural en el mundo antiguo. Actas de la reunión realizada en Zaragoza los días 2 y 3 de junio de 2003*. Barcelona: Publicacions Universitat de Barcelona. 137–49.

————. 2004b. "Theodor Mommsen und die römische Epigraphik aus der Sicht Hundert Jahre nach seinem Tod." *Epigraphica* 66: 217–45.

————. 2005. "Inschriften und Biographie in der römischen Welt." In K. Vössing (ed.), *Biographie und Prosopographie. Internationales Kolloquium zum 65. Geburtstag von Prof. Dr. Anthony R. Birley, 28. September 2002, Schloss Mickeln, Düsseldorf*. Stuttgart: Franz Steiner Verlag. 29–52.

Ando, C. 2000. *Imperial Ideology and Provincial Loyalty in the Roman Empire*. Berkeley: University of California Press.

Avi-Yonah, M. 1940. *Abbreviations in Greek Inscriptions (The Near East 200 B.C.–A.D. 1100)*. Jerusalem: Quarterly of the Department of Antiquities of Jerusalem.

Barrett, J. C. 1993. "Chronologies of Remembrance: The Interpretation of Some Roman Inscriptions." *World Archaeology* 25: 236–47.

Beard, M. 1998. "Documenting Roman Religion." In C. Moatti (ed.), *La Mémoire perdue. Recherches sur l'administration romaine. Actes de la seconde table ronde organisé sur les archives dans l'histoire romaine*. Rome: École française de Rome. 75–101.

Biró, M. 1975. "The Inscriptions of Roman Britain." *Acta Archaeologica Academiae Scientiarum Hungaricae* 27: 13–58.

Bodel, J. 2001. "Epigraphy and the Ancient Historian." In J. Bodel (ed.), *Epigraphic Evidence. Ancient History from Inscriptions*. London: Routledge. 1–56.

Borg, B., and C. Witschel. 2001. "Veränderungen in Repräsentationsverhalten der römischen Eliten während des 3. Jhs. n. Chr." In G. Alföldy and S. Panciera (eds.), *Inschriftliche Denkmäler als Medien der Selbstdarstellung in der römischen Welt*. Stuttgart: Franz Steiner Verlag. 47–120.

Buraselis, K. 2007. *ΘΕΙΑ ΔΩΡΕΑ. Das göttlich-kaiserliche Geschenk. Studien zur Politik der Severer und zur Constitutio Antoniniana*. Vienna: Verlag der Österreichischen Akademie der Wissenschaften.

Carrié, J.-M., and A. Rousselle. 1999. *L'Empire romain en mutation des Sévères à Constantin 192–337*. Paris: Éditions du Seuil.

Champlin, E. 1991. *Final Judgments. Duty and Emotions in Roman Wills 200 B.C.–A.D. 250*. Berkeley: University of California Press.

Chaniotis, A. 2003. "The Perception of Imperial Power in Aphrodisias: The Epigraphic Evidence." In L. de Blois, P. Erdkamp, O. Hekster, G. de Kleijn, and S. Mols (eds.), *The Representation and Perception of Roman Imperial Power. Proceedings of the Third Workshop of the International Network Impact of Empire (Roman Empire, c. 200 B.C.–A.D. 476), Netherlands Institute in Rome, March 20–23, 2002.* Amsterdam: J. C. Gieben. 250–60.

———. 2009. "Travelling Memories in the Hellenistic World." In R. Hunter and I. Rutherford (eds.), *Wandering Poets in Ancient Greek Culture: Travel, Locality, and Panhellenism.* Cambridge: Cambridge University Press. 249–69.

Cherry, D. 1995. "Refiguring the Ancient Epigraphic Habit." *Ancient History Bulletin* 9: 143–56.

Corbier, M. 2006. *Donner à voir, donner à lire. Mémoire et communication dans la Rome ancienne.* Paris: CNRS Éditions.

Crawford, M. (ed.). 1996. *Roman Statutes.* London: Institute of Classical Studies.

———. 1998. "How to Create a *Municipium*: Rome and Italy after the Social War." In M. Austin, J. Herries, and C. Smith (eds.), Modus Operandi: *Essays in Honour of Geoffrey Rickman.* London: Institute of Classical Studies. 31–46.

Davies, P. J. E. 2000. *Death and the Emperor. Roman Imperial Funerary Monuments from Augustus to Marcus Aurelius.* Cambridge: Cambridge University Press.

de Brestian, S. 2008. "Interrogating the Dead. Funerary Inscriptions in Northern Iberia." In R. Häussler (ed.), *Romanisation et épigraphie. Études interdisciplinaires sur l'acculturation et l'identité dans l'Empire romain.* Montagnac: Éditions Monique Margail. 267–79.

Delmaire, R. 2005. "Un genre en voie de disparition: les cursus épigraphiques au Bas-Empire." In J. Desmulliez and C. Hoët-Van Cauwenberghe (eds.), *Le Monde romain à travers l'épigraphie: Méthode et pratiques. Actes du XXIVᵉ Colloque International de Lille (8–10 novembre 2001).* Lille: Presses de l'Université Charles-de-Gaulle-Lille. 247–70.

Derks, T. 1998. *Gods, Temples and Ritual Practices. The Transformation of Religious Ideas and Values in Roman Gaul.* Amsterdam: Amsterdam University Press.

Devijver, H. 1996. "Local Elite, Equestrians and Senators: A Social History of Roman Sagalassos." *Ancient Society* 27: 105–62.

Duncan-Jones, R. 1982. *The Economy of the Roman Empire: Quantitative Studies.* 2nd ed. Cambridge: Cambridge University Press.

Eck, W. 1984. "Senatorial Self-Representation: Developments in the Augustan Period." In F. Millar and E. Segal (eds.), *Caesar Augustus: Seven Aspects.* Oxford: Clarendon Press. 129–67.

———. 1987. "Römische Grabinschriften. Aussageabsicht und Aussagefähigkeit im funerären Kontext." In H. von Hesberg and P. Zanker (eds.), *Römische Gräberstrassen. Selbstdarstellung—Status—Standard.* Munich: Verlag C. H. Beck, and Bayerische Akademie der Wissenschaften. 61–83.

———. 1988. "Aussagefähigkeit epigraphischer Statistik und die Bestattung von Sklaven im kaiserzeitlichen Rom." In P. Kneissl and V. Losemann (eds.), *Alte Geschichte und Wissenschaftsgeschichte. Festschrift für Karl Christ zum 65. Geburtstag.* Darmstadt: Wissenschaftliche Buchgesellschaft. 130–39.

———. 1989. "Religion und Religiosität in der soziopolitischen Führungsschicht der Hohen Kaiserzeit." In W. Eck (ed.), *Religion und Gesellschaft in der römischen Kaiserzeit. Kolloqium zu Ehren von Friedrich Vittinghoff.* Cologne: Böhlau Verlag. 15–51.

———. 1992. "Ehrungen für Personen hohen soziopolitischen Ranges im öffentlichen und privaten Bereich." In H.-J. Schallen, H. von Hesberg, and P. Zanker (eds.), *Die römische*

*Stadt im 2. Jahrhundert n. Chr. Der Funktionswandel des öffentlichen Raumes.
Kolloquium in Xanten vom 2. bis 4. Mai 1990.* Cologne: Rheinland-Verlag. 359–76.

———. 1994. "Statuendedikanten und Selbstdarstellung in römischen Städten." In Y. Le
Bohec (ed.), *L'Afrique, la Gaule, la religion à l'époque romaine. Mélanges à la mémoire
de Marcel Le Glay.* Brussels: Latomus. 650–62.

———. 1995. "'Tituli honorarii,' curriculum vitae und Selbstdarstellung in der Hohen
Kaiserzeit." In H. Solin, O. Salomies, and U.-M. Liertz (eds.), *Acta Colloquii Epigraphici
Latini Helsingiae 3.–6. sept. 1991 habiti.* Helsinki: Finnish Society of Arts and Letters.
211–37.

———. 1997a. "Lateinische Epigraphik." In F. Graf and M. Beard (eds.), *Einleitung in die
lateinische Philologie.* Stuttgart: B. G. Teubner. 92–111.

———. 1997b. "Der Euergetismus im Funktionszusammenhang der kaiserzeitlichen
Städte." In M. Christol and O. Masson (eds.), *Actes du Xᵉ Congrès international
d'épigraphie grecque et latine, Nîmes, 4–9 octobre 1992.* Paris: Publications de la
Sorbonne. 305–31.

———. 1997c. "Administrative Dokumente: Publikation und Mittel der Selbstdarstellung."
In W. Eck, *Die Verwaltung des römischen Reiches in der Hohen Kaiserzeit. Ausgewählte
und erweiterte Beiträge 2.* Basel: F. Reinhardt. 359–81.

———. 1998. "Grabmonumente und sozialer Status in Rom und Umgebung." In P. Fasold,
T. Fischer, H. von Hesberg, and M. Witteyer (eds.), *Bestattungssitte und kulturelle
Identität. Grabanlagen und Grabbeigaben der frühen römischen Kaiserzeit in Italien
und in den Nordwest-Provinzen. Kolloquium in Xanten vom 16. bis 18. Februar 1995:
Römische Gräber des 1. Jhs. n. Chr. in Italien und den Nordwestprovinzen.* Cologne:
Rheinland-Verlag. 29–40.

———. 2000. "Provincial Administration and Finance." In A. Bowman, P. Garnsey, and
D. Rathbone (eds.), *The Cambridge Ancient History XI. The High Empire, A.D. 70–192.*
2nd ed. Cambridge: Cambridge University Press. 266–92.

———. 2001. "Grabgrösse und sozialer Status." In M. Heinzelmann, J. Ortalli, P. Fasold,
and M. Witteyer (eds.), *Römischer Bestattungsbrauch und Beigabensitten in Rom,
Norditalien und den Nordwestprovinzen von der späten Republik bis in die Kaiserzeit
(Culto dei morti e costumi funerari romani, Roma, Italia settentrionale e province nord-
occidentali dalla tarda Repubblica all'età imperiale). Internationales Kolloquium, Rom
1.–3. April 1998.* Wiesbaden: Dr. Ludwig Reichert Verlag. 197–202.

———. 2004. "Straßen und ihre Denkmäler." In R. Frei-Stolba (ed.), *Siedlung und
Verkehr im römischen Reich. Römerstraßen zwischen Herrschaftssicherung und
Landschaftsprägung. Akten des Kolloquiums zu Ehren von Prof. H.E. Herzig vom 28. und
29. Juni 2001 in Bern.* Frankfurt: Lang. 17–39.

Edmondson, J. 2002. "Writing Latin in the Province of Lusitania." In A. E. Cooley
(ed.), *Becoming Roman, Writing Latin? Literacy and Epigraphy in the Roman West.*
Portsmouth, R.I.: Journal of Roman Archaeology. 41–60.

Edmondson, J., T. Nogales Basarrate, and W. Trillmich. 2001. *Imagen y Memoria.
Monumentos funerarios con retratos en la Colonia Augusta Emerita.* Madrid: Real
Academia de la Historia, Museo Nacional de Arte Romano.

Eich, P. 2005. *Zur Metamorphose des politischen Systems in der römischen Kaiserzeit. Die
Entstehung einer "personalen Bürokratie" im langen dritten Jahrhundert.* Berlin:
Akademie Verlag.

Eilers, C. 2002. *Roman Patrons of Greek Cities.* Oxford: Oxford University Press.

Étienne, R. 1974. *Le Culte impérial dans la péninsule ibérique d'Auguste à Dioclétien.* Paris: E.
de Boccard.

Feraudi-Gruénais, F. 2003. *Inschriften und Selbstdarstellung in stadtrömischen Grabbauten.* Rome: Edizioni Quasar.

Forbis, E. 1996. *Municipal Virtues in the Roman Empire: The Evidence of Roman Honorary Inscriptions.* Stuttgart: B. G. Teubner.

Giorcelli Bersani, S. 2004. *Epigrafia e storia di Roma.* Rome: Carocci Editore.

Gordon, R., and J. Reynolds. 2003. "Roman Inscriptions 1995–2000." *Journal of Roman Studies* 93: 212–94.

Guarducci, M. 1967. *Epigrafia Greca I. Caratteri e storia della disciplina. La scrittura greca dalle origini all'età imperiale.* Rome: Librario dello stato.

Haensch, R. 2007. "Inscriptions as Sources of Knowledge for Religions and Cults in the Roman World of Imperial Times." In J. Rüpke (ed.), *A Companion to Roman Religion.* Oxford: Blackwell. 176–87.

Harris, W. V. (ed.). 1993. *The Inscribed Economy. Production and Distribution in the Roman Empire in the Light of* instrumentum domesticum. *The Proceedings of a Conference Held at the American Academy in Rome on 10–11 January 1992.* Ann Arbor: University of Michigan Press.

Häusle, H. 1980. *Das Denkmal als Garant des Nachruhms. Beiträge zur Geschichte und Thematik eines Motivs in lateinischen Inschriften.* Munich: Verlag C. H. Beck.

Häussler, R. 1993. "The Romanisation of the *Civitas Vangionum.*" *Bulletin of the Institute of Archaeology* 15: 41–104.

———. 1998. "Resta, viator, et lege: Thoughts on the Epigraphic Habit." *Papers from the Institute of Archaeology* 9: 31–56.

———. 2002. "Writing Latin—From Resistance to Assimilation: Language, Culture and Society in N. Italy and S. Gaul." In A. E. Cooley (ed.), *Becoming Roman, Writing Latin? Literacy and Epigraphy in the Roman West.* Portsmouth, R.I.: Journal of Roman Archaeology. 61–76.

Herrmann, P. 1968. *Der römische Kaisereid. Untersuchungen zu seiner Herkunft und Entwicklung.* Göttingen: Vandenhoeck and Ruprecht.

Hölkeskamp, K.-J. 1996. "*Exempla* und *mos maiorum.* Überlegungen zum kollektiven Gedächtnis der Nobilität." In H.-J. Gehrke and A. Möller (eds.), *Vergangenheit und Lebenswelt: Soziale Kommunikation, Traditionsbildung und historisches Bewusstsein.* Tübingen: Narr. 301–38.

Hope, V. M. 1997. "Words and Pictures: The Interpretation of Romano-British Tombstones." *Britannia* 28: 245–58.

———. 2000a. "Inscription and Sculpture: The Construction of Identity in the Military Tombstones of Roman Mainz." In G. J. Oliver (ed.), *The Epigraphy of Death. Studies in the History and Society of Greece and Rome.* Liverpool: Liverpool University Press. 155–85.

———. 2000b. "Fighting for Identity: The Funerary Commemoration of Italian Gladiators." In A. E. Cooley (ed.), *The Epigraphic Landscape of Roman Italy.* London: Institute of Classical Studies. 93–113.

———. 2001. *Constructing Identity: The Roman Funerary Monuments of Aquileia, Mainz and Nîmes.* Oxford: Hedges.

———. 2003. "Trophies and Tombstones: Commemorating the Roman Soldier." In R. Gilchrist (ed.), *World Archaeology 35.1: The Social Commemoration of Warfare.* London: Taylor and Francis. 79–97.

Hopkins, K. 1978. *Conquerors and Slaves. Sociological Studies in Roman History 1.* Cambridge: Cambridge University Press.

Horster, M. 1998. "Ehrungen spätantiker Statthalter." *Antiquité Tardive* 6: 37–59.

————. 2001. *Bauinschriften römischer Kaiser. Untersuchungen zu Inschriftenpraxis und Bautätigkeit in Städten des westlichen Imperium Romanum in der Zeit des Prinzipats.* Stuttgart: Franz Steiner Verlag.

Høtje, J. M. 2005. *Roman Imperial Statue Bases from Augustus to Commodus.* Aarhus: Aarhus University Press.

Kajanto, I. 1968. "On the 'Freedom of Expression' in Latin Epitaphs." *Latomus* 27: 185–86.

Kelly, C. 1998. "Emperors, Government and Bureaucracy." In A. Cameron and P. Garnsey (eds.), *The Cambridge Ancient History XIII. The Late Empire, A.D. 337–425.* Cambridge: Cambridge University Press. 138–83.

Khanoussi, M., and L. Maurin. 2002. *Mourir à Dougga. Recueil des inscriptions funéraires.* Bordeaux and Tunis: Ministère de la Culture (Tunisie), Institut National du Patrimoine (INP).

Kokkinia, C. 2000. *Die Opramoas-Inschrift von Rhodiapolis: Euergetismus und soziale Eliten in Lykien.* Bonn: Rudolf Habelt Verlag.

Lassère, J.-M. 2005. *Manuel d'épigraphie latine.* Paris: A. et J. Picard.

Lattimore, R. 1962. *Themes in Greek and Latin Epitaphs.* Urbana: University of Illinois Press. Reprint of 1942 edition.

Lendon, J. E. 1997. *Empire of Honour. The Art of Government in the Roman World.* Oxford: Clarendon Press.

Lepelley, C. 1979. *Les Cités de l'Afrique romaine au Bas-Empire I.* Paris: Études Augustiniennes.

Le Roux, P. 2001. "La 'Crise' des élites hispano-romaines (IIIe-IVe siècles)." In M. Navarro Caballero and S. Demougin (eds.), *Élites hispaniques.* Bordeaux: Ausonius. 45–61, 261–275.

Liebeschuetz, J. H. W. G. 2001. *Decline and Fall of the Roman City.* Oxford: Oxford University Press.

Liertz, U.-M. 1998. *Kult und Kaiser. Studien zu Kaiserkult und Kaiserverehrung in den germanischen Provinzen und in Gallia Belgica zur römischen Kaiserzeit.* Rome: Institutum Romanum Finlandiae.

MacMullen, R. 1976. *Roman Government's Response to Crisis A.D. 235–337.* New Haven: Yale University Press.

————. 1982. "The Epigraphic Habit in the Roman Empire." *American Journal of Philology* 103: 233–46.

————. 1986. "Frequency of Inscriptions in Roman Lydia." *Zeitschrift für Papyrologie und Epigraphik* 65: 237–38.

Mann, J. C. 1985. "Epigraphic Consciousness." *Journal of Roman Studies* 75: 204–6.

Mayer, M. 2003. "Usos epigráficos singulares: la epigrafia para una ocasión." In M.G. Angeli Bertinelli and A. Donati (eds.), *Serta antiqua et mediaevalia: Usi e abusi epigrafici. Atti del colloquio internazionale di epigrafia latina (Genova 20–22 settembre 2001).* Rome: "L'Erma" di Bretschneider. 255–77.

McLean, B. H. 2002. *An Introduction to Greek Epigraphy of the Hellenistic and Roman Periods from Alexander the Great down to the Reign of Constantine (323 B.C.–A.D. 337).* Ann Arbor: University of Michigan Press.

Meyer, E. A. 1990. "Explaining the Epigraphic Habit in the Roman Empire: The Evidence of Epitaphs." *Journal of Roman Studies* 80: 74–96.

————. 2004. *Legitimacy and Law in the Roman World.* Tabulae *in Roman Belief and Practice.* Cambridge: Cambridge University Press.

Millar, F. 1977. *The Emperor in the Roman World (31 BC–AD 337).* London: Duckworth.

————. 1983. "Epigraphy." In M. Crawford (ed.), *Sources for Ancient History.* Cambridge: Cambridge University Press. 80–136.

Mouritsen, H. 2005. "Freedmen and Decurions: Epitaphs and Social History in Imperial
　　Italy." *Journal of Roman Studies* 95: 38–63.
Mrozek, S. 1973. "À propos de la répartition chronologique des inscriptions latines dans le
　　Haut-Empire." *Epigraphica* 35: 113–18.
———. 1988. "À propos de la répartition chronologique des inscriptions latines dans le
　　Haut-Empire." *Epigraphica* 50: 61–64.
———. 1994. "Épigraphie latine et évolution vers l'abstrait." *Ktema* 19: 319–27.
———. 1998. "La Répartition chronologique des inscriptions latines datées au IIIᵉ siècle
　　ap. J.-C." In E. Frézouls and H. Jouffroy (eds.), *Les Empereurs illyriens. Actes du colloque
　　de Strasbourg (11–13 octobre 1990) organisé par le Centre de Recherche sur l'Europe
　　centrale et sud-orientale.* Strasbourg: AECR. 11–20.
Mrozewicz, L. 1999. "Zwischen Normalität und Bedrohung. Epigraphik der Umbruchzeit.
　　Die Moesischen Provinzen angesichts der Krise der römischen Welt." In S. Panciera
　　(ed.), *XI Congresso Internazionale di Epigrafia Greca e Latina (Roma 18–24 settembre
　　1997), Atti I.* Rome: Edizioni Quasar. 461–72.
Nielsen, H. S. 1996. "The Physical Context of Roman Epitaphs and the Structure of 'the
　　Roman Family.'" *Analecta Romana Instituti Danici* 23: 35–60.
———. 1997. "Interpreting Epithets in Roman Epitaphs." In B. Rawson and P. Weaver
　　(eds.), *The Roman Family in Italy. Status, Sentiment, Space.* Oxford: Clarendon Press.
　　169–204.
Niquet, H. 2003. "Inschriften als Medium von 'Propaganda' und Selbstdarstellung im 1. Jh.
　　n. Chr." In G. Weber and M. Zimmermann (eds.), *Propaganda—Selbstdarstellung—
　　Repräsentation im römischen Kaiserreich des 1. Jhs. n. Chr.* Stuttgart: Franz Steiner
　　Verlag. 145–73.
Noreña, C. 2001. "The Communication of the Emperor's Virtues." *Journal of Roman Studies*
　　91: 146–68.
Peachin, M. 2006. "Rome the Superpower: 96–235 CE." In D. S. Potter (ed.), *A Companion
　　to the Roman Empire.* Oxford: Blackwell. 126–52.
Pleket, H. W. 1999. "Greek Inscriptions in the Roman Empire: Their Strength, Deficiencies
　　and (In)accessibility." In S. Panciera (ed.), *XI Congresso Internazionale di Epigrafia
　　Greca e Latina (Roma 18–24 settembre 1997), Atti II.* Rome: Edizioni Quasar. 77–91.
Pobjoy, M. 2000. "Building Inscriptions in Republican Italy: Euergetism, Responsibility,
　　and Civic Virtue." in A. E. Cooley (ed.), *The Epigraphic Landscape of Roman Italy.*
　　London: Institute of Classical Studies. 77–92.
Potter, D. S. 1994. *Prophets and Emperors. Human and Divine Authority from Augustus to
　　Theodosius.* Cambridge, Mass.: Harvard University Press.
———. 2004. *The Roman Empire at Bay AD 180–395.* London: Routledge.
Prag, J. R. W. 2002. "Epigraphy by Numbers: Latin and the Epigraphic Culture in Sicily."
　　In A. E. Cooley (ed.), *Becoming Roman, Writing Latin? Literacy and Epigraphy in the
　　Roman West.* Portsmouth, R.I.: Journal of Roman Archaeology. 15–31.
Pucci, G. 2001. "Inscribed *Instrumentum* and the Ancient Economy." In J. Bodel (ed.),
　　Epigraphic Evidence. Ancient History from Inscriptions. London: Routledge. 137–52.
Ratté, C., and R. R. R. Smith. 2004. "Archaeological Research at Aphrodisias in Caria,
　　1999–2001." *American Journal of Archaeology* 108: 145–86.
Revell, L. 2009. *Roman Imperialism and Local Identities.* Cambridge: Cambridge University
　　Press.
Reynolds, J. 1982. *Aphrodisias and Rome.* London: Society for the Promotion of Roman
　　Studies.
Rodà, I. 1999. "Foros y epigrafía: algunos ejemplos de Hispania Citerior." *Histria Antiqua* 5:
　　121–30.

Roddaz, J.-M. 2005. "Auguste et la transmission du message idéologique." In A. Bresson, A.-M. Cocula, and C. Pébarthe (eds.), *L'Écriture publique du pouvoir*. Paris: de Boccard. 35–44.

Roller, M. B. 2004. "Exemplarity in Roman Culture: The Cases of Horatius Cocles and Cloelia." *Classical Philology* 99: 1–56.

Roueché, C. 1989. *Aphrodisias in Late Antiquity*. Leeds: Society for the Promotion of Roman Studies.

Rowe, G. 2009. "Epigraphical Cultures of the Classical Mediterranean: Greek, Latin, and Beyond." In A. Erskine (ed.), *A Companion to Ancient History*. Oxford: Blackwell. 23–36.

Saller, R., and B. Shaw. 1984. "Tombstones and Roman Family Relations in the Principate: Civilians, Soldiers, and Slaves." *Journal of Roman Studies* 74: 124–56.

Salomies, O. 1994. "Observations on the Development of the Style of Latin Honorific Inscriptions during the Empire." *Arctos* 28: 63–106.

Schmidt, M. G. 2004. *Einführung in die lateinische Epigraphik*. Darmstadt: Wissenschaftliche Buchgesellschaft.

Spannagel, M. 1999. Exemplaris principis. *Untersuchungen zu Entstehung und Ausstattung der Augustusforums*. Heidelberg: Verlag Archäologie und Geschichte.

Spickermann, W. 2003. *Germania Superior. Religionsgeschichte des römischen Germanien I*. Tübingen: J. C. B. Mohr.

———. 2008. "Romanisierung und Romanisation der germanischen Provinzen." In R. Häussler (ed.), *Romanisation et épigraphie. Études interdisciplinaires sur l'acculturation et l'identité dans l'Empire romain*. Montagnac: Éditions Monique Margail. 307–20.

Taylor, L. R. 1961. "Freedmen and Freeborn in the Epitaphs of Imperial Rome." *American Journal of Philology* 82: 113–32.

Thomas, E., and C. Witschel. 1992. "Constructing Reconstruction: Claim and Reality of Roman Rebuilding Inscriptions from the Latin West." *Papers of the British School at Rome* 60: 135–77.

Van Nijf, O. M. 1997. *The Civic World of Professional Associations in the Roman East*. Amsterdam: J. C. Gieben.

von Hesberg, H., and S. Panciera. 1994. *Das Mausoleum des Augustus. Der Bau und seine Inschriften*. Munich: Bayerische Akademie der Wissenschaften.

von Hesberg, H., and P. Zanker. 1987. "Einleitung." In H. von Hesberg and P. Zanker (eds.), *Römische Gräberstrassen. Selbstdarstellung—Status—Standard*. Munich: Verlag C.H. Beck, and Bayerische Akademie der Wissenschaften. 9–20.

Wallace-Hadrill, A. 1981. "The Emperor and his Virtues." *Historia* 30: 298–319.

———. 1982. "Civilis Princeps: Between Citizen and King." *Journal of Roman Studies* 72: 32–48.

———. 1990. "Roman Arches and Greek Honours: The Language of Power at Rome." *Proceedings of the Cambridge Philological Society* 216: 143–81.

———. 2003. "The Streets of Rome as a Representation of Imperial Power." In L. de Blois, P. Erdkamp, O. Hekster, G. de Kleijn, and S. Mols (eds.), *The Representation and Perception of Roman Imperial Power. Proceedings of the Third Workshop of the International Network Impact of Empire (Roman Empire, c. 200 B.C.–A.D. 476), Netherlands Institute in Rome, March 20–23, 2002*. Amsterdam: J. C. Gieben. 189–206.

Wightman, E. M. 1985. *Gallia Belgica*. London: B. T. Batsford.

Witschel, C. 1999. *Krise—Rezession—Stagnation? Der Westen des römischen Reiches im 3. Jahrhundert n. Chr*. Frankfurt: Buchverlag Marthe Clauss.

———. 2002. "Meilensteine als historische Quelle? Das Beispiel Aquileia." *Chiron* 32: 325–93.

————. 2006. "Der *epigraphic habit* in der Spätantike: Das Beispiel der Provinz *Venetia et Histria*." In J.-U. Krause and C. Witschel (eds.), *Die Stadt in der Spätantike— Niedergang oder Wandel? Akten des internationalen Kolloquiums in München am 30. und 31. Mai 2003*. Stuttgart: Franz Steiner Verlag. 359–411.

Woolf, G. 1996. "Monumental Writing and the Expansion of Roman Society in the Early Empire." *Journal of Roman Studies* 86: 22–39.

————. 1998. *Becoming Roman. The Origins of Provincial Civilization in Gaul*. Cambridge: Cambridge University Press.

Yavetz, Z. 1984. "The Res Gestae and Augustus' Public Image." In F. Millar and E. Segal (eds.), *Caesar Augustus: Seven Aspects*. Oxford: Clarendon Press. 1–36.

Zanker, P. 1992. "Bürgerliche Selbstdarstellung am Grab im römischen Kaiserreich." In H.-J. Schallen, H. von Hesberg, and P. Zanker (eds.), *Die römische Stadt im 2. Jahrhundert n. Chr. Der Funktionswandel des öffentlichen Raumes. Kolloquium in Xanten vom 2. bis 4. Mai 1990*. Cologne: Rheinland-Verlag. 335–58.

Zimmer, G. 1992. "Statuenaufstellung auf Forumsanlegen des 2. Jahrhunderts n. Chr." In H.-J. Schallen, H. von Hesberg, and P. Zanker (eds.), *Die römische Stadt im 2. Jahrhundert n. Chr. Der Funktionswandel des öffentlichen Raumes. Kolloquium in Xanten vom 2. bis 4. Mai 1990*. Cologne: Rheinland-Verlag. 301–13.

CHAPTER 10

COMMUNICATING WITH TABLETS AND PAPYRI

ANDREA JÖRDENS

INTRODUCTION

> As legal documents of last will and testament we must accept every sort of
> material: therefore, whether the documents are of wood or of some other
> material, or whether of papyrus or parchment, or even of the skin of some
> animal, they will rightly be called binding legal documents. (Ulp., *Dig.* 37. 11. 1 pr.)

THIS chapter will examine the abundant variety of everyday written correspondence that still survives from Roman antiquity. There is no other type of source
material from this period that affords such an immediate or wide-ranging glimpse
into quotidian habits of communication and interaction as do these written tes-
timonials. Legal instruments, like those upon which Ulpian touches above, along
with administrative records of many sorts, represent an essential and important
part of this corpus of evidence. More essential for the present purposes, however,
are letters. This is especially the case, because in antiquity the epistle was consistently employed in many more contexts than that of simple private communication. To give but one example, the letter was the typical vehicle for numerous kinds
of request to various different administrative authorities.

It is also well to recognize, however, that pretty well none of the missives to
be discussed here was intended to leave a record for posterity; hence, such documents do not usually evince quite the same kinds of aesthetic or rhetorical goals

that underlie many an inscribed (on stone or bronze) text, or that inform the literary production of Graeco-Roman antiquity. In short, we here shall investigate the
remains of daily affairs. We shall look especially at the ways individuals attempted,
by writing letters to one another, or to various officials of the state, to get their day-
to-day problems and affairs satisfactorily resolved.

Now, although Egypt, because of the large number of papyrus texts preserved
by her sands, is the ancient locale most typically associated with quotidian writing, numerous archaeological discoveries from regions once scarcely known for their
extensive written output have also (especially in recent decades) considerably widened our knowledge of these habits. An early example came from the archives of the
cohors XX Palmyrenorum (the twentieth cohort of soldiers from Palmyra), which
were discovered at Mesopotamian Dura Europos in 1931–32 (*P. Dura*), and which
rendered highly visible the world of the Roman military. Just recently, several significant new finds from Mesopotamia, and especially Palestine (in particular, the
documents unearthed in several caves near the Dead Sea), have added much to our
knowledge of routine communications (Cotton, Cockle, and Millar 1995). In addition, documents that correspond with those unearthed in the drier desert regions
are increasingly coming to light in the northwestern provinces, despite the adverse
climatic conditions there prevalent. The best known of these, because they are the
most spectacular, are the so-called Vindolanda tablets, discovered in the excavation
of a second-century AD Roman military camp at Chesterholm, on Hadrian's Wall
(*T. Vindol.*). Similarly important are the small tablets from the sanctuary of Minerva
at Aquae Sulis, in southern England, or, to cross to the continent, the tablets from
Vindonissa in Switzerland, or those found long ago at Alburnus Maior in Romania
(*T. Sulis, T. Vindon.*, or *T. Dacia*, respectively). The Vindonissa tablets—like a significant body of *ostraka* (small pieces of broken pottery used as writing tablets) from
the Libyan frontier zone (*O. BuDjem*), or those from the Red Sea stone quarries (esp.
O. Claud.; cf. also *O. Berenike* or, most recently, *O. Krok.*), or also the Vindolanda
tablets—once again tell us much about the military sphere. The Alburnus Maior
documents, on the other hand, are mainly commercial in their nature, as are many of
the archives preserved by the eruption of Vesuvius in AD 79 (e.g., *TPSulp.*).

This very brief sketch of the nature of our extant documentation makes it clear
that written communication in Roman antiquity was far more widespread than the
often coincidental, always selective finds from military camps, shrines, or special
places of refuge might otherwise seem to indicate. In view of their vast quantity and
great variety, however, it is simply impossible to offer anything like a thorough presentation of these source materials in this chapter. Thus, only a few telling examples
will be introduced. It also should at this point be made clear that the Greek-language
papyri of Egypt, in view of their preponderance and indisputable importance, will
necessarily be central to the following discussion. All in all, the sampling offered
below intends to provide a lucid sense of the ways in which, and the kinds of matter
about which, individuals in Roman antiquity communicated with one another on a
daily basis via papyri and tablets. This tantalizing glimpse of workaday intercourse
may also perhaps inspire further investigation of these valuable written sources.

PHYSICAL DESCRIPTION OF TABLETS AND PAPYRI

Before we examine the content of the documents in question, and thus, various kinds of daily interactions, it is best to say something about the types of material that were most usually written on, the tools used to effect that writing, and the styles of writing themselves. Now, one marked feature of the documents here to be examined is their physical variety, for in the provinces of the Roman Empire, quite a wide range of different writing materials was in common use. The language, too, varied according to provenance; only in the military was the spoken and written language throughout the empire principally Latin. But even among the soldiers, one adjusted the choice of writing material to local customs, depending, in the end, on the available resources of the region. Thus, the extent of overlap one finds with respect to the manner, content, and character of the documents the empire over is rather astonishing. Nor should it be forgotten that in some areas, writing was a long-established habit, whereas elsewhere, people lived (and had long lived) in near absolute illiteracy.[1] Nonetheless, there is an unmistakable convergence in the nature of our surviving documents—in their forms, and even in their scripts. Indeed, by late antiquity, the mere style of script and locution, which had heretofore allowed a geographical location of most documents, is scarcely any longer sufficient to distinguish whether a document came from (say) Egypt, Palestine, or Asia Minor; only the indications of provenance supplied by proper names (for these were largely peculiar to given locales) are now of assistance (Mitthof and Papathomas 2004). Thus, the following discussion will be organized neither geographically nor according to the type of writing material (viz., e.g., papyrus as versus wooden tablets)— the two standard organizational methods for scholars dealing with these kinds of documents. Instead, it is much preferable to examine given forms of social interaction, which then, as now, differed according to whether one was dealing with an administrative bureau, interacting with a business partner, or writing to members of one's close family. Let us begin with a few remarks concerning the various materials written on, the tools with which one set down these texts, as well as the varieties of script.

In Rome itself, everyday texts were typically produced using a stylus, with which one side of a wax-coated tablet was inscribed (Meyer 2004). Two of these tablets would then be bound together, into a so-called *diptychon*, to protect the writing on the inside. In the case of legal contracts, a third tablet was added to form a *triptychon*, thus guarding against subsequent tampering with the text. The *diptychon* would be tied and sealed, which meant that the 'original' copy of the text was closed and protected, while the copy on the third tablet remained accessible. With additional, usually two-sided tablets, this basic system could further be extended to the so-called *polyptycha* (a many-sided tablet), allowing for significantly longer texts. With these tablets, ink was used only for the exposed sides, if at all.

---

1. On literacy in the ancient world, see Harris 1989; also Humphrey 1991.

With respect to the use of ink, there had long been a tempting conclusion, namely, that in the West this form of writing tended to be the exception. This notion is now, however, belied by the wooden tablets from Vindolanda. These thin and narrow tablets, which are almost reminiscent of modern-day postcards, and which were inscribed directly in ink, could be folded and then tied shut. If necessary, for longer messages, they could be tied together, accordion-style, by means of holes punched in the narrow sides.

A third kind of tablet was something significantly different from the wax or wooden ones just described. This third sort was called an *album*, and in question here were large boards, which were painted white (hence, the name *album—albus*, in Latin, meaning 'white'), and then written upon. These instruments were intended for public communication of official acts, or news. An *album*, given its physical nature, and given the type of text it held, no longer quite falls under the category of everyday writing, and will thus not be further discussed here.

One last type of tablet, though, was very much the bearer of everyday writings: lead tablets. These were widespread throughout the ancient world, and were highly popular for magical uses. The technique involved scratching a text onto a small strip of lead foil, rolling this up, and then concealing this potent document in an appropriate place (cf. Rives in this volume).

A situation, rather different from that just described, was to be found in the Near East, where the papyrus plant, native to the Nile Delta, offered the most convenient writing material. It is true that early on in these regions, other media were often preferred for the everyday text: cuneiform texts, for example, were produced on clay tablets; and as we see from the famous finds from the Dead Sea area, animal skins often served as surfaces for writing.[2] Parchment, which was not tanned, but cleansed in a lime bath, and thus whitened, was reserved for more important texts. However, with the Roman conquest of the Ptolemaic Kingdom, Egyptian papyrus found completely new markets. The sheets, made of two sets of the fibrous strips from cut papyrus plants, which were then laid at right angles on top of one another, could be worked into long rolls, which were inscribed in single columns running from left to right. To have writing surfaces for letters, one cut off strips of the desired size, which were then rolled, or folded, and, if necessary, secured with a seal. During the imperial era, the text normally ran parallel to the fibers; turning the sheet 90° and inscribing it *transversa charta* (against the grain) became popular only in late antiquity. As a cheaper variant of this, and thus mainly for brief notes, one could always use the ubiquitous *ostraka*. These were shards of broken pottery, which were written upon with ink.

Now, the fact that papyrus is an organic, and above all moisture-sensitive, material explains the generally lamentable state of its archaeological preservation: while the overwhelming mass of surviving papyrus texts come from the Egyptian interior (the so-called *chora*, 'countryside'), only very few documents are now known from the Nile Delta, or from Alexandria. Texts that originated in these latter

2. With regard to writing on leather, see now Baratta 2008.

areas survived only if by some special circumstance they made their way out to the *chora*—perhaps because some administrator, after leaving office, took them back with him to his home town—or if, because of a fire, they were charred, and thus preserved, as happened in the case of the 'Villa dei papiri' in Herculaneum (Sider 2005). Most important for the present purposes is the realization that, because the chronological distribution of papyrus finds from Egypt is largely a happenstance of their discovery, no significant conclusions can be drawn from these documents with respect to the actual geographical spread of writing, or as to the overall frequency of written correspondence (fundamental now is Habermann 1998).

Although thus far tens of thousands of such Greek papyri from Egypt have been made widely available, here too there is a marked imbalance, which must always be kept in mind—just like the sporadic nature of papyrus finds from provinces other than Egypt. Even more striking for the present discussion than the widespread lack of documents from the Delta, is the almost total lack of non-literary sources from Alexandria; thus, despite the Alexandrian upper classes having been so intimately intertwined with Roman society, their exact relationship to Rome and the Romans is extremely difficult to grasp. Indeed, we get a clearer view of this interaction in the *chora* (countryside), where Romans appear as traders, landowners, veterans, and, not least, as governmental officials; although, of course, not everyone who had Roman citizenship and access to the *tria nomina* (i.e., the typical form of nomenclature belonging to Roman citizens) was Italic, or even truly Roman. Nevertheless, the Egyptian source material reveals a good deal about contacts and interchange that cannot be gleaned in such detail for any other province, and that thus may after all throw some light on the questions here at hand.

ORDERING LIFE VIA LETTERS

The wealth of information about daily interactions yielded by the sands of Egypt is especially valuable and interesting with respect to the realm of administration, and the ways in which peoples' lives were configured by interactions with the various branches of the government, for in the ancient world, administration always involved significant amounts of communication. If our perception of oral communication is greatly influenced by literary representations, it is the papyri that give us our unique conceptions of the intense written interchange among various officials, and between officials and the populace. There are as yet, however, no systematic studies of this issue, and here, too, a few brief introductory suggestions will have to suffice. Still, a couple of recent works now throw light on communications between the governor of Egypt (the *praefectus Aegypti*) and his subordinate officials, as well as on the prefect's communications with cities of his province (Thomas 1999; Jördens 2006). Likewise noteworthy are the attempts that have been made to evaluate the social standing of the interlocutors from their use of bureaucratic language

(Kruse 2002: 879ff.). Also, a brief word about the administrative structure typical of the province Egypt, which even had a well-defined notion of 'official channels' of communication, is in order.

The highest authority in Roman Egypt was the *praefectus Aegypti* (the governor of the province), a Roman knight, who, like the procurators entrusted with special duties, had his office in Alexandria. The *epistrategoi*, officials responsible for the three—and later four—large divisions of the province, were likewise knights, while the four dozen nomes (smaller territories within the province) were governed by functionaries called *strategoi*, who as a rule came from the Alexandrian upper class. Then, ranked just below the *strategos* in each nome, was the so-called royal scribe (the *basilikos grammateus*), while the village scribes made up the lowest rank of local officials. With the exception of the prefect (i.e., the *praefectus Aegypti*), these were all purely civil officials, reinforced and supported, of course, by numerous functionaries with special duties—tax farmers, persons performing liturgies, as well as other assistants of all kinds.

Now, given the extant documentation, it must be said that we know these lowest levels in the administrative hierarchy best, while for the higher authorities we are limited essentially to chance finds. Nevertheless, this generally does not pose a terrible problem for the questions to be discussed here, since even isolated attestations of correspondence can potentially claim to be representative. Two arbitrarily chosen examples will suffice to illustrate this. They stem not only from about the same time—the middle of the second century AD—but pertain coincidentally to the same subject: the flight from their communities of liturgists, that is, people who were required to undertake certain temporary and unpaid public duties.

The first case concerns a dossier apparently put together by a *strategos* (again, the chief administrator of a nome) on the occasion of his turning over his office to his successor. According to the dossier, the *strategos* had reported to the *praefectus Aegypti*, apparently already quite some time before, regarding the flight of two liturgists; after futile attempts to locate the fugitives in his own district (nome), the *strategos* had secured from the prefect an edict allowing for an advertisement of the search throughout the entire province. Apparently, this, too, showed no results for a long time (*P. Berl. Leihg.* II 46; after April 1, 136). The second example is a collection of letters sent by the *strategoi* of several other nomes to their colleague in the Oxyrhynchite Nome, inquiring about the possible presence of fugitive liturgists (*P. Oxy.* LX 4060; AD 160/61). Evidently this relates to the very step in the process by which, according to the dossier, the prefect's edict had empowered the first *strategos* to conduct a province-wide search: thus, the search appears to have amounted to a survey among the colleagues of the *strategos* of *P. Berl. Leihg.* The lesson here is that a lively written communication underlay the quotidian ordering of society's affairs in the Egyptian countryside.

Now, in contrast to the first case above, where the *praefectus Aegypti* was approached by a subordinate official, the second case involves a written exchange between officers of equal rank, and the tone of the writing is correspondingly different. In his request to the governor, the *strategos* weaves in a respectful "Sir" and, as a precaution, even uses the formula "if it please your Divine Spirit"; but, when addressing his colleagues, he uses the polite, but long ossified, address, *philtate*. That this is merely a formulaic phrase, corresponding roughly to our "My dear," can be seen from the highly regularized sequence of greeting, request for official help, and complimentary close:

> Calpurnius Artemidorus, alias Ptolemaeus, *strategos* of the Onuphite (nome), to his dear Phocion, *strategos* of the Oxyrhynchite (nome), greetings. In response to a report to him by me about the undermentioned persons [the names and reasons are given] Volusius Maecianus, the most glorious prefect, gave orders for them to be searched for. I have written to you, therefore, my dear (colleague), that you may order the search for them to be made in your district, too, and if these persons shall be found, that you may act accordingly and notify me. (*P. Oxy.* LX 4060, 82–89)

The closing, also, which reads literally, "I pray for your health, my dearest (colleague)," would probably better be rendered in English as a more formulaic, "farewell, my dear." The prefect, on the contrary, abstains entirely from any empty courtesies; notably, moreover, instead of using the otherwise customary *euchomai* ("I pray"), he always uses the much less obliging *boulomai* ("I want"). In short, the ways in which these individuals corresponded with one another regarding these matters of everyday business reflect, in mirror-like fashion, their relative positions in the social and administrative hierarchy (cf. Kruse 2002: 884 ff.).

Even the interaction of private individuals with state officials did not always require grand diction. The death notice, for example, which one filed with the authorities to prevent further tax demands upon the deceased, typically ended with a simple, "therefore, I request that he/she be inscribed in the list of the dead, as is fitting." In some cases, these requests were supported by an oath.[3] Here, it is the form of the initial salutation in which a (social) difference is apparent. According to standard practice, the correspondence between those of equal rank, be it in the official or in the private realm, would begin with the address formula, "A to B, greetings"; however, in writing to superiors or to administrative officials, the recipient is typically the first named: "to B from A, greetings." Once again, the niceties of prestige and rank are manifested even in such mundane correspondence, and merely by the ordering of the names.

Much more eloquently worded, on the other hand, were the petitions with which inhabitants turned to civil, as well as military—the choice would generally depend upon whom one might expect to offer the most effective support in a particular case—officials for help.[4] If there did not happen to be a military unit stationed nearby, whose commander one could therefore approach, then the commonest path led the Egyptian petitioner to the *strategos* in the capital city of the

---

3. For this type of document, cf. Casarico 1985.

4. Cf., e.g., White 1972; in general, also Hobson 1993. For a somewhat later period, cf. now Feissel and Gascou 2004.

nome. Sometimes, however, neither cost nor trouble were spared to take some concern directly to the prefect himself. Still, one did not always have to travel all the way to Alexandria for this, since the governor made himself available at the *conventus* (a kind of province-wide circuit court) in the countryside every spring (Haensch 1997). In Egypt, as contrasted with other provinces, this meant not only that a court day was held, but that the local administration was subjected to a review, hence the Greek designation of the Latin *conventus* as *dialogismos* (i.e., an accounting). Nevertheless, the prefect was also available to hear the complaints of the populace even when he was not conducting the *conventus*. Be that as it may, during one *conventus* visit at Arsinoe (the capital of a nome in middle Egypt) of scarcely three days, the prefect is recorded to have received 1804 petitions (*P. Yale* I 61, 208–10 [May 22, 209?]). Various processes were developed to cope with such an onslaught of business (cf. Haensch 1994); thus, for example, a large portion of the judicial workload was already delegated on the spot to subordinate local authorities, or to special *iudices pedanei* (deputy judges).

As we can see in the recently published petitions from the middle Euphrates (Gascou and Feissel 1995), neither the style of such complaints nor their handling was a phenomenon peculiar to Egypt. This holds true already on the level of form, given that on the far eastern edge of the empire, too, the extant petitions always begin with the customary, "to B from A, greetings." It may also be noted that the recitation of the facts of the case, introduced with a participial phrase, is punctuated throughout by interjections of the honorific *despota* (Master) or *kyrie* (Sir), that the complainant's own defenselessness before the injustice done him or her is, as in Egypt, carefully highlighted, and that again, just as in Egypt, the addressee is apostrophized as the only help available in a desperate situation. Here, by way of example, is one of the Euphrates documents:

> Since, therefore, Sir, I cannot obtain satisfaction anywhere, if your Fortune does not graciously nod my way—because I am oppressed by Bathsabbatha, my father's creditor, to whom the aforementioned vineyard is also mortgaged—so I bid and entreat you, when it please your Fortune, through your *subscriptio* (subscription, i.e., reply), to order the procurator Claudius Ariston in Appadana—or whomever your Fortune pleases…but also to order that he hand over the income for the period in which he harvested the crop. Because in this way I, a humble man, will by your Fortune be spared harassment and not robbed of what is mine, and I will forever owe you a debt of thanks. (*SB* XXII 15497, 13–19; AD 244–250)

Like in Egypt, the requested *subscriptio* consisted merely of a laconic referral to a subordinate authority. Precisely this can be gathered from a second example, which had probably been placed in the records:

> *Subscriptio* (reply) of Julius Priscus, *vir perfectissimus* ('most perfect man'—a title of rank), Prefect of Mesopotamia, deputy consul: Ariston, *vir egregius* ('outstanding man'—a title of rank, lesser than *vir perfectissimus*), will review your request. (*SB* XXII 15496, 19–21; August 28, 245)

Whether the following Latin subscript *legi* (I have read it) came from him personally—in this case, that is, from the emperor's brother, Julius Priscus, who was the acting governor of the province—or whether it is merely a registrar's endorsement from Priscus' office, as the subsequent page numbering "209" might suggest, is open to question. One thing that we see clearly, though, from such a petition and response, is that a lowly person might have managed to place his or her personal affairs in the hands of the highest authority in the world, namely, the emperor (or here, the emperor's brother).

In any case, the form of such petitions finally came to influence the style even of private contracts, as shown by the so-called *hypomnema* (memorandum) developed in the Fayum district, west of the Nile. Traditional private deeds, the so-called *cheirographa*, conformed to the style of ordinary letters, and so began likewise with the usual, 'A to B, greetings,' and differed only in having a date instead of a complimentary closing at the end (Wolff 1978: 106ff.). But for the *hypomnema* of the imperial era, the address 'to B from A' once again became typical, just as we have observed in applications to administrative officials, and particularly in the petitions. Here is one example:

> To Flavia Petronilla, alias Titanias, with her guardian, her husband Gaius Valerius
> Pansa, ex-gymnasiarch, from Kan- and Heries, his brother. We desire to lease
> from you the palm garden called that of Herennius, belonging to you in the area
> of the village of Hephaestias…And I will pay the rent at the time of the gathering
> without delay. I, the lessee, shall be responsible for all the acts of cultivation—the
> gathering, fertilization, irrigation, circumvallation, a third share of embanking
> canals, and a half share of cleaning them, and I will pay 2 *artabae* of…(Signed) I,
> Gaius Valerius Pansa, have made the lease as above, and so long as there is no
> higher offer, the aforesaid lease shall continue secured to you. (*P. Ryl.* II 172, 1–9,
> 15–33; September 14, 208)

As in this example, the *hypomnema* was preferentially used in agricultural matters, and is never encountered in relation to purchases or loans. Originally, then, it will have had to do merely with lease offers to absentee landlords, which became legally binding only through the signature of the lessor. It is thus hardly surprising that this type of deed originated in the second-most fertile region of Egypt after the Delta (Wolff 1978: 114ff.; most recently, Yiftach-Firanko 2007).

That social rank did play a role in selecting the type of document in a given instance seems evident from a special form of the obviously stylized private protocol; these begin with an emphasized, 'they have acknowledged to one another,' and only then introduce the names. Thus, in these types of documents, the parties express mutual respect, where typically such acknowledgment would come only from the weaker party. This form appears to have been used especially when deputizing a liturgist, as one such agreement in the form of a *cheirographon* (attested declaration) shows:

> The Aurelii Sarapammon, son of Heras and Isidora, chosen *dekanos*, and Paulus,
> son of Horion and Helena, both from the illustrious and most illustrious city of

the Oxyrhynchites with Aurelius Horion son of Horion of the same city as surety
for their presence and appearance for the following service, to each other
greetings. We agree, I, Paulus, on the one hand, to go instead of you,
Sarapammon, wherever I may be commanded, with the asses and camels and
wand-bearers handed over to me, and to undertake and fulfill the position of you
the *dekanos*…and (I agree) that I shall make you Sarapammon free of any
corporal harm and annoyance in all matters in general pertaining to the service of
dekanos. I, Sarapammon, on the other hand, (agree) to approve on these
conditions and to pay the wages found to have accrued in full. If any inquiry in
any way whatsoever arises about (?)…(to) the *dekanoi*, I, Sarapammon (shall…)
in accordance with the share falling on me and (I agree) that you, Paulus, will be
free from trouble in this matter…(*P. Oxy.* XXXVIII 2859, 1–8, 18–25; November
10, 301)

Of course, contracts were not always promptly fulfilled. If one did not want
to trust to a mere petition with a request for legal protection, one could also make
good one's claims with the help of a summons, or a lien. In contrast to public deeds,
however, it appears that privately drawn-up deeds, such as those just mentioned,
could not be produced in court as evidence. Thus, whoever, either for convenience
or to limit expense, had foregone the exhibition of the contractual document before
the *archidikastes* in Alexandria,[5] at a notary public, or at a bank (Wolff 1978: 91ff.,
81ff., and 95ff. respectively) had first to undergo the troublesome process of the
so-called *demosiosis* (public declaration), in order to make the contract potentially
valid in a court of law. For this, the creditor had personally, or through a middleman, to submit a corresponding petition to the *archidikastes* in Alexandria, including a complete and exact copy of the contract, and likewise had to pay the prescribed
fees, whereupon two duplicates of the contract were deposited in the Alexandrian
archives. One copy of this file was forwarded to the local authorities, who then, for
their part, had to inform the other party of it. For the forwarding itself, however, the
creditor was once again responsible.[6]

One would assume that this time-consuming and expensive process would be
resorted to only in dire circumstances, when all other possibilities for an amicable
settlement had been exhausted, and even in such situations, only when considerable sums were involved. But such is not the case in a surprising papyrus from the
year AD 258/59, which contains the notification of the *strategos* by the *archidikastes*
concerning a completed *demosiosis* (*P. Mich.* XI 614). As usual, all the earlier steps
of the process are itemized in this protocol, among them the initial petition of the
creditor—two brothers—together with the original (privately drawn-up) loan contract. From this it appears that the brothers' father had almost a quarter of a century earlier loaned six and one-half artabs of wheat, that is, somewhat more than

5. Literally, the *archidikastes* was the 'chief judge,' the head of a special notary's office.
The *archidikastes* is not to be confused with the high-ranking *iuridicus* or *dikaiodotes* (also a
judicial official), a Roman procurator.

6. On this whole procedure, see Primavesi 1986. On the archives, cf. also Cockle 1984
and Burkhalter 1990.

what two donkeys, or a camel, would be able to carry. This was a fairly significant quantity of grain. If the brothers had no family, they could easily have lived off the income from this for some months, the more so because the interest, which ought to have come to the same amount as the original loan, was still accruing; and in addition to that, there was a surcharge of half as much again in case of default. On the other hand, the brothers had to lay out the costs for their middleman to travel to Alexandria; and even if this was not his only purpose in going there, and even if he dealt with their affair only incidentally, still they will have had to pay him some compensation, and they had also to pay the *demosiosis* fees. Doubtless, the subsequent process of issuing a warning was also not without expense, to say nothing of the time and annoyance involved. In short, one wonders if all this—the more so after 23 years!—stands in any kind of proportionality to the loss, or whether one should suspect some other motivation in the background. It is notable that no maturation date was agreed upon for the original loan, and likewise that the brothers' grandfather and the debtor both bear the name Papontheus. Was the loan perhaps a favor among relatives, that was suddenly redirected in order to satisfy quite other demands? In any case, although we can hardly doubt that contracts first and foremost were intended to obviate litigation, it is not to be questioned that in case of need, they could perfectly well be brought to bear on extrinsic fields, and might thus serve completely different purposes.

Thus, we may seem here to be in the presence of a fairly litigious society; and indeed, this aspect of the society is amply revealed to us by the many papyrus documents such as this one. But one should keep in mind also that when things are going well, usually there is little noise. Put another way, the smooth running of affairs generally has, as one of its chief characteristics, that it leaves no obvious traces in the extant papyrological record.

On the other hand, when events did turn sour, there might be different results. Here, it seems fair to stress that litigation and violence are the two methods generally engaged when disputes arose, and that these represent markedly different reactions to an altercation.[7] That having been said, it must also be stressed that disputes between neighbors in Egypt seem to have had a special tendency to degenerate into pitched legal battles. Perhaps the most striking example of this is the years-long dispute between the priests Satabus and Nestnephis from the small town Soknopaiu Nesos, a squabble whose origins remain obscure (Jördens 2005: 45–46; recently, Schentuleit 2007: esp. 103–7). The first we hear of it is a complaint by Nestnephis against Satabus, who had acquired a house, along with a building site, from a third priest. Suspiciously, however, the complaint was first lodged three years after the purchase, when Satabus had already made considerable investments in the property. The claim of Nestnephis, that the acquired property did not belong to the seller at all, but was "abandoned," and therefore state property, in any case immediately brought the responsible official—here the *idios logos* (an official at Alexandria responsible for the handling of deserted properties)—into the picture; and he

7. On the latter, cf., e.g., Bagnall 1989. See also Fagan (on violence) in this volume.

entrusted a centurion with the task of investigating the accusation (the nome officials, though likewise informed, seem to have played no active role). Because the
sanctuary elders called in to testify at least partly confirmed Nestnephis' version of
things, Satabus was ultimately forced, despite his apparently legitimate purchase, to
make a further payment to the *idios logos* for a part of the building site. Whether he
ever attempted to recover his losses from the seller remains unknown.

The dispute, however, did not end there, though this question of property
ownership certainly remained central to it. Rather, the two rivals turned to other
venues for a vigorous exchange of blows. Thus, Satabus reports to the *strategos*
the theft of a mortar by Nestnephis, who had set upon him in a night ambush to
steal it. Naturally, Satabus does not hesitate to complain bitterly before the afore-
mentioned centurion, and even to the prefect. The families of the two priests also
became involved. A son of Satabus takes legal action against Nestnephis, with an
accusation of several offenses at once, each one outweighing the last—usurpation
of "abandoned" land, temple robbery, tax evasion. An oath was demanded more
than twenty years later from another son, to the effect that the payment to the *idios
logos* by the father had actually been made. The dispute must thus have run on
for decades, ramifying in both families, although the sources provide no further
evidence for this.

On the other hand, one can equally find evidence in the papyri of people using
every means to intercede on behalf of others. Thus, among the papers of a *strategos*
from early in the reign of the emperor Hadrian (AD 117–138), we also come upon the
letters of recommendation that were so characteristic of Roman society altogether
(Kim 1972; Cotton 1981). This genre, which likewise appears in literary contexts, has
a number of continually recurring elements—the identification of the person recommended, the habit of relying on a personal nexus, the emphasis on the person's
good character and trustworthiness, to mention only a few; but among individual
attestations there are also some notable variations. This is especially evident from
two (undated) letters that happen to concern the same person. While the second text
comes from the higher ranking *epistrategos*, the sender of the first letter is unknown:

> Faberius Mundus to the *strategos* Apollonius, greetings. Ulpius Malchus, the
> *beneficiarius* (a military aide) of Rammius, our noble Prefect, who is to concern
> himself with the area under your control, a quite excellent man, I recommend to
> you. I do hope that he will make an effort to stand by you, as I have assured you
> he will. I have also written to him, though, so that when you have gotten in touch
> with him, he will make himself available to you with even greater alacrity.
> Farewell, most revered brother. (*P. Brem.* 5)

> Flavius Philoxenus to the *strategos* of Heptakomia, Apollonius, greetings. I am
> quite sure you already know that Malchus is my (friend); therefore, treat him as if
> he were a part of my very self. What more should I write to you? You know full
> well where I stand. Farewell. (*P. Brem.* 6)

Given the extremely important role played by patronage in Roman society, such
letters as this were both common, and crucial (cf. Leunissen 1993).

In contrast to this case, there were also many attempts to exert influence not simply to elicit favors, but even to circumvent the legal framework, especially where familial concerns were involved. Thus, Tabetheus despairingly implores her brother, Claudius Tiberianus, to do everything he can to protect her son, Satornilos, from a murder charge. This would have been no small undertaking, inasmuch as a homicide in the imperial era was a crime, whose adjudication was reserved for the prefect himself. Hope for some accommodation between the families, as had been possible under the Ptolemies, with an expiatory payment following Greek custom, would scarcely any longer have existed. Tabetheus nevertheless beseeches her brother, in a highly oblique, and thus not easily understood, letter, that he might at least make the attempt:[8]

> ...I want you to write concerning a friend; deliver them to him immediately. I was much annoyed...When I went down from our home at Tonis and came to Saturnilos' lodging and saw our things—may the evil eye not touch them, I did not approve that he, my son, should trust Menas. And after he had killed him, he told me not to be distressed; I told Saturnilos that I was sleepless from worry. Since you caused me damage to the extent of twelve hundred drachmai, let them go to my son's ransom. And I went down to Alexandria with my son. For this reason, a madness took hold of him, because he did not approve that he [i.e., Menas] and his family should consume the rations. If god wills and you receive the rations that I put up for you, do not you also...them. Concerning last year's rations, I did not prepare them;...prepared them last year. I sent them from Alexandria as late as the second shipment upstream. And he became ill. I was tortured with the grief that he caused me, but I was utterly happy that he remained alive. I have insistently urged him, 'Take a taste of Alexandria,' and he says to me, 'I don't want to.' I thank the gods that he is like you; no one can mock him. Salute all your people, each by name. How much damage have I incurred this past year on account of Saturnilos! Neither was he (?) liable for it nor was I, but I have incurred damage on every side. Farewell. (*P. Mich.* VIII 473, 8–9, 12–33; early second century AD)

Whether Claudius Tiberianus, as the salutation suggests, was really Tabetheus' own brother, and a native Egyptian, or just a friend, whom she called 'brother,' or her husband, as has recently been suggested (Strassi 2008), is admittedly unclear; the close relation between the correspondents could have some entirely different basis. Nevertheless, it is not altogether unlikely that they were siblings, all the more so since his children, as another letter mentions, bore the Egyptian names Isidoros and Segathis. Since we know from his correspondence, which was conducted partly in Latin, that he served as a *speculator* (scout), and later settled as a veteran in Karanis, in middle Egypt, it is probable that he was native to this province, and owed his Roman name purely to his military service. Be that as it may, this letter demonstrates the kinds of desperate situation that could descend upon people, and one of the many ways in which escape might be sought.

8. See now Strassi 2008: 128ff. on this document.

Claudius Tiberianus' status as a Roman citizen, however, raises another matter that is both well known and extremely important, namely, the rise to citizen status via military service. This process is very nicely illustrated, on a very personal level, by the oft-cited letter that the sailor Apion sent from the gulf of Naples to Philadelphia, in middle Egypt:

> Apion to Epimachus, his father and lord, very many greetings. Before all else I pray for your health, and that you may always be well and prosperous, together with my sister and her daughter and my brother. I thank the lord Serapis that when I was in danger at sea he straightway saved me. On arriving at Misenum I received from Caesar three gold pieces for travelling expenses. And it is well with me. Now I ask you, my lord and father, write me a letter, telling me first of your welfare, secondly of my brother's and sister's, and enabling me thirdly to make obeisance before your handwriting, because you educated me well and I hope thereby to have quick advancement, if the gods so will. Give many salutations to Capiton, and my brother and sister, and Serenilla, and my friends. I have sent you by Euctemon a portrait of myself. My name is now Antonius Maximus, my company the Athenonica. I pray for your health. P.S.: Serenus son of Agathodaemon salutes you, and…and Turbo son of Gallonius, and…(BGU II 423; second century AD. Translation: Sel. Pap. I 112)

Of course, it was not always necessary that members of the military leave their families behind while they were on active duty. In any case, the documents from Vindolanda around the year AD 100 provide a different picture, at least where officers were concerned. According to these records, there was regular contact between Claudia Severa, whose husband, C. Aelius Brocchus, was later to be transferred to Pannonia as commander of a cavalry unit, and Sulpicia Lepidina, the wife of the cohort commander, Flavius Cerialis. Thus, Sulpicia is invited to her friend's birthday party:

> Claudia Severa to her Lepidina, greetings. On the third day before the Ides of September, sister, for the day of the celebration of my birthday, I give you a warm invitation to make sure that you come to us, to make the day more enjoyable for me by your arrival, if you are present (?). Give my greetings to your Cerialis. My Aelius and my little son send him (?) their greetings. I shall expect you, sister. Farewell, sister, my dearest soul, as I hope to prosper, and hail. (T. Vindol. II 291)

Egyptian invitations, however, were more terse, as a rule being limited to the absolute essentials. This seems not to have been merely a matter of the different language—in other words, Greek, as opposed to the Latin of Claudia Severa's invitation. That is to say, there seem to have been regional differences in the etiquette of such invitations. Here is an example from Egypt:

> Herais requests your company at dinner in celebration of the marriage of her children at her house tomorrow, the 5th at 9 o'clock. (P. Oxy. I 111; third century AD)

Such invitations from Egypt demonstrate, however, something more wide-ranging, namely, that it was not only in administrative correspondence, in exchanges between private individuals and governmental authorities, or in contracts, but also in the purely private realm that typical conventions and relatively fixed formulas were used for particular needs. If one takes all the evidence together, one might indeed be tempted to conclude that personal letters, like that of Tabetheus, or that of Apion, with their very specific concerns, should rather be viewed as exceptions to the rule. If such individual letters have nonetheless served to shape our overall perception of the private letter in antiquity, this is not least the fault of the preference for including especially colorful examples in the various modern collections of papyri. The average letter was, however, much more prosaic. This is especially true of business correspondence, where even the salutation was sometimes omitted, if it was just a matter of brief informational notes:

> From Alypios. The two oxen that the manager Horion announces to you, feed regularly, so that he can come back on the second. Farewell. To Heroneinos, the manager, from Thraso. 13th Year, 8th of Phamenoth. (*P. Flor.* II 149; March 4, 266)

Since this letter belongs to the so-called Heroneinos Archive, from which at present almost 500 papyri have been published, the correspondents and their milieu are well known. This document is a message sent from the capital of the nome to the local steward in Theadelphia by the manager responsible for an entire estate in the Fayum, which belonged to an Alexandrian grandee. It was common for many such letters to travel back and forth in a given week, demonstrating an intensive exchange among the individual management units; such exchange happened similarly with respect to people, animals, and goods (Rathbone 1991). Thus, in a context like this, one might with a good conscience forgo the polite formulas. That these routine documents were an everyday medium is also demonstrated plainly by their rapid reuse for other purposes; thus, the back of the above-cited letter was soon used for a statement of wages (*SB* XIV 11556; after AD 268).

In the private arena, the ratio of concrete information to wholly generic statements of goodwill being transmitted was nearly the reverse. Often enough, the request to get something for the sender, or the corresponding reply, was the only content of a letter, when it did not actually consist entirely of salutations and polite formulas:

> Serapias to her father and lord Ammonius, many greetings. I do obeisance on your behalf to the lady Philotera (i.e., the goddess of the place). I received from Nestereus six loaves of bread. If I come to Myos Hormos, as I announced to you, I shall send you a jar of fish-sauce with the first donkeys. For I care as much about you as if you were my own father. And if I find the linen for you I shall buy it. If you have a drinking-cup, send it to me. My brother salutes you. P.S.: Don't forget to send me the scalpel. PP.S.: Receive 1 jar and write to me about yourself. Greet Proklos. (*SB* XXII 15453; second century AD)

> [- - -]renos to Ptolemaios, my brother, very many greetings. Before all else I pray for your health and make your obeisance before the gods here, praying that the best things in life be yours. Greet Diogenes and Ptolemaios and all your people by name. I pray for your good health, brother. (*SB* XXIV 16334; first century AD)

The situation in Britain was no different:

> Sollemnis to Paris, his brother, very many greetings. I want you to know that I am
> in very good health, as I hope you are in turn, you neglectful man, who have sent
> me not even one letter. But I think that I am behaving in a more considerate
> fashion in writing to you…to you, brother…my messmate. Greet from me
> Diligens and Cogitatus and Corinthus and I ask that you send me the
> names…Farewell, dearest brother (?). (*T. Vindol.* II 311; around AD 100)

The friendly tone of this letter—the names may even suggest that the correspondents were slaves—leaves little doubt that the reproach against the dilatory letter
writer for cutting off communication, and thus being a *homo impientissimus* (a
most impious man), is here meant only in fun. Of course, there will also have been
instances where communication truly was completely withdrawn, but inevitably
these are more seldom found reflected in the extant documents. This can, however,
be observed in situations of conflict, where an imbalance of social status made it
seem inadvisable to confront a rival directly. In such cases, one readily resorted to
the roundabout route, via the gods, who could better be trusted to bring about the
desired consequences:

> Kronos, you who suppress the grudges of all men: suppress the grudge of
> Hori, whom Maria bore, and let him not speak against Hatros, whom Taesis
> bore. And I beseech you by the finger of the god, he should not open his
> mouth against him, for he is subject to Kronos' son and to Kronos. Let him
> not speak against him, neither night, nor day, nor one hour. (*PGM* O.1; late
> imperial)

Sometimes, however, even this option was unavailable, because one was not in a
position to name the enemy, as might be the case in reporting a theft. Numerous
examples of this survive, above all from Aquae Sulis (present-day Bath) in Southern
England. In this text, we see how one might threaten the perpetrator of the wrong
on durable lead tablets deposited in the temple of Minerva:

> (The person) who has lifted my bronze vessel is utterly accursed. I give (him) to
> the temple of Sulis, whether woman or man, whether slave or free, whether boy
> or girl, and let him who has done this spill his own blood into the vessel itself. I
> give, whether woman or man, whether slave or free, whether boy or girl, that thief
> who has stolen the property itself (that) the god may find (him). (*T. Sulis* 44; ca.
> AD 175–275)

The lettering here ran from right to left, which doubtless was done to enhance the
effectiveness of the curse. There may have been an even greater hope of success,
however, when one expedited the god's efforts with some remuneration, which one
promised to the god, as well as to the honest finder of the lost object—as seen here
at Oxyrhynchos in middle Egypt:

> If anyone on the 7th of Hathyr found a set of brown children's clothes, he should
> give them to the crier in the Thoereion of the oracle gods, for which he will

receive from her 16 drachmas; and to the goddess (go) two drachmas. (*P. Heid.* IV 334; probably second century AD)

If, on the contrary, one had two alternatives, allowing a clear Yes or No—for example, if there were already a certain suspicion regarding the perpetrator—then, in Egypt, one usually opted to consult an oracle. In this case, two largely identical versions—one positive, one negative—were turned in at the temple, and of these, the correct one would be given back. In the same way, other pivotal questions could also be answered when the need arose:

> To the very great and mighty god Soknopaios, from Asklepiades son of Areios. If it is not granted to me to live together with Tapetheus, the daughter of Marres, and she never becomes my wife, show it to me and confirm this piece of writing for me. In the past, Tapetheus was the wife of Horion. Year 35 of Caesar, 1st of Pachon. (*W. Chr.* 122; April 26, 6)

The less restrained might sometimes even try to enforce the communication by magical means, as here on a triangular lead tablet of unknown provenance (cf. Betz 1986):

> *Sit koum aeioyô iêaê iêo yo ieô aiêoy ey iaê iaô aeyia iôa iêô êa iaô ôai* (magical gibberish). I request and beseech your power and your authority, *êkiaeoy asôr askatanthiri setônekoii* (magical gibberish), drive Termoutis, whom Sophia bore, to Zoel, whom Droser bore, with mad and unceasing, imperishable love, now, quickly. (*Suppl. Mag.* I 41; third/fourth century AD)

The texts presented above certainly indicate that there was little limit to the variety of everyday forms of communication in the imperial period. They likewise demonstrate, however, a very high intensity of written interchange. Women were included in these forms of written exchange, and naturally took part in this aspect of life. Nor was this true merely for the wives of Roman officers, but also for Egyptian mothers who were simply looking after their families. They certainly need not always have taken up the stylus themselves, as there were always professional scribes easily available. And there is no question that many people (men as well as women) could not write at all, while others perhaps regarded doing their own writing as beneath their station (cf. McDonnell 1996). This can at least be inferred from the ready inclusion of closings written in a different hand at the ends of letters, which, in better circles, as well as among the upper levels of the administration, was actually the rule. The empty and clichéd written formalities may well be explained by the fact that, even in the case of private letters, one so often made use of scribes, who tended to fall back upon a limited stock of fixed formulas for the greeting, introduction, conclusion, and closing of any given missive. At the same time, however, such permutations of the standard phrasing—for example, the reversal of the greeting, or the variation of epithets or the closing formula—could then be interpreted as significant, and were to be seen as an expression of the social relationship of the parties involved. Relative social rank, of course, was always lurking here.

CONCLUSIONS

As witnesses to the daily life of the Roman Empire, papyri from Egypt had long enjoyed a kind of privileged status; that there were, now and then, similar findings of such unassuming documents from outside Egypt as well was known mainly to specialists. More recently, however, various surprising discoveries from several different provinces of the empire have increasingly opened our eyes to a world that previously had been apparent only through the lens of other material finds. Now, these other provinces are speaking to us as had previously only Egypt, telling us with significantly more clarity about the lives of the 'little' men and women. What has been especially surprising, perhaps, is the high level of written culture that more and more emerges as having been prevalent the empire over. The materials that one relied upon to create written documents, of course, varied in accord with the locally available natural resources. In the densely forested areas of the North, wood was the material of choice; leather or parchment in the East; papyrus in Egypt; and wax tablets pretty well everywhere. And yet, whether stylus or ink was used to make the writing, the character of the texts was everywhere quite similar, revealing ancient society in all its panoply.

The needs, feelings, and fears of that population are all here richly on display. One can see, for example, that even secondary legal transactions were readily put in writing, and this by no means only in Egypt, which has traditionally been regarded as an exception in this regard. The level and variety of written communication is shown even more clearly by the great richness of private correspondence. There is thus, as a rule, no sign that communication was limited to important informational content only, much less to just what would have been absolutely necessary. On the contrary, we again and again find an abundance of incidental details, scribbled notes, or well-formed courtesies in the extant documentation. The presence of proper family archives, in which one readily finds collected and preserved not only legal documents, but also private papers of all kinds, likewise testifies to the high esteem with which written texts were generally regarded.

Thus, these kinds of text are of unparalleled value for the social history of Graeco-Roman antiquity. It might even be argued that such documents are most particularly important for revealing the areas beyond the world of daily and family life. As just one example, because of the new documentary finds, in particular, we are learning more and more about relationships between Roman citizens and the other residents of the empire's provinces. Nor does the administrative system of that world any longer feel like an anonymous monolith, but now exudes much more the sense of an intensely communicative social process. This is especially the case where petitions are concerned, for they increasingly reveal a network of governmental officials, all the way up to the emperor himself, who were in principle available to the subjects of the realm. All of this must have given the individual a distinct feeling that his needs were heeded—and that must have contributed greatly to an overall sense of contentment.[9]

9. This is largely the argument made by Ando 2000.

The significance of social interactions and the careful attention paid to questions of status are matters well on display in the realm of private law, and all of this is intimately revealed by the kinds of document we have considered here. For example, we see that contracts were entered into not only for the sake of establishing a secure legal position, should litigation arise, but also precisely to avoid the kinds of conflict that might result in a courtroom battle. And then, all the same, we have examples of years-long legal strife, arguments that often arose over relatively small sums; this seems to have been particularly the case when the members of a family, or neighbors, were involved. Such documents take us directly into the homes, the streets, the neighborhoods of the Greeks and Romans.

Thus, letters of recommendation, pleas for help, and notes from soldiers to the folks back home all open up vistas onto all the variants of social life and social mobility in the Roman world. But the extent to which written communication in and of itself was of crucial importance is demonstrated perhaps nowhere better than in the letters that carry little more than a greeting. In short, we are increasingly aware of an idiosyncratic world that existed under the Roman Empire, a world that stretched from Britain to the Euphrates, and from the Libyan desert to Germany—a world in which written communication of every conceivable variety was one of most salient hallmarks of daily life.

SUGGESTED READING

For general introductions to the field of papyrology, see Montevecchi 1988, Rupprecht 1994, (repr. 1999), or Pestman 1994; cf. also Turner 1973. Bagnall 1995 is very useful in coordinating the field of papyrology with historical study. On the history of Egypt, see Bowman 1986. To get a sense of the full integration of the available documentary source material under discussion here, and the kind of socio-historical results that can be obtained from it, see Lewis 1983, or Bowman 1994. With respect to communications of various kinds via letter as this emerges from the papyri, see Winter 1933, White 1986, Rowlandson 1998, and Bagnall and Cribiore 2006. Finally, for the writing materials and the history of the book in antiquity, see Schubart 1921, Blanck 1992, Mazal 1999, and Turner 1987, with plates.

BIBLIOGRAPHY

Ando, C. 2000. *Imperial Ideology and Provincial Loyalty in the Roman Empire.* Berkeley: University of California Press.

Bagnall, R. S. 1989. "Official and Private Violence in Roman Egypt." *Bulletin of the American Society of Papyrologists* 26: 201–16 = Bagnall, R. S. 2003. *Later Roman Egypt: Society, Religion, Economy and Administration.* Aldershot: Ashgate.

———. 1995. *Reading Papyri, Writing Ancient History.* London: Routledge.

Bagnall, R. S., and R. Cribiore. 2006. *Women's Letters from Ancient Egypt, 300 BC–AD 800.* Ann Arbor: University of Michigan Press.

Baratta, G. 2008. *"Pelles scriptae*: Inschriften auf Leder und Lederwaren." In M. Hainzmann and R. Wedenig (eds.), *Instrumenta Inscripta Latina II. Akten des 2. Internationalen Kolloquiums, Klagenfurt, 5.–8. Mai 2005*. Klagenfurt: Geschichtsverein für Kärnten.

Betz, H. D. 1986. *The Greek Magical Papyri in Translation, Including the Demotic Spells*. Chicago: University of Chicago Press.

Blanck, H. 1992. *Das Buch in der Antike*. Munich: Verlag C. H. Beck.

Bowman, A. K. 1986. *Egypt after the Pharaohs. 332 BC–AD 642, from Alexander to the Arab Conquest*. Berkeley: California University Press.

———. 1994. *Life and Letters on the Roman Frontier. Vindolanda and Its People*. London: British Museum Press.

Burkhalter, F. 1990. "Archives locales et archives centrales en Égypte romaine." *Chiron* 20: 191–216.

Casarico, L. 1985. *Il controllo della popolazione nell'Egitto romano, 1. Le denunce di morte (C. Pap. Gr. II)*. Azzate: Tipolitografia Tibiletti s.n.c.

Cockle, W. E. H. 1984. "State Archives in Graeco-Roman Egypt from 30 BC to the Reign of Septimius Severus." *The Journal of Egyptian Archaeology* 70: 106–22.

Cotton, H. 1981. *Documentary Letters of Recommendation in Latin from the Roman Empire*. Königstein/Ts.: Verlag Anton Hain.

Cotton, H. M., W. E. H. Cockle, and F. G. B. Millar. 1995. "The Papyrology of the Roman Near East: A Survey." *Journal of Roman Studies* 85: 214–35.

Feissel, D., and J. Gascou (eds.). 2004. *La pétition à Byzance*. Paris: Association des Amis du Centre d'Histoire et Civilisation de Byzance.

Gascou, J., and D. Feissel. 1995. "Documents d'archives romains inédits du moyen Euphrate (IIIᵉ s. après J.-C.)." *Journal des Savants*: 65–119.

Habermann, W. 1998. "Zur chronologischen Verteilung der papyrologischen Zeugnisse." *Zeitschrift für Papyrologie und Epigraphik* 122: 144–60.

Haensch, R. 1994. "Die Bearbeitungsweisen von Petitionen in der Provinz Aegyptus." *Zeitschrift für Papyrologie und Epigraphik* 100: 487–546.

———. 1997. "Zur Konventsordnung in Aegyptus und den übrigen Provinzen des römischen Reiches." *Akten des XXI. Internationalen Papyrologenkongresses. Berlin 13.–19. 8. 1995*. Stuttgart-Leipzig: B. G. Teubner. 320–91.

Harris, W. V. 1989. *Ancient Literacy*. Cambridge, Mass.: Harvard University Press.

Hobson, D. W. 1993. "The Impact of Law on Village Life in Roman Egypt." In B. Halpern and D. W. Hobson (eds.), *Law, Politics and Society in the Ancient Mediterranean World*. Sheffield: Sheffield Academic Press. 193–219.

Humphrey, J. H. (ed.). 1991. *Literacy in the Roman World*. Ann Arbor: Journal of Roman Archaeology.

Jördens, A. 2005. "Griechische Papyri in Soknopaiu Nesos." In S. L. Lippert and M. Schentuleit (eds.), *Tebtynis und Soknopaiu Nesos—Leben im römerzeitlichen Fajum*. Wiesbaden: Harrassowitz. 41–56.

———. 2006. "Der *praefectus Aegypti* und die Städte." In A. Kolb (ed.), *Herrschaftsstrukturen und Herrschaftspraxis: Konzeption, Prinzipien und Strategien der Administration im römischen Kaiserreich*. Berlin: Akademie Verlag. 191–200.

Kim, Ch.-H. 1972. *Form and Structure of the Familiar Greek Letter of Recommendation*. Missoula: Society for Biblical Literature.

Kruse, Th. 2002. *Der Königliche Schreiber und die Gauverwaltung. Untersuchungen zur Verwaltungsgeschichte Ägyptens in der Zeit von Augustus bis Philippus Arabs (30 v. Chr.–245 n. Chr.)*. Munich: K. G. Saur.

Leunissen, P. M. 1993. "Conventions of Patronage in Senatorial Careers under the Principate." *Chiron* 23: 101–20.

Lewis, N. 1983. *Life in Egypt under Roman Rule*. Oxford: Clarendon Press.

Mazal, O. 1999. *Griechisch-römische Antike (Geschichte der Buchkultur, 1)*. Graz: Akademische Druck- und Verlagsanstalt.

McDonnell, M. 1996. "Writing, Copying, and Autograph Manuscripts in Ancient Rome." *Classical Quarterly* 46: 469–91.

Meyer, E. A. 2004. *Legitimacy and Law in the Roman World. Tabulae in Roman Belief and Practice*. Cambridge: Cambridge University Press.

Mitthof, F., and A. Papathomas. 2004. "Ein Papyruszeugnis aus dem spätantiken Karien." *Chiron* 34: 401–24.

Montevecchi, O. 1988. *La papirologia*. 2nd ed. Milan: Vita & Pensiero.

Pestman, P. W. 1994. *The New Papyrological Primer*. 2nd ed. Leiden: E. J. Brill.

Primavesi, O. 1986. "P.Cair.inv.10554 r: Mahnverfahren mit Demosiosis." *Zeitschrift für Papyrologie und Epigraphik* 64: 99–114.

Rathbone, D. 1991. *Economic Rationalism and Rural Society in Third-Century A.D. Egypt. The Heroninos Archive and the Appianus Estate*. Cambridge: Cambridge University Press.

Rowlandson, J. (ed.). 1998. *Women & Society in Greek & Roman Egypt. A Sourcebook*. Cambridge: Cambridge University Press.

Rupprecht, H. A. 1994. *Kleine Einführung in die Papyruskunde*. Darmstadt: Wissenschaftliche Buchgesellschaft.

———. 1999. *Introduzione alla papirologia*. 2nd ed. Turin: G. Giappichelli Editore.

Schentuleit, M. 2007. "Satabus aus Soknopaiu Nesos: Aus dem Leben eines Priesters am Beginn der römischen Kaiserzeit." *Chronique d'Égypte* 82: 101–25.

Schubart, W. 1921. *Das Buch bei den Griechen und Römern*. 2nd ed. Berlin: Walter de Gruyter.

Sider, D. 2005. *The Library of the Villa dei Papiri at Herculaneum*. Los Angeles: J. Paul Getty Museum.

Strassi, S. 2008. *L'archivio di Claudius Tiberianus da Karanis*. Berlin: Walter de Gruyter.

Thomas, J. D. 1999. "Communication between the Prefect of Egypt, the Procurators and the Nome Officials." In W. Eck (ed.), *Lokale Autonomie und römische Ordnungsmacht in den kaiserzeitlichen Provinzen vom 1. bis 3. Jahrhundert*. Munich: R. Oldenbourg Verlag. 181–95.

Turner, E. G. 1973. *The Papyrologist at Work*. Durham: Duke University Press.

———. 1987. *Greek Manuscripts of the Ancient World*. 2nd ed. London: University of London—Institute for Classical Studies.

White, J. L. 1972. *The Form and Structure of the Official Petition: A Study in Greek Epistolography*. Missoula: Society of Biblical Literature.

———. 1986. *Light from Ancient Letters*. Philadelphia: Fortress Press.

Winter, J. G. 1933. *Life and Letters in the Papyri*. Ann Arbor: University of Michigan Press.

Wolff, H. J. 1978. *Das Recht der griechischen Papyri Ägyptens in der Zeit der Ptolemaeer und des Prinzipats, II: Organisation und Kontrolle des privaten Rechtsverkehrs*. Munich: Verlag C. H. Beck.

Yiftach-Firanko, U. 2007. "The Rise of *Hypomnêma* as a Lease Contract." *Proceedings of the 24th International Congress of Papyrology. Helsinki 1.–7. 8. 2004*. Helsinki: Societas Scientiarum Fennica. 1051–61.

CHAPTER 11

COINS AND COMMUNICATION

CARLOS F. NOREÑA

INTRODUCTION

THE primary function of coinage in the ancient world was economic. Like other types of currency—for example, cattle, slaves, agricultural produce, metals—coins might serve as an accumulation of material wealth, an index of value, or a medium of exchange for goods and services (Polanyi 1968; Howgego 1995: 12–23; Harris 2008). Coinage, in other words, is a particular form of money, as Aristotle recognized (*Pol.* 1256b–1258a), but not the only one. Two features that distinguished ancient coins from other types of money were their adherence to a standard, which reduced transaction costs, and the fact that they bore designs indicating a minting authority, which in principle guaranteed their monetary value. Both features maximized the monetary utility of coinage, and both reflect the critical role of the state in producing it. In fact, the minting of coinage was, in practice, the near-exclusive prerogative of the state. There can be little doubt that the main reason for minting coinage in the ancient world was to facilitate state expenditure (Crawford 1970). But ancient states could also mint new coins in order to affirm status; to replace older coins that were worn or overvalued; or even to facilitate private trade (Howgego 1990).

It is important to keep these economic functions in mind when considering coinage as a medium of communications in the ancient world. Three points deserve particular emphasis. First, the designs on coins, usually some combination of type and legend, not only identified the issuing authority, but could also be employed to convey a wide range of messages. As a result, coins were commodities in which two different regimes of value, the economic and the symbolic, converged and reinforced one another. Second, coins were official documents. Though many details of mint operations are obscure to us, we can say that state control over the production of coins invested the messages they conveyed with a high degree of formal authority. And third, the use of coins for state expenditure required production on a near-industrial scale, which ensured constant circulation in both the public and private spheres. In no other medium were simple messages transmitted under state authority so regularly, and so extensively communicated to so many individuals. It was this distinctive combination of official status, simultaneous embodiment of economic and symbolic value, and mass production, then, that made coinage such a potentially powerful medium of communications in a pre-industrial world.

The purpose of this chapter is to examine how Roman coinage worked as a medium of communications in the Roman world. The term 'Roman coinage' embraces all coins minted in areas under Roman administrative control. This includes both the coinage produced under the authority of the central state, mainly in the city of Rome, and the numerous civic and regional coinages produced under local authority in the provinces. We may refer to the former as the 'central' coinage and the latter as 'local' coinage. It should be noted, however, that for the period after 31 BC, it is now conventional to refer to the one as the 'Roman imperial coinage' and to the other as the 'Roman provincial coinage,' even though there is some overlap between the two categories (Burnett 2005: 171–73; Metcalf 2006).

Rome began to produce bronze and silver coinages in the late fourth or early third century BC. The year 211 BC saw the introduction of the silver *denarius*, which henceforth formed the basis of the denominational system for the central coinage. For most of the republic, the central coinage consisted of the *denarius* and various bronze denominations, gold not being introduced on a large scale until 46 BC. This system was overhauled and stabilized under Augustus. Denominations were still based on the *denarius*, but now included a regular gold multiple, the *aureus* (1:25), and regular 'bronze' (*aes*) fractions, the *sestertius* (4:1) and *dupondius* (8:1), both struck from an *orichalcum* alloy, and the *as* (16:1), *semis* (32:1), and *quadrans* (64:1), all made of copper. The most important subsequent denominations, introduced under the duress of inflation and debasement, include the silver *antoninianus* (twice the face-value but only 1.5 times the weight of the *denarius*), issued by Caracalla in AD 215, and the gold *solidus* (about 3/5 the weight of the early-imperial *aureus*), issued by Constantine ca. 309.

Gold coins were struck exclusively, and silver coins primarily, by the central state, and both circulated throughout the whole of the empire. For most of our period, the main central mint was located in the city of Rome, but from 12 BC to AD 64 it was in Lugdunum (Metcalf 1989). In addition, a series of 'provincial' mints in the east, especially at Alexandria, Antioch, and Caesarea in Cappadocia, produced silver and bronze coins on behalf of the central state (cf. Butcher 2004). The bronze coins produced by the central state circulated mainly in Italy and the western empire, supplemented through the early Julio-Claudian period by various base-metal coinages produced under local authority and not conforming to a uniform standard. In the east, by contrast, virtually all base-metal coins, also struck to a variety of standards, were supplied by local and regional mints, which continued in operation through the late third century AD.

It is this unwieldy mass of different coinages, all treated under the rubric of 'Roman coinage,' that forms our subject. In order to assess this coinage as a medium of communications, we may begin with a classic model of communications developed by the American political scientist Harold Lasswell (1948). The 'Lasswell formula' is based on a simple question, "Who says what in which channel to whom with what effect?" Though this model does not address some important questions that will require attention, especially those of intentionality, feedback, the slow diffusion of messages over the long term, and the effects of multiple channels operating simultaneously in a complex network of communications, it nevertheless serves as a useful way to break down a complicated process into its main constituent parts. These will be considered under the headings of 'agency' (*Who*), 'messages' (*says what*), 'medium' (*in which channel*), 'audience' (*to whom*), and 'impact' (*with what effect?*).

Agency

The first step in understanding communication by means of coins is to examine the administration of the mints, with particular attention to the questions of output and the selection of designs.

The administration of the central mint under the republic is tolerably clear (*RRC*: 598–620). Though new denominations and standards were normally authorized by statute (cf. Plin. *Nat.* 23. 46), it was the senate that controlled the state's finances (Polyb. 6. 13. 1). In practice this meant annual calculation of revenues and authorization of expenditure, which was made from some combination of old and new coin. The production of new coin was the responsibility of the *triumviri monetales*, or 'moneyers,' annually elected magistrates who served in colleges of three. How and by whom it was decided how this new coin was to be allocated among the various denominations is unknown, but patterns in type selection indicate that it was the moneyers themselves who chose the designs on the coins they struck. Who did what in the mint of the imperial period is less clear (cf. Carson 1956). The office of *triumvir monetalis* survived at least through the Severan period (*ILS* 1181), but by the early second century AD, the central mint was administered by an equestrian *procurator monetae* (*CIL* VI 1607, 1625), and it was the *a rationibus* who seems to have determined total mint output (Stat. *Silv.* 3. 3. 103–5). As under the republic, state expenditure was made both from old and from new coin. So who chose the designs on the new coins? Several references point to the intervention of the emperor (Suet. *Aug.* 94. 12, *Nero* 25. 2; Eus. *VC* 4. 15. 1; Soc. *HE* 3. 17; Soz. *HE* 5. 19. 2), but these are hardly sufficient to prove regular imperial selection of designs

(Wolters 1999: 262–64). Routine type selection was likely in the hands of the higher ranking mint officials (which would mean that the subject matter appearing on coins issued by the central government was determined by men of equestrian status; cf. Peachin 1986).

Organization of the many local mints throughout the empire varied considerably (Weiss 2005). The production of new coins was normally authorized by a decree of the local council, which presupposed central approval (or, perhaps more likely, acquiescence). In one region, Asia Minor, extensive sharing of dies between different cities implies the regular use of private workshops for the production of civic coins (Kraft 1972). Most civic coins include an ethnic identifier ('of the Ephesians,' 'of the Laodiceans,' etc.), indicating the minting authority; some also include the names of individuals, mainly local magistrates, indicating, it seems, responsibility for a particular issue. Designs must have been chosen either by these magistrates or by the local council as a whole.

In all cases, then, it was the state, whether central or local, that regulated the production of coins, and it was ultimately the state that guaranteed their economic value. Actual decisions about output and design were taken—again, insofar as this can be determined—by specific collectivities (the Roman senate and local councils) and by authorized individuals (moneyers, magistrates, mint officials, emperors). It was these actors, and not states as such, that used coins to communicate messages. And they did so with varying degrees of self-assertion, sometimes allowing themselves to be effaced by the state, sometimes aggressively pressing their own claims, but always acting under the umbrella of state authority. What degree of organization may, or may not, have been involved in all this is no longer clear. In any case, the question of who, exactly, chose this or that denomination or coin type is, at least in the present context, unimportant. What matters is that those making these decisions belonged to the political elite, and that the coins themselves were authoritative objects which literally bore the stamp of some form of state authority. As we will see when we turn to the typology of Roman coin designs, the extent to which collectivities and individuals could employ the coinage to communicate messages in their own interests depended on underlying social and political conditions and structures of power.

MESSAGES

Messages on coins were conveyed through designs. Designs normally comprised both image (type) and text (legend), and were deployed on both faces of the coin. The obverse usually identified the minting authority, while the reverse usually communicated an additional message about, or under, that authority. In different periods and contexts, either the obverse or the reverse bore most of the discursive force of the coin's message, with most of the expressive work done either by the type or the legend, but the full message of the coin depended on the image and text on both faces, and it is therefore vital to 'read' the entire coin as a single, composite whole (Wallace-Hadrill 1986: 67–70).

The designs on republican coins mark a long trajectory from the advertisement of the Roman state to the commemoration of individual aristocrats (Alföldi 1956; *RRC*: 712–44; Hölscher 1982; Flower 1996: 79–88). The earliest Roman coins bore little specifically Roman content and were hardly distinguishable from their Greek models. With the adoption of the *denarius* in 211 BC came a new typology, unambiguously Roman, that endured with little variation for the next seventy-five years. On the obverse appeared the helmeted head of Roma, and on the reverse the Dioscuri on horseback, glossed by the legend ROMA; subsequent variants of the reverse include Luna or Victoria in a biga (see fig. 11.1). During this first phase of the republican *denarius* coinage, the identity of the moneyers was normally marked by symbols or by abbreviated versions of their names, but the primary purpose of the designs was to identify the coins as Roman.

Signs of modest self-assertion on the part of the moneyers begin to appear on bronze coins in the first half of the second century BC, but the critical rupture came in 137 BC, when Tiberius Veturius minted a *denarius* with Mars instead of Roma on the obverse, and with an oath-taking scene on the reverse (see fig. 11.2). Both sides of the coin publicized Veturius' family: Mars alluded to Tiberius Veturius Philo, who had been *flamen Martialis* (priest of Mars) in 204 BC, while the oath scene not only recalled the treaty of the Caudine Forks, when Veturius' ancestor was consul (321 BC), but also referred to the Numantine treaty of 137 BC, negotiated by Veturius' relative, Tiberius Gracchus (*RRC* p. 226). For the first time, then, a Roman *denarius* transmitted a set of messages promoting an individual family, rather than the state as a whole. This departure from tradition ushered in a new phase in the typology

(a)   (b)

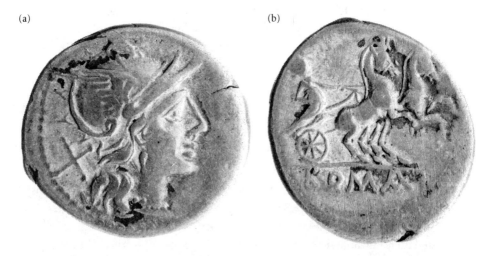

Figure 11.1. Denarius, 179–70 BC. *RRC* 158/1. Photo courtesy American Numismatic Society, 1944.100.240.

(a)   (b)

Figure 11.2. Denarius, 137 BC. *RRC* 234/1. Photo courtesy American Numismatic Society, 1941.131.57.

of the republican coinage, characterized by designs that increasingly served to commemorate the aristocratic families of individual moneyers. Commemoration sometimes took the form of allusion to divine ancestry, such as Sextus Julius Caesar's *denarius* of 129 BC depicting Venus, mythical ancestress of the Julii, on the reverse (*RRC* 258); more often, the designs celebrated the achievements of the moneyers' more recent relatives, especially in the areas of warfare (e.g., *RRC* 263/1, 269/1, advertising the military exploits of the Metelli) and monumental building (e.g., *RRC* 291, showing an aqueduct begun by Marcus Aemilius Lepidus in 187 BC). Perhaps the most important aspect of this new typology was, simply, that the designs were constantly changing. This was a revolutionary development in the use of coinage as a medium of communications; for the static typology of the early coinage— an inheritance from the Greek model—gave way to remarkable variety, a defining feature of Roman coinage from the 130s BC down to the early fourth century AD. This paradigm shift was triggered by contemporary developments in the political sphere, as moneyers sought increased publicity in the face of more acute electoral competition, and in the cultural sphere, as aristocratic families looked for new ways to 'monumentalize' their status (Meadows and Williams 2001; cf. also Flower in this volume). The underlying message of each of these designs, taken individually, was that the family concerned possessed a distinguished lineage, had served the state over multiple generations, and therefore deserved its position of honor and authority; taken as a group, these coins also asserted aristocratic superiority in general, and justified the collective dominance of the senatorial oligarchy as a whole.

The political use of the coinage as a medium of communications intensified over the course of the first century BC. Designs focused less on families across several generations, and more on living individuals. This process can be traced from the rise of the late-republican 'dynasts' through its culmination under Augustus. Both Marius and Sulla, for example, are represented, while alive, as triumphing generals (*RRC* 326/1; 367/3). Pompey is celebrated through a more elaborate symbolic program. The reverse type of one *denarius* depicts three small wreaths for Pompey's three triumphs, a large wreath for the golden crown awarded in 63, the stern of a ship for the command against the pirates, a stalk of grain for the *cura annonae* of 57, and a large globe for world conquest (see fig. 11.3). But the watershed moment on the road to monarchic symbolism came with Caesar. Particularly dramatic is a *denarius* with complex symbolism on the reverse (an axe, globe, caduceus, fasces without an axe, and clasped hands, alluding, respectively, to Caesar's pontificate, world conquest, *felicitas*, *libertas*, and *concordia*), a potent obverse legend (CAESAR DICT(ATOR) PERPETUO—'Caesar, the dictator in perpetuity'), and, most striking, a portrait of Caesar himself on the obverse (see fig. 11.4). Caesar was the first living individual to be portrayed on a Roman coin, an arresting conflation of state and individual that paved the way for the typology of the imperial coinage. Yet the trend toward the autocratic monopolization of the coinage was temporarily interrupted in the early triumviral period. While Antonius and Octavian both strove to publicize an association with Caesar (cf. *RRC* 488; 490/2), Cassius and Brutus produced designs emphasizing the republican ideal of *libertas* (*RRC* 498–508). By the later years of the triumviral period, however, designs on Roman coins were reduced to expressing the competing claims of Antonius and Octavian, and the latter's victory at Actium in 31 BC ultimately extinguished the typological and ideological polyvalence that had defined the republican coinage since the 130s. Indeed, the advent of monarchy is fully reflected in the coinage of Augustus (Wallace-Hadrill 1986; Trillmich 1988), dominated by the regular appearance of Augustus' portrait on the obverse and the prevalence of key Augustan themes on the reverse: honors voted by the senate, for example, the golden shield displaying his virtues (see fig. 11.5); 'constitutional' matters, illustrated by the recently discovered *aureus* of 28 BC with the reverse legend LEGES ET IURA P[OPULI] R[OMANI] RESTITUIT ('he restored the statutes and customary laws of the Roman people'—cf. Rich and Williams 1999); victory over foreign enemies (e.g., *RIC* 1², 275a, AEGVPTO CAPTA—'Egypt Captured'); 'personal' deities such as Apollo (e.g., *RIC* 1², 170); and dynastic arrangements (e.g., *RIC* 1², 207, depicting Gaius and Lucius Caesar).

Though aristocratic, family-oriented designs continued through the late republic, their messages were eventually overwhelmed by those publicizing the achievements and power of living individuals. These designs nevertheless continued to link the dynasts to the state as a whole. An equestrian statue of Sulla, for example, is depicted on a *denarius* with an obverse portrait of Roma, which underlines Sulla's association with the state (*RRC* 381), while the bronze coinage of Augustus carried the prominent legend S[ENATUS] C[ONSULTO] ('by decree of the senate'), initially intended to indicate authorization of the new denominational structure of the Augustan coinage (Bay 1972; *contra* Burnett 1977), but with the effect of symbolically authorizing the whole Augustan regime. One major element in the typology of coin designs that did change was the disappearance of the moneyers. Many of the most striking designs from the late republic and early Augustan period were

Figure 11.3. Denarius, 56 BC. *RRC* 426/4b. Photo courtesy American Numismatic Society, 1944.100.2621.

(a)   (b)

Figure 11.4. Denarius, 44 BC. *RRC* 480/6. Photo courtesy American Numismatic Society, 1935.117.23.

(a)   (b)

Figure 11.5. Denarius, 20–19 BC. *RIC* 1², Augustus 52b. Photo courtesy American Numismatic Society, 1937.158.408.

formally produced and signed by moneyers unrelated to the individuals celebrated on the coins; but, by the end of the first century BC, the moneyers were no longer represented, either by type or legend, and the entire discursive content of the coins was henceforth monopolized by Augustus and his successors.

The designs on Roman imperial coins produced by the central mint over the first three centuries AD expressed a relatively stable constellation of imperial ideals and values.[1] The underlying typology, however, was based on a bewildering variety of types and legends, especially on the reverses. One way to approach this immense body of material is to focus on those designs that were highly topical and surely intended to convey specific messages. Dynastic politics loomed large on such designs. Some announced successors to the throne, such as Vespasian's series depicting Titus and Domitian (e.g., *RIC* 2. 2), others publicized members of the imperial family (cf. Gaius' *sestertius* showing his three sisters, Agrippina, Drusilla, and Julia, *RIC* 1^2. 33), but most celebrated immediate imperial predecessors, normally deified (cf. Septimius Severus' CONSECRATIO—i.e., consecration as a god—types for both Pertinax, *RIC* 4. 1. 24A, and Commodus, 4. 1. 72A). Especially pointed were Hadrian's coins declaring ADOPTIO ('adoption'), which sought to legitimize his somewhat dubious accession (see fig. 11.6). Civil war contexts also called forth topical designs. Most often these proclaimed concord within the state, especially between the legions. Contenders for the throne in 69 and in 193–97 propagated virtually identical messages (cf. Vitellius in 69, FIDES EXERCITUUM—'loyalty of the armies'—*RIC* 1^2. 28, and Clodius Albinus in 195–7, FIDES LEGIONUM—'loyalty of the legions'—*RIC* 4. 1. 19). Designs were also employed to announce various types of civic benefaction, including new or restored buildings, such as the Trajanic issues representing the Column (see fig. 11.7), the Basilica Ulpia (*RIC* 2. 246), the Forum Traiani (255), and the Circus Maximus (571); new policies, such as Nerva's remission of *vehiculatio* (road tax) costs in Italy (*RIC* 2. 93), or institution of the *alimenta* (food supply) program (*RIC* 2. 92: TUTELA ITALIAE—'guardianship of Italy'); and above all cash handouts (*congiaria*). But the most regular topical designs were those announcing military victories. These were a leitmotif of the imperial coinage, with coins commemorating, for example, the victories (real or imagined) of Gaius over Germania (e.g., *RIC* 1^2. 57); Claudius over Britannia (*RIC* 1^2. 30); Vespasian over Judaea (*RIC* 2. 424); Domitian over Germania (*RIC* 2. 252); Trajan over Dacia (*RIC* 2. 96), Arabia (94), Parthia (324), Armenia and Mesopotamia (642); Marcus Aurelius over Sarmatia (*RIC* 3. 340); Septimius Severus over Parthia (*RIC* 4. 1. 142); Decius over Germania (*RIC* 4. 3. 43), and so forth.

What all these designs have in common is their topicality and short-term resonance. But communications could also occur over the long term. It must be emphasized that Roman imperial coins often remained in circulation for over a century (cf. Howgego 1994). As a result, most of the messages they bore were very

---

1. Mattingly's introductions to the individual volumes of *BMCRE* remain the best overall introduction to the designs on the imperial coinage from Augustus through Severus Alexander; for the second century, Strack 1931–37 is also basic.

Figure 11.6. Denarius, AD 117. *RIC* 2, Hadrian 3. Photo courtesy American Numismatic Society, 1978.8.1.

Figure 11.7. Sestertius, AD 112–114. *RIC* 2, Trajan 601. Photo courtesy American Numismatic Society, 1944.100.44747.

slowly diffused throughout the Roman world. In order to appreciate this long-term diffusion, it is necessary to focus not on the topical or the spectacular—the emphasis of most research on imperial coin designs—but rather on the ocean of standard and repetitive designs in circulation at any one moment. One approach is to undertake quantitative analysis of the relative frequencies of the different designs (Noreña 2001). Such analysis of all *denarii* minted at Rome between 69 and 235 reveals that personifications were the most common iconographic category (55%), followed by deities (29%). Among personification types, some designs represented abstract ideals, of which the most frequent were Pax (Peace), Felicitas (Happiness), Concordia (Harmony), and Victoria (Victory) (see fig. 11.8), and others represented

Figure 11.8. Aureus, AD 193. *RIC* 4.1, Septimius Severus 22. Photo courtesy American Numismatic Society, 1944.100.81382.

personal virtues, of which the most frequent were Aequitas (Equity), Pietas (Piety), Virtus (Virtue), Liberalitas (Generosity), and Providentia (Foresight). The message of these mostly generic, non-topical designs was that the emperor had brought about favorable conditions in the empire, and that he had done so both through military conquest and through his own paradigmatic character. And it was the long-standing iconographic idiom of the coinage itself that reinforced this message, since the benefits and virtues depicted on the reverse were almost always collocated with a portrait of the reigning emperor on the obverse (cf. Bastien 1992–94; King 1999)—the symbolic conflation of monarch and state being the core message of the imperial coinage as a whole.

The typology of the imperial coinage remained stable through most of the third century, and it would be difficult to discern from the designs alone that the state was suffering a political and military 'crisis.' With the Tetrarchy (AD 293–305), however, the iconographic variety that had characterized the Roman coinage since the 130s BC was curtailed, and topical designs became less frequent. The main innovation of the fourth century was the emergence of Christian symbolism (see fig. 11.9).

The designs on local coins minted in the Roman provinces were as varied as the cities that produced them (Harl 1987; Butcher 1988; Howgego 2005; Heuchert 2005). In the western empire, where local mints ceased producing coins during the reigns of Tiberius, Gaius, and Claudius, the designs developed from a local to an increasingly Roman imperial typology. In the Iberian peninsula, for example, most coins minted through the early first century BC look decidedly non-Roman, partly in iconographic terms, through the use of non-Roman symbols, but especially in linguistic terms, through the use of Greek, Punic, Celtiberian, Lusitanian, and other local languages for the legends (see fig. 11.10); by the early first century AD, by contrast, most local coins included portraits of emperors on the obverse and standard imperial imagery on the reverse (cf. Ripollès 2005). This shift is paralleled

Figure 11.9. Bronze, AD 350–353. *RIC* 8, Magnentius 188. Photo courtesy American Numismatic Society, 1944.100.20533.

throughout the western Mediterranean, marked most emphatically by the total displacement of local languages by Latin on legends (Burnett 2002). The underlying message of such designs was one of assimilation to Rome. In the eastern empire, with its long, pre-Roman tradition of civic coinages, designs on coins continued to promote distinctive, local identities down through the late third century AD. The most common format included a portrait of the reigning emperor on the obverse, usually glossed by an identifying legend, in Greek, and on the reverse a design of local significance, often from the religious sphere, again with a Greek legend. A coin from Laodicea in Asia, showing Augustus on the obverse and Tyche on the reverse,

(a)   (b)

Figure 11.10. As, AD 14–37. *RPC* 1, 125. Photo courtesy American Numismatic Society, 1969.222.3501.

glossed by the legend LAOKIDEŌN ('of the Laodiceans'), is a typical example
(see fig. 11.11; but cf. fig. 11.12 for an example of more exotic imagery). In addition to
civic deities and personifications of place, common reverse designs included local
buildings (especially temples), references to local games and festivals, and symbols alluding to elements of local mythology, almost always with Greek legends.
Normally bearing a portrait of the emperor on the obverse, such coins conveyed a
dual message of imperial integration and civic distinction—the twin pillars of local
identity in the Roman east (Howgego 2005).

(a)   (b)

Figure 11.11. Tetradrachm, 27 BC–AD 14. *RPC* 1, 4382.2. Photo courtesy American
Numismatic Society, 1944.100.66331.

Figure 11.12. Dichalkon, AD 126–27. Photo courtesy American Numismatic Society,
1988.59.1.

MEDIUM

In assessing coins as vehicles for the transmission of messages, it is important to remember that they were always embedded within larger networks of communications. Coins were distinctive in several respects, but their messages belonged to semiotic systems that transcended individual media. It is not surprising, then, that the messages themselves were neither distinctive nor unusual. In the middle republic, for example, the designs on coins mirror the public monuments in their focus on the state as a whole (Hölscher 1980: 269–71), while in the late republic they not only contributed to the rising tide of individualism visible in all media (Hölscher 1982, 1984), but also reflect the contemporary interest in monumentalizing the past (Meadows and Williams 2001). During the imperial period, when all official media of communications were monopolized by the imperial regime, the messages on coins could be coordinated with those in other media to maximize the impact of a public statement. Two examples from the reign of Vespasian illustrate such coordination. The well known IUDAEA CAPTA ('Judaea Captured') type of 71 was only minted intensively between May and July of that year, surely in conjunction with the triumph over Judaea in June (Kraay 1978). And in 75, the dedication of the Templum Pacis and the extension of the *pomerium* were commemorated in part by a dramatic increase in the volume of *denarii* advertising Pax (Noreña 2003). In both cases, the coinage was skillfully employed to reinforce messages transmitted by other means. Local coinages, too, often operated in harmony with other media. This is especially clear in the symbolic association of Roman imperial power and local identity, reflected both in the typology of the coins, with their regular collocation of imperial portraits and images of local significance, and in the characteristic mixing of Roman and Greek elements in local festivals, sculpture, monuments, and public space (Howgego 2005: 15; Heuchert 2005: 44).

One feature of coinage as a medium of communications that is sometimes overlooked is the discursive flexibility enabled by the minting of multiple denominations. This flexibility is most apparent on the Roman imperial coinage, with its wide-ranging and relatively stable denominational structure, where we find some intriguing correlations between message and denomination. Imperial *congiaria* (distributions of cash to the urban plebs), for example, tended to be commemorated by elaborate distribution scenes on *sestertii*, and by the personification of imperial generosity (*liberalitas*) on *aurei* and *denarii* (Metcalf 1993)—a literal message for the base metal coins, in other words, and an abstract one for the precious metal coins. And on the coinage of Vitellius, certain legends were confined to precious metal coins (e.g., FIDES EXERCITUUM, PONT[IFEX] MAXIM[US]), while others were confined to base metal coins (e.g., SECURITAS P[OPULI] ROMANI, LIBERTAS AUGUSTI, ANNONA AUG[USTA/I] (Hekster 2003). The potential significance of such correlations between message and denomination becomes clear when we turn to the question of audience.

AUDIENCE

Anyone who handled coins in the Roman world was a potential recipient of the messages they conveyed. Though the extent to which the economies of the Roman world were monetized cannot be determined with precision, and though the use of money in forms other than coin, such as bullion (Howgego 1992: 8–12) and credit (Harris 2006), may have been widespread, we can say with some confidence that coin use was regular in urban centers and not uncommon in rural areas (Howgego 1992: 16–22), and that nearly everyone in the Roman world used coins at one time or another.

Reaching such a large audience was made possible by the mass production and far-flung circulation of coins. In the case of imperial coins, which circulated among tens of millions of users, there are some hints of attempts to reach specific cross-sections of the population. The patterning in representations of imperial *congiaria* discussed above may point to an effort to pitch the same message differently to different social classes: abstract idealism for the wealthy, educated users of high-value coins, pedestrian literalism for the masses carrying small change. Similar calculations might have governed the choice of legends for the coins of Vitellius: political ideals for the upper classes, and social ideals for the lower classes. There are also some geographical patterns. The concentration in mid-second-century Britain of coins depicting Britannia, for example, may indicate an attempt to appeal to provincial identity (cf. Walker 1988). In these and similar cases, however, it is difficult to prove intent. Perhaps we should look instead to the targeting of soldiers. After all, most newly minted coins were put into circulation through state payments (see below), most of the imperial budget was devoted to the army—as high as 77%, according to one estimate (Duncan Jones 1994: 33–46)—and much of the iconography of the imperial coinage, especially the portraiture of the emperor (Bastien 1992: 235–80; King 1999: 133), was martial in nature. Or maybe the designs on imperial coins were chosen with a view to pleasing a single person, the emperor (Levick 1982).

But did these messages have any demonstrable effect on the thinking or behavior of emperors or soldiers? Or of the coins' millions of other users? Were the messages intelligible? Did anyone even notice them?

IMPACT

These questions have been the subject of intense debates for over fifty years now (initiated by Jones 1956), but there is no consensus in sight (Wolters 1999: 255–339; Levick 1999). Let us begin with the problem of the intelligibility of coin designs. Instead of declaring that these designs either were or were not intelligible, we should think in terms of a spectrum of intelligibility. At one end of the spectrum is the *denarius* coinage of the middle republic (c. 211–137 BC), when coins with a simple and largely static design (see fig. 11.1) circulated mainly in Rome and peninsular Italy among users who must have been familiar with Roman iconography. Most of the designs on local coinages also fall on this 'more intelligible' end of the spectrum. These coins feature multiple images (cf. figs. 11.10–11.12), to be sure, but they were drawn from a traditional, local repertoire, and the coins usually circulated locally (Jones 1963: 313–24). At the other end of the spectrum are the coins from the late Roman Republic. Many of the designs seem intentionally obscure—recall the complex symbolism of the coins of Tiberius Veturius, Pompey, and Caesar (see figs. 11.2–11.4)—aimed at the elite and perhaps even designed to exclude the masses from full understanding (cf. Hölscher 1984). Indeed, it is difficult to escape the conclusion that most of the nuances of these designs were lost on the majority of the coins' users. Somewhere in the middle of the spectrum is the Roman imperial coinage. On the one hand, the obverse portrait of the emperor was a standard and easily comprehended image, and the reverse designs employed a limited pictorial vocabulary (cf. figs. 11.5–11.9); on the other hand, the designs varied constantly, the coins circulated from one end of the empire to the other (and beyond), and not everyone could read the Latin legends. In general, what was necessary in order to understand the designs on coins was a basic level of visual and cultural literacy. And this must have been very high in the Roman world, characterized, as it was, by the omnipresence of public images in everyday life (Hölscher forthcoming). The intelligibility of individual coins should be assessed on a case-by-case basis, of course, but it seems safe to say that most users of coins understood most of the messages conveyed by their designs.

Even if most of the designs on coins were broadly intelligible to most of the coins' users, it is nevertheless very difficult to demonstrate their specific effects, if any. The literary sources offer little guidance. There are some mentions of numismatic imagery (e.g., the *New Testament* passages on the emperor's image on coins, *Matthew* 22: 19–21, *Mark* 12: 15–17, *Luke* 20: 22–25; Epictetus on differing reactions to coins of Trajan and Nero, *Ench.* 3. 4. 5), and even a handful of well-known references to specific designs (Dio on Brutus' famous EID MAR—'the Ides of March'—type, Dio. 47. 25. 3; Suetonius on Augustus' capricorn type, *Aug.* 94. 12; Socrates on the reaction in Antioch to Julian's 'pagan' bull type, *HE* 3. 17), but these passages cannot by themselves sustain the proposition that designs were regularly noticed. Material and documentary evidence is more illuminating. Patterns in type selection on the imperial coinage itself, for example, indicate that earlier designs could influence later ones. This is most evident in the explicit 'restoration' types of the first two centuries AD (Komnick 2001), but can also be perceived in other cases, as under Vespasian, when the central mint issued a whole series of imitation types (Buttrey 1972). These are good examples of what communications theorists refer to as a 'feedback loop,' a recursive process in which the medium has an effect upon its source (cf. Westley and MacLean 1957). On local coinages, too, we can discern the influence of imperial coins. The mint of Alexandria, for example, issued a series of designs emphasizing mythology and place from the late first to the mid-second century AD, roughly when these themes became prominent on the imperial coinage (Howgego 2005: 14–15). Another potential indicator is art in the private sphere. For the Augustan period, at least, it has been shown that the spread of official imagery from the public sphere to domestic contexts was extensive (Hölscher 1984: 20–32; Zanker 1988: 265–95), and we may reasonably infer that the coinage played an important role in the process. The epigraphic record also provides some insights. The initial appearance of certain superlative epithets in provincial honorific inscriptions for the emperor follows closely behind the initial appearance of the related virtues on the coinage (Wallace-Hadrill 1981: 23–24), and quantitative analysis reveals that long-term fluctuations in the relative frequencies of these virtue types are mirrored in the frequencies with which the epithets are cited in these inscriptions (Noreña 2011: chpt. 5).

There are several avenues for investigating the impact of the designs on coins, then, all of them promising and in need of further research. But it is vital to keep in mind that the messages transmitted by coins were very similar, and often identical, to those conveyed by other media, most of which (unlike the coins) are no longer extant. It may not be possible, in other words, to pinpoint the specific role played by coins in the overall transmission of particular messages.

We come finally to the question of whether or not coinage in the Roman world should be seen as a vehicle of propaganda (Levick 1999: 50–52; Wolters 2003). Much of the discussion on this contentious issue has concentrated on the imperial coinage, and has focused on whether individual designs advanced what Ellul has called 'agitation propaganda,' the intense, aggressive, and often subversive attempt to change attitudes (1973: 71–75). Missing from the debates about agency and intent in the selection of designs is sufficient attention to the mechanics of coin production and circulation, which virtually preclude the possibility of coins being used in this way on a regular basis. As far as we know, most new coin was put into circulation through state payments (cf. Harl 1996: figs. 9.1–4), but we do not know what proportion of such expenditure was made from newly minted coins (Howgego 1990: 11–15). There are some reasons to suspect that it was low. The costs involved in the physical movement of coin between the provinces and the treasury at Rome will have been considerable (Millar 2004: 89–104), making regular, large-scale recycling of old coin unlikely. And quantitative studies of mint output from the first two centuries AD suggest that new coin accounted for a low percentage of state expenditure—perhaps as low as 10% (Carradice 1983 on Domitian, with Burnett 1987: 95; Duncan-Jones 1994: 46, 111–12). Even more important, all newly minted coins will have been swallowed up by the bulk of old coins already in circulation (cf. Howgego 1994), with the result that their messages, unless carefully coordinated with those in other media, will have been diluted almost immediately. For these reasons, coins were ill-suited to function as weapons in concerted campaigns of 'agitation' propaganda.

If, however, we consider what Ellul has called 'integration propaganda,' which is diffuse, subtle, and intended to bolster existing attitudes (1973: 75–76), and if we concentrate not on individual designs, but rather on the mass of coins in circulation, then we may conclude that the coinage had a major impact. Though the specific effect of messages on coins is difficult to document, as we have seen, the distinctive features of the coinage as a medium of communications ensured that coins played a crucial role in shaping public discourse—critical for the maintenance of any configuration of power. Consider the function of the coinage in the Roman Empire. Over the course of the second century AD, according to one estimate, the central mint produced over 15 million *denarii* per year, and as many as 500 million under Septimius Severus alone (Duncan-Jones 1994: 165). No other commodity in the Roman world was produced on that scale. And coins were portable. As a result of their mass production and portability, coins were everywhere, constantly crossing back and forth between the public and private spheres. The rise of the imperial portrait as a standard feature of both the central and the local coinages is only the most conspicuous example of the cumulative effect of coins. It was above all the regular appearance of the emperor's image on coins that made this image ubiquitous, in the forum and in the private home alike, from one end of the Roman world to the other. This proliferation of the imperial image was perhaps the key development in the emergence of the 'imagined community' that was the Roman Empire. In a world without modern technologies of mass communications, the only medium capable of such a deep impact was the coinage.

SUGGESTED READING

The best introduction to coinage in the ancient Greek and Roman world is Howgego 1995. For the Roman coinage, Burnett 1987 covers the central coinage, and Butcher 1988 the local coinages of the empire; shorter introductions include Pobjoy 2006 (republican coinage) and Metcalf 2006 (imperial and provincial coinage). The major reference works on the central coinage are, for the republic, Crawford (*RRC*), and for the empire, *Roman Imperial Coinage* (*RIC*) and *Coins of the Roman Empire in the British Museum* (*BMCRE*). The most important current research project on Roman coinage is the multi-volume *Roman Provincial Coinage* (*RPC*), of which several volumes have appeared; updates to the project, as well as a database with images, can be found at the *RPC Online: Roman Provincial Coinage Project* site: http:// rpc.ashmus.ox.ac.uk/project/.

BIBLIOGRAPHY

Alföldi, A. 1956. "The Main Aspects of Political Propaganda on the Coinage of the Roman Republic." In Carson and Sutherland 1956: 63–95.
Bastien, P. 1992–94. *Le Buste monétaire des empereurs romains*. 3 vols. Wetteren: Édition Numismatique Romaine, Essais, recherches et documents 19.
Bay, A. 1972. "The Letters *SC* on Augustan *aes* Coinage." *Journal of Roman Studies* 62: 111–22.
Burnett, A. 1977. "The Authority to Coin in the Late Republic and Early Empire." *Numismatic Chronicle* 137: 37–63.

———. 1987. *Coinage in the Roman World*. London: Seaby.

———. 2002. "Latin on Coins of the Western Empire." In A. E. Cooley (ed.), *Becoming Roman, Writing Latin? Literacy and Epigraphy in the Roman West*. Portsmouth, R.I.: Journal of Roman Archaeology, Supplement 48. 33–40.

———. 2005. "The Roman West and the Roman East." In Howgego, Heuchert, and Burnett 2005: 171–80.

Butcher, K. 1988. *Roman Provincial Coins: An Introduction to the 'Greek Imperials.'* London: Seaby.

———. 2004. *Coinage in Roman Syria: Northern Syria, 64 BC–AD 253*. London: Royal Numismatic Society.

Buttrey, T. V. 1972. "Vespasian as Moneyer." *Numismatic Chronicle* 7th ser. 12: 89–109.

Carradice, I. 1983. *Coinage and Finances in the Reign of Domitian AD 81–96*. Oxford: British Archaeological Reports.

Carson, R. A. G. 1956. "System and Product in the Roman Mint." In Carson and Sutherland 1956: 227–39.

Carson, R. A. G., and C. H. V. Sutherland (eds.) 1956. *Essays in Roman Coinage presented to Harold Mattingly*. Oxford: Oxford University Press.

Crawford, M. 1970. "Money and Exchange in the Roman World." *Journal of Roman Studies* 60: 40–48.

Duncan-Jones, R. 1994. *Money and Government in the Roman Empire*. Cambridge: Cambridge University Press.

Ellul, J. 1973. *Propaganda: The Formation of Men's Attitudes*. New York: Vintage Books.

Flower, H. 1996. *Ancestor Masks and Aristocratic Power in Roman Culture*. Oxford: Clarendon Press.

Harl, K. 1987. *Civic Coins and Civic Politics in the Roman East A.D. 180–275*. Berkeley: University of California Press.

———. 1996. *Coinage in the Roman Economy 300 B.C. to A.D. 700*. Baltimore: Johns Hopkins University Press.

Harris, W. V. 2006. "A Revisionist View of Roman Money." *Journal of Roman Studies* 96: 1–24.

———. (ed.). 2008. *The Monetary Systems of the Greeks and Romans*. Oxford: Oxford University Press.

Hekster, O. 2003. "Coins and Messages: Audience Targeting on Coins of Different Denominations?" In L. De Blois, P. Erdkamp, O. Hekster, G. de Kleijn, and S. Mols (eds.), *The Representation and Perception of Roman Imperial Power*. Amsterdam: J. C. Geiben. 20–35.

Heuchert, V. 2005. "The Chronological Development of Roman Provincial Coin Iconography." In Howgego, Heuchert, and Burnett 2005: 29–56.

Hölscher, T. 1980. "Die Geschichtsauffassung in der römischen Repräsentationskunst." *Jahrbuch des Deutschen Archäologischen Instituts* 95: 265–321.

———. 1982. "Die Bedeutung der Münzen für das Verständnis der politischen Repräsentationskunst der späten römischen Republik." In T. Hackens and R. Weiller (eds.), *Actes du 9ème Congrès International de Numismatique*. Louvain-la-Neuve: Association Internationale des Numismates Professionnels. 269–82.

———. 1984. *Staatsdenkmal und Publikum: vom Untergang der Republik bis zur Festigung des Kaisertums in Rom*. Konstanz: Konstanzer althistorische Vorträge und Forschungen 9.

———. Forthcoming. *Visual Power in Ancient Greece and Rome*. Berkeley: University of California Press.

Howgego, C. 1990. "Why did Ancient States Strike Coins?" *Numismatic Chronicle* 150: 1–25.

————. 1992. "The Supply and Use of Money in the Roman World 200 BC to AD 300." *Journal of Roman Studies* 82: 1–31.

————. 1994. "Coin Circulation and the Integration of the Roman Economy." *Journal of Roman Archaeology* 7: 5–21.

————. 1995. *Ancient History from Coins*. London: Routledge.

————. 2005. 'Coinage and Identity in the Roman Provinces.' In Howgego, Heuchert, and Burnett 2005: 1–18.

Howgego, C., V. Heuchert, and A. Burnett (eds.). 2005. *Coinage and Identity in the Roman Provinces*. Oxford: Oxford University Press.

Jones, A. H. M. 1956. "Numismatics and History." In Carson and Sutherland 1956: 13–33.

Jones, T. B. 1963. "A Numismatic Riddle: the so called Greek Imperials." *Proceedings of the American Philosophical Society* 107: 308–47.

King, C. E. 1999. "Roman Portraiture: Images of Power?" In Paul and Ierardi 1999: 123–36.

Komnick, H. 2001. *Die Restitutionsmünzen der frühen Kaiserzeit: Aspekte der Kaiserlegitimation*. Berlin: Walter de Gruyter.

Kraay, C. 1978. "The Bronze Coinage of Vespasian: Classification and Attribution." In R. A. G. Carson and C. Kraay (eds.), *Scripta Nummaria Romana: Essays Presented to Humphrey Sutherland*. London: Spink and Son. 47–57.

Kraft, K. 1972. *Das System der kaiserzeitlichen Münzprägung in Kleinasien*. Berlin: Gebr. Mann Verlag.

Lasswell, H. 1948. "The Structure and Function of Communication in Society." In L. Bryson (ed.), *The Communication of Ideas*. New York: Institute for Religious and Social Studies.

Levick, B. 1982. "Propaganda and the Imperial Coinage." *Antichthon* 16: 104–16.

————. 1999. "Messages on the Roman Coinage: Types and Inscriptions." In Paul and Ierardi 1999: 41–60.

Meadows, A., and J. Williams. 2001. "Moneta and the Monuments: Coinage and Politics in Republican Rome." *Journal of Roman Studies* 91: 27–49.

Metcalf, W. E. 1989. "Rome and Lugdunum Again." *American Journal of Numismatics* 1: 51–70.

————. 1993. "Whose Liberalitas? Propaganda and Audience in the Early Roman Empire." *Rivista italiana di numismatica e scienze affini* 95: 337–46.

————. 2006. "Roman Imperial Numismatics." In D. S. Potter (ed.), *A Companion to the Roman Empire*. Oxford: Blackwell. 35–44.

Millar, F. 2004. "Cash Distributions in Rome and Imperial Minting." In H. Cotton and G. Rogers (eds.), *Government, Society, & Culture in the Roman Empire*, vol. 2 of *Rome, the Greek World, and the East*. Chapel Hill: University of North Carolina Press. 89–104.

Noreña, C. F. 2001. "The Communication of the Emperor's Virtues." *Journal of Roman Studies* 91: 146–68.

————. 2003. "Medium and Message in Vespasian's Templum Pacis." *Memoirs of the American Academy in Rome* 48: 25–43.

————. 2011. *Imperial Ideals in the Roman West: Representation, Circulation, Power*. Cambridge: Cambridge University Press.

Paul, G. M., and M. Ierardi (eds.). 1999. *Roman Coins and Public Life under the Empire: E. Togo Salmon Papers II*. Ann Arbor: University of Michigan Press.

Peachin, M. 1986. "The Procurator Monetae." *Numismatic Chronicle* 146: 94–106.

Pobjoy, M. 2006. "Epigraphy and Numismatics." In N. Rosenstein and R. Morstein-Marx (eds.), *A Companion to the Roman Republic*. Oxford: Blackwell. 51–80.

Polanyi, K. 1968. "The Semantics of Money-Uses." In G. Dalton (ed.), *Primitive, Archaic and Modern Economies: Essays of Karl Polanyi*. Garden City: Doubleday Anchor. 175–203.

Rich, J., and J. Williams. 1999. "*Leges et iura P.R. restituit*: A New Aureus of Octavian and the Settlement of 28–27 BC." *Numismatic Chronicle* 159: 169–213.

Ripollès, P. 2005. "Coinage and Identity in the Roman Provinces: Spain." In Howgego, Heuchert, and Burnett 2005: 79–93.

Strack, P. 1931–1937. *Untersuchungen zur römischen Reichsprägungen des 2. Jahrhunderts.* 3 vols. Stuttgart: W. Kohlhammer.

Trillmich, W. 1988. "Münzpropaganda." In M. Hofter (ed.), *Kaiser Augustus und die verlorene Republik*. 474–528. Mainz: Philipp von Zabern.

Walker, D. R. 1988. *Roman Coins from the Sacred Spring at Bath*. Oxford: Oxford University Committee for Archaeology.

Wallace-Hadrill, A. 1981. "Galba's Aequitas." *Numismatic Chronicle* 141: 20–39.

———. 1986. "Image and Authority in the Coinage of Augustus." *Journal of Roman Studies* 76: 66–87.

Weiss, P. 2005. "The Cities and Their Money." In Howgego, Heuchert, and Burnett 2005: 57–68.

Westley, B., and B. MacLean. 1957. "A Conceptual Model for Mass Communication Research." *Journalism Quarterly* 34: 31–38.

Wolters, R. 1999. *Nummi Signati: Untersuchungen zur römischen Münzprägung und Geldwirtschaft*. Munich: Verlag C. H. Beck.

———. 2003. "Die Geschwindigkeit der Zeit und die Gefahr der Bilder: Münzbilder und Münzpropaganda in der römischen Kaiserzeit." In G. Weber and M. Zimmermann (eds.), *Propaganda—Selbstdarstellung—Repräsentation im römischen Kaiserreich des I. Jhs. n.Chr.* Wiesbaden: Franz Steiner Verlag. 175–204.

Zanker, P. 1988. *The Power of Images in the Age of Augustus*. Ann Arbor: University of Michigan Press.

PART IV

COMMUNAL CONTEXTS FOR SOCIAL INTERACTION

CHAPTER 12

ELITE SELF-REPRESENTATION IN ROME

HARRIET I. FLOWER

INTRODUCTION

ELITE self-representation informs much, if not most, of the Roman culture to which we have access via literary texts and artistic monuments. It was the wealthy and educated who had the leisure and resources to produce or commission creative works in most media; and, given the political concerns of their world, they were highly motivated to create memorials of their achievements and values that might last well beyond their own generation. Consequently, anyone who studies the culture of the Romans must start from the realization that the majority of citizens (i.e., those who did not belong to the very small elite) left little or nothing for posterity. Our understanding of Rome and its people is, therefore, a partial and biased one. This observation applies to prose and verse texts, art, architecture, numismatics, and many epigraphical records. It is likewise necessary to realize that the urban image of the city of Rome, a powerful political and cultural capital of a world empire, was projected by the ancient elites, and most often also read and interpreted by elites in later ages. By contrast, we have only limited access to anything that could be termed a plebeian culture (*cultura della plebs*) although we know that such a popular culture flourished in the ancient city (Horsfall 2003). It was the elites who defined Rome, its character and place in the world, and within the European cultural imagination.

This essay will consider the nature of such elite Roman self-representation in the specific cultural context of ancient society. There is no room here to discuss the way Roman self-construction was interpreted and imitated by later ages. Rather, the present focus will be on the elites of antiquity and the function of their self-representation within the Rome of their own times. Nearly all the ancient literary texts that have come down to us can be interpreted as some form of elite self-representation, with the exception of the very earliest authors. Plautus, Ennius, and Terence do not fit into this category, since they were foreigners, who had come to Rome as slaves or traveling players. The earliest literature in Latin that we know of seems to have been mostly written by freedmen, but this pattern changed during the second century BC. Despite the fact that many Roman slaves were highly literate and well educated in a wide range of disciplines, literary production in most genres became associated with the elites and with their particular cultural concerns. The reason for this may be connected with the fact that so much literature was produced with a view to some form of performance, within a city that thrived on spectacle and celebration. However, this essay will concern itself with the broader aspects of elite self-representation, rather than with the history of literature written in Latin (on which, see Conte 1994, and Walter 2004).

In Rome, as in so many societies, political and social influence resided in the means and methods of communicating and representing that influence. Communication had very direct effects in terms of power and prestige. Rome originated as a city-state and continued to cultivate aspects of this original condition throughout its long history. Roman politics grew within a defined urban space and under conditions of a tightly knit, face-to-face community. In this context, Romans of all backgrounds saw and watched each other regularly, even as they also cultivated an image of their city to present to a wider world, first in Italy, and then beyond (Morstein-Marx and Rosenstein 2006). Self-representation, especially in the form of spectacle and the visual media, was as important as any activity for those who wanted to be recognized as leaders in the city (Hölkeskamp 2001). Communication of various sorts, therefore, provided the essential bond between fellow members of the elite, between the elite and the masses, and between Romans and foreigners, particularly elites in other cities and communities. This short essay will focus on the city of Rome and its elite, although Rome's expanding influence fostered and clashed with a variety of elite cultures throughout the Mediterranean world.

Now, the identity of Rome's elites was shaped by the rituals and symbols they employed, several of which endured over many generations. In this sense, elite self-representation should not simply be seen in terms of propaganda imposed by the powerful on the rest of society. Rather, leading Romans were expected to conform to inherited patterns of behavior and achievement within a traditional social setting. Under these conditions, politics was the ultimate and only way to achieve elite status, and career paths became increasingly elaborate and hierarchical. At the same time, spectacles, such as the triumphal procession, the games, and theatrical performances, provided spheres within which Romans of all backgrounds interacted freely, communicated ideas openly, and shared a sense of community and common identity (Flower 2004). In this sense, Roman elite self-representation nearly always addressed the traditional status and character of the community as a whole, at the same time as it was designed to celebrate its leaders, rather than stressing social distance or differences in material wealth. Self-representation also depended in important ways on an appreciative and present audience, which reacted quickly and publicly to rituals and monuments.

This discussion will now proceed to examine three different examples of elite self-representation in Rome: the political culture of the republican office-holding class (the *nobiles*) (second—first centuries BC); Augustus' self-representation when he defined himself as a single leader in relation to the traditional modes of self-representation long favored by the republican elites (late first century BC—early first century AD); and the changed world of elite culture depicted in detail in the letters of Pliny the Younger (early second century AD).

IMAGE MAKING AND THE CHARACTER
OF ROMAN REPUBLICAN POLITICS

Recent scholarly debates about the nature of Roman politics, especially in the republican period, have focused in a particular way on the question of popular participation in political decision making and on the real locus of power, on the tacit assumption that such a locus can indeed be identified. Many scholars had tended to describe the republic, and indeed any constitutional form of government, as essentially an oligarchy, either more or less disguised by political rhetoric and public relations exercises depending on the prevailing political climate (following Syme 1939). By contrast, the last twenty years have witnessed a serious and well-argued attempt to present Rome as a type of democracy, in which the ordinary voters (adult male citizens, present in person at the voting) had the ultimate say in choosing leaders and in deciding policies (esp. Millar 1998, 2002). Others have countered with a variety of observations about the limits on popular power and participation inherent in Roman practices (Jehne 1995; Hölkeskamp 2004a and 2004b; Flaig 2003). One should especially note the following factors: the limited number of citizens who could vote in person at Rome on any given day; the lack of free political debate and any right to public speech or assembly; evidence from extant sources that citizens tended frequently to endorse elite proposals and elect candidates from the same families over many generations; the significant powers of magistrates in office (all of whom were wealthy and many of whom came from traditional political families), including their ability to orchestrate the voting and electoral assemblies over which they presided; and ultimately, the huge influence on Roman society of the republican senate, composed of former magistrates who were members for life. For our present purposes, it is highly significant to note that this lively and on-going debate really involves, to a significant degree, the nature and impact of elite self-representation as one of its most central concerns.

Both sides in the present debate have invoked the intensity and importance of elite communication with ordinary citizens as evidence in support of their own interpretation of Rome's political structures. The basic conditions of the Roman Republic involved the need for elites to seek political offices through repeated electoral successes (Nicolet 1980). Similarly, policy decisions were also subject, at least formally, to the ratification of the voters. Did the elaborate self-advertisement and status seeking of the Roman politician reflect his genuine dependence on these voters, or was it the means by which he influenced ordinary citizens and achieved an elaborately staged consensus, at the expense of what a modern political theorist would classify as genuine debate and deliberation? A situation of voting, whether in an election or concerning a piece of legislation, can be interpreted as an expression of popular will or as a carefully orchestrated ritual of consensus, in which the elites enjoyed the traditional and anticipated acquiescence of ordinary citizens. Studies of electioneering and of political speeches (*contiones*) have shed further light on the interaction of Roman elites with ordinary citizens (Yacobson 1999 and 2004; Morstein-Marx 2004; also Pina Polo in this volume). The importance accorded to rhetoric, which was the essential component of elite education next to military training, reflects the need to persuade and to influence one's fellow citizens both in political and in forensic contexts.[1]

Among a number of significant issues that have emerged from this debate is the central importance of the elites and their image within society. They were the ones who staged political discourse, with all its rituals and images, as well as creating the very notion of a society that was 'republican,' in other words one in which there was a public airing and settling of issues of common concern to the whole community (Mouritsen 2001). The history of Rome, which was written in both Greek and Latin by senators during the republican period, seems to have been consistently and stridently anti-monarchical, while celebrating the society and imperial aspirations of the Roman people and of their senate (Walter 2004). The Roman community was known as *Senatus Populusque Romanus (SPQR)*, the senate and the Roman people, a phrase that put the political elite first but that stressed a partnership working together in a harmonious political community (Bonnefond-Coudry 1989; Ryan 1998); moreover, the story of Rome as a community was often equated with the stories of individual political leaders and of their families' service to the state (Hölkeskamp and Stein-Hölkeskamp 2000). But in the end, the celebration of merit, achievement, and harmony within society supported the overall position of the political elites, while still connecting them closely with ordinary Romans, whom they interacted with frequently both in the city and during military campaigns.

As things stand, there has been no clear resolution of the question of what exactly to call the Roman political system in terms of modern political theory. It is

---

1. On the place and importance of the rhetorical education in Roman society, see Connolly in this volume.

notable that the Romans themselves did not develop a terminology for their system of government. The label *res publica* (the public thing), from which we get our term 'republic,' was always vague and could refer to the state or the citizen body, as well as to the constitution, which was never written down. The rhetoric of traditional values, identified closely with the customs of the ancestors (*mos maiorum*), masked a society that was dynamic and subject to continual change, whether due to external influences (especially from Greek culture) or to internal political debates. The development of the hierarchy of magisterial offices (*cursus honorum*) provides just one obvious example of evolution within the republican context (Beck 2005). The importance of group deliberation, whether in the senate or in public, can be attested early in Rome, both in the role of the senate and in that of the informal circle of advisers often invoked by elite Romans (*consilium*). At the same time, compromise was highly valued and could reap distinct political rewards, both for individual politicians and for groups within society. But whether the Roman idea of consensus and societal harmony really corresponds by analogy to any more modern political system remains an open question. In sum, the political life of ancient Rome relied very heavily on communication within the city of a particular set of elite self-representations. The resultant understandings of the elite, but also of the community as a whole, then set the tone for political life and, much more, within the community.

Augustus and Self-Representation

The man who eventually called himself by the new name of Augustus remains arguably the most discussed figure from Roman history (Galinsky 1996, 2005; Eck 2007). No investigation of elite self-representation would be possible without some reference to him. There are hardly any other examples, from any period of world history, of a leader who seized power so violently and unconstitutionally, but who nonetheless managed to (re)integrate himself into a new society that was to a large extent his own creation (Osgood 2006). In 2 BC, Augustus was hailed as father of his country (*pater patriae*) and restorer of traditional values and civic life, a figure who would serve as an exemplar to all later Roman rulers. At the same time, the change to a new system of one man rule inevitably affected the nature of Rome's elite and how they could represent themselves to their various audiences of peers and fellow citizens, not least to the leading citizen himself (*princeps*), who had effective command of most of Rome's armies (Eck 1984; Eck and Heil 2005). Indeed, during the imperial period, Rome's ruler, whether more or less autocratic in his personal style of government, soon become the ultimate addressee of the art, architecture, inscribed texts, and literary creations of elite Romans.

At the very beginning of this imperial period, Augustus' claim to preeminence, however specious it may sometimes appear, was overtly based on the assertion he made in the account of his achievements that was published throughout the empire at the time of his death in AD 14 (*Res Gestae Divi Augusti* 34. 3, Scheid 2007): *Post id tempus auctoritate omnibus praestiti, potestatis autem nihilo amplius habui quam ceteri, qui mihi quoque in magistratu conlegae fuerunt* (After that time I excelled all others in *auctoritas*, but I did not have any more formal power than others who were my colleagues in each magistracy). In other words, after the year 27 BC, when Augustus asserted that he had handed the Roman state back to the senate and the people, he described his own situation as leader simply in terms of *auctoritas*, which can be translated as 'influence,' or 'stature,' or 'prestige.' This very concept of the universal recognition of a political leader who is above everyone else in society simply by common consent reveals the importance of image making and rituals of societal consensus for the Romans.

Thus, Augustus himself seems to assert that it is his image that is most important, rather than his formal powers. His political settlement has been described as a carefully constructed façade that masked his real power (Syme 1939). Yet he himself sometimes seems to admit and to advertise this situation, even as he claims that his image, and the status he acquired gradually through a variety of honors, represented his influence and described his position in Roman society. In other words, the new system of one-man rule created by Augustus was overtly and explicitly based on self-representation, albeit that dissimulation (most notably of his military powers) also had a role to play.

How, then, did Augustus create this new image of preeminence for himself in Rome? The answer is simple: he used, appropriated, and adapted the traditional habits and rituals of self-representation that had been cultivated by the *nobiles*, the elected political elite of the traditional republic (Zanker 1988). Since the time when the political struggle between patricians and plebeians (often referred to as the Conflict of the Orders) was resolved during the course of the fourth century BC, the new elite, who were defined by the political offices to which they had been elected, developed a range of ways to advertise and to maintain their self-image before the eyes of the citizen voters (Hölkeskamp 1987; Gruen 1990, 1992; Hölscher 1978, 1980, 1990, 2001). Augustus' use of these various means of gaining and advertising merit and achievement served as his personal commentary on the political culture that had come before his new age. Consequently, the political revolution that he created was represented in terms of traditional honors and values, just as it was accompanied by a special attention to Rome's early history and to a general program of cultural renewal.

Modern scholars naturally tend to study Augustus primarily as an innovator and as a person who set a highly influential agenda for his various successors, whom we refer to as 'emperors.' He himself declared his ambition to found a stable and admired constitution, which would be considered best for Rome (Suet. *Aug.* 28). However, he did so in terms of past political habits and customs. As a result, his age can serve as a kind of mirror that provides a reflection of what came before, particularly in terms of self-representation in the public sphere within the city of Rome.

The following aspects of public life came to be dominated by Rome's leading man, even as they represented his need for a leading role in, and sometimes a monopoly of, the most important existing *loci* of self-representation, since he was now the patron and the ultimate father figure in Roman society.

The triumph (after a military victory) (Itgenshorst 2005; Beard 2007)

Public building and the inscriptions that labeled such buildings in Rome (Alföldy 1991; Favro 1996)

Honorific statues in the city (Sehlmeyer 1999)

The public games and entertainments (Bernstein 1998)

Public religion as expressed by important state cults (Beard, North, and Price 1998)

Coinage (Crawford 1974)

The calendar (Feeney 2007)

The elaborately staged funerals of the political families (Flower 1996; Flaig 2003)

The position of patron of the inhabitants of the city, especially in their local neighborhoods (Lott 2004)

Literature and art (Galinsky 1996; Conte 1994; Flower 2004)

While it is notable that Augustus did not want to dominate the political scene by becoming a dictator or by holding the highest political office, the consulship, every year, he did not exhibit the same scruples in other spheres of Roman life. The development of his own image also involved that of his family, so that the emergence of a leading man was accompanied by the recognition and representation of his family (who were very cautious in their habits of intermarriage with other families) as the first family in Rome (*domus Augusta*).

Particularly striking is Augustus' decision to become a member of every major priestly college, although only Caesar had held more than one such priesthood before. Augustus' position as *pontifex maximus* (after 12 BC) was an important step in his self-definition, and undoubtedly gave the office an aspect beyond what it had enjoyed before. Soon, the emperor and his family members were the principal people to be seen in scenes of sacrifice and ritual in Roman state art. Indeed, the new name of Augustus that he adopted in 27 BC was essentially a religious rather than an overtly political one. Similarly, he cultivated the religious life of ordinary Romans, including especially of freedmen, in the local neighborhoods (*vici*) of the city, through financial gifts, administrative reforms, and general patronage. Yet he did not put his statues in these local neighborhoods, as some revolutionary political leaders of earlier ages had done (e.g., Marius Gratidianus). Augustus was always a nuanced and thoughtful reader of republican precedents; his priorities reflect the importance of various aspects of public ritual and image that had been traditional in Rome.

At the beginning of his time as sole ruler, the new *princeps* had called upon the traditional political elites to help him in restoring public buildings, roads, monuments of various kinds, and in celebrating Roman victories in triumphal processions. These men had the resources to help and many had traditional family connections to structures or roads that had been originally built by one of their ancestors. However, all this gradually changed in the first ten years of the new order, the years leading up to the celebration of the New Age in the magnificent *ludi saeculares* (secular games) of 17 BC. From now on it was the emperor who would either restore or build new buildings in the city. While he would not always put his own name on every building, he certainly ensured that very few others had the chance. In tandem with these activities, the Augustan age saw a huge increase in the number of inscribed texts put up in the city and elsewhere, inscriptions on bronze and on marble, many of which named the emperor or celebrated some aspect of his cultural program (Alföldy 1991; Corbier 2006). Every milestone along a new or refurbished Roman road would now name the emperor. Augustus' boast that he had found Rome a city of brick and recreated her a city of marble is one of his most telling statements (Suet. *Aug.* 28; Dio 56. 30. 3). At the same time, he himself secured central control of the marble trade, particularly of the Italian marble from Luna (Carrara), which was to become the hallmark of so many of his public projects.

Republican statues of leading Romans were moved outside the city limits, while Augustus represented himself as the culmination of Roman history in the center of his new forum, surrounded by selected earlier Roman heroes, many in triumphal dress (Zanker 1968). The ritual of the triumph had traditionally represented the ultimate celebration of empire and the culmination of a politician's career. Beyond the highest political office, the triumph allowed the general to receive a supreme accolade from the whole city, after being voted this recognition of his victory by his peers in the senate. But after 19 BC, no person outside the imperial family was to celebrate a triumph in Rome. As a result, a type of victory celebration that had at one time been common, with some years even seeing several such parades, became very rare and exclusively associated with the emperor's role as preserver or builder of Rome's overseas empire. The triumph would, it seems, have become even rarer, perhaps even obsolete, if Augustus' advice had been followed by subsequent generations, for he left specific instructions that the Roman Empire should not be expanded beyond what he considered to be its natural boundaries (Dio 56. 33. 2–6). This policy can also be read as Augustus' reaction to the destabilizing effect of rapid expansion, especially in the generation after Sulla, when Pompey and Caesar added vast areas to the Roman Empire, celebrated with many days of victory parades. Subsequently, emperors such as Claudius would expand into new provincial areas and would celebrate their conquests with splendid triumphs.

Augustus' choice to set stringent new limits on the triumph surely suggests some of the political and social impact that these rituals had accumulated over the generations (Hickson 1991). While other religious rites in the city were being renewed or expanded, this most splendid one in honor of Jupiter Optimus Maximus was to become very rare indeed, at the same time as its venerable history was commemorated in the long list of Roman triumphs set up in the forum. Augustus did not want other leading Romans to celebrate a triumph, for they might pose threats to his position of preeminence. Furthermore, he did not himself wish to celebrate more of these parades, for he did not desire the image of a leader whose position was primarily founded on military campaigning and warfare. His triple triumph in 29 BC was designed as a culmination of his military prowess, and he distanced himself more and more from his earlier image as triumvir and warlord in the tradition of Caesar and Pompey.

By contrast with the triumphal procession, Augustus did not feel able or willing to deprive the political families of their right to celebrate their traditional funerals in public, and to display the prestige of their relatives before the whole city. During the republican period, politicians who had been elected to the office of aedile, praetor, consul, or censor had the right to be represented by a wax mask (*imago*) worn by an actor at their funerals and at the funerals of their family members (at first only for men, then also for women). The actor would wear the *imago* mask and the garb of the highest political office held by the man, or triumphal dress, if the deceased had celebrated a triumph during his lifetime. At such a funeral, to which all the citizens were invited, the body of the deceased was accompanied by all his office-holding ancestors (represented by actors in masks and costume, with attendants) to the forum. There the funeral oration was given by a family member, often a young son. The 'ancestors' would sit on their ivory chairs of office to listen, with the citizens likewise present, to a eulogy that praised the deceased and also rehearsed the careers and achievements of the previous office-holders in the family, and in related families. The spectacle celebrated family prestige over the generations in the most public way possible, even as the famous men of the past reappeared again to walk through the city and to take part in this public ceremony. A wide variety of ancient authors attest to the importance of these funerals, and they stress the fact that ordinary people also participated, sometimes even coming into town especially for the occasion. These events had the effect of joining the entire Roman community in a ritual that served to reaffirm the political order itself, as well as the fact that certain individuals, certain families, and certain values were supreme within that order.

Such funerals continued to be celebrated well into the imperial period in Rome. When not in use at a funeral, the masks of the ancestors were kept in labeled cupboards in the *atrium* of houses belonging to family members. Thus, in this perhaps slightly more private context, they served on a daily basis the same purposes as they did on the less frequent and more public occasions of funerals.

As a response to this very republican funeral culture, which celebrated the individual family but also the whole class of office holders and the prestige conferred on them by election to high office, Augustus designed a new type of imperial funeral to mark off his family as the leading one in Rome. He appropriated the ancestors of other families, who were not related to him either by blood or by marriage. In this way the funerals he staged for his family members, as well as his own funeral in AD 14, included much longer processions of masked actors, who represented a wide variety of Roman heroes, including some from before the republican period. This homage suggests something of the effects created by the spectacle of funeral processions. Augustus was not known as a frequent public speaker in Rome, but he did deliver the funeral oration for members of his own family who died during his lifetime, and he did so in contravention of the usual custom, which had favored a member of the next generation rather than an older relative or sibling. The *princeps'* relatives were buried in the new monumental mausoleum that he built on the Campus Martius, a heroic marker of his family's status, which was surrounded by a public park, and whose entrance was flanked by two columns bearing the brazen inscription recording his achievements (Hesberg and Panciera 1994).

In short, the Roman citizens were now surrounded by images of their new leader, the revered one (Augustus), on coins and inscriptions, in literature and oratory, in the new urban image of the city of Rome, and in a complex calendar of festivals and anniversaries, which included the new month of August named in his honor. The prominence of his image inevitably replaced the previous culture of publicity, which had celebrated a variety of individuals, families, and political or religious messages. To name but one (more) telling fact, during the republican period, portraits of living men had not appeared on Roman coins minted in the city.

On the other hand, and in contravention to his usurping center stage in most aspects of communal life, Augustus also claimed credit for refusing honors, avoiding public celebrations, and not inscribing his name everywhere. He dressed in simple clothes, which were made in his own household, and he lived in a house that looked like that of other members of the senatorial elite, on the Palatine, where republican politicians had chosen to live for many generations (Wiseman 1987). He cultivated his image as a patrician, since he had been adopted by Julius Caesar, but he also made new patricians and promoted many men from non-traditional backgrounds. His power was ultimately based on the army, but the soldiers who guarded his home and ensured his safety appeared in plain clothes and carried their weapons concealed. These members of the Praetorian Guard did not have a military camp of their own in or near the city during Augustus' lifetime. Consequently, the complexity and subtlety of his self-representation suggests not only his own preferences, but a shrewd and practical appreciation for the central importance of image and influence within the city of Rome.

PLINY IN HIS OWN WORLD

So far, this essay has focused almost exclusively on elite self-representation within the sphere of public life—and the ways in which that vein of self-representation actually served to form the political community. As the position of the Roman emperor developed, an emperor who came to live in a splendid palace by the end of the first century AD, Roman senators and others sought prestige and influence for themselves in a more private sphere, outside the political world that had come to be so overshadowed by one man (Talbert 1984). Competing with the emperor was dangerous and often futile, so that his loyal supporters sought recognition beyond their relationship to his policies (Roller 2001). A glimpse of such a world of senatorial image making can be found in the letters of the younger Pliny (esp. books 1–9), which were published in regular installments between the late 90s and his death around AD 113. Born under Nero, Pliny had lived under the reigns of, and been promoted by, a series of emperors from the Flavians to Trajan. In this politically unstable and changing world, he offers a carefully crafted and reassuring picture of intellectual rigor, scrupulous honesty, professional expertise, and personal cultivation in contexts in which the emperor only rarely makes a direct appearance (Radicke 1997; Hoffer 1999; Henderson 2002; Castagna and Lefèvre 2003). His exchange of letters with Trajan, to be found in book 10, seems to have been published after his death.

Pliny takes pride in his professional qualifications and achievements in the law, in finance, and in administration. He has had a distinguished political career, but not one based on popular elections, since those had now been moved to the senate, a forum in which the emperor's nominees were directly designated for high office. Pliny represents himself as a faithful and professional administrator of the empire, and of 'good' emperors. Meanwhile, he longs for escape from the city to one of his several remarkable villas, where he can pursue a leisured existence based on intellectual pursuits, especially reading and writing. He appears as much defined by his use of his own time (*otium*), as by the time he spends on the law or administration. His carefully crafted intellectual life, supported by vast wealth and extensive use of slave labor, takes place away from Rome in various rural or seaside settings, in the company of a select group of chosen friends. He maintains close connections with his hometown of Comum in northern Italy and with local elites there, among whom he finds a wife.

Pliny, the senator from an equestrian background, desires and creates his own status within a separate intellectual and cultural world. In the sphere of his villa he meets only his invited friends, and is not directly dependent on the politics of representation in front of a crowd, or on the direct patronage of the emperor. The value of self-determination in a private elite sphere had clearly evolved in response to the new political climate in Rome. It is interesting that Pliny wants to portray such a wide variety of aspects of this world in his 'letters,' ostensibly addressed to his friends, but actually written as essays or opinion pieces designed to be read by an educated readership. The letters construct an image of Pliny himself, but also of his milieu, values, and aspirations. In these texts he seeks affirmation for his life-style and interests, while encouraging others of his social class to imitate him. Elements of satire sometimes criticize behavior Pliny does not approve of, but the tone is rarely harsh or bitter. Rather, the picture of Pliny's world is idealized and idealistic, free from the intense competition of republican senators or from insistent nostalgia for a better past age. Pliny knows that his family has only risen to real prominence in the generation of his parents, and he aims to make the most of this social mobility and subsequent new-found affluence. The private sphere he describes in such detail would not necessarily have seemed very familiar to mid-republican senators of his consular rank, yet like them, he is eager to represent for posterity his own prestige in a literary medium of his choice, even as he seeks to set the tone for elite society and even for the emperor in Rome.

CONCLUSIONS: ELITE SELF-REPRESENTATION AND THE EVOLUTION OF ROMAN SOCIETY

Elite self-representation dominates our picture of ancient Roman society and consequently its evolution also traces for us the outlines of political change in Rome as we can now understand it. As a result, the political culture of republican Rome is best defined and understood through the image of the *nobiles*, who described themselves in terms of martial valor, public service, and fidelity to ancestral traditions and values (*mos maiorum*). The traditional character and pervasiveness of this manner of self-representation helps to explain the success of republican Rome and of its political leaders over many generations of conquests abroad and political unity behind senatorial leadership at home. The continuing influence of received forms of republican self-representation is demonstrated in their use by Augustus, who defined his position as the first emperor largely in terms of aristocratic values and of traditional spheres and rewards for achievement. However, the very pervasiveness and rigidity of elite life caused some Romans to seek different modes of existence outside the city, even during the later second century BC. By the time of the high empire, in the second century AD, the dominant role played by the emperor in city life and politics meant that leading senators like Pliny the Younger sought recognition and prestige in the image of a much more private kind of elite life, far from Rome and from public business. In this new sphere, elite status was reflected in personal taste and cultural pursuits in the setting of the country villa and in the presence of a select audience of chosen friends. It is his literary interests and personal culture of leisure that Pliny chooses to dwell on, rather than writing the history of his times or a detailed account of his professional career and accomplishments as a lawyer, politician, or civil servant.

SUGGESTED READING

The topic, indeed the whole field of topics covered in this chapter, is very broad and somewhat amorphous. I have focused on senators in Rome from the republic to the high empire. Many other elites in different times and places could fruitfully be discussed. Good general places to start reading would be Stein-Hölkeskamp and Hölkeskamp 2006 and Zanker 1988. Flower 1996 and 2006 offer a variety of perspectives on memory, commemoration, self-presentation, and political censure in Roman culture from early times to late antiquity. Individual subject bibliographies can be found cited in parentheses in the text above.

BIBLIOGRAPHY

Alföldy, G. 1991. "Augustus und die Inschriften: Tradition und Innovation." *Gymnasium* 98: 289–324.

Beard, M. 2007. *The Roman Triumph*. Cambridge, Mass.: Harvard University Press.

Beard, M., J. North, and S. Price. 1998. *Religions of Rome*. 2. Cambridge: Cambridge University Press.

Beck, H. 2005. *Karriere und Hierarchie. Die römische Aristokratie und die Anfänge des* cursus honorum *in der mittleren Republik*. Berlin: Akademie Verlag.

Bernstein, F. H. 1998. *Ludi Publici: Untersuchungen zur Entstehung und Entwicklung der öffentlichen Spiele im republikanischen Rom*. Stuttgart: Franz Steiner Verlag.

Bonnefond-Coudry, M. 1989. *Le Sénat de la république romaine de la guerre d'Hannibal à Auguste: pratiques délibératives et prise de décision*. Rome: École française de Rome.

Castagna, L., and E. Lefèvre (eds.). 2003. *Plinius der Jüngere und seine Zeit*. Munich: KG Saur Verlag.

Conte, G. B. 1994. *Latin Literature: A History*. Baltimore: Johns Hopkins University Press.

Corbier, M. 2006. *Donner à voir, donner à lire. Mémoire et communication dans la Rome ancienne*. Paris: CNRS.

Crawford, M.H. 1974. *Roman Republican Coinage*. 2 vols. Cambridge: Cambridge University Press.

Eck, W. 1984. "Senatorial Self-Representation: Developments in the Augustan Period." In F. Millar and E. Segal (eds.), *Caesar Augustus, Seven Aspects*. Oxford: Oxford University Press. 129–67.

———. 2007. *The Age of Augustus*. 2nd ed. Oxford: Blackwell.

Eck, W., and M. Heil (eds.). 2005. *Senatores populi romani. Realität und mediale Präsentation einer Führungsschicht*. Stuttgart: Franz Steiner Verlag.

Favro, D. G. 1996. *The Urban Image of Augustan Rome*. Cambridge: Cambridge University Press.

Feeney, D. C. 2007. *Caesar's Calendar: Ancient Time and the Beginnings of History*. Berkeley: University of California Press.

Flaig, E. 2003. *Ritualisierte Politik: Zeichen, Gesten und Herrschaft im Alten Rom*. Göttingen: Vandenhoeck and Ruprecht.

Flower, H. I. 1996. *Ancestor Masks and Aristocratic Power in Roman Culture*. Oxford: Clarendon Press.

———. (ed.). 2004. *The Cambridge Companion to the Roman Republic*. Cambridge: Cambridge University Press.

———. 2006. *The Art of Forgetting: Disgrace and Oblivion in Roman Political Culture*. Chapel Hill: University of North Carolina Press.

Galinsky, K. 1996. *Augustan Culture: an Interpretive Introduction*. Princeton: Princeton University Press.

———. 2005. *Cambridge Companion to the Age of Augustus*. Cambridge: Cambridge University Press.

Gruen, E. S. 1990. *Studies in Greek Culture and Roman Policy*. Leiden: E. J. Brill.

———. 1992. *Culture and National Identity in Republican Rome*. London: Duckworth.

Henderson, J. 2002. *Pliny's Statue. The Letters, Self-Portraiture and Classical Art*. Exeter: University of Exeter Press.

Hesberg, H. von, and S. Panciera. 1994. *Das Mausoleum des Augustus: der Bau und seine Inschriften*. Munich: Bayerische Akademie der Wissenschaften.

Hickson, F. V. 1991. "Augustus *triumphator*: Manipulation of the Triumphal Theme in the Political Program of Augustus." *Latomus* 50: 124–38.

Hoffer, S. E. 1999. *The Anxieties of Pliny the Younger.* Atlanta: Scholars Press.

Hölkeskamp, K.-J. 1987. *Die Entstehung der Nobilität. Studien zur sozialen und politischen Geschichte der römischen Republik im 4. Jhdt. v. Chr.* Stuttgart: Franz Steiner Verlag.

———. 2001. "Capitol, Comitium und Forum. Öffentliche Räume, sakrale Topographie und Erinnerungslandschaften der römischen Republik." In S. Faller (ed.), *Studien zu antiken Identitäten.* Würzburg: Ergon. 97–132.

———. 2004a. *Rekonstruktionen einer Republik. Die politische Kultur des antiken Rom und die Forschung der letzten Jahrzehnte.* Munich: R. Oldenbourg Verlag.

———. 2004b. Senatus populusque romanus: *die politische Kultur der Republik: Dimensionen und Deutungen.* Wiesbaden: Franz Steiner Verlag.

Hölkeskamp, K.-J., and E. Stein-Hölkeskamp (eds.). 2000. *Von Romulus zu Augustus. Große Gestalten der römischen Republik.* Munich: Verlag C. H. Beck.

Hölscher, T. 1978. "Die Anfänge römischer Repräsentationskunst." *Mitteilungen des Deutschen Archäologischen Instituts (Röm. Abt.)* 85: 315–57.

———. 1980. "Römische Siegesdenkmäler der späten Republik." In H. A. Cahn and E. Simon (eds.), *Tainia, R. Hampe zum 70. Geburtstag.* Mainz: von Zabern. 351–71.

———. 1990. "Römische Nobiles und hellenistische Herrscher." In *Akten des XIII. Internationalen Kongresses für Klassische Archäologie Berlin 1988.* Mainz: von Zabern. 73–84.

———. 2001. "Die Alten vor Augen. Politische Denkmäler und öffentliches Gedächtnis im republikanischen Rom." In G. Melville (ed.), *Institutionalität und Symbolisierung. Verstetigung kultureller Ordnungsmuster in Vergangenheit und Gegenwart.* Cologne: Böhlau. 183–211.

Horsfall, N. M. 2003. *The Culture of the Roman Plebs.* London: Duckworth.

Itgenshorst, T. 2005. *Tota illa pompa. Der Triumph in der römischen Republik.* Göttingen: Vandenhoeck and Ruprecht.

Jehne, M. (ed.). 1995. *Demokratie in Rom? Die Rolle des Volkes in der Politik der römischen Republik.* Stuttgart: Franz Steiner Verlag.

Lott, J. B. 2004. *The Neighborhoods of Augustan Rome.* Cambridge: Cambridge University Press.

Millar, F. G. B. 1998. *The Crowd in Rome in the Late Republic.* Ann Arbor: University of Michigan Press.

———. 2002. *Rome, the Greek World, and the East 1: The Roman Republic and the Augustan Revolution.* Ed. H. M. Cotton and G. M. Rogers. Chapel Hill: University of North Carolina Press.

Morstein-Marx, R. 2004. *Mass Oratory and Political Power in the Late Roman Republic.* Cambridge: Cambridge University Press.

Morstein-Marx, R., and N. Rosenstein (eds.). 2006. *A Companion to the Roman Republic.* Oxford: Blackwell.

Mouritsen, H. 2001. *Plebs and Politics in the Late Roman Republic.* Cambridge: Cambridge University Press.

Nicolet, C. 1980. *The World of the Citizen in Republican Rome.* London: Batsford.

Osgood, J. 2006. *Caesar's Legacy: Civil War and the Emergence of the Roman Empire.* Cambridge: Cambridge University Press.

Radicke, J. 1997. "Die Selbstdarstellung des Plinius in seinen Briefen." *Hermes* 125: 447–69.

Roller, M. B. 2001. *Constructing Autocracy: Aristocrats and Emperors in Julio-Claudian Rome.* Princeton: Princeton University Press.

Ryan, F. 1998. *Rank and Participation in the Republican Senate*. Stuttgart: Franz Steiner Verlag.

Scheid, J. 2007. *Res Gestae Divi Augusti*. Paris: Les Belles Lettres.

Sehlmeyer, M. 1999. *Stadtrömische Ehrenstatuen der republikanischen Zeit. Historizität und Kontext von Symbolen nobilitären Standesbewußtseins*. Stuttgart: Franz Steiner Verlag.

Stein-Hölkeskamp, E., and K.-J. Hölkeskamp (eds.). 2006. *Erinnerungsorte der Antike. Die römische Welt*. Munich: Verlag C. H. Beck.

Syme, R. 1939. *The Roman Revolution*. Oxford: Clarendon Press.

Talbert, R. J. A. 1984. *The Senate of Imperial Rome*. Princeton: Princeton University Press.

Walter, U. 2004. Memoria *und* res publica. *Zur Geschichtskultur im republikanischen Rom*. Frankfurt am Main: Verlag Antike.

Wiseman, T. P. 1987. "*Conspicui postes tectaque digna deo*: The Public Image of Aristocratic and Imperial Houses in the Late Republic and Early Empire." In *L'Urbs: espace urbain et histoire (1er siècle av. J.-C.—IIIe siècle ap. J.-C.)*. Rome: École Francaise. 393–413.

Reprinted in Wiseman, T. P., *Historiography and Imagination: Eight Essays on Roman Culture*. Exeter: University of Exeter Press. 98–115.

Yacobson, A. 1999. *Elections and Electioneering in Rome. A Study in the Political System of the Late Republic*. Stuttgart: Franz Steiner Verlag.

———. 2004. "The People's Voice and the Speaker's Platform: Popular Power, Persuasion, and Manipulation." *Scripta Classica Israelica* 23: 201–12.

Zanker, P. 1968. *Forum Augustum, das Bildprogramm*. Tübingen: Wasmuth.

———. 1988. *The Power of Images in Augustan Rome*. Ann Arbor: University of Michigan Press.

CHAPTER 13

PUBLIC SPEAKING IN ROME: A QUESTION OF *AUCTORITAS*

FRANCISCO PINA POLO

INTRODUCTION: THE *CONTIO* AS VENUE FOR POLITICAL COMMUNICATION WITH THE PEOPLE

IN republican Rome, the *contio* (a rough equivalent of the modern American town hall meeting) was the only institutionalized venue in which an orator might directly address the public as his primary audience. Whereas the *comitia* (the popular voting assemblies) were convened to undertake deliberations that would ultimately result in a vote on a given set of matters at hand, the *contio* was by definition a gathering that could come to no such conclusion; indeed, those who attended were organized neither by tribe nor century, as was the case in the popular voting assemblies (Gel. 13. 16. 3). On the other hand, since the *contio* was an officially sanctioned meeting of the people, it could be convened only by a magistrate (though not by a promagistrate), or by a tribune of the plebs.[1] The individual who summoned such a meeting of the people then presided, and was expected to address those assembled—he possessed the so-called *potestas contionandi* (the power to convene a *contio* along with the right to speak there). He also had the power to turn the platform over to other individuals,

---

1. One source (Fest. p. 38L) includes priests as having possessed the power to convene *contiones*; however, such a prerogative is otherwise unattested for them, and seems improbable.

if he so chose (*contionem dare*), and he could likewise summon individuals chosen by him, either private persons or magistrates, to address the assembly (*producere in contionem*). The convener furthermore decided the order of speakers, along with the amount of time allotted to each person who would address the meeting.

In the republican period, such *contiones* were held quite frequently—indeed, even more assiduously than the popular voting assemblies—and they were convened for various purposes. Thus, for example, a proposed law had initially to be debated for a period of three market days (i.e., at least two weeks) in the context of such *contiones*. The proposer of the legislation in question, those who desired to support it, as well as any who were opposed, were expected to attend these deliberatory meetings. Before the creation of the several standing courts in the late republic, any trial before the people (*iudicium populi*) was also conducted in the context of a *contio*. In such a case, the arguments for prosecution and defense took the form of a public debate, after which the presiding magistrate would convoke the popular voting assembly, where a verdict would ultimately be rendered. Aside from these kinds of meeting, which were preparatory to a full convocation of the popular voting assembly, there were also any number of *contiones* held over the course of a given year, whose only purpose was to inform the populace regarding various matters of communal importance. At such gatherings the edicts of magistrates or decrees of the senate, for example, were read aloud to the public. Military victories, and defeats, were likewise announced to the people in *contiones*; it was here that victorious generals, after their triumphs, told of their great deeds on the field of battle. Here, too, were recited eulogies for the community's most eminent men. It was at *contiones* that magistrates were sworn into office, and gave a reckoning of service upon laying down an official post. In short, the *contio* was probably the Roman community's most important venue for the transaction of official business of all kinds, and for the transmission of important news concerning the *res publica* (the body politic).

The most important of these meetings were those involving politics. Given that this was the only venue in which an officially sanctioned contact could be established between individuals who desired a political career and the mass of the people, these meetings quickly became the principal instrument of self-representation for those who desired to embark on the *cursus honorum* (the series of state offices that constituted a political career). Matters of immediate public consequence could be raised in these *contiones*, and it was here that political campaigns were carried on. In this context, an individual might flaunt his own positions, and attack those of his enemies.

In short, the *contiones* were an absolutely central element of Roman political life—as the chief medium available to individuals for acquiring popularity, but also as the main point of contact between the senate (and senators) and the people, this contact mediated by the oratory of magistrates. Thus, the *contio* served as a conduit of communal information, and as the principal locus of official public debate; and in Rome's 'face-to-face' society, most of the acts that would affect communal life were discussed before the people. However, were these matters considered with the people's input, or with the populace functioning more as an audience?

In 138 BC the Roman state faced a significant increase in the price of grain. Curiatius, who was then tribune of the plebs, brought the consuls Brutus and Scipio Nasica before a *contio*, where he hoped to force them to agree to propose to the senate that a quantity of wheat should be purchased and made available by the state, to regulate the price of this basic commodity (V. Max. 3. 7. 3). When Nasica began to offer his arguments against the tribune's plan, the crowd brought him up short with its shouts. Nasica pleaded with the people for quiet, arguing that he knew better than they what was in the interest of the community. According to our source for this series of events, Valerius Maximus, this stopped the people in their tracks. They quickly became respectfully silent, since they accorded much more weight to the *auctoritas* (the political clout) of the orator than they did to the grain problem at hand.

Valerius Maximus also relates how Carbo, another tribune of the plebs, caused Scipio Aemilianus, just after the latter's victory over Numantia in Hispania, to ascend the orator's tribunal (V. Max. 6. 2. 3). Carbo then asked Scipio what his opinion was with respect to the recent death of Scipio's brother-in-law, Tiberius Gracchus. Carbo was obviously hoping to force Scipio, in a public forum, to condemn the murder of Gracchus. Nonetheless, Scipio responded that Gracchus had been killed justifiably. Those present at the assembly exploded in protest, to which the orator reacted in a cutting fashion: "You keep quiet, you to whom Italy is a step-mother." The crowd was immediately silenced, though not because of any fear instilled in them by the great man; rather, we are told that they felt acutely the deep respect that Scipio and his ancestors had waked in them.

The attitudes toward the people demonstrated by these two Scipios are exceptional in their publicly displayed lack of respect; nevertheless, they encapsulate an entire ideology held deeply by the Roman republican aristocracy. An orator presenting an argument to the people was of course expected to select those points he considered most persuasive. Yet, along with the actual arguments, indeed, even above and beyond them, there was deployed a more essential thing: the *auctoritas* of the man speaking, in other words, his reliability and capacity to lead, given the fact that he was a member of Rome's social elite. For this reason, one was not seeking, in the context of a *contio*, a true consensus based on a real debate with the populace. Rather, one expected the people to accept the judgment of those who claimed to be its betters. Such acceptance, of course, did not always come easy, and confrontation was occasionally the order of the day. Still, on the whole, the people were very largely excluded from intervening in the actual ordering of the *res publica*.

The logical consequence was that not everyone at Rome had free access to making a speech before the public. Instead, the magistrate in charge of a given assembly had the exclusive right to decide who might speak there. Addressing the public in such a context, then, was the prerogative of a magistrate, and did not constitute one of the rights of citizens generally. In theory, no Roman, whatever his social status, was excluded from addressing a gathering of the citizenry. But the actuality presented us by the available sources, with very few exceptions, shows that during the period of the republic, those who addressed the public were members of the social elite, generally acting magistrates, otherwise ex-magistrates; and many of these were men who had been consul. Thus, nearly every man known to have addressed a gathering of the Roman people was a senator, and as such, each of these men was endowed with the *auctoritas* that membership in the senatorial order entailed. The right to deliver a speech from the tribunal thus derived largely from the *potestas* (official authority) with which the orator (as acting magistrate) was invested, or from the level of *auctoritas* generally recognized to accrue to the individual in question. And so, at a *contio*, just as in the senate, the right to speak was doled out in close accord with the hierarchies that characterized Roman society generally. And this meant, in turn, that the effectiveness of an orator depended heavily on his social status, and on the civil and military (and also religious) offices and accomplishments to which he could lay claim. To put the matter plainly: in republican Rome, some citizens were more highly regarded, because of the qualifications just mentioned, than others, and the weight of the spoken word in a public political setting was tied intimately to the status of the person who uttered it.

It is thus precisely to the *auctoritas* that emanated from the orator's tribunal that Cicero referred, when he wanted to justify the fact that during the first twenty years of his own political career, he had intervened in not a single *contio*. At the start of his defense of the Manilian law in 66 BC, Cicero (who was then praetor) defined the orator's tribunal as "the most important place for the conduct of public business, the most distinguished place for public speaking." He went on to say that he had previously not dared to address the public from that platform because his personal *auctoritas* had not yet reached the level appropriate to that venue: "Previously, on account of my age, I did not dare aspire to such a place of authority, and I had determined to appear there only when my talents were perfected." (Cic. *Man.* 1)

The society of the Roman Republic was one in which oral, as opposed to written, communication performed a centrally important function, and *contiones* were absolutely fundamental to this orally communicative world. However, the limitations placed by Rome's aristocratically oriented political regime on speaking in public resulted in public political communications following a one-way street, namely, from the elite down to the rest of the population. Those who attended a *contio* had the right to be informed about the details of a projected piece of legislation, or regarding important news that affected the community, or the opinions of the great men on some matter of pressing importance. The people could expect often to witness a regular oratorical duel between members of the elite; however, the understood rules of the game left no space for active interventions by the people in these debates. Political discussion took place, then, in full view of the people, yet without their active participation. There simply existed no regulated mechanism for the public to make its opinion known in a *contio*, even though that public could indicate its will by applause, silence, shouting and the like, just as it might in other venues, for example, the theater.

This lack of institutionalized conduits for the people to make its will known forced the populace to turn to exceptional measures, to reach the leaders of the

society.[2] The result was that more violent actions, of one kind and another, ultimately became the only method available to the people for demonstrations of
political desires. This clearly added to the generally high level of violence present
in Roman republican society (on which, see Fagan in this volume). Again, all of
this was played out in the *contiones*, which became, especially in the late republic,
important instruments for mobilizing the urban *plebs*. Thus, the *contio* came to be
associated with the rabble rousers (*seditiosi*), who in this later period were perceived
as endangering the very existence of the Roman state.

The Topography of Public Oratory

The combination of qualities such as *potestas*, *dignitas*, and, in the end, *auctori-*
tas, which orators were expected to possess, was reflected in the very topography
of oratory before the people. There were several places where *contiones* were most
usually held. At times, the spaces that fronted on certain temples—that of Castor in
the Forum, of Jupiter on the Capitoline, or of the goddess Bellona in the Campus
Martius—were engaged for this purpose. We also hear of *contiones* put on in the
Circus Flaminius. This particular spot was especially useful, since it lay outside the
sacred boundary of the city. Thus, persons who were functioning as magistrates
with *imperium* (the legal right to command troops), and who could therefore not
legally enter the city, or those who were awaiting a triumph and were likewise forbidden to enter the city limits, could attend public meetings there. The legislative
contiones, held just before a vote was to be taken on a matter of public business in
the *comitia centuriata*, were, like the popular voting assembly itself, convened in the
Campus Martius, again, just beyond the sacred city limits.

Still, all of these locales were exceptional, given that the typical place from which
an orator addressed the public was the Rostra, in the Forum Romanum. The name
of this monument derived from the ship beaks, captured in the battle at Antium in
338 BC by Caius Maenius, who then had these trophies affixed to the front of the
platform. This was just one of various physical transformations that the speaker's
platform experienced over the course of time. But be that as it may, the Rostra stood
on the same spot for its entire republican history; it separated the Comitium from
the Forum, and faced the senate house, thus serving as a kind of physically symbolic
meeting point between the senators and the rest of the populace. In 44 BC, however, Caesar had a new tribunal constructed at the far western end of the Forum;
this was soon thereafter rebuilt and expanded by Augustus. It was from this stage,
or from the *rostra* attached to the temple of the Divine Julius Caesar, that orators of

2. Cicero, for example, considered it seditious for orators to ask specific questions of
those attending a *contio*, something that appears to have happened only exceptionally anyhow. See Cic. *Sest.* 126, *Q. fr.* 2. 3. 2.

the imperial period would address the public. In any case, until the middle of the second century BC, the orators had faced their audiences in the Comitium, thus speaking in the direction of the senate house. From that point on, they would speak facing the Forum, a much larger space. The public, in both instances, remained standing, a circumstance considered most propitious by Cicero, who thought that the Greek custom of sitting in theaters for assembly meetings led only to the taking of bad decisions (Cic. *Flac.* 16; *Agr.* 2. 13).

Whatever the locale chosen for a given *contio*, though, the disposition of orator to public was always the same. The man speaking always stood above his audience, pronouncing his words from 'a higher place,' whether this was the podium of a temple, or the speaker's tribunal.[3] This up-down physical arrangement in the *contio* represented the type of communication desired in those gatherings; it symbolized the moral and political authority of the aristocracy, and it helped to reaffirm hierarchically the validity of the oration held. The importance of all this is captured in an episode narrated by Cicero. In 62 BC, Caesar was presiding over a *contio*, which he, in his capacity as praetor, had called. He refused to authorize Catulus, at that moment a man of consular rank (and thus, in terms of the *cursus honorum*, his superior), to take the speaker's platform. Caesar ultimately did not stop his opponent from speaking, but was able to force him to talk from a physically less elevated position (*ex inferiore loco*) (Cic. *Att.* 2. 24. 3). Caesar's action was a public declaration of his disdain for Catulus and, at the same time, was a method of robbing his opponent's address of its strength, regardless of what the actual arguments may have been.

The *auctoritas* of the orator's tribunal was intensified by the fact that the structure itself had the status of a sacred space (*templum*).[4] This was a consecrated place—like, in fact, the podiums of temples, from which *contiones* could also be directed, and also like the senate house, which watched over, in a sense, the speaker's platform (cf. Cic. *Flac.* 57). This sacral character served symbolically to reaffirm the authority of those who spoke from this tribunal, and gave their words the sort of force that would normally emanate from a place inhabited by the gods, and presided over by the Roman state religion (Cic. *Man.* 71). What is more, the Rostra, which was in its original nature a kind of triumphal monument commemorating the victory over the Latins, came ultimately to be a physical record of the history of the Roman state. Here were erected statues of prominent Romans, which stood as exemplary of the virtues that had contributed to forming the 'tradition of the elders' (*mos maiorum*), which in turn embodied the superiority of Rome over other civilizations, and gave legitimacy to Rome's empire. Thus, the Rostra came to be a place

---

3. Cicero, for example writing about the idea of persuading individuals that an honorable death can be desirable, says (*Tusc.* 1. 117): "Be that as it may, one must employ the greatest eloquence, just as if one were holding a *contio* from a height raised above the audience, so that those listening either begin to hope for death, or, at the very least, that they begin to desist from fearing it."

4. Both Liv. 8. 14. 12 and Cic. *Vat.* 24 call the Rostra a *templum*.

of collective memory for the Romans, a symbol of the continuity and efficacy of a political system that worked constantly to legitimate the power of the aristocracy; and it was from this same spot that the aristocrats monopolized public communication with the people.

THE POLITICAL SIGNIFICANCE OF *CONTIONES*

Now, the fact that the people was not authorized to participate directly in political debates does not mean that its opinions, even if manifested in a rough and tumble manner (indeed, at times via organized claques), could simply be ignored.[5] All who desired could attend a *contio*; there were no legal restrictions. In practice, and depending on the expectations awakened by the topic at hand, or by the orators who would make presentations, there might be a crowd of some hundreds, or even thousands, these all usually being inhabitants of Rome. But however many people actually attended (and a large crowd could easily be interpreted by the man who convoked the *contio* as popular approbation of his position on the matter at hand), the persons present were taken to represent the Roman people as a whole, despite the fact that they quite certainly were never more than a fraction of Rome's actual citizen population. A large crowd of this kind at a given *contio* was likely to generate rumors, which would quickly spread to the various quarters of the city, and could thereby materially affect the political climate of the city. In any case, it was a matter of utmost importance for any aspiring Roman politician to appear at *contiones*, and thus to make himself visible in Rome. In this way he would find favor with the people. What is more, it was from the tribunal that a man might stoke ill will against his enemies, thus leading to the ruin of their prestige.

The possibility of gaining a large political following via success at the *contiones* meant that these gatherings became more and more important as the republic began to wane; this was particularly so, given the role these meetings would play in the political strategy of Clodius during the 50s BC. The events just subsequent to the Ides of March in 44 BC also exemplified perfectly the importance of public opinion as manifested in the *contiones*. In the days following the assassination of the *dictator*, the murderers of Caesar were intent upon winning public support for their deed. Using their power as praetors to convoke *contiones*, Brutus and Cassius held several public discourses, in the Forum as well as on the Capitolium, regarding the slaying of Caesar.[6] The people's response was negative, or indifferent. On the other

---

5. Cic. *Sest.* 106 presents the *contio* as one of the venues in which popular sentiment could be expressed. On the other hand, his distaste for those who attended such meetings, as opposed to the "true Roman people" (*verus populus Romanus*), is demonstrated on various occasions in the corpus of his writings, e.g.: Cic. *Att.* 1. 16. 11; *Amic.* 95.

6. Dio 44. 20–21, 34. 1–3; App. *BC* 2. 121–22, 137–41; Plut. *Brut.* 18. 10.

hand, Lepidus and especially Antony were able quite successfully to play to the public by giving speeches in which they mixed excoriation of the assassins with calls for reconciliation, to avoid a fresh civil war. With such messages, and these joined to the promise to maintain the acts of Caesar, they were able to win over the populace, and to deprive Caesar's murderers of any significant support at Rome. In short, their credibility turned out to be greater than that of the assassins. The result was that Brutus and Cassius had to flee the Forum, and take refuge on the Capitoline citadel; later, they would find it necessary to leave the city altogether, and eventually, they saw themselves forced to abandon Italy. Their inability to communicate directly with the populace, and thus the collapse of their leadership, led inevitably to their loss of the battle for Rome. Antony first took advantage of this situation—in spite of the efforts of Cicero to incite a war against him via the Phillippic orations, various of these held before the populace—and then later so did Octavian.

In the process that led from his being an upstart to his arriving at the station of *princeps*, Octavian took full advantage from the very first of oratory before the people. Each of his interventions in a public assembly represented an important advance in his attempt to win for himself the support of the populace. At the moment of Caesar's death, Octavian was practically unknown, and his only political capital consisted of having been named the adoptive son of the now-dead dictator. In such circumstances, to be seen by the *plebs* as Caesar's legal heir was fundamentally important, not merely due to the symbolic importance of going by the name Caius Iulius Caesar, but also because this signified the control of his adoptive father's wealth. Thus, any realization of the testamentary promises made by Caesar, many of which would affect the urban population greatly, depended on the goodwill of Octavian. Given all of this, when Octavian first arrived in Rome, in May 44, since he was not yet a senator, and therefore could not himself take part easily in a meeting of the senate, he had the tribune L. Antonius call a *contio* for him. There, Octavian addressed the people, presented himself as the only legitimate successor of Caesar, and affirmed that he would fulfill all of the promises made in his testament by Caesar. He thus gained much political capital from his adoption.[7] And it must be said that his speaking in a *contio* implied Octavian's membership in the political elite, despite the fact he had as yet done nothing to gain either reputation (*fama*) or esteem (*dignitas*), much less *auctoritas*.

Several months later Octavian appeared again before the people, at a *contio* called for him by the tribune Cannutius.[8] In his speech, Octavian now openly condemned Antony's political course, proclaimed himself the rightful political successor to Caesar, affirmed that he hoped to achieve the same position as his adoptive father, and gestured suggestively to the nearby statue of the dictator. After the final defeat of the assassins of Caesar and the foundation of the Triumvirate, it remained to be seen who would ultimately take power. This struggle occurred to a large degree on the field of battle. However, in the city there quickly arose a

7. Cic. *Att.* 14. 20–21, 15. 2. 2–3.
8. Dio 45. 6. 3, 48. 14. 4; App. *BC* 3. 41–42; Cic. *Att.* 16. 15. 3.

parallel fight to win the support of the urban *plebs*, and once again, the *contiones* would play a significant role in this struggle. In this venue, Octavian revealed himself as the master at gaining the people's backing. He artfully disengaged all of his principal rivals. Sextus Pompeius was revealed by Octavian as the individual who allowed the pirates to disrupt the flow of grain to Rome (App. *BC* 5. 77). Antony was painted as the turncoat cavorting with a foreign queen, Cleopatra (Dio 50. 4. 1; Plut. *Ant.* 54–55). Thus did Octavian justify in the public eye the two wars which came to their ends in the battles of Naulochus and Actium; and in doing so, he presented himself as the one who would save the republic, rather than as the initiator of hostilities.

However, Octavian's ultimate victory, which ushered in a new political regime, put an end to the great era of Roman public oratory. Yet paradoxically, his speeches before the public were emblematic of the potential of persuasion. They demonstrated forcefully the power of the spoken word, and they indicated clearly not only how important it was to control the city, but also the absolute necessity for any prospective political leader of establishing a presence for himself as an orator before the people. During the thirties BC, Octavian alone was able to take advantage of the tribunal to address the people, since his enemies were absent from Rome. With his public discourses, he was able to convert his personal enemies into enemies of the people, and of the state, while simultaneously fashioning himself as the only possible protector of Rome, Italy, and indeed, the entire West. It must be granted that the Roman *plebs* was not the decisive element in the final struggle for power. However, in the *contiones* where he addressed this audience, Octavian was able to air publicly all of his political programs and objectives, which culminated ultimately in his achieving the status at *princeps*.

THE EMPEROR SPEAKS TO THE PEOPLE

With the principate having been established, *contiones* did not disappear, though they seem to have been held significantly less frequently than they had been previously. As before, these meetings continued to be one of the principal venues for contact between state officials and the *populus*, the place where citizens received public news and information. Nonetheless, the new political order meant that these public assemblies would now be dominated by the emperor, since true political debate was no longer a real possibility. Under the principate, there was no room in the *contiones* for true controversy, nor was the podium turned over to speakers other than the prince. In general, these gatherings were now initiated by the emperor, and he would use the meetings to communicate matters that he considered important, issues that might stand as proof of his good rule and magnanimity. It was only during the civil war of 68/69 that the *contiones* partially recovered their earlier significance. During this brief interlude, the opposing parties attempted to sway public opinion at Rome via such town hall meetings.[9] In the end, though, this struggle, too, was decided by the armies.

The majority of the few imperial age *contiones* about which we hear were presided over by emperors, who generally were the only persons to speak. This is logical, given the emperor's position altogether, but also because his *auctoritas* was so much greater than anyone else's. Though we have not a single text of an imperial speech held before the populace (though we do know of such orations held both before the senate and among the troops), almost all the emperors engaged in this kind of communication: Augustus, Tiberius, Caligula, Claudius, Otho, Vitellius, Nerva, Trajan, Hadrian, Septimius Severus, and Severus Alexander. This last emperor, for example, convened a gathering of the people on the Capitolium, to announce his victory over the Persians and the concomitant circus games (*HA Sev. Alex.* 57. 1). No doubt, purely informative *contiones*, like this one, continued to be necessary under the principate. Nonetheless, it seems likely that emperors themselves will have made an appearance only when especially important business was at hand, otherwise leaving the consuls or the prefect of the city to address the crowd. Just as in the republican period, public funeral laudations also took place in the context of a *contio* spoken from the Rostra. During the empire, though, most public funerals were held for members of the imperial family.

Aside from such funeral laudations, the type of imperial age *contio* best attested by our sources is that convened to introduce the new consuls of each year. At these gatherings, the newly installed consuls would swear an oath to obey the laws, and the outgoing pair would likewise adjure that they had faithfully adhered to these statutes during their terms of office. These assemblies thus continued a republican tradition, though now, the emperors were again most often the chief protagonists. Caligula took his oath as consul from the Rostra, and Claudius did the same (Dio 59. 13. 1, 60. 10. 1). This was obviously an act of, essentially, political propaganda, with the emperor presenting himself to the people as a *bonus princeps*, one who would submit himself to the rule of law, just like any other decent citizen. It is just this aspect of being emperor that Pliny, in his *Panegyric* to the emperor Trajan, repeatedly stresses. As Pliny puts it, "the Prince does not stand above the laws, but they above him. And by the same token, as consul he is allowed no more than the other consuls." Then, as Pliny goes on to say, "Caesar, you subjected yourself on the Rostra with reverence to laws, which were not made to bind a Prince." (Plin. *Pan.* 65)

Naturally, the public attending such meetings had no function other than to serve as spectators and witnesses to the event, that is, to affirm by its presence the legitimacy of certain public acts. This was the case, for example, with the adoption of Trajan by Nerva. For this purpose, Nerva convened a *contio* on the Capitolium, to announce that he would have a new son, hence, an intended successor (Plin. *Pan.* 8. 3). It may be that we can observe a sort of precedent for this procedure in a notice

9. On Galba as orator, see Tac. *Hist.* 1. 39. On Vitellius: Suet. *Vit.* 15. 2–3; Tac. *Hist.* 3. 36, 68. On Otho: Tac. *Hist.* 1. 90.

transmitted by Suetonius, who writes that Augustus swore, in a *contio*, that he had adopted Tiberius for the good of the state (Suet. *Tib.* 21. 3). In any case, Nerva's action is on the whole exceptional, and must be understood as a calculated political gesture, as a mechanism for establishing a closer relationship with the people and in contrast to the recent 'tyranny' of Domitian.

In this context are to be understood the coins and reliefs of Trajan and Hadrian, in which these emperors are represented addressing the people. Under the empire, a typical iconographic representation on the coinage involved speeches by the emperor to his soldiers (we find such scenes on the coins of Caligula, Nero, Galba, Nerva, Trajan, and Hadrian). These coin types display the emperor, wearing his military uniform, as he communicates with the army. These representations of the *adlocutio* (address) to the soldiers do not find a counterpart for the civilian realm. We have no preserved representation of a civil *contio* until the age of Trajan.

Nonetheless, a few coins (*sestertii*) minted during the reign of Trajan do present, on their reverses, the emperor dressed in the toga (i.e., his civilian costume), standing on the orator's tribunal, and accompanied by another person, who also wears a toga.[10] Here, Trajan raises his right hand, a gesture well recognizable to all Romans as characteristic of an orator delivering a speech, just as we see in the famous Arringatore statue from the republican period, a statue that now stands as the iconographic paradigm for the civilian orator (see fig. 13.1). Before the emperor are several toga-clad Romans, raising their hands in acclamation of him. The scene is completed on the left by inclusion of the turning post from the circus, upon which stands a figure, perhaps the divine spirit of the place (*Genius loci*). The legend that accompanies this image is SPQR OPTIMO PRINCIPI SC (The Senate and the Roman People to the Best Prince by Decision of the Senate; see fig. 13.2). The scene depicted on this coin reflects an announcement made by the emperor regarding the circus (perhaps his speech even took place there), perhaps concerning the celebration of games, perhaps regarding a project of construction or reconstruction of that edifice (cf. Plin. *Pan.* 51. 3–5).

Hadrian had two distinct series of coins minted, both sporting depictions of civil *contiones*.[11] In both series the emperor appears on the reverse. He stands on a tribunal decorated with ships' beaks, behind which rises a temple with Corinthian columns. The prince raises his right hand, as several citizens standing below him raise their hands toward him in acclamation. The tribunal is presumably the *rostra* of the temple of the Divine Julius Caesar. The difference in the two series is that while in the one Hadrian appears alone on the tribunal, with the legend COS III SC (consul for the third time, by decision of the senate; see fig. 13.3), in the other series he is accompanied by children, again with the legend SC. Thus, these two series must be referring to two distinct matters. In the first case, we have no evidence that

10. *RIC* II, p. 283, no. 553; Strack 1931: 133, fig. V 363; *BMCRE* III, p. 175, nos. 827–28.

11. *RIC* II, p. 424, nos. 639–41; Strack 1933: 113–15, fig. IX 599; *BMCRE* III, p. 433, nos. 1309–11.

Figure 13.1. Statue of Aulus Metellus, so-called L'Arringatore. First century BC. Museo Archaeologico Nazionale di Firenze.

Figure 13.2. Reverse, sestertius of Trajan speaking to the people. *RIC* II p. 283 no. 553. Photo courtesy of the American Numismatic Society: ANS 1964.183.1.rev.1735.

Figure 13.3. Reverse, Hadrian on a tribunal. *RIC* II p. 424 nos. 639–41. Photo courtesy of the American Numismatic Society: ANS 1977.284.5.rev.1735.

would allow us to identify the scene; perhaps the matter at hand was an assembly celebrated after Hadrian's return from his first trip to the eastern Mediterranean, or it could be that we are here dealing with the announcement of some benefaction made by the emperor. As far as the second type is concerned, we must obviously presume some matter involving children. We are most probably dealing with Hadrian's extension of the alimentary program for the Italian youth, which Trajan before him had promoted (*HA Had.* 7. 8).

From roughly the same period, we also have sculptural reliefs depicting the act of addressing the populace. In the so-called Anaglypha, whose attribution to Trajan or Hadrian is not entirely secure, we find on one side the emperor represented as he stands on the *rostra* of the temple of Caesar. He is togate, is accompanied by several other togate personages, and is holding an oration (see fig. 13.4). Given that to the right of those attending the assembly we see a monument that symbolizes the alimentary program, the suggestion has been made that the relief depicts the creation of this program by Trajan, or its expansion by Hadrian. On the other hand, since there are no children to be seen in this relief, some have thought that we are here dealing with the announcement of some other kind of benefaction for the people. Be that as it may, the relief clearly serves to record an act of generosity by the Prince, which was announced to the public at a *contio*.

Finally, a relief from the so-called Arch of Portogallo shows Hadrian standing on a tribunal, and addressing the public, which is represented by a semi-nude figure (see fig. 13.5). Just beneath the tribunal one sees a child, whom many are inclined to identify as Lucius Verus. Now, given that this relief was accompanied, on the original monument, by another relief that portrayed the apotheosis of Hadrian's wife Sabina, it has been thought that the Portogallo relief depicts the funeral oration held in honor of Sabina. Nonetheless, given that two other figures stand on

Figure 13.4. Relief of the so-called Anaglypha Traiani. Rome, Forum Romanum. Second century AD. Photo DAI Rome 1968.2784, photo Felbermeyer.

Figure 13.5. Relief belonging to the so-called Arch of Portogallo, Rome, depicting Hadrian addressing the populace. Second century AD. Rome, Musei Capitolini. Archivio Fotografico dei Musei Capitolini. Inv. MC 809/S.

the tribunal alongside the emperor (who is holding a roll in his left hand), and given that the youth standing beneath the tribunal shows no overt sign of being an aristocratic child, there remains the possibility that we are dealing here with an official act, perhaps again, one connected with the alimentary system. In any case, the scene is much less realistic than the others thus far described here, and might therefore intend to represent the emperor symbolically in his function as orator before the people.

This concentration, during the reigns of Trajan and Hadrian, of coins and reliefs that depict civil *contiones* demonstrates, on the one hand, the vivacity of this type of assembly as a method of communication between the emperor and the populace during the early principate. These representations are also, though, a mechanism of self-representation for the emperor. That is to say, we understand these portrayals as part of the propaganda intended to create an image of the *optimus princeps* (the ideal emperor) and of the *civilis princeps*. Whatever the exact historical circumstances that may have lain behind the scenes just observed, these representations place significant emphasis on the relationship between the emperor and his subjects. The very act of calling an assembly, and there addressing the people directly, was in itself a gesture of respect and generosity toward the common folk. It is this approach to the people that the iconography of the coins and reliefs was attempting to emphasize; and the enthusiastic response of the crowd formed a decisive part of the apologetic propaganda for the *princeps*, this modeled, nonetheless, on the usual hierarchical pattern, in other words, speech from a higher place and acclamation from below.

In his correspondence with Marcus Aurelius, Fronto insists on the importance of rhetorical training for a good emperor, given that eloquence would be indispensable just generally in public life, and especially for dealings with, and in, the senate. Nor does Fronto neglect the matter of speaking in popular assemblies as a requisite for him, who would govern properly (Fro. *Amic.* 141. 22 Naber = Haines 2. p. 58). Indeed, we know that Marcus Aurelius participated in various *contiones*, and that Fronto praised his ex-student for the outstanding oratorical skill displayed on these occasions.[12] The author of the *Historia Augusta* considered Marcus to be a paradigmatically good emperor, one endowed with virtues similar to those attributed by Pliny in his *Panegyric* to Trajan; among these virtues was the habit of comporting himself like a private citizen (*civiliter*), along with his personal concern for the people (*HA Marc. Ant.* 7. 1, 8. 1, 8. 5, 8. 9, 12. 1, 26. 3). We encounter something similar in the case of Severus Alexander, whom the *Historia Augusta* author presents as being a good prince, in the mold of Trajan, Hadrian, or Marcus Aurelius. One of the virtues attributed to Alexander is that of frequently addressing the populace: "he held many *contiones* in the city, much like the tribunes and consuls of old" (*HA Sev. Alex.* 25. 11).

---

12. Fro. *Amic.* 40. 7 Naber = Haines 1 p. 52. For other instances of Marcus Aurelius participating in *contiones*, see *HA Marc. Ant.* 7. 11 and Dio 72. 32. 1.

There can be no doubt that the acts of communication and interaction with the populace in the context of *contiones* became, under the early empire, one of the chief characteristics of the good emperor. Thus, the iconographic type of the *princeps* speaking to the people came to represent the emperor's magnanimity (*liberalitas*), while simultaneously being a symbol of his obligation to behave as a simple citizen (*civilitas*). It showed that he was close to his subjects, and would always protect them. Likewise here was a demonstration of his competence in leading; and this image lent his governance a certain sheen of respect for the venerable republican traditions.

CONCLUSION

At Rome, public oratory had always played a central role in politics; however, speaking before the people had also never been a right of every citizen, and never formed part of freedom (*libertas*) as it was construed by the Romans. Speaking to the people was, rather, one of the constituent elements of the power of magistrates, and it went hand in hand with the *auctoritas* wielded by certain members of the society. In practice, to speak before the populace was a privilege reserved for the social elite, and this entailed, then, effective control of most of the political information in the community. This right belonged to the entire aristocracy during the republic, and was then taken over by the emperor, in whose person was concentrated effectively all formal political power (*potestas*) as well as all political clout (*auctoritas*). The emperor's word came to be the only one that really mattered. Be this all as it may, the *contiones* always had been, and always remained, an absolutely essential mechanism of societal communication, even if they always did work from top to bottom in the society. These meetings also served, of course, to gain favor and popularity for the orators with the populace at Rome. The *contio* was a vehicle for debate and persuasion before the Roman people, who functioned simultaneously as witness and spectator. For as Cicero claimed, without the public, there could be no orator (Cic. *de Orat.* 2. 338, *Brut.* 192).

SUGGESTED READING

In the main, ancient sources have been used to support arguments in this chapter. The larger bibliography just below will help the reader to become oriented in this topic more broadly. The most significant works, though, are these. For public speaking and its effects during the period of (especially) the late republic, one should consult Pina Polo 1989 and 1996, Hölkeskamp 1995, Laser 1997, Millar 1998, Mouritsen 2001, Morstein-Marx 2004, and Hiebel 2009. For the imperial period, Yavetz 1969 is still an essential study, though it can now be well supplemented by Bell 2004.

BIBLIOGRAPHY

Aldrete, G. S. 1999. *Gestures and Acclamations in Ancient Rome*. Baltimore: Johns Hopkins University Press.

Arce, J. 1990. *Funus Imperatorum: los funerales de los emperadores romanos*. Madrid: Alianza Editorial.

Bell, A. 2004. *Spectacular Power in the Greek and Roman City*. Oxford: Oxford University Press.

Benner, H. 1987. *Die Politik des P. Clodius Pulcher: Untersuchungen zur Denaturierung des Clientelwesens in der ausgehenden Romischen Republik*. Stuttgart: Franz Steiner Verlag.

Bennett, J. 1997. *Trajan Optimus Princeps: A Life and Times*. London: Routledge.

Boatwright, M. T. 1987. *Hadrian and the City of Rome*. Princeton: Princeton University Press.

Botsford, G. W. 1968. *The Roman Assemblies*. 2nd ed. New York: MacMillan.

Cameron, A. D. E. 1974. *Bread and Circuses: The Roman Emperor and his People. Inaugural lecture in Latin language and literature at King's College*. London: King's College.

Carafa, P. 1998. *Il comizio di Roma dalle origini all'età di Augusto*. Rome: "L'Erma" di Bretschneider.

Champlin, E. 1980. *Fronto and Antonine Rome*. Cambridge, Mass.: Harvard University Press.

Coarelli, F. 1977. "Il Comizio dalle origini alle fine della Repubblica. Cronologia e topografia." *Parola del Passato* 32: 202–7.

———. 1985. *Il Foro Romano. II. Periodo repubblicano e augusteo*. Rome: Edizioni Quasar.

Döbler, C. 1999. *Politische Agitation und Öffentlichkeit in der späten Republik*. Frankfurt: Peter Lang.

Gilbert, R. 1976. *Die Beziehung zwischen Princeps und stadtrömischer Plebs im frühen Prinzipat*. PhD Thesis, Universität Bochum.

Hiebel, D. 2009. *Rôles institutionnel et politique de la contio sous la République romaine (287–49 av. J.-C.)*. Paris: De Boccard.

Hölkeskamp, K-J. 1995. "*Oratoris maxima scaena*. Reden vor dem Volk in der politischen Kultur der Republik." In M. Jehne (ed.), *Demokratie in Rom? Die Rolle des Volkes in der Politik der römischen Republik*. Stuttgart: Franz Steiner Verlag. 11–49.

———. 2001. "Capitol, Comitium und Forum. Öffentliche Räume, sakrale Topographie und Erinnerungslandschaften der römischen Republik." In S. Faller (ed.), *Studien zu antiken Identitäten*. Würzburg: Ergon. 97–132.

Jehne, M. 2000. "Rednertätigkeit und Statusdissonanzen in der späten römischen Republik." In Chr. Neumeister and W. Raeck (eds.), *Rede und Redner. Bewertung und Darstellung in den antiken Kulturen*. Möhnesee: Bibliopolis. 167–89.

Koeppel, G. M. 1986. "Die historischen Reliefs der römischen Kaiserzeit. IV. Stadtrömische Denkmäler unbekannter Bauzugehörigkeit aus Hadrianischer bis Konstantinischer Zeit." *Bonner Jahrbücher* 186: 3–23.

Kühnert, B. 1991. *Die plebs urbana der späten römischen Republik*. Berlin: Akademie Verlag.

Laser, G. 1997. Populo et scaenae serviendum est. *Die Bedeutung der städtischen Masse in der späten römischen Republik*. Trier: Wissenschaftlicher Verlag Trier.

Millar, F. 1977. *The Emperor in the Roman World (31 BC–AD 337)*. Ithaca: Cornell University Press.

———. 1984. "The Political Character of the Classical Roman Republic, 200–151 B.C." *Journal of Roman Studies* 74: 1–19.

———. 1986. "Politics, Persuasion and the People before the Social War (150–90 B.C.)." *Journal of Roman Studies* 76: 1–11.

———. 1989. "Political Power in Mid-Republican Rome: Curia or Comitium?" *Journal of Roman Studies* 79: 138–50.

————. 1995. "Popular Politics at Rome in the Late Republic." In I. Malkin and
    W. Z. Rubinsohn (eds.), *Leaders and Masses in the Roman World. Studies in Honour of
    Z. Yavetz.* Leiden: E. J. Brill. 91–113.

————. 1998. *The Crowd in Rome in the Late Republic.* Ann Arbor: University of Michigan Press.

Morstein-Marx, R. 2004. *Mass Oratory and Political Power in the Late Roman Republic.*
    Cambridge: Cambridge University Press.

Mouritsen, H. 2001. *Plebs and Politics in the Late Roman Republic.* Cambridge: Cambridge
    University Press.

Nicolet, C. 1976. *Le metier de citoyen dans la Rome républicaine.* Paris: Editions Gallimard.
    English: *The World of the Citizen in Republican Rome.* London: Batsford 1980.

Paterson, J. R. 2000. *Political Life in the City of Rome.* Bristol: Bristol Classical Press.

Pina Polo, F. 1989. *Las contiones civiles y militares en Roma.* Zaragoza: Departamento
    Ciencias de la Antigüedad, Universidad de Zaragoza.

————. 1991. "*Civilitas Principis*: las asambleas populares en monedas y relieves de la época
    de los Antoninos." *Habis* 22: 187–202.

————. 1995. "Procedures and Functions of Civil and Military *contiones* in Rome." *Klio*
    77: 203–16.

————. 1996. Contra arma verbis. *Der Redner vor dem Volk in der späten römischen
    Republik.* Stuttgart: Franz Steiner Verlag.

————. 2004. "Die nützliche Erinnerung: Geschichtsschreibung, *mos maiorum* und die
    römische Identität." *Historia* 53: 147–72.

————. 2005. "I Rostra come espressione di pottere della aristocrazia romana." In G. Urso
    (ed.), *Popolo e potere nel mondo antico.* Pisa: Edizioni ETS. 141–55.

Purcell, N. 1994². "The City of Rome and the *Plebs Urbana* in the Late Republic." In
    J. A. Crook, A. Lintott, and E. Rawson (eds.), *Cambridge Ancient History, Vol. 9, The
    Last Age of the Roman Republic, 146–43 B.C.* Cambridge: Cambridge University Press.

Seelentag, G. 2004. *Taten und Tugenden Traians. Herrschaftsdarstellung im Principat.*
    Stuttgart: Franz Steiner Verlag.

Strack, P. L. 1931. *Untersuchungen zur römischen Reichsprägung des zweiten Jahrhunderts.
    I. Die Reichsprägung zur Zeit des Traian.* Stuttgart: W. Kohlhammer.

————. 1933. *Untersuchungen zur römischen Reichsprägung des zweiten Jahrhunderts. II. Die
    Reichsprägung zur Zeit des Hadrian.* Stuttgart: W. Kohlhammer.

Tatum, W. J. 1999. *The Patrician Tribune: Publius Clodius Pulcher.* Chapel Hill: University of
    North Carolina Press.

Taylor, L. R. 1949. *Party Politics in the Age of Caesar.* Berkeley: University of California Press.

————. 1966. *Roman Voting Assemblies.* Ann Arbor: University of Michigan Press.

Torelli, M. 1982. *Typology and Structure of Roman Historical Reliefs.* Ann Arbor: University
    of Michigan Press.

Ulrich, R. B. 1994. *The Roman Orator and the Sacred Stage: The Roman Templum Rostratum.*
    Brussels: Latomus.

Vanderbroeck, P. J. J. 1987. *Popular Leadership and Collective Behavior in the Late Roman
    Republic (ca. 80–50 B.C.).* Amsterdam: J. C. Gieben.

Vasaly, A. 1993. *Representations. Images of the World in Ciceronian Oratory.* Berkeley:
    University of California Press.

Veyne, P. 1976. *Le pain et le cirque. Sociologie historique d'un pluralisme politique.* Paris:
    Seuil.

Will, W. 1991. *Der römische Mob. Soziale Konflikte in der späten Republik.* Darmstadt:
    Wissenschaftliche Buchgesellschaft.

Yavetz, Z. 1969. *Plebs and Princeps.* Oxford: Clarendon Press.

CHAPTER 14

....

THE SECOND
SOPHISTIC

....

THOMAS A. SCHMITZ

I⊤ is difficult to provide a satisfactory definition of the term 'Second Sophistic.' It was coined by a Greek intellectual of the third century AD, Philostratus.[1] His *Lives of the Sophists*, an anecdotal, highly idiosyncratic history of the movement, defines the phenomenon in a functional, transhistorical way (Whitmarsh 2005: 4–5). Philostratus claims that the history of the Second Sophistic began in the fourth century BC with the Attic orator Aeschines (*VS* 481–82); but he also includes sophists such as Gorgias, Protagoras, or Hippias of Elis, all active during the fifth century BC, in his account. Whenever the movement may be taken to have begun, for Philostratus, improvised declamation is the decisive factor for defining the Second Sophistic. Ultimately, though, he is interested in establishing (or constructing) a classical pedigree for the sophists of the imperial era. Hence, his anecdotal account provides a wealth of information on the historical, political, and social circumstances of the sophists, but does not answer the question as to why a revival of sophistic-style learning and oratorical display became such a prominent social and intellectual phenomenon during the second and third centuries AD.

This lack of a clear definition may offer a (partial) explanation of the fact that modern scholars have been much divided about the scope and the importance

---

1. There are several authors by the name of 'Philostratus'; two of them are mentioned in the *Lives of the Sophists*; neither of them is the author of this work. While we can be confident that at least two different individuals must have contributed to the corpus of works transmitted under this name, we cannot hope to obtain certainty concerning the attribution of individual works to these authors, but one may consult: Solmsen 1941; Rothe 1989: 1–5; Flinterman 1995: 5–14; and de Lannoy 1997. On Philostratus, see now Bowie and Elsner 2009.

of the Second Sophistic. What exactly do we mean when we speak of the 'Second Sophistic'? Some scholars have taken seriously Philostratus' claims that sophistic oratory had always been prominent in Greek culture; they conclude that there was nothing special about imperial sophists, and have even denied the existence of the Second Sophistic as a historical phenomenon.[2] Others have accepted a much wider definition of the term; for them, the Second Sophistic is the dominant and most characteristic phenomenon of the entire culture of the second and third centuries AD.[3] This essay will focus on the Second Sophistic in the narrow sense of the word: we shall take this phenomenon to have been a cultural movement that gained particular prominence in the second and third centuries AD, and that was characterized by linguistic classicism, improvised declamations on historical and judicial topics, and professional performers who would often come from the highest echelons of society in the eastern half of the Roman Empire.

There can be no doubt that most of the ingredients of the Second Sophistic were not completely new phenomena, but had their origins in late classical and Hellenistic Greek culture (and that to this extent, Philostratus' account is accurate). Imitation of classical models (μίμησις) can be traced back to the early Hellenistic period,[4] and the Alexandrian scholars established canons of classical orators and made collections of pure Attic words.[5] With Caecilius of Calacte and Dionysius of Halicarnassus (in the first century BC), these trends developed into a full-blown ideology of classicism (Hidber 1996). Moreover, declamation on historical or fictional topics had been a staple of Greek rhetorical training since the earliest stages of the development of rhetoric in Greek cities (Russell 1983: 3–20).

But, while these individual intellectual ingredients of the Second Sophistic have a long history within Greek culture, their social function seems to undergo fundamental changes in the second century AD. Evidence for this development can be seen in the epigraphical and numismatic record.[6] So, for example, a growing number of individuals from the upper strata of society in the eastern provinces

2. The most outspoken and radical formulation of this approach can be found in Brunt 1994, who calls the entire Second Sophistic a "bubble;" for a direct reply, see Flinterman 1996.

3. See, e.g., Swain 1991: 149, and Swain 1996: 1; cf. formulations such as "the world of the second sophistic" (Borg 2004a), or "the period of the second sophistic" (Pearcy 1993).

4. Orators such as Charisius (Cic. Brut. 286) and Hegesias (Cic. Orat. 226) claimed to follow Lysias' model, even though later rhetoricians considered Hegesias the worst offender against the ideals of classical Atticism.

5. Aristophanes of Byzantium and Istrus, a student of Callimachus, both wrote Ἀττικαὶ λέξεις (lists of pure Attic diction), and Attic Greek played a dominant role in the grammatical theories of Philoxenus (cf. Pfeiffer 1968: 198–201; Dihle 1977; Dihle 1992: 1173; and Jackson 2000). Worthington 1994 has maintained that our canon of ten Attic orators originated as late as the first century BC, with Caecilius of Calacte; against this view, see Smith 1995, who argues for an Alexandrian origin; cf. also Wisse 1995 and O'Sullivan 1997.

6. On 'sophistic' inscriptions, see Schmitz 1997: 15, and Puech 2002; cf. also Swain 1991: 152. On coins, see Münsterberg 1915, and Weiß 2004.

find it important to emphasize their status as *rhetores* (orators) or *sophistai* (sophists) in honorary and funerary inscriptions, and on coins; terms such as 'education' (παιδεία) and 'eloquence' (λόγοι) become ubiquitous.

This agrees with what we observe in other sources: sarcophagi of this period often emphasize their owners' education (Borg 2004b); novels invariably depict their protagonists as paragons of virtue and *paideia*;[7] and tools such as Atticist lexica and treatises on rhetoric demonstrate the growing pressure for all members of the upper classes to acquire and display competence in linguistic classicism (Alpers 2001). How can we account for these new social functions that traditional aspects of Greek culture acquired in the second and third centuries AD?

The first important factor we have to consider involves the dramatic social and economic changes in the eastern part of the Roman Empire during this period. The eastern provinces, especially mainland Greece, suffered enormously from the Roman civil wars in the first century BC; most of the major battles took place in Greece, and Roman armies constantly ravaged the land for several decades. Augustus' ascendancy and the resultant (relative) stability triggered an economic recovery (Alcock 1993). Two aspects were here especially momentous. First, Augustus and subsequent emperors continued to foster a political development that had already begun under Caesar's dictatorship: the provincial elites were admitted into the administration of the empire and could rise to the highest political functions.[8] Since some of the emperors of the first and second centuries were particularly Hellenophile, the number of senators and other dignitaries from the Greek East was constantly rising (Halfmann 1979, 1982; Oliver 1982). Second, and in tandem with the developments just described, the social and political influence of the provincial dignitaries within their local and regional spheres grew. Members of the social elite benefited most from this economic recovery; they accumulated land and wealth and monopolized the most important and prestigious functions in local administrations.[9]

These developments favored the emergence of a new class of local magnates in the eastern provinces. Most of them came to possess Roman citizenship. While they remained firmly rooted in their respective city-states, and held important civic offices, their outlook extended well beyond this regional frame: many of them would spend time in Rome with influential Roman friends, and serve in the imperial administration; many of these families were also linked to each other by marriage, formalized friendship, or common interests. Alcock (1993: 78) is right to call this elite a "supra-civic landowning class."

The (re-)emergence of this wealthy 'leisure class' and its members' awareness of their heightened social status, both within their local and regional communities and within the context of the Roman Empire as a whole, explains why these dignitaries

---

7. On this, see Bowie 1991: 188–92, Bowersock 1994: 41–42, and Swain 1996: 117–18.

8. To begin to get a sense of this process, which has received much renewed discussion (and debate) in recent years, see (e.g.) Bowersock 1965; Ando 2000; MacMullen 2000; Ostenfeld 2002.

9. See: Stahl 1978; Alcock 1993: 70–71; Quass 1993; Stephan 2002.

began to look for new ways of demonstrating and performing their superiority. It is important to keep in mind that in ancient society, different areas of excellence (such as political power, informal influence, economic privilege, educational excellence, or personal 'virtue') were not considered separable, but tended to reinforce and intensify each other. We should not think of cultural distinction as a mere reflection of its bearer's social status and power, but as an integral feature of this social status that contributed to his or her position of power.

A number of routes were open to members of the social elite for such performative manifestations of their privileged status.[10] As mentioned above, holding public office was a particularly visible area; honorific inscriptions, with their long lists of titles and offices, bear witness to the fact that many members of the elite accumulated such positions. Another important area was the so-called euergetism: members of the upper class spent large sums of money on benefactions for their fellow citizens, which could be used for, for example, public buildings, adornment of festivals, donations, or undertaking costly public services (such as embassies) out of their own purse.[11] Such benefactions were heavily publicized and served to enhance the renown and the social position of the donor. These gifts also provided an outlet for the pervading competitiveness that was typical of the upper classes in the Hellenized world. Euergetism thus offered a supplementary means (in addition to holding local, regional, or imperial offices) of acquiring social prestige; we know that some members of the elite were so eager to strive for this sort of distinction that they squandered their entire wealth on such benefactions.[12]

It is in the context of these social circumstances that the Second Sophistic should be viewed. Education (*paideia*) was another area in which members of the upper classes were able to demonstrate their superiority and to compete with each other, and it is no coincidence that inscriptions often combine praise for holding important offices, dispensing largesses, and excelling as sophists.[13] The usual competitive vocabulary such as "holding first place" (πρωτεύειν), "excelling" (διαπρέπειν), or being "second to none" (οὐδενὸς δεύτερος) is often applied to the realm of education, especially to sophistic oratory.[14] Two particular aspects of the usual Greek education need, however, to be emphasized.

First, in the absence of a publicly funded schooling system, providing education for one's children always depended on private initiative. This demanded considerable expenses, which only relatively few families were able to afford and were willing

10. For an overview of the phenomenon of elite self-representation, see Flower in this volume.

11. On euergetism in general, see Veyne 1990; for a particularly striking example, see Coulton 1987 and Kokkinia 2000. The practice was of course not restricted to the Eastern provinces; see Lomas and Cornell 2003.

12. See Rostovtzeff 1957: 2, 589–90; MacMullen 1974: 61–62; Panagopoulos 1977: 207–9; Sartre 1991: 162.

13. For examples, see *IGRR* IV 1630; *MAMA* VIII 501, 564.

14. For example, *SEG* 32 (1982) 1261; *TAM* V,1 62; *IG* II[2] 4211.

to spend.[15] Hence, attainment of the canonical education always served as a marker of class distinction (cf. Hedrick in this volume).

Second, this social aspect of *paideia* was reinforced by its public, performative aspect. The ancient educational system mostly lacked formal signs of achievement, such as diplomas, official titles, or incorporation into reserved associations. Hence, members of the upper classes had to demonstrate their *paideia* by performative acts. Proper use of language, proper table manners, proper gait, bearing, or clothing could all serve as performative displays of education (Gleason 1995; and cf. Connolly and Hahn in this volume).

Members of the social elite tended to describe *paideia*, then, not as a laboriously acquired, external attribute, but instead as a natural characteristic that was part of their entire personality. This is especially obvious in inscriptions that join words denoting education (such as παιδεία or λόγοι) with concepts referring to the general 'excellence' (ἀρετή, καλοκἀγαθία) or the 'character' (ἤθη) of the individual being honored.[16] Such a view of education as being a 'natural' component of an individual's identity can be understood as reinforcing social distinctions, and thus legitimizing the political hierarchy. This function of education becomes especially clear when we consider that in contemporary ideology, a certain kind of cultivated erudition was an indispensable prerequisite for partaking in political power (Schmitz 1997: 44–50).

It is nonetheless difficult to assess to whom this performative display of education, as a marker of social status, was primarily addressed. For while inscriptions spoke, at least potentially, to all who could read, many scholars have found it difficult to accept the claims made by members of the Second Sophistic themselves that their declamations reached mass audiences.[17] Scholars who are more skeptical about this argue that only educated members of the upper classes were capable of recognizing the linguistic, stylistic, historical, and dramatic niceties of a sophistic performance. Yet, even if this be so, it must be recognized that for those who constituted the other strata of society, the bare fact that these people had the competence to perform or appreciate cultural feats that were beyond their own reach could be seen as proof of their 'natural' superiority and thus help legitimize their elevated social position and political power.

Within the upper classes, sophistic declamations also served as an outlet for the all-embracing competitive spirit (φιλοτιμία) that pervaded Greek society—and indeed, Roman imperial society altogether. *Paideia* (intellectual cultivation) was a field for formal competition especially for younger members of the social elite; rhetorical *agones*

---

15. Harris 1989 has rightly cautioned against the assumption that high percentages of the population of the ancient world were literate; for a discussion of his arguments, see Beard 1991, and Bowman and Woolf 1994.

16. Examples: ἤθος, παιδεία, and ἀρετή (*TAM* V 976); ῥήτωρ and καλοκἀγαθία (*AE* 1968, 475); λόγος, ἤθος, and πᾶσα ἀρετή (*TAM* II 422). See also Schmitz 1997:136–46.

17. See, e.g., Philostr. *VS* 619; Aristid. *Or.* 51. 31–32. On the audiences for sophistic declamations, see Korenjak 2000.

(contests) existed at school level and at a number of local and regional festivals.[18] There were also rhetorical and 'sophistic' competitions for adults.[19] However, the area where we can see the competitive value of *paideia* most clearly is not in formalized *agones*, but rather in the general combative atmosphere that surrounded sophistic declamations. Numerous anecdotes and accounts provide a consistent picture:[20] performances were usually followed by discussions about linguistic, stylistic, or historical details that often became heated and acrimonious. One-upmanship was a standard attribute of sophists, and exposing a rival as ignorant or putting an attacker to shame with a witty and devastating retort was part of a sophist's job;[21] thus, Philostratus (*VS* 491) considers involvement in such professional quarrels a hallmark of the real sophist. Other social events presented more intimate occasions to perform one's *paideia* and thus demonstrate that one was a worthy member of the educated social elite, the πεπαιδευμένοι (*pepaideumenoi*—the cultivated, educated individuals): during private dinner parties, learned discussions about linguistic, rhetorical, and historical questions were a regular form of entertainment for members of the upper classes, as the idealized accounts of such parties in Aulus Gellius, Plutarch, or Athenaeus as well as their parody in Petronius demonstrate.[22] Undoubtedly, such debates were an outlet for the competitive spirit of one-upping one's peers; at the same time, however, they also created awareness of social cohesion by providing a common playing field that restricted access to the competition to members of one social class only. Again, the social function of *paideia* can be described as being analogous to euergetism: both areas allow the competitive display of social status on a field that is inaccessible to actors from the lower strata of society.

This cohesive, centripetal function of the Second Sophistic is even more visible in an area that has attracted a great deal of scholarly attention during recent years: the classicizing outlook of *paideia*, the exclusive focus on the glorious past of Athens, and the strict canonization of the classical Attic dialect as the only proper form of Greek speech (Ἑλληνισμός) all contribute to a definition of 'Greekdom' that proved particularly attractive in the wide and complex universe of the Roman Empire.[23] Again, it is easy to see that the developments leading to this cultural definition of a Greek identity date back to the Hellenistic period: after the conquests of Alexander the Great and the establishment of the Hellenistic kingdoms, the ruling elites of Macedonian expatriates tended to construct a specific Greek identity less in ethnic than in cultural terms.[24] At the same time, these constructions allowed the

18. See Ziebarth 1914: 136–47; Schmitz 1997: 101–10.

19. See, e.g., *AE* (1969/1970) 587; cf. Schmitz 1997: 110–12.

20. Examples abound in Philostratus' *Lives of the Sophists* and Lucian's satires.

21. Some examples are quoted in Anderson 1993: 55–64.

22. See Frazier 1994, Braund and Wilkins 2000, Jacob 2005, and Holford-Strevens and Vardi 2005.

23. Only a few of the most important contributions can be quoted here: Said 1991; Woolf 1993–94; Flinterman 1995; Goldhill 2001; Whitmarsh 2001; Ostenfeld 2002; Stephan 2002; Borg 2004.

24. See Kuhrt and Sherwin-White 1987; Hall 2002.

(non-Greek) local upper classes to consider themselves *Hellenes* as well because they subscribed to similar values in terms of philosophy, culture, religion, and political outlook. This facilitated the emergence of a large group of people who, regardless of their ethnic descent, considered themselves *Hellenes*.

These trends continued in the Second Sophistic. What is distinctly new, however, is the unprecedented emphasis on just one relatively brief period of Greek history, the 'classical' Athens of the fifth and fourth centuries BC.[25] It was this relatively brief period that was, time and again, reenacted and resurrected in sophistic declamations;[26] knowledge of the political events and cultural production of this time as well as perfect mastery of the Attic dialect spoken and written during this period were regarded as the most important aspects of *paideia*.

It should be noted that this cultural definition of Greek identity never completely replaced older, ethnic models of perception. One of the most important factors in fostering an 'official' definition of Greek identity was the Panhellenion, founded by Hadrian in 131; admission to this prestigious organization was restricted to cities that could prove their 'pure' Greek origin.[27] However, this ethnic definition was again deeply intertwined with cultural aspects, since proof of Greek origin was mainly demonstrated by referring to foundation narratives, mythical ancestors, and kinship with eminent Greek cities such as Athens or Sparta. Hence, cities that applied for access to the Panhellenion encouraged writers to scrutinize and collect myths about their origins; as inscriptions show, such myths were often publicized in sophistic declamations.[28] This was again an area in which members of the social elite could demonstrate their *paideia* and prove its worth in political matters.[29]

One factor that has been discussed intensely (maybe to an undue extent) is the relationship between this Greek identity and the fact that these Greeks were living in the political reality of the Roman Empire. As we have seen, the historical outlook of the Second Sophistic is decidedly Hellenocentric; in many texts, Rome and Roman domination are not mentioned at all. Hence, some scholars have concluded that the Second Sophistic is "perfectly harmless on the surface but anti-Roman in its implications, since its intent was the reassertion of Hellenism" (MacMullen 1966: 244). Others maintain that "the kind of Hellenism" the Second Sophistic "preaches is one that does not conflict with Roman supremacy, but is approved by the Romans" (Jones 1978: 35, on Dio Chrysostomos).

When we weigh the arguments of the two opposing camps (which Jones 2002: 365 has aptly termed "accommodationists" and the school of "spiritual resistance"),

25. See Schmitz 2007.

26. See Schmitz 1999.

27. On the Panhellenion, see Spawforth and Walker 1985, Spawforth and Walker 1986, Jones 1996, and Romeo 2002; on the 'ethnic' aspect of Greek identity, see Lund 2005.

28. E.g., *TAM* II,1 174; for another example and a reconstruction of the cultural and political background, see Robert 1987: 78–90.

29. On such "kinship diplomacy," as Jones 1999 aptly calls it, see Weiß 1984, Scheer 1993, Schmitz 1997: 181–96, 206–9, Weiß 2000.

it is difficult to avoid the trap of anachronism; terms such as 'nationalism' or 'colony' are loaded with modern connotations that may get in our way when we endeavor to explore mentalities in the ancient world. Seen from our modern perspective, the ancient testimonies may indeed appear to be contradictory. On the one hand, sophistic texts such as some of Lucian's satires are critical of what they perceive as a lack of education and civilization in the Romans.[30] On the other hand, most members of the social elite held Roman citizenship, some rose to high offices in the imperial service, and texts such as Aristides' *On Rome* demonstrate that they had found some satisfactory arrangement with Roman domination; and of course, the fact that they constituted the part of Greek society that profited most from the economic opportunities and the political stability of the *pax Romana* certainly helped them find their peace of mind. We have to accept these contradictions and must understand that for members of the social elite, it was possible to have (at least) a 'Greek' and a 'Roman' identity (just as many of them used the Roman *tria nomina*— the combination of three names that only Roman citizens were permitted to use— as well as traditional Greek names).[31] According to the demands of the situation, they might emphasize their Greek identity and ignore the political realities of the Roman Empire (or even disparage the Romans), or they might proudly highlight their status as Roman citizens and speak of the Roman Empire as 'we' (as opposed to external enemies). Such inconsistencies were less important to the actors in the social field of the Second Sophistic than they are to the modern observer since their discourse was primarily addressed to their peers who would share the same allegiances and the same political and cultural outlook.

To sum up, the Second Sophistic has for a long time been regarded as a problem. Its classicizing ideology and seemingly useless rhetorical fantasy were extremely difficult to interpret. Some scholars have emphasized the importance of sophists as ambassadors for (Bowersock 1969), or have seen them as 'propagandists' of, the Roman Empire (Sirago 1989); others have rejected such interpretations and consider the Second Sophistic an expression of escapism that allowed members of the Greek elite to forget their powerlessness in the huge Roman Empire (Bowie 1970). All such interpretations, however, ultimately failed to take into account the social dimension of this cultural phenomenon. The portrayal delineated above is now shared by a majority of scholars working in this field. They see the Second Sophistic as one facet of a semiotic system that allowed a performative expression and reinforcement of values and attitudes of the social elite in the Greek part of the Roman Empire. The overt display of status, the zealous competition in a restricted field of endeavor, and the establishment of a cultural identity that provided a supremely positive self-perception can all be understood as part of a social 'habitus' as described by

30. See especially his *Nigrinus* and *On Salaried Posts.*; cf. Peretti 1946; against this anti-Roman interpretation, see Forte 1972: 371–90, Nutton 1978, and Sirago 1989. The most outspoken version of this 'resistant' reading of the Second Sophistic is found in Fuchs 1938; the year of its appearance is certainly not a coincidence. Cf. Walbank 1972.

31. On the tension between these identities, see Alcock 2007 and Connolly 2007.

Bourdieu (1986). It is thus impossible to separate the social from the cultural repercussions of the Second Sophistic.

SUGGESTED READING

Whitmarsh 2005 provides an up-to-date introduction to many aspects of the Second
Sophistic. More specialized studies are Gleason 1995 (esp. on the role of gender in sophistic oratory) and Schmitz 1997 (on the social and political aspects). The prosopographical
overview in Bowersock 1974: 35–40 is still useful; it is now supplemented by the collected
epigraphical evidence in Puech 2002. One aspect that has attracted a great deal of scholarly attention during the past decades is the creation of a Greek identity in sophistic
oratory and related literary production. Woolf 1993–94 is a seminal study; more recent
contributions can be found in Goldhill 2001, Whitmarsh 2001, Ostenfeld 2002, and Borg
2004.

BIBLIOGRAPHY

Alcock, S. 1993. *Graecia Capta. The Landscapes of Roman Greece.* Cambridge: Cambridge
    University Press.
———. 2007. "Making Sure You Know Whom to Kill: Spatial Strategies and Strategic
    Boundaries in the Eastern Roman Empire." *Millennium* 4: 13–20.
Alpers, K. 2001. "Lexikographie B. I Griechische Antike." In G. Ueding (ed.), *Historisches
    Wörterbuch der Rhetorik*, vol. 5. Tübingen: Niemeyer. 194–210.
Anderson, B. 1993. *The Second Sophistic. A Cultural Phenomenon in the Roman Empire.*
    London: Routledge.
Ando, C. 2000. *Imperial Ideology and Provincial Loyalty in the Roman Empire.* Berkeley:
    University of California Press.
Beard, M. (ed.). 1991. *Literacy in the Roman World.* Ann Arbor: Journal of Roman
    Archaeology.
Borg, B. (ed.). 2004a. *Paideia. The World of the Second Sophistic.* Berlin: Walter de Gruyter.
———. 2004b. "Glamorous Intellectuals: Portraits of *pepaideumenoi* in the Second and
    Third Centuries AD." In Borg 2004a: 157–78.
Bourdieu, P. 1986. *Distinction: A Social Critique of the Judgement of Taste.* London:
    Routledge [French original 1979].
Bowersock, G. W. 1965. *Augustus and the Greek World.* Oxford: Clarendon Press.
———. 1969. *Greek Sophists in the Roman Empire.* Oxford: Oxford University Press.
———. 1994. *Fiction as History. Nero to Julian.* Berkeley: University of California Press.
Bowersock, G. W. (ed.). 1974. *Approaches to the Second Sophistic. Papers Presented at
    the 105th Annual Meeting of the American Philological Association.* University Park:
    American Philological Association.
Bowie, E. 1970. "Greeks and Their Past in the Second Sophistic." *Past and Present* 46: 3–41.
    (Reprinted in M. I. Finley (ed.), *Studies in Ancient Society.* London: Routledge 1974.
    166–209.)

———. 1991. "Hellenes and Hellenism in Writers of the Early Second Sophistic." In Said 1991: 183–204.

Bowie, E., and J. Elsner (eds.). 2009. *Philostratus*. Cambridge: Cambridge University Press.

Bowman, A. K., and G. Woolf (eds.). 1994. *Literacy and Power in the Ancient World*. Cambridge: Cambridge University Press.

Braund, D. C., and J. Wilkins (eds.). 2000. *Athenaeus and His World: Reading Greek Culture in the Roman Empire*. Exeter: University of Exeter Press.

Brunt, P. A. 1994. "The Bubble of the Second Sophistic." *Bulletin of the Institute of Classical Studies* 39: 25–52.

Connolly, J. 2007. "Being Greek/Being Roman. Hellenism and Assimilation in the Roman Empire." *Millennium* 4: 21–42.

Coulton, J. 1987. "Opramoas and the Anonymous Benefactor." *Journal of Hellenic Studies* 107: 171–78.

Dihle, A. 1977. "Der Beginn des Attizismus." *Antike und Abendland* 23: 162–77.

———. 1992. "Attizismus." In G. Ueding (ed.), *Historisches Wörterbuch der Rhetorik*, vol. 1. Tübingen: Niemeyer. 1163–76.

Flinterman, J.-J. 1995. *Power, Paideia, and Pythagoreanism. Greek Identity, Conceptions of the Relationship between Philosophers and Monarchs and Political Ideas in Philostratus' Life of Apollonius*. Amsterdam: J. C. Gieben.

———. 1996. "De tweede sofistiek: een portie gebakken lucht?" *Lampas* 29: 135–54.

Forte, B. 1972. *Rome and the Romans as the Greeks Saw Them*. Rome: American Academy in Rome.

Frazier, F. 1994. "Deux images des banquets de lettrés: les *Propos de tables* de Plutarque et le *Banquet de Lucien*." In A. Billault and A. Buisson (eds.), *Lucien de Samosate. Actes du colloque international de Lyon organisé au Centre d'études romaines et gallo-romaines les 30 septembre–1er octobre 1993*. Lyon: Centre d'études romaines et gallo-romaines. 125–30.

Fuchs, H. 1938. *Der geistige Widerstand gegen Rom in der antiken Welt*. Berlin: Walter de Gruyter.

Gleason, M. W. 1995. *Making Men. Sophists and Self-Representation in Ancient Rome*. Princeton: Princeton University Press.

Goldhill, S. (ed.). 2001. *Being Greek under Rome. Cultural Identity, the Second Sophistic and the Development of Empire*. Cambridge: Cambridge University Press.

Halfmann, H. 1979. *Die Senatoren aus dem östlichen Teil des Imperium Romanum bis zum Ende des 2. Jahrhunderts n. Chr.* Göttingen: Vandenhoeck & Ruprecht.

———. 1982. "Die Senatoren aus den kleinasiatischen Provinzen des römischen Reiches vom 1. bis 3. Jahrhundert (Asia, Pontus-Bithynia, Lycia, Pamphylia, Galatia, Cappadocia, Cilicia)." In *Atti del Colloquio Internazionale AIEGL su Epigrafia e ordine senatorio Roma, 14–20 maggio 1981*. Rome: Edizioni di storia e letteratura. 603–50.

Hall, J. B. 2002. *Hellenicity: Between Ethnicity and Culture*. Chicago: University of Chicago Press.

Harris, W. V. 1989. *Ancient Literacy*. Cambridge, Mass.: Harvard University Press.

Hidber, T. 1996. *Das klassizistische Manifest des Dionys von Halikarnass: die Praefatio zu De Oratoribus Veteribus*. Stuttgart: B. G. Teubner.

Holford-Strevens, L., and A. Vardi (eds.). 2005. *The Worlds of Aulus Gellius*. Oxford: Oxford University Press.

Jackson, S. B. 2000. *Istrus the Callimachean*. Amsterdam: Hakkert.

Jacob, C. 2005. "'La table et le cercle': sociabilités savantes sous l'Empire romain." *Annales histoire, sciences sociales* 60: 507–30.

Jones, C. P. 1978. *The Roman World of Dio Chrysostom*. Cambridge, Mass.: Harvard University Press.

———. 1996. "The Panhellenion." *Chiron* 26: 29–56.

———. 1999. *Kinship Diplomacy in the Ancient World*. Cambridge, Mass.: Harvard University Press.

———. 2002. Review of Goldhill 2001. In *Mouseion, Journal of the Classical Association of Canada* 3: 362–65.

Kokkinia, C. 2000. *Die Opramoas-Inschrift von Rhodiapolis*. Bonn: Rudolf Habelt Verlag.

Korenjak, M. 2000. *Publikum und Redner. Ihre Interaktion in der sophistischen Rhetorik der Kaiserzeit*. Munich: Verlag C. H. Beck.

Kuhrt, A., and S. Sherwin-White (eds.). 1987. *Hellenism in the East: Greek and Non-Greek Civilizations from Syria to Central Asia after Alexander*. Berkeley: University of California Press.

Lannoy, L. de. 1997. "Le Problème des Philostrate (état de la question)." *Aufstieg und Niedergang der römischen Welt* II 34.3. Berlin: Walter de Gruyter. 2362–449.

Lomas, K., and T. Cornell (eds.). 2003. *"Bread and Circuses": Euergetism and Municipal Patronage in Roman Italy*. London: Routledge.

Lund, A. A. 2005. "Hellenentum und Hellenizität: zur Ethogenese und zur Ethnizität der antiken Hellenen." *Historia* 54: 1–17.

MacMullen, R. 1966. *Enemies of the Roman Order. Treason, Unrest, and Alienation in the Empire*. Cambridge, Mass.: Harvard University Press.

———. 1974. *Roman Social Relations 50 B.C. to A.D. 284*. New Haven: Yale University Press.

———. 2000. *Romanization in the Time of Augustus*. New Haven: Yale University Press.

Münsterberg, R. 1915. "Die Münzen der Sophisten." *Numismatische Zeitschrift* 48: 119–24.

Nutton, V. 1978. "The Beneficial Ideology." In P. Garnsey and C. R. Whittaker (eds.), *Imperialism in the Ancient World. The Cambridge University Research Seminar in Ancient History*. Cambridge: Cambridge University Press. 209–21.

Oliver, J. H. 1982. "Roman Senators from Greece and Macedonia." In *Atti del Colloquio Internazionale AIEGL su Epigrafia e ordine senatorio Roma, 14–20 maggio 1981*. Rome: Edizioni di storia e letteratura. 583–602.

Ostenfeld, E. N. (ed.). 2002. *Greek Romans and Roman Greeks*. Aarhus: Aarhus University Press.

O'Sullivan, N. 1997. "Caecilius, the 'Canons' of Writers, and the Origins of Atticism." In W. J. Dominik (ed.), *Roman Eloquence. Rhetoric in Society and Literature*. London: Routledge. 32–49.

Panagopoulos, C. 1977. "Vocabulaire et mentalité dans les *Moralia* de Plutarque." *Dialogues d'Histoire Ancienne* 3: 197–235.

Pearcy, L. T. 1993. "Medicine and Rhetoric in the Period of the Second Sophistic." *Aufstieg und Niedergang der römischen Welt* II 37.1. Berlin: Walter de Gruyter. 445–56.

Peretti, A. 1946. *Luciano. Un intellettuale greco contro Roma*. Florence: La Nuova Italia.

Pfeiffer, R. 1968. *History of Classical Scholarship from the Beginning to the End of the Hellenistic Age*. Oxford: Clarendon Press.

Puech, B. 2002. *Orateurs et sophistes grecs dans les inscriptions de l'époque impériale*. Paris: J. Vrin.

Quass, F. 1993. *Die Honoratiorenschicht in den Städten des griechischen Ostens. Untersuchungen zur politischen und sozialen Entwicklung in hellenistischer und römischer Zeit*. Stuttgart: Franz Steiner Verlag.

Robert, L. 1987. *Documents d'Asie mineure*. Paris: Ecole Française Athènes.

Romeo, I. 2002. "The Panhellenion and Ethnic Identity in Hadrianic Greece." *Classical Philology* 97: 21–40.

Rostovtzeff, M. 1957. *The Social and Economic History of the Roman Empire*. 2nd ed. Oxford: Clarendon Press.

Rothe, S. 1989. *Kommentar zu ausgewählten Sophistenviten des Philostratos. Die Lehrstuhlinhaber in Athen und Rom*. Heidelberg: Julius Groos.

Russell, D. A. 1983. *Greek Declamation*. Cambridge: Cambridge University Press.

Said, S. (ed.). 1991. Έλληνισμός. *Quelques jalons pour une histoire de l'identité grecque. Actes du Colloque de Strasbourg 25–27 octobre 1989*. Leiden: E. J. Brill.

Sartre, M. 1991. *L'Orient romain. Provinces et sociétés provinciales en Méditerranée orientale d'Auguste aux Sévères (31 avant J.-C.–235 après J.-C.)*. Paris: Seuil.

Scheer, T. S. 1993. *Mythische Vorväter. Zur Bedeutung griechischer Heroenmythen im Selbstverständnis kleinasiatischer Städte*. Munich: Editio Maris.

Schmitz, T. A. 1997. *Bildung und Macht. Zur sozialen und politischen Funktion der zweiten Sophistik in der griechischen Welt der Kaiserzeit*. Munich: Verlag C. H. Beck.

——. 1999. "Performing the Past in the Second Sophistic." In M. Zimmermann (ed.), *Geschichtsschreibung und politischer Wandel im 3. Jahrhundert n. Chr. Kolloquium zu Ehren von Karl-Ernst Petzold (Juni 1998) anläßlich seines 80. Geburtstags*. Stuttgart: Franz Steiner Verlag. 71–92.

——. 2007. "Die Erfindung des klassischen Athen in der zweiten Sophistik." In A. Steiner-Weber, M. Laureys, and T. A. Schmitz (eds.), *Bilder der Antike*. Göttingen: Bonn University Press: 71–88.

Sirago, V. A. 1989. "La seconda sofistica come espressione culturale della classe dirigente del II sec." In *Aufstieg und Niedergang der römischen Welt* II 33.1. Berlin: Walter de Gruyter. 36–78.

Smith, R. M. 1995. "A New Look at the Canon of the Ten Attic Orators." *Mnemosyne* 48: 66–79.

Solmsen, F. 1941. "Philostratos 8–12." *RE* 20.1: 124–77.

Spawforth, A. J., and S. Walker. 1985. "The World of the Panhellenion. I. Athens and Eleusis." *Journal of Roman Studies* 75: 78–104.

——. 1986. "The World of the Panhellenion. II. Three Dorian Cities." *Journal of Roman Studies* 76: 88–105.

Stahl, M. 1978. *Imperiale Herrschaft und provinziale Stadt. Strukturprobleme der römischen Reichsorganisation im 1.–3. Jh. der Kaiserzeit*. Göttingen: Vandenhoeck & Ruprecht.

Stephan, E. 2002. *Honoratioren, Griechen, Polisbürger. Kollektive Identitäten innerhalb der Oberschicht des kaiserzeitlichen Kleinasien*. Göttingen: Vandenhoeck & Ruprecht.

Swain, S. 1991. "The Reliability of Philostratus's *Lives of the Sophists*." *Classical Antiquity* 10: 148–63.

——. 1996. *Hellenism and Empire. Language, Classicism, and Power in the Greek World, AD 50–250*. Oxford: Oxford University Press.

Veyne, P. 1990. *Bread and Circuses. Historical Sociology and Political Pluralism*. London: Penguin. (Original French version Paris: Seuil 1976.)

Walbank, F. W. 1972. "Nationality as a Factor in Roman History." *Harvard Studies in Classical Philology* 76: 145–68.

Weiß, P. 1984. "Lebendiger Mythos. Gründerheroen und städtische Gründungstraditionen im griechisch-römischen Osten." *Würzburger Jahrbücher für die Altertumswissenschaft* 10: 179–211.

——. 2000. "Eumeneia und das Panhellenion." *Chiron* 30: 617–39.

————. 2004. "Städtische Münzprägungen und zweite Sophistik." In Borg 2004a: 179–200.

Whitmarsh, T. 2001. *Greek Literature and the Roman Empire. The Politics of Imitation.* Oxford: Oxford University Press.

————. 2005. *The Second Sophistic.* Oxford: Oxford University Press.

Wisse, J. 1995. "Greeks, Romans and the Rise of Atticism." In J. G. J. Abbenes, R. Simon Slings, and I. Sluiter (eds.), *Greek Literary Theory after Aristotle. A Collection of Papers in Honour of D. M. Schenkeveld.* Amsterdam: Vrije University Press. 65–82.

Woolf, G. 1993–94. "Becoming Roman, Staying Greek: Culture, Identity and the Civilizing Process in the Roman East." *Proceedings of the Cambridge Philological Society* 40: 116–43.

Worthington, I. 1994. "The Canon of the Ten Attic Orators." In I. Worthington (ed.), *Persuasion. Greek Rhetoric in Action.* London: Routledge. 244–63.

Ziebarth, E. 1914. *Aus dem griechischen Schulwesen. Eudemos von Milet und Verwandtes.* 2nd ed. Leipzig: B. G. Teubner.

CHAPTER 15

ROMAN SOCIETY IN THE COURTROOM

LEANNE BABLITZ

ANCIENT Rome was a city of hierarchies, contests, and performances, not the least of which could be found on most days within its courtrooms. Although the Roman elite has left the most prominent body of evidence on Rome's justice system, the city's courts brought together individuals of highly diverse social status in a wide variety of interactions. As such, the courts are a valuable source of information on the social history of Rome. Whereas our contemporary court system is largely removed from the everyday lives of most of the population, in Rome the law involved many, particularly as judges, but also as advocates, litigants, and, of course, audience. Indeed, in the imperial era Rome was pulsing with courts, and the workings of justice played out on various 'stages' throughout the city.

The visibility of the courts was a matter of both pragmatics and ideology. The sheer volume of cases dictated that hearings take place in numerous locations, but the extent to which the populace could observe these usually public displays also served to reinforce several levels of state and social function. Wrongdoings and injustices could be exposed and put right, while the overarching 'presence' of the emperor was linked to this complex judicial apparatus, implying or openly demonstrating his direction of the state.

THE LOCATIONS OF COURTROOMS AT ROME

The first step in appreciating the wide-ranging presence of Rome's courtrooms in the fabric of Roman society is to gain a sense of their physical locations. At the heart of the Roman legal system were the praetors, elected magistrates who oversaw the administration of private and public law within the city; the *praetor urbanus* (urban praetor) and the *praetor peregrinus* (foreign praetor) presided over their respective courts. There were also several *quaestiones perpetuae* (standing courts), as well as other praetorial tasks presided over by lesser officials.[1] We can locate these several courts with mixed success.

Overall, we are correct to envision a city that on most days was alive with the sights and sounds of court activities. The Forum Romanum saw the bulk of these events during the first 200 years of the imperial period. The urban praetor occupied the east end for the first three decades of Augustus' reign, later moving to the Forum of Augustus. The court of the *praetor peregrinus* likewise was first located in the Forum Romanum and then moved, with the *praetor urbanus*, to the Forum of Augustus in the early part of Augustus' reign. As the volume of cases continued to grow, and even the addition of the Forum of Julius Caesar as a venue for court cases was insufficient, the Forum of Augustus was added to accommodate the praetors as well as the *quaestiones perpetuae*.[2] Likely used to capacity in the first century, the Forum of Augustus was supplemented by the Forum of Trajan (once it began to be opened in AD 113), where the courts of the *praefectus urbi* (prefect of the city) and of consuls can plausibly be located; built over a hundred years after the completion of the Forum of Augustus, the massive size and similar design of Trajan's complex would have lent itself well to legal activities.[3] Meanwhile, the court of the emperor was largely nomadic, having no standard location. After Augustus, most emperors appear to have used the Forum Romanum, the Forum of Augustus, as well as the imperial residence and gardens to hear cases.[4] Thus, it appears that these four large

---

1. This article is based on my book *Actors and Audience in the Roman Courtroom* (Bablitz 2007). For further discussion on the various topics here presented I would suggest that the reader first consult that work. In the notes below I provide some direction to other modern scholarship on various topics, and I cite my own work only for especially contentious issues. For discussion of the development, jurisdiction, and procedure of the praetors' courts, see Greenidge 1901: *passim*; Crook 1967: 68–97; Frier 1985: 42–78; Camodeca 1996: 172–73; Brennan 2000: 133–35, 461–65. For discussion of the development, jurisdiction, and procedure of the *quaestiones perpetuae*, see Greenidge 1901: 415–504; Gruen 1968: 258–62; Jones 1972: 48–97; Robinson 1995: 1–14; Brennan 2000: 235–38, 365–70, 416–24, 465–75.

2. Castagnoli 1950: 75–77; Richardson 1973; Coarelli 1985: 166–80; Giuliani and Verduchi 1987: 95–102; David 1995: 377–82; Carnabuci 1996: 29–90; Metzger 2005: 155–63.

3. Anderson 1984: 161–66; Packer 1997: 244, 431.

4. Sen. *Apoc.* 7. 4; Suet. *Aug.* 33. 1, *Claud.* 33. 1, *Dom.* 8; Tac. *Ann.* 11. 2–3; Dio 55. 33. 5, 57. 7. 2, 60. 4. 3, 66. 10. 5, 68. 10. 2, 69. 7. 1, 76. 11. 1; *Acta Isidori. Rec. B Col. 2; Acta S. Laurentii; Acta S. Marcelli; Acta S. Crescentii; Acta S. Susannae*. For the martyr acts, see Musurillo 1972.

areas—the Forum Romanum, and the fora of Augustus, Julius Caesar, and Trajan—
were teeming with the bustle and commotion of court hearings throughout the
early imperial period. Other areas in the city would also have lent themselves to
hosting court activities. The Portico of Livia, the Temple of Peace, the Temple of the
Divine Claudius, and the Basilica Aemilia all had suitable space. Few courts were
anchored to a specific location; instead, facilities were used interchangeably as needs
arose, and places could be used on a daily basis for various legal proceedings. The
workings of the law were thus very public, and scarcely to be avoided by anyone living or doing business within the city of Rome.

What, then, would one of these publicly placed courts have looked like?
Although no one arrangement could have suited all types of hearings, it is possible
to reconstruct a 'standard' courtroom for a public case or an important private case,
and thereby to envision the interactions of the various participants within it. Those
present would have included one or more (perhaps as many as forty-five) persons
judging, the litigants, their advocates with various assistants, the witnesses, and a
diversely composed audience.[5]

Unlike modern courts, those in Rome typically involved frequent participation of and interaction between advocates, litigants, supporters, and members of
the audience. Thus, first to note is the absence of physical barriers: the Roman
courtroom was not an enclosed space, but rather, some area of a large public space
reserved for legal activities at a given time. Thus, contact was possible between
litigants and judges (for example, clasping the judges' knees was encouraged by
Quintilian and mentioned by Seneca the Elder), and individuals could easily wander from one side of the court to the other (opposing) side.[6] We also know that
advocates needed to address both the judges and opposing counsel while trying
to avoid turning their backs to these people.[7] Taking into account these and other
factors, the most suitable arrangement seems to be a more or less square area, with
the benches of the litigants and their advocates facing each other, the presiding
magistrate and judge (or judges) on a third side of the square, while supporters of
the litigants and, farther back, members of the audience were arranged on benches
in a semi-circle extending behind the litigants and across from the judge(s). More
peripheral audience members could have stood and/or walked around all sides of
this arrangement (see fig. 15.1).[8]

Given the structural acoustics and the number of persons present, the noise
level would have been considerable. But apart from the sounds generated within a
given courtroom, when courts were held contiguously—such as the four tribunals

---

5. For the argument regarding a panel size of forty-five judges see Bablitz 2007:
99–100.

6. Sen. *Controv.* 9. 6. 12, 10. 2. 3; Quint. *Inst.* 6. 1. 34, 39.

7. Quint. *Inst.* 11. 3. 127.

8. David 1992: 484 produced a drawing based on late republican evidence. The
similarities are striking.

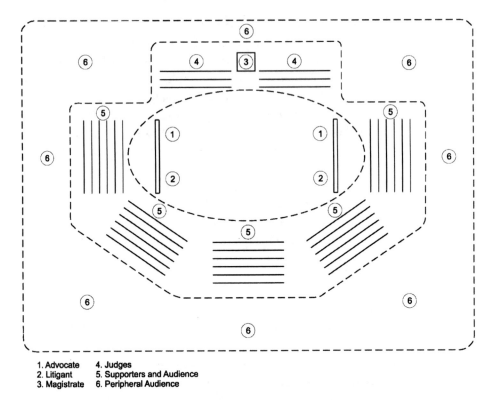

1. Advocate   4. Judges
2. Litigant   5. Supporters and Audience
3. Magistrate   6. Peripheral Audience

Figure 15.1. Reconstructed layout of a large Roman courtroom.

of the centumviral court, which were set up right next to one another—interference from other nearby venues was an added challenge to judges, advocates, and audience alike.[9] Galerius Trachalus apparently possessed the ideal voice for such circumstances:

> Certainly I remember that, when he was speaking in the Basilica Julia before the first court, and the four courts were convened, as is usual, and the whole place was in uproar with shouting, not only was he heard and understood, but also he was commended (a thing which was most insulting to the other speakers) by all four courts (Quint. *Inst.* 12. 5. 6).[10]

Doubtless, making oneself heard amid the hubbub of most Roman courtrooms was often a significant challenge.

---

9. For continued discussion of the centumviral courtroom see my forthcoming article, which advances beyond what is presented in Bablitz 2007: 61–70.

10. *Certe cum in basilica Iulia diceret primo tribunali, quattuor autem iudicia, ut moris est, cogerentur atque omnia clamoribus fremerent, et auditum eum et intellectum et, quod agentibus ceteris contumeliosissimum fuit, laudatum quoque ex quattuor tribunalibus memini.* All translations are my own unless otherwise noted.

THE LITIGANTS

Who were the litigants in this noisy array of Roman courtrooms, and what was the experience like for them? Unfortunately, the evidence for the imperial period is less than satisfying. However, we can find some specifics as well as draw more general inferences. Both men and women appear as litigants, in a roughly four-to-one ratio. Male litigants in the surviving sources are involved in cases of murder and treason, assault, loans, inheritances, forgery, insult (*iniuria*), adultery, and Christianity. Female litigants are usually mentioned in cases of murder or inheritance, but also loans and adultery. Interestingly, even in the small sample (114 collected from mostly literary sources) of identifiable litigants in the early imperial period, the status of these people ranges from royalty and imperial family to senator, equestrian, citizen, non-citizen, free, and freed.[11] Wealthy litigants appear more frequently, which is likely because they had more time resources for seeking legal redress and more property and interests over which to argue in the first place.

Although we know even less about litigants who arrived from outside of Rome—a pity, as the surviving evidence indicates that vast numbers came and went each year—we can surmise that these individuals were likely to have had some wealth, given the cost of traveling to and staying in Rome. We do, though, know of at least one case in which a woman came to Rome to prove her status as the daughter of a former slave. Others from another range of the social spectrum included royalty, such as Archelaus, the king of Cappadocia, and Berenice, sister to Agrippa II, the king of Judaea. Entire communities also brought litigation to Rome, either before the senate or in the emperor's court, although we can deduce frustratingly little about the nature of these cases.[12]

Money, not surprisingly, seems to have been both the most common cause of disputes and a highly significant factor—tied in with status—affecting the experience of litigants in the courtroom. Having wealth and influence in Roman society provided a measure of protection against litigation, either by discouraging the other party from proceeding with the case or by enabling the wealthier litigant to marshal superior forces—advocates, client supporters, a claque, and so forth. Seneca describes the case of a poor man who believed his father to have been murdered by a rich enemy. Rather than sue, the son dressed in mourning and followed the wealthy man around the city; when the latter lost an election, he sued the former for *iniuria* (unlawful harm to his reputation). The rich man asked the son, "*Cur me non accusas, non postulas?*" (Why don't you accuse me, lay charges against me?). The response is telling: "*Pauper divitem, lugens candidatum ego accusem?*" (Am I, a poor

---

11. For the complete lists see Bablitz 2007: 221–23.

12. Petronia: Pugliese Carratelli 1948: nos. 13–15; Archelaus: Suet. *Tib.* 8. 1; Dio 57. 17. 3; Berenice: Quint. *Inst.* 4. 1. 19.

man, to accuse a rich man, am I, mourning, to accuse a candidate for office?) (Sen. *Controv.* 10. 1. 2).

On the other hand, those with public reputations were indeed vulnerable to litigious attack by persons who stood to gain from the former's general demise. We must remember that Roman courtrooms did not have our modern limitations on what 'evidence' could be introduced, and the darkest aspects of people's lives could be dragged into the glare and scrutiny of the public court. Those with wealth and influence doubtless had more leverage, but were by no means entirely immune to being targeted via litigation.

For most individuals, regardless of their status, litigation was in many cases a risky and tiring undertaking. In addition to withstanding a public besmirching of their reputation, litigants might be expected to participate actively in the courtroom, through displaying appropriate facial expressions and posturing, answering questions from the judge, or even physically embracing the judge's knees in supplication. And all this could be witnessed by family, friends, clients, enemies, creditors, even the emperor, as well as the general public. Yet many still elected to initiate litigation in Rome's imperial courtrooms.

THE JUDGES

Litigation, of course, necessitates judges, so who exactly were the men judging all of these cases? The evidence is not always as rich as we would like it to be, but we do know that being a judge in Rome was a job taken on by a greater proportion of the population than it is today in Western judicial systems.

Judges served either in panels or individually, sometimes as a function of the individual's particular public office, and in other situations as selected from a list of prospective qualified judges. What type of judge—single or panel—would be used was sometimes determined by the case type, and sometimes determined by litigants when they selected the court in which to present their dispute. One's status could also have an effect on the type of judge one faced.

In the case of panels, we have the most evidence on the Roman standing public courts, or *quaestiones perpetuae*, each of which handled a specific category of crime. Judges for these courts were chosen from the *album iudicum*, a list of men who met particular qualifications, including financial and moral. One had to be between twenty-five and sixty years of age, possess substantial wealth (a minimum of 200,000 sesterces—roughly 200 times the annual wage of a legionary soldier), not have been found guilty of a crime or ejected from the senate, and pass a character examination. However, no legal training was required. From Caligula's reign onward, one did not even have to be from Italy, and we have evidence that men even in the lowest financial category of the *album* traveled from distant provinces to judge in the capital. Seneca and Pliny both comment on judges coming from distant places to hear relatively minor cases.[13] The surviving sources indicate men with origins in Spain, Mauretania, Numidia, Gaul, Pannonia, Bithynia, and other regions in the western provinces, while the less Romanized eastern provinces are not mentioned.[14] It is interesting to ponder the potential social and cultural dynamics, and challenges, that might have ensued when judges from distant lands sat in judgment over inhabitants of Rome.

Such panels of judges, though, were less in use than single individuals, the most common of which was the *unus iudex* (the solitary judge). Men in this role likely heard the majority of legal cases in Rome. Provided with a formula that described the main theoretical point of contention in a particular case, the *unus iudex* heard the evidence and decided which litigant best fit the terms of the formula, applying his understanding and reasoning rather than specialized knowledge. Punishment was predetermined according to each formula, giving the judge limited powers of discretion. Notwithstanding this level of structure, the judge could be scrutinized for his adherence to procedure and assessed penalties if he were found to have erred.[15]

Selection of the *unus iudex* for a particular case fell to the litigants, who were to work out between them a mutually agreed upon judge. Apart from the judge being male, at least twenty years old, and not a slave, there appear to have been no other restrictions in terms of residency, wealth, or other criteria. Although it is likely that those men listed on the *album iudicum* were also asked to work as single judges, the role of *unus iudex* probably drew a relatively broad cross-section of individuals into the process of administering justice within Rome.

Perhaps not surprisingly, deficiencies in the judges' education caused some Romans frustration, as witnessed in passages from Quintilian and Juvenal; the former complains of the shortcomings of inexperienced judges from the "countryside" while the latter refers to "cattledriver judges."[16] Quintilian is mordant in criticizing the intellectual and educational shortcomings of some judges:

> We, on the other hand, have to compose speeches for others to judge, and often speak before people who are quite ignorant and certainly untrained in the arts of rhetoric; and unless we can entice them with delights, drag them along by the

---

13. Plin. *Nat.* 29 .8. 18; Sen. *Ira* 3. 33. 1.

14. For Africa see Pflaum 1969; for Gaul see Burnand 1974; Spain: e.g., *CIL* II 2079 = *ILS* 2713, *CIL* II 4211 = *RIT* 271 = *ILS* 6936; Sardinia: *CIL* X 7518 = *ILS* 6764; Sicily: *Zeitschrift für Papyrologie und Epigraphik* 151 (2005) 193–21, *CIL* X 7507 = *ILS* 6772; Pannonia: e.g., *CIL* III 726 = *ILS* 1419, *CIL* III 6476 = *AE* 1987, 820; Asia: *AE* 1924, 82, *AE* 1972, 573 = *AE* 1969/70, 595b; Bithynia and Pontus: *IGRR* III 63 = *OGIS* 528; Lycia and Pamphylia: *IGRR* III 778 = *OGIS* 567.

15. This is a problematic topic. See Kelly 1966: 102–17 and Robinson 1999.

16. Quint. *Inst.* 4. 2. 45; Juv. 7. 116–17.

strength of our pleading, and sometimes disturb them by emotional appeals, we cannot make even a just and true case prevail...(Quint. *Inst.* 5. 14. 29)[17]

For some judges coming from outside the capital, Latin might even have been a second language; add this to the more general unfamiliarity of those from the Italian countryside or the provinces with the ways of Rome, and the courtrooms might at times have been rather 'multicultural.' As it was not unusual for a judge to seek in his deliberations the aid of an *assessor* (advisor)—a man of political and/ or legal experience—gaps in a judge's Latin, knowledge, or background would not necessarily have hindered his ability to preside over a case. Claudius, though, is known to have acted quite severely against a judge who did not have a decent grasp of Latin: "He not only struck from the list of potential judges a man distinguished by his birth, a leading citizen of the Greek province, though verily ignorant of the Latin language, but even revoked the man's Roman citizenship" (Suet. *Claud.* 16. 2).[18] Perhaps the reality lay somewhere in between the ideal and the critics' invective.

Inevitably, the question of judges' integrity also arises. While impartiality was viewed as a laudable trait, the favoritism that ran throughout Roman society was nonetheless a factor in the courtroom as well. A judge was not required to recuse himself if a conflict of interest existed, although he had the option to do so. Praetors could reject cases without offering any explanation. The possibility was always there for a judge to be swayed by ties of friendship, by a litigant's higher status, or by bribes. Still, surviving evidence does not leave us with the impression that Rome's judiciary was rife with corruption.

Considering these various factors and pressures, did men welcome or shun the duty to serve as judges? Individuals such as senators and old-money equestrians with active political careers likely viewed judging as a duty to be borne—and perhaps avoided whenever possible. On the other hand, equestrians without such careers, or those who were advancing in years and sought to maintain both involvement and reputation in Rome, likely saw judicial service as a valuable opportunity. Likewise, those from outside the capital, and seeking to establish themselves there, appear to have coveted inclusion in the *album iudicum*; for some, this marked the pinnacle of their achievements. Those men asked to serve as single judges were presumably honored by the request, as well as aware of their visibility during these highly public cases; being perceived as a fair judge, and one not devoid of *clementia* (mildness), could significantly enhance one's general reputation. Nonetheless, serving as a judge in Rome likely was a time-consuming and sometimes draining activity for many. A far greater portion of the population than today would have been directly involved in meting out justice to their fellow men, further underscoring the prevalence of court proceedings in imperial Rome.

---

17. *Nobis ad aliorum iudicia componenda est oratio, et saepius apud omnino imperitos atque illarum certe ignaros litterarum loquendum est, quos nisi et delectatione adlicimus et viribus trahimus.* I follow the translation of Russell (2001) for the second half of this passage.

18. *Splendidum virum Graeciaeque provinciae principem, verum Latini sermonis ignarum, non modo albo iudicum erasit, sed in peregrinitatem redegit.*

THE AUDIENCE

Before turning to consider the advocates, who would have been in the most direct and sustained dialogue with Rome's judges, it is worth reconstructing the audience in public courtrooms. These individuals were both potential participants in the event and recipients of the court's various 'messages'—on justice, class, status, the cost of transgressions, the value of clemency, the art of rhetoric, and a multitude of other explicit and implicit points.

Within the audience, we find a wide range of individuals. The advocate would typically be accompanied by various assistants—junior counsel, clerks, and other attendants. These could include young Roman aristocrats, who could be expected to be present as part of their overall education, to observe the skills of great orators and learn the ways of court procedures.[19]

Litigants would also have their own support teams, consisting of family, friends, and for higher-placed individuals, clients. It appears from surviving sources that only defendants, not plaintiffs, brought in family members as reinforcements, likely because persons were viewed as instrumental in attempting to rouse pity in a judge. However, both sides would frequently have other supporters, who likely occupied the benches immediately behind those of the litigant, his advocate, and the rest of their litigation team. Indeed, given the public nature of most proceedings and the importance of status in Roman society, being able to muster a large and impressive group of supporters could make a positive impression on those judging, as well as the rest of the audience.

Apart from these individuals linked to the advocates, litigants, or both, who else comprised the audience? Evidence is not plentiful, but we can identify some and speculate on others. As already noted, most courts were held in public areas that would have experienced high volumes of foot traffic; so, anyone in Rome who happened to be going by could have paused to observe the latest happenings before continuing on. There would also have been those who elected to stay and watch, rather than simply passing by in the course of other business. Such individuals would have been either unemployed or able to take a break from their labors and perhaps be entertained by the goings-on in one of the city's numerous venues. Seats were sometimes available, offering rest and some shelter from the weather, be it rain or the intense summer sun. If one were lucky, the case might offer excitement, too. Creditors, according to Juvenal, could find the courts useful for tracking down delinquent debtors. Individuals of wealth and leisure also attended, presumably out of general interest and—in the case of those such as Quintilian and Pliny the Younger—to observe prominent orators and the evolving dynamics of the courts.[20]

---

19. Quint. *Inst.* 6. 4. 9, 8. 5. 21, 10. 5. 19, 11. 3. 131, 12. 3. 2–4; Tac. *Dial.* 2. 1; Plin. *Ep.* 2. 14. 9–11, 4. 16. 2, 6. 6. 3; Fronto *Ad Am.* 1. 27. 1.

20. Quint. *Inst.* 12. 5. 6; Juv. 7. 106–10; Plin. *Ep.* 1. 16. 1.

Paid audience members constituted a different category of attendees. Some of these were clients, who were expected as part of the services for their *sportula* (stipends) to provide enthusiastic audible support for their patrons. Others were unconnected with the case participants, hired *ad hoc* as necessary. Such claques appear to have been common and were probably paid for by the advocates. That this occurred suggests an interesting shift in courtroom emphasis—namely, from the merits of the case to the merits of the advocate. Martial provides us with a vivid illustration of how such paid enthusiasm could have operated: "Take Selius, who holds out a net for dinner, to praise [you], if you are reading aloud or pleading a case: 'Good going! Weighty hit! And swift! And nasty! Well done! Beautiful! That is what I wanted!' 'You have now got your dinner, be quiet'" (Mart. 2. 27).[21] Evidence also suggests that these claques moved from court to court; if this was indeed so, then the relative transparency of this commissioned praise must have added to the theatrical—as distinct from judicial—qualities of Rome's courtrooms. In addition, this financial aspect to being an audience member must have contributed to socio-economic diversity in the onlookers, and various sources confirm that the 'rank-and-file' of Rome, as well as the privileged and elite, both witnessed and participated in courtroom business.

Many claque members do seem to have been directly tied to case participants, in an extension of the Roman institution of patronage. Clients in the imperial period continued to accompany their patrons to court as part of their obligations, providing strength in numbers and in some cases emotional impact—for instance, by dressing in mourning garb and effecting grief-stricken demeanors and facial expressions. Hence, there seems to have been a blending in the courtroom of the traditional social hierarchy and its central vehicle (patronage), along with a capitalism in which praise could conceivably go to the highest bidder.[22]

Consideration of these claques also highlights how, in a manner very different from modern courtrooms, audience members could engage themselves in a case. Rhetoric teachers took it for granted that their pupils needed to learn to speak amid a significant, ongoing din—the very public nature of most courtrooms would have meant a more or less constant hum of activity and voices. But audience members also were free to vocalize their opinions, and did so frequently—even in the presence of the emperor. Suetonius records an instance in Claudius' court when an audience member shouted that a man just convicted of forgery should have his hands cut off; the emperor concurred and ordered this to be carried out.[23] Insults and obscene language were not uncommon, nor was raucous laughter. Approval in

---

21. *Laudantem Selium cenae cum retra tendit / accipe, sive legas sive patronus agas: / 'Effecte! graviter! cito! nequiter! euge! beate! / hoc volui!' 'Facta est iam tibi cena, tace.'*

22. The best description of the courtroom claque is found in Plin. *Ep.* 2. 14. 4–8. See also Quint. *Inst.* 11. 3. 131; Mart. 2. 27, 2. 74. For discussion of non-courtroom claques and their workings, see Aldrete 1999 especially chapters 4 and 5, and Cameron 1976: 235–49.

23. Suet. *Claud.* 15. 2.

the form of clapping, however, does not appear to have been used, perhaps exactly because more specific and expressive vocal input was not discouraged.

Advocates were also known to use audience members as 'props.' Apart from coaching the family or clients of the defendant to appear woebegone, disheveled, and generally victimized, advocates could involve other onlookers in the courtroom drama. One advocate is reported to have feigned terror and hidden among audience members when his opponent produced the sword with which the defendant had allegedly committed murder: "*subito ex subselliis ut territus fugit et, capite ex parte velato cum ad agendum ex turba prospexisset, interrogavit, an iam ille cum gladio recessisset*" (suddenly [he] fled from the benches as if in terror, and then, when he was to speak, peeked out from among the crowd, with his head partly covered, and inquired whether that man with the sword had now left) (Quint. *Inst.* 6. 1. 48).

Sometimes, however, audience members enlisted in advance by the advocate did not function quite as planned. Quintilian relates one such incident in which poor preparation backfired rather spectacularly:

> Another advocate, defending a woman, thought it a good idea to display a portrait of her husband; this repeatedly raised a laugh, because the persons entrusted with handing him the portrait, not knowing when the epilogue was coming, let it be seen whenever he turned their way, and when it was finally put on display it proved so hideous (it was the old man's wax death mask) that it ruined also the effect of the effect of the preceding speech. (Quint. *Inst.* 6. 1. 40)[24]

Clearly, it paid to spend proper time preparing one's 'planted' participants. The audience was a potentially effective weapon that could, however, through miscalculation or oversight, swiftly be turned against the ill-prepared advocate.

Extant sources leave no doubt, then, that the Roman audience was a lively element in the courtroom, and thus had a role in the judicial system. When even the emperor himself was not deaf to input from the general public, lesser judges would have needed to be particularly focused and resolute if they wished to draw conclusions based on reason alone, rather than on the antics of vocal, biased spectators.

THE ADVOCATE

At the centers of these semi-orchestrated maelstroms were the advocates, a group which appears to have been diversifying during the early imperial period. In the republican period, advocates were typically upper-class patrons of the parties in

---

24. *Alius imaginem mariti pro rea proferre magni putavit, at ea risum saepius fecit. Nam et ii quorum officii erat ut traderent eam, ignari qui esset epilogus, quotiens respexisset patronus offerebant palam, et prolata novissime deformitate ipsa (nam senis cadaveri cera erat infusa) praeteritam quoque orationis gratiam perdidit.* Translation of Russell 2001.

litigation; however, the literary evidence suggests that men of other wealth, education, status, and geographical origin were beginning to enter the arena, shifting the class composition of advocates and gradually reshaping the role into that of a 'professional.' Increasingly, men from outside the upper echelons and immigrants from the provinces were transforming what it meant to be an advocate in Rome.

One significant change involved remuneration. Traditionally, a patron would provide legal services to his clients for no monetary fee, as part of the patronage system; indeed, receiving pay for such services was long informally prohibited. Instead, for his legal aid the patron received what we would now term 'symbolic capital'— the continued gratitude and aid of his client (in both senses of the term), which in turn enhanced the patron's overall reputation and *auctoritas* (socio-political clout). However, as early as the second century BC, legislation was being enacted to enforce this custom, which suggests that at least some individuals were exchanging money for such services and no patron/client relationship existed. By Cicero's time the paying of advocates was effectively an open secret. Claudius finally established a fee limit, effectively acknowledging the shift of a cultural practice into a profession and regulating it.[25]

With advocacy now offering the incentive of an income, many men of lower social standing were drawn to the activity. In addition, it could be a channel for social advancement, as advocacy was still perceived as a highly respectable activity. Successful advocates from outside Rome could even gain a footing in Roman society. Not surprisingly, there was a degree of backlash from the upper class, many of whom claimed the vocation was being dragged down by inferior upstarts. These developments coincide with declarations by various authors of the time that a 'decline in oratory' was taking place. The reality may have been that the old nobility saw its hegemony in the courtroom being encroached upon by those beneath them in the social hierarchy, and since they could do little to stem the tide, authors such as Juvenal, Pliny, and Tacitus resorted to vitriol and disparagement instead. Certainly, the changes taking place in advocacy were indicative of other changes taking place within Rome's social hierarchy during the first century AD.[26]

Rather predictably, though, these non-aristocratic advocates have left few traces in the extant records, and it is therefore difficult to say much about the types of cases they undertook. We may be correct to infer that the Roman class system would have been conservative, and that advocates of lower social standing therefore represented similar individuals in the hierarchy and worked on relatively minor cases in lower courts, as compared with the nobility. On the other hand, with advocacy becoming a way for those of even humble origins to climb the ladder of wealth and power, we cannot assume that class divisions were remaining rock-solid in other respects.

25. Cic. *De off.* 69, *Pro Mur.* 8; Tac. *Ann.* 11. 5–7; Plin. *Ep.* 5. 9. 4; Dio 54. 18. 2; Berger 1953: 549; Pani 1986: 318–24; Rich 1990: 195; David 1992: viii–ix, 121–37; Crook 1995: 148–49.

26. For discussion of these various issues, see: Neuhauser 1958: *passim*; Kennedy 1972: 446–64; Kennedy 1994: 186–92; Levick 1983: 114; Braund 1992: 81; Crook 1995: 146–58, 176–80; Gleason 1995: *passim*; Clarke 1996: 100–108.

In general, it is safe to say that an advocate would have weighed several factors when taking on cases. Status—his own and his potential client's, if there was not a patron/client relationship between them—was one; ties of friendship (cf. Verboven in this volume) were also significant considerations, as was the potential for gratitude and other symbolic capital; the character of the litigant was not to be disregarded, if one wished to preserve a reputation for integrity and sound judgment; and if one were doing this for a living, the likelihood of being paid—and how much—had to be factored in. Family go virtually unmentioned in the literary sources, presumably because it was taken for granted that an advocate would represent his relatives.

An advocate would in some instances have elected to refuse a case if the opposing litigant—or those connected with him/her—was influential and could do him harm, particularly if the advocate was not linked to the potential client by a patron/client relationship, which made it much easier to refuse a potentially dangerous undertaking. Taking on one's superiors was a very risky business in Roman society, and to be avoided unless success was virtually guaranteed.

Once a case was undertaken, the advocate became the center of energy. How much time and effort he would have to invest of course varied widely, depending on the nature of the case, the parties involved, and the skill of the advocate. A well-reputed advocate with an established 'practice' could anticipate long work-days involving a wide variety of activities and numerous social interactions.

Naturally, the courtroom was his main stage, where the outcome of hours or days of preparation could hang upon his performance before the judge(s) and audience. In relatively minor matters, he could afford to rely primarily on the solidity of the case he had built. But in issues of greater consequence, the successful advocate was a master of managing his interactions with all those present. So much more hinged on his success than simply the interests of his client; his own esteem, influence, and power could be enhanced or damaged in these courtrooms. If a prosecution went awry, the advocate could find himself charged with *calumnia* (wrongful prosecution), with dire professional and social consequences if found guilty. On the other hand, victories could lead to celebrity even beyond the walls of Rome. As Aper describes in Tacitus' *Dialogus*: "The reputation and fame of what other profession can compare to the glory of oratory?...Visitors...and non-residents even, when they first step into the city ask about, and, as it were, are very eager to become acquainted with those whom they have heard about in their cities and colonies" (Tac. *Dial.* 7. 2, 7. 4).[27] Interestingly, as we move from the late republican to the early imperial period, we find that audience approbation held an increasingly important place in advocates' success, with the result that many orators now 'played to the audience' more than to the judges. The net effect was that these audiences were also becoming more and more pivotal in the creation and demise of men's reputations— an unmistakable shift from the Rome of Cicero and his successors. Thus, Quintilian

27. *Fama et laus cuius artis cum oratorum gloria comparanda est?...advenae...et peregrini iam in municipiis et coloniis suis auditos, cum primum urbem attigerunt, requirunt ac velut agnoscere concupiscunt.*

complains, "*Pendemus ex laude atque hanc laboris nostri ducimus summam. Ita, quae circumstantibus ostentare volumus, iudicibus prodimus*," (We attach great value to praise and we consider this to be the highest goal of our labor. So, what we wish to display to the audience, we betray to the judges) (Quint. *Inst.* 4. 2. 127).

Criticisms notwithstanding, the challenge of the advocate's job should not be underestimated. Of all those present in the courtroom, he had to keep everyone else in mind. Who was the opposing counsel, and how formidable an opposition did he constitute? We have seen that successful advocates could garner significant reputations, while there was also a long-term trend toward greater penetration of the profession by relative social 'outsiders'; the identity of one's opposition thus had always to be taken into some consideration. Who was judging? Would he—or the panel—be from Rome, familiar with the city's ways but also part of its intricate social network, leading to potential bias or other repercussions? Or would the judge be from outside the capital, perhaps even from the provinces, a comparative rustic whose Latin was not necessarily polished? Then there were the members of the advocate's own ensemble and wider circle, including junior as well as senior colleagues who would be taking note of his words, gestures, facial expressions, and tactics. Would his performance meet their expectations or fall short? Would he be the talk of the town for his eloquence or for an embarrassing gaff?

Quintilian describes an instance of advocate maneuvering that illustrates the importance of strategy:

> Once, an advocate led across to the opposing benches a girl, who was alleged (for the dispute was over this point) to be the sister of the opposing litigant, as if to leave her in the arms of her brother, but the brother, previously instructed by me, had moved from his seat. The advocate, normally at no loss for words, was struck dumb by this unexpected turn of events and took his little girl back again, the effect having been lost. (Quint. *Inst.* 6. 1. 39)[28]

A large proportion of the people present likely would have had no direct connection with the case. Yet while these individuals could not be relied on to have much, or perhaps any, specialist knowledge, they expected entertainment, and their displeasure was not to be incurred lightly. What happened in Rome's courtrooms clearly circulated via the grapevine.

And of course, the litigant could not be forgotten! The skilled advocate needed to prepare the client for his or her role in the case, providing coaching as to dress, demeanor, and responses to potential questions from a judge, or maneuvers by opposing counsel. Ultimately, the course of the litigant's future hinged on the advocate's performance, and even the most seasoned advocate must have felt the weight of this responsibility as he juggled multiple variables and challenges within the courtroom.

---

28. *Transtulit aliquando patronus puellam, quae soror esse adversarii dicebatur (nam de hoc lis erat), in adversa subsellia, tamquam in gremio fratris relicturus; at is a nobis praemonitus discesserat. Tum ille, alioqui vir facundus, inopinatae rei casu obmutuit et infantem suam frigidissime reportavit.*

Conclusion

The courts of imperial Rome held a measure of physical, social, political, and cultural centrality that might well be measured against the roles played by the emperor, or by the games. The ubiquity and predominantly public nature of the city's courtrooms made them impossible to disregard, and augmented the benefits and damages stemming from the streams of litigation that increasingly flowed through these civic spaces. While the success or failure of a legal case was the basic issue for both the participating litigants and advocates as well as the judge(s) hearing the case, the publicity of these activities (for which the audience's attendance was necessary) made it possible for far more to be at stake than just the winning or losing of a case. The publicity, in fact, was critical—without an audience, the impact was not nearly as deep. The extent to which participation in the courts could affect one's status within Roman society was determined almost completely by the activity being entirely public. If a merchant who sued a customer of higher social standing than himself for non-payment of a bill won his case, he could hold his head up just a little higher among his fellow merchants, and to that same degree the defeated customer lost some of his own status, having lost the case.

Likewise the advocate's ability to achieve success in the courtroom affected far more than just his case statistics. Victory could mean that more people would know who he was and this knowledge could translate, for example, into cases for individuals of still higher social status or more votes for him when he ran for public office in the next elections. A less successful advocate might be able to weather one or two defeats without any harm to his standing, but if the number got too high, he might find himself becoming ever more desperate for cases just to maintain his livelihood.

Judges, too, had much to gain from participating. Being chosen for the task by either the litigants or a superior official was an honor in itself. Overseeing the hearing in a prominent public location provided still further advertisement of this appointment since all who passed by the court, from slaves running errands to senators on their way to a senate meeting, could see the judge(s) and realize their role. However, there could be negative effects as well. If a judge was seen as having given an unfair verdict, his reputation could suffer. It would not be surprising if at least some litigants betrayed their frustration at losing their cases by publicly questioning the judge's general intelligence and fairness, and in some circumstances there may have been some truth in the attack.

The balance of power, authority, and reputation was always swinging back and forth in the courtroom—for every victor there was a loser; for every increase in authority for one there was a decrease for another. And it was for this that some of the audience came, to watch this constant oscillation back and forth from case to case. For those audience members of the servile or lower classes watching two aristocratic litigants attack each other, there surely was comfort either in seeing the foot of the victorious in the face of the defeated or realizing just how easily someone could be toppled and made the fool. Little was entirely permanent, and even the rich and powerful could discover that there was someone richer and more powerful. This was perhaps slightly cold comfort for the lower echelons, but comfort nonetheless. Audience members were not always merely disinterested onlookers seeking entertainment; they could have a variety of ties to the performers at hand, from anxious clients hoping to bolster their patron's cause, to distraught family members seeking clemency or restitution, to observers of rhetoric, intent on studying the techniques of the advocates. Ultimately, the Roman courtroom was highly diverse in its size, procedures, participants, and dramas, but consistently powerful in its impact on Roman social relations.

SUGGESTED READING

For the physical aspects of Rome's courts, as well as discussion regarding the use and manipulation of public space, see Anderson 1984, Vasaly 1993, Millar 1998, and Bablitz forthcoming. Very interesting discussion of gesture and movement is found in Aldrete 1999 and Corbeill 2004. On rhetoric, see Kennedy 1994 and Clarke 1996, and on its connection to masculinity, see Gunderson 2000 and 2003. The scholarship on Roman law is immense. Some works that succeed at linking the law with daily life and, therefore, are my favorites, are Greenidge 1901, Kelly 1966 and 1976, Crook 1967 and 1995, and Metzger 2005.

BIBLIOGRAPHY

Aldrete, G. S. 1999. *Gesture and Acclamations in Ancient Rome*. Baltimore: Johns Hopkins University Press.
Anderson, J. C. 1984. *The Historical Topography of the Imperial Fora*. Brussels: Latomus.
Bablitz, L. 2007. *Actors and Audience in the Roman Courtroom*. London: Routledge.
———. Forthcoming. "Some Letters, a Relief, and the Centumviral Court." In W. V. Harris and F. De Angelis (eds.), *Spaces of Justice in the Roman World*. Leiden: E. J. Brill.
Berger, A. 1953. *Encyclopedic Dictionary of Roman Law*. Philadelphia: American Philosophical Association.
Braund, S. H. 1992. "Juvenal—Misogynist or Misogamist?" *Journal of Roman Studies* 82: 71–86.
Brennan, T. C. 2000. *The Praetorship in the Roman Republic*. Oxford: Oxford University Press.
Burnand, Y. 1974. "Les juges des cinq décuries originaires de Gaule Romaine." In *Mélanges d'Histoire Ancienne: offerts à William Seston*. Paris: E. de Boccard. 59–72.
Cameron, A. 1976. *Circus Factions: Blues and Greens at Rome and Byzantium*. Oxford: Clarendon Press.
Camodeca, G. 1996. "La ricostruzione dell'élite municipale ercolanese degli anni 50–70: Problemi di metodo e risultati preliminari." *Cahiers Glotz* 7: 167–78.

Carnabuci, E. 1996. *I Luoghi dell'Amministrazione della Giustizia nel Foro di Augusto*. Naples: Jovene.

Castagnoli, F. 1950. "Roma nei versi di Marziale." *Athenaeum* 28: 67–78.

Clarke, M. L. 1996. *Rhetoric at Rome: A Historical Survey*. 3rd ed. London: Routledge.

Coarelli, F. 1985. *Il foro Romano: Periodo republicano e Augusteo*. Rome: Quasar.

Corbeill, A. 2004. *Nature Embodied: Gesture in Ancient Rome*. Princeton: Princeton University Press.

Crook, J. A. 1967. *Law and Life of Rome, 90 BC AD 212*. Ithaca: Cornell University Press.

———. 1995. *Legal Advocacy in the Roman World*. Ithaca: Cornell University Press.

David, J.-M. 1992. *Le Patronat judiciaire au dernier siècle de la République Romaine*. Rome: École française de Rome.

———. 1995. "Le tribunal du préteur: contraintes symboliques et politiques sous la République et le début de l'empire." *Klio* 77: 371–85.

Frier, B. 1985. *The Rise of the Roman Jurists*. Princeton: Princeton University Press.

Giuliani, C. F., and P. Verduchi. 1987. *L'Area central del Foro Romano*. Florence: L. S. Olschki.

Gleason, M. W. 1995. *Making Men: Sophists and Self-Representation in Ancient Rome*. Princeton: Princeton University Press.

Greenidge, A. H. J. 1901. *The Legal Procedure of Cicero's Time*. Oxford: Oxford University Press.

Gruen, E. S. 1968. *Roman Politics and the Criminal Courts, 149–78 BC*. Cambridge: Cambridge University Press.

Gunderson, E. 2000. *Staging Masculinity: The Rhetoric of Performance in the Roman World*. Ann Arbor: University of Michigan Press.

———. 2003. *Declamation, Paternity, and Roman Identity: Authority and the Rhetorical Self*. Cambridge: Cambridge University Press.

Jones, A. H. M. 1972. *The Criminal Courts of the Roman Republic and Principate*. Oxford: Oxford University Press.

Kelly, J. M. 1966. *Roman Litigation*. Oxford: Clarendon Press.

———. 1976. *Studies in the Civil Judicature of the Roman Republic*. Oxford: Clarendon Press.

Kennedy, G. 1972. *The Art of Rhetoric in the Roman World*. Princeton: Princeton University Press.

———. 1994. *A New History of Classical Rhetoric*. Princeton: Princeton University Press.

Levick, B. 1983. "The Senatus Consultum from Larinum." *Journal of Roman Studies* 73: 97–115.

Metzger, E. 2005. *Litigation in Roman Law*. Oxford: Oxford University Press.

Millar, F. 1998. *The Crowd in Rome in the Late Republic*. Ann Arbor: University of Michigan Press.

Musurillo, H. 1972. *The Acts of the Christian Martyrs*. Oxford: Clarendon Press.

Neuhauser, W. 1958. *Patronus und Orator: eine Geschichte der Begriffe von ihren Anfängen bis in die augusteische Zeit*. Innsbruck: Universitätsverlag Wagner.

Packer, J. E. 1997. *The Forum of Trajan in Rome: A Study of the Monuments*. Berkeley: University of California Press.

Pani, M. 1986. "La remunerazione dell'oratoria giudiziaria nell'alto principato: una laboriosa accettazione sociale." *Miscellanea Greca et Romana* 10: 315–46.

Pflaum, H.-G. 1969. "Les juges des cinq décuries originaires d'Afrique Romaine." *Antiquités Africaines* 2: 153–95.

Pugliese Carratelli, G. 1948. "Tabulae Herculanenses II." *Parola del Passato* 3: 165–84.

Rich, J. W. 1990. *Cassius Dio: The Augustan Settlement (Roman History 53–55.9)*. Warminster: Aris and Phillips.

Richardson, L., Jr. 1973. "The Tribunals of the Praetors of Rome." *Mitteilungen des Deutschen Archäologischen Instituts (Römische Abteilung)* 80: 219–33.

Robinson, O. F. 1995. *The Criminal Law of Ancient Rome*. Baltimore: Johns Hopkins University Press.

———. 1999. "The 'Iudex qui litem suam fecerit' explained." *Zeitschrift der Savigny-Stiftung für Rechtsgeschichte (Romanistische Abteilung)* 116: 195–99.

Russell, D. A. 2001. *Quintilian: The Orator's Education*. 5 vols. Cambridge, Mass.: Harvard University Press.

Vasaly, A. 1993. *Representations: Images of the World in Ciceronian Oratory*. Berkeley: University of California Press.

CHAPTER 16

PUBLIC ENTERTAINMENTS

KATHLEEN M. COLEMAN

INTRODUCTION

IN AD 12, Augustus was due to celebrate the Ludi Martiales, a celebration closely related to his own position as the adopted son of Julius Caesar, whose death he had avenged under the aegis of Mars Ultor ("the Avenger"). He was therefore anxious that the games in honor of this deity should go smoothly. But he was faced with a quandary: what was to be done with his wife's twenty-year-old grandson, the future emperor Claudius, whose father was Livia's son by her first marriage? Suetonius quotes a letter to her from Augustus, written in a colloquial mixture of Latin and Greek (*Cl.* 4. 2–3, trans. Edwards): "If…we suspect that he is lacking and impaired in the wholeness both of his mind and of his body, we should not provide those people who are apt to mock and laugh at such things with opportunities to ridicule both him and ourselves…I do not wish him to watch the circus games from the imperial box, for he would be conspicuous, exposed at the front of the spectators."

This is a rare opportunity for us to overhear an emperor thinking aloud. Augustus' concerns revolve around the key issues determining social relations in places of public entertainment in the Roman world: visibility, hierarchy, and freedom of expression. Like Suetonius' eavesdropping quotation, much of the evidence is anecdotal, and a full compendium would far exceed the scope of a summarizing article. But some broad trends can be illustrated with selective examples. The metropolitan bias of our evidence tends to privilege interaction concerning the

Roman emperor; in what follows I shall try to put this focus within the broader context of civic life empire-wide.

Apart from obvious factors affecting visibility and audibility—the varying size of the venues, differences in seating regulations, and the presence or absence of a verbal component in the performance—the types of social interaction that are documented for the spectacles of the circus, theater, and amphitheater follow similar patterns. Rather than treating these venues separately, therefore, I shall treat them together, structuring my analysis in order to emphasize the mechanisms of social interaction. The phrase 'entertainment facilities,' where it occurs, is shorthand for 'circus, theater, and amphitheater.'

ENTERTAINMENT FACILITIES

The monumental remains of Roman entertainment buildings scattered around the Mediterranean world may blind us to the very humble and temporary nature of their earliest predecessors. In Rome, the first spectators at the site of the Circus Maximus sat on the slopes of the Palatine; the earliest theatrical audiences perched on the steps in front of the temple of the deity in whose honor a play was being performed; the onlookers at the funerals at which the earliest gladiatorial combats were staged watched from the upper stories of the basilicas in the Forum or sat on temporary bleachers (or simply stood within view but out of range). In the rest of Italy, however, and in the provinces—especially in the Eastern Empire, with its rich theatrical tradition inherited from Greek culture—some of the monumental spectacle buildings were older than those in the capital.

Like Rome's first permanent theater, dedicated by Pompey in 55 BC, her first amphitheater was also a late development, built by Statilius Taurus in 29 BC out of the *manubiae* (spoils of war) awarded to him for securing Africa for Octavian during the civil war (Tac. *Ann.* 3. 72. 1). As gladiatorial combat and staged hunts spread around the empire, local theaters and stadia, where they existed, were adapted to host violent spectacles safely and efficiently.[1] Everywhere these structures comprised some of the most striking buildings in their communities, and in their tiers the spectators were massed together in proper order, united in watching the spectacle in the presence of the gods and deceased benefactors—the invisible members of the Roman community.

---

1. For the origins of the circus, see Humphrey 1986: 60–67; for republican theaters in Italy, Sear 2006: 48–53; for republican amphitheaters, Welch 2007: 72–101. For a summary of the evolution of spectacle buildings in the city of Rome, see Coleman 2000. For adapted theaters in the Eastern Empire, see Welch 2007: 163–85.

ABSENT PRESENCE: GODS AND BENEFACTORS

Simply put, "going to the theater [or circus or amphitheater] was one of the great collective experiences in the Roman city" (Clarke 2003: 130). Entertainment buildings were designed so that all the spectators could see the show. This meant that they were also visible to one another. As Ovid neatly puts it (speaking, in fact, of women at the theater, although the point transcends gender): "They come to see and to themselves be seen" (*Ars* 1. 99). Where all the people sat and what they wore advertised their relative status. The assembled throng also included surrogates for the absent: not only deceased luminaries, but also the gods. Little is known about the religious aspect of the amphitheater, but entertainments in the theater and circus were staged in the context of religious festivals, and images of the gods were displayed, either throughout or at least on days involving sacrifices (Gebhard 1996: 118). The display of images of the gods in the circus probably began very early; the evidence of Sinnius Capito, writing in the first century BC, is quoted by the lexicographer Festus (p. 500 Lindsay): "They say that *tensa* is the name given to a vehicle in which the emblems of the gods are carried to the *pulvinar* (dais) in the circus during the *ludi circenses* (circus games)."

Most of our evidence for religious display in the theater comes from the empire, when the development of the imperial cult had blurred the line between human benefactors and the divine, so that, for instance, at Ephesus in AD 103/4 a foundation established by a prominent citizen, C. Vibius Salutaris, decreed arrangements to display images of the reigning emperor and his wife (Trajan and Plotina) alongside the gods, as well as personifications of the constituent elements of Roman and Ephesian society: the Roman Senate and people, and the *boule* (city council), *gerousia* (council of elders), *ephebeia* (youth brigade), *demos* (people), and six civic tribes of Ephesus.[2] Since the distinct elements of the Ephesian community were presumably represented there in person as well, their symbolic presence in the form of personified images underlines the importance of representing the entire hierarchy of Ephesian society: the gods, the ruling Roman power, and the local community. The images, usually set up on the stage or in the orchestra, were here placed in the auditorium, sharing the viewing space with the live audience (Gebhard 1996: 121–23).

The structures themselves memorialized the patrons who had provided them for the community. For those who could read, dedicatory inscriptions commemorated the founders. The *duoviri* (pair of chief magistrates) of the Roman colony at Pompeii built the amphitheater "for the colonists" (*CIL* X 852 = *ILLRP* 645 = *ILS* 5627). Toward the end of the first century AD at Casinum in central Italy (modern Cassino), the formidable Ummidia Quadratilla, the dissolute grandmother of the younger Pliny's friend (*Ep.* 7. 24), dedicated the amphitheater and a "temple," *templum*—perhaps a shrine inside the amphitheater (*CIL* X 5183 = *ILS* 5628 = *EAOR* IV 46 = Caldelli 2004: app. I, no. 2a). She also restored the theater, dating from

2. *IEph* I 27; improved text and accompanying translation in Rogers 1991: 152–85.

the Second Triumvirate, which had been embellished by her father (*AE* 1946, 174, brilliantly supplemented by Fora 1992); perhaps it was originally constructed by a member of the same family. The large theater at Pompeii still contains the base for a seated statue of M. Holconius Rufus, *duovir* (chief magistrate) five times in the Augustan period (*CIL* X 837), and an inscription marking the seat of honor granted to him in the *ima cavea* (the lowest band of seating) to commemorate his fifth term of office (*CIL* X 838); together with his son, M. Holconius Celer, he financed extensions to the theater, which dated from the second century BC (Sear 2006: 131). The patronal ties of single families over several generations formed one strand of the social relations that were played out within these structures.

Further inscriptions from the amphitheater at Pompeii during the reigns of Augustus and Nero commemorate eight more *duoviri* who contributed areas of permanent stone seating in the upper portions of the *cavea* (auditorium) to replace the previous accommodation, whether wooden bleachers or even just the earth embankment itself (Caldelli 2004: app. I, nos. 5–12). Usually the scale of generosity is modestly conveyed by the phrase "with his/her own money" (*sua pecunia*); sometimes an actual sum is mentioned, as at Luca (modern Lucca, in Tuscany), where Q. Vibius, who occupied the distinguished office of *duovir quinquennalis* (censor) sometime between AD 50 and 150, donated 100,000 sesterces for ten years to construct the amphitheater, and then left a further amount in his will to finish it, in order to save the public funds that had been set aside for this purpose (*CIL* XI 1527 = *EAOR* II 63 = Caldelli 2004: 138, app. II, no. 4). An aedile, Sex. Iulius Ianuarius, donated 500 *loca* (seats) to the circus at Lyons, probably in the second century AD (*CIL* XIII 1919 = *ILS* 5659). These were very likely stone seats intended for dignitaries, since much of the circus seems to have been built of wood; most benefactions in circuses endow installations more glamorous than wooden bleachers, such as the turning posts at each end of the track or the platform for the judges (Humphrey 1986: 398–99, 428). All such legible reminders of past generosity entrenched the culture of patronage and reciprocal generosity that permeated public entertainment in Roman society (Edmondson 2002: 56–57).

SYMBOLS OF THE SOCIAL ORDER: SEATING, CLOTHING, AND *MISSILIA*

Seating appears to have been indiscriminate in the circus, at least insofar as men and women sat together, although by AD 5 the senators and *equites* (knights) sat apart from everyone else, and from each other (Dio 55. 22. 4, 60. 7. 3).[3] Further

---

3. *Pace* Humphrey 1986: 70, sources attesting separate seating for senators by the early second century BC clearly refer to *ludi theatrales* (theatrical performances) rather than *ludi circenses* (circus games), even if they disagree about the precise occasion: see Briscoe on Livy 34. 44. 5.

reiterations of these privileges may simply introduce finer distinctions, or may be re-enactments necessitated by erosion of the privileges in the meantime (Humphrey 1986: 101–2). In the theater, however, Augustus' seating regulations, which justifiably dominate all discussions of theatrical seating at Rome, reflect his concern for stiffening Rome's moral fiber and establishing proper order in Roman society. But, long before the Augustan legislation was enacted, there is ample evidence, both epigraphic and architectural, for segregated seating at theatrical events in Italy and the western provinces.

At Capua in 94 BC, in recompense for repairing a public portico, by decree of the local *pagus* twelve named freedmen in official posts (*magistri*) were to receive seats in a designated section of the theater "as though they had sponsored games," *tamqua(m) sei {sei} ludos fecissent* (*CIL* X 3772 = *ILLRP* 719). This gesture privileging freedmen (*liberti*) foreshadows the privileges that Augustus granted to the Augustales, the priestly college attached to his cult that afforded an outlet for the civic ambitions of the freedman class (T. Jones 2009: 131). Or, to take another example, the architecture of the amphitheater at Pompeii clearly reveals variations in the accommodation: five rows of seats, more spacious than the rest and marked off from them by a retaining wall, were accessible from underneath; this meant that the spectators seated there, presumably the Roman colonists, did not have to rub shoulders with the rest on their way in and out (Bomgardner 2000: 43–47). These developments reflect the terms of paragraph 126 of the foundation charter for the Roman colony of Urso in Spain, dated to 44/43 BC, whereby, in addition to general seating regulations for spectacles of all types, seating in the theater was to be regulated by a decree of the decurions (town council) according to status: *coloni* (colonists), *incolae* (resident aliens), *hospites* (official guests), and *adventores* (casual visitors) (*CIL* II²/5. 1022 = *ILS* 6087 = Crawford 1996: no. 25; T. Jones 2009: 129–30).

Under the *lex Iulia theatralis*, promulgated by Augustus, the spectators in the theater, and probably also the amphitheater, were divided according to status (free vs. servile, soldiers vs. civilians), class (senators vs. equestrians vs. plebs), gender (men vs. women), marital status (married vs. unmarried), and age (men vs. boys); in addition, there were separate seats for the boys' *paedagogi* (Suet. *Aug.* 44).[4] The seats were allocated from front (most illustrious) to back (least illustrious). Senators sat farthest forward, in at least some instances not even in the *cavea* but on freestanding seats (*subsellia*) placed around the edge of the orchestra, which must have been much more comfortable and, therefore, were a mark of status. Behind them, in accordance with the *lex Roscia* of 67 BC, promulgated when theaters in Rome were still temporary structures, the first fourteen rows of the *cavea* ("the XIV") were reserved for the *equites*, and became a byword for jealously guarded privilege. *Equites* who, through no fault of their own, failed to meet the census requirement of

---

4. The *locus classicus* for discussion of theatrical seating is Rawson 1987. The sketch above is drastically simplified; details are very complex, and much remains unclear. For further discussion of female seating, and a useful list of post-Augustan seating inscriptions, see T. Jones 2009: 132–33, 135–36.

400,000 sesterces were relegated to a specially designated area, thereby saving face to the extent that they were not forced to sit with the *plebs* (Cic. *Phil.* 2. 44).[5] Augustus demonstrated empathy by allowing people who had been bankrupted in the civil wars to remain in the XIV, if they or their fathers had ever met the census requirement (Suet. *Aug.* 40. 1);[6] his gesture illustrates the growing tendency for the emperor to bypass legal provisions by disbursing privilege, thereby superimposing a vertical axis of power over the diagonal graph of republican society.

Within the distinct classes, special categories occupied their own seats. For example, a citizen who had been awarded the *corona civica* (a distinction for saving the life of a fellow citizen in battle) sat immediately behind the senators, and it was customary for the entire audience, senators included, to rise when he entered (Plin. *Nat.* 16. 11–13); *viatores tribunicii* ('tribunician' messengers), who belonged to the *apparitores*, a group of freeborn and *liberti* that ranked among the upper echelons of the free *plebs*, were seated immediately behind the *equites* (Tac. *Ann.* 16. 12); the *sodales Augustales*, a board of senators in charge of the cult of the deified Augustus, had their own reserved *subsellia* (*Tabula Hebana* = Ehrenberg and Jones 1976: no. 94a, lines 52–53); Vestal Virgins sat opposite the praetor's tribunal (Suet. *Aug.* 44. 3).

The transition from republic to empire opened seams in the tightly woven social structure. When a certain Sarmentus, a witty and handsome *libertus* (freedman), usurped the privileges of an *eques* and sat in the XIV, the audience shouted for his removal; he was charged in court with usurping rank, but when he revealed that he had been manumitted by Maecenas, one of Augustus' most trusted advisers, the charge was dropped (*scholion* to Juv. 5. 3, Treggiari 1969: 271–72). The emperors would not infrequently grant honors to individuals that gained them the right to occupy a seat above their actual station (Edmondson 1996: 105–6).

It is not clear how long Augustus' regulations remained in force, and how far they spread, or whether they applied to the amphitheater as well. But there is independent evidence for stratified seating in amphitheaters: inscriptions from the seats at Nemausus (Nîmes) stipulate separate seating for boatmen on the Rhône and its tributaries, a purely local requirement (*EAOR* V 43–44); inscriptions from Lugdunum (Lyons), probably from the amphitheater, specify seats for people from two other communities in Gallia Narbonensis, Glanum (St-Rémy) far to the south and Antipolis (Antibes) far to the south-east, and for visitors, perhaps merchants, from Macedon (*EAOR* V 78. 6–8); risers in the Colosseum specify reserved seating for ambassadors from Gades (modern Cadiz). One way in which the inhabitants could demonstrate pride in their community was to show it off to others; in this

---

5. Although it has been supposed that these seats were among the XIV (Reinhold 1971: 281), Cicero, addressing Antony, makes it clear that the special area was separate from them: *illud tamen audaciae tuae quod sedisti in quattuordecim ordinibus, cum esset lege Roscia decoctoribus certus locus constitutus* (it was a mark of your audacity that you took a seat among the fourteen rows, although by the lex Roscia a specific place had been fixed for debtors).

6. Surely a gesture of calculated *clementia*, rather than—as assumed by Reinhold 1971: 281—simple willingness to allow ineligible persons to occupy empty seats.

sense, specifying accommodation for *adventores* in a spectacle building was no different from naming them among the groups who were to benefit from a bath building (*CIL* IX 5074–75; T. Jones 2009: 130).

Presence and visibility are key to understanding what was at stake, as is demonstrated by the case of Julius Caesar. By a decree of the senate, he was granted use of a *sella curulis*, equivalent to a throne, everywhere except in the theater, where he was to sit on a *subsellium* (seat), like the tribunes; only *flamines* (priests) seem to have been allowed a *sella curulis* in the theater. But, by another decree, he was granted a golden chair in the theater with a golden wreath on it. Unless one decree canceled out the other, the latter privilege seems to have been reserved for Caesar's absences from Rome, so that the golden chair and wreath were a symbolic substitute for him, an honor derived from Near Eastern practices of placing honorific chairs to represent absent VIPs (gods, or leaders absent or deceased) (Weinstock 1957: 149–51).

By comparison, 'trading down' in the hierarchy of seating could be a bid for popularity, as when Trajan foreswore the *pulvinar* in the circus to take his seat among the people; Pliny is quick to pick up the cue, emphasizing the people's joy at seeing the emperor's actual person instead of just the structure sheltering him (*Pan.* 51. 4–5). Pliny's implicit comparison is with Domitian, but even an emperor as sensitive to the performative aspects of his role as Nero reclined in an enclosure (*cubiculum*) at the amphitheater, peering through gaps between the hangings (Suet. *Nero* 12. 2). For the audience to know that the emperor was invisibly present, and potentially keeping an eye on those who could not see him, must have unsettled notions of the reciprocal visibility of the ideal ruler; it is significant that Nero later gave up this practice to sit in full view (Hekster 2005: 171).

The absent Caesar's golden wreath is an extreme example of distinctive apparel. Clothing marked out those with privilege from those without, both groups and individuals. By the *lex Iulia theatralis* spectators dressed in dark colors (*pullati*) were relegated to the back of the theater (Suet. *Aug.* 44. 2). Under Caligula, senators were allowed cushions at the circus for the first time, and felt hats "in the Thessalian fashion," τὸν Θετταλικὸν τρόπον, both visible marks of extra comfort and, hence, privilege (Dio 59. 7. 8). After his defeat of Mithradates, Pompey was granted the privilege of wearing triumphal dress—*toga picta* (an embroidered toga) and golden wreath—to the circus (normally it was permitted on the day of the triumph alone), while as a former consul he wore the *toga praetexta* (a toga with a purple stripe) and laurel wreath to the theater (Vell. 2. 40. 4, Dio 37. 21. 4); after his victory in the civil war, Caesar, by contrast, was granted the privilege of wearing triumphal dress at all public events (App. *BC* 2. 106, Dio 43. 43. 1). Some of the emperors 'dressed down' to seem more egalitarian: when he re-dedicated Pompey's Theatre in AD 41, Claudius, although eligible to wear the *toga picta* throughout, instead wore a *toga praetexta*, except while conducting a sacrifice (Dio 60. 6. 9). Dio recounts this detail immediately after mentioning that Claudius had his own name carved upon the stage building, with the implication that this carried a whiff of *hubris*. Possibly Claudius' choice of attire was designed to deflect accusations of megalomania.

Among the spectators, the visual impact of the white-clad ranks of citizens could be manipulated for symbolic effect, as at the gladiatorial combat sponsored by Augustus in memory of Agrippa, where everyone except Augustus and the sons of Agrippa wore black (Dio 55. 8. 5). On this occasion, the venue was also selected to honor the commemorand, since the spectacle took place in the Saepta, the voting enclosures that Agrippa had built on the Campus Martius. By such departures from the norm, a leader could position himself as the spiritual heir to a popular figure and the guarantor of his memory, a move calculated, in this case, to appeal exclusively to the masses, since the elite, regarding Agrippa as an upstart and complicit in the erosion of their privileges, boycotted his funeral altogether (Dio 54. 29. 6).

The highly stratified seating arrangements in entertainment facilities encouraged cheating: in AD 89 the emperor Domitian, tightening up the regulations that reserved the XIV for *equites* with the proper census qualification, employed bouncers to keep out usurpers (Mart. 5. 8, 14, 23, 25, 27, 35). Seating arrangements also provided a means for displaying personal grants of social privilege, since promotion to a higher station became instantly apparent from the seat that a person occupied, for instance as a result of having been awarded *ornamenta* (formal honors) of various types; but being invited to occupy a special seat was in itself a conspicuous honor, even without the formal privileges of *ornamenta*, so that the emperors instantly, if temporarily, elevated persons whom they invited to sit in the imperial box (Edmondson 1996: 105–6). An emperor of ill repute like Caligula is accused of undermining the social structure by inciting the *plebs* to usurp the seats of the *equites* (Suet. *Cal.* 26. 4); this may be merely a telling rumor (Edmondson 2002: 54), or it may indicate that the status distinction that Domitian tried to restore had long been eroding (Reinhold 1971: 282).

It was appropriate for the visible stratification among the spectators to be matched by a properly hierarchical distribution of tokens of the sponsor's generosity: the *missilia* that were distributed at public spectacles in the West, and the equivalent ῥίμματα in the Eastern Empire, deriving from an independent Greek tradition going back at least to the fifth century BC (Robert 1969). These were small edible items, or tokens to be cashed in for larger prizes, which were scattered among the spectators. In more sophisticated contexts, the distribution was enabled by a mechanism suspended above the spectators' heads (Killeen 1959). This procedure caused a scrum—Seneca recommends leaving the theater before the distribution starts (*Ep.* 74. 7)—and on one notorious occasion Domitian had to do it again, scattering 500 tokens, respectively, where the senators and *equites* were sitting, to redress an imbalance that had occurred the day before, when too many tokens had been caught by the *plebs* (Suet. *Dom.* 4. 5). Suetonius' deadpan method of reporting does not betray whether or not he approved of Domitian's attempt to counter fate, but the anecdote plausibly conveys the notion that there should be a correlation between scale of generosity and status of recipient; public entertainment visibly reinforced Roman ideas of propriety in social relations.

EUERGETISM

As in Rome, so in Italy and the provinces public entertainment is a chief tool for establishing a pecking order within the community. In this context, we hear little of dramatic productions and chariot races; instead, gladiatorial displays (*munera*) and beast hunts (*venationes*) dominate the record. Inscriptions numbering in the hundreds record, with great pride, spectacles mounted by local grandees. The spectacles are of very modest dimensions, compared with the dazzling extravaganzas put on by the emperors at Rome, yet the claim to be the first person in the local community ever to have mounted a show of a particular type or on a particular (albeit modest) scale testifies to the inflationary pressures of euergetism in a Roman city.[7] The claim to be "first person of all" (*primus omnium*), found also in the context of distributions of grain and food, peaks in the second century AD; its subsequent decline suggests that the financial difficulties of the third century may also have affected the relationship of dependency between community and patron that is so strikingly evident at public entertainments (Mrozek 1971). These shows earned the sponsor a statue in his community, usually by vote of the town council but sometimes expressly at the request of the people (*postulante populo*, or some similar phrase), a visible and lasting token of gratitude from his fellow citizens and symbolic recompense for his financial outlay.

Sometimes the sponsors are *liberti*, for whom the shows are an outlet for their wealth and a stepping-stone to the prestige in the community that their social origins would preclude them from achieving by any other route, since they were barred from serving on the town council by their servile origins. Hence, we find *liberti*, as well as natives of other communities, being given honors in exchange for acts of euergetism, including the provision of shows (Kleijwegt 1992), or else receiving the honor indirectly, in the form of political office for a son, who might still be a small child (Gordon 1931). 'Munificence' (*munificentia*) is a recurrent term in the context of civic benefactions, implying a spontaneity that probably disguises pressure from the recipients.[8] Some of the shows are liturgies incumbent upon the occupant of a particular office, especially priesthoods of the imperial cult. Neither piety nor self-abnegation is a qualification for such an office but, rather, the sponsor's financial capacity to perform its obligations.[9]

One of the difficulties of contextualizing what we know about the dealings between emperor and people at the games in Rome is that we have very little to

7. The concept of 'euergetism,' from Greek εὖ, *eu* (= well) and ἔργον, *ergon* (= deed), is above all associated with Veyne 1990. For a detailed study of its workings in the Roman cities of Asia Minor, see Zuiderhoek 2009.

8. The claim by Zuiderhoek 2009: 108–9 that a letter of Antoninus Pius to the Ephesians proves that communities might actually reject acts of munificence is based on a supplement to the Greek text that has been emended by Kokkinia 2003: 204 to prove the opposite.

9. For a succinct account of the mechanisms for funding public entertainment, see Edmondson 2002: 54–58.

compare it with. But, as more archaeological evidence comes to light, specifically inscriptions, we are slowly acquiring enough information about random individuals to be able to pursue case studies. It is clear from the amenities listed on advertisements for spectacles at Pompeii (Sabbatini Tumolesi 1980) that, if these amenities were an index of the sponsor's generosity and forethought, their absence would brand him as mean. Three brief examples may illustrate the scope of this approach, two from Italy and one from the East:

1. Sculptural reliefs on the tomb of the *libertus* C. Lusius Storax at Chieti (ancient Teate Marrucinorum, in central Italy near the Adriatic coast) show the man himself in a dignified posture on a raised platform in the middle, flanked by servants and other dignitaries, with the arena band tilting their instruments toward him as they play a fanfare, and even some animated spectators depicted in the background; but Storax himself is the focus of attention and ritual (Clarke 2003: 145–52). Naturally, the relief idealizes Storax's position; even so, it gives a vivid impression of the social recognition that a freedman could acquire by sponsoring a public spectacle.

2. Arguably the most prominent citizen in Pompeii at the time of the eruption of Vesuvius was Cn. Alleius Nigidius Maius, whose generous sponsorship of gladiatorial shows in every post that he occupied brought him public acclaim, as is amply attested by graffiti hailing him in terms such as "chief of sponsors" (*princeps munerariorum, CIL* IV 7990). A civic amenity described as *opus tabularum* (lit., "a work comprising panels"), which he dedicated with a further lavish show in the amphitheater (*CIL* IV 138), was probably the series of elaborate paintings around the podium wall in the amphitheater itself that survives in a copy made by the nineteenth-century French artist Charles François Mazois before the original crumbled away (Franklin 1997: 442–44). Public entertainments, and the amenities for mounting them, are a means for acquiring the civic endorsement that leads to prominence in the community.

3. Beyond Italy, in Oenoanda in Lycia (south-eastern Turkey), a distinguished *eques*, C. Iulius Demosthenes, founded a four-yearly agonistic festival in AD 125, comprising contests in rhetoric, music, poetry, drama, and athletics. His plans, set out in detail down to the last drachma, were endorsed by the reigning emperor, Hadrian.[10] The composite document recording these plans and the procedural stages of their corroboration pulses with civic pride. The competition between

10. Communities gained extra prestige by posting up copies of letters of witness from emperors (*martyriai*) endorsing the generosity of individual citizens (Kokkinia 2003). Foundations established for mounting games minted coins to commemorate the imperial privilege granting the city the right to spend their wealth on *munera* and *venationes* (Nollé 1992–93).

communities to adorn themselves with buildings and cultural institutions establishes the conditions in which a sponsor like Demosthenes can describe his benefactions in terms that today sound nauseatingly self-congratulatory ("as I have loved my dearest homeland since earliest youth, and have not only maintained but thoroughly surpassed the generosity of my ancestors towards it," etc.); but the tenor of the proposal made by the city council to adopt Demosthenes' plans sounds just the same ("Iulius Demosthenes, our most excellent citizen who also founded the festival, a man of the greatest distinction, outstanding in reputation, ancestry, and character not only in his home city but also in the province…the council has praised…for his continuous good will to the city and for his present patriotic zeal and his unsurpassed great-heartedness and for his devotion to the emperors…" (trans. Mitchell 1990: 185). The benefit that the foundation would bring to the community in both prestige and economic terms earned the sponsor these lavish tributes in return for his investment.

The flip side of a culture of generosity is the potential for extortion. In the reign of Tiberius, the *plebs* of Pollentia (Pollenzo, in Piedmont) would not allow the funeral of a chief centurion to go ahead until by force (*per vim*) they had extracted from his heirs the promise of a gladiatorial display. Tiberius sent in two cohorts, and the majority of the citizens and councillors of the town were thrown into prison for life (Suet. *Tib.* 37. 3). Predictably, the funerary associations of gladiatorial combat created a culture of expectation that caused class tension, or at least isolated the donor; it is clear in this case that the councillors connived with the populace. Possibly blackmail of this sort explains the testamentary provisions for gifts of games, food, and similar legacies by deceased donors (C. P. Jones 1999: 592); such provisions may have been a form of insurance against disruption, delay in burial being not only an indignity but also, in the absence of modern mortuary practices, a health hazard.

Expression of the Popular Will: Allusion and *Acclamatio*

In his speech on behalf of Sestius (56 BC), Cicero, newly returned from exile, claims that there are three places where the judgment and will of the people is expressed: at a public assembly, at the polling station, and at games and gladiatorial shows.[11] He goes on to argue at length that it is only in the third category that the people have been able to demonstrate their true (i.e., positive) feelings about him: the news

---

11. Cic. *Sest.* 106: *etenim tribus locis significari maxime de <re publica> populi Romani iudicium ac voluntas potest, contione, comitiis, ludorum gladiatorumque consessu.*

that the senate had passed a decree to recall him from exile prompted the audience in the theater to spontaneous applause, which they renewed when members of the senate arrived; and, when the presiding consul sat down, they spontaneously stood up, palms raised in the posture of grateful supplication (*Sest.* 117). By contrast, when Cicero's arch-enemy Clodius arrived, the audience insulted him with abusive verses from the play they were watching, whereas the chief actor gained repeated ovations for his pointed delivery of verses appropriate to Cicero's own situation (*Sest.* 118–23). Cicero's comment is significant (*Sest.* 118, trans. Nicolet [Falla]): "among many and varied reflections in the comedy, there was never a passage seeming, from the poet's words, to have some bearing on our times, where either the whole people failed to grasp the special point or where the actor himself failed to make it clear." And, at gladiatorial contests in the Forum, the arrival of Sestius, Cicero's own champion, roused unanimous applause from spectators sitting as far away as the slopes of the Capitoline (*Sest.* 124).

The speed and subtlety with which Roman audiences picked up allusions in the theater is an astonishing feature of their culture. It has been suggested that the sponsors of theatrical events would select plays that allowed scope for innuendo complimentary to their partisans or derogatory of their enemies, so that the plays that were performed at the Floralia of 57 BC, described by Cicero in the quotation above (the *Eurysaces* and *Brutus* by Accius), were deliberately chosen by the pro-Ciceronian faction in the senate, at the behest of the aediles, to give his supporters scope for promoting his cause (Nicolet 1983: 170). Conversely, there is evidence that sponsors would try to censor a politically inflammatory choice, as evidently happened after the assassination of Julius Caesar, when arrangements were being made for the celebration of the Ludi Apollinares in July 44: Mark Antony chose to replace Brutus' choice of (again) Accius' *Brutus* with his *Tereus*; both Brutus and Antony were *praetor urbanus* in 44 BC, and Brutus was evidently hoping to enhance his reputation as a liberator by staging a classic play about his heroic forefather (Nicolet 1983: 171). The social relations that were played out at the theater could be subtly manipulated in advance.

The picture that Cicero paints of intense political engagement among spectators at the games in the last decades of the republic helps to show why the emperors paid so much attention to theater audiences, and why their biographers devote such scrutiny to their interactions with the crowd. Even without television and the Internet, public figures were instantly recognizable—it is easy to forget how small the Roman elite was (the senate was reduced to 600 under Augustus, which was the size it had been half a century earlier under Sulla; the Equites probably numbered ca. 2,000[12])—so that, for example, the younger Cato (Uticensis) famously left the theater during a celebration of the Floralia, in order that his presence should not inhibit the performance by nude actresses at this ribald festival. Cato's gesture was undoubtedly calculated to gain respect, in which it succeeded, since his departure was received with enormous applause (V. Max. 2. 10. 8, Mart. 1 *praef.*). On the other hand, his forebear, Cato the Censor, was famously uncompromising: a former

---

12. Rawson 1987: 105; Slater 1994: 130.

consul whom he and his fellow censor had expelled from the senate, L. Quinctius Flamininus, gained popular sympathy by sitting as far away as possible from the senatorial seats at the next theatrical performance, whereupon the people called so vociferously for his restoration that he finally resumed his former place (Plut. *Cat. mai.* 17. 6, *Flam.* 19. 4; V. Max. 4. 5. 1).

The noise from the crowd is often emphasized in our sources. In Greek, βοάω (shout), the word that Plutarch uses in both versions of his account of Flamininus' reception, also occurs in the context of the chanted *acclamationes* (acclamations) that were a powerful tool in the expression of popular will in the entertainment facilities of antiquity. There is no equivalent in modern Western society to these spontaneous, concerted expressions of complex and specific sentiments, which probably depended upon rhythm for their momentum. They were regularly regarded as authentic expressions of popular opinion; our modern suspicion that the people were only mouthing what they were told to say, rather than what they really thought, is probably an anachronism (Roueché 1984). To appreciate the potency of entertainment facilities as conduits of social interaction, it is necessary to consider the effect of the *acclamationes* upon the authorities at which they were directed.

The show itself would prompt either approval or criticism, although we tend to hear more about the latter. Pompey's approval rating did not improve—and may even have dropped—when the display of elephants at the opening of his theater in 55 BC prompted sympathy for the beasts (*misericordia*), although this rare instance of an anecdote that survives in five different versions is a prime example of the distortions that accrue in the re-telling.[13] We may suspect that the crowd's sympathy for the elephants was expressed precisely by *acclamatio*, the formula "have pity" being attested later on (in both Latin and Greek) in the context of Christian martyrdom (examples at Potter 1996: 141). Public entertainment, in other words, provided a context for eloquent confrontation between the people and their patrons.

AUDIENCE INITIATIVE

The guaranteed presence of the sponsor at a show provides the ideal opportunity for asking him things—or telling him. Under the republic, the recorded instances tend to illustrate the spectators' reaction against a particularly zealous application

---

13. The eyewitness account, by Cicero (*Fam.* 7. 1. 3), simply says that the crowd showed "much astonishment, but no enjoyment" (*admiratio magna...delectatio nulla*). Some time before AD 65, Seneca (*Dial.* 10. 13. 6–7) focuses on the elephants' human victims. Before AD 79, the elder Pliny (*Nat.* 8. 21) says that the people cursed Pompey; ca. AD 100 Plutarch portrays the spectators as simply awestruck (*Pomp.* 52. 4). A century later Dio (39. 38) implies that the people interpreted Pompey's action as a violation of a sacred promise to the animals that they would come to no harm.

of law or precedent by the sponsor or another authority, as with the reaction against the demotion of L. Quinctius Flamininus from the senate (cited above, under "Expression of the Popular Will"). Under the empire, when authority is vested in a single person, the stakes are higher: one man has the capacity to provide for all. Modern cynicism is a barrier to appreciating the combination of trust and expectation that this increasingly engendered in the emperor's subjects (Nutton 1978). Ancient audiences came to the shows and spectacles in Rome and beyond with high hopes and a boisterous attitude.

With the disenfranchisement of the people that accompanied the establishment of the Principate, the theater has been called Rome's "parliament" (Hopkins 1983: 16). Insofar as it implies a formal and legitimate structure for democratic debate and accommodation, this is a misleading term. But, with the advent of autocracy at the end of the republic, the theaters became something of a bastion of free speech, more or less constrained by the personality and self-confidence of the ruler but simultaneously rendering him exposed. In the theater, gestures from the audience could contribute a *double entendre* to an actor's script: when the mime librettist Laberius declaimed, "Come on, citizens, we have lost our freedom!" and "He whom many fear must fear many," the entire audience turned to stare at Julius Caesar, who had stripped him of his equestrian rank by forcing him to act in one of his own mimes. According to the fifth-century author Macrobius, the audience noted that "[Caesar's] impotence was assaulted by this impudence" (*impotentiam eius hac dicacitate lapidatam*, Macr. 2. 7. 4–5); if this is not an anachronistic impression being read back into the incident by Macrobius himself, the notion that Caesar, under the circumstances, was powerless suggests that the traditional *theatralis licentia*[14] was perceived to render the powerful vulnerable.

Such license had destabilizing potential. Tacitus records that, under Tiberius, soldiers and a centurion were killed and a military tribune wounded when they intervened to curb "insults against magistrates and dissension among the *plebs*" (*probra in magistratus et dissensionem vulgi*), leading to a debate in the senate and measures that prevented *equites* from consorting with actors and gave the praetors the power to exile citizens who caused trouble (Tac. *Ann.* 1. 77). Other emperors, less heavy-handed, were more successful in calibrating their reactions to popular pressure. Augustus had learned the importance of appearing to share the people's pleasures from the animosity that Julius Caesar had aroused by taking paperwork with him to the games (Suet. *Aug.* 45. 1).[15] He also learned to turn criticism to his advantage: when an *eques* at a public spectacle persisted in demanding the abolition of the Augustan marriage laws, the emperor gestured to the children of his step-grandson Germanicus who were sitting with him, and indicated that the spectators

14. Frank and boisterous behavior sometimes degenerating into violence: cf. Tac. *Ann.* 1. 77. 1 *theatri licentia*, Suet. *Dom.* 8. 3 *licentiam theatralem*—hence the title of the classic study of theatrical unrest at Rome by Bollinger 1969.

15. For the sensitivity (or insensitivity) of other emperors to the necessity of attending games, see Edmondson 1996: 84.

should follow the fecund example of this father of six (Suet. *Aug.* 34. 2). We do not know whether Augustus said anything on this occasion; the eloquence of his gesture may have been enough.

The practical and symbolic value of the theater as a place to rally opposition and express frustration made it a crucial location for negotiating the relationship between emperor and people. A grain shortage late in the reign of Tiberius almost caused a revolt, and in the theater for days on end numerous demands were hurled at the emperor with more license than usual (Tac. *Ann.* 6. 13). Finally, Tiberius got the Senate to issue a decree rebuking the people; the fact that he did not rebuke them himself was taken not as behavior suitable for a citizen (*civile*), as he had intended, but pride (*superbia*). Whether it is to be regarded as coincidental spontaneity or an orchestrated protest, there is occasional evidence of an individual request being made in several venues simultaneously: under Galba, the successor of Nero, audiences in "all the theatres and stadia" demanded the punishment of Nero's confidant, Tigellinus, until Galba issued an edict saying that Tigellinus was dying, and that the people should not try the patience of the government or force it to behave in a tyrannical fashion (Plut. *Galba* 17. 4).

Sometimes, to avoid violence, the emperor gave in: when Tiberius took away the *Apoxyomenos* of Lysippus (a statue of an athletic youth scraping himself with a strigil), removing it from the *thermae* of Agrippa to his private quarters and replacing it with a substitute, the people protested in the theater with such intransigence (*contumacia*) that in the end he gave it back (Plin. *Nat.* 34. 62). Pliny, citing the episode to illustrate the genius of Lysippus, portrays this as a tussle between art lovers, but it has been plausibly suggested that there may have been a moral component: if Agrippa's *thermae* (warm baths) offered the facilities of a Greek gymnasium, which up until now had been shunned at Rome for its immoral connotations, that would explain why (i) Agrippa had deemed the *Apoxyomenos* appropriate decoration, (ii) Tiberius removed this symbol of a decadent Greek practice out of public view, and (iii) the *populus Romanus* demonstrated so persistently for its return—prompted, probably, by claques of the *iuvenes* (young men) who indulged in gymnastic exercises.[16]

With the Praetorian Guard ready to do their bidding, the emperors could have quashed any revolt that might erupt in the theater. Caligula did just that, most brutally, with a protest against taxes; the Jewish author Josephus, who recounts this episode, prefaces it with a revealing ethnographic comment about the chariot races (*AJ* 19. 24, trans. Feldman): "This is a kind of spectator sport to which the Romans are fanatically devoted. They gather enthusiastically in the circus and there the assembled throngs make requests of the emperors according to their own pleasure. Emperors who rule that there can be no question about granting such petitions are by no means unpopular." Indeed, any public exchange between people and emperor

16. Cf. Slater 1994: 137–38, who finds it "perhaps incredibl[e]" that the destination for the statue was the emperor's own bedroom; but that was presumably the only place where Tiberius could guarantee that it would be truly out of sight.

was so politically charged that most emperors went out of their way to avoid violent confrontation. Nero is reported to have tolerated all sorts of cheeky behavior, even letting an actor get away with miming the actions of drinking and swimming during a performance of the popular song, "Farewell father, farewell mother," a clear allusion to Nero's role in the deaths of Claudius and Agrippina (Suet. *Nero* 39. 3). It has been observed that emperors who infringed the theatrical license accorded to free speech have gone down in history as 'bad' emperors, namely, Caligula and Domitian, each of whom executed an actor for a *double entendre* (Suet. *Cal.* 27. 4, *Dom.* 10. 4; Cameron 1976: 160).

Imperial Control

Public entertainment gave the people the opportunity to observe the emperor's personality and behavior at first hand. There is no equivalent in Greek for the Roman concept of *civilitas*, the capacity to behave like a *civis*, a citizen among citizens (Cameron 1976: 177, Wallace-Hadrill 1982: 42–44). This is what Tiberius was trying to do in displaying behavior that was *civile*, when he refrained from speaking his mind to the people during the grain shortage mentioned above (under "Audience Initiative"). But the emperor's status as a *civis* is reminiscent of *Animal Farm*: some *cives* were more equal than others. The emperor was *primus inter pares*; he had to maintain a balance between equality and majesty. To a certain extent, stooping toward the lower classes was *de rigueur*; when senatorial sources praise the emperor for displaying *comitas* (affability) by sharing in the pleasures of the crowd at the theater or the baths, this behavior must fit the "ritually required pattern of condescension" (Wallace-Hadrill 1982: 42). Condescension it may have been, but the emperor's willingness to let the people voice their opinions and desires at the games entailed risk, too; doubtless, he usually anticipated their concerns and did not let their requests become too importunate, but there was always the possibility that he might be caught on the wrong foot (Cameron 1976: 173).

Arbitrary or arrogant behavior transgressed the social boundaries, the most rigid of these being the distinction between spectator and performer. The *senatus consultum* (senatorial decree) from Larinum shows the preoccupation with keeping erstwhile members of the upper classes off the stage and out of the arena, where to receive payment for such an appearance would entail *infamia*: social and legal ostracization (see Leppin in this volume). 'Erstwhile' is key here, since the decree specifies persons who had ever met the census requirement (i.e., including those who had since failed to do so). This has led to speculation that *equites* who were banned from the XIV for some minor infraction, thereby losing their equestrian status, deliberately engineered this loss of status so that they could perform with impunity on the stage or in the arena for substantial financial gain and popular following (Slater 1994: 140–43). Such behavior not only infringed Roman notions of hierarchy and privilege, but also endangered public safety, if it is plausible to suppose that it was performers formerly possessed of equestrian status who incited their fellows in the XIV to start the riots mentioned above (under "Audience Initiative") at the beginning of Tiberius' reign (Slater 1994: 122–40).

Augustus' preoccupation with shaping a properly ordered society, which is visible in his marriage legislation as well as the *lex Iulia theatralis*, partly rests on the premise that social reputation can compensate for loss of political power. It is therefore important to recognize that he promoted the senatorial and equestrian classes, and did not undermine their status by prompting immoral performances that would subject them to the disabilities entailed by *infamia* (Horsmann 2008). Later emperors, however, were not so scrupulous. Emperors who sent members of the upper classes into the arena were demonstrating their absolute power; the sources are quick to identify the class of the victim, since victims from the lower classes did not matter. Two passages in Dio neatly illustrate this prejudice: describing Nero's funeral games for Agrippina, he fulminates at the scandal of female participants from the upper classes (Dio 61. 17. 3, trans. Cary), "There was another exhibition that was at once most disgraceful and most shocking, when men and women not only of the equestrian but even of the senatorial order appeared as performers in the orchestra, in the Circus, and in the hunting-theatre, like those who are held in lowest esteem," whereas, describing the opening of the Colosseum, his sigh of relief at the negligible status of the women involved is almost audible (66. 25. 1), "a total of nine thousand animals, both tame and wild, were despatched, and women, although not distinguished ones (γυναῖκες, οὐ μέντοι ἐπιφανεῖς), participated in despatching them."

Entertainment facilities clearly tempted the emperors to demonstrate their absolute authority. But, conversely, it was expedient for an emperor to allow the people to get their own way on occasion, even if there was no threat of violence. Fronto, advising the emperor on rhetorical strategy, cites an analogy from the amphitheater (*Ad M. Caes.* 2. 2. 2, p. 18 van den Hout): "At the request of the people (*populo postulante*), you honor or set free men who have put all their energy into killing wild animals—they may be criminals and condemned prisoners, but, at the request of the people, you give in. As a result, everywhere the people rule, they prevail, they come out on top. So, you will act and speak in such a way as to make the people happy." Of course, a canny emperor could plant agents in the crowd to incite them to make demands that he wanted to fulfill. If Titus, hailed on his demise as *amor ac deliciae generis humani* ("beloved favorite of the human race," Suet. *Tit.* 1), wanted to get rid of somebody, he allegedly posted agents in the theaters and military barracks to call for that person's punishment (Suet. *Tit.* 6. 1); the collocation of theaters and barracks in Suetonius' remark (*per theatra et castra*) makes it clear that the place to engage civilians *en masse* was at a public spectacle.

An emperor attuned to popular opinion could make strategic use of theatrical occasions to increase his political credibility. Before sending them into exile, Titus paraded *delatores* (informers) in the Colosseum in a grand gesture symbolizing a 'new broom sweeps clean' policy (Mart. *Spect.* 4–5, Suet. *Tit.* 8. 5). After the intervening reign of Domitian, whose reliance on these hated figures was notorious, Trajan repeated the gesture (Plin. *Pan.* 34. 1, 35. 4; Coleman 1999, 2006: 54–58, Rutledge 2001: 302–6). Pliny describes how the victims' heads were twisted back so that their features were visible to all—a nice reversal, in that they were notorious for pursuing their loathsome activities in secret. The architecture of the Colosseum, with its towering *podium* wall, emphasized an 'us and them' divide between the *cavea* and the arena. The resulting humiliation of the *delatores* may have been part of their punishment.

INTERNATIONAL RELATIONS

We have already seen (under "Symbols of the Social Order") the importance of making provision for contingents from other communities at public spectacles. On the international level, public entertainment could showcase complex diplomatic relations. The disgraceful loss of three Roman standards in Crassus' ill-fated expedition against Parthia in 53 BC was finally redressed in 20 BC, when Phraates IV of Parthia returned them to Augustus. Some time later, for reasons that are not altogether clear, he sent his four sons to Rome, where Augustus first paraded them in the arena at a gladiatorial show and then seated them immediately behind him to watch it, so that they were simultaneously symbols of Roman hegemony and honored guests (Suet. *Aug.* 43. 4); the full scope of their honorific treatment becomes clear from the term for where they were seated, *secundo subsellio*, which, in addition to specifying the row behind Augustus' own seat, also shows that the princes sat on free-standing chairs (*subsellia*), which, as we have seen, conveyed special prestige.

More than half a century later, under Nero, a dispute arose with the Frisians, a Germanic tribe who had moved onto land on the bank of the Lower Rhine that the Roman army felt entitled to use (Tac. *Ann.* 13. 54). Two Frisian ambassadors, arriving in Rome, were given the standard tour. When they entered Pompey's Theatre and, in response to their enquiries about the seating arrangements, were told that the foreigners seated among the senators were being granted a conspicuous honor in recognition of their *virtus*[17] and their friendship (*amicitia*) with the Roman people, they immediately sat there too, on the basis that the Germans were second to none in *arma aut fides* (military prowess and loyalty). The spectators were impressed by this show of old-fashioned spunk and competitive spirit, and Nero granted the pair Roman citizenship—although to oust the Frisians from the wetlands beside the Rhine he had to use force in the end. The capacity of Roman auditoria to organize society in a quintessentially Roman hierarchy

---

17. Manly qualities of physical and moral courage.

could evidently be hijacked by foreign competitors in a game of diplomatic one-upmanship.[18]

THE ULTIMATE SOCIAL CHASM

The social distance between the spectators in the *cavea* and the protagonists in the arena was played out in contexts in which the spectators had the power to influence the outcome of the spectacle, either by determining the fate of a defeated gladiator or by determining the degree of humiliation and suffering visited upon prisoners condemned to capital punishment. With the famous—if disputed—gesture of the "turned thumb" (*pollice verso*),[19] the spectators conveyed to the sponsor whether they thought that a defeated gladiator deserved a reprieve (*missio*) or death, thereby enacting the ultimate distinction in social relations—power over the life of the subordinate party. Since gladiators were slaves, or free persons who had taken the *auctoramentum* (oath of obedience) that forfeited their free status, the spectators effectively exercised the prerogative of a slave owner, who had the absolute right of life and death over his property, whether animal or human. When the anxieties of the *senatus consultum* from Larinum (mentioned above, under "Imperial Control") are seen in this light, the threat posed to the social order by aristocratic performance in the arena becomes starkly obvious.

Spectacular forms of execution, primarily the enactment of *damnatio ad bestias* (condemnation to the beasts), are vividly documented for us in the accounts of Christian martyrdom in the arena. The spectators, safely separated from the fate of the condemned by the barrier of the *podium*, were nevertheless in some sense the arbiters of justice. They were present to see justice done, and to monitor *how* it was done. Hence, the interventions by the spectators sometimes mock the protagonists but sometimes criticize their treatment, as in the account of the martyrdom of Perpetua and Felicitas at Carthage in AD 203. When Perpetua and Felicitas were brought into the arena naked and entangled in nets, the spectators were appalled and sent them back to be dressed in tunics, thereby indicating that propriety had been violated (*Pass. Perpet.* 20. 2–3). Yet, the crowd acknowledged the bloody mauling of the martyr Saturus with a slogan from the baths, "Well washed!" (*salve lotum!*), a salutation that smacks of sadism, whether or not the spectators were deliberately alluding to the Christian rite of baptism (*Pass. Perpet.* 21. 2). Ultimately, when the martyrs, mortally wounded, were about to be removed to have their throats slit, the spectators insisted that they be executed in full view

18. A doublet of this story set in the reign of Claudius (Suet. *Cl.* 25. 4) somewhat undermines its credibility (Edmondson 2002: 43).

19. Probably turned to point aggressively upward: see Corbeill 1997, slightly expanded in Corbeill 2004: 41–66.

(*Pass. Perpet.* 21. 2, 7), a demand predicated on the ancient belief that justice is to be carried out in public and seen by the community to have taken its proper course (Coleman 1990: 44–49). It was one of the responsibilities of a properly ordered society to patrol its social boundaries.

CONCLUSION

In AD 12, when Augustus was fretting about the ridicule that the imperial house might attract, if the palsied Claudius were to watch the circus games from the *pulvinar*, the republican tradition of *theatralis licentia* still informed the reactions of the Roman audience. Nearly two centuries later, Dio and the other senators in the stands chewed laurel leaves from their wreaths to suppress their nervous laughter at the sight of Commodus brandishing the severed head of an ostrich in the arena to indicate that he could do the same to them (Dio 73. 21. 2). Visibility still governed relations in the entertainment facilities of the Roman world; but the equilibrium of the republican hierarchy had been over-balanced by the increasingly autocratic structure of the Principate, fatally liable to exploitation by megalomaniac rulers; and freedom of expression was no longer a reciprocal privilege. An *eques* who had been rebuked by Augustus for drinking in his seat could retort that the emperor did not have to fear losing his, if he went home for lunch (Quint. *Inst.* 6. 3. 63); the senators watching Commodus could not risk any response at all. Throughout Rome's history, public entertainment provided a forum where the entire community—gods, benefactors, senators, *equites*, *plebs*, *liberti*, slaves—witnessed and participated in social and political exchange. No other institution reflects with such clarity the shifting dynamics of Roman social relations.

SUGGESTED READING

Fundamental on the relations between emperor and audience is the chapter entitled "The Emperor and His People at the Games" in Cameron 1976: 157–92. The canonical treatment of the Augustan seating regulations by Rawson 1987 should be read against the evidence for pre-Augustan arrangements collected by T. Jones 2009. Social relations more broadly are tackled for the amphitheater by Hopkins 1983, Edmondson 1996, and Edmondson 2002. The role of the theater in political life in the late republic is masterfully sketched by Nicolet 1983: 361–73. The use of theatrical allusion as a form of protest is analyzed by Bartsch 1994: 63–97, the destabilizing potential of upper-class performers by Slater 1994. For acclamations, see the important discussions by Roueché 1984, Potter 1996, and Aldrete 1999: 101–64. Relations with the gods are suggestively explored by Gebhard 1996.

BIBLIOGRAPHY

Aldrete, G. S. 1999. *Gestures and Acclamations in Ancient Rome*. Baltimore: Johns Hopkins University Press.

Bartsch, S. 1994. *Actors in the Audience: Theatricality and Doublespeak from Nero to Hadrian*. Cambridge, Mass.: Harvard University Press.

Bollinger, T. 1969. *Theatralis licentia. Die Publikumsdemonstrationen an den öffentlichen Spielen im Rom der früheren Kaiserzeit und ihre Bedeutung im politischen Leben*. Winterthur: Hans Schellenberg.

Bomgardner, D. L. 2000. *The Story of the Roman Amphitheatre*. London: Routledge.

Caldelli, M. L. 2004. "Le élites locali fanno spettacolo negli edifici di spettacolo." In M. Cébeillac-Gervasoni, L. Lamoine, and F. Trément (eds.), *Autocélébration des élites locales dans le monde romain. Contextes, images, textes (IIe s. av. J.-C. / IIIe s. ap. J.-C.)*. Clermont-Ferrand: Presses universitaires Blaise Pascal. 129–55.

Cameron, A. 1976. *Circus Factions: Blues and Greens at Rome and Byzantium*. Oxford: Clarendon Press.

Clarke, J. R. 2003. *Art in the Lives of Ordinary Romans*. Berkeley: University of California Press.

Coleman, K. M. 1990. "Fatal Charades: Roman Executions Staged as Mythological Enactments." *Journal of Roman Studies* 80: 44–73.

———. 1999. "'Informers' on Parade." In B. Bergmann and C. Kondoleon (eds.), *The Art of Ancient Spectacle*. Washington, DC: National Gallery of Art. 231–45.

———. 2000. "Entertaining Rome." In J. Coulston and H. Dodge (eds.), *Ancient Rome: The Archaeology of the Eternal City*. Oxford: Oxford University Committee for Archaeology. 205–52.

———. 2006. *M. Valerii Martialis Liber Spectaculorum: Edited with Introduction, Translation, and Commentary*. Oxford: Oxford University Press.

Corbeill, A. 1997. "Thumbs in Ancient Rome: *Pollex* as Index." *Memoirs of the American Academy in Rome* 42: 1–21.

———. 2004. *Nature Embodied: Gesture in Ancient Rome*. Princeton: Princeton University Press.

Crawford, M. H. (ed.). 1996. *Roman Statutes*. London: Institute of Classical Studies, School of Advanced Study, University of London.

EAOR. 1988–. *Epigrafia anfiteatrale dell'Occidente romano*. 6 vols. to date. Rome: Edizioni Quasar.

Edmondson, J. C. 1996. "Dynamic Arenas: Gladiatorial Presentations in the City of Rome and the Construction of Roman Society during the Early Empire." In Slater 1996: 69–112.

———. 2002. "Public Spectacles and Roman Social Relations." In *Ludi Romani. Espectáculos en Hispania Romana*. Mérida: Museo Nacional de Arte Romano. 43–63.

Ehrenberg, V., and Jones, A. H. M. (eds.). 1976. *Documents Illustrating the Reigns of Augustus & Tiberius*. 2nd enlarged ed., with addenda by D. L. Stockton. Oxford: Clarendon Press.

Fora, M. 1992. "Ummidia Quadratilla ed il restauro del teatro di Cassino (per una nuova lettura di AE 1946, 174)." *Zeitschrift für Papyrologie und Epigraphik* 94: 269–73.

Franklin, James L., Jr. 1997. "Cn. Alleius Nigidius Maius and the Amphitheatre: *Munera* and a Distinguished Career at Ancient Pompeii." *Historia* 46: 434–47.

Gebhard, E. R. 1996. "The Theater and the City." In Slater 1996: 113–27.

Gordon, M. L. 1931. "The Freedman's Son in Municipal Life." *Journal of Roman Studies* 21: 65–77.

Hekster, O. 2005. "Captured in the Gaze of Power. Visibility, Games and Roman Imperial Representation." In O. Hekster and R. Fowler (eds.), *Imaginary Kings: Royal Images in the Ancient Near East, Greece and Rome.* Stuttgart: Franz Steiner Verlag. 157–76.

Hopkins, K. 1983. "Murderous Games." In K. Hopkins, *Death and Renewal.* Cambridge: Cambridge University Press. 1–30.

Horsmann, G. 2008. "Public Performances by Senators and Knights and the Moral Legislation of Augustus." In J. Nelis-Clément and J.-M. Roddaz (eds.), *Le Cirque romain et son image.* Bordeaux: Ausonius. 475–80.

Humphrey, J. H. 1986. *Roman Circuses: Arenas for Chariot Racing.* Berkeley: University of California Press.

IEph. 1979–84. H. Wankel (ed.). *Die Inschriften von Ephesos.* 8 vols. Bonn: Kommission für die Archäologische Erforschung Kleinasiens bei der Österreichischen Akademie der Wissenschaften, Österreichisches Archäologisches Institut, Institut für Altertumskunde der Universität Köln.

Jones, C. P. 1999. "Interrupted Funerals." *Proceedings of the American Philosophical Society* 143: 588–600.

Jones, T. 2009. "Pre-Augustan Seating in Italy and the West." In T. Wilmott (ed.), *Roman Amphitheatres and* Spectacula: *A 21st-Century Perspective.* Oxford: Archaeopress. 127–39.

Killeen, J. F. 1959. "What Was the *Linea Dives* (Martial, VIII,78,7)?" *American Journal of Philology* 80: 185–88.

Kleijwegt, M. 1992. "The Value of Empty Honours." *Epigraphica* 54: 131–42.

Kokkinia, C. 2003. "Letters of Roman Authorities on Local Dignitaries: The Case of Vedius Antoninus." *Zeitschrift für Papyrologie und Epigraphik* 142: 197–213.

Mitchell, S. 1990. "Festivals, Games, and Civic Life in Roman Asia Minor." *Journal of Roman Studies* 89: 183–93.

Mrozek, S. 1971. "*Primus omnium* sur les inscriptions des municipes italiens." *Epigraphica* 33: 60–69.

Nicolet, C. 1983. *The World of the Citizen in Republican Rome.* Trans. P. S. Falla. Berkeley: University of California Press = *Le métier du citoyen dans la Rome républicaine.* 2nd ed. 1979. Paris: Gallimard.

Nollé, J. 1992–93. "Kaiserliche Privilegien für Gladiatorenmunera und Tierhetzen. Unbekannte und ungedeutete Zeugnisse auf städtischen Münzen des griechischen Ostens." *Jahrbuch für Numismatik und Geldgeschichte* 42–43: 49–82.

Nutton, V. 1978. "The Beneficial Ideology." In P. D. A. Garnsey and C. R. Whittaker (eds.), *Imperialism in the Ancient World.* Cambridge: Cambridge University Press. 209–21.

Potter, D. 1996. "Performance, Power, and Justice in the High Empire." In W. J. Slater (ed.), *Roman Theater and Society.* Ann Arbor: University of Michigan Press. 129–59.

Rawson, E. 1987. "*Discrimina ordinum*: The *Lex Julia theatralis.*" *Papers of the British School at Rome* 55: 83–114 = *Roman Culture and Society: Collected Papers.* Oxford: Oxford University Press 1991. 508–45.

Reinhold, M. 1971. "Usurpation of Status and Status Symbols in the Roman Empire." *Historia* 20: 275–302.

Robert, L. 1969. "Inscriptions d'Athènes et de la Grèce Centrale. IV. Sur le décret d'Acraiphia pour l'évergète Épaminondas." *Archaiologikè Ephemeris* 34–9 = *Opera Minora Selecta. Épigraphie et antiquités grecques.* Vol. 7. Amsterdam: Adolf M. Hakkert 1990. 740–45.

Rogers, G. M. 1991. *The Sacred Identity of Ephesos. Foundation Myths of a Roman City.* London: Routledge.

Roueché, C. 1984. "Acclamations in the Later Roman Empire: New Evidence from Aphrodisias." *Journal of Roman Studies* 74: 181–99.

Rutledge, S. H. 2001. *Imperial Inquisitions: Prosecutors and Informants from Tiberius to Domitian.* London: Routledge.

Sabbatini Tumolesi, P. 1980. *Gladiatorum paria. Annunci di spettacoli gladiatorii a Pompei.* Rome: Edizioni di Storia e Letteratura.

Sear, F. 2006. *Roman Theatres: An Architectural Study.* Oxford: Oxford University Press.

Slater, W. J. 1994. "Pantomime Riots." *Classical Antiquity* 13: 120–44.

———. (ed.). 1996. *Roman Theater and Society.* Ann Arbor: University of Michigan Press.

Treggiari, S. 1969. *Roman Freedmen during the Late Republic.* Oxford: Clarendon Press.

Veyne, P. 1990. *Bread and Circuses: Historical Sociology and Political Pluralism.* Trans. Brian Pearce. London: Penguin. Abridged trans. of *Le Pain et le cirque: sociologie historique d'un pluralisme politique.* Paris: Seuil 1976.

Wallace-Hadrill, A. 1982. "Civilis Princeps: Between Citizen and King." *Journal of Roman Studies* 72: 32–48.

Weinstock, S. 1957. "The Image and the Chair of Germanicus." *Journal of Roman Studies* 47: 144–54.

Welch, K. E. 2007. *The Roman Amphitheatre: From Its Origins to the Colosseum.* Cambridge: Cambridge University Press.

Zuiderhoek, A. 2009. *The Politics of Munificence in the Roman Empire: Citizens, Elites, and Benefactors in Asia Minor.* Cambridge: Cambridge University Press.

CHAPTER 17

SOCIALIZING AT THE BATHS

GARRETT G. FAGAN

To contemporary Western sensibilities, bathing revolves around the rather private matter of getting clean. Shared or public baths, of course, are not unknown—think of saunas, Turkish baths, or hot tubs; but for the most part people today do not consider these places routine venues for their ablutions, nor do they, as a rule, associate the act of bathing with the act of socializing. For the Romans, the opposite was the case. So social was Roman bathing that even so-called private baths attached to the houses and villas of the elite were actually places where host and guests would gather to relax (e.g., Petr. 72–73). By the empire's heyday in the second century AD, public baths were practically ubiquitous. Any Roman settlement worth its salt had them, and their ruins have survived in abundance, from the vast leisure complexes of the capital to a humble wooden establishment associated with a temporary marching camp on the Rhine frontier (Bosman 1999). Clearly, then, public baths were a linchpin of Roman social life. But why? Who used them? What did people do there? What went on, exactly? In short, what role did the baths play in Roman social relations?

THE ROMAN BATH

Public bathing was not a prominent feature of Near Eastern culture (Killebrew 1997; note the absence even of an entry for 'baths' in Redford 2001). Prior to the Romans, the practice had flourished among the Greeks, in city baths (called *balaneia*) or the washing facilities attached to gymnasia or palaestrae (termed *loutra*). Such places were communal in access and could certainly accommodate complex activities, from strigiling (scraping off oil and dirt with instruments called *strigiles*) to hot-water bathing to sweating in intense heat; some archaic facilities accommodated showers (Tölle-Kastenbein 1990). By the second century BC, the hip bath had become *de rigeur* in most Greek bathing establishments, to the point that it is considered by modern researchers diagnostic of such structures. The hip (or *Sitz*) bath was an individual tub with a raised seat at one end on which the bather sat to have hot water poured over him or her (there is some evidence that sections of Greek hip bath complexes could be reserved for women). In the evolved form of the *balaneion* (such as those identified at Eleusis, Eretria, Olympia, Oeniadae, or the Piraeus) such tubs were arrayed around the inside wall of a chamber, usually a rotunda, so that the bathers would sit in close proximity and would interact socially. But the Greek bathing routine was generally loose and unsystematic, and few Greek baths offered any great variety of bathing options under one roof (Delorme 1960; Ginouvès 1962; Hoffmann 1999). An exception is the unique third-century BC structure in the sanctuary of Asclepius at Gortys in Arcadia, which allowed for hot-water bathing in hip baths and full immersion tubs (features drawn from the traditional *balaneion*), as well as bathing at basins set into the walls and a sweat bath (drawn from the traditional *loutron*; see Ginouvès 1959). How typical such structures were in the Greek world, however, is far from clear. If the confident hand of the architect implies some familiarity with this genre of building, few examples comparable to that at Gortys have been securely identified in the surviving record, although some recently found establishments at Olympia, Thessaloniki, and Pella seem to echo the bathing system used at Gortys (e.g., Sinn et al. 2003; Trümper 2007: 225–74 and 2009). Greek baths in Magna Graecia (e.g., at Megara Hyblaea, Gela, or Syracuse) display some complexity in ground plan, although the functions of the non–hip-bath chambers are less obvious than at Gortys (DeLaine 1989; Broise 1994). We may also note that, to suit their requirements, the Greeks developed rudimentary techniques of underfloor heating (the so-called *hypocaust*) as well as water supply and drainage systems (Nielsen 1985; Manderscheid 2000: 467–84).

What made Roman baths distinctive against this Greek background is less the technology needed to operate them, as one body of scholarly opinion insists (DeLaine 1988: 14–15; Benedum 1967; Nielsen 1985; Wikander 1996; Thébert 2003: 45–122), and more the systematic and complicated nature of the bathing routine they catered to. Roman bathing procedures entailed light exercise in a palaestra (a designated work-out area), followed by progression through a sequence of heated spaces, from cold room (*frigidarium*), to medium-hot room (*cella media* or *tepidarium*), to hot room (*caldarium*). An extra hot room (*laconicum* or *sudatorium*) was optional, as were rooms for special activities, such as massage or strigiling. In some or all of these spaces the bather was invited to participate in true communal bathing, not in individual hip baths on the Greek model, but in shared pools of cold or heated water (called *alvei* or *solia*). The sequence of variously heated spaces and bathing in communal pools are the defining characteristics of the Roman system.

While the origins of such baths have been much disputed and no scholarly consensus has emerged (for recent discussions, see Fagan 2001; Thébert 2003: 45–122), they seem to have been firmly established by approximately 200 BC, when baths of this type are alluded to in the plays of Plautus (most clearly at *Rud.* 382–85); complex Roman baths appear in the archaeological record not long afterward, at places like the Central Baths at Cumae in about 180 BC or the Stabian Baths at Pompeii, around 140–120 BC (Nielsen 1993: 1, 25–36).

The Roman bathing ritual, firmly established by the early second century BC, was therefore complicated. The linear deployment of bathrooms in early facilities purposefully channeled the bather through a set sequence of rooms, from cold to hot, and back out again through the same spaces, which reinforces the systematic nature of the procedures the buildings were designed to accommodate. Later on, when a greater variety of room arrangements was common, the bather was still required to proceed through several activities that combined exercise and strigiling, sweating and cooling in appropriately heated spaces, and immersion in hot, tepid, and cold water (Nielsen 1993: 1, 67–73). It is evident that these procedures, when effected even during a truncated visit, necessitated sustained close contact over a prolonged period with other bathers, most especially in the communal pools, where several bathers wallowed in the same water simultaneously. The inherent sociability of experiencing heated space and/or water with other people has been recognized by other cultures (compare the Islamic *hammam*, the American hot tub, or the Finnish sauna), but rarely has the requirement of sharing both been so methodically allied as in the Roman bathhouse. The ubiquity of the bathhouse from the first century BC well into the Byzantine era therefore marks it as one of the central *loci* of social contact in the Roman world. This is one reason the baths have attracted so much scholarly attention in recent decades (Manderscheid 1988, 2004). Not only are they interesting in architectural, technological, and artistic/decorative terms, their apparent functional mundanity affords us a glimpse at Romans interacting socially in an informal context and in a manner that is rarely appreciable from other circumstances (e.g., Manderscheid 1981; Brödner 1983; Heinz 1983; Pasquinucci 1987; Yegül 1992; Nielsen 1993; Weber 1996; Fagan 1999a; Yegül 2010). It is to this social aspect of the Roman bathing experience that the rest of this essay addresses itself.

The Baths as Loci of Social Intercourse

Given the ubiquity of the Roman bath and its centrality in daily life, the pertinent written sources are abundant. Virtually every genre of Roman literature contains useful information in the form of anecdotes, allusions, and metaphors drawn from the bathing experience. A large body of verse inscriptions praise the pleasures of bathing (Dunbabin 1989: 12–18; Busch 1999). Inscriptions too are plentiful and, of course, there are the remains of the buildings themselves. The main problem is that rarely do these different classes of evidence mesh together neatly, nor is the typicality of any specific datum readily apparent. The audience that Roman literature addressed was already familiar with the baths, so that knowledge of the conditions there, both physical and social, could be assumed by authors. Thus, when confronted with a bath-related story, the modern student usually has to read between the lines to deduce norms from what an author says (or does not say); even with that done, the applicability of deductions to bathing conditions in other times and places remains debatable (Fagan 1999b).

A good example of all this is a tale Cicero spins in the *Pro Caelio*, a forensic speech delivered in April 56 BC on behalf of the young senator M. Caelius Rufus, who stood accused of various heinous crimes, one of which was an attempt to poison a prominent noblewoman, Clodia. As Cicero would have it, Clodia was a prime mover behind the case against Caelius, who had until recently been Clodia's lover (or, at least, one of her lovers). Clodia was a member of the immensely wealthy and powerful Claudian clan, and was the sister of the noxious demagogue P. Clodius Pulcher, himself Cicero's political archenemy. Cicero therefore spends a good portion of his defense of Caelius demonizing Clodia. At one point (Cic. *Cael.* 56–69), he addresses the charge of attempted poisoning in which public baths feature prominently. The prosecution had alleged that Caelius plotted with slaves inside Clodia's household to poison her. Caelius arranged for a friend of his, one P. Licinius, to meet Clodia's slaves and hand over the poison. But the slaves revealed all to Clodia, who craftily ordered the slaves to go along with the plot and to meet Licinius in the Balneae Seniae (the Senian Baths), located somewhere in Rome. She then contracted some of her own friends (*amici*) to lay an ambush in the baths, and to apprehend Licinius as he was handing over the poison. Unfortunately for Clodia, the trap was sprung prematurely, and Licinius escaped with the poison.

Cicero, in addressing these allegations, makes a farce out of the prosecution's scenario, and in doing so he tells us much about the social scene in a set of public baths in mid-first-century BC Rome. The first thing to note is that Cicero names the Senian Baths without any further elaboration. He apparently expected the elite jurymen to recognize the place readily, if not this particular establishment, then at least the genre of facility it represented. He also assumed the jury was sufficiently familiar with conditions inside such a building to follow his demolition of the prosecution's case: he asks such things as how fine young men in street clothes would go unnoticed once they left the vestibule and went inside the baths proper. Moreover, where would they hide—in a bathtub? Cicero (and the jury) knew that a general state of undress prevailed inside the baths (and was unremarkable in itself, requiring no further comment), and that the bathrooms afforded few hiding places outside the communal pool; Cicero, of course, discounts the possibility that the ambushers could conceal themselves in the throng of other bathers. Cicero heaps mockery on the fine young dandies who constituted Clodia's force of spies, but not for their mere presence in the Senian Baths. Rather, he takes them to task for marching on the orders of a woman (Cic. *Cael.* 67). Had public baths been places of ill repute, not usually visited by noble youths like these, Cicero would surely have deployed that ammunition in his comedic fusillade. That he does not is therefore highly significant in reconstructing elite attitudes toward public baths in late republican Rome. Even more significant is this fact: upper-class youths, such as Licinius or Clodia's friends, could apparently be seen at the Senian Baths in close association with Clodia's slaves, without attracting unwanted notice. This fact is central to the prosecution's scenario, and it is readily assumed by Cicero also.

The Ciceronian snapshot of life at the Senian Baths illustrates how instructive an allusive anecdote can be about social attitudes and practice. Public baths are revealed as unremarkable features in Rome's cityscape, familiar both to Cicero and to the elite jury he was addressing; they were venues for social intercourse, where privileged young men might be seen in close association with slaves (or, at least, slaves of the privileged), and so they were places where people of different classes interacted at close quarters. At the same time, however, deducing the wider implications of the story is not absolutely straightforward. For instance, it could be asked, do we know with certainty that access to the Senian Baths was open to all, or was it restricted to the elite (and their servants)? If the latter, perhaps the close communication across classes required by Cicero's tale was not typical of other bathhouses in this era. Whether Clodia's slaves were present as customers or were masquerading as attendants to one of Clodia's friends is also unclear. Indeed, was it normal for slaves in general to use public baths as customers? Was nakedness the norm? Or was some other state of undress habitual? Cicero's evidence, addressed to people clearly familiar with such establishments, understandably leaves such matters as this open, and that makes extrapolating from this specific anecdote to normal bathing practice appear inadvisable. Problems like this dog careful interpretation of much of the literary evidence about bathing culture, since it is so often indirect and evocative rather than straightforward and descriptive.

The best procedure is to avoid getting bogged down in all the possibilities raised by a specific datum, unless there is some good reason to suspect that one or more of these scenarios was indeed the case. So, where the Senian Baths are concerned, there is no explicit reason to suppose that this establishment was somehow special or unusual, or that conditions there differed markedly from those prevailing at comparable bathhouses. Various possibilities are certainly conceivable, but not warranted on the face of it—and other evidence suggests that, for instance, general nakedness and a striking social mix was normative in Roman public baths, if not necessarily in a uniform manner and at every single facility. In fact, there is no evidence, even from graffiti, that baths were formally segregated on a social basis, that is, that certain baths restricted access *de iure* to certain classes of clientele. This is not to say that *de facto* exclusivity could not be effected by various means—location, entrance prices, bouncers at the door, and so forth. It seems a stretch to imagine that the fabulous Baths of Claudius Etruscus in Flavian Rome, praised fulsomely by both Martial (*Ep.* 6. 42) and Statius (*Silv.* 1. 5), would have admitted dirt-encrusted construction workers. But gross social segregation when it came to bathing seems to have been frowned upon. The sheer quantity of allusions to baths and bathing conditions in the surviving record make the silence with regard to separating bathers of different classes striking. Had, for instance, exclusive baths for senators or knights or decurions been standard in Roman cities, surely some indication of that fact would filter through the abundant surviving sources. Yet none does. On a positive note, Valerius Maximus (9. 5 ext. 4) regards it as symptomatic of the *insolentia* of Carthage's rulers that they bathed separately from the general populace, which implies that the opposite was expected of the Roman elite, an expectation echoed in shocking stories of arrogant Roman officials clearing out local baths for their own use (Gel. 10. 3. 1–3) or notices that some emperors bathed with the *populus* (Suet. *Tit.* 8. 2; *HA Had.* 17. 5–7, *Heliogab.* 17. 9, *Alex. Sev.* 42. 1; Merten 1983). The *Digest* defines a man's domicile for tax purposes as the place where he farms, visits the forum, the theater, and the baths (*Dig.* 50. 1. 27. 1). The person the law had in mind was clearly wealthy, the owner of multiple properties in different districts, and it is plainly regarded as normal for such a person to be found in the local bathhouse. This observation is in turn corroborated by Pliny, who, in extolling the virtues of one of his villas, comments that a nearby village (*vicus*) boasted no less than three *balnea meritoria* (baths that charged an entrance fee), which he would use if it were inconvenient to heat his villa's private suite (Plin. *Ep.* 2. 17. 26). The un-self-conscious, casual manner in which Pliny makes this comment is perhaps its single most revealing feature: it was clearly not considered improper among his peers (who made up his readership) for a senator of Pliny's rank to be found in simple, small-town bathhouses of the sort in this village.

In general, the social mix at the baths has long been noted by scholars: as Russell Meiggs (1973: 404) commented, "A visit to the baths was the favourite recreation of almost all classes of society." Examples could be multiplied, but the point is clear. Despite an obsession even with the minutest of status grades, a mass of vignettes, anecdotes, and allusions in ancient writers makes it clear that the baths were frequented by all manner of people from across the social spectrum. To argue, therefore, that the Senian Baths somehow differed from this norm, without any indication given by Cicero that they did, runs counter to the preponderance of other data. Consider this anecdote from the letters of Pliny the Younger (writing in the late first, early second centuries AD). Pliny (*Ep.* 3. 14. 6–8) tells how Larcius Macedo, an ex-slave who had risen to the praetorship, was once visiting a public bath in Rome (which bath is not specified). As he moved about, Macedo had a slave out front, clearing a path through the crowds. This slave had the temerity to touch a Roman knight, who spun around and, in trying to land a blow on the impertinent slave, in fact struck Macedo with such force that he was bowled over. (Macedo was later murdered by his own slaves in his private bathing suite; baths were clearly unlucky places for him, notes Pliny darkly.) This one vignette shows that the baths at Rome were so crowded that a slave was needed to clear the way, and it places a praetorian senator, a knight, and a slave within an arm's length of each other. As with Cicero's tale in the *Pro Caelio*, Pliny assumes the social mix at the baths in a story he tells for other purposes.

A host of comparable evidence locates pretty much the whole gamut of Roman society in the baths, often together, and apparently in close proximity: senators, knights, commoners, governors, provincials, and even slaves (the main material is collected and discussed in Fagan 1999a: 189–206). For instance, inscriptions commemorating the gift of free bathing sometimes specify the different classes of people to whom the gift applied: *coloni* (Roman citizen settlers), *municipes* (non-citizen members of the community), *incolae* (inhabitants of the territory attached to the community), *hospites* (official guests), *adventores* (travelers), and even *servi* and *ancillae* (their slaves and handmaidens) (e.g., CIL I² 1903a = ILS 5671; CIL V 376 = InscrIt 10. 3. 71; CIL XI 4100; CIL XIV 2979 = ILS 5672). Such inscriptions do not indicate that the clientele of the favored baths was habitually restricted to any of these groups; rather, they state quite explicitly that the benefaction of free bathing extended to all these different classes of people. It can be presumed that, first, these classes would normally use the facility, but had to pay, and, second, that during the operation of the benefaction, other classes of people continued to enjoy access, but likewise had to pay. On either interpretation, the range of customers found at the baths is revealing. And, once more, nothing suggests that these bathing facilities were unusually profligate in welcoming bathers from so many status grades. Most inscriptions recording gifts of free bathing merely note the benefaction or denote the recipients vaguely as 'the people' (*populus*), a category that embraced many classes (see examples in Fagan 1999a: 300–308).

Finally, there are the remains of the buildings themselves, where no indication of social segregation can be found, beyond imprecise inferences drawn from the location of some baths. For instance, the Baths of Caracalla in Rome were sited near lower-class neighborhoods, so it has been suggested that they were intended to serve the lower orders, so as to win them over to the emperor (Heinz 1983: 124). But it can also be noted that these baths stood right outside the Porta Capena, near the Via Appia on a new road that led directly to the nearby Circus Maximus, and in an area of the city that housed camps for the urban cohorts and *vigiles* and has also yielded evidence of at least some elite residences (DeLaine 1997: 13–15). Given all of this, it can just as plausibly be supposed that the facility would have attracted a spectrum of customers from diverse backgrounds, travelers who happened by prominent among them. For the most part, public baths are to be found in the busiest parts of towns: at gates, in or near the forum, on the main streets. At Pompeii, for instance, the old Republican Baths sat just outside the entrance to the Triangular Forum, and so in close proximity to the theater and the odeon; the Stabian Baths occupied the corner of a busy crossroads that led to gates in all four directions; the (unfinished) Central Baths likewise sat on a crossroads; the Forum Baths and (unfinished) Sarno Baths lay adjacent to the Forum; the Suburban Baths were found just outside the Porta Marina and close to the docks; and the Balneum Venerium et Nongentum was in the Praedia Juliae Felicis, near the Amphitheater (Fagan 1999a: 56–68). At Herculaneum, the location of the Forum Baths is self-evident, while the Suburban Baths stood near the docks and a large hotel. At Ostia, one was never more than a few yards from a public bathhouse, and they too clustered at gates, near the forum, and on main roads (Meiggs 1973: 404–20). Locations like these suggest that attracting the widest possible customer base, not catering to restricted classes, was the prime motive in siting public baths.

As to the ground plans, the earliest baths, notes Varro (*Ling. Lat.* 9. 68), had separate bathing wings for men and women, an observation corroborated by archaeology (see, e.g., the Stabian Baths at Pompeii). But this is a gender, not a class, distinction. Later bath designs gave up even this division (although separate facilities, or different bathing hours for men and women, were possible; DeLaine 1992; Yegül 1992: 48–91; Nielsen 1993: 1, 1–118). Lucian's famous description of a fancy bathhouse (*Hipp.* 5) includes a room "larger than is appropriate for a bath, but necessary for the reception of the rich." Such rooms are hard to identify in surviving remains, but they may be referred to in inscriptions as *basilicae (thermarum)* (*CIL* VII 287 = *ILS* 2548, *CIL* XII 4342 = *ILS* 5685). Whatever the case about that, Lucian's comment entails two reasonable deductions. First, for such a room even to exist, less affluent bathers must also have been present, otherwise the exclusivity of the reception room would be meaningless. Second, the room seems only to have served the purpose of *receiving* the rich. As the privileged bathers moved from this room through the rest of the facility, they would have mingled with the establishment's common patrons. Once more, the social mix and close proximity of bathers from different classes appears to have been the norm. Before assessing the social meaning of this circumstance, we should briefly address what, besides bathing, went on inside the Roman bathhouse.

WHAT WENT ON?

It must be said that, on the issue of what the Romans got up to inside their baths, the sources are less informative (presumably because everyone knew this sort of thing already). A passage very often cited in this connection is the famous complaint by Seneca (*Ep.* 56. 1–2) about the noises emanating from a bathhouse, over which he had an apartment. Seneca, like any upstanding Roman of substance, was keen to devote his leisure time to worthwhile literary pursuits, but the cacophony from below thwarted his best efforts: the huffing and puffing of those exercising, the slap and crack of the masseur's hand, the shouting out of ball-game scores, the pitiless bathroom singer, the splash of the wallower, the tumult attending the arrest of a thief, the cries of the depilator outstripped only by the yelps of his customer-victims, and the calls of the food stand snack sellers. It is a lively aural tableau, evocative of the varied and vibrant atmosphere that must have been common to most public baths.

For more specific information, useful material is provided by the novelists and satirists, such as Petronius, Apuleius, Martial, and Juvenal. While the fictive or satiric nature of these works adds extra layers of difficulty to the interpretation of their evidence, to enjoy any traction, novels and satire must connect to the familiar. The satirist may lampoon and exaggerate, but he lampoons and exaggerates a recognizable reality. That, in fact, is the whole point of the endeavor. The novelist tells a gripping tale that embellishes and distorts, but to have any impact such distortions must be rooted in a context shared by novelist and audience alike. For these reasons, despite the difficulties of interpretation, the content of satire and fiction affords us a unique ground-level view of Roman society, and so provides invaluable insights into all sorts of matters of interest to the social historian (Saller 1980; Millar 1981; note also my essay on violence in this volume). What they tell us about the baths is no exception.

Since optimal bathing hours fell during the early to mid-afternoon (sources collected and discussed by Nielsen 1993: 1, 135–38), it was normal for the bath to precede the main evening meal (*cena*). This had the social consequence of dinner parties convening at nearby public baths (Martial favored the Baths of Stephanus near his house, *Ep.* 11. 52. 1–4) or emerging spontaneously from a meeting of friends at the bathhouse (Anonymous, *Life of Aesop* 38–41). When the heroes of Petronius' *Satyricon* first encounter the gauche freedman Trimalchio, whose *cena* forms the main event of the surviving text, it is in a bathhouse, where the host is meeting his guests and playing ball games (Petr. 26–28). The bath, in fact, was practically an *hors d'oeuvre* to the dinner that followed, and this gave rise to a delicious situation, ripe for satire. Martial parodies the deeply unpopular aspiring dinner-guest Menogenes, a man shunned by polite society and a friend to no one, who haunts the public baths in a sycophantic grand tour to secure himself a place on someone's— anyone's—dinner couch (Mart. 12. 82; cp. 1. 23, 1. 59, 2. 14, 5. 44). Echoes are found in Plutarch, when he evinces the predicament of the 'shadow,' the man invited to someone else's dinner party by one of the guests. The unfortunate 'shadow' cannot go to the party directly without his sponsor, but he likewise does not wish to act as that sponsor's attendant at the baths beforehand (Plut. *Mor.* 707E). The custom of bathing before the evening meal was thus both rife with social etiquette and mined with potentially embarrassing situations.[1]

Graffiti from Herculaneum suggest other pleasures available at the baths: "Apelles, chamberlain of the emperor, and Dexter had lunch here most pleasantly— and fucked at the same time," reads a graffito scribbled on the walls of the Suburban Baths at Herculaneum (*CIL* IV 10677). Another vigorous visit is recorded in this note: "Two companions were here and, since they had a thoroughly terrible attendant called Epaphroditus, threw him out onto the street not a moment too soon. They then spent 105½ sesterces most agreeably when they fucked" (*CIL* IV 10675). We know from other sources that prostitutes could be found at the baths (e.g., Amm. Marc. 28. 4. 9; *Dig.* 3. 2. 4. 2), and since both of the graffiti just mentioned (and others, no more refined) were found in the same little room in this establishment, it may reasonably be supposed that it served as a bath-based brothel. We must not over-emphasize the prevalence of sex at the baths, and certainly not on the dubious testimony of bathroom-wall graffiti; but, for some bathers, at least, it does seem to have been on the agenda (see also McGinn in this volume).

---

1. With regard to dining, see the essay in this volume by Dunbabin and Slater.

A famous epitaph from Rome celebrates 'baths, wine, and sex' as the essence of life (*CIL* VI 15258 = *ILS* 8157), which adds another entry to the roster of potential pastimes in the bath—drinking. Martial comments on Aper, a stern critic of bathroom topers when he was indigent but now, having come into some money, a fellow who cannot leave the baths sober (*Ep.* 12. 70). Trimalchio at the baths is surrounded by slaves who drink wine and squabble (Petr. 28), and moralizers liked to rail at drinkers in the tubs (Sen. *Ep.* 122. 6; Pliny *Nat.* 14. 140). But as with sex, none of this can be taken too literally or applied too uniformly. If some bathers over-indulged, that does not transform public baths into Roman drunk tanks.

Entertainments could be staged in the baths, as mosaics of athletic contests from some facilities make clear. Beginning with the Baths of Trajan (opened in AD 109), the outside enclosure (*peribolos*) of the imperial baths in Rome included rows of viewing benches. Famous mosaics from the Baths of Caracalla (completed in AD 217) depict professional athletes, some clutching the palm frond of victory, and suggest what was viewed from these stands (Blake 1940: 111–12; Insalaco 1989; Newby 2005: 67–78). Evidence for libraries at baths is a little ambiguous, but the possibility is real that forms of recreation beyond the corporeal were also on offer (Nielsen 1993: 1, 165–66; Houston 1996).

The baths were thus leisure palaces just as much as (if not more than) they were places to get clean. Again, regional and temporal variation should be borne in mind here, so that all of these activities were not necessarily practiced or offered in every facility. The sources, partial and patchy as they are, allow only a generalized impression of the sorts of non-bathing activities the baths had to offer.

THE ROLE OF THE PUBLIC BATHHOUSE IN ROMAN SOCIETY

All in all, the baths positively hummed with social activity. That said, the precise degree of inter-class mingling in the bathhouse is not a matter directly commented on by the sources. What little we do hear tends to the lewd or off-putting. The satirists, unsurprisingly, like to linger on sexual themes, such as the bather Laecania, who liked to bring along a well-endowed attendant to wash her in the pools; she might like to adjourn and enjoy his attributes in private, suggests Martial (*Ep.* 7.35). The story of Larcius Macedo incurring a powerful blow while making his way through the crowds is echoed in other notices of people struck inside the bath (Sen. *Dial.* 4. 32. 2; Lib. *Or.* 1. 21; Galen *Meth. Med.* 10. 2 = 10. 672 K). Tensions appear to have run a little high in the confines of the pools and bathing spaces, especially at peek hours of operation. Nevertheless, the social mix at the baths and the physical proximity of the customers in informal and crowded conditions make the atmosphere there appear remarkably free of the constraints often imposed on the interactions of Roman status groups. So it is understandable that scholars have often interpreted the baths as places where the normal rules of social engagement were relaxed, if not put into full abeyance, then at least greatly attenuated. On this view the baths represented a 'democratic' or egalitarian element in the otherwise stiflingly oppressive Roman class system or, as one as one author puts it, they were "a hole in the ozone layer of the social hierarchy" (Toner 1995: 57; see also, e.g., Dyson 1992: 174, Stambaugh 1988: 205, Yegül 1992: 32).

The apparent prevailing nakedness of the bathers adds further weight to this interpretation. Although the Latin word *nudus* denotes as state of improper dress as well as outright nakedness, a variety of vignettes do suggest that Roman bathers went completely naked; satirists in particular comment cruelly and explicitly on the physical features, or failings, of their fellow bathers (e.g., Cic. *Cael.* 62; Mart. 1. 23, 3. 3, 3. 51, 3. 68, 3. 72, 6. 93; Ov. *Fast.* 4. 133–64; Plut. *Cato Maj.* 20. 8; Sen. *Ep.* 122. 6). It seems from such allusions that nakedness was not uncommon. In such conditions the apparent equalizing impact of the public bath would have been strengthened, as it would be hard to avoid the gaze of the critic when stripped down to the skin. "When you wish to inquire into man's true worth, and to know what manner of man he is, look at him when he is naked," writes Seneca (*Ep.* 76. 32). A naked senator looks very much like a naked plebeian. That said, an iron rule of nakedness ought not to be envisioned at the baths (see the interesting comments on Roman attitudes to nudity in Bonfante 1989). Even if it was common to go naked in the baths, that custom could change over time or vary by region, or even by bathhouse within a community. A spectrum of options was probably available to the Roman bather, as seems likely with so many particulars of the bathing habit for which ambiguous or contradictory evidence survives, such as male-female mixed bathing or degrees of ambient luxury (Bowen Ward 1992; Sommer 1996). Variety, it seems likely, was the only constant, so that different bathhouses earned reputations for different virtues or vices. And Seneca, in writing about true worth revealed by nudity, is making a philosophical point about the trappings of estate covering a man's true soul, not a sociological point about the imagined equalizing consequences of nakedness.

Yet even in a context of prevailing nakedness, it is unnecessary to conclude that the social atmosphere was necessarily more egalitarian than it was in various other venues. The Roman upper classes, obsessed with status and the fine distinctions between grades, were not likely to have built, restored, adorned, patronized, and visited public bathhouses if they were places of social tension where their public standing (*dignitas*) risked being sullied or undermined (as argued forcefully by Toner 1995: 53–64). There is little doubt that the conditions in the bathhouse placed particular demands on the status-minded, but there was no shortage of ways to declare rank. For instance, important bathers arrived in style, trailed by a retinue of servants and dependents. Ammianus Marcellinus (28. 4. 8–9) reports retinues of fifty following late imperial aristocrats into the baths of Rome. An arrival like that would leave few doubts about relative status. Lucian, as we have noted, comments on a special reception hall reserved to the rich. And slave retinues were not left at the entrance, or in the vestibule. They followed their owner into the bathhouse, as clothes guards, water pourers, washers, anointers, masseurs, carriers of towels and instruments, servers of wine and food, and way clearers (Wissemann 1982; Bruun 1993). To bring a personal staff to the bath, while others relied on personnel hired from the facility or on friends, was enough in itself to shout status from the bathtubs. Fine accoutrements (*instrumenta balnei*) also separated the quality from the *hoi polloi*, as would be clear when finely perfumed unguents were poured from delicate vials (Juv. 7. 129–31), or skin was scraped with silver strigils (*Dig.* 34. 2. 40. 1) and dried with fluffy woolen (rather than rough linen) towels, or when the finest wines were dispensed into gold or silver goblets (Petr. 28). Multiple changes of clothes and jewelry, as well as bearing and accent, also made social distinctions clear.

When Martial confronts us with the indigent bather putting on airs at the bath, his raggedy clothes carried by ratty servants and his body anointed by a single drop of oil, we get to the point of it all (Mart. 12. 70). The baths were places to be seen, and how one was seen in the Roman world all but determined social rank. Public appearance and status were practically synonymous. Against this backdrop, far from being 'democratic' or leveling in their social spirit, the baths provided yet another stage for the establishment of rank and were arguably the primary vehicle for its daily display. Thus can Juvenal (7. 129–31) mock the aspirant who risks bankruptcy by keeping up appearances at the baths—a situation that makes little sense in a supposedly egalitarian bathhouse. The heroes of the *Satyricon* recognize the stranger Trimalchio instantly by the way he appears to them in the bath (Petr. 28), and Clement of Alexandria could identify affluent women in the baths on sight (*Paid.* 3. 31. 1–33. 3). The Mishnah (*m. Maks.* 2: 5) assumes that "a gentile of high estate" will be readily recognizable in the baths. Social distinctions were not masked in the bath; they were emphasized. The social message of the baths, in fact, was probably particularly raw. Even here, in an environment of prevailing nakedness, or at least undress, social distinctions nevertheless persisted. The rich Roman bather was, in effect, saying that he was better than the rest, even when unclothed.

We must use our imaginations to envision what transpired when Pliny the Younger showed up unannounced at one of the three *balnea meritoria* in the *vicus* near his Laurentine villa. Here, a consular and a senator, a local magnate, would hardly have 'mucked in' with the locals on an equal footing. He would certainly not have contemplated going to such places if they were theaters of social ambiguity where his *dignitas* risked being tarnished. It is far more likely that when Pliny appeared, space was cleared. Lesser souls moved aside (or were shunted aside?) and enjoyed the show of the great man in their midst, in all his bathing finery. Inscriptions record the construction (or repair) of a town's bathhouse by the *domi nobiles*, the local elite. These inscriptions would be prominently displayed on the buildings themselves, or on the bases of honorific statues of the benefactor set up in the forum or some other notable spot in town (Fagan 1999a: 128–75). Such benefactors would be well known locally, and their families undoubtedly enjoyed trans-generational recognition. The baths they had built could be named after them (e.g., *AE* 1961, 109 = *SupplItal* 3, 144–445, no. 8). One can imagine what transpired when such people made an appearance at the facility they were responsible for, what deference was displayed, and what stage management took place.

Pliny (*Ep.* 9. 15) complains of being swamped by petitioners when he visited one of his rural estates. The magnate at his ablutions may have presented an ideal opportunity to bring a petition or approach for a favor (compare Suet. *Ves.* 21), but the interaction would not have been conducted as if between equals, and the appropriate distinctions were meticulously maintained. Visiting the baths was folded into the daily routine of elite Romans, who would move from the forum in the morning, to the baths in the afternoon, and on to dinner in the evening, all the while trailed by slaves, dependents, and hangers-on. The purpose of this routine was to be seen in public as an important person, and the baths played their role in the daily pageant. The visit to the baths marked the transition from relatively open accessibility in the forum to more limited accessibility at the dinner party, which was populated by invited guests only. This circumstance is what gave rise to the parasites who sought to break into the more exclusive social context of the dinner by fishing for invitations (part of the joke on these wretches is that, as their quest took them to the finer and then to the lesser baths of Rome, the quality of their potential dining experience, and the eminence of their hosts, declined in proportion). As transitional social spaces, the baths would engender a certain amount of informal or even relaxed mingling with the lower orders, but it was surely not open and unrestricted, 'egalitarian' and 'democratic.' The confines of the bath may have been more crowded (at least in the non-imperial facilities) than in the open piazzas of the forum, but personal attendants could always keep undesirables at bay and, if necessary, mild violence would discourage or punish unwanted contact.

In sum, public baths were places where Romans gathered regularly in close proximity, but they did not do so in a spirit of equality across class lines. Bathers were not physically distinguished from each other by class in the manner of, say, audiences at spectacles (Rawson 1987) or diners at public banquets (Dunbabin 2003: 72–102; Donahue 2004); but that does not imply that they mixed and mingled as equals at the baths, or even that an ethos of egalitarianism informed bathing culture (in fact, no evidence for such an ethos exists). The baths stressed solidarity within a Roman community by admitting everyone, but the differing ways the bathers conduced their ablutions and interacted with each other ensured that everyone knew his place. The younger Pliny once raised the possibility that the gradations of class and rank might be abolished, only to conclude aghast that "nothing is more unequal than the resulting equality" (*Ep.* 9. 5. 3). He is unlikely to have thought differently when soaking in the tubs of one of the *balnea meritoria* down the road from his Laurentine villa.

SUGGESTED READING

Fundamental are general treatments of baths: see Krencker et al. 1929, Yegül 1992, and Nielsen 1993. These works center around architectural and technological issues and are lavishly illustrated. For a consideration of socio-historical matters and pertinent epigraphy, see Fagan 1999a. More focused works can be readily traced via DeLaine 1988 and in Manderscheid's eminently useful bibliographies (1988, 2004).

BIBLIOGRAPHY

Benedum, J. 1967. "Die Balnea Pensilia des Asklepiades von Prusa." *Gesnerus* 24: 93–107.

Blake, M. E. 1940. "Mosaics of the Late Empire in Rome and Vicinity." *Memoirs of the American Academy in Rome* 13: 81–130.

Bonfante, L. 1989. "Nudity as Costume in Ancient Art." *American Journal of Archaeology* 93: 543–70.

Bosman, A. V. A. J. 1999. "Possible Baths at the Fort of Velsen I: A Provisional Interpretation." In J. DeLaine and D. E. Johnston (eds.), *Roman Baths and Bathing*. Portsmouth, R.I.: Journal of Roman Archaeology. 2, 245–50.

Bowen Ward, R. 1992. "Women in Roman Baths." *Harvard Theological Review* 85: 125–47.

Brödner, E. 1983. *Die römischen Thermen und das antike Badewesen: Eine kulturhistorische Betrachtung*. Darmstadt: Wissenschaftliche Buchgesellschaft.

Broise, H. 1994. "La practique du bain chaud par immersion en Sicile et dans la péninsule italique à l'époque hellénistique." *Xenia Antiqua* 3: 17–32.

Bruun, Ch. 1993. "*Lotores*: Roman Bath-Attendants." *Zeitschrift für Papyrologie und Epigraphik* 98: 222–28.

Busch, S. 1999. Versus Balnearum: *Die antike Dichtung über Bäder und Baden im römischen Reich*. Stuttgart: Franz Steiner Verlag.

DeLaine, J. 1988. "Recent Research on Roman Baths." *Journal of Roman Archaeology* 1: 11–32.

———. 1989. "Some Observations on the Transition from Greek to Roman Baths in Hellenistic Sicily." *Mediterranean Archaeology* 2: 111–25.

———. 1992. "New Models, Old Modes: Continuity and Change in the Design of Public Baths." In H-J. Schalles, H. von Hesberg, and P. Zanker (eds.), *Die römische Stadt im 2. Jahrhundert n. Chr.: Der Funktionswandel des öffentlichen Raumes*. Bonn: Rudolf Habelt Verlag. 257–75.

———. 1997. *The Baths of Caracalla: A Study in the Design, Construction, and Economics of Large-Scale Building Projects in Imperial Rome*. Portsmouth, R.I.: Journal of Roman Archaeology.

Delorme, J. 1960. *Gymnasion: Étude sur les monuments consacrés à l'éducation en Grèce*. Paris: de Boccard.

Donahue, J. F. 2004. *The Roman Community at Table during the Principate*. Ann Arbor: University of Michigan Press.

Dunbabin, K. M. D. 1989. "*Baiarum Grata Voluptas*: Pleasures and Dangers of the Baths." *Papers of the British School in Rome* 57: 6–46.

———. 2003. *The Roman Banquet: Images of Conviviality*. Cambridge: Cambridge University Press.

Dyson, S. L. 1992. *Community and Society in Roman Italy*. Baltimore: Johns Hopkins University Press.

Fagan, G. G. 1999a. *Bathing in Public in the Roman World*. Ann Arbor: University of Michigan Press.

———. 1999b. "Interpreting the Evidence: Did Slaves Bathe at the Baths?" In D. E. Johnston and J. DeLaine (eds.), *Roman Baths and Bathing*. Portsmouth, R.I.: Journal of Roman Archaeology. 1, 25–34.

———. 2000. "Hygienic Conditions in Roman Baths." In G. C. M. Jansen (ed.), *Cura Aquarum in Sicilia*. Leuven: Peeters. 281–87.

———. 2001. "The Genesis of the Roman Public Bath: Recent Approaches and Future Directions." *American Journal of Archaeology* 105: 403–26.

Ginouvès, R. 1959. *L'établissement thermal de Gortys d'Arcadie*. Paris: J. Vrin.

———. 1962. *Balaneutikè: Recherches sur le bain dans l'antiquité grecque*. Paris: de Boccard.

Heinz, W. 1983. *Römische Thermen: Badewesen und Badeluxus im Römischen Reich*. Munich: Hirmer Verlag.

Hoffmann, M. 1999. *Griechische Bäder*. Munich: tuduv-Verlagsgesellschaft.

Houston, G. W. 1996. "Onesimus the Librarian." *Zeitschrift für Papyrologie und Epigraphik* 114: 205–8.

Insalaco, A. 1989. "I mosaici degli atleti dalle Terme di Caracalla: Una nuova indagine." *Archeologia Classica* 41: 293–327.

Killebrew, A. 1997. "Baths." In E.M. Meyers (ed.), *The Oxford Encyclopedia of Archaeology in the Near East*. Oxford: Oxford University Press. 1, 283–85.

Krencker, D., E. Krüger, H. Lehmann, and H. Wachtler. 1929. *Die trierer Kaiserthermen*. Augsburg: Filser.

Lafon, X. 1991. "Les bain privés dans l'Italie romaine au IIe siècle av. J.-C." In *Les thermes romains. Actes de la table ronde organisée par l'École française de Rome, Rome 1988*. Rome: École française de Rome. 97–114.

Manderscheid, H. 1981. *Die Skulpturenausstattung der kaiserzeitlichen Thermenanlagen*. Berlin: Mann.

———. 1988. *Bibliographie zum römischen Badewesen unter besonderer Berücksichtigung der öffentlichen Thermen*. Munich: DB Drucken.

———. 2000. "The Water Management of Greek and Roman Baths." In Ö. Wikander (ed.), *Handbook of Ancient Water Technology*. Leiden: E. J. Brill. 467–535.

———. 2004. *Ancient Baths and Bathing: A Bibliography for the Years 1988–2001*. Portsmouth, R.I.: Journal of Roman Archaeology.

Meiggs, R. 1973. *Roman Ostia*. 2nd ed. Oxford: Clarendon Press.

Merten, E. W. 1983. *Bäder und Badegepflogenheiten in der Darstellung der* Historia Augusta. Bonn: Rudolf Habelt Verlag.

Millar, F. 1981. "The World of the Golden Ass." *Journal of Roman Studies* 71: 63–75.

Newby, Z. 2005. *Greek Athletics in the Roman World: Victory and Virtue*. Oxford: Oxford University Press.

Nielsen, I. 1985. "Considerazioni sulle primi fasi dell'evoluzion dell'edificio termale romano." *Analecta Romana* 14: 81–112.

———. 1993. *Thermae et Balnea: The Architecture and Cultural History of Roman Public Baths*. 2nd ed. 2 vols. Århus: Århus University Press.

Pasqinucci, M. 1987. *Terme romane e vita quotidiana*. Modena: F. C. Panin Editore.

Rawson, E. 1987. "*Discrimina Ordinum*: The *Lex Julia Theatralis*." *Papers of the British School in Rome* 55: 83–114 (= E. Rawson (ed.), *Roman Culture and Society*. Oxford: Clarendon Press 1991. 508–45).

Redford, D. B. (ed.) 2001. *The Oxford Encyclopedia of Ancient Egypt*. 3 vols. Oxford: Oxford University Press.

Saller, R. P. 1980. "Anecdotes as Evidence for Roman Imperial History." *Greece & Rome* 27: 69–83.

Sinn, U., C. Leypold, and Chr. Schauer. 2003. "Olympia: Eine Spitzenstellung nicht nur im Sport. Eine neuentdeckte Badeanlage der hellenistischen Zeit." *Antike Welt* 34: 617–23.

Sommer, C. S. 1996. "Waren Frauen in der Römerzeit schmutziger als Männer? Überlegungen zur Eintrittspreisgestaltung in römischen Thermen." *Fundberichte aus Baden-Württemberg* 2: 301–6.

Stambaugh, J. E. 1988. *The Ancient Roman City*. Baltimore: Johns Hopkins University Press.

Thébert, Y. 2003. *Thermes romains d'Afrique du Nord et leur contexte méditerranéen: Études d'histoire et d'archéologie*. Rome: École française de Rome.

Tölle-Kastenbein, R. 1990. "Duschen in archaischer Zeit." *Schriftenreihe der Frontinus-Gesellschaft* 14: 191–201.

Toner, J. P. 1995. *Leisure and Ancient Rome*. Cambridge: Polity Press.

Trümper, M. 2007. *Die "Agora des Italiens" in Delos: Baugeschichte, Architektur, Ausstattung und Funktion einer späthellenistischen Porticus-Anlage*. Rahden/Westfalen: Verlag Marie Leidorf.

———. 2009. "Complex Public Bath Buildings of the Hellenistic Period: A Case-Study in Regional Differences." In M.-F. Boussac, T. Fournet, and B. Redon (eds.), *Le bain collectif en Égypte. Études urbaines* 7: 139–79.

Weber, M. 1996. *Antike Badekultur*. Munich: Verlag C. H. Beck.

Wikander, Ö. 1996. "Senators and Equites VI: Caius Sergius Orata and the Invention of the Hypocaust." *Opuscula Romana* 20: 177–82.

Wissemann, M. 1982. "Das Personal des antiken römischen Bades." *Glotta* 62: 80–89.

Yegül, F. 1992. *Baths and Bathing in Classical Antiquity*. Cambridge, Mass.: MIT Press.

———. 2010. *Bathing in the Roman World*. Cambridge: Cambridge University Press.

PART V

MODES OF INTERPERSONAL RELATIONS

CHAPTER 18

ROMAN HONOR

J. E. LENDON

INTRODUCTION

"Vengeance, fathers! Vengeance, brothers! Vengeance, husbands!" Thus the Roman professor of rhetoric, his eyes a-bulge with counterfeit rage, offering an approved sentiment to his well-fed students. His theme—*The Man Who Raped Two Girls*—was one of those contrived moral puzzles so beloved of Roman declaimers. Both of the rapist's two victims claim their rights under the imaginary law governing this topic: the one demands to marry the rapist; the other demands his death. What is to be done? The professor calls for death: "He was getting ready for a third rape, but he ran out of night!"

Such a theme takes us from the cool white porticos of our imagined Rome to the shouting streets of a Mediterranean village. And the collective contributions of Roman declaimers on this theme are an eerie tutorial upon the conceptions of honor and shame we associate with Mediterranean village life. "On the next day there was weeping in the girl's house, as the mother bewailed her lost hopes." Will killing the rapist avenge both girls, or will it further insult the one who wants to marry him? Was the girl demanding marriage even raped, or is she just a conniving slut? And the girl who wants the rapist to die: is she—the tramp!—just jealous that he did not confine his attentions to her?[1]

My thanks to Elizabeth Meyer, Garrett Fagan, and the editor of the volume. Remaining errors are mine alone.

1. Sen. *Contr.* 1. 5, quoted 1. 5. 1. The declaimers are Porcius Latro (*Vindicate patres, vindicate fratres, vindicate mariti* = the first quotation), and Mento. There is considerable literature on the relationship between declamation and Roman values, traceable through Corbeill 2007. Similarly hard-edged honor-and-shame themes are rehearsed in fable, Bloomer 1997: 73–109, and in the *Sententiae* of Publilius Syrus, on which Morgan 2007: 95–96, 197.

Since the 1960s, ethnographers and anthropologists have systematically described the conceptions of honor and shame that prevail—or did until recently—around the Mediterranean littoral.[2] The self-image of the man of honor consists chiefly of what he imagines his community thinks of him.[3] He feels shame at, and dreads, anything that detracts from that public perception; thus his sense of shame operates as his main social control, enforcing exacting codes of behavior. He regards the public's perception of him as unstable and in need of protection, and so he reacts strongly to any perceived attack upon his honor, taking revenge for it. The particular vulnerability of his honor (the most acute potential source of his shame) lies in the sexual purity of the women under his protection—his wife, his daughters—and he is quick to avenge threats to their virtue for the sake of his honor.

That ancient Greeks had a sense of honor similar to that frequently found in the modern Mediterranean has long been understood,[4] and countless Roman moments—like rehearsing *The Man Who Raped Two Women* in the schoolroom—show that the Romans did so as well, even down to the common metaphors of stains to honor and billy goats for cuckolds.[5] It is easy to staff the whole opera of Mediterranean honor and shame from Latin writings.[6] The Mediterranean honor model has proved useful for understanding the emotions Romans express in their literature, and so helps us to interpret that literature, as well as Roman manners,

2. For a concise history of the concept of Mediterranean honor, see C. S. Stewart 2001; the literature is conveniently gathered by Horden and Purcell 2000: 489–523, who also intervene in the arid dispute over whether a shared culture of honor and shame can be regarded as giving a sociological unity to the Mediterranean region, ignored here: we are interested in commonalities (which have been amply demonstrated) for purposes of comparison, not whether all Mediterranean peoples share such a culture (they do not) nor whether similar cultures of honor exist outside that region (they do). For Rome, the most important contribution to the anthropological literature is Pitt-Rivers 1966 (cf. Evans Grubbs 1995: 212; McGinn 1998: 12), because, unlike later authors who concentrated on the honor of humble persons, Pitt-Rivers contrasted plebeian and aristocratic forms of honor—and in Rome it is mostly the honor of high persons that is visible to us. The study of European upper-class honor has been the province of historians rather than anthropologists: see esp. Neuschel 1989, Muir 1993, and McAleer 1994. Wyatt-Brown 2002 surveys historical writings about honor.

3. F. H. Stewart 1994: 12–14 collects definitions of honor.

4. And subject to ferocious controversy, which can be traced through Fisher 2000, Herman 2006, Brüggenbrock 2006, and McHardy 2008. The main ground for debate is the lack of pervasive violence arising from Greek honor, something Greek honor shares with Roman (see below).

5. For stains, *OLD s.v. inquino, maculo*, with Pitt-Rivers 1966: 35. Goats, e.g., Catul. 37. 5 with Blok 2001.

6. Cohen 1991. Newbold 2001a and 2001b gathers the vocabulary of revenge in Tacitus, Suetonius, Ammianus Marcellinus, and the *Historia Augusta*, showing what a pervasive theme revenge is in Latin historical writing.

customs, and law.[7] Mediterranean honor has also been called in repeatedly to explain the social background of the New Testament.[8] But at the same time the honor of the social strata we see most clearly (the upper classes of the late republic and the early Roman Empire) *differs* in many respects from what the norms of Mediterranean honor and shame would lead us to expect.[9] And understanding the distinctiveness of Roman honor, and the reasons for that distinctiveness, is if anything more useful for understanding the actions and institutions of the Romans.

ROMAN HONOR AS MEDITERRANEAN HONOR: REVENGE

"You will compel me…to have a mind for my own dignity [*dignitas*]," says Cicero. "No-one ever brought the tiniest suspicion on me whom I did not overturn and wreck" (Cic. *Sul.* 46). Although philosophers might complain about it, Romans expected to take revenge for insults.[10] Seneca defines the very emotion of anger as "the lust to avenge insult," and clemency as not taking vengeance when one can.[11] To Cicero, the law of nature consists of six elements. One of them, ranked alongside piety to the gods and parents, is the duty of vengeance.[12] We see this duty of revenge in particular in the way the Roman law authorized men to deal with the sexual misconduct of their wives and daughters: the Augustan Adultery Law of 18 or 17 BC allowed (under limited circumstances) the private killing of daughters and their lovers, and of the lovers of wives. In the second century BC the killing of adulterous wives had also been accepted.[13]

7. Emotions, Barton 2001; and also for the words Romans used to describe their sense of shame, Kaster 2005. Manners, customs, and law: see, e.g., Saller 1994: 133–53 on Roman horror of being struck; Kneppe 1994: 315–26 on élite manners and dress; Wlosok 1980: 160–65 on the censorship; Evans Grubbs 1989 on the law of abduction marriage; Evans Grubbs 1995: 321–30 on Constantine's marriage legislation; McGinn 1998 on the law of prostitution; Corbeill 1996: 65–68 on *cognomina*; van Hooff 1990 and Hill 2004 on suicide.

8. Lawrence 2003 and Jewett 2003 gather the considerable literature; add now Hellerman 2005.

9. For what can be known about the honor of less exalted persons, see Lendon 1997: 95–103 and Barton 2001: 11–14.

10. For revenge among the Romans, Thomas 1984, Flaig 2003, and Rivière 2006; for the philosophical critique, Harris 2001: 201–28; also Hahn in this volume.

11. Anger, Lactantius, *de Ira Dei* 17, quoting a lost passage of Sen. *de Ira*, alluded to at 1. 3. 1. Clemency, Sen. *Clem.* 2. 3. 1.

12. *De Inv.* 2. 66, *vindicatio*; cf. *Top.* 90.

13. For the law, Cantarella 1991, and for the honor-and-shame ethical background, Cohen 1991.

Outside the household, the normal venue of revenge for upper-class Romans was lit-igation, for a victory in court was honorable to the victor and shaming to the defeated:[14]

> [my client, Publius Quinctius] begs you that that reputation [*existimatio*], that honor [*honestas*] which he brought into your court...he be allowed to carry away again from this place; that he whose dutifulness [*officium*] no one ever doubted may not in the sixtieth year be branded with shame [*dedecor*], disgrace [*macula*; lit. "spot, stain"] and the basest ignominy [*turpissima ignominia*]; that Sextus Naevius [his opponent] not abuse my client's honorable distinctions [*ornamenta*] as spoils of victory; that you allow my client to carry that reputation [*existimatio*] which he has borne into his old age, even to his grave.[15]

Not only will Quinctius lose honor if he loses the case, but his prosecutor, Naevius, is conceived as carrying Quinctius' honor away as spoil to enjoy himself. And not only one's own matters of honor were pursued in court: it was a duty of *pietas* for a young man to prosecute his father's enemies—even more so, his father's murderer.[16] Marcus Cotta, on the very day he assumed the *toga virilis* (a transition to manhood made at around age fourteen) prosecuted the man who had convicted his father (Val. Max. 5. 4. 4). Such prosecutions were a characteristic Roman behavior: "it is also said that Cato [the Censor], meeting a young man passing through the forum after a case at law in which he had secured a verdict of loss of citizenship against an enemy of his dead father, greeted the youth and said, '*these* are the things we must sacrifice to our ancestors: not lambs and baby goats, but the tears and condemna-tions of their enemies.'"[17]

The Roman law of *iniuria*, insult, was expansive, and evokes a very touchy sense of honor: action for insult lay not only against those who insulted oneself, but also against those who insulted anyone "under our power," including slaves or children; or those who were "objects of our affection," that is, wives or daughters-in-law; or the corpse of a man who had made one his heir (Ulpian *Dig.* 47. 10. 1. 3–6). Beatings, shouted abuse, and written libels naturally constituted insults, but so did house-break-ing (although a case could not be brought by a man residing temporarily in a brothel), taking action—like sealing up his house—that implied a solvent debtor would not pay, preventing a man from fishing, taking a victim's son into a low cook-shop, or contumeliously blowing smoke at those living in higher apartments.[18] Appropriately,

---

14. For honor in Roman courts, Kelly 1976; Meyer 2006: 171–74. On the atmosphere generally in Roman courts, see also Bablitz in this volume.

15. Cic. *Quinct.* 99, a particularly interesting case because it takes the form of a *sponsio*, see below.

16. Luzzatto 1934; Thomas 1984: 69, 74.

17. Plu. *Cato Maj.* 15. 3; cf. Plu. *Luc.* 1. 1–2. On hereditary vengeances pursued in court, David 1983; Epstein 1987: 43.

18. Beating and shouting, Ulpian *Dig.* 47. 10. 1. 1–2; writings, Ulpian *Dig.* 47. 10. 5. 9–10; housebreaking, Ulpian *Dig.* 47. 10. 5. *pr.*; debtor, Ulpian *Dig.* 47. 10. 15. 32–33; Modestinus *Dig.* 47. 10. 20; fishing, Ulpian *Dig.* 47. 10. 13. 7; cookshop, Paulus *Dig.* 47. 10. 26; smoke, Javolenus *Dig.* 47. 10. 44. On the law, Smith 1951; Daube 1951; Pólay 1986.

the punishment of those convicted of insult under the *Lex Cornelia de iniuriis* (as well as for other crimes) was *infamia*, 'infamy,' a legally defined state of disgrace that might deprive one of certain legal rights and ranked one with gladiators, whores, and actors: those with no honor because they had no sense of shame.[19] Insults that did not rise to the level of *iniuria* might be repelled by a *sponsio*, a type of action at law reserved for questions of honor: a litigant offered a wager on a statement, "that I am a better man than you," for example, or "that the Carthaginian fleet was defeated under my (rather than your) command," and challenged his opponent to take up the challenge. If the opponent did, then a judge decided between them; if he demurred, he was deemed to be admitting that his opponent's position was the true one. Thus when Cicero insultingly accused Piso of having crept into Rome by the Caelimontane gate upon his return from a disgraceful governorship, Piso promptly responded with the *sponsio*, "That I entered by the Esquiline Gate," and Cicero could not respond.[20]

Failing access to or success in court, all the *iniuriae* (insults) against which the law inveighed could be mobilized for purposes of revenge. From their distant past the Romans inherited ritualized shaming behavior, *occentatio*, singing abusive songs at the house door, and *flagitatio*, shouting one's grievance in public in the presence of the person to be shamed. House doors might be pelted with stones, rude ditties posted, or accusing writings circulated.[21] Like the pot-banging Mediterranean *charivari* in its many forms, shaming by a community could be organized and elaborate: a whole town in first-century AD Gaul once subjected a senator of Rome to a mock funeral, complete with facetious groaning and lamentations. Or an individual could simply follow the man to be shamed around, silent, but dressed in mourning.[22] In extreme cases the characteristic Roman institution of revenge suicide could be resorted to- suicide calculated and organized to bring obloquy upon its target, a measure especially employed to shame misbehaving emperors.[23] Insult bred insult in return, and the two parties might descend into a state of long-term mutual abuse, *inimicitia* (enemyship), punctuated, where opportunity offered, by legal or political attacks.[24] These were the methods employed by élite Romans who could not command armies. But if the very strong felt that their honor could not be defended within the institutions of the city because those institutions were commanded by their enemies, they might resort to civil war. The rebel Catiline wrote to a friend that he was

---

19. On *infamia*, Greenidge 1894; Kaser 1956; Gardner 1993: 110–54. Gladiators and prostitutes are treated in this volume: Leppin and McGinn.

20. Quoted, Gel. 14. 2. 21 (paraphrasing slightly); Val. Max. 2. 8. 2; Cic. *Pis.* 55. On the *sponsio*: Crook 1976; Churchill 2000.

21. Usener 1900; Fraenkel 1961; Manfredini 1979; Veyne 1983. For catalogues of Roman forms of abuse, Richlin 1983: 81–104; Peachin 2001: 140–41.

22. Mock funeral, Tac. *Hist.* 4. 45. Follow in mourning, Sen. *Contr.* 10. 1; Ulpian *Dig.* 47. 10. 15. 27 with Lintott 1968: 16–20.

23. Grisé 1982: 88–89; Plass 1995: 81–134; Hill 2004: 207–12; Edwards 2007: 113–43.

24. On *inimicitia* arising from insult, Epstein 1987: 34–38, carried on by insult, 76.

stirred up by insults and slights, because, robbed of the fruit of my labor and zeal
I could not obtain a position of honor [*dignitas*]...It is not that I could not pay
my debts...but rather that I saw unworthy men honored with office [*non dignos
homines honore honestatos*] and myself an outcast by false suspicion. For this
reason, honorable enough [*satis honestas*] in my situation, I have followed my
present course in the hope of preserving what honor [*dignitas*] I have left.[25]

This might seem a quixotic pose, a bizarre motivation for beginning a rebellion, had
not Sulla likewise justified his march on Rome in terms of revenge (App. *Civ.* 1. 77),
and had Julius Caesar not defended in eerily similar terms his decision to cross the
Rubicon and take up arms against Pompey and the senate.

Caesar summoned his soldiers to assembly. He reminded them of all the insults
[*iniuriae*] his enemies had inflicted upon him at any time, and complained that
those enemies had corrupted Pompey and led him astray because of Pompey's
envy and detraction of Caesar's glory [*laus*]; Caesar, on the other hand, had
always supported and aided Pompey's honor [*honor*] and dignity [*dignitas*]....He
exhorts them...to defend the honor [*existimatio*] and dignity [*dignitas*] of their
commander from his enemies.[26]

Evidently Caesar assumed an audience for his work on the *Civil War*—in which
he made this claim—sympathetic to his claim that he needed to take revenge on
those who had insulted him, as his soldiers had been when he addressed them.
And the similar motivation of Augustus, in avenging the murder of his adoptive
father Julius Caesar, was memorialized in his vast temple to Mars the Avenger (*Mars
Ultor*), whose titanic ruins can still be seen in Rome, and which he vowed during the
war of Philippi against Brutus and Cassius.[27]

Revenge not only played its role in creating the Roman principate, it also posed
a perennial threat to Roman emperors.[28] Caligula's strange and monstrous conduct
was not itself enough to get him killed. Rather, his murderer, the tribune of the
guard Cassius Chaerea, was moved to kill him because the emperor

was accustomed to abuse him with every kind of insult as soft and effeminate,
although he was quite advanced in age, and when he asked for the watchword the
emperor would give him "Priapus" or "Venus," and when he offered his hand to
kiss—when Chaerea was thanking him for some reason—he gestured and moved
it in an obscene fashion.[29]

Caracalla died for the same reason, and Nero thwarted a conspiracy that included
members, including the poet Lucan, who were driven to plot against him by his
insults to them.[30]

25. Sal. *Cat.* 35. 3–4 (trans. draws from Rolfe).
26. Caes. *Civ.* 1. 7 (trans. draws on Peskett), with Strasburger 1953: 243–44.
27. Suet. *Aug.* 29. 2 for the vow; see Amiotti 1998.
28. Lendon 1997: 13.
29. Suet. *Gaius* 56. 2; see also Dio 59. 29. 2; Jos. *AJ* 19. 21, 29–32.
30. Caracalla: Herod. 4. 12. 1–2, 4. 13. 1–2, 5. 1. 3. Nero, the Pisonian conspiracy: Tac. *Ann.*
15. 48–51; Suet. *Vit. Luc.*

At Roman revenge's most elevated level, the Roman state itself sought in foreign war revenge against insult. As the Greeks did their cities, so Romans regarded Rome anthropomorphically, as a gigantic person; thus Rome, like a person, had honor, and slights against that honor had to be avenged. In 107 BC, the tribe of the Helvetii had defeated a Roman army. When Julius Caesar commanded a Roman army in Gaul fifty years later, he was eager "to exact in war punishment for the old *iniuriae* of the Helvetii to the Roman people," and when the Helvetii tried to push into Roman territory in southern Gaul, he sensed another *iniuria*, and made war upon them.[31] Catching one canton of the Helvetii isolated from the rest by a river, he slaughtered them, remarking with satisfaction,

> This canton had in the memory of our fathers marched out alone and slain the consul L. Cassius, and sent his army under the yoke. Thus whether by chance or the judgment of the immoral gods, that part of the Helvetian community that had inflicted so striking a calamity on the Roman people was the first to pay the penalty. By this event Caesar avenged [*ultus est*] not only public *iniuriae*, but private as well, because the grandfather of his father-in-law L. Piso, the legate L. Piso, the Tigurini had slain in the same battle as L. Cassius.[32]

From Rome's semi-mythic early days—from the war against Tarentum, undertaken (the Romans said) because a Tarentine shat upon the toga of a Roman envoy—through the wars with Carthage, the republic's wars in the East, and on into the wars of the Roman Empire in both East and West, revenge was always powerful in directing Roman arms.[33]

DISTINCTIVE QUALITIES OF ROMAN HONOR

Lack of Violence

But where are the Roman Capulets and Montagues? Where is the day-to-day violence over honor in the streets of the city? What about dueling, and blood feud, and slights on the street avenged in blood?[34]

---

31. Defeated, Caes. *Gal.* 1. 7, old *iniuriae*, quoted 1. 30, new *iniuria*, 1. 14.

32. Caes. *Gal.* 1. 12. That Caesar could claim, presumably not expecting the claim to inspire mockery, to avenge the killing of his wife's great-grandfather, indicates at what a distant relationship revenge could still be regarded as being due. But this is, so far as I know, a unique case.

33. Tarentum, Dion. Hal. 19. 5; App. *Samn.* 7. 2; for revenge in Roman foreign affairs, Mattern 1999: 185–94, 216–22.

34. This puzzle goes back to Treggiari 1991: 313; cf. McGinn, 1998: 12–14. On the lack of feuding in Roman society, see also Fagan in this volume.

"I serve as good a man as you."

"No better."

"Yes, better, sir."

"You lie!"

"Draw, if you be men!"

Most honor societies know violence like this, and violence over honor was an acute public order problem in the cities of the Italian Renaissance—and at many Southern U.S. universities until the Civil War. "The ultimate vindication of honour lies in physical violence," writes the anthropologist, on evidence both ethnographic and historical, from all social levels, from many centuries and many countries.[35] But at Rome such violence, if it existed at all, was not a phenomenon large enough for contemporaries to remark upon. Romans went unarmed in their cities. Seneca's *de Constantia*, *de Ira*, and *de Clementia* largely concern the ethics of honor and vengeance, but even he, eager to present revenge in the worst possible light, does not associate vengeance with violence.[36] Killing those who insult you, as one of Seneca's imaginary interlocutors admits, is largely a satisfaction confined to the imagination (Sen. *Ira* 3. 43. 3–4). And where insult did occasionally elicit violence in Roman society—Nero's father once gouged out an equestrian's eye for abusing him—the violence is signaled out as inappropriate, even bizarre.[37] In most honor societies there is more talk of killing for honor than there is of actual violence: a discontinuity exists between society's standards as expressed and as lived in practice.[38] But Rome stands out because even at the level of talk, offenses to honor between men—even violent ones—were not usually expected to elicit violence in return.[39] Had it been otherwise, a master of invective like Cicero would hardly have made it

35. Pitt-Rivers 1966: 29.

36. For exceptions, Sen. *Ira* 1. 1. 1–2 (temporary madness), *Clem.* 1. 7. 4 (humble persons).

37. Suet. *Nero* 5. 1; similarly bizarre was having one's retainers beat an insolent peasant to death, Gel. 10. 3. 5–6; cf. Philostr. *VS* 2. 10 (587–8).

38. F. H. Stewart 1994: 115–18, 123–24.

39. To Barton 2001: 18, "[t]he suppression of the vendetta depended above all on the self-mastery (*decorum, disciplina, modestia, temperantia*) and the sense of honor (*pudor, fides*) of the inhabitants, quickened by a fear of losing face and a dizzy horror of disgrace"; and to Harris 2001: 14, 201–28, 401–8 it depended upon a powerful ideology of anger control (and see Hahn in this volume for the contribution of philosophical education to this ideology), explanations both of which are good as far as they go, but which fail to explain the exceptional quality of Greek and Roman avoidance of violence over honor. Why does (in Barton's theory) honor prevent violence at Rome, where elsewhere it requires violence? Whence anger control? F. H. Stewart 1994: 67–68 proposes that Greek and Roman honor was not "reflexive," that is, it lacked the rule that "if A impugns B's honor, then B's honor is *ipso facto* diminished or destroyed, unless B responds with an appropriate counterattack on A" (64), but Stewart is wrong (see Cic. *Inv.* 2. 86; Sen. *Ira* 2. 33. 1; *Clem.* 1. 7. 3; Publilius Syrus 99, 231, 240, 285, 645 (Friedrich); cf. for Greece Arist. *NE* 1126a), although the diminution might be a small one because of the texture of Roman honor (see below). Some reaction was required: but not a violent one. That's the puzzle.

alive out of his teens. Roman dinner parties, the special home of witty abuse, would have ended in bloodshed. Nor, if insult had led to wounding and death, could the Roman culture of gorgeous literary slander—Catullus, Horace, Juvenal, Persius, Martial—have burgeoned.[40]

Within the household, as the rhetorician's cry for vengeance suggests, violence over honor was at least imaginable. Killing of adulterous wives and daughters and their lovers occurred in fact: imperial rescripts refer to actual cases.[41] Valerius Maximus does as well, in his collection of *exempla* for the use of orators. In his pages, exemplary of severity to unchastity is Pontius Aufidianus, who, upon discovering that a slave of his had debauched his daughter, slew both daughter and slave.[42] But if so unextravagant an instance ranks as an *exemplum*, can such killing have been very usual? In fact, the more one looks into the historical evidence (which records countless cases of unchastity), the less killing one encounters: in the late republic and early empire morals were easy at the top of society, and if adultery had demanded killing, there would have been a general slaughter among the aristocracy. No actual instances of a husband killing an adulterous wife or her lover are known in the literary record of this era. Indeed, by this period of Roman history the adultery of aristocratic wives tended to result not in murder, but in divorce, when it was not simply tolerated.[43] And the divorcing husband of a proved adulteress was entitled to an additional increment of merely one twenty-fourth of her dowry as compensation.[44] The centrality of the chastity of wives and daughters to male honor has been taken as the defining quality of Mediterranean honor: "[t]hroughout the Mediterranean area, male honor derives from the struggle to maintain intact the shame of kinswomen; and this renders male reputation insecurely dependent upon female sexual conduct." This describes the legendary world of Lucretia and Verginia, and the fantasy world of the declaimers; it does not describe Roman aristocratic values of the late republic and empire.[45] By then the honor of men and women, at least of the aristocracy, had become to a great degree independent of each other, and the

40. For abuse at Roman dinners, Peachin 2001.

41. Rescripts, Marcus Aurelius in Macer *Dig.* 48. 5. 33[32]. *pr.*, Marcus Aurelius and Pius in Papinian *Dig.* 48. 5. 39[38]. 8, *CJ* 9. 9. 4 (Alexander Severus); *Coll.* 4. 6 (Severus and Caracalla in Paulus).

42. Val. Max. 6. 1. 3; also 6. 1. 6.

43. Treggiari 1991: 275; cf. Evans Grubbs 1995: 212–13; Edwards 1993: 54–56. Related is the strange (from a comparative perspective) upper-class Roman lack of anxiety about the legitimacy of their children, Edwards 1993: 49–50.

44. Hallett 1984: 236–39.

45. Quoted, Gilmore 1987a: 4. It cannot be stated with certainty whether the tales of blood revenge in archaic Rome reflect real practices or later imagination, but the survival of vengeance vocabulary (*ulcisci* "to take revenge," *vindicare* "to avenge") in Classical Latin and in legal parlance (e.g., *vindex* "avenger" for legal representative) (see Thomas 1984: 68) may imply that such violence was historical and that Rome had made a historical transition away from it. It may also be significant that the Twelve Tables made slander a capital offence (Cic. *Rep.* 4. 12).

honor of women no longer a fragile treasure at the center of male honor, but separate and structurally similar to male honor.[46] The honor of women was not confined to their chastity, but they too took pride in glorious lineage, wealth, and worthy deeds.[47] The honor of aristocratic women and men relates less like that of man and wife or father and daughter in the Mediterranean tradition, and more like that of Roman brothers—concerned for each others' reputation, which has an impact on their own, but fundamentally independent entities in the world of honor.[48]

The measures on killing adulterers in Augustus' adultery law confirm the picture of a society in which such killing was extremely rare. The *Lex Julia* was directed at the discouragement and punishment of adultery. It made adultery a publicly punishable offense, and it endeavored to compel husbands to divorce adulterous wives—if they failed to do so, they could be prosecuted for pimping. In this context we naturally expect the strongest reinforcement of husbands' and fathers' rights to deal sternly with adultery themselves. Nor should we imagine that the avenger of Julius Caesar, the builder of the temple of Mars Ultor, had set himself against vengeance in principle. Yet in fact, the right of husbands and fathers to kill adulterers was constrained by so many conditions in the *Lex Julia* as to render it almost purely theoretical. A father could kill his daughter and her lover only if (1) he was *sui iuris* and she was still under his power, and (2) he caught her in the very act of adulterous sexual intercourse, in his house or her husband's, fell upon the lovers immediately, and killed both of them.[49] A husband could not kill his wife.[50] He could kill her lover only if he caught his wife and the adulterer in the act, in his own house, and the lover belonged to a degraded social category, was a slave, one of their freedman, a pimp, an actor, or similar (Macer *Dig.* 48. 5. 25(24). *pr.*).

46. Treggiari 1991: 311–13. For lack of concern about women's chastity in a modern aristocracy much concerned with honor, Pitt-Rivers 1966: 64–71. For parallels to the tendency toward disentanglement of men's and women's honor, Davis 1987: 26; Gilmore 1987b: 98–100.

47. Women's honor, see esp. *ILS* 8393 = Wistrand 1976; Tac. *Ann.* 13. 45. Although not indispensable to the honor of élite women, chastity remained important as a positive distinction, Barton 2001: 37–38; Langlands 2006: 37–77. Honor from acts, e.g., Plin. *Ep.* 3. 16, 6. 24. Cf. Pitt-Rivers 1966: 71, "women of high birth are accorded on that account a right to the kind of pride which is a male attribute, an element of masculine honour."

48. Wives share in husbands' honor, Apul. *Met.* 2. 3; *HA Aelius* 5. 11. Husbands in wives', Tac. *Agric.* 6; male relations in a woman's honor, Cic. *Rosc. Am.* 147. This independence is confirmed by the imperial juristic writing on insult (*Dig.* 47. 10): no special category of insult to wives and daughters is envisioned; the jurists are not terribly interested in it, compared, for example, to their fascination with insults to, through, and by slaves. Women may sue in their own right if insulted, Ulpian *Dig.* 47. 10. 1. 9; Paulus *Dig.* 47. 10. 18. 2; but note that wives may not sue if their husbands are insulted, Paulus *Dig.* 47. 10. 2.

49. Summarizing Treggiari 1991: 282–3.

50. Whether the husband lost this power under the *Lex Julia* (Cantarella 1991: 231–32) or never in theory had it (Treggiari 1991: 265–74) is disputed and uninteresting, since it is clear from Cato (Gel. 10. 23. 5) that it was not expected that any effective sanction would be applied to the murdering husband, whatever the law.

Why all the limitations? Evidently despite Augustus' severe purpose—his intention (as he describes his moral legislation in his *Res Gestae*) "to restore many exemplary practices of our ancestors now fallen into disuse"—vengeance killing had become so exotic by the Augustan Age that it could hardly be contemplated at all.[51] All Augustus could do to stem the rising tide of laxity was to carve out a narrow exception for the bouts of uncontrollable rage—what we might call temporary insanity—brought on by actually coming upon adulterers in the act. His was a society that had come to countenance blood revenge only as a dish that had to be eaten unbearably hot.

Among the Romans, a people with a strong sense of honor and a lively conception of revenge, insults between men were not expected to end in violence and did not do so in fact. Where the chastity of women was involved, violence was imagined (confirming the membership of the Romans in the wider culture of Mediterranean honor) but lethal violence rarely occurred in fact, and had come to be understood by Augustus' day as a form of temporary loss of mental control—far from the deliberate, cold planning of blood vengeance.[52] And where violence over honor did occur, it seems to have had limited social ramifications—no extended violent feuds between families, no Hatfields and McCoys. Oddly, Romans were prepared to launch civil wars to defend their honor, and foreign wars to defend that of Rome, but were not prepared to strike their next-door neighbors.

A Culture of Invective

A Roman peculiarity related to the lack of violence over honor at Rome was the Roman tolerance of hearty and enthusiastic verbal abuse in the public sphere—in politics and especially in the law courts.[53] With every appearance of pride Cicero reports on an exchange of invective—he calls it an ἀγών, a contest—with his *bête noir* Clodius on the very floor of the Roman Senate (I paraphrase freely): "You were at a hot-spring! (you decadent swine)." "Is that like saying I snuck into the mysteries (like *you* did)?" Ha ha! "What does a rube from Arpinum know about hot water?" Ha ha! "You bought a house! (you fat bastard)." "But you bought a jury!" Ha ha! "The jurors didn't trust what you said on oath." "To the contrary! Twenty-five trusted me, and thirty-one didn't trust you: they made sure to get their bribe money is advance!" Roars (Cic. *Att.* 1. 16. 10). Although the Romans had no concept of parliamentary privilege, there is no sign that remarks like these were prosecuted as *iniuriae*, although *iniuriae* they were emphatically intended to

---

51. *RG* 8. 5. Cf. Treggiari 1991: 293, "I lean rather to the view that Augustus was trying to deter potential adulterers by reviving alleged ancient custom."

52. For anger of vengeance as madness, cf. Sen. *Ira* 1. 1.

53. This puzzle goes back to Crook 1967: 254–55; 1976: 136–37; and Kelly 1976: 98–102. Generally, on the culture of invective at Rome, see Corbeill 1996; on invective in Latin literature Koster 1980; for the scholarly interpretation of invective in rhetoric, Powell 2007: 19–20.

be. Nor prosecuted were the astonishing things said about opponents in court—
yokel! greedy-guts! temple-breaker! murderer! pimp! rotten lump of carrion!
swamp vulture!—where the *vituperatio*, the blackening of an opponent's reputation, was a perfectly normal part of litigation, even small-stakes civil litigation.[54]
How could such practices arise and survive in a society where men were tender
about their honor? Who, faced with the prospect of such treatment, would take
someone else to court or enter the senate? Was abuse in politics and the courts
somehow set outside the world of honor?[55] Were remarks made in such special
contexts presumed to have no effect on the honor of the participants? Or did the
audience merely judge the torrent of mutual abuse as a joyful contest between the
orators, dismissing the accusations that made it up as purely rhetorical?[56] But, in
fact, such abuse did have an effect on honor—an orator might restrain himself
in the interests of the *existimatio* of an opponent[57]—as the very existence of the
phenomenon also implies: for if such abuse had no effect on reputation, why
engage in it?[58] And if invective was a competition, why should that particular form
of competition take root in a world where men cared for their reputations? The
great orator Hortensius, something of a dandy, sued a man for *iniuria* for jostling
him and disarranging his toga.[59] But like all other Romans of the ruling class, he
put up with constant *iniuriae* in politics and the courts. Just as with the Roman
reluctance to strike those who insulted them, this is hardly what we expect in a
society preoccupied with honor.

In the private sphere as well—we see it especially in the context of dinner parties (*convivia*)—the Romans appear to have had a very high tolerance for mockery.
Hosts teased guests, guests derided each other, and jesters were hired and sharp-
tongued slaves trained to make fun of the diners.[60] Is the Roman *convivium* another
narrow realm where the laws of honor were suspended? Or can we offer a better
explanation for why the Romans could both value honor and tolerate abuse?

The Masonry of Honor

The anthropologist Julian Pitt-Rivers offered a celebrated distinction between what
he called honor as virtue, "honour which derives from virtuous conduct," and
honor as precedence, "honour which situates an individual socially and determines

54. *Vituperatio*, Kelly 1976: 99–101. For invective in Cicero, Craig 2004, 2007; and the
essays collected in Booth 2007.
55. The implication of Crook 1967: 255.
56. Riggsby 1997: 247–48; adjusted by Craig 2004: 195–96.
57. Kelly 1976: 102, analyzing Cicero's *pro Tullio*; cf. van der Wal 2007 on the *pro
Murena*.
58. Corbeill 1996: 5 and Powell 2007: 3 are right in taking seriously the intended impact
of such abuse on the target's honor.
59. Macrob. *Sat.* 3. 13. 5.
60. Peachin 2001: 137–39.

his right to precedence."[61] This second variety of honor, of which elevated Romans especially partook, necessarily admits gradations in quantity, gradations that define social rank. But what especially characterizes the Roman outlook is the tendency to view such honor as a stable commodity, an objective, concrete possession, capable of being added to or subtracted from in small quantities, granted by one person (or honorable entity, for not only persons possessed honor) to another, imported from outside the circle of rivals for honor, and hoarded over the generations. This curious solidity of Roman honor is alluded to in Aulus Gellius' approving paraphrase of Theophrastus:

> A small and minor shame [turpitudo] or disgrace [infamia] should be undergone if by so-doing a great benefit be obtained for a friend. For the slight loss incurred to damaged honor [honestas] is repaid and compensated for by the greater and profounder honor [honestas] that inheres in helping a friend. And the small blemish or hole, as it were, in one's reputation [fama] is shored up by the fortification formed by the benefits gained for the friend (1. 3. 23).

Not for the Romans, evidently, the Spanish dictum that "glass and a man's honor shatter at the first blow." To Gellius the first blow, or any number of slight blows, may be willingly accepted, since the walls of honor are easily repaired later. Roman honor is not like glass; it is like masonry: slow to build, and slow to crumble. This was especially true of those at the top of society, who could be indifferent to the opinions of others:

> Those who are eminent from inherent prestige (οἰκείᾳ ἀξιώσει) neither seek signs of approval from anyone, nor, should they be lacking, censure those who failed to provide them, knowing full well that they are not being scorned. On the other hand, those whose grandeur is acquired [Sejanus is meant] seek such things very eagerly, as necessary to fill up their prestige (οἱ δὲ ἐπακτῷ καλλωπίσματι χρώμενοι πάντα ἰσχυρῶς τὰ τοιαῦτα, ὡς καὶ ἐς τὴν τοῦ ἀξιώματός σφων πλήρωσιν ἀναγκαῖα) and should they fail to get them, are as irritated as if they were being slandered, and as peeved as if they were being insulted (Dio 58. 5. 3).

"The inherent prestige" of the true grandee depends chiefly upon the apprehension of his lineage and property. The honor an aristocrat of an ancient family with great estates drew from those sources was incontrovertible; he possessed it whatever an individual might say, and could afford to be relatively indifferent to insult.[62]

---

61. Pitt-Rivers 1966, quoted 36, cf. 23–24, 50–55, 62–71. But "no man of honour ever admits that his honour = precedence is not synonymous with his honour = virtue. To do so would be to admit himself dishonoured. For him there is only one concept, his honour" (37). F. H. Stewart 1994: 54–63 makes the same distinction between "vertical" and "horizontal" honor, and of types of the former singles out especially "rank honor" and "competitive honor." The seeming lack of common ground between conceptions of honor constitutes part of Herzfeld's 1980: 341–42 objection to the vagueness of the term 'honor.'

62. Cf. Pitt-Rivers 1966: 62, the "social position" of an upper-class Andalusian "is a matter of birth and wealth, and is therefore, in a sense, impregnable to gossip." On Roman methods for keeping lineage and the glories of ancestors in the public eye, Flower 1996; Rawson 1990.

Those whose honor was not unassailable were more anxious to protect it, more anxious to avoid slander and insult and humiliation. But the relative solidity of Roman aristocratic honor means that it was not amenable to catastrophic loss.[63] We can see this because behaviors associated with such permanent loss in other societies are not common at Rome: Romans sometimes committed suicide at the prospect of shame—after a conviction in court or loss of a battle—but much less when the shame they feared had actually come upon them, when they had been sent into exile or captured.[64] Nor did Romans, when humiliated, usually withdraw permanently from society in the manner of the emperor Tiberius on Capri.[65] The greatest humiliation of Cicero's career was his exile, and his expressions of mortification in his letters are moving and authentic: "Nothing is more wretched, more vile, more unworthy of us than this. I am prostrated by shame as well as misery."[66] But although in his shame he "cannot abide crowds, flees the company of men, and can hardly bear to look upon the light" (and even contemplates suicide), he intrigues relentlessly for his recall, and when it happens, it never strikes him not to return, not to retake his place in society and politics with his honor, he says, completely restored.[67] Cicero's honor had been "obscured" as he put it (*Red. Pop.* 4), not blotted out for good. The honor of Roman aristocrats seems to have been nearly impossible to exterminate entirely, and always amenable to repair.[68] This durable quality of Roman honor helps to explain the Roman custom of attacking the tombs and mutilating the cadavers of the dead (guarded against in so many Roman epitaphs) and the post-mortem shaming of the executed: the destruction of their houses, and most famously, *damnatio memoriae*, the destruction of their statues and removal of their names

63. Although it could be imagined to be so, e.g., Sen. *Clem.* 1. 22. 1, *nemo dignitati perditae parcit* (nobody is sparing of honor when it has been lost); cf. Publilius Syrus 520 (Friedrich); but see Cic. *ad Fam.* 4. 7. 2, *victi sumus igitur; aut, si vinci dignitas non potest, fracti certe et abiecti* (and so we are defeated; but if honor cannot be defeated, then certainly we are broken, and cast down): men can be broken, but not *dignitas*.

64. Grisé 1982, collecting suicides after conviction or defeat 62–67 (and, of course, not only dishonor was anticipated by the convicted and defeated) and from actual shame at 67–68; cf. Hill 2004: 197–202; van Hooff 1990: 107–20. Van Hooff (85) attributes to shame or its expectation 32% of the 923 Greek and Roman suicides whose motives are commented on in the sources.

65. There are enough instances to show that Tiberius was not unique, but that the practice was not common, Cic. *Sul.* 74, *de Orat.* 2. 249, with Barton 2001: 257–58, 261.

66. Quoted, *ad. Fam.* 14. 3. 2; cf. *ad Att.* 3. 10. 2, 3. 19. 1, 3. 20. 1. For the motif of the shamed being unable to look upon the light, cf. Livy 9. 7. 3 with Barton 2001: 79, 114, 254, who notices that Livy's (imaginary in its details) depiction of the Roman soldiers sent under the yoke at the Caudine Forks (9. 5–7) is a tutorial on Roman shame behavior.

67. Quoted, Cic. *ad Att.* 3. 7. 1. Suicide, Cic. *ad Att.* 3. 3, 3. 7. 2, 3. 26; restored, Cic. *Red. Sen.* 1–2; *Red. Pop.* 4; *Att.* 4. 1. 3.

68. This provides an alternative explanation for the phenomenon studied by Rosenstein 1990, the successful careers of defeated Roman generals. For the reintegration of the shamed into society, cf. Barton 2001: 274.

from public monuments.[69] Not even a shameful death could destroy a Roman's honor—so the process of shaming had to continue after death.

Here, then, we have an appealing explanation—in the peculiar chemistry, as it were, of Roman aristocratic honor—for the lack of violence over Roman honor, and Roman tolerance of abuse in politics and the courts. It is not that insult did a great Roman no harm in his honor—in that case Cicero's invectives would have been a waste of breath—but it did not do much harm. It did not threaten the destruction of his honor; it merely knocked a few bricks off the edifice. And even Romans who had undergone the most profound shame found ways to rebuild their honor. The imperviousness of Roman honor to permanent damage made Rome, like New York, a city of second chances. The future historian Sallust was a turbulent tribune in 52 BC, and was expelled from the Senate in 50. He joined Caesar's faction, participated in the civil war, was praetor in 46, and then Caesar's governor of Africa. There he conducted himself badly, incurred (in Cassius Dio's words) "the most shameful disgrace," was prosecuted upon his return to Rome, and had no future in politics.[70] But rather than stew in mortification, Sallust turned to the writing of history, as an alternative road to honor:

> It is a glorious thing to serve one's country in deeds; but to do so with words is not to be despised. One can become renowned [*clarum fieri*] in both peace and war. Many are praised who act, but also those who have written the acts of others. And although the same amount of glory [*gloria*] hardly attends the writer as the doer of deeds, nonetheless to write about events is extremely arduous.[71]

Despite his previous disgrace, Sallust does not depart the struggle for honor. He simply chooses another method of seeking it. And he succeeded brilliantly: for Sallust's adoptive son, his father's distinction as an historian threw open the gates to the highest offices.[72] As a second-chancer, Sallust finds his parallel under the empire in the poet Silius Italicus, who (Pliny the Younger reports), "damaged his reputation [*fama*] under Nero—it was believed that he accused people willingly—but he conducted his friendship with [the emperor] Vitellius wisely and tactfully, brought back honor [*gloriam reportaverat*] from his proconsulate in Asia, and wiped out the stain to his honor [*macula*] that his previous [political] activity had inflicted, by a praiseworthy leisure"—his verse (Plin. *Ep.* 3. 7. 3).

The masonry of Roman honor was not only amenable to repair, but it could also be built higher.[73] Anthropologists sometimes class honor as a limited good, which, if it can be gained, can be increased only by despoiling competitors for honor

---

69. Tombs and cadavers, Visscher 1963: 139–58; Thomas 1984: 67–68; post-mortem shaming of executed, Mustakallio 1994; Flower 2006.

70. On Sallust's career, Syme 1964: 29–39; quoted, Dio 43. 9. 3.

71. Sal. *Cat.* 3. 1–2 (trans. adapted from Rolfe).

72. Tac. *Ann.* 3. 30; he preferred, however, not to pursue a senatorial career.

73. On the quest for honor, esp. Wiseman 1985.

of it.[74] Although Roman honor could be taken from another and made one's own in court or civil war, no traces of a sense of its ultimately being limited in quantity can be found among the Romans.[75] To the Roman mind, honor could not only be accumulated within the community of the honorable, but also be imported from outside. Thus Silius Italicus' ability to "bring back" glory from Asia.[76] We might well dismiss this as a metaphor gotten out of hand, if the empire's subjects did not take so seriously their role in providing their rulers with honor to cart back to Rome, and if those rulers did not devote themselves so earnestly to gaining provincial honors. The provincials themselves met to vote their governors countless honorific decrees in their cities and provincial councils, and erected thousands of statues to the officials placed over them.

This reveals another aspect of the constitution of Roman honor: it was regarded as divisible into small, durable quanta—'honors' (*decora, honores,* τιμαί…)—and those quanta were granted by one entity that possessed honor (without thereby losing its own) to another, by a process of 'honoring' (*honorare,* τιμάω).[77] This could be done by honorable individuals—one could be "praised by a praiséd man"[78]—with complimentary words, invitations to dinner, flattering letters (the 'signs of approval' Sejanus sought above), by cities, especially with their resolutions and seats of honor and statues, and by corporate bodies of any type: provincial councils, guilds, military units, or the Roman Senate.[79] Regimes of honors are known in many aristocratic states—even now the British crown publishes its 'honours list'—but what sets the Roman Empire apart is the multiplicity of fonts of honor whose honors were valued, and the fact that so many of those fonts were collectivities rather than individuals. If in aristocratic societies honor exists in a tension between ascription by the community at large ('reputation') and by discrete acts of honoring ('distinctions'), the upper classes of the Roman Empire appear to have been attracted to the later understanding of honor to an historically unusual degree.

74. For literature see Gilmore 1987b: 90; the classic statement is Foster 1965: 300–301. Even gloomier is the outlook of the Icelandic sagas, where the amount of honor in the world is declining, Miller 1990: 30.

75. Court, see above n. 16; civil war, Dio 41. 56. 3, the εὔκλεια of the defeated becomes that of the victor. Habinek 2000: 266–77 argues for a historical transition between a zero-sum *gloria* (glory) of the republic, and a non-zero-sum *claritas* (distinction) under the empire.

76. Cf. Plin. *Ep.* 8. 24. 8, *onerat te quaesturae tuae fama, quam ex Bithynia optimam revexisti* (that fame of your quaestorship, which you brought back from Bithynia, is weighing you down). The 'importation' metaphor is used of generals as well, e.g., Livy 3. 3. 10, 3. 10. 1.

77. On the puzzling relationship between honor and honors, Pitt-Rivers 1966: 22–23. F. H. Stewart 1994: 30–31 discards the concept of 'honors' from the study of honor as an accident of English usage, but as a lexical accident shared by Latin, Greek, and many modern languages, an understanding of honor must include it.

78. Symmachus, *Ep.* 9. 110, *laudari ab laudato viro vetus dictum est.*

79. For the honor of corporate bodies, cf. Pitt-Rivers 1966: 35–36, 56–57; for cities and corporate bodies in the empire, Lendon 1997: 73–77; for cities cf. Maupai 2003.

What about the honor of those further down in society? Cicero notes that the orator is to make different kinds of appeals to the lofty and to the low:

> Who pursues honor, glory, praise, and any distinction as keenly as he flees ignominy and discredit and contumely and disgrace? [*quis enim honorem, quis gloriam, quis laudem, quis ullum decus tam umquam expetat quam ignominiam, infamiam, contumeliam, dedecus fugiat?*] ...In addressing well-educated people [i.e., members of the élite] we shall speak most of praise and honor [*de laude et de honestate*]....Whereas if we are speaking to uneducated and ignorant people [i.e., humble persons], profits, rewards, pleasures, and avoidances of pain should be put forward; and ignominy and contumely [*contumeliae atque ignominiae*] should be added, for no one is so rustic that ignominy and contumely [*contumelia...et dedecus*] do not greatly move him, even if honor [*honestas*] itself moves him less.[80]

The honor of the grandee is something that can be sought after, accumulated, piled up. The humble man, by contrast, is considered to be concerned about preserving, not increasing, his honor. Haughty Cicero, peering down from his vast height, does not expect the humble man to seek positive distinction, but merely to react to dishonor, like an amoeba fleeing a tiny prickle: to defend the honor that being a free man conveys in a world of honorless slaves. No matter how low its possessor, that honor is tender. "Demonstrate," Cicero advises the orator, "that the insult (*iniuria*) was such as could not be tolerated not merely by a man of rank, but by any free man at all."[81] The poor man's honor, Cicero implies, is a treasure to be kept, or lost, and arguably not as stable as the honor of the aristocrat.[82] Yet if Cicero's contrast were strictly true, we might expect violence over honor among the humble, of which there is only the most exiguous traces, an absence sufficient to exclude the likelihood of sanguinary Renaissance Verona operating underneath the world of high Romans we are privileged to see clearly.[83] In fact, when we can see the honor of the lowly at work—when they come together to form guilds and associations, for example, which leave inscriptions—the honor of the humble seems to have the same composition as that of the grand, consisting of an accumulation of quanta, of "honors," however small or even ridiculous those might seem to an aristocrat.[84] No glass honor here: humble honor is a brickwork, just like the honor of the lofty. But, alas, we do not see the honor of the Roman humble clearly enough to come to any firm conclusions about its nature.

80. Cic. *Part.* 91–92 (trans. adapted from Rackham).

81. Cic. *Inv.* 2. 84. Rome shares the line between the honorable free and the honorless slave (Saller 1994: 133–53) with other slave societies (esp. Patterson 1982), but such a line exists only in the minds of free men: slaves, of course, are motivated by their own honor, Lendon 1997: 96–97.

82. Cf. Pitt-Rivers 1966: 23–24, 61–63, 72, the rich man has honor-as-precedence, the humble man honor-as-virtue. Among the grand, "[h]onour is a question of class honour and personal precedence rather than sex which dominates the honour of the *pueblo*" (65).

83. But see Sen. *Clem.* 1. 7. 4 for a suggestion that the humble did get into fights over matters of revenge.

84. Lendon 1997: 97–98.

Roman Honor as a Constructive Force

From a comparative perspective, Roman honor was singular in two ways. It was not, under normal conditions, and at any social level, socially disruptive, and it was, at least among the higher classes for whom we have evidence, a fairly stable possession or acquisition.[85] It is appealing to posit that these two singularities are related—that is was the very stability of Roman honor that rendered it comparatively pacific, since Romans did not feel that their whole honor was apt to be lost at a single reproach not energetically repulsed.

These singularities in the Roman conception of honor had, moreover, gigantic consequences in the Roman world. Cicero depicts the Roman man of honor as defensive in his outlook, more anxious to defend his existing honor than to add to it: in this huddling, nervous figure we recognize the archetypal Mediterranean man of honor. But what sets the élite Roman apart from that model is that once his existing honor was established and protected, he went out into the world to make a systematic career out of accumulating more of it. "We are by nature...as zealous and as hungry as possible for honor (*honestas*)...and there is nothing we are not prepared to endure and suffer in order to obtain it."[86] "Honor (*honos*) nourishes the arts, and all men are fired up to zeal by fame (*gloria*)," and we have seen that men of talent could gain honor by cultural pursuits, poetry, history, and above all oratory, the queen of arts under the Roman Empire.[87] Not only was courtroom advocacy highly honorable, but eloquence performed as public entertainment was the most prominent form of high culture, and especially in the Greek East, virtuoso display orators—sophists—were men of prodigious fame (cf. Schmitz in this volume). Honor might also be pursued by the cultivation of a great clientage, and by ostentation in appearance, retinue, and domicile.[88]

Until the first century BC the glory of courage in war had been an indispensable element of Roman honor: it explains in part the army-ant quality that permitted the Romans to triumph over peoples so much richer and more sophisticated than they were. Sallust puts the rise of Roman power in a nut-shell: "once liberty was obtained, the city grew great very quickly, such was the lust for glory [*gloria*] that

---

85. Habinek 2000: 268–72 argues for a transition from a destructive concept of honor under the late republic, manifested in the civil wars, to a non-destructive concept under the empire: I would argue that with the exception of the civil wars (an anomaly), Roman honor was not, by historical standards, socially destructive in any recoverable generation: the problem was not with republican honor, but with republican institutions which had lost their ability to confine honor conflicts within them.

86. Cic. *Tusc.* 2. 58. Lendon 1997: 35; Barton 2001: 37.

87. Quoted, Cic. *Tusc.* 1. 4. Oratory, Plin. *Ep.* 6. 29. 3; history, Herod. 1. 1. 1; poetry, Tac. *Dial.* 5; so similarly a theoretical knowledge of the law, Cic. *Off.* 2. 65; Tac. *Ann.* 3. 75.

88. Tac. *Ann.* 3. 55, and, e.g., Petronius, Tac. *Ann.* 16. 18; Mucianus, Tac. *Hist.* 2. 5. Still in the fourth century, Amm. Marc. 14. 6. 9. On the aristocratic house, Wiseman 1987. Cf. for conspicuous consumption as a contributor to honor in early modern Italy, Burke 1987: 132–49.

possessed them."[89] Under the empire, military command was still highly honorable, and an aristocrat might choose to pursue honor as an officer in the Roman army. But military service was usually slotted into a career of civilian office holding, because in imperial Rome and the cities of the empire the most usual way honor was pursued was by running for office, and significantly the most usual Latin word for a political office is *honor*.[90] "Julius Naso seeks an office [*honores*]. His opponents are both many and worthy. To overcome them is as glorious [*gloriosum*] as it is difficult" (Plin. *Ep.* 6. 6. 1). So strong was this urge for political advancement that offices in the cities of the Roman Empire, rather than being remunerative, were highly expensive, both because of the public generosity expected of candidates, and because of the sums—often formally set out—an office-holder was expected to contribute to his city upon election. For the quest for honor through office was closely entwined with another: the quest for honor through public generosity.[91] A great proportion of the day-to-day expenses of cities under the empire, not to mention great projects like the building of temples and theaters, was met not from tax revenues, but from the contributions of towns' richer inhabitants. Indeed, the cities of the empire could not function without public benefaction; where generosity flagged (or poverty overwhelmed it) the government had to step in to require it. But public benefaction did not arise from governmental fiat; it arose out of the benefactors' desire for the honors their city bestowed upon those benefactors, for praises chanted in the assembly, for statues, monuments, and local offices. It arose, in short, out of élite Romans' competition with one another for honor.[92] Apuleius describes such a benefactor in his *Golden Ass*:

> Thasius…was a native of Corinth, which was the leading city in the entire province of Achaea. As his lineage and honor [*dignitas*] demanded, he had proceeded in order through all the local magistracies and had now been appointed to hold the office of *duumvir quinquennalis* [the highest office in a Roman town]. To repay the town for his appointment, he had munificently promised a three-day gladiatorial show. In his zeal for public glory [*gloria*] he had even traveled to Thessaly to buy the most noble beasts and notorious gladiators.[93]

First Thasius protects his honor by doing what is expected of persons of his lofty rank—holding all the offices in his town. Then he seeks to add to his honor by sponsoring unusually opulent games. It is upon the cumulativeness and durability of Roman honor that so much of what we consider characteristic of Roman civilization is consequent: the relentless spectacles, the great buildings and the public amenities unmatched again in the West until the nineteenth century, so many of them private works erected for the love of honor, with the donor's name in stone-cut letters, man-high.

89. Sal. *Cat.* 7. 3. On the glory of war under the republic, Harris 1979: 17–34.
90. In Greek the most usual word for office is τιμή, which means the same, Lendon 1997: 276. For honor and office, Lendon 1997: 176–94.
91. Lendon 1997: 78–89.
92. In Greek the sentiment that inspires these benefactions is φιλοτιμία, 'honor love.'
93. Apul. *Met.* 10. 18 (trans. adapted from Hanson).

The same drive to accumulate the Roman Empire's curiously substantial honor played its role too in the empire's most striking quality: its stability. Roman rule depended upon the cooperation of the cities of the empire, and of the chief men of each city. An important part of how that cooperation was gained was by the emperor and his governors granting honors to, or withholding honors from, the grandees and cities of the empire. This was a powerful technique:[94]

> When the emperor looked benevolently upon his [Opramoas'] policy, and by the manner of his reply encouraged the other magistrates to the same zeal, and encouraged the man himself to increase his enthusiasm for virtue—for the praise of a mighty emperor can do this, who encourages the spirits of those who strive towards highest reputation, and thus provides for the cities an abundance of good men—then Opromoas, exalted by the divine [imperial] replies, showed his generosity.[95]

At the same time, and no less important to the peace of the provinces, the provincials—who did not, of course, choose their governors—regulated the behavior of those placed over them by conferring honors upon good governors and withholding them from bad.[96] The stern Thrasea Paetus grumped at the power this gave provincials over their rulers: "now we court foreigners, and we flatter them...let false praise and praise elicited by begging be restrained like evildoing or cruelty...The early days of our magistrates are usually better, and they decline when their tenures draw to a close when, just like candidates, we are gathering up votes."[97] One rather suspects that provincials did not share the Stoic saint's suspicion of the best way they had—other than prosecuting the worst offenders—of getting governors to rule in their interests rather than in the governors' own.

CONCLUSION

An upper-class Roman went about with three different codes of honor in his mind. The first was the hot-blooded, fragile honor of the rhetorical schools, where insult and unchastity were avenged with killing. This conception of honor is closest to the anthropologist's understanding of honor in traditional Mediterranean village society. But the Roman knew that the world of the schools was a fantastic Never-Never Land, a world of sister-seizing pirates and virgin-ravishing tyrants. He did not live by the code of the schools: his reaction to insult, or to his daughter's creeping out

---

94. Lendon 1997: 129–68, 201–35; Meyer-Zwiffelhoffer 2002: 307–26.
95. *TAM* 2. 905 ch. 66 = Kokkinia 2000: nr. 67.
96. Lendon 1997: 194–201; Meyer-Zwiffelhoffer 2002: 187–222.
97. Tac. *Ann.* 15. 21 (trans. adapted from Jackson).

at night, was more subdued. Quietly confident that the honor he possessed was, in fact, in no great danger of loss, he guarded it primarily with good manners, and his day-to-day thoughts about honor had to do with increasing it, not merely protecting it. The lived honor of high-placed Romans was therefore not very like traditional Mediterranean honor, or, given the lack of violence over it, to European aristocratic honor before the decline of dueling. It was similar to, and perhaps in part derivative of, the honor of the Classical Greeks. Yet lying between the glass honor of declamation and the building-block honor of daily life was a third honor, the honor Romans aspired to, the honor the Romans wished they had: neither as bloody as the honor of the schools, nor as stolid and acquisitive as the honor of daily life in the forum. This is the honor we see when an orator adduces idealized claims of honor to appeal to a real audience, or when philosophers discuss the rights and wrongs of revenge. When Seneca in his *de Constantia* and *de Ira* argues that the wise man should be indifferent to insult, it is primarily at the vengeful precepts of the honor Romans aspired to, rather than the honor Romans lived, that he aims: in real life insult did not tend to produce the uncontrollable and undignified rage against which he warns. The Romans, in short, felt they should be, or in the case of philosophers, should guard against being, more touchy about matters of honor than they actually were. Accordingly, they often feared that their honor was more fragile than it actually was, dreading the more absolute shame that they imagined patrolled the honor they aspired to. This is suggested by their habit of committing suicide at the prospect of shame, Cicero's extravagant grief at the disgrace of his exile, and by his surprise upon his return that people treated him exactly as they had before he went: "I have obtained to a degree beyond my hopes what I thought it would be the most difficult to recover," he writes to Atticus a few days after his return, "my public distinction, my dignity in the Senate, and my influence among the aristocracy."[98] An élite Roman, moreover, was always tugged some way toward the bloody honor of the schools by the code of honor Romans aspired to, which is why he might go to law over his reputation, or, if he had an army and the courts were closed to him, launch a civil war to defend his honor. And, as a collectivity, Romans operated by the crueler honor they aspired to rather than the honor they lived by in the streets of the city: that is why revenge is a larger theme in Roman foreign relations than in Roman politics, as Carthage and Corinth had cause to rue.

The deepest historical significance of Roman honor lies in how it was lived from day to day, not in the declaimers' honor, nor in the touchier honor Romans wished they had. In some societies, like old Albania, the violence born of honor made government impossible. In others, like Renaissance Venice, a wobbly serenity was achieved by turning all the powers of order against honor: noble violence was severely punished, nobles' insults of one another—likely to lead to violence—were vigorously prosecuted by the state, and the Venetians strictly controlled the forms of aristocratic ostentation, such as armorial insig-

---

98. *Ad Att.* 4.1.3, *splendorem nostrum illum forensem et in senatu auctoritatem et apud viros bonos gratiam.*

nia and large banquets, which touched off fights elsewhere.[99] Elsewhere still, as in Germany before WWI, honor and the state have existed side by side, rarely touching, since approaching the state over a matter of honor was to sacrifice one's honor, given that "appeal to a court of law was interpreted as a groveling confession of assailability and weakness."[100] In other societies yet, like nineteenth-century Corsica, revenge could be sought by violence or through the courts, indifferently.[101] Things were otherwise at Rome. Roman honor, as in Classical Athens, did not usually lead to violence, and disputes over honor were often settled, among the classes we can see, through the institutions of the city state, and especially in court.[102] Rather than the world of honor being opposed to the world of the city, or independent of the world of the city, or parallel to the world of the city, honor lived in the city, and powered the city like an electrical grid, driving men to excel in what the city desired: service to the city, expenditure for the city, and service to the empire. It could do so because Roman honor, rather than being a fragile bauble to be protected, was strong, durable, and amenable to increase by increments—increments that could be granted by the city. Honor is one of history's strong forces, like greed or the lust for power. Opposed to the state, it can thwart the state, destroy the state, or make the state impossible. Independent of the state, it can create a baroque and spectacular world of its own—that of classical Spanish drama, or duelists in the mists of the *Bois de Boulogne*. But placed at the service of the community, honor can create, and preserve, an empire.

SUGGESTED READING

On the subject of Roman honor in general, Lendon 1997 and Barton 2001 offer contrasting treatments, the former a conventional monograph approaching honor historically and investigating its significance in government, the latter a post-modern prose poem evoking the subjective experience of Roman honor and shame, at once fascinating and infuriating. The most systematic attempt to understand Roman values in terms of an anthropological honor model is Cohen 1991. For Roman revenge behavior Thomas 1984 is indispensable.

99. Ruggiero 1980, control of noble violence, 66–68 (noting the fact that the aristocracy still committed a disproportion of crimes of speech and assault), 74; punishment of insults, 69, 126, 131–32, 134. Control of ostentation, Muir 1993: 52, 89–90.

100. Quoted McAleer 1994: 30; cf. Pitt-Rivers 1966: 30; F. H. Stewart 1994: 79–81.

101. Wilson 1988: 265–93.

102. In late antiquity, the terminology of revenge comes conventionally to be used for punishments imposed or threatened by the Roman state, e.g., the "avenging sword" of execution, Rivière 2006: 31–40.

BIBLIOGRAPHY

Amiotti, G. 1998. "Augusto e il culto di Marte Ultore." In M. Sordi (ed.), *Responsabilità perdono e vendetta nel mondo antico*. Milan: Vita e Pensiero. 167–74.

Barton, C. A. 2001. *Roman Honor. The Fire in the Bones*. Berkeley: University of California Press.

Blok, A. 2001. "Mediterranean Totemism: Rams and Billy-Goats." In A. Blok, *Honour and Violence*. Malden, Mass.: Blackwell. 173–209. A revision of "Rams and Billy-Goats: A Key to the Mediterranean Code of Honor." *Man* (n.s.) 16 (1981): 427–40.

Bloomer, W. M. 1997. *Latinity and Literary Society at Rome*. Philadelphia: University of Pennsylvania Press.

Booth, J. (ed.) 2007. *Cicero on the Attack. Invective and Subversion in the Orations and Beyond*. Swansea: Classical Press of Wales.

Brüggenbrock, C. 2006 *Die Ehre in den Zeiten der Demokratie: das Verhältnis von athenischer Polis und Ehre in klassischer Zeit*. Göttingen: Vandenhoeck & Ruprecht.

Burke, P. 1987. *The Historical Anthropology of Early Modern Italy*. Cambridge: Cambridge University Press.

Cantarella, E. 1991. "Homicides of Honor: The Development of Italian Adultery Law over Two Millennia." In D. I. Kertzer and R. P. Saller (eds.), *The Family in Italy from Antiquity to the Present*. New Haven: Yale University Press. 229–44.

Churchill, J. B. 2000. "*Sponsio quae in verba facta est*? Two Lost Speeches and the Formula of the Roman Legal Wager." *Classical Quarterly* 50: 159–69.

Cohen, D. 1991. "The Augustan Law on Adultery: The Social and Cultural Context." In D. I. Kertzer and R. P. Saller (eds.), *The Family in Italy from Antiquity to the Present*. New Haven: Yale University Press. 109–26.

Corbeill, A. 1996. *Controlling Laughter. Political Humor in the Late Roman Republic*. Princeton: Princeton University Press.

———. 2007. "Rhetorical Education and Social Reproduction in the Republic and Early Empire." In W. Dominik and J. Hall (eds.), *A Companion to Roman Rhetoric*. Oxford: Blackwell. 69–82.

Craig, C. 2004. "Audience Expectations, Invective, and Proof." In J. Powell and J. Paterson (eds.), *Cicero the Advocate*. Oxford: Oxford University Press. 187–213.

———. 2007. "Self-Restraint, Invective, and Credibility in Cicero's *First Catilinarian Oration*." *American Journal of Philology* 128: 336–39.

Crook, J. 1967. *Law and Life of Rome*. Ithaca: Cornell University Press.

———. 1976. "*Sponsione Provocare*: Its Place in Roman Litigation." *Journal of Roman Studies* 66: 132–38.

Daube, D. 1951. "*Ne quid infamandi causa fiat*. The Roman Law of Defamation." In G. Moschetti (ed.), *Atti del Congresso Internazionale di Diritto Romano e di Storia del Diritto*. Milan: Giuffrè. 3, 413–50. Reprinted in D. Daube, *Collected Studies in Roman Law*. D. Cohen and D. Simon (eds.). Frankfurt: Vittorio Kloserman. 1991. 1, 465–500.

David, J.-M. 1983. "Sfida o vendetta, minaccia o ricatto: l'accusa pubblica nelle mani dei giovani romani alla fine della repubblica." In E. Pellizer and N. Zorzetti (eds.), *La paura dei padri nella società antica e medievale*. Rome: Laterza. 101–12.

Davis, J. 1987. "Family and State in the Mediterranean." In D. D. Gilmore (ed.), *Honor and Shame and the Unity of the Mediterranean*. Washington: American Anthropological Association. 22–34.

Edwards, C. 1993. *The Politics of Immorality in Ancient Rome*. Cambridge: Cambridge University Press.

———. 2007. *Death in Ancient Rome*. New Haven: Yale University Press.

Epstein, D. F. 1987. *Personal Enmity in Roman Politics, 218–43 BC*. London: Croom Helm.

Evans Grubbs, J. 1989. "Abduction Marriage in Antiquity: A Law of Constantine (*CTh* IX.24.1) and Its Social Context." *Journal of Roman Studies* 79: 59–83.

———. 1995. *Law and Family in Late Antiquity*. Oxford: Clarendon Press.

Fisher, N. R. E. 2000. "Hybris, Revenge and Stasis in the Greek City-States." In H. van Wees (ed.), *War and Violence in Ancient Greece*. London: Duckworth. 83–123.

Flaig, E. 2003. *Ritualisierte Politik. Zeichen, Gesten und Herrschaft im Alten Rom*. Göttingen: Vandenhoeck & Ruprecht.

Flower, H. I. 1996. *Ancestor Masks and Aristocratic Power in Roman Culture*. Oxford: Clarendon Press.

———. 2006. *The Art of Forgetting. Disgrace and Oblivion in Roman Political Culture*. Chapel Hill: University of North Carolina Press.

Foster, G. M. 1965. "Peasant Society and the Image of Limited Good." *American Anthropologist* 67: 293–315.

Fraenkel, E. 1961. "Two Poems of Catullus." *Journal of Roman Studies* 51: 46–53.

Gardner, J. F. 1993. *Being a Roman Citizen*. London: Routledge.

Gilmore, D. D. 1987a. "Introduction: The Shame of Dishonor." In D. D. Gilmore (ed.), *Honor and Shame and the Unity of the Mediterranean*. Washington: American Anthropological Association. 2–21.

———. 1987b. "Honor, Honesty, Shame: Male Status in Contemporary Andalusia." In D. Gilmore (ed.), *Honor and Shame and the Unity of the Mediterranean*. Washington: American Anthropological Association. 90–103.

Greenidge, A. H. J. 1894. Infamia: *Its Place in Roman Public and Private Law*. Oxford: Oxford University Press.

Grisé, Y. 1982. *Le suicide dans la Rome antique*. Paris: Les Belles Lettres.

Habinek, T. 2000. "Seneca's Renown: *Gloria, Claritudo*, and the Replication of the Roman Elite." *Classical Antiquity* 19: 264–303.

Hallett, J. P. 1984. *Fathers and Daughters in Roman Society*. Princeton: Princeton University Press.

Harris, W. V. 1979. *War and Imperialism in Republican Rome, 327–70 BC*. Oxford: Clarendon Press.

———. 2001. *Restraining Rage. The Ideology of Anger Control in Classical Antiquity*. Cambridge, Mass.: Harvard University Press.

Hellerman, J. H. 2005. *Reconstructing Honor in Roman Philippi*. Cambridge: Society for New Testament Studies.

Herman, G. 2006. *Morality and Behaviour in Democratic Athens*. Cambridge: Cambridge University Press.

Herzfeld, M. 1980. "Honour and Shame: Problems in the Comparative Analysis of Moral Systems." *Man* (n.s.) 15: 339–51.

Hill, T. D. 2004. Ambitiosa Mors. *Suicide and Self in Roman Thought and Literature*. London: Routledge.

Horden, P., and N. Purcell. 2000. *The Corrupting Sea*. Oxford: Blackwell.

Jewett, R. 2003. "Paul, Shame, and Honor." In J. P. Sampley (ed.), *Paul in the Greco-Roman World. A Handbook*. Harrisburg: Trinity Press International. 551–74.

Kaser, M. 1956. "*Infamia* und *Ignominia* in den römischen Rechtsquellen." *Zeitschrift der Savigny-Stiftung für Rechtsgeschichte, Romanistische Abteilung* 73: 220–78.

Kaster, R. A. 2005. *Emotion, Restraint, and Community in Ancient Rome*. Oxford: Oxford University Press.

Kelly, J. M. 1976. "'Loss of Face' as a Factor Inhibiting Litigation." In J. M. Kelly, *Studies in the Civil Judicature of the Roman Republic*. Oxford: Oxford University Press. 93–111.

Kneppe, A. 1994. Metus temporum. *Zur Bedeutung von Angst in Politik und Gesellschaft der römischen Kaiserzeit des 1. und 2. Jhdts. n. Chr.* Stuttgart: Franz Steiner Verlag.

Kokkinia, C. 2000. *Die Opramoas-Inschrift von Rhodiapolis*. Bonn: Rudolf Habelt Verlag.

Koster, S. 1980. *Die Invektive in der griechischen und römischen Literatur*. Meisenheim am Glan: Hain.

Langlands, R. 2006. *Sexual Morality in Ancient Rome*. Cambridge: Cambridge University Press.

Lawrence, L. J. 2003. *An Ethnography of the Gospel of Matthew*. Tübingen: Mohr Siebeck.

Lendon, J. E. 1997. *Empire of Honour. The Art of Government in the Roman World*. Oxford: Clarendon Press.

Lintott, A. W. 1968. *Violence in Republican Rome*. Oxford: Oxford University Press.

Luzzato, G. I. 1934. "Sull'obbligo degli eredi di vendicare l'uccusione dell'ereditando." In E. Albertario (ed.), *Studi in memoria di Umberto Ratti*. Milan: Giuffrè. 545–89.

Manfredini, A.D. 1979. *La diffamazione verbale nel diritto romano*. Milan: Giuffrè.

Mattern, S. P. 1999. *Rome and the Enemy. Imperial Strategy in the Principate*. Berkeley: University of California Press.

Maupai, I. 2003. *Die Macht der Schönheit. Untersuchungen zu einem Aspekt des Selbstverständnisses und der Selbstdarstellung griechischer Städte in der Römischen Kaiserzeit*. Bonn: Rudolf Habelt Verlag.

McAleer, K. 1994. *Dueling. The Cult of Honor in Fin-de-Siècle Germany*. Princeton: Princeton University Press.

McGinn, T. A. J. 1998. *Prostitution, Sexuality, and Law in Ancient Rome*. Oxford: Oxford University Press.

McHardy, F. 2008. *Revenge in Athenian Culture*. London: Duckworth.

Meyer, E. A. 2006. "The Justice of the Roman Governor and the Performance of Prestige." In A. Kolb (ed.), *Herrschaftsstrukturen und Herrschaftspraxis*. Berlin: Akademie Verlag. 167–80.

Meyer-Zwiffelhoffer, E. 2002. Πολιτικῶς ἄρχειν. *Zum Regierungsstil der senatorischen Statthalter in den kaiserzeitlichen griechischen Provinzen*. Stuttgart: Franz Steiner Verlag.

Miller, W. I. 1990. *Bloodtaking and Peacemaking: Feud, Law, and Society in Saga Iceland*. Chicago: University of Chicago Press.

Morgan, T. 2007. *Popular Morality in the Early Roman Empire*. Cambridge: Cambridge University Press.

Muir, E. 1993. *Mad Blood Stirring. Vendetta and Factions in Friuli during the Renaissance*. Baltimore: Johns Hopkins University Press.

Mustakallio, K. 1994. *Death and Disgrace. Capital Penalties with* Post-Mortem *Sanctions in Early Roman Historiography*. Helsinki: Suomalainen Tiedeakatemia.

Neuschel, K. B. 1989. *Word of Honor. Interpreting Noble Culture in Sixteenth-Century France*. Ithaca: Cornell University Press.

Newbold, R. 2001a. "Pardon and Revenge in Tacitus and Ammianus." *Electronic Antiquity* 6.

———. 2001b. "Pardon and Revenge in Suetonius and the *Historia Augusta*." *Prudentia* 33: 41–58.

Patterson, O. 1982. *Slavery and Social Death*. Cambridge, Mass.: Harvard University Press.

Peachin, M. 2001. "Friendship and Abuse at the Dinner Table." In M. Peachin (ed.), *Aspects of Friendship in the Graeco-Roman World*. Portsmouth, R.I.: Journal of Roman Archaeology. 135–44.

Pitt-Rivers, J. 1966. "Honor and Social Status." In J. G. Peristiany (ed.), *Honour and Shame: The Values of Mediterranean Society*. Chicago: University of Chicago Press. 21–77.

Plass, P. 1995. *The Game of Death in Ancient Rome: Arena Sport and Political Suicide*. Madison: University of Wisconsin Press.

Pólay, E. 1986. Iniuria *Types in Roman Law*. Trans. J. Szabó. Budapest: Akademiai Kiadó.

Powell, J. G. F. 2007. "Invective and the Orator: Ciceronian Theory and Practice." In J. Booth (ed.), *Cicero on the Attack. Invective and Subversion in the Orations and Beyond*. Swansea: Classical Press of Wales. 1–23.

Rawson, E. 1990. "The Antiquarian Tradition: Spoils and Representations of Foreign Armour." In W. Eder (ed.), *Staat und Staatlichkeit in der frühen römischen Republic*. Stuttgart: Franz Steiner Verlag. 157–73. Reprinted in E. Rawson, *Roman Culture and Society: The Collected Papers of Elizabeth Rawson*. Oxford: Clarendon Press, 1991. 582–98.

Richlin, A. 1983. *The Garden of Priapus. Sexuality and Aggression in Roman Humor*. New Haven: Yale University Press.

Riggsby, A. M. 1997. "Did the Romans Believe in their Verdicts?" *Rhetorica* 15: 235–51.

Rivière, Y. 2006. "Pouvoir impérial et vengeance. De *Mars Ultor* à la *divina vindicta* (Ier-IVe siècle ap. J.-C.)." In D. Barthélemy, F. Bougard, and R. Le Jan (eds.), *La vengeance, 400–1200*. Rome: École française de Rome. 7–42.

Rosenstein, N. 1990. Imperatores Victi. *Military Defeat and Aristocratic Competition in the Middle and Late Republic*. Berkeley: University of California Press.

Ruggiero, G. 1980. *Violence in Early Renaissance Venice*. New Brunswick: Rutgers University Press.

Saller, R. P. 1994. *Patriarchy, Property and Death in the Roman Family*. Cambridge: Cambridge University Press.

Smith, R. E. 1951. "The Law of Libel at Rome." *Classical Quarterly* 1: 169–79.

Stewart, C. S. 2001. "Honor and Shame." In N. J. Smelser and P. B. Baltes (eds.), *International Encyclopedia of the Social and Behavioral Sciences*. New York: Elsevier. 10, 6904–7.

Stewart, F. H. 1994. *Honor*. Chicago: University of Chicago Press.

Strasburger, H. 1953. "Caesar im Urteil seiner Zeitgenossen." *Historische Zeitschrift* 175: 225–64. Reprinted as *Caesar im Urteil seiner Zeitgenossen*. Darmstadt: Wissenschaftliche Buchgesellschaft 1968.

Syme, R. 1964. *Sallust*. Berkeley: University of California Press.

Thomas, Y. 1984. "Se venger au forum. Solidarité familiale et procès criminel à Rome (premier siècle av.—deuxième siècle ap. J.-C.)." In A. Lemaire, C. Malamoud, J. P. Poly, J. Svenbro, and Y. Thomas (eds.), *La vengeance. Études d'ethnologie, d'histoire et de philosophie*. Paris: Editions Cujas. 3, 65–100.

Treggiari, S. 1991. *Roman Marriage. Iusti Coniuges from the Time of Cicero to the Time of Ulpian*. Oxford: Clarendon Press.

Usener, H. 1900. "Italische Volksjustiz." *Rheinisches Museum* 56: 1–28. Reprinted in id., *Kleine Schriften*. Osnabrück: Zeller, 1965. 4, 356–82.

van der Wal, R. L. 2007. "'What a Funny Consul We Have!' Cicero's Dealings with Cato Uticensis and Prominent Friends in Opposition." In J. Booth (ed.), *Cicero on the Attack. Invective and Subversion in the Orations and Beyond*. Swansea: Classical Press of Wales. 183–205.

van Hooff, A. J. L. 1990. *From* Autothanasia *to Suicide. Self-Killing in Classical Antiquity.* London: Routledge.

Veyne, P. 1983. "Le folklore à Rome et les droits de la conscience publique sur la conduite individuelle." *Latomus* 42: 3–30.

Visscher, F. de 1963. *Le droit des tombeaux Romains.* Milan: Giuffrè.

Wilson, S. 1988. *Feuding, Conflict and Banditry in Nineteenth-Century Corsica.* Cambridge: Cambridge University Press.

Wiseman, T. P. 1985. "Competition and Co-operation." In T. P. Wiseman (ed.), *Roman Political Life, 90 B.C.–A.D. 69.* Exeter: University of Exeter Press. 3–19.

———. 1987. "*Conspicui postes tectaque digna deo*: The Public Image of Aristocratic and Imperial Houses in the Late Republic and Early Empire. In *L'Urbs: Éspace urbain et histoire (Iᵉʳ siècle av. J.-C.–IIIᵉ siècle ap. J.-C.).* Rome: École française de Rome. 393–413. Reprinted in T. P. Wiseman, *Historiography and Imagination.* Exeter: University of Exeter Press 1994. 98–115.

Wistrand, E. 1976. *The So-Called* Laudatio Turiae. Göteborg: Acta Universitatis Gothoburgensis.

Wlosok, A. 1980. "*Nihil nisi ruborem*: Über die Rolle der Scham in der Römischen Rechtskultur." *Grazer Beiträge* 9: 155–72.

Wyatt-Brown, B. 2002. "Honor's History across the Academy." *Historically Speaking* 3.5 (June). 13–15.

CHAPTER 19

FRIENDSHIP AMONG THE ROMANS

KOENRAAD VERBOVEN

INTRODUCTION: ROMAN VIEWS

FRIENDSHIP loomed large in the Roman mind, and was much reflected upon. Greek philosophy—not surprisingly, perhaps—usually provided the intellectual framework.[1] Aristotle had distinguished three types of friendship (*philia*) based on three different grounds for affection: utility, pleasure, and virtue. Only the last was constant because it was based on love for the 'absolute good' that friends perceived in each other. Friendship based on utility or pleasure endured only so long as it was useful or pleasant, and was ultimately based on self-love. Therefore, *philia* based on virtue was primary, and provided the standards by which this kind of relationship should be judged altogether. Nevertheless, Aristotle rejected the idea that only *philia* based on virtue was 'real,' because this was in conflict with observed reality (*EE* 1236b 21: *biazesthai ta phainomena*—what is apparent constrains [us]).[2]

Epicurus argued that all friendship could be traced back to the universal human need for others: "All *philia* is a virtue in itself, but draws its origin from assistance" (*Sent. Vat. 23*). The Stoics, on the other hand, reaffirmed the primacy of virtue as the only basis of true friendship. Now, although neither school denied that affection

---

1. With regard to philosophy and Roman education, hence, the Roman worldview, see Hahn in this volume.

2. Friendship is extensively treated in the *Ethica Eudemia* (book 7), the *Ethica Nicomachea* (book 8), and the *Magna Moralia* (book 2).

was essential, the Epicureans believed that this arose in response to the expected assistance from others, while Stoics thought that it was a response to the perception of virtue.

Roman intellectuals, then, usually adopted either the Epicurean, or a (miti-gated) version of the Stoic viewpoint. Cicero's influential essay *Laelius de amicitia* defined friendship as an "agreement (*consensio*) with goodwill (*benevolentia*) and affection (*caritas*) on all things divine and human" (Cic. *Amic.* 20). The source of goodwill was *amor* (love), from which the word *amicitia* (friendship) derived (Cic. *Amic.* 26). We should also note that the idea of friendship based on *consensio* was widespread. Sallust's Catiline asserts that "to want and not want the same thing, that is truly firm friendship" (*Cat.* 20. 4).

Cicero added that true friendship could exist only between virtuous men (*boni viri, Amic.* 18). However, he rejected the Stoic contention that because true friendship depended on virtue, and only the wise were truly virtuous, only wise men could truly be friends. Theoretically yes, Cicero acknowledged, but the Stoic definition of wisdom was such that no mortal man had ever reached this ideal (*Amic.* 18). Cicero's ideas, however, were not always so straightforward, nor were they accepted by everyone (Fiore 1996). Social practice was often presented as being in conflict with ideals and philosophy. Thus, the *Laelius* claimed to be about "true and perfect" (*vera et perfecta*) friendship, not the "vulgar or ordinary" sort (*Amic.* 22). Usual practice was to love those friends most from whom one expected to reap the greatest benefit (*Amic.* 79). And so, in his *De Inuentione*, Cicero included *amicitia* because it was useful, and could be sought after for the material rewards it entailed. "Some people believe that *amicitia* is desirable only for its usefulness, others for itself only, again others for itself and its useful-ness...in oratory friendship should be sought for both reasons" (*Inv.* 2. 167). In his oration for Roscius Amerinus, Cicero affirms that friendships were formed "to manage a common advantage (*commune commodum*) through mutual services (*mutuis officiis*)" (*Rosc. Am.* 111). Elsewhere, namely, in his *Laelius*, Cicero con-tended that friendship should be sought after because it was delightful in itself, as generosity was desirable for its own sake and not for the *gratia* (goodwill) it engendered (*Amic.* 31). Aulus Gellius tells us that Cicero was criticized for this passage because the motives behind generosity were often dubious. He concluded that Cicero spoke only in a philosophical sense (Gel. 17. 5. 10: *ita ut philosophi*— just like the philosophers).

Leaving Cicero behind, we find the idea that *amicitia* consisted in the exchange of gifts and services to be ubiquitous in Roman literature. Terence, for example, very early on had spoken of "procuring friends by services rendered" (*Eu.* 148). Fronto distinguishes *amor* from *amicitia* because the latter exists only through the exchange of *officia* whereas the former arises rather from impulse than from calculation (*Aur.* 1. 3. 5: *impetus potius quam ratione*).

What emerges from the ancient sources, then, are roughly two veins of thought regarding the origins, or the nature, of friendship. On the one hand, it could be argued that true *amicitia* derived from the longing of all human beings for comradeship.

Here, virtue, in one or another of its manifestations, would lie at the heart of the relationship. Others, however, claimed to see a more unsentimental kind of bond as predominant. According to such views, one sought friends not because of affinity, or as the result of a moral estimation of the potential friend, but instead, because of the usefulness that might arise from the connection.

MODERN VIEWS

Modern scholars are divided in their approaches to the ancient testimony. In his epoch-making study on the Roman nobility, Matthias Gelzer classified Roman friendship, together with patronage and *hospitium*, as "(reciprocal) relations of closeness and loyalty" (*[gegenseitiger] Nah- und Treuverhältnisse*), all of these based on *fides* (good faith, trust) and *officium* (duty), not affection (Gelzer 1969: 65–68).[3] Gelzer argued that the nobility controlled political institutions through their networks of friends and clients. His thesis lay at the origin of the prosopographic approach to Roman political history. Ronald Syme would subsequently write that "*amicitia* was a weapon of politics, not a sentiment based on congeniality" (Syme 1939: 157), while Lily Ross Taylor argued that *amicitia* was simply "the old Roman substitute for party" (Taylor 1949: 7–8).

A similar view prevailed outside the field of political history. Wilhelm Kroll thought that the idea of emotional friendship was a Greek invention (Kroll 1933: 55–60). Of course, Romans were not incapable of feeling friendly affection for each other, but such emotions were irrelevant in forming or maintaining friendship relations, which instead were founded on mutual interests and obligations. Genuine affection was a plus, not a must.

Then, in the 1950s, the instrumental approach to *amicitia* was theoretically underpinned by the anthropological concept of gift exchange. This notion became particularly popular among Greek historians under the influence of Moses Finley, whose *World of Odysseus* laid the basis for explaining *philia* (friendship) as an instrumental relation based on gift exchange. The legal historian Jacques Michel thus compared the moral obligations of *amicitia* and *gratia* described by Roman authors to those described by anthropologists for gift exchange relations in 'primitive' cultures (Michel 1962: 433–595). Richard Saller would some twenty years later argue that "the ideals of common interests and selfless service represent a philosophical view of *amicitia*…in the common view *amicitia* was expected basically to entail reciprocal exchange of *officia* (favors, debts, obligations) and *beneficia* (benefits, kindnesses)" (Saller 1982: 13; cf. recently Burton 2004).

Current research is still very largely dominated by this anthropological paradigm, which usually reduces the emotional discourse of *amicitia* to the conventional

---

3. On Roman notions of hospitality, see Nicols in this volume.

underpinning of the principle of altruism evoked in gift exchange. The view of *amicitia* as a gift-exchange relationship finds support in the fact that instrumental friendship is very common in comparative perspective. Anthropologists tend to assume that instrumental friendship is pervasive in non-modern cultures (e.g. Schmidt et al. 1977; Pitt-Rivers 1973; Wolf 1966). Beyond this, modern historians have stressed the instrumental nature of friendship in early modern Europe (e.g., Kettering 1986 and 1992).

A sweeping critique, however, was formulated by Peter Brunt in 1964, who defended Cicero's view of affection as the basis of friendship (Brunt 1988a). Of course, the language and poses of friendship were often used to cover up instrumental motives, but that is quite a different matter. More recently, David Konstan, in a number of publications since the early 1990s, has seriously challenged the instrumental view of ancient friendship. He believes that "(*philia*) constituted in principle, as modern friendship, a space of personal intimacy and unselfish affection distinct from the norms regulating public and commercial life." The ancient world and modern society "perhaps for entirely different reasons—did produce a space for sympathy and altruism under the name of friendship that stands as an alternative to structured forms of interaction based on kinship, civic identity, or commercial activity" (Konstan 1997: 5–6). Few social historians as yet have accepted Konstan's argument in its entirety, but his work is important because it ties the study of ancient friendship to the growing field of the history of emotions.

THE ETHICS OF ROMAN FRIENDSHIP

Let us leave aside, for the moment, the question of how genuine the affection was that Roman friends claimed to feel, and look at the enunciated norms and ideals underlying *amicitia*. What we want to see, precisely, is what the Romans told themselves they were doing when they formed and fostered relationships that involved friendship.[4]

Benevolentia (Goodwill) and *Benignitas* (Kindness, Generosity)

According to Cicero *benevolentia* is essential in *amicitia*. One could conceivably remove goodwill from kinship, as he thinks, but not from friendship (*Amic.* 19). Contrary to kinship, friendship is a voluntary (an 'achieved') relation. *Benevolentia* itself is inseparable from another quality, namely, *benignitas*. The former denotes a feeling, while the latter denotes this feeling in action. Working from this stance, Cicero then holds that *benignitas* and *iustitia* (justice) are the two most important virtues underpinning society; *iustitia*

---

4. More fully in Verboven 2002: 35–48.

makes a person abstain from evil, while *benignitas* induces him to do good (*Off.* 1. 20). *Benignitas* denotes the disposition (or as the Romans would say, the virtue) from which *benificia* (favors, benefactions) spring. It implies voluntariness, sincerity, and altruism. Or, as Seneca the Younger would put things, "Whoever gives *beneficia* imitates the gods, whoever asks for a return (imitates) usurers" (Sen. *Ben.* 3. 15. 4 ; cf. Cic. *Am.* 31).

Now, if *benevolentia* was essential to friendship and *benignitas* inseparable from it, then friendship could not exist without the exchange of *beneficia*. Accordingly, *benignitas* was a duty for friends; and in turn, in any true friendship, *beneficia* (voluntary acts of kindness) were also *officia*—in other words, acts of duty, symbolizing goodwill and affection (Saller 1982: 15–21). *Beneficia/officia* thus signified a commitment on the part of the giver, serving as a pledge for future services: "To have received is an entitlement to receive again" (*Avoir reçu est un titre à recevoir encore*: Michel 1962: 454). Pliny the Younger made a very similar remark ages before: "The merit of a bygone service (*veteris officii meritum*), seemed in need of being preserved by a new one. For it is the case, that you subvert older kindnesses when you do not add later ones to them" (Plin. *Ep.* 3. 4. 6).

Gratia (Goodwill, Kindness)

Beneficia were by definition gratuitous, but failure to return a good deed was shameful and impermissible for a decent man (*viro bono*, Cic. *Off.* 1. 48). However, *gratia* lay not in the act, as such, of returning a kindness. Like *benignitas*, *gratia* was primarily a state of mind. While *benignitas* was the disposition generating *beneficia*, *gratia* was the disposition that ensured a response to *beneficia*. The point was that regardless of a friend's material ability to return a kindness, his disposition should be the same: he should feel genuinely obliged. "For even a poor man, provided he is a good man, even though he cannot return *gratia*, can surely have it" (Cic. *Off.* 2. 69).

Gratia could, or should, also be expressed symbolically. The philosopher Artemidorus received financial aid from Pliny when he was exiled by Domitian. After his return, he seized every occasion to praise his benefactor, thereby expressing his *gratia* and increasing Pliny's reputation. "The benign nature of our Artemidorus is such that he extols the dutiful services from his friends (*officia amicorum*) too much" (Plin. *Ep.* 3. 11. 1). Such praise, especially when offered in a public context, was worth roughly its weight in gold to a man like Pliny.

Conversely, *gratia* obligations did not end with the delivery of a return gift, or a service. Seneca warns that one should be more careful about the persons from whom one accepted *beneficia* than about those from whom to request a loan. For financial debts extinguish once they are repaid, whereas a debt of *gratia* never expires: "For I owe (still) when I have returned, start again, but friendship stays" (*Ben.* 2. 18. 5; cf. Cic. *Off.* 1. 69).

Dutiful acts of kindness were thus thought to bring friends closer together. The parties involved became bound by *gratia*, or it could be said that they were tied together by favors (*beneficiis devincti*). Cicero put things this way: "Great indeed is that union (*communitas*) that is forged from good deeds bestowed and received in turn, which, while they are mutual and pleasing, bind in firm partnership those between whom they are given" (Cic. *Off.* 1. 56). Seneca refers to the most sacred law (*sacratissimum ius*) of *beneficia*, from which *amicitia* is born (*Ben.* 2. 18. 5). Moreover, because *beneficia* were (ideologically) gratuitous acts of kindness, return gifts and favors were themselves *beneficia*: "There are two kinds of generosity (*liberalitas*), one that consists in giving a *beneficium*, the other of returning one" (Cic. *Off.* 1. 48).

Fides (Trust, Good Faith)

Whether as cause or as consequence, *amicitia* just could not exist in Roman eyes without the exchange of gifts and services. Even Cicero's *Laelius* affirmed that it was a distinctive feature of friendship "to give and receive deserved favors (*meritis*)" (*Amic.* 26). Ideologically, however, what was being 'exchanged' were not gifts and services, as such, but tokens symbolizing a package of dispositions that inevitably resulted in actions. Thus, the object of the exchange always included the confirmation of the friendship bond.

Time was an essential ingredient in this bond. Friendship itself was by definition open-ended and ideally enduring. Accordingly, the exchange signifying this bond was never immediate. The time lag between the reception of a gift/service and the bestowal of a counter-gift/service signified the trust and solidarity required of friends. Romans expressed this by the concept of *fides*, which signified both trust and trustworthiness.

In the context of friendship, *fides* denoted the faith friends had in each other's *benignitas* and *gratia*. Conversely, *fides* implied solidarity, which had to be shown by acts of kindness that in turn generated *gratia*. *Fides* guaranteed that obligations were upheld. Therefore, any *beneficium* signified *fides*, as well as *benignitas* and/or *gratia*.

Fides was, however, a broad concept. According to Cicero *fides* was the very "foundation of justice" (*fundamentum iustitiae, Off.* 1. 23). There was, then, a common *fides* owed to all mankind, and a more specific sort of *fides*, which was owed to fellow citizens. *Fides* underlay and guaranteed international treaties and private contracts. It expressed both a debtor's creditworthiness and his moral credibility (Verboven 2002: 40–41).

Most of all, however, *fides* was the cement of personal relations in general, and of friendship in particular. "*Fides* alone is the rennet of friendship" (Pub. *Sent.* 249). It is the "prop of the stability and constancy we seek in friendship" (Cic. *Amic.* 65). Or, as Cicero put this elsewhere, "As a place without a port cannot be safe for ships, so a soul with no *fides* cannot be steadfast for friends" (Cic. *Inv.* 1. 47).

Amor (Affection, Love)

The ultimate source of goodwill (*benevolentia*), according to Cicero, was affection (*amor*), from which the word *amicitia* was derived (*Amic.* 26). We already saw that philosophers agreed on the importance of affection, but disagreed on where this affection came from. Did it originate from the perception of virtue in the other (as Cicero and the Stoics believed), or was it generated by the awareness that the other was helpful or useful to oneself (as the Epicureans believed)? This matter was resolved neither by the ancients nor has it been resolved by modern scholars studying the Romans.

Be that as it may, affection was subject to certain types of social regulation. *Amici* were simply and plainly *expected* to feel affection (*amor*, in some sense) for each other. This norm of affection was inextricably bound up with the norms of reciprocity, solidarity, and loyalty. Pliny the Younger claimed that the emperor Trajan had so great a capacity to put his friends under an obligation that only an ingrate could fail to love him (Plin. *Pan.* 85. 8). Seneca noted that love in response to favors was part of the natural order of things; even wild beasts were induced to love those who cared for them (*Ben.* 1. 2. 5). In turn, affection had to manifest itself in *beneficia* that would kindle *gratia* in the receiver.

Amicitia, in other words, was a complex relationship, in which reciprocity, affection, and loyalty were mingled, and advantage and altruism intertwined, all of these together producing, and being produced by, acts of kindness. To receive a *beneficium* was thus gratifying, and had to kindle *amor* and *gratia*. Dionysius from Halicarnassus notes that whoever loves another favors the one he loves, and whoever is favored loves the one who favors him (D.H. 8. 34. 1).

No doubt friendly affection was often shallow ('liking' rather than truly 'loving'), and sometimes was surely feigned (as it is today). But such manipulation was (and is) possible only because the norm of affection—as that of reciprocity—was (and is) generally acknowledged. As a modern sociologist has put it, "A minimal element of affect remains an important ingredient in the relation. If not present, it must be feigned. When the instrumental purposes of the relation clearly take the upper hand, the bond is in danger of disruption" (Wolf 1966: 13).

Thus, the practical implications of this 'norm of affection' should not be underestimated. The anthropologist Pitt-Rivers noted that appeals to the obligation to reciprocate are not permitted in friendship, because they violate the 'amity' underlying the relation (Pitt-Rivers 1973: 96–97). However, appeals to affection *are* allowed, both among the people in modern Andalusia studied by Pitt-Rivers and among the ancient Romans. They are common, for instance, in Cicero's letters of recommendation, which play heavily upon the idea that mutual affection has to be shown through mutual services, and that services received will both (re-)confirm and kindle affection. Cicero often presents the recommendation itself as due to the *commendatus* on account of the affection between himself and the recommender: "I love Precilius dearly for his modesty, humanity, character and exceptional love for me" (*Fam.* 13. 15. 1); "Curius, who does business in Patrae, is loved by me for many important reasons" (*Fam.* 13. 17. 1).

Existimatio (Reputation)

The ethical norms described above served as guidelines for how friends should behave, and as standards by which their behavior was judged. The honorable man was *benignus* (generous), *gratus* (appreciative), *fidus* (faithful), and *benevolens* (well-wishing) with respect to his friends. Stinginess, ingratitude, disloyalty, or indifference destroyed a person's reputation—and such a loss of face, in Cicero's opinion, was worse than death (*Quinct.* 49; 98; *Q. Rosc.* 16). No one desired *amicitia* with a person who was reputedly *illiberalis* (stingy), *ingratus* (unappreciative), and *infidus* (treacherous) (Michel 1962: 589–90). Honor and prestige depended on a person's ability to live up to social obligations, and to do so in the ways we have been sketching. Consequently, the exchange of sentiments and services between friends put one's reputation (*existimatio*) on the line, and hence (in Roman eyes), one's honor (on which, see Lendon in this volume).

The emphasis on honor and obligation thus added strength to friendships that might otherwise have been emotionally rather shallow. This is why friendship was so often publicly expressed and insisted upon, even for relations that were patently 'political.' In order for reputation and honor to be effective in consolidating instrumental friendship, it had to be made public. Only when the existence of an *amicitia* was publicly recognized, and gifts and services were known to have been exchanged, could public opinion be called upon to censure breach of faith, ingratitude, and indifference.

A Web of Expectations

There is no such thing as *the* 'real' Roman friendship. For *amicitia* to be genuine, *beneficia*, as tokens of goodwill, gratitude, trust, solidarity, and affection, were indispensable, and put the reputations of the partners at stake. Some friendships were very intimate; in others affection was more a question of liking than loving; still others were primarily instrumental relations in which affection was accessory; others again were primarily pleasurable. *Amicitia* was not genuine without goodwill and concern, but friendship in which goodwill and concern were not made manifest by an exchange of *officia* was unreal.

Providing our data are sound, we can sometimes distinguish friendships that were (more) affectionate from ones that were (more) instrumental, but simply to distinguish between emotional and instrumental friendship, let alone to discard one or the other as an anachronism or a sociologist's illusion, is to ignore the complexity of Roman friendship. *Amicitia* presupposed an exchange relationship subject to the rules of *gratia*, but the bond was never *only* an exchange relationship. He who merely failed to return a gift was an ingrate; he who failed to do so as a friend was mean, ungrateful, disloyal, and selfish. What we must recognize, then, is that Roman friendship continuously evolved in a complex web of expectations and obligations (Verboven 2002: 35–48). Specific relations and interactions may be situated at various points in this web, but only the web as a whole defined the constraints and possibilities inherent in *amicitia*.

Now, the question of sincerity (another important requirement) needs to be factored into this perspective. Inevitably, in friendship a tension existed between the principles of altruism and self-interest. Attitudes regarding *beneficia* and *gratia* were ambiguous, though, because the same actions could be motivated by altruism or self-interest. The norms of *amicitia* were therefore inherently ambivalent, having an internal psychological side (feeling goodwill, feeling grateful, trusting in, feeling affection, caring for one's reputation) and an outward social side (exchanging *beneficia*, showing solidarity, showing concern, living up to one's obligations).

Voluntariness and altruism were insisted upon, but the system was prone to manipulation. It was not difficult to hold that "[only] vile or stupid persons think *beneficia* are gifts" (*Pub. Sent.* B37). And the proverbial image of gifts as bait on an angler's hook is commonly found in authors such as Martial, Horace, and Pliny (e.g., Mart. 5. 18. 7–10; Hor. *Ep.* 1. 7. 73; *S.* 2. 5. 25; Plin. *Ep.* 9. 30). Cicero's letters of recommendation contain frequent hints about *gratia* and the favors expected to be returned (e.g., *Fam.* 13. 65. 2; *Att.* 16. 16a. 5). And so, in what might be called the typical Roman fashion, calculation in friendship was generally disapproved of, while commonly practiced. And in the end, the positive emphasis on reciprocity, reputation, and status added considerable stability and weight to instrumental or emotionally shallow friendships.

FRIENDSHIP AND PATRONAGE

The relationship between *amicitia* and patronage is ambiguous. Despite the ideal of equality prescribed for friendship, some friendships were very unequal. Moreover, such inequality was not limited to differences in status or age that inevitably imposed an element of deference in the 'lesser' or younger friend toward the 'greater' or older friend, but could also result from differences in wealth or access to resources, that affected the possibilities for exchange of *officia*.

Now, a typical feature of gift exchange is that it is competitive. The recipient of a gift or favor who is unable to return one becomes morally bound. In the words of Publilius Syrus, "To accept a kindness (*beneficium*) is to sell your liberty" (*Pub. Sent.* B5). If a balance could not be struck, friendship became asymmetrical. Richard Saller has thus argued that such 'lop-sided' friendships could more rightly be called patron-client relations (Saller 1982 and 1989). Other scholars reject this idea, and stress the uniqueness of Roman patronage as a historical and cultural phenomenon (Eilers 2002: 1–83).

The debate is confusing because the two sides tend to use different concepts of patronage. In sociology, patronage denotes a specific *type* of exchange relation, or system, that occurs in different forms in different cultural contexts. The Roman concepts of *patrocinium* (being a patron) and *clientela* (clientship), however, denote a specific type of interpersonal relationship in Roman society and culture, with its own symbols, rituals, and history. The sociological concept of patronage may thus provide an analytical perspective to study Roman *patrocinium-clientela*, but the uniquely Roman cultural construct of *patrocinium-clientela* cannot be reduced to the theoretical construct of 'sociological' patronage. The contribution of sociology should be seen to lie in the possibility of cross-cultural comparison and the analysis of social dynamics, not in the re-definition of ancient concepts.

But even so, difficulty remains. Except in the case of municipal or collegial patronage, or of patron-freedmen relations, the *patrocinium-clientela* complex, despite its cultural specificity, was not a formally defined relationship. All attempts to postulate formal initiation rites for private patron-client relations have failed. *Clientela* was a matter of public avowal and voluntary submission. Of course, social opinion could pressure a person to accept the role of client, and the ideology of patronage prescribed that the relationship could not honorably be broken; but these were generally understood moral constraints, not formal rules. Like *amicitia*, the *patrocinium-clientela* bond implied *benignitas*, *fides*, and *gratia*. Inevitably, the borderline between *patrocinium-clientela* and *amicitia* remained much less than clear-cut.

Patrocinium-clientela was a question of role patterns that could be adopted, rejected, or (morally) imposed by public opinion. Cicero notes that the rich and powerful often refused to acknowledge that they were *beneficio obligati* (obligated by a favor), because they feared to be labeled *clientes* (clients—*Off.* 2. 69). According to Fronto, his friendship with Gavius Clarus was so intimate that Clarus did not hesitate to do for Fronto everything a client or a faithful freedman would do for his patron (*Ver.* 2. 7. 2). The implication is that such hesitation would not have been unnatural. Clarus was a senator of praetorian rank at the time and would surely have objected to being labeled Fronto's client, although clearly Fronto was Clarus' senior and outranked him.

The businessman M' Curius, who lived in Patrae, was an intimate (*familiaris*) of Atticus, who recommended him to Cicero as a possible host for the return journey from Cilicia, where Cicero had been governor. Curius took the opportunity to oblige Cicero by writing him into his will, and by taking care of Cicero's favorite freedman, Tiro, who had fallen ill and had to stay behind. An *amicitia* ensued between Cicero and Curius, and the friendship subsequently lasted many years. Cicero seems genuinely to have liked Curius, but the difference between them in status, wealth, and influence was unbridgeable. Curius appropriately addressed Cicero as *amice magne* (my great friend) and *patrone mi* (my patron), although he insisted that Atticus would always take pride of place (*Fam.* 7. 29; cf. Verboven 2002: 215; Deniaux 1993: 487–89).

The principle of equality in friendship, then, did not imply social or political equality, but the effective irrelevance of such inequalities. Thus, *amicitia* and *clientela* were not mutually exclusive, but the language of friendship was preferable to that of patronage, which implied inferiority and dependency. The greater the factual inequality between friends was, the more difficult it was credibly to claim a principle equality between them.

Friendship in Social Practice

Amicitia was, to put the matter simply, essential for participation in Roman society. A Roman's social life was firmly set in his circle of friends. Friends dined and wined together, went to the baths and games together, acted as witnesses to wills and contracts for one another, asked each other's opinions on betrothals and marriages, wrote when absent to exchange news and gossip.[5] In short, friends were enmeshed in webs of social obligations signifying reciprocal commitments of goodwill, assistance, loyalty and affection.

However, the services provided by *amici* far exceeded the boundaries of mere sociability. Reading Cicero's letters, for instance, we find that friends were expected to provide services that we would hardly dare to ask even from our parents. Friends could legitimately expect each other to lend assistance in court, to use influence in administrative or political affairs, to help pay off debts, and so forth. Non-delivery constituted a breach of faith and jeopardized the relation itself.

As a corollary of all this, the tension between private obligations and universal or public obligations was very real (Veyne 1976: 411). The question of how much friends could rightfully expect from each other is expressly addressed in Cicero's *Laelius*, which emphasizes respect for institutions and universalist ethical norms. However, the dictates of friendship might at any moment weigh quite heavily on any and all other considerations.

Politics

Scholars now generally agree that *amicitia* and *clientela* were not substitutes for political parties under the republic. Networks built on 'friendship' and patronage were inherently unstable alliances that rarely set the political agenda, were incapable of generating long-term common action, and could not control popular assemblies (Yakobsen 1999: 65–123). However, although *amicitia* did not dictate Roman politics, those who lacked 'friends' and followers were politically impotent and doomed to suffer a short-lived career.

The Roman state almost completely lacked an effective institutional and administrative apparatus to regulate the distribution and delegation of power or the allocation of positions and resources. Personal networks and recommendations were pretty well the only means available to obtain official positions, to influence political decisions, or to petition for government or administrative action (Cotton 1981; Cotton 1986; Deniaux 1993; Verboven 2002: 324–29). Saller showed that the same mechanisms prevailed under the empire. The only difference was that instead of the

---

5. Dinner parties, the baths, the games, and the law courts as places where social relationships were cultivated are all treated in this volume. See Dunbabin and Slater, Fagan, Coleman, and Bablitz, respectively.

numerous competing noble families of the republic, there was now one undisputable *summus amicus* (supreme friend) or patron, namely, the emperor (Saller 1982).

At the level of the senatorial and equestrian elites, though, things continued much as before. Thus, Fronto describes how, as governor of Asia, he formed his staff by appealing to his relatives and friends (*Ant.* 8), just as his republican predecessors had done. The young jurist, Trebatius Testa, was introduced by Cicero to Caesar (*Fam.* 7. 5. 3), just as Pliny introduced his protégé Voconius Romanus to his friend Priscus (*Ep.* 2. 13).

A young politician, then, whether he lived during the republic or the empire, started his career under the protection of a senior politician, who was expected to use his influence on his protégé's behalf, and to introduce the young man into the 'friendship' of others. A classic example is that of M. Caelius Rufus, who was entrusted by his father into the care of Cicero, and thence quickly made his way in society circles. Cicero himself had been similarly introduced to the circle of Scaevola the Augur. Pliny the Younger's early career was promoted by the influential Q. Corellius Rufus (Plin. *Ep.* 4. 17).

But aside from the obvious realm of personal political careers, minor political decisions could likewise be obtained or obstructed through the use of 'friends.' And so, when the city of Salamis on Cyprus desperately needed a loan, but found that a Gabinian law forbade loans to foreign ambassadors, their patron, M. Brutus, used his influence (*gratia*) to obtain two *senatus consulta* (decrees of the senate) granting an exception to the law (*Att.* 5. 21. 10–13).[6]

Access to courts of law and legal proceedings, too, could be facilitated or blocked through the use of friends. Cicero wrote several letters of recommendation for M. Fabius Gallus in connection with a legal dispute between Gallus and his brother. Cicero asked Caelius Rufus to act as court patron (*Fam.* 2. 14), and he asked the *praetor*, Curtius Peducaeanus (who would preside the case), to facilitate Gallus as much as possible (*Fam.* 13. 59). Papirius Paetus was asked to use his influence to reconcile the two brothers and avert the case's coming to court (*Fam.* 9. 25. 2–3).

Private Affairs

Most gifts between *amici* were purely symbolic. Valuable gifts are recorded primarily in a (sociologically) patronal context. Pliny, for instance, donated 300,000 sesterces to Romatius Firmus, so that Firmus could achieve equestrian status, and added that their longstanding friendship assured him that Firmus would dutifully remember this gift (*Ep.* 1. 19). Between friends of equal standing, valuable gifts occur mainly in times of crisis. Cicero, for example, received very considerable amounts of cash from his friends when he left Rome to go into exile—Atticus alone gave 250,000 sesterces (Nep. *Att.* 4. 4; Cic. *Att.* 3. 19. 3; 20. 2).

6. On the implications of the case, see Braund 1989a: 143–45. For the complete dossier, see Migeotte 1984: 254–59.

What we must recognize, though, is that assistance to friends in need was absolutely vital in a world without religious charity or social security. The expectation that friends would help to overcome financial difficulties was so self-evident that satirical authors construed an ancient version of insurance fraud on it. Tongilianus bought a house for 200,000 sesterces. When it burned down, his friends raised a million in compensation. And so, the satirist could with effect put the question, "Pray would you not yourself seem to have set fire to it, Tongilianus?" (Mart. 3. 52; cf. Iuv. 3. 220).

Posthumous gifts, in the form of legacies and inheritances, were strongly expected from friends. Cicero claimed, in 43 BC, that over the years he had received 20 million sesterces in legacies and inheritances (*Phil.* 2. 40). Several testators are known from his letters. Cluvius from Puteoli, for instance, instituted Cicero, Caesar, and a Campanian businessman, T. Hordeonius, as heirs. Cicero acquired part of a building block with shops yielding 100,000 sesterces a year, besides a large amount of cash and silverware (*Att.* 13. 45. 3; 14. 9. 1; 10. 3; 11. 2). Cluvius had acted as financial middleman for Cicero and Pompey, and thus owed his fortune partly to these great friends. In a letter of recommendation Cicero describes him as "very attentive to me" (*valde me observat*) and very "intimate with me" (*valde mihi familiaris*) (*Fam.* 13. 56).

The *officia testamentaria* (duties in connection with inheritances) were not limited to legacies and inheritance shares. At least as important was guardianship over the testator's under-age children and the women subject to his *patria potestas*. It was customary that a testator appointed several of his closest friends as *tutores* (guardians). Such an appointment was highly honorable. It signified the deepest possible trust in a friend's *fides*. Great men (senators, important knights, and municipal nobles) were typically also the guardians of many of their deceased friends' children. Most *tutores* were honorary guardians, and were not involved in the daily operations of their pupil's affairs. But, they were expected to supervise the overall administration of those matters, and their help and influence would be called upon if necessary.

The businessman P. Iunius appointed four guardians for his son: his brother Marcus, his friend P. Titius, his business partner L. Rabonius, and the noble M. Claudius Marcellus. When Rabonius struck a deal with the infamous Verres to defraud young Iunius, the other guardians convened, and Marcellus was called in—in vain as it turned out. Much to Marcellus's dismay Verres refused to yield, and young Iunius was forced to pay an extortionate amount of 'damages' for adjustment works on the temple of Castor and Pollux that his father had contracted to repair (Cic. *Ver.* 1. 130–156). Cicero himself was *tutor* of the young T. Pinnius, whose father had probably been a private banker (*faenerator*) in the East. Cicero wrote a letter of recommendation on behalf of his pupil to the governor of Bithynia regarding a debt of 8 million sesterces, which the city of Nicaea owed to Pinnius (*Fam.* 13. 61). Cicero was hardly the person to keep the records of debts owed to his ward. However, when it came time to collect from an important community that was indebted to Pinnius, then the influential guardian would naturally step in.

Loans were traditionally part of the exchange between friends, although they were not always interest-free (Verboven 2002: 120–25). The examples we have of free loans occur mostly either in a patron-client context, or in an obviously political context. Crassus and Caesar, for example, built their political power bases by extending 'friendly' loans to their political *amici* (Sal. *Cat.* 48. 5; Suet. *Jul.* 27. 1). The thus-created economic connection bound the 'friends' even more tightly to one another. Cato is said to have used an inheritance from a cousin to extend loans to his friends (Plut. *Cat. Min.* 6. 4). Otherwise, free loans occur primarily in contexts of crisis, and differ little from expressly labeled gifts. Cicero gave his friend Axius' son a free loan despite being short of cash himself, and agreed grudgingly to accord a remission of payment when the debt became due (Cic. *Att.* 10. 11. 2; 15. 4).

More important than loans were personal securities, which were often provided by *amici*. The close link between creditworthiness (*fides*) and honor meant that to sustain a friend's *fides* vis à vis the world at large was an imperative duty. And even when no formal security was given, friends could be called upon for financial assistance. Cicero, for example, paid the debts of Tullius Montanus, because he considered that to be his duty (*pertinet ad nostrum officium*—it is [part of] my duty toward him, Cic. *Att.* 12. 52. 1).

Friends played a role also in the management and supervision of each other's patrimony. They served as agents and representatives in cases where slaves and freedmen would be less suitable to undertake these tasks. *Mandata* (contractual commissions), in particular, were considered *officia amicorum* (the dutiful service of friends). The jurist Paulus asserted that "there is no *mandatum* unless it is unremunerated, because it springs from personal duty (*officium*) and friendship, and payment is opposed to duty" (*Dig.* 17. 1. 1. 4). As *procuratores* (managers), friends supervised the general management of estates or affairs in the absence of their owner, or assisted the latter even when he was present. Atticus, for instance, was *procurator* for the Cicerones, M. Cato, Q. Hortensius, and A. Torquatus, as well as for numerous Roman knights (Nep. *Att.* 15. 1–3).

To turn to yet another practical matter, letters of recommendation illustrate the importance of *amicitia* to sway influence. Approximately 25–30% of Cicero's recommendations concern businessmen (Deniaux 1993; Cotton 1986). These individuals received introductions, help in enforcing contracts, official positions, and so forth from the pen of Cicero. The businessman M. Scaptius obtained a *praefectura* (a command) and a cavalry squadron from the governor of Cilicia, Appius Claudius, to force the city of Salamis to pay the debt it owed to Scaptius and his associate P. Matinius. Brutus—who was the city's real creditor, and who was hiding behind Scaptius and Matinius, subsequently asked Appius' successor, Cicero, to renew Scaptius' command, and to help 'persuade' the city. Cicero refused that request, but mediated nonetheless, and eventually forbade Salamis to deposit the sum due in a temple, thus leaving the matter to his successor.

It would be pointless to continue to list the many more ways in which friends assisted and accommodated each other in private affairs of every kind. They would only further illustrate the same basic reality; *amicitia* bypassed formal procedures and provided help where formal institutions and family ties failed, or as Saller put it, "Roman friendship was a corollary of the underdevelopment of rational, impersonal institutions for the provision of services" (Saller 1982: 14). But what also must be said is that this all took place in a highly formalized atmosphere. Friends did not simply, out of the goodness of their hearts, or spontaneously, do these kinds of favors for other friends. Rather, the whole nexus of friendship, as comprehended by the Romans, placed expectations on friends that were tantamount to being compulsory.

Amicitia in International Relations

Contrary to the (private) *patrocinium-clientela* relationship (reputedly instituted by Romulus), *amicitia* did not have a foundation myth, or legend, although it was central to many very ancient Roman stories. Nonetheless, the language of *amicitia* was commonly used metaphorically to describe deep-rooted social and political relations that had little to do with interpersonal friendship.

Thus, *amicitia* was a central notion in the political discourse of international relations. Allied kings and nations were bestowed with the title *amicus sociusque* (friend and ally). Such formal *amicitiae* obviously lacked anything like real emotional content, but as ideological constructs, these friendships served a clear purpose. The title *amicus* carried with it—just as was the case in interpersonal relationships—the idea (and responsibilities) of equality and sovereignty, but also of goodwill, trust, and solidarity. It implied that the moral obligations and sanctions of *amicitia* could be appealed to, and that assistance was owed beyond what might generally be stipulated in formal treaties.

Did Roman Friendship Have a History? Some Conclusions

A last and difficult question is whether Roman friendship had a history. Did *amicitia* change over the centuries? Did its moral imperatives change? David Konstan has argued that the notion of friendship changed in late antiquity under the influence of Christianity, which led to a greater emphasis on self-disclosure between friends (Konstan 1997: 149–73). This may be true, but over the roughly 500 years that separate Plautus from the triumph of Christianity, we find very little apparent change in how Romans thought about *amicitia*.

The lack of privacy, the manifold tokens affirming and 'publicizing' friendship, the link with honor and reputation, the emphasis on practical assistance, and the tension between altruism and self-interest mark Roman friendship over the ages.[7] To the extent, then, that Roman friendship was distinct, that was not, perhaps, because Roman *amicitia* in itself was profoundly different from friendship in other cultures, but rather, because it occupied such an especially central position in Roman social cul-

---

7. With respect to publicizing friendship, cf. Nicols in this volume on hospitality, and the tablets that served to make those relationships known; and on honor, cf. Lendon in this volume.

ture overall. Roman friendship was intimately linked to one of Roman culture's most basic premises: total personal moral accountability toward the community (*existimatio*), rather than to (say) a transcendent God or his representatives on earth. Put simply and plainly, a Roman's personal identity was predominantly determined by the gaze of his or her community, and that gaze was very largely fixed on how that person dealt with his or her friends. Roman culture and society was, then, in a very essential way, friendly. We must understand that friendliness, however, in Roman terms.

SUGGESTED READING

The literature on *amicitia* is vast, and the following notes can do no more than offer a few starting points. They may be used in combination with the 'bibliographical essay' found in Konstan 1997: 174–76. The only recent general introduction to ancient friendship in English is Konstan 1997, which is also the best place to start for learning more about affection in ancient friendship. Brunt's superb essays on *amicitia* and *clientela* (1988a and 1988b) remain indispensable for aristocratic friendship in the late republic. Michel 1962 is still important for its detailed comparison of the morality of *gratia* and *amicitia* with anthropological data from 'primitive' cultures. Saller 1982 provides a good introduction to *amicitia* as a reciprocity relation. More recently, Burton 2004 offers a good example of how Bourdieu's theory on gift-exchange relations may be useful. For a critical view of friendship and gift exchange, see Konstan 1995, Konstan 1997 *passim*, and (although focused on the Greek world) Konstan 1998. Michel's study of the role of *amicitia* in the development of Roman law has (to my knowledge) never been surpassed. On the impact of *amicitia* in the law of obligations and inheritances, Verboven 2002 will be useful, and also a good access point for the role of *amicitia* in private social practice. For *amici* as testators, Champlin 1991: 131–54 provides a good introduction. There is no general up-to-date reassessment of the role played by *amicitia* in republican politics, but Brunt 1988a is still relevant, and Yakobsen 1999: 64–123 provides valuable insights. Saller 1982 is indispensable for the principate. On the relation of *amicitia* with patronage Saller 1989, Konstan 1995, and Verboven 2002: 49–62 2003 will be useful. For the use of (the discourse on) *amicitia* in international relations, Badian 1958 remains fundamental, together with Braund 1984. A good introduction to client kings for undergraduates may be found in Braund 1989b.

BIBLIOGRAPHY

Badian, E. 1958. *Foreign clientelae (264–70 B.C.)*. Oxford: Clarendon Press.
———. 1968. *Roman Imperialism in the Late Republic*. 2nd ed. Ithaca: Cornell University Press.
Braund, D. C. 1984. *Rome and the Friendly King. The Character of the Client Kingship*. London: Croom Helm.
———. 1989a. "Function and Dysfunction: Personal Patronage in Roman Imperialism." In A. Wallace-Hadrill (ed.), *Patronage in Ancient Society*. London: Routledge. 137–52.

———. 1989b. "Client Kings." In D. C. Braund (ed.), *The Administration of the Roman Empire*. Exeter: University of Exeter Press.

Brunt, P. A. 1988a. "Amicitia in the Late Roman Republic." In P. A. Brunt, *The Fall of the Roman Republic and Related Essays*. Oxford: Clarendon Press. 352–81. (Originally published in *Proceedings of the Cambridge Philological Society* 11, 1965: 1–20.)

———. 1988b. "Clientela." In P. A. Brunt, *The Fall of the Roman Republic and Related Essays*. Oxford: Clarendon Press. 382–441.

Burton, P. J. 2004. "Amicitia in Plautus: a Study of Roman Friendship Processes." *American Journal of Philology* 125: 209–43.

Champlin, E. 1991. *Final Judgments. Duty and Emotion in Roman Wills. 200 B.C.–A.D. 250*. Berkeley: University of California Press.

Cotton, H. M. 1981. "Military Tribunates and the Exercise of Patronage." *Chiron* 11: 229–38.

———. 1986. "The Role of Cicero's Letters of Recommendation: 'iustitia' versus 'gratia'?" *Hermes* 114: 443–60.

Deniaux, E. 1993. *Clientèles et pouvoir à l'époque de Cicéron*. Rome: Ecole Française de Rome.

Eilers, C. 2002. *Roman Patrons of Greek Cities*. Oxford: Oxford University Press.

Finley, M. I. 1954. *The World of Odysseus*. New York: Viking Press.

Fiore, B. S. J. 1996. "The Theory and Practice of Friendship in Cicero." In J. T. Fitzgerald (ed.), *Greco-Roman Perspectives on Friendship*. Atlanta: Scholars Press. 59–76.

Gelzer, M. 1969. *The Roman Nobility*. Trans. with intro. Robin Seager. Oxford: Blackwell.

Kettering, S. 1986. *Patrons, Brokers and Clients in Seventeenth-Century France*. Oxford: Oxford University Press.

———. 1992. "Friendship and Clientage in Early Modern France." *French History* 6: 139–58.

Konstan, D. 1995. "Patrons and Friends." *Classical Philology* 90: 328–42.

———. 1997. *Friendship in the Classical World*. Cambridge: Cambridge University Press.

———. 1998. "Reciprocity and Friendship." In C. Gill, N. Postlewaith, and R. Seaford (eds.), *Reciprocity in Ancient Greece*. Oxford: Oxford University Press. 279–302.

Kroll, W. 1933. *Die Kultur der Ciceronischen Zeit. I. Politik und Wirtschaft*. Leipzig: Dieterich'sche Verlagsbuchhandlung.

Michel, J.-M. 1962. *Gratuité en droit romain*. Brussels: Latomus.

Migeotte, L. 1984. *L'emprunt public dans les cités grecques. Recueil des documents et analyse critique*. Paris: Les Belles Lettres.

Pitt-Rivers, J. 1973. "The Kith and Kin." In J. Goody (ed.), *The Character of Kinship*. Cambridge: Cambridge University Press.

Saller, R. P. 1982. *Personal Patronage under the Early Empire*. Cambridge: Cambridge University Press.

———. 1989. "Patronage and Friendship in Early Imperial Rome: Drawing the Distinction." In A. Wallace-Hadrill (ed.), *Patronage in Ancient Society*. London: Routledge. 49–62.

Schmidt, S., L. Guasti, C. H. Landé, J. C. Scott (eds.). 1977. *Friends, Followers and Factions: A Reader in Political Clientelism*. Berkeley: University of California Press.

Syme, R. 1939. *The Roman Revolution*. Oxford: Clarendon Press.

Taylor, L. R. 1949. *Party Politics in the Age of Caesar*. Berkeley: University of California Press.

Verboven, K. 2002. *The Economy of Friends. Economic Aspects of Amicitia and Patronage in the Late Republic*. Brussels: Latomus.

———. 2003. "Review of Eilers 2002." *Bryn Mawr Classical Review*, http://ccat.sas.upenn.edu/bmcr/2003/2003–06–19.html

Veyne, P. 1976. *Le pain et le cirque. Sociologie historique d'un pluralisme politique*. Paris: Editions du Seuil. (Abridged and trans. as P. Veyne, *Bread and Circuses: Historical Sociology and Political Pluralism*. Intro. Oswyn Murray; trans. Brian Pearce. London: Allen Lane 1990.)

Wolf, E. S. 1966. "Kinship, Friendship, and Patron-Client Relations in Complex Societies." In M. Banton (ed.), *The Social Anthropology of Complex Societies*. London: Tavistock.

Yakobsen, A. 1999. *Elections and Electioneering in Rome*. Stuttgart: Franz Steiner Verlag.

CHAPTER 20

HOSPITALITY AMONG THE ROMANS

JOHN NICOLS

INTRODUCTION

THE conventions surrounding the social institution called *hospitium* (hospital-ilty, or guest-friendship) by the Romans provided a means by which members of different communities, either individually or as a group, might find a way to deal with one another to the *mutual* advantage of both parties; the alternative, hostility, inevitably led to the disadvantage of one, if not of both parties. Though it cannot be explicitly demonstrated from the extant sources, there are many indications that the practice of hospitality in many forms was ubiquitous in the ancient world, and that it was universally viewed in a positive light. Indeed, the conventions surrounding hospitality were probably critical in the mitigation of conflict generally.

Now, we must first of all realize that the word *hospitium* covers a range of meanings. So, for example, in reference to the earliest events in Roman history, the sources generally refer to *hospitium* in the context of social connections established between individuals of different states. We may call this kind of rela-tionship *hospitium privatum* (private hospitality). In practice, this entailed some kind of explicit agreement between the two parties not only to offer an outsider amenities (lodging, material support, conceivably entertainment), but also to show care for his interests and safety. It is implicit in these relationships that the parties, though of different communities, are socially rough equals, and that

I gratefully acknowledge the contribution of my research assistant, Annika Copp Noble.

each is capable of offering similar services to the other.[1] During the course of the republic, these private arrangements also acquired a public dimension, in that one of the partners to the arrangement was a collective. Hereafter, this form will be referred to as *hospitium publicum* (public hospitality). Moreover, and already during the early period, *hospitium* also is applied to the actual structures devoted to providing hospitality; thus, *hospitium* may refer both to public buildings for entertaining visitors and guest houses. During the last decades of the republic, and perhaps connected to the extension of citizenship to all Italians, *hospitium* was applied to include 'hospitable' arrangements even between Roman citizens.[2] In late antiquity, which is beyond the scope of this contribution, *hospitium* evolved to encompass also the compulsory quartering of soldiers. Despite the variations listed here, there is ample evidence that the word continued to be used in the traditional sense throughout Roman history, in other words, with respect to friendly relationships between two individuals, or an individual and some community.

THE NATURE OF THE EVIDENCE

References to traditional *hospitium* appear throughout Latin literature, and they continue well into the principate. The chronological context of these references is preponderantly, however, the republic. Livy is of course a major contributor, but Cicero employs the term extensively to describe contemporary social relationships. From the later period, Pliny the Elder provides a good number of references, Tacitus fewer. In sum, though, the literary evidence indicates that *hospitium*, in its many forms, continued to be practiced throughout the central period of Roman history (roughly, the third century BC through the third century AD).

The epigraphical evidence is also extensive, but unevenly distributed in both geographical and chronological terms. Some inscriptions with evidence related to *hospitium* are found in all periods of Roman history in Italy and North Africa, but few in the Rhine/Danube areas. The Iberian Peninsula is the most important single source of material. As a good number of the inscriptions originating there were written in Celtic, it is a reasonable conclusion that the institution was already well established in that region (and presumably elsewhere) before the Romans arrived.

1. Mommsen 1864 remains the most important contribution to the study of *hospitium*. The lexicon article by Leonhard (1913) offers a brief overview. See the section on suggested reading at the end of this article for some other specialized studies.

2. Cic. *Balb.* 43 suggests that Balbus, now a Roman citizen, was considered the *hospes* of his hometown of Gades—that is, Balbus retained the affection of his home state and defended its interests as *sanctissimum hospitem*.

Proxenia and Hospitium

The Romans made a nearly complete identification between Greek *proxenia* (guest-friendship) and Latin *hospitium*. To the Greeks *Zeus Xenios* (Zeus the Hospitable) himself guaranteed the relationship, just as did Jupiter for the Romans (see below); and indeed, the Greek expression *proxenos*, with its many variants, is widely attested in literary and epigraphical sources.[3] Be that as it may, educated Romans knew their Homer, and knew that Homer strongly endorsed the civilizing value of *hospitium* (i.e., *proxenia*) in book 6 of the *Iliad*. For when Diomedes and Glaukon meet on the field of battle, they recognize the guest-friendship that existed since the time of their fathers; the two therefore exchange (n.b., a significant element of *hospitium*) armor, that others may know of their relationship, and they both resolve to seek glory elsewhere. Many stories with similar motifs also survive in Roman literature. Philip of Macedonia, so Seneca explains, was outraged when he learned that Pausanius mistreated one of his *hospites*, a man who had even once saved Pausanius' life—this plainly demonstrated that Pausanius was *ingratissimus* (most ungrateful), and not only to the man who had saved his life, but also to that man's guest-friend, Philip (Sen. *Ben.* 4. 37. 2–4). As will be argued below, despite any and all similarities between Greek *proxenia* and Roman *hospitium*, the Romans tended to treat this kind of relationship more formally and legally than did the Greeks (cf. Mommsen 1864: 330–31).

So too did the Romans easily apply the term *hospitium* to relations between non-Romans. Thus, for example, the German tribes could be described as having been originally formed by a synthesis of new arrivals and *hospites* (Tac. *Ger.* 2. 1). Or we are told that Syphax (the Numidian chief) and Hasdrubal (the Carthaginian leader) were guest-friends (*hospites*) when the former sought marriage to the daughter of latter (Liv. 29. 23. 3). What episodes of this sort indicate is that the Romans viewed guest-friendship both as an institution 'shared' not only with the Greeks, but with most other peoples—yet also as a form of relationship that lent itself to distinct Roman variations.

The Sacred Character of Hospitium

The sources are in agreement about the fundamental dynamics of the relationship. Formal or informal, public or private, *hospitium* was, as Cicero explains, *quod sanctissimum est* (a most hallowed thing—Cic. *Ver.* 2. 2. 110), devised by the gods to benefit humans. Seneca concurs: *duo sacratissima inter homines...hospitium et adfinitas* (two things are most sacred amongst men...hospitality and

---

3. On the breadth of the phenomenon, see the important article by Gschnitzer 1973.

close relationships—*Con.* 8. 6. 17). The tendency to place *hospitium* in a religious or quasi-religious sphere takes two forms. Most notably, the Romans variously viewed *hospitium* as the special responsibility of a particular manifestation of the god Jupiter (namely, *Jupiter Hospitalis*), who stood as the guarantor or protector of the relationship, and of the parties to the relationship (Cic. *Verr.* 4. 22; *Q. fr.* 2. 12; *Deiot.* 6; cf. also 2 *Maccabees* 6). From an expression in Plautus (*deum hospitalem ac tesseram mecum fero*—I always keep my hospitality god and tablet with me; *Poen.* 5. 1. 25), it has been deduced that this *tessera* (a tablet, which recorded the relationship of hospitality) bore the image of *Jupiter Hospitalis*.[4] Other authors note a more generalized divine responsibility, as is suggested by references to *dii hospitales* (hospitality gods; see Tac. *Ann.* 15. 52; also in Liv. 39. 51 and Ov. *Met.* 5. 45; cf. further Serv. *ad Aen.* 1. 140). Such references to gods, who appear to oversee relationships of hospitality, seem to place *hospitium* completely outside the Roman legal framework. Certainly for much of the classical period, and in reference to *hospitium privatum*, that was probably the case; *hospitium publicum*, however, had to involve some form of communal/legal action (see below).

In this respect, we might note some other significant variations on the subject. Cicero (*Cael.* 51 and 54) observes that it was especially heinous (he talks of a *magnum crimen*—a colossal crime) to incite slaves to murder their master's *hospes*. Pliny the Elder equates the relationship between children and parents to that between *hospites*—a very suggestive passage because the inequality of the parties would then be undeniable (Plin. *Nat.* 2. 144).

Did the Romans take these expressions of sanctity seriously? Various references in the sources indicate that the maintenance of *hospitium* was considered part of the natural order; indeed, there are several stories related by mainstream Roman authors that assume that even animals understood and respected the *iura hospitium* (the rules of guest-friendship). Aristotle, so Pliny notes, described scorpions that spare *hospites*, but kill indigenous peoples (*Nat.* 8. 229; also 4. 91). The same author records that when some *hospites* of Medus were murdered, all the ravens flew away from the Peloponnesus (*Nat.* 10. 33). Pliny also includes the story of a snake mother who killed her own child when the latter had violated the rules of hospitality (*Nat.* 10. 208). Of course, these stories need to be understood as metaphors; nonetheless, they do indicate that popular culture in the ancient world took it for granted that *hospitium* was an element of the natural order, something that could be understood and respected even by animals.

Certainly there are no indications that anyone expected Jupiter or any of the gods necessarily to intervene directly to punish a man who was ungrateful or unfaithful (Plin. *Nat.* 2. 117). Moreover, though the open abuse of *hospitium*

---

4. It is possible that the portrait embedded in one *tabula hospitalis* (from Castro) is indeed Jupiter; still, the fact that the portrait is of a beardless man probably suggests that this is not the case. Be that as it may, portraits were attached to most of the *tabulae* that have been found in Spain, and this was perhaps also the case elsewhere.

may not have been an indictable offense, publicly violating its conventions was perceived to be uncivilized or, more accurately, something only a wild beast would do. Indeed, this is one of the main charges that Cicero levels against Verres: *Sed quid ego hospitii iura in hac immani belua commemoro?* (But why should I even speak of the rules of hospitality with regard to this tremendous monster?—*Ver.* 2. 5. 109). Cicero certainly presumed that he could damage the reputation of Verres by dwelling on those actions that violated the *ius hospitalis*, and other writers concur (see below).

On the Initiation of the Relationship

Hospitium is extended by a formal invitation, by a decree of the local senate, if it is public, or by an individual, who offers lodging and victuals, if it is in the private sphere. In both cases, the formula is clear (respectively): *invitare eum publice tecto ac domo* (to invite him publicly into house and home; *Ver.* 2. 4. 25); *vocare in hospitium* (to offer hospitality; Liv. 24. 16. 16), *eum domum suam invitare* (to invite him into one's home; *Ver.* 2. 2. 89), or, *hospitio invitabit* (he will offer a hospitable relationship; Cic. *Phil.* 12. 35). Depending on how formal the relationship was, a token (*tessera*, or later a *tabula*—see figs. 20.1 and 20.2 for representative examples) might be prepared to commemorate the occasion.[5] The occasion might also be marked by the formal exchange of gifts, or by sacrificing and consuming an animal (cf. Stat. *Ach.* 1. 843: *munera...signum hospitii*, gifts which are a mark of hospitality). Alternatively, an alliance might also be the basis of a *hospitium publicum*; and thus, Caesar indicates that the Aedui enjoyed the *hospitium amicitaque populi Romani* (the hospitality and the friendship of the Roman people; *Gal.* 1. 31).

The most important episode for this process is Livy's story about Roman ambassadors (*legati*) on their way to Delphi to bring a gift to the god Apollo. When they came to Lipari, the chief magistrate, Timasitheus, entertained them *in publicum hospitium* (surely to be understood here as a public building specifically intended, at least in part, for entertaining important guests), and assisted the legates on their voyage to and from Delphi. After the legates had returned safely to Rome, a covenant of hospitality was made with Timasitheus by a decree of the senate, and gifts were presented to him in the name of the state (Liv. 5. 28. 4–5). Here we find almost all the ingredients of the relationship: a chance encounter, a party in need, protection offered, the use of public facilities, mutual obligation, a senatorial decree authorizing *hospitium publicum*, and the arrangement for gifts to be provided at public expense.

5. Balbín Chamorro 2006. This important study also includes an excellent set of plates with the most important *tesserae* and *tabulae*.

Figure 20.1. This is a good example of the developed form of the *tessara* or *tabula hospitalis*. Note the pentagonal form and the portrait bust at the top. The text dates to AD 28, and is distinctive because the two parties, both apparently Celtic (from northwestern Spain) chose to use the Latin language to record *hospitium publicum*. The basic publication for the Tillegus text is *AE* 1961, 96. Photo courtesy of Armin U. Stylow.

THE *TESSARAE HOSPITALES* (TOKENS OF GUEST-FRIENDSHIP)

The earliest *tesserae* (tokens) may have been of earthenware, having the head of Jupiter Hospitalis stamped upon them (Pl. *Poen.* 5. 1. 25; 2. 87–99). More common in the late republic and early principate was the use of metal *tesserae* and *tabulae*, especially in those cases involving the conclusion of a *hospitium publicum*. These objects are sometimes in the form of animals, for example, a pig, perhaps to commemorate an animal slaughtered as part of a ritual meal confirming the relationship.[6] The *tesserae* at least in some cases appear to be deliberately broken in

6. Balbín Chamorro 2006. Dozens of such items are to be found in Balbín Chamorro's plates, pp. 249ff. Fish and a variety four-legged, domesticated examples may be found. Note also the much published pig from Pisuerga (plate no. 53).

Figure 20.2. This is a good example of the quadratic and 'classical' form of the *tabula hospitalis*. Note the handle suggesting a concern for portability. This inscription records the establishment of *hospitium* and of *clientela* between a prominent member of the equestrian order, Q. Licinius Silvanus Granianus, and the Roman city of Baetulo (Barcelona). It dates to the late AD 90s. *AE 1936, 66 = RIT 288, 289.* Photo courtesy of Armin U. Stylow.

half, or constructed with interlocking parts, so that the two parties could recognize one another on a subsequent occasion by fitting the pieces together again.[7] Later bronze tablets tend to take either a pentagonal or quadratic form.[8] Though there are many variations, all record at least the names of the *hospites*, their intention to

7. Balbín Chamorro 2006: plate no. 38. This one appears to be manufactured to achieve the same result.

8. Balbín Chamorro 2006: plates 54 and 55 for examples of rectangular items; nos. 58, 72, 73 for the pentagonal.

formalize a relationship, and the intention that the relationship should continue to future generations (...*liberis posterisque*—for their children and descendants; also in literary texts, e.g., Liv. 27. 16). In many cases, *hospitium* is brought into connection with other social relationships—most notably with forms of patronage that would seem to undermine (n.b.) an otherwise implicit equality of status and services (see below).

Another way to formalize such a relationship was the transmittal of clasped right hands as a sign/symbol of *hospitium* (so, e.g., *miserat civitas Lingonum vetere instituto dona legionibus dextras, hospitii insigne*—The community of the Lingones had, in accord with an ancient custom, sent gifts to the legions, namely, clasped right hands, which was a sign of hospitality; Tac. *Hist.* 1. 54. Cf *Hist.* 2. 8. 11, where Syrian legions sent a similar gift to the praetorians). Tacitus is here explicit that this was a Lingonian practice.[9] In this case, the reference is clearly to *hospitium publicum*. Significant is the fact that the references from Pliny the Elder, from Statius, and from Tacitus confirm the archaeological record, namely, that *hospitium* continued to be initiated in a fairly conventional way well into the second century AD.

HOSPITIUM AND ROMAN LAW

As noted above, Roman law did not regulate *hospitium*. That is, disappointed *hospites* could not take legal action to claim damages when a guest-friend did not act as was expected. The agreement depended, then, upon the continuing goodwill of both parties, and more subtly, on the damage to reputation that might result from betraying guest-friends (examples follow). There is, however, one important exception to this rule, and it is instructive in its own right. The *lex Ursonensis* (ch. 131) does indeed regulate the manner by which Julian colonies (assuming, of course, that this document reflects what was general practice among these colonies) might conclude a contract of *hospitium publicum*. It is important to recognize what this paragraph does and does not do. It does specify the manner by which an individual may be accorded the honor of guest-friendship, and it defines his status (e.g., *sine imperio privatus*—a private person, not holding a Roman magistracy), but it says nothing about the obligations of either party. This paragraph assumes that such appointments could be controversial, and that during the civil wars probably were, as the history of Urso itself indicates. In sum, the only known legal document regulating *hospitium* concerns *hospitium publicum* and the requirements for a valid legal action; it does not regulate performance of service.

9. Balbín Chamorro 2006: plates 1, 24, 41. There is some reason to believe that the symbol *signum hospitalis* may have originated in Persia (cf. Xen. *An.* 2. 4).

WHO WERE THE *HOSPITES*? *HOSPITIUM*
PUBLICUM AND *PRIVATUM*

As noted above, *hospites* might be individuals or collectives. Typically, the *hospites* belonged to different communities. As Rome evolved, and especially after (though not necessarily because of) the unification of Italy, *hospitium* also described hospitable arrangements and included partners, both of whom might be Roman citizens but from different Roman communities. On the whole, we have much more information about *hospitium publicum*, an arrangement of guest-friendship in which at least one of the sides involved was a collective. Though private parties may also have had reasons to memorialize this sort of relationship, they apparently did not do so in the kind of formal/official way employed by communities. Moreover, in private contracts, the variability of expectations and formalities was presumably much greater.

In any case, as just mentioned, if one of the parties to the arrangement was a collective, then it is appropriate to speak of *hospitium publicum*. So, as noted above, in AD 69, the Lingones, originally a Celtic group in the northeast of France, concluded *hospitium* with the legions stationed nearby, a clear case of both parties being collectives. Epigraphical references confirm that the groups that engaged in this kind of association might also be clans or other associations.[10]

Much more common in the surviving records, however, are cases in which one of the parties is a collective, or a local head of state, and the other is an individual (frequently an aristocratic Roman). The two best examples of this phenomenon are preserved by inscriptions (*ILS* 6102 and 6104), both of which use variations on the standard language: in one case the expression *hospitium renovavit* (he renewed the guest-friendship) occurs, suggesting that a long-standing relationship was renewed; in the other, we read that *hospitalem tesseram fecit* (he made a token of guest-friendship). Both cases involve communities as one party and an individual of some importance and/or official status from another community. In the latter case many, though by no means all, of these *hospites* were Roman magistrates with some official function in the province.

There is one rather well-known *tessara hospitalis* from Munigua (lying between Sevilla and Cordoba), and it provides a good example of this phenomenon. In this case, we read that *Sex. Curvius Silvinus quaestor pro praetor hospitium fecit cum senatu populoque Muniguensi Hispaniae ulterioris* (Sextus Curvius Silvinus the quaestor and propraetor established guest-friendship with the senate and people of Munigua in Further Spain; *AE* 1972, 263). Silvinus was, then, a Roman senator with an official function in the province. He is also here revealed as the active partner (*fecit*—he

---

10. Balbín Chamorro 2006: *tabulae* 47, 48, 49, and 50 are good examples of the range; here an *oppidum*[?] (town), *gentilitas* (ethnic community), *civitas* (city), and a *castellum* (fort), respectively.

established); nonetheless, the community provided the commemorative inscription and sent ambassadors (*legati*) to deliver it to Silvinus. This inscription was found in Munigua itself, and as *legati* are mentioned, it may be that two copies were prepared, one for the local archives, and a second to be delivered to the *hospes* (cf. *CIL* V 4919–22 for an analogous case).

We should not be too legalistic, though, in applying these concepts, a point that is confirmed by Cicero's statements on his own relationship to Syracuse. Cicero indicates that though Roman governors were traveling on public business, they were ideally given the wherewithal to travel without having to impose on provincials for material support and comforts. Nonetheless, it is readily apparent in the *Verrines* that both Verres and Cicero himself concluded *hospitium publicum* and *privatum* in various Sicilian communities. So, for example, Cicero notes that when he came to Syracuse to collect material for the case against Verres, a formal decree of the city extended to him and to his brother *hospitium publicum*. The decree was recorded on bronze: *id* (the decree) *non modo tum scripserunt verum etiam in aere incisum nobis tradiderunt* (nor did they merely write the decree, but indeed, they brought it to me cut into bronze; Cic. *Ver.* 2. 4. 145). Nonetheless, though he might have stayed in a public building, given both his position as governor and his now-formalized relationship of guest-friendship with the city, Cicero decided to lodge with his personal *hospites*. That is, at least some towns did have hospices in the sense of publicly owned buildings for lodging their official guests (see, e.g., Liv. 5. 28. 4; Plin. *Ep.* 10. 81). At Rome, for example, visitors might be lodged in a *villa publica* (Liv. 30. 21. 12). In other cases, the leading citizens of the host community could arrange among themselves to distribute the burden, and would entertain the public guest-friends in their private residences.

Probably equally common, though not nearly as well documented, were connections of hospitality established between individuals. I have published elsewhere a table summarizing Cicero's various private *hospites* in Sicily (Nicols 2001: 100). That table, which collects the evidence from the *Verrines*, provides our best indication of the variety of hospitable arrangements concluded between Roman magistrates and locals. One may presume that prominent Romans enjoyed such relations with many individuals and families in the provinces they had once governed.

There was, however, a wide range of activity that could be implied when the words *hospes* or *hospitium* were used. Cicero, for example, employs the word *hospitium* in respect to offering 'hospitality' at Arpinum to his good friend Atticus. Clearly we cannot interpret this to mean that the two friends were *hospites* in the sense that Scipio Africanus and the Numidian king, Masinissa (Cic. *Cato* 34), or Scipio and Polybius (Cic. *Rep.* 4. 3) were. Moreover, we need to be cautious that we do not discount the frequency of private arrangements simply because the material evidence does not provide an extensive record for such connections.

The Exchange of Gifts

It is not clear to what extent gifts—aside from, say, the tokens that recorded *hospitium*—were exchanged in this process. Cicero observes that a certain Sthenius had collected objects of marvelous artistic value, not so much for his own pleasure but especially to impress his friends and *hospites* (*Ver.* 2. 2. 83). This collection aroused the interest (and cupidity) of many Romans, and thus enabled Sthenius to acquire an illustrious group of *hospites* at Rome (Cic. *Ver.* 2. 2. 110). It may well be, then, that Verres' abuse of the normal rules of hospitality is to be connected with his expectations regarding gift giving. Sthenius, for example, lost all those items assembled for this purpose to the rapacity of his *hospes*, the notorious Verres.

For the most part, though, the gifts might be more accurately categorized as generous or lavish expenditure in support of the visiting *hospes*, support that a sensitive and thoughtful visitor understood as a burden on the host. Cicero and Livy were well aware of this problem (cf., e.g., Liv. 42. 1). In Messana, for example, Cicero had his cousin put up in another household, apparently in order to reduce the costs to his own *hospes* (Cic. *Ver.* 2. 4. 25; also *Fam.* 7. 23). Note also the expression of relief in *o hospitem non gravem!* (Oh you guest who is not so burdensome!—Cic. *Fam.* 9. 20), or Seneca's comment that the body is not a permanent dwelling (*domus*), but a kind of inn (*hospitium*), suitable for a brief stay, but something that might become cumbersome (*gravis*) to the host (Sen. *Ep.* 120. 14). In other cases, the exchange appears to involve items of fairly minor commercial value. Cicero, for example, sent a copy of a speech (a *munusculum*—i.e., a small gift—as he puts it) to an old *hospes et amicus* in return for the little gifts he had received (Cic. *Fam.* 9. 12; also *Fam.* 9. 16. 7, where *hospitium* and *amicitia* are complementary, and the notion of transaction/debt is explicit).

Services

Aside from providing for the comforts of visitors, *hospites* also provided services, some of which are not at all easily distinguishable from those provided by patrons and clients. The evidence, which is primarily epigraphical, indicates that the Romans were not particularly troubled by the implications of combining relationships that had very different ramifications with respect to equality or inequality of status and of service. Indeed, a significant number of *tesserae* and *tabulae* record not only the establishment of *hospitium*, but also of *patrocinium/clientelae* (patronage/clientship); the type of document, in other words, cannot necessarily indicate the specific type of relationship thereupon recorded.[11] Moreover, these texts are explicit in saying that both relationships—in other words, hospitality and patronage—are

11. For detailed account of the issue, see Balbín Chamorro 2006.

being established at the same time. Though much scholarly ink has flowed on this issue, the evidence is consistent in at least two respects, namely, that (a) the Romans and their counterparts in the provinces did not see the two relationships (again, hospitality and patronage) as mutually exclusive, and (b) an individual could thus simultaneously be both a *hospes* and a *cliens/patronus*, even though the former sort of bond could be seen as assuming equality between the parties involved, and the latter inequality. There is not much sense in trying to bring (what we would perceive as) order to the system. One may guess that the circumstances dictated (in a fashion perfectly clear to a Roman) whether one responded as a guest-friend, as a patron, or as a client. Furthermore, the flexible nature of the structure may have made it more attractive to all the participants, allowing each to stress what seemed most important at any given moment.[12] That is, inferiors might assuage their inferiority by emphasizing that they were truly *hospites*, while the superior party might also perceive of, and claim, the other party as a client.

To lend this all a bit more clarity, it is worth listing some of the services recorded as having been proffered in such relationships. The list is not meant to be all-inclusive, but rather, to demonstrate the range of activity possible in this realm.

1. In general, Cicero notes that he provided his *hospes*, Hegesaretus of Larissa, with benefactions during his consulship, and the latter had shown himself to be *gratus* (grateful) and *diligentissumus* (most attentive) in responding thereafter (Cic. *Fam.* 13. 25).

2. One of the more frequent references to *hospitium* in the sources relates to the exchange of information between *hospites*. So, for example, it was through *privatis hospitiis* (private connections of hospitality) that information was conveyed to Rome about the impending revolt of the Latins (Liv. 8. 3). However, such exchanges of information can also involve fairly simple matters, like guiding a stranger through one's town (Cic. *Ac.* 1. 9).

3. In terms of providing protection (often legal):
   a. Cicero mentions that L. Plaetorius appeared in court in a case involving the latter's *hospes*, Vibius Cappadox. Cappadox was living in the house of his *familiaris* (close acquaintance) and *hospes* when he died intestate. The protection of Cappadox's estate is the issue. In another case, Cicero aides his *hospes* to protect the latter's property by writing to the provincial governor (Cic. *Fam.* 13. 37).

---

12. Cic. *Cato* 32 notes Cato's on-going obligations to friends, clients, and *hospites*. Cf. also Cic. *Fam.* 9. 16. 7, where *hospitium* and *amicitia* (friendship) are complementary; and *Fam.* 13. 25, where Cicero commends Hegesaretus of Larissa as his *hospes* and *familiaris* (close acquaintance), and also as a grateful and good man, the first in his state. One might think also of C. Avianus Philoxenus, whom Cicero calls *antiquus hospes meus* (my long-standing guest-friend), and also *familiaris* (intimate acquaintance); as a favor to Cicero, Caesar made Philoxenus a citizen of Comum (Cic. *Fam.* 13. 35); *amici, vicini,* and *hospites* of Cluentius hope for his restoration (Cic. *Clu.* 202). Cicero offers *hospitium* to Atticus, clearly a generalized meaning here (Cic. *Att* 2. 16. 4).

b. A legionary in the army of Vitellius defends his *hospes*, a workman, against a charge of fraud (Tac. *Hist.* 2. 66).

4. Recommendation/commendation: Avianius Philoxenus, whom Cicero calls an old *hospes meus* (guest-friend of mine), is honored with citizenship in Comum, because Cicero recommends Philoxenus to Caesar (Cic. *Fam.* 13. 35).

5. The following references do not lend themselves to neat categories, but rather illustrate the range of attitudes about *hospitium*:

   a. Syphax admits to madness in putting aside all *hospitia privata et publica foedera omnia* (Liv. 30. 13. 11).

   b. Aeneas is *hospes* to Latinus; the alliance between them was a *foedus publicum*, one that became private with the marriage (Liv. 1. 1. 9). Tarquinus has a similar relationship with the Latins (Liv. 1. 49).

   c. Polybius, though technically a hostage, was also the *hospes* of Scipio (Cic. *Rep.* 4. 3).

   d. Syphax offers *hospitium* to both Scipio and to Hasdrubal (Liv. 28. 18), and hopes to use the occasion to reconcile them. Scipio notes that he had no personal animosity toward the Carthaginian, but could not negotiate without having been ordered to do so by the senate. There are implications here: third party *hospitium* might lead to negotiations between enemies, but official concerns ultimately dominate over private ones.

   e. Cicero writes to the propraetor P. Servilius on behalf of his *necessarius and hospes*, Andro of Laodicea (Cic. *Fam.* 13. 67). Even after leaving his province, Cicero continues to remember and to show his gratitude to his *hospes*. Also: Cic. *Fam.* 13. 37.

FAILURE TO RESPECT *HOSPITIUM*

This contribution has focused primarily on the descriptions of *hospitium* in which the institution functions successfully. The sources also provide many examples to illustrate that *hospitium* sometimes also failed to meet the expectation of one or the other of the parties to the relationship. In general, these examples do not indicate that *hospitium* failed as an institution; there are simply too many examples of it working effectively. Rather, the 'failures' illustrate especially clearly the fact that *hospitium* was nowhere legally enforceable, but depended on the continuing goodwill of both parties.[13] That is, we know of no case in which anyone threatened legal action against a *hospes* for violating the 'rights of hospitality' (*iura hospitii*); indeed,

---

13. I have a fuller discussion of this element in the article published in Nicols 2001.

the word 'rights' here is somewhat misleading as a legal term.[14] Nonetheless, as the following passages indicate, there are numerous cases in which parties were disappointed, and surely there were many more in which the relationship ceased because neither of the parties wished to continue it:

1. Pliny the Elder notes that *infida hospitia* (untrustworthy arrangements of hospitality) were a characteristic feature of dangerous times (Plin. *Nat.* 2. 117). This opinion is echoed in many places by Tacitus (e.g., Valens polluted *hospitium* by his adulteries and debaucheries in the homes of his *hospites*—Tac. *Hist* 3. 41).
2. Tiberius (allegedly) tortured and eventually killed his *hospes* from Rhodes because he feared the latter would talk about the bad treatment he had received from his guest and thereby diminish Tiberius' reputation (Suet. *Tib.* 62. 1).
3. Deiotarus, the king of Galatia in Anatolia, saw Caesar as his *hostem et hospitum* (enemy and guest-friend; Cic. *Div.* 2. 79). Caesar was received *magnificentissumo hospitio* (with the most splendid hospitality), yet ultimately left his royal host despoiled.

There are, then, two forces that encouraged the respect of *hospites*. First, in periods that were more stable and peaceful, *hospites* might share the firm belief that the services performed by one party would yield corresponding benefits over the short and long term. In times of crisis, however, when alliances might have life-or-death significance, expectations of reciprocity were inevitably lower, and the effectiveness of the institution suffered correspondingly. Hence, Tacitus could express astonishment that, during the civil wars of AD 69, there were indeed some examples in which *fides* (good faith) was respected (*Hist.* 1. 3). Second, our sources are consistent in stressing that the reputation for being a faithful *hospes* was an important and positive component of one's reputation. So, too, acquiring a reputation as a faithless *hospes* could undermine one's reputation. Thus, the effectiveness of the relationship depended on how useful it was to each party to sustain or expand it.

CONCLUSIONS

In sum, the practice of *hospitium* is widely attested in literary and epigraphical documents well into the high imperial period. While what remains of the histories of Livy might suggest that it was most common in the earlier part of Roman history, and by implication declined as the republic collapsed and was replaced by the principate, the continued, frequent, and consistent use of the term in the works of Cicero,

---

14. The words are Cicero's and quoted above in reference to Verres. On the different meanings of *ius/iura*, see Berger 1953: ad loc.

Caesar, Seneca, Pliny, and Tacitus, and in the inscriptions dating to the principate, all indicate that the institution was widely understood and used by the ancients, both Romans and peregrines, throughout the central period of Roman history.

That having been said, it must also be noted that, with one exception, the practice of *hospitium* remained outside the purview of Roman law. That is, Roman municipal law (at least during the late republic) did establish some formal constraints to be followed in initiating *hospitium publicum*. And the fact that so many of the *tabulae* establishing *hospitium* take the form of municipal decrees suggests that Roman communities did continue to see a legal dimension to this institution, at least in respect to the establishment of *hospitium publicum*. Otherwise, though, the practice of *hospitium* remained outside the sphere of matters potentially governed by the courts, and could be 'regulated' only via the goodwill and reputation of the parties involved. In this sense, the exercise of *hospitium* easily took on an aspect of sacrosanctity.

For the society overall, *hospitium* in principle provided a mechanism by which outsiders might find protection, support, lodging, guidance, and friendship in a foreign community. Theoretically, the full range of services provided was available to both parties. In fact, however, the unequal status and resources of each party effectively meant that one party was usually 'superior' to the other. This reality was expressed in the formulae that easily combined *hospitium* with *clientelae* on the 'contracts' (*tabulae* and *tesserae*) that commemorated the establishment of the relationship. Nonetheless, the continued use of *hospitium* throughout the central periods of Roman history suggests that the institution was indeed pervasive and indeed valued by Romans and peregrines alike. We may reasonably conclude that in most cases, *hospitium* met the needs and expectations of both parties successfully.

SUGGESTED READING

There is no systematic account of Roman hospitality available in English. For the early period, Bolchazy 1977 is a good place to start. Badian 1958 deals with one important aspect of the relationship during the Roman Republic and serves also as a good introduction to the institution. Still fundamental is Mommsen 1864.

BIBLIOGRAPHY

Badian, E. 1958. *Foreign clientelae (264–70 B.C.)*. Oxford: Oxford University Press.
Balbín Chamorro, P. 2006. *Hospitalidad y Patronato en la península Ibérica Durante la Antigüedad*. Salamanca: Junta de Castilla y León.
Beltrán, F. 2001. "Los pactos de hospitalidad de la Hispania Citerior: una valoración histórica." In L. Hernández, L. Sagredo, and J. M. Solana (eds.), *Actas del I Congreso*

Internacional de Historia Antigua: La Península Ibérica hace 2000 años, (Valladolid, 23–25 de noviembre de 2000). Valladolid: Universidad de Valladolid. 393–99.

Berger, A. 1953. *Encyclopedic Dictionary of Roman Law*. Philadelphia: American Philosophical Society.

Bolchazy, L. J. 1977. *Hospitality in early Rome*. Chicago: Ares.

Cagnat, R. 1900. "Hospitium militare." In Ch. Daremberg and E. Saglio (eds.), *Dictionnaire des antiquités grecques et romaines, tome troisiéme, premiére partie (H-K)*. Paris: Librairie Hachette. 302–3.

d'Ors, A. 1953. *Epigrafía jurídica de la España romana*. Madrid: Instituto Nacional de Estudios Jurídicos.

Étienne, R., P. Le Roux, and A. Tranoy. 1987. "*La tessera hospitalis* instrument de sociabilité et de romanisation dans la Péninsule Ibérique." In F. Thélamon (ed.), *Sociabilité, pouvoirs et société*. Rouen: Université de Rouen. 323–36.

Gschnitzer, F. 1973. "Proxenos." In *RE* Suppl. XIII, 629–730.

Harmand, L. 1957. *Un aspect social et politique du monde romain: Le patronat sur les collectivités publiques des origines au Bas Empire*. Paris: Faculté des Lettres de l'Université de Clermont.

Leonhard, R. 1913. "Hospitium." In *RE* VIII.2, 2493–98.

Mangas, J. 1983. "*Hospititum y patrocinium* sobre colectividades públicas: ¿terminos sinónimos? (de Augusto a fines de los Severos)." *Dialogues d'histoire ancienne* 9: 165–84.

Mommsen, Th. 1864. "Das römische Gastrecht und die römische Clientele." In Th. Mommsen, *Römische Forschungen I*. Berlin: Weidmann. 321–90.

Nicols, J. 1980. "*Tabulae patronatus*: A Study of the Agreement between Patron and Client-Community." In *Aufstieg und Niedergang der römischen Welt II.13*. Berlin: Walter de Gruyter. 535–61.

———. 2001. "*Hospitium* and Political Friendship in the Late Republic." In M. Peachin (ed.), *Aspects of Friendship in the Graeco-Roman World*. Portsmouth, R.I.: Journal of Roman Archaeology. 99–108.

Rouland, N. 1979. *Pouvoir politique et dépendance personelle dans l'Antiquité romaine*. Brussels: Latomus.

....

CHAPTER 21

ROMAN DINING

....

KATHERINE M. D. DUNBABIN

AND WILLIAM J. SLATER

INTRODUCTION

....

Two contradictory pieces of evidence from the Graeco-Roman world reveal the confusion of antiquity in facing its own dining customs. Philostratus writes in the early third century AD about a visit of the wise man Apollonius to the Indians in the time of the emperor Tiberius (*VA* 3. 27. 3): "...the cups did the rounds as in a drinking party; and they reclined as in a collegial banquet (*sussition*), not with the king in a superior position,—this is an important point for Greeks and Romans—but at random, where anyone found a place." Much earlier, in 67 BC, a typical decree of an association of farmers in Hellenistic Egypt honors their benefactor Paris, who had given them land for a clubhouse and banquet room, with a place at high table in their banquets (*SEG* VIII 529, line 28): "it is decreed that he be welcomed and honored with two portraits which will be placed in the gymnasium and in the clubroom and that these be crowned on the eponymous days when we get together to sacrifice in the name of the kings; and that he be offered the first couch [*protē klisia*] for life..." According to the principles prevailing in antiquity, collegial banquets are supposed to be models of equality; yet not only is it accepted that pride of place in seating is highly regarded in all society, but paradoxically honors may be awarded to benefactors by the members of an association, so entrenching inequality in their banquets.

The contradiction reflects a fundamental tension in the ideology and practice of formal dining, even more marked in Roman society than in Greek. Older studies (e.g., Marquardt 1886; Friedländer 1922) sought to produce a positivist normative view of the Roman *convivium* (banquet, social dining); more modern studies have emphasized that the Roman custom of dining together brought with it the cultural baggage of centuries, particularly Greek idealism concerning the social values of equality, freedom, and communal participation, already firmly fixed in thinking and literature before the particular rituals of the Roman *convivium* developed (see esp. Vössing 2004: 253–64). Behind this admirable facade, Roman society also inherited from the Greeks the simple reality that equality was unobtainable in an unequal society, where slaves, freedmen, and citizens of different types and backgrounds, not to forget old men, young men, and women, jostled each other; and the entrenched Roman systems of hierarchical patronage relations only exacerbated the paradox. The historian must be vigilant in distinguishing fact and claims, reality and idealism, in the often biased and contradictory sources.

Moreover, text-based studies have tended to concentrate too exclusively on Rome, its literature, and its elite politics.[1] But there exists also a wealth of epigraphic evidence, in Latin and Greek, for the banquets of associations, which represent indirectly a different but coherent quasi-democratic tradition that flourished throughout the Roman Empire. This material includes trade and religious associations, sometimes of freedmen and slaves, as well as more politically visible groups; communal dining was central to their social networking and their importance in activities such as the imperial cult. In a sense, the empire was dependent for its cohesion on such organized gatherings that met in regular session, employing similar mechanisms of commensality to express their community and integration into the larger framework of society. Meanwhile, the archaeological remains of urban houses and country villas throughout the empire offer a glimpse, through the design, layout, and decoration of rooms for dining and reception, of the practices of the elite and sub-elite in the provinces, for whom written evidence is often limited. And art, with its many scenes of dining, in different contexts, also illustrates the attitudes, the assumptions, and the ideologies of a similar wide section of Roman and Graeco-Roman society.

Certain broad categories can be distinguished within the spectrum of Roman dining; but the distinction between them was never sharp, and there is considerable overlap. Similarly, Roman technical vocabulary is never precise, and most terms could be used flexibly or changed their significance. Our sources, of all sorts, tell us very little about 'ordinary' familial/domestic dining, nor do they even make clear whether it was indeed the norm, at any level of society, for families to eat together on a daily basis.[2] In contrast, the written sources have most to say about social dining by the elite, or wealthier members of the sub-elite (like Petronius' fictional freedman Trimalchio), entertaining a group composed primarily of friends and associates in what we would consider private circumstances; this is also the form best reflected in the architectural remains of houses and villas. There was also much public banqueting, where a benefactor (in Rome, under the empire, often the

---

1. E.g., Stein-Hölkeskamp 2005 (reviewed by Slater 2006); cf. also Salza Prina Ricotti 1983. Such text-based studies are also usually limited geographically to Rome and Italy, and chronologically to the late republic and early principate.

2. Bradley 1998. The limited evidence refers almost entirely to the elite. The urban poor seem to have obtained much of their hot food at taverns and cookhouses: see Kleberg 1957.

emperor) entertained large groups of people in public. Between these two forms, and not always clearly to be distinguished from them, was the peculiarly Roman practice of a patron entertaining his clients. The corporate dining of associations, recorded especially in inscriptions, covered a wide social range, from magistrates to groups of working men. Numerous religious groups, again of all social levels, also dined together regularly.[3] Finally, communal dining was also an important part of the cult of the dead, at funerals and on recurring anniversaries.

HISTORY

At dinner most Romans usually lay down on couches to eat and drink, and so, in requiring that they be served by menials, created by contrast a power position of freedom and superiority for themselves. Varro (*De vita populi Romani* fr. 30a, ed. Riposati) implies that reclining to dine was a relatively new and decadent custom, which was presumably contrasted with the simplicity of an idealized earlier rural Latin life. In fact, this type of dining posture was probably first introduced in the archaic period from the Etruscan elite, and encouraged by Greek culture to the south, from which the banquet derived its ideals. The development in the earlier and mid-republic is largely unknown.[4] With the establishment of Roman hegemony in the Hellenistic East from approximately 200 BC onward, the refinements of contemporary Greek dining practices were disseminated, and the practice of reclining was normalized, insofar as it was not already established; but there were distinct variants from earlier Greek fashions. During the empire, many different customs could coexist. Dining fashions can be traced particularly in the architecture of urban houses and villas, which reveal a standardized pattern over much of the empire by AD 100, with progressive development into the sixth century. The custom of reclining then disappears and was forgotten until sixteenth-century scholars rediscovered it, in their search for the historicity of the Last Supper (Dunbabin 2003a: 199–202; Rossiter 1991).

3. On Christian commensality, for example, see Becker in this volume. On the ritualized dining of a Roman priestly college, the Arval brethren, see Scheid in this volume. See further below, the section on corporate dining.

4. For the Roman literary construction of their earlier eating habits, see Purcell 2003. On the Roman banquet in the archaic period (sixth century BC), and its Etruscan origins, see Zaccaria Ruggiu 2003. She believes that the rituals of formal banqueting, including the practice of reclining, disappeared from Rome after the expulsion of the Tarquin kings, and there was then a profound break before their reintroduction, together with the wider habits of luxurious living, in the second century BC. But the evidence does not support such a claim; see the review by Terrenato 2004.

While the main outlines are easy to sketch, it is extremely difficult to detail and interpret the variants, always susceptible to changes in fashion, class hierarchies, ethnic differences, and personal taste. On holidays, ordinary Romans, like all the ancient world, could recline to eat in the countryside, as at the shrine of Anna Perenna outside Rome (Ov. *Fast.* 3. 523–42), whereas the wealthy could recline on the ground at hunting parties, but would then illustrate their superiority by luxurious apparatus or the quality of their slaves. In particular, while the importance attached to seat placement is attested, the actual order was determined both by the different shapes of the dining room and by the nature and number of the gathering, and could therefore be modified or even neglected for reasons usually obscure to us. Likewise, though a dinner meeting of eastern merchants might observe different rules from a gathering attended by the Roman magistrates in the same Campanian town, conversely we find that the magistrates of Asian cities begin early in the empire to adopt dining habits derived from Italy. Exceptions can be found to almost every general rule, and we have no means of quantifying our data—except perhaps the architectural—that would be acceptable for a modern historian. We are particularly ill-informed about elite Greek dining in Hellenistic times, as at Alexandria, despite its direct influence on Rome.

Social Dining: Architecture
and Placement

The usual Latin word for dining room, *triclinium,* means primarily a three-couch arrangement, or an intimate room with three couches for dining.[5] Greek dining rooms usually held more than five couches, and at least in the earlier Greek pattern the couches were smaller, normally for one or two diners, each with its own table. But by the end of the republic, Romans lay normally at a maximum of three to a standard couch, and four was considered crowded.[6] A couch was on average about 2.5 meters long by 1.5 meters deep, with a raised headrest (*pluteus*);[7] the three couches were placed in the form of the Greek letter Π, save that the left leg would be longer, leaving space for a single small table in the middle. Examples in masonry that survive in Pompeii illustrate this pattern, with minor variations (Dunbabin 1991: 123–24, with references; see fig. 21.1). The depth and size of the couch require that a Roman would lie at a more oblique angle than a Greek. The guests reclined on their left elbow, eating food portions with their right hand from the table set in the center. The main literary evidence

---

5. *Triclinium* is in origin Greek for three-couches. More general terms, such as *cenatio* and *cenaculum,* are also found: see Leach 1997: 67–68; Vössing 2004: 197, 561–66.

6. It is not clear when this pattern was adopted; a sixth-century Etruscan terracotta from Acquarossa is unique at this date in showing three per couch: Small 1971: 42–43 pl. XXIa.

7. For the meanings of *pluteus* and *fulcrum* (the ornamented front of the headrest), see Vössing 2004: 547–54.

Figure 21.1. Pompeii I.6.2–4, House of the Cryptoporticus. Masonry *triclinium* showing traditional arrangement of three couches around single small table; the ledge along the front, and the additional benches at the ends, are unusual. AD 62–79. Photo KMDD.

for this standard late republican pattern is Horace's account of Nasidienus' dinner for Maecenas (*Sat.* 2. 8), along with municipal law codes that restrict the number of guests to nine per *convivium* (*Lex Coloniae Genetivae,* ch. CXXXII, line 23, Crawford 1996: 417).

Banqueters are said to be above (*supra*) the guests lying to their right, in front of them, and below (*infra*) those at their backs, to their left. In accordance with these designations, the three couches (*lecti*) were called highest, middle, and lowest (*summus, medius, imus*), and the three guests on each couch would also be in the same pattern; thus, a guest who was *summus in imo* (highest on the lowest couch) would be the third person of the nine from the left for anyone entering the dining room (see fig. 21.2). Contrary to a common view, there is no evidence that these place terms were applied generally or particularly to social standing, although seating placement could be important (Sen. *de ira* 3. 37. 4; Amm. Marc. 28. 4. 21). In more formal dinners a servant called *vocator* or *nomen-clator* was in charge of placement and supervision, while a tricliniarch organized the staff and service. An over-sensitive guest could be annoyed at being placed on the *imus* instead of the *medius* couch (Sen. *de constantia sapientis* 10. 2), and another might insist on lying on the *medius* when placed on the *summus* (Plu. *Bru.* 34. 8). Nonetheless, a guest could be asked where he wanted to lie, if there was a possible problem (Plu. *Cat. Mi.* 37. 3–4), or guests could simply ignore the *nomenclator* (Ath. 2. 47 E). The formal place of honor in the standard triclinium

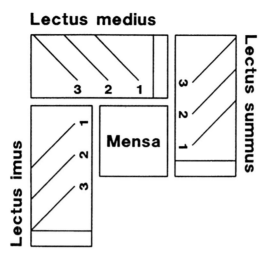

Figure 21.2. Plan of the layout of a traditional Roman *triclinium* in the late Republic and early Empire, for nine guests; 1, 2, 3 on each couch are respectively *summus, medius,* and *imus.* After H. Thédenat, *Pompéi.* Paris: H. Laurens Éditeur 1910. Fig. 44.

banquet is number 3 on the middle couch, *imus in medio,* known also as the consular or praetorian place, next to, in other words, superior to, the usual place for the host at *summus in imo.* For family or dependents of the host, the *imus* couch was usually reserved.[8]

This traditional three-couch structure continued, but also developed into something very different under the empire. It had always been possible to accommodate larger numbers by simply multiplying the number of triclinia in a series of rooms or in a larger room. This process is described as dining by *triclinia,* and was common especially for public or corporate gatherings. But even by the end of the republic, private dining luxury demanded the larger numbers common in Greece, and developed longer couches (probably from Hellenistic Greek precedents), with the architecture to accommodate them; such an arrangement would still be termed *triclinium.* Already Trimalchio's banquet in the mid-first century AD has at least fourteen guests, with the placing of the host in a (or 'the') new fashion (Petr. 31. 8). More important, excavation reveals that many houses throughout the empire, by the second century AD, possessed grand rooms marked out by the design of their mosaic pavement for much longer couches, set in a regular Π shape. These rooms, easily able to accommodate twenty diners, are sometimes distinguished by fine views through the open side, often to fountains in the peristyle. This should be regarded as the normal mode of luxurious formal dining in a private setting during the imperial period; examples survive throughout the Mediterranean area, especially in the North African and Spanish provinces of the empire (see fig. 21.3). Accordingly, places on the couches in these rooms must have been allocated on a

8. References for the overall arrangement are collected in Marquardt 1886: 302–6. Place of honor: Plu. *Moralia* 619 B–F (= *QC* 1. 3), with differing explanations for its preference.

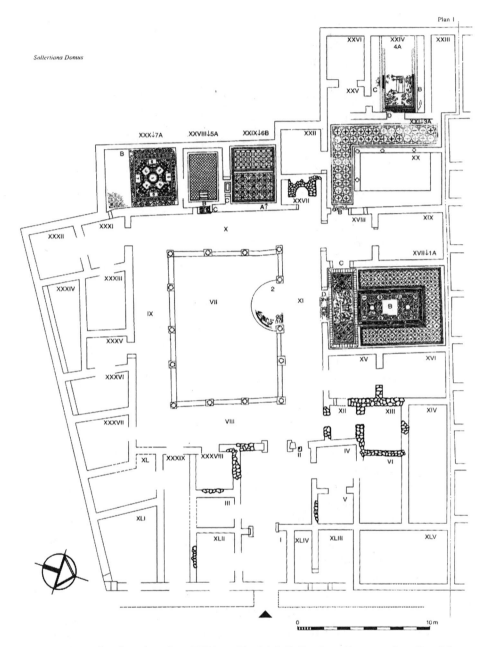

Figure 21.3. Thysdrus (modern El Djem, Tunisia), Sollertiana Domus, plan. On right, *triclinium* marked out by mosaic pavement in T + U design for long couches holding numerous guests. Late second to early third century AD. After C. Dulière, H. Slim, et al., *Corpus des mosaïques de Tunisie* III. *Thysdrus (El Jem)* 1. *Quartier sud-ouest.* Tunis: Institut national d'archéologie et d'arts 1996. Plan I.

Figure 21.4. Volubilis (Morocco), House of the Ephebe. View from *triclinium*
with mosaic pavement marked out in T + U, into peristyle beyond.
Early third century AD. Photo KMDD.

different and less intimate system, which is not clear to us. A single table would no
longer have sufficed, and the space allows for several small tables, or for ledges in
front of the couches on which to set food and drink. Room must be made for the
movement of servants in front of the couches, and in larger rooms for servants to
move behind them also. Performance areas meant for entertainers are often left open
before the couches, with the space marked out by the pattern of the mosaic pavement (see fig. 21.4).[9] Different dining rooms could exist together in the same house,
for different social groups; the greater the house, the more dining rooms it will have,
for winter or summer, as well as for larger and smaller gatherings, with correspondingly different claims to public prestige or private comfort. Undoubtedly, we are
missing many grand dining rooms in upper stories (i.e., of buildings that have long
since collapsed), with spectacular views and cooling breezes.

A further development was the semi-circular couch, Greek *stibadium*, originally
in the form of cushions at ground level, or made of piled-up leaves out of doors.
A single example in masonry is found in a Pompeian garden, and further outdoor
stibadia appear in the second century AD, notably the magnificent example in the

9. This is known as a T + U design, with the "U" representing the space for the couches
around three sides of the room, the "T" the space in the center and at the entrance for service
and entertainment: Dunbabin 1991: 125–28; Dunbabin 2003a: 41–43.

Serapeum of Hadrian's villa at Tivoli; the younger Pliny gives a detailed description of one in the garden of his Tuscan villa (*Ep.* 5. 6. 36–37). These so-called *sigma* couches—named from the Greek letter C—provided a more intimate setting, with seven or eight guests maximum and with eventually a different placement hierarchy (Dunbabin 1991: 128–32; Dunbabin 2003a: 43–46, 144–46, 169–74). The *sigma* is attested by Martial (*Ep.* 10. 48; 14. 87) in the late first century AD, apparently as indoor furniture; but interior rooms designed to house this fashion are difficult to locate until the third and especially fourth century, when they become extremely popular in large villas and palaces. By this date the originally more informal fashion has developed its own formality, and such rooms are often imposing and luxurious. The couch itself, instead of the central table, may even be equipped with fountains like that in the fourth/fifth-century villa at Faragola in Apulia (Dunbabin 2003a: 169–70; Volpe 2006; see fig. 21.5). Three *sigmas* set in apses on three sides of a square constitute the luxury room called a triconch, again a means to overcome the constraints of numbers. Sidonius (*Epistulae* 1. 11. 10–16) describes in detail a banquet with the emperor Majorian on a *sigma* in AD 461. Here, as in all examples on the *sigma* where we can determine it for certain, the place of honor was the 'lowest,' having the best view forward, on the right horn (*dextro cornu*), in other words, on the viewer's left;

Figure 21.5. Faragola (Puglia, Italy), villa. Dining room with semicircular
sigma couch in masonry, with fountain basin in center instead of table.
Late fourth to fifth century AD. Photo courtesy of G. Volpe.

Figure 21.6. Constanza (Romania), Tomb of the Banquet. Funerary painting showing five diners reclining on a *sigma* couch, served by two servants with wine and water. Mid-fourth century AD. Photo courtesy of A. Barbet.

Christ is (anachronistically) shown in this position in late antique scenes of the Last Supper, such as the mosaic in S. Apollinare Nuovo in Ravenna.[10] Food was provided from a round or horseshoe-shaped table fitting into the center of the *sigma*. *Sigma* dining appears as the typical form of conviviality in many paintings and mosaics from the later centuries of the empire, including both pagan and Christian funerary paintings (Dunbabin 2003a: 164–69, 175–87; see fig. 21.6; also fig. 21.14).

The large *triclinia* of the imperial period would seem to have little in common with the intimate *triclinia* of the older republic, designed in origin for the family and a few guests; though both could serve to entertain and make a public display. It is self-evident that larger groupings make a desirable communal conversation more difficult to achieve, something on which our sources comment. The ideal numbers for intimacy were traditionally between the Graces and the Muses, in other words, between three and nine persons;[11] and the fashion for the *sigma* couch represents

10. Dunbabin 2003a: 191–202. There are some indications in the art that the central position on the *sigma* may at some point have been the more prestigious.

11. Gel. 13. 11, in the mid-second century AD, still quotes this ideal, but he is following the dictum of Varro (*Sat.* 333 Ast.) from the late republic.

an answer to this criticism. On the other hand, the undeniable trend to larger and more exotic banqueting rooms also suggests not just a need to accommodate greater numbers, but a desire for open space, to be connected to the importance of entertainment in banqueting. Similarly the late *sigma* room also has space before the couch for performance, and the multiplication of *sigmas* in the triconch leaves this playing space while preserving intimacy. We can therefore see the development of private dining-room architecture as offering solutions to opposing social pressures: intimacy in conversation versus performance space.

While Roman normative banqueting fashions and architecture spread through the empire, nonetheless other local traditions survived, and could spread through trade or cultic links. Greek customs may have persisted in the Eastern Empire, and in other Greek areas, including parts of southern Italy. In oriental cults and associations there was a tradition of a high table, *protoklisia*, which contradicted the usual Graeco-Roman insistence on equality.[12] It is possible that this mark of social elevation was employed by Hellenistic rulers and by emperors in some circumstances. How far these traditions affected private dining we cannot tell. But it is best to assume considerable diversity outside of the Roman aristocracy, which was itself capable of putting on spectacular dinners in game parks and aviaries or picture galleries (Var. *R.* 1. 59; 3. 5. 9–17).

WOMEN AND CHILDREN

One of the classic differences between Roman and Greek dining practices was the presence of women of all classes at social banquets (Nep. *Praef.* 6–7; cf. Cic. *Ver.* 2. 1. 26. 66). Whereas respectable Greek women seem to have been absent from normal formal *symposia*, and sat when present, Etruscan women did lie down to dinner, perhaps normally so in familial circumstances. The presence of distinguished Roman women at social banquets can be assumed from the early republic, and probably they reclined with their husbands, as they normally did in the last period of the republic and afterward.[13] But the finer nuances of this behavior cannot be determined in view of the minimal evidence; thus, it is not clear whether it was regarded as socially avant garde for a woman to be placed beside someone not her husband. Certainly the less respectable but famous mistresses of the wealthy could participate as equals at the

12. Some Eastern cults also had large rectangular rooms with high stone podia for reclining, and even pillars on the front of the podia: Schwarzer 2002.

13. Roller 2006: 96–98, 153–56, argues against the conventional view (transmitted by Val. Max. 2. 1. 2 and Isid. *Orig.* 20. 11. 9, quoting Varro) that women sat to dine in the good old days and believes that women also reclined from a very early date. Vössing 2004: 225–26, disagrees, but thinks it is not clear when they began to recline. Certainly it was normal for them to do so by the late republic.

highest level of society dinners, though Cicero was somewhat surprised to find himself dining with the most glamorous mime actress of his day (*Fam.* 9. 62). Women might also dine formally together, without men, though we have little information about behavior on such occasions. Children are found both seated and reclining in formal family gatherings, but boys would have moved to recline when they officially achieved manhood (Roller 2006: 157–79). The custom of sitting may have been more prevalent in some parts of the empire; and anyone might choose, for reasons of age or propriety, to sit on a seat placed by a couch.

Preparation and Apparatus

Before dining, it was customary to take a bath and exercise.[14] In later antiquity the guests might betake themselves to the library to relax with games and reading, while all assembled (Sidonius *Epistulae* 2. 9. 4–6; cf. 9. 13. 3). Earlier, the custom (originally Greek) of permitting guests to bring their hangers-on (*umbrae*) must have made it difficult to organize a guest list in the modern manner, and our evidence suggests that invitations were usually delivered on short notice. To begin dinner before the ninth hour (mid-afternoon) was thought unseemly (Mart. 4. 8. 6; Juv. 1. 49), and to arrive late was snobbish and caused resentment (Plu. Q.C. 726B). Roman banquets, unlike classical Greek, did not separate wine and food; both were served throughout. A further difference was that each guest took his wine as he wished, by asking personally for water to be mixed into his winecup.[15] A luxury banquet afforded the choice of cold (even snowy) or boiling hot water, prepared in a special heater (*authepsa*), and also a choice of wines, the Romans being more connoisseurs of fine old wines than were the Greeks (wine: Tchernia 1986). Food was prepared and served by the slaves, and the successive dishes presented with ceremony to the assembled company; it was then frequently brought to the guests in individual servings. The range of foodstuffs available under the empire was very large, with the produce of the empire pouring into Rome in various forms; some products, like the cherry, were introduced into Italy from Asia Minor, whereas others, like the highly valued spices, came from as far away as India and Indonesia.[16] A number of recipes survive, mostly for elaborate ways of preparing often exotic foods and sauces, especially the collection preserved under the name of the first-century AD gourmet Apicius (Flower and Rosenbaum 1958). The number of courses naturally varied, and musical and dramatic entertainments could be offered in the intervals. At a grand

14. For the social nexus of bathing among the Romans, see Fagan in this volume.

15. See Dunbabin 1993; Greek practice at the *symposion* (drinking party) emphasized communal mixing of the wine for all guests alike.

16. Food: see the articles in Wilkins, Harvey, and Dobson 1995; Wilkins and Hill 2006. For the literary treatment of food, see Gowers 1993.

dinner, the service and the apparatus themselves could become a spectacle, with silver and gold cups on display, valuable serving dishes, and handsome servants in elegant dress. Paintings and mosaics record the importance of such display, while numerous elaborate vessels of silver and other materials have survived (see figs. 21.7 and 21.8).[17] Moralists reject as indecent the efforts expended on competitive display, on rare food and expensive furniture and slaves, of which long and perhaps misleading accounts are preserved, and praise the joys of the simple banquet. Convivial behavior offers easy moral targets, and many of the ancient accounts, for example, in Seneca, must be considered exaggerated and untypical; especially untrustworthy are descriptions of the dining habits of emperors to whom the tradition was hostile, like Gaius or Nero.[18]

Figure 21.7. Pompeii, Tomb of Vestorius Priscus. Painting of table with display of silverware for banquet. Approximately AD 70/71. Photo DAI Rome 31.2529.

17. Silver vessels: Pirzio Biroli Stefanelli 1991; Painter 2001. Servants: D'Arms 1991; Dunbabin 2003b.

18. On the dining habits of emperors, and their presentation in the historiographical tradition, see Vössing 2004: esp. 533–39.

Figure 21.8. Thysdrus (El Djem, Tunisia). Mosaic pavement from *triclinium*
with display of varied foodstuffs that might be set before guests,
and other items related to banqueting, including scene of dice players.
Third century AD. Tunis, Musée du Bardo Inv. 3197. Photo KMDD.

Entertainers and Frivolities

It was considered desirable that the guests entertain themselves, but both the Greeks and Etruscans employed professional entertainers to enliven their dinner parties, and the Romans at festive days and public banquets did likewise. In houses, the smaller Roman republican format must have made it more difficult to accommodate anything other than musical accompaniment at first. As dining rooms increased in size to allow more guests and staff, and conversation accordingly became less unified, the role of entertainment increased and was integrated into the dinner, in more elaborate occasions as a spectacle (Jones 1991; Dunbabin 2008). The wilder developments of this kind of dining are parodied by Petronius, and often criticized (and doubtless exaggerated) by the moralists wishing to demonstrate more cultured taste. Pliny (*Ep.* 5. 19) speaks with respect and affection of his own house musician and actor, the freedman Zosimos, but with contempt for house buffoons who might enjoy more freedom of expression than was deemed appropriate; yet such clowns are attested for Tiberius' dinners. Particularly offensive to the more serious were the young house slaves (*pueri minuti*), who were encouraged to amuse the guests with ribald language, a taste imported from Alexandria, along with dwarfs and other oddities. Larger dining rooms with space before the couches allowed for performances of drama, usually extracts, Menander being especially appreciated by cultivated Greek speakers, while comedy, music, mime, and dancing appealed to the Romans, even between courses (see fig. 21.9). These entertainments ideally were supposed to stimulate participation by those present, just as Martial's friend Stella expects his guests to be able to compose verses (Mart. 9. 89). More cultivated guests might also be expected to listen to poetry recitations by the host, or even works of prose and scholarship, which would provoke general discussion. Such reports suggest that considerable demands could be made on the sophistication and general knowledge of a guest hoping to participate in higher society, quite apart from the convivial skills required.

Public Banquets

Alongside normal social dining, much Roman dining involved banquets offered in public by a benefactor to a large group of people. The concept of convivial equality was absent from such events; Seneca emphasizes that the diners were in no real sense the fellow guests (*convivae*) of the donor (*Ben.* 1. 14). These banquets, in Latin called by terms such as *epulum* or *cena publica*,[19] are well attested epigraphically in

19. Other terms used are *convivia publica, strationes publicae, epulae*; cf. Vössing 2004: 188–96, 270–73; Vössing 2005.

Figure 21.9. Mosaic of a banquet in the open air, Detroit Institute of Arts 54.492.
Founders Society Purchase, Sarah Bacon Hill Fund; photo © 1999, the Detroit
Institute of Arts. Six guests are reclining at a *sigma*-style couch, outdoors,
under an awning, while entertained by dancers and music; in front, servants
prepare food and drink. Possibly from Ostia, probably fourth century AD.

many parts of the empire in imperial times, and are known in Rome from republican times, where they formed a public benefaction (*munus*), or part of one, given to
the people by a wealthy sponsor on the occasion of a funeral, or a triumph, or the
dedication of a building. Ambitious politicians could win popular approbation by
such means; Julius Caesar is specifically said to have made major use of such banquets. Under the empire, the emperors monopolized the giving of such banquets
in Rome itself, and these events played an important part in the public relations of
many emperors.[20] Austerity in apparatus was never appreciated by the recipients,

20. Republic: Landolfi 1990. Caesar's banquets: D'Arms 1998. Emperors: Vössing 2004:
esp. 265–90.

and in Rome these assemblies traditionally took place in public in the forum, usually the Forum Boarium and the sanctuary of Hercules, but also by city ward. Caesar in 46 BC feasted the people at 22,000 *triclinia*, and the following year in his private gardens; emperors did so in the larger public buildings and stoas (D'Arms 1999; D'Arms 2000a). Domitian hosted the people and the higher orders in the Flavian amphitheater with a buffet meal (Stat. *Silv.* 1. 6. 28–50; cf. Suet. *Dom.* 4. 5). Such massive liberality would have required renting and hiring staff and apparatus in large quantity via so-called *macellarii* (literally, meat-market men) (Suet. *Vesp.* 19. 1).

Following Caesar, wealthy municipal magistrates in the cities of Italy, such as P. Lucius Gamala at Ostia, offered comparable largesse to their public. Sponsored banquets of this sort took place under the empire in every city in Italy, and in many of the western provinces; they are recorded in numerous inscriptions.[21] These municipal benefactions range from special dinners for the magistrates to detailed largesse for the entire city, and specific sums of money were regularly distributed to the banqueters during the meal, according to their class; the inscriptions often distinguish minutely between the superior honors to be given to the members of the decurionate as compared with the Augustales or, even more so, the plebs. The occasions for such benefactions may be the erection of a statue, or a birthday, or simply a gift from a grateful and distinguished citizen. The banquet is sometimes described as being held in public, in the forum, or in a stoa, or a basilica, but can be assumed to be so even if not expressed. Occasionally, it is specified that the banqueters, or some of them, are to recline. A relief sculpture from Amiternum, in central Italy, which clearly celebrates such a benefaction, shows one group of men reclining to dine, while another group is seated: evidently two different status groups who receive distinct treatment (Dunbabin 2003a: 79–84; see fig. 21.10). The distinctions between the various forms of benefaction are difficult to understand in detail, but lying down to eat in *triclinium* style, formally called a *cena recta*, was the most prestigious and expensive; less prestigious forms included the *prandium* (brunch), *epulae* (meals), or *sportulae* (handouts); *mulsum et crustulum*, rough wine and biscuits, were reserved for the lowest class. Many such occasions would involve sacrifice, barbecues, and distributions of meat in the open air in a public place.[22]

These donated banquets are not always clearly separated from the regular public dining by civic officials, which was not normally a matter of record. In Rome, magistrates and senators traditionally dined communally at public banquets (Cic. *Pis.* 65), a right specifically upheld for the senate by Augustus (Suet. *Aug.* 35. 2). It is sometimes evident that the dinner of the municipal officials was meant to be public in the sense that the people could watch the spectacle and appreciate the generosity of a benefactor; they could also observe the public display of hierarchical class structures, given that some form of prestige ordering evidently governed the seating

---

21. See Donahue 2004, with the review of Vössing 2005; Mrozek 1987; Wesch-Klein 1990: 33–37. Gamala: D'Arms 2000a.

22. Mrozek 1987: esp. 33–62, on categories of distribution. Sacrifice: Scheid 1985.

Figure 21.10. Amiternum (Abruzzi), funerary relief of a public banquet with
two groups of diners, one reclining (left), one seated (right). Probably mid-first century
AD. Pizzoli, church of Santo Stefano. Photo DAI Rome 84.VW 935, photo Fittschen.

at such events.[23] Municipal laws (*Tabula Heracleensis* lines 133–34, 139; Crawford
1996: 368) accordingly forbid those marked by *infamia* (legally inflicted disgrace)
from attendance at such *convivia publica*.

Patronal *Convivia*

The clarity of the public/private definition, however, is illusory, especially in regard
to the elite at Rome. Already in 64 BC, indiscriminate hospitality was forbidden
as a means of soliciting votes (Cic. *Mur.* 67); and Pliny (*Ep.* 6. 19) shows that candidates were still in his day ignoring such laws against extensive *convivia*. Indeed,
the municipal laws forbid those canvassing for office to hold *convivia*, presumably

23. Cf. Sidonius' assertion (*Ep.* 7. 12) that the lowest on the first table was higher than
the highest on the second. However, the populace did not appreciate public dining by officials at public expense when not legitimized by ritual or when the people was not involved—
Vössing 2004: 192.

of this kind, since they specifically allow (obviously more modest) *convivia* for the standard nine guests (*Lex Coloniae Genetivae*, ch. CXXXII, line 23. Crawford 1996: 417). In any case, it was normal for the ambitious to hold such large *convivia* for friends and clients on any suitable occasion, for example, on the host's birthday; this custom did not represent an official public benefaction, and would not be recorded in inscriptions. Common aspects of the public *munus*, such as a cash distribution, might also evidently be found in very large dinners, privately motivated; these might be in a semi-public form, since it was possible for instance to entertain large numbers in one's own atrium with the main doors open to the street, or in one's gardens, as well as in a more explicitly public place. Pliny (*Ep.* 10. 116), in his concern for public order in Bithynia, specifically asks about the permissible size of such invitations when money is distributed to the local town council and other citizens, citing marriages, dedications of buildings, and magistrates' entry into office as occasions for such gatherings with a thousand or more guests. It is wisest to assume that a spectrum of public and semi-public banqueting existed, and that these affairs could range from the privately motivated dining of large numbers, principally of clients and friends, to the public dining of the entire people in the forum; the funding could be public or private, as could the setting (D'Arms 1998; D'Arms 1999: 307–8). The desire for absolute distinctions here can lead us only to violate the realities of the Roman world.

The socially entrenched grouping, whereby a patron maintains, by food-money (*sportula*) and personal support, a group of clients, who will in turn support him in public life, is a hallmark of Roman society.[24] The *sportula*, originally food, became a fixed sum of money, normal by the time of Nero, and connected usually with the morning *salutatio* (a ritualized greeting of the patron by his clients), at which guests for a later dinner might be selected (Sen. *Ep.* 19. 11). Unfortunately our evidence is insufficient to sketch a picture of the legislative changes brought in by emperors, who, in order to assert their own privilege, at times forbade patronal *cenae rectae* (formal dinners) for clients, especially in the first century AD. But the definition of this client relation was not itself clear. A particular difficulty for understanding the implications of these dinners by patrons is that the gift of food is often expressed in terms of money, and vice versa (cf. Vössing 2004: 191 n. 2), so that we cannot be sure whether dinner consisted of a cash distribution or its edible equivalent, or both combined; this is a difficulty with corporate dining as well. For example, Martial (*Ep* 12. 29) can speak of being invited by word of mouth to dinner "at 20 sesterces"; he rejects the invitation, preferring hunger—that is, he apparently does not wish to be considered a client. Yet, on the other hand, Martial (*Ep.* 10. 27) alleges that handouts (*sportulae*) of a specific monetary value could be given even to senators and knights reclining at large *convivia* offered by a private individual of lesser status, probably a wealthy freedman, on his birthday. Here there can be no question of client/patron

---

24. See D'Arms 1984; Vössing 2004: 187–94, 240–44, and 281–88 on the problems of imperial restrictions on these forms of patronage.

relations, only of the quasi-public *convivia* that possibly concealed bribery, of the type that worried legislators and Pliny (*Ep.* 10. 116). Obviously to be invited to dinner 'at XX sesterces' (or the equivalent) did not always imply client/patron relations. Client relationships could be fluid, and it seems that the mechanisms, such as money distributions, that distinguished the public *convivia* and client handouts were being employed more widely.

Several authors single out for criticism the unequal treatment to which humbler clients might be subjected at a patronal *convivium*: served inferior food and drink, or singled out for insult or neglect by the slaves and other hangers on.[25] There is an element of convention about these accounts, and the writers invariably have their own axe to grind; nevertheless, it is clear that these occasions could lead to a peculiar tension between the display of status and traditional ideals of equality at dinner. It was also always normal for a patron to bring along members of his entourage (*umbrae*) to a dinner invitation, even if they had not been invited, as Maecenas did to the dinner of Nasidienus in Horace's account (Hor. *Sat.* 2. 8. 21–22; cf. *Ep.* 1. 5. 28). When Caesar visited Cicero at Puteoli, his retainers had to be fed in separate *triclinia* (Cic. *Att.* 13. 52. 2).

CORPORATE DINING

This term describes the formal banquets of private or exclusive associations (*collegia*), of businessmen and merchants, but also of more restricted religious and social groups, which are scarcely to be separated from them and might overlap with those holding *convivia publica*.[26] Two commonly attested official groups are the Augustales, associations of freedmen, who looked after the imperial cult, and the *collegia iuvenum*, associations of young men (D'Arms 2000b; Jaczynowska 1978). These groups are distinguished not only by restricted access, but by the traditional equality of the members, who democratically appoint their officers and patrons, and whose language imitates that of an autonomous city. Related groups are the priests and municipal officers, who dine formally together (Rüpke 2002; Wesch-Klein 1990: 35–37). Dining together on fixed occasions was the essence of this communal life, and is reflected in the numerous inscriptions that record it. Typical is an association for the worship of Diana and Antinous at Lanuvium, which consisted of slaves and freedmen (*CIL* XIV 2112 = *ILS* 7212); the inscription lays out regulations for the conduct of the members, financial subscriptions, elections, and banqueting rules, including costs for provisions and penalties for misbehavior. More

---

25. Plin. *Ep.* 2. 6. 1–5; Juv. 5; Mart. 3. 60; Lucian *Merc. Cond.* 26–27; see D'Arms 1990.

26. On corporate and religious dining, see Ausbüttel 1982: 55–59; van Nijf 1997: 149–88; Egelhaaf-Gaiser 2000: 272–329. Again, there is also relevant material in the articles of Becker, Perry, and Scheid in this volume.

exceptional is the long fragmentary series of inscriptions recording the meetings of the Arval Brothers, an exclusive aristocratic club gathering for religious purposes at their temple between Ostia and Rome, which was equipped with dining rooms and a racecourse (Scheid 1990). They record in ritual detail their banquets both there and in Rome for several hundred years. The banqueting of higher priestly groups could be part of state cult, and at Rome, as elsewhere, these often involved notoriously elaborate apparatus. Christian communities early developed their own habits of communal dining, derived from the Graeco-Roman tradition; basic practices, such as reclining, corresponded to those of contemporary secular dining, and specifically Christian features developed only slowly.[27]

Several groups of merchants constructed elaborate masonry *triclinia* in their headquarters at Ostia, like those in the Building of the Triclinia (I 12. 1), seat of the carpenters' guild (see fig. 21.11), while wealthy Augustales could build a dining room into their imperial temples, as at Misenum (Bollmann 1998; D'Arms 2000b). Only the wealthiest of these associations would be able to construct their own club rooms, and we should assume that facilities for major regular banqueting were improvised in rented space, or in temples or basilicas, as well as in private houses, not only in dedicated buildings. The Last Supper, for example, can be viewed as the reclining banquet of a small religious group in Roman Judaea, meeting in an upstairs rented room. There is no technical name for these club rooms, though the word *schola* is often used in modern discussion. The costs of banqueting came from community funds, supported by testamentary legacies, and could be the subject of detailed regulation.

FUNERARY BANQUETS

Statius (*Silv.* 5. 1. 235–37) describes the burial of his wealthy friend Priscilla on the Appian Way: "Attendants stand around, a mob used to obedience, then couches and tables are carefully made ready according to custom. It is a *domus*, a *domus!*" Statius' description emphasizes that the tomb, like a normal house, needs dining facilities, and such arrangements are known in both Greek and Roman areas to allow for repeated dining by families and friends at the memorial. In the cemetery of Ostia at Isola Sacra, for instance, several tombs have masonry couches inside, or at their entrance, and some have provisions for cooking (Egelhaaf-Gaiser 2000: 294–300, 319–21; Dunbabin 2003a: 127–29; see fig. 21.12). While no associations existed for the specific purpose of paying for members' funerals, this function was very much a

27. See Smith 2003. No specifically Christian architectural forms existed for these meetings until the third century, and the claim sometimes made, that the *sigma* was peculiarly Christian, is erroneous. For the development of the Eucharist as a separate ritual from the regular communal meal, see White 1998: esp. 180–81.

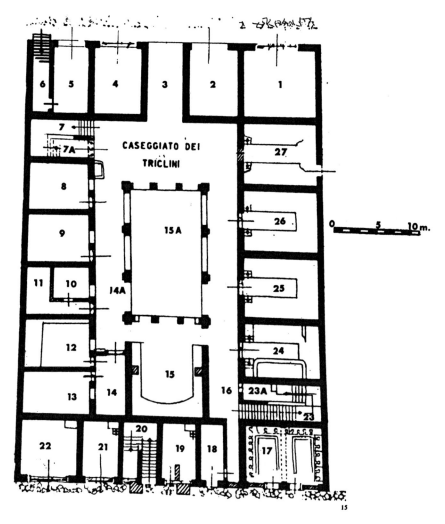

Figure 21.11. Ostia, Building of the Triclinia (I 12. 1). Plan showing four
masonry *triclinia*, for banquets of the carpenters' guild, installed in rooms on
right side (24–27). Building ca. AD 120, *triclinia* installed later in second century. After
J. Packer, *The Insulae of Imperial Ostia*. Rome: American Academy in Rome 1971. Plan 15.

part of corporate life, so that grave plots could be acquired for the members, with
corresponding facilities. This was especially suitable for the poorer elements in society, and the slaves of the great.

Funeral dining emphasizes community with the dead, regarded as the fellow
guest of the living. Scenes of dining are among the most common images used as
funerary decoration, for individual grave monuments or painted decoration of the
tomb itself. The dead man or woman may be shown alone, or with his or her spouse,
dining on a couch (the so-called *Totenmahl*), or convivial groups may appear, dining in current fashion (Dunbabin 2003a: 103–32; Roller 2006: 22–45, 123–53; see
fig. 21.13; also fig. 21.6). The significance of such scenes is multivalent, ranging from

Figure 21.12. Isola Sacra (Ostia), tomb with dining couches
at entrance. Second century AD. Photo KMDD.

the pleasures of life, through allusion to the funerary banquet, to the hope that
such pleasures will continue after death. Christians in turn used similar scenes, with
similarly multivalent significance—for instance, the groups of banqueters on the
sigma couch found in the decoration of several of the Roman catacombs. These
depictions sometimes differ very little from those in contemporary scenes of secular
dining (Dunbabin 2003a: 175–91, with references; see fig. 21.14).

IDEALS AND ETHICS

Literature attests to the ancient awareness of the *convivium* as culturally important
for society and for the individual, both in theory and practice. Varro (*Sat.* 333–41
Ast.) already presented in the mid-first century BC a now largely lost account of
the ideals associated with a Roman banquet, which clearly derive from a Greek
philosophical source; the fragments deal with practical matters, such as numbers
of guests, but also with the central importance of good conversation, which should
combine pleasure with utility. Plautus (*Mil.* 635–48), doubtless translating a Greek
original, describes the ideal symposiast as a *cavillator facetus*—a witty critic—and
an easy *conviva* (fellow diner), because he does not interrupt or argue, and knows
when to talk and when to keep quiet. He does not spit, clear his throat, or snuffle

Figure 21.13. Rome, funerary altar of Q. Socconius Felix, shown with his wife
reclining on a couch, and served wine by young servants beside the table. Second half
of first century AD. Photo DAI Rome 63.755, photo Felbermeyer.

(or worse). Clearly one's behavior and conversation at such a central social institution as the *convivium* were universally recognized as providing precise and immediate criteria for others to make a judgment of character, taste, and sophistication.
Therefore, much effort was expended on both analysis and description of this interaction (in Latin, *conversatio*), and especially how best to promote its desirable qualities, since it was accepted, again in the tradition of the Greeks, that to come together
for dinner (*convivere*) was in a sense the essence of civilized life (*vivere*), and that
how people interact and converse with one another at table can be understood as a
microcosm of the joys and problems of society altogether (cf. Cic. *Fam.* 9. 24. 3; *De
Sen.* 13. 45). Philosophers were accordingly preoccupied with the attempts to define
and illustrate the goals of such an ideal gathering, seeking with terms such as *urban-
itas, humanitas,* or *libertas* to convey the spirit of an open-minded and civilized
contribution to a communal endeavor. Likewise, the conversational ideals focus on
that elegant language of wit, which amuses but does not offend (*lepos*, charm or
grace; *facetiae*, cleverness), while displaying the critical spirit that befits a gathering
of free people (*cavillatio*, repartee or badinage). Conversely, a common concern,
expressed even in collegial laws, is that inappropriate jokes may give offense and

Figure 21.14. Rome, catacomb of SS. Peter and Marcellinus. Painting showing four men
reclining on a *sigma* couch, and served wine by a maidservant from a hot-water heater to left.
An inscription addresses the servant and tells her to mix the wine. Probably end of third to
early fourth century AD. Photo Pontificia Commissione di Archeologia Sacra, Lau L45.

lead to brawling, or that untimely and tasteless criticism (*petulantia*) may spoil the
atmosphere of commonality.

Much attention is devoted, therefore, to those conversational subjects and
mechanisms that will be productive of this desirable atmosphere of well being.
A general rule is to maintain a balance between the serious and the frivolous, but
there is much diversity of opinion as to what this exactly means, and how it is to
be promoted. For example, conversation could be structured by the host in terms
of questions or themes—philosophical, scientific, philological, historical—to
which solutions could then be proposed by the guests. Many such discussions
are preserved, especially in Plutarch's model *Convivial Questions*, and in Aulus
Gellius' reported conversations. Notable is the avoidance of real political issues
in our surviving sources from the imperial period, and the emphasis is not so
much on scientific discussion, which in excess might be considered too serious
and unsuitable, but rather on civilized contribution by cultivated amateurs. (One
should recall that riotous dinners are not likely to be models for our philosophical
sources; for those poets and epigrams provide some substitute.) Bons mots by the
political elite in convivial company were much appreciated, but when repeated
in society, dangerous even in the republic, and potentially lethal in the empire.
However, the *convivia* of the associations, whether of religious groups or trades-
men and merchants, appear to have preserved more of the dangerously free spirit
of democratic banter than would have been tolerable among the Roman elite,

especially under the empire. Otherwise, it would not be necessary for the worshippers of Diana and Antinous at Lanuvium to forbid their members from rising
from their couches to start a fight (*CIL* XIV 2112 = *ILS* 7212, column II, line 25),
or even the very distinguished citizens of Hadrianic Athens to have had bouncers
('horses,' as the Athenians called them) at their Iobacchic ceremonial dinners (*SIG*
1109, line 145).

The ethics promoted within private *convivia* derive from the general antique
antithesis of *otium* (leisure) to *negotium* (business): the enjoyment of leisure in an
intimate setting of friends is contrasted with the external pressing demands of public life. This attitude expresses itself in a hedonistic logic that views the delights of
the *convivium* as real living in opposition to the futile worries of civic business, and
ultimately opposes the impermanent present joys of the *convivium* to the inevitability of death itself, an old folk motif immortalized in Horace's dictum *carpe diem*
(*Carm.* 1. 11. 8). Much convivial poetry pursues this argument by detailing both the
delights of an ideal *convivium*—true friendship, comfort, wine, absence of envy,
good order, and so forth—and from the opposite angle the temporality of all things
human and the certainty of their end. The ideal *convivium* can therefore act as a
model for the well-ordered society and its desirable virtues: a resolution of the real
tensions reflected elsewhere in our sources.

SUGGESTED READING

No single work covers all aspects of Roman dining, and the increase in archaeological data
renders earlier generalization suspect. Thus, older works, such as Marquardt 1886 (297–340),
concentrate on the social dining of the elite, with a collection of written sources that is still
useful. Among modern approaches, an important series of articles by D'Arms (1984–2000),
which exploit our epigraphic evidence, concentrates on the public banquet and on the life
of associations. Dunbabin 2003a shows what can be derived from art, and in a number of
articles (1991–2003) illustrates specific developments. Smith 2003 gives a useful comprehensive view emphasizing Christian and Jewish material, but cannot be trusted in detail. The
bibliography in Vössing 2004 is notable.

BIBLIOGRAPHY

Ausbüttel, F. 1982. *Untersuchungen zu den Vereinen im Westen des römischen Reiches.*
    Kallmünz: M. Lassleben.
Bollmann, B. 1998. *Römische Vereinshäuser. Untersuchungen zu den Scholae der römischen
    Berufs-, Kult-, und Augustalen-Kollegien in Italien.* Mainz: von Zabern.
Bradley, K. 1998. "The Roman Family at Dinner." In I. Nielsen and H. Sigismund Nielsen
    (eds.), *Meals in a Social Context. Aspects of the Communal Meal in the Hellenistic and
    Roman World.* Aarhus: Aarhus University Press. 36–55.

Crawford, M. (ed.). 1996. *Roman Statutes* I–II. London: Institute of Classical Studies.

D'Arms, J. 1984. "Control, Companionship, and *Clientela*: Some Social Functions of the Roman Communal Meal." *Échos du monde classique/Classical Views* 28, n.s. 3: 327–48.

———. 1990. "The Roman Convivium and the Idea of Equality." In O. Murray (ed.), *Sympotica. A Symposium on the Symposion*. Oxford: Clarendon Press. 308–20.

———. 1991. "Slaves at the Roman Convivium." In Slater 1991: 171–83.

———. 1998. "Between Public and Private: The *epulum publicum* and Caesar's *horti trans Tiberim*." In M. Cima and E. LaRocca (eds.), *Horti Romani*. Rome: "L'Erma" di Bretschneider. 33–43.

———. 1999. "Performing Culture: Roman Spectacle and the Banquets of the Powerful." In B. Bergmann and C. Kondoleon (eds.), *The Art of Ancient Spectacle*. New Haven and London: National Gallery of Art, Washington, D.C. 301–19.

———. 2000a. "P. Lucius Gamala's Feasts for the Ostians and Their Roman Models." *Journal of Roman Archaeology* 13: 192–200.

———. 2000b. "Memory, Money, and Status at Misenum: Three New Inscriptions from the *Collegium* of the Augustales." *Journal of Roman Studies* 90: 126–44.

Donahue, J. F. 2004. *The Roman Community at Table during the Principate*. Ann Arbor: University of Michigan Press.

Dunbabin, K. 1991. "Triclinium and Stibadium." In Slater 1991: 121–48, figs. 1–36.

———. 1993. "Wine and Water at the Roman Convivium." *Journal of Roman Archaeology* 6: 116–41.

———. 2003a. *The Roman Banquet: Images of Conviviality*. Cambridge: Cambridge University Press.

———. 2003b. "The Waiting Servant in Later Roman Art." *American Journal of Philology* 124.3: 115–40, figs. 1–25.

———. 2008. "Nec grave nec infacetum: The Imagery of Convivial Entertainment." In K. Vössing (ed.), *Das römische Bankett im Spiegel der Altertumswissenschaften*. Stuttgart: Franz Steiner Verlag. 13–26.

Egelhaaf-Gaiser, U. 2000. *Kulträume im römischen Alltag*. Stuttgart: Franz Steiner Verlag.

Flower, B., and E. Rosenbaum. 1958. *The Roman Cookery Book. A Critical Translation of the Art of Cooking by Apicius*. London: Harrap.

Friedländer, L. 1922. *Darstellungen aus der Sittengeschichte Roms*. 10th ed. Ed. G. Wissowa. Leipzig: S. Hirzel.

Gowers, E. 1993. *The Loaded Table. Representations of food in Roman Literature*. Oxford: Clarendon Press.

Jaczynowska, M. 1978. *Les associations de la jeunesse romaine sous le haut-empire*. Wroclaw: Polska Akademia Nauk.

Jones, C. P. 1991. "Dinner Theater." In Slater 1991: 185–98.

Kleberg, T. 1957. *Hôtels, restaurants et cabarets dans l'antiquité romaine*. Uppsala: Almqvist & Wiksells.

Landolfi, L. 1990. *Banchetto e società romana. Dalle origini al I. sec. a.C.* Rome: Edizioni dell'Ateneo.

Leach, E. W. 1997. "Oecus on Ibycus: investigating the vocabulary of the Roman house." In S. Bon and R. Jones (eds.), *Sequence and Space in Pompeii*. Oxford: Oxbow. 50–72.

Marquardt, J. 1886. *Das Privatleben der Römer*. 2nd ed. Ed A. Mau. Leipzig: S. Hirzel.

Mrozek, S. 1987. *Les distributions d'argent et de nourriture dans les villes italiennes du Haut-Empire romain*. Brussels: Latomus.

Nijf, O. van. 1997. *The Civic World of Professional Associations in the Roman East.*
   Amsterdam: J. C. Gieben.

Painter, K. 2001. *The Insula of the Menander at Pompeii.* IV: *The Silver Treasure.* Oxford:
   Clarendon Press.

Pirzio Biroli Stefanelli, L. 1991. *L'argento dei Romani. Vasellame da tavola e d'apparato.*
   Rome: "L'Erma" di Bretschneider.

Purcell, N. 2003. "The Way We Used to Eat: Diet, Community, and History at Rome."
   American Journal of Philology 124.3: 1–30.

Roller, M. B. 2006. *Dining Posture in Ancient Rome. Bodies, Values, and Status.* Princeton:
   Princeton University Press.

Rossiter, J. 1991. "Convivium and Villa in Late Antiquity." In Slater 1991: 199–214.

Rüpke, J. 2002. "*Collegia sacerdotum*: religiöse Vereine in der Oberschicht." In U. Egelhaaf-
   Gaiser and A. Schäfer (eds.), *Religiöse Vereine in der römischen Antike.* Tübingen: Mohr
   Siebeck. 41–67.

Salza Prina Ricotti, E. 1983. *L'arte del convito nella Roma antica.* Rome: "L'Erma" di
   Bretschneider.

Scheid, J. 1985. "Sacrifice et banquet à Rome: quelques problèmes." *Mélanges de l'École
   française de Rome: Antiquité* 97.1: 193–206.

———. 1990. *Romulus et ses frères. Le collège des frères arvales, modèle du culte public dans
   la Rome des empereurs.* Rome: École française de Rome.

Schwarzer, H. 2002. "Vereinslokale im hellenistischen und römischen Pergamon." In
   U. Egelhaaf-Gaiser and A. Schäfer (eds.), *Religiöse Vereine in der römischen Antike.*
   Tübingen: Mohr Siebeck. 221–60.

Slater, W. (ed.). 1991. *Dining in a Classical Context.* Ann Arbor: University of Michigan
   Press.

———. 2006. "A Great Public Dinner of the Gentle-People." *Journal of Roman Archaeology*
   19: 484–93 (review of Stein-Hölkeskamp 2005 and Vössing 2004).

Small, J. P. 1971. "The Banquet Frieze from Poggio Civitate (Murlo)." *Studi Etruschi* 39:
   25–61.

Smith, D. E. 2003. *From Symposium to Eucharist: The banquet in the Early Christian World.*
   Minneapolis: Fortress Press.

Stein-Hölkeskamp, E. 2005. *Das römische Gastmahl: eine Kulturgeschichte.* Munich: Verlag
   C.H. Beck.

Tchernia, A. 1986. *Le vin de l'Italie romaine. Essai d'histoire économique d'après les amphores.*
   Rome: École française de Rome.

Terrenato, N. 2004. "Banquet and Society in Archaic Central Italy." *Journal of Roman
   Archaeology* 17: 526–30 (review of Zaccaria Ruggiu 2003).

Volpe, G. 2006. "*Stibadium e convivium* in una villa tardoantica (Faragola—Ascoli
   Satriano)." In M. Silvestrini, T. Spagnuolo Vigorita, and G. Volpe (eds.), *Studi in onore
   di Francesco Grelle.* Bari: Edipuglia. 319–49.

Vössing, K. 2004. *Mensa Regia. Das Bankett beim hellenistischen König und beim römischen
   Kaiser.* Leipzig: K. G. Saur.

———. 2005. "Epulum publicum. Das Mahl in der städtischen Öffentlichkeit." *Journal of
   Roman Archaeology* 18: 572–76 (review of Donahue 2004).

Wesch-Klein, G. 1990. *Liberalitas in rem publicam. Private Aufwendungen zugunsten von
   Gemeinden in römischen Afrika bis 284 n. Chr.* Bonn: Rudolf Habelt Verlag.

White, L. M. 1998. "Regulating Fellowship in the Common Meal: Early Jewish and
   Christian Evidence." In I. Nielsen and H. Sigismund Nielsen (eds.), *Meals in a Social*

Context. Aspects of the Communal Meal in the Hellenistic and Roman World. Aarhus: Aarhus University Press. 177–205.

Wilkins, J., D. Harvey, and M. Dobson. 1995. *Food in Antiquity*. Exeter: University of Exeter Press.

Wilkins, J., and S. Hill. 2006. *Food in the Ancient World*. Oxford: Blackwell.

Zaccaria Ruggiu, A. 2003. *More regio vivere. Il banchetto aristocratico e la casa romana di età arcaica*. Rome: Quasar.

CHAPTER 22

VIOLENCE IN ROMAN SOCIAL RELATIONS

GARRETT G. FAGAN

INTRODUCTION

SOMETIME in the mid-first century BC, M. Terentius Varro, the esteemed scholar, had an appointment with a sacristan at a temple of Tellus near Rome. Varro showed up with a group of three friends and relatives. The sacristan was late. As the group held a learned conversation to while away the time, a freedman appeared, visibly upset. He reported that his master, the sacristan, had been stabbed to death in a crowd at Rome, apparently by mistake. Varro comments that "we went our separate ways, lamenting more the vicissitudes of the human lot than being surprised that such a thing had happened at Rome" (Var. *R*. 1. 69. 4).

Aulus Gellius (Gel. 10. 3. 1–3), citing earlier authorities, documents the reprehensible behavior of Roman officials among subject peoples. The wife of one consul, he recounts, insisted on bathing in the men's facilities at Teanum Sidicinum in south-central Italy and then had the local magistrate—a respected pillar of his community—beaten at a post in the forum because the baths were not clean enough. The

I'd like to thank Ted Lendon for bringing my attention to the curious absence of feuding and dueling in Roman society during his visit to Penn State in 2006. Some interesting points made by a graduate student (Ashley Kunsa) in her paper on feuding for my seminar on cruelty and violence in the ancient world (spring 2007) have been adapted and deployed in this chapter, with her kind permission. The editor, Michael Peachin, as well as Paul Harvey Jr., Jill Harries, Werner Riess, and Ted Lendon read the entire chapter and provided many valuable suggestions, corrections, and pointers. Errors that remain, and opinions expressed, are not their fault.

magistrate of a nearby town avoided the prospect of impending humiliation by applying violence to himself—he threw himself from the city walls. Gellius also reports how a curious rustic in Asia jokingly asked to see inside the litter of a traveling Roman, a noble youth not even yet a magistrate; the young nobleman ordered the chap beaten to death on the spot for his impertinence (Gel. 10. 3. 5).

When a sitting praetor angered the city's bankers by reviving an ancient law against usury and then favoring debtors in court, he paid a heavy price. While pouring a libation at the Temple of Castor and Pollux in the Roman forum, someone threw a stone that hit him. He then made a dash for the Temple of Vesta to seek asylum, but was blocked by a mob and chased into a tavern. There an incumbent magistrate of the Roman people had his throat cut (Liv. Per. 74; App. B.C. 1. 54; V. Max. 9. 7. 4). A comic actor who made provocative remarks during a performance was dragged from the stage and lynched by the audience (D.S. 37. 12).

Augustus liked to watch street brawlers in action; apparently they were readily rounded up from the byways of the city (Suet. Aug. 45. 2). Drusus, son of the emperor Tiberius, liked his violence. Because of his unseemly devotion to gladiatorial spectacles, he earned the nickname 'Castor'—the name of a popular gladiator of the age—for slapping a knight in public (Dio 57. 14. 9; see Hor. Ep. 1. 18. 19 for Castor). But when Drusus-Castor slapped a certain other knight in the face, it proved a fatal mistake, for this knight was L. Aelius Sejanus, Tiberius' immensely powerful Praetorian Prefect. Sejanus harbored the grievance for years and ended up allegedly orchestrating Drusus' murder (or so the story went—Tac. Ann. 4. 3–12).

Pliny the Younger tells how the ex-praetor Larcius Macedo was punched to the ground when his slave had the temerity to touch a Roman knight in a crowded public bath (Plin. Ep. 3. 14. 6–8). The second-century doctor Galen comments nonchalantly how one of his patients, on leaving a "gymnasium" (by which Galen means one of Rome's large imperial bathhouses), encountered some friends engaged in a fight outside and had to separate the battling parties. Galen states that quarrels like this were pretty standard among bathing youths, though violence was not necessarily the inevitable outcome (Galen Meth. Med. 10. 3 = 10. 672K). Indeed, a sort of youthful boisterousness and tomfoolery, often of a violent bent, was considered standard fare for the Roman iuventus, young men aged from their mid-teens to early twenties (Eyben 1993: esp. 107–12 and 121–23). But youths were not the only troublesome bathhouse customers. A first-century petition from Egypt claims that a fracas in a bath between four women and two men led to the petitioner's wife and mother-in-law losing valuable golden jewelry (P. Ryl. 2. 124).

Tradition had it that Nero's natural father, Cn. Domitius Ahenobarbus, was not a nice man. One day, as he was driving his chariot along the Appian Way, he spotted a child playing by the roadside. Ahenobarbus accelerated and ran the youngster down. On another occasion, he gouged out the eye of a Roman knight during an argument in the forum (Suet. Nero 5. 1).

These scattered snapshots suggest a level of violence in ancient Rome that modern readers are likely to find disconcerting. Apart from the randomness of Varro's sacristan's murder, the disproportionality in many of the incidents is remarkable:

a rustic beaten to death for simple curiosity; a punch thrown in reaction to an inadvertent touch; murder plotted to avenge a slap; a local squire publicly thrashed and humiliated for dirty bathrooms. The historicity and precise details of each case are less significant than the attitudes and assumptions the stories seem to lay bare: a hair-trigger readiness to slap, cuff, beat, humiliate, and even murder. In this chapter, we focus not on the big-ticket violence of the Roman world—warfare, gladiatorial spectacles, political murder, mob riots, and the like—but rather on the sort of offhand, even 'casual' violence suggested by these vignettes. In a nutshell, how violent was Roman society? Or, to refine the question a little, how often and how readily did individual members of the Roman community resort to acts of violence in their interactions with one another?

Having posed these apparently simple and straightforward questions, it needs to be appreciated that we cannot answer them—at least not in the manner of modern social science, with thorough documentation and quantification. The paltry material left to us from the Roman era precludes such an approach: the required demographic material is just not there. Whether for rates of domestic violence, or muggings, or bandit/pirate raids, or even violent conflicts between supposedly 'law-abiding' inhabitants of the empire, no statistics can be generated, nor can regional or chronological variations be traced. So we are forced back on likelihoods and probabilities drawn from an interpretation of the available evidence. But since that evidence is open to divergent interpretation, the best we can hope for is to arrive at a kind of Roman 'etiquette of violence,' insofar as we can glimpse the sort of violence that was done, by whom and to whom, and under what circumstances. Even if the quantification of violence in Roman social relations proves an impossible task, its typology and the milieu that generated and facilitated it can be perceived from the sources. Before proceeding, a brief consideration of those sources is therefore in order.

SOURCES

Our evidence for the 'ground-level' of Roman social interactions is pitifully sparse and diffuse. The high literature of the day may contain the occasional anecdote or allusion (as documented above), but a systematic picture of life among the common people is harder to reconstruct from such sources (but see Horsfall 2003 for a sterling attempt). Far more useful are those genres that address themselves to the everyday: satire, the novel, and fables. All are fiction, of course, which seems at first to undercut their value for the historian: such material is inevitably characterized by exaggeration and sensationalism for effect. But following the interpretive lead of Saller (1980), Millar (1981), Hopkins (1993), or Riess (2001: 348–76), ancient anecdotes and fiction can act as mirrors that reflect social attitudes, assumptions, and realities, even if the immediate context is highly dubious or even fantastical. This is because in order to be effective, satires or novels have to present their audience with recognizable social paradigms (Harries 2007: 121–23). Fergus Millar succinctly summarizes the situation: "The invented world of fiction may yet represent—perhaps cannot help representing—important features of the real world" (1981: 75).

This is all the more so when a work explicitly claims to be offering social observations, as when the satirist Juvenal states, "Whatever people do—their hopes, fears, angers, and pleasures, their joys and comings and goings—this forms the medley of my book" (Juv. 1. 85–6; cp. Apul. *Met.* 9. 13). Likewise, fables, which on the surface are little more than fairy tales populated by talking animals and plants, are expressly linked to patterns of real-world human behavior by the inclusion of a 'moral' at the beginning or end, or by explicit statements in the prologues. Thus the fabulist Phaedrus (writing in the Augustan Age or shortly thereafter) notes that "double is the dowry of this little book: it moves one to laughter, / and by wise counsel gives life advice to the prudent" (Phaed. 1. *prol.* 3–4). Elsewhere he comments that "nothing else is sought through fables / than that the mistakes of mortals be corrected" or asserts that fables "show life itself and people's ways" (id. 2. *prol.* 2–3 and 3. *prol.* 50; cp. Ach. Tat. 2. 20–22 where characters recount their own behavior in fables; for socio-historical readings of the genre, see Christes 1979; Holzberg 2002: 46–50). The social symbolism embedded in fables was clearly meant to be appreciated by their audience. In light of this, the usefulness of such material for peering into the dank basements of Roman society cannot be denied (see, e.g., Bradley 1987: 150–53; Horsfall 2003: 20–30).

A particularly good example is provided by Apuleius' novel *The Golden Ass*. Composed in the early second century AD and set in Greece of some indeterminate era, it concerns itself with marvelous and magical doings, not least the transformation of the narrator into an ass. Yet these amazing events are set against a realistic backdrop that appears to reflect the society of Apuleius' own time and place (second-century Madaurus in North Africa; Millar 1981; Riess 2001). This is a Roman wolf (or ass?) in Greek clothing. Such a conclusion is bolstered by comparing Apuleius' version with Lucian's "Lucius, or The Ass" (both probably derived from a third author, Lucius of Patras), which contains less social detail—and is also notably less violent. In what follows we shall refer to Apuleius' novel extensively, though a wide variety of corroborating sources are on offer (a sampling of them will be cited where pertinent). Especially worth noting is the consistent attitude of nonchalance, even of normalcy about interpersonal violence across these and other sources, which may suggest that even if the quantity of everyday violence is exaggerated in *The Golden Ass*, the novel nevertheless reveals something qualitative about the assumptions and attitudes that underpinned the uses of violence in Roman social relations.

The story of *The Golden Ass* is simple enough. Lucius, a well-heeled youth who is visiting the town of Hypata in Thessaly, is accidentally transformed into an ass by his lover. He then embarks on a series of (mis)adventures that takes him far and wide, until the goddess Isis restores him to human form. Along the way, Lucius interacts with representatives of all levels of Roman society, from local aristocrats and their servants, to errant soldiers, to common bakers, to criminals and bandits. The degree of violence that pervades the interactions of these diverse characters is striking. The evidence is best presented in tabulated form (table 22.1). The table includes only the violent acts perpetrated, related, contemplated, threatened, or dreamed. Not included are the violent metaphors, such as imagery drawn from war or gladiatorial combat to describe sexual encounters (e.g., Apul. *Met.* 2. 15–17; sexual-military metaphors also feature heavily Achilles Tatius' second-century AD novel, *Leucippe and Clitiphon*).

STATE-SANCTIONED VIOLENCE

Three types of state-sanctioned violence appear particularly pertinent to the matters addressed in this chapter: spectacular, judicial, and magisterial violence. All three make an appearance in Apuleius' *The Golden Ass* (see table 22.1) and are attested in a variety of other sources.

Spectacular violence, especially that associated with the arena, has been much studied in recent years. One explanatory model for the prevalence and popularity of arena violence is that it sought to defuse, or at least channel, the aggressive impulses of the watching populace (Plass 1995: 3–77). In a related vein, it has been argued by some that a general level of violence in their society probably contributed to the Romans' readiness to accept it as a form of mass entertainment (e.g., Hopkins 1983; Coleman 1998). But that observation cuts both ways: the culture of violent mass entertainment—whether in circus, theater, or amphitheater—surely fed into behaviors on the Roman 'street.' This suggestion, however, cannot be securely tested and is controversial even when applied to the modern mass media; but at a basic psychological level, Roman spectacular violence arguably told the audience that it was all right if enemies of the state, social outcasts, and deviants were treated in the most brutal imaginable fashion—for fun. All of which is to say that arena games can be read as a tacit acknowledgment, even if unconscious, that a generally high level of violence permeated Roman society. Yet, if the same argument were made from the content of the mass media for modern society, it would clearly be misleading, since most people live their whole lives without encountering anything like the sort of lurid atrocity that so fascinates the purveyors of violent films, television, and 'infotainment.' So the relationship of Roman spectacular to societal violence is best read not in any quantifiable sense, but rather as a vague ideological buttress for the notion that violence could be justifiably inflicted on certain classes of person.

This suggestion is amply borne out by the way violence was folded into the Roman judicial system. Torture was routinely applied to slaves and others of low standing to gain information; under the emperors, it was applied even to senators

Table 22.1. Acts of Violence in Apuleius' *The Golden Ass*

Category	Act	Perpetrator	Victim	Reference
Spectacular	Gladiatorial games	n/a	n/a	1.7
	Gladiatorial games		Gladiators, beasts, huntsmen, criminals	4.13
	Display of catamite priests: self-mutilation with swords, knuckle-bone scourging	Catamite priests	Catamite priests	8.27–28
	Three-day gladiatorial spectacle	Thiasus	Beasts and gladiators	10.18
	Rape of woman in gladiatorial spectacle	Ass-Lucius	Condemned woman	10.23
Criminal	Throat cut	Brigands	Arignotus, Diophanes' brother	2.14
	Murder	Gang of noble youths	Random	2.18
	Murder	Thrasyleon, brigand dressed as bear	Guards, doorman	4.18
	Mugging	Brigands	Socrates, a traveler	1.7
	Assault in tavern room (stabbing, urination on face)	Two crones	Aristomenes and Socrates, travelers	1.11–13
	Throttling	Alcimus, brigand leader	Old woman	4.12
	Murder	Brigands	Husband of Charite, kidnapped girl	4.27
	Murder	Psyche	Evil sisters	5.27
	Burning, exposure to beasts, crucifixion, torture to death, sewn up inside ass	Brigands	Charite, kidnapped girl	6.31–32
Personal	Beating	Thelyphron	Fine lady's hired goons	2.26–27
	Kicking	Horse and ass in the stable	Ass-Lucius	3.26
	Beating with huge piece of wood	Lucius' slave	Ass-Lucius	3.27
	Beating with cudgels; cutting of flanks	Brigands	Ass-Lucius	3.28–29

Beating	Youth guarding vegetable garden	Ass-Lucius	4.3
Beating, cutting of hamstrings, thrown off cliff	Brigands	An ass	4.5
Arm hacked off	Brigands	Lamachus, brigand leader	4.11
Suicide	Lamachus, brigand leader	n/a	4.11
Torture	Venus	Psyche	6.9
Beating	Venus	Psyche	6.10
Beating	Brigands	Ass-Lucius	6.25
Kicking	Ass-Lucius	Old woman	6.27
Beating	Horses	Ass-Lucius	7.16
Beating to the point of ulceration; ball of thorns tied to tail	Boy-drover	Ass-Lucius	7.17–19
Beating	Traveler	Ass-Lucius	7.25
Murder	Thrasyllus	Tlepoleumus	8.5
Suicide	Charite	n/a	8.14
Suicide	Thrasyllus	n/a	8.14
Attack dogs sent in and rocks thrown from rooftops	Farmhands	Fleeing slaves and Ass-Lucius	8.17–18
Beating with cudgels	Farmhands	Ass-Lucius	8.21
Suicide	Bailiff's wife and baby	n/a	8.22
Flogging with kunckle-bone scourge	Catamite priests	Ass-Lucius	8.30
Beating	Mill workers	Ass-Lucius	9.11
Endemic beatings and floggings	Master and agents	Mill workers	9.12
Regular whipping	Baker's wife	Ass-Lucius	9.15
Sodomized, strung up, buttocks beaten with rod, beaten	Baker	Wife's lover	9.28
Murder by hanging	Mysterious woman	Baker	9.30

(continued)

Table 22.1. (continued)

Category	Act	Perpetrator	Victim	Reference
	Threats, harassment, killing of livestock	Wealthy landowner	Poor neighbor	9.35
	Dogs trained to attack passers-by	Wealthy landowner	Random	9.36
	Dog attack	Wealthy landowner	Villagers (one dies)	9.36–37
	Transfixed with spear	Wealthy landowner	First brother of murdered villager	9.37
	Killed with sword	Second brother of murdered villager	Wealthy landowner	9.38
	Suicide	Second brother of murdered villager	n/a	9.38
	Suicide	Father of dead brothers	n/a	9.38
	Struck with vine stick, attempted murder	Centurion	Market-gardener	9.39
	Murder by poison	Evil stepmother	Son	10.2–5
	Strung up, flogged, murdered by having white-hot branding iron inserted into privates	Wife	Sister-in-law	10.24
	Double murder by poison	Wife	Husband and a physician	10.25–26
	Double murder by poison	Mother	Own daughter and physician's wife	10.27–28
	Suicide	*Aristomenes*	*n/a*	*1.16*
	Kicking to death	*Ass-Lucius*	*Photis*	*3.26*
	Suicide	*Charite, kidnapped girl*	*n/a*	*4.24–25*
	Burying alive	*Old woman*	*Charite, kidnapped girl*	*4.25*
	Suicide	*Ass-Lucius*	*n/a*	*4.4*
	Suicide	*Psyche*	*n/a*	*6.12, 6.17*
	Murder	*Brigands*	*Ass-Lucius*	*6.26*
	Suicide	*Ass-Lucius*	*n/a*	*7.24*
	Suicide	*Charite*	*n/a*	*8.7*

Note: Italicized items are acts of violence that are threatened, contemplated, dreamed, or requested but not actually carried out.

in cases of conspiracies against the emperor, whether real or imagined (Peters 1985: esp. 1–36). Ammianus (Amm. Marc. 22. 16. 23) laments of the Egyptians: "It has thus far been impossible to find any torture violent enough to make a hardened bandit of that region say his own name against his will." In Achilles Tatius (Ach. Tat. 7. 12. 2), a man convicted of murder is about to be subjected to torture, in order to give evidence with respect to another case, when he is saved by the intervention of a priest of Artemis. Torture, however, was more commonly employed punitively, as enhancements to legal penalties. Roman torture included such unpleasantness as beating (with cudgels or whips), scourging, racking, and searing with hot plates. As a matter of principle, the severity of judicial punishment was gradated according to social status, with the more degrading and brutal procedures reserved to slaves and the lower orders of the freeborn. A broadening in both the savagery of punishments and the spectrum of society subject to them is observable over time (Garnsey 1968; Wiseman 1985: 5–10; MacMullen 1986; Dossey 2001; Riess 2002). The legal imperative behind all this is enunciated clearly in the *Digest* (*Dig.* 48. 19. 10. 1): "In the case of slaves, the rule is observed that they are punished after the fashion of men of low rank." The wording is revealing: the "men of low rank" (*humiliores*; a term that gained legal potency after AD 212) represent the measure against which the punishment of slaves is to be calibrated. Legally, the two classes came to be considered interchangeable, and both together constituted a significant chunk of the empire's population (see further Garnsey 1970: 103–52).

The schoolbook (*colloquium*) of a Roman child, probably between seven and eleven years old, tabulates a daily routine in order to teach important vocabulary. At one point the child accompanies his father to the forum, where a trial is in progress:

> The defendant brought into court is a bandit. He is questioned as he deserves; he
> is tortured, the interrogator beats him, his chest is pummelled, he's strung up,
> stretched, lashed with rods, thrashed thoroughly, he goes through the whole series
> of torments, and still he denies his guilt. He must be punished: the sentence is
> death, and he's led away to the sword [i.e., to be executed] (Dionisotti 1982: 105
> [§75]).

The next defendant is a rich man, and he manages to talk his way to acquittal; no thrashing, pummeling, or stringing up for him. The public and open nature of the judicial tortures—they take place right in the court itself, as the trial progresses—is especially noteworthy, as is the exposure of mere schoolchildren to such horrors as an occurrence routine enough for inclusion in their workbooks (see *Dig.* 48. 18. 1 on the uses and abuses of torture; note also Clark 2006). The context of this vignette warrants some notice, since it is hardly irrelevant that schoolchildren were themselves victims of violence in the classroom. "Apply yourself, boy, or you'll be flogged" is the endearing message one schoolboy was forced to write out repeatedly on a surviving tablet from Roman Egypt (Bonner 1977: 61). Horace and Martial comment on the liberal application of beatings, often with a knotted stick (*ferula*), administered by teacher to pupil (Hor. *Ep.* 2. 1. 69–72; Mart. 10. 62, 14. 80), and a wall-painting from Pompeii shows a schoolroom punishment—apparently called "The Horse"—in which the victim is stretched over the shoulder of one boy as another holds his ankles and the teacher (or his proxy) lashes his exposed buttocks with a rod (García y García 2005: 44–47). The law held teachers accountable only for excessive brutality—judicious brutality was fair game, especially if the intent was to correct (*Dig.* 9. 2. 6). So both the content and the context of the *colloquia* were marred by violence. Apprenticeship was not much better, it seems. Roman jurists debated the difficult question as to whether a shoemaker was liable for damages after hitting his apprentice so hard with a last that the boy lost an eye (*Dig.* 9. 2. 5. 3).

Roman magistrates could order violence done to the obdurate to compel obedience without anything even vaguely resembling our concept of due process (Peachin 2007a). Pliny (*Ep.* 10. 96. 3) revealingly comments that when he was interrogating accused Christians, if they persisted in their denials, he had them led away to execution, "for whatever they admit to, I have no doubt that their stubbornness and unbending obstinacy deserved punishment." The guilt or innocence of the accused is reckoned secondary to their defiance of Pliny's magisterial authority. Recall that Pliny was a mild-mannered man as Romans go, and yet here he orders people killed merely because he took umbrage at their recalcitrance. In the *Acts of the Pagan Martyrs* the emperor Trajan displays similar impatience at the tone adopted by those brought before him: "You must be eager to die, having such contempt for death as to answer me with insolence" (Musurillo 1954: 48). According to Ammianus (Amm. Marc. 22. 16. 23), failure to pay tribute in Egypt resulted in a whipping, and victims exhibited their stripes as badges of honor. C. Gracchus, via Aulus Gellius (Gel. 10. 3. 5), notes that the Roman noble youth who ordered a rustic beaten to death for asking what was inside his litter "had yet to attain any magistracy," which stresses the perpetrator's youth but also suggests that a magistracy would somehow mitigate, or at least make more understandable, the brutality of his action.

The mere existence of spectacular violence, of judicial torture and violent punishment, and of Roman magistrates' right to assault and humiliate those who came before them likely fed into a tolerance of violence in Roman private interactions. The state's willingness to engage in or endorse varieties of violent behavior stamped a sort of official imprimatur on it and, arguably at least, loosed more of it among the general population. Roman magistrates, whether provincial or local, were drawn from the elite and all enjoyed enhanced social status as a result of holding office (see, e.g., Curchin 1990: esp. 71–84; Cébeillac-Gervasoni 1998: 203–52). Their capacity to inflict violence on those who ranked below them would naturally be reproduced in the way such elites treated their social inferiors in general. It would be fruitless to seek a linear causality between public and private actions in this regard and more helpful just to recognize that the same attitudes likely pervaded the milieu of the privileged.

CRIMINALITY AND POPULAR JUSTICE

Common criminality was a standing source of violence in the Roman world. Lucius, as an ass, becomes the property of a band of brigands, whose multifarious acts of skullduggery are recounted around the camp fire (for citations, see table 22.1). Brigandage and piracy were perennial problems in the Roman world, especially for travelers. The memoranda of Theophanes of Hermopolis in Egypt, preserved on papyri, recount a business journey of some six months' duration from his hometown to Antioch in Syria and back again in approximately AD 320. Theophanes traveled with a substantial retinue. One of the many expenses recorded in the memoranda is the hiring of six Sarmatians for the last part of the outward journey. The horsemen probably functioned as an escort/bodyguard for Theophanes' final push to Antioch, after he had left his main party behind in the interests of speed (Matthews 2006: esp. 50–51). Traveling alone was to invite disaster, so the Sarmatians were a necessary expense. Galen (*Anat. Admin.* 1. 2 = 2. 221–22K) recalls once seeing a bandit's body lying unburied by the roadside, the man killed by a traveler who fought back. Other travelers fared not so well. Inscriptions record the fate of those on the road "killed by bandits" (*interfectus a latronibus*; see, e.g., *ILS* 2646, *CIL* III 14587 = *ILS* 8504, *CIL* VI 20307 = *ILS* 8505). A commemorative inscription from Lambaesis relates the mission of army engineer Nonius Datus to inspect a botched aqueduct channel at Saldae in the reign of Antoninus Pius (AD 138–160): "I set out, and on the road I fell victim to bandits; naked and injured, I escaped with my retinue (*cum meis*) and arrived at Saldae" (*CIL* VIII 2728 = 18122 = *ILS* 5795). Even though Datus was an imperial official traveling with a retinue, his security on the road was not guaranteed. Pliny famously reports (*Ep.* 6. 25) the disappearance of two elite travelers—one a mere 40 miles from Rome; at least one of them, he expressly states, was accompanied by a retinue of slaves, but it can be reasonably assumed in the case of the other. These real-world data dovetail with the fictional fate of the characters in Achilles Tatius' novel, who are captured by Egyptian bandits and severely beaten, only to be rescued by a company of soldiers later on (3. 9–13; cp. 3. 20, 5. 7, 7. 3 and Dio 71. 4; on ancient bandits, see further MacMullen 1966: 255–68; Flam-Zuckerman 1970; Isaac 1984; Shaw 1984, 1993; McGing 1998; Riess 2001, 45–246; Grünewald 2004; Blumell 2007; and Riess in this volume).

Piracy—basically, brigandage on the sea—was also a perennial problem. In Achilles Tatius (Ach. Tat. 2. 16–18) the hero's sister is carried off by armed fishermen who moonlight as pirates. Later, another crew of fishermen-pirates abducts the heroine Leucippe and (apparently) behead her in cold blood when Clitiphon gives chase (Ach. Tat. 5. 7). Rape is considered the natural consequence of capture by pirates (Ach. Tat. 6. 21. 3). The dual role of the fishermen-pirates is itself noteworthy, as it blurs the distinction between 'criminal' and 'law-abiding' inhabitants of the Roman Empire. This in turn led, for instance, to a very broad definition of who exactly were 'brigands' or 'pirates' (both termed *latrones*). Essentially, anyone could be so designated, if their use of violence was deemed illegitimate (Shaw 1984; also Riess in this volume). Despite Pompey's supposed eradication of Mediterranean piracy in 67 BC, the problem persisted throughout the Roman era, largely because it was conducted on a small and localized scale, as reflected in Achilles Tatius' novel. Pompey may have eliminated the large pirate fleets, but falling victim to small-scale raiding was a risk of maritime and coastal life (see Ormerod 1924; Monaco 1996: 5–31; de Souza 1999; Rauh 2003).

Violent crime was not the sole preserve of the untracked interstices between Roman communities. Urban crime was no less endemic than rural brigand-age. Before transforming into an ass, Lucius comes home drunk from a party and encounters what he thinks are three thieves attempting to break into his host's house (Apul. *Met.* 2. 30, 3. 6). Accepting the situation on its face, he engages the 'thieves' and kills all three (they turn out to be inflated animals skins). Later, among the brigands, Ass-Lucius overhears the villains recounting armed break-ins in town that didn't go as planned because the householders fought back (Apul. *Met.* 4. 10–21). Juvenal sketches the drunken bully, who can find sleep only after a brawl, but who gives wide berth to the important man attended by a large retinue. The thug, however, will way-lay the unaccompanied traveler and pick a fight. Juvenal writes, "Such is the liberty of the pauper: after being pummelled and cut in fights, he begs and prays to be allowed to go home with a few teeth in his head" (Juv. 3. 279–301; quote at 299–301). But the empty-handed traveler can sing in the bandit's face, since he offers no prospect of gain (ibid. 10. 19–22). As we saw above, Augustus liked to watch street-brawlers. Even a well-to-do out-of-towner, like Sextus Roscius of Ameria, a town not far from Rome, could be murdered on the streets of the capital as he made his way home from a din-ner party at night (Cic. *Q. Rosc.* 18). People of substance felt the need to go about with retinues of slaves for protection (Cic. *Mil.* 10; Nippel 1995; Hopwood 1999). Augustus saw fit to post guards around the city during show days, on the apparent assumption that deserted streets were the natural habitat of prowlers (*grassatores*; Suet. *Aug.* 43. 1 and Crook 1967: 69). In general, the relative absence of effective policing in ancient Rome gave a wider scope of action to the criminally inclined.

The minimal state-sponsored policing and the long-established and accepted principle of self-help (see below) led to what might be termed popular justice, a phenomenon that nicely illustrates the relatively attenuated distinction between the public and private spheres in the Roman world. Once again, *The Golden Ass* offers a good starting point. A brigand leader is pushed out of a window by an old woman whose hovel he was in the process of ransacking (Apul. *Met.* 4. 12). When the bandits attack one rich household they meet fierce resistance on the part of the householder and his slaves, who set dogs on them and counterattack with cudgels, lances, and swords (Apul. *Met.* 4. 19–21). Ass-Lucius occasionally defends himself against assault by kicking or defecating on his tormentors (Apul. *Met.* 4. 3, 7. 28). While these instances of self-defense may seem a case apart, they are best set on a continuum with the more openly retributive actions taken by some characters. Ass-Lucius' gang of brigands finally come to grief at the hands of a mob of townsfolk, who butcher them with swords, or worse, arrest them and then hurl them into a gorge. There is no trial, no due process, just instant lynching (Apul. *Met.* 7. 12–13).

The legality (or not) of the action is a secondary matter; the lynching itself, and the attitudes that it lays bare, is what concerns us here (Riess 2001: 99, 319). When Ass-Lucius escapes from some herdsmen who were planning to castrate him, a traveler commandeers him. But the herdsmen appear to reclaim their ass. The traveler resists and is beaten to a pulp for his trouble, clapped in chains, and then handed over to magistrates (Apul. *Met.* 7. 25–26)—a combination of popular and 'official' justice. Later, townspeople accost the catamite priests with whom Ass-Lucius is then traveling and beat, chain, and imprison them on charges of theft (Apul. *Met.* 9. 9). All of this is consistent with the practice of calling for help when under assault, in the full expectation that violence would be done to the assailant (Lintott 1999: 11–16; see Apul. *Met.* 4. 10–11 for an example).

Mob justice, especially stoning, is amply attested in the sources (see the *loci* assembled by MacMullen 1974: 171 n.30; stoning is threatened at Apul. *Met.* 1. 10 and Ach. Tat. 8. 14. 5). The people expected to see violence done in the name of justice, as Cicero notes in relation to a pirate leader captured at Syracuse but sequestered away by the villainous C. Verres, whom Cicero was prosecuting:

> The maritime people of Syracuse, who had often heard that leader's name and trembled at it, wanted to feast their eyes and sate their souls with his torture and execution, but the ability to glimpse him was denied to all...There is no surer evidence of victory than to see those whom one has frequently feared led off in chains to execution. (Cic. *Verr.* 2. 5. 65–66)

Such attitudes most obviously fed into the phenomenon of arena spectacles, but they would also underlie acts of popular justice. If the authorities did not do their part, the mob could always step in or, better yet, pre-empt due process entirely.

Before proceeding, a brief word needs to be said about religious violence. Aside from the ethno-religious riots that occasionally marred relations between Christians, Jews, and pagans in Alexandria and other eastern cities, as well as the sort of small-scale violence the early Christian proselytizers encountered on their travels (see *Acts*), there is little evidence for this brand of violence until the later empire (Hahn 2004; Gaddis 2005). In Apuleius, Ass-Lucius is threatened with sacrifice (Apul. *Met.* 7. 22), which was an occupational hazard of being an animal among ancient pagans. When human sacrifice makes an appearance in the classical literary sources, it is always carried out by foreigners and cited as a measure of their barbarity (e.g., Tac. *Ann.* 1. 61. 3, 14. 30. 3; Ach. Tat. 3. 15–17; sources assembled and discussed in Isaac 2004: *passim*; see also Rives 1995).

Interpersonal Violence

If the level of interpersonal violence in Roman social relations cannot be securely quantified, some contours of its application do stand out. Under the right conditions—and those conditions are notably broad in scope—violence appears to have been seen as a perfectly valid option when dealing with certain classes of people. It goes without saying that where disputes arose between parties, the potential for violence increased markedly. For example, in Apuleius' *The Golden Ass*, a conflict between a wealthy land-owner and a poor farmer is charted (Apul. *Met*. 9. 35–38). It is immediately notewor-thy that there is a significant status differentiation between the disputing parties—the landowner is a local squire, while his victim is a lowly smallholder. In order to drive the simple farmer off his land, and so increase his large estate, the squire through his goons harasses the farmer, attacks him in his cottage, kills his livestock, and tramples his crops. Intimidatory violence is the squire's first resort.

It is revealing that violence also marks the poor farmer's response. He does not appeal to local magistrates or seek redress through the legal system, but instead gathers a group of friends to resist. When the squire shows up, he reacts violently to this show of defiance and sets his sheep dogs on the farmer's group. The dogs tear apart a young man, one of three brothers. The two surviving siblings charge the squire in a stone-throwing rage, but one of them is transfixed with a spear, which tells us that the landowner (or his goons) came to the meeting armed. The one sur-viving brother feigns injury to lure the landowner in close. Falling for the trick, the squire draws his sword and charges, but the brother puts up sudden resistance and murders his assailant with a sword (whether the squire's or his own is not immedi-ately obvious); he then kills himself with a dagger. The father of the three brothers, on hearing of this tragedy, kills himself with a cheese knife in despair.

Apuleius' sensational tale is echoed in reports of very real small-town rival-ries, often vicious and violent, that are reported in, say, Cicero's speeches *Pro Roscio Amerino* or *Pro Cluentio Habito* (see also MacMullen 1974: 1–27). Valuable material is found also in papyri, particularly from Egypt, where personal letters, petitions to magistrates, and other documents recount various acts of violence (Winter 1933: 113–16; Musurillo 1954; Bagnall 1989, 2004; Alston 1994; Parca 2002). A typical text (dated AD 296 from the village of Karanis) reads: "Since I have suffered violence and unlawful assault and have been deprived of my property by my father's brother Chairemon…and find this situation intolerable, I have come to seek the protec-tion of the laws" (*P. Cair. Isid*. 63). Another (*P. Oxy*. II 237) documents a vicious dispute between a father, a daughter, and her husband involving money, property, and alleged acts of violence. In cases like these, anger and resentment at landholding arrangements, inheritances, and convoluted family relationships leads to criminal-ity, violence, and even death. (And note that, while Apuleius' tale may be fictional, the social interactions he reports are quite real.) Private disputes, especially where a social disparity applied, could (and did) end in violence (see Peachin 2007b). However, the extent to which violence regularly entered such disputes between Romans is beyond our capacity to measure.

In Apuleius, violence comes to permeate the life of the novel's main character once he has become an ass. In human form he had experienced some unpleasant-ness (such as his 'trial' during the Festival of Laughter for the killing of imaginary thieves at his host Milo's house), but it pales into insignificance beside the sustained violence he experiences as an ass. He is beaten, lashed, cudgeled, punched, kicked, bitten, and sliced by all and sundry: his various owners and minders, servants and drovers, rival horses, and even his very own horse and stable boy. So appalling is the level of violence meted out to Ass-Lucius that he contemplates suicide at least three times as a means of escaping his travails. Indeed, the readiness and regularity with which characters in the novel resolve on suicide to escape current difficulties, not to mention those who actually go through with it, is itself a noteworthy feature of the work. Violence may bring discomfort and despair, but, as often as not, it also offers a ready solution.

The most banal conclusion to draw from all this is that pack animals had a hard time of it in the Roman world. No doubt they did. But a deeper symbolic current might well be seen as flowing through Ass-Lucius' brutal treatment at the hands of almost a dozen characters in the novel. A strong impression left by the ancient evidence is that the Roman system of rigid status differentials contributed to the infliction of interpersonal violence, in a top-down direction. As an ass, Lucius has passed beneath the very lowest echelon of the human social hierarchy (although Bradley (2000) argues that, as an ass, he becomes assimilated into slave status). He is beyond consideration, by anybody. His lot is worse even than that of slaves at the hands of a cranky owner (on whom, see below). Indeed, slaves and mere boys feel free to beat and humiliate him at will. The hierarchy, in other words, even extends into the animal kingdom. Horses, a more elevated form of equine than the humble ass, also beat and humiliate him. A telling moment occurs when the newly transformed Lucius is put into Milo's stable, which he now shares with his own horse, another ass, and a stable boy. In a harbinger of things to come, this trio immediately beats him (*Met.* 3. 26–27, cp. 7. 16). Meting out and incurring violence appears as a sort of status marker: those higher up in the hierarchy feel free to cuff, beat, and otherwise maltreat those beneath them.

This deduction from *The Golden Ass* is borne out in other sources. Seneca identifies three main fears in life: want, disease, and "what comes from the violence of those more powerful than us," with the last deemed the most terrifying of the three. He goes on to list the horrid paraphernalia of violence—the prison, the cross, the rack, the hook, and the stake driven up through the body and out the mouth. He ends by advising: "Let's see to it, then, that we don't give offence" (Sen. *Ep.* 14. 3–6). As a senator, Seneca naturally had in mind those more powerful than himself—emperors or well-connected officials—but his observations apply no less, and arguably more so, to humbler Romans, who peered up from the lower rungs of the social ladder. The violent, public procedures of magistrates, reviewed above, were only one manifestation of this principle. It bled into private interactions as well: moderate violent punishments administered by patrons to their freedmen (and, by extension, to other inferiors) were seen as appropriate and were embraced by law (*Dig.* 47. 10. 7. 2). This does not mean that all patrons smacked their dependents about as a matter of course, but it does show that elite attitudes deemed such chastisement valid and legal.

Other sources help fill out the picture. Surviving Greek novels (mostly of Roman date) tend not to portray quite so much graphic violence as does *The Golden*

Ass, although fragments of a novel by Lollianos called *Phoinikika* (possibly of the second century AD) include such delights as a bandits' lair that resembles a charnel house, human sacrifice, and cannibalism (Stephens and Winkler 1995: esp. 314–57 for Lollianos). A good example of the extant Greek novel is Achilles Tatius' *Leucippe and Clitophon*. This, being a romance, is considerably less violent than *The Golden Ass*, but its world is no pacific utopia either. A mother wishes rape upon a daughter who has apparently sold her virginity too cheaply (Ach. Tat. 2. 24). As in *The Golden Ass*, characters repeatedly contemplate or threaten suicide as an escape from their difficulties (Ach. Tat. 2. 26. 2, 2. 30. 2, 3. 16. 1, 5. 8. 1). When a ship carrying the heroes founders, a brutal fight breaks out between the crew (who are armed) and the passengers (Ach. Tat. 3. 2–3). A husband given up for dead returns and instantly beats the new husband of his wife (Ach. Tat. 5. 23. 5–7; cp. 7. 14. 3). A jilted lover resolves on murdering his rival (Ach. Tat. 7. 1. 1–2; cp. 8. 1. 3–4).

In Phaedrus' fables we encounter violence repeatedly and, consonant with our observations above, it is usually dished out by powerful parties (wolves, lions, eagles, hunting dogs) to the less powerful (sheep, doves, deer). Thus a wolf manufactures a fight and then lacerates a lamb, just because it can (Phaed. 1. 1); a once powerful lion, as it lies dying, is gored and kicked by a vengeful boar, a bull, and an ass—the lion's loss of status manifested in its violent treatment (Phaed. 1. 21); a panther wreaks vengeance on her tormentors (Phaed. 3. 2); the cuckold unwittingly murders his own son (with a sword) and then commits suicide in despair (Phaed. 3. 10); the ass is worked and beaten to death—and then converted into tambourines to be beaten *after* death (Phaed. 4. 1); and so on. More of the same is found in Juvenal's *Satires*. Tankards fly at a dinner party and cause the lowly client to staunch his wounds with his napkin (Juv. 4. 24–29). There is the poor client who has to endure the condescending insults of his patron and is thus deemed worthy of slapping and flogging by the poet (Juv. 5. 171–73). Or the woman who lays about her humble neighbors with whips and cudgels because their barking dog keeps her awake at night: "Quickly with the cudgels," she says, "thrash the owner first, then the dog" (Juv. 6. 413–18). The experience of a guilty conscience is expressed as the lashes and blows of torture (Juv. 13. 193–95).

Papyri are also informative. The documented violence is usually inflicted by social peers on each other, by social superiors on inferiors, and by officials on civilians. The petitions are naturally outraged in tone and usually seek not punishment of the perpetrator but restitution of some sort (Bagnall 1989; Hobson 1993). The documents are rhetorically nuanced, as we'd expect from their purpose, and one rhetorical strategy stands out: the accusation that the perpetrator is 'powerful' and has wronged a humbler plaintiff. This claim is made even if the facts of the case disprove it. Bagnall (1989: 211–12) notes one instance where a former magistrate (and so a local squire) lays this charge at the feet of mere fishermen. Resort to the claim of powerlessness in the face of hubristic violence was obviously seen as a winning formula. This is probably because, as one scholar has put it, from the legal perspective, "violence was a crime of the powerful, inflicted on the powerless" (Harries 2007: 106–32, quote at 116). Recognition of this fact means we cannot read such papyri at face value as unproblematic evidence for systematic depredation visited by the upper classes on the lower. The acts of violence themselves are noteworthy, but we must again be aware of the context: a petition seeks to persuade, and the possibility, if not likelihood, of exaggeration or even outright fabrication cannot be overlooked (analogous discourse strategies mark Athenian forensic orations pertaining to cases involving violence; see Cohen 1995). And, as always, the petitions are too singular to be interpreted quantitatively. So, when we read of an unfortunate woman in mid-first century Oxyrhynchos who was twice attacked by other women and beaten so severely as to suffer two miscarriages (*P. Oxy.* II 315–16 and 324 = *SB* X 10239, 10244–45; cp. *P. Mich.* 5. 228), we cannot say how typical or common or frequent assaults like this were—she just may have been very unlucky.

If the privileged felt they enjoyed the right to lay hands on their inferiors, the converse was seen as a shocking deviation. Indeed, it may be argued that much violence branded 'criminal' in the Roman world was criminal only because it did not respect the proper social distinctions: contrast Cicero's moral outrage at the crucifixion of a Roman citizen by the rogue governor of Sicily, C. Verres (Cic. *Verr.* 2. 5. 160–72) with his nonchalant noting of a slave crucified by a prior governor for carrying a hunting spear (Cic. *Verr.* 2. 5. 7). In *The Golden Ass*, when a centurion encounters one of Ass-Lucius' owners (a market-gardener), the soldier hits the gardener with his vine stick, commandeers the ass, and then decides on murder to cover up his behavior. (Note, by the way, that precisely this situation—a soldier taking a donkey—is also described by Epictetus, but in the *real* world; see Epict. *Diss.* 4. 1. 79 with Mitchell 1976 and Hermann 1990 for other examples.) The gardener ill-advisedly fights back in self-defense, beats up the centurion, steals his sword, and flees. The centurion then returns with comrades, hunts down the gardener, and brings him to court. Ass-Lucius leaves the gardener awaiting execution (Apul. *Met.* 9. 40–42). The gardener's fatal sin was to fight back against a soldier, a person of superior status to himself. Juvenal, in assessing the "rewards of happy soldiering" (*felicis praemia militiae*), lists as his very first example the fact that "no civilian will dare beat you; indeed, even if beaten himself, he will ignore it and not show the praetor his knocked-out teeth, or the black and blue lumps on his face" (Juv. 16. 8–12).

All of this evidence fleshes out our typology of violence in Roman social relations: violence was inflicted in interpersonal conflicts, as a status marker in circumstances where power differentials were made salient, as an act of revenge, as an expression of popular justice, or on oneself as an escape from present troubles.

ATTITUDES AND CIRCUMSTANCES

Lintott has noted how violence was an accepted part of the self-help principle of Roman law (Lintott 1999: 6–34). As far back as the Twelve Tables (449 BC), citizens were often left to themselves to beat back attackers or intruders. For instance, it was declared lawful to kill a thief at night, but not during the day, unless the thief put up armed resistance (Table VIII. 13). This theme is echoed almost a millennium later in the *Digest* (*Dig.* 4. 2. 7. 1), which includes an entire section (*Dig.* 43. 16) of interdicts against "force and armed force" (*de vi et vi armata*); these are overwhelmingly concerned with the forcible ejection of possessors from their possessions (Labruna 1971). Violent revenge was also legal in some instances, such as adulterers caught in the act: they could be flogged, lynched, or castrated (Hor. *Sat.* 1. 2. 41–46). The use of violence to repel violence (*vim vi repellere licet*—*Dig.* 43. 16. 1. 27) and summary, on-the-spot revenge (e.g., *Dig.* 47. 10. 11. 1) were accepted standards in Roman legal and social thought, and we see precisely their effects playing out in *The Golden Ass*, the fables of Phaedrus, Achilles Tatius, and the other sources reviewed above. The persistence of self-help principles and a highly attenuated law-enforcement system that rendered almost invisible the policing apparatus of the state contributed to a blurring of the distinction between the legitimate and illegitimate uses of violence. As a result, Roman attitudes toward the use of violence in social relations were far looser than we would consider normative today.

An important circumstantial question raises its head at this point: did Romans routinely go about armed? The situation in the city of Rome itself is well-known—a total ban on manufactured arms within the official boundary (the *pomerium*). But what about the situation in provincial cities, or in the countryside? The issue is important, as it might suggest a ready resort to violence, perhaps not infrequently lethal, that was common and accepted. Once more, however, the evidence is not interpreted easily. Brunt (1975) noted that among the interdicts on acquiring or carrying arms, specific instances are singled out: no arms at public meetings or in court; no stores of arms, unless acquired as part of an inheritance or for commercial purposes; no carrying concealed weapons with intent to murder or steal. The assumption is that in instances other than those specified, being armed was legal. Perhaps so, but legal boundaries do not encompass the full gamut of social reality, and the legal right to carry weapons does not mean Romans routinely availed themselves of it. A useful comparison here is how the legal rights of the *paterfamilias* to beat, sell, or kill is children appear to have been minimally acted on in real life. Heavy cultural restrictions stayed the hand of even the crabbiest head of a household (Saller 1991, 1994: 133–53; Harris 1986). The speed with which rebels, riotous city dwellers, or even private citizens could equip themselves may seem to suggest that arms were readily available. But crucial here is what constituted 'arms.' The *Digest*'s definition is notably broad: "all weapons, that is, cudgels and stones, and not only swords, spears, and lances" (*Dig.* 43. 16. 3. 2). By that standard, anyone could be armed instantly by merely picking up a rock.

There were circumstances in which being armed with genuine weapons was advisable. The prevalence of brigands between settlements prompted travelers to go armed, the richer ones accompanied by a bodyguard of escorts (MacMullen 1966: 255–68). Shepherds usually had spears to fend off wolves, whether animal or human (Cic. *Verr.* 2. 5. 7). In *The Golden Ass*, Lucius, a stranger in his host's town, returns home from a party and is clearly armed, as he kills three supposed intruders (Apul.

Met. 2. 30). Later in the novel, when the house of a wealthy local is attacked by brigands, the slaves turn out in numbers armed with swords, spears, and clubs—here a
man with much to lose keeps a cache of defensive arms in his house (Apul. *Met.* 4.
19). Later still, when the squire threatens the small farmer, the latter has no trouble
raising a band of armed resistors—nor the squire a gang of armed thugs, for that
matter (Apul. *Met.* 9. 35–38). But the arms expressly identified in this case are notable: the commoners appear to have mostly rocks, and possibly one sword; the squire
has a spear and a sword (Apul. *Met.* 9. 35–38). Other sources hint at a ready access
to weapons. Juvenal imagines a personal enemy coming at a rival with a sword or
a club (Juv. 9. 97–99) or a cuckold killing the debaucher of his wife with a sword
(Juv. 10. 311–17). He also reports that a brawl between two Egyptian villages in AD
127 escalated from insults and fisticuffs to stone throwing and then to swords, bows,
and arrows (Juv. 15. 51–74). A similar progression from insults to swords is charted
by Tacitus when describing the riot in Pompeii's amphitheater in AD 59 (Tac. *Ann.*
14. 17). The legal ruling "whoever comes at us with arms, we can repel with arms;
but this must be done at once and not after an interval" (*Dig.* 43. 16. 3. 9) assumes
that weapons were immediately available. In all the body of Roman law, no attempt
is made to disarm the populace systematically, if we except politically suspect or
recently conquered populations, who were sometimes denied access to arms (though
not permanently: see Juv. 8. 121–25). In any case, it would also have been practically
impossible to enforce a comprehensive ban on private arms (Brunt 1975). It is reasonable to conclude, therefore, that the Roman populace, if not routinely armed in
the street or on the farm, enjoyed easy access to weapons, once the term 'weapons' is
defined broadly enough. Aside from staves, cudgels, and stones, we may imagine that
most manufactured weapons in circulation were not strictly military in character (as
was, say, the *pilum*, the standard legionary javelin) but were primarily designated for
other tasks, such as hunting or defending livestock from predators.

   Another pertinent circumstantial matter is the routine application of violence
to slaves, who were omnipresent at all levels of Roman society. "Crucify that slave,"
demands Juvenal's callous harridan of her long-suffering husband, without giving
any good reason (Juv. 6. 219–24). The satirist portrays the sexually frustrated woman
taking out her anger on her slaves with rod and whip, tearing out a handmaid's hair,
and keeping an executioner on annual retainer (Juv. 6. 475–93). The master super-
vises preparations for a dinner party with whip in hand (Juv. 14. 59–64; cp. 9. 107–12),
and the dour owner thrashes a slave merely for licking a pastry (Juv. 9. 5). Even the
soft-hearted romantic Clitophon repeatedly punches an Egyptian slave in the face
and then imprisons him, all for accidentally drugging his love, Leucippe (Ach. Tat.
4. 15. 6; cp. 5. 17. 6, 5. 18. 4, 6. 20–22), and a slave girl threatened with torture flees
(Ach. Tat. 2. 25. 3–27). The *Life of Aesop*, an anonymous Egyptian composition of the
first century AD, documents the relationship between the slave Aesop and his owner
Xanthippus. Aesop lives under constant threat of violence, whether it be a beating
or fully fledged torture; the same is true of the cunning slaves in Plautine plays.
Petronius' novel includes numerous instances of violence meted out or threatened
to slaves (e.g., Petr. 28. 7, 30. 5–11, 34. 2, 49, etc.). Violence was simply part and parcel

of the slave's lot, which Cicero characterized as a matter of coercion and breaking of the spirit (Cic. *Rep.* 3. 37) and symbolized by with the whip, the hook, and the cross (Cic. *Rab. Perd.* 16; for violence against slaves, see Daly 1961; Bradley 1987: 113–37; Parker 1989; Bradley 1994: esp. 28–29, 165–70).

These are the types of violence that marred Roman social interactions, particularly when status disparities were involved. In legal punishments, freeborn commoners were subjected to the same harsh treatment as slaves. The violence and scale of Roman arena and circus spectacles contributed to the high visibility of violence in Roman society, while the violence routinely meted out to slaves, to schoolboys by teachers, or to suspects and convicts by the authorities sanctioned it as an expression of power and status. Now imagine the effects on a child raised in such a societal environment, where violence was casually applied to persons deemed worthless at home (Saller 1991; Cutler 2006) and differentially applied in public to social inferiors according to their status—such a child would surely have become accustomed to the violent treatment of those he saw as lessers with a slap, a cuff, or some other brand of humiliation (Dionisotti 1982). Indeed, Juvenal makes this very point in his fourteenth *Satire* (esp. Juv. 14. 14–24). Augustine (*Ep.* 153. 16) conceives of institutionalized violence as a continuum from the emperor at the top through judicial authority, warfare, owners correcting their slaves, and on down to fatherly strictness at the bottom. The vector of his analysis can be easily reversed.

A general analogue for all we have seen thus far is offered by conditions in early modern Western Europe (roughly 1500 to 1800). It does seem that in these years—particularly in England, France, Germany, and Italy—violence was far more common than in subsequent centuries. Men went about armed. Until the eighteenth century, aristocrats maintained large private arsenals, up to and including artillery pieces. Private plaintiffs, not the state, pressed charges against wrongdoers. Violence was a common feature of domestic life, of relations between peasants and soldiers, between the state and its subjects, and between people of all classes over matters of honor ('honor' being both your view of yourself and everyone else's view of you). To be violated in any way, even verbally, demanded a response, and most generally a physical one. Failure to respond validated the violation. This gave rise to the prevalence of feuds, duels, and vendettas in a variety of European societies in these years. Gradually, the growing power of the state sought to curb private violence by confiscating private arsenals, limiting access to arms, training professional and disciplined state armies, expanding judicial regulation of social interactions, and banning such rituals as duels. Despite these efforts, however, violence remained a stock feature of many European societies down to 1800, not least because policing systems remained woefully inadequate (Hale 1972; Muir 1993; Amussen 1995; Evans 1996; Ruff 2001).

Any historical comparison is naturally more suggestive than probative, since regional variation over time is no less likely for the early modern era than it is for the Roman. Nevertheless, when it comes to violence, instructive echoes bounce between these eras (see Riess 2002 for an enlightening comparandum between these same two eras in the matter of torture). Romans had ready access to arms. Policing as we understand it was all but non-existent (Nippel 1995; but see, *contra*, Brélaz 2005 and Fuhrmann 2005). Criminal cases were prosecuted by aggrieved private citizens, not the state (see the petitions preserved on papyrus). Soldiers, even the professionalized forces of the imperial age, could victimize civilians at will. Do these coincidences mean that the Roman era was comparably violent to the early modern period? We cannot say for certain. The differences matter just as much as the similarities. Unlike the early modern period, the sword was not a status symbol among the Romans, so there was less incentive to wear it routinely; images in Roman art of civilian males show them unarmed. We also cannot meaningfully gauge the degree of domestic violence at Rome, even among the well-attested elites (Treggiari 1991: 430). It does seem, however, that wife beating was not broadly condoned and offered valid grounds for divorce or other legal action (Quint. *Inst.* 7. 4. 11; *CJ* 5. 17. 8. 2; *P. Oxy.* VI 903, L 3581). In the early modern era, wife beating was celebrated as a necessity among the lower classes. If wives were spared, the Roman domestic scene was nevertheless sullied by casual or punitive violence applied liberally to slaves. After the late republic, aristocrats could not maintain large arsenals or raise private armies without risking their lives as challengers to the emperor's authority, although wealthy householders were allowed to maintain modest armories to defend against plunderers (*Dig.* 48. 6. 1–2). The comparison with early modern Europe is therefore suggestive, but hardly conclusive. The best we can say is that, broadly speaking, certain conditions comparable to those in early modern Europe may have generated an inclination toward violence among the Romans, but how frequently that inclination was indulged remains an open question.

A final point pertinent to the Roman etiquette of violence is worth noting. It is, in fact, a negative point, the curious absence of a widespread habit in Mediterranean societies that one might expect to find at Rome, but which does not show up. This is the blood feud, vendetta, or duel over matters of honor. Most of the social conditions that generate such behavior are to be found in ancient Rome: an obsession with honor (*dignitas*; see Lendon 1997: esp. 30–55), a clan- and family-oriented social organization, a large population of elite youths (*iuvenes* or *iuventus*, often organized into clubs), attenuated state policing, and ready access to weapons, to name only a few (Herlihy 1972; Black-Michaud 1975: 1–32; Boehm 1984: 65–89; Wilson 1988: 61–176). Against this background, it might reasonably be expected that, say, Clodius would have called out his archenemy Cicero to settle their interpersonal dispute definitively with a duel, or that the murders inflicted by the Scipiones Nasicae and the Opimii on the Gracchi, or the Cassii and Bruti on the Iulii Caesares would have generated lasting blood feuds between these families, but this did not happen. Why not?

Feuds, by commonly accepted definition, take place between peers, since social inferiors are regarded as unworthy of such attention, and social superiors are attacked only at one's peril. They are therefore examples of socially 'horizontal' patterns of violence. A strong sense of egalitarianism pervades feuding cultures. Reciprocal killing and maiming marks the course of the blood feud. Matters progress according to established sets of rules. The goal of the feud is to enhance individual or group prestige within the community, not to inflict loss on the opponent(s). By striking back at each other, the feuding parties seek to redress the temporary status imbalance established by their rivals' prior action. The duel may be seen as a subset of these behaviors, in that it comprises a potentially lethal, rule-based encounter to settle a matter of honor between individuals, and so to maintain one's prestige and reputation within a community (see the sources cited in the preceding paragraph).

While it is true that the Romans preferred to administer violence through proxies, rather than in person (Galen *Anim. Pass.* 4 = 5. 17K; Gel. 10. 3. 5; Cic. *Cluent.* 176–77), or that they played out their enmities ritualistically in the public gaze—via elections, the courts, euergetistic rivalry, and so forth—rather than privately by means of violence (Epstein 1987: esp. 74–126; Flaig 2003: esp. 137–54; compare the situation at Athens: Cohen 1995; *contra* Herman 2006), it is far less clear why this should have been the case. The centrality of parallel status in the blood feuding ethos may provide a key to unlocking an answer. As we have seen throughout this chapter, violence done to social equals in the Roman world was frowned upon, while violence done to inferiors was more acceptable. The exceptions to these rules were self-defense (meeting force with force) or, to a lesser extent, instant vengeance, meted out to one who had done you some serious and tangible wrong—but on the spot. Waiting to exact vengeance, as would be required by a feud or a duel, was not condoned (see above). No less significant is that blood feuding requires public submission to the passions. Burning emotions of vengeance are put on open display in acts of reciprocal violence (a study of feuding in Renaissance Italy is entitled *Mad Blood Stirring*; see Muir 1993). As one scholar puts it, in feuding societies "the passion for revenge is embedded in a way of life that revolves around the notion of honor, and in which 'boiling blood' is a socially recognized category" (Elster 1990: 871). Such public display of violent emotion, however, would contravene the Roman elite's norms of solemnity (*gravitas*) and self-control (*disciplina, temperantia*) in public demeanor. The virtue of restraining, not indulging, powerful passions was valued by the Roman upper classes (Harris 2001; Kaster 2005: esp. 84–103). That tensions boiled just below the surface is suggested by what happened when society's lid blew off, as during the late republican proscriptions. In an atmosphere of pervasive violence temporarily sanctioned by the state, old scores were settled (e.g., Cic. *Rosc*; Plut. *Sulla* 30–31; App. *B.C.* 1. 71–73). Appian (*B.C.* 4. 5–51) assembles a dossier of harrowing triumviral proscription tales that includes not only numerous cases of 'horizontal' violence among peers, but also of inferiors (like slaves) gleefully seeing to the murder of their betters. The stories illustrate the irregularity of these types of violence since, by depicting the proper order turned upside down, they seek to induce horror in the reader. As such, they offer evidence for a powerful abhorrence of any such actions under normal conditions.

These observations apply to the elite, for whom we have the best evidence. The situation among the lower orders is less obvious. Here conditions conducive to feuding may well have led to some form of vendetta and blood revenge. Cicero documents longstanding and nasty rivalries resulting in violence in the small towns of Ameria, not far from Rome (Cic. *Rosc.* 16–20, 84–97), or at Larinum in Apulia (Cic. *Pro Cluentio*). Juvenal (15. 33–83) refers to an ancient and long-nurtured hatred (*vetus atque antiqua simultas, / immortale odium…ardet*) between the towns of Ombi and Tentyra in Upper Egypt that eventually blossomed into an armed confrontation. Juvenal's account can be set against late antique and Byzantine papyri from Egypt that document actual cases of comparable village-on-village violence (see examples cited in Winter 1933: 116 nn. 2 and 4). One suspects that much of the violence alleged in surviving petitions on papyri stemmed from ongoing disputes, the details of which are no longer recoverable from the snapshot view of events the surviving documents afford us. One (*P. Mich.* 6. 423–24), for instance, claims a campaign of attacks on persons and agricultural property by two brothers, and another (*P. Ryl.* 2.124) describes an (apparently unprovoked) assault in a village bathhouse. Apuleius, a man of some material wealth and social standing, was engaged in a running dispute with his in-laws that eventually saw the author put on trial for his life (Apul. *Apol.*; Bradley 1997). It is quite possible, then, that among the lower orders some form of violent feuding was more common than was the case with the elite, but the entire matter remains something of a puzzle (see Lendon, in this volume, on the whole matter of feuding).

Conclusions

What emerges from our analysis is that violence marred some social relations among the Romans more than it did others. Among the elite, aside from occasional spasms of horror during republican proscriptions or imperial witch hunts, violence was not a condoned mode of interaction. Blood feuding and dueling were absent, in part because the Roman upper classes valued restraint over succumbing to the passions, especially anger. If a senator like Cn. Domitius Ahenobarbus lost his temper in a dispute and put out the eye of a Roman knight in the forum (Suet. *Nero* 5. 1), this was something to be frowned upon, not admired. The Roman protocols of violence did not condone violence done by and to elite peers, or near peers.

It was a different story when it came to the treatment of social inferiors. Elite obsessions with status and authority allowed the expression of those qualities through violent treatment of subordinates when circumstances were felt to warrant it. Slaves were maltreated by everybody as a matter of course. This whole ethos of violently manifesting status and authority was given an official imprimatur through state-sanctioned institutional violence in the arena and circus, in judicial torments and punishments, and during examinations before magistrates. Yet, to conceive of Roman social relations as habitually governed by brutishness would be unrealistic. Indeed, a recent sociological study of violence argues that it is generally rare as a means of resolving interpersonal conflict and that people usually seek to avoid it

(Collins 2008). The Romans identified violence as an act worthy of legal sanction as early as the Twelve Tables, a precedent that endured in subsequent Roman law. In this connection, we note the swine L. Veratius who amused himself by going about in public hitting freemen in the face and then ordering a slave, who followed along behind, to dole out to the victim the fine stipulated in the Twelve Tables: 25 asses, a pittance in Veratius' day (Gel. 20. 2. 12–13). But if most Romans did not follow Veratius' bad example and routinely hit each other, they did show a certain readiness to lay hands on social inferiors when they felt justified in doing so. The disapproval of Veratius' behavior in Gellius' report stems in no small part from the fact that he specifically targeted freemen. Would Gellius have been similarly censorious if Veratius had only slapped slaves?

The situation among the lower orders is naturally murkier, but the available sources, especially the novels and papyri, point to violent tendencies, perhaps even in the form of feuding and vendettas, especially when disputes involving property and family relationships were concerned. That said, the nature of the sources for these social strata—sensationalizing fiction and instances of conflict that reached the attention of the authorities—cautions against reading them as necessarily reflective of general patterns of behavior or even of widely shared attitudes. Criminality stalked the countryside (bandits), the sea (pirates), and the darker urban recesses (gangs, muggers, and belligerent drunks). In Rome, as today, the lower orders were probably more likely to be victims of violence than the upper classes. Their deplorable living conditions may have heightened tensions and made people that little bit tetchier (Yavetz 1958; Scobie 1986).

So how violent was Roman society? We cannot say for sure. None of the material discussed here can be securely quantified. We simply cannot tell how many inhabitants of the empire were victims or perpetrators of violence during their (relatively brief) lives. Indeed, it is possible to argue from much the same evidence as that surveyed here that the Roman Empire offered a relatively peaceful environment, the sort of place where—just to take the matter of travel and banditry—the wealthy regularly trundled unmolested between their city and country residences, where a Christian like Tertullian could praise efforts to suppress banditry (Apol. 2. 8), or, for that matter, where the characters in Acts of the Apostles could move about quite freely from town to town. The anecdotes about violence cited at the opening of this chapter can all be read as reporting situations that were rare and exceptional (though the nonchalant tone of most may suggest otherwise). It is therefore perfectly reasonable to imagine that most Romans went about their daily business unscathed by interpersonal violence. An exception can be made in the case of slaves, whose lot was characterized by the capricious application of various forms of violence and humiliation. But even then, we cannot even begin to assess what proportion of the vast slave and ex-slave population felt the back of the hand or the cut of the lash, or how frequently they did so. We are working off impressions, and impressions can be misleading. If a miasma of violence seems to hang over Roman social relations, like any fog it presents a shifting and indistinct aspect.

SUGGESTED READING

The fullest treatment of violence in the Roman world in English remains Lintott 1999 (a second edition of a 1968 original), but it is restricted to the republic. A comparable work on the imperial period has yet to appear, although MacMullen 1966 and 1974 are full of illuminating detail. The best treatment of banditry remains Shaw 1984. Millar 1981—supplemented now by Riess 2001—is fundamental for making a case for historical realities embedded in ancient fiction.

BIBLIOGRAPHY

Africa, T.W. 1971. "Urban Violence in Imperial Rome." *Journal of Interdisciplinary History* 2: 3–21.

Alston, R. 1994. "Violence and Social Control in Roman Egypt." In *Proceedings of the 20th International Congress of Papyrologists, Copenhagen, 23–29 August, 1992.* Copenhagen: Museum Tusculanum Press. 517–52.

Amussen, S. D. 1995. "Punishment, Discipline, and Power: The Social Meaning of Violence in Early Modern England." *Journal of British Studies* 34: 1–34.

Bagnall, R. S. 1989. "Official and Private Violence in Roman Egypt." *Bulletin of the American Society of Papyrologists* 26: 201–16.

———. 2004. "Women's Petitions in Late Antique Egypt." In D. Feissel and J. Gascou (eds.), *La pétition à Byance.* Paris: Centre de Recherche d'Histoire et Civilisation de Byzance. 53–60.

Black-Michaud, J. 1975. *Cohesive Force: Feud in the Mediterranean and the Middle East.* New York: St. Martin's Press.

Blumell, L. H. 2007. "'Beware of Bandits': Banditry and Land Travel in the Roman Empire." *Journeys* 8: 1–20.

Boehm, C. 1984. *Blood Revenge: The Anthropology of Feuding in Montenegro and Other Tribal Societies.* Lawrence: University of Kansas Press.

Bonner, S. F. 1977. *Education in Ancient Rome, from the Elder Cato to the Younger Pliny.* Berkeley: University of California Press.

Bradley, K. R. 1987. *Slaves and Masters in the Roman Empire: A Study in Social Control.* Oxford: Oxford University Press.

———. 1994. *Slavery and Society at Rome.* Cambridge: Cambridge University Press.

———. 1997. "Law, Magic and Culture in the *Apologia* of Apuleius." *Phoenix* 51: 202–23.

———. 2000. "Animalizing the Slave: The Truth of Fiction." *Journal of Roman Studies* 90: 110–125.

Brélaz, C. 2005. *La sécurité publique en Asie Mineure sous le Principat (Ier-IIIème s. ap. J.-C.).* Basel: Schwabe.

Brunt, P. A. 1975. "Did Imperial Rome Disarm Her Subjects?" *Phoenix* 29: 260–70 = Brunt, P. A., *Roman Imperial Themes.* Oxford: Oxford University Press 1990. 255–66.

Cébeillac-Gervasoni, M. 1998. *Les magistrats des cités italiennes de la seconde guerre gunique à Auguste: le Latium et la Campanie.* Paris: École française de Rome.

Christes, J. 1979. "Reflexe erlebter Unfreiheit in den Sentenzen des Publilius Syrus und den Fabeln des Phaedrus: Zur Problematik ihrer Verifizierung." *Hermes* 107: 199–220.

Clark, G. 2006. "Desires of the Hangman: Augustine on Legitimized Violence." In
    H. A. Drake (ed.), *Violence in Late Antiquity*. Burlington: Ashgate. 137–46.

Cohen, D. 1995. *Law, Violence, and Community in Classical Athens*. Cambridge: Cambridge
    University Press.

Coleman, K. M. 1998. " 'The Contagion of the Throng:' Absorbing Violence in the Roman
    World." *Hermathena* 164: 65–88.

Collins, R. 2008. *Violence: A Micro-sociological Theory*. Princeton: Princeton University Press.

Crook, J. A. 1967. *Law and Life of Rome*. Ithaca: Cornell University Press.

Curchin, L. A. 1990. *The Local Magistrates of Roman Spain*. Toronto: University of Toronto
    Press.

Cutler, A. 2006. "The Violent Domus: Cruelty, Gender, and Class in Roman Household
    Possessions." In E. D'Ambra and G. P. R. Métraux (eds.), *The Art of Citizens,
    Soldiers and Freedmen in the Roman World*. BAR International Series 1526. Oxford:
    Archaeopress. 103–14.

Daly, L. W. 1961. *Aesop without Morals*. New York: T. Yoseloff.

de Souza, P. 1999. *Piracy in the Graeco-Roman World*. Cambridge. Cambridge University
    Press.

Dionisotti, A. C. 1982. "From Ausonius' Schooldays? A Schoolbook and Its Relatives."
    Journal of Roman Studies 72: 83–125.

Dossey, L. 2001. "Judicial Violence and the Ecclesiastical Courts in Late Antique North
    Africa." In R. Mathisen (ed.), *Law, Society, and Authority in Late Antiquity*. Oxford:
    Oxford University Press. 98–114.

Elster, J. 1990. "Norms of Revenge." *Ethics* 100: 862–85.

Epstein, D. F. 1987. *Personal Enmity in Roman Politics, 218–43 B.C.* London: Croom Helm.

Evans, R. J. 1996. *Rituals of Retribution: Capital Punishment in Germany, 1600–1987*. Oxford:
    Oxford University Press.

Eyben, E. 1993. *Restless Youth in Ancient Rome*. London: Routledge.

Flaig, E. 2003. *Ritualisierte Politik: Zeichen, Gesten und Herrschaft im Alten Rom*. Göttingen:
    Vandenhoeck und Ruprecht.

Flam-Zuckermann, L. 1970. "À propos d'une inscription de Suisse (*CIL* XIII 5015): étude du
    phénomène de brigandage dans l'empire romain." *Latomus* 29: 451–73.

Fuhrmann, C. J. 2005. *Keeping the Imperial Peace: Public Order, State Control, and Policing
    in the Roman Empire, AD 100–300*. Chapel Hill: PhD Thesis, University of North
    Carolina.

Gaddis, M. 2005. *There Is No Crime for Those Who Have Christ: Religious Violence in the
    Christian Roman Empire*. Berkeley: University of California Press.

García y García, L. 2005. *Pupils, Teachers and Schools in Pompeii: Childhood, Youth and
    Culture in the Roman Era*. Rome: Bardi.

Garnsey, P. 1968. "Why Penalties Become Harsher: The Roman Case." *Natural Law Forum*
    13: 141–62.

———. 1970. *Social Status and Legal Privilege in the Roman Empire*. Oxford: Clarendon
    Press.

Grünewald, T. 2004. *Bandits in the Roman Empire*. London: Routledge.

Hahn, J. 2004. *Gewalt und religiöser Konflikt: Studien zu den Auseinandersetzungen zwischen
    Christen, Heiden und Juden im Osten des Römischen Reiches (von Konstantin bis
    Theodosius II)*. Berlin: Akademie Verlag.

Hale, J. R. 1972. "Violence in the Late Middle Ages: A Background." In L. Martines (ed.),
    Violence and Civil Disorder in Italian Cities, 1200–1500. Berkeley: University of
    California Press. 19–37.

Harries, J. 2007. *Law and Crime in the Roman World*. Cambridge: Cambridge University Press.

Harris, W. V. 1986. "The Roman Father's Power of Life and Death." In W. V. Harris and R. S. Bagnall (eds.), *Studies in Roman Law in Memory of A. Arthur Schiller*. Leiden: E. J. Brill. 81–95.

———. 2001. *Restraining Rage: The Ideology of Anger Control in Classical Antiquity*. Cambridge, Mass.: Harvard University Press.

Herlihy, D. 1972. "Some Psychological and Social Roots of Violence in the Tuscan Cities." In L. Martines (ed.), *Violence and Civil Disorder in Italian Cities, 1200–1500*. Berkeley: University of California Press. 129–54.

Herman, G. 1994. "How Violent was Athenian Society?" In R. Osborne and S. Hornblower (eds.), *Ritual, Finance, Politics. Athenian Democratic Accounts Presented to David Lewis*. Oxford: Oxford University Press. 99–117.

———. 2006. *Morality and Behaviour in Democratic Athens: A Social History*. Cambridge: Cambridge University Press, 2006.

Hermann, P. 1990. *Hilferufe aus römischen Provinzen: Ein Aspekt der Krise des römischen Reiches im 3. Jhdt. n. Chr.* Hamburg: Joachim Jungius-Gesellschaft der Wissenschaften.

Hobson, D. W. 1993. "The Impact of Law on Village Life in Roman Egypt." In B. Halpern and D. W. Hobson (eds.), *Law, Politics and Society in the Ancient Mediterranean World*. Sheffield: Sheffield Academic Press. 193–219.

Holzberg, N. 2002. *The Ancient Fable: An Introduction*. Bloomington: Indiana University Press.

Hopkins, K. 1983. *Death and Renewal*. Cambridge: Cambridge University Press.

———. 1993. "Novel Evidence for Roman Slavery." *Past and Present* 138: 3–27.

Hopwood, K. (ed.). 1999. *Organised Crime in Antiquity*. London: Duckworth.

Horsfall, N. 2003. *The Culture of the Roman Plebs*. London: Duckworth.

Isaac, B. 1984. "Bandits and Judaea and Arabia." *Harvard Studies in Classical Philology* 88: 171–203.

———. 2004. *The Invention of Racism in Classical Antiquity*. Princeton: Princeton University Press.

Kaster, R. A. 2005. *Emotion, Restraint, and Community in Ancient Rome*. Oxford: Oxford University Press.

Labruna, L. 1971. *Vim fieri veto: Alle radici di una ideologia*. Naples: Jovene.

Lendon, J. E. 1997. *Empire of Honour: The Art of Government in the Roman World*. Oxford: Clarendon Press.

Lintott, A. 1999. *Violence in Republican Rome*. 2nd ed. Oxford: Oxford University Press.

MacMullen, R. 1966. *Enemies of the Roman Order: Treason, Unrest, and Alienation in the Empire*. Cambridge, Mass.: Harvard University Press.

———. 1974. *Roman Social Relations, 50 BC to AD 284*. New Haven: Yale University Press.

———. 1986. "Judicial Savagery in the Roman Empire." *Chiron* 16: 147–66 = MacMullen, R., *Changes in the Roman Empire: Essays in the Ordinary*. Princeton: Princeton University Press 1990. 204–17.

Martines, L. (ed.). 1972. *Violence and Civil Disorder in Italian Cities, 1200–1500*. Berkeley: University of California Press.

Matthews, J. 2006. *The Journey of Theophanes: Travel, Business, and Daily Life in the Roman East*. New Haven: Yale University Press.

McGing, B. C. 1998. "Bandits, Real and Imagined, in Greco-Roman Egypt." *Bulletin of the American Society of Papyrologists* 35: 159–83.

Millar, F. 1981. "The World of the *Golden Ass*." *Journal of Roman Studies* 71: 63–75.

Mitchell, S. 1976. "Requisitioned Transport in the Roman Empire: A New Inscription from Pisidia." *Journal of Roman Studies* 66: 106–31.

Monaco, L. 1996. Persecutio Piratarum: *Battaglie ambigue e svolte costituzionali nella Roma repubblicana*. Naples: Jovene.

Muir, E. 1993. *Mad Blood Stirring: Vendetta and Factions in Friuli during the Renaissance*. Baltimore: Johns Hopkins University Press.

Musurillo, H. A. 1954. *The Acts of the Pagan Martyrs:* Acta Alexandrinorum. Oxford: Clarendon Press.

Nippel, W. 1995. *Public Order in Ancient Rome*. Cambridge: Cambridge University Press.

Ormerod, H. A. 1924. *Piracy in the Ancient World: An Essay on Mediterranean History*. Liverpool: University of Liverpool Press. (Reprint 1997, Baltimore: Johns Hopkins University Press.)

Parca, M. 2002. "Violence by and against Women in Documentary Papyri from Ptolemaic and Roman Egypt." In H. Melaerts and L. Mooren (eds.), *Le rôle et le statut de la femme ne Égypte Hellénistique, Romaine et Byzantine*. Leuven: Peeters. 283–96.

Parker, H. 1989. "Crucially Funny or Tranio on the Couch: The *Servus Callidus* and Jokes about Torture." *Transactions of the American Philological Association* 119: 233–46.

Peachin, M. 2007a. "Angriffe und Erniedrigungen als alltägliche Elemente der kaiserzeitlichen Regierungspraxis." In R. Haensch and J. Heinrichs (eds.), *Herrschen und Verwalten. Der Alltag der römischen Administration in der Hohen Kaiserzeit*. Cologne: Böhlau. 122–31.

———. 2007b. "Petition to a Centurion from the NYU Papyrus Collection and the Question of Informal Adjudication Performed by Soldiers." In A. J. B. Sirks and K. A. Worp (eds.), *Papyri in Memory of P.J. Sijpesteijn*. Oakville: American Society of Papyrologists. 79–97.

Peters, E. 1985. *Torture*. Oxford: Blackwell.

Plass, P. 1995. *The Game of Death in Ancient Rome: Arena Sport and Political Suicide*. Madison: University of Wisconsin Press.

Rauh, N. K. 2003. *Merchants, Sailors and Pirates in the Roman World*. Stroud: Tempus.

Riess, W. 2001. *Apuleius und die Räuber. Ein Beitrag zur historischen Kriminalitätsforschung*. Stuttgart: Franz Steiner Verlag.

———. 2002. "Die historische Entwicklung der Römischen Folter- und Hinrichtungspraxis in Kulturvergleichender Perspektive." *Historia* 51: 206–26.

Rives, J. 1995. "Human Sacrifice among Pagans and Christians." *Journal of Roman Studies* 85: 65–85.

Ruff, J. R. 2001. *Violence in Early Modern Europe, 1500–1800*. Cambridge: Cambridge University Press.

Saller, R. P. 1980. "Anecdotes as Historical Evidence for the Principate." *Greece & Rome* 27: 69–83.

———. 1991. "Corporal Punishment, Authority, and Obedience in the Roman Household." In B. Rawson (ed.), *Marriage, Divorce, and Children in Ancient Rome*. Oxford: Oxford University Press. 144–65.

———. 1994. *Patriarchy, Property, and Death in the Roman Family*. Cambridge: Cambridge University Press.

Scobie, A. 1986. "Slums, Sanitation, and Mortality in the Roman World." *Klio* 68: 399–433.

Shaw, B. D. 1984. "Bandits in the Roman Empire." *Past and Present* 105: 3–52.

———. 1993. "The Bandit." In A. Giardina (ed.), *The Romans*. Chicago: University of Chicago Press. 300–41.

Stephens, S. A., and J. J. Winkler. 1995. *Ancient Greek Novels: The Fragments*. Princeton: Princeton University Press.

Treggiari, S. 1991. *Roman Marriage*: Iusti Coniuges *from the Time of Cicero to the Time of Ulpian*. Oxford: Clarendon Press.

Wilson, S. 1988. *Feuding, Conflict and Banditry in Nineteenth-Century Corsica*. Cambridge: Cambridge University Press.

Winter, J. G. 1933. *Life and Letters in the Papyri*. Ann Arbor: University of Michigan Press.

Wiseman, T. P. 1985. *Catullus and His World: A Reappraisal*. Cambridge: Cambridge University Press.

Yavetz, Z. 1958. "The Living Conditions of the Urban Plebs." *Latomus* 17: 500–17 = R. Seager (ed.), *The Crisis of the Roman Republic*. Cambridge: Heffer 1969. 84–92.

PART VI

SOCIETIES WITHIN THE ROMAN COMMUNITY

CHAPTER 23

ORGANIZED SOCIETIES: *COLLEGIA*

JONATHAN S. PERRY

THE 'FAMILIAL LIFE' OF THE *COLLEGIA*: BEFORE THE 1970S

THE study of 'social relations' within, and in connection to, the Roman *collegia* (organized societies, of various sorts) may be among the oldest, and perhaps the liveliest, represented in this volume. Scholarship in this vein was first undertaken by the remarkable J.-P. Waltzing, who composed what is still, after a full century and more, the standard book on these institutions. Surveying the phenomenon while perched atop the industrial powerhouse of fin-de-siècle Belgium, Waltzing surmised that it was only natural for workers, whether in the past or the present, to organize themselves. After all, he observed, we human beings, in every place and time, "like to associate ourselves with people of similar occupations, of equal social conditions, who have the same ideas and interests" (Waltzing 1895–1900: I, 265). Here, as throughout the four-volume *Étude historique sur les corporations professionnelles chez les Romains*, Waltzing underscored the obvious advantages of "la vie familiale dans les collèges," for after the work-week is done, people instinctively and spontaneously enjoy coming together and sharing in their accustomed "divertissements," thus making their lives "easier and more pleasant" (Waltzing 1895–1900: I, 322). Whether in Rome or in Liège, workers do not really desire to assemble, on their days off, to discuss collective bargaining, poor working conditions, or higher wages. Rather, they are merely seeking a break from the daily routine, a chance to divert their attention and improve their minds.

While Waltzing may have been somewhat naïve about the intentions of the labor organizers in his own city, his conception of them reveals an important trend in the history of scholarship regarding the *collegia*, in other words, that they have almost universally been evaluated in comparison to 'similar' organizations in the scholar's own society.[1] This avenue of approach became a particularly urgent matter in the late nineteenth and early twentieth centuries, when industrialization was demanding new 'social relations' among groups in Western European societies, and when, coincidentally, due to the ongoing compilation of the *Corpus Inscriptionum Latinarum*, the critical primary source material for this subject was suddenly becoming more widely available. By the late 1890s, roughly 1500 inscriptions, naming nearly 200 distinct *collegia*, had been identified; and the rapid appearance of this sizable corpus of relevant texts, illuminating the inner workings of these organizations in a key period of their development, would revolutionize the study of *collegia* well into the following century.[2] Prior to this point, students of Roman society had been dimly aware of the existence of *collegia*, a set of associations that usually appeared, in the extant sources, in the context of official licensing and/or restriction. In fact, while still a law student at Kiel in 1843, Theodor Mommsen had, himself, published the first systematic analysis of these institutions (Mommsen 1843), in terms of the legal texts and literary references that were then available. While it essentially launched modern study of the *collegia*, Mommsen's *De collegiis et sodaliciis Romanorum* is also famous for preserving, in its final pages, the first glimmers of the *CIL* project. In turn, as the individual volumes of *CIL* began to appear in print, students in the 1880s and 1890s quickly realized that they could be mined for dissertations—albeit, dissertations of varying quality and sophistication.[3]

Nevertheless, most investigations, excepting Waltzing's mammoth catalogue[4] and commentary, continued, until very recently, to turn primarily on juridical matters—a trend best exemplified in L. Schnorr von Carolsfeld's truncated book on the "juristische Person" of the members of such *collegia*, and the long and productive career of

1. Further, on this theme, see Perry 2006, which addresses the development of scholarship on *collegia* from the mid-nineteenth century (introduction and chapter 1) through Waltzing and his milieu (chapter 2), to scholars working—often with the support, or even the participation, of their government—in Fascist Italy (chapters 3, 4, and 5), and from 1945 to the present (chapter 6).

2. Some of the excitement of epigraphic research is reflected in Marc Bloch's classic *The Historian's Craft*. This son of the Greek epigraphist Gustave Bloch observed, "I have before me a Roman funerary inscription carved from a single block, made for a single purpose. Yet nothing could be more variegated than the evidences which there await the probing of the scholar's lancet" (Bloch 1953: 145).

3. See, among these, Maué 1886 and Schiess 1888. Not all students were sufficiently aware, at the time, of the potential of this material. Thus, French legal theses continued to be written, generally with very little reference to epigraphic sources (for examples, see Perry 2006: 64–67 and Tran 2001).

4. Which has recently been updated, but only for Roman Italy, in Mennella and Apicella 2000.

Francesco Maria De Robertis (1910–2003).[5] A rather sinister detour in this scholarly progression merged the study of *collegia* with the principles of Fascist 'Corporativismo' in 1930s Italy, culminating in the 1939 treatise *Dalla Corporazione romana alla Corporazione fascista*. Published by the Fascist Minister of National Education Giuseppe Bottai, and under the auspices of the Istituto di Studi Romani (reconfigured after the war as the still-functioning Istituto Nazionale di Studi Romani), this work is no mere historical oddity from a failed regime. Rather, through both itself and its German translation— amply documented in a fascinating set of archival documents—it casts light on the intersection of contemporaneous racial theory and the famous '*Romanità*' theme of the Fascists between 1938 and 1942. In similar fashion, larger historical and intellectual trends have continued to act upon Roman collegial studies since 1945. As Marxist conceptions and paradigms began to rise to the fore, in many academic disciplines, classicists have addressed the 'social' aspects of the associative phenomenon in ever greater depth. While Marxist theory influenced some of these studies—though not to an overwhelming extent, even in Communist Eastern Europe and the U.S.S.R.—postwar analyses have moved beyond the juristic studies of their predecessors, opting instead to weigh the degree of sociability detectable among members of these ancient institutions.

THE COLLEGIA IN MACMULLEN AND ALFÖLDY

Within this context, it is important to note that in the masterworks that initiated the contemporary study of Roman social relations, Ramsay MacMullen and Géza Alföldy yielded considerable pride of place to the *collegia*. In the process, they made a sharp break with the juridical approach favored in previous eras, stressing instead the 'sociable' aspects that had created and maintained these institutions. Accordingly, it is critical not only to understand how thoroughly, and in what specific ways, *Roman Social Relations (RSR)* and *Römische Sozialgeschichte (RSG)* transformed our contemporary understanding of *collegia*, but also to acknowledge the misunderstandings that might have been engendered by this approach to frustratingly incomplete and haphazardly collected evidence. As such, the much-tilled field containing the *collegia* is by no means exhausted—one simply needs to dig elsewhere, and with different tools.

Presumably aware of the general thrust of scholarship on the topic in previous decades, MacMullen insisted, early in *RSR*, that "[a]ny analogy with a medieval guild or modern labor union is wholly mistaken. Rather, their purpose is social in the broadest sense."[6] In fact, he delineated this "broad sense" with broad humor,

5. Schnorr von Carolsfeld 1933 and De Robertis 1938, 1955, and 1971.

6. With their wealth of religious confraternities, guilds, and other associations, medieval societies have also been evaluated increasingly in terms of social relations by contemporary scholars. See, for example, Rosser 1994, a study of commensality among English confraternities in the late Middle Ages.

alluding to "the party mood" that seems to have prevailed among a group of diners who were "beautifully drunk and dizzy with the noise and dancing" (MacMullen 1974: 19). This image of joyful carousers masks a serious point, however. In MacMullen's estimation, the demands and interests of sociability *took precedence over* those of economic advancement, in spite of the shared profession one might presume among the college's membership. In other words, any benefits of collective association in an economic sense were, in MacMullen's view of things, *incidental* and *unintended* consequences of the groups' principal purpose, which was to gather together with one's peers. As he sketched out the phenomenon, "Quite to the contrary, a great deal suggests that a friendly, gossipy atmosphere prevailed among people who saw each other every day, worked at the same job in the same neighborhood, and shared all the same ups and downs. Trade associations were the result" (MacMullen 1974: 72–73).[7] Thus, because "[o]rganization of some sort was inevitable" (MacMullen 1974: 41) among people in this, as in any other, society, the challenge to the researcher is to uncover the social relations that actually prompted collective association, rather than to focus exclusively on the members' titles and thus their presumed daily work.

This approach led directly to some of the most useful and original sections of *RSR*, most notably the appendix A.2, on "Crafts' Localities." Here, MacMullen listed those urban districts that seem to have derived their names from the craftsmen's associations that congregated there. In other words, it was the primarily social act of human association that tied a type of profession to a certain locale, and not vice versa. Alföldy took a similarly optimistic view of the benefits and results of this type of lower-class interaction. He placed his analysis of *collegia* within the context of the lower strata, specifically within the empire's cities. As he noted, the prospects of the urban, as opposed to those of the rural, poor were much brighter, leaving as they did "more scope for a public life, more largesse and, not least, better chances of entertainment than in the countryside" (Alföldy 1985: 134). Like Waltzing and MacMullen, then, he drew attention to the 'social benefit' of collegial association, which brightened up an otherwise drab and wretched existence. While membership in a college provided opportunities for social advancement, it was "still more important…that the *plebs urbana* was regularly provided with grain" (Alföldy 1985: 135). Furthermore, he adds, "A bonus was the availability of entertainment, particularly at shows in the amphitheatre, circus and theatre…And there were also the other opportunities for the pleasure-seeker provided by a city—like a visit to a brothel: 28 brothels are attested at Pompeii alone."[8]

7. One might compare the wry comments of a former Socialist organizer in Ignazio Silone's 1936 novel *Bread and Wine*: "But the point is that those [Red] leagues were not political. The poor peasants…joined the league for the sake of company and protection. To them socialism meant getting together. The ideal of the boldest spirits among them was to have work and be able to eat their fill" (Silone 1986: 141–42).

8. On this final point, McGinn (2004: 267–90) has recently compiled a rather larger catalogue of 40+ "possible brothels" at Pompeii.

Thus, both MacMullen and Alföldy attempted to detect the essentially social motivations for association, employing imaginative reconstructions of the lives of the ordinary urban day-laborer to do so. They were, in these conclusions, aided by the nature of the evidence that has survived from antiquity. MacMullen (1974: 18) traced the source of confusion about *collegia* to a misinterpretation of the evidence in this regard: "The associative principle looks like an economic one simply because a barely literate society naturally put on paper only things like contracts and receipts." However, one remarkable, and often-noted, feature of collegial inscriptions—by far the most plentiful source of information on their existence—is how *little* economic detail is contained in them. The stress, throughout these documents, is instead on banquets, the creation of monuments, the recognition of patrons, burials of members or friends of the group, the announcement of officers, in other words, phenomena that are indeed what MacMullen has called "social in the broadest sense." But one must admit that these documents might be obscuring more than they reveal. If, for example, a *collegium* were agitating for better working conditions, would it be likely to have inscribed a document demanding a redress of grievances by the city's power elite? And even more important, are we justified in expecting them to have shared their most intimate deliberations with the larger society in an inscribed monument? By far the bulk of the material we possess concerning *collegia* is either dedicatory (and generally in honor of a patron) or else funerary. It may simply not have been normal—or, indeed, rational—procedure to inscribe the detailed minutes of their sessions, for the prying eyes of those highly placed community members who were literate.

Nevertheless, together with this new approach to collegial inscriptions has come a new way of evaluating social relations within these communities. Here, MacMullen and Alföldy veered away from Marxist paradigms of class struggle. If, after all, the *collegia* were not primarily economic engines of financial advancement, then their existence does not reflect class-bound interests, and they therefore cannot conform to classical Marxist models. If, alternatively, there was a struggle inherent in collegial organization, it was for relative status (on the one hand, among the members within the *collegium* itself, and on the other hand, for the members within the broader society), rather than for financial gain. Alföldy (1985: 149) concluded that a class-based model of social protest is fundamentally inappropriate in the Roman context:

> A social class grows up on the foundation of a common relationship between its members and economic production. In simple terms, this relationship depends upon the ownership or non-ownership of the means of production (in an ancient society, inevitably, land and workshops with the requisite equipment), on the division of labour and on the distribution of the goods produced.

By its very nature, then, the Roman social system, which "offered many openings for social advancement" (Alföldy 1985: 152), precluded the outbreak of class-based revolts, and its elites pursued a subtle strategy of preventing the rise of shared discontent, based upon economic class interests. As Alföldy observes, "The particular groups of the lower population were bound to the upper strata in a variety of ways, and, therefore, often pursued very different courses: nor were there any clear social divisions within the lower strata. No universal revolutionary class could thus develop" (Alföldy 1985: 153).

MacMullen concurred in this analysis, maintaining that modern paradigms are not at all applicable to this society. In short, while one might have expected a united force of workers, organized in *collegia*, to have exerted some measurable pressure on their upper-class patrons and governmental elites, the evidence for this simply does not exist. As he notes, "But what is striking about Roman crafts in operation is not that they pushed their interests as defined in a modern sense but that they did so only very rarely indeed" (MacMullen 1974: 75). Nothing in the ancient documents suggests that *collegia* ever called for a strike to secure their interests—though here one should compare Waltzing's brief comment on an inscribed edict from Asia Minor that might be so read[9]—nor are we ever told of attempts to bolster wages, to regulate practitioners of the craft, or to lobby for better working conditions. In fact, MacMullen observes that both the rural and urban poor were fundamentally resigned to their lot in life, with "passivity, silence, and deference." In short, they did not see signs of change in their relative status, did not question their condition, and had no expectation of rising beyond the stratum into which they had been born.

However, such a perspective must always be seen in relative terms. Again, MacMullen employed imaginative reconstruction to envisage these diminished, at least to our eyes, prospects (MacMullen 1974: 119):

> Like ourselves, the Roman in his one-room shop, in the back of which he and his wife and children slept and in the front of which he spent the day making and selling (let us say) articles of felt, did not look forward to a future altogether without prospects. He could realistically aim at an apprenticeship for his son and the lad's help in the business later. He could realistically aim at the secretaryship of his craft's local guild.

Indeed, MacMullen continues, these crafty organizations did manage to make themselves profitable in a certain, more social, sense. By organizing themselves into defined groups, they could "command the patronage of really important persons," tying themselves to these patrons financially and in terms of mutual obligations. An individual worker would never have been so honored by the haughty elite. United with others of his type, though, he was empowered to exchange favors with local officials—and, on rare occasions, even to bask in the attention of the emperor and/or the senate. The ideal desideratum would be the

9. This "exemple curieux" concerns a group of bakers who, having threatened to strike, forced the governor and local senate to make concessions. On the basis of this document, Waltzing concludes: "Cet édit prouve que les boulangers de Magnésie étaient associés et que l'association les avait mis en état d'affamer la ville et de troubler l'ordre" (Waltzing 1895–1900: I, 192).

extension of government recognition of the *collegium*, but, perhaps, attention might even be welcome on those occasions when the government specifically banned the association.

In this context, MacMullen stressed that the *collegia* seem to have pursued honor and status, rather than explicitly financial advantage. Accordingly, they may have adhered to the same basic patterns laid out by J. E. Lendon for upper-class "communities of honor," in which status and social prestige were distinct from, and not merely a consequence of, wealth.[10] Like many other kinds of groups in their society, they recognized the power of a unified stance in the acquisition of status, for which everyone in the Roman world was, both individually and communally, so eager. Rather than pressing for paid time off and a living wage, these craftsmen were desirous of "[p]ure comradeship. Friends liked to get together of an evening to eat, drink, and be merry. Moralists grumbled that they ate too much, to the point of inflating prices in the food markets; worse, that they drank too much..." (MacMullen 1974: 77).

Accordingly, the subtle dance between the two societal groups depended on the broadly social interests of both partners, and each followed, and sometimes mimicked, the other's steps with great interest. Alföldy analyzed the complex interaction in this way: "The members of such associations enjoyed a certain corporate identity: in the government of these associations they might imitate the role of civic dignitaries. At the same time these associations could finance better meals and a proper burial for their members out of membership dues and the donations of wealthy citizens" (1985: 134). Thus, collegiate association improved the social status of the membership, while also providing a welcome break from a grinding daily routine.

Therefore, as suggested by the pioneering works in the field of Roman social relations, there would seem to be two especially productive and illuminating avenues to pursue, specifically in respect to the *collegia*. First, we might ask how the members of these associations created their own 'mini-societies,' forming new networks of social interaction among these generally lower-stratum individuals. And second, we might explore how these societies interacted with other similar groupings in their cities, and particularly with the elites, who possessed most of the social goods that the urban poor coveted. If we concede that the *collegia* were organized for broad social advancement, rather than for narrow financial gain, how did they then set out to accomplish this, and, more important, what concessions were made by both parties to the exchange? As will become clear, the best approaches to the available evidence have sought to combine two basic methods—evaluating on the one hand the interior and on the other hand the exterior dynamics relating to *collegium* members.

10. Lendon 1997: 54–55. Lendon also cites the regulations of *collegia* for examples of how "communities of honor" could be found far beneath the ranks of the aristocracy. Even within these groups, however, there seem to have been sharp gradations between those possessing more or less 'honor.'

RELATIONS WITHIN THE *COLLEGIA*

In recent decades, several studies have attempted to describe the internal relationships of Roman *collegia*, though, as always, they are subject to the limitations inherent in the available evidence. Most of these studies have focused upon the 'official' items contained in the inscriptions, in other words, the decisions made by the magistrates who presided over the collective group, and especially on the magistrates themselves. The best of these studies have rigorously examined the surviving documents of organizations within some particular city (e.g., More 1969 on the *fabri tignarii*, carpenters, in Rome), of one particular type of *collegium* (Liu 2004 on *centonarii*—who were, until recently, identified as provincial firemen), or in terms of the collegial magistrates named in their records (Royden 1988). Alternatively, scholars have set the *scholae*, the central structures and meeting places built by the membership, within the spatial geography of their cities, and have attempted to uncover the unspoken assumptions that may have motivated these construction projects (Bollmann 1998). Others have built upon the findings of nineteenth-century 'Christian archaeologists' (especially De Rossi 1864–1877) to trace the possible connections between the *collegia* and communities of early Christians.[11]

However, the most profitable approach here might be to evaluate the funerary records of the associations, which constitute a sizable proportion of the total records that have survived. Among these the most revealing, and most instantly familiar, of all *collegia* inscriptions—that of the *cultores Dianae et Antinoi* (the Worshippers of Diana and Antinous) at Lanuvium—can be particularly helpful. This text (*CIL* XIV 2112) purports to be the by-laws of the organization, which were approved by those members assembled on June 9, 136.[12] Among other pronouncements, the members of this *collegium* unanimously voted that the initiation fee for the club would be 100 *sesterces*, plus an amphora of "good" wine, and that monthly dues would be assessed at 5 *asses*. Upon death, if the member was paid up and in good standing, his heirs would receive 250 *sesterces*, to be used for provision of the elements of an appropriate funeral. The by-laws went on to specify what would happen in the cases of death more than twenty miles distant from Lanuvium, intestacy, slave status, and suicide;[13] but a large portion of the document also deals with expected and proper conduct at the college's banquets and

11. Among others, see especially Harland 2003, Seland 1984, and McCready 1996. On early Christian communities, see Becker in this volume.

12. A. E. Gordon suggested that the connection with Antinous was probably a result of fortuitous timing. Noting that there does not seem to have been a physical temple of Antinous at Lanuvium, he argued thus (Gordon 1938: 44–46): "It looks...as though the society, happening to be founded soon after the death of Hadrian's favorite, had taken as its 'patron saints' not only Diana, who...was often thus honored, but Antinous as well..."

13. For an analysis of this last stipulation, within its wider philosophical context, see Mentxaka 2003.

celebrations. For example, any member who made too much noise when moving from one place to another would be fined 4 *sesterces*, anyone who spoke abusively or caused a disturbance at dinner would be fined 12, and anyone who verbally assaulted a "*quinquennalis*" of the club would be fined 20.

Attracted by "the detailed legal formalism" revealed here, Keith Hopkins, in *Death and Renewal*, extracted even more sociological inferences. For example, the very detail of the by-laws, which may be somewhat "surprising to find so low in the social scale," implies that the membership only trusted the permanence of formal and explicit expectations of behavior. Moreover, it is obvious, judging by their rules, that this was primarily a social club, boasting regular feasts, business meetings, and admonitions against drunkenness, among other stipulations. Given the preponderance of this sort of evidence, Hopkins (1983: 214) suggested, "Perhaps commemoration of the dead was merely an excuse for a good party." Or, again, we may be witnessing the phenomenon MacMullen identified, namely, that the social prerogatives of association, and the maintenance of proper standards of decorum, predated and continued to be of more importance than the putative business of burying the membership.

An analysis of the specifically funereal role of *collegia* has been extended to the analysis of columbaria monuments (Hasegawa 2005), as *collegium* members attempted, literally, to carve a niche for themselves in death, as well as in life. Or, as I attempted to demonstrate in my dissertation, the *collegium*, particularly in funerary contexts, might have served as a supplemental or replacement family for the deceased.[14] A remarkable instance of familial language in a collegial context concerns the *matres* (mothers) of *collegia*, who seem to occupy a position distinct from the more elevated berth of patronesses. Unlike patronesses, women who presumably reached down to the *collegia* from within the elite, the "mothers" seem to have been "social climbers from within the ranks of the *collegia*," in the estimation of Emily Hemelrijk.[15] Familial terminology would thus reinforce bonds among the members, while also conferring a bit of prestige upon a woman marked out for this title. Identified as an (or perhaps the) "mother" of the group on a commemorative plaque, she was accorded a special place among them. Moreover, the "vie familiale," which Waltzing identified in the 1890s, could also have been simulated at the moment of death—especially in those instances in which the *collegium*, as a group, assisted a blood relative in burying a deceased member.

Nevertheless, it must be conceded that the evidence we possess does not document the day-to-day deliberations that would help cast light on the social goals and interactions within these groups. One would wish for something like the minutes of the American Communist Party—a truly fringe group that has been studied with great interest in recent decades—or of a twentieth-century labor union; but such

14. Perry 1999 and Perry 2002, for a specific application of this notion.

15. Hemelrijk 2008. It should be noted that the number of *matres*, conveniently compiled by Hemelrijk into a table, is very small (twenty names), and the number of patronesses even smaller (fourteen).

detail is sorely lacking for the Roman *collegia*.[16] What has survived may lend itself more profitably to an analysis from the perspective of the urban elite, and especially with regard to how that elite interacted with the *collegia* in its midst. And, in this respect, truly innovative and thought-provoking work has been offered in the 1990s by John R. Patterson and Onno M. van Nijf, work that has been effectively summarized in a recent article by Koenraad Verboven. The general thrust of this scholarship, however, has developed an optimistic picture of this interaction—in other words, the work points in the direction of collegial organization as a means of social mobility and social advance vis-à-vis the urban elite.

Relations between the *Collegia* and Their Patrons

While Guido Clemente had contributed a lengthy analysis of patronage networks in Italy in 1972, the appearance of Patterson's article "The *Collegia* and the Transformation of the Towns of Italy in the Second Century AD" in 1994 launched several new points for discussion. This paper dealt directly with the *collegia*, within the context of urban life in Roman Italy, tracing their development over several centuries, and highlighting their enhanced status and importance over that period. They boasted, and capitalized upon, their close connections with civic leaders, and their internal organization mirrored that of local governmental elites. Succinctly and compellingly put, Patterson argues that, "As well as engaging in their normal festive and funeral activities, we thus find the *collegia* playing an increasingly important role in civic life; setting up statues to the emperors and benefactors, for example, and thus acting on behalf of the populace as a whole…" (Patterson 1994: 235). The notion that the *collegia* "increasingly" engaged in such activities appears crucial to his analysis, as he has continued to address the role of *collegia* in terms of social mobility in his latest contribution (Patterson 2006). In Patterson's view, existing collegial structures "helped to socialize the upwardly mobile into the civilised nexus of patronage, benefaction, and reciprocal honours that characterized the Roman city, and allowed their members to participate in civic affairs to their own benefit and that of the community more generally" (Patterson 2006: 262). Thus, a rising tide lifted all boats, and "the comparatively well off" were gradually encouraged to participate in civic life in more public ways, enhancing their own collective status while also assisting the wider community.

16. Upon his defection from the party, Whittaker Chambers commented on the important role played by certain "Mothers," who had been generally adopted by the membership (Chambers 1952). For the mechanics and internal deliberations of the Communist Party in the United States during the 1930s, see Ottanelli 1991.

In this vein, van Nijf has recently proposed that *collegia* be understood primarily within the nexus of social connections. And more specifically, if we are to understand the funerary activities of the *collegia*, we must be prepared to see that burial by a college "was less a necessity than a conscious choice. If we want to be able to explain why people chose to be buried by a *collegium*, and why they emphasised their membership of *collegia* at death, we must open up the discussion. In order to understand the funerary activities of *collegia*, we need to place them within their social and historical context" (van Nijf 1997: 33). In the remainder of the book, van Nijf traces the influence of this "social context" on the activities of the *collegia* in the eastern provinces of the empire. His approach is particularly fruitful in the matter of commensality (communal dining), a feature of life in many *collegia* that underscores the sociable desires and priorities of these groups. Public banquets and distributions should be seen as revealing indicators of status and degree of participation in the hierarchical structures of eastern cities. In short, "The evidence shows a clear social pattern behind the organisation of public food-giving and food-sharing rituals. Participation in these rituals was negotiated through membership of one or more subsections of the city, treated differently according to their standing in society" (van Nijf 1997: 246–47). Accordingly, the rituals reinforced existing patterns of organization, and, by mimicking the epigraphic habits of their social betters, the leaders of *collegia* "internalised and reproduced" the hierarchy of their cities.

In subsequent work, van Nijf has continued to employ this approach to the evidence, suggesting the means by which collegial members were incorporated into the social structures of their cities. Specifically, in analyzing the *collegia* of *fabri*, *centonarii*, and *dendrophori*[17] (van Nijf 1999), he examined the intersection of collegial sociability and civic ritual within their larger civic hierarchies. Through sections on the "Stedelijke identiteit van collegia" (civic identity of the *collegia*) and their "Feesten en rituelen" (feasts and rituals), he demonstrates how these *collegia*, some of the most frequently represented in the inscriptional record, were deliberately included in civic rituals and ceremonies and thus represented the harmonious hierarchies of which they were a part. This perspective is also reflected in his 2003 article entitled "Les élites comme patrons des associations professionnelles dans l'Orient Romain." Here, van Nijf detected, in the honorary inscriptions offered by *collegia* to their patrons, a manifestation of "leur solidarité avec les valeurs essentielles de la cité" and a means of presenting themselves as loyal citizens, "dévoués à l'ordre social et politique" (van Nijf 2003: 315). By identifying themselves with the city's leading citizens, they also identified themselves with the city itself, often employing the patriotic language appropriate to their situation (van Nijf 2003: 316). The terminology assured that their civic identity would be recognized and guaranteed, as being a "partie intégrante" of the local political hierarchy (van Nijf 2003: 317–18).

17. The precise identification of the roles and responsibilities of each of these groups remains controversial. On the *dendrophori*, see most recently Faoro 2004.

By selecting and nurturing patronage relationships, therefore, members of *collegia* engaged in a none-too-subtle campaign for increased social status. In his recent study of *collegiati* attested in inscriptions from Italy and Gaul during the empire, Nicolas Tran has similarly developed the theme of "leur mobilité dans la hiérarchie sociale," tracing the interior and exterior means of acquiring "respect-abilité" in this context (Tran 2006: 97). Again, he stresses the positive elements of this exchange: drawing on his experience as a small-scale elite within the hierarchy of the organization, the successful *collegiatus* would then seek out patrons within the wider civic elite. In the process, "De conditions inégales, les *collegiati* cherchent à gagner en dignité: par le collège, des hommes de métier et des affranchis acquièrent une respectabilité qui pouvait leur faire défaut, et quelques-uns atteignent un réel prestige social" (In a situation of unequal social conditions, the members of the *collegium* hope to improve their standing: and so, via the college, working men and freedmen acquire a level of respectability, that might otherwise have escaped them, and some secure real social prestige) (Tran 2006: 48). Accordingly, the desire to secure the patron possessing the highest possible status coincided with the overall goals of social mobility. In the process, members of *collegia* who engaged in such behavior expropriated a tool of elite privilege for their own use: "Dans le dessein d'organiser leur promotion par eux-mêmes, les *collegiati* s'approprient, à travers le patronat, un instrument de la supériorité d'une élite qui aspire parfois à les compter parmi ses obligés" (With the goal of organizing their own promotion, the members of the *collegium* appropriate to themselves, via the patronage of a great man, an instrument of superiority usually engaged by an elite that aspires, for its part, to retain those *collegiati* as its clients) (Tran 2006: 459).

Some of this approach has also been incorporated into a thought-provoking recent article by Koenraad Verboven. Building on previous arguments in favor of the "importance of the associations in structuring social life" in the empire's cities, Verboven focuses attention on those businessmen who had been singled out as col-legial patrons, asking, essentially, why the businessmen would choose to show their generosity toward specific, mostly professional, associations (Verboven 2007: 870). Notice that he has shifted attention away from the colleges' interests in identify-ing and ingratiating themselves with prospective patrons, and instead toward the options of a businessman, concerning *which* organization to patronize with his con-nection. Underlying this approach, however, is the notion that association with a *collegium*—and more specifically, with a certain *collegium*—would confer enhanced status upon the patron who named it in an inscription. By listing his patronage of a prestigious local organization, among his other civic duties, an elite figure gained whatever prestige the association had to offer:

> The *collegia* provided the business elites with the platform and social capital they needed to acquire public esteem and in some cases to push through into the civic elites. Not coincidentally if we look at inscriptions of businessmen, we find that the business elite affirms its position and communicates its claims to social status mainly through the different degrees of belonging to a (mostly) professional *collegium*. (Verboven 2007: 872)

As Verboven develops his argument, the trick would seem to have been to determine *which* college offered the *most* status to a prospective patron, and he posits a hierarchical relationship *among* colleges, all vying for the attention of powerful patrons. "Obviously," he notes, "not every association enjoyed the same esteem. The associations themselves were hierarchically related, according to their aims and size, and the wealth and influence of their members" (Verboven 2007: 875). The difficulty here, though, is how to determine the precise gradation of status among a town's available *collegia*. While it seems perfectly reasonable to assume that patrons would weigh relative status in their selection process, as part of a general plan of action "to rise (eventually) into the aristocracy itself" (Verboven 2007: 888), how would we go about proving this? Given the status of the evidence, how are we to reconstruct the patron's thought process? Verboven suggests that patronage of a college of *centonarii* would confer high status, given the public service they provided (whether or not this extended to firefighting services).[18] However, it must be admitted that most cities seem not to have possessed a college of *centonarii*, and that each city, if not each individual citizen, would likely have possessed a different notion of which *collegia* were most prestigious, in the general opinion of the community. One might compare the ambitions of a prominent American businessperson, struggling up the corporate ladder, while also attempting to cut a figure for him/herself within the larger community. Does s/he attend the chamber of commerce function next Tuesday morning, or does s/he beg off that commitment in favor of another club's pancake breakfast? Many factors might enter into this decision, such as which local politician would be likely to see one there, or how many minutes one would be allowed to speak before the assembled membership. Again, it seems to me, the sources are silent on these points.

CONCLUSION: ANOTHER APPROACH?

I would suggest that there is another, far less optimistic, but perhaps more realistic, way to evaluate the interaction of *collegia* and elites. If the members of a *collegium* went out of their way to imitate the elite, might this not be perceived as an instance of their *subjection* to the local hierarchy, and an attempt by that hierarchy to reinforce the lower status of this group? Consider, for example, a intriguing historical parallel that van Nijf has introduced (in a 2002 Festschrift article in honor of H. W. Pleket) illuminating the possible connections between private associations and civic hierarchies. Comparing the Dutch civic guards (the "schutters") of the sixteenth and seventeenth centuries, he concluded that membership in groups of

---

18. It is generally agreed today that there is no solid evidence for the firefighting services rendered by the *collegia centonariorum*, as was claimed in the late nineteenth century and until quite recently. Nevertheless, one can still, at times, find claims along these lines, e.g., Lafer 2001.

this sort provided an outlet for self-expression and "a focus for their sociability'" for men of middle rank, who were effectively forbidden access to the higher reaches of the civic aristocracy (van Nijf 2002). However, by shifting our focus and evaluating this interaction from the top down, might one conclude that the civic elite had other motives in mind while allowing this sociable group a wide berth? Seen from this angle, particularly telling is the fact that city authorities offered the schutters subsidies for clothes, sashes, and drink, on the occasions of their parades (van Nijf 2002: 321). One might wonder whether these concessions were deliberately designed to stress their *subordinate* relation to the elite, in case their sociability made them think too much of themselves.

Again, perhaps Waltzing had already hit upon the truth, those many decades ago. In his estimation, through the first three centuries AD, *collegia* were free to enroll whomever they wished, to select their own officers, and to offer dedications to whatever patrons they chose to honor via association with themselves (Waltzing 1895–1900: I, 335–37). Even on the rare occasions when an emperor or governor intervened in the process (by licensing or recognizing the association in some way), the government never attempted to regulate the college's interior workings. As a consequence, a great variety of internal arrangements became the norm, throughout the empire, and the laissez-faire attitude of the authorities made the *collegium* more and more attractive to a larger subset of urban workers. The inevitable result of this was immense goodwill toward the emperor, expressing itself in general and heartfelt gratitude to the leader who had allowed them freedom in this regard. Such enthusiasm was natural, "because [the *collegia*] demonstrated the loyalty of the popular classes and their attachment to the Empire." As demonstrated by their flattery of the emperor in their collegial decrees, "the people were satisfied with the imperial regime."[19]

Thus, collegial association may have been a tool, not created but ultimately wielded by the elite, in order to organize and control a potentially restive urban population, engendering loyalty, of a sort, in the process. These lessons were not lost on the government of Fascist Italy: throughout the country, "Dopolavoro" organizations were instituted, to provide relaxation, moral uplift, and, of course, ideological indoctrination, 'after work.'[20] One might compare the 'clubs' of employees that are sometimes formed by a modern corporation, perhaps in order to divert attention from a dwindling pot of resources and to improve—or to monitor?—staff morale. One wonders how much consolation such associations can provide as the Domitianic thunderbolts of lay-offs assault a present-day corporation.

19. Waltzing 1895: I, 494: "…parce qu'ils prouvent le loyalisme des classes populaires et leur attachement à l'Empire…le peuple était satisfait du régime impérial." Ando (2000: chapter 4) may be identifying the same phenomenon, in the creation of a "consensus" in respect to Roman government, especially in his analysis of imperial communications on the provincial level. The perception of leniency—coupled with the personal attention afforded by the imperial bureaucracy—may have redounded to the emperors' benefit in the form of loyal, or at least quiescent, subjects.

20. On this subject, see above all De Grazia 1981.

SUGGESTED READING

The best brief survey of the evidence, and the complications regarding its interpretation, is Ausbüttel 1982. While it is centered in the Roman East, van Nijf 1997 is a superb introduction to the fundamental themes regarding the social relations of the *collegia*. Perry 2006 is a survey of the literature on *collegia*, up to the twenty-first century, though it is concentrated in the early twentieth, and deals only with social relations, per se, in the final chapter. However, the essential book is still, despite its age, Waltzing 1895–1900; the *Étude historique* desperately needs a full update, incorporating new inscriptional evidence and more contemporary interpretations of it.

BIBLIOGRAPHY

Alföldy, G. 1984. *Römische Sozialgeschichte*. 3rd ed. Wiesbaden: Franz Steiner Verlag.

———. 1985. *The Social History of Rome*. Trans. D. Braund and F. Pollock. London: Croom Helm.

Ando, C. 2000. *Imperial Ideology and Provincial Loyalty in the Roman Empire*. Berkeley: University of California Press.

Ausbüttel, F. M. 1982. *Untersuchungen zu den Vereinen im Westen des römischen Reiches*. Frankfurt: Laßleben.

Bloch, M. 1953. *The Historian's Craft*. Trans. Peter Putnam. New York: Alfred A. Knopf.

Bollmann, B. 1998. *Römische Vereinshäuser: Untersuchungen zu den Scholae der römischen Berufs-, Kult- und Augustalen-Kollegien in Italien*. Mainz: Philipp von Zabern.

Bottai, G. 1939. *Dalla Corporazione romana alla Corporazione fascista*. Rome: Istituto di Studi Romani.

Chambers, W. 1952. *Witness*. New York: Random House.

Clemente, G. 1972. "Il patronato nei collegia dell'impero romano." *Studi Classici e Orientali* 21: 142–229.

De Grazia, V. 1981. *The Culture of Consent: Mass Organization of Leisure in Fascist Italy*. Cambridge: Cambridge University Press.

De Robertis, F. M. 1938. *Il diritto associativo romano dai collegi della Repubblica alle corporazioni del Basso Impero*. Bari: Laterza.

———. 1955. *Il fenomeno associativo nel mondo romano, dai collegi della Repubblica alle corporazioni del Basso Impero*. Naples: Libreria Scientifica.

———. 1971. *Storia delle corporazioni e del regime associativo nel mondo romano*. Bari: Adriatica.

De Rossi, G. B. 1864–1877. *La Roma sotterranea cristiana*. Rome: Cromo-litografia pontificia. Repr. Frankfurt: Minerva 1966.

Faoro, D. 2004. "I *collegia* professionali nel Bellunese: Il caso dei *dendrophori*. Stato degli studi e proposte di riflessione." *Archivio storico di Belluno, Feltre e Cadore* 324: 5–18.

Gordon, A. E. 1938. *The Cults of Lanuvium*. Berkeley: University of California Press.

———. 1964. *Album of Dated Latin Inscriptions*. Berkeley: University of California Press.

Harland, P. A. 2003. *Associations, Synagogues, and Congregations: Claiming a Place in Ancient Mediterranean Society*. Minneapolis: Fortress Press.

Hasegawa, K. 2005. *The Familia Urbana during the Early Empire: A Study of Columbaria Inscriptions*. Oxford: Archaeopress.

Hemelrijk, E. 2008. "Patronesses and 'Mothers' of Roman *Collegia.*" *Classical Antiquity* 27: 115–62.

Hopkins, K. 1983. *Death and Renewal, Sociological Studies in Roman History 2*. Cambridge: Cambridge University Press.

Lafer, R. 2001. *Omnes collegiati, "concurrite"!: Brandbekämpfung im Imperium Romanum.* Frankfurt: Peter Lang.

Lendon, J. E. 1997. *Empire of Honour: The Art of Government in the Roman World.* Oxford: Clarendon Press.

Liu, J. 2004. *Occupation, Social Organization, and Public Service in the Collegia Centonariorum in the Roman Empire (First Century BC–Fourth Century AD).* New York: PhD Thesis, Columbia University.

MacMullen, R. 1974. *Roman Social Relations, 50 B.C. to A.D. 284.* New Haven: Yale University Press.

Maué, H. 1886. *Die Vereine der fabri, centonarii und dendrophori im römischen Reich.* Frankfurt: Mahlau & Waldschmidt.

McCready, W. O. 1996. "*Ekklēsia* and Voluntary Associations." In J. Kloppenborg and S. Wilson (eds.), *Voluntary Associations in the Graeco-Roman World.* London: Routledge. 59–73.

McGinn, T. 2004. *The Economy of Prostitution in the Roman World. A Study of Social History and the Brothel.* Ann Arbor: University of Michigan Press.

Mennella, G., and G. Apicella. 2000. *Le corporazioni professionali nell'Italia romana: un aggiornamento al Waltzing.* Naples: Arte tipografica.

Mentxaka, R. 2003. "La cláusula '*item placuit: quisquis ex quacumque causa mortem sibi adsciveri[t], eius ratio funeris non habebitur*' de CIL 14, 2112 y sus hipotéticos fundamentos." *Revue Internationale des droits de l'Antiquité* 50: 217–47.

Mommsen, T. 1843. *De collegiis et sodaliciis Romanorum, accedit inscription lanuvina.* Kiel: Schwers'sche Buchhandlung.

More, J. H. 1969. *The Fabri Tignarii of Rome.* Cambridge, Mass.: PhD Thesis, Harvard University.

Ottanelli, F. M. 1991. *The Communist Party of the United States: From the Depression to World War II.* New Brunswick: Rutgers University Press.

Patterson, J. R. 1994. "The *collegia* and the transformation of the towns of Italy in the second century AD." In *L'Italie d'Auguste à Dioclétien, Actes du colloque international organisé par l'École française de Rome (Rome, 25–28 mars 1992).* Rome: École française de Rome. 227–38.

———. 2006. *Landscapes and Cities: Rural Settlement and Civic Transformation in Early Imperial Italy.* Oxford: Oxford University Press.

Perry, J. S. 1999. *A Death in the Familia: The Funerary Colleges of the Roman Empire.* Chapel Hill: PhD Thesis, University of North Carolina.

———. 2002. "*CIL* 6.16932: The Creation of a Detached Signum?" *Zeitschrift für Papyrologie und Epigraphik* 138: 245–48.

———. 2006. *The Roman Collegia: The Modern Evolution of an Ancient Concept.* Leiden: E. J. Brill.

Rosser, G. 1994. "Going to the Fraternity Feast: Commensality and Social Relations in Late Medieval England." *The Journal of British Studies* 33: 430–46.

Royden, H. L. 1988. *The Magistrates of the Roman Professional Collegia in Italy from the First to the Third Century A.D.* Pisa: Giardini.

Schiess, T. 1888. *Die römischen collegia funeraticia nach den Inschriften.* Munich: Theodor Ackermann.

Schnorr von Carolsfeld, L. 1933. *Geschichte der juristischen Person, erster (einziger) Band, Universitas, Corpus, Collegium im klassischen römischen Recht.* Munich: Verlag C. H. Beck. (Reprint, Aalen: Scientia Verlag, 1969.)

Seland, T. 1984. "Collegium Kai Ekklesia: Nyere Synspunkter på de Gresk-romerske foreninger som modell for og parallell til de urkristne forsamlinger." *Ung Teologi:* 49–65.

Silone, I. 1986. *Bread and Wine.* Trans. Eric Mosbacher. New York: Penguin Books.

Tran, N. 2001. "Le collège, la communauté et le politique sous le Haut-Empire romain. Remarques sur l'histoire du droit à la fin du XIXe siècle et la 'tradition sociologique.'" *Cahiers du Centre Gustave Glotz* 12: 181–98.

———. 2006. *Les membres des associations romaines. Le rang social des collegiati en Italie et en Gaules, sous le Haut-Empire.* Rome: École française de Rome.

van Nijf, O. M. 1997. *The Civic World of Professional Associations in the Roman East.* Amsterdam: J. C. Gieben.

———. 1999. "Verenigingsleven en stedelijke identiteit: de rol van *fabri, centonarii* en *dendrophori.*" *Lampas* 32: 198–210.

———. 2002. "*Collegia* and Civic Guards: Two Chapters in the History of Sociability." In W. Jongman and M. Kleijwegt (eds.), *After the Past. Essays in Ancient History in Honour of H. W. Pleket.* Leiden: E. J. Brill. 305–39.

———. 2003. "Les élites comme patrons des associations professionnelles dans l'Orient Romain." In M. Cébeillac-Gervasoni and L. Lamoine (eds.), *Les élites et leurs facettes: Les élites locales dans le monde hellénistique et romain.* Rome: École française de Rome. 307–21.

Verboven, K. 2007. "The Associative Order: Status and Ethos of Roman Businessmen in [the] Late Republic and Early Empire." *Athenaeum* 95: 861–93.

Waltzing, J.-P. 1895–1900. *Étude historique sur les corporations professionnelles chez les Romains, depuis les origines jusqu'à la chute de l'Empire d'Occident.* 4 vols. Louvain: Peeters.

CHAPTER 24

THE ROMAN ARMY

DAVID POTTER

INTRODUCTION

FOR centuries prior to the emergence of the principate the army was the only institution supported by the Roman state that incorporated large numbers of Roman citizens. The creation of a single commander in chief who would also direct civilian affairs in the course of the first century BC (the *princeps*) was the third major transition of Roman society for which the needs of the army may be seen as the driving force. The first major reform was the transition from a military force based upon the *gentes* (extended families) of archaic Rome to one based upon the centuries of the *comitia centuriata*—the voting groups of one of the popular assemblies. The second was the result of the defeat of the Latins in the late fourth century BC, which changed the way that the Roman state incorporated non-Roman units into its army. Both of these earlier reforms had significant impact on the definition of the state as a whole. Whatever the truth may be about the tale of the expulsion of the kings, the government of the Roman Republic was defined by the power of the *comitia centuriata* to elect its own generals and make laws governing society as a whole. The reformed military of the fourth century, based now upon bilateral treaty obligations, made it possible for Rome to incorporate the manpower of subordinate states with unrivalled efficiency and to exploit that manpower to fight the wars that would eventually result in the creation of the Mediterranean empire.

The Roman army did not cease to evolve in the centuries after the emergence of the *princeps*. After the experiments of Sulla and Caesar failed to bring stability, the first successful *princeps*, Augustus, recognized that he needed not only to control access to commands, but also to define a new role for the military. In so far as there was any theory at all governing the affairs of the republic, the army was seen primarily as an instrument of conquest; the post-Augustan army, however, was primarily seen as an instrument of occupation. The purpose of the post-Augustan army was to support the position of the emperor, and, as the army settled into new quarters on the frontiers in the course of Augustus' long reign, it soon became apparent that the use of the singular to describe this entity was no longer appropriate, as, indeed, it had not been appropriate in the years prior to Augustus when units had been raised on an ad hoc basis to serve under magistrates appointed to command them. Thus, although an army of the Roman people, the force that Julius Caesar commanded in Gaul in 53 BC had no direct administrative connection with the army of the Roman people that the legates of Gnaeus Pompey commanded in Spain, or that Crassus commanded at Carrhae.

As the post-Augustan legions acclimatized to their quarters they came to take on distinctively regional identities. Perhaps the most significant difference between the armies of the imperial period and those of the pre-Augustan age was that in the imperial force senior officers were centrally appointed, and that subaltern officers moved from unit to unit in the course of their careers. This provided a unity at the command level that was not present at the level of the common soldier, whose loyalty was primarily focused not on a local commander but rather on the distant figure of the *princeps*.

The tension between regionalism and centralization defines the history of the Roman army in the three centuries after Augustus. In the fourth century, the emergence of multiple courts shifted the balance decisively in favor of regionalism. As the eastern and western governments went their separate ways during the fifth century, the armies of east and west played significant roles in defining the paths that the respective regions took. Chronic disorganization and factionalism made the western army ineffective, while that of the east, albeit not without some difficulty, maintained a sufficient degree of cohesion to maintain its emperor. It is symbolic of the way that the politics of military faction came to dominate the west that the last Italian emperor (actually the son of Attila the Hun's secretary, a Pannonian) handed over power to the German commander of German troops (also a previous servant of Attila) in his nominal employ.

The surrender of the western empire to a German general underscores one of the crucial questions in considering the social history of the army: where did the soldiers come from, and what was their connection to the population of the Roman state as a whole? That is to say, since the Roman army was always perceived as being Roman society in microcosm, it is imperative that we understand what kind of society that army was, as well as how it related to the broader Roman society, at any given moment in time.

THE EARLIEST ARMIES

Although there is no direct evidence for the Roman army of the regal period, there is some evidence from other parts of Italy to suggest that armed forces of the seventh and sixth centuries BC were essentially warbands that coalesced around individual aristocrats—the sixth-century dedication from Satricum by the "sodales of Poplios Valesios" to the god Mamars is probably the product of just such an organization (*CIL* I² 2832 a). So, too, legends connected with two of the great *gentes* (extended families) of the republic—the Fabii and the Claudii—may be combined with stories about the brothers Caeles and Aulus Vibenna in company with a character named Mastarna from the Etruscan city of Vulsci, as well as the Lars Porsenna of Clusium, who seems to have terrorized central Italy at the end of the sixth century BC (Dion. Hal. *Ant. Rom.* 7. 3–11), to reflect a society in which there was as yet no clear division between 'state-sponsored' warfare and contests between individual familial groups (Cornell 1995: 133–41). Appius Claudius, for instance, was welcomed into the Roman community because he brought thousands of followers with him, while some 300 Fabii were annihilated at Cremara with 4000–5000 dependents in 477.[1] Although there are difficulties with each individual piece of evidence—not the least of which being that both the actions of Appius Claudius and the Fabii are placed well after the traditional date for a new form of political institution connected with a very different style of military organization—the notion that pre-republican military organization should be connected in some way with the *gentes* that seem to have dominated the earliest Rome is not inherently incredible. Perhaps as significant is the fact that the practice of raising armies from bands of dependents would not cease even throughout the republican period. In the historical period, we know, for instance, that Scipio Africanus used volunteers from his Spanish army for the invasion of North Africa in 204, and that Scipio Aemilianus took 4000 dependents in the army that served under him at Numantia in 133 BC (Liv. 29. 1; App. *Iber.* 84). It would also seem likely that Scipionic support explains why a significant numbers of Africanus' veterans did not object to serving Flamininus, an ally of Scipio, in 199 BC, although others from the same army had violently objected to the same assignment a year earlier under the consul Villius, who had no such connection with Scipio.[2] In communities that would become allies of Rome, recruitment by members of local elites would remain the norm until the end of the republic (and, in the provinces, would continue in the case of auxiliary units into the later first century AD). Elsewhere in Italy, armed bands, such as the 200 Lucanian exiles who are found in the company of Alexander of Epirus in 325 BC, and mercenary bands, such as that under Decius the Campanian who seized Rhegium, or the Campanian

---

1. Suet. *Tib.* 1; Liv. 2. 48–50; Dion. Hal. *Ant. Rom.* 9. 15–20, with C. S. Smith 2006: 42, 290–95. See also Dion. Hal. *Ant. Rom.* 9. 5. 4, possibly reflecting a similar tradition in Etruria.

2. Liv. 32. 9. 2; Plut. *Flam.* 3. 3. Contrast Liv. 32. 3. 3; and see also Briscoe 1973: 32–33.

group (the so-called Mamertines, or adherents of Mars) that seized Messene in the early third century (Liv. 8. 24. 6; Polyb. 1. 7. 7, 1. 7. 2), might reflect similar styles of organization.

The *dilectus* (draft) upon which the army under the Servian system was based, may be seen as a system that, intentionally or otherwise, attenuated direct links between bands of troops and gentilician leaders. The best analysis of the system attributed to Servius Tullius, prior to the foundation of the republic, is that it describes the structure of the legion that Rome could muster against its enemies. According to this system the Roman people were ultimately divided into five *classes* (divisions) according to their wealth. Wealth, in turn was equated with the style of armament that members of each *classis* could afford, and thus the role of the *classis* in battle; each *classis* was divided into a number of centuries. The number of centuries was then calculated to reflect the political power of the *classis*. There were, then, eighteen centuries for the cavalry (*equites*), eighty centuries for the first *classis*, whose members were instructed to equip themselves with breastplates and spears, relatively expensive equipment. The second through fourth *classes*, whose members were progressively less heavily (i.e., less expensively) armored, were constituted of twenty centuries each; and the fifth *classis*, of thirty centuries, was armed with simple projectiles of various sorts. Those who fell below a minimum property qualification were formed into a single century, while specialists—musicians and engineers—were divided into two centuries apiece (C. S. Smith 2006: 280–90, noting as well that the developed system described here may not belong to the sixth century). This organization also provided the structure of the assemblies in which Romans elected magistrates whose primary function in this period may have been to command the army in battle, and to vote on issues of community importance. Among the most significant of these decisions would be whether to go to war with their neighbors. One decision that might also have been made, even at this stage, was about who would serve as unit officers within the legion. Polybius states that centurions were elected by the men who served in their century (Polyb. 6. 24. 2), and there is no reason to think that this was not very ancient practice by the middle of the second century BC. The ability to elect officers, even at the unit level, gave the Roman military a perpetual 'citizen militia' aspect. The image of a centurion at this period is reflected in Livy's Spurius Ligustinus, who spoke up for other centurions during the levy of 171 BC: he claims to have been born in a hut on a minuscule estate of two *iugera*, and to have made his way in the service through his valor, earning the respect and patronage of various generals along the way (Liv. 42. 34).

The most important aspect of the Servian system was that gentilician divisions would not govern the command structure of the army. Men from different *gentes*, even if they were not brigaded into the same units (there is absolutely no evidence on this point), would at least serve side by side with men from other *gentes*, and overall command would be exercised by an official who was a community, and precisely not a gentilician, leader. Decisions on war and peace were also hedged with religious ritual. Indeed, the Romans people did not vote for war, it seems, but rather for the dispatch of fetial priests who would demand redress of grievance from an offending state (*rerum repetitio*). The fetial would demand that whatever this redress happened to be should be made within thirty days. If no redress was forthcoming by the end of that period, the fetial would announce that a state of war would exist if the redress was not made within three days and, failing action, would return at the end of those three days to throw a spear into what was now enemy territory (the *denuntatio belli*). The effect of this formula was not only to establish, before the gods, the fact that Rome was not at fault, but also to establish that whatever individual loss had occasioned the initial vote to send the fetial was taken up as a community issue (Watson 1993: 29). All Roman wars were thus defensive wars (at least in theory), and this may have contributed to the willingness of the legion to place itself in harm's way.

In the ideal world the Romans would not go to war on their own. After the battle of Lake Regillus, traditionally dated to 493 BC, Rome struck a treaty with the defeated peoples of Latium—the *Foedus Cassianum*—according to the terms of which the Latins would contribute troops to aid the Romans in those years in which the Romans determined that an army needed to be raised. The Romans would exercise overall command, but it also seems to have become established practice that the Latins would be brigaded separately from the Romans and, possibly, that individual units would serve under their own commanders as part of the Latin force (Cornell 1995: 297–98). Thus, from a very early stage in the history of the republic, Rome's army, like her society, was a conglomerate of Romans and allies.

THE ERA OF CONQUEST

The Servian army appears to have been similar to the hoplite armies of contemporary Greece. This hoplite-like army was humiliated at the battle of Allia in 390 (or 387) BC by a band of Gauls who went on to capture the city of Rome. The catastrophe does not seem to have led to any immediate change in Roman military habit (possibly because the political system was so closely connected with it), but in the third quarter of the fourth century the army did change. The proximate cause was likely the prospect of long-term engagement with the people of Samnium; in a crucially important passage, originally composed by the Sicilian historian Philinus, and known to us through various later quotations, a Roman ambassador says that the Roman military art evolved through contact with foreign peoples and that the adoption of the "shields" (a metaphor for tactics) in the contemporary army stemmed from the Samnites (*FGrHist* 839. 3; see also Meyer 1924: 226–31). Soldiers of the fourth century were spearmen—at least as can be seen in the painting on the Esquiline Tomb where we find spearmen that resemble Samnite representations of warriors—and the new system was clearly based upon a reorganization of spear-wielding infantry in the Roman army (for typical Samnites, see Saulnier

1983). The *gladius* (sword), the characteristic hand-to-hand weapon of the legions in the period of Mediterranean conquest, would not be adopted until the second half of the third century.

The new legion was divided into four divisions of maniples, whose membership was now determined by years of experience rather than wealth. The four divisions were the *velites*, or light troops, who would skirmish ahead of the main battle line, the *hastati*, who, as their name suggests, engage with spears, probably employing a mixture of throwing weapons with heavier spears that could be used in hand-to-hand combat, the third division, or *principes*, were so named it seems because it was expected that they would play the decisive role in winning the victory. In the third century it appears that they might, at least on occasion, be armed with pikes. Finally there were the *triarii*, experienced men who would only play a role in battle if things were going desperately wrong—hence, we are told, the proverb "things have descended to the *triarii*" indicated a very unpleasant situation (Liv. 8. 8. 11, with Oakley 1998: 474; see also Rawson 1971: 29). The elimination of class divisions within the army is a striking development, though one that is paralleled by other developments in the middle of the fourth century, including the admission of plebeians to all magistracies and priesthoods, the end of enslavement for debt, and more extensive use of colonization. The organization of the military and the socio-political communities were, so it seems, evolving in tandem.

The first major victory of the 'new model' Roman army was arguably in the Latin war of 340–338 BC. Although details of the war are largely lacking, it is not unreasonable to think that the Roman victory was due, at least in part, to superior command of a new tactical system (assuming that there is at times some smoke from a real fire in a Livian narrative) (Liv. 8. 10. 4–6). As a result of the settlement of this war Rome abandoned the practice—in place since the time of the *foedus Cassianum*—of treating with the Italian states as a collective and, instead, made separate treaties with each place (Liv. 8. 14 with Oakley 1998: 538–59). At the same time, the Roman state created two varieties of partial citizenship: the *ius Latii* (Latin rights) and *civitas sine suffragio* (citizenship without the vote), the first of which guaranteed certain protections of Roman citizenship to people who remained citizens of their own communities, the other a framework within which states lost their independence, became part of the Roman polity with restricted rights, though they could at some point obtain full citizenship. The creation of these statuses enabled the significant expansion of the Roman state and did so in a way that was genuinely different from that employed by other aggressive powers in fourth-century Italy, such as the Samnites and the Tarentines, both of whom used what might be seen as more 'traditional' methods of control—outright conquests and occupation or subordinate alliances that provided no opportunity of inclusion in the community of the victor (Afzelius 1942: 136–75). The new statuses, which may derive from the longstanding Roman custom of extending different legal rights—for example, the right to hold office—across the community of citizens, were fundamental to the process of colonization in the fourth century.

The establishment of colonies involved the institution of new Roman communities at strategic points in central Italy. These communities tended to draw their members, as far as we can tell, from among the less fortunate at Rome, and offered the classes that populated the legions tangible long-term benefits for service. Somewhere between 20,000 and 30,000 men were resettled with their families on land taken from conquered states, while some 70,000 men, with their families, received land grants in the nineteen Latin colonies founded between 334 and 264 BC (Cornell 1995: 380–81). These communities may also have enabled members of Italian elites to form connections with leaders of Roman society. It is in any case striking that the image from the Esquiline tomb, perhaps the most important surviving piece of contemporary evidence for this period, combines the image of a Roman named Fabius grasping the hand of a person who is evidently the leader of an Italian community in a gesture of *fides*. The image of the two men joined in peace is accompanied in this painting with images of warfare, reflecting the notion that those joined in *fides* (good faith) would wage war together to their joint advantage.

The combination of a revolutionary diplomatic system that allowed for the incorporation of defeated peoples within the Roman state, and a new style of warfare, symbolized in the surviving image from the Esquiline tomb, enabled Rome to overcome the Samnite league, which in 340 BC was virtually the equal of Rome in terms of territory and population. It is likely that the ability of Rome to offer a more attractive option to the smaller states of central Italy contributed as much to the ultimate victory as any superiority in warfare. As the Roman system of alliances grew in strength, the ability of its enemies to resist grew progressively less, until Rome won two massive victories—over the Etruscans, Umbrians, and Gauls at Sentinum in 295 and over the Samnites at Aquilonia in 293 BC. Once Tarentum was subdued (in 272 BC), the Roman state was the sole major power in mainland Italy, and it has been something of a truism from the time of Polybius onward, that it could dispose of military force unmatched by any other Mediterranean power. This statement seems plausible, as the potential manpower of the Roman alliance, which Polybius puts around 700,000 men, certainly exceeds, by a wide margin, the military power available to the Seleucid or Ptolemaic regimes in the east, and even that of Carthage in North Africa (Polyb. 2. 24, with Walbank 1957: 196–203). Even if these numbers are exaggerated, the actual number of men put in the field during the first years of the Hannibalic war (217–215 BC)—roughly 225,000—is staggering not only by the standards of any ancient state, but also as a proportion of total available manpower (assuming that Polybius' number reflects an official reckoning of all men of military age). The number of men enlisted thus amounts to something like 33% of the total pool, which is a very high percentage when compared with other states at the time, and far greater even than the demands upon Roman manpower at the peak periods of the First Punic War when, if Rome actually did actually put 300 quinquiremes in the water as Polybius on occasion suggests, somewhere around 200,000 men may have been required (Polyb. 1. 25, with Walbank 1957: 82–84; though see *ILLRP* 319 suggesting that many warships were triremes). Although these numbers are imprecise, they are still valuable as indications of the scale of the Roman war effort as compared with that of other states and of the efficiency of the Roman system in deploying available resources. Thus, while the Roman state was certainly not the most populous at this time—the total population of Roman Italy appears to have been about 3,000,000 at this point, while the population of the Seleucid empire around the middle of the third century was about 30,000,000 and of the Ptolemaic empire in the vicinity of 3,000,000 to 4,000,000—the system of alliances constructed by the Romans made it possible to mobilize the available manpower of Italy far more effectively than was possible in any other major state (for Ptolemaic and Seleucid populations, see Aperghis 2004: 35–58). A society characterized by the incorporation of outsiders was, then, mirrored by an army constructed in similar fashion; and this idiosyncratic manner of operation goes a long way toward explaining the fact that the Romans built the empire they did.

THE ERA OF REVOLUTION

The demands upon the manpower of Italy declined during the course of the Hannibalic war, as the Romans avoided costly large-scale encounters in Italy itself, and Scipio was leading Roman armies to victory in Spain. In the last decade of the third century, the number of men under arms was probably around 150,000; but this was still an achievement well beyond the capacity of any other ancient state, especially if one takes into consideration the losses at Trebbia (218 BC), Trasimene (217 BC), and Cannae (216 BC). The fact that Rome could accomplish such a feat is testimony to the way that military service shaped the experience of not only the youth of Italy, but also members of the elite for whom military service was a significant component in attaining the qualification for office. War also had the effect of providing employment for large numbers of young men in the first half of the following century, with numbers ranging from around 200,000 at the height of the war with Antiochus III (192–189 BC) to around 120,000 in average years. The number dropped to around 90,000 a year after the middle of the second century, and the resulting unemployment might have contributed somewhat to a sense of economic malaise that, combined with the actual unpopularity of military service in provincial garrisons, might have contributed to the enthusiasm with which the agrarian proposals of Tiberius Gracchus were received in the countryside. There is no evidence to support the claims of Gracchus that slaves had replaced free peasants as the engines driving the rural economy, and the evidence for the availability of peasant soldiery in the next generation positively belies the assertion. When the Social War broke out in 90 BC, the two sides put (on a low estimate) a total of 200,000 men in the field and, on a higher estimate, possibly as many as 300,000 (Brunt 1971: 435–40).

Between the time of Gracchus and the outbreak of the Social War there had been a change in the way that the *dilectus* was held, and a change in the structure of the legion. These involved (a) the restructuring of the legion internally so that the cohort of roughly 500 men became the main tactical unit, and (b) the recruitment of men who had previously been regarded as being too poor to enlist. It is easy to overestimate the significance of these changes and to underestimate the importance of a practice that appears to have become standard in the course of the Social War itself. The number of the destitute recruited into the *supplementum*—an extra force, levied to build up legions already in the field—that Gaius Marius raised for his army in North Africa in 108 BC was likely very small, and there is little evidence that generals would willingly look to the urban poor as a source for soldiers in anything but the most extreme emergency (Sal. *Jug.* 86. 2–3, with discussion in de Light 2007: 124–27). Likewise, the move from maniple to cohort was an ongoing process in the course of the second century and was never, it seems, officially sanctioned by any central authority; at this period, organizing a legion this way was a matter of choice that appears to have been left up to a general. It may be that after Marius' success against the Cimbrians and Teutons in 103 and 101 BC, cohorts became de facto the norm, just as the use of the eagle as the symbol for a legion seems to have been normalized by Marius; but that is far less significant than the fact that, unlike in the early part of the century, soldiers seem no longer to have been electing their officers, who were now increasingly drawn from the equestrian or municipal aristocracy, and they tended to be recruited by locale. Marius' legions seem even at this time to have been recruited heavily from Etruria (Plut. *Mar.* 41. 2; App. *BC* 1. 67. 305; Harmand 1967: 252; Brunt 1962: 79; R. E. Smith 1958: 51). During the Social War (91–87 BC) we hear of Minatius Magius, who recruited a legion from his native town of Hirpinum with which he helped in the capture of Herculaneum (Vell. 2. 16. 1); and Gnaeus Pompey's recruitment of two legions a few years later to assist Sulla, or the twenty cohorts raised by Domitius Ahenobarbus to fight Caesar in 49 BC (Plut. *Pomp.* 8; Caes. *Civ.* 1. 15. 7), may have been unexceptional acts for a local magnate of this period. Certainly Ahenobarbus' father had deep connections with the aristocrats of this region—even those who took up arms against Rome in 90 BC (Cic. *Phil.* 12. 27). Settlement of troops in colonies such as those founded by Sulla after his victory in 81 simply served to strengthen connections between individual magnates and particular regions of Italy.

The practice of constituting legions out of troops raised from specific districts had probably always been a feature of the levy as it affected Italian communities. But in the first century BC it became standard practice for the army as a whole. Caesar's army in the fifties, for instance, was recruited almost exclusively from Cisalpine Gaul. Long service in a province also acclimatized troops to particular local conditions so that, for instance, Pompey's army in Spain had, according to the hardly unbiased observation of Caesar, become scarcely Roman by 49 BC (Caes. *Civ.* 1. 44. 1–2). Prejudiced as Caesar's testimony might be, the statement needs nonetheless to have been believable.

Another development of this period, namely, the use of indigenous units from provinces as auxiliaries, seems also to have become standard. Much of the fighting, for instance, against Aristonicus in Asia Minor after the creation of the Roman province in 133 BC was carried out by local forces, while both Caesar and Pompey raised very large provincial forces to support their legions in the civil war that broke out in 49 BC (Dreyer and Engelman 2003: 35). The civil wars of the period after the assassination of Caesar hastened the separation of the army from its Italian roots as the massive armies recruited first for the war between Caesar's heirs and his assassins—there were a total of sixty-six legions in service in 43—and then by Mark Antony cannot have been more than nominally Roman; even though we may presume that the officer corps was largely Italian, and the language of command was Latin, there is no reason to think that there were anything like enough people of citizen background to fill the ranks of those armies (Brunt 1971: 480–88). Some glimpses of the process can be obtained from references such as that regarding the Spanish War, where we encounter a *legio vernacula* (a legion made up of indigenous people) on the Pompeian side that is contrasted with the *legio ex colonis* (a legion of men from the colonies—i.e., Romans) (*B. Hisp. 7. 4* see also Caes. *Civ.* 2. 20. 4); or one thinks of Pompey, who recruited provincials into his army in 48, or Labienus, who did the same in 46 (Caes. *Civ.* 3. 4; *B. Afr.* 19. 4), events noted by Caesar, who liked to stress the lack of *romanitas* among his enemies' troops. But Caesar was not himself immune to the charge—his *legio V Alaudae* was famously recruited from Transalpine Celts, and it is likely that the same is true of the legion later known as *legio V Galllica*; the 'emergency legions' raised to fight Pharnaces in 47 BC were likewise provincial (*B. Alex.* 34. 5), while the troops employed on Caesar's behalf by P. Sittius in 46 BC likely included many ancestors of the P. Sittii who later show up in the epigraphy of Cirta—a telltale sign of mass enfranchisement upon (the earlier) recruitment (App. *BC* 4. 54; Plin. *Nat.* 5. 22; Mann 1983: 3). The two legions that Brutus raised in Macedonia in 42 BC were, it seems, Roman in name only, while Mark Antony was short of Italian soldiery when he opened the Actian campaign (App. *BC* 3. 79, 4.75; Cic. *Phil.* 10. 13, 11.27 on Brutus; Jos. *AJ* 14. 448; *BJ* 1. 323–24 on Antony). The fact that many men in his legions came from the provinces originally may have made it more practical for Augustus to settle them in provincial *coloniae* when he demobilized them (Mann 1983: 6).

The armies of the late republic were notoriously loyal to their generals and disloyal to their state, but this in many ways reflected the longstanding tradition that the Roman army was the representative of the political will of the Roman people. Caesar, for instance, shows himself often in the position of convincing his men that they should do what he asks, or, on occasion, reprimanding them for not doing as he might have wished. He presents himself as a politician working the crowd when he deals with his men, and there is no reason to think that this picture is of a uniquely Caesarian understanding of his position—the army of Afranius and Petreius, for instance, was just about ready to vote with its feet and join Caesar when their general intervened to stop them. The question that the men were asking outside of Ilerda was essentially whether Caesar was a good man to work for (Caes. *Civ.* 1. 74). When Caesar's troops (or those of Augustus) mutinied, Caesar with remarkable speed convinced his men to return to their proper obedience (Suet. *Caes.* 69–70, *Aug.* 17. 3). It should be noted as well that he could not readily have had recourse to mass punishment, even though it is said that he punished individual acts of desertion or sedition with severity (Suet. *Caes.* 67. 1, *Aug.* 24. 2). Superb as some of the armies of the late republic were on the battlefield, they were still very much a militia in which the latent tendencies of militia service—especially the notion that officers served at the discretion of their men, and that the soldiers might well sense their primary allegiance to belong to commanders whom they respected—remained very much alive.

The Post-Augustan Army

With provincialization came professionalization. In the period after Actium the function of the Roman army was transformed from a representative of the will of the Roman people to a force devoted to the protection of the reputation of the *princeps*. The process was gradual under Augustus, whose first task was to reduce the size of the military—about half the men in service in 31 BC had been released by 27. His second priority was to find a task for an army that, at twenty-eight legions, was 25% larger than the army of twenty-one legions that had existed in 50 BC, but also responsible for a great deal more territory. Indeed, by the end of the Augustan Age, the population of the empire was somewhere in the vicinity of 50,000,000 people, and the available manpower of military age (18–40 years) was somewhere in the vicinity of 12,500,000, meaning that an army of some 500,000 men encompassed 4% of the people who might have been eligible for service. Indeed, one of the significant features of Roman military history is that the ratio of men in service to those available is not a constant. The significant decline in this ratio might go a long way toward accounting for the economic success of the empire after Augustus.

The imperial system of service evolved gradually in the course of Augustus' reign, and it was only after the conquest of the Balkans in the penultimate decade of Augustus' life that a regular disposition of legions as garrisons in different parts of the empire began to become clear. The bulk of the army began to settle in the areas that had borne the brunt of Augustan military activity—the Rhine and Balkan lands—at this point. In AD 6, Augustus took the crucial step of establishing the *aerarium militare* (military treasury—with an associated inheritance tax to keep it full), which stabilized a much longer period of service—now twenty years for members of the legions, twenty-five for soldiers in auxiliary cohorts—than had been the norm in previous centuries, while also guaranteeing that men who survived their term of service would become people of standing in whatever community they joined (Aug. *Anc.* 17. 2; Dio 55. 25. 2–6; Suet. *Aug.* 49. 2; Corbier 1977). Those communities—when not the one into which a given soldier had been born—were very often ones that developed in proximity to the camps in which these men had served for most of their lives (Mann 1983: 28–35).

Indeed, as the Julio-Claudian period progressed, several trends became clear. The first—and this was already the case under Augustus—is that Italians were increasingly rare as recruits. It is striking that when a *dilectus* (levy) was held in AD 9 in Italy, after the massacre of Varus' legions in the Teutoberg Forest in Germany, poor soldiers were said to have been drafted even from the city (Tac. *Ann.* 1. 31; Dio 57. 5). The implication of this is plainly that Rome itself rarely provided recruits in normal times. Epigraphic evidence likewise suggests that Italy became ever less important as the point of supply for the roughly 8,000 men required each year to keep the legions up to strength. This same category of evidence furthermore suggests that as time past, men tended to go from specific areas of the empire into service in areas where others from their district had gone before. The military force in Britain, for instance, seems to show a disproportionate number of men from Spain and southern France; and while the North African garrison seems to have been largely constituted from men who had grown up in the area, the Danubian legions were largely constituted from the Balkans and the eastern legions reveal very few men of western extraction (Mann 1983: 54–61). Most men were also volunteers rather than recruits—in the third century, Arrius Menander noted that "in the past" men who resisted the *dilectus* (levy) would be reduced to slavery, but that "now" capital punishment was not inflicted because the number of recruits was made up by volunteers (*Dig.* 49. 16. 4. 10; Mann 1983: 55–58).

Although the men who served in the legions were, then, increasingly local, their officers were not. Centurions of the late republic had largely, it seems, been drawn from the local ruling classes in the areas from which their men had been recruited. This may not even have been true by the end of the reign of Augustus, when, in the mutiny of AD 14, there is evidence of considerable hostility between enlisted man and centurions. As 'normative' equestrian careers came into being during the first century AD, the centurionate often appears as the first rung on a ladder, and we are told of men—the rhetorician Valerius Probus is a case in point—who could not win admission to that order (Suet. *Gramm.* 24. 1). Centurions also tended to move from legion to legion. The result was to create an administrative class of officer that was separated from the common soldier in terms of both social and geographic origins.

The change in the army between the point at which Caesar initiated the round of civil wars that brought about the creation of the Augustan system and the end of the Julio-Claudian army is vividly illustrated by Tacitus' discussion of the motivation of armies in the course of the civil war of AD 69. The forces driving the soldiers are shown as being quite distinct from the positions taken by their officers. Vitellius, for example, will manage a revolt because he wants to be emperor; on the other hand, the soldiers will rebel not because they are devoted to Vitellius, but rather because they are angry at Galba, who they feel has not treated them with respect. The legions on the Danube will join Vespasian not because they are devoted to the cause of Vespasian, but rather because they feel that they were dishonored by the summary execution of a number of their officers (Tac. *Hist.* 1. 53, 2. 60). More than a century later, in AD 193, when Septimius Severus raised the standard of rebellion in Pannonia, it appears that soldiers were convinced to rebel because they thought that they had been slighted; so, too, in 218, when *legio III* proclaimed Elagabalus emperor, the reason then being the soldiers' discontent with Macrinus (Potter 2004: 101–2, 150–51).

But no rebellion could be undertaken unless the mood of the troops had been tested beforehand, yet another sign that the interests of the officer class were distinct from those of the soldier. When provincial leaders provided support for a rebellion, it was not to express solidarity with the troops, but rather to obtain influence with a future ruler. Indeed, what set two early third-century rebellions apart—those of Maximinus against Alexander Severus and of Gordian I against Maximinus in AD 235 and 238, respectively—is the fact that one seems to have begun on the initiative of troops, who held the emperor in contempt, and the other was begun by aristocrats who held the emperor in contempt. Maximinus never secured the loyalty of the empire as a whole, and Gordian fell victim to the garrison of the neighboring province (Campbell 1984: 413; Potter 2004: 167–70). Julius Caesar's men followed him because they believed that their best interests were directly served by his success; by the third century, however, it was with a view to the interests of distant emperors, either reigning or would-be, that the loyalty of troops on the fringes of the empire would sway and be swayed.

The soldiers of the imperial period, then, although usually stationed near the areas where they were born, do not seem to have viewed themselves as representatives of the local population. Papyri from Egypt, along with inscriptions from various provinces, reveal that soldiers tended rather to act as a privileged class apart from and above the civilians, whom they saw themselves as ruling (see, e.g., *P. Oxy.* II 240, with discussion in Campbell 1984: 248–49; also, Isaac 1990: 86)—a distinction that, at least symbolically, was enhanced into the early third century by the fact that soldiers were not allowed to contract legal marriages before they left the service. Military administration as a whole appears, then, as a pair of marginally intersecting spheres of interest between officers and men. The average soldier seems to have viewed himself as a member of an elite group that ruled the area in which he served, even though he did not necessarily regard himself a member of the local aristocracy (Pollard 1996; Rathbone and Alston 2007: 194–95). The officer corps, from the rank of centurion upward (all of whom were allowed to marry), saw appointment to individual units as a series of stepping-stones that would lead either to a lateral move into an equestrian civil service position or to a more significant social position altogether.[3] Given such attitudes, it is impossible to postulate any specific military agenda; officers and men reacted to events in terms of what they understood to be their best interests, a point well made by Tacitus in his account of the surrender of Cremona (Tac. *Hist.* 3. 31).

3. Note that in the reign of Septimius Severus, the range of pay within the centurionate was between 36,000 sesterces for a regular centurion and a 140,000 sesterces for a centurion of the first rank (*primus pilus*), while a junior procurator (i.e., a junior official in the civilian bureaucracy) was paid 60,000 sesterces (which was the rough equivalent of the anticipated income of an estate valued at 1,000,000 sesterces). For these figures, see Speidel 1992: 102–3; Rathbone and Alston 2007: 161; Duncan Jones 1982: 21.

Moreover, differences in class were matched by differences in language. It appears that soldiers recruited into the legions, and indeed also into auxiliary units, would have used Latin in their professional lives. Soldiers would tend, as it seems, to acquire a rudimentary command of the language, while their officers would have varying degrees of proficiency. The prefect in command of the cohort at Vindolanda near Hadrian's wall, even though he was from a provincial background, appears generally to have been quite fluent; and he may be roughly representative of others at this level. His junior officers, and centurions who might, for instance, have tried their hand at poetry (as did some in the camp at Bu Njem in North Africa), might be less good. Still, for all these men, some command of Latin appears to have been significant. For officers it would be a sign that they were ready to move upward in the hierarchy; for soldiers it differentiated them from the people over whom they ruled—and they seem to have desired this sort of differentiation (Adams 1995: 128–31; Adams 1999: 133–34; Isaac 1994: 168).

THE ARMY AFTER DIOCLETIAN

The traditional Roman army was largely destroyed in a series of military disasters between AD 250 and 260. Although legions remained, they had suffered very heavy losses in the battles that saw the death of the emperor Decius, the capture of Antioch on the Orontes, and the seizure of the emperor Valerian. The legionary force was not thereafter brought back up to anything like its previous strength, and units that might previously have been termed 'auxiliary' appear to have been raised in status to 'legionary,' if that is the right way to interpret the lists of units found in the *Notitia Dignitatum*, a list of imperial officials and units that was compiled around AD 400. In the *Notitia* we encounter, for instance, among the *legiones palatinae* (those in theory attached to the emperor) the *Tongrecani seniores, Pannoniciani seniores, Moesiaci seniores,* and *Lanciarii Sabarienses*, while among the *legiones comitatenses* (again, troops serving the emperor directly) of the western empire are found groups such as *Septimani seniores, Pacatianenses, Vesontes, Mattiarii iuniores,* and *Mauri cetrati*. All of these units are distinguished by an ethnic appellation, the hallmark of auxiliary forces in the earlier empire. Furthermore, according to the *Notitia*, these soldiers were mingled with such obvious survivals of the early empire as the *Tertio Augustani* and *Tertiani Italica* (descendents, respectively of Augustan and Severan legionary foundations). In other words, the army of this later period was to a much greater degree an ethnic mix than had been its earlier predecessor.

The army that came into being in the second half of the fourth century AD, though no larger, it seems, than the previous one, differed significantly from the Severan army in that it was divided less by status—in other words, legionary versus auxiliary troops—than by function. The basic division was thus between troops who were stationed in a frontier zone—those now called *limitanei*—under the command of a *Dux* (as the commanders of frontier zones, that now included several of the subdivided provinces of the post-Diocletianic empire, were called) and those assigned to the *comitatus* (the 'central' army, responsible directly to the emperor), which was commanded in each prefecture by an official (or officials) with the rank of *magister* (Isaac 1988; Elton 2007: 306–7). The change in the command structure was in many ways the crucial factor in the role that the army would play in politics, and also in the role that it would play in society.

As a result of the changes that took place in government at the beginning of the fourth century, especially the newly created division between civilian and military government, a gap opened increasingly widely between civilian and military administration. This division was compounded by significant ethnic divisions between the general staff and the bureaucracy. And so, although the empire had been saved in the third century by officers of Balkan extraction, who may not, at least in the cases of Claudius II, Aurelian, and Probus (to say nothing of Diocletian and his colleagues), have been able to trace citizen ancestors prior to the *constitutio Antoniniana* (Caracalla's grant of near universal citizenship in AD 212), military service appears truly to have lost much of its traditional cache in the course of the fourth century. The result was that men whose extra-Roman ancestry was within a generation of their assumption of high office were moving into significant positions in the hierarchy. In the fourth century they did so as commanders of Roman units, rather than as commanders of units derived from their native tribes. After the essential failure of the effort to control the Goths, who had entered the empire in AD 375 (and afterward), Germanic units under their own commanders became far more obvious. The result was often severe tension between members of the civilian aristocracy and the military—and these tensions derived both from the different types of service being provided by the two groups, and from the fact that they were ethnically dissimilar. In short, the civil and the military spheres were rapidly becoming two distinct societies.

Tension between the civilian and military sectors was not devoid of openly racist elements. Germans were physically and linguistically distinctive in most provinces of the empire, and there is some reason to think that Germanic officers were in many ways more loyal to the empire than the empire was to them. Gainas, the *magister militum* of the east who tried to exploit ethnic tensions between Goths and others in AD 405, was an exception rather than the rule. More typical may have been the attitude of Honorius, who refused to deal with Alaric in AD 410, when he might have been brought into Roman service, and who banned people from wearing German attire in the city of Rome (*CTh* 14. 10. 2–4). Even though Athaulf, who replaced Alaric after his death in AD 411 as the leader of the band that would become known as the Visigoths, expressed the desire to replace "Romania" with "Gothia," he nonetheless married an imperial princess, by whom he fathered a son whom he named Theodosius, anticipating, perhaps, that he would be the father of a future emperor (Oros. *Hist.* 7. 43. 5; Heather 2006: 238–41). There were plainly some Goths who were disturbed by the thought of assimilation, but they seem to have been less numerous than those who sought respect from the imperial regime.

It is notable that we hear of ethnically motivated pogroms against Germanic troops, but not the reverse (e.g., Amm. Marc. 31. 16. 8; Zos. 5. 35. 5). When Goths looted and pillaged, it was by and large because they needed sustenance rather than because they simply wanted to kill Romans (a distinction that no doubt was irrelevant to their victims).

A far more serious problem, for Rome at least, than the German question, was the fact that the state had lost the ability to put bigger armies in the field. This stemmed from the collapse of civil authority, and the inability to control the costs of warfare. It surely is telling that although Rome controlled more territory in AD 455 when Geiseric sailed from Carthage to sack Rome than Rome had controlled when it first went to war with Carthage in 264 BC, he faced no coherent opposition. There was no Roman fleet to intercept him, no Roman army to resist him. The Vandal occupation of North Africa in AD 439 may reasonably be taken as the last straw that broke the back of the elderly camel that was then the western administration; but to say this begs the question as to why that administration was simply incapable of deploying the potentially great resources that were available to the business of government. There is no single or obvious explanation for this failure, but the *Theodosian Code* and other documents suggest that significant factors included the following: the unwillingness of large landholders to allow people on their estates to be conscripted; extreme hostility between soldier and civilian, compounded by a decline in the real value of army pay, which meant that service no longer boosted a person's status; and the disjuncture between civil and military authority (Fear 2007: 427–37). The civilian authorities were expected to furnish recruits to the military, and civilian officials were more likely to be sympathetic to the complaints of aristocrats, far more of whom now had connections of their own within the imperial administration (Heather 2006: 116–18), whose goodwill they needed to obtain if they were to advance their careers. The progressive decline in the fortunes of the western administration after the first decade of the fifth century may also have inclined many of these same aristocrats incline to make accommodation with barbarian leaders whom they saw as more potent characters in their own areas (Heather 2006: 434).

CONCLUSIONS

One of the persistent issues in the history of ancient Rome is the contest between the state—as the Romans put it, the *res publica*—and individual members of the aristocracy for control; and that issue, more so than the tale of Rome's wars, defines the history of the Roman army. Rome grew powerful in Italy when institutions were created that could harness the ambitions of the leaders of the *gentes* to the service of the collective good. So long as this understanding stood firm, so, too, did the republic. And during this whole period, it can plausibly be maintained that the

Roman army was indeed the voting populace under arms. That is, the society of the army was, broadly speaking, the civilian society, though dressed and functioning, momentarily, differently. The principate emerged out of the imbalance between the power of individuals, who were able to exploit provincial commands that were subject to utterly inadequate control by the limited governmental structure of the republic, uniting in a new way the interests of an individual with claims regarding the welfare of the state. The army of this period was no longer a mirror of the Roman community. It was, rather, a kind of parallel society. Nonetheless, the focal point for the military collective, like that for the rest of the population, was the emperor, who now embodied the state (the *res publica*). For about three centuries, these two societies, the one martial and the other civilian, coexisted in parallel, yet continually intersecting orbits around the *princeps*. This cosmos would come to ruin when individual stake holders once again were able to emerge as the dominant force in Roman society—that is to say, when individuals leading groups of loyal followers could once again advance meaningful claims to control of the state. It is in some ways fitting that a terminal date for the Western Empire should be that on which the army of Italy essentially privatized itself by declaring its leader to be its king.

SUGGESTED READING

For studies of the social aspects of service in the Roman army, a topic that has not been treated in any detail here, see Harmand 1967, Campbell 1984, Davies 1989, Wesch-Klein 1998, Phang 2001, and Phang 2008. A topic that has been much in vogue in recent years involves the ways in which Roman soldiers interacted with civilian populations. On this, see Isaac 1990, Kennedy 1996, and Pollard 2000.

BIBLIOGRAPHY

Adams, J. N. 1995. "The Language of the Vindolanda Writing Tablets: An Interim Report." *Journal of Roman Studies* 85: 86–134.
———. 1999. "The Poets of Bu Njem: Language, Culture and the Centurionate." *Journal of Roman Studies* 89: 109–34.
Afzelius, A. 1942. *Die römische Eroberung Italiens (340–264 v. Chr.)*. Copenhagen: Aarhaus University Press.
Aperghis, G. G. 2004. *The Seleukid Royal Economy: The Finances and Financial Administration of the Seleukid Empire*. Cambridge: Cambridge University Press.
Briscoe, J. 1973. *A Commentary on Livy Books XXXI–XXXIII*. Oxford: Clarendon Press.
Brunt, P. A. 1962. "The Army and the Land in the Roman Revolution." *Journal of Roman Studies* 52: 69–86 = Brunt 1988: 240–80.
———. 1971. *Italian Manpower 225 BC–AD 14*. Oxford: Clarendon Press.

————. 1988. *The Fall of the Roman Republic*. Oxford: Clarendon Press.

Campbell, J. B. 1984. *The Emperor and the Roman Army*. Oxford: Clarendon Press.

Corbier, M. 1977. "L'aerarium militare." In, *Armées et fiscalité dans le monde antique: [actes du colloque national]*, Paris, 14–16 octobre 1976. Paris: Éditions du Centre national de la recherche scientifique. 197–234.

Cornell, T. 1995. *The Beginnings of Rome: Italy and Rome from the Bronze Age to the Punic Wars (c. 1000–264 BC)*. London: Routledge.

Davies, R. 1989. *Service in the Roman Army*. New York: Columbia University Press.

de Light, L. 2007. "Roman Manpower and Recruitment during the Middle Republic." In P. Erdkamp (ed.), *A Companion to the Roman Army*. Malden: Blackwell.

Dreyer, B., and H. Engelman. 2003. *Die Inschriften von Metropolis*. Bonn: Rudolf Habelt Verlag.

Duncan Jones, R. 1982. *The Economy of the Roman Empire: Quantitative Studies*. Cambridge: Cambridge University Press.

Elton, H. 2007. "Military Forces." In Sabin, van Wees, and Whitby 2007: 2, 270–309.

Fear, A. T. 2007. "War and Society." In Sabin, van Wees, and Whitby 2007: 2, 424–58.

Goldsworthy, A. 1996. *The Roman Army at War*. Oxford: Clarendon Press.

Harmand, J. 1967. *L'armée et le soldat à Rome de 107 à 50 avant notre ère*. Paris: Éditions A. et J. Picard et Cie.

Heather, P. 2006. *The Fall of the Roman Empire*. Oxford: Oxford University Press.

Isaac, B. 1988. "The Meaning of *limes* and *limitanei* in Ancient Sources." *Journal of Roman Studies* 78: 125–47 = Isaac 1998: 345–87.

————. 1990. *The Limits of Empire: The Roman Army in the East*. Oxford: Clarendon Press.

————. 1994. "Inscriptions from Southern Jordan." *Scripta Classica Israelica* 13: 163–68 = Isaac 1998: 334–42.

————. 1998. *The Near East under Roman Rule: Selected Papers*. Leiden: Brill.

Kennedy, D. L. (ed.). 1996. *The Roman Army in the East*. Ann Arbor: Journal of Roman Archaeology.

Mann, J. C. 1983. *Legionary Recruitment and Veteran Settlement during the Principate*. London: Institute of Archaeology Occasional Publication n. 7.

Meyer, E. 1924. "Das römischen Manilpularheer, seine Entwicklung und seine Vorstuffen." *Kleine Schriften*. 2nd ed. Halle: M. Niemeyer. 2, 231–85.

Oakley, S. 1998. *A Commentary on Livy Books VI–X*. Vol. 2. Oxford: Clarendon Press.

Phang, S. E. 2001. *The Marriage of Roman Soldiers (13 BC–AD 235): Law and Family in the Imperial Army*. Leiden: E. J. Brill.

————. 2008. *Roman Military Service. Ideologies of Discipline in the Late Republic and Early Empire*. Cambridge: Cambridge University Press.

Pollard, N. 1996. "The Roman Army as 'Total Institution' in the Near East? Dura-Europus as a Case Study." In Kennedy 1996: 212–27.

————. 2000. *Soldiers, Cities, and Civilians in Roman Syria*. Ann Arbor: University of Michigan Press.

Potter, D. S. 2004. *The Roman Empire at Bay AD 180–395*. London: Routledge.

Rathbone, D., and R. Alston. 2007. "Warfare and the State." In Sabin, van Wees, and Whitby 2007: 2, 158–97.

Rawson, E. 1971. "The Literary Sources for the Pre-Marian Army." *Papers of the British School in Rome* 39: 13–31 = E. Rawson, *Roman Culture and Society*. Oxford: Clarendon Press 1991: 34–57.

Sabin, P., H. van Wees, and M. Whitby (eds.). 2007. *The Cambridge History of Greek and Roman Warfare*. 2 vols. Cambridge: Cambridge University Press.

Saulnier, C. 1983. *L'armée et a guerre chez les peuples Samnites (viie–ivᵉs.)*. Paris: De Boccard.

Smith, C. S. 2006. *The Roman Clan*. Cambridge: Cambridge University Press.

Smith, R. E. 1958. *Service in the Post-Marian Roman Army*. Manchester: Manchester University Press.

Speidel, M. P. 1992. "Roman Army Pay Scales." *Journal of Roman Studies* 82: 87–106.

Walbank, F. 1957. *A Historical Commentary on Polybius*. Vol 1. Oxford: Clarendon Press.

Watson, A. 1993. *International Law in Archaic Rome: War and Religion*. Baltimore: Johns Hopkins University Press.

Wesch-Klein, G. 1998. *Soziale Aspekte des römischen Heerwesens in der Kaiserzeit*. Stuttgart: Franz Steiner Verlag.

CHAPTER 25

GRAECO-ROMAN CULTIC SOCIETIES

JOHN SCHEID

INTRODUCTION: NO ONE RELIGION—MANY CULTIC SOCIETIES

THE religions of the Graeco-Roman world were collective by nature, or, to put the matter the other way around, pretty well every social grouping was at the same time a cultic community. Whatever cult one considers, it was always celebrated within the setting of a congregation structured by, and subject to, a collective logic; and whenever one is confronted with an essentially secular grouping, this, too, was invariably brought together around a common divinity and a set of common religious obligations. Graeco-Roman religious activity was, then, essentially a collective enterprise, even if any given religious act might remain individual (Veyne 2005: 419–541).

Religious practices thus had an incontrovertibly unifying function in the ancient world: it was through religion that one belonged to a community, and it was in large part through its cultic traditions that one community distinguished itself from others. Individual religiosity was surely developed in this setting, yet it was always as a member of a collective that an individual encountered the gods. Moreover, the gods themselves were members of these groups. Independently of their supernatural lives, which cultivated people did not neglect, and which they tried to define in their speculations, the earthly life of the gods took its course in relation to these communities, and the blessings the gods bestowed, or the punishments they inflicted, concerned above all the communities of which they were a part.

Now, these communities were at once diverse and autonomous. Despite their frequent physical proximity and interconnections, each cultic community obeyed its own authority, and thus defined which would be its gods, and what would be the religious obligations owed those deities. It is also true that the religious culture and customs of many of these communities were quite similar to one another; however, these different communities were not the mere parts of something like a single religion, nor were they determined by some one common religious tradition. This, then, is another of the fundamental principles of the religions of Graeco-Roman antiquity, namely, that they did not belong to anything like a universal religion.

That notwithstanding, historians, philosophers, or ethnologists of antiquity do frequently speak of 'the religion' of the Greeks, of the Romans, or of (say) the Athenians. But it is important to stress that *the* religion of the Romans simply did not exist; one can speak only of religions, plural (Beard, North, and Price 1998). Even to say this, though, is to operate at the level of generality, and should not be taken to signify that these (plural) religions were themselves unified wholes, each having a simple 'pantheon,' a prescribed doctrine, or some absolute authority. Indeed, given that these religions were not revealed, yet were connected via intricate social structures, they really could not be subsumed under some form of central religious control. For example, the priests of Rome, of Ephesus, or of Antioch did not supervise the religious lives of Roman citizens, of the citizens of Ephesus, or of Antioch. In each case, these priests were in charge of only a very particular area of the religion of the Roman, Ephesian, or the Antiochene community. What individuals did outside their participation in state cultic activities was entirely their own concern.

There also crops up, now and again, a tendency to consider the Roman *pontifex maximus* as a sort of pope of the Roman religion, in other words, to see this state official as the religious patriarch of all Roman citizens, and of all Roman religious practice. This, too, is just false. In fact, even in the context of the public religion of Rome, the *pontifex maximus* directed only the college of pontiffs, and the latter served principally to counsel the senate and the magistrates on questions of patrimony and the cult of Rome's public gods. The *pontifex* had no say whatsoever in the 1001 religious communities of the Romans, which were not within his domain. The only aspect of his activity, and of that of the pontiffs, that could directly concern all citizens of Rome, was the management of the necropoleis. So, for example, a correctly installed tomb was theoretically protected under law, and in order to move or modify it, authorization from the pontiffs was required. But this authority was necessarily limited by the expanse of the Roman Empire. It could not be materially exercised in the provincial cities, and even in towns of Italy it is doubtful that the pontifical college of Rome ever took charge of these types of problems. In similar fashion, the power of the priests of Athens, or of Antioch, ceased at the territorial limits of these poleis—and at the doors of their citizens' homes. This basic characteristic of Graeco-Roman religious communities, namely, that they were highly fragmented, and highly regionalized, held true for all the locales of that world.

Thus, even the numerous communities throughout the Mediterranean region that worshiped the goddess Isis, which can appear to have been quite similar from one province to another, were formally separate. This is why Apuleius' hero Lucius, who had already been initiated into this cult in Greece, had to undergo another initiation at Rome toward the end of his journey. In short, there was no one, pan-Mediterranean religion of Isis. There were, instead, many separate communities, which participated variously in the cultic veneration of this deity. And this cultic community (or better, these cultic communities) of Isis can be understood as representative of cultic organization generally in the Graeco-Roman context.

It is only later, in the fifth century AD, that the last 'pagans' sought to maintain and preserve all the temples and cults that had survived Christianization, and thus gave the impression of attempting to defend one single religion, which stood in singular opposition to Christianity. In fact, more all-encompassing cults had only existed in the context of the provinces of the Roman Empire. From the beginning of the empire, collective altars and temples of their respective provinces were created in major provincial urban centers, at Lyon, Ephesus, Tarragona, and so forth. Every year, a collective cult of Rome and Augustus was celebrated by elected delegates from the different cities of the province at these centralized sites (Price 1984). However, despite the integrative character of this imperial cult, which seems to have united (at least in this type of worship) entire areas of the Roman world, there still can be no vision here of something akin to a 'religion of empire'—namely, one religion that might define the status of a citizen of the Roman Empire. These particular manifestations of the imperial cult were, instead, only one element of the collective cults of Rome, and of the cities of her empire.

Thus, when all is said and done, the cities of a given province formed, through their delegates, an eminent cultic community (viz., of the Roman imperial cult); however, this was not *the* religious community of those people, but merely *a* religious community, analogous to many other religious communities in existence, and to which the same people will have belonged. In short, cult was very often community, and the cultic communities were many and varied.

The Hierarchy of the Groups

If one considers the whole panoply of religious communities that existed in the Roman Empire, one readily discerns a hierarchy among them that was determined by their socio-political standing. At the top, because it was the most all-embracing, and also because it wielded the most power and resources, was the community formed by the city. Whether in Roman or Latin colonies or municipalities (*municipia*), or in peregrine cities, the civic religious community was plainly the most eminent. The ritual obligations performed by these communities as a group constituted the public religion of the place, and public in the sense that this was the religion of the *ciuitas*, of the *polis*, of the *populus*, or of the *demos*.[1]

The religious duties of the civic communities had their beginnings in the foundation of the cities by their temporal authorities, and they remained a ritual obligation for all citizens of the city concerned. Such civic cults were generally overseen by the magistrates and the priests of the place. Thus, the civic cult could be celebrated only in places designated as appropriate for public worship, in the open air, that is, in places accessible to all. Given that, communal cultic rituals would very often be carried out in front of the religious edifices of the city, for example, on plazas fronting the temples of the gods. In Rome, and in Roman cities, the obligation and the right to celebrate the public cult—that is, to participate in the sacrifices and in the public games, and to sacrifice for the good of the people— was likewise a matter for those regularly residing in these cities (the *incolae*). In the peregrine cities, the rules could vary, and non-citizens of those places might find themselves excluded or limited in the exercise of the cult—so, for example, at the Temple in Jerusalem, the *goyim* were not allowed to enter the interior spaces of the edifice, nor to offer their sacrifices directly, but only to do so through an intermediary from the Jewish clergy.

Now, while in the cities of the Greek world the cultic community was strictly limited to the freeborn, in Roman cities, it also included freedmen and slaves. The example of the Arval Brethren, which is especially well represented by our extant sources, reveals the collaboration of all members of the community, regardless of their social status. Under Augustus, the brotherhood of Arvals had become one of the public priestly colleges of Rome. The twelve priests themselves were, by regulation, of senatorial rank. However, at their side officiated assistants, who were freedmen, as well as public slaves. Moreover, boys, the children of senators, worked with the priests during the religious services celebrated in the urban residence of the fraternal *magister* (the head of the priestly college). In short, the sequence of cultic activities demonstrates clearly that the brotherhood formed a complex group, involving all members of the (secular) community.

The religious service performed by the Arvals included a banquet, during which (between the first and second course—*mensa prima et secunda*), the Arvals made a sacrifice to the divinity the brotherhood was bound to honor each year. Thus, on May 30, AD 84, the secretary of the brotherhood notes that "the Arval brethren met to perform the sacrifice to *dea Dia*, and during the meal, the president Tiberius Tutinius Severus, Tiberius Iulius Candidus Marius Celsus, Aulus Iulius Quadratus, Lucius Veratius Quadratus…made a sacrifice of incense and wine…"[2] Now, on the

---

1. The Latin word *civitas* and the Greek word *polis* both mean 'community,' or 'city/ town,' while *populus* (Latin) and *demos* (Greek) both indicate the people, generally the legally defined citizens of the town or community.

2. Scheid 1998: no. 53, lines 17–20. The inscription is damaged, and the lacunae, represented here with dots, cannot be restored with certainty

basis of this inscription, one would be inclined to conclude that only the named senators officiated. However, because of the chance find of a later document, from the May 20, AD 91, we get a more precise description of the scene. Thus, we now know that

> the Arval brethren dined with the president Lucius Veratius Quadratus at his home, to perform the sacrifice to *dea Dia*, and during the meal the president Lucius Veratius Quadratus…Publius Sallustius Blaesus, Lucius Pompeius Vopiscus Arruntius Catellius Celer, Lucius Iulius Marinus Caecilius Simplex made sacrifices of incense and wine, assisted by the same boys having father and mother still living as on the 17th of May. And the boys, clad in a *ricinium* [a shawl, worn on this occasion] and wearing the *toga praetexta* [the special toga worn by boys before they came of age], carried the offerings to the altar with the aid of the *calatores* [the assistants of the priests] and the public slaves. They touched the *tuscanicae* [vases, apparently] with lighted torches, and had them carried to their homes by the *calatores*.[3]

We can see, therefore, that beneath the apparent simplicity of the service was hidden a complex collaboration of diverse members of the small community of Arvals. The priests are the ones who act on behalf of the city of Rome, as is befitting of senators. But in fact, their action consists only in their authority over the religious service, and in the orders they give; the ritual activity itself is effected by four boys, the sons of senators—minors, then, but of eminent social rank. And as befits people of this high social rank, these boys, in turn, do not themselves perform the 'manual labor' involved in the cultic act. Instead, this is realized by the public slaves belonging to the college, with the help, which is to say, under the control, of the *calatores*, freedmen who served as lictors for the Arvals. As a result, the ritual gives each member of the fraternity his own place, and each member executes the acts appropriate to his social station. The cultic society, in other words, very closely reflects the larger society, both in the way it was structured and in the ways the members of the group function together.

Thus, the only ones who matter ritually were the Arvals themselves, in other words, the senators. We possess some reports of the brotherhood that are more attenuated, and these mention the priests alone, which indicates that authority was theirs and theirs alone. Indeed, the earlier inscription says explicitly that it is the priests—in other words, again the senators—who sacrifice, even if they remain reclining on their couches throughout the ritual. It is worth noting that the subordinate members of the cultic community, they who are of lesser social distinction, are not deemed worthy of mention in the text from AD 84—the boys by reason of their age, and the others because they are freedmen or slaves. Thus, only the fortuitous discovery of a second inscription (that of AD 91) reveals the much more complex structure of the ritual, and the collaboration of all the members of this little community in it (Scheid 1990: 539–41).

3. Scheid 1998: no. 59, column II, lines 15–24.

CULT AND MEMBERSHIP IN THE COMMUNITY

The respective places that individuals occupied, or might occupy, in the celebration of cultic rites served largely to define their social status in the community concerned. Thus, in Greece and in Rome, participation in a particular set of cultic rites signified membership in the community with which these were associated, for example in the civic community. At public sacrifices, for example, each citizen had a right to a specified portion of the victim, which was sometimes fixed by individualized rules, and sometimes simply by the status of the individual concerned. In the Latin-speaking world of the imperial age, such portions were generally expressed in monetary terms (Toller 1889), with variations allocated according to the recipient's official social status: at Rome, this had likewise to do with social standing, whether a person was of senatorial, equestrian, or simple citizen status; and in the municipalities beyond the capital, the matter was handled according to one's rank as *decurio* (member of the local aristocracy), *Augustalis* (one of those who officiated over the local imperial cult), or simple citizen. The peregrine cities had their own hierarchy of participation, which in Greece was generally defined by rules known from our epigraphic evidence.[4] It even appears that in Rome a part of the vocabulary for defining social relations came from this sacrificial distribution (*particeps*, *princeps*, etc.; cf. Scheid 2005: 264–74).

Women occupied a particular place in this organization. In theory, they were excluded from the primary roles, which were reserved for men. In the name of their ritual incapacity, they were thus subordinated to men (for Greece, Bruit Zaidmann 1991; Frei-Stolba and Bielman 1998; Frei-Stolba et al. 2003; for Rome, Cazanove 1987; Scheid 1991; Scheid 2003a). Nevertheless, it is evident that things were not so simple. Leaving aside feminine sacerdotal functions, it must be noted that women officiated regularly for the good of the people in the name of the community of matrons, and that they were capable of celebrating certain public rites alongside the men. In this context, too, the reports, and certain rules, seem designed more to construct the subordination of women to men than to describe an actual secondary role reserved for women.

Now, a public calendar defined the annual religious duties of the civic community, and these obligations were divided among the dignitaries and groups of citizens. Certain festivals were celebrated by the magistrates or the priests, others by the collective heads of families (in Rome, for example, the Quirinalia or the Parentalia). In support of these rites, the cities constructed and maintained temples and other places of public worship, which were principally devoted to the public cults. These places of worship were located either in the urban center of the city or in the surrounding rural territory that belonged to those urban centers; and it was often the case that the large cultic sites of regional importance were controlled by the most

---

4. In the Greek cities, for example in Cos, in the context of the sacrifices to Zeus Polieus, it depended on the local context whether the magistrates, who were also the priests, received specific parts of the victim—there was no universal rule.

important city of the region. Thus, the famous sanctuary of the Clitumnus Springs was taken from the Umbrians after the conquest in 241 BC, and was annexed to the Latin colony of Spoletium; under Augustus it was given to the new Roman colony of Hispellum. It is also important to note that cities similarly financed the needs of cult by providing, for example, the sacrifical victims.

These civic cults addressed a specific set of gods who enjoyed the status of public divinity ('our' gods), and modern historians often designate these deities collectively by the term 'pantheon'—we talk, that is, about the pantheon of some particular town. The gods of a given community themselves also formed a community, at least if one reads the poets (for example, Ov. *Met.* 1. 170–76). Such a list could evolve over time, but only the supreme authorities of the various communities—in Rome the senate, and in Roman municipalities the counsel of *decuriones*—could induct a new divinity into the group that the civic body already honored in regular cult. With the exception of the Near Eastern religions, where divinities had a very different rank and status, the relations with the gods in the Graeco-Roman world were those that the community could maintain through its most eminent citizens, its patrons. The gods were accorded the highest rank, with extraordinary homage and respect, but only their immortality and their formidable power distinguished them, so far as the Greeks or Romans were concerned, from other (mortal) members of the community. The gods were not the creators of the community; rather, they were treated as if they had been invited to join it by the founders and authorities of the commonwealth.

Although it was the most eminent of the various ancient religious communities, we must recognize that the city was not the only religious frame of reference for the inhabitants of the Graeco-Roman world. By virtue of his or her social relations, the individual was caught up in a whole network of other religious communities. And so, the first community to which an individual belonged was that of the home. Each family had its own religion, created by the familial ancestors, and more or less different from the family cult of the neighbors. Nor did any higher authority prescribe this or that particular religious conduct for these families. Communal opinion, in its way, demanded that one have such a familial religion, and that one continue to celebrate the religion of one's ancestors, rather than looking abroad for one's devotions; but even this was only true for natives. Foreigners residing in the cities of the Graeco-Roman world had, for their part, the right, and even the duty, to honor the divinities of their own families. Each father was, then, the 'priest' of his family. With the other males of the family, he determined and controlled the ritual obligations and their execution, and in the context of the cult, it was the father, or one of his sons, who officiated.

This familial autonomy can be observed most clearly in funerals. The deceased were not interred by the priests of the city, but by the members of the family, with the oldest male presiding. The pontiffs and other priests did not even have the right to attend funerals. They were involved only if the deceased was a member of their own family; and in this case, they appear to have officiated in their capacity as father or child, not as pontiff or augur.

Now, the family community included all members of the family, both free and slave, though the latter could play only a secondary or delegated role. Thus the *villicus* (bailiff) of Cato the Elder was in charge of the cult in the family domain when the master was absent—but only in the master's place, and only for a certain number of prescribed services. The *uillica* (the bailiff's wife) likewise replaced the mistress of the home in such situations. In addition, the slaves belonging to any given household (*familia*) participated as assistants in that family's cultic tasks. In theory, the mother of the family occupied a secondary role in religious matters, and in Rome, it seems that she was not allowed to sacrifice for the family community. Nonetheless, while she could not take the place of the father as head of the familial cult, still it is clear that the father required his wife's assistance in various cultic matters and she was in charge of the domestic rites reserved for female members of the family. The epigraphic record reveals, in addition, that women were often among those who left votive offerings in places of cultic worship, which proves that they had considerable religious autonomy.

If we move out of the familial community, we find that every individual belonged to one or another subdivision of the city, which again involved participation in a particular cultic group, or groups. He or she resided in a quarter (*vicus*), perhaps in a housing complex (*insula*), or beyond the city limits in one of the rural districts. Each of these subdivisions of the population had its own cultic identity. The quarter in Roman cities included places of collective cult worship, located at the crossroads (*compita*), where the neighborhood community would meet on specific dates to perform sacrifices, and would even hold collective games in honor of their patron deities. These rites of the Compitalia are well known; and it is by participation in these cults that the inhabitants of a quarter acquired their local identity. The same kind of phenomenon is attested in certain housing developments (*insulae*) at Rome and Ostia. Archeology reveals collective cult sites there, and occasional inscriptions attest that it was the proprietor of the *insula* who built such a site (see, e.g., *CIL* VI 65–67 = *ILS* 3500–3501a). And in the rural districts of the cities, the developed areas celebrated collective cults that gave the rustics a place in the urban fabric of their city.

Beyond the family, and beyond the neighborhood, individuals frequently belonged also to organized colleges, or associations, or *thiasoi* (guilds—cf. also Perry in this volume). Each of these associations, whatever its purpose or objective, formed in fact, and in the first place, a cultic community (Veyne 2005: 467). Whether it was a college of functionaries, of merchants, of transporters, of people from the same region, or of military units, each of these communities had one divine 'member,' who defined and protected the mortal associates; sometimes this divinity was the genius of the organization (i.e., the divinization of the group's potency), but in other cases, the association actually named itself after the divinity, who now functioned as the group's 'patron.' Such was the situation in Rome with, for example, the college of Aesculapius and Hygieia, whose function was to assure funerals and proper funerary rites to its members, most of whom apparently lacked families (*CIL* VI 10234 = *ILS* 7213). Each of these associations had religious obligations, which often defined the group's annual calendar; and sometimes one is even tempted to consider this or that *thiasos*, whose ritual calendar happens to be known, as a religious community prefiguring the Christian communities (on which, see Becker in this volume).

In fact, then, the religious aspect was an absolutely integral element of every Graeco-Roman association, and more than the 'profane' trait or label that characterized the group's members, it was the patron divinity and the collective cultic practices that ultimately defined the college (see Belayche and Mimouni 2003). And so, a college of sacerdotal lictors, for example, might honor a divinity closely linked to its activities: such was the case with Jupiter Epulo, who received a consecration from the *kalatores* (assistants) of the *VIIviri epulonum* (a college of priests; see AE 1936, 95).

Cultic Community

The last example shows, in fact, precisely how every community in the Graeco-Roman world was ultimately a ritual community. The Greeks and the Romans, and the inhabitants of the Graeco-Roman world more generally, organized themselves collectively into communities modeled on the larger urban centers, and notably around communal divinities and ritual obligations that gave each individual community its identity. These devotions must not be considered as an indication of a special inclination toward one god or goddess, or even an exclusive consecration to a divinity or to some particularly religious lifestyle, since the cult and the divinity were in fact bound to the very structure of collective life in the ancient world. Nor are we to take the belonging of individuals to such groups to intimate some special relations of the worshippers and a deity. This is why the religious aspect of associative, familial, and civic communities never elicits comment from our sources; it was taken completely for granted. The communal cults, then, served principally as expressions of the collective structures, and were not chiefly representative of some devotion to or passion for the religious. It is difficult, for example, to imagine that the philosophical sects, which likewise had their cults and religious calendars, saw themselves as pietist groups (Koch Piettre 2005: 44–45).

It is likewise evident, as we have come to realize more clearly in recent years, that the different levels of integration overlapped. That is to say, the ancients passed from one collective practice to another without dwelling on the transition. Thus, the magistrate who was engaged during his term of office with celebrating the public religious services of his position added here and there a sacrifice for himself and his family. It is impossible to count the private, individual, and familial or associative devotions that took place in the large and small sites of public cults, for aside from the major public services, the temples stood open to non-public religious life. Similarly, the magistrates, and even the emperor, could make consecrations other than those of the public cult at such sites.

Even more telling for our subject is the wider religious community that established itself around certain sites of collective cults. We are ill informed, for example, about the frequenting of major public temples by the faithful of other religions, or religious practices. Nevertheless, it is undeniable that in Rome the *compita* (street-corner shrines in the quarters), or other little sanctuaries, also attracted religious communities that were not directly involved in the cults for which these sanctuaries were principally set up. For example, the anonymous *vicus* of the via della Marmorata, between the western side of the Aventine and the Monte Testaccio, demonstrates this. Right next to the *schola* (meeting place) of the *compitum* (street-corner shrine), with its inscribed calendar, and its public and private consecrations, there was a *mithreum* (a small chamber where the god Mithras was worshipped).[5] And if one climbs the slope of the Aventine, one finds near S. Alessio a large Dolichenum (a temple of the Syrian god, Baal) likewise situated near the public sanctuary of the *vicus Armilustri* (Merlat 1960: 147ff.; Hörig and Schwertheim 1987: 221–63). In Trastevere, the Palmyrene cult of the gods Aglibôl and Malakbêl took up residence—with authorization from the pontiffs—in the Gardens of Caesar, next to a sanctuary of Hercules, and in a spot devoted to the cult of Sol, the Roman sun god (Palmer 1981: 368–97). Still more interesting, the third satire of Juvenal (*Sat.* 3. 10–20) may be understood to say that between the temple of Mars and the Porta Capena, in the sacred grove of the Camenes, and near other areas of cultic springs, there was a *proseuche* (a location where Jews met to pray). The text is certainly ambiguous, but it appears fairly certain that the Jews had agreed to develop part of the sacred grove of the Camenes in order to establish a place of prayer there, and that the Romans saw no problem in this (Friedländer 1865: 191; contra Leon 1995: 137). As with the sanctuaries of the *vici*, we again see how foreign communities with foreign gods established themselves on, or near, the sites of traditional Roman cults. It would appear that proximity to a Roman cultic site was perhaps even a desideratum for these foreigners.

Where the Christians are concerned, our evidence is less good. Nevertheless, there is one clear example of the same desire for proximity to a Roman cultic site. Five miles from the Porta Portuensis, on the banks of the Tiber, was the ancient, public, sacred grove of Dea Dia. The location of this grove was, in the time of Augustus, at the very outer fringes of Rome's suburban territory. The shrine's traditional activity comes to a halt toward the middle of the third century AD; the last piece of evidence dates to the early fourth century AD. Then, in this rural environment, encompassing numerous empty spaces, a group of Christians chose to establish a catacomb, with its *martyrium* at the top of the hill just above where the ancestral sacred grove was spread out. It is clear that they sought out the same symbolic site, and its religious context, to mark their own presence.

All these examples show that such cultic sites functioned as meeting points and crossroads for the various religious communities that sprang up at Rome, and in the Roman world. These sites quickly became rather thoroughly multi-cultural,

5. See Rodríguez Almeida 1984: 45–106; Degrassi 1963: 90–98; *CIL* VI 33–35, 588, 760, 30855; *IGVR* 106–8.

potentially harboring groups from several different religious traditions. And so, the various religions rubbed elbows with each other, and the religious communities interacted and intermixed, despite sporadic pogroms and periodic persecutions. It was only with the Christian repression of religions other than Christianity that, in the long run, the number and diversity of religious communities at Rome dwindled.

SUGGESTED READING

As general introductions to religions in the Roman world, four books in particular may be suggested: Beard, North, and Price 1998; Ando 2003; Scheid 2003a; and the relevant chapters in the *Cambridge Ancient History*. Further reading on cultic communities and identity: Belayche and Mimouni 2003, with further literature; Riemer and Riemer 2005.

BIBLIOGRAPHY

Ando, C. (ed.). 2003. *Roman Religion*. Edinburgh: Edinburgh University Press.

Beard, M., J. North, and S. Price. 1998. *Religions of Rome*. 2 vols. Cambridge: Cambridge University Press.

Belayche, N., and S. Mimouni (eds.). 2003. *Les communautés religieuses dans le monde gréco-romain. Essais de définition*. Louvain: Brepols.

Bruit Zaidmann, L. 1991. "Les filles de Pandore. Femmes et rituels dans les cités." In G. Duby and M. Perrot (eds.), *Histoire des femmes en Occident. L'Antiquité*. Paris: Plon. 363–403.

Cazanove, O. de. 1987. "Exesto. L'incapacité sacrificielle des femmes à Rome (À propos de Plutarque, Quest. Rom. 85)." *Phoenix* 41: 159–74.

Degrassi, A. 1963. *Inscriptiones Italiae. XIII, 2. Fasti anni Numani et Iuliani*. Rome: Unione Accademica Nazionale.

Detienne, M., and J.-P. Vernant (eds.). 1979. *La cuisine du sacrifice en pays grec*. Paris: Gallimard.

Dubourdieu, A. 1986. "Cinctus Gabinus." *Latomus* 45: 3–20.

Fasold, P., Th. Fischer, H. von Hesberg, and M. Witteyer (eds.). 1998. *Bestattungssitte und kulturelle Identität*. Bonn: Rudolf Habelt Verlag.

Fasold, P., and Witteyer, M. (eds.). 2001. *Tradition und Wandel im Grabbrauch Rätiens und Obergermaniens während der frühen Kaiserzeit. Römischer Bestattungsbrauch und Beigabensitten*. Wiesbaden: L. Reichert.

Fasold, P., M. Struck, and M. Witteyer (eds.). 2007. *Körpergräber des 1.–3. Jahrhunderts in der römischen Welt*. Frankfurt: Archäologisches Museum.

Frei-Stolba, R., and A. Bielman (eds.). 1998. *Femmes et vie publique dans l'Antiquité géco-romaine*. Paris: Etudes de Lettres. 1, 33–50.

Frei-Stolba, R., A. Bielman, and O. Bianchi (eds.). 2003. *Les femmes antiques entre sphère privée et sphère publique*. Bern: Peter Lang.

Friedländer, L. 1895. *D. Iunii Iuvenalis Saturarum libri V*. Leipzig: B. G. Teubner Verlag.

Georgoudi, St., R. Koch Piettre, and Fr. Schmidt (eds.). 2006. *La cuisine et l'autel. Les sacrifices en questions dans les sociétés de la Méditerranée ancienne*. Louvain: Brepols.

Grottanelli, C., and L. Milano (eds.). 2004. *Food and Identity in the Ancient World*. Padova: S.A.R.G.O.N.

Grottanelli, C., and N. Parise (eds.). 1998. *Sacrificio e società nel mondo antico*. Bari: Laterza.

Heinzelmann, M., et al. (eds.). 2001. *Römischer Bestattungsbrauch und Beigabensitten: in Rom, Norditalien und den Nordwestprovinzen von der späten Republik bis in die Kaiserzeit. Culto dei morti e costumi funerari romani: Roma, Italia settentrionale e province nord-occidentali dalla tarda Repubblica all' età imperiale*. Wiesbaden: L. Reichert.

Hörig, M., and E. Schwertheim. 1987. *Corpus cultus Iouis Dolicheni* (E.P.R.O. vol. 106). Leiden: E. J. Brill.

Jouin, M., and P. Méniel. 2001. "Les dépôts animaux et le fanum gallo-romain de Vertault (Côte-d'Or)." *Revue Archéologique de l'Est* 50: 119–216.

Kajava, M. 1998. "Visceratio." *Arctos* 32: 109–31.

Koch, C. 1932. "Mola salsa." In *RE* XV, 2, col. 2016ff.

Koch, R. 2005. *Comment peut-on être dieu ? La secte d'Épicure*. Paris: Belin.

Krause, C. 1931. "Hostia." In *RE, Supplementband* 5, cols. 236–82.

Latte, K. 1914. "Immolatio." In *RE* s.v.

———. 1960. *Römische Religionsgeschichte*. Munich: Verlag C. H. Beck.

Legouilloux, M. 2000. "L'hécatombe de l'ekklesiaterion de Posidonia-Paestum. Le témoignage de la faune." In St. Verger (ed.), *Rites et espaces en pays celte et méditerranéen. Etude comparée à partir du sanctuaire d'Acy-Romance (Ardennes, France)*. Rome: De Boccard-Bretschneider. 341–51.

Leon, H. 1995. *The Jews of Ancient Rome*. 2nd ed. Philadelphia: Hendrickson.

Martens, M., and G. De Boe (eds.). 2004. *Roman Mithraism. The Evidence of the Small Finds*. Brussels: Museum Het Toreke.

Merlat, P. 1960. *Jupiter Dolichenus. Essai d'interprétation*. Paris: Presses Universitaires de France.

Nouilhan, M. 1989. "Les lectisternes républicains." In A.-Fr. Laurens (ed.), *Entre hommes et dieux. Le convive, le héros, le prophète*. Paris: Les Belles-Lettres. 27–40.

Ortalli, J. 2001. "Il culto funerario della Cispadana romana." In Heinzelmann et al. 2001: 215–42.

Palmer, R. E. A. 1981. "The Topography and Social History of Rome's Trastevere (Southern Sector)." *Proceedings of the Cambridge Philological Society* 125: 368–85.

Prescendi, Fr. 2007. *Décrire et comprendre le sacrifice. Les réflexions des Romains sur leur propre religion à partir de la littérature antiquaire*. Stuttgart: Franz Steiner Verlag.

Price, S. 1984. *Rituals and Power: the Roman Imperial Cult in Asia Minor*. Cambridge: Cambridge University Press.

Reverdin, O., and J. Rudhardt (eds.). 1980. *Le sacrifice dans l'Antiquité* (Entretiens sur l'Antiquité classique, vol. 27). Geneva: Fondation Hardt.

Riemer, U., and P. Riemer. 2005. *Xenophobie-Philoxenie. Vom Umgang mit Fremden in der Antike*. Stuttgart: Franz Steiner Verlag.

Robinson, M. 2002. "Domestic Burnt Offerings and Sacrifices at Roman and Pre-Roman Pompeii, Italy." *Vegetation History and Archaebotany* 11: 93–99.

Rodríguez Almeida, E. 1984. *Il Monte Testaccio: ambiente, storia, materiali*. Rome: Quasar.

Ryberg, I. S. 1955. *Rites of the State Religion in Roman Art*. Rome: American Academy in Rome.

Santini, Cl. 1998. "Il lessico della spartizione nel sacrificio romano." In C. Grottanelli and N. Parise (eds.), *Sacrificio e società nel mondo antico*. Bari: Laterza. 293–302.

Scheid, J. 1990. *Romulus et ses frères, modèle du culte public dans la Rome des empereurs.* Rome: De Boccard-Bretschneider.

———. 1991. "D'indispensables 'étrangères.' Les rôles religieux des femmes à Rome." In G. Duby and M. Perrot (eds.), *Histoire des femmes en Occident. I. L'Antiquité.* Paris: Plon. 405–37.

———. 1995 (1998). "Græco ritu: A Typically Roman Way of Honouring the Gods." *Harvard Studies in Classical Philology* 97: 15–31.

———. 1998. *Commentarii fratrum arvalium qui supersunt. Les copies épigraphiques des protocoles annuels de la confrérie arvale (21 av.–304 ap. J.-C.).* Rome: De Boccard-Bretschneider.

———. 2003a. "Les rôles religieux des femmes à Rome. Un complément." In R. Frei-Stolba, A. Bielman, and O. Bianchi (eds.). *Les femmes antiques entre sphère privée et sphère publique.* Bern: Peter Lang. 137–51.

———. 2003b. *An Introduction to Roman Religion.* Edinburgh: Edinburgh University Press.

———. 2004. "Interdits et exclusions dans les banquets sacrificiels romains." In C. Grottanelli and L. Milano (eds.), *Food and Identity in the Ancient World.* Padua: S.A.R.G.O.N. 123–39.

———. 2005. *Quand faire c'est croire. Les rites sacrificiels des Romains.* Paris: Aubier.

———. 2007. "Körperbestattung und Verbrennungssitte aus der Sicht der schriftlichen Quellen." In Fasold et al. 2007: 19–26.

Schnegg-Köhler, B. 2002. *Die augusteischen Säkularspiele.* Leipzig: B. G. Teubner.

ThesCRA *Thesaurus cultus et rituum antiquorum,* I. *Processions, sacrifices, libations, fumigations, dédications;* II. *Purification, Consecration, initiation, héroisation et apothéose, banquet, danse, musique, rites et activités relatives aux images de culte.* Los Angeles: J. Paul Getty Museum. 2004.

Toller, O. 1889. *De soectaculis, cenis, distributionibus in municipiis Romanis Occidentis.* PhD Thesis, Altenburg, University of Leipzig.

Turcan, R. 1980. "Le sacrifice mithriaque: innovations de sens et de modalités." In Reverdin and Rudhardt 1980: 343–58.

———. 1989. *Les cultes orientaux dans le monde romain.* Paris: Les Belles-Lettres.

Van Andringa, W., and S. Lepetz. 2003. "Le ossa animali nei santuari: per un' archeologia del sacrificio." In de O. Cazanove and J. Scheid (eds.), *Sanctuaires et sources dans l'Antiquité.* Naples: Centre Jean-Bérard. 85–96.

Veyne, P. 2005. *L'empire gréco-romain.* Paris: Seuil.

Wissowa, G. 1912. *Religion und Kultus der Römer.* Munich: Verlag C. H. Beck.

CHAPTER 26

ANCIENT JEWISH SOCIAL RELATIONS

SETH SCHWARTZ

INTRODUCTION

THE basic problem of all Jewish social history is integration. To what extent did Jewish communities possess an inner-Jewish social structure? Were local communities connected to one another by social ties? To what extent were they integrated socially into their various environments?

In attempting to answer these questions for antiquity, we may begin with what are, conceptually speaking, the most elementary observations. The very designation of a collectivity as Jewish implies its inner social cohesion, either because the constituents' social interactions are especially concentrated, or because they consensually attach peculiar significance to such interaction as occurs. In other words, their social cohesion may be thick, thin, or essentially symbolic or imaginary—a kind of intersubjective fiction—but that it exists is true practically by definition; if it were not, the collectivity would be no collectivity but merely a random agglomeration of individuals possessing no special label. Similarly, all Jewish collectivities must be socially integrated in their environment—no human group can exist in total isolation—though such integration may, once again, be thick, or thin, or largely mediated through a pivotal individual or a small group of intermediaries.

The investigator's task then is to try to locate his/her subject somewhere along these spectra of integration, and then to flesh out the resultant broad sketch with situationally specific detail. In practice, however, while almost every political, cultural, and religious history of the ancient Jews presupposes a social history, social history *stricto sensu* is still in its infancy among scholars of ancient Judaism, not-withstanding the groundwork laid by such early endeavors as the first volumes of Salo Baron's pioneering *Social and Religious History of the Jews* (18 volumes, Philadelphia: Jewish Publication Society, 1952–83, esp. volumes 1–2; first edition, 1939). To be sure, in recent decades first-century Galilee has, for obvious reasons, received considerable social-historical attention from New Testament scholars, but much of this work is eccentric from the perspective of 'mainstream' Roman social history (the same is true *mutatis mutandis* of much 'Talmudic' social history; see below). Nevertheless, valuable work has been done on the ancient Jews, even if those doing it have not always considered themselves primarily social historians. Before providing a survey, though, it will be helpful to specify who it is, precisely, we are talking about.

JUDAISM AND THE PROBLEM OF INTEGRATION

By the time substantial numbers of Jews came under Roman rule, following Pompey's conquest of the eastern Mediterranean basin in 63 BC, Judaism had already assumed its familiar classical ancient form. Ideally, it focused on the sacrificial worship of Yahweh, the one god of Israel, in the temple of Jerusalem, in accordance with the laws of the Pentateuch (or Torah)—the first five books of the Hebrew Bible. By the first century BC many, probably even most, Jews lived outside their ancestral homeland in Palestine, and for them Judaism, again ideally, involved a modified, non-sacrificial, form of worship frequently centered in prayer houses (*proseukhai*) or synagogues, plus—as in Palestine—observance of the Pentateuchally ordained practice of abstaining from work one day out of seven (in an environment in which the week was not yet common), and the biblical food laws, to mention only the most conspicuous practices. Some such Jews continued to regard Jerusalem as their metropolis and its temple as the center of their religious life. Even during the Roman Republic they consequently sent donations to Jerusalem and aspired to visit it for one of the three annual pilgrimage festivals—an aspiration that became real-istic only with the establishment of the principate (which eased travel) in 27 BC and Herod's expansive rebuilding of the temple in 20 BC (which enabled the accommo-dation of huge numbers of visitors).

For the present purposes it is worth emphasizing that the Torah prescribed for the Jews a life lived in the profoundest possible state of separation from their neighbors. Jews were not to worship their neighbors' gods, eat their food, or marry their sons or daughters. The Torah implies, further, that the Jews are to avoid formal relationships of social dependency with pagans (unless, biblical books like Ruth seem to suggest, the latter are willing to abandon their gods). Furthermore, the Jews' inner social constitution is meant to be egalitarian and characterized by unconditional corporate solidarity; even among themselves

Jews were supposed to avoid vassalage, clientele, or any relation that institution-alizes social dependency: Israelites are God's vassals, not men's (Leviticus 25.42, 55). Hence the importance of charity (especially Leviticus 25; Deuteronomy 15)—obligatory, ideally anonymous, redistribution of resources benefiting the general corps of the poverty-stricken, intentionally designed to suppress the development of institutionalized individual social dependency (Weinfeld 1995; Hamel 1990). It is this thoroughly utopian ideological complex, as it were, hard-wired into Judaism, that has always generated the peculiar texture of the Jews' problems of integration, both external and internal.

HISTORY AND GEOGRAPHY

From the sixth century BC there was a large and important concentration of Jews living outside what would become the Roman world, in central and southern Mesopotamia, about whom very little is known before late antiquity. But Roman Jewry was probably more numerous and is certainly much better known.

Throughout the Roman imperial period, possibly as late as the Muslim con-quests of the 630s, the main concentration of Jews in the Mediterranean basin and adjacent lands was located in Palestine (surveys: Schürer 1973–87; Horbury et al. 1999; Smallwood 1981; Avi-Yonah 1984). Between 63 BC and the outbreak of the first Jewish revolt against Rome in AD 66, Palestine was ruled in part by native Jewish vassals, first by warring branches of the priestly Hasmonean family, which had assumed power in the second century BC in the wake of the protracted decline of the Seleucid kingdom. In 40 BC the Roman senate named Herod, an aggressive retainer/friend of the Hasmoneans, king, and he soon ruled the entire area west of the Jordan River. After his death, in 4 BC, Palestine (roughly half of whose pop-ulation of, say, 600,000–1,000,000 was Jewish, according to the most responsible guesses; Broshi 1979; McGing 2002) was ruled, in accordance with a complicated and frequently altered set of arrangements, by a prefect or procurator—who was a personal agent of the emperor—together with a member of the Herodian family, the high priest of the Jerusalem temple, and the Roman governor of Syria (Gabba 1999). This period of explosive growth and irrepressible ferment ended with rebel-lion, led at its outbreak in 66 by a loose coterie of charismatic individuals who con-verged on Jerusalem as the Romans re-conquered the non-Judaean districts of the country from late 67 to early 70.

The revolt ended with a disastrous siege of Jerusalem in the spring and sum-mer of 70, culminating in the destruction of the city and its temple, the death by starvation and arms of, certainly, tens of thousands of the besieged (Josephus gives the impossible figure of 1,100,000), and the capture and sale of further tens of thou-sands (Josephus: 97,000). In the aftermath of the revolt, Palestine was 'normalized' as a Roman province, provided with a *legatus Augusti pro praetore* first of praetorian and then of consular rank as the provincial garrison was increased around 120 from one to two legions.

The long-term demographic and economic impact of the failed revolt was surprisingly slight. Such an inference is necessary to explain the outbreak of a massive uprising, led by one Simon bar Kosiba (or Bar Kokhba) only two generations after the end of the first revolt (132–135). Archaeology has done little to refute Cassius Dio's claim that the revolt ended in the decimation of the population of Judaea, and probably of Idumaea as well. Galilee once again escaped serious damage and from 135 until the sixth or seventh century was home to the main concentration of Jews in the Roman world (Baras and Tsafrir 1982–84). It must be emphasized, though, that however many Jews lived in the Roman Empire in the first century (McGing [2002] is properly skeptical), by the middle of the second, after three devastating revolts (see below on the diaspora revolt of 115–117), their numbers were necessarily greatly reduced.

For several centuries the Jews of northern Palestine, now stripped of political and legal autonomy, lived to all appearances as 'normal' Roman subjects, and, after 212, as citizens, concentrated in the territories of the two Galilean cities, Tiberias and Sepphoris, and in the un-urbanized area of Upper Galilee immediately to the north. But in the third, and more conspicuously in the fourth, century, renewed trappings of a specifically Jewish life began to reappear. A so-called patriarch—originally the dynastic leader of the nascent rabbinic movement but by the third century an increasingly powerful, and officially recognized, Jewish grandee—ruled the Jews from his base in Tiberias. Rabbis, scholars of Torah who had received judicial appointment either by the patriarch or by rabbinic elders, began to exert influence—though they did not yet exercise control—over the Jews of northern Palestine. The Christianization of the empire, furthermore, forced the Jews both in Palestine and elsewhere to choose between continued integration at the cost of conversion to Christianity, and continued adherence to Judaism (whose legality, and the authority of whose clergy including the patriarch, was consistently affirmed by the Christian emperors) at the cost of social withdrawal. The consequence was a late antique re-emergence, palpable in both archaeological and literary remains, of a specifically Jewish public life and culture (Schwartz 2001: 179–289). This development was probably abetted by demographic recovery.

DIASPORA

Jews living outside Palestine faced a different set of social problems. Though there were very large communities at Alexandria, Rome, and perhaps Antioch and a few other cities (Corinth, Ephesus, Sardis), most Jews lived in small groups, probably not exclusively in cities. At any rate, rural Jewish communities are attested for Syria, Asia Minor, and especially Egypt. Palestinian Jews were overwhelmingly agrarian, not mercantile (to the extent that the biblical Hebrew word for merchant is the proper noun *kena'ani*, which means 'Phoenician'), so that non-servile emigrants may often have preferred the life of a smallholder, day laborer, or tenant farmer to anything more urban. These were indeed the chief occupations of Jews resident in Hellenistic and early Roman Egypt—the only place for which detailed information is available (Tcherikover, Fuks, and Stern 1957–64; Modrzejewski 1997). However, we cannot know how many diasporic Jews were emigrants from Palestine or their descendants, as opposed to converts to Judaism and *their* descendants.

Whether urban or rural, Jews sometimes were organized as ethnic/religious corporations and tried to claim the right to follow their own laws when these were in conflict with local norms. Though such efforts were often partly successful, they sometimes led to conflict, when city councils tried to compel Jews to participate in the public municipal religion, or in public works or trials conducted on the Jewish Sabbath. Contrary to the recent arguments of Erich Gruen (1998, 2002), Jewish life in the diaspora was far from tension-free, and the rate of attrition from Judaism was probably high in all periods (Bohak 2002, and see below).

In fact, tensions reached a peak in some of the largest diaspora communities in the first century of Roman rule. The Hellenistic rulers of Egypt had regarded Jews, like all immigrants, as 'Hellenes'—subjects who enjoyed privileges native Egyptians lacked—and some Jewish residents of Alexandria concurrently came to regard themselves as citizens. This was no mere legal nicety: both papyrological and literary evidence indicates that many Jews in Egypt eagerly identified with the Greek ruling classes, speaking Greek, using Greek names and even Greek, rather than Jewish, civil law (Modrzejewski 1997). Some Alexandrian Jews, perhaps especially the wealthiest, attained a high level of acculturation: their Torah was written in Greek, not Hebrew, and some few, at least, received thorough Greek educations. Alexandrian Jewish writers like Pseudo-Aristeas (second-first century BC) and Philo (d. ca. AD 50) were the earliest and are still among the most compelling theorists of Jewish life in the diaspora, whose work deserves to be read alongside Maimonides's *Guide to the Perplexed* (published in Fustat, Egypt, 1200) and Moses Mendelssohn's *Jerusalem* (Berlin, 1783). Both Alexandrians argued in effect that the Jews' Torah and the greatest philosophers of the Greeks promoted the same ideals—a fact that for them justified the Jews' continued devotion to some aspects of their peculiar lifestyle (Pseudo-Aristeas and Philo both downplayed the Jews' particularism).

These integrationist elites came under increasing pressure when Egypt came under Roman rule, both from local 'Greeks' and from the Roman state. A period of rioting that had begun in Alexandria in AD 38 ended in 41 with a crushing defeat for the Jews when the emperor Claudius declared that though the Alexandrian Jews had the right to follow their own laws without disturbance, they were not citizens of Alexandria, and (probably) that they were henceforth to be placed in the same legal category as native Egyptians (Barclay 1996; Schäfer 1997; Gruen 2004). When the Palestinian Jews rebelled in 66, some Jews tried to foment a rebellion in Alexandria, and possibly in some cities of Syria. In 115, under circumstances that are very poorly understood, a massive disturbance erupted among the Jews in Egypt, which apparently was both a war against the Greeks and a rebellion against the state. The rising spread to other North African cities, and to Crete and Cyprus. Little is known about this rebellion, but it is surely striking that, henceforth, identifiable Jews virtually disappear from the papyrological evidence until the end of the third century (Pucci 1981; Goodman 2004). The maximalist view, that Jewish life in Egypt and elsewhere was largely destroyed in the wake of the revolt, is not implausible.

The Jewish life that gradually re-emerged in the late antique Roman diaspora (fourth–sixth centuries) is known mainly from scattered brief references in literary texts and from archaeological remains, also scattered, so little can be said about it with any certainty. It may be fair to conclude that there was never again until the rise of Islam a counterpart to the Jewry of early imperial Alexandria, either in terms of size, or of political or cultural ambitions. To be sure, late antique Rome was home to at least eleven synagogues (a word that may, in epigraphical texts, refer to communities/congregations rather than buildings), and Jews in Sardis, Aphrodisias, Antioch, and Apamea built large and conspicuous synagogue structures, and counted some prominent citizens among their members and supporters (Levine 2005: 250–309). Clearly Jews in such places had learned to cope in an environment, first pagan and then Christian, that was by no means invariably friendly. In John Chrysostom's Antioch (AD 386–96) the Jews celebrated their festivals exactly as pagans and Christians did, with lively processions in the city's forum (Wilken 1983). Probably influential non-Jewish supporters, sometimes known as *theosebeis* (God-worshipers), played a crucial role in furthering the Jews' ambivalent integration (even the rabbis, generally regarded as highly separatist, warned Jews living in mixed settlements to support the gentile poor, celebrate gentile marriages, and mourn the gentile dead, "because of the ways of peace"—in other words, to win not converts but friends; Schwartz 2005). But the only places where we have tolerably reliable evidence that late antique Jews played leading roles in civic life are tiny settlements like Venusia in southern Italy (Williams 1999a) and Magona in the Balearics (Bradbury 1996).

SOCIAL RELATIONS IN ROMAN PALESTINE: 63 BC TO AD 70

As indicated above, the bulk of scholarship on Jewish society and culture in the first century has been produced by people who by training and inclination are theologians or New Testament scholars. Some such work—for example, the vast library of 'social scientific readings' of the New Testament—is outside the purview of this chapter. Of what remains in this category, the most important and influential single book is surely by Sanders (1992), which, though not self-consciously a social history is, as its sub-title indicates, heavily concerned with a core social-historical and social-anthropological problem, the relation between ideology and praxis (these are not terms whose use Sanders himself would be likely to endorse). I shall have more to say about Sanders below.

Of scholarship that is more self-consciously social-historical, most has the advantages and disadvantages of immersion in archaeological and exegetical detail—the main disadvantage being parochialism. For many such scholars the most important development of recent years has been the excavation at Sepphoris, in southwestern Galilee, of extensive Roman-period remains. This, together with a meticulous, but in economic-historical terms inconclusive, analysis of the diffusion of locally produced Galilean pottery (Adan-Bayewitz 1993), has led many to bizarre conclusions about the wealth, cosmopolitanism, and sophistication of the Galilee of Jesus' youth (Nazareth is six kilometers from Sepphoris)—neglecting the fact that Sepphoris was a mere village during Jesus' childhood, and that even at its late imperial height it was no metropolitan center but one of many hundreds of small Roman towns in the Eastern Empire (Chancey [2002] surveys this scholarship with refreshing skepticism; cf. Udoh 2005). Others remain committed to a vision of Galilee as a rural idyll, in which the egalitarian ethos preached in the Gospels was lived out on the soil (Edwards and McCollough 1997; it is not easy to see how such a view could survive a reading of Josephus's autobiography). The best of this sort of work (Freyne 1980; Horsley 1996; Horsley and Hanson 1985) must be taken seriously, though it is still hard to avoid the sense that it is too positivistic, that Galilee is so small and poorly attested a region that its history can be reconstructed only episodically and with great uncertainty. Surely it cannot reward the attention that scholars continue to pay to it.

GOODMAN

In attempting to explain the initial failure of Roman rule in Palestine, Martin Goodman (1987)—probably the first Jewish historian to absorb and exploit the assumptions and methods of Finleyite ancient social and economic history—produced an account that constituted a quantum leap forward from such formerly standard works as the naively positivistic and unsophisticated Jeremias (1969). I will therefore use an analysis of Goodman's work as a way of surveying the topic as a whole.

For Goodman, Roman rule empowered groups of Jews, especially members of the Herodian family and leading priests of the Jerusalem temple, whose rise generated a social and economic crisis. They, and the temple they controlled, accumulated vast quantities of wealth in a way that tended to push Judaean smallholders off their land and into lives of debt, penury, and brigandage. The Jews lacked the practices of rural patronage and urban euergetism, which might have provided a measure of social stability for some farmers and artisans, and instead practiced charity, which kept the poor alive, numerous, unhappy, and socially unmoored.

Goodman's more or less explicit intention was to rescue first century Judaea from theologians, by 'normalizing' the Jews as Roman subjects. He tried to demonstrate that there was no essential misfit between Judaism and Roman rule, only an accidental crisis generated primarily by the Romans' improvident promotion of Jewish *novi homines* (Pastor [1997] writes critically of Goodman but adopts a highly simplified version of his argument).

However, if we read Goodman's Judaean provincial history in the context of precisely the sort of Finleyite social history he sought to embrace (especially Saller 1982; Wallace-Hadrill 1989; Avidov 1996), his Judaeans seem far less normal, and have much more in common with the theologians' Jews, than he supposed (as he practically concedes, 1987: 97–108). This is because in Goodman's view (though not in his language), the only thing actually integrating the Judaeans was ideology—a shared devotion to the Jerusalem temple and to the Torah. They had no networks of social dependency, reciprocity having given way to the contract as the basis of exchange (cf. Mauss 1990, originally published in 1924—as if these were mutually exclusive; see Bloch and Parry 1989), and patronage to charity. If all states are in some measure imagined communities (Anderson 1991), Judaea, with its over-centralized economy but fundamental lack of materially based social cohesion, constituted a community far more imagined than most. In fact, it proved to be remarkably fragile, shattering under Roman pressure into competing little groups of extremists, since religious sectarianism and ideological extremism offered the only realistic forms of social cohesion available. Goodman's account, then, explores the dark, dysfunctional side of the Pentateuch's utopian legislation.

In arguing for the Jews' normality as Roman subjects, Goodman paradoxically greatly over-stated their abnormality (cf. especially Shaw 1989, partly conceded in Goodman 2002). In particular, much of Goodman's ethnography or religious history proceeds by treating prescriptive texts as descriptive: the Jews' holy books were obsessed with purity, *ergo* real-life Jews were so obsessed; the Torah enjoins charity and disapproves of patronage, so the Jews did, too, and so forth. But this prejudges the crucial and very complex question of the relation between the Jews' core religious ideology and their *culture*—their workaday attitudes, practices and social institutions (see below).

Nevertheless, Goodman's account remains the best sustained treatment available, and parts of it may be salvaged: though he could not explain why, the conditions of the first century *were* unusual because it was only then—in the wake of the Hasmoneans' Judaization of Palestine, and due to the relative ease and safety of travel caused by the Roman pacification of the Mediterranean basin, and due also to Herod's massive reconstruction of the Jerusalem temple, and construction of a grand Mediterranean port at Caesarea Maritima (Richardson 1996; Raban and Holum 1996)—that Jerusalem and its temple became massive silver magnets, courtesy in part of a greatly expanded pilgrimage trade. This, in turn, is indeed likely to have made life more difficult for small farmers, because rising wealth in

Jerusalem led inexorably to rising land prices in its Judaean hinterland, which in their turn rendered traditional grain, olive, and grape farming unprofitable and so unsustainable. There is indeed relatively little evidence for the diffusion of patronage in Judaea (as opposed to Galilee: Schwartz 1994), though it must be said that there is even less evidence for charitable institutions (for euergetism the evidence is abundant, but it took a highly distinctive form: Schwartz 2008; Judaean patronage requires further study). Though Goodman himself provides extensive evidence that many Judaeans had conventionally Graeco-Roman attitudes to power and to political alliances (1987: 198–227; cf. Shaw 1993), divisive ideological extremism certainly was unusually important. In sum, whatever their relation to the Revolt of 66, there is good reason to believe that economic and social conditions in first century Judaea were unusually unstable: the district was massively richer and apparently far more populous than ever before, but the benefits of this new situation were highly unequally distributed, a state perhaps not meaningfully mitigated by such compensatory redistributive institutions as may have existed.

SANDERS

Ed P. Sanders has spent his long career investigating the Jewish context of the careers and teachings of Jesus and Paul. What distinguishes him from most other scholars of primarily theological orientation is the thoroughness and untendentiousness of his immersion in his topic, his interest not just in religious ideas but in practice, his sophisticated approach to his sources (in particular his admirable caution when confronting rabbinic literature), and his avoidance of crude and deterministic deployment of imperfectly comprehended sociological models (cf. Saldarini 1988, using Lenski 1966, and Horsley 2004, using Scott 1990, to mention only the best work of this type).

The massive Sanders 1992 is perhaps his most important work, and has certainly been his most influential. In this book Sanders tried to recover what he called 'common Judaism,' the religious system of the mass of non-elite first-century Jews, especially those who did not join a sect. He argues that the fundamental element of this system was 'covenantal nomism'—the notion that Pentateuchal laws must be observed because the Jews had an enduring, as it were contractual, agreement with their God to do so. The bulk of the work is devoted to an exploration of the practical implications of covenantal nomism, an inquiry complicated by the fact that no pre-rabbinic text directly confronts the issue, that the evidence, both literary and archaeological, tends to be suggestive rather than probative (for example, was the great first-century Judaean limestone vessel industry generated by the Jews' concern with ritual purity—Deines 1993–or by the ubiquity of limestone in Judaea and the development of the technical means to work it quickly and cheaply?), and by the apparent absence of any single centralized interpretive authority. The result, in effect an ethnography of first-century Jews, was impressive, though debatable in many details; like Goodman, Sanders sometimes moves too easily from prescription to description.

But as an ethnography, Sanders' account raises serious questions. Sanders seems tacitly to have assumed that Judaism was co-extensive with the *culture* of the Jews. Since his sources provided little realistic information about land tenure, kinship groups, non-kinship-based social institutions except for sects, the agrarian economy, or indeed about the sorts of popular or agrarian semi-religious praxis Redfield 1960 called "the little tradition" (Sanders neglected apocalypticism, since he regarded it as the province of sectarian groups, and, more problematically, its disreputable cousin magic), Sanders barely mentioned them, thereby implying that they were of little significance for the Jews. As a result, for all its richness and complexity, his account of 'common' Jews seems to some extent idealizing. Like Goodman's Judaeans, Sanders' Jews are bound together only by their Judaism, though unlike Goodman, Sanders provides much compelling detail about the powerful sense of community this could sometimes entail, for example, during pilgrimage festivals. Sanders' Jewish society is thus far more functional than Goodman's and, though perhaps unrealistic in its optimism, is still, due to its profusion of detail, a bit more realistically described (except inasmuch as Sanders did not consider the impact of Roman rule on the Jews).

BAUMGARTEN

Albert Baumgarten (1997) provided an account of Jewish sectarianism that was to some extent complementary to Sanders' account of non-sectarian Judaism. He began by supposing that the most effective way of making sense of the profusion of religious sects in ancient Palestine might be through comparison-fueled structural functionalism (the notion that societies can be understood as functioning organisms, whose features can, in a rough and often complicated way, be best understood in relation to each other). Baumgarten argued that seventeenth-century England provided a useful comparandum to ancient Palestine: in particular, ancient like early modern sectarians tended to come from relatively well-to-do though normally non-aristocratic backgrounds; although sectarian ideologies were often rigoristic and totalizing, the organizations were highly porous, and many individuals belonged serially to several different groups; because the sects offered similar products to more or less a single group of consumers, they tended to generate and to place great emphasis on 'small differences'; the sects tended to have strongly dualistic theologies, and to embrace millenarianism, but in both England and Palestine this was the result not of the desperation of the members, but of their 'cognitive dissonance'—in other words, their small-scale dissatisfactions. Baumgarten carried the argument further: Jewish sectarianism was not only phenomenologically but genetically similar to English sectarianism. It too was a product of demographic and economic growth, rising literacy rates, and galloping urbanization, all of which destabilized traditional social arrangements and contributed to a sense of dislocation especially among the relatively well off (Baumgarten did not explain what those traditional arrangements had consisted of in Palestine).

Baumgarten's work was partly successful. His promotion of comparison and of an eclectic approach to sociology and social anthropology both served as important correctives to almost all other scholarship in the field. The phenomenological portion of his account is especially important in convincingly refuting the naïve Marxizing views commonplace among scholars of Jewish sectarianism: that apocalypticism was a product of poverty and oppression, sectarians were marginal and persecuted extremists reacting to foreign—or to profoundly corrupt native Jewish—rule, and so on. But his genetics of sectarianism must be regarded as a failure, partly because of insufficiently cautious use of comparative material. In fact, at no time in antiquity did Palestine experience the sort of exponential growth that occurred in England in the seventeenth and eighteenth centuries, certainly not in the second century BC, which is when Baumgarten dated it. It did, however, experience limited growth in the first century—the date of most of Baumgarten's evidence!—for reasons explored above, and this may be relevant to the history of sectarianism in ways that remain to be clarified (a very preliminary attempt: Schwartz 2001). Furthermore, Baumgarten's early dating of the rise of sectarianism freed him from the need to consider the impact of Roman rule, another issue awaiting clarification.

PALESTINE AFTER THE REVOLTS

There is a substantial corpus of social and economic historiography concerning the Jews in post-70 Palestine, much of which suffers from the same deficiencies, *mutatis mutandis*, as New Testament social and economic history—problematic immersion in a single literary source (in this case, rabbinic literature), and a pervasive parochialism and lack of verisimilitude. There are exceptions, distinguished by a more cautious approach to the rabbinic texts, a better grasp of Roman history, and a higher level of theoretical self-consciousness: once again Martin Goodman (1983) is prominent among them, followed by Hezser (1997), and Lapin (2001). But such scholarship, because of its cautious skepticism, must confront the fact that evidence for social and economic conditions in second through seventh century Palestine is poor, and that its results must inevitably be very limited, though there is surely room for further progress. Since I have provided a detailed account of these issues in Schwartz 2002, I will say no more about them here.

DIASPORA: PROBLEMS OF EVIDENCE

While the evidence for Jewish Palestine, especially in the first century, is rich enough to support a body of plausible social historical speculation, evidence for Jewish life in the diaspora is highly fragmentary. Indeed, there is a still more fundamental problem that has received insufficient attention. Outside Palestine, and the exceptional diasporic environment of early Roman Alexandria, the Jews lived in scattered, small, and, one must suppose, highly unstable groups. All Jewish communities necessarily experienced attrition: individuals, groups, or even entire communities lost all sense of separate identity and merged into their pagan environments.[1] The few such individuals mentioned in literary sources—Tiberius Julius Alexander, scion of the leading Jewish family of Alexandria, who enjoyed the most distinguished career available to a Roman knight, as prefect of Egypt in 66, and of the praetorian cohorts under Vespasian (Etienne 2000); and the descendants of the Hasmonean-Herodian prince Alexander and the Cappadocian princess Glaphyra who served first as eastern client kings and then as Roman senators—were almost by definition atypical.[2] And only very rarely can such people be detected in epigraphical or papyrological remains—Niketas, the mid-Hellenistic period 'Hierosolymite' (Jerusalemite) donor to the Dionysia at Iasos (Ameling 2004, no. 21), the enigmatic "former Jews" (Judaeans?—"oi pote Ioudaioi") who nevertheless retained a strong enough sense of group cohesion to have made a large joint donation to a municipal festival in second century Smyrna (Ameling 2004, no. 40; cf. Horbury and Noy 1992, nos. 21–22).

Furthermore, among surviving literary artifacts, writing by marginal, or weakly or non-self-identifying Jews is hard to detect. Almost all surviving pre-Christian texts—even if they survive only in fragments—can be assigned unambiguously to either Jews or pagans: there is thus no doubt that Philo, Aristeas (notwithstanding its author's pagan literary persona), Artapanus, and so on are Jewish texts while Diodorus, Plutarch, and Tacitus are not (Jewish and Christian texts cannot always be so neatly distinguished—note, for example, the debate over *Joseph and Aseneth*; Bohak 1996; Kraemer 1998). Texts by ambiguous, radically non-normative, or lapsed Jews are unknown (outside the New Testament) and if they existed probably could not be identified.

What this all implies is that evidence for diaspora Judaism misleadingly concerns the Jewish hard-core, the most strongly self-identified members of Jewish

---

1. On the opposite process, pagans slipping into Judaism, see, e.g., Barclay (1996: 310–19); Goodman (1994). However much notice this attracted from disapproving Roman writers, its demographic significance cannot be assessed; it is at any rate *a priori* unlikely to have outweighed attrition from Judaism.

2. Very occasionally a writer gives us a glimpse of large, less aristocratic, groups of lapsed Jews—Suet. *Dom.* 12. 2. The conversion of Jewish individuals and groups to Christianity in the late empire is relatively well attested—for a well-known, though not necessarily accurately reported, case, see Bradbury (1996).

religious corporations or communities, and not Jews who failed to leave recogniz-able material evidence of their Jewishness, either because they lived outside com-munal frameworks, or were weakly self-identified, or practiced varieties of Judaism we cannot easily recognize as such, or concealed their Jewishness, or abandoned it. Furthermore, scholars tend to conflate evidence for diasporic Judaism, which is in fact scattered both temporally and geographically. It is, for example, possi-ble to produce a history of the Jews of Graeco-Roman Egypt (e.g., Modrzejewski 1997); but the illusion of continuity created thereby elides the fact that for many communities—like those of Athribis or Xenephyris (Horbury and Noy 1992, nos. 24, 27–28)—we have only one or two items of evidence apiece, and so we cannot know whether their strategies of corporate survival were actually successful or not (Bohak 2002). By neglecting such problems, historians have produced an account of Jewish life in the diaspora that is far too static and normative, one might say far too optimistic. In reality, it is overwhelmingly likely that in many periods it had (like most Jewish life in better attested periods) a much more volatile and improvisatory character than the standard literature suggests.

While very few accounts engage seriously with such concerns, the Roman diaspora, even outside the larger Egyptian settlements, is not completely resistant to investigation, most successful when either highly localized and non-generalizing, or alternatively—since wherever self-defining Jews lived in the Roman Empire, includ-ing much of Palestine, they confronted broadly similar pressures—conducted at a very high level of abstraction (though this is rarely done in a responsible way).

EGYPT

Not unexpectedly, early imperial Egypt has been most extensively discussed, and has proved most controversial. But, as for Palestine, social history in the strict sense has been largely neglected—papyrological evidence for Jews in Egypt is far richer for the Hellenistic period. Instead, scholars have concentrated on the relatively well-attested period of rioting and rebellion that began in 38 and ended crushingly in 117. The debate about the background of the events of 38 and 41 has profound social historical implications since it immediately concerns the question of inte-gration. According to the view that has enjoyed something like consensual sup-port since Tcherikover 1945 (and cf. Tcherikover, Fuks, and Stern 1957–64), the masses of the Jews in both Alexandria and the Egyptian countryside had long since adapted to the cultural norms of the privileged Greek minority, and not those of the native Egyptian majority; concurrently, they sought political identification with the Greeks, in the form of 'Hellenic' status in the countryside and citizenship in Alexandria, while continuing to retain some measure of religious and social separa-tion (contrast Kasher 1985). The best known representative of this position was the Alexandrian philosopher Philo—a wealthy man who was profoundly well educated in Greek literature and philosophy, and participated enthusiastically in most of his city's civic and cultural activities, yet remained a pious Jew who dedicated his life to the study and philosophical explication of the Torah, and to the defense of the religious and political interests of his community (Barclay 1996: 158–80).

Obviously, few Alexandrians—Greek, Egyptian, or Jewish—were as rich, literate, and well connected as Philo. But it seems not unlikely that many or most Egyptian Jews in broad terms supported his politics of integration and acculturation, at least until the early Roman period. Why this tradition of accommodation quickly failed under Roman rule is less clear: was it deeply ingrained Graeco-Egyptian anti-Semitism (Schäfer 1997), or the result of a set of contingencies not symptomatic of any deeper problem (Gruen 2004) or of disastrous Roman policies that managed to alienate all residents of Egypt—Greek, Egyptian and Jewish—simultaneously, in a way that led both to the flourishing of anti-Roman agitation and to inter-communal violence? Barclay (1996) has argued—in a detailed and generally excellent treatment—that the disturbances of 38 and 41 reflect among other things social divisions within Alexandrian Jewry between wealthy and acculturated integrationists like Philo, and the poor Jewish masses, who were less acculturated and indifferent or opposed to integration. While this may not be completely wrong, it is probably a premature judgment, and is certainly too baldly formulated: many poor Jews were demonstrably as acculturated as Philo, to judge from papyrological evidence, just not as well educated, and some of them may have had a lot to gain from a grant of Alexandrian citizenship. For their part, some wealthier Jews—among them immigrants from Judaea—were conceivably far less acculturated. Perhaps more important, political or religious orientation certainly had no simple relationship to cultural orientation, as Barclay's study itself amply demonstrates.

OUTSIDE EGYPT

For reasons already specified, no substantial large-scale synthesis is possible for the non-Egyptian diaspora, notwithstanding the recent publication of several excellent editions of primary sources, especially inscriptions (Lüderitz 1983; Reynolds and Tannenbaum 1987 [with the revisions and corrections of Chaniotis 2002]; Noy 1993; Ameling 2004, to mention only the most important; note also Pucci Ben-Zeev 1998), and of locally specific syntheses (Trebilco 1991; Rutgers 1995), not to mention scores of more detailed studies (e.g., Rajak 2002; Williams 1994, 1999a, 1999b; van der Horst 1998; Millar 1992, 2004). At most, a few not unimportant general points may be regarded as basically established: especially before the fifth and sixth centuries, but to some extent even then, even the most strongly self-identified Jews—in other words, the ones about whom we have some information—were fairly highly acculturated in their Roman environments. For example, all used Greek, and in some places Latin, not only for routine communication (this is admittedly a guess since we have no records of routine communication) but also for liturgical and other religious purposes: until the fifth century there is almost no evidence for Hebrew prayer or Torah study. Inscriptions from Asia Minor, Italy, and elsewhere quote the Septuagint, not a different Greek translation. All synagogue buildings so far discovered use decorative and design elements borrowed from their Roman environments (Levine 2005). Furthermore, by the fourth century, at latest, many Jewish communities used language and practices derived from the widespread urban social institution modern scholars call euergetism (Rajak and Noy 1993). In some places there is evidence for the role that well-to-do gentiles played in the political integration and economic welfare of Jewish communities (e.g., Trebilco 1991; Chaniotis 2002). Finally, there is the peculiar fact that almost all archaeological evidence about these communities comes from the fourth century and later, presumably demonstrating some heightened tendency to Jewish separation (or a shift in modes of political and economic integration) in the Christian Empire (Schwartz 2001; Kalmin and Schwartz 2003).

CONCLUSION

No simple characterization of the Jews' experience in antiquity is adequate. The Jews as discrete national group were unintegrable in the Roman world, a fundamental fact that explains the devastating consequences of the three revolts against the Roman state. Concurrently, some Jews gradually developed a social institution, the local religious community, which fostered limited acculturation but also enabled moderate separatism. Even this did not completely defuse the tensions in some respects inherent in the relations between Judaism and Rome's relative interventionism. Nevertheless, the local community did sometimes work, especially in the later empire, since Christian emperors were inclined to treat the Jews as members of a separate, inferior but legitimate, religious community/church. It was in this decentralized form that the Jews were subsequently incorporated into the kingdoms of Rome's Christian and Muslim successor states.

SUGGESTED READING

The best treatments of ancient Jewish social relations and of the Jews' problematic integration in their ancient environments are Goodman 1987; Shaw 1989 and 1993, who provides an important corrective to Goodman on many points; Sanders 1992; and Baumgarten 1997. The only large-scale treatment of the latter topic for the post-70 period is Schwartz 2001.

BIBLIOGRAPHY

Adan-Bayewitz, D. 1993. *Common Pottery in Roman Galilee: A Study of Local Trade*. Ramat-Gan: Bar-Ilan University Press.

Ameling, W. 2004. *Inscriptiones Judaicae Orientis, Vol. 2: Kleinasien*. Tübingen: Mohr Siebeck.

Anderson, B. 1991. *Imagined Communities: Reflections on the Origins and Spread of Nationalism*. 2nd ed. London: Verso.

Avidov, A. 1996. *Processes of Marginalization in the Roman Empire*. PhD Thesis, Cambridge University.

Avi-Yonah, M. 1984. *The Jews under Roman and Byzantine Rule: A Political History of Palestine from the Bar Kokhba War to the Arab Conquest*. New York: Schocken Books.

Baras, Ts., and Y. Tsafrir. 1982–84. *Eretz Israel from the Destruction of the Second Temple to the Muslim Conquest*, 2 vols. Jerusalem: Izhak Ben-Zvi Institute.

Barclay, J. 1996. *Jews in the Mediterranean Diaspora from Alexander to Trajan (323 BCE–117 CE)*. Edinburgh: T. & T. Clark.

Baumgarten, A. 1997. *The Flourishing of Jewish Sects in the Maccabean Era: An Interpretation*. Leiden: E. J. Brill.

Bloch, M., and J. Parry (eds.). 1989. *Money and the Morality of Exchange*. Cambridge: Cambridge University Press.

Bohak, G. 1996. *"Joseph and Aseneth" and the Jewish Temple in Heliopolis*. Atlanta: Scholars Press.

———. 2002. "Ethnic Continuity in the Jewish Diaspora in Antiquity." In J. Bartlett (ed.), *Jews in the Hellenistic and Roman Cities*. London: Routledge. 175–92.

Bradbury, S. 1996. *Severus of Minorca: Letter on the Conversion of the Jews*. Oxford: Oxford University Press.

Broshi, M. 1979. "The Population of Western Palestine in the Roman-Byzantine Period." *Bulletin of the American Society of Oriental Research* 236: 1–10.

Chancey, M. 2002. *The Myth of a Gentile Galilee*. Cambridge: Cambridge University Press.

Chaniotis, A. 2002. "The Jews of Aphrodisias: New Evidence and Old Problems." *Scripta Classica Israelica* 21: 209–42.

Deines, R. 1993. *Jüdische Steingefässe und pharisäische Frömmigkeit: ein archäologisch-historischer Beitrag zum Verständnis von Joh 2.6 und der jüdischen Reinheitshalacha zur Zeit Jesu*. Tübingen: Mohr Siebeck.

Edwards, D., and C. McCollough (eds.). 1997. *Archaeology and the Galilee: Texts and Contexts in the Greco-Roman and Byzantine Periods*. Atlanta: Scholars Press.

Etienne, S. 2000. "Reflexion sur l'apostasie de Tibérius Julius Alexander." *Studia Philonica Annual* 12: 122–42.

Freyne, S. 1980. *Galilee from Alexander the Great to Hadrian, 323 BCE to 135 CE: A Study of Second Temple Judaism*. Wilmington: University of Notre Dame Press.

Gabba, E. 1999. "The Social, Economic and Political History of Palestine 63 BCE–CE 70." In Horbury et al. 1999: 94–167.

Goodman, M. 1983. *State and Society in Roman Galilee*. Totowa, N.J.: Rowman and Allanheld.

———. 1987. *The Ruling Class of Judaea: The Origins of the Jewish Revolt against Rome, AD 66–70*. Cambridge: Cambridge University Press.

———. 1994. *Mission and Conversion: Proselytizing in the Religious History of the Roman Empire*. Oxford: Clarendon Press.

———. 2002. "Current Scholarship on the First Revolt." In A. Berlin and J. A. Overman (eds.), *The First Jewish Revolt: Archaeology, History and Ideology*. London: Routledge. 15–25.

———. 2004. "Trajan and the Origins of Roman Hostility to the Jews." *Past & Present* 182: 3–29.

Gruen, E. 1998. *Heritage and Hellenism: The Reinvention of Jewish Tradition*. Berkeley: University of California Press.

———. 2004. *Diaspora: Jews amidst Greeks and Romans*. Cambridge, Mass.: Harvard University Press.

Hamel, G. 1990. *Poverty and Charity in Roman Palestine, First Three Centuries CE*. Berkeley: University of California Press.

Hezser, C. 1997. *The Social Structure of the Rabbinic Movement in Roman Palestine*. Tübingen: Mohr Siebeck.

Horbury, W., et al. (eds.). 1999. *The Cambridge History of Judaism. Volume Three. The Early Roman Period*. Cambridge: Cambridge University Press.

Horbury, W., and D. Noy. 1992. *Jewish Inscriptions of Graeco-Roman Egypt*. Cambridge: Cambridge University Press.

Horsley, R. 1996. *Archaeology, History and Society in Galilee: The Social Context of Jesus and the Rabbis*. Valley Forge: Trinity Press.

———. (ed.). 2004. *Hidden Transcripts and the Arts of Resistance: Applying the Work of James C. Scott to Jesus and Paul*. Atlanta: Society of Biblical Literature.

Horsley, R., and J. Hanson. 1985. *Bandits, Prophets, and Messiahs: Popular Movements in the Time of Jesus*. Minneapolis: Continuum International.

Jeremias, J. 1969. *Jerusalem in the Time of Jesus: An Investigation into Economic and Social Conditions during the New Testament Period*. Philadelphia: Fortress Press.

Kalmin, R., and Schwartz, S. (eds.). 2003. *Jewish Culture and Society in the Christian Roman Empire*. Leuven: Peeters.

Kasher, A. 1985. *The Jews in Hellenistic and Roman Egypt: The Struggle for Equal Rights*. Tübingen: Mohr Siebeck.

Kraemer, R. 1998. *When Aseneth Met Joseph: A Late Antique Tale of the Biblical Patriarch and His Egyptian Wife, Reconsidered*. Oxford: Oxford University Press.

Lapin, H. 2001. *Economy, Geography, and Provincial History in Late Roman Palestine*. Tübingen: Mohr Siebeck.

Lenski, G. 1966. *Power and Privilege: A Theory of Social Stratification*. New York: McGraw-Hill.

Levine, L. 2005. *The Ancient Synagogue: The First Thousand Years*. 2nd ed. New Haven: Yale University Press.

Lüderitz, G. 1983. *Corpus jüdischer Zeugnisse aus der Cyrenaika*. Wiesbaden: Reichert.

Mauss, M. 1990. *Gift: The Form and Reason for Exchange in Archaic Societies*. Trans. W. Halls. London: Routledge.

McGing, B. 2002. "Population and Proselytism: How Many Jews Were There in the Ancient World?" In J. Bartlett (ed.), *Jews in the Hellenistic and Roman Cities*. London: Routledge. 88–106.

Millar, F. 1992. "The Jews of the Graeco-Roman Diaspora between Paganism and Christianity." In J. Lieu, J. North, and T. Rajak (eds.), *The Jews among Pagans and Christians in the Roman Empire*. London: Routledge. 97–123.

———. 2004. "Christian Emperors, Christian Church and the Jews of the Diaspora in the Greek East, CE 379–450." *Journal of Jewish Studies* 55: 1–24.

Modrzejewski, J. 1997. *The Jews of Egypt from Rameses II to Emperor Hadrian*. Princeton: Princeton University Press.

Noy, D. 1993. *Jewish Inscriptions of Western Europe*. 2 vols. Cambridge: Cambridge University Press.

Pastor, J. 1997. *Land and Economy in Ancient Palestine*. London: Routledge.

Pucci, M. 1981. *Rivolta ebraica al tempo di Traiano*. Pisa: Giardini Editori.

Pucci Ben-Zeev, M. 1998. *Jewish Rights in the Roman World: The Greek and Roman Documents Quoted by Flavius Josephus*. Tübingen: Mohr Siebeck.

Raban, A., and K. Holum (eds.). 1996. *Caesarea Maritima: A Retrospective after Two Millennia*. Leiden: E. J. Brill.

Rajak, T., and D. Noy. 1993. "Archisynagogoi: Office, Title, and Social Status in the Greco-Jewish Synagogue." *Journal of Roman Studies* 83: 75–93.

Rajak, T. 2002. *The Jewish Dialogue with Greece and Rome: Studies in Cultural and Social Interaction*. Leiden: E. J. Brill.

Redfield, R. 1960. *The Little Community, and Peasant Society and Culture*. Chicago: University of Chicago Press.

Reynolds, J., and R. Tannenbaum. 1987. *Jews and God-Fearers at Aphrodisias: Greek Inscriptions with Commentary*. Cambridge: Cambridge Philological Society.

Richardson, P. 1996. *Herod: King of the Jews and Friend of the Romans*. Columbia: Continuum International.

Rutgers, L. 1995. *The Jews in Late Ancient Rome: Evidence of Cultural Interaction in the Roman Diaspora*. Leiden: E. J. Brill.

Saldarini, A. 1988. *Pharisees, Scribes and Sadducees in Palestinian Society: A Sociological Approach*. Wilmington: Wm. B. Eerdmans.

Saller, R. 1982. *Personal Patronage under the Early Empire*. Cambridge: Cambridge University Press.

Sanders, E. P. 1992. *Judaism: Practice and Belief, 63 BCE–66CE*. Philadelphia: Trinity Press.

Schäfer, P. 1997. *Judaeophobia: Attitudes toward the Jews in the Ancient World*. Cambridge: Harvard University Press.

Schürer, E. 1973–87. *History of the Jewish People in the Age of Jesus Christ (175 BC–AD 135)*. 3 vols. (rev. and ed. by G. Vermes, F. Millar, et al.). Edinburgh: T. & T. Clark.

Schwartz, S. 1994. "Josephus in Galilee: Rural Patronage and Social Breakdown." In F. Parente and J. Sievers (eds.). *Josephus and the History of the Greco-Roman Period: Essays in Memory of Morton Smith*. Leiden: E. J. Brill. 290–306.

———. 2001. *Imperialism and Jewish Society from 200 BCE to 640 CE*. Princeton: Princeton University Press.

———. 2002. "Historiography on the Jews in the 'Talmudic Period,' 70–640 CE." In M. Goodman (ed.), *Oxford Handbook of Jewish Studies*. Oxford: Oxford University Press. 79–114.

———. 2005. "Roman Historians and the Rise of Christianity: The School of Edward Gibbon." In W. V. Harris (ed.), *The Spread of Christianity in the First Four Centuries: Essays in Explanation*. Leiden: E. J. Brill. 145–60.

———. 2008. "Euergetism in Josephus and the Epigraphical Culture of First Century Jerusalem." In H. Cotton et al. (eds.). *From Hellenism to Islam: Cultural and Linguistic Change in the Roman Near East*. Cambridge: Cambridge University Press. 75–92.

Scott, J. 1990. *Domination and the Arts of Resistance: Hidden Transcripts*. New Haven: Yale University Press.

Shaw, B. 1989. Review of Goodman. *Journal of Roman Studies* 79: 246–47.

————. 1993. "Tyrants, Bandits and Kings: Personal Power in Josephus." *Journal of Jewish Studies* 44: 176–204.

Smallwood, E. M. 1981. *The Jews under Roman Rule from Pompey to Diocletian: A Study in Political Relations*. Leiden: E. J. Brill.

Tcherikover, V. 1945. *The Jews in Egypt in the Hellenistic-Roman Age in the Light of the Papyri*. Jerusalem: Hebrew University Press (in Hebrew).

Tcherikover, V., A. Fuks, and M. Stern (eds.). 1957–64. *Corpus Papyrorum Judaicarum*. 3 vols. Cambridge, Mass.: Harvard University Press.

Trebilco, P. 1991. *Jewish Communities in Asia Minor*. Cambridge: Cambridge University Press.

Udoh, F. 2005. *To Caesar What Is Caesar's: Tribute, Taxes, and Imperial Administration in Early Roman Palestine, 63 BCE–70 CE*. Providence: Brown Judaic Studies.

van der Horst, P. 1998. *Hellenism, Judaism, Christianity: Essays on their Interaction*. Leuven: Peeters.

Wallace-Hadrill, A. (ed.). 1989. *Patronage in Ancient Society*. London: Routledge.

Weinfeld, M. 1995. *Social Justice in Ancient Israel and the Ancient Near East*. Minneapolis: Fortress Press.

Wilken, R. 1983. *John Chrysostom and the Jews: Rhetoric and Reality in the Late Fourth Century*. Berkeley: University of California Press.

Williams, M. 1994. "The Jews of Corycus—a Neglected Diasporan Community from Roman Times." *Journal for the Study of Judaism* 25: 274–86.

————. 1999a. "The Jews of Early Byzantine Venusia: The Family of Faustinus I, the Father." *Journal of Jewish Studies* 50: 38–52.

————. 1999b. "The Contribution of Jewish Inscriptions to the Study of Judaism." In Horbury et al. 1999: 75–93.

CHAPTER 27

CHRISTIAN SOCIETY

ADAM H. BECKER

Introduction

In Carthage, in AD 203—according to a document, part of which purports to be a first-hand account by the subject herself—a young woman who had recently given birth shamed her father by rejecting his pleas that she acquiesce to Roman authority and the Roman gods, and willingly allowed herself to be mauled to death by a cow. The account of this event is one of the more famous early Christian documents, and the martyr, Perpetua, has become decidedly popular in recent years among historians, as well as within certain contemporary Christian circles.[1] The *Martyrdom of Perpetua and Felicitas*, extant in both Latin and Greek versions, is one of several martyrological texts deriving from pre-Constantinian Christianity. In this text, we discern a social sub-group with new forms of commitment rejecting traditional notions of family and civic belonging in its calls for allegiance to the group and its God. Closer analysis of this text also shows that the members of this particular Christian group were Montanists—that is, they belonged to a movement that continued to engage in the practice of prophesying long after it had ended in the rest of the church. On account of this, Montanism was condemned by many at the time, and was eventually eradicated. In other words, Perpetua and her comrades were a sub-group within a sub-group.

Despite these idiosyncrasies, the growth of the Christian community at Carthage may be set within the on-going religious history of Roman North Africa,

---

1. See, for example, the recent scholarly conference "Perpetua's Passions: Pluridisciplinary Approaches to the Passio Perpetuae et Felicitatis (3rd century AD)," Sonderforschungsbereich: Transformationen der Antike, July 9–11, 2007, Humboldt-Universität, Berlin. There are a number of contemporary Christian uses of this text, including a church play based upon it. For a full-length historical study, see Salisbury 1997.

and may be perceived as the conclusion to a long-developing process (Rives 1995: 173–249). Furthermore, this text depicting resistance to temporal power serves as an example of how Christians engaged in an intensification, to the point of inversion, of contemporary discourses on gender, the body, and power (Shaw 1996). A text such as the *Martyrdom of Perpetua* demonstrates, in other words, how early Christians were part of the broader ancient world, while at the same time understanding themselves, especially in the pre-Constantinian period, as positioned directly against it.

Now, looking at Christianity within Graeco-Roman society raises the same questions asked in the historical analysis of any innovative social movement, for example, how new was it? How different? And this line of questioning corresponds with a further question: How socially integrated were the Christians within ancient society? To talk of 'Christian social relations' or 'Christian society' is to suggest that this was a group distinct from the wider community of the Mediterranean basin at the time. To be sure, Christians had a specific ideology of, and particular modes of interacting with, the non-Christian world, but in emphasizing Christian social relations, we must not lose sight of how thoroughly integrated Christians were within the Roman Empire (at least most of the time, and in most places). Indeed, the success of Christianity at spreading, and at convincing non-Christians that the new message was relevant, and that the new believers were a group worth associating with, points to the Christians' proximity to the larger society, both ideologically and in quotidian practice.

It is also the case that, while early Christian literature was composed for the Christian community, the participation in common public rhetorical strategies and the use of a standard philosophical *koine* in this literature suggests that the Christian community, as a whole, and despite its own self-perception—which has historically misled scholars—was integrated into the broader social world of the Roman Empire. Like Jews, most early Christians would probably not have stood out within the social, economic, and cultural diversity of the Roman Empire; and in fact, their literature reflects precisely this integration of the individuals themselves. Thus, even those texts that seem so clearly to reject Graeco-Roman norms, such as the second- and third-century Apocryphal Acts, attest to, for example, a world of shared notions of family, as well as some common masculine anxieties (Cooper 1996).

Furthermore, the social composition of this religious movement was varied. To be sure, the earliest Christians did not belong to the broader society's aristocracy, but nor were they generally from among the lowest echelons of society, such as landless peasants, or the class of oppressed slaves, who worked in agriculture. In fact, Christianity functioned to confound class boundaries, and may even have brought people together in new ways. Wayne Meeks has suggested that the Pauline churches may be characterized by a mixing of status, and by instances of status inconsistency; one thinks, for example, of the rich freedmen who were prominent in these communities (Meeks 2003: 51–73). Nor should we lose sight of the fact that Christians would have belonged to many of the social categories addressed in this volume. Despite the rhetoric, then, membership within the *ecclesia* did not necessarily exclude one from other social groupings, including, as we shall see, the synagogue.

Still, while individual Christians might well have seemed like perfectly normal members of the wider society, the Christian community itself constituted a social group with a markedly new kind of commitment. This innovative social bond was not quite like the one we find in Judaism, nor, for example, was it comparable with the affiliations established in and by the voluntary associations (*collegia*) of antiquity—or at least, this is the picture we have from the Christians' highly ideological texts, which constitute the overwhelming majority of our extant sources. In fact, one could argue that in the long process, whereby 'religion' has become disembedded from various overlapping social, ideological, and material spheres, a process that comes to fruition in modernity, the formation of the Christian community is an important early step (e.g., Boyarin 1999: 18; Rives 2007: 208). Of course, Christianity in the Roman Empire can probably better be understood by comparing it with other institutions and social groups of the day, yet the level of violence Christians occasionally suffered, due to their intransigence toward the basic political theology of Rome, is impossible to understand without taking seriously the oppositional rhetoric espoused by this religious movement from the moment of its earliest literary production onward (1 *Cor.* 1: 26–31; *Revelation*). Moreover, Christians conspicuously tended to frown upon some (highly respected) occupations, such as military service, and the teaching of classical literature; and Church elites banned attendance at public spectacles and games, occasions that served to express and to advertise the banding together of the community (e.g., Tertullian, *De Spectaculis*). Such tendencies, and especially when these were conjoined with an avoidance of traditional public religious festivals, would have removed Christians from some of the typical public experiences of the ancient world. However, we do not know how often the laity abided by such restrictions.

In short, then, Christians and the Christian community were simultaneously integrated into and alienated from the broader society of the early Roman Empire. The following pages will trace the ways in which vacillating adhesion to and disaffection from the surrounding world characterized the position of Christians and Christian society in this period.

JESUS AND HIS FOLLOWERS

Though the historical Jesus cannot be reconstructed definitively, and any attempt to describe him will be based on probability and speculation, nevertheless we should briefly address his possible role in the development of the *ecclesia* as a social movement. Much of the scholarship of the past twenty years has emphasized the local significance of the Galilee (e.g., Freyne 1988), and archeology has become an important tool for the historical reconstruction of the early Jesus movement (e.g., Chancey 2006). Modern scholars have posited numerous social roles for Jesus of Nazareth. He has been understood as a wonder worker, a rabbi with a circle of disciples, a prophet of reform and revival, an eschatological prophet, and a Cynic philosopher. Some evidence, particularly the manner of his death, ties him to bandits and anti-Roman revolutionaries. The scholarship, in short, is massive despite the paucity of sources. The ambiguities of the evidence, as well as the mutual inclusivity of these various social roles, suggest that several, if not all, may be accurate in some way. In the face of such historical ambiguity, then, we might first simply ask, did Jesus play much of a role at all? Or is the early history of the movement and its slow but striking success due to its social formation and not necessarily due to the charisma of its first leader?

For example, it is disputed whether Jesus himself promulgated the idea of 'the twelve,' that is, the symbolic number of his followers corresponding to the number of Israelite tribes and perhaps therefore signifying the mustering of all of Israel (e.g., Mk. 3: 14). Nevertheless, the early prevalence of this idea shows the macro-thinking already characteristic of what was originally just a handful of followers. Furthermore, it is possible that Jesus himself enjoined his followers to go out and seek others, another act that had a significant influence on the social composition and style of the movement, since proselytism was essential from early on, first to fellow Jews, but soon after to Gentiles.

This was a movement that seems to have broken down norms, calling for a reformulation of the present world and a conversion of others to its cause. A new social constitution developed, based upon the removal of certain social boundaries and the concomitant inclusion of those on the margins of the social order. The practice of open commensality—that is, dining with all, including tax collectors and other disreputable people—would have been an embodied performance of social revolution (Crossan 1992).[2] Jesus, as he is depicted in the Gospels, provided both women and Gentiles access to the movement, in a manner that may not have corresponded to the mores of local Palestinian culture. However, as there are multiple versions of Jesus within the diversity of early sources, so also there is no single position on the role of women within these sources (D'Angelo and Kraemer 1999). As so often where Jesus and his doings are concerned, it is difficult to go much beyond a *non liquet*. A new form of social access may be directly due to Jesus' role as an apocalyptic prophet with a deeply eschatological worldview. Whether it is the case or not that such openness was due to Jesus himself—this is disputed by scholars—it is clear that the early Jesus movement was motivated by apocalyptic and eschatological expectations, and that his followers' sense of the imminence of the end-time (e.g., Mk. 9: 1) guided the movement for some time to come.

The poverty of the Galilee and the deprivation of pre-modern non-elite society may have helped to create a context for such a breakdown of norms, though the destitute were certainly not Jesus' only adherents. The identification with the poor

2. For a sense of the typical aspects of Roman commensality, see the essays of Dunbabin and Slater, and Perry (who discusses dining in the context of *collegia*) in this volume.

that we find in sources deriving from the Galilee, the later Jerusalem church, and beyond has been understood as a critique of the exploitative political economy of the day. Such a critique may be seen as part of a larger trend attested elsewhere, for example, by the revolutionaries described by Josephus, who happens to be our main source for details on the broader political, economic, and social context of Judaea at this moment in time.

THE EARLY MOVEMENT: Q, JERUSALEM, AND THE PAULINE HOUSE-CHURCH

The evidence is extremely sparse for the early period after Jesus' death and into the 50s, when the first extant documents, the letters of Paul, were written. This Jewish messianic movement, with a pressing awareness of the imminent end-time, seems to have spread rapidly through synagogues of the Jewish diaspora within the first few decades. Unfortunately, our sources, especially those on Jesus and events in Palestine, derive from decades later. Early on, the larger communities were in Jerusalem and the Galilee, the former led by Jesus' brother, James. In the past, scholars thought that a culture of wandering prophets and apostles quickly came into existence in the Galilee, associated with what we find in Q, the hypothetical Gospel used by both Matthew and Luke; but the reality of this has been challenged in recent scholarship, which encourages us to not be deceived by what may be only the rhetorical positioning of the sources (Arnal 2001; see also Draper 1998). Apostles traveled from city to city, as is best attested by Paul, but this also had a precedent in the synagogue emissaries and the various traveling religious experts of the time.

The early Jerusalem community, attested by documents such as Paul's *Letter to the Galatians*, the much later book of *Acts*, and perhaps the *Letter of James*, is often described as 'Jewish'; but such a categorical distinction is anachronistic for this early period, since this was a Jewish movement overall, even despite the participation of Gentiles. As *Acts* 11: 26 famously notes, it was not until mid-century that the term 'Christian' was first used in Antioch, and the significance of this strange Latinate Greek appellation remains disputed. It may in fact reflect legal usage, which would suggest that 'Christians' were already in trouble, perhaps as rabble-rousers within the Jewish community (in order to preserve the nuance, one scholar has suggested rendering 'Christianus' with 'Christ-nik'). This is parallel to what we find in, for example, Suetonius' reference to the troublesome followers of "Chrestus" (*Claud.* 15).[3] In any case, the Jerusalem community lost its early dominance after the siege

---

3. The label also resembles the tags given to the (n.b.) political followers of some Roman dynasts during the waning years of the republic, and then in the civil wars of AD 68/69: *Caesariani, Pompeiani, Galbiani, Othoniani, Vitelliani*. On this, see Schumacher 2006: 28.

of the city during the Jewish war (66–73), and because of the destruction caused by the Bar Kochba Revolt (132–35), though also as a result of the rapid spread of this new Messianic movement across the eastern Mediterranean region.

Though the Jesus movement spread originally through synagogues, as is depicted—perhaps historically—in *Acts*, the central Christian place for ritual gathering was what is commonly known as the house church (*domus ecclesia*). Such a social circle seems to be the basis of the Pauline communities (e.g., 1 *Cor.* 16: 19; *Rom.* 16: 5; *Phlm.* 1; cf. *Col.* 4: 15). Our earliest sources represent this secondary stage of the movement, when it had moved out of Palestine into the Greek-speaking communities of the eastern Mediterranean, as well as to Rome itself. That Christians gathered in small domestic architectural settings in part explains why little remains of pre-Constantinian church building. Another reason for this phenomenon seems to be that Christians did not develop a strong localization of the holy until the fourth century. For the period prior to this, there is little evidence of Christian holy sites, public processions and festivals, or of the notion that Palestine was the 'holy land.' These all became common later, with the rise of the cult of saints (Brown 1981).

The house church was the basic Christian communal unit in the early period, as this new religious movement spread through and beyond the Jewish diaspora. Early Christian communities have often been compared to the voluntary associations typical of the Hellenistic and Roman periods, such as we find with the mystery religions and burial societies (e.g., Ascough 2000; Harland 2003). Gathering in houses has been understood as a measure taken to protect Christians from a persecuting Roman imperial government. However, gathering in houses was not uncommon, for example, among Jews of the day (e.g., Rajak 2002). Paul's communities have received close scholarly scrutiny and have now been well contextualized within the cities of the Roman Empire (e.g., Meeks 2003;[2] Ascough 1998). However, there remains no settled opinion on Paul's message and its corresponding audience, both because of the difficulty of the sources, and as a result of their ongoing theological importance.

It has been commonly assumed that Christianity's inherent universalism allowed for Gentiles to participate in this new religious movement, in contrast to the supposed particularism of Judaism. While it is true that Paul's Gospel provided easier access to Gentiles, since he argued explicitly that Gentiles did not need to become Jews to join the movement—even that Christ's death had a special significance for Gentiles in particular—nevertheless historians often locate the social origins of the Gentile mission among the 'God fearers' of antiquity. These Gentiles, who were engaged with Judaism in varying degrees, from performing certain rituals to sometimes eventually converting, are most famously attested in the Aphrodisias synagogue inscription from the third century AD (Reynolds and Tannenbaum 1987). They may be the biblically literate Gentile audience assumed by Paul's letters. Much scholarship on Paul remains highly theological, and only exceptional works have fruitfully applied what we know about the broad socio-historical context to his works (Stowers 1994). In any case, the decision to allow Gentiles into the movement under the dispensation of a special Gospel for the Gentiles (e.g., *Gal.* 2: 7–8) would prove to be a major turning point in the long run. Out of this, a plainly new social movement would evolve, as the mission to the Jews, already in trouble in Paul's day (e.g., *Rom.* 11), withered away.

COMMUNAL PRACTICES AND OFFICES

The pre-Constantinian sources for most Christian rituals, including liturgy, are also sparse, and reconstruction is often highly speculative (e.g., Nodet and Taylor 1998). There was certainly variation in practice. For example, while most texts advocate full body immersion for baptism, catacomb art and architectural remains suggest smaller gestures, such as a simple pouring on the head. The meaning of such ritual practices also varies in the sources.

Baptism clearly derives from a similar Jewish practice, as mediated through the reconfiguration advocated by John the Baptist, and has parallels in ancient Greek and Roman religions. This was the central initiation ritual into various Graeco-Roman cultic communities, as it would become for Christians in later periods. While baptism's stated purpose was, among other things, to 'wash' the initiate of his or her sin, and to identify him or her with Christ (*Rom.* 6: 3–4), it functioned as an important boundary between those inside and those outside the group. Indeed, by the second and third centuries we see the development of the catechumenate, a kind of halfway group of acolytes in transition to Christian status, who were not yet baptized.

Another of the earliest Christian practices, one for which Jesus may have set a precedent, and which seems to have been central for proselytism, is healing. This corresponds to the important role healing played in ancient religion generally, such as we find in the cult of Asclepius. Scholars have applied cultural anthropological approaches to Jesus' and his followers' miracles, which in themselves fundamentally challenge an Enlightenment historical perspective. In any case, miracles, particularly those of healing, are common in the sources, where they are used to explain the growth of the movement (MacMullen 1984: 25–42). That is to say, miracles convinced possible converts of the genuineness of the apostles and their mission.

The Christian collective ritual par excellence was (and remains) the Lord's Supper, or Eucharistic meal. Banquets and communal eating were common to voluntary associations, burial societies, philosophical circles, and cultic gatherings in antiquity, although the various symbolic meanings attributed to the Eucharist were specific to Christianity (1 *Cor.* 11: 23–25; *Mk.* 14: 22–25). Inclusion in the meal signified and confirmed inclusion in the group, and from early on exclusion was a tool to control deviance (e.g., 1 *Cor.* 11: 27–34). The most famous outsider source for early Christian ritual gatherings is Pliny the Younger (d. ca. 113), who tells us what he himself was told by a Christian in Bithynia:

They affirmed, however, that the whole of their fault or error had been this: they were accustomed to come together on a fixed day before the light of day and sing in turn a hymn to Christ as if to a god, and to bind themselves by an oath (*sacramento*) not for some crime, but rather neither to commit theft, robbery, or adultery, nor to fail in trust, nor to refuse to return what was entrusted when approached. When these acts were done, it was their practice to depart and to gather again to take food, but ordinary and harmless food. (*Ep.* 10. 96)

Pliny's account points to two areas we know little of for the early period: prayer and liturgy. In addition to formal rituals, moral exhortation and public scriptural reading (and interpretation, no doubt) also functioned to integrate the group socially, as well as to create and maintain boundaries against outsiders, and those Christians who differed in practice and/or belief. At such ritual gatherings, Christians engaged in the 'holy kiss,' a gesture taken from Roman family and erotic practice, and well attested in the sources (Penn 2005). This ritual marked off as family those who were considered within the community.

Another common practice was fasting, which would become an important part of Christian personal and public piety in later centuries (e.g., Shaw 1998). In some congregations certain 'gifts,' such as the ability to prophesy and speak in tongues (*glossolalia*), created problems of authority. Such practices, however much they were ritualized and corresponded to ancient notions of divine communication, were threatening to institutional structures at various points in Christian history, and thus were often quashed as deviant behavior (e.g., Nasrallah 2003).

Christianity also derived an ideology of the book from its Jewish matrix. Such an emphasis on books and literacy made the early church a textual community, not only for its intellectual elites, but also for the congregation who listened to scriptural lections, exegesis, and homilies. This also led to the creation of a Christian literature, and eventually to new forms of literacy, such as in Coptic and Syriac (Koester 1995; Gamble 1995; Young et al. 2004; for a recent study of second and third century, see Rhee 2005).

Along with the development and maintenance of ritual practices, an important part of Christian institutionalization was the creation of offices within the *ecclesia*. Though the titles appear early (*episkopos*, *presbyteros*, and *diakonos*), a formal hierarchy of ecclesiastical positions developed slowly and inconsistently. The letters of Ignatius of Antioch (d. early second century AD) are commonly cited as an early attestation of the singular rule of one bishop over a city, and of the strong emphasis on the subordination of the whole community to this officer analogized to Christ. However, it is not precisely clear when all major churches were locked into this system. Not only did resistance continue for some time, but various charismatic figures would continue to pose a threat to the hierarchical authority for centuries to come. Even for the period mainly covered in this volume, we might mention the following as examples of figures who could explicitly or implicitly challenge the authority of the bishop: rich lay patrons, itinerant apostles, prophets such as we find among the Montanists, and 'Confessors,' that is, those people who confessed their faith, but happened to survive un-martyred during the persecutions of the third century. Furthermore, we should consider how charismatic figures often helped to confirm institutional authority, and how there were attempts to balance the relationship between these different kinds of authority, as we find in *Didache* 11–13, 15, which relegates apostles, prophets, and office-holders, such as bishops, to specific spheres, each demanding its own respect. Even before the rise of the imperial church, an important function of the bishop, lending him social power within the community, was his duty of caring for the poor (Brown 2002).

The rise of the bishop to a dominant position within the community took time, and was fully achieved only in the fourth century, when bishops received the support of the state (Rapp 2005). However, there clearly was a shift from the kind of charismatic authority we find in the writings of Paul to the kind of authority advocated by Ignatius. Further vantage points on the development of the growing authority of the bishop are offered by the figures of Cyprian of Carthage (ca. 200–258) and Paul of Samosata (Bishop of Antioch ca. 260–268). The career of the latter provides an extreme example of the episcopal power that was to come.

New Models of/for a New Community

In conceptualizing the early Christian community, we should not imagine a small, solitary group of followers growing over time, but rather, a tendency within Judaism that spread among both Jews and those God-fearing Gentiles, who had already been at times engaged with Judaism in various ways. This tendency was then taken up more broadly and transformed by Gentiles involved in the diverse religious, cultural, social, economic, and political world of the ancient Mediterranean littoral and beyond. This is not, then, the creation of a community *ex nihilo*, but the gradual consolidation of new forms of community out of a pre-existent social congeries. The diversity of early Christianity thus reflects, at least in part, the diversity of, as well as the complex pagan interaction with, the Judaism of the day.

The Christian community, especially as it developed over time and became more and more a Gentile movement, required models for understanding and mobilizing itself, all the more so in the apologetic context, where Christians were maligned by some, and considered bizarre by many. In other words, a Jewish sect with many Gentile adherents worshipping a man who suffered a degrading form of capital punishment seemed dangerous. Christians borrowed from the institutions of the—not mutually exclusive—Graeco-Roman and Jewish worlds to understand themselves as a group. For example, military metaphors are not uncommon in early Christian sources. Even the word *sacramentum*, the Latin equivalent to the Greek *mysterion*, may derive from an originally military usage (the *sacramentum* was the oath, sworn by Roman soldiers, to their commanders). At the end of the period under review, we find this application of military metaphor most explicitly in Pachomius' foundation of coenobitic monasteries, which were based upon the model of a Roman military camp. Such metaphors helped an extremely diverse social movement define itself locally, while simultaneously connecting itself to the broader community. Even in early Christian texts, for example, *ecclesia*, the Greek word for a city-state's popular assembly, which was used in Jewish texts to translate *qahal*, a Hebrew term for the religious congregation, is employed to designate both the local group and the community at large (*Acts* 9: 31).

The Christian Family/'Family'

Christianity's challenge, as well as its acquiescence to and borrowing from ancient social norms, is well attested by the Christian ideology and practice of family (Balch and Osiek 2003; Osiek and Balch 1997; cf. also Osgood in this volume). Many Christian texts reject traditional concerns about the family (e.g., *Mk.* 3: 31–35), while 'family' was employed as a central metaphor for talking about the new community. Christians were to be a new family, and were expected to relate to one another as brothers and sisters, and to be obedient like children. Despite a potential for a total disruption of family life, especially in the early, highly eschatological period (cf. 1 *Cor.* 7), we find in some early Christian sources the standard model of the family that can be traced back to Book I of Aristotle's *Politics*. For example, the so-called household codes (*Col.* 3: 18–4: 1; *Eph.* 5: 21–26: 9; 1 *Pet.* 2: 18–37) essentially maintain Aristotle's posited three relations constitutive of the family: parent-child, husband-wife, and master-slave. However, Christianity created new roles for women within the community, some of which did not survive the first generation of the movement (Osiek and MacDonald 2006). Such innovations were noted by non-Christian society (MacDonald 1996). Furthermore, new notions of the feminine proliferated, both in how women were imagined, but also in a diversity of formulations for gendering the divine (D'Angelo and Kraemer 1999).

Ascetic concerns about the body, which led to the full growth of monasticism from the early fourth century onward, took hold early in the Jesus movement (Vaage and Wimbush 1999; Brown 2008). One innovation which would have longterm significance was the development of a social group of celibates, sometimes consisting of widows, at other times of those who took special vows, often analogized in the sources to the Nazirites of the Hebrew Bible. There were even some groups, such as the so-called Encratites, who held celibacy to be a *sine qua non* of Christian life. There were some precedents to this religious celibacy in Graeco-Roman cults and Second Temple Judaism, such as among the Therapeutae (the ascetic "philosophers" living by Lake Mareotis near Alexandria, described by Philo of Alexandria). However, non-Christians never created the types of formalized celibacy that Christians would eventually develop from the late third century onward with the rise of monasticism.

Early Christians differed from the broader society regarding marriage on two main issues: secondary marriage and divorce, both of which were forbidden, with only minor exceptions. Marriage with non-Christians, despite recommendations against it, was not uncommon (cf. 1 *Cor.* 7: 39). Furthermore, despite the preference shown to celibacy (cf. 1 *Cor.* 7), basic marriage patterns remained the same, and most innovations, for example, a focus on certain symmetrical relations between wife and husband in marriage, can also be found in the moral philosophy of the day (e.g., Musonius Rufus). Like Jews, Christians looked down upon abortion and the abandonment of children, but such practices were also sometimes criticized by Graeco-Roman moralists.

Relationships within the traditional household were transformed little by Christianization. Rather, Christians made original contributions to these institutions by re-interpreting and endorsing them in Christian terms. In other words, Christians transformed institutional discourses while differentiating themselves from the broader society. However, in that differentiation they often did not change the status quo. For example, the equality of soul posited by Christianity led to criticisms of slavery, but there is little evidence of Christians making any attempt to abolish the actual practice of slavery, or even of having manumitted their own slaves for Christian purposes. Instead, we find Christian authors at times using Christian terms to emphasize the need for servile obedience (1 *Pet.* 2: 18–25).

THE PROBLEM OF SELF-DEFINITION

In the mid-second century, Justin Martyr (d. ca. 165), a Christian of perhaps Samaritan origin, attired in the philosopher's gown, proffered himself as a Christian teacher in Rome. Justin's oeuvre provides a basic schema of the Christian discursive and rhetorical strategy of self-definition, which would continue into the Constantinian period. His *Dialogue with Trypho*, the first fully extant anti-Jewish text, attempts to define the limits between Judaism and Christianity, and to demonstrate how the former was superseded by the latter. Justin's two *Apologies*, the first of an on-going Christian genre, takes its title from Socrates' famous defense, and depicts Christians as, like Socrates, if not beneficial, at least harmless to society at large. Justin argues that the many similarities between Graeco-Roman religion and Christianity are intentional perversions created by demons in order to mislead human beings. Finally, Justin is also one of the first Christian authors to engage in what modern scholars call heresiology, that is, the science of categorizing aberrant forms of Christianity; he employed the scholastic term, *haíresis*, which originally meant the school of thought one 'chose' (in Greek, *haireîsthai*) to follow, to refer to those groups who missed the theological mark. These three elements of Justin's literary corpus are attempts to address what ultimately reflects social confusion within the Christian community. Justin tried to establish the correct relations between often overlapping social groups, by setting up categorical boundaries between what he deemed authentic Christianity and the rest. This is the point where the internal politics of the group and its external relations with others meet: a major aim of much early Christian literature is to determine who is in and who is out, where the one community ends and another begins. In the following, I will employ the three issues that concerned Justin—Jewish-Christian relations, apologetics, and heresy— as primary categories of social analysis for pre-Constantinian Christianity.

THE PARTING OF THE WAYS?

Just as the question of Christian social relations raises questions about Christian integration into the broader society, a further problem arises when we address Jewish-Christian relations, especially in the pre-Constantinian period. To put it simply, scholarly conversation has in recent years subverted our once stable notions of who was a Jew and who was a Christian (and who were the odd, hyphenated hybrids in between) (Becker and Reed 2007; Jackson-McCabe 2007). Some people thought of themselves as Jews, yet understood Jesus to be the Messiah, while others saw themselves as Christians, but did things that look to us, and to many of their contemporaries, as thoroughly Jewish. This is not a matter of hazy boundaries at the time of origin. Among certain communities, such ambiguities in communal boundaries and self-definition continued long past the time of Constantine.

The traditional model of Jewish-Christian relations held that Jesus, or at least Paul, created a new religious movement that soon broke out of Judaism, a relatively monolithic entity, and formed a new religion, wholly distinct from its predecessor. According to a more recent model, ambiguities remained for some time, but the destruction of the Jewish Second Temple in Jerusalem in AD 70, and the subsequent Bar Kochba revolt (AD 132–135), were the final points in the process of differentiation. From now on there were two different religious communities, Rabbinic Judaism and Christianity. Several factors, including the recognition of its inherent theological foundation, have made the older model difficult to maintain. For example, the Dead Sea Scrolls discovered at Qumran and the Coptic codices found at Nag Hammadi in Upper Egypt have respectively problematized the notion that Judaism and Christianity were singular entities in this period. It turns out the Jewish matrix of Christianity was diverse, and that within the diversity of Judaism a diversity of Christianities emerged. This model better reflects our sources, but may itself not go far enough in its recognition of the pluralism of ancient Judaism and Christianity.

A problem with the model of the 'parting of the ways,' as the more recent model is called, is that it treats both Judaism and Christianity as linearly evolving entities, discrete from one another. However, it may be that the 'Judaism' and 'Christianity' of the sources were never lived by all those within the diverse religious communities of the ancient (and modern?) world. Rather, these two 'religions' may be constructs invented by religious elites. Rabbis and bishops advocated exclusive belonging, but our evidence suggests that there were often people in between. Furthermore, Jews and Christians often shared the same social spaces and discursive realms. Therefore, even where they constituted autonomous communities, they were responding to one another through self-distancing and differentiation. Not only did Judaism remain pluriform into late antiquity, but Christianity remained deeply imbricated within Second Temple Jewish concerns (e.g., Boyarin 2004).

Those Christians who wanted to force the separation from Judaism competed with Jews even for the very title 'Israel.' From the second century onward, Christians argued that they were the true Israel. In contrast, the Jews, so it was argued, had lost their dispensation after they rejected Christ. They were now a people cursed and rejected by God, a fact confirmed by the destruction of the Second Temple in AD 70. This led to a Christian revision of sacred history: Christians were the spiritual descendents of the ancient Israelites or Hebrews. Texts such as the second-century *Epistle of Barnabas*, building on Second Temple Jewish allegorical methods, argue that the Jewish law was never intended to be observed literally, and Christian readings of scripture often aimed to show how the Jews never accurately understood their own texts.

Within this competitive framework, Christians imagined themselves to be the new people of God. For example, the second-century *Epistle to Diognetus* argues that Christians, spread throughout the lands, are in fact aliens foreign to the earth (e.g., 5. 5). Furthermore, being neither Jews nor Gentiles, they are a third race, an anomaly, and they relate to this world as a soul does to a body. This kind of ethnic reasoning makes sense especially in a society where religion and ethnicity were often bound together, and it allowed for Christians to fit themselves squarely within the ancient world (Buell 2005).

PAIDEIA AND APOLOGETICS

Christian apologetics was an important tool for educated elites and sub-elites, who used this device to negotiate between their Christianity and their *paideia*, that is, the pedigree of learning and social deportment, which bound them to the dominant culture of the Graeco-Roman world. In turning Christianity into a form of philosophy, and even Socrates and Plato into proto-Christians, early Christian writers naturalized the Christianization of elite classical culture, while responding to criticisms of this errant Jewish sect. Much of this apologetic engagement with classical culture relied on earlier attempts by Jews to justify their own 'barbarian wisdom,' and also reflected classical engagement with Near Eastern culture, such as we find in Numenius of Apamea's famous second-century comparison: "For what is Plato but Moses Atticizing?" (Stern 1976–84: II. 363, a–e). Furthermore, the modern theological concern about the relationship between Christ and culture, as well as the sociological question of the relationship between Christianity and classical culture, both ultimately go back to Christian concerns expressed in this apologetic literature.

As stated above, Jesus' original circle of followers may be understood as a circle of students around a rabbi. Whether this is accurate or not, the image of Jesus as a teacher, and Christianity as a form of pedagogy, was not uncommon in the early Church, and would later be a basis for Christian institutions of learning from late antiquity deep into the Middle Ages (Rousseau 2002: 124–52). Though the use of pedagogical language was usually metaphorical, at times concrete circles of learning formed around Christian learned masters. The most famous instance of this is the so-called School of Alexandria, a title that may in fact be misleading. Rather, Christian 'schools' were informal study circles. For example, a circle seems to have formed in Alexandria and later in Caesarea around Origen (ca. 185–ca. 251), whose oeuvre played a central role in the development of Christian thought, and in the Egyptian desert around St. Antony (ca. 251–356), toward the end of the period here under review.

ORTHODOXY AND HERESY

The role of heresiology and the discourse of orthodoxy have received close attention from a number of scholars over the past thirty years (and going back further to Walter Bauer in the 1930s), but the synthesizing of such an analysis has only begun (Iricinschi and Zellentin 2008). The proliferation of diversity within the traditional heresiological model must be re-cast, and this bears upon how we understand early Christian social diversity in general. "Early Christianity was diverse from the beginning" has become a mantra in some quarters, though it does not always guide the scholarship. The model of a single, unidirectional movement toward greater and greater diversity needs to be replaced by one that allows for expansion and contraction simultaneously as Christianity spread.

The sectarianism of Second Temple Judaism continued in early Christianity, and a unitary early Church is only a theological fantasy. Dissension is attested in the earliest documents, and continues especially until Constantine. In the pre-Constantinian period, Christians were unable to use state violence to maintain unity and eradicate deviant behavior. This may in part explain the focus on literary persuasion from early on, as well as the standard Graeco-Roman practice of maintaining bonds of friendship and patronage. To put it simply, how does one tell people what to do across immense distances in a pre-modern society when one does not have the support of the state? Parallel to this, diversity can be seen in the indeterminacy of a formal canon through this period, and the formalization of the

Christian biblical canon only in the fourth century (Gamble 1985). The problem of diversity and the construction of 'heresy' is most often addressed in the recent scholarship on the category 'gnostic' and so-called gnosticism (Williams 1999; King 2003). Scholars now see the work of authors such as Irenaeus of Lyons (d. ca. 202), in his so-called *Adversus haereses*, as constructing the limits of a proto-orthodox Christianity, in order to shut out those members of both his own community and the broader *ecclesia* with whom he disagreed.

PERSECUTION AND SOCIAL FORMATION

An enduring myth central to the Christian understanding of the early history of Christianity is the tale of the confessing Church and persecuting Rome (Frend 1965; Castelli 2004). It is often taken for granted that Rome persecuted Christians, while it is at times forgotten that, with the Christianization of the Roman Empire in the fourth and fifth centuries, the Church itself engaged in social coercion on a much broader scale. A scholarly chicken-and-egg question exists for the origins of Christian oppositional rhetoric and the state-sponsored violence perpetrated against Christians. The Jewish community, despite its antiquity and integration into the Graeco-Roman culture of the Mediterranean, at times experienced a certain precariousness. Such conditions were all the more precarious for Christians, who were associated with the Jews, but lacked an ancient ethnic pedigree, as well as a reputation for its own philosophical character, both of which Judaism had acquired by the Roman period. Scholars have noted that persecution was sporadic until the third century, when the emperor Decius demanded universal participation in the Roman cult, thus beginning the period of the worst violence suffered by Christians.

CHRISTIANIZATION AND CONSTANTINE'S CONVERSION: REVOLUTION OR CONTINUING TRENDS?

One of the fundamental questions regarding early Christianity, going back to Edward Gibbon's famous attempt to understand the 'decline and fall of the Roman Empire,' concerns Christianization. In fact, this has for some time been a standard question in scholarship on late antiquity (e.g., Brown 2003; MacMullen 1984). The issue remains unresolved, and scholars continue to discuss what should be understood as a multi-causal phenomenon (Harris 2005). The American sociologist Rodney

Stark, however, has made a controversial contribution to this discussion (Stark 1996).[4]

The actual rate of Christianity's demographic expansion remains disputed. However, it is clear that Christians were still a relatively small minority, even at the time of Constantine's conversion. The earliest Christian populations were in Asia Minor, Syria-Palestine, and Egypt. Rome and Carthage were the major centers in the West, the latter being the center of Christian Latin literary production in the early centuries. Part of Christianization also seems to have entailed the gradual homogenization of Christian practice and belief, as churches in different regions with local particularities, especially before the rise of the imperial church in the fourth century, slowly succumbed to the tendencies of the broader institution. Furthermore, on the way to a Christian empire, there was a renegotiation of classical norms, rather than an eradication of classical culture (Brown 1992).

The problem of Christianization is directly related to the question of the role played by Constantine's conversion and the rise of the imperial church in the eventual transformation of the classical world. The conversion of Constantine provided the church with the power to guide government policy, toward not only non-Christians but also Christians deemed 'heretical' by the 'orthodox' who were in power. This change in the balance of power has important historiographical implications as well, since texts and communal histories were purged of what did not fit the orthodox line.

CONCLUSIONS

Every form of social analysis, or perhaps, rather, all analysis, requires some kind of reification. Early Christianity creates a heuristic predicament, because it is a social entity thoroughly belonging to the ancient world, and yet its expansion and the Christian usurpation of both power and the classical tradition (for we owe the majority of what remains of the latter to Christianity) demonstrate the difference that Christianity did in fact make. From Jesus and his followers through the early movement and its gentilization we see clearly the process of the partial assimilation of a Jewish sectarian movement to dominant cultural norms. This new social group relied on traditional and innovative forms of social maintenance, both practical and ideological, while forcing into view robust notions of religious and political autonomy. This led to the real and imagined differentiation of Christians from state and society, but in the end it also allowed for their active and intentional appropriation of various forms of power.

Apart from such problems of conceptualization, the historiography of early Christianity continues to be hindered by disparities in the coverage of the diversity

---

4. See the assessment and critique of his work in *Journal of Early Christian Studies* 6 (1998), especially Hopkins 1998.

of sources. Because of the understandable Christian focus on the canonical New Testament, and therefore on the first and early second centuries in general, a gap still exists between scholarship on the New Testament and that on pre-Nicene Christian literature (second to fourth centuries), a gap wider than that found between scholarship focusing on pre-Nicene and that on post-Nicene Christianity. It is only in certain areas, such as gender and sexuality, that more complex analysis has been done for the period after the canonical New Testament texts. The multiple social scientific approaches applied to the New Testament have not been applied nearly as much to later Christian literatures, despite the paucity of the evidence for the earlier period and the greater wealth of sources for the later one (Malherbe 1983; Malina 1996; Stegemann et al. 2002; Blasi et al. 2002). As with most historiography, there is often a lag between the development of social theory and its application to the early Christian sources. It is rare for works that use sociology and anthropology in the study of early Christianity to employ cutting edge social theoretical tools (e.g., Gager 1975; Theissen 1978). However, scholars of the New Testament have long been interested in social issues: the *Sitz im Leben* approach of traditional New Testament scholarship is implicitly sociological (if reductionistic).

Late nineteenth and early twentieth discussions of myth, ritual, and the origins of religion are foundational to the modern social scientific study of religion and society. The Christian Eucharistic meal served as a paradigmatic exemplar and prototype in much of this scholarship, where it served as the ritual of social maintenance par excellence. In addressing Christianity in a volume such as this, in which historians of various stripes use the category of the 'social,' we are coming full circle, inasmuch as the early Christian community's ritual of weekly gatherings lies at the foundation of how we imagine group interaction and ritual. Behind Durkheim's and Freud's totem lies both implicitly and explicitly the Christian cross, and the totemic meal is the Eucharistic one. A similar circularity appears when scholars employ Weber's typology of authority without being conscious of his reliance on the historiography of early Christianity in his theorization. Thus, early Christianity is not a separate entity of social analysis, but is implicated in the very formation of such an analysis.[5]

SUGGESTED READING

The bibliography is immense, especially for the period covered by the canonical New Testament. I have limited references throughout this essay to more recent work in English. Blasi et al. 2002 is a recent, wide-ranging work for the New Testament period. However, certain social issues, such as Jewish-Christian relations and heresiology, have sizeable bibliographies. For the question of Christianization deep into the Middle Ages, begin with Brown 2003.

5. For a discussion of method and the application of social theory to early Christianity, see Blasi et al. 2002: 3–79.

BIBLIOGRAPHY

Arnal, W. E. 2001. *Jesus and the Village Scribes: Galilean Conflicts and the Setting of Q.* Minneapolis: Fortress Press.

Ascough, R. S. 1998. *What Are They Saying About the Formation of Pauline Churches?* New York: Paulist.

———. 2000. "The Thessalonian Christian Community as a Professional Voluntary Association." *Journal of Biblical Literature* 19. 2: 311–28.

Balch, D. L., and C. Osiek (eds.). 2003. *Early Christian Families in Context: An Interdisciplinary Dialogue.* Grand Rapids: Eerdmans.

Becker, A. H., and A. Y. Reed (eds.). 2007. *The Ways That Never Parted: Jews and Christians in Late Antiquity and the Early Middle Ages.* 2nd ed. Minneapolis: Fortress Press.

Blasi, A. J., J. Duhaime, and P.-A. Turcotte (eds.). 2002. *Handbook of Early Christianity: Social Science Approaches.* Walnut Creek: AltaMira.

Boyarin, D. 1999. *Dying for God: Martyrdom and the Making of Christianity and Judaism.* Stanford: Stanford University Press.

———. 2004. *Borderlines: The Partition of Judaeo-Christianity.* Philadelphia: University of Pennsylvania Press.

Brown, P. R. L. 1981. *The Cult of the Saints: Its Rise and Function in Late Christianity.* Chicago: University of Chicago Press.

———. 1992. *Power and Persuasion in Late Antiquity: Towards a Christian Empire.* Madison: University of Wisconsin Press.

———. 2002. *Poverty and Leadership in the Later Roman Empire.* Hanover: University Press of New England.

———. 2003. *The Rise of Western Christendom.* 2nd ed. Oxford: Blackwell.

———. 2008. *The Body and Society: Men, Women, and Sexual Renunciation in Early Christianity.* 2nd ed. New York: Columbia University Press.

Buell, D. K. 2005. *Why This New Race: Ethnic Reasoning in Early Christianity.* New York: Columbia University Press.

Castelli, E. 2004. *Martyrdom and Memory: Early Christian Culture-Making.* New York: Columbia University Press.

Chancey, M. A. 2006. *Greco-Roman Culture and the Galilee of Jesus.* Cambridge: Cambridge University Press.

Cooper, K. 1996. *The Virgin and the Bride: Idealized Womanhood in Late Antiquity.* Cambridge, Mass.: Harvard University Press.

Crossan, J. D. 1992. *The Historical Jesus: The Life of a Mediterranean Jewish Peasant.* San Francisco: Harper San Francisco.

D'Angelo, M. R., and R. S. Kraemer (eds.). 1999. *Women and Christian Origins.* New York: Oxford University Press.

Draper, J. A. 1998. "Weber, Theissen and 'Wandering Charismatics' in the *Didache*." *Journal of Early Christian Studies* 6.4: 541–76.

Frend, W. H. C. 1965. *Martyrdom and Persecution in the Early Church: A Study of a Conflict from the Maccabees to Donatus.* Oxford: Blackwell.

Freyne, S. 1988. *Galilee, Jesus and the Gospels: Literary Approaches and Historical Investigations.* Philadelphia: Fortress Press.

Gager, J. G. 1975. *Kingdom and Community: The Social World of Early Christianity.* Englewood Cliffs: Prentice-Hall.

Gamble, H. Y. 1985. *The New Testament Canon: Its Making and Meaning.* Philadelphia: Fortress Press.

————. 1995. *Books and Readers in the Early Church: A History of Early Christian Texts.* New Haven: Yale University Press.

Harland, P. A. 2003. *Associations, Synagogues, and Congregations: Claiming a Place in Ancient Mediterranean Society.* Minneapolis: Fortress Press.

Harris, W. V. (ed.). 2005. *The Spread of Christianity in the First Four Centuries: Essays in Explanation.* Leiden: E. J. Brill.

Hopkins, K. 1998. "Christian Number and Its Implications." *Journal of Early Christian Studies* 6. 2: 185–226.

Iricinschi, E., and H. Zellentin (eds.). 2008. *Heresy and Identity in Late Antiquity.* Tübingen: Mohr Siebeck.

Jackson-McCabe, M. 2007. *Jewish Christianity Reconsidered: Rethinking Ancient Groups and Texts.* Minneapolis: Fortress Press.

King, K. L. 2003. *What Is Gnosticism?* Cambridge, Mass.: Harvard University Press.

Koester, H. 1995. *Introduction to the New Testament: Vol. 2, History and Literature of Early Christianity.* 2nd ed. Berlin: Walter de Gruyter.

MacDonald, M. Y. 1996. *Early Christian Women and Pagan Opinion: The Power of the Hysterical Woman.* Cambridge: Cambridge University Press.

MacMullen, R. 1984. *Christianizing the Roman Empire: AD 100–400.* New Haven: Yale University Press.

Malherbe, A. 1983. *Social Aspects of Early Christianity.* 2nd ed. Philadelphia: Fortress Press.

Malina, B. J. 1996. *The Social World of Jesus and the Gospels.* London: Routledge.

Meeks, W. 2003. *The First Urban Christians: The Social World of the Apostle Paul.* 2nd ed. New Haven: Yale University Press.

Nasrallah, L. 2003. *An Ecstasy of Folly: Prophecy and Authority in Early Christianity.* Cambridge, Mass.: Harvard University Press.

Nodet, E., and J. Taylor. 1998. *The Origins of Christianity: An Exploration.* Collegeville: Liturgical Press.

Osiek, C., and D. L. Balch. 1997. *Families in the New Testament World: Households and House Churches.* Westminster: John Knox.

Osiek, C., and M. Y. MacDonald. 2006. *A Woman's Place: House Churches in Earliest Christianity.* Minneapolis: Fortress Press.

Penn, M. P. 2005. *Kissing Christians: Ritual and Community in the Late Ancient Church.* Philadelphia: University of Pennsylvania Press.

Rajak, T. 2002. "Synagogue and Community in the Graeco-Roman Diaspora." In J. R. Bartlett (ed.), *The Jews in the Hellenistic and Roman Cities.* London: Routledge. 22–38.

Rapp, C. 2005. *Holy Bishops in Late Antiquity: the Nature of Christian Leadership in an Age of Transition.* Berkeley: University of California Press.

Reynolds, J. M., and R. F. Tannenbaum. 1987. *Jews and Godfearers at Aphrodisias.* Cambridge: Cambridge University Press.

Rhee, H. 2005. *Early Christian Literature: Christ and Culture in the Second and Third Centuries.* London: Routledge.

Rives, J. B. 1995. *Religion and Authority in Roman Carthage from Augustus to Constantine.* Oxford: Clarendon Press.

————. 2007. *Religion in the Roman Empire.* Oxford: Blackwell.

Rousseau, P. 2002. *The Early Christian Centuries.* London: Longman Pearson.

Salisbury, J. 1997. *Perpetua's Passion: The Death and Memory of a Young Roman Woman.* London: Routledge.

Schumacher, L. 2006. *Corpus der römischen Rechtsquellen zur antiken Sklaverei. Teil VI. Stellung des Sklaven im Sakralrecht.* Stuttgart: Franz Steiner Verlag.

Shaw, B. 1996. "Body/Power/Identity: Passions of the Martyrs." *Journal of Early Christian Studies* 4. 3: 269–312.

Shaw, T. M. 1998. *The Burden of the Flesh: Fasting and Sexuality in Early Christianity.* Minneapolis: Fortress Press.

Stark, R. 1996. *The Rise of Christianity: A Sociologist Reconsiders History.* Princeton: Princeton University Press.

Stegemann, W., B. J. Malina, and G. Theissen. 2002. *The Social Setting of Jesus and the Gospels.* Minneapolis: Fortress Press.

Stern, M. 1976–84. *Greek and Latin Authors on Jews and Judaism.* Jerusalem: Israel Academy of Sciences and Humanities.

Stowers, S. 1994. *A Rereading of Romans: Justice, Jews, and Gentiles.* New Haven: Yale University Press.

Theissen, G. 1978. *Sociology of Early Palestinian Christianity.* Trans. John Bowden. Philadelphia: Fortress Press.

Vaage, L. E., and V. Wimbush. 1999. *Asceticism and the New Testament.* London: Routledge.

Williams, M. A. 1999. *Rethinking "Gnosticism": An Argument for Dismantling a Dubious Category.* Princeton: Princeton University Press.

Young, F., et al. (eds.). 2004. *The Cambridge History of Early Christian Literature.* Cambridge: Cambridge University Press.

PART VII

MARGINALIZED PERSONS

CHAPTER 28

SLAVES IN ROMAN SOCIETY

LEONHARD SCHUMACHER

INTRODUCTION: SLAVERY AS A SPECIFIC FORM OF LACK OF FREEDOM IN CLASSICAL ANTIQUITY

GRAECO-ROMAN antiquity was a slave-keeping society, and owners were able, in principle, to deploy their slaves in any and all fields of life. One exception was military service, including naval service (Welwei 1988). There were no 'galley slaves' in antiquity. When there was rowing to be done, it was the duty of free sailors. And so, to put the matter plainly, the impressive film scenes in *Ben Hur* are simply anachronistic. Of course, certain activities did presuppose appropriate qualifications of a physical or of an intellectual kind (Schumacher 2001a; Bellen and Heinen 2003). An illiterate person, for example, was not suitable to be a secretary, an elocutionist hardly qualified as a field worker, an agricultural laborer was little suited to serve at banquets. In the textile trade, female slaves predominated at spinning wheels and on looms, while male slaves toiled in fulleries and felting shops. In short, any demanding activities required a training, which was financed by slave owners as an investment in one of their operating resources—in Roman terms, the slave could be viewed as a so-called *instrumentum vocale* (speaking tool).[1]

In this connection, the definition of a slave continues to be disputed. Under global sociological aspects, and above all in light of current findings on slavery, a general definition is nowadays preferred. Slavery is "the complete domination of

---

1. See Var. *R.* 1. 17. 1, and on Varro, see Hübner 1984; Roth 2007.

one person by another for the purpose of economic exploitation."[2] In its essence, of course, this also applies to Roman conditions; however, a far richer spectrum emerges for that world. Not every person directly subject to another's power, even if he was economically exploited, was necessarily enslaved; on the other hand, it cannot be assumed that every slave was also being economically exploited. Personal and social status were simply not identical. Thus, for example, wives in the *manus* (literally, the hand) of their husbands, or children (both sons and daughters) in the power of their fathers (here an institution called *patria potestas* was involved) were legally free persons with Roman citizenship, although they were *alieni iuris*, in other words, (like slaves) without the legal right of self-determination. A certain type of loan bound the debtor (as *nexus*) legally to his creditor, and such persons were then economically exploited by those creditors—even though they remained free citizens (Var. *L.* 7. 105), performed military service (Liv. 2. 24. 6), and had the right themselves to bring a lawsuit (V. Max. 6. 1. 9). The situation of the *coloni* (tenant farmers) of late antiquity appeared similar; these were people who performed agricultural work while bound to the soil, but were not slaves (Sirks 1993). The same is also true for the so-called decurions and other occupational groups of this epoch (*CTh* 9. 45. 3; *Nov. Valent.* 35. 3; Schumacher 2006: 33–35). Even with regard to the under-privileged and exploited rural population of the *chora* (countryside) in Egypt, despite all the peculiarities specific to their situation, one still has to have doubts about their (oft-supposed) slave status (Lewis 1983: 65–83; Bagnall and Frier 1994). Conversely, slave status is attested for numerous functionaries within the imperial administration, without any idea of a general exploitation imposing itself here.

Under these conditions, then, a more abstract definition is desirable, to achieve a better understanding of slavery in the Roman period. Wanted is an understanding that does not excessively accentuate economic exploitation through the forcibly coerced performance of work and services, but rather, one that concentrates upon the individual's legal status. According to this, the unrestricted and permanent subjection to the direct power of a master (*dominus*) characterizes the Roman slave as being the property of an individual person or of some corporate body. In the case of corporate property, the exercise of power over the slave could in practice be delegated. If the holder of power dropped out of the group, his rights as master passed to his legal successor. This unlimited power, even beyond the death of the individual or the corporate body, which was functioning as master, was constitutive for the social condition of the slave, and distinguished him from other persons subject to authority of some kind. The termination of the status of being a slave could take place only through the free manifestation of the owner's will, not through his demise.

In his manual of Roman law, the *Institutiones*, written around the middle of the second century AD, the jurist Gaius initially established a fundamental differentiation between free men (*homines liberi*) and slaves (*servi*), in order subsequently to

2. See Bales 2004: 6; also Bales 2000, Zeuske 2009, and Flaig 2009. Long ago, a differentiation more appropriate to the Roman situation was presented by Kloosterboer 1960.

put the legal position of slaves more precisely as being "subject to alien law" (*alieno iuri*). This "alien law" is put into more concrete terms as the "power of their masters" (*potestas dominorum*): "Slaves are thus in the power of their masters" (Gaius *Inst.* 1. 9, 48, 52). As a consequence of this constellation, the slave was never a legal personality, but always just a legal object, as was indicated just above.[3] Thus, Gaius gives us the Roman slave; and such legal distinctions must always be kept in mind when dealing with slaves in the Roman world.

The Slave and His or Her Social Relations

The Slave 'Family' (*Familia Servorum*)

Since slaves were without the right of self-determination, they could not, of course, enter into a legally binding marriage (*matrimonium*). Cohabitation unions (*contubernia*), with the master's approval, were tolerated as being the custom (*mos*), but remained legally irrelevant. For the master, the smallest organizational element was thus the group of slaves within his 'household' (*domus*), which the younger Pliny (*Ep.* 8. 16. 2), in a bold analogy, but by no means sarcastically with respect to the slaves, likened to the political community of free citizens. Seneca (*Ep.* 47. 14) used similar wording, albeit with respect to former times. For the slaves, he wrote, the *domus* was a "small-size state" (*pusilla res publica*), and they were designated as "members of the household" (*familiares*) by their masters. Dispensing with humanitarian interpretations, in our connection it suffices to comment that, as a rule, in Roman linguistic usage 'household' (*domus*) designated the 'extended family,' including the agnate and also cognate (*FIRA* II² 631–34) relatives, the freedmen and slaves, the clients, and also substantive goods: in brief, a master's entire property (Saller 1994: 74–101; Saller 1997). For the slaves, as a whole, within this constellation, Classical authors (e.g., Cato *Agr.* 56–59; Cic. *Caec.* 55; *Dig.* 47. 9. 1 pr.) preferred the term 'family' (*familia*)—not, of course, in the modern sense of a father-mother-child(ren) relationship, but simply to designate the collective of all those under the owner's power (Flory 1975). At times, the owner (*dominus*) of the slave 'family' would be named, so as thereby to designate the group (*CIL* VI 7395, 23548, 38711, *CIL* VIII 12833; *CIL* X 3995). Also, the *familia* could be specified under local or functional aspects—as being, for example, urban (*urbana*: *CIL* VI 1747; Amm. 14. 6. 17), rural (*rustica*: *CIL* X 3028; *Dig.* 50. 16. 166 pr.), public (*publica*: *CIL* VI 2342; *CIL* X 4856; *AE* 1903, 186), belonging to the aqueduct system (*aquaria*: Fron. *Aq.* 166), or gladiatorial (*gladiatoria*: Cic. *Sul.* 54; *CIL* VI 29681; *CIL* XII 727). In a functional respect, freed slaves (*liberti*) could also be subsumed under the term *familia* (*CIL* VI 479, 8456;

---

3. On this, see Buckland 1908; Kaser 1971: I, 283–302 (§§ 67–71); II, 124–150 (§§ 209–13); Watson 1987; Corbino 1990: 243–62.

Dig. 50. 16. 195); but as a rule, a differentiation was made between the *liberti* and the *familia servorum* (*B. Hisp.* 33. 3; *CIL* VI 11998, 26197). In modern literature the term *familia Caesaris* (family of the emperor) is used in the comprehensive sense for the emperors' slaves and freedmen as a whole, a term for which there actually is, however, no ancient evidence.[4]

Now, the arguably constitutive element of Roman society overall was the dominant position of the *pater familias* (the father of the family). He alone had power to dispose over the assets (*patrimonium*) of the agnate extended family (*Dig.* 50. 16. 195. 2; *CJ* 6. 38. 5 pr.); until his death, or the destruction of his existence as an upstanding member of the Roman community (*capitis deminutio*), he held power over his wife (*in manu*) and his children (*in patria potestate*).[5] Originally subject just to the control exerted by social pressure, the father's absolute powers, especially the right of putting to death members of his family (*ius vitae necisque*), would over the course of time be restricted normatively—for instance, through a legally mandated criminal procedure before a 'domestic court' (*consilium*: see Kunkel 1974). However, in principle, the father's autocratic power of disposition over the assets, to which the slaves simply belonged, remained. Their situation was determined much more elementarily than that of the 'household children' by the holder of power, in other words, by their master (*dominus*); thus, in order to make the difference clear, a differentiation between *patria potestas* (the power of the father over both his slaves and his relatives) and *dominica potestas* (the power of the father just over his slaves) is to be recommended.

As already emphasized, this latter power did not expire with the death of the *dominus*, but passed to his legal successor. The slave thus always remained property until a formal manumission had occurred, and state authorities intervened in this sphere only if the existence of the community appeared somehow threatened. When the state did engage in expropriations of slaves, this was aimed at instrumentalizing the slaves against their masters—for example, to take testimony from the slave against the master. Apart from arbitrary measures adopted by political rulers, such as the proscriptions of Sulla and the Triumvirate (Hinard 1985), in the republic these actions involved only three particular situations, in which the master was guilty of some misdeed: religious sacrilege (*incestus*), high treason (*coniuratio*), and internal insurrection (*vis publica*). From Augustus on, the concept of 'lèse-majesté' (*crimen maiestatis*) would come to dominate those situations in which the state would take a person's slaves; though as time went by, adultery by women (*adulterium*) and tax fraud (*fraus census*) were also added as criminal offenses that could result in the loss of slave property (Schumacher 1982). The reason given in any such

4. Weaver 1972: 299–300. The term is also discussed by Winterling 1999: 23–26. See further Schumacher 2001b: 333–34 with note 11.

5. From the end of the republic, at the latest, wives *in manu* were an exceptional occurrence; cf. Treggiari 1991: 16–36. For the power of the *pater familias*, cf. Crook 1967 and Saller 1994: 102–32. The impact of patriarchy on Roman political mentality seems to be exaggerated by Lacey 1980.

case for the expropriation of the convicted person's slaves was the 'common weal' (*utilitas publica*). Imperial decrees ordering the compulsory sale of slaves, who had fled for a justified reason (*iusta causa*) into a recognized asylum or to a statue of the emperor, were motivated by regulatory political considerations (*Dig.* 1. 6. 2; 21. 1. 17. 12–13; Bellen 1971; Gamauf 1999; Klingenberg 2005).

The legislation of late antiquity did not in principle question the masters' free power of disposition over their slaves as their property either—with the exception, of course, of the criminal offenses just referred to. However, drastic restrictions did affect the Jews. Initially, they were forbidden to acquire Christian slaves (*CTh* 16. 9. 2), ultimately even to possess them (*CJ* 1. 10. 2; *Nov. Just.* 37. 7; Linder 1987; Schumacher 2006: 43–45). Heretics were also included in this ban, but it was obviously aimed principally at Jewish masters. We might also note in this context that Hadrian had already placed the forced circumcision of slaves, which was regarded as equivalent to castration, under the threat of capital punishment (*Dig.* 48. 8. 4. 2; 48. 8. 11 pr.).

The protection of private property, carefully guaranteed by the Roman state over the centuries, certainly contributed to the stabilization of slavery as an institution. However, slaves were human beings, and their yearning for individual freedom is undisputed; indeed, violent insurrections had been cruelly suppressed during the slave wars of the republic (Bradley 1989; Urbainczyk 2008). Association with potentially powerful politicians, such as Sex. Pompeius, as a road to freedom proved likewise illusory (Aug. *Anc.* 25; App. *BC* 5. 131. 544–5). Put simply, taking flight within the imperial frontiers offered only minimal opportunities. Therefore, the best hope for freedom lay in manumission (*manumissio*), which was certainly not an impossibility for some slaves, above all those in the service sector (Fabre 1981; Waldstein 1986). However, the fact that the slaves did, it is true, bemoan their personal situations, but never did, so far as we can tell, call slavery as an institution into question, appears more decisive to me. Apart from senators, knights, and decurions, no social group had more slaves at their disposal than the freedmen, who did not by any means think of manumitting their own slaves out of sympathy (Treggiari 1969; Duff 1928). These slaves had, of course, been bought by these freedmen mainly *post manumissionem*; however, it should also be recognized that these freedmen could already have possessed a number of slaves of their own, the so-called *servi vicarii*, when they were still serving as slaves themselves (Erman 1896; Reduzzi Merola 1990). If even slaves might own slaves, then one can begin to get a sense of the level of acceptance of slavery as an institution in Roman society.

Now, a manumission presupposed 'good conduct.' In this respect, the masters had developed a very complex system for enforcing this 'good behavior.' Basically, discipline comprised two components: a carrot and a stick (Bradley 1984). The carrot consisted primarily in the prospect of manumission itself, though it also involved the toleration of personal relationships (*contubernia*) among the slaves (*familia*), and the granting of separate property (*peculium*) for use on their own responsibility (Pólay 1967; Flory 1978; Friedl 1996: 75–85; Brinkhof 1978; Zeber 1981; Schumacher 2001a: 239–48, 265–76). The stick was put into concrete form with the withdrawal of these privileges, and rigorous punitive measures, ranging from corporal punishment to cruel execution (Schumacher 2001a: 276–91). Such measures found their limits at best in the masters' economic interests, insofar as slaves represented business capital, though sometimes also via the state's interest to safeguard public order—for dissatisfied slaves were known sometimes to start revolts. Unreasonable cruelty (*saevitia*) was punished only in exceptional cases. Augustus did not even withhold his friendship from Vedius Pollio, who had one of his slaves fed to his morays (Dio 54. 23. 2; Sen. *De ira* 3. 40. 3). The punishment by the emperor Hadrian of a woman named Umbricia, who had tormented her slaves excessively, remained rather unique (*Dig.* 1. 6. 2). Crucifixion, as a usual form of execution for slaves (*AE* 1971, 88 II 8–10), served mainly as a deterrent—and was above all intended to discourage any attempt by slaves to murder their masters. Representative, for instance, is the S(*enatus*) C(*onsultum*) *Silanianum* of the year AD 10, which decreed the execution of all those slaves who had been in the victim's house (*sub eodem tecto*) at the time of the attack (*Dig.* 29. 5. 1. 26–29; Tac. *Ann.* 13. 32. 1). Its application with regard to the assassination of the prefect of the city (Rome), Pedanius Secundus (Tac. *Ann.* 14. 42–5), of Larcius Macedo (Plin. *Ep.* 3. 14. 1–4), and of Afranius Dexter (Plin. *Ep.* 8. 14. 12–15) is attested (Schumacher 1990).

Slaves in Society

Integrated—in the literal sense—into their master's *familia* (extended family) and *domus* (household), slaves were deployed in all sectors of production, services, and administration. The bulk of them, including women (Var. *R.* 2. 10. 6; Col. 12. 3. 6), worked in agriculture and shepherding (Staerman 1969; Samson 1989; Scheidel 1990a; Graßl 1990; Schumacher 2001a: 95–107). In spite of their economic significance, these persons are only poorly documented as social groups, for they themselves lacked the funds for tombstones (generally the best type of source we have for people of the lower classes), and beyond their circle there was no perceived need to cultivate their memory. Nonetheless, according to Varro (*R.* 2. 10. 10–11), one shepherd (*pastor*) in Illyria could care for about 80–100 sheep, whereas herds of horses would need four times that number. The elder Pliny (*Nat.* 7. 135) estimated a rich freedman's estate as being worth 60,000,000 sesterces in cash, 257,000 head of cattle, plus 7200 teams of oxen, and 4116 slaves, most of whom must have been employed as shepherds. With respect to other types of agricultural activity, and the numbers of slaves engaged therein, there are only comparable indications for wine growing and olive cultivation (Var. *R.* 1. 18. 1–5).

These groups were highly restricted in their interpersonal contacts, generally being in touch only with other persons of a similar station, or perhaps with a few free wage laborers (*mercennarii*) in the same field of activity. The men might be permitted, as a special privilege, to have personal relationships with their fellow female slaves—though this was certainly done in part with the objective of increasing the number of slaves (Var. *R.* 2. 1. 26). Manumissions only seldom took place in these sectors, and had little effect on the deployment of herdsmen and laborers in the fields. In the early imperial period, Columella (1. 8. 19) recommended the manumission of women who had given birth to three (surviving) children, as a reward; the children themselves, however, would remain enslaved (*Dig.* 1. 5. 5. 1; Hermann-Otto 1994).

The interpersonal contacts of slaves in the manufacturing trades developed in a more varied manner, since here the relations to suppliers and customers, as well as the proximity to urban settlements, played a role. In larger undertakings, such as ceramic production, fulling, and dye shops, the outside contacts were less than in the crafts, or in the retail trade, where the deployment of labor was organized to a certain degree by the slaves themselves. The objective always remained, of course, the earning of profits for the master. The granting of separate property (*peculium*) for the slaves' own use, and the permission to enter into a partnership (*contubernium*) with a female slave in one's own *familia* (*CIL* XIII 447; *AE* 1977, 54) created incentives. Separate property allowed to a slave might also include female slaves, who are in some instances attested in personal relationships with their un-free masters (*CIL* VI 8687; *CIL* XI 6078).

It should be recognized that slaves in the service sector, or in the areas of administration and trade, stood better chances of being granted privileges. Here the tasks required a constant interaction with social groups outside of the *familia servorum*: with Roman citizens (*cives Romani*) and non-Romans (*peregrini*), with other slaves and freedmen, and not least with the slave's own master or his agents. In individual cases, the separate property controlled by these slaves could increase to considerable dimensions. For example, the physician Decimius Merula in Assisi had paid his master 50,000 sesterces for his manumission (*CIL* XI 5400)—an amount that constituted 50% of the annual salary of a (centenary) procurator of equestrian status. Actors (*histriones*), charioteers (*aurigae*), and other specialists are known to have paid far higher sums in order to obtain their liberty (Plin. *Nat.* 7. 128; Kudlien 1986: 92–152; Leppin 1992: 84–90; Horsmann 1998: 146–66). A certain Musicus, slave to the emperor Tiberius, traveled with a retinue of sixteen under-slaves (*vicarii*) to Rome, in order to report on his keeping of accounts in the province of Gallia Narbonensis (*CIL* VI 5197). On the other hand, simple slaves in the crafts and trades had really to scrimp and save the money to buy their freedom (Sen. *Ep.* 80. 4; Horsmann 1986). The liberation of relatives, who had been left behind in servile status, then once again required considerable financial efforts.

It is no wonder, then, that great profits were to be made, on the one hand, in the slave trade, and on the other with prostitution, which can only be touched on (Harris 1980; Stumpp 1998; Schumacher 2001a: 54–65, 232–38; and cf. McGinn in this volume). Very few persons from these fields of business are known by name. Free slave-dealers (*mangones*) were, for instance, Toranius Flaccus in Rome (Plin. *Nat.* 7. 56), the Helvetian C. Domitius Carassounus (*ILS* 4851), Aeschines Flavianus from Miletus (*AE* 1922, 135), and Alexander from Thyatira (*TAM* V 2, 932). The well-known (Cn. Cornelius) Lentulus Batiatus (Plu. *Crass.* 8. 2), who ran a school of gladiators in Capua, is to be ascribed at least to the world of the freedmen, as is L. Valerius Zabda (*CIL* VI 33813). When his freedman, Aries, described his patron as a slave-trader (*mercator venalicius*), we can presume that he would also have been employed in this trade. That status, along with occupation in the slave trade, are likewise attested for A. Caprilius *A(uli) l(ibertus)* [the freedman of Aulus] Timotheus through his (Greek) funerary inscription from Amphipolis (*AE* 1946, 229), where he is described as a "seller of bodies" (in Greek, *somatemporos*), and for P. Poetellius *P(ubli) l(ibertus)* [the freedman of Publius] Syrus (*CIL* VI 10200), whose business as *lanista* (gladiatorial trainer) in Rome corresponded to Lentulus' function in Capua. It is highly probable that these freedmen continued in the slave trade for their own account as they had previously engaged in it as *servi* on their masters' behalf.

Comparable with the *lanista*, but legally much more sharply defined, the professional pimp (*leno*), who bought girls and boys and trained them for prostitution (*Dig.* 3. 2. 4. 2), was socially ostracized. In contrast to slave trading, this activity was flatly regarded as 'dishonorable' (*infamis*).[6] This explains why the organization of prostitution, above all the actual running of brothels, was without exception the responsibility of slaves (*Dig.* 3. 2. 4. 3) or freedmen (*CIL* IX 2029), who were usually former prostitutes themselves. M. Sempronius Nicocrates, who boasted that he had become so rich with the trade in beautiful women that he could afford a splendid sarcophagus decorated with the muses (*IGUR* 1326), fits into this picture; he had lost his civic rights anyway after a (failed) career as a professional musician. Otherwise, freedmen restricted themselves to the financing of, and having a (silent) partnership in, prostitution.

Slaves' services in the field of administration were, on the other hand, 'honorable.' At the lowest level, this was a matter of the organization of the running of estates, especially the management of enslaved productive forces, and in case of need, even of free wage laborers (Cato *Agr.* 1. 3; Var. *R.* 1. 17. 2; Bürge 1990). The duties of the cattle master (*magister pecoris*) in pasturing (Var. *R.* 1. 2. 14) corresponded to those of the bailiff of an estate (*vilicus*) in the fields and in horticulture. In the master's absence—and this was already the rule in the second century BC—the *vilicus* bore the responsibility in practice for an increase in his estate's earnings. Cato (*Agr.* 5. 1) brought these obligations down to the simple formula: *disciplina bona utatur, . . . sua servet diligenter*—"he should see to a good working discipline, . . . fulfill his duties conscientiously." The details need not be discussed here (see Kaltenstadler 1978; Aubert 1994: 117–200; Carlsen 1995: 57–101; Roth 2007). The prerequisites were a good physical condition, absolute loyalty toward the owner, and detailed knowledge in the theory and practice of agriculture (Col. 11. 1. 7–9). A female companion, assigned to him by the master, was responsible in her function as the bailiff's wife (*vilica*) for the organization of the kitchen and household (Cato *Agr.* 143; Col. 12. 1. 1–6; Roth 2004). So long as the *vilicus* exercised his function, he as a rule remained a slave, since he could be better supervised in this status.[7] Cicero's fictitious anecdote

6. *CIL* I² 593, lines 123–24 (*Tabula Heracleensis*) = Crawford 1996: I, 355–91 (no. 24), lines 122–23; cf. *Dig.* 23. 2. 43 pr.-9; Leppin 1992: 71–83; Horsmann 1998: 42–44; Stumpp 1998: 306–29.

7. Some exceptions (*CIL* III 7147; *AE* 1980, 229) do not falsify the rule; divergently, however, Scheidel 1990b. His arguments (*CIL* III 5616; *Dig.* 40. 5. 41. 15; 32. 97) are not as valid as he claims; on these problems see Schumacher 2010.

(*Ver.* 2. 3. 119) of the fraudulent estate bailiff is significant in its substance. More decisive, however, was the legal capacity to act, given that Roman law did not provide for the direct representation of the master by a person who was *sui iuris* (Kaser 1971–75: I, 260–61; II, 99–100; Schäfer 1998: 21–26). As in the analogous case of a *dispensator* (household manager, treasurer), a manumission almost always presupposed the end of the slave's duties (Schumacher 2010).

The question of pension provision after a long period of fulfillment of duty (*CIL* X 5081) touches on the problem of slaves' separate property (*peculium*) during their active phase in a servile status. Details are hardly documented, so that effectively only inferences by analogy can be offered (Roth 2005). But, for example, if slave herdsmen have stocks of animals of their own (Var. *R.* 1. 2. 17; 2. 10. 5), and if un-free overseers (*praefecti*) of the estate could be granted *peculium* and *contubernium* as rewards (Var. *R.* 1. 17. 5), it does seem reasonable to assume that *vilici* were just as privileged as these slave herdsmen or un-free overseers, particularly inasmuch as the *vilici* might be allowed a female partner in the *vilica* anyway. Thus, as a rule, they also had a separate property at their disposal that they retained, including their *vicarii servi* (*Dig.* 33. 7. 12. 44), in the event of their manumission (*Dig.* 15. 1. 57. 1; 20. 1. 32). Admittedly, narrow limits were probably put on any increase to the *peculium*, since larger commercial transactions were ruled out (Col. 1, 8, 13) by the requirement for the bailiff's regular presence on the estate (Cato *Agr.* 5. 3; Var. *R.* 1. 16. 5; Col. 11. 1. 23). Even the urban *vilici* were mainly slaves, although imperial freedmen are also attested in this function (*CIL* VI 8650, 33761). However, like the *vilici* on the imperial domains, the holders of these posts were subject to controls other than those that bound the slave administrators of private estates.

The divergence of personal status and social prestige becomes particularly clear in the employment of slaves in public administration. Two sectors are to be sketched out here: the *servi publici* (public slaves) in the communal sector, and the *familia Caesaris* (the emperor's slaves) in the central administration (Weiß 2004; Weaver 1972: 224–66; Schumacher 2001b: 342–52). The situation in the capital, the imperial household, and the emperor's domains around the empire must be disregarded here, in order not to go beyond the limits of this article. Just as Rome's state representatives—censors, consuls, governors—had un-free staff (*servi publici*) at their disposal (Liv. 43. 16. 13; Plu. *Galba* 8. 5; *OGIS* 487; Eder 1980), this institution is also attested from the time of the late republic on for magistrates at Rome—for example, aediles and quaestors (*CIL* 1² 594, line 62; *AE* 1986, 333, lines 19–20). Here, these assistants are designated as being municipal slaves (*servi communes*), some of whom were especially privileged as *limocincti* (the magistrate's personal attendants: *CIL* XIII 8334). Their duties involved mainly clerical work, carrying out correspondence, keeping the accounts, and administration at the lowest level. The fact that they could also influence decisions was made clear by Cicero (*Q. fr.* 1. 2. 3) when he rebuked his brother Quintus because the latter, as governor of Asia, had granted his (private) slave Statius more liberties in official matters than appeared proper.

In addition to the slaves who worked for magistrates at Rome, municipalities also had a contingent of publicly owned slaves at their disposal, who could be employed in practically all administrative matters, and who were even able to take some decisions at the lower levels in their sector. A certain influence did, of course, also result from these competences. In the financial administration (*arca publica*), the *arcarii* (treasurers: *TP Sulp.* 56) and *dispensatores* (managers/treasurers: Gaius *Inst.* 1. 122) were occupied with managing the treasury, the *actores* (managers) with contracts of lease, real estate transactions, and the acquisition of slaves (*CIL* XI 2714; *CIL* IV 3340, 143). *Tabularii* (accountants) were responsible for the filing of records (*CIL* V 8850). Other functions carried out by them involved overseeing market-places (*CIL* XI 1231) and storehouses for grain (*CIL* IX 1545), the maintenance of aqueducts (*AE* 1964, 138), as well as, above all in the East, the safeguarding of order (Plin. *Ep.* 10. 19. 1) and ritual matters (*CIL* X 3941; Bömer and Herz 1981). This wide spectrum of fields of employment presupposed specialized knowledge of various kinds, which, especially in the case of financial transactions, could also be utilized to the advantage of the slaves' own separate property (*peculium*). In the event of a manumission, the now ex-slaves of course retained these assets (*Dig.* 40. 3. 3), and they could dispose of half of their *peculium* by testament while still in their servile status (*CIL* X 4687; Ulp. *Reg.* 20. 16). Of course, these slaves also possessed under-slaves (*vicarii*), as has been repeatedly documented (*CIL* XI 6073; *CIL* XII 4451). Foundations, which could become quite expensive, particularly characterize per-sonal wealth and a, relatively speaking, higher social position respectively (*SEG* 38, 1445; *CIL* IX 4112; *CIL* XI 5375). The municipal slaves as a whole, including the freed-men (*CIL* XI 2656, 3780) described themselves as a *familia publica* (a public family: *CIL* XIV 32, 255). Their number would have corresponded to the municipalities' requirements: an estimate of between fifteen and fifty persons, depending upon the town, seems realistic to me.

The imperial administration, with its *familia Caesaris*, was considerably more extensive, and can not at all be assessed in its full dimensions. Nonetheless, it is perfectly clear that slaves and freedmen in these circles sometimes advanced to the very centers of power. With the reign of Claudius, the freed slaves' sway certainly reached a climax, thereafter to decline again gradually. However, hardly anything changed in these persons' potential influence on politics and society, although the palace eunuchs' power did not become excessive again until the fourth century AD (Schlinkert 1996: 237–84).

If we concentrate here on (say) the central imperial offices of the financial administration (*a rationibus*), the (administrative) correspondence (*ab epistulis*), and the petitions (*a libellis*), an extensive staff is to be reckoned with in each of these departments (Wolf 1965; Wachtel 1966: 17–107; Boulvert 1970; Boulvert 1974). The first signs of this development date back already to the time of Julius Caesar (Suet. *Jul.* 76. 3; Just. *Epit.* 43. 5. 11–12; Malitz 1987). Augustus, when rendering his testamentary account, referred to the names of freedmen and slaves from his *familia* who could furnish information on the state finances (Suet. *Aug.* 101. 4); for a time, he had intended to entrust the poet Horace with the running of his chancery (Suet. *Vit. Hor.* 45). Under Claudius, several highly influential freedmen are known to have played very significant roles at the very highest levels: Pallas as *a rationibus*, Narcissus as *ab epistulis*, and Polybius as *a studiis* within the department of the *a libellis* (Suet. *Cl.* 28; Sen. *Dial.* 11. 6. 5; Seitz 1969). Their personal loyalty to the emperor was just as proverbial as were their wealth and their arrogance (Dio 60. 34. 4–5; Plin. *Ep.* 8. 6. 1–10). From the beginning of the second century AD on, however, these offices were turned over to members of the equestrian order (Schumacher 2001b).

Of greater interest in the present context are the functionaries at a lower and intermediate level, in so far as slaves were there deployed. Rather complex and disparate findings emerge here. Still, it looks as if governmental service led, by middle age, to a sort of automatic manumission. With the exception of the treasurers (*dispensatores*), slaves aged between thirty and forty could mainly reckon with obtaining their freedom, although exceptions (*CIL* VI 8449; *CIL* VIII 12607) confirm the rule (Schumacher 2010). In most cases, the *manumissio* took place when the slaves, after subaltern positions as *vicarii* (managers: *CIL* VI 64), *arcarii* (treasurers: *CIL* VI 8719), and *tabellarii* (record-keepers: *CIL* VI 9052) were designated for higher duties, in other words, on the level of the *adiutores* (assistants), *optiones* (assistants), *tabularii* (account-keepers), *praepositi* (overseers), or *proximi* (personal assistants; Weaver 1972: 200–258). Their further careers continued in accordance with their aptitude, or by virtue of special promotion, to the post of *procurator* (high-level manager). These conditions explain why the auxiliary functions are not included in the inscriptions of successful freedmen; for the need to mention such low-level positions had now, with their social and professional rise, become inconsequential. Thus, as a rule, the careers of these men, as those careers are depicted in inscriptions of various sorts, begin with the position that they held at the time of their manumission (see, e.g., *CIL* VI 8428, 8608, 10233; *ILS* 1518).

Like other slaves, the *servi Caesaris* (the emperor's slaves) would frequently have property at their disposal, to which under-slaves (*vicarii*) could belong—and in fact, these under-slaves could also own slaves (*vicari vicarii*—under-slaves of under-slaves: *CIL* XV 1003; cf. Schumacher 2001a: 270–75). Now, the entire imperial household of slaves was provided with its resources by the emperor (Corbier 1980: 61–95 and esp. 66–68; Bürge 1993), and we know well that the imperial slave might use his *peculium*, above all, to redeem himself or his relatives from servile status, or, if he so chose, as provision for old age (Chantraine 1973). The amount of these slaves' financial emoluments (Sen. *Ep.* 80. 7) probably corresponded roughly to the remuneration of slaves in the *familia publica* (Fron. *Aq.* 118; Rodgers 2004: 302–5); however, they were deprived of the privileges of the *servi publici*. There is record of an annual salary of 40,000 sesterces for one group of freedmen, namely, the *proximi a memoria* (assistants to the *a memoria*) (*CIL* VI 8619); the procurator Euphrates, also an imperial freedmen, who boasted annual earnings of 100,000 sesterces (*CIL* XIV 2087), was drawing a salary equivalent to the remuneration of the *procurator Alexandriae*, who was a high-level official of equestrian status (*AE* 1972, 574; Boulvert 1981: 31–41; Pflaum 1982: 24–26, no. 70).

Of course, *peculium*, salary, and other privileges depended on the masters' decisions. And so, in all the sectors touched on above, the slave was not the subject, but rather the object of legal regulation. On the other hand, since slaves were often quite active, either on behalf of themselves or in the place of their masters, they could thus become the subjects, rather than the objects, of legal regulation. In the case of business actions, an initial authorization by the master (*voluntas domini*) was an indispensable pre-requisite (*Dig.* 50. 17. 107; Gaius *Inst.* 4. 14). With regard to any property possessed by the slave, his freedom of action was bound to the express permission for disposal (*libera administratio peculii*) granted by the master (*Dig.* 2. 14. 28. 2; Buti 1974: 48–70), for every acquisition by a slave became, at least initially, the master's property (Gaius *Inst.* 2. 87). This applied to an even higher degree to dispositions in the master's interest. Pledges took place in the form of the so-called verbal contract (*stipulatio*), the wording (*sponsio*) of which could establish or convert a debt (Gaius *Inst.* 3. 92–93; *Dig.* 12. 2. 21; Scherillo 1930; Gröschler 1997: 154–55).

One particular stipulated promise to pay by September 15, AD 39 (*TP Sulp.* 68) documents the proceeding. The contracting parties were the grain merchant C. Novius Eunus, as debtor, and the imperial slave Hesychus, acting for his master (the emperor Caligula) as creditor. The closing formula of the contract with the stipulation read: "…*stipulatus est Hesychus C(ai) Caesaris Augusti ser(vus), spopondi C(aius) Novius Eunus*" (Hesychus, slave of the [emperor] Caius Caesar Augustus, got the pledge [of redemption of the loan], and I, Caius Novius Eunus, did pledge so). Problems could arise in court if the slave was acting as a litigant on his master's behalf. In the first phase of Roman civil proceedings before the magistrate (*praetor*)—the second phase of the proceedings for the taking of evidence before the jurors (*iudices*) can be disregarded here—the taking of an oath (*iusiurandum*) played a considerable role. With regard to slaves, only the result need be mentioned here: his oath, in such a situation, was at all events binding. No distinction was made in this respect between slaves and free persons (Amirante 1954: 142–51; Schumacher 2006: 18–23).

This finding deserves notice because a slave's oath was not simply accepted in all situations. In a criminal trial, for example, the testimony of a slave had to be elicited by torture, to ascertain the truth of the evidence (*Dig.* 48. 18. 1–22). The slave's oath, with which, prior to his manumission, he had promised to perform certain daily tasks (*operae*) for his master, was not by itself valid, at least from the time of the late republic onward (*Rhet. Her.* 2. 19). Only the repetition of that promise once he had become a freedman would make the commitment legally effective (*Dig.* 40. 4. 36; 40. 12. 44 pr.). These examples show that the acceptance of the slave's oath taken in a civil trial did not somehow represent an improvement in his legal position, but simply served the purposes of adjudication. Precisely in the interaction of the slave with free persons, the interests of the latter took priority.

Apart from such individual interactions between slaves and free persons, their social relations are well documented, too, in the context of several different kinds of multilateral groups to which slaves might belong. These associations (*collegia*), insofar as they were authorized by the state, offered a wide field for networks between slaves and, especially, freedmen (Ausbüttel 1982; Fisher 1988; Kloppenborg and Wilson 1996; and cf. Perry in this volume). The express approval by the master (*voluntas domini*) was, as usual, the pre-requisite for a slave's membership in such an organization (*Dig.* 47. 22. 3. 2). In addition to numerous artisans' guilds (*Dig.* 50. 6. 6. 12; *CIL* IX 2213; van Nijf 1997; Dittmann-Schöne 2001; Zimmermann 2002), cult associations are also documented, which are subsumed under the term *collegia tenuiorum* (associations of insignificant people). This particular designation points to a category of associations, the establishment of which generally required approval by the senate or emperor (*Dig.* 47. 22. 1. 1; *AE* 1983, 181).

The broad documentation of the activities of such associations concentrates on three spheres of life: the cult itself, with its attendant feasts and banquets; measures for mutual support; and burial, with subsequent care for the grave. Apart from the professional *collegia*, membership was as a rule determined not by personal status, but by common interests and objectives. However, freedmen are represented in a markedly greater number in these associations than are slaves (*CIL* VI 30983); and in most cases, freedmen also carried out the executive functions in the *collegia*— they were the chairmen (*magistri*) or the members of the board (*curatores*), and they also managed the joint coffer (*arca*).

The organizational structure was stipulated in statutes of association (*leges*), of which only one example, this for a burial club, expressly took slaves as one of its themes (*CIL* XIV 2112 II 3–10; Schumacher 2006: 26–30). Apart from the general conditions laid out in this constitution, certain burial procedures were also regulated. According to the stipulations laid out, after their deaths, un-free club members were allowed to have only a mock funeral (*funus imaginarium*), if their masters had not manumitted their corpses for burial. In the case of manumission, however, an amphora of good wine was to be donated by the former master. Membership fees, which were to be paid monthly, were within modest bounds: the total amounted to just 15 sesterces a year. The expenses for the burial of members were assessed correspondingly restrictively.

However, these regulations for burial did not ultimately represent the main purpose for the founding of the club—there were not any burial associations (*collegia funeraticia*) in this sense. More decisive were the social support during lifetime, and the social activities and joint feasts held on cultic occasions. The costs for arranging banquets were financed partially by endowments (*CIL* VI 8826; *CIL* VI 10234, lines 17–19), and were partially assumed by the organizers of the events (*magistri cenarum*) (*CIL* XIV 2112, column II, lines 8–10). The club life of the lower classes, including that of slaves, thus reflected the social life of the *res publica Romana*.

Conclusions: The Social Differentiation of Slaves

The one criterion common to all slaves was the permanent subjection to the unrestricted power of another person, or to that of an institution. All personal and social links, all business activities and social relations were determined, in principle, by the master (whether an individual or a corporate entity) as owner; and the master's interests were aimed primarily at the exploitation of the slaves' manpower in the production process, in trade, or in the services sector. Exploitation of slaves in the interpersonal field of sexual relations, between those holding power and those subjected to power (and particularly when the exploitation did not involve prostitution), does not need to be taken as a separate theme in our connection of social interactions.

On account of their particular status, then, slaves were usually excluded from civil society. They formed a group that was homogeneous in its deprivation of rights, but otherwise heterogeneous. Three factors mainly determined the social situation of slaves: their duties; their nearness (in the sense of their personal relationship) to or distance from the master; and finally, the latter's social status. The consequences resulting from this will be sketched out here by way of conclusion.

Slaves engaged in agriculture and shepherding had only slight chances of distinguishing themselves, or finding other means of earning a living. If they did gain their liberty at all, it was usually at an advanced age, and in most cases they remained, after manumission, in their previous field of activity, though now as wage laborers (*mercennarii*), or as tenant farmers (*coloni*) (Bürge 1990; De Neeve 1984). While still slaves, they could perhaps hope for assignments as overseers (*praefecti*), or as bailiffs of an estate (*vilici*). Commerce, trade, and the service sector offered more favorable conditions, on account of the slave's practical knowledge and craft skills. Manumission, generally linked with the commitment to subsequent daily tasks performed for the previous master (*operae*), took place in both the master's and the slave's interest, and was also promoted through personal relations, in other words, nearness to the master. The freedman (*libertus*) now worked for himself (Maxey 1938), though his former owner (*patronus*) participated in the profit through the post-manumission obligations (*operae*). However, the possible competition between freedmen and free-born persons in the fields of handicrafts or trade might have had a negative effect on the potential income of the lower classes altogether.

We dealt above with the *vilici*, the municipal slaves (*servi publici*), and a part of the *familia Caesaris* in more detail as representative within the sphere of administration. Their fields of competence were considerable, as was their social prestige in the realm of public service, and so, too, their influence on decisions taken at the higher levels of the imperial administration. The basis of their powers in each case, however, was approval by the master (*voluntas domini*), whose own social position also determined that of his slaves. So, for example, in the master's absence, the bailiff of the estate was responsible for the entire organization of the agricultural holding. He could, it is true, reckon just as little with a manumission as could the public finance officials (*dispensatores/actores*); however, this shortcoming was compensated by the demanding range of duties. The reasons for this disinclination to manumit lay less in worries about embezzlement than in the matter of legal capacity to contract: since Roman private law had not developed a system of direct agency by free persons, a freedman would not have been able to discharge these duties (Schumacher 2010).

The public slaves (*servi publici*) of Rome and other cities were especially privileged. Together with the slaves of the imperial house (*servi Caesaris*), they formed the top of the 'slave hierarchy.' Both groups could also reckon with manumission, though in the case of the imperial slaves, the subsequent career chances were significantly better. Administrative personnel and slaves at court are not to be differentiated in this respect (Dio 54. 21. 3–8; *CIL* XI 3612). The decisive criterion was the nearness to the emperor.

With respect to the social stratification of slaves altogether, different criteria have to be taken into account. In the private sphere, it is best to divide these persons into two main groups: the *familiae rusticae* and *urbanae*. Slaves in agriculture formed the lowest level, in which the bailiffs of estates had a special status. Slaves in urban households were mostly in a better position; however, in addition to the opportunities, personal risks could certainly also result from proximity to the master. Slaves in trade and commerce should also be included in this intermediate level. In these groups' internal structure, the slaves born in the master's house (*vernae*) were regarded as being more respectable than the purchased slaves (*empticii*) (*CIL* VI 8919), presumably because they could be better trained. For the children of a *vilicus* (bailiff), or for those who issued from a master's union with his slave (*CIL* VI 19749, 27280), a better position is quite likely on account of the emotional link.

As already mentioned, the public and imperial slaves ranked at top level in the social grading. In these groups, too, the *vernae* had a special position. Finally, we have also to mention the under-slaves (*vicarii*). They are documented in particularly large numbers in the *familia Caesaris*; in most cases they followed their un-free masters (*servi ordinarii*) in their functions when the latter were manumitted. The fact that under-slaves could also have slaves at their disposal (*vicari vicarii*) within the framework of their *peculium* has already been mentioned. Such constellations are also attested for private spheres (*CIL* VI 7295; *Dig.* 9. 14. 19. 2). These *vicarii* with their under-slaves ranked at the lower end of their respective group within the hierarchy. The prospect of manumission, for which ordinary slaves of the intermediate and higher levels could quite realistically hope, was extremely slight in their case.

In patent imitation of Roman society otherwise, then, the slave society itself came to be structured hierarchically. That notwithstanding, everyone belonging to this group, whether (s)he was the emperor's favorite, or the lowliest slave of a humble slave, was markedly separated from the all the rest of the population—first by virtue of the fact that every one of these individuals was technically under the utter dominance of someone else, and second because these persons were not held legally to be persons, but things. Thus, slaves were propelled, in absolutely tangible fashions, to the very fringes of Roman society. And yet, a slave might come to be fabulously wealthy and powerful as one of the emperor's favorites, or might be (say) personal doctor and 'friend' to the most highly placed of senators, might become, in other words, colossally richer and more influential than the freeborn citizen who labored as (say) a blacksmith.

The marginality of a Roman slave, then, is a thing that must be approached with nuance. Some were just plain pushed to the outer fringes, and remained firmly there. Others, while technically degraded and even dehumanized, due to their strict legal status, largely led the life of Riley. We must reckon, in other words, with a potentially very significant amount of social dissonance when we consider the lot of the Roman slave. The various shadings of that potential dissonance have, I hope, been sufficiently delineated in the preceding paragraphs.

SUGGESTED READING

For general overviews of slavery in the Roman world, one may best consult Bradley 1984 and Schumacher 2001a. With respect to the legal regulation of slaves and slavery, Buckland 1908 and Watson 1987 are standard. On the subject of slaves at work, see Maxey 1938; Buti 1974; Eder 1980; Aubert 1994; Carlsen 1995; Roth 2007. The emperor's slaves are well treated by Weaver 1972. On public Slavery, see Weiß 2004. Bellen and Heinen 2003 provide much more literature on all matters to do with slaves and slavery.

BIBLIOGRAPHY

Amirante, L. 1954. *Il giuramento prestato prima della litis contestatio nelle legis actiones e nelle formule*. Naples: Jovene Editore.

Aubert, J.-J. 1994. *Business Managers in Ancient Rome. A Social and Economic Study of Institores, 200 BC—AD 250*. Leiden: E. J. Brill.

Ausbüttel, F. M. 1982. *Untersuchungen zu den Vereinen im Westen des Römischen Reiches*. Kallmünz: Verlag Michael Lassleben.

Bagnall, R. S., and B. W. Frier. 1994. *The Demography of Roman Egypt*. Cambridge: Cambridge University Press.

Bales, K. 2000. *New Slavery: A Reference Handbook*. Santa Barbara: ABC–CLIO.

———. 2004. *Disposable People: New slavery in the Global Economy*. 2nd ed. Berkeley: University of California Press.

———. 2005. *Understanding Global Slavery: A Reader*. Berkeley: University of California Press.

Bellen, H. 1971. *Studien zur Sklavenflucht im römischen Kaiserreich*. Wiesbaden: Franz Steiner Verlag.

Bellen, H., and H. Heinen (eds.). 2003. *Bibliographie zur antiken Sklaverei*. Stuttgart: Franz Steiner Verlag.

Bömer, F., and P. Herz. 1981. *Untersuchungen über die Religion der Sklaven in Griechenland und Rom I. Rom*. 2nd ed. Wiesbaden: Franz Steiner Verlag.

Boulvert, G. 1970. *Esclaves et affranchis impériaux sous le Haut-Empire romain. Rôle politique et administratif*. 2nd ed. Naples: Jovene Editore.

———. 1974. *Domestique et fonctionnaire sous le Haut-Empire romain. La condition de l'affranchi et de l'esclave du prince*. Paris: Les Belles Lettres.

———. 1981. "La carrière de Tiberius Claudius Augusti libertus Classicus." *Zeitschrift für Papyrologie und Epigraphik* 43: 31–41.

Bradley, K. R. 1984. *Slaves and Masters in the Roman Empire. A Study of Social Control.* Brussels: Latomus.

——. 1989. *Slavery and Rebellion in the Roman World* 140–70 BC. Bloomington: Indiana University Press.

Brinkhof, J. J. 1978. *Een studie over het peculium in het klassieke romeinse recht.* Meppel: Krips Repro B. V.

Buckland, W.W. 1908. *The Roman Law of Slavery. The condition of the slave in private law from Augustus to Justinian.* Cambridge: Cambridge University Press.

Bürge, A. 1990. "Der mercennarius und die Lohnarbeit." *Zeitschrift der Savigny-Stiftung für Rechtsgeschichte. Romanistische Abteilung* 107: 80–136.

——. 1993. "Cibaria. Indiz für die soziale Stellung des römischen Arbeitnehmers?" In M. J. Schermaier and Z. Végh (eds.), *Ars boni et aequi. Festschrift für Wolfgang Waldstein zum 65. Geburtstag.* Stuttgart: Franz Steiner Verlag. 63–78.

Buti, I. 1974. *Studi sulla capacità patrimoniale dei servi.* Naples: Jovene Editore.

Carlsen, J. 1995. *Vilici and Roman Estate Managers until AD 284.* Rome: "L'Erma" di Bretschneider.

Chantraine, H. 1973. "Außerdienststellung und Altersversorgung kaiserlicher Sklaven und Freigelassener." *Chiron* 3: 307–29.

Corbier, M. 1980. "Salaires et salariat sous le Haut-Empire." In *Les "devaluations" à Rome. Époque républicaine et impériale II.* Rome: École Française de Rome. 61–95.

Corbino, A. 1990. "Servitù (diritto romano)." *Enciclopedia del Diritto* 42: 243–62.

Crawford, M. H. (ed.). 1996. *Roman Statutes.* 2 vols. London: Institute of Classical Studies, University of London.

Crook, J. A. 1967. "Patria potestas." *Classical Quarterly* 17: 113–22.

De Neeve, P. W. 1984. *Colonus. Private Farm-Tenancy in Roman Italy during the Republic and the Early Principate.* Amsterdam: J. C. Gieben.

Dittmann-Schöne, I. 2001. *Die Berufsvereine in den Städten des kaiserzeitlichen Kleinasiens.* Regensburg: Verlag Roderer.

Duff, A. M. 1928. *Freedmen in the Early Roman Empire.* Oxford: Oxford University Press. (Reprint, Cambridge: W. Heffer & Sons. 1958).

Eder, W. 1980. *Servitus publica. Untersuchungen zur Entstehung, Entwicklung und Funktion der öffentlichen Sklaverei in Rom.* Wiesbaden: Franz Steiner Verlag.

Erman, H. 1896. *Servus vicarius. L'esclave de l'esclave romain.* Lausanne: Rouge. (Reprint, Naples: Jovene Editore 1986).

Fabre, G. 1981. *Libertus. Recherches sur les rapports patron—affranchi à la fin de la République romaine.* Rome: École Française de Rome.

Fisher, N. R. E. 1988. "Roman Associations, Dinner Parties, and Clubs." In M. Grant and R. Kitzinger (eds.), *Civilization in the Ancient Mediterranean.* New York: Scribner. 1199–1225.

Flaig, E. 2009. *Weltgeschichte der Sklaverei.* Munich: C. H. Beck Verlag.

Flory, M. B. 1975. *Family and Familia: A Study of Social Relations in Slavery.* PhD Thesis, Yale University.

——. 1978. "Family in *familia.* Kinship and Community in Slavery." *American Journal of Ancient History* 3: 78–95.

Friedl, R. 1996. *Der Konkubinat im kaiserzeitlichen Rom: von Augustus bis Septimius Severus.* Stuttgart: Franz Steiner Verlag.

Gamauf, R. 1999. *Ad statuam licet confugere. Untersuchungen zum Asylrecht im Prinzipat* Frankfurt: Peter Lang Verlag.

Graßl, H. 1990. "Zur Rolle der Frau in antiken Hirtenkulturen." *Laverna* 1: 13–17.

Gröschler, P. 1997. *Die tabellae—Urkunden aus den pompejanischen und herkulanensischen Urkundenfunden*. Berlin: Duncker & Humblot.

Harris, W. V. 1980. "Towards a Study of the Roman Slave Trade." *Memoirs of the American Academy in Rome* 36: 117–40.

Herrmann-Otto, E. 1994. *Ex ancilla natus. Untersuchungen zu den "hausgeborenen" Sklaven und Sklavinnen im Westen des römischen Kaiserreiches*. Stuttgart: Franz Steiner Verlag.

Hinard, F. 1985. *Les proscriptions de la Rome républicaine*. Rome: École Française de Rome.

Horsmann, G. 1986. "Die *divi fratres* und die *redemptio servi suis nummis.*" *Historia* 35: 308–21.

———. 1998. *Die Wagenlenker der römischen Kaiserzeit*. Stuttgart: Franz Steiner Verlag.

Hübner, W. 1984. *Varros instrumentum vocale im Kontext der antiken Fachwissenschaften*. Wiesbaden: Franz Steiner Verlag.

Kaltenstadler, W. 1978. *Arbeitsorganisation und Führungssystem bei den römischen Agrarschriftstellern: Cato, Varro, Columella*. Stuttgart: Gustav Fischer Verlag.

Kaser, M. 1971–75. *Das römische Privatrecht*. 2 vols. 2nd ed. Munich: C. H. Beck Verlag.

Klingenberg, G. 2005. *Servus fugitivus*. Stuttgart: Franz Steiner Verlag.

Kloosterboer, W. 1960. *Involuntary Labour since the Abolition of Slavery. A Survey of Compulsory Labour throughout the World*. Leiden: E. J. Brill.

Kloppenborg, J. S., and S. G. Wilson (eds.). 1996. *Voluntary Associations in the Graeco-Roman World*. London: Routledge.

Kudlien, F. 1986. *Die Stellung des Arztes in der römischen Gesellschaft*. Stuttgart: Franz Steiner Verlag.

Kunkel, W. 1974. "Das Konsilium im Hausgericht." In W. Kuhnkel, *Kleine Schriften*. Weimar: Hermann Böhlaus Nachfolger. 117–49.

Lacey, W. K. 1980. "Patria potestas." In B. Rawson (ed.), *The Family in Ancient Rome. New Perspectives*. London: Croom Helm. 121–44.

Leppin, H. 1992. *Histrionen. Untersuchungen zur sozialen Stellung von Bühnenkünstlern im Westen des Römischen Reiches zur Zeit der Republik und des Prinzipats*. Bonn: Rudolf Habelt Verlag.

Lewis, N. 1983. *Life in Egypt under Roman Rule*. Oxford: Oxford University Press.

Linder, A. 1987. *The Jews in Roman Imperial Legislation*. Detroit: Wayne State University Press.

Malitz, J. 1987. "Die Kanzlei Caesars—Herrschaftsorganisation zwischen Republik und Prinzipat." *Historia* 36: 51–72.

Maxey, M. 1938. *Occupations of the Lower Classes in Roman Society*. Chicago: Chicago University Press. (Reprint, New York: Arno Press 1975).

Pflaum, H.-G. 1982. *Les carrières procuratoriennes équestres sous le Haut-Empire romain. Supplément*. Paris: Librairie Orientaliste Paul Geuthner.

Pólay, E. 1967. *Die Sklavenehe und das römische Recht*. Szeged: Facultas Scientiarum Politicarum et Juridicarum Universitatis Szegediensis.

Reduzzi Merola, F. 1990. *Servo parere. Studi sulla condizione giuridica degli schiavi vicari e dei sottoposti a schiavi nelle esperienze greca e romana*. Naples: Jovene Editore.

Rodgers, R. H. 2004. *Frontinus de aquaeductu urbis Romae*. Cambridge: Cambridge University Press.

Roth, U. 2004. "Inscribed Meaning: The Vilica and the Villa Economy." *Papers of the British School at Rome* 72: 101–24.

———. 2005. "Food, Status, and the *Peculium* of Agricultural Slaves." *Journal of Roman Archaeology* 18: 278–92.

———. 2007. *Thinking Tools—Agricultural Slavery between Evidence and Models*. London: Institute of Classical Studies, University of London.

Saller, R. P. 1994. *Patriarchy, Property and Death in the Roman Family*. Cambridge: Cambridge University Press.

———. 1997. "Roman Kinship: Structure and Sentiment." In B. Rawson (ed.), *The Roman Family in Italy. Status, Sentiment, Space*. Oxford: Clarendon Press. 7–34.

Samson, R. 1989. "Rural Slavery, Inscriptions, Archaeology and Marx." *Historia* 38: 99–110.

Schäfer, C. 1998. *Spitzenmanagement in Republik und Kaiserzeit. Die Prokuratoren von Privatpersonen im Imperium Romanum vom 2. Jh. v. Chr. bis zum 3. Jh. n. Chr*. St. Katharinen: Scripta Mercaturae Verlag.

Scheidel, W. 1990a. "Feldarbeit von Frauen in der antiken Landwirtschaft." *Gymnasium* 97: 405–31.

———. 1990b. "Free-Born and Manumitted Bailiffs in the Greco-Roman World." *Classical Quarterly* 40: 591–93.

Scherillo, G. 1930. "Sulla stipulazione del *servus* e del *filius familias*." In *Studi in onore del Pietro Bonfante V*. Milan: Fratelli Treves Editori. 205–41.

Schlinkert, D. 1996. *Ordo senatorius und nobilitas. die Konstitution des Senatsadels in der Spätantike*. Stuttgart: Franz Steiner Verlag.

Schumacher, L. 1982. *Servus index. Sklavenverhör und Sklavenanzeige im republikanischen und kaiserzeitlichen Rom*. Wiesbaden: Franz Steiner Verlag.

———. 1990. Review of J. G. Wolf, *Das Senatusconsultum Silanianum und die Senatsrede des C. Cassius Longinus*. Heidelberg: Winter Universitäts-Verlag 1988. In *Zeitschrift der Savigny-Stiftung für Rechtsgeschichte. Romanistische Abteilung* 107: 641–45.

———. 2001a. *Sklaverei in der Antike. Alltag und Schicksal der Unfreien*. Munich: C. H. Beck Verlag.

———. 2001b. "Hausgesinde—Hofgesinde. Terminologische Überlegungen zur Funktion der familia Caesaris im 1. Jh. n. Chr." In H. Bellen and H. Heinen (eds.), *Fünfzig Jahre Forschungen zur antiken Sklaverei an der Mainzer Akademie, 1950–2000. Miscellanea zum Jubiläum*. Stuttgart: Franz Steiner Verlag. 331–52.

———. 2006. *Corpus der römischen Rechtsquellen zur Sklaverei. Teil VI: Stellung des Sklaven im Sakralrecht*. Stuttgart: Franz Steiner Verlag.

———. 2010. "On the Status of Private *Actores, Dispensatores* and *Vilici*." In U. Roth (ed.), *By the Sweat of Your Brow. Roman Slavery in Its Socio-Economic Setting*. London: Institute of Classical Studies of the University of London. 31–47.

Seitz, W. 1969. *Studien zur Prosopographie und zur Sozial- und Rechtsgeschichte der großen kaiserlichen Zentralämter bis hin zu Hadrian*. PhD Thesis, Universität München.

Sirks, B. 1993. "Reconsidering the Roman Colonate." *Zeitschrift der Savigny-Stiftung für Rechtsgeschichte. Romanistische Abteilung* 110: 331–69.

Staerman, E. M. 1969. *Die Blütezeit der Sklavenwirtschaft in der römischen Republik*. Wiesbaden: Franz Steiner Verlag.

Stumpp, B. E. 1998. *Prostitution in der römischen Antike*. Berlin: Akademie Verlag.

Treggiari, S. 1969. *Roman Freedmen during the Late Republic*. Oxford: Clarendon Press.

———. 1991. *Roman Marriage. Iusti Coniuges from the Time of Cicero to the Time of Ulpian*. Oxford: Clarendon Press.

Urbainczyk, T. 2008. *Slave Revolts in Antiquity*. Berkeley: University of California Press.

van Nijf, O. M. 1997. *The Civic World of Professional Associations in the Roman East*. Amsterdam: J. C. Gieben.

Wachtel, K. 1966. *Freigelassene und Sklaven in der staatlichen Finanzverwaltung der römischen Kaiserzeit von Augustus bis Diokletian*. Berlin: Deutsche Akademie der Wissenschaften.

Waldstein, W. 1986. *Operae libertorum. Untersuchungen zur Dienstpflicht freigelassener Sklaven*. Stuttgart: Franz Steiner Verlag.

Watson, A. 1987. *Roman Slave Law*. Baltimore: Johns Hopkins University Press.

Weaver, P. R. C. 1972. *Familia Caesaris. A Social Study of the Emperor's Freedmen and Slaves.* Cambridge: Cambridge University Press.

Weiß, A. 2004. *Sklave der Stadt. Untersuchungen zur öffentlichen Sklaverei in den Städten des Römischen Reiches.* Stuttgart: Franz Steiner Verlag.

Welwei, K.-W. 1988. *Unfreie im antiken Kriegsdienst. III. Rom.* Stuttgart: Franz Steiner Verlag.

Winterling, A. 1999. *Aula Caesaris. Studien zur Institutionalisierung des römischen Kaiserhofes in der Zeit von Augustus bis Commodus. 31 v. Chr.–192 n. Chr.* Munich: R. Oldenbourg Verlag.

Wolf, M. 1965. *Untersuchungen zur Stellung der kaiserlichen Freigelassenen und Sklaven in Italien und den Westprovinzen.* PhD Thesis, Universität Münster.

Zeber, I. 1981. *A Study of the Peculium of a Slave in Pre-classical and Classical Roman Law.* Wrocław: Wydawn, Wrocławskiego Uniwersytetu.

Zeuske, M. 2009. *Globalgeschichte der Sklaverei. Menschen als Ware gestern und heute.* Zurich: Rotpunktverlag.

Zimmermann, C. 2002. *Handwerkervereine im griechischen Osten des Imperium Romanum.* Mainz: Römisch-Germanisches Zentralmuseum.

CHAPTER 29

WOMEN IN ROMAN SOCIETY

KRISTINA MILNOR

IN his autobiographical *On Prognosis*, which chronicles the author's rise through Roman society from unknown immigrant to imperial caregiver, the second-century doctor Galen offers us a work that is "extremely important for the understanding of the intellectual and social history of the second century...the most detailed single source for a doctor's career" (Nutton 1979: 146). It is thus not, perhaps, surprising that he also provides us with snapshot-like portraits of a number of different Roman women, who appear in the text as patients, fellow medical professionals, and potential patrons. These women include the wife of the former consul Flavius Boethus, who was suffering from "female flow"; too modest to seek the care of male doctors, she sought out the best midwives, yet received no relief. Galen was called in by her husband, but instead of speaking with her directly, he at first discusses her symptoms only with her attendants. It is only when an emergency arises and the nurses are at a loss that the doctor intervenes and treats the patient directly (8. 2–7).[1] At the other end of the spectrum is a certain Annia Faustina, a member of the imperial family, who arrives with one of Galen's rivals in tow as the author is in the midst of treating the emperor's son Commodus for a fever.[2] She begins by aggressively questioning the treatment being provided to the boy, goes on sarcastically to compliment Galen's skill, mock the practices of her own attendant, insult the boy's tutor, and drive off in her carriage, leaving Galen irritated and complaining (12. 5–9). In contrast with the wife of Boethus, who is ashamed to take any role

---

1. Galen is always cited here from Nutton 1979.
2. This seems to be Annia Fundania Faustina, cousin of Commodus' father Marcus Aurelius. See Nutton 1979: 223 and Hekster 2002: 33 n. 87.

in her own medical care, Annia Faustina not only interferes with Galen's treatment of Commodus, but shows in her comments a real familiarity with the schools of medical thought and their different practices. *On Prognosis* thus offers a view of the wide range of social relationships and roles that women could have in second-century Rome, from the sheltered wife most comfortable in the company of other women, to the imperious relative of the emperor who engages as an equal with the philosopher-doctors who are the heroes of the text. More shadowy, but still present, are the midwives who were first called in to treat the wife of Boethus, with whom Galen works to seek a cure, and one of whom he praises as "thoroughly knowledgeable about her business" (8. 8).

Of course, Galen's text is very much a product of its time. Two hundred years earlier, before the advent of imperial rule in Rome, Annia Faustina would not have had her role in the emperor's household to give her status—although it is clear that elite women in ancient society always lived very different lives from their poorer sisters. Indeed, Roman women's history almost inevitably gets told as a series of stories about famous individuals who emerge onto the stage of history at least in part because they are related to socially or politically prominent men. This is an artifact of our sources as much as of Roman reality: the fact of the matter is that ancient authors did not conceptualize what we would term social history or the history of marginalized groups. For them, history was the story of (male) society, culture, and politics, and when women do play a role in that story, it is generally treated as a disruption of the normal course of events. For this reason, 'incidental' information, like that provided by Galen in *On Prognosis*, is extremely important to our ability to write about female social relations in ancient Rome. Yet even he, it should be noted, preserves the tropes of traditional historical writing: the undifferentiated group of midwives surrounds the patient identified only as "the wife of Boethus," while, in contrast, Annia Faustina not only has her own name, but plays an important and active role in the progress of the narrative. She is also the only woman who actually speaks in the course of the text. In part, to be sure, she is given a voice here because she has the education and knowledge to articulate—albeit in a manner not particularly friendly to Galen—some of the conflicts that he is trying to explore and explain for the reader. She has this knowledge because she comes from a class and family background that supported a certain level of formal education for its female members. Thus, there are 'real' historical reasons why elite Roman authors, or ones like Galen who are trying to join the elite, show a preference for depicting women like Annia Faustina: they speak the same language (Hallett 1989).

The reality is, however, that women as a group were certainly among the 'marginalized' of Roman society, even if certain individuals among them were able to make a place for themselves in Roman history. In general terms, the reasons for this marginalization are fairly clear: the Romans, like many other pre-modern cultures, saw women as naturally suited to, and therefore representative of, the private or domestic sphere, the world of the family, of daily household tasks, of other marginalized groups like children and slaves. While adult citizen men were expected to hone their skills for participation in politics and the military, women were praised for their focus on the world of the home. Funerary epitaphs are revealing, if not of the total reality of women's lives, then of the ideals against which they were measured; much is made on tombstones for women of the nursing of children, love of husbands, and household tasks such as working with wool (Lattimore 1942: 294–300; cf. Forbis 1990). But this was not, for the Romans, the stuff of history, the stuff worth remembering as part of the community's shared record as it is represented in literary texts, public inscriptions, institutions, and so on. The funeral epitaph of a certain Murdia, the inscribed record of the speech, or *laudatio*, which her son delivered at her funeral sometime during the reign of Augustus, is remarkably telling in this context: having listed all of the traditional virtues that she displayed, from chastity (*pudicitia*) to hard work (*diligentia*), Murdia's son notes that "[women's] natural goodness, preserved by its own guardianship, does not require a proliferation of words…it is difficult to find new kinds of praise for a woman, since their lives are disturbed by little variation" (…*naturalia bona propria custodia servata varietates verborum non desiderent…adquirere novas laudes mulieri sit arduom, quam minoribus varietatibus vita iactetur…: CIL* VI 10230). Because the domestic world, the work necessary to make it function, and the virtues that were associated with accomplishing that work, were all static and unchanging, there was (according to Murdia's son) very little that should or even could be said about the life of a good Roman woman.

In some senses, Murdia's son here sounds something like Pericles in Thucydides' version of his funeral oration, where he makes one of the great paradigmatic statements about the social role of ancient Athenian women: "the greatest glory of a woman is to be least talked about by men, whether they praise you or blame you" (Th. 2. 45. 2). For Pericles, any visibility in public is bad for women; like Murdia's son, he sees them as fundamentally other to the world inhabited by men and described in their communal discourse. On the other hand, it is worth noting the different contexts of these statements. Pericles has essentially only this to say about women (although he does also advise them not to be any weaker than they can help), but the son makes his statement within a speech specifically in praise of his mother, in which he offers not just a list of her virtues but a fairly extensive description of her life and the consequences of her death. In other words, despite his caveat that he could find little to say, he actually said a great deal. Not only did he say it in the oration, but he also (as was traditional) had the text inscribed and set up as part of his mother's grave monument. Murdia's domestic virtues, far from being hidden from sight inside her home, were both described in a public space and made part of the public landscape of the ancient city. In this way, the son's memorial of his mother stands as an important reminder to us, first that paradoxes certainly existed in the representation and reality of ancient Roman women's lives, but also that one key to understanding those paradoxes may lie within the very mechanics of Roman history and society. *Laudationes* for women were not uncommon; Livy preserves the story that the honor was given to them in 390 BC as a reward for having donated their personal jewelry to pay the tribute demanded by the Gauls (Liv. 5. 50. 7). The public-spirited gesture made by the women, it would seem, demanded a publicly visible repayment; because they were willing and able to take action during a crisis in the state, they were given a small rhetorical space in civic life. This story, in the same way as Murdia's epitaph, thus exposes the tension between domestic virtues and their representation, whether in the pages of Roman history or on the stage of Roman social life.

We may note, however, that there is again a strong class element here: the women who ransomed the city in 390 BC were those who had gold jewelry to donate; Murdia is remembered fondly by her son at least in part because she made sure that he received his due share of her property. One of the significant differences between the social circumstances of ancient Athenian and ancient Roman women was that the latter could and did possess property, something that clearly had an influence on both the actual and imagined roles that they played in Roman society and culture (Gardner 1986: 163–203; Van Bremen 1983). Although it was only under the Augustan social legislation that women could become formally *sui iuris*—that is, able to conduct their own business without the oversight of a (male) *tutor* or guardian—in practice, it is clear that women frequently took charge of their own affairs. The history of the late republic, particularly, contains many stories of business transacted between men and women, such as the property bought by Servilia from Caesar at a discount, nastily insinuated by Cicero to have been part of the price paid for Servilia's youngest daughter (Suet. *Jul.* 50. 2). Crassus is also supposed to have been acquitted of adultery with Licinia, a Vestal virgin, when it was revealed that his frequent visits to her had only been in order to negotiate a better price on a property that she owned in the suburbs (Plu. *Crass.* 1. 2). Cicero speaks admiringly of Caecilia Metella, who assisted the destitute Sextus Roscius of Ameria with both her influence and her funds (*S. Rosc.* 27). The orator himself apparently borrowed money in 45 BC from a certain Caerellia, with whom he had a somewhat rocky friendship and of whose lending practices Atticus apparently did not approve (*Att.* 12. 51. 3). One of the best-remembered episodes of the Second Triumvirate was when the Triumvirs attempted to raise funds by taxing the property of Rome's wealthiest women, a move that was successfully opposed by a group headed by a certain Hortensia, who confronted the magistrates in the Forum Romanum and delivered a speech that was read and praised by later generations (Quint. *Inst.* 1. 1. 6). Although we unfortunately do not possess the text of that oration, the second-century historian Appian offers a version in which Hortensia is made to argue that the possession of property is one of women's inalienable rights, and that by attempting to tax it the Triumvirs are attempting to "degrade [the women] to a position unworthy of [their] station, customs, and womanly nature" (App. *BC* 4. 32).

The fact that these stories proliferate remarkably during the late republic, however, should serve to warn us against falling into the temptation to talk about the history of Roman women as though it were trans-historical, not subject to the influence of time, chance, and changes in other, apparently unrelated, social institutions. It is clear, for instance, that the social and political turmoil that afflicted the Roman state during the last century BC had significant implications for the roles of certain Roman women (Cluett 1998). On the one hand, the close association between women and domestic life meant that as power became concentrated in the hands of fewer and fewer aristocratic families, female influence within and between those families took on greater and greater importance. A mother's traditional role in helping to arrange a daughter's marriage, for example, could have real political implications (Dixon 1983). Similarly, the role of 'grieving widow' could be put to real political use, as when Fulvia dramatically revealed the body of her assassinated *popularis* husband, P. Clodius Pulcher, in an effort to whip up the emotions of the crowd against his optimate enemies.

On the other hand, the conventional separation between the domestic and civic worlds meant that women were, to a certain extent, protected from the vagaries of political life that afflicted Roman men. Since they were not formally subject to exile or proscription, they often remained behind in Rome, the center of political power, while their male relatives were forced to flee elsewhere. Thus, during Cicero's exile in 58 BC, he relied on his wife Terentia to manage his financial affairs while he was absent from Italy; the wife praised in the so-called *Laudatio Turiae* interceded with the triumvir Lepidus on behalf of her proscribed husband; the female relatives of the tyrannicides were of crucial importance in protecting and furthering the interests of their husbands, sons, and brothers after 44 BC. It is worth noting, certainly, that our sources are better with later periods: our ability to write the history of any group of Romans, let alone a marginalized one, during the early republic is limited at best. So it is not entirely surprising that as we have more and different kinds of historical information generally for the late republic and empire, we also have more to say about the women of those periods. Nevertheless, it cannot be denied that the enormous overall changes in Roman politics and society during the civil wars and afterward had real and permanent effects on the lives of Roman women.[3]

Despite these advantages, however, it is evident that politically ambitious women of even the late republic and empire were confined by the moral discourse that saw performance of conventional 'domestic' virtues as the highest measure of a woman's success, and that correspondingly associated public visibility with moral transgression (Hillard 1992). Perhaps the most famous example of this effect is Fulvia, who (in Plutarch's formulation) "gave no attention to a woman's domestic duties," wanting only "to rule a ruler and command a commander" (*Ant.* 10. 2). Fulvia goes down in history as both power hungry and sexually rapacious, two qualities that are often associated in Roman depictions of bad women. An epigram is preserved in Martial, in which the Perusine War is represented as Fulvia's revenge for sexual rejection by Octavian: she is made to say to him, "*aut futue, aut pugnemus*" (Either fuck, or let's fight!: Mart. 11. 20. 7. Cf. Hallett 1977). It has been persuasively argued that, at least in part, this depiction of Fulvia should be attributed to later propaganda favorable to Octavian, which sought to contrast Fulvia's wicked womanhood with the heroic femininity of Octavia, Antony's subsequent wife and sister to Octavian (Delia 1991). It is certainly true that the negative picture of Fulvia

3. For an overview of the changes in Roman society unleashed by the progress from republic to empire, see Ando in this volume.

found in Cicero's *Phillipics* (e.g., 2. 48, 99, 113) is part of a strategy to depict her husband, Antony, as weak and immoral; in this way, the orator is employing the same tactic that he used previously with great success in the *Verrines*, where he described the ways that Verres was completely under the sway of the *meretrix* (prostitute) Chelidon (e.g., *Ver.* 2. 1. 120). The immorality of women thus is used as both cause and proof of the immorality of the men with whom they were associated (Hillard 1989). Similarly, Sallust remarks on the female followers of Catiline that they were led to him through their indebtedness: "they had first managed their vast expenditures by means of prostituting their bodies, but afterwards, when age had put a limit on their profitability but not on their desire for luxury, they had acquired substantial loans" (*quae primo ingentis sumptus stupro corporis toleraverant, post, ubi aetas tantummodo quaestui neque luxuriae modum fecerat, aes alienum grande conflaverant*: Sal. *Cat.* 24. 4). Among these women is a certain Sempronia: "everything was dearer to her than her honor and modesty; you could not easily tell whether she was less sparing of her money or her reputation; her licentiousness was such that she more often sought out men than was sought by them" (*Sed ei cariora semper omnia quam decus atque pudicitia fuit; pecuniae an famae minus parceret, haud facile discerneres; lubido sic accensa, ut saepius peteret viros quam peteretur*: Sal. *Cat.* 25. 3).

Sallust's final remark in this passage points to one reason why the behavior of women like Sempronia was problematic for most Roman men: by not comporting herself as a proper woman (i.e., passively, as represented in the verb *peteretur*), she threatens to take over the proper role of a Roman man (i.e., to become active, as with the verb *peteret*). Indeed, in an earlier sentence, Sallust attributes to her a "masculine daring" (*virilis audacia*: 25. 1). Moreover, Sempronia's masculinity is matched by a dangerous femininity displayed by the corrupted men around her, whose bodies and minds have been "feminized" (*effeminat*: *Cat.* 11. 3) by luxury and greed (Boyd 1987). In a similar vein, Fulvia is memorialized by Velleius Paterculus as "having nothing womanly except her body" (*nihil muliebre praeter corpus gerens*: Vell. 2. 74) because, as is depicted with more verve in Cassius Dio (Dio 48. 10), during the Perusine War she girded on a sword and attempted to give orders to the soldiers. Horace tars Cleopatra's followers with a similar brush in *Epode* 7, when he associates them with *spadones rugosi* ("wrinkled eunuchs": 13–14) because they freely follow a woman's authority. These women thus appear as individual, 'historical' examples of the general principle apparently articulated by Cicero in *de Re Publica* 5, where the orator-turned-philosopher criticizes Plato's vision of a communal society: "indeed, he does not even debar women from the senate house, and allows them to be in the military, and in the magistracies, and in supreme command. How great will be the misfortune of that city, in which women assume the offices of men!" (*quin etiam feminis curiam reservavit, militiam et magistratus et imperia permisit. quanta erit infelicitas urbis illius, in qua virorum officia mulieres occupabunt!*: Lact. *Epit.* 33. 4–5). Women must be confined to the domestic sphere because to allow them a place in public business would be to take that place away from Roman men.

Recent scholarship has made much of the important, and sometimes precarious, position that the 'correct' performance of masculinity held for Roman men, particularly in the area of rhetorical performance. Roman civic life was always fiercely competitive, a 'zero-sum game' in which the triumph of one man's position or authority meant the defeat of another's. Perhaps somewhat ironically, this was true not only under the republic, in which contests in the law court or senate house could have real effects on the future of the Roman state, but also under the empire, when one's position in the social hierarchy was all that was at stake. At any rate, it is clear that by a certain point in Roman history, manliness was something that could be seen and judged in a person's affect, the way in which he carried himself, gestured, and spoke (Gleason 1995; Connolly 1998; and cf. Connolly in this volume). A man who did not perform his gendered self to the satisfaction of his countrymen ran the risk of being labeled effeminate, that is, not a real man who was able and willing to shoulder the responsibilities of a Roman citizen. Thus, as I noted above, the threat posed by 'masculine' women was a real one: since Roman men were constantly faced with the need to prove their manliness in the theater of public life, it was vitally important to maintain the strong boundary between it and the world of women.

It is worth noting, however, that we do know of significantly many women who did hold a kind of 'public' position in Roman society, namely, they worked outside their homes. It is true that we have little evidence of women employed in the professions—the occasional appearance of women before law courts, speaking on their own or others' behalf, is worth noting, but probably does not indicate that this was their main wage-earning activity.[4] There is some scanty evidence of women bankers, but it probably points more to their role as private or semi-private moneylenders (Gardner 1986: 233–37). Some examples of this are a certain Otacilia Laterensis, who attempted to claim back a fraudulent loan from a former lover (V. Max. 8. 2. 2) and a case in the *Digest* where a Manilius is trying to recover some money placed on deposit with an unnamed woman (*Dig.* 2. 13. 4. 10). On a smaller scale is a certain Faustilla, who seems to have worked as a moneylender and pawnbroker in Pompeii (*CIL* IV 4528, 8203, 8204). Far more common, however, are women engaged in the medical profession, like the midwives in Galen's *Prognosis*. Although they are most frequently found specializing in the care of women, we do have evidence that points to female practitioners of general medicine—even the aunt of the fourth-century poet Ausonius, Aemilia Hilaria, who was "expert with the medical arts in the manner of men" (*more virum medicis artibus experiens*: Aus. *Parentalia* 6. 6). But as we work down the social scale to skill in crafts and small mercantile businesses, especially those relating to food production, women grow increasingly common. Female proprietresses of, for instance, cookshops and market stalls are well represented in both the epigraphic and visual record. Yet, such women, especially those who worked in the notoriously dissolute *cauponae* or *tabernae* (taverns or inns), were often seen as morally compromised, so that, for instance, they were considered under Roman law to have the same status as prostitutes (Gardner 1986: 130, 132–33). Indeed, the

4. On professional advocates generally, see Crook 1995.

emperor Constantine went so far as to distinguish between a woman who owned or managed a tavern, who was allowed the same status as a Roman *matrona*, and those who actually served the patrons, and were therefore considered to live degraded lives (*CJ* 9. 9. 28).

This final distinction underscores two important points: first, that it was the 'public' nature of a working woman's role that made it problematic for Roman culture; the owner of the tavern is less implicated in immorality because she does not expose herself directly to customers. Second, however, it also shows how clearly and directly these moral standards map onto class differences: the proprietress of the cookshop is seen to have a higher status because her greater wealth (as the owner of the business rather than one of its workers) allows her to maintain that status. Thus, there is significant evidence that the performance of traditional domestic virtues was simultaneously more important and more possible for women of higher social status, creating a neatly closed system in which the display of 'domesticity' was both evidence of and a contribution to maintaining a particular position in the social hierarchy. Natalie Kampen has analyzed a wide range of visual depictions of women engaged in mercantile activities and concludes that there is little difference between the iconographic tropes employed to show male and female small-scale vendors; once we move into the world of the rich merchant or artisan, however, we find no images of businesswomen, despite the fact that we know from other sources that women did participate in business at this level. Nevertheless, women appear in these representations alongside their merchant husbands only engaged in 'domestic' activities such as spinning or having their hair dressed (Kampen 1982). A similar effect may be seen in funerary monuments, for example, one in which the wife of a certain butcher is claimed to be *casta, pudens, volgei nescia, feida viro* ("pure, chaste, ignorant of the crowd, and faithful to her husband") on a grandiose and elaborately carved stone; both the scale of the monument and its announcement of domestic virtues are attempting to claim a certain social status for the deceased and her (at the time of its production, still living) husband (*CIL* I 1011). The moral marginalization of women—their isolation in the domestic sphere away from the public business of men—thus had an important role to play in the creation and maintenance of class distinctions in Roman society.

On the surface, then, dominant ideology in Rome seems to display a real investment in the confinement of women to traditional domestic roles, virtues, and values. What is curious, however, is that women's adoption of men's virtues is not always represented in a negative light. Take, for instance, the remarks of Valerius Maximus on the story of Lucretia, whose rape and suicide famously motivated the overthrow of the Etruscan kings in Rome and the foundation of the Roman Republic. Book 6 of Valerius' catalogue of historical exempla, *Memorable Words and Deeds*, opens with praise of Lucretia's signal quality, her *pudicitia* (chastity), which Valerius describes as *virorum pariter ac feminarum praecipuum firmamentum* ("the most important foundation of men and women equally": V. Max. 6. 1. pr.). He exemplifies this with the story of Lucretia:

Dux Romanae pudicitiae Lucretia, cuius virilis animus maligno errore fortunae muliebre corpus sortitus est, a Sex. Tarquinio regis Superbi filio per vim stuprum pati coacta, cum gravissimis verbis iniuriam suam in concilio necessariorum deplorasset, ferro se, quod veste tectum adtulerat, interemit causamque tam animoso interitu imperium consulare pro regio permutandi populo Romano praebuit. (V. Max. 6. 1. 1)

The foremother of Roman chastity, Lucretia, to whose female body a male spirit fell through an unhappy mistake of fortune, was forcibly raped by the son of the king Sextus Tarquinius Superbus, and when she had poured out her injury with the most serious words in a meeting of her relatives, she killed herself with a sword which she had brought, concealed under her clothing—and by such a courageous death she gave the Roman people a cause to substitute the authority of consuls for that of the king.

The opening statement, that chastity is as important to men as to women, is somewhat ambiguous: are men imagined to rely on women's chastity, or are they supposed to be chaste themselves? The example of Lucretia seems to support the former interpretation, as Valerius focuses on her role as a willing martyr to the expulsion of the kings and the republican revolution. Lucretia is ironically and unwillingly brought out into the sphere of politics by her *pudicitia*, a traditional feminine domestic virtue; her allegiance to that virtue has a profound and positive effect on the public affairs of Rome. Because of this strange circumstance, Valerius labels her a hybrid of male and female, a *virilis animus* (manly spirit) in a *muliebre corpus* (female body). Yet, his words do not imply criticism; rather, he seems to be praising the (masculine) strength and courage that she was able to display in her adherence to the (feminine) virtue of *pudicitia*.

Of course, it should not be forgotten that, although the episode that Valerius is discussing notionally took place in 509 BC, he is describing it during the early years of the principate—a period in which the domestic roles of certain women were being given unprecedented prominence in Roman politics. With the rise of the *domus Caesaris* the central political unit of the Roman state, imperial women's 'household' influence over their male relatives took on real public significance: in the same way that republican women could further their own public careers through their relationships with politically important men, the 'domestic' influence that, for example, Livia exercised over her husband Augustus and son Tiberius translated directly to political clout. Indeed, by the time of the Severan dynasty (AD 193–235), we find women acting in a very real sense as 'kingmakers,' identifying which of their male relatives would be next to succeed to imperial power (Fantham 1994). In part, they were able to do this because of the traditional power that women had in family matters, but they were also assisted by a real, historical circumstance: from the very beginning of imperial rule, the lives of men close to the throne were often cut short by death on the battlefield or assassination (Corbier 1995). Imperial women, on the other hand, could live through several generations of male relatives, surviving to see a son or even grandson inherit the throne. This meant that women could be an important binding link between reigns: emperors like Claudius, Hadrian, and Marcus Aurelius were able to cement their positions by marrying women more closely related to previous emperors than they were themselves. In part, one suspects, because imperial women's domestic roles were found to be useful to imperial men, we find them quickly institutionalized under the early empire. Livia and her sister-in-law Octavia were designated both *sui iuris* (legally independent) and *sacrosanctae* (protected by the gods) in 35 BC, meaning that their persons were considered inviolate under Roman law, an honor that had long been confined to tribunes of the plebs. They and other imperial women also served as patrons of significant building projects, which gave them real, material public visibility, and after Augustus' death in AD 14, Livia was given the title *Augusta*, which would continue to be given to imperial women as a semi-formal mark of their power.

At the same time, however, scholars have often pointed out that the political roles that imperial women were called on to play were often assimilated to traditional ideals of female behavior (Fischler 1994). Livia's public acts, for instance, were understood as arising out of her domestic roles: the shrine that she built to *Concordia* (Harmony) looks to the traditional 'fellowship' between husband and wife, and she is portrayed as exercising toward the Roman people the kind of benevolence that befits a nurturing mother (Flory 1984; Purcell 1986). Similarly, Velleius Paterculus' comment on Livia's death is: *eminentissima... femina, cuius potentiam nemo sensit nisi aut levatione periculi aut accessione dignitatis* ("[she was] a very eminent woman, whose power no one felt except for the alleviation of danger and the elevation of rank": Vel. 2. 130. 5). The recently published *SC de Cn. Pisone patre* from the reign of Tiberius makes explicit the connection between her role as mother in the emperor's household and her public benevolence, expressing the senate's gratitude to her, "not only for the birth of our emperor, but also for her many and great kindnesses towards all ranks of men" (*non partu tantum modo principis nostri, sed etiam multis magnisq(ue) erga cuiusq(ue) ordinis homines beneficis*: lines 116–17). The inscription goes on to remark that the senate is pleased to accede to her request to spare Plancina, the wife of the traitorous Piso, particularly because "although she rightly and deservedly should be able to exercise the highest influence over what she requests from the Senate, she uses that right most sparingly" (*cum iure meritoq(ue) plurumum posse in eo quod a senatu petere<t> deberet, parcissume uteretur eo*: lines 117–18). This emphasis on restraint is echoed in the extensive praise of the imperial household—especially its female members—for the 'moderation' (*moderatio*) of their grief over the death of Germanicus, as they waited for the senate's verdict in the case against Piso and took no dramatic action. These imperial women's influence on public life is profound, but it is made rhetorically acceptable by an emphasis on their restraint in using it.

What is especially ironic about the complex public-and-private position accorded to imperial women is that it originates during the age of Augustus, an era that took some pains to announce itself as a return to traditional Roman values. This is particularly clear in ideological moves such as the passage of the Augustan social legislation, which in 18–17 BC formally outlawed adultery, prohibited intermarriage between certain social classes, and insisted—through a series of economic and political rewards and penalties—that adult Roman citizens must marry and produce children. The social legislation has long been seen as a reaction against a pervasive immorality that had crept into Roman society during the last years of the republic. Thus, for example, scholars in the past often assumed that the adultery legislation testified to the existence of an increasingly large elite 'demi-monde,' in which liaisons between married and unmarried men and women were common-place (Field 1945; Williams 1962). Evidence of this social sphere is often found in literary texts such as those by the Roman elegists, in which poets seem to celebrate their affairs with loose-living women. More recently, however, it has been recog-nized that poetry of any kind, perhaps especially elegy, has a complex relationship with historical reality, and that the depiction of women therein may be at once a form of 'counter-cultural feminism'—an attempt to challenge traditional ideas about the correct relationship between the sexes (Hallett 1984)—and a literary game in which the poet plays with power, gender, and the dynamics of 'publication' (McCarthy 1998). It is true that many Roman authors display a concern about the decline of women's morality, as when Juvenal laments that "poverty made Latin women chaste in the old days, hard work and a short time to sleep...kept their humble homes from being corrupted by vice" (Juv. 6. 287). Yet, this seems to be a part of a more general, and conventional, anxiety about the effect of wealth and imperial success on Roman society—a 'real' concern in rhetorical terms but not necessarily a reflection of actual historical circumstances.[5]

In fact, it would seem that an increased concern with female morality in the early empire may have been less an attempt to marginalize women within the sphere of the household than an implicit recognition of the ways that women's domestic virtues could and did have real impact on the lives of Roman men. After all, the stories of Lucretia and other women had long been part of Roman his-tory; it seems likely, although it is difficult to prove, that they took on greater sig-nificance during the transition from republican to imperial governance, but they were already there to be exploited. In this sense, we should probably note that the Romans seem always to have possessed a sense of the importance of the family, and women within it, as social institutions: one of the originary myths of the Roman state, for instance, was that of the Sabine women, who were kidnapped from a neighboring community by the Romans but went on to form an important bond between their captor-husbands and their original natal families. In the Romans' sense of their own history, therefore, from the very beginning domestic and civic life were intertwined—even as there existed a parallel gendered discourse that tried to keep separate the public world of men and the private one of women. At the same time, however, it is clear that the collapse of the Roman Republic and the rise of imperial governance had significant implications for both the representation and reality of women's lives. As the imperial family became one of the central insti-tutions of Roman politics, domesticity and the domestic sphere took on increasing civic significance. Although there always remained moral and ideological barriers

5. On the whole issue of literary texts as a mode of communication, and thus being perhaps employed to create social or political consensus, see Hedrick in this volume.

to women's appearance in public, the fact that at the highest level of Roman society, the boundary between their world and that of men had become porous meant that certain women, at least, were able to play real and important roles on the stage of Roman history.

SUGGESTED READING

Scholarship on ancient women generally, and Roman women in particular, has changed a great deal over the past four decades. Some of the most comprehensive overviews and introductions to the social lives of ancient Roman women, however, can still be found in work from the early years of the women's history movement in the 1970s and 1980s, for example, Finley 1968, Pomeroy 1975, Cantarella 1981, and Gardner 1986. The first publication of Lefkowitz and Fant (the still-standard collection of primary sources) was in 1975. More recent overviews can be found in Fantham et al. 1995 (the standard text book for Women in Antiquity courses) and D'Ambra 2006. Some valuable essays that trace the influence of first-, second-, third-, and fourth-wave feminism on Roman studies are the introductions to Dixon 2001, Rabinowitz and Richlin 1993, and McClure 2002. Readers seeking a more theoretical approach are also encouraged to consult the older but still valuable Blok 1987 and Richlin 1993.

BIBLIOGRAPHY

Blok, J. 1987. "Sexual Asymmetry: A Historiographical Essay." In J. Blok and P. Mason
    (eds.), *Sexual Asymmetry: Studies in Ancient Society*. 1–57. Amsterdam: J. C. Gieben.
Boyd, B. W. 1987. "Virtus Effeminata and Sallust's Sempronia." *Transactions of the American
    Philological Association* 117: 183–201.
Cantarella, E. 1981. *Ambiguo malanno: condizione e immagine della donna nell'antichità
    greca e romana*. Rome: Eniaudi Scuola.
Cluett, R. G. 1998. "Roman Women and Triumviral Politics, 43–37 BC." *Echos du Monde
    Classique/Classical Views* 42, n.s. 17: 67–84.
Connolly, J. 1998. "Mastering Corruption: Constructions of Identity in Roman Oratory."
    In S. R. Joshel and S. Murnaghan (eds.), *Women and Slaves in Greco-Roman Culture*.
    London: Routledge. 130–51.
Corbier, M. 1995. "Male Power and Legitimacy through Women: the Domus Augusta under
    the Julio-Claudians." In R. Hawley and B. Levick (eds.), *Women in Antiquity: New
    Assessments*. London: Routledge. 178–93.
Crook, J. A. 1995. *Legal Advocacy in the Roman World*. Ithaca: Cornell University Press.
D'Ambra, E. 2006. *Roman Women*. Cambridge: Cambridge University Press.
Delia, D. 1991. "Fulvia Reconsidered." In S. B. Pomeroy (ed.), *Women's History and Ancient
    History*. Chapel Hill: University of North Carolina Press. 197–217.
Dixon, S. 1983. "A Family Business: Women's Role in Patronage and Politics at Rome 80–44
    BC." *Classica et Mediaevalia* 34: 91–112.
———. 2001. *Reading Roman Women*. London: Duckworth.

Fantham, E. 1994. "Women of the High and Later Empire: Conformity and Diversity." In E. Fantham et al. 1995: 345–94.

Fantham, E., H. P. Foley, N. B. Kampen, and S. B. Pomeroy (eds.). 1995. *Women in the Classical World: Image and Text*. Oxford: Oxford University Press.

Field, J. A. 1945. "The Purpose of the Lex Iulia et Papia Poppaea." *Classical Journal* 40.7: 398–416.

Finley, M. I. 1968. "The Silent Women of Rome." In M. Finley, *Aspects of Antiquity: Discoveries and Controversies*. London: Chatto & Windus. 129–42.

Fischler, S. 1994. "Social Stereotypes and Historical Analysis: The Case of the Imperial Women at Rome." In L. J. Archer, S. Fischler, and M. Wyke (eds.), *Women in Ancient Societies*. London: Routledge. 115–33.

Flory, M. B. 1984. "*Sic exempla parantur*: Livia's Shrine to Concordia and the Porticus Liviae." *Historia* 33: 309–30.

Forbis, E. P. 1990. "Women's Public Image in Italian Honorary Inscriptions." *American Journal of Philology* 111.4: 493–512.

Gardner, J. F. 1986. *Women in Roman Law and Society*. Bloomington: Indiana University Press.

Gleason, M. W. 1995. *Making Men: Sophists and Self-Presentation in Ancient Rome*. Princeton: Princeton University Press.

Hallett, J. P. 1977. "Perusinae Glandes and the Changing Image of Augustus." *American Journal of Ancient History* 2.2: 151–71.

———. 1984. "The Role of Women in Roman Elegy: Counter-Cultural Feminism." In J. Peradotto and J.P. Sullivan (eds.) *Women in the Ancient World*. Albany: State University of New York Press. 241–62.

———. 1989. "Women as Same and Other in Classical Roman Elite." *Helios* 16.1: 59–78.

Hekster, O. 2002. *Commodus. An Emperor at the Crossroads*. Amsterdam: J. C. Gieben.

Herrmann, C. 1964. *Le rôle judiciaire et politique des femmes sous la République romaine*. Brussels: Latomus.

Hillard, T. 1989. "Republican Politics, Women, and the Evidence." *Helios* 16.2: 165–82.

———. 1992. "On the Stage, Behind the Curtain: Images of Politically Active Women in the Late Roman Republic." In B. Garlick, S. Dixon, and P. Allen (eds.), *Stereotypes of Women in Power*. New York: Greenwood Press. 37–64.

Joshel, S. R. 1992. *Work, Identity, and Legal Status at Rome: A Study of the Occupational Inscriptions*. Norman: University of Oklahoma Press.

Kampen, N. B. 1982. "Social Status and Gender in Roman Art: The Case of the Saleswoman." In N. Broude and M. D. Garrard (eds.), *Feminism and Art History*. New York: Harper and Row. 63–78.

Lattimore, R. 1942. *Themes in Greek and Latin Epitaphs*. Urbana: University of Illinois Press.

Lefkowitz, M., and M. Fant. 2005. *Women's Life in Greece and Rome: A Source Book in Translation*. 3rd ed. Baltimore: Johns Hopkins University Press.

McCarthy, K. 1998. "Servitium Amoris: Amor Servitii." In S. R. Joshel and S. Murnaghan (eds.), *Women and Slaves in Greco-Roman Culture*. London: Routledge. 174–92.

McClure, L. K. 2002. *Sexuality and Gender in the Classical World*. Oxford: Blackwells.

Nutton, V. 1979. *Galen: On Prognosis*. Berlin: Akademie Verlag.

Pomeroy, S. B. 1975. *Goddesses, Whores, Wives, and Slaves*. New York: Schocken Books.

Purcell, N. 1986. "Livia and the Womanhood of Rome." *Proceedings of the Cambridge Philological Society* 32: 78–105.

Rabinowitz, N. S., and A. Richlin (eds.). 1993. *Feminist Theory and the Classics*. London: Routledge.

Richlin, A. 1993. "The Ethnographer's Dilemma and the Dream of a Lost Golden Age." In Rabinowitz and Richlin 1993: 272–303.

Van Bremen, R. 1983. "Women and Wealth." In A. Cameron and A. Kuhrt (eds.), *Images of Women in Antiquity*. Detroit: Wayne State University Press. 223–42.

Williams, G. 1962. "Poetry in the Moral Climate of Augustan Rome." *Journal of Roman Studies* 52: 28–46.

CHAPTER 30

CHILDREN IN THE ROMAN FAMILY AND BEYOND

JENS-UWE KRAUSE

INTRODUCTION: DEMOGRAPHIC CONDITIONS

PROCREATION was considered by most Romans to constitute the most essential purpose of wedlock; and, according to ancient moral philosophers, that purpose alone justified sexuality within a marriage (Plu. *Moralia* 140B). Thus, Romans wed (at least ideally) in order to have children—and the Latin formulaic expression *liberorum quaerendorum causa* (for the purpose of begetting children) was to be found in most Roman marriage contracts. This desire for children seems generally to have arisen from several different needs: to secure the continuance of the family name; to provide heirs to the family property; or, especially among those of lesser wealth or status, to ensure a system of support in old age. To be sure, there is the occasional reference in ancient literature to family happiness, to the outright joy afforded parents by small children (e.g., Lucr. 3. 894–911). However, this is rarely mentioned as a reason for begetting a child. Rather, offspring were principally intended to guarantee the survival of the family: *oikos* (household) for the Greeks, *domus* (household) or *familia* (family) for the Romans.

Thus, remaining childless was considered a significant evil, and was feared in particular by the head of the household. On the other hand, we possess many sources that attest to what may have been reasonably widespread childlessness (Parkin 1992: 114). Pliny the Younger, to name but one example, remained childless, despite three marriages. His third wife, Calpurnia, did become pregnant, but had a miscarriage (Plin. *Ep.* 8. 10, 8. 11). Many divorces were, therefore, the result of a marriage's lack of issue.

An extremely high mortality rate for children caused many a Roman not to have immediate heirs. Probably about 25–30% of newborns died within the first year of life; by way of comparison, in modern industrialized countries, infant mortality amounts to just about 1%. Of the Roman children who survived their births, about 50% died before reaching the age of ten (for the statistics, see Frier 1982, 1999, 2000). Therefore, the number of surviving children remained low, despite an apparently high rate of pregnancies. Because of this high child mortality, families with many offspring were the exception in antiquity. And so, to name but one example, the Roman emperor Marcus Aurelius and his wife Faustina had at least twelve children; yet, only one son, the later emperor Commodus, survived his father. Given, then, the great likelihood of losing one's children in their formative years, the opinion is frequently voiced by scholars, that Roman parents could not risk investing too many feelings in their children. At first sight, this thesis seems to be supported by the fact that deceased infants were often not even buried properly; and it is true that, generally speaking, children are underrepresented on the gravestones of the imperial period (Shaw 1991). However, such an utter lack of emotional ties between parents and children is contradicted by many literary sources, which show that parents were much distressed by the death of their children, even of small children and infants (Golden 1988).

In any case, because of high and unpredictable mortality rates, Roman families were, unlike many of today's, significantly different from each other. For example, in present-day Western Europe, most married couples have one or two children, who are mostly born relatively soon after the parents' wedding, and who, as a rule, reach adulthood. As soon as the desired number of children has been reached, effective modes of contraception are practiced. This was different in Rome. To secure descendants, Roman parents were often forced to produce children until comparatively late in their lives. As a result, the age difference between parents and children tended to be much larger than in most contemporary European families (Krause 1994–95, 1: 33–34). This applied similarly to the age difference between siblings. It could lie in the vicinity of two or three years, but the census declarations preserved from Egypt show that siblings were frequently separated by ten years or more. Such age differences could be even more significant between step-siblings.

In short, then, the high and completely unpredictable rates of child mortality led to significantly diverse family settings in the Roman Empire. Marriages would often last just a few years. When children were born, no predictions at all could be made as to whether they would survive their parents. Families without surviving children must have been commonplace; and if there was only a surviving daughter, then property would likely be transferred from her family to that of her husband. On the other hand, if a large number of children in a given family unexpectedly survived, thus beating the odds, that family's property would have to be distributed among them. This could lead to a significant social decline for the next generation, and in the worst case scenario, to impoverishment. Therefore, in Rome, the number of surviving children could well decide the rise or fall of a given family.

Consequently, finding oneself confronted with a large number of surviving children could easily prove to be just as undesirable as could a dearth of children. Moreover, since Roman inheritance law did not follow the principle of primogeniture, it was desirable to keep the number of children small, and thus to avoid splitting the family property amongst too many heirs. Contemporaries were well aware of the risk of a large progeny, who might easily become a financial burden. And so, under Tiberius' reign, for example, Hortensius Hortalus, who came from a distinguished senatorial family, fell into severe financial difficulties; he no longer possessed the minimum wealth required of a senator. One of the reasons cited for his predicament were his many children—he had four (Suet. *Tib.* 47).

Now, assuming that a child did survive, then his education required great investments that, in the best case, found some return only late in life. The state developed merely a tentative social policy, which was intended to lessen the burden of educating children for members of the society's lower strata. Thus, the emperor Trajan offered monies to less-well-to-do parents and their children, which could be used for the purposes of education. Moreover, loans from the central government were also made available to Italian landowners; then, the interest payments on these loans were administered and used by the local communities to assist parents, at least partially, with the costs of educating their children. Such alimentary programs supported girls to the age of thirteen or fourteen, and boys for a few years longer (Duncan-Jones 1964; Woolf 1990; Wierschowski 1988; Rawson 2001; see also Horster in this volume).

But in spite of any and all such programs, it is clear that there was significant interest in limiting the number of children. However, just which methods of family planning were most often used, and how efficient they ultimately were, remains unclear. Ancient medical texts describe a number of contraceptive practices (Hopkins 1965–66; Parkin 1992: 126–27). The techniques, as they are portrayed in these texts, were based equally on methods involving magic and medicine. Now of course, some of these operations will surely have been effective, but it is questionable whether the difference between successful and useless methods was terribly well realized. And in fact, what would appear to be the simplest form of contraception, *coitus interruptus*, is not at all mentioned in our ancient texts.

Aside from contraception, the ancient medical texts also list a number of medications and surgical procedures that would lead to abortion; once again, we find a mix of effective and completely unsuitable approaches. Nonetheless, there were certainly successful abortions; and while doctors discussed the legitimacy of abortion well into the imperial period, this procedure did not pose a legal problem. Abortion was not considered criminal—unless it might serve to impede a father's right to a legitimate potential heir. Given that concern, however, it was illegal for a wife to pursue an abortion without her husband's consent; should she do so, then she was perceived to be interfering with her husband's absolute prerogative to determine his child's destiny. Abortion with a father's consent, on the other hand, was completely legal (*Dig.* 47. 11. 4; 48. 19. 39).

Abortion, though, posed very great risks to a mother's health; thus, the abandonment of children offered a less dangerous method of family planning. The decision to forsake a child was usually made right after birth and lay within the jurisdiction of the head of the family, the *pater familias*. Now, while we are in no position to quantify cases of abandonment, ancient authors routinely consider this a frequent practice (Boswell 1988; Harris 1994; Corbier 1999: 1261–73; Corbier 2001). Poverty, of course, was a continual motive for the abandonment of children. According to Plutarch, the poor often chose not to raise their children because they were concerned that they would not be able to provide them with an adequate education (*Moralia* 497E). But even the rich got rid of surplus children; in such circles, the exposure of the child was usually intended to avoid splitting the inheritance among too many offspring, a circumstance already encountered above.

Compared to abortion, the abandonment of children had the advantage that it could be used in a much more targeted fashion. And so, for example, while it is difficult to quantify this exactly, it would appear that girls were abandoned in higher numbers than boys (Apul. *Met.* 10. 23). For while sons began to contribute early to the economic well-being of a family through their work, daughters had to receive a considerable dowry at the time of their weddings. Thus, sons were generally perceived as being instrumental for the financing of old age; daughters tended to be, instead, a financial burden. Furthermore, it was through the offspring of sons that the family line would be continued.[1]

Often, children were abandoned at a crossing, or in front of a temple, in the hope or expectation that some passer-by would take care of the child. Thus, a few abandoned children had the chance to be raised as foundlings, and, consequently, the abandonment of children cannot be exactly equated with homicide. Abandonment of children was also most likely one of the more important resources for the slave supply. The well-known grammarian Melissus, for example, had been abandoned by his parents as a newborn, was brought up as a slave, received a superior education, and was given as a gift to Maecenas. Later, his mother demanded that he be freed; Melissus, however, preferred to remain a member of Maecenas' household— even if as a slave (Suet. *Gram.* 21. 1–2).

In short, then, Roman demographic realities posed serious hazards for parents and children alike. The vicissitudes of both child survival rates and the available methods of family planning always entailed great risks. Insofar as the latter is concerned, the options available (contraception, abortion, abandonment) were likewise treacherous for mothers and for those children who were forsaken. On the other hand, should parents produce too few children altogether, then the high mortality rates might easily bear another, more far-reaching danger: early deaths of the few born could lead to the family's extinction outright. And yet again, in the case of too many children, fragmentation of the familial property might threaten the economic well-being of subsequent generations. Thus, as we saw at the outset, the desire for children, and for enough surviving children to guarantee familial stability

---

1. And for the abandonment of disabled children, see Stahl in this volume.

in various senses, was great. In short, children were highly valued, and producing children was a well-recognized social virtue. Nevertheless, the desire to control family size and make-up, and the lack of modern technologies for doing so, meant that precarious methods of family planning were widely tolerated. The forces of both nature and nurture, in the end, tended to result in a rather precarious existence for Roman children.

FROM BIRTH TO COMING OF AGE

Usually, the birth of a child took place in the father's house, but in a much less private atmosphere than is usually the case nowadays. First, it was customary to have a midwife present. In the lower classes of society, neighbors often took over the midwife's function. Frequently, other women, mostly relatives of the couple, attended the birth. The midwife was the first person to examine the newborn, and therefore made a preliminary decision as to whether the child was fit to live. However, it was the father who had to decide whether the newborn was to be raised or to be abandoned.

On the *dies lustricus*, the ninth day after the birth of a boy, the eighth after the birth of a girl, the child of an elite family would be named. This delay can probably be explained by a very high rate of perinatal mortality, and the caution it must have generated. Until the *dies lustricus*, the child was, as it were, in a transitional phase. It was only after a few days had passed that it could realistically be determined whether the baby had an actual chance of survival. In any case, assuming that the child did survive, on the *dies lustricus* the newborn would also receive the so-called *bulla*, a leather locket containing amulets that was worn by aristocratic children until they reached adulthood, and that served an apotropaic function. Aside from the *bulla*, an aristocratic youth also wore a particular garment, namely, the *toga praetexta*, a toga with a purple border stripe, until he attained manhood.

In the upper strata of society, it was typically a wet nurse who fed the baby and was responsible for the child's earliest upbringing. In larger households, such wet nurses were primarily slaves; however, there were also poor free women who made a living this way (Joshel 1986; Bradley 1994; Corbier 1999: 1274–80). It is impossible to make generally valid statements about the duration of the nursing. In Roman Egypt, contracts with paid nurses were frequently set up for two years, and doctors generally recommended that babies should be nursed at least until they developed their first teeth, in other words, until at least their sixth or seventh month.

Even after the weaning process, the wet nurse would usually remain with the child. She possessed great influence on her ward's personal development. These relationships with wet nurses often lasted a lifetime, and sometimes reached a level of stability that did not exist in the parent-child relationship. Pliny the Younger, for example, gave his wet nurse the gift of a country estate, valued at 100,000 sesterces, to support her in her old age (Plin. *Ep.* 6. 3). The philosopher Favorinus opposed the practice of using wet nurses, complaining that, among other things, the mutual love between mother and child was bound to suffer as the children developed closer loving relationships with their wet nurses (Gell. 12. 1. 22–23). We can only speculate as to the effects of employing wet nurses (and later teachers) upon the relationships of children with their mothers. At least in the upper classes, wives were only loosely tied into their husband's family through the task of raising their children, and of this occupation they were mostly relieved by slaves. This might partially explain the comparatively high number of divorces in the Roman Empire. Hardly ever does the divorced wife's separation from her children, who normally remained in their father's household, seem to have posed a problem.

As soon as the child was older, a slave, who would function as a teacher, was assigned to him. This person would accompany the child everywhere, not only to school, but, for instance, also to the circus or the theater. This slave-teacher was of very great importance for the child's socialization (Bradley 1985a). Consequently, wet nurse and teacher shared, at least in the upper classes, the tasks of a child's most basic early education. Especially the father, it would seem, had very little contact with his small children. Thus, Seneca comforts a father regarding his son's early death with the argument that the wet nurse had anyhow known the child much better than did the father (Sen. *Ep.* 99. 14). Very young children in Roman aristocratic families, then, had caregivers beyond father and mother, and these individuals were of potentially greater importance than were the parents during those children's formative years.

Still, there could well be input, early on, from the adult members of the family. In Roman houses, at least insofar as the available archaeological evidence would indicate, there were no rooms specifically intended for use by children. Youngsters simply lived and played among the adults. Indeed, many probably shared sleeping quarters with the slaves, who were assigned to take care of them. Thus, when Roman authors do show us children at play, the scenario is not in a children's room of any sort, but in the central living area and parlor of the house, namely, the atrium. To this extent, then, a Roman aristocratic child was pretty well constantly under the vigilance of his or her mother and father.

With respect to care-giving by the parents, it was generally expected that the mother would look after the small children. A son's education, starting at about the age of seven, was preferably the father's task, for it was an old republican principle that boys and young men were supposed to learn primarily from their father's example. However, as soon as the boys reached the stage of early adolescence, they were entrusted to one or more experts, mostly relatives or friends of the family, whose example they were likewise expected to imitate (Tac. *Dial.* 34). With the Roman adoption of the Greek school system, beginning in the second century BC, the educational system changed completely. In upper-class families, the children were now usually educated at home by a slave or freedman, primarily of Greek origin, who was well versed in literature. However, only few parents could afford such private tutors. The alternative was to have the children attend a school. While Quintilian, in his handbook on rhetoric, stresses the importance of education within the family, he, as opposed to many of his contemporaries, prefers schools over private education at home (*Inst.* 1. 2. 4–5).

In poorer circles, childhood ended quickly. Boys were expected, from a young age, to contribute to the family's support. In agriculture, for example, children were utilized to herd small animals (Var. *R.* 2. 10. 1; Col. 8. 2. 7; Ov. *Fast.* 4. 511). From Roman Egypt, we have sources documenting children as substitute workers during the olive harvest; they received up to four obols per day, while the daily payment for adults amounted to six obols (*P. Fay.* 102, ca. AD 105). Boys learned a trade very early—at the age of twelve or thirteen—and were soon in a position to supplement the family finances. So, for example, the writer Lucian was originally supposed to learn such a trade; it was planned that he would become a stone-mason. This education was not as costly as one that would lead to the intellectual professions, and the son would be able to help support the family much more quickly (Lucian *Somn.* 1–4). Quite correctly, research has insisted on the immense importance of children for their parents' support in old age, and this especially among the lower classes. Their early professional training, then, should be seen in this context (Bradley 1985b: 327–30; Saller 1988: 405–6; Wiedemann 1989: 153–55).

Coming of age for elite boys was marked by the exchange of the *toga praetexta*, again, a boy's special toga, for the *toga virilis* (the manly toga). There was no absolutely fixed point in time for this ceremony; however, boys were between fourteen and sixteen years old when they received their adult clothing. For the girls, marriage was the point in time that separated childhood from adulthood, and Roman girls could legally marry from the age of twelve.

THE FATHER'S ROLE

Children simply belonged to their father—they took his name and they received his social status. The Romans talked of the power of the father (*patria potestas*), but not that of the parents. There were only loose legal ties with the mother's family—indeed, with the mother herself. And in many areas, such as inheritance law, or with regard to the arranging of a guardianship, agnatic relationships were all-important.

In short, *patria potestas* was arguably the most distinctive characteristic of the Roman family (and was similarly important in the law; see Kehoe in this volume). It encompassed the physical structure of the house with everything that belonged to it, the free members of the family, the slaves, and the assets. This power was almost unlimited, and the *pater familias* was technically entitled to kill his slaves as well as his children without suffering any punishment—he possessed the so-called right of life and death (*ius vitae necisque*) over these members of the household. This right to kill applied not only to the newborns, but even to an adult son, who continued to be subject to this *patria potestas*. Legally, there was almost no difference between a slave's and a son's position with regard to the head of the family.

During his lifetime, the father (again, technically) controlled the economic activities of the children, who were under his *potestas*. He could give them an allowance (*peculium*), but was not obligated to do so. Legally, the children did not own anything so long as they were subject to this fatherly power. This *patria potestas* must have been especially oppressive because there was no definite coming of age that ended it. It simply lasted until a father's death. Only then did children become legally independent (*sui iuris*).

The demographic conditions of the Roman world (especially the high mortality rates), however, created a situation in which adult children must rarely have remained under their fathers' power. When young women married, often shortly before they turned twenty, in all likelihood half of them had already lost their fathers. Men would marry (ideally) at about the age of thirty; at this point in their lives, perhaps only a quarter of them would still be under their fathers' *patria potestas*. In short, given the mortality rates that must have been operative in that world, only a small fraction of adult Romans will have had very long to tolerate a father, who was still alive, and who thus still controlled the family fortune.

There were yet further mechanisms that weakened *patria potestas*. For example, an institution called *emancipatio* was a fictive sale, via which a *pater familias* released his son or daughter from his power. The father 'sold' his child to a third party. This person then freed the child; but instead of gaining freedom and full legal rights, the child fell back into the father's power. This process was performed three times, and after the third 'sale' the child would be released entirely from the father's power. Until the early imperial period, though, *emancipatio* was most likely not a regular practice. This might have changed in late antiquity. This may be so, given that one of Constantine's laws mentions the coming of age, and says that this usually released children from paternal power (*CTh* 8. 18. 2, AD 319). In other words, what previously had been an irregular practice seems by Constantine's day to have become quite normal.

Furthermore, *patria potestas* could be moderated by the grant of a *peculium*, in other words, a specific set of assets (sometimes plain cash), which legally remained part of the father's property but could nonetheless be used relatively freely by a son; daughters sometimes received such grants, but this was rare. While the father could theoretically rescind a *peculium* he had granted, such a situation, or the various problems that might conceivably have resulted, play hardly any role whatsoever in the Roman legal sources. It was obviously common to allow a dependent the use of such a *peculium* once granted, and to withdraw it only for very important reasons. In most cases, the *peculium* was more than mere pocket money. It was generally large enough for sons to be able to enter contracts, even large enough to serve as security for obligations vis à vis the state. And so, with the *peculium*, a son received the opportunity to form and run his own household, and to live according to his social status. This institution thus served a double purpose—it led to a certain independence for the individual granted such a *peculium*, yet, at the same time, it continued the financial dependency on the father (Thomas 1982).

The alternative to granting funds that a son could himself administer was the payment of an annuity, which allowed him to live in accord with his social station. Like a *peculium*, such an annuity continued the economic dependency on a father. Some young men were not satisfied with the monies supplied by their fathers, and therefore sought loans from willing lenders. The resultant indebtedness of youths still under their fathers' *potestas* posed a continuous problem. Apart from fathers, who often tended to be frugal, or outright stingy, with regard to their children, there were others who favored a more liberal educational style. The existence of such liberal fathers must have made the situation of those who were dependent on a frugal father far into their adult lives even more difficult.

All of this, of course, raises the question as to just when a Roman reached adulthood, and just how the Romans understood the attainment of adult status. More important, really, than attaining a particular age was the family situation, in other words, whether a person was still dependent on a father or not; and the described Roman family structures led to considerable inequalities. The son of a long-lived father would remain under *patria potestas* potentially far into his life, and all the while did not possess full legal capacity; and yet, many far younger men became, due to their fathers' earlier deaths, much sooner the heads of their households. The potential for conflict here is obvious.

We may now turn to the matter of provision for the heirs upon a father's death. Even from early on, the custom of establishing a will was widely common in Rome.[2] It should be noted, however, that the standard rule of inheritance, namely, that children would be instituted as heirs, could be modified through individual arrangements. This gave wealthy fathers the possibility to exert pressure on their children by threatening them with disinheritance. While the children would have the right to contest an unfounded disinheriting via a prescribed legal procedure (the *querela inofficiosi testamenti*), it was still possible for a father to leave his children with the legal minimum, namely, a fourth part. Clearly, then, there were important reasons for a son to obey his father. Nevertheless, certain limitations had to be observed. Due to considerable social pressures, a father could not afford to disinherit his son without a clear cause. It was generally assumed that each legitimate child, both male and female, should receive an equal, or at least a substantial, portion of the inheritance. Reasons for excluding a child completely from an inheritance had to be very convincing. And while disinheriting was pretty certainly fairly rare, a hint toward a future inheritance may well have served as a means to achieve obedience and respect from children.

Another institution, that of a domestic court that was presided over by the *pater familias*, and in which he could render judgments over his family members, continued to exist into the imperial period. In this context, the power of the father over his son, the husband over his wife, and the proprietor over his slave was lent a

---

2. On Roman testamentary habits generally, see Champlin 1991.

quasi-legal sanction. Crimes committed within a family were mostly not brought
before public courts, but instead were handled in this more private realm. And
while the context was more private-seeming, the decisions rendered in such a family court could be quite effective. The power of a household head over his children
included, as we have already noted, his ability to put them to death (the so-called
ius vitae necisque). No public court was needed to exercise this prerogative; it was,
however, customary for a father to consult with a group of relatives, serving as a
board of advisors (in Latin, a *consilium*), before he rendered such a judgment.

That having been said, it must nonetheless be realized that there are very few
sources supporting the actual utilization of this *ius vitae necisque* by Roman fathers
(Thomas 1984; Harris 1986). Indeed, during the reign of Augustus, people in Rome
almost lynched a father who had whipped his son to death—public opinion tended
to be hostile toward any excessive use of paternal force (Sen. *Cl.* 1. 15. 1). Obviously,
a simple right to kill was, at least in the early imperial period, no longer undisputed,
and future enactments limited its scope further. For example, the emperor Hadrian
(AD 117–138) deported a father who killed his son during a hunting trip because the
son had engaged in an affair with his wife, the son's stepmother. Hadrian supported
his decision by stating that the father had killed his son in the manner of a robber,
rather than according to paternal law. The point was that a father's power was supposed to be based on dutiful respect (in Latin, *pietas*—*Dig.* 48. 9. 5, Marcianus),
and the father in question had, apparently, acted simply out of anger. By the fourth
century, at the latest, a father's right to kill his children had been abolished.

But despite any and all limitations, the *ius vitae necisque* was, so long as it survived, not entirely without meaning. It existed as a threat, and must have had an
according psychological effect on children. In sum, then, a father's power became
legally more limited over the imperial period. Still, this power did continue to exist,
and the basic patriarchal family structures were never seriously questioned (Arjava
1998).

Now, the legal documents that provide much of this picture are not necessarily
well suited to describe the daily realities of family life. They determined only what
which was legally possible. Thus, a father could indeed disinherit his children, and
he could kill them without being punished, but that does not mean that most or
many fathers acted that way. The relations between fathers and children were, just
as one would expect, multifarious. There were strict as well as liberal fathers, fathers
who spoiled their children, and stingy fathers. Indeed, it would appear that Romans
increasingly expected fathers to show not only qualities such as strictness, but also
benevolence, interest, or tender love. Furthermore, our literary sources repeatedly
hint at the educational role of the father. Relations between parents and children
were ultimately, and ideally, to be formed on the basis of *pietas*, and *pietas* had to be
understood reciprocally. It was owed to the father by the son, but also to the children by the father (Eyben 1991; Saller 1991; Saller 1994).

The important thing to remember, in the end, is that for all the variety of
relationships that will have existed between Roman fathers and their children, in
the background always loomed the institutions of *patria potestas* and the *ius vitae*

necisque. We cannot quantify the effects of these on the relationships in question. However, effects there must surely have been.

THE MOTHER'S ROLE

A woman who had entered a *sine manu*-marriage (a particular legal category of marriage, which was more liberal toward the wife) was by law bound to her husband's family only loosely. A mother never shared in the *patria potestas*, even when her husband was not up to the task of overseeing the family. Indeed, even after her husband's death, she did not gain any such power over her children. As a rule, she guided their education, should the father not be able to, but a guardian had to be appointed to administer the children's financial concerns. The mother was not entitled to become the legal guardian.

So long as a marriage continued, the mother bore very little financial responsibility for the children's support; principally, it was the husband's task to take care of this. However, the proceeds from the dowry could be used for the support and education of common children. As early as in republican times, a husband was entitled to keep a share of the dowry on behalf of the children in the case of a divorce initiated by his wife or her *pater familias*. Therefore, a mother had a certain financial responsibility for her children, and this potentially continued even after the end of her marriage. Proceedings after the death of a wife were similar to those after a divorce. In that situation, the dowry (or more exactly, the dowry specifically given by the bride's father, in Latin, the *dos profecticia*) went back to the wife's father, minus one-fifth for each surviving child; in other words, the support of the children had to be co-financed from the deceased mother's property. In the case of the husband's death, the entire dowry was at the wife's disposal (or that of the person with legal powers over her). The children's support, however, was to be financed solely with the deceased husband's assets; or in any case, this was the legal perspective on the matter.

In the imperial period we can observe a tendency to give greater legal weight to the cognatic than the agnatic relationship. Such a strengthening of the blood relationship implied an acknowledgment by the jurisprudents of closer relationships between mothers and their children. This was true in particular for inheritance law, the rights of custody upon a divorce, and regulations regarding guardianship.

Thus, beginning in the second century AD, children and their mothers possessed the mutual right to inherit on intestacy (by virtue of the *senatus consultum Tertullianum* and the *senatus consultum Orfitianum*). Now, while it was a general rule that children of divorced parents would grow up with their fathers, legal developments of the imperial period allowed the mother greater influence with regard to the children's education. In certain critical circumstances, for example, a divorced mother might even be allowed to gain guardianship (Wacke 1980). According to classical Roman law, the administration of fatherless children's property was their guardian's affair alone, while a mother was simply not entitled to that role. Nonetheless, even in the early imperial period, a mother had a certain influence over the administration of the property, which could lead to conflicts with the guardian. In late antiquity, a mother could become the guardian of her children officially, especially in cases when no agnatic relative was available (*CTh* 3. 17. 4 = *CJ* 5. 35. 2, AD 390; Krause 1994–95: 3, 113–29). Thus, while the law increasingly took close relationships between mothers and children into consideration, the Romans were always far from treating mother and father equally in this regard.

However, once again, it must be admitted that the law simply does not reflect the entire reality of the situation. While there was no maternal equivalent for the *patria potestas*, on which the mother could have based a (legal) right to respect from her children, she might very well be the object of love and respect for her children—a mother was at least thought to be owed *pietas*, in the same fashion as was a father.

One of the most important tasks of a wife was the education of the children (cf. Osgood in this volume). She was primarily responsible for the young children. For them, the mother was the most important contact in the nuclear family; however, this depended on the family's social status. In the upper strata of society, parents were assisted in the education of their children by various household personnel, slaves, but also by professional educators and teachers from outside the household (see Horster in this volume). Among the lower classes, it is a likely guess that mother-child relationships were, for better or for worse, on the whole, closer. While the rich seem generally to have handed newborns over to a wet nurse, the mothers in poorer families will have raised their children by themselves. In any case, apart from the care for young children, mothers were also in charge of the education of their daughters, who remained in their mothers' care until marriage.

But even with regard to the sons' education, mothers possessed a certain influence. In some cases, both parents made basic decisions with regard to their children's upbringing. For example, the choice of a marriage partner for one's offspring lay within the father's domain, but it was generally common to consult the mother as well, and over the imperial period her influence in this regard seems to have grown.

Ancient literature frequently mentions the different educational styles of fathers and mothers. Fatherly strictness is commonly contrasted with a mother's greater indulgence. Seneca points out that fathers usually insisted that the children pursue their studies, while mothers nursed and pampered their offspring (*Prov.* 2. 5). It was usually thought to be a father's task to reprimand and discipline a son. It may be that we are simply dealing here with literary topoi; however, there may also be a kernel of reality in such stories.

Now, the fact that a wife in a Roman marriage frequently possessed her own property served actually to strengthen her position toward her children. Larger expenses on behalf of the children were often afforded by using the mother's assets. This provided the mother with, for example, some influence over her children's education. And just as a father could threaten his children with disinheritance, so a mother could exert some pressure by hinting at her will. Given the property distribution within Roman families, it was therefore important for children to court their mothers as well as their fathers.

The role of the mother in the Roman family clarifies, then, how purely legal strictures and social reality could lie some distance apart. According to Roman law, while a mother belonged to her husband's family only loosely, and although connections between mothers and children were strengthened legally only in the imperial period, there was no question that in Roman society generally, a mother's responsibility for and connection to her children was very large, both within a marriage and after its dissolution.

ORPHANS

Probably about 40% of all Roman children lost their fathers before they reached the age of 15. These youths would then be put under guardianship (*tutela*), usually of a close (male) relative. If the father had died intestate, the closest agnatic male relative would usually become guardian (this was called *tutela legitima*); the guardian was, as a rule, a paternal uncle, or an older brother of the now-fatherless child. This *tutela legitima* fell to a person who could legitimately inherit the ward's assets, with the exception that a woman was entitled to such an inheritance but was not permitted to serve as guardian. Boys were freed from guardianship when they turned fourteen; however, at that point, they did not gain full legal capacity. They continued to be subordinate to a person who would look after their interests (in Latin, a *curator*) and whose agreement was necessary with regard to all business transactions; however, as opposed to a guardian, a *curator* was not legally in charge of his ward's property.

A mother's possibilities to influence financial decisions were legally fairly limited. Single women were hardly considered capable of controlling their own property. Even less was there any willingness to trust women with the administration of a third party's property, even in the case of the woman's own children. Therefore, a mother was not at all in any position to make autonomous decisions with regard to all the important issues affecting her children after her husband's death.

As a rule, and as has been indicated, the mother took a lead in her children's education, while a guardian would be in charge of their property. Especially after the death or remarriage of a mother, orphans were frequently taken in by other relatives (e.g., grandparents, or uncles and aunts). As just one of many possible examples, Octavian, subsequently the emperor Augustus, grew up on his grandfather's estate; and his education was guided by his maternal grandmother, Julia, upon the remarriage of his mother. After his grandmother's death, Octavian moved to his mother and stepfather's house; he was then twelve. The young Caligula, son of Germanicus, seems to have lived with his great-grandparents over periods of time while his parents were still alive. After his father's death, he at first lived with his mother, and after her exile, with his great-grandmother, Livia. When Livia died, he was sent to his paternal grandmother, Antonia, and finally moved to Tiberius' household on Capri at the age of nineteen (Krause 1994–95: 3, 49–77).

Thus, grandmothers and aunts often had an important function with regard to the education of children. Children were, on occasion, and even while a father was still alive, but especially after a mother's death, transferred to the grandparents, often enough to the grandmother, or perhaps to an aunt. This was an experience shared not only by those who had lost both parents, for children who had lost a father were often sent to their grandparents, or uncle and aunt, even while their mother was still alive. Especially if the mother remarried, such a solution was preferred to the children's inclusion in a stepfamily. Thus were kinships beyond the core family often groomed.

Frequently enough, maternal relatives assisted with the education of orphaned children. A widowed mother was usually perceived only with difficulty to be able to take on the education of her children alone, and women in this position often sought out the support of their own parents or a sister (a maternal aunt of the orphans). Thus, while the general preference was to give orphans into the care of paternal relatives, nevertheless, the engagement of maternal relatives was a possibility. Even after the dissolution of a marriage, close contacts and relations between the children, who technically belonged to their deceased father's *familia*, and their maternal relatives could remain in existence.

STEPPARENTS AND STEPSIBLINGS

The Roman family is characterized just generally by the following distinctive features, among others: the inconstancy of marriage and its easy disintegration; the frequent early death of one partner; and the availability of a surviving partner for a new marriage. In short, the Roman family formed a dynamic unit, which could be continuously dissolved and newly reconstituted (Bradley 1987, 1991a). And that, of course, will have had its effects on the upbringing and socializing of children.

Men who had been married once before, in other words, were widowed or divorced, tended to prefer younger women for their second marriages, since a young woman would be better suited to producing children. When a man married again, it was thus possible that the marriage partners belonged to very different generations, and that the second wife was possibly little older, or potentially even younger, than the children from the man's first marriage.

Upper-class families in particular were not based on marriage connections of terribly great permanency; children could not count on their parents' marriages lasting until their deaths at an old age. A fairly large number of men and women married at least twice during adulthood. Proportionally, many more children than in (say) modern Western society may well have been confronted with stepparents and stepsiblings. It is difficult to guess the emotional consequences of such marriage patterns. In ancient literature, we continually encounter the motif of the bad stepmother (Gray-Fow 1988; Noy 1991; Watson 1995). This hints at frequent 'real-life' tensions between children and stepparents. There is evidence for quite a few 'good' stepmothers; however, they do not dominate the overall picture drawn of stepmothers in Roman society. In Roman literature, the topos of the bad stepfather is not quite as prominent as the one of the bad stepmother, primarily because most children lived in their father's household upon a divorce, and thus were confronted with a stepmother rather than a stepfather. If we believe ancient sources, not only relationships between stepparents and stepchildren were strained, but relationships between stepsiblings were usually distant. Financial matters especially are often portrayed as having caused disputes; so, for instance, it was considered a certain risk that a mother might neglect the children from her first marriage when distributing her wealth.

CONCLUSIONS

Given all of the above, it seems safe to put things as follows. The group in which a Roman child was raised and socialized was very often more broadly cast than the core family consisting of father, mother, and children. Indeed, it would appear that a significantly small percentage of children in antiquity experienced (at least for all of their childhood) something like an intact core family. Rather, the Roman family, at least in the upper echelons of the society, seems to have been much more fluid. This was the result, on the one hand, of the natural mortality rates, and on the other hand of the socially determined frequency of divorce, and the consequences thereof, for children's living conditions. In short, very many children grew up in heterogeneous families, with stepparents and stepsiblings.

Apart from their parents, and others of their relatives, there were various caregivers with whom Roman children must frequently have established close emotional relationships. For the aristocratic child there were female wet nurses and male slaves, who frequently supervised the children's education. Though we obviously cannot gauge exactly the effects of such an upbringing, it seems hard to imagine that these different persons did not exert influence over the being of their young wards.

The 'typical' Roman family was, therefore, quite different from (say) the typically perceived modern Western core family. The latter has an expected format. Two partners, almost equal in age, form a new household; there are relatively few children; these children are reasonably close in age; adult children leave the household, generally in their late teens or early twenties; and parents are, at that point, left by themselves. The period of post-paternal companionship in a marriage, then, may possibly last for decades. Such a model is certainly not at all suited to describe the Roman family.

The result of this all is that in several ways one might consider children (or in any case, many children) in the Roman world to have been marginalized by their society. Clearly, they were not outsiders in anything like the sense that magicians, or bandits, or prostitutes were. Yet, one can easily enough point to similarities between the positions of slaves and children, which might encourage a much less than optimistic picture of the life of a Roman child. Thus, it is well worth considering just exactly what the place of these young people in Roman society was.

Within the family, children were, one might argue, instrumentalized, to perpetuate the *gens*, or to support their elders. Furthermore, the fact that there often was a whole range of persons who saw to the care and upbringing of children could perhaps also be thought to have isolated these young people in various ways. That a child was subject to exposure, indeed to every whim of a father wielding the *patria potestas*, has also caused some despair about the plight of Roman children. Indeed, there was a quite influential ancient intellectual trend to perceive children as being absolutely irrational, hence, in many ways excluded from the 'inside' of Roman society. As one scholar has recently put it:

> A moral and philosophical tradition ranked children, like women and irrational animals, among outsiders excluded from the male social hierarchy. Children still had to develop the qualities that would turn them (or a tiny minority of them) into full-fledged, independent Roman aristocrats. They still lacked the ability to act in a morally correct way. They were unable to control anger and other emotions, they did not speak in a rhetorical style, they were weak and infirm, and, above, all, irrational.[3]

What is more, a forceful current in social history generally has perceived childhood in pre-modern European society as having been altogether dismal, as having been largely characterized by an utter lack of any recognition for this as a particular and discernable (not to say fragile) stage of the human life cycle (e.g., Ariès 1962).

Most recently, however, there has been a tendency to see things otherwise. A significantly more affective model of the Roman family, and thus of the place of children within that family, has largely gained sway (see now esp. Rawson 2003). To name but one fundament of the more recent scholarly trend, the use and effectiveness of the quintessentially Roman institution of *patria potestas* has been called seriously into question (Saller 1994). In short, it is nowadays much more difficult than it once was to think of Roman children as outsiders, or as

3. Laes 2007: 37. What Laes demonstrates overall, however, is that this particular 'literary' or 'intellectual' discourse on children was radically different from the kind of talk (and emotion) that appears on the tombstones of Roman children. He posits, at least in part, a difference in attitude owing to the difference in genres of writing/communication. Note that there are several other articles in this volume on children and the perception of them in the Roman world (H. Sigismund-Nielsen, J. Huskinson, and R. Redfern).

marginalized by their society. Nonetheless, it is important to realize that there was a time when, and there were scholars among whom, Roman children could indeed be viewed as little more than slave-like creatures, as truly marginalized figures in their community. Nowadays, though, we would do much better to see these young people as having been "welcome and valued and visible in Roman society" (Rawson 2003: 1).

SUGGESTED READING

Recently Beryl Rawson has produced a very good and convenient overview of children in the Roman world (Rawson 2003). This is probably the best place to begin reading about this subject. And as mentioned just above, she argues against the idea that Roman children were marginalized by their society. Keith Bradley's various writings (see just below in the bibliography) on Roman children are likewise most valuable. Saller 1994 is the most important work in recent years on the subject of *patria potestas*, and Frier 2000 provides a brief, but excellent introduction to demography in the Roman world.

BIBLIOGRAPHY

Ariès, P. 1962. *Centuries of Childhood. A Social History of Family Life*. New York: Vintage Books. (Orig. *L'Enfant et la vie familiale sous l'Ancien Régime*. Paris: Plon 1960.)

Arjava, A. 1988. "Paternal Power in Late Antiquity." *Journal of Roman Studies* 88: 147–65.

Balla, P. 2003. *The Child-Parent Relationship in the New Testament and Its Environment*. Peabody, Mass.: Hendrickson.

Boatwright, M. T. 2005. "Children and Parents on the Tombstones of Pannonia." In George 2005: 287–318.

Boswell, J. 1988. *The Kindness of Strangers: The Abandonment of Children in Western Europe from Late Antiquity to the Renaissance*. New York: Pantheon Books.

Bradley, K. R. 1985a. "Child Care at Rome: The Role of Men." *Historical Reflections / Réflexions Historiques* 12: 485–523 = Bradley 1991a: 37–75.

———. 1985b. "Child Labour in the Roman World." *Historical Reflections / Réflexions Historiques* 12: 311–30 = Bradley 1991a: 103–24.

———. 1987. "Dislocation in the Roman Family." *Historical Reflections / Réflexions historiques* 14: 33–62 = Bradley 1991a: 125–55.

———. 1991a. "Remarriage and the Structure of the Upper-Class Roman Family." In B. Rawson (ed.), *Marriage, Divorce, and Children in Ancient Rome*. Oxford: Oxford University Press. 79–98 = Bradley 1991b: 156–76.

———. 1991b. *Discovering the Roman Family*. Oxford: Oxford University Press.

———. 1994. "The Nurse and the Child at Rome. Duty, Affect and Socialisation." *Thamyris* 1: 137–56.

———. 2005. "The Roman Child in Sickness and in Health." In George 2005: 67–92.

Champlin, E. J. 1991. *Final Judgements. Duty and Emotion in Roman Wills 200 BC–AD 250.* Berkeley: University of California Press.

Corbier, M. 1999. "La petite enfance à Rome: lois, normes, pratiques individuelles et collectives." *Annales* 54: 1257–90.

———. 2001. "Child Exposure and Abandonment." In S. Dixon (ed.), *Childhood, Class and Kin in the Roman World.* London: Routledge. 52–73.

Dasen, V. (ed.). 2004. *Naissance et petite enfance dans l'Antiquité. Actes du colloque de Fribourg, 28 novembre–1ᵉʳ décembre 2001.* Fribourg: Academie Press.

Dixon, S. 1988. *The Roman Mother.* Norman: University of Oklahoma Press.

———. 1999. "The Circulation of Children in Roman Society." In M. Corbier (ed.), *Adoption et fosterage. Actes du colloque international, Paris, 4 et 5 juin 1993.* Paris: De Boccard. 217–30.

———. (ed.). 2001. *Childhood, Class and Kin in the Roman World.* London: Routledge.

Duncan-Jones, R. P. 1964. "The Purpose and Organisation of the Alimenta." *Papers of the British School in Rome* 32: 123–46.

Evans, J. K. 1991. *War, Women and Children in Ancient Rome.* London: Routledge.

Eyben, E. 1986. "Sozialgeschichte des Kindes im römischen Altertum." In J. Martin and A. Nitschke (eds.), *Zur Sozialgeschichte der Kindheit.* Freiburg: Verlag Karl Alber. 317–63.

———. 1991. "Fathers and Sons." In Rawson 1991: 114–43.

French, V. 1991. "Children in Antiquity." In J. M. Hawes and N. R. Hiner (eds.), *Children in Historical and Comparative Perspective. An International Handbook and Research Guide.* New York: Greenwood Press. 13–29.

Frier, B. W. 1982. "Roman Life Expectancy: Ulpian's Evidence." *Harvard Studies in Classical Philology* 86: 213–51.

———. 1999. "Roman Demography." In D. S. Potter and D. J. Mattingly (eds.), *Life, Death, and Entertainment in the Roman Empire.* Ann Arbor: University of Michigan Press. 85–109.

———. 2000. "Demography." In A. K. Bowman, P. Garnsey, and D. Rathbone (eds.), *The Cambridge Ancient History 11: The High Empire, A.D. 70–192.* 2nd ed. Cambridge: Cambridge University Press. 787–816.

Garnsey, P. 1991. "Child Rearing in Ancient Italy." In Kertzer and Saller 1991: 48–65.

George, M. (ed.). 2005. *The Roman Family in the Empire. Rome, Italy, and Beyond.* Oxford: Oxford University Press.

Golden, M. 1988. "Did the Ancients Care When Their Children Died?" *Greece & Rome* 35: 152–63.

Gray-Fow, M. J. G. 1988. "The Wicked Stepmother in Roman Literature and History: An Evaluation." *Latomus* 47: 741–57.

Harlow, M., and R. Laurence. 2002. *Growing Up and Growing Old in Ancient Rome. A Life Course of Approach.* London: Routledge.

Harris, W. V. 1986. "The Roman Father's Power of Life and Death." In R. S. Bagnall and W. V. Harris (eds.), *Studies in Roman Law in Memory of A. Arthur Schiller.* Leiden: E. J. Brill. 81–95.

———. 1994. "Child-Exposure in the Roman Empire." *Journal of Roman Studies* 84: 1–22.

Hopkins, K. 1965–66. "Contraception in the Roman Empire." *Comparative Studies in Society and History* 8: 124–51.

Huskinson, J. 1996. *Roman Children's Sarcophagi. Their Decoration and Its Social Significance,* Oxford: Oxford University Press.

Joshel, S. R. 1986. "Nurturing the Master's Child: Slavery and the Roman Child-Nurse." *Signs* 12: 3–22.

Kertzer, D. I., and R. P. Saller (eds.). 1991. *The Family in Italy from Antiquity to the Present.* New Haven: Yale University Press.

Kleijwegt, M., and R. Amedick. 2004. "Kind." *Reallexikon für Antike und Christentum* 20: 865–947.

Kneissl, P., and V. Losemann (eds.). 1988. *Alte Geschichte und Wissenschaftsgeschichte. Festschrift für Karl Christ zum 65. Geburtstag.* Darmstadt: Wissenschaftliche Buchgesellschaft.

Krause, J.-U. 1994–95. *Witwen und Waisen im Römischen Reich.* 4 vols. Stuttgart: Franz Steiner Verlag.

Laes, C. 2007. "Inscriptions from Rome and the History of Childhood." In M. Harlow and R. Laurence (eds.), *Age and Ageing in the Roman Empire.* Portsmouth, R.I.: Journal of Roman Archaeology. 25–37.

McWilliam, J. 2001. "Children among the Dead: The Influence of Urban Life on the Commemoration of Children on Tombstone Inscriptions." In Dixon 2001: 74–98.

Néraudau, J.-P. 1984. *Etre enfant à Rome.* Paris: Payot.

Noy, D. 1991. "Wicked Stepmothers in Roman Society and Imagination." *Journal of Family History* 16: 345–61.

Parkin, T. G. 1992. *Demography and Roman Society.* Baltimore: Johns Hopkins University Press.

Rawson, B. (ed.). 1991. *Marriage, Divorce, and Children in Ancient Rome.* Oxford: Clarendon Press.

———. 1997. "The Iconography of Roman Childhood." In B. Rawson and P. Weaver (eds.), *The Roman Family in Italy. Status, Sentiment, Space.* Oxford: Clarendon Press. 205–32.

———. 2001. "Children as Cultural Symbols. Imperial Ideology in the Second Century." In Dixon 2001: 21–42.

———. 2003. *Children and Childhood in Roman Italy.* Oxford: Oxford University Press.

Saller, R. P. 1988. "*Pietas*, Obligation and Authority in the Roman Family." In Kneissl and Losemann 1988: 393–410.

———. 1991. "Corporal Punishment, Authority, and Obedience in the Roman Household." In Rawson 1991: 144–65.

———. 1994. *Patriarchy, Property and Death in the Roman Family.* Cambridge: Cambridge University Press.

Shaw, B. 1991. "The Cultural Meaning of Death: Age and Gender in the Roman Family." In Kertzer and Saller 1991: 66–90.

Thomas, Y. 1982. "Droit domestique et droit politique à Rome. Remarques sur le pécule et les honores des fils de famille." *Mélanges d'Archéologie et d'Histoire de l'école Française de Rome, Antiquité* 94: 527–80.

———. 1984. "Vitae necisque potestas. Le père, la cité, la mort." In *Du châtiment dans la cité. Supplices corporels et peine de mort dans le monde antique.* Rome: École Française de Rome. 499–548.

Wacke, A. 1980. "Elterliche Gewalt im Wandel der Jahrtausende. Zum Sorgerecht der geschiedenen Mutter nach römischem Recht." In W. Eck, H. Galsterer, and H. Wolff (eds.), *Studien zur antiken Sozialgeschichte. Festschrift Friedrich Vittinghoff.* Cologne and Vienna: Böhlau. 417–34.

Watson, P. A. 1995. *Ancient Stepmothers. Myth, Misogyny and Reality.* Leiden: E. J. Brill.

Wiedemann, Th. 1989. *Adults and Children in the Roman Empire*. New Haven: Yale University Press.

Wierschowski, L. 1988. "Die Alimentarinstitutionen Nervas und Traians. Ein Programm für die Armen? " In Kneissl and Losemann 1988: 756–83.

Woolf, G. 1990. "Food, Poverty and Patronage. The Significance of the Epigraphy of the Roman Alimentary Schemes in Early Imperial Italy." *Papers of the British School in Rome* 58: 197–228.

CHAPTER 31

ROMAN PROSTITUTES AND MARGINALIZATION

THOMAS A. J. MCGINN

INTRODUCTION: MARGINALIZED PERSONS

THAT prostitutes in ancient Rome were marginalized persons seems like an obvious point. More than the most casual consideration of their marginal status, however, yields a fair harvest of contradiction, if not outright confusion. We can say that prostitutes were marginalized in some ways but not in others, a generalization that does not, however, communicate much of sense or of substance. To come to grips with this problem, an analytical approach is preferable, and it is better, in fact, to pursue more than one such approach simultaneously.

Our main axis of interpretation thus takes the following track. First, we will look at how prostitutes were marginalized. What mechanisms were deployed to remove them to the edges of Roman society? Next, we will ask what we mean by 'marginalization' when speaking of Roman prostitutes. Does it refer to absolute exclusion, or something less than this, so that they are integrated into society while being held at some distance from the center? Finally, why were prostitutes marginalized? Are the Roman reasons for situating prostitutes, in a legal and social sense, at the edges of the community really so obvious, given that their marginalization is something common to many societies? Because marginalization is a cultural construct, if anything is, we would do well not to make facile assumptions in this regard, taking for granted that such treatment of prostitutes is inevitable, for example.

Beyond this, we will examine some very familiar categories of experience. These include political and social life, law, the economy, and even the topography of the Roman city. We focus chiefly on female prostitutes, in large part because the evidence for them is better, but include some consideration of male prostitutes, as well as male and female pimps, when it is convenient to do so.

MEANS OF MARGINALIZATION

Prostitution in Classical Rome

Prostitution in ancient Rome was widespread, and constituted an important aspect of the economy in terms of upper-class investment, state revenue, and female employment. Highly exploitative in nature, it also enjoyed great symbolic importance. The vast bulk of the legal, literary, documentary, and archaeological evidence derives approximately from the period 200 BC–AD 250, and most of this by far concerns the prostitution of women, again, the focus of this essay. The literary and legal evidence is by and large Rome-centered, while some of the most important documentary sources, such as inscriptions, hail from the periphery of the empire. It is also important to recognize that the highest concentration of material remains is found in Pompeii. Thus, in general terms, the evidence for Roman prostitution is scattered and composite in its nature, which makes for no small challenge in its interpretation.

Participation in Cultic Practices

Gender at Rome was a well-differentiated category in a number of respects, including civic status. Female prostitutes were far from the social equals of respectable women, as their role in cult, separate and inferior, demonstrates clearly. They were by implication banished from certain rituals performed by respectable women, such as those of the Bona Dea and of Ceres. Evidence suggests a fundamental exclusion of prostitutes from any role as official celebrants in cult (see Sen. *Con.* 1. 2 *thema*).

More significant perhaps is the positive aspect, the relegation of prostitutes to a separate cult, either by themselves or among a group of non-respectable women. Examples are the rites of Venus Erycina, celebrated by *meretrices* (prostitutes) outside the Porta Collina, whereas respectable women worshiped the goddess in the center of the city, on the Capitoline, and the contrasting cults of Fortuna Virilis and Venus Verticordia. *Mulieres humiliores* (less respectable women), a category that must have included prostitutes, were assigned to the first of these two latter cults, while *mulieres honestiores* (more respectable women) were associated with the second. The feast of the Nonae Capratinae was celebrated by the *feriarum ancillae* (slave women of the religious festival), a group considered by moderns to have included both slaves and women of servile origin; it no doubt included prostitutes as well. Prostitutes were prominent participants in public religious celebrations that were evidently attended by the entire community, such as the Floralia. An analogy may be sought in the participation of prostitutes in religious festivals and other public occasions in parts of late medieval Europe. Sacred prostitution, on the other hand, was at no time a Roman practice (McGinn 1998: 24–26; see also Karras 1999: 165).[1]

A nice illustration of participation by prostitutes in religious festivals, and the range of social meanings that can be associated with this practice, comes from Germany in the period of transition from the very late medieval period to the very early modern. At the *Jakobidult*, or Fair of St. James, held in Munich each year, a race was held in which prostitutes competed for a piece of linen, a typical item in a woman's dowry. This usage developed after 1488, the year in which the town council granted permission for prostitutes to marry. Historians have noted that the race took place very near the convent of a religious order, the Poor Clares, to which a pilgrimage took place immediately following the festival. In 1562 the city authorities abolished the race and, before the end of the century, closed the municipal brothel as well. Half of the inmates of this institution then entered convents, while the rest sought husbands, after collecting money for a dowry from the city (Strasser 2004: 59, 63).

It seems easy to explain these developments as spurred by the changes in religious doctrine and practice produced by the Reformation, though it is worth noting first, that they are more than a little self-contradictory in themselves, and second, that they occurred in Bavaria, a region that remained thoroughly Catholic in its confessional allegiance during this period. Repression of prostitution was a policy enthusiastically advocated by many Protestant Reformers, and not adopted, certainly in such an extreme form, in some other areas of Europe, such as Italy, that, like Bavaria, remained Catholic. So, the Reformation can serve as only a partial explanation of these events. Of particular interest in this case is the fact that integration of prostitutes into the ceremonial life of the community not only suggests great complexity in its motivation(s), but experienced dramatic changes in a relatively short span of time.[2]

This comparative evidence suggests both the importance of participation by prostitutes in cult for the question of their integration into society and the need for great caution in assessing its precise significance. It is also good to exercise care in comparing such usages in Christian and post-Christian cultures with those in pre-Christian ones. We can safely conclude, all the same, that the precise articulation of the role of Roman prostitutes in the religious life of the community placed them at

---

1. Skepticism over the existence of sacred prostitution in antiquity has in recent years extended to Greece and the Near East: Beard and Henderson 1998; Budin 2006.

2. It is useful to note that the period of Reform in Bavaria and elsewhere saw increasing marginalization of nuns as well as prostitutes. See Strasser 2004: 79–81.

its margins, but did not utterly exclude them, a practice that finds parallels in other societies.

Law and Public Policy

In other aspects of civic status, matters were more complex, though consistently tending to the disadvantage of female prostitutes. All women were barred from office-holding and political activity in general. Male prostitutes and pimps were excluded from such participation as a matter of routine, as well as from service in the army. Under the republic, they appear to have received consistently negative attention from the censors, the officials charged with a sort of moral oversight of Roman society. What this means is that their status as citizens was effectively compromised, though it is worth remarking that they were not automatically excluded from the citizen body. For female prostitutes, such disabilities flowed from the fact of their gender, rather than that of their profession, which arguably renders their status as citizens more complicated and difficult to characterize, at least initially.

Prostitutes and pimps of both genders were disadvantaged in terms of the role they were allowed to play in the civil and criminal courts. In principle, they were barred from making pleas on behalf of others (or more generally, from representing others) in the Praetor's court (the main forum for private law litigation in Rome), from bringing criminal accusations, or from acting as witnesses. Prostitutes and pimps suffered from a very low position viewed from the perspective of both legal disability and social prejudice, and so were assigned to a core category of disgrace that included a very few other types, such as actors and gladiators (McGinn 1998: 21–69; see also Leppin in this volume).

Statute law also regulated the status of practitioners of prostitution in a very direct manner; most notable here is the marriage and adultery legislation from the reign of the emperor Augustus. The first enactment, actually two laws passed in 18 BC and AD 9, prohibited marriage between freeborn Romans and a small number of socially despised types, including prostitutes and pimps. Thus, it made into a legal rule what had previously been subject to severe social disapproval, backed up by censorial sanction. It is doubtful that the law had much relevance for upper-class spouse selection. In any case, Augustus was careful not to punish prostitutes overmuch, even allowing the unmarried among them to receive as much as one-fourth of a decedent's estate through testamentary bequest.[3] Liability for adultery and criminal fornication under the Augustan adultery law, passed in 18 or 17 BC, was grounded in the respectable status of the female partner. This meant by contrast that sexual relations with some types of women deemed non-respectable, including prostitutes and procuresses, were exempt from the statutory penalty. At the same time, the law created non-respectable statuses for the complaisant husband, who

---

3. I find unpersuasive the recent reexamination of this problem by Tellegen-Couperus 2003.

was now to be punished as a criminal pimp, and the adulteress, who was assimilated to a prostitute, most visibly through the imposition of the toga, the prostitute's badge of shame. Augustus was, in short, quite adept at exploiting the symbolic power of prostitution for his moral and political purposes (McGinn 1998: 70–104, 140–215; McGinn 2002).[4]

A later piece of legislation, passed by the senate in AD 19, forbade members of the senatorial and equestrian orders, the top ranks of Roman society, from practicing prostitution. The incident that sparked this law occurred when a member of the senatorial order, named Vistilia, attempted to register as a prostitute in order to escape prosecution for adultery. The senate closed this statutory loophole, and punished Vistilia for adultery (see Tac. *Ann.* 2. 85. 1–3; Suet. *Tib.* 35. 2; Pap. *Dig.* 48. 5. 11[10]. 2; McGinn 1998: 216–19).

The state also taxed prostitution, a fiscal initiative that was introduced by the emperor Caligula in AD 40, and continued long afterward. Caligula's purpose, at minimum, was to raise as much money for the state as possible, a goal realized in such abundance that, where possible, responsibility for collection of the tax was transferred from civilian tax collectors to the military, evidently for reasons of security. The rate of the tax was set at the price of one sexual encounter per day, though a different rate prevailed in Egypt, where civilian tax collectors continued to operate, as we know they did in Palmyra, on the eastern fringes of the empire. The tax on prostitutes had three major implications for Roman society, regarding profitability, legitimacy, and social control. It generated enormous revenues for the state, legitimized (deliberately or not) the practice of venal sex, and facilitated, especially after transfer of the responsibility for collection to the military, a closer surveillance of the business. For Christian critics, a further implication was that the tax configured the state as a kind of pimp (McGinn 1998: 248–87).

Roman private law granted an extraordinary protection for a master who did not want his or her slave to be prostituted by a new owner after sale. It recognized the 'real' validity of a restrictive covenant on sale—namely, "that a slave woman not be prostituted"—which was enforced by penalties of re-acquisition by the original master, or of freedom for the slave. It seems that emperors and jurists extensively elaborated and aggressively applied the rules for this covenant, though we cannot know how often it was actually invoked by masters selling their slaves. A Roman version of the honor-shame syndrome best explains how an owner might retain an interest in the sexual integrity of a slave even after alienation, that is, after transfer of property (i.e., the slave) to a new owner (McGinn 1998: 288–319). Rules relating to prostitutes and prostitution also arose in other areas of the private law, ranging from inheritance to theft. The major concerns voiced by the jurists in this connection are grounded in questions of honor and economics, meaning in the latter instance both

---

4. Olson 2002 has a rather confused critique of my argument on the dress of prostitutes and adulteresses. Its difficulties cannot be disentangled here, however.

the exploitation of prostitutes for profit, and extravagant, wasteful behavior with regard to them (McGinn 1998: 320–37).

Members of the elite regarded brothels as places of dirt and disorder, and so it is not surprising that these establishments were subject to the oversight of public officials—in Rome, the aediles. There is some very tenuous evidence that regulations governed the hours of operation for brothels. For the Romans, a large part of maintaining public order regarding the practice of prostitution lay in the policing of status distinctions between respectable women and prostitutes and in collecting taxes and payments for the lease of public property where sex was sold. There were exceptional circumstances, such as a water-theft scandal in the mid-first century BC, that invited a relatively high level of official intervention. And contrary to what has sometimes been assumed, Roman public policy did not dictate the location of brothels, removing them to side streets and out-of-the-way places, in a form of the 'moral zoning' so familiar from cultures in later periods. Some property owners may have had scruples about operating a venue for the sale of sex on their premises; but in general terms, a desire for profit determined the number and location of brothels, an interest shared, as we have seen, by the state itself (McGinn 2004: 78–166).[5]

The lack of evidence for moral zoning of brothels suggests an important truth about the regulation of prostitution by the Roman authorities. Nowhere is it possible to discover a 'law of prostitution.' Legal rules situated prostitutes and pimps at the margins of society through the imposition of a series of civic and legal disabilities, whose function was to place practitioners outside the pale of the community of honor, which alone enjoyed a claim to rank and its privileges. Prostitutes and pimps were two of a very small set of marginal types who found themselves, when they did possess citizenship, in this penumbra of Roman citizen status. They fell just inside the line separating the citizen community and those who did not belong to this, some of whom, even as *peregrini* (resident aliens), might have a better claim to recognition of honorable status than practitioners of prostitution. Exceptions, of course, were the many prostitutes who were themselves not Roman citizens, but even they were less marginalized than groups such as *latrones* (bandits), who were totally excluded from society (see Riess in this volume).

There is, then, both a broad diversity in the legal approaches taken toward prostitution and a complexity that characterizes the status of prostitutes. The status of a prostitute depended, apart from considerations of gender, first on her assignment to

5. That there was no moral zoning of bars, a category that partly overlaps with that of brothels, has been conclusively demonstrated to my mind by Ellis 2004. Varone 2005 is in substantial agreement with me on this subject, though I would not use the anachronistic phrase 'red-light district,' even in jest, to describe the topography of Roman prostitution. The arguments of Ray Laurence on moral zoning, which I criticize in McGinn 2004 and elsewhere, have now been refined in the second edition of his book on Roman Pompeii, which takes into account my views. Though we seem closer than before, there are still significant points of variance: see Laurence 2007: 82–101.

one of the fundamental classifications of peregrine, slave, freed, or freeborn. These women do not appear to have possessed, qua prostitutes, a unified status before the law, that is, a coherent ensemble of rights and duties, or even of disabilities, that are laid out with clarity and precision in the legal sources.

Economics

The sale of sex in the Roman world was a cash-rich enterprise that provided investors with relatively large profits, compared with the costs incurred in setting up such a business. Chief among these were the cost of urban real estate, whether leased or purchased, and, if it was necessary to purchase slaves to work as prostitutes, their price. Members of the upper classes had good reason to avoid identification as pimps, because of the social censure and civic disabilities this entailed, but such evasion was fairly easy to accomplish through the use of slaves and others as middlemen. Prostitution was widespread, associated with a number of places and events that drew large numbers of potential clients, such as circuses, baths, festivals, and circuit courts. The male consumer found purchased sex to be both readily available and relatively inexpensive. Employment opportunities for women in the Roman economy were bleak at best, and it is persuasive that some women were drawn into the profession by the lack of realistic alternatives, and the lure of some level of material ease. If this was indeed the case, it is just as likely that this prospect, however modest, was an illusory one, given the highly exploitative character of venal sex in the Roman world. To be sure, many, if not most, female prostitutes were probably vulnerable to compulsion by slave owners and aggressive pimps, and that goes a long way toward explaining why they entered prostitution in the first place, and remained in it afterward (McGinn 2004: 14–77).

The vast bulk of our material evidence for prostitution comes from Pompeii, an Italian town buried by an eruption of Mt. Vesuvius in AD 79. Though the state of this evidence presents great challenges to the identification of brothels and other venues where sex was sold, scholars have located, with varying degrees of confidence, at least forty-one possible brothels, of which about half seem more certain than the rest, and thirteen possible *cellae meretriciae*, or cribs, which are one-room venues for sex, lying off a street or in the back of a bar. Three sub-types of brothel emerge from the archaeological remains at Pompeii: (a) the purpose-built subtype, with a lone specimen that also stands out as our most certain example of a brothel anywhere in the Roman world; (b) the tavern subtype, featuring rooms in the back and/or upstairs, and evidently the most numerous of the three; and (c) a sub-type associated with lower-class lodgings, but without a tavern. Sex was very likely sold in or near other well-frequented locations in the city, such as bath complexes, some of which were associated in turn with brothels (see Fagan in this volume). Scholars have also identified brothels in a number of other Roman towns, including Rome itself, Dura-Europos on the eastern border of the empire, Ostia (the port of Rome), and Sayala in Lower Nubia, though varying degrees of uncertainty attend these identifications as well. None of this evidence provides convincing support for theories of moral zoning, a point raised above. In other words, the marginalization of Roman prostitutes did not depend on their physical isolation within the Roman city.

Late Antiquity and the Repression of Pimping

Perhaps the most striking development in the period of the late antique Roman Empire (here defined as approximately AD 250 to 550) regarding female prostitution is the promulgation of a series of laws intended to repress certain aspects of venal sex, especially pimping. The first of these statutes, enacted by the emperor Constantius in 343, regulated the sale of Christian slave women (*CTh* 15. 8. 1). Once prostituted, they could be sold only to a recognized Christian. The law does not strictly forbid their prostitution, nor does it concern free Christian prostitutes or non-Christian slave prostitutes. A law of Theodosius II in 428 prohibited the forced prostitution of daughters-in-power by their *patres familias* and of slave women by their owners, under severe penalties (*CTh* 15. 8. 2 = *CJ* 11. 41. 6 = [abbreviated] *CJ* 1. 4. 12). The authorities were also permitted to intervene under this statute in the case of persons who hired out their sexual services on account of poverty. Theodosius makes no distinction here between Christians and non-Christians, nor do his successors.

The same emperor suspended collection of the tax on prostitution for the city of Constantinople in 439, at least from pimps, who were now forbidden to ply their trade there (*NTh* 18). In the mid-fifth century, Leo forbade the procuring or pimping by anyone of male or female slaves and free persons, not even if they were stage performers (*CJ* 1. 4. 14 = [?] 11. 41. 7). He also prohibited the collection of the tax on prostitutes from pimps, and apparently not only at Constantinople; Leo seems to have intended the scope of his measures to be empire-wide. This is certainly true for a statute that Justinian promulgated in 535 containing an absolute ban on pimping (*Nov.* 14). Despite the sympathy for prostitutes that is at least implicit in this series of laws, which configure them as vulnerable victims of exploitation, we have to wait until the reign of this last emperor until any disposition is made for them after they are freed from the snares of pimps (see Proc. *Build.* 1. 9. 1–10).

None of these laws, at least as they are preserved, define 'prostitute' or 'prostitution,' though Justinian does describe the activities of pimps in some detail. A series of new post-classical rules in the fields of marriage and adultery law suggests that the legal conception of what it was that defined a prostitute underwent a profound change in this period. These rules arise in the first case in a statute enacted by Constantine on marriage partners, a follow-up by Marcian, and a passage from a late antique juristic treatise (*CTh* 4. 6. 3 = [with modifications] *CJ* 5. 27. 1 [AD 336]; *Nov. Marc.* 4 [AD 454]; *Tit. Ulp.* 13). In the second, they derive from a law of Constantine on liability for adultery and another post-classical juristic text on the same subject (*CTh* 9. 7. 1 = [with modifications] *CJ* 9. 9. 28 [29]; *PS* 2. 26. 11). In substance, these rules create a series of analogues for 'prostitute': the woman who worked in a tavern, the woman who sold merchandise to the general public, the daughter of a pimp, the daughter of a tavern worker, as well as the woman manu-mitted by a pimp or procuress. In each case, the new rule can be explained as the assimilation of a longstanding social prejudice into law (McGinn 1997).[6] The effect of these changes in the law was most likely to intensify the social, as well as legal, marginalization of a broad range of lower-class women, who, in this period, were mostly Roman citizens, if they were not slaves (see Neri 1998: 215).

We are poorly informed about the enforcement of the laws repressing pimping, and we simply cannot know how effective they were. What evidence we do possess suggests that prostitution continued to flourish in this later period. But be that as it may, the sympathy expressed, even if implicitly, for prostitutes in the anti-pimping legislation was not shared, certainly not fully, by many Christian authorities, and prostitutes found themselves excluded in important respects from participation in the life of the community (Neri 1998: 223, 227, 231). Despite the evident unease of at least some Christian emperors over the tax on prostitutes, and its implicit official endorsement of the sale of sex, the state continued to collect the tax until its abolition by Anastasius in 498. One curiosity from the late antique period is the information in the Regionary Catalogues that fourth-century Rome sported forty-five or forty-six brothels. We do not know whether these numbers refer to all brothels, large brothels, purpose-built brothels, or even state-owned brothels. Only on a restrictive interpre-tation would such numbers hold much sense for a city the size of Rome, however (McGinn 2004: 167–73, 221–22). Finally, we should note that not all Christians in late antiquity thought that prostitution should be repressed. A famous text by Augustine offers a rationale for regulating prostitution through zoning, the real impact of which was not felt until centuries later, when we can be certain that such physical segregation of this business was in fact undertaken. Worth noting is that Augustine's concern with marginalizing prostitutes was social as much as topographical (*Ordine* 2. 12 *CCSL* 29. 114; McGinn 2004: 93–111). Zoning can, of course, be contrasted with a policy of repression, which seeks to drive prostitutes and prostitution out of a society altogether, and which may have been attempted, or at least advocated, at this time.

THE MEANING OF MARGINALIZATION FOR ROMAN PROSTITUTES AND PROSTITUTION

What precise significance did marginalization have for female Roman prostitutes, and why were they thus marginalized? We have already seen an outline of an answer to these questions. In this context, however, it is well to raise a couple of general

---

6. It is important to recognize that in Marcian's law, the category of notional marriage partners described as "low and degraded" (*humiles abiectaeque*) persons stands as an exam-ple of the importation of social values into law. Cf. Humfress 2006: 184–89, who seems to regard it as a purely legal classification.

points. First, the debate in the scholarly literature as to whether marginality entails total exclusion from a society or placement on its extreme outer edge is irrelevant for female prostitutes, who can be located firmly within any reasonably well-defined boundaries set for Roman society and the various civic statuses this contained (see Germani 1980: 8, 46; Neri 1998: 8–9). Second, despite differences of opinion in the scholarship, marginality and social stratification are, at least in an ideal sense, analytically distinguishable. In Roman society, however, the two were, from an elite perspective, typically conflated (Germani 1980: 7, 23–27; Geremek 1985: 71; Weiler 1988a: 18; McGinn 1998: 15–16; Neri 1998: 9–11, 16–17). Here too, we can state with confidence that while female prostitutes ranked very low indeed in terms of social stratification, they were as a group set apart from other categories or types whose status was low but not, in any meaningful sense, marginal, such as the poor in general. In sum, they were indeed a part of Roman society but were placed on its outermost edges. The Romans denied them economic clout, social prestige, and political power (see Germani 1980: 47).

The marginality of Roman female prostitutes was, as we have seen, multidimensional in its manifestations. Its full implications are somewhat obscured, however, by the moralism of the ancient sources. What might be termed the composite nature of their marginality also inhibits understanding. Cumulating statuses—above all gender-based, socio-legal, and economic in nature—conspired to deprive them of the means to full participation in the political and social life of the community. As women, they were excluded from voting or holding public office, for politics was the preserve of male members of the elite. Moreover, the vast majority of female prostitutes were slaves, ex-slaves, or lived in social conditions that were close to slavery. Vulnerable to exploitation, they were in overwhelming numbers plagued by poverty. Many free prostitutes were non-citizens and/or immigrants, though it is difficult to be certain to what extent the sheer marginalization of prostitutes may have contributed to perceptions of them as 'foreign' (McGinn 2004: ch. 2).[7] So, in the person of a prostitute, one might often have seen a woman, who was a slave, or perhaps free, but an ex-slave or not a citizen, and who was, in addition, usually poor. In short, prostitutes' exclusion from active participation in politics, indeed, from the kind of existence led by members of the Roman elite, was so overdetermined that it was unnecessary to devise a set of rules specific to the purpose of excluding such women, qua prostitutes, from political life.

At the same time, prostitutes, in actual Roman lived experience, as opposed to the categories constructed by ancient moralists and modern historians, might have been difficult at times to distinguish clearly from other disadvantaged groups and individuals (see Neri 1998: 21). For that matter, we are not well positioned to assess the extent to which prostitution was for many women a temporary expedient, that allowed, at least from a non-elite perspective, eventual re-integration (if this was

---

7. In fact, most of the adult male citizen population found itself excluded from any real role in politics under the principate. See Morley 2006: 34.

in fact necessary) into the ranks of the working poor.[8] Prostitution was, for those members of the Roman elite who have succeeded in communicating their views to us, a permanent condition, a label linked to a person's moral nature, or what we might in modern terms describe as an 'identity' (see Karras 1999: 161–64).

The difficult and controversial relationship between marginality and poverty merits some comment here. We at once encounter problems of definition: if anything, defining 'poor' is even more difficult than defining 'marginal.' Societies that show little social differentiation tend to place the poor on the edges. That seems unlikely to have been true, however, for the Romans (Neri 1998: 10–11; Morley 2006: 27–36; Scheidel 2006: 54–59). Members of the Roman elite, it is true, were in the habit of characterizing poverty, and the poor, in moralizing terms suggestive of a group on the margins of society (Neri 1998: 7; Morley 2006: 29–30, 39). But if the distinction between marginality and stratification has any sense, the poor should be located at the bottom of a society, at least in the case of one that shows the degree of status differentiation Rome does, not at its outermost edges. Thus, poverty may contribute to marginal status, but does not imply this by itself (Germani 1980: 7, 23–27; Geremek 1985: 71; Neri 1998: 9–11, 16–17). As Bronislaw Geremek puts it, "Le pauvre n'est pas un marginal…" (the poor person is not a marginal one) (Geremek 1985: 76). This does not mean, however, that certain important groups within the overall category of 'poor' might not qualify as marginalized, both to the modern mind and even from an ancient perspective. These include the homeless, beggars, the seriously ill and/or disabled (Holman 2006: 444–45, 452–53; Mayer 2006: 467–71).

Wealth remains relevant to the question of marginalization all the same. Members of groups resident in or near Roman communities, but who did not count as citizens of those places, such as *incolae* (resident aliens), *hospites* (guests), and *adventores* (visitors), might soften the implications of their marginal status through the accumulation of material assets (Mrozek 1988). By the same token, wealthy freedmen might see the effects of their social and legal marginality considerably effaced (Weber 1988). In this way, the possession of significant economic resources contributed, in a number of cases, to a situation of 'status dissonance.' For those already disadvantaged, on the other hand, the effect of a lack of material assets tended to be cumulative. Thus, the poverty of prostitutes was a factor in their marginalization, a fact that seems to receive increasing recognition in late antiquity (see now Mayer 2006: 471).

Participation in the religious life of the community shows a different pattern of exclusion. Women in general played an important part here, one that was largely separate from that of men. Their participation was structured along various status cleavages, including that of respectable versus non-respectable, as we have seen above. The fact that female prostitutes were assigned a role in cult is highly significant, because it shows clearly that their marginalization from Roman

---

8. On 'temporary marginality,' see the observations of Weiler 1988a: 19; Neri 1998: 22.

society was not total. The same holds for the position defined for them by the Augustan marriage and adultery legislation. Under the first category of law, they were forbidden to marry freeborn Roman citizens, though they were allowed (and one might even say tacitly encouraged, at least to some extent) to marry freedmen. The second category, by exempting them from liability for adultery and criminal fornication, granted them recognition as an approved extramarital sexual outlet for men. By compelling them to register with public officials and (perhaps) to wear the toga as a badge of shame, alongside of convicted adulteresses (we do not have to assume that either measure was strictly enforced, at least for very long), the state sought to assure them a key role in safeguarding the chastity of respectable women. In part, they were made to provide a highly visible negative exemplum. This granted the practice of prostitution a certain legitimacy, as did their liability to taxation from Caligula onward (as payers of a direct tax, prostitutes and pimps were initially set apart from more privileged citizens, but this distinction lost its force over time). The potency of the latter point is illustrated by the considerable embarrassment caused, at least to some Christian emperors, by this tax. Their response was to attempt to repress pimping, on the one hand, and, on the other hand, eventually to abolish the tax.

Let us turn, for a moment, from society's attitudes about prostitutes, to these women themselves. Just how they might have viewed themselves? To what extent can we recover any sense of their lived experience? As with Roman women in general, direct testimony from female prostitutes is almost completely lacking. Our only source appears to be the graffiti that survive, above all from Pompeii, in which prostitutes advertise their prices and services (if these epigraphs are not insults leveled at them). Did they view themselves as an outcast group? Did they share a common culture of sorts, possess a group identity, or a sense of belonging to an anti-society at odds with the values of the mainstream culture? We can never be certain, of course, though the graffiti, if we understand them correctly, would tend to suggest that prostitutes were very far from subscribing to the rules, written and unwritten, that governed the sexual conduct of respectable women.[9] Various types of deviance were associated with sexual deviance, an attitude originating in bias and/or perceptions on the part of respectable society, but one that to a degree may have reflected actual experience. The sources do permit us to see that many prostitutes lived and worked in an atmosphere redolent not only of poverty, but of disorder and criminality as well, factors that would have heightened their sense of social isolation. In particular, they appear not infrequently to have been involved with crimes against property, such as theft; though prostitutes, like other Romans mired in poverty, might be victims as well as perpetrators (McGinn 2004: ch. 2;

---

9. On the importance of culture as a criterion in determining marginality, see Geremek 1985: 70–71. For Rome we lack access to the sort of archives generated by courts and police so important to historians of more recent periods as more or less direct evidence of the experience of marginality. In this respect, see Geremek 1985: 74.

also Geremek 1985: 73–76; Neri 1998: 21–23; Karras 1999: 169; Morley 2006: 33 for the general point).

It is significant that, aside from one very partial exception, female prostitution was never criminalized at Rome. That exception is itself worth remarking on, since it suggests just how uninterested the Romans were in such a policy of repression. The decree of the senate mentioned above, forbidding prostitution by members of the senatorial and equestrian orders, was passed in response to a highly exceptional episode, in which Vistilia, a woman of senatorial rank, attempted to register with the aediles as a prostitute in order to escape prosecution for adultery, a singular occurrence, as far as we know. There is no good evidence that Vistilia herself, or any other member of the two upper orders, ever practiced prostitution. Actual prostitutes, as opposed to adulteresses, were left free by the law to ply their trade, acting albeit under various forms of legal and extra-legal compulsion to sell sex. The local authorities took an interest in them insofar as they were associated with petty criminality (especially theft), or public disorder, or insofar as they were liable to paying the Caligulan tax. Thus, Tertullian includes pimps among those groups—including thieves working in the baths (*fures balnearum*) and Christians—whose members were found on the registers kept by soldiers (*matrices*) listing persons liable to paying a tax and/or who were vulnerable to extortion, evidently because of their association with criminal activity (Tert. *Fuga* 13. 3 *CCSL* 2. 1154–55). All the same, the contrast with late antiquity, with its repression of pimping and male prostitution, could not be clearer (for the latter, see just *Coll. Leg. Mos.* 5. 3 [AD 390]).

Apart from exclusions of a political/legal, economic, or cultural/social nature, there is the important category of spatial or topographical marginality.[10] That no official policy relegated prostitutes out of certain areas of a city and into others is sometimes difficult to comprehend from a modern perspective. What is clear is that the spatial management of prostitution was a far different matter in pre-Christian antiquity than it has been since the Middle Ages and later. Prostitutes were excluded from the center of society, but they were excluded in plain sight. They, as well as venues for the sale of sex, were found in various places in the Roman city, many of them both central and visible. This helps us to understand the (by now obvious) point, that prostitutes were far from being placed utterly outside of society. It also sheds important light on the precise nature of their marginalization. Prostitutes were regarded as necessary elements of society. There was no obvious sense among the Romans that prostitutes and prostitution ought to be eliminated; nor were prostitutes viewed just as sexual outlets for Roman males. Rather, they were made to serve as highly visible living lessons for Roman women with claims to respectability. Thus, just as no true understanding of freedom in Roman society was utterly independent of the idea of slavery, so the understanding of honor was incomplete without being informed by considerations of shame. These binary moral calculuses helped construct each other.

---

10. These categories are an adaptation of those offered by Geremek 1985: 70–71. See also Neri 1998: 14.

CONCLUSIONS

Marginality of any one group within a society, such as female prostitutes, should ideally be viewed in historical terms as part of a much larger process (see Geremek 1985: 72). Prostitution and its practitioners are not marginalized to the same extent in every society. Nor is prostitution always marginalized in the same way; indeed, there are sometimes differences in the degree or kind of marginalization even within the same culture, especially over time (see Neri 1998: 14–15). The structure of the economy, especially the gendered division of labor, as well as large-scale events, such as a war, or a series of wars, often have important marginalizing consequences for broad sectors of a society. Whatever the numbers and destinies of individual prostitutes, or the sheer dimensions and distribution of the business of prostitution, however, there appears to have been a broad consistency in the social experience of the female Roman prostitute as sociological type over time. Prostitutes remained more or less where they had been positioned from the start, that is to say, marginalized in plain sight, possessed of the paradoxical status of "deviant insiders."[11]

Finally, why were female prostitutes thus marginalized in Roman society? The traditional response to this question has been to offer misogynistic bromides about 'the oldest profession' and the like. We cannot simply assume, however, that the marginalization of prostitutes, though common, is going to have the same causation across cultures. It is a curious, but important, fact that we are not always well-informed about the reasons behind the exclusion of groups by societies much closer in time to us than are the Romans (Geremek 1985: 78). Given that the study of marginality in a culture amounts to the study of the society and its values as a whole (Neri 1998: 29; Karras 1999: 162), it does seem possible to read the rationale for exclusion, in a kind of inverse manner, from the behavioral prescriptions set for the mainstream. This is why the study of respectable women and respectable society overall is so essential for the understanding of the place of prostitutes and prostitution, and vice versa. All the same, the causes and effects of marginalization are often difficult to tease apart (Geremek 1985: 79). Were prostitutes, for example, marginalized because they were shameful—or were they shameful because they were marginalized?

The easy answer is that both are true. Certainly the second alternative reflects a certain self-reinforcing aspect of marginalization that, while perhaps not inevitable, is still very common. It is the first, however, that claims a certain priority. One can fruitfully understand the social prejudice against female prostitutes at Rome as the expression of what anthropologists have defined as a syndrome of honor and shame. This was a Roman version of a set of prescriptions regarding sexual behavior (and some behavior we would not identify as strictly sexual) that assigns roles and status on the basis of a gendered division of labor, in which the man protects the family's—or household's—(sexual) honor, while the woman conserves her (sexual)

11. The phrase is used to describe the status and role of prostitutes in sixteenth-century Seville by Perry 1985: 143. See McGinn 1998: 341; Neri 1998: 12.

purity. The honor of the family or household pertains to every one of its members, and is collective in nature. Such a syndrome is found in various manifestations in various cultures, and has been especially common among traditional societies in the Mediterranean (see McGinn 1998: 10–14).[12]

One can, then, if armed with a perspective informed by considerations of honor and shame, better understand some of the most important root causes of the prejudice against Roman female prostitutes that resulted in their social marginalization. In order to do this, it is useful to compare some behaviors ascribed to them with ideals associated with married women (but that were, in principle, extended to all respectable Roman women, whatever their marital status). Let us focus on three elements in a list not meant to be exhaustive. First, prostitutes were promiscuous, while wives were supposed to be sexually loyal to their husbands (and respectable unmarried women were supposed to be sexually inactive). Second, prostitutes demanded payment, typically in advance, for sex, while wives ideally avoided any appearance of such direct material reward, to the extent that they brought dowries to a marriage as a guarantee of the seriousness and respectability of the relationship, and gifts of any value between spouses were banned by law. Third, the bond between spouses was regarded, at its best, as affective and almost spiritual in nature (again, I emphasize that I am speaking of ideals here), while transactions with prostitutes were something very different.[13]

In sum, prostitution was supposed to be as far from marriage as any sexual relationship could be, and the prostitute herself functioned as a kind of anti-wife. She was despised for this, and also perhaps for serving as a constant, visible reminder of male weakness and need. Certain behaviors, to which any woman might be deemed prone, led to the assignment of a permanent, degraded status to some women, and to the construction of the prostitute as a highly defined type, with implications for all (see Karras 1999: 169–71). The prostitute was cast on the margin of society, where she might more safely serve a double function, from a Roman point of view, both of distracting male sexual interest from respectable women and of serving as a warning to the latter of the cost of transgressing against society's established rules for female behavior.

SUGGESTED READING

The most relevant and up-to-date literature on prostitution has already been cited in the treatment above. One might name the following, however, as some of the central discussions of the topics here delineated: Flemming 1999; McGinn 1997; McGinn 1998; McGinn 2002; McGinn 2004; and Neri 1998.

12. For a recent restatement of some by now familiar objections to Mediterraneanist conceptions of honor and shame, see Harris 2005: 26–29, 39. Note also Lendon in this volume.

13. On Roman marriage ideal(s), see just Mod. *Dig.* 23. 2. 1, with Treggiari 1991: 183–319.

BIBLIOGRAPHY

Atkins, M., and R. Osborne (eds.). 2006. *Poverty in the Roman World*. Cambridge: Cambridge University Press.

Beard, M., and J. Henderson. 1998. "With This Body I Thee Worship: Sacred Prostitution in Antiquity." In M. Wyke (ed.), *Gender and the Body in the Ancient Mediterranean*. Oxford: Blackwell. 56–79.

Bowden, W., et al. (eds.). 2006. *Social and Political Life in Late Antiquity*. Leiden: E. J. Brill.

Budin, S. L. 2006. "Sacred Prostitution in the First Person." In Faraone and McClure 2006: 77–92.

Ellis, S. J. R. 2004. "The Distribution of Bars at Pompeii: Archaeological, Spatial, and Viewshed Analyses." *Journal of Roman Archaeology* 17: 371–84.

Faraone, C. A., and L. K. McClure (eds.). 2006. *Prostitutes and Courtesans in the Ancient World*. Madison: University of Wisconsin Press.

Flemming, R. 1999. "*Quae Corpore Quaestum Facit*: The Sexual Economy of Female Prostitution in the Roman Empire." *Journal of Roman Studies* 89: 38–61.

Geremek, B. 1985. "L'image de l'autre: Le marginal." In *XVI Congrès international des sciences historiques (Stuttgart, 25 Août–1 September 1985): Rapports*. Stuttgart: Le Comité International des Sciences Historiques. 1: 67–81.

Germani, G. 1980. *Marginality*. New Brunswick: Transaction Books.

Harris, W. V. 2005. "The Mediterranean and Ancient History." In W. V. Harris (ed.), *Rethinking the Mediterranean*. Oxford: Oxford University Press. 1–42.

Holman, S. R. 2006. "Constructed and Consumed: The Everyday Life of the Poor in 4th Century Cappadocia." In Bowden et al. 2006: 441–64.

Humfress, C. 2006. "Poverty and Roman Law." In Atkins and Osborne 2006: 183–203.

Karras, R. M. 1999. "Prostitution and the Question of Sexual Identity in Medieval Europe." *Journal of Women's History* 11.2: 159–77.

Laurence, R. 2007. *Roman Pompeii: Space and Society*. 2nd ed. London: Routledge.

Mayer, W. 2006. "Poverty and Society in the World of John Chrysostom." In Bowden et al. 2006: 465–84.

McGinn, T. A. J. 1997. "The Legal Definition of Prostitute in Late Antiquity." *Memoirs of the American Academy in Rome* 42: 73–116.

———. 1998. *Prostitution, Sexuality, and the Law in Ancient Rome*. New York: Oxford University Press.

———. 2002. "The Augustan Marriage Legislation and Social Practice: Elite Endogamy vs. Male 'Marrying Down.'" In J.-J. Aubert and A. J. B. Sirks (eds.), *Speculum Iuris: Roman Law as a Reflection of Social and Economic Life*. Ann Arbor: University of Michigan Press. 46–93.

———. 2004. *The Economy of Prostitution in the Roman World: A Study of Social History and the Brothel*. Ann Arbor: University of Michigan Press.

Morley, N. 2006. "The Poor in the City of Rome." In Atkins and Osborne 2006: 21–39.

Mrozek, S. 1988. "Die epigraphisch belegten sozialen Randgruppen in den Städten Italiens (Prinzipatszeit)." In Weiler 1988b: 243–55.

Neri, V. 1998. *I marginali nell'Occidente tardoantico: Poveri, 'infames' e criminali nella nascente società cristiana*. Bari: Edipuglia.

Olson, K. 2002. "*Matrona* and Whore: The Clothing of Women in Roman Antiquity." *Fashion Theory* 6.4: 387–420 = K. Olson. 2006. "*Matrona* and Whore: Clothing and Definition in Roman Antiquity." In Faraone and McClure 2006: 186–204.

Perry, M. E. 1985. "Deviant Insiders: Legalized Prostitution and a Consciousness of Women in Early Modern Seville." *Comparative Studies in Society and History* 27: 138–58.

Scheidel, W. 2006. "Stratification, Deprivation and Quality of Life." In Atkins and Osborne 2006: 40–59.

Strasser, U. 2004. *State of Virginity: Gender, Religion, and Politics in an Early Modern Catholic State.* Ann Arbor: University of Michigan Press.

Tellegen-Couperus, O. 2003. "A Clarifying *Sententia* Clarified: On *Institutio Oratoria* VIII.5.19." In O. Tellegen-Couperus (ed.), *Quintilian and the Law: The Art of Persuasion in Law and Politics*, 213–221. Leuven: Leuven University Press.

Treggiari, S. 1991. *Roman Marriage: Iusti Coniuges from the Time of Cicero to the Time of Ulpian.* Oxford: Clarendon Press.

Varone, A. 2005. "Nella Pompei a luci rosse: Castrensis e l'organizzazione della prostituzione e dei suoi spazi." *Rivista di Studi Pompeiani* 16: 93–109.

Weber, E. 1988. "Freigelassene—Eine diskriminierte Randgruppe?" In Weiler 1988b: 257–65.

Weiler, I. 1988a. "Soziale Randgruppen in der antiken Welt." In Weiler 1988b: 11–40.

———. (ed.). 1988b. *Soziale Randgruppen und Außenseiter im Altertum: Referate vom Symposion "Soziale Randgruppen und antike Sozialpolitik" in Graz (21. bis 23. September 1987).* Graz: Leykam.

CHAPTER 32

BETWEEN MARGINALITY AND CELEBRITY: ENTERTAINERS AND ENTERTAINMENTS IN ROMAN SOCIETY

HARTMUT LEPPIN

INTRODUCTION

IT is a truism that actors and gladiators were simultaneously among the most despised and the most revered persons in Roman society. Thus, marginality is one prominent aspect of their social position, celebrity another. Marginalization seems to have arisen at least in part because entertainers functioned in a public sphere that could not be entirely controlled by the Roman elite. On the one hand, Rome's urban masses assembled in the *comitia* (assemblies of the people) and *contiones* (political town-hall meetings), where members of the elite did indeed hold sway over them (see Pina Polo in this volume). However, the people could also come together in the theaters, in the circuses, or in the amphitheaters. Here they would enjoy the games, but they would also express their (often political) wishes; they would praise or belittle members of the elite—or the emperor himself (cf. Coleman in this volume). In addition to expressing their own desires, though, the masses that congregated for these public amusements were precariously exposed to the influence of the entertainers, who thus potentially could exercise significant power. And so, these places of public entertainment were dangerous in the eyes of the Roman elite, who constantly lived with the fear that the social order might be shaken because the constellations that arose in the context of these public entertainments might easily encourage *licentia* (wantonness) among the masses. In short, the fact that spectacles to a fair degree eluded control by the elites helped to inspire those same elites to marginalize entertainers.

Yet, despite the risks they posed, the games were simply indispensable to Roman society. First, the *ludi* (games) formed an essential element of various religious festivals. That made criticism of these diversions nearly impossible; and so, only certain types of behavior during the spectacles tended to come under attack. Moreover, such criticism as was voiced typically emerged in the moralistic tone so often characteristic of senatorial historiography. But in addition to the protective mantle of religion, there must have been very many people who simply liked the games (indeed, probably the majority of the Romans—both elite and non-elite). This disposition of the population shaped the political function of *spectacula* (public entertainments). Individual members of the elite, who acted as *editores* (sponsors), gladly used the games to win popularity. This was just another aspect, then, of Roman euergetism, and another expression of the competitiveness that so largely characterized the Roman elite. The *editor*, who presided over the games he had sponsored, was the center of attention during the spectacle, which itself abundantly demonstrated his *liberalitas* (generosity) and *magnificentia* (grandeur). Julius Caesar, for example, is notorious for using this chance to win popularity early in his career (and for incurring heavy debts in the process). As a result, Roman emperors tended to monopolize the organization of important games, and they often would attempt to host games that surpassed those of their predecessors. Even in the provinces, the giving of more sumptuous games required imperial assent. Emperors, in other words, were not willing to be outdone in the matter of entertaining their subjects.

Given such worries, and given again the highly competitive inclinations of the typical Roman aristocrat, it is no wonder that the senate long avoided erecting permanent theaters or an amphitheater at Rome, for such structures would have kept their founders' names, and reputations, in the public eye for centuries. Instead, Rome knew only wooden constructions until the end of the republic and the beginning of the principate (Holleran 2003: 51–53). Outside the center of power, however, in Italy and in some provinces, theaters and amphitheaters had been built much earlier. In any case, this aristocratic competitiveness, which frequently expressed itself in the underwriting of *spectacula*, engendered a tendency to make games bigger and ever more inventive. That resulted in considerable amounts of resources being tied up in these affairs. In short, the Roman Empire was marked by an extremely rich culture of festivals, not only in Rome itself, but also in the provinces and provincial towns, where members of local elites competed with each other, often in an economically ruinous way.

Contemporaries observed the importance of *panem et circenses* (bread and circuses) for the Roman people (cf. Juv. 10. 81). These words, articulated in the context of a moralizing discourse, have long been interpreted as an expression of the decadence of the Roman people; yet, this phenomenon, the feeding and entertaining of the urban populace, was indeed extremely important to the social cohesion of Roman society. Thus, the Roman games were marked by tensions between religious concerns, the ambitions of individual members of the elite, and various constraints on the elite as a whole. These tensions are in turn reflected by the inconsistent status of the performers, who were on the one hand popular, and could form friendships with high-standing individuals, but who were simultaneously discriminated against by law, and often widely reviled as well. This ambiguity will be further highlighted in the second section of this chapter; the first part will deal with the different venues where performers appeared, since these could do much to determine the perceived status of the entertainers.

Before proceeding, however, it is well to say something of our documentation for the topic at hand. First and foremost, it must be realized that sources for Roman spectacles are quite diverse. In many literary texts, particularly in historiography, entertainers are mentioned more or less casually, and for the most part in a negative context, because the moralistic discourse of the senatorial tradition predominated. Therefore, literary sources that do not inscribe themselves in this discourse are of special interest—medical texts would be an example. Other sources even show sympathy for entertainers and entertainment. Several inscriptions praise certain celebrities (mainly gladiators and pantomimes), and texts such as Suetonius' biographies of the Roman emperors illustrate the author's interest in innovative *spectacula*. Epigraphic documents are extremely helpful, mostly for illuminating the social position of entertainers and the organization of the games (see as exemplary studies Sabbatini Tumolesi 1988: 127–140; Fora 1996; Roueché 1993). Archaeological sources provide a certain impression of the popularity of Roman-style entertainments in the provinces (e.g., Weber-Hiden 2005), although the respective buildings could have been used otherwise, for example as cult theaters. Papyri are relevant for a few aspects of the agonistic world. What the entertainers thought and said about themselves, though, is almost completely lost; only a very few inscriptions provide us with some inkling of this (Hope 2000).

Venues of Performance

To examine entertainers as a quasi-unified class is roughly justified by certain common factors in their social position. Nonetheless, there were marked differences between the various groups of entertainers, whose composition depended more on the context in which they performed, and on regional cultural differences, than it did on their respective specialties. So, for example, a tragedian who participated in

an *agon* (Greek-style contest) in the Greek East was much respected, even generally
honored by his society, whereas a tragedian who appeared on the stage in the context
of Roman *ludi* (games) was subject to *infamia* (disgrace), a specific category of juristic
discrimination, among Roman citizens.[1] Therefore, it is essential to comprehend the
different venues in which entertainers might find themselves before an audience.

Ludi (Public Entertainments)

Ludi, best translated as public entertainments writ large, were often regarded by
Romans as institutions that had been transferred from a foreign culture, namely,
from the Etruscan society just to Rome's north. Different possible interpretations
of their introduction at Rome were handed down by Roman historians, and are
also suggested by archaeological evidence. During the Roman Republic, the number and the range of festivals, which chiefly occasioned the holding of *ludi*, grew in
a steady course (fundamental: Bernstein 1998). This was justified on the one hand
by religious needs—during many crises the Roman elite reacted by institutional-
izing new festivals—but was also an expression of aristocratic competition. These
games (especially the *ludi scaenici*—theater entertainments) were often enriched
with Greek elements, which, however, were then integrated with the Roman context. In the imperial period, the expansion in the number of festivals, hence, entertainments, did not come to an end; many festivals that celebrated special events
(imperial victories, birthdays, etc.) were performed at least temporarily. *Munera*
(gladiatorial shows) were introduced into the official calendar, and Greek *agones*
(contests) would also be established in the West. The crisis of the third century,
however, engendered a reduction of performances throughout the empire. Then,
Christianization, starting in the early fourth century AD, would gradually have its
effect on *ludi* and *munera*. The latter were finally abolished in the fifth century,
whereas *ludi scaenici* survived into Byzantine times, when *ludi circenses* (horse and
chariot races) enjoyed immense popularity.

Ludi Circenses *(Horse and Chariot Races)*

Ludi circenses were the oldest games in Rome. The Circus Maximus, the arena in
Rome that was home to these entertainments, was traced back to the regal period.
In 329 BC a permanent building is mentioned for the first time. The stone monument was erected under Caesar and Augustus, and was gradually enlarged so as to
offer space for 150,000 to 180,000 spectators. Claudius introduced special seats for
senators; Nero did the same for *equites*.

Chariots drawn by two horses (*bigae*) were the early standard. In imperial times
quadrigae (rigs drawn by four horses) were mostly in use, and often even larger

---

1. See below for an extended discussion of *infamia* as it was suffered by entertainers and
affected their lives. Indeed, this legalized ill repute was arguably the essence of their social
position altogether.

chariots were presented to the public. It was usual that on one day of chariot racing several races were given, and we know that certain charioteers took part in thousands of races during their careers. However, as chariot races were extremely expensive, they were given only rarely.

Individual charioteers were supported by so-called circus factions (*factiones*), usually named after certain colors (e.g., the Blues, the Greens). Being much more than fan groups, these factions had vast resources at their disposal, which they used to buy horses, to finance 'stables,' to train the charioteers, and to provide the drivers with suitable vehicles (still fundamental: Cameron 1976). Individual charioteers could change their factions, and were sure to make known on their inscriptions for which faction they had been successful.

The social origins of these charioteers are generally quite difficult to establish (Horsmann 1998). A large group, probably the majority, was of slave origin, but had a good chance of being manumitted. Common Roman charioteers were affected, though, by *infamia* (a legalized status of disgrace), whereas the Greek charioteers who performed in Greek *agones* were socially respected (see above). Many of these charioteers gained huge notoriety, and we still possess for quite a few of them inscriptional evidence to that effect. On the one hand, elaborate epigraphic monuments were set up in their honor, which show that among certain groups the charioteers were regarded as people on a par with members of the elites, while humble graffiti likewise attest to their considerable attraction for a yet wider audience.

In the *circi* athletic competition was also performed as well as chariot racing, but the former had much less importance; performers seldom appear in our sources (see Mann 2002; König 2005: 205–253 for the perception of athletic competitions in the West). Although what was performed in the circus at first glance looks very similar to competitions in the East, the differences remain vital.

Ludi Scaenici *(Theatrical Entertainments)*

Roman tradition placed the beginning of *ludi scaenici* in the fourth century BC, when Etruscan actors, who performed simple scenes, were fetched to Rome for religious reasons. The introduction of Greek drama, which was said to have taken place after the First Punic War, brought much more complexity to this form of entertainment. The dramas performed could play a role in the self-representation so conspicuously practiced by Roman aristocrats, but they were not seen as an essential element of education, and were in fact more often interpreted as expressions of *luxuria* (over-indulgence), and as perniciously seductive for young people.

Theater performances were long given in improvised theaters, which nonetheless could be equipped splendidly. Only during the late republic were stone buildings erected. Rome ultimately possessed three stone theaters, though they together supplied room for much smaller audiences than did the circuses and the amphitheaters: the theater of Pompey (completed in 55 BC) with around 12,000 seats; the theater of Balbus (Augustan) with 6000 to 7000 seats; and the theater of Marcellus (Augustan) with 10,000 seats. Being less costly, theater productions were held much more often than were chariot races. Many Italian and provincial towns possessed theaters, which were used for religious and other public events as well as for plays.

But the show on the stage was not the only performance taking place during a given set of *ludi scaenici*. Elite Romans attached great importance to the seating order in the theater from at least the beginning of the second century BC onward (Rawson 1987 [1991]). There they not only could see, but could be seen. In imperial times, the first fourteen rows were reserved for *equites* and senators; women and slaves were restricted to the uppermost seats. However, this regulation, which was renewed several times, does not seem to have worked well. Nevertheless, the insistence on this order confirms that the Roman elite perceived the theater as a place where the social order should be highlighted.

Actors were classified according to the type of performance in which they specialized. There were tragedies and comedies, these more or less based on Hellenistic models, in addition to the more traditional, comic forms, such as Atellana (farce) or mime, and pantomime, introduced at the beginning of the empire. During the imperial period, tragedy and comedy lost much of their importance, whereas pantomime and mime came to the fore. While pantomime was extremely artful, and required an intense training, mime was less sophisticated and included improvisations. Mime also was the only theatrical form where women performed, though these actresses were often identified with prostitutes. In general, mime actors had the worst reputation, and thus the weakest social position, among stage entertainers.

The social background of actors was generally low to begin with. Many of them were of slave origin, because only slave holders could afford the expensive education of a specialist, such as a pantomime artist, whereas sufficiently rich free fathers would prefer a more respectable profession for their children. Correspondingly, among the mimes, who did not need a specialized training, there seem to have been more people of free origin (citizens and non-citizens) than in other areas of performance. The importance of Greeks among actors should not be over-estimated, because they had to speak Latin well.

But, while it could generally be expected that an actor would be of lowly social background, there are several mentions of knights and senators performing as actors. The most notorious of these was the emperor Nero. Apart from the fact that most of these high-status performers appeared in Greek-style *agones*, which were not subject to *infamia* (again, a legal category of disgrace), this phenomenon could not have been too frequent, because otherwise the sources would have been less alarmed (Wiedemann 1992: 102). However, it seems to have grown in frequency at the time of the transition from republic to empire, when the elites were enlarged overall, and many traditional values were shattered. The *SC Larinense* (a decree issued by the senate), from AD 19, provides a vivid impression of the awareness of the Roman senate in this regard (*AE* 1978, 145; new texts and contexts in Levick 1983, and Lebek 1990 and 1991).

Actors are also known to have given private performances. Several, mainly comedians, are attested serving as private teachers for voice training. This kind of activity could easily enhance their chances to make fruitful contacts, and thereby eventually perhaps to improve their social standing. Still, and as with common Roman charioteers, most actors were subject to *infamia*, with the exception of those participating in *agones*. In exceptional circumstances, actors—pantomimes in particular—became rich, and even received honorific inscriptions.

Munera (Gladiatorial Combats)

Gladiatorial combats (*munera*) are the embodiment of Roman spectacles in modern perspective, yet they were added to the official festival program only late. In contrast to *ludi* they were never part of the public cult. At first, gladiatorial combats, which seem to have originated in Campania (see Welch 1994), were a kind of memorial service, put on by private persons as part of the funeral ritual for relatives. The first recorded gladiatorial combat came in 264 BC. Initially, very few fighters were involved, but the number of participants increased over the course of time, in accordance with the general growth of expenditure on public entertainments generated by rivalries among the Roman aristocracy. Although *munera* were given to honor deceased relatives, their dates were often arranged so as to coincide with election campaigns. Thus, in the waning years of the republic numerous laws attempted to restrict expenditure of this sort. And while these contests never did become the duty of any magistrate, gladiatorial combats nevertheless soon came to play a significant role in the world of Roman *spectacula*.[2]

In the imperial period emperors often changed the regulations on *munera*. The general tendency was to guarantee annual *munera*, to be held by magistrates, *praetores* or *quaestores*, in part from their own means, which was considered a heavy burden. The possibility that magistrates might host lavish games was constrained by imperial regulations (see *ILS* 5163, 9340; see further, Carter 2003), which aimed both at protecting the sponsors' property and at preventing them from rivaling the emperor.[3]

The most impressive spectacles, then, were always those under-written by the emperor. On some occasions emperors provided thousands of gladiators fighting against each other; the connection to funerals was by now infrequent. Many innovative ways of fighting—sea battles (*naumachiae*), for example, are well-attested (Coleman 1993)—were invented. In general, these events took place much more rarely than theatrical exhibitions, and were more popular.

Even provincial *munera* were usually connected with the emperor, since they were typically given in the context of imperial festivals. In the western provinces *munera* were widespread and typically organized on the municipal level (see the

2. Traditionally, 105 BC is regarded as the year in which gladiatorial combats were provided by magistrates for the first time; see, however, Baltrusch 1988. The first official gladiatorial combats seem to have been given after Caesar's death, and thus, as a part of the governmental apparatus, are a phenomenon of the imperial period.

3. It is controversial whether *lanistae* (owners of gladiatorial training schools) could act as *editores* (sponsors of games). On this, see Chamberland 1999: 615.

broad documentation in EAOR and Fora 1996). Gladiatorial combats were frequent even in the East and not only within Roman *coloniae* (Robert 1940; Nollé 1992–93).

Gladiatorial combats could be performed in improvised buildings—some even erected in the Forum Romanum—but they were typically presented in elliptical *amphitheatra* (amphitheaters). The first amphitheater in Rome was built under Augustus by a private individual, Statilius Taurus. The Colosseum was built only by the Flavian dynasty and officially inaugurated in AD 80 by Titus. In several provincial towns *amphitheatra* were erected, and in many eastern towns theaters were used for gladiatorial combats and even transformed to allow exhibitions of this kind.

Being a central element of the self-representation carried on by emperors, gladiatorial combats were deeply connected with the Roman ideology of victory. Since the *editor* (sponsor) decided in concert with the spectators about the fate of those gladiators who had given up, and thus who could be killed or delivered, they were able publicly to display their consensus about central Roman values, such as *virtus* (manly courage), *disciplina* (proper conduct), *clementia* (clemency), and *iustitia* (justice) (Flaig 2000; see also Wiedemann 1992: 1–54, who stresses the idea that victory over death was symbolized in gladiatorial combats). The cruelty of the exhibitions, as such, was hardly criticized among traditional Romans, whereas Christians condemned it sharply. Nevertheless, these spectacles were abolished only at the beginning of the fifth century AD.

The social origin of gladiators seems to have been, on the whole, more diverse than that of most other entertainers. There were slaves and freedmen among them, but also a substantial number of *ingenui* (freeborn persons). Criminals (who sometimes were forced to 'perform' in gruesome mythological role-plays, see Coleman 1990), prisoners of war, and barbarians were often condemned to fight as gladiators. Nonetheless, volunteers are attested, too (their importance is stressed by Barton 1993; Veyne 2001). Female gladiators, though rare, are also on record (Coleman 2000; Schäfer 2001; Brunet 2004). Free-born persons who chose to fight as gladiators obliged themselves by a special oath to endure a slave-like dependency, agreeing via this oath to be burned, chained up, killed, and so forth in dedication to their chosen career (Sen. *Ep.* 37. 1–2). Gladiators, too, were subject to *infamia*.

Gladiators were grouped together in *familiae* (troupes) by *lanistae* (owners of training schools); they trained and lived together in so-called *ludi* (training schools). The owner of the school hired out the gladiators of his 'family' to those who desired to sponsor games. In the empire, imperially owned training camps for gladiators were established inside and outside Rome, but private *familiae* still wandered across the empire. They were looked after by doctors and were expected even to keep to a special diet. Among these gladiators there were specialists for various kinds of fighting. On their inscriptions, many of them defined themselves precisely according to their fighting specialties, thus, as *secutores* (pursuers), *retiarii* (netters), and so forth—anyhow, not as gladiators just generally. Indeed, there existed an internal hierarchy among these gladiators that determined their respective prices, and that must have been important for their self-perception (Carter 2003; a prosopographical analysis of gladiators is lacking, though some observations on their social status are to be found in Hope 2000).

Fighting as a gladiator was, of course, very dangerous; many will have met their ends at a young age (but for another view of such matters, see Carter 2006). Those who survived could be freed from their status by the award of a *rudis* (a special wooden 'retirement' sword), which was in general presented after three years of service; however, the veterans often stayed in the school as trainers. Even individuals who had committed some crime, and were resultantly condemned *ad ludos* (i.e., to fight as gladiators), might be pardoned if they fought bravely in the arena.

Especially at the beginning of the principate, members of the elite could be found participating in gladiatorial combats, in part because they were forced to do so by emperors, in part voluntarily. A special, apparently isolated case was the emperor Commodus (AD 180–92), who set out to perform as a gladiator and a *venator* (hunter; Dio 72. 17–20 is the account of a terrified eyewitness). This was the most extreme case of an emperor setting the stage for victory by means of gladiatorial combat, thus bringing about his downfall (see, however, the nuanced analysis of this aspect of Commodus' reign by Hekster 2002: 146–62).

Gladiators, though, were not the only entertainers in Roman spectacles. Animal fights (*venationes*) were usually held in the Circus Maximus. Initially belonging to the category of *ludi*, in the course of time they became ever more connected with *munera*, sometimes even serving to meld these two types of entertainment. These animal shows were frequently enriched by the presentation of exotic animals. Condemnation of convicted malefactors *ad bestias* (to the animals) meant that the victims were thrown to wild animals and thereby executed, but there were also professional *venatores* (hunters). However, in contrast to gladiators, it was acknowledged that *venatores* who did not hire themselves out for fighting were not subject to *infamia* (*Dig.* 3. 1. 1. 6).

Agones (Greek-Style Contests)

Agones were a distinctly Greek institution, less because of their content than their social setting. Having originally been connected with elite festivals in archaic times, they were gradually ever more professionalized. Nevertheless, participating in *agones* remained a respected, even an honorable business; and the contestants in these events continued through the Roman imperial period to be socially acceptable in the East. Thus, within the Roman Empire, two different cultures of public spectacles persisted, at least in principle, the one Greek in origin and nature (*agones*), the other Etrusco-Roman (*ludi*).

Agones were differentiated according to the prizes offered to the contestants. In *agones hieroi* (sacred contests) or *stephanitai* (crowned games) the prize to the victor was a crown (which could have indirect material consequences, since the crowns themselves were often made of precious metals); in *agones thematikoi* (contests involving valuable prizes) or *chrematitai* (contests involving cash prizes) material prizes were offered. Of these various types of contest, the first sort was the more prestigious.

A further differentiation was based on the types of performance. There were *agones mousikoi* (musical), *athletikoi* (athletic), and *hippikoi* (riding contests). To make things even more complicated, certain types of performance could be exhibited in Roman *ludi* as well as in Greek *agones*—tragedies or chariot races, for example. Yet, there was a sharp distinction between these institutions, and this was reflected even in Roman law, which expressly exempted contestants who participated in *agones hieroi* (sacred games) from *infamia* (Leppin 1992: 78–82; cf. Horsmann 1998: 44–50).

Now, in origin *agones* were typically local festivals, and were celebrated at specific intervals (most usually every fourth year, the so-called penteteric *agones*). During the empire, the dates of the festivals—or at least, the dates of the more important ones—had to fit into a rich schedule of festivals, to allow the *agonistai* (contestants) to travel around and to participate in as many festivals as possible. These contestants joined together in large associations, the so-called Dionysiac *technites* (artists) for the musical contests and the *xystikoi* (athletes) for the sporting contests. These organizations had developed in the Hellenistic period and had initially met on a local level. Their members were granted many privileges that entitled them to travel around the whole East. It seems likely that the associations themselves controlled which performers were admitted to agonistic festivals. During the empire, the local associations merged into ecumenical organizations. They even conducted diplomatic relations with the emperor, as did the Greek city-states (Millar 2001: 456–63), and their headquarters were moved to Rome, probably at the beginning of the second century AD (Pleket 1973: 207–27).

This process is an aspect of the hybridization of the Greek and Roman cultures of spectacle in imperial times. Another aspect is that regular *agones* were introduced in the West. Such Greek-style games were first put on at Naples, a town that was largely Hellenic, in the Augustan period. Nero later introduced an agonistic festival at Rome, and named the games after himself—they were called the *Neronia*. These games, though, came to an end with Nero's demise. Domitian instituted a permanent agonistic festival in Rome, the penteteric *Kapitolia*, which were soon counted among the most prestigious festivals in the agonistic world (Caldelli 1993; Rieger 1999). Other *agones* instituted in the West by emperors, or on a local basis, remained less important (König 2005: 221–25).

Another element of this hybridization was that pantomimes, whose dancing had taken a form that was regarded as Italian (Ath. 1. 20 D/E; Suda, s.v. Πυλάδης), became part of the agonistic festival program in the West and occasionally even in the East (Slater 1995). Although the artists involved were typically of lowly origins, they were nonetheless awarded the title of *hieronikes* (winner in an *agon hieros*). Yet in general, these performers kept true to their traditions, at least until the culture of festivals broke down with the demise of paganism around AD 400.

Although *agonistai* were not discriminated against by being branded with *infamia*, participating in *agones* was in principle unacceptable to members of the Roman elite, with some notorious exceptions. Thus, Nero's various performances are to be understood against the background of the agonistic world. He obviously

wanted to show his excellence in this field, both as a musical artist and as a chari-
oteer; and it must be said that he tried, albeit in vain, to fulfill his aim in a sensitive
way (Champlin 2003: 53–83; Meier 2008). To that end, his initial performances were
in private contexts. Then, during the first *Neronia*, he was awarded a crown without
actually competing. It was in Naples that he made his first public performance, in
64. In the context of the second installment of the *Neronia*, probably in 65, he made
his exhibitions on a public stage in Rome itself. That the emperor himself appeared
in the capital as an *agonistes* caused a great stir. Shortly thereafter, in the course of
his tour through Greece, during 66 and 67, he won all the important *agones*, and
returned to Rome in the guise of a *hieronikes* (a victor in the sacred games). Such
actions lost him the allegiance of the Roman elite, and alienated most of the military. All of this led to his downfall. Nero probably believed that a performance in
an *agon*, which was legally not connected with *infamia*, was not defamatory, but
showed his prowess. However, his literary reception in the historiographical sources
demonstrates that the difference between *agones* and *ludi* was deliberately ignored
by the senatorial tradition.

This short overview may make clear that the conditions for entertainers were
very different, depending upon their respective professions and the cultural context
in which they performed. Thus, any generalizing sketch of their social position is
only with difficulty laid out. Nevertheless, there are some common elements that
will be highlighted in the next paragraphs.

THE SOCIAL STATUS OF ENTERTAINERS

The Roman perspective on *spectacula*, and the entertainers who staffed these spectacles, seems to be contradictory. On the one hand, these entertainments formed an
integral part of Roman festivals; on the other hand, they were considered foreign to
Roman tradition. Thus, the entertainers were indispensable, but also regarded with
mistrust. This contradiction coincided with another problem. In this one clearly
defined social field—again, the games—entertainers had a certain power. They
could communicate directly and forcefully with large masses, even so as broadly to
influence public opinion. They actually could embarrass members of the elite, for
example, by pointing to them in some suggestive fashion in the course of a drama. In
this regard, actors were especially privileged among the entertainers, since they could
make use of spoken communication, and thus were able to voice their political commentary more plainly. On the other hand, the same people were excluded from any
political career by their infamous state. Entertainers, in other words, had no legitimate claim on political power, yet clearly were able in certain situations to exert real
influence—a situation that led the elite to regard these people with great distrust.

Let us, then, sketch several aspects of the social situation of entertainers, with
the reservation (which will be often repeated) that the perspective of our sources is

extremely one-sided. Because the documentation available to us represents pretty well only the perspective of traditionally oriented members of the elite, it is very strongly biased to stress the avowedly deviant behavior of entertainers. This means that our sources, when they do talk of entertainers, magnify their popularity to fabulous proportions, whereas, on the whole, the poor, despised, truly marginalized entertainers hardly ever feature in those same sources. In short, these persons are little talked about, but when they are discussed, it is not nicely.

Infamia (Legal Disgrace)

Infamia, again, a legally inflicted state of ill-repute with real-world consequences, was first of all a social fact. Entertainers were despised persons in the traditional discourse that is preponderant in our literary sources.[4] They were not regarded as suitable for social intercourse or marriage. If they became powerful, rich, and respected, this was considered a symptom of decadence. The scorn for actors was even more serious, as they, male and female alike, had the reputation of being prostitutes (Edwards 1997). As physical attractiveness was an important quality in actors, this will not have been completely unfounded. However, this perception of them only added an extra layer of disrepute.

Although the authors of literary sources acrimoniously bemoan the emergence of rich and powerful entertainers, this phenomenon should not be over-stated. If these cases had been truly regular and widespread, they would most likely have received less attention. It is probably also safe to assume that the majority of entertainers fell victim to every kind of discrimination in everyday life, and in death, just as was the case in the literary representations of them.[5] Socio-legal *infamia*, in other words, will have had a very great impact on the lives of entertainers.

Yet, regional differences are also to be expected. Whereas traditionalist Romans despised all entertainers alike, in Greece, and undoubtedly in certain milieus of the Roman world, they were respected. For example, such persons are known to have received honorary citizenship in southern Italian municipalities during Cicero's lifetime (Cic. *Arch.* 10).

Infamia was also a category of legal status in Roman law, which in principle affected only Roman citizens. It was not a clear-cut general concept, but was instead mentioned in several legal documents, which addressed certain social groups—not always the same ones—with varying terminology (still fundamental is Kaser 1956; also see Edwards 1997: 69–76; Hugoniot 2004). Two types of legal *infamia* are, in any case, to be distinguished: (a) praetorian *infamia*, based on the praetorian edict,

---

4. It may be that there were some exceptions to this rule in earlier times, on which see Leppin 1992: 71–72.

5. There seem to have been, for example, special cemeteries for gladiators. See Knibbe and Thür 1995: 42–46; Hope 2000: 99. Or note the inscription marking the burial spot, at Rome, of an organization (*societas*) of mimes (*CIL* VI 10109 = *ILS* 5217). These must have been the luckier ones, as they could at least afford membership in this association.

which developed in republican times and was fixed under Hadrian; and (b) the *infamia*, which was pronounced in various laws issued subsequent to the republican era, and which contained catalogues of persons who would be subject to this disgrace. This form of regularized marginalization resulted in multifarious inhibitions, the most important of which are the following:

> Certain types of legal procedures were not available to them. Entertainers could not bring a legal claim before a magistrate for second parties, nor did they have the right to lay an accusation in a public court. Thus, they could not appear in court for friends or for a community, which hindered them from winning prestige by their activity in trials.
>
> Their eligibility for various public functions was severely reduced: *expressis verbis*, they were forbidden to become *decuriones*, magistrates in local municipalities. There was obviously no chance whatsoever that they should become Roman knights or senators.
>
> Some individual rights were severely limited. They were forbidden to marry freeborn persons or members of the elite. Should they commit adultery, they were significantly less protected against spontaneous retribution by the offended party. They were probably subject to restrictions in inheritance law.

This list is certainly not complete, and not every group of entertainers was affected by every single measure in the same way. However, the general impression remains that entertainers were excluded from many of the most basic rights of Roman citizens. This extends to all groups of entertainers, with the exception of the *agonistai*, who (at least allegedly) did not compete for money. Such discrimination did not change in imperial times, and, indeed, under Augustus it was even more formalized.

Restrictions imposed by *infamia*, however, affected mostly those entertainers who aspired to conduct themselves like members of the elite. They had less of an effect on entertainers who wanted to lead a normal, more or less respectable life. And, again, it should be stressed that these latter persons are rarely visible in the literary sources. Still, when they do come into the light, it would appear that many of them led relatively normal lives. Even gladiators, with their risky jobs, are attested, for example, to have had wives and children (Wiedemann 1992: 114–16).

Approximation to High Status

When *ludi* and *munera* were given, vast crowds would assemble to witness them. As long as the entertainers performed, drove, and fought successfully, they enjoyed the admiration of the populace—and, it must always be stressed, of numerous members of the elite. Yet, this kind of popularity was difficult to transfer to the normal conditions of life beyond the theaters. Entertainers exercised influence in the sense that they could allude to broad political problems, or to the personal defects of elite persons, when they were performing. Entertainers and their supporters were thus quite capable of causing unrest, but they were by no means competent to intervene in political debates in any officially sanctioned sense. However, precisely the fact that they could exercise influence over the political life of the community at an 'improper' junction made them dangerous in the eyes of the elite. It is characteristic that on several occasions entertainers were altogether driven from Rome after instances of trouble at a spectacle.

That having been said, the popularity of certain actors, and their status as celebrities, is well attested by inscriptions executed by their fans. Many a graffito at Pompeii, for example, reveals the huge popularity of the gladiators. The retinue that might accompany an entertainer when he appeared in the public—a symbol, take note, of popularity, prestige, and status—could be quite large.[6] Their funerals, a foremost expression of *gloria*, could be celebrated in a most honorific way (Plin. *Nat.* 7. 186; Mart. 10. 50. 1–4).

Still more important were the personal contacts that entertainers might establish with members of the elite. Contemporary authors abhorred the sexual attractiveness that they perceived as a significant factor in the formation of such contacts. Gladiators and pantomimes were regarded as major objects of sexual fantasies entertained by Roman women of high status (e.g., Juv. 6. 82–114). Indeed, at one point things reached such a pitch that senators were not allowed to visit the homes of pantomimes and knights were prohibited from accompanying these performers when they went out in public (Tac. *Ann.* 1. 77. 4).

The relationships between actors and leading members of society attracted a great deal of (negative) attention in Roman sources. The presence of actors in their entourage is a topos employed by senatorial historiography to characterize bad emperors—they were made bad, at least in part, by their bad counselors. Nonetheless, the well-understood code of proper imperial behavior demanded that the prince demonstrate interest in *spectacula*, and even that he should be on friendly terms with certain actors. Thus, Augustus is depicted as having tolerated a limited frankness on the part of the pantomime Pylades (Dio 54. 17. 5; Macr. 2. 7. 19). It is also worth remarking that many of the most prominent pantomimes were imperial *liberti* (freed slaves) and, thus, in a longstanding personal relationship with the emperor. Still, special contacts between emperors and entertainers of this kind were observed warily by members of the elite, who always suspected that undue influence was being exerted by these persons on the emperor. This may have been true in certain cases. Some entertainers may have received personal privileges, but this did not change the basic structures of power in the empire. It is just another expression of the general importance of personal relationships in Roman society altogether.

Occasionally, entertainers received honorary inscriptions from public institutions, and thus were treated like *honesti* (members of the upper classes). Very rarely, however, did actors actually become local dignitaries (Leppin 1992: 103–6; Horsmann 1998: 124–35). And while an entertainer might on rare occasions manage to become part of a local elite, not a single instance is attested in which an

---

6. See Plin. *Nat.* 29. 9, mentioning pantomimes and a certain group of charioteers, who were accompanied by throngs of admirers when they went out on the streets of Rome.

entertainer rose to the two upper orders of Roman society; no senator or *eques* who previously had been a professional entertainer is reliably documented (although polemical texts written by traditionalists often insinuated that certain persons had once exercised such an infamous profession).[7]

Another significant factor in the matter of status was wealth, which several entertainers notoriously enjoyed. The sources provide many figures to illustrate just how much an entertainer could earn, but these sums are given precisely because they are unexpectedly high. Very rarely are poor entertainers mentioned, although some passages (e.g., Sen. *Ep.* 80. 17–18; *HA Alex.* 34. 2) demonstrate that they were much more representative. Nevertheless, the widespread perception in our elite sources tended to be that entertainers were unduly wealthy and, thus, had overmuch political and/or social sway.

Those texts that provide an impression of the way entertainers represented themselves, namely, a number of longer inscriptions, show that these people identified, on the whole, with the values of their society, aiming at being the first among their equals (Leppin 1992: 121–34). Interestingly, pantomimes tried to create their own professional tradition by taking over famous names (as, for example, Apolaustus) from their predecessors. Although their marginalization never ended and their behavior was typically depicted as deviant, they were not a group within Roman society that set out to create some new set of values. Everything points to them as striving, rather, for integration in Roman society.

In sum, then, popularity, friendship with people in high places, and wealth brought entertainers into a position that often seemed to be (or could be represented as) comparable to that of members of the elite. Their status remained precarious, not infrequently depending to a high degree on the emperor's sympathies. Correspondingly, there is no visible or lasting upward mobility for these troupes of entertainers. Nor is this merely a problem of the sources. Although the children of those troupes would not stress their origin, their enemies would. Apparently, some approximation to high status did not lead to a sustained improvement of the social position of the entertainers or their offspring.

CONCLUSIONS

The social position of Roman entertainers is difficult to assess because the traditionalist elite Roman discourse considered the desired marginalization of this group as threatened by the success of certain individuals. Readers of the texts that displayed this kind of prejudice were expected to react with indignation to such incidences. Yet exactly this shows that the marginalization of entertainers was deeply rooted in

---

7. Roscius is an exception, but he was shown quite plainly just how precarious his status was. See Leppin 1992: 241–44.

Roman society; legal *infamia* became more formalized in the principate and was never abolished. And in fact, this kind of socio-legal disgrace for entertainers was even aggravated with the Christianization of the Roman Empire. True, entertainers were at some moments and in some ways the objects of admiration, but this never served so as to put an end to their social stigma.

Even successful entertainers—the celebrities of the ancient world—enjoyed only an inconsistent status. They might be rich, they might boast the *amicitia* of high-born people, even of the emperor, but they were still subject to *infamia*. In very few cases do we see actors who became municipal dignitaries, and there is no dependable evidence for a senator of such origins. Those members of the elite who strove to perform in the public sphere remained exceptions. Some (most famously Nero) are perhaps to be seen in the context of the agonistic world, where *infamia* was not relevant. Nonetheless, social prejudices always lurked in the background.

On the other hand, indicators of high status, which unquestionably were attainable for entertainers, in a certain way necessitated their marginalization even more urgently. Entertainers were persons who, by means of their power during the *spectacula*, their physical attractiveness, or their wealth could put into question the very status of the elite. Therefore, the senate had to attach importance to the preservation of their legal and social marginalization, and, in the end, was quite successful at this.

To sum up, the glory of the entertainers is a recurrent theme in Roman literature, exactly because it was so disturbing to the elite, who were principally the authors of that literature. The study of Roman entertainers, then, is not only a study of a marginalized group, but also a study of the fears and worries of the Roman elite, concerned for the preservation of their own status—and this more than ever in a period when an emperor could endanger everything and everybody.

SUGGESTED READING

There seems to be no good scholarly general introduction into Roman games. Auguet 1994 (de facto 1970) is outdated, and concentrates on gladiatorial combats and chariot races. The best general introduction to Roman entertainers is Potter 1999. An elegant essay, putting the Colosseum in its social and cultural context, is Hopkins and Beard 2005, which highlights many modern misunderstandings. Wiedemann 1992 and Teyssier 2009 are fundamental for gladiators. Several essays in Rawson 1991 provide a good idea of the importance of Roman games. My own book (Leppin 1992) deals with the social position of stage actors.

BIBLIOGRAPHY

Auguet, R. 1994. *Cruelty and Civilization. The Roman Games*. London: Routledge.
Baltrusch, E. 1988. "Die Verstaatlichung der Gladiatorenspiele." *Hermes* 116: 324–37.

Barton, C. 1993. *The Sorrows of the Ancient Romans: The Gladiator and the Monster.* Princeton: Princeton University Press.

Bernstein, F. 1988. *Ludi publici. Untersuchungen zur Entstehung und Entwicklung der öffentlichen Spiele im republikanischen Rom.* Stuttgart: Franz Steiner Verlag.

Bollinger, T. 1969. *Theatralis licentia: Die Publikumsdemonstrationen an den öffentlichen Spielen im Rom der frühen Kaiserzeit und ihre Bedeutung im öffentlichen Leben.* Winterthur: Schellenberg.

Brunet, S. 2004. "Female and Dwarf Gladiators." *Mouseion* 3.4: 145–70.

Caldelli, M. L. 1993. *L'Agon Capitolinus: Storia e protagonisti dall'istituzione domizianea al IV secolo.* Rome: Istituto Italiano per la Storia Antica.

Cameron, A. 1976. *Circus Factions: Blues and Greens at Rome and Byzantium.* Oxford: Clarendon Press.

Carter, M. 2003. "Gladiatorial Ranking and the SC DE PRETIIS GLADIATORUM MINUENDIS (CIL II 6278 = ILS 5163)." *Phoenix* 57: 83–114.

———. 2006. "Gladiatorial Combat with 'Sharp' Weapons (ΤΟΙΣ ΟΞΕΣΙ ΣΙDΗΡΟΙΣ)." *Zeitschrift für Papyrologie und Epigraphik* 155: 161–75.

Chamberland, G. 1999. "The Organization of Gladiatorial Games in Italy." *Journal of Roman Archaeology* 12: 613–16. (Review of Fora 1996.)

Champlin, E. 2003. *Nero.* Cambridge, Mass.: Harvard University Press.

Coleman, K. M. 1990. "Fatal Charades: Roman Executions Staged as Mythological Enactments." *Journal of Roman Studies* 80: 44–73.

———. 1993. "Launching into History: Aquatic Displays in the Early Empire." *Journal of Roman Studies* 83: 48–74.

———. 2000. "Missio at Halicarnassus." *Harvard Studies in Classical Philology* 2000: 487–500.

EAOR 1988–. *Epigrafia anfiteatrale dell'Occidente romano.* Rome: Edizioni Quasar.

Easterling, P., and E. Hall (eds.). 2002. *Greek and Roman Actors: Aspects of an Ancient Profession.* Cambridge: Cambridge University Press.

Edwards, C. 1997. "Unspeakable Professions: Public Performance and Prostitution in Ancient Rome." In J. P. Hallett and M. B. Skinner (eds.), *Roman Sexualities.* Princeton: Princeton University Press. 66–95.

Flaig, E. 2000. "An den Grenzen des Römerseins: Die Gladiatur aus historisch-anthropologischer Sicht." In W. Eßbach (ed.), *Wir, ihr, sie: Identität und Alterität in Theorie und Methode.* Würzburg: Ergon. 215–30.

Fora, M. 1996. *I munera gladiatoria in Italia. Considerazioni sulla loro documentazione epigrafica.* Naples: Jovene.

Golvin, J.-C., and C. Landes. 1990. *Amphithéâtres et Gladiateurs.* Paris: Presses du CRNS.

Hekster, O. 2002. *Commodus: An Emperor at the Crossroads.* Amsterdam: J. C. Gieben.

Herz, P. 1990. "Die musische Agonistik und der Kunstbetrieb der Kaiserzeit." In J. Blänsdorf (ed.), *Theater und Gesellschaft im Imperium Romanum.* Tübingen: Francke. 175–95.

Holleran, C. 2003. "The Development of Public Entertainment Venues in Rome and Italy." In K. Lomas and T. J. Cornell (eds.), *Bread and Circuses: Euergetism and Local Patronage in Roman Italy.* London: Routledge. 46–60.

Hope, V. 2000. "Fighting for Identity: The Funerary Commemoration of Italian Gladiators." In A. Cooley (ed.), *The Epigraphic Landscape of Roman Italy.* London: Institute of Classical Studies. 93–113.

Hopkins, K. 1983. *Death and Renewal.* Sociological Studies in Roman History 2. Cambridge: Cambridge University Press.

Hopkins, K., and M. Beard. 2005. *The Colosseum.* Cambridge, Mass.: Harvard University Press.

Horsmann, G. 1998. *Die Wagenlenker der römischen Kaiserzeit.* Stuttgart: Franz Steiner Verlag.

Hugoniot, C. 2004. "De l'infamie à la constrainte. Evolution de la condition sociale des comédiens sous l'empire romain." In C. Hugoniot, F. Hurlet, and S. Milanezi (eds.), *Le statut de l'acteur dans l'Antiquité grecque et romaine.* Tours: Presses Universitaires François-Rabelais. 213–40.

Humphrey, J. H. 1986. *Roman Circuses: Arenas for Chariot Racing.* London: Batsford.

Kaser, M. 1956. "Infamia und ignominia in den römischen Rechtsquellen." Zeitschrift der Savigny-Stiftung für Rechtsgeschichte. *Romanistische Abteilung* 73: 220–78.

Knibbe, D., and Thür, H. 1995. V*ia Sacra Ephesiaca II: Grabungen und Forschungen 1992 und 1993.* Vienna: Schindler.

König, J. 2005. *Athletics and Literature in the Roman Empire.* Cambridge: Cambridge University Press.

Lebek, W. D. 1990. "Standeswürde und Berufsverbot unter Tiberius: Das SC der Tabula Larinas." *Zeitschrift für Papyrologie und Epigraphik* 81: 37–96.

———. 1991. "Das SC der Tabula Larinas: Rittermusterung und andere Probleme." *Zeitschrift für Papyrologie und Epigraphik* 85: 41–70.

Leppin, H. 1992. *Histrionen: Untersuchungen zur sozialen Stellung von Bühnenkünstlern im Westen des Römischen Reiches während der Republik und des Principats.* Bonn: Rudolf Habelt Verlag.

Levick, B. 1983. "The Senatus Consultum from Larinum." *Journal of Roman Studies* 73: 97–115.

Mann, C. 2002. "Griechischer Sport und römische Identität: Die certamina athletarum in Rom." *Nikephoros* 15: 125–58.

Meier, M. 2008. "Qualis artifex pereo: Neros letzte Reise." *Historische Zeitschrift* 286: 561–605.

Millar, F. 2001. The Emperor in the Roman World. 3rd ed. London: Duckworth.

Nollé, J. 1992–93. "Kaiserliche Privilegien für Gladiatorenmunera und Tierhetzen: Unbekannte und ungedeutete Zeugnisse auf städtischen Münzen des griechischen Ostens." *Jahrbuch für Numismatik und Geldgeschichte* 42/3: 49–82.

Pleket, H. W. 1973. "Some Aspects of the History of the Athletic Guilds." *Zeitschrift für Papyrologie und Epigraphik* 10: 197–227.

Potter, D. 1999. "Entertainers in the Roman Empire." In D. Potter and D. Mattingly (eds.), *Life, Death and Entertainment in the Roman Empire.* Ann Arbor: University of Michigan Press. 256–325.

Rawson, E. 1981. "Chariot-Racing in the Roman Republic." *Papers of the British School at Rome* 49: 1–16. = Rawson 1991: 389–407.

———. 1985. "Theatrical Life in Republican Rome and Italy." *Papers of the British School at Rome* 53: 97–113. = Rawson 1991: 468–87.

———. 1987. "Discrimina ordinum: The Lex Julia theatralis." *Papers of the British School at Rome* 55: 83–114. = Rawson 1991: 508–45.

———. 1991. *Roman Culture and Society: Collected Essays.* Oxford: Clarendon Press.

Rieger, B. 1999. "Die Capitolia des Kaisers Domitian." *Nikephoros* 12: 171–203.

Robert, L. 1940. *Les gladiateurs dans l'Orient grec.* Paris: E. Champion.

Roueché, C. 1993. *Performers and Partisans at Aphrodisias in the Roman and Late Roman Periods.* London: Society for the Promotion of Roman Studies.

Sabbatini Tumolesi, P. 1988. *Epigrafia anfiteatrale dell'occidente Romano I.* Roma. Rome: Casa Editrice Quasar.

Schäfer, D. 2001. "Frauen in der Arena." In H. Bellen and H. Heinen (eds.), *Fünfzig Jahre Forschungen zur antiken Sklaverei an der Mainzer Akademie 1950–2000.* Stuttgart: Franz Steiner Verlag. 243–68.

Slater, W. J. 1995. "The Pantomime Tiberius Iulius Apolaustus." *Greek, Roman and Byzantine Studies* 36: 263–93.

Stefanis, I. E. 1988. *Dionysiakoi technitai: Simboles stin prosopografia tou theatrou kai tis mousikis ton archaion Ellinon.* Iraklion: Panepistimiakes Ekdoseis Kritis.

Teyssier, E. 2009. *La mort en face: le dossier gladiateurs.* Arles: Actes sud.

Thomas, R. 2001. "Aurigae und agitatores: Zu einer Wagenlenkerstatuette im Römisch-Germanischen Museum Köln." *Kölner Jahrbuch* 34: 489–522.

Veyne, P. 2001. "Histoire et sociologie de la gladiature romaine." In J.-L. Fabiani (ed.), *Le goût de l'enquête: pour Jean-Claude Passeron.* Paris: L'Harmattan. 119–63.

Ville, G. 1981. *La gladiature en Occident des origins à la mort de Domitien.* Rome: Ecole Française de Rome.

Weber-Hiden, I. 2005. "Gladiatorendarstellungen auf Terrasigillata: Kann die Terrasigillata ein Hinweis für die Beliebtheit von Gladiatorenkämpfen sein?" In F. Beutler and W. Hameter (eds.), *Eine ganz normale Inschrift.* Vienna: Österreichische Gesellschaft für Archäologie. 595–608.

Welch, K. 1994. "The Roman Arena in late-Republican Italy." *Journal of Roman Archaeology* 7: 59–80.

Wiedemann, Th. 1992. *Emperors and Gladiators.* London: Routledge.

Wistrand, M. 1992. *Entertainment and Violence in Ancient Rome: The Attitudes of Roman Writers of the First Century A.D.* Gothenburg: Acta Universitatis Gothoburgensis.

CHAPTER 33

MAGICIANS AND ASTROLOGERS

J. B. RIVES

INTRODUCTION

MAGICIANS and astrologers display, in a particularly acute form, the ambiguity that so often characterized marginalized groups in the Roman world. Like actors and gladiators (see Leppin in this volume), they provided specialized skills and services that endowed them with considerable popularity and even a degree of social power, while simultaneously restricting them to the margins of polite society. At the same time, they were often regarded as subversive of public order, and so like bandits (see Riess in this volume) were subject to coercive actions on the part of political authorities, even though the characterization of someone as a magician or astrologer was a slippery one that, again like the category 'bandit,' depended to a certain extent on the perceptions of the people involved. Yet caution is necessary. Although these contradictions were real enough, the stark form in which I have presented them here results to a certain extent from a longstanding scholarly tendency to conflate magic and astrology in a way that obscures some crucial differences.

That there are good reasons for treating magicians and astrologers together is nevertheless clear enough. We can readily identify three characteristics that they had in common. First, and perhaps most obvious, both groups were ethnically marked, having strong associations with foreign, and specifically eastern, traditions. These eastern associations were partly genuine and partly, it seems, a reflection of complex cultural attitudes. Astrological learning is demonstrably Mesopotamian in origin, with a significant infusion from Egyptian tradition, even if the theoretical framework was considerably elaborated in Greek contexts. Ancient awareness of its Mesopotamian origin is indicated by the fact that one of the most common terms for 'astrologer' in both Greek and Latin was *Chaldaios/Chaldaeus*, which properly denoted a native of southern Mesopotamia. Similarly, recent research has revealed some striking continuities between older Mesopotamian and Egyptian traditions and the 'magical' practices of Graeco-Roman culture. The term *magos/magus* was itself of eastern origin, in this case Persian, and originally denoted a Persian wise man or priest. The word retained its primary meaning in both Greek and Latin throughout antiquity, although from an early date people applied it more loosely to figures whom they regarded as religious quacks, and it eventually acquired a meaning similar to that of the modern 'magician.'

The history of the word *magos/magus*, with its frequently negative connotations, is a reminder of the ambivalence that marked Greek and Roman attitudes toward 'oriental' traditions. On the one hand, there was the fear and suspicion that many people feel toward an alien and in some respects incomprehensible culture, compounded by contempt for peoples who were perceived as slavish or (in the case of the Persians) by hostility for enemies. As a result, we can at times identify a tendency to characterize practices that in fact had a good Greek or Italian pedigree as 'oriental' in origin, as a way to denigrate them and separate them from 'proper' Graeco-Roman culture. On the other hand, there was respect and even awe for traditions widely regarded as much more ancient than Greek and Roman culture and much more adept in the secrets of the cosmos, a sentiment that actual practitioners of magic and astrology at times attempted to exploit. Although writers of the imperial period typically published astrological treatises under their own names, the earliest astrological literature in Greek, now known only from citations and adaptations in these later texts, seems to have been largely pseudepigraphic, attributed to Egyptian sages such as Hermes Trismegistus, the legendary pharaoh Nechepso, and his high priest Petosiris; other texts circulated under the names of Jewish and Persian figures, for example, Seth, Abraham, Solomon, Zoroaster, and Ostanes (Gundel and Gundel 1966: 9–66). Likewise, in the magical tradition we can detect a tendency, developing in the eastern Mediterranean perhaps in the late Hellenistic period and eventually spreading throughout the Roman Empire, to adopt the trappings of eastern wisdom; for example, both the papyrus texts uncovered in Egypt and a number of the 'curse tablets' found throughout the empire ostentatiously incorporate names and phrases of Jewish and especially Egyptian origin.

A second feature common to both magicians and astrologers was the mastery of esoteric technical knowledge that was considered both especially efficacious and generally inaccessible. In this respect we can locate them in a much wider group of free-lance ritual experts (diviners, initiators, purifiers) whom the elites of the classical Graeco-Roman world often marginalized and sometimes employed. Yet we can also identify a significant development. Astrologers differed from earlier types of diviners in being more systematic, more invested in observation, and, in a word, more 'scientific'; in this respect they had more in common with physicians than with oracle-mongers or haruspices (cf. Barton 1994b). Although magicians did not advance 'scientific' claims of this sort, the gradual incorporation of more exotic elements that I noted above did allow them to transform what was in origin a generally accessible body of folk practices into an esoteric and technical discipline that required specialized study. For both magicians and astrologers, it was precisely their claim to possess otherwise unavailable skills that gave them a degree of social power, since people turned to them for help that they could not obtain, at least not as effectively, elsewhere. Hence, the obvious concern among both groups was to maintain the social value of their specialized knowledge by confining it to a small group of professionals. The composers of both astrological treatises and magical texts often presented themselves as addressing select students or initiates, whom they adjured not to impart their learning to the unworthy crowd. The fact that some astrologers wrote instructional treatises at all might seem at odds with this desire to keep their learning secret, but careful analysis of some extant examples suggests that these texts were intended more as epideictic displays of their authors' learning than as tools for imparting practical skills (Barton 1994a: 114–42). But the claim of these groups to otherwise inaccessible knowledge and power was also what caused the socio-economic elite to regard them with suspicion and often outright hostility, because it made them at least potentially a rival source of social power.

This brings us to the third feature shared by magicians and astrologers, namely, the fact that both groups were liable to legal restrictions and even at times capital punishment. The precise nature and motivation for these legal restrictions has been the topic of considerable scholarly investigation, much of which has focused on the hostility of the ruling classes to these groups. Thus, Ramsay MacMullen included magicians and astrologers among the 'enemies of the Roman order,' along with Stoic aristocrats, philosophers, the urban mob, and bandits (MacMullen 1966); more recently, Marie Theres Fögen argued that they fell afoul of an increasingly monopolistic imperial claim to the proper interpretation of the cosmos, as did also Manichees, haruspices, and wonder-workers (Fögen 1993).

Although analyses of this sort are useful for delineating large-scale patterns, they also run the risk of devolving into vague generalizations. As I have already suggested, more detailed analysis also reveals some significant differences between magicians and astrologers that have important implications for their social and legal status. Above all, astrology was a clearly defined and generally respectable branch of learning, whereas magic was not so much a distinct discipline as a highly flexible label that people could attach to practices, and practitioners, that they viewed with suspicion, fear, or disdain. In order to have a more precise understanding of the social role of magicians and astrologers, therefore, we need to consider the two groups separately.

ASTROLOGERS

Astronomy was from an early date a crucial part of Graeco-Roman culture; knowledge of the heavenly bodies and their movements was essential to both the calendar and navigation. But the practice of casting horoscopes, that is, of making predictions about individuals based on the positions of the heavenly bodies at the time of their birth, was Babylonian in origin, although the earliest preserved cuneiform horoscope dates only to 410 BCE, and the bulk of them belong to the period of Greek rule. The conquests of Alexander facilitated the spread of this practice to the west, and during the Hellenistic period it seems to have flourished especially in Egypt; I noted above the pseudepigraphic Graeco-Egyptian astrological literature that was apparently produced at this time. The Hellenistic period was also the great age of Greek astronomy, in terms of both its theoretical development and its wider dissemination, especially through the poetry of Aratus. Astrology developed in tandem with astronomy; indeed, ancient writers tended to use the two terms interchangeably. The astronomer Ptolemy wrote companion treatises on what we now distinguish as astronomy and astrology (conventionally known as the *Almagest* and the *Tetrabiblos*), which he himself conceived as two branches of the same discipline: the former allowed people to chart the complex but systematic relationship of the heavenly bodies to each other, the latter to understand the impact that these patterns of heavenly bodies have on earthly events.

That the Graeco-Roman elite took astrology very seriously is obvious. Soon after its introduction into the Greek world, it became a common topic in philosophical debates over the role of fate and the validity of divination, a discussion that apparently began in the second century BC but gained intensity in the second century AD (Long 1982). By that time, astrology was widely recognized as a distinct intellectual discipline, as indicated not only positively by treatises like that of Ptolemy, but also negatively by the fact that the great skeptic Sextus Empiricus ranked it with grammar, rhetoric, geometry, arithmetic, and music in his scathing attack on all those who professed to teach certain knowledge. Astrology was also deemed respectable enough to be expounded in verse, as Aratus had done for astronomy. The earliest extant treatise on astrology is that of the Latin poet Manilius, from the early first century AD, whose example was later followed by the Greek poets Dorotheus of Sidon and Manetho.

Yet, the most important endorsement of astrology as a discipline came not from the intellectual elite, but from the social elite.[1] Already in the mid-first century BC, the king Antiochus I of Commagene created a monumental complex that included an elaborate relief depicting the constellation Leo and the planets Jupiter, Mercury, and Mars; this conjunction seems to commemorate the date at which his rule was confirmed by Pompey the Great (Neugebauer and Van Hoesen 1959: 14–16). Much better known, and having far greater impact, was Augustus' use of astrology in the validation of his rule. According to Suetonius (*Aug.* 94. 12), Augustus as a young man received such a glorious horoscope that as emperor he made it public and issued coins with the image of his birth sign Capricorn. That Augustus ensured the wide distribution of the image of Capricorn is clear enough from its appearance on numerous extant coins, from both Roman and provincial mints, as well as antefixes,

---

1. On the intellectual elite as a sub-group of the broader social elite, see Hahn in this volume.

glass-paste cameos, and gems. Since Capricorn was not in fact Augustus' sun sign, scholars have debated its exact role in his horoscope; what is not debated, though, is the fact that Augustus' propagation of it amounted to a tacit endorsement of astrology (Barton 1994b: 40–47, 1995).

After Augustus, astrology retains a notable place in narratives of Roman emperors. Tiberius was renowned for his friendship with the astrologer and scholar Thrasyllus, and left a reputation for being a skilled astrologer himself. The astrologer Ti. Claudius Balbillus (possibly the son of Thrasyllus) was favored by emperors from Claudius to Vespasian, and his daughter married Antiochus Epiphanes, son of the last king of Commagene. An astrologer helped persuade Otho to conspire against Galba, and another advised Vespasian in his own bid for power. Domitian is said to have learned from astrologers not only the year and day, but the very hour of his death, knowledge that his assassins exploited in laying their plans. An actual horoscope of Hadrian survives, which was originally included by the second-century writer Antigonus of Nicaea in his collection of historical horoscopes (Neugebauer and Van Hoesen 1959: 90–91; cf. Cramer 1954: 162–68).

These interconnections between astrology and Roman political power have attracted considerable scholarly interest over the years. The most comprehensive study is that of Frederick Cramer (1954), which covers Roman history down to the Severan dynasty (the promised second volume, which was to cover the period from Diocletian to Justinian, never appeared). But Cramer's work, although it remains essential as a collection of the evidence, is in many ways unsatisfactory, uncritical in its use both of the evidence and of modern analytical categories. Cramer viewed astrology as a faith; for him, the turning point was not Augustus' promotion of his birth sign, which he interpreted as merely the political exploitation of popular superstitions, but rather his conversion late in life to a 'syncretistic scientific mysticism' whose apostle was Thrasyllus (Cramer 1954: 82–99; quotation from 99). More recent work has attempted to examine in less anachronistic terms the relationship between astrology and political power. Andrew Wallace-Hadrill, for example, has interpreted the shift from earlier forms of divination to astrology as part of a larger shift from traditional to scientific discourse that Augustus employed in formulating, and exploiting, a new paradigm of Roman culture (Wallace-Hadrill 2005: 64–65). Tamsyn Barton has called into question the entire conceptual framework of science and pseudo-science that informed earlier studies like that of Cramer, and has instead drawn attention to the mutually reinforcing way that Augustus and later emperors validated astrology as a legitimate form of knowledge, while at the same time invoking its authority to validate their own rule (Barton 1994b: 27–62). Most recently, Alfred Schmid, in a very detailed study, has explored the idea that astrology reflected a new understanding of the cosmos that also found expression in a monarchic construction of society, so that the coincidence in the spread of astrology and the development of the empire was no mere accident (Schmid 2005).

However we explain them, the interconnections between astrological knowledge and imperial power endowed astrology with considerable social power; they also made it potentially very dangerous. We find a paradigmatic example of its dangers in the fate of M. Scribonius Libo Drusus, a young man of illustrious family who allegedly conspired against Tiberius, and was said to have consulted Chaldaeans, magi, and dream interpreters (Tac. *Ann.* 2. 27. 2), presumably in order to obtain information about future events that would be useful to his plans; Libo was tried in AD 16, but killed himself before the trial ended. Similar cases followed: in 20, Aemilia Lepida was charged with adultery, poisoning, and 'making inquiries of Chaldaeans about the emperor's household' (Tac. *Ann.* 3. 22. 1); in 49 Lollia Paulina was similarly charged with 'questioning Chaldaeans, magi, and the oracle of Clarian Apollo concerning the emperor's marriage' (Tac. *Ann.* 12. 22. 1); in 66 P. Anteius was arrested and committed suicide after an informer reported to Nero that he had consulted an astrologer named Pammenes (Tac. *Ann.* 16. 14). We should note that in the cases of Libo Drusus and Lollia Paulina astrologers are lumped together with other free-lance diviners and even the perfectly respectable oracle of Apollo at Claros. What this suggests is that what attracted legal reprisal was not the particular form of divination, for example, astrology as opposed to haruspicy, but rather, the nature of the inquiry: anything that might be interpreted as having a bearing on imperial power elicited absolutely punctilious scrutiny and control. Nevertheless, astrology, because of its popularity and perceived effectiveness, often played an especially prominent role in such episodes.

But what of actual astrologers? It is first of all worth noting that, because of the high profile of astrology as an intellectual discipline, not everyone who knew about or even wrote on the subject was someone whom we would label 'an astrologer': Manilius, for example, or even Ptolemy. Most working astrologers who appear in our texts are instead anonymous 'Chaldaeans,' presumably lower-class professionals. It is likely enough that many of these were, or at least affected to be, eastern in origin. The astrologer consulted by P. Anteius, for example, had the Egyptian name Pammenes, and another, executed by Domitian, apparently also had an Egyptian name, Ascletarion (Sijpesteijn 1990). We get some insight into the lives of these professionals from the writings of Vettius Valens of Antioch, who composed his *Anthologies*, one of the chief surviving compendia of astrological learning, in the mid-second century AD. He was of modest background, although his name suggests that he may have held Roman citizenship, and seems to have supported himself by collecting fees from clients and students: his text contains some 130 actual horoscopes, most of them presumably cast by himself, and is addressed to a pupil named Marcus. But it would be too schematic to posit a simple dichotomy between elite expounders and lower-class practitioners. Ti. Claudius Balbillus, for example, whom I mentioned above, held several important positions in the equestrian cursus, but was also the author of several astrological treatises and, it seems, a practicing astrologer. The crucial social distinction was presumably not whether one actually practiced or not, but, as so often, whether one made a living from it by charging fees for one's services.

Although in the trials discussed above it was their high-status clients, and not the astrologers themselves, who are the focus of attention, there is ample evidence that professional astrologers could also suffer because of their art's dangerous power. Tacitus notes that in the wake of Libo Drusus' trial "*senatus consulta* were passed expelling astrologers and magi from Italy," and that two such men, both apparently Roman citizens, were formally executed (*Ann.* 2. 32. 3). Similar expulsions took place later in the century, under Claudius and Vitellius certainly, and perhaps under Vespasian and Domitian as well (Cramer 1954: 233–48). We also hear about punishments of individual astrologers: the Pammenes consulted by P. Anteius was already in exile, although Tacitus does not reveal the reason, and Domitian executed Ascletarion in order to disprove his claims to knowledge (according to Suetonius, *Dom.* 15. 3, he failed). The main reason that astrologers were liable to these sorts of reprisals was the same as for their elite clients, the threat to imperial power posed by their perceived access to otherwise unobtainable information. By the early third century AD, it was an established legal principle that making inquiries about the emperor, or other important political matters, was a capital offense, a principle of which astrologers themselves were no doubt keenly aware. Thus, Firmicus Maternus, in the handbook of astrology that he wrote in the mid 330s, urges the would-be astrologer never to entertain questions about the emperor, explaining that such questions are not only criminal but pointless, because the emperor is in fact exempt from the power of the stars (*Mathesis* 2. 30. 4–7).

Despite the high profile they have in the historical record, however, it is very unlikely that the vast majority of professional astrologers, men like Vettius Valens, had much reason to be concerned about such perilous political inquiries. Judging by the material in the extant treatises, most of their clients would have had much more mundane concerns: career, health, marriage, children, and family relations (MacMullen 1971). Yet, there is evidence that even astrological inquiries unrelated to questions of imperial power could result in criminal charges. Augustus evidently forbade all inquiries about deaths, and later juristic writers confirm that inquiries about people's health, even one's own, were punishable acts. None of our sources articulate the underlying concern in policies such as these, but it was presumably felt that access to such information could lead to scheming, and thus social disruption.

As a field of learning, then, astrology was by the imperial period well established and (in principle) highly respectable. Practicing astrologers could be found in the highest levels of Roman society (the very highest, if we count the emperor Tiberius), although the bulk of them were no doubt professionals of relatively low status, probably eastern in origin, charging modest fees for their services to clients of probably equally modest rank. In all cases, however, the perceived ability of astrologers to provide reliable information about future events both endowed them with a degree of social power and concomitantly caused them to be viewed with suspicion. Although in the historical record the political dimensions of astrological knowledge receive the most attention, in reality more mundane concerns with private affairs were no doubt much more common; in both areas, especially the former, injudicious inquiries could result in criminal charges.

MAGICIANS

Astrology as a discipline is fairly easy to define; if there are complications in applying the label 'astrologer' to particular individuals, these have more to do with issues of social status than with the simple meaning of the term. The situation is very different when we turn to magicians, since magic is by no means easy to define. For most scholars working in the late nineteenth and the early twentieth centuries, however, that problem did not arise. They tended to work with an implicit 'common-sense' understanding of what 'magic' meant, an understanding that usually involved a contrast with both religion and science: magic was presumed to differ from the former in that it seeks to manipulate or control rather than supplicate superhuman forces, and from the latter in that the forces that it seeks to manipulate do not in fact exist. But the lack of a more sophisticated analytical framework did not much matter, since much of the work done in this period was primarily philological, concerned chiefly with collecting, editing, and explicating individual documents. Investigation of the social aspects of magic was minimal, the chief exception being the study of Roman laws on magic. Here, however, analytical weakness proved to be a real hindrance; even though useful work was done in gathering the key evidence (Pharr 1932; Massonneau 1934: 136–241), the authors generally concluded little more than that the Romans made magic illegal, and they did so because magic was antisocial: the magician "wished to gain certain personal advantages at the public expense" (Pharr 1932: 270). At most, people made a distinction between 'black' (i.e., antisocial) magic, which was always condemned, and 'white' magic (particularly healing charms), which was allowed, despite the absence of any evidence for such a classification in the ancient sources.

Starting in the 1970s, however, scholars of the ancient world, partly under the influence of anthropological approaches, began to critique earlier assumptions about the definition of magic and to study it more as a polemical label than as an objectively definable type of human activity. This reorientation had a profound effect on the study of ancient magic, since it necessarily required researchers to maintain a much keener sensitivity to social and cultural context. In one of the earliest of such studies, Peter Brown reinterpreted accusations of magic in late antiquity not as evidence for the growth of superstition, but rather as a response to changes in the structure of social power: people whose power lay in clearly articulated governmental positions brought charges of magic against those whose power derived from less easily definable forms of social prestige (Brown 1970). Similarly, G. E. R. Lloyd, working on the other end of antiquity, argued that starting in the fifth century BC, Greek thinkers who were struggling to articulate a new understanding of the cosmos (what we would now describe as 'rational' or 'scientific') disparaged their more traditional competitors as *magoi*, using a term that properly denoted foreign peddlers of mumbo jumbo (Lloyd 1979: 10–58; for a more detailed discussion of the early Greek use of this term, see Bremmer 1999: 1–9). Scholars of early Christianity likewise adopted this new approach. Morton Smith examined the evidence for charges of magic against Jesus, reaching the controversial conclusion that such accusations were in fact fundamentally correct (Smith 1978; see in general Phillips 1986: 2711–32 for a valuable discussion of scholarly trends in the 1970s and early 1980s).

The study of magic as a rhetorical construct, a weapon that people employed in complex strategies of social and cultural positioning, is now well established; as a recent example, we may note Francisco Marco Simón's study tracing the growth of the concept of magic in Rome as the encapsulation of everything regarded as alien and contrary to proper Roman mores (Marco Simón 2001; cf. Gordon 1999: 191–210). A major focus for current research of this sort is gender. It has long been observed that the image of the witch is one of the most striking stereotypes in Latin literature, from Horace to Apuleius. This image of an all-powerful, often sexually voracious female figure can easily be seen as an embodiment of male anxieties about the secret influence of women, as well as a strategy for associating women with negative cultural values. The stereotype would be all the more striking if in reality women were more often the victims than the perpetrators of erotic magic, as some people have suggested; but the situation seems to have been less clear than that (Dickie 2000; on magic and gender, see now Stratton 2007).

But the investigation of magic as a label has not obscured the fact that people in the Roman world did engage in practices involving spells, potions, and rituals that have traditionally been labeled as 'magic.' Whether this label is a help or a hindrance to historical analysis has been much discussed (Versnel 1991a; Smith 1995; Bremmer 1999: 9–12). Many of those who currently study these 'magical' practices continue to use the term for the sake of convenience, albeit with a cautious awareness of its ideological baggage (e.g., Faraone 1999: 16–18). A wide range of practices come under this category, perhaps most conveniently classified by their areas of concern: bodily and mental health, sexual and affective relationships, financial prosperity, and so forth. Recent study of these practices tends to be more concerned with social context than that of earlier generations, perhaps in consequence of the intensive focus on the social implications of the term 'magic.' It is impossible here to survey the full range, but a few examples will serve as illustration.

One of the best attested magical practices is that of producing and depositing small sheets of lead inscribed with verbal formulae intended to bring superhuman forces to bear on another person or persons. These sheets are usually known by the Latin term *defixiones* or, in English, curse tablets and binding spells, and many hundreds of them have been discovered (Gager 1992). While the language in these tablets is typically very violent, close examination reveals more than a generic human tendency to hostility. Christopher Faraone, for example, argued that the primary purpose of such spells was not to kill or maim but rather to bind or restrain rivals in various well-defined competitive contexts, for example, commercial activities, love, court cases, and athletics (Faraone 1991). H. S. Versnel identified what he regarded as a fundamentally different category of tablet, which he labeled 'judicial prayers': appeals to superhuman agents to provide the petitioners with justice against those who have harmed them, most commonly thieves (Versnel 1991b). In both cases, although in rather different ways, the technology of what we call magic was used to express or even to structure certain types of social relationships.

While these relationships all happen to be negative, similar practices figured in the construction of positive relationships as well; in this connection, erotic magic has attracted particular attention. In one of the most ambitious treatments of this topic, Christopher Faraone has proposed that Greek love magic played a significant part in the construction of both gender and erotic relationships (Faraone 1999). He identifies two distinct classes of ritual: those used generally by men to inspire passion in women, and those used generally by women to increase affection in men; the former were used to obtain new sexual partners, and the latter to ensure the fidelity of existing partners. This taxonomy implies a belief that, in contrast with the stereotypes often found in literary texts, women were endowed with a natural modesty and chastity, which men had to overcome by artificial means, and men were naturally passionate and promiscuous, and thus needing to be tamed by women. Although Faraone's thesis has been criticized for being overly schematic, it provides an important model for the way that study of ancient magical practices can help us understand social relationships.

If there were magical practices, then there were naturally practitioners, whom *prima facie* we might reasonably describe as magicians. But as with astrology, it would be misleading to describe everyone who engaged in some form of magic as a magician. It seems clear that some of the techniques usually included under the rubric 'magic' were folk practices, in which almost anyone could engage. To turn again to *defixiones*, one of the greatest single caches of such tablets has been found in the sacred pool of the goddess Sulis Minerva at Bath (Tomlin 1988). All the tablets that can be deciphered fall into Versnel's category of judicial prayers: petitions addressed to the goddess invoking her help against thieves. Recent excavations have uncovered a cache of similar tablets in the temple of Isis and Magna Mater at Mainz (Blänsdorf 2005). In both cases the diversity of hands, the invocation of familiar and public deities, and the use of stereotyped but fairly simple formulae suggest that the people who produced these tablets were ordinary folk who drew on traditions that were in general circulation. Nor do we have any reason to think that these individuals suffered any negative social consequences because of their occasional resort to these practices.

Other sources, by contrast, reveal highly complex and self-consciously recherché traditions. These are represented most strikingly in the papyrus collections of formularies and ritual prescriptions discovered in Egypt, conventionally known as the Greek magical papyri (although some include also texts in Egyptian Demotic). Many of these abound in complex and precise ritual instructions, elaborate verbal formulae, long lists of exotic and unintelligible words and names, learned allusions to Jewish and Egyptian deities and wise men, and other deliberately esoteric material. The fact that formulae very similar to, and in some cases identical with, those found in the papyri also occur in *defixiones* suggests that working magicians, presumably professionals, actually employed these collections in preparing materials for clients; so, for example, a cache of tablets from third-century AD Athens includes some twenty examples apparently produced by the same scribe working from a single handbook (Jordan 1985). Although the scribe in question seems not to have been particularly expert in the formulae that he copied, others presumably devoted substantial amounts of time to the mastery of these traditions.

We must thus posit a range of practitioners, from ordinary people who may now or then have written up a simple *defixio* or prepared a simple amulet, to highly specialized adepts who regarded themselves as the guardians of a lofty and esoteric tradition. In between there is likely to have been a number of fairly low-level professionals, people with enough specialized knowledge that they could charge for their services. Some of these were perhaps not even full-time 'magicians,' but people who combined a number of roles: professional scribes who had a side-line in preparing *defixiones*, for example, or midwives who could provides amulets or love potions (see especially Dickie 2001; cf. the more ordered taxonomies of magical practitioners sketched by Gordon 1999: 178–91 and especially Frankfurter 2002). Some of these professionals apparently exploited the exotic elements of the skills that they provided; David Frankfurter, for example, has argued that traditional Egyptian priests of the imperial period may have deliberately re-fashioned themselves to become the *magoi* of the Graeco-Roman imagination (Frankfurter 1998: 198–237).

Given this range of practices and practitioners, older assumptions about the general illegality of magic (or even of 'black' magic) have become increasingly problematic. Indeed, in an important critique of earlier work, Robert Phillips argued that the lack of a generally accepted definition of magic in antiquity precluded any comprehensive law; he proposed that we should instead subsume the legal repression of 'magic' within the larger and more historically accurate category of repression of unsanctioned religious activity (Phillips 1991). More recent work has indeed tended either to focus on the social concerns that motivated some people to bring charges of magic against others (e.g., Graf 1997: 61–88) or to pay more careful attention to what exactly was at issue in particular legal contexts (Gordon 1999: 243–65). In my own work on this topic, I have tried to analyze in detail what are usually regarded as laws against magic, and to determine the specific types of actions with which they were concerned; in some cases, we can see that the application of these laws was gradually extended, so that, for example, the act of killing another person by means of a clandestine ritual came to be regarded as actionable under the law against poisoning. But alongside these specific laws there also developed in practice a more fluid charge of 'magic,' which was more concerned with a general sense that certain people were socially subversive. Such trials, of which that involving Apuleius is the best known, depended not on formal statutes, but on the executive power of magistrates, and they functioned in effect as forums in which Roman officials and interested parties could thrash out the limits of acceptable social and religious behavior (Rives 2003, 2006).

CONCLUSIONS

In terms of marginalization, we must thus make a fundamental distinction between astrologers and magicians. Astrology was a clearly defined discipline, one that was, moreover, socially respectable. What led to the marginalization of individual astrologers was the specific way that this discipline was applied in practice. The political potential of astrology receives the most stress in our sources, and it is clear that this enabled a few astrologers to become powerful and influential, while making many others liable to periodic repressive measures. But for most astrologers, the political dimension was probably of little significance. What led to their marginalization was instead the ethnically marked nature of their discipline (something that individual astrologers might exaggerate for effect), their operation as fee-charging professionals, their typically low social status, and their potential for creating social disturbances.

The overall situation of magic is essentially different. There was indeed a wide range of practices that we can conveniently label 'magical,' and that contemporary actors, at least at times, also labeled 'magical.' We can reasonably regard many of these practices as marginal, even if they were widespread, insofar as they tended to be private, even secretive, and concerned especially with personal and sometimes anti-social desires. Yet 'magic' as such was marginal by definition, since it did not so much designate a defined discipline as function as a label for marking off certain activities and behaviors as dangerous or fraudulent or somehow unacceptable. To call someone a magician was thus *ipso facto* to marginalize that individual.

Nevertheless, in practice similar factors must have affected the elite's attitude toward professional magicians and astrologers alike. In both cases, individuals who were for the most part from outside the socio-economic elite claimed to have otherwise inaccessible knowledge and skills that allowed them to bypass or subvert the normal channels of social power. Both groups were associated with 'foreign' traditions, an association that magicians and astrologers themselves sometimes exploited for their own ends, but that their enemies might equally exploit against them. In the end, just as with most other marginalized groups, both magicians and astrologers were in various ways central to life in the Roman world.

SUGGESTED READING

Barton (1994a) and Beck (2007) provide useful recent introductions to ancient astrology, Pérez Jiménez (2001) a comprehensive bibliography. Cramer 1954 is the most detailed discussion of social and legal issues, but unsatisfactory in many respects; Barton 1994b: 27–71 is sketchier but more stimulating. Introductory books on magic include Graf 1997, Janowitz 2001, Martin 2005, and Collins 2008, with guides to earlier work; further bibliography in Calvo Martínez 2001.

BIBLIOGRAPHY

Barton, T. 1994a. *Ancient Astrology*. London: Routledge.
———. 1994b. *Power and Knowledge: Astrology, Physiognomics, and Medicine under the Roman Empire*. Ann Arbor: University of Michigan Press.
———. 1995. "Augustus and Capricorn: Astrological Polyvalency and Imperial Rhetoric." *Journal of Roman Studies* 85: 33–51.

Beck, R. 2007. *A Brief History of Ancient Astrology*. Oxford: Blackwell.

Blänsdorf, J. 2005. "The Curse Tablets from the Sanctuary of Isis and Magna Mater in Mainz." *Mene* 5: 11–26.

Bouché-Leclerq, A. 1899. *L'astrologie grecque*. Paris: E. Leroux.

Bremmer, J. 1999. "The Birth of the Term 'Magic.'" *Zeitschrift für Papyrologie und Epigraphik* 126: 1–12. (Reprinted in revised form in J. N. Bremmer and J. R. Veenstra (eds.), *The Metamorphosis of Magic from Late Antiquity to the Early Modern Period*. Leuven: Peeters 2002. 1–11 and 267–71.)

Brown, P. 1970. "Sorcery, Demons and the Rise of Christianity: From Late Antiquity into the Middle Ages." In M. Douglas (ed.), *Witchcraft Confessions and Accusations*. London and New York: Tavistock. 17–45. (Reprinted in P. Brown, *Religion and Society in the Age of Saint Augustine*. London: Faber and Faber 1972. 119–46.)

Calvo Martínez, J. L. 2001. "Cien años de investigación sobre la magia antiqua." *Mene* 1: 7–60.

Collins, D. 2008. *Magic in the Ancient Greek World*. Oxford: Blackwell.

Cramer, F. H. 1954. *Astrology in Roman Law and Politics*. Philadelphia: American Philosophical Society.

Dickie, M. W. 2000. "Who Practiced Love-Magic in Classical Antiquity and in the Late Roman World?" *Classical Quarterly* n.s. 50: 563–83.

———. 2001. *Magic and Magicians in the Greco-Roman World*. New York: Routledge.

Faraone, C. A. 1991. "The Agonistic Context of Early Greek Binding Spells." In Faraone and Obbink 1991: 3–32.

———. 1999. *Ancient Greek Love Magic*. Cambridge, Mass.: Harvard University Press.

Faraone, C. A., and D. Obbink (eds.). 1991. *Magika Hiera: Ancient Greek Magic and Religion*. Oxford: Oxford University Press.

Fögen, M. T. 1993. *Die Enteignung der Wahrsager: Studien zum kaiserlichen Wissensmonopol in der Spätantike*. Frankfurt: Suhrkamp Verlag.

Frankfurter, D. 1998. *Religion in Roman Egypt: Assimilation and Resistance*. Princeton: Princeton University Press.

———. 2002. "Dynamics of Ritual Expertise in Antiquity and Beyond: Towards a New Taxonomy of 'Magicians.'" In P. Mirecki and M. Meyer (eds.), *Magic and Ritual in the Ancient World*. Leiden: E. J. Brill. 159–78.

Gager, J. G. 1992. *Curse Tablets and Binding Spells from the Ancient World*. Oxford: Oxford University Press.

Gordon, R. 1999. "Imagining Greek and Roman Magic." In B. Ankarloo and S. Clark (eds.), *Witchcraft and Magic in Europe: Ancient Greece and Rome*. Philadelphia: University of Pennsylvania Press. 159–275.

Graf, F. 1997. *Magic in the Ancient World*. Trans. F. Philip. Cambridge, Mass.: Harvard University Press. (First published as *La magie dans l'antiquité gréco-romaine*. Paris: Les Belles Lettres 1994.)

Gundel, W., and H. G. Gundel. 1966. *Astrologumena: Die astrologische Literatur in der Antike und ihre Geschichte*. Wiesbaden: Franz Steiner Verlag.

Janowitz, N. 2001. *Magic in the Roman World: Pagans, Jews and Christians*. London: Routledge.

Jordan, D. R. 1985. "*Defixiones* from a Well near the Southwest Corner of the Athenian Agora." *Hesperia* 54: 206–55.

Lloyd, G. E. R. 1979. *Magic, Reason and Experience: Studies in the Origins and Development of Greek Science*. Cambridge: Cambridge University Press.

Long, A. A. 1982. "Astrology: Arguments Pro and Contra." In J. Barnes et al. (eds.), *Science and Speculation: Studies in Hellenistic Theory and Practice*. Cambridge: Cambridge

University Press. (Reprinted in A. A. Long, *From Epicurus to Epictetus: Studies in Hellenistic and Roman Philosophy*. Oxford: Clarendon Press 2006. 128–55.)

MacMullen, R. 1966. *Enemies of the Roman Order: Treason, Unrest, and Alienation in the Empire*. Cambridge, Mass.: Harvard University Press.

———. 1971. "Social History in Astrology." *Ancient Society* 2: 105–16.

Marco Simón, F. 2001. "Sobre la emergencia de la magia como sistema de alteridad en la Roma del siglo I d. C." *Mene* 1: 105–32.

Martin, M. 2005. *Magie et magiciens dans le monde gréco-romaine*. Paris: Editions Errance.

Massonneau, E. 1934. *La magie dans l'antiquité romaine*. Paris: Librairie du Recueil Sirey.

Neugebauer, O., and H. B. Van Hoesen. 1959. *Greek Horoscopes*. Philadelphia: American Philosophical Society.

Pérez Jiménez, A. 2001. "Cien años de investigación sobre la astrología antiqua." *Mene* 1: 133–204.

Pharr, C. 1932. "The Interdiction of Magic in Roman Law." *Transactions of the American Philological Association* 63: 269–95.

Phillips, C. R., III. 1986. "The Sociology of Religious Knowledge in the Roman Empire to A.D. 284." *Aufstieg und Niedergang der römischen Welt*. Berlin: Walter de Gruyter. II. 16. 3, 2677–773.

———. 1991. "*Nullum Crimen sine Lege*: Socioreligious Sanctions on Magic." In Faraone and Obbink 1991: 260–76.

Riley, M. 1987. "Theoretical and Practical Astrology: Ptolemy and His Colleagues." *Transactions of the American Philological Association* 117: 235–56.

Rives, J. B. 2003. "Magic in Roman Law: The Reconstruction of a Crime." *Classical Antiquity* 22: 313–39.

———. 2006. "Magic, Religion, and Law: The Case of the *Lex Cornelia de sicariis et veneficiis*." In C. Ando and J. Rüpke (eds.), *Religion and Law in Classical and Christian Rome*. Stuttgart: Franz Steiner Verlag.

Schmid, A. 2005. *Augustus und die Macht der Sterne: Antike Astrologie und die Etablierung der Monarchie in Rom*. Cologne: Böhlau Verlag.

Sijpesteijn, P. J. 1990. "The Astrologer Ascletarion." *Mnemosyne* 43: 164–65.

Smith, J. Z. 1995. "Trading Places." In M. Meyer and P. Mirecki (eds.), *Ancient Magic and Ritual Power*. Leiden: E. J. Brill. 13–27.

Smith, M. 1978. *Jesus the Magician*. San Francisco: Harper and Row.

Stratton, K. B. 2007. *Naming the Witch: Magic, Ideology, and Stereotype in the Ancient World*. New York: Columbia University Press.

Tomlin, R. 1988. "The Curse Tablets." In B. Cunliffe (ed.), *The Temple of Sulis Minerva at Bath, Vol. 2: The Finds from the Sacred Spring*. Oxford: Oxford University Committee for Archaeology. 59–277.

Versnel, H. S. 1991a. "Some Reflections on the Relationship Magic-Religion." *Numen* 38: 177–97.

———. 1991b. "Beyond Cursing: The Appeal to Justice in Judicial Prayers." In Faraone and Obbink 1991: 60–106.

Wallace-Hadrill, A. 2005. "*Mutatas Formas*: The Augustan Transformation of Roman Knowledge." In K. Galinsky (ed.), *The Cambridge Companion to the Age of Augustus*. Cambridge: Cambridge University Press. 55–84.

CHAPTER 34

THE ROMAN BANDIT (*LATRO*) AS CRIMINAL AND OUTSIDER

WERNER RIESS

INTRODUCTION: DEFINING THE ROMAN *LATRO*

THE first person ever thrown to the animals in the Forum Romanum was, so we are told, a bandit (Str. 6. 2. 6). It is hardly surprising that this novel method of execution, which enlisted popular entertainment as an integral element of punishment, was conceived of and put into practice by Augustus. He, as the first Roman emperor, who had finally brought the civil wars to an end, found it urgently necessary to stabilize his fledgling regime. In order to accomplish that, he had to make it clear, both outside of and especially within his empire, that he was in control, that his world was in order. Hence, a gruesome display of communal revenge against a social outcast could become an extremely useful instrument of governance.

But regardless of the way in which Augustus employed that particular malefactor, our current knowledge of bandits (in Latin, *latrones*—singular, *latro*) in the Roman world results from something like thirty years of research. To comprehend what is now generally thought about bandits and banditry in the Roman world, it is necessary to have some sense of the course this scholarship has taken. An initial stimulus came from the French Annales school, which effectively created the fields of social history and the history of mentalities. But aside from this scholarly impulse, the student unrest of the late 1960s set in motion a real paradigm shift in the directions taken by historical research. Resultantly, from the 1970s onward, an interest in the historical phenomena of violence and crime was emerging. Into this context must be fit any examination of Roman-era banditry (in Latin, *latrocinium*).

Because of (at least at first sight) a lack of adequate sources, historical work on the Graeco-Roman world tended for some time to lag behind comparable research on criminality in early modern Europe. Given the archival and various other source materials available for the early modern period, it was possible to write fairly detailed criminal histories of several European cities and regions (Frank 1995; Schwerhoff 1991). Indeed, quite broad-ranging, comprehensive studies of violence and crime are no longer rare for Europe in this period (Ruff 2001; Emsley 1996; Sharpe 1984).

Where the Roman world is concerned, various marginalized groups and outsiders have by now, in spite of a slow start, managed to attract significant attention.[1] Moreover, we are finally beginning to discern the lineaments of a history of Roman criminality (Krause 2004; Wolff 2003; Riess 2001; Neri 1998; Nippel 1995; Nippel 1988). It should further be noted that, given a particularly favorable source situation for Roman Egypt, in other words, the large numbers of extant papyrus texts, crime in that particular region has now become an object of fruitful research (Peachin 2006; Bauschatz 2005; McGing 1998; Aubert 1995; Alston 1994; Hobson 1993; Bagnall 1989; Davies 1989; Drexhage 1988a and 1988b; Baldwin 1985). Following in the footsteps of work on social discipline during the early modern period, quite a few studies have also been published on Roman attempts to combat crime; and these studies, especially given the fact that nothing like a modern-style police force existed among the Romans, have raised a number of basic questions about the functioning of Roman society in general.[2] Thus, we are beginning to have a decent socio-historical background, against which the phenomenon of banditry in the Roman world can be considered.

In spite of differing theoretical approaches and research goals concerning banditry, there has been agreement among scholars that the term *latro* encompasses a broad semantic field, which could also be used metaphorically (Riess 2001: 89; van Hoof 1988; Burian 1984; van Hoof 1982; MacMullen 1963). Given the relatively narrow definitions, however, which Roman jurists attributed to the term, the question arises as to how and why this well-defined term came to designate, from quite early on, not only highwaymen and bandits, but also guerilla fighters, political opponents,

---

1. On the ancient world, see Hopwood 2002; Hopwood 1999; Graßl 1988; Kneppe 1988; Weiler 1988a, 1988b, 1985, and Weiler and Graßl 1988. Basic still is Shaw 1984. For a legal-historical approach, see Bauman 1996. With regard to some parallels from the Middle Ages and early modern period, see von Hippel 1995; Roeck 1993; Hartung 1986.

2. For broad studies, see Fuhrmann 2005 and Kelly 2002. Petraccia Lucernoni 2001 examines the role of *stationarii* (low-level military officials) in fighting crime. Stoll 1997 offers similar work on another group of soldiers (*beneficiarii*) who carried out similar tasks. Crime fighting in several different areas of the Roman Empire has also won some attention: Brélaz 2005 (Asia Minor); Nippel 1988 and 1984 (Rome); Bauschatz 2005, Aubert 1995, and Bagnall 1989, 1982, 1977 (Egypt); older but still useful are Hirschfeld 1913a and 1913b as well as Rostovtzeff 1905.

usurpers, and barbarians. This semantic finding must be analyzed with regard to its social causes and socio-political implications. As we shall see, the essential characteristic of this linguistic usage is the expression of utter disdain and reprobation for the person or activity thereby distinguished. We shall use, in what follows, the one English word 'bandit'; however, it must always be kept in mind that behind this term lurks the Latin word *latro*, with all of its broader connotations.

Any engagement with the *latrones* of the Roman Empire is nonetheless well advised to begin with the narrow legal definitions just alluded to. The Roman jurists wrote from the perspective of the ruling elites and might even be perceived as the mouthpieces of the emperor and the upper classes, who ultimately held an absolute monopoly with respect to establishing both legal and societal norms. We might put things this way: the jurists were intimately involved in the formation and the enunciation of the norms embraced by the leading strata of Roman society. Let us, then, see what these writers have to say.

First of all, our sources generally understand robbery to be theft with the application of violence (cf. Riess 2001: 99). More specifically, though, the Roman jurists almost invariably attribute to the person labeled as a *latro* the use of armed force (*vis armata*), criminal intent (*dolus malus*), and the formation of gangs (e.g., Marcian *Dig.* 48. 19. 11. 2). Hence, in the juristic literature, the term *latro* tends to be reserved for the person who, as part of a band or group, commits what we would call aggravated robbery. Additionally, the legal authors are careful to distinguish the *latro* from the largest group of those who acted violently overall, in other words, officially declared 'enemies' of the state (in Latin, such a person was called a *hostis*): "Enemies (*hostes*) are those against whom the Roman people have publicly declared war, or they, who have declared war on us. The rest are called bandidos (*latrunculi*), or brigands (*praedones*)" (Ulpian *Dig.* 49. 15. 24 pr.; cf. Pomponius *Dig.* 50. 16. 118 pr.).[3] A significant point to be made here is that those defamed as bandits would lose any conceivable legal rights at international law, whereas those categorized as enemies of the state would not. Semantic studies have furthermore demonstrated that *latrocinium* (viz., a malicious act carried out by a *latro*) could be used to isolate a particular kind of conflict with state enemies, namely, guerilla war (Riess 2001: 14; Grünewald 1999: 59ff.; Rosenberger 1992: 153–54). In short, since guerilla tactics were often employed by opponents, who were not as strong as the Romans on the open field of battle—for example, by tribes fighting in clans—and because the Romans also tended to perceive these groups as lacking in civilization, such enemies were not accorded the status of an equal foe.

The various punishments for *latrocinium*, irrespective of the exact malefaction in question, also indicate that the perpetrators were viewed as beyond the pale of society and civilization. And even though *latrocinium* was not considered to be an

---

3. Note that *latrunculus* is a diminutive form of *latro*, and thus has an air of contempt about it. As we shall see, all those characterized as *latrones* are simultaneously stigmatized as outsiders, of one sort or another. The diminutive simply adds a further layer of contempt.

offense quite on the same level with *homicidium* (homicide), the punishment for
latrocinium was nevertheless of equal severity (*CJ* 9. 2. 11, AD 292). Depending on
the circumstances, the punishment could even be intensified. Infamous bandits, the
so-called *latrones famosi*, were executed either by the *furca* (a machine built to break
the neck) or by crucifixion, or they might be thrown to the animals (Callistratus,
Dig. 48. 19. 28. 15; *Coll. Leg. Mos.* 1. 6). These kinds of punishment, especially given
that they are prescribed by jurists, demonstrate clearly that the *latro* is being constructed as the 'other,' the outsider par excellence. Those who robbed temples or
graves, or who were caught as highwaymen or kidnappers, formed specific subcat-
egories of this sort of criminal (Riess 2001: 105–13). Cattle rustling (in Latin, *abig-
eatus*), another crime often associated with *latrones*, was likewise punished quite
strictly (Herz 1988).

The individuals who established Roman society's norms often stigmatized any
use of violence—or indeed, any malefaction—they considered illegitimate as *latrocinium*, and punished accordingly. This method of procedure implies a process of
'labeling,' which will be discussed in more detail below. But the essential point for
the moment is that one can hardly posit something like a homogenous criminal
class in the Roman Empire—which, nonetheless, was often a presupposition of
Marxist theory on class warfare (see, e.g., Günther 1953).

The broad classification of certain malefactors as *latrones* reflects the attitudes
of the ruling elites, and this practice likewise betrays some of that elite's strategies
to maintain its own position of power (Riess 2001: 240ff.). From this perspective,
all those could be stigmatized as *latrones*, hence marginalized, who, for whatever
reasons, resisted the monopoly on power, government, and societal standards fixed
by the Roman elite. Following the lead of recent research on outsiders, we might
imagine a society shaped in concentric circles. The ruling classes always form the
center of society. The next circle is populated by fully integrated groups. Further out
we find the partially or half-integrated portions of society, and, finally, the clearly
marginalized groups and outsiders.

In the case of Rome, we must bear in mind that the elite produced and shaped
the majority of the historical sources at our disposal. The members of society's
lower strata were generally too poor to provide lasting testimony of their concerns
and needs, or to make themselves individually heard. Furthermore, the information modern historians have access to is frequently ideologically tinged, biased, and
highly selective. Since the source-producing upper classes barely knew the world of
the lower classes, hence, the environment of the *latrones*, we must constantly reckon
with distortions and crass misrepresentations in (especially) the literary sources. As
a result, the literary descriptions of bandits, in particular, are so full of topoi that we
can legitimately speak of a standardized 'bandit discourse.'[4] Comparison with the
early modern period (e.g., Ruff 2001; Emsley 1996; Frank 1995; Lange 1994; Roeck
1993; Schwerhoff 1991; Danker 1988; Beattie 1986; Sharpe 1984), in conjunction with

---

4. Cf. Riess 2001: 12–28 on source-related problems. On bandits in the ancient novel, see
Riess 2001; Hopwood 1998; Winkler 1980.

recourse to sociological theory regarding deviant behavior (Lamnek 1997; Lamnek 1996; Becker 1963; Cloward and Ohlin 1960; Merton 1938), can assist us in correcting our image. By engaging such comparanda, we can perhaps break through the 'polysemous imperialistic discourse' that otherwise impedes a proper historical understanding of *latrones* in the Roman world (Clavel-Lévêque 1976; 1978: 17–28).

THE SOCIOLOGY OF DEVIANT BEHAVIOR AND THE NATURE OF ROMAN BANDITRY (*LATROCINIUM*)

In order to investigate specific phenomena involving banditry more closely, sociologists concentrating on deviant behavior usually divide such malefactors into two groups; they differentiate between the 'anomic' perpetrators, and 'labeled' criminals. This distinction also possesses heuristic value for ancient studies. Both groups will be delineated and discussed in what follows.

The theory of anomic behavior searches for structural causes of deviation in a given society, though it does not necessarily attempt to determine that society's norms. The American sociologist Robert Merton developed a general theory of deviant behavior (Merton 1938), which has been significantly modified and extended since (Lamnek 1996: 106–42), but his basic assumptions will suffice here. According to Merton, social reality is divided into a cultural and a social structure. Within the first structure, culturally determined goals, and the legitimate means to attain these goals, play a significant role. In the Roman context, such goals were circumscribed by several factors: a subsistence economy, settledness, landownership, and social ascent that would usually require the passing of several generations. Decisive, nonetheless, is the overall social structure.

Within any given society, not everyone possesses the legitimate means to achieve the culturally defined and valued goals, for access to the requisite means is usually distributed unevenly. The disadvantaged thus experience frustration, to which they can react in various ways. One type of reaction is a turn toward violence and crime, in order to obtain through force what society withholds. The less equally a society distributes opportunities, the more anomic will that society be, and the more pronounced are the anomic experiences of the under-privileged.

In the Roman context, delinquents driven by such anomic conditions were those who, because of their poverty, understood their living circumstances overall as anomic, and who sought a way out of their desperate situation by engaging in criminal behavior. Obviously, the poor in antiquity might also attempt initially to counter their misery in a peaceful way—for instance, by finding work as day laborers, prostitutes, or by begging. Indeed, since the majority of such anomic malefactors are indeed rooted in the society—the point is that they generally begin by attempting to achieve their society's cultural goals, though ultimately in vain—they frequently shy away from the use of violence, and are first satisfied by non-violent theft. Force tends to remain a last resort.

In the Roman Empire, however, violent lawbreaking was endemic, and the origins of the malefactors are roughly comparable to those of bandits in the early modern period. Their degree of separation from society varied, some being sedentary fringe groups, others temporary vagabonds, and yet others itinerants. Those most susceptible to this kind of misconduct in the Roman context, were people fleeing crop failures, tax burdens, and wars. In other words, fugitives (often debtors), army veterans and deserters, gladiators and runaway slaves (the so-called *servi fugitivi*), that is to say, people who had learned to survive through violence, who had easy access to weapons, in other words, 'illegitimate' means, and who could no longer be integrated into 'civil' society, were those who tended to become *latrones*. Usually, an accumulation of unfortunate factors, which are typical in periods of crisis in pre-modern societies, threw such people off course. They found their only chance for survival to reside in leading a vagrant life, and in resorting to violence. On occasion, they joined other 'drop-outs' for a limited period of time, or even permanently, as a means of empowerment. The most significant groups of bandits, who seem generally to have acted out of a necessity imposed by poverty, may now be described.

In pre-modern times, most farmers eked out their lives constantly on the verge of destitution. Given the lack of organized systems of social support, they were left exposed to misfortunes, such as crop failures, natural catastrophes, and wars. And since it was almost impossible for most to accumulate any financial reserves, even minor financial burdens could lead to situations in which these people could no longer supply themselves with the basics, were reduced literally to starvation, and thus found themselves forced to give up their normal lives, and to wander off in search of livelihood. In such circumstances, they might well resort to criminality, and violence.

Given the nature of the extant papyrological and epigraphic evidence, the phenomenon of those who fled their land can best be examined in Egypt and Asia Minor. An exemplary case from Egypt illustrates how the accumulation of internal and external factors might lead to a crisis-like escalation of an individual's financial situation. The sensational Thmouis papyrus shows us the instability of living conditions in one of the richest provinces of the empire, and similar conditions can probably be assumed for the other provinces as well. The papyrus lists, in reverse order, tax accounts of one nome from AD 169/70 to 228. Beginning in the 160s, we see an increasing desertion of farms. We are aware of catastrophic fluctuations of the Nile's flood at that time, which led to crop failures. This meant that the farmers were neither able to pay their taxes nor to complete their liturgies. Simultaneously, the emperor Marcus Aurelius had to fend off substantial external threats from the north and east of the empire. The costs of those wars were huge, and the Roman Empire began quickly to feel their pressure. In this tense situation, the authorities could not relinquish tax income, and so were unwilling to grant amnesties or remissions. Many farmers must have been significantly late with their payments, and seem to have resorted to deserting their properties, which only then worsened their living conditions.

However, can we simply suppose that many of these now-itinerant persons drifted together, grew prone to violence, and perhaps joined already-existing bandit gangs? Indeed, an endemic problem in Egypt was *anachoresis* (flight from one's property), and in the edicts of some prefects of Egypt, we hear about such fugitives, who supposedly chose a criminal way of life. The most famous prefectural edict is that of Marcus Sempronius Liberalis (*BGU* II 372 = *WChrest* Nr. 19), who in AD 154, even before the major crisis, tried to induce those leaving their land to return. Should they refuse, he threatened, they were to be treated as bandits.

With regard to indebtedness, there is an interesting parallel to Roman Egypt. In Judaea, a specific debt problem led, via its connection with certain political and religious unrest, to the catastrophic Jewish War. Martin Goodman argues that the war was brought about by—along with a bundle of other factors—the significant indebtedness of wide sectors of the local population. Many insolvent Jews thus decided to turn to banditry. That debt was indeed one of the main impulses for the Jewish War becomes obvious through the symbolic destruction of the records of debt in Jerusalem, which was ultimately the signal for the start of the uprising (Goodman 1982; and cf. Schwartz in this volume).

There also existed an intimate connection between the army and banditry, something well documented throughout pre-modern times.[5] Bandits were sometimes forced to join the army, the hope being that they would thus be socialized (*HA Aur.* 21. 7; Burian 1960). Indeed, civilians, who suffered not only from attacks by foreign armies, but also from the requirements to house and feed Roman soldiers, as well as to supply vehicles and beasts of burden for those soldiers' transportation needs, largely considered these military men as potential criminals. It frequently was only his official legitimation that distinguished the Roman legionary from a mere bandit. And of course, hostile troops, who happened to have been denied the distinction as enemies of the Roman state, could always be stigmatized as *latrones*. It must likewise be remembered that in the Roman professional army, in which legionaries and members of auxiliary troops served for decades without pause, many forgot their original (professional) skills, and, having entered the army at a young age, upon discharge, might know nothing but the military trade.

In the army, training with weapons and killing were part of the daily routine. The resultant brutalization led, in those instances when these veterans were unable or unwilling upon discharge from active service to re-integrate in civil life, to terrible consequences for society. If their severance pay was insufficient, some simply turned to banditry and continued to practice their learned violent trade, though no longer in any sanctioned capacity. Considerably more precarious than the situation of the veterans was that of deserters, or of soldiers, who had fought on the losing side in a civil war, and whose units were thereupon dismantled by the victorious

---

5. For the Roman period, see, e.g., Liv. 8. 34. 7–11; Dio 52. 27; 75.2; *CTh* 7. 20. 7 (353 A.D.); *CJ* 12. 46. 3 (353 AD).

emperor (Giuffrè 1981). The connection between war altogether and roaming bands of bandits is quite well documented for antiquity. Indeed, the misdeeds of the gangs, which cropped up after the Thirty Years' War, hardly surprises any more than does the 'pirate' Sextus Pompeius, who was active after the civil wars of the late republic (Aug. *Anc.* 25. 1; Plin. *Nat.* 16. 7; App. *BC* 5. 132), or one might think of the 'defectors' and 'rebels,' whom Septimius Severus had to fight for years after the civil war he had won (*CIL* III 10471–73 = *ILS* 1153 = *AE* 1890, 82). How difficult it was to gain control over these groups, and how long the fight against them could last—for example, in Bavaria, after the Thirty Years' War, apparently half a century—is reflected in the elaborate legend written by Cassius Dio about the bandit chief Bulla Felix, who for years on end managed to lead the emperor Septimius Severus around by the nose (Dio 77. 10). Still, it is highly unlikely that significantly large (Bulla Felix's band, for example, is supposed to have comprised several hundred men), well-organized robber bands were common, since such groups would easily have been located and decimated by Roman cohorts. We can assume, rather, that the formation of such gangs, in so far as this happened altogether, took place in concentric circles, comparable to some groupings in civil society. That is to say, a small core of uprooted, highly mobile bandits might sporadically be joined by other loose groups of criminals, who were partially or even entirely integrated in the local society, but who might also occasionally have engaged in criminal activities. Such comings and goings of gang members would result in loosely formed and ever mutating bands. In short, the transitions between the fringes of 'civil' society and the outcast criminal environment were quite fluid. Such occasional bandits resided between the orbit of the hardcore 'professional' criminals, who were completely excluded from society, and the realm of the 'honorable' citizens, and thereby formed a kind of periphery to the more permanent bandit gangs.

Soldiers no longer fighting in units officially sanctioned by the government, for example, deserters and veterans now lacking economic wherewithal, were easily at risk of becoming *latrones*. A three-step descent from *miles* (soldier) via *desertor* (deserter) to *latro* can be found as a stereotype used by ancient authors—so, for instance, with regard to Spartacus (Flor. *Epit.* 2. 8. 8). The potential danger posed by such battle-tested vagabonds is illustrated by the reports about the 'war of the deserters' under Commodus (Alföldy 1989). Even though this struggle might involve, just as in the case of Bulla Felix, a romanticizing fictionalization of contemporary problems, we can still see which social group was considered likely to have managed major actions, such as the siege of the legionary camp at Argentorate, and a subsequent trek to Italy, including a supposed assassination attempt on the emperor Commodus. Thus, when our ancient sources stereotypically speak of such bands recruiting all evil people—a category that always included deserters—regardless of the generally defamatory tone of the comments, they were describing the actual pool of recruits drawn upon by these bandit gangs; they were describing, in short, what we know rather well from the early modern period in Europe.

Aside from rootless soldiers and escaped gladiators (who were just as given to violence as were the soldiers), fugitive slaves could also function as cohesive groups prone to banditry. Thanks to Heinz Bellen's study (Bellen 1971; cf. also Kudlien 1988), we are aware of the close connection that existed between bandits and slaves, of the fact that there were apparently no large bandit gangs that did not possess a component of fugitive slaves, and that Apulia and Calabria were particular trouble spots, not just in late antiquity, but also in the early imperial period, as well as during the third century AD. This assures the continuity of the problematic situation in southern Italy from the Gracchi to the legal efforts of Valentinian and Honorius (Riess 2006).

Bandits set loose by anomic conditions equally illustrate the importance of the social construction of reality. And despite the fact that the law-abiding population often suffered at the hands of the criminals, bandit gangs regularly gained support from integrated members of society, who had become involved with those more criminal elements. Indeed, without ties to the more settled community, no drop-out was able to exist for long. Therefore, the complete outsider is an artificial construct of those who fixed the society's norms; it was a construct geared toward motivating and sanctioning opposition against those who broke the rules. This is one of the reasons that romanticizing ideas of social bandits, who steal from the rich to give to the poor (Hobsbawm 1972, 1971), have to be relegated to the sphere of literary fiction (Riess 2001: 161–66, 168–71).

Now, a basic distinction has to be drawn between the (actual) bandits brought into existence by anomic conditions, and those groups, who were merely *labeled* as *latrones*, and who will hardly have thought of themselves as criminals of some sort. These latter were delinquents only in the eyes of the standard-prescribing Roman authorities, and were labeled as criminals because their traditional way of life and their actions were opposed to the interests of the Roman elite. It is obvious that these labeling processes were based on issues of power (MacMullen 1963). People thus stigmatized, therefore, did not consider themselves as criminals, but instead tended to see the superior power (implicitly, for instance, Fl. Jos. *BJ* 2. 8. 1; *AJ* 18. 1. 1ff.) as something that needed to be resisted. And thus, in a sort of reversal of this labeling trend, tax collectors were frequently equated by local populations with bandits (cf. Isaac 1984: 177).

In the case of the Roman Empire, people labeled as bandits frequently belonged to bellicose, nomadic groups, who could not, or would not, adapt to the ideal of the Mediterranean urban way of life. 'Banditry,' in their case, was a method of providing themselves with additional income, and was essential to their livelihood. For such people, the decisive clash with the Roman authorities would invariably come at the time of a census, when populations were expected to be stationary, so that they could be evaluated for the purposes of tax collection. At such a moment, entire villages and tribes might feel threatened in their accustomed way of life, and might simply withdraw into the mountains and begin guerilla wars against the Romans. The mighty Celtic tribe of the Salassi, for instance, which had developed a high level of civilization in the Alps, and had almost been extinguished by Augustus, had not behaved any differently under this emperor than they had during the generations before his time. However, the Salassi stood in the way of the Augustan exploration and reorganization of the Alpine region, were thus quickly labeled as *latrones* and, therefore, were abandoned to annihilation (Riess 2001: 51). The same is true of the North African sheik Tacfarinas, who, with his nomadic people, offered resistance to Tiberius for years (Gutsfeld 1989; Metzler 1988; Shaw 1982b).

Political unrest, in particular, was frequently labeled as *latrocinium* at Rome; and such disturbances could, as already mentioned, involve a guerilla war. In various regions of the Roman Empire, repeatedly troublesome zones were to be found—places where the Roman state was not able to establish its power monopoly with significant permanence. Some regions de facto never, or only temporarily, belonged to the Roman dominion, largely because they simply could not be controlled efficiently by the central government. Indeed, specific geographic and cultural conditions brought about different varieties of predatory lifestyles, so that the affected regions were considered trouble spots throughout Roman history. Yet, despite various differences, these regions shared certain common features. Members of these—to the Romans' taste—foreign cultures were hardly outsiders in their own worlds; in and of themselves, they formed full-fledged legitimate societies. They existed only in certain areas, and there formed the basic supply of perpetually available 'permanent bandits'; such groups were especially troublesome because banditry was part of their traditional way of life. It must be recognized that they were outlaws only from the Romans' point of view. The integration of such peoples caused the Romans serious difficulty, since their values and norms were diametrically opposed to those of the Romans. It would appear that such groups were often initially indifferent to Rome, and that opposition developed only at the point when Rome began to criminalize their values and ways of life, and to use force against them.

Here, it is essential to disentangle the strongly ideological discourse of Roman imperialism. 'Bandits' (i.e., *latrones*), such as those just described, were primarily a Roman and Hellenistic phenomenon, precisely because Roman and Hellenistic territorial expansion had caused a clash of cultures in the first place (Briant 1976). Since specific geographical regions evinced specific situations of this type, however, it is well worth surveying these briefly.

REGIONAL MANIFESTATIONS OF
ORGANIZED BANDITRY

In Anatolian Isauria, there was a strong cultural gap between the Hellenized inhabitants of coastal towns and the bellicose shepherds of the mountains, who still spoke their native languages, and seemed strange and threatening to townspeople along the coast (cf. Feld 2005; Mitchell 1999; Hopwood 1999; 1989b; 1983; Zimmermann 1996; Lewin 1991; Shaw 1990; Syme 1987; 1968; Hellenkemper 1986; Minor 1979; Rougé 1966). Despite a longstanding, mainly peaceful coexistence, there were regular infringements by both sides. The sense of cultural superiority on the part of the Hellenes, and their constant fear of the mountain populations, resulted in a lopsided system of justice—there was no hesitancy to torture and execute strangers from the mountain areas, with hardly a trace of legal proceedings; this only served to promote mutual prejudice and estrangement. The timing of the various conflicts with these highland inhabitants shows clearly that they were not the usual bandits aroused by anomic conditions. Pompeius' fight against the Cilician pirates, as well as Cicero's dubious activities in the region, formed only the beginning of Rome's confrontation with the obstinate mountain people (n.b., further unrest is documented for AD 6/7, 36, 42, 260/68, 354, 359, and 368). The fact that the governor of Isauria, during late antiquity, held an unusual combination of civil and military powers leads to the assumption that Isauria was a highly militarized province at that time, and that Rome controlled it only de jure. Ultimately, all attempts at pacification proved vain. Early in the fifth century AD, Isaurians plundered Pamphylia, Lycia, Cyprus, Lycaonia, Cappadocia, and Pontus.

Similar difficulties seem to have existed in the Balkans, more specifically in Dardania (cf. Wolff 1998; Mócsy 1968). Here as well, the bellicose mountain peoples were a thorn in the Romans' side. The Dardanians and their herds had always led a poor existence in the mountains. For them, chance banditry, especially in the form of highway robbery, was apparently a necessary form of sustenance. Only with the arrival of the Roman state, which laid claim to a monopoly on the use of force, was the private use of force pushed into the criminal sphere. Just how similar the Dardanian conditions were to those in Anatolian Isauria becomes apparent through an inscription, which reveals that a 'catcher of bandits' had been brought from Isauria to Dardania specifically in order to apply his knowledge and expertise (*CIL* III 14513). Marcus Aurelius finally mastered the situation by recruiting many shepherds into his army, a step that was part of a standard repertory of 'integrational measures' aimed at bandits.

From the area of Palestine, many rabbinical sources report the presence of 'bandits' (cf. Shaw 1993b; Freyne 1988; Horsley 1981, 1979; Horsley and Hanson 1985; Isaac 1984; Sperber 1970). But, apart from actual criminality brought about by anomic conditions, persons who appear simply to have been labeled as bandits are equally well documented. Still, distinctions are not easily made, given that the Greek word (*lestes*) engaged by Flavius Josephus, who is our main source for Palestinian banditry, has a wide semantic range, like the Latin word *latro*, which is very broad. The ambiguous Greek term *lestes* can be used to describe both ordinary highwaymen, as well as guerilla fighters (Hengel 1976: 42–47). Josephus labeled even members of the radical war party of the zealots as *lestai* (Hengel 1976: 44). These zealots, who formed the radical wing of the pharisaic group, were much influenced by eschatological prophesy, and therefore interpreted their fight against Rome as involving the ultimate fate of the world; there was nothing here in common with ordinary banditry. This indicates that Jews will hardly have been willing to grant the Romans the privilege of labeling them criminals, that they considered the Roman reign a tyranny, and, consequently, that they in turn stigmatized the Romans as 'bandits.' As has already been said, such processes of distributing guilt involved relative levels of power. It is obvious that certain groups within the Roman Empire did not accept such a unilateral setting of norms by the Romans and, therefore, would also hardly accept at face value the Roman claim to rule over them.

A particular group of shepherds, who engaged in banditry, and who mounted a political resistance to Rome in a fashion similar to that of the Jewish guerillas, are documented for Egypt, and were there called the Boukoloi, in other words, the Cattlemen (see, e.g., Alston 1999). Our sources are quite contradictory as to the exact location of the conflicts in question (X. Eph. 3. 12.; Ach. Tat. 3. 9–18; 4. 12; Hld. 1. 5ff.; 2. 17–18; 6. 2–12; Str. 17. 1. 6; 17. 1. 18ff.; Dio 71. 4; HA. Aur. 21; HA, Avid. 6). Be that as it may, this unrest is documented for the year AD 172. These so-called Boukoloi murdered a Roman centurion and thus initiated an uprising. They defeated the Roman troops initially sent against them, almost conquered Alexandria, and were just barely subdued by Avidius Cassius. Nevertheless, such sparse details do not provide enough evidence to posit something like a national Egyptian resistance movement, as one scholar has done (Winkler 1980). In fact, the evidence supplied by the novelist Achilles Tatius, along with the recently found Thmouis papyrus, brings us closer to a solution of the Boukoloi question. Achilles Tatius stresses that the Boukoloi were ethnically distinct from the Egyptians. This fact alone, if indeed we accept it, would render the notion of the Boukoloi as Egyptian freedom fighters little likely. Further, Achilles Tatius mentions in his novel, though he is the only author to do so, that the town Nikochis was a shelter for the Boukoloi. This would not appear to be particularly relevant, were it not for the fact that the tax list on the Thmouis Papyrus brings up the town of Nikochis in the context of severe upheavals at precisely the same time (167/168 AD). The tax list mentions Roman troops, who intervened and killed almost all the inhabitants of those villages in which the unrest had begun. Additionally, 'godless Nikochites' are claimed to have attacked three villages, burned them down, and killed most of the villagers. Given the congruity of time and place, it seems reasonable to identify the Boukoloi in Achilles Tatius' Nikochis with the 'godless Nikochites' of the papyrus. The violent acts mentioned in the Thmouis papyrus would then be precursors of the unrest in AD 172. Thus, the hatred of the Nikochites/Boukoloi, who were ethnically different from the Egyptians, was directed equally against Egyptian villages and Roman rule. Given the present lack of adequate sources, their ultimate goals will have to remain obscure.

Once more, however, the coincidence of internal and external problems is conspicuous. As observed in conceivably parallel situations elsewhere in the empire, the Boukoloi might have been an ethnically and culturally separate shepherd population, whose lifestyle was—because of their secluded position in the Nile Delta—distinctly different from that of other inhabitants of the province. At certain moments, then, as around AD 170, when the empire was shaken by attacks from the outside and a devastating pestilence from the inside, the Boukoloi, just like the Isaurians, did not hesitate to attack larger cities, thus bringing on a confrontation with Rome.

Shepherds, who lived quasi-nomadic lives, suffered from such a low reputation (see in general Shaw 1982a) that they were often labeled *latrones*, even in core parts of the empire, in other words, in middle and southern Italy, as well as on Sicily. The great landowners of these regions bred extensive herds of livestock on their estates, and they employed slaves to tend those herds. Such shepherd-slaves and their animals followed ancient paths, which led them up to cooler areas in the Abruzzi mountains during the summer, and down to the warmer plains of Apulia during the winter. These Italian shepherds (to whom Varro dedicated a literary monument) did not number among those exposed to severely anomic conditions, but were, due to their mobile and manifoldly exposed way of life, discriminated against as bandits. This is illustrated by the assumption, common throughout the entire imperial period, that they were able to raise children beyond their own. That is, many poor city-dwellers assumed there to be enough prosperity among these shepherds that children (the so-called *nutriti*) were sent out to the countryside, there, it was hoped, to be raised in better circumstances. In reality, the putative guardians of these children were neglected by their owners to such a degree that they often were forced to resort to banditry in order to survive. The masters knew this, and condoned their shepherds' kidnapping and cattle rustling. However, the situation could get out of control when the shepherd-slaves turned against their owners. There was no end to the unrest caused by slave wars from the second century BC through late antiquity (n.b., the lack of literary sources for the third century can be made up for, in this regard, by epigraphic evidence—see Riess 2006). It is obvious that in nearly all periods of unrest in Italy, be it during the civil wars of the late republic, the Spartacus revolt, or the Catilinian conspiracy, Italian shepherds played an eminent role in the trouble (Metzler 1988).

CONCLUSIONS

It goes without saying that a heuristic division, such as that employed here, of bandits (*latrones*) into two large groups—those driven to actual criminality by anomic conditions and those labeled as criminals because they were considered outsiders—provides us a static and idealized view of things. Clearly, these categories will constantly have overlapped in actuality. On the one hand, bandits called forth by anomic conditions were also exposed to labeling processes, and on the other hand, groups simply labeled as bandits will sometimes have acted out of real desperation. This surely applies, for instance, to the pirates of antiquity, for whom buccaneering was a traditional way of life, but one that could at least partially be attributed to poverty (see De Souza 1999; Ferone 1997; Pohl 1993; Braund 1993; Clavel-Lévêque 1978; Ziehbarth 1929; Ormerod 1924). This was similarly the case for the above-mentioned shepherd cultures of central and southern Italy (see Riess 2006; Manfredini 1992; Deman 1988; Russi 1988; 1986; Milan 1979–80; Capozza 1974–75; De Robertis 1974, 1972–1980).

Even more than the theoretical approach that uses anomie as a model, the labeling approach shows how the construction of reality is conditioned by society, and to what an immense degree the relationship of a society to its marginalized groups exposes underlying shortcomings within the society itself. Therefore, not only does deviant behavior, as in the case of anomic bandits, lead to discrimination, stigmatization, marginalization, and, finally, exclusion, but so too does the labeling of criminality by the elites, who set the norms of their society.

The result is twofold. On the one hand, the several varieties of malefactors, who might be called *latrones*, all stood in opposition to the interests of the political and social elites forming the center of society. They challenged the monopoly on violence, power, and definition, to which the Roman elites saw themselves entitled. This is why these bandits were bitterly repressed. On the other hand, and paradoxically, the Roman Empire needed violent outsiders for its continuance. Punishment of them had to illustrate visibly and palpably to all that monopoly on violence, and the absolute power of the elites. Cruel, publicly staged executions symbolically justified, strengthened, and perpetuated the claim to power by the elites. At the same time, the games were a form of communication between the upper classes and the *plebs*. The theatrically staged executions (see Coleman 1990, and in this volume also Fagan) served not only as entertainment, but had a highly political character. In the realm of legitimizing the imperial system, the theater and the circus played significant roles as political venues for the plebs, who were in these contexts enabled, as a group, to communicate via a set of unwritten rules with the organizer of the event, primarily the emperor, and thus to express their consent to, or their criticism of, his rule. The emperor was likewise dependent on this form of political participation by the people, and he knew how to present himself through the games' glamour, and how to engage the audience in his favor. The games, therefore, had to take place to make the system of imperial legitimacy feasible. A constant supply of criminals was necessary.

The choreography of the seating in an amphitheater also reflected the order of Roman society. The delinquents in the arena were excluded altogether from the circles of the honorable citizens, who were now the audience. The respectable citizens, the spectators, were able to look down upon (both literally and figuratively) those excluded and doomed to death. The state's power was demonstrated symbolically via the bodies of the condemned. As we have seen, the phenomenon of banditry was endemic, at least in part because the Roman governmental apparatus was insufficient for anything like an organized attempt to prevent or fight crime. But, as so often was the case, Rome managed to turn a deficit into an advantage. The Roman elites were to a degree dependent upon the endemic character of brigandry, to justify their claim to power as well as their military actions against dissidents and any opponents of their regime. Bandits were constructed as enemies, whose suppression served the purposes of internal integration.

Thus, not unlike the discourse about barbarians, the discourse concerning bandits forms a significant part of Rome's political economy. For the purposes of establishing a positive self-image, and for the legitimization of imperialistic ambitions, one needs the constant presence of an enemy, who has to be obliterated. Bandits, from whom it was easy to distance oneself, since they represented values radically opposed to those cherished by established Roman society, allowed for a convenient avenue to self-definition, and provided the certainty that, by repressing them, one was absolutely in the right.

Any collective search for identity is usually based on processes of demarcation, and thus, of exclusion and marginalization. Since marginalization is dependent on stigmatization, which again requires the use of stereotypical clichés, a close connection between stereotyping and marginalization is necessary. This explains the essentializing description of brigands by elite authors in antiquity. The distribution of gruesome fairy tales about bandits and other marginal groups was part of a political strategy of exclusion. Not only does the spread of irrational fears make integrated groups move more closely together, but it also, possibly unintentionally so, drives a wedge between those within the system and those outside of it. Such a process widens and hardens the gap between the socially integrated and the outsiders, in other words, the discourse clearly fulfills the function of stabilizing the existing power structure.

Let us return to our original question. The socio-politically essentializing use of the word *latro*—whose broad semantic range, let us remember, was fundamental to the ways this word was manipulated—means that the discourse on banditry painted many groups with the same brush. The Roman elites made no effort to understand distinctions among those they considered marginal. Thus, by means of an informal use of language, invading barbarians, bellicose peoples within the empire, nomads, highwaymen, shepherds, and political enemies could all be lumped together as deviants, and, therefore, these large social groups could be isolated whole hog from Roman society. This, in turn, only aggravated the anomic circumstances that had led, in the first place, to the existence of some of these groups. Through such ignorance and intolerance, wide circles of the population of the Roman Empire were labeled as *latrones*, and thus criminalized, hereby serving to justify Rome's own imperialistic claims and feelings of cultural superiority. Rome needed bandits, barbarians, and strangers to more easily see herself in a favorable light. This leads to the conclusion that the centrifugal forces in Roman society were so strong that the society became dependent on creating an identity through exclusion. The thus-created identity was supposed to strengthen the feeling of belonging together, and to guarantee the cohesion of the multi-ethnic state.

Bandits did not destroy the Roman Empire, they outlived it. With them the discourse on banditry, which was a marked component of the pre-modern *longue durée*, survived the political collapse of the Imperium Romanum, and found continuity in medieval and early modern sources, especially in hagiography. Early Christianity, it must be said, also needed *latrones* as ideal objects of proselytization. The conversion especially of a bandit, who could be perceived as the archetypal sinner, proved beyond any possible doubt the spiritual power of a saint (Sulp. Sev. *Mart.* 11. 4–5; Wortley 1996; Giardina 1983).

The prolific field of the history of criminality, which took shape about thirty years ago, is far from being completely explored. Potential topics for future work can only be hinted at. Sources from antiquity will have to be further analyzed theoretically. Detailed studies of individual authors, legal documents, inscriptions, and papyri promise an abundance of relevant results. Ancient law, in particular, is still lacking an interpretation from the perspective of social anthropology and cultural history. A prosopographic collection of all known ancient bandits and gang leaders could lead to a new typology for the phenomenon of gangs. Which bandits were remembered by name, and why? Can their nomenclature be explained semantically? What messages did their names have?

Another urgently necessary approach would involve comparative regional studies, which take into consideration the entire corpus of our extant source materials, especially epigraphic documents (such as the confession inscriptions of western Asia Minor). The different forms of transhumance in Italy and Asia Minor, for instance, have never been compared. How did the structures of cattle rustling in Spain differ from those in Italy? Why, contrary to the Italian case, do we not encounter the development of mafia-like structures in Spain? The examination of endemic phenomena, which are often characteristic of the *longue durée*, should especially be continued down into the modern period. Here we find splendid opportunities for cooperation with the neighboring disciplines of modern and contemporary history, anthropology, and the social sciences. Such undertakings could, for instance, contribute in a substantial manner to a broader historical foundation of research concerning the mafia. Given the abundance of available data, a criminal history of Italy could surely be completed in the near future, and could itself provide a significant building block for a history of conflict in antiquity.

In order to allow a synchronous and ultimately a diachronic historiography of marginality in the future, the interactions between integrated and marginalized portions of society will have to be illuminated much better than has been done in the past. In a history of marginality, topography and space in general will gain special importance. Which spaces were outsiders banished to, and what, in fact, did the fringes of society look like topographically? A social topography for antiquity, if it were to look at archeological materials from a culturally comparative and social-anthropological perspective, could offer important information on the perception of space, as well as on the structuring of space in antiquity in general.

The construction of borders through marginalization, or exclusion, separates the world into 'inner' and 'outer' spaces. The long-neglected connections between 'inner' and 'outer' should also lead to a closer connection of social history to political history and even the history of international relations, and thus, should clear the path for a more integrated historiography.

SUGGESTED READING

The essential foundation for any work on bandits and banditry in antiquity is still Shaw 1984. This essay poses the decisive questions that have shaped research on this topic down to the present. In his survey of 1993(a), Shaw offers an accessible and concise overview of banditry in the Roman Empire. Extensive and of high quality is his contribution to the second edition of the *Cambridge Ancient History* (Shaw 2000). MacMullen, in his 1966 book, compiled in the appendix "Brigandage" almost all of the extant literary source material on banditry in the Roman Empire. This still unsurpassed work offers a solid introduction into the world of all those who did not accept Roman power. To what extent bandits were dependent on the support of leading circles, how they formed an integrative part of the Roman social system, with its many structures of dependency and patronage, is illuminated by Hopwood 1989a. The phenomenon of banditry sharply gains in profile through this integration in societal structures. Riess 2001 presents an overall interpretation of Roman bandits, integrating all the available types of sources, and also employing the methods of inter-cultural comparison, as well as the sociology of deviant behavior.

BIBLIOGRAPHY

Alföldy, G. 1989. "Bellum Desertorum." In G. Alföldy, *Die Krise des römischen Reiches.* Stuttgart: Franz Steiner Verlag. 69–80.

Alston, R. 1994. "Violence and Social Control in Roman Egypt." In A. Bülow-Jocobsen (ed.), *Proceedings of the 20th International Congress of Papyrologists, Copenhagen, 23–29 August, 1992.* Copenhagen: Museum Tusculanum Press. 517–21.

———. 1999. "The Revolt of the Boukoloi: Geography, History and Myth." In K. Hopwood (ed.), *Organised Crime in Antiquity.* London: Duckworth. 129–53.

Aubert, J.-J. 1995. "Policing the Countryside: Soldiers and Civilians in Egyptian Villages in the Third and Fourth Centuries A.D." In Y. LeBohec (ed.), *La hiérarchie (Rangordnung) de l'armée romaine sous le Haute-Empire. Actes du Congrès de Lyon (15–18 septembre 1994).* Paris: de Boccard. 257–65.

Bagnall, R. 1977. "Army and Police in Roman Upper Egypt." *Journal of the American Research Center in Egypt* 14: 67–86.

———. 1982. "Upper and Lower Guard Posts." *Chronique d'Égypte* 57: 125–28.

———. 1989. "Official and Private Violence in Roman Egypt." *Bulletin of the American Society of Papyrologists* 26: 201–16.

Baldwin, B. 1985. "Crime and Criminals in Graeco-Roman Egypt." In B. Baldwin, *Studies on Greek and Roman History and Literature.* Amsterdam: J. C. Gieben. 505–12 = *Aegyptus* 43, 1963: 256–63.

Bauman, R. 1996. *Crime and Punishment in Ancient Rome.* London: Routledge.

Bauschatz, J. 2005. *Policing the Chora: Law Enforcement in Ptolemaic Egypt.* PhD Thesis, Duke University.

Beattie, J. 1986. *Crime and the Courts in England: 1660–1800.* Princeton: Princeton University Press.

Becker, H. 1963. *Outsiders. Studies in the Sociology of Deviance.* New York: Free Press.

Bellen, H. 1971. *Studien zur Sklavenflucht im römischen Kaiserreich.* Wiesbaden: Franz Steiner Verlag.

Braund, D. 1993. "Piracy under the Principate and the Ideology of Imperial Eradication." In J. Rich and G. Shipley (eds.), *War and Society in the Roman World.* London: Routledge. 195–212.

Brélaz, C. 2005. *La sécurité publique en Asie Mineure sous le Principat (Ier–IIIème s. ap. J.-C.). Institutions municipales et institutions imperiales dans l'Orient romain.* Basel: Schwabe.

Briant, P. 1976. "Brigandage, dissidence et conquête en Asie achéménide et hellénistique." *Dialogues d'histoire ancienne* 2: 163–258.

Burian, J. 1960. "Latrones milites facti (Ad SHA Marc. 21,7)." *Eunomia*: 47–49.

———. 1984. "Latrones. Ein Begriff in römischen literarischen und juristischen Quellen."
Eirene 21: 17–23.

Capozza, M. 1974–75. "Il brigantaggio nelle fonti della prima rivolta servile siciliana." *Atti
dell'Istituto Veneto di Scienze* 133: 27–40.

Clavel-Lévêque, M. 1976. "A propos des brigands: discours, conduites et pratiques
imperialistes." *Dialogues d'histoire ancienne* 2: 259–62.

———. 1978. "Brigandage et piraterie: représentations idéologiques et pratiques
impérialistes au dernier siècle de la République." *Dialogues d'histoire ancienne* 4: 17–31.

Cloward, R., and L. Ohlin. 1960. *Delinquency and Opportunity. A Theory of Delinquent
Gangs.* Glencoe: Free Press.

Coleman, K. 1990. "Fatal Charades: Roman Executions Staged as Mythological
Enactments." *Journal of Roman Studies* 80: 44–73.

Danker, U. 1988. *Räuberbanden im Alten Reich um 1700: ein Beitrag zur Geschichte von
Herrschaft und Kriminalität in der frühen Neuzeit.* 2 vols. Frankfurt: Suhrkamp Verlag.

Davies, R. 1989. "The Investigation of Some Crimes in Roman Egypt." In R. Davies, *Service
in the Roman Army.* New York: Columbia University Press. 175–85 and 281–83 = *Ancient
Society* 4, 1973: 199–212.

Deman, A. 1988. "Bergers transhumants et mouvements de resistance en Italie depuis
les Gracques jusqu'à Caesar." In T. Yuge and M. Doi (eds.), *Forms of Control and
Subordination in Antiquity.* Leiden: E. J. Brill. 209–25.

De Robertis, F. 1972–80. "Prosperità e banditismo nella Puglia e nell'Italia meridionale
durante il basso impero." In M. Paone (ed.), *Studi di storia pugliese in onore di
Giuseppe Chiarelli I.* Galatina: Congedo Editore. 197–232.

———. 1974. "Interdizione dell'Usus equorum e lotta al banditismo in alcune costituzione
dell basso impero." *Studia et Documenta Historiae et Iuris* 11: 67–98.

De Souza, P. 1999. *Piracy in the Graeco-Roman World.* Cambridge: Cambridge University Press.

Drexhage, H. 1988a. "Eigentumsdelikte im römischen Ägypten (1.–3. Jh. n. Chr.). Ein
Beitrag zur Wirtschaftsgeschichte." *Aufstieg und Niedergang der Römischen Welt* II 10, 1.
Berlin: Walter de Gruyter. 952–1004.

———. 1988b. "Einbruch, Diebstahl und Straßenraub im römischen Ägypten unter
besonderer Berücksichtung der Verhältnisse in den ersten beiden Jahrhunderten n.
Chr." In Weiler and Graßl 1988: 313–23.

Emsley, C. 1996. *Crime and Society in England 1750–1900.* 2nd ed. London: Longman.

Feld, K. 2005. *Barbarische Bürger: die Isaurier und das Römische Reich.* Berlin: Walter de
Gruyter.

Ferone, C. 1997. *Lesteia. Forme di predazione nell'Egeo in età classica.* Naples: Procaccini.

Frank, M. 1995. *Dörfliche Gesellschaft und Kriminalität. Das Fallbeispiel Lippe 1650–1800.*
Paderborn: Ferdinand Schöningh.

Freyne, S. 1988. "Bandits in Galilee: A Contribution to the Study of Social Conditions
in First-Century Palestine." In J. Neussner (ed.), *The Social World of Formative
Christianity and Judaism. Essays in Tribute to Howard Clark Kee.* Philadelphia: Fortress
Press. 50–68.

Fuhrmann, C. 2005. *Keeping the Imperial Peace: Public Order, State Control and Policing
in the Roman Empire in the First Three Centuries.* PhD Thesis, University of North
Carolina at Chapel Hill.

Giardina, A. 1983. "Banditi e santi: un aspetto del folklore gallico tra tarda antichità e
medioevo." *Athenaeum* 71 (N.S. 61): 374–89.

Giuffrè, V. 1981. "Latrones desertoresque." *Labeo* 27: 214–18.

Goodman, M. 1982. "The First Jewish Revolt: Social Conflict and the Problem of Debt." *Journal of Jewish Studies* 33: 417–27.

Graßl, H. 1988. "Grundsätzliches und Methodisches zur historischen Randgruppenforschung." In Weiler and Graßl 1988: 41–46.

Grünewald, T. 1999. *Räuber, Rebellen, Rivalen, Rächer.* Stuttgart: Franz Steiner Verlag.

Günther, R. 1953. *Das Latrocinium als eine besondere Form des Widerstands der unterdrückten Klassen und Barbaren im römischen Sklavenhalterstaat während des Prinzipats.* PhD Thesis, Universität Leipzig.

Gutsfeld, A. 1989. *Römische Herrschaft und einheimischer Widerstand in Nordafrika: Militärische Auseinandersetzungen Roms mit den Nomaden.* Stuttgart: Franz Steiner Verlag.

Hartung, W. 1986. "Gesellschaftliche Randgruppen im Spätmittelalter. Phänomen und Begriff." In B. Kirchgässner and F. Reuter (eds.), *Städtische Randgruppen und Minderheiten.* Sigmaringen: Jan Thorbecke. 49–114.

Hellenkemper, H. 1986. "Legionen im Bandenkrieg—Isaurien im 4. Jh." In *Studien zu den Militärgrenzen Roms III. 13. Intern. Limeskongreß in Aalen 1983.* Stuttgart: Konrad Theiss Verlag. 625–34.

Hengel, M. 1976. *Die Zeloten. Untersuchungen zur jüdischen Freiheitsbewegung in der Zeit von Herodes I. bis 70 n. Chr.* 2nd ed. Leiden: E. J. Brill.

Herz, P. 1988. "Latrocinium und Viehdiebstahl. Soziale Spannungen und Strafrecht in römischer Zeit." In Weiler and Graßl 1988: 221–41.

Hippel, W. von. 1995. *Armut, Unterschichten, Randgruppen in der Frühen Neuzeit.* Munich: R. Oldenbourg Verlag.

Hirschfeld, O. 1913a. "Die Sicherheitspolizei im römischen Kaiserreich." In O. Hirschfeld, *Kleine Schriften.* Berlin: Weidmann. 576–612 = *Sitzungsberichte der Berliner Akademie* 1891: 845–77.

———. 1913b. "Die ägyptische Polizei der römischen Kaiserzeit nach Papyrusurkunden." In O. Hirschfeld, *Kleine Schriften.* Berlin: Weidmann. 613–23 = *Sitzungsberichte der Berliner Akademie* 1892: 815–24.

Hobsbawm, E. 1971. *Primitive Rebels. Studies in Archaic Forms of Social Movement in the 19th and 20th Centuries.* 3rd ed. Manchester: Manchester University Press.

———. 1972. *Bandits.* Harmondsworth: Penguin.

Hobson, D. 1993. "The Impact of Law on Village Life in Roman Egypt." In B. Halpern and D. W. Hobson (eds.), *Law, Politics and Society in the Ancient Mediterranean World.* Sheffield: Sheffield Academic Press. 193–219.

Hooff, A. Van. 1982. "Latrones famosi." *Lampas* 15: 171–94.

——— 1988. "Ancient Robbers. Reflections behind the Facts." *Ancient Society* 19: 105–24.

Hopwood, K. 1983. "Policing the hinterland. Rough Cilicia and Isauria." In S. Mitchell (ed.), *Armies and Frontiers in Roman and Byzantine Anatolia. Proceedings of a colloquium held at University College, Swansea, in April 1981.* Oxford: British Archaeological Reports. 173–87.

———. 1989a. "Bandits, Elites and Rural Order." In A. Wallace-Hadrill (ed.), *Patronage in Ancient Society.* London: Routledge. 171–87.

———. 1989b. "Consent and Control. How the Peace Was Kept in Rough Cilicia." In D. French and C. Lightfoot (eds.), *The Eastern Frontier of the Roman Empire.* Oxford: British Archaeological Reports. 191–201.

———. 1998. "All that May Become a Man: The Bandit in the Ancient Novel." In L. Foxhall and J. Salmon (eds.), *When Men Were Men. Masculinity, Power and Identity in Classical Antiquity.* London: Routledge. 195–204.

———. 1999. "Bandits between Grandees and the State: The Structure of Order in Roman Rough Cilicia." In K. Hopwood (ed.), *Organised Crime in Antiquity*. London: Duckworth. 177–206.

———. 2002. "Aspects of Violent Crime in the Roman Empire." In P. McKechnie (ed.), *Thinking Like a Lawyer: Essays on Legal History and General History for John Crook on His Eightieth Birthday*. Leiden: E. J. Brill. 63–80.

Horsley, R. 1979. "Josephus and the Bandits." *Journal for the Study of Judaism* 10: 37–63.

———. 1981. "Ancient Jewish Banditry and the Revolt against Rome." *Catholic Biblical Quarterly* 43: 409–32.

Horsley, R., and J. Hanson. 1985. *Bandits, Prophets and Messiahs. Popular Movements in the Time of Jesus*. Minneapolis: Winston Press.

Isaac, B. 1984. "Bandits in Judaea and Arabia." *Harvard Studies in Classical Philology* 88: 171–203.

Kelly, B. 2002. *The Repression of Violence in the Roman Principate*. D Phil Thesis, Oxford University.

Kneppe, A. 1988. "Die Gefährdung der securitas: Angst vor Angehörigen sozialer Randgruppen der römischen Kaiserzeit am Beispiel von Philosophen, Astrologen, Magiern, Schauspielern und Räubern." In Weiler and Graßl 1988: 165–76.

Krause, J.-U. 2004. *Kriminalgeschichte der Antike*. Munich: Verlag C. H. Beck.

Kudlien, F. 1988. "Zur sozialen Situation des flüchtigen Sklaven in der Antike." *Hermes* 116: 232–52.

Lamnek, S. 1996. *Theorien abweichenden Verhaltens*. 6th ed. Munich: Fink Verlag.

———. 1997. *Neue Theorien abweichenden Verhaltens*. 2nd ed. Munich: Fink Verlag.

Lange, K. 1994. *Gesellschaft und Kriminalität. Räuberbanden im 18. und frühen 19. Jahrhundert*. Frankfurt: Peter Lang.

Lewin, A. 1991. "Banditismo e civilitas nella Cilicia antica e tardoantica." *Quaderni di Storia* 76: 167–80.

MacMullen, R. 1963. "The Roman Concept Robber—Pretender." *Revue Internationale des droits de l'Antiquité* sér. 3, 10: 221–25.

——— 1966. *Enemies of the Roman Order. Treason, Unrest and Alienation in the Empire*. Cambridge, Mass.: Harvard University Press. (Reprint London: Routledge 1992.)

Manfredini, A. 1992. "Municipi e città nella lotta ai latrones." *Annali dell'Università di Ferrara* 6: 23–34.

McGing, B. 1998. "Bandits, Real and Imagined, in Greco-Roman Egypt." *Bulletin of the American Society of Papyrologists* 35: 159–83.

Merton, R. 1938. "Social Structure and Anomie." *American Sociological Review* 3: 672–82.

Metzler, D. 1988. "Widerstand von Nomaden gegen zentralistische Staaten im Altertum." In T. Yuge and M. Doi (eds.), *Forms of Control and Subordination in Antiquity*. Leiden: E. J. Brill. 86–95.

Milan, A. 1979–80. "Ricerche sul latrocinium in Livio I: Latro nelle fonti preaugustee." *Atti dell'Istituto Veneto di Scienze* 138: 171–97.

Minor, C. 1979. "The Robber Tribes of Isauria." *Ancient World* 2: 117–27.

Mitchell, S. 1999. "Native Rebellion in the Pisidian Taurus." In K. Hopwood (ed.), *Organised Crime in Antiquity*. London: Duckworth. 155–75.

Móscy, A. 1968. "Latrones Dardaniae." *Acta Antiqua Academiae Scientiarum Hungaricae* 16: 351–54.

Neri, V. 1998. *I Marginali nell'Occidente Tardoantico. Poveri, 'Infames' e Criminali nella nascente società cristiana*. Bari: Edipuglia.

Nippel, W. 1984. "Policing Rome." *Journal of Roman Studies* 74: 20–29.

————. 1988. *Aufruhr und 'Polizei' in der römischen Republik.* Stuttgart: Klett-Cotta.

————. 1995. *Public Order in Ancient Rome.* Cambridge: Cambridge University Press.

Ormerod, H. 1924. *Piracy in the Ancient World. An Essay in Mediterranean History.* Liverpool: Liverpool University Press. (Reprint 1978.)

Peachin, M. 2006. "Petition to a Centurion from the NYU Papyrus Collection and the Question of Informal Adjudication Performed by Soldiers." In A. Hanson (ed.), *Miscellanea in Honour of P.J. Sijpesteijn.* Chippenham: American Society of Papyrologists. 77–95.

Petraccia Lucernoni, M. 2001. *Gli stationarii in età imperiale.* Rome: "L'Erma" di Bretschneider.

Pohl, H. 1993. *Die römische Politik und die Piraterie im östlichen Mittelmeer vom 3. bis zum 1. Jh. v. Chr.* Berlin: Walter de Gruyter.

Riess, W. 2001. *Apuleius und die Räuber. Ein Beitrag zur historischen Kriminalitätsforschung.* Stuttgart: Franz Steiner Verlag.

————. 2006. "Hunting Down Robbers in 3rd Century Central Italy." In C. Wolff (ed.), *Les exclus dans l'Antiquité. Conference Proceedings series of the Centre d'Études et de Recherches sur l'Occident Romain.* Lyon: De Boccard. 195–213.

Roeck, B. 1993. *Außenseiter, Randgruppen, Minderheiten.* Göttingen: Vandenhoeck & Ruprecht.

Rosenberger, V. 1992. *Bella et Expeditiones. Die antike Terminologie der Kriege Roms.* Stuttgart: Franz Steiner Verlag.

Rostovtzeff, M. 1905. "Die Domänenpolizei in dem römischen Kaiserreiche." *Philologus* 64 (N.F. 18): 297–307.

Rougé, J. 1966. "L'Histoire Auguste et l'Isaurie au IVᵉ siècle." *Revue des Études Anciennes* 68: 282–315.

Ruff, J. 2001. *Violence in Early Modern Europe 1500–1800.* Cambridge: Cambridge University Press.

Russi, A. 1986. "I pastori e l'esposizione degli infanti nella tarda legislazione imperiale e nei documenti epigrafici." *Mélanges d'Archéologie et d'Histoire de l'École Française de Rome* 98: 855–72.

————. 1988. "Pastorizia e brigantaggio nell'Italia centro-meridionale in età tardo-imperiale (a proposito di C.Th. IX 30, 1–5)." *Miscellanea greca e romana* 13: 251–59.

Schwerhoff, G. 1991. *Köln im Kreuzverhör. Kriminalität, Herrschaft und Gesellschaft in einer frühneuzeitlichen Stadt.* Bonn: Bouvier.

Sharpe, J. 1984. *Crime in Early Modern England 1550–1750.* London: Longman Group.

Shaw, B. 1982a. "Eaters of Flesh, Drinkers of Milk. The Ancient Mediterranean Ideology of the Pastoral Nomad." *Ancient Society* 13: 5–31.

————. 1982b. "Fear and Loathing: The Nomad Menace and Roman Africa." In G.-M. Wells (ed.), *L'Afrique romaine-Roman Africa.* Ottawa: University of Ottawa Press. 29–50.

————. 1984. "Bandits in the Roman Empire." *Past & Present* 105: 3–52.

————. 1990. "Bandit Highlands and Lowland Peace: The Mountains of Isauria-Cilicia." *Journal of the Economic and Social History of the Orient* 33: 199–233; 237–70.

————. 1993a. "The Bandit." In A. Giardina (ed.), *The Romans.* Chicago: University of Chicago Press. 300–341.

————. 1993b. "Tyrants, Bandits and Kings: Personal Power in Josephus." *Journal of Jewish Studies* 44: 176–204.

————. 2000. "Rebels and Outsiders." In G. Bowersock, P. Garnsey, and D. Rathbone (eds.), *The Cambridge Ancient History XI. The High Empire, AD 70–192.* 2nd ed. Cambridge: Cambridge University Press. 361–403.

———. 2001. "Räuberbanden." In *Der Neue Pauly X*. Stuttgart: J. B. Metzler. 758–63.

Sperber, D. 1970. "On Pubs and Policemen in Roman Palestine." *Zeitschrift der Deutschen Morgenländischen Gesellschaft* 120: 257–63.

Stoll, O. 1997. "Die Benefiziarier—Rangordnung und Funktion. Einige Bemerkungen zur neueren Forschung." *Laverna* 8: 93–112.

Syme, R. 1968. "Isauria." In R. Syme, *Ammianus and the Historia Augusta*. Oxford: Clarendon Press. 43–52.

———. 1987. "Isaura and Isauria. Some Problems." In E. Frézouls (ed.), *Sociétés urbaines, sociétés rurales dans l'Asie Mineure et la Syrie hellénistiques et romaines. Actes du colloque organisé à Strasbourg (novembre 1985) par l'Institut et le Groupe de Recherche d'histoire romaine et le Centre de Recherche sur le Proche-Orient et la Grèce antiques.* Strasbourg: AECR. 131–47.

Weiler, I. 1985. "Zur Geschichte sozialer Randgruppen in der Alten Welt." In E. Weber and G. Dobesch (eds.), *Römische Geschichte, Altertumskunde und Epigraphik*. Wien: Österreichische Gesellschaft für Archäologie. 659–72.

———. 1988a. "Soziale Randgruppen in der antiken Welt. Einführung und wissenschaftsgeschichtliche Aspekte. Ausgewählte Literatur zur historischen Randgruppenforschung." In Weiler and Graßl 1988: 11–40.

———. 1988b. "Abweichendes Verhalten von Außenseitern und sozialen Randgruppen. Ansätze zu einer Theoriebildung im Altertum." In Weiler and Graßl 1988: 177–89.

Weiler, I., and H. Graßl (eds.). 1988. *Soziale Randgruppen und Außenseiter im Altertum*. Graz: Leykam.

Winkler, J. 1980. "Lollianos and the Desperadoes." *Journal of Hellenic Studies* 100: 155–81.

Wolff, C. 1998. "Les brigands de Dardanie au IIe siècle ap. J.-C." *Rivista Storica dell'Antiquità* 28: 121–33.

———. 1999. "Comment devient-on brigand?" *Revue des Études Anciennes* 101: 393–403.

———. 2003. *Les brigands en Orient sous le Haut-Empire romain*. Rome: de Boccard.

Wortley, J. 1996. "De Latrone Converso: The Tale of the Converted Robber (BHG 1450 Kb 25 861)." *Byzantion* 1: 219–43.

Ziebarth, E. 1929. *Beiträge zur Geschichte des Seeraubs und Seehandels im alten Griechenland*. Hamburg: Friedrichsen, Walter de Gruyter.

Zimmermann, M. 1996. "Probus, Carus und die Räuber im Gebiet des pisidischen Termessos." *Zeitschrift für Papyrologie und Epigraphik* 110: 265–77.

CHAPTER 35

PHYSICALLY DEFORMED AND DISABLED PEOPLE

JOHANNES STAHL

INTRODUCTION

JUST exactly what the word 'disabled' nowadays actually means, or might involve, is not altogether easy to settle, given that the term can be used, and viewed, in many ways. In Roman antiquity, it would appear that there was an even more vague concept of what it might mean to be disabled. We can approach this matter initially from the angle of language.

Now, it is first important to realize that the Latin word *debilis* sometimes corresponds to the English 'disabled,' yet it can also simply mean 'weak.' Nor were particular designations for specific types of disability employed very precisely; in fact, ancient language use partly arose from a lack of understanding regarding the causes of such impairment altogether. For example, in Latin one always finds a very strong differentiation between *mutus* (mute) and *surdus* (deaf); therefore, a particular phenomenon of this type of ailment, which is nowadays well delineated—namely, that hearing loss can lead to a deficiency in language acquisition, what we call deaf-muteness—remained absolutely unrecognized in Roman times.

For the present purposes, then, it is advisable to follow the WHO definition, and thereby to establish a coherent sense of the ramifications of the term 'disabilitiy.' This definition lays out, and then differentiates among, three aspects of disability, namely, (a) bodily impairment, (b) functional disability, and (c) social handicap, and is now widely employed by research in disability studies (Cloerkes 2001: 4–5; cf. Albrecht et al. 2001). Thus armed, we may turn to the Roman world.

The discussion here will be concerned with those individuals from Roman antiquity who were impaired according to the definition just given. Others, who would not naturally fall into this group but whose physical appearance nonetheless provoked a distinct and regularly negative reaction, will also be considered. It is also well to point out that the focus of this present account, given the nature of this volume in which it appears, does not involve the medicinal or technical side of the subject—it may simply be said that the various resources, which disabled persons could count on, corresponded largely with those available in other pre-industrial societies (see, for example, Bliquez 1996)—but rather lies in the social realm. We shall primarily be involved, then, with the attitudes Roman society had regarding the disabled, and the kinds of reaction generated by those attitudes. Furthermore, because the subjects of the present discussion practically never themselves speak in our extant source material, and are instead described by the non-disabled majority, and because our sources altogether are indelibly stamped by the perspective of Roman society's dominant stratum, the image we are left with can hardly be considered objective. Nonetheless, the picture drawn below will at least be quite revealing as to the views held by the social group that monopolized public discourse in the Roman world.

ATTITUDES REGARDING DISABILITIES
AND THE DISABLED

If one sets out to examine the attitudes of the broad public in Roman times regarding the disabled, it is sensible to differentiate between how the disabilities themselves, as fundamental physical phenomena, were viewed, and how disabled persons, as individuals, were perceived. Concerning the evaluation of disabilities, three principal factors played a role: the functional impairment that the disability involved, the aesthetic impairment, and the more far-reaching connotations with which the disability was invested.

Now, with respect to functional impairment, suitability for service in the military was the most important evaluative criterion in Roman society. And yet, no absolute principles were ever established as to which disabilities would make an individual unsuitable as a soldier. Rather, this decision remained a matter of ad hoc judgment, and lay within the discretion of the person carrying out the physical examination at the time of a levy—the consul, for example, during the republic. In contrast, the ability to work (at some handicraft, or as a laborer—i.e., the kinds of occupation principally available to those not of the elite) was generally a secondary concern in marking disability, precisely because the socially dominant groups themselves were altogether negatively disposed toward physical labor.

One particular type of disability, in any case, was frequently a significant impairment in the Roman world. Because that society cultivated a widely oral culture, inability to hear or to speak counted as a significant functional deficiency. Thus, apart from any and all jokes about the speech-impaired, deaf individuals were plainly disadvantaged in a crucially pragmatic manner, namely, before the law. This was so because many legal acts required of the actor some spoken expression, or the ability to hear and register something said (Küster 1991). Among the Romans, no allowance was made for those who could not speak or hear the necessary words. Such persons would simply be unable to take advantage of the law on the matter in question.

Furthermore, various distinguishing bodily characteristics were often enough disdained by the social environment, even though these did not constitute a substantial functional impairment. Thus, for example, a missing eye or a pronounced facial scar could easily result in abuse and rejection by one's peers. Here, a certain aesthetic sensibility played a decisive role. And while a purely visual malformation like this was perhaps preferable to a functional impairment (Cels. 7. 9. 1), these deformities were still perceived by those burdened with them as particularly loathsome—and all the more if the blemish were distinctly visible at first glance.

Along with the aspects of function and aesthetics should be included a third, one that is perhaps somewhat surprising from a contemporary viewpoint: the farreaching implications that a particular disability might involve. So, for example, we would probably tend to think that it is wholly irrelevant for the abilities and appearance of a person, whether the left or the right leg is paralyzed. Yet in Roman times, a right-sided paralysis was much more negatively judged than was one on the left side of the body, and an encounter with someone crippled on the right side was held to be an evil omen. Similar such beliefs—for example, that a given disability was caused by magic, or conversely, that a disability bestowed magical capabilities on the person afflicted with it—were quite widespread. Notions of this kind gained credence not only by means of mythical stories, in which (say) people were struck blind by the gods, but also as a result of the broad distribution of curse tablets, by means of which the writer attempted, at least temporarily, physically to incapacitate his adversary (cf. Rives in this volume).

Indeed, it must be said just generally that beliefs concerning disabilities appear to have been enthusiastically associated with mythical and venerable historical figures, so that for each kind of disability there might exist an exemplary and representative 'ancestor': hence, Mucius Scaevola for a missing hand, Hannibal for a missing eye, Horatius Cocles or Vulcan for a limp, or Homer for blindness (cf. Delcourt 1957; Esser 1961). In short, disabilities, to the mind of an ancient Roman observer, were not merely matters of physiological origin and concern, but involved what we would tend to label magical, or superstitious, or religious causes and effects. Also on display here is the deep-seated Roman predilection to comprehend phenomena of all kinds on the basis of highly significant exemplary manifestations of those phenomena.

ATTITUDES REGARDING DISABLED INDIVIDUALS

Despite the fact that (as we have just seen) a Roman might entertain certain fixed notions about any given handicap, the type of disability itself was not solely decisive in producing attitudes toward the person afflicted with it; indeed, various attendant circumstances also played a crucial role in the formation of opinion about the disabled individual. First of all, contemporaries largely reckoned that hardly anybody was physically perfect: "How few are really beautiful" is the sober conclusion reached by Cicero (*N.D.* 1. 79). It was, then, in principle via deviation from an ideal of absolute beauty that an individual might be saddled with what was known as a personal *nota* (a mark, or stigma; see V. Max. 8. 11. *ext.* 3). Such bodily traits could also play a role in the naming of persons, as was often the case with *cognomina* (roughly, nicknames). In other words, by this component of their names, individuals might be indelibly marked in accord with some aspect of their appearance or character. Severe physical impairments were especially favored as *cognomina*; thus, we get people with names such as Luscus (the One-eyed), Surdus (the Deaf), or Balbus (the Stutterer). Despite the seemingly pejorative nature of these names, they were evidently consciously adopted or accepted by those who bore them. And despite the fact that they could be used derisively (Cic. *Inv.* 2. 28–29), pride in the name might well prevail, as one can see for example in the aristocratic name P. Furius Crassipes (Fat Foot). On the occasion of his aedileship in 84 BC, Crassipes had a coin minted, on which a small clubfoot was represented (*RRC* I, p. 371, no. 356). Many such examples come, however, from a time when these surnames were not conferred individually, but rather were inherited within a family—and the pride of noblemen in their (perhaps unsavory) names toward the end of the republic is largely connected to the fact that these names were associated with the achievements of venerable ancestors. On the other hand, we should not be misled: monikers such as these are not to be taken as evidence of a positive attitude toward bodily affliction in Rome.

The attitude toward a disabled person also depended decisively on how and when he had acquired his disability. A fictional legal case from Quintilian (*Decl.* 297), in which the following situation was constructed, may clarify. There was a law that stipulated that any person who blinded another person would be deprived of his own vision or else serve from then on as the guide to the person whom he had made blind. Now, in the case related by Quintilian, a war hero had struck out the eyes of a prostitute. While she demanded that he serve her as a guide, he preferred to be blinded—for it would have been unbearably shameful for him to be observed serving such a woman. The accuser, however, brings into consideration the fact that the blindness of the hero, if it came to pass, would be less glorious as well: "This disability would not be of the kind as it would be if you had suffered it in war," says the prostitute. In short, a blinding inflicted in combat was heroic; the same malady, if inflicted in punishment by a prostitute, was disgraceful. And, of course, we are led to presume that the distinction would somehow be both remembered and advertised.

Furthermore, if a disability were able to be interpreted as the result of one's own wrongdoing, the disabled person could await only a minimum of sympathy at best (Arist. *EN* 1114a 23–31). Thus, for example, the blinding of a drinker could be ascribed to his own alcohol consumption, and correspondingly derided (Hor. *S*. 2. 7. 15–18; Mart. 6. 78); and gout, which led to paralysis, was generally seen as the result of a dissolute lifestyle (Lucian, *Ocyp., Trag.*).

For the most part, however, the cause of disability was not, in the Roman world, unambiguously identifiable. And so, in cases of doubt, society indeed often sought guilt in the person himself, rather than in external circumstances. It will come as no surprise, then, that in hopes of preventing discrimination, afflicted persons might try to place a positive spin on their troubles, as did Plautus' Curculio, who passed off the loss of his eyesight, which actually resulted from the throwing of a mug in a tavern, as a considerably more glorious battle wound—even though his version of events did not find much approbation (Pl. *Cur.* 392–400). And just as the manner in which someone became disabled would play a role in establishing society's attitude toward the person's affliction, so too could the moment when the hardship befell the person play such a role. Thus, congenital disabilities were counted as particularly severe, whereas disabilities that appeared in later life were seen as attendant circumstances of old age, and were mostly accepted out of necessity (Parkin 2003: 57–89).

Finally, gender, social status, and personal relations are also to be considered in this context. Where women are concerned, for example, the rules just delineated would, in principle, apply; however, given their position in society, there might be some differences in emphasis. In other words, while physical suitability for the military was the most basic criterion for establishing the functional normality of Roman men, for women, the ability to give birth played a similar role. Accordingly, infertility in women amounted, for all intents and purposes, to a disability, and was treated as such. Thus, the reportedly first case of divorce in the Roman Republic, initiated by a certain Sp. Carvilius Ruga, was founded on the inability of his wife to provide him with children (Gel. 4. 3. 2; 17. 21. 33). Aesthetic blemishes in women were also greater impairments than these were for men, especially since the chances for an advantageous marriage could easily be dashed by such a 'handicap' (Luc. *Tox.* 24–26).

A person's social position, and this often in intimate association with that individual's career, likewise played an important role in the overall perception of his disability. Despite the fact that bodily work often led to injuries of various sorts (Rosner 1955: 362–63), and that such injuries would often be perceived among the Romans as deformities, some of the handicrafts practiced in that world, and in particular those that could be exercised while sitting (Hp. *Art.* 53), allowed some deformed persons at least the possibility of gainful employ. It thus appears that disabled persons were generally over-represented in these professions, and indeed that certain types of disability came to be seen as going hand in hand with certain types of work. So, for instance, in a play of Plautus we find the following (*Aul.* 72–73): "Like a lame shoemaker, he sits around at home all day long."

But since working with one's hands was frowned upon altogether (and especially among the upper classes), the disabled person who (precisely because of his bodily condition) took up such a career was reduced to being doubly despised, on the one hand for his 'choice' of work, and on the other hand for his physical condition. Here, one might think of the god Vulcan—for example, as he appears in Lucian (*DDeor.* 8, 17). He is the lame blacksmith, who is continually mocked by his fellow divinities both because of his bodily fault (he limps) and as a consequence of the 'profession' he practices (he is a simple, dirty craftsman). To most observers, then, the career and the disability seemed somehow to belong together, though, of course, either one was shameful enough by itself. As to how disabled craftsmen were viewed by their non-disabled peers in the profession, that is a question that must remain open. Our sources simply reveal nothing in this regard.

One also thinks, in this context, of the disabled slave. It seems that here the main concern had to do with the individual's capacity to carry out the tasks envisioned for him or her by the master; aesthetic flaws appear generally to have been less crucial where slaves were involved. Indeed, it looks as if bodily blemishes were habitually felt to be simply characteristic of slaves. But again, any disability that hindered the slave from performing the duties expected of him or her would lessen the slave's value for the master, and that could easily result in a worsening of the slave's situation overall. The extant legal sources are thus repeatedly insistent about determining the physical condition of slaves (e.g., Ulp. *Dig.* 21. 1. 1. 1).

When it came to judging a stranger who happened to be disabled, it would appear that the degree to which the disability was conspicuous played a very significant role in the formation of opinion regarding that individual. In contrast, if there already existed any kind of social relationship to the person, then other criteria might play a greater role, and the significance of the disability could be relativized. Thus, emotional affection for a person could cause his or her bodily defects eventually to be minimized or fully overlooked—the cliché 'love is blind' was already widespread in antiquity (Lucr. 4. 1153–69), as was the observation that parents often fundamentally regard their children as handsome (Hor. *S.* 1. 3. 43–48).

Inversely, a negative judgment of a person, this reached, let us say, independently of that person's disability, could easily lead to the physical characteristic stepping into the foreground, and being made into an external sign of an inner defect. So, for example, one might think of L. Valerius Catullus Messalinus, a notorious informer under the emperor Domitian, who had incurred the hatred of many of his peers. Messalinus went blind in old age. Then, after his death, he was aggressively attacked by Pliny (*Ep.* 4. 22. 4–6) and Juvenal (4. 113–22), among others; a very prominent feature of these attacks was his blindness. That is, the fact that he went blind demonstrated the fact that he was a bad person. Such substantial attacks against the blind are otherwise very unusual in Roman literature, and this instance is surely to be explained by the fact that the man attacked here was already an independently hated figure. Hence, the necessity arose at the beginning to establish his blindness in the foreground as a negative characteristic.

REACTIONS TO DISABLED PERSONS

When it comes to everyday interactions between those with and those without disabilities, attitudes toward the disabled not only represent abstract opinions, but bear concrete effects as well. The range of possible reactions on the part of the physically unimpaired is rather broad, moving from aggressive rejection, to ignorance, to sympathy and affection. It is well worth considering the nature of these responses to the phenomenon of disability.

Reactions: Physical Violence, Aggressive Rejection, and Fear

The most extreme form of reaction to disability was physical violence, and the indirect, or even intentional, murder of disabled people. This was, however, the absolute exception, and occurred only in very particular circumstances. One of these was the moment directly after the birth of a child.

Now, for the parents of a child born disabled, there existed the simple option of not accepting that child, that is to say, of abandoning it; there was no penalty for such an action (cf. Krause in this volume). Abandonment of a disabled newborn was not, though, automatic, or required; instead, it was a singular decision in each case. In other words, there was no legal duty, as there reputedly was in Sparta (cf. Schmidt 1983–84), to abandon children because of functional or social weaknesses. Nonetheless, there did exist some pressure to abandon or kill children born with particularly serious deformities, such as missing or extra limbs. This had to do, on the one hand, with their reduced life expectancy. Even more important, as it would seem, was the fact that such a disability was likely to be recognized as a *prodigium*, in other words, as an unfavorable omen for the whole state, which surely involved a disturbance in the relationship of the community to the gods. This was, to Roman sensibilities, a very serious situation. Thus, an actual duty to abandonment in republican Rome could apply, though only in the cases of these severely disabled children. Our evidence for this comes from the Twelve Tables (Cic. *Leg.* 3. 19), and also from a comment of Seneca (*Dial.* 3. 15. 2).

If, on the other hand, a child was taken into a family, that child could not merely be abandoned at some later point in time. Hermaphrodites and persons of uncertain gender could, however, as older children or as adults, become the victims of murder, should they be labeled as a *prodigium* (see, e.g., Liv. 27. 37. 5). Again, the danger they were perceived to pose for the community lay behind such harsh treatment. Other types of disability, so long as their sufferers were not perceived as *prodigia*, were not handled so severely. Nor do we have any evidence that old, disabled, or terminally ill people might be put to death as a reaction to their conditions. In contrast with these persons, however, slaves were seriously threatened by abandonment or death, should they be afflicted by any disability. In fact, it was evidently a widespread custom to abandon sick or enfeebled slaves on the island of Asclepius (the god of healing) in the Tiber River. The emperor Claudius attempted to limit this practice by granting freedom to all slaves who were abandoned there; thus, should the there-abandoned slave regain his health, he would not be required to return to his master. In addition, Claudius stipulated that the killing of an infirm slave might be prosecuted as murder (Suet. *Cl.* 25. 2; Dio 60. 29).

Now, while those with particular disabilities were not always subjected to physical violence, they might nonetheless be feared, and thus suffer serious rejection, for an encounter with such a person was regarded as a bad sign. This kind of treatment might befall those with one eye, or dwarves, among others; but in particular, epileptics and people lame in the right foot were regularly shunned. An encounter with a person belonging to one of the last two groups was regarded as particularly portentous, and so, one tried to avoid any and all contact with them, almost as if a contagious illness were involved. Should it so happen that contact with such a person could not be avoided, one might protect oneself by spitting in front of, or on, the person in question (cf. Plin. *Nat.* 28. 35; Apul. *Apol.* 44; cf. Wohlers 1999: 132–36). In any case, this kind of fear, and the reactions it caused, remained limited to particular disabilities, and usually to particular situations.

Reactions: Curiosity and Sensation Mongering

Disabilities did not always elicit fear. On the contrary, a few kinds of physical qualities, which had an either extraordinary or strange character, exerted instead a compelling fascination for the beholder. In particular, under the Roman Empire there prevailed a marked curiosity regarding people who were physically conspicuous in certain ways, and this curiosity was satisfied by presenting the individuals, sometimes with these persons' own volition, sometimes by compulsion, to large audiences. The individuals in question were above all persons of extreme physical size—for example, the gigantic man who was given as a 'present,' in conjunction with the signing of a treaty, by the Parthian king Artabanus to the Roman emperor Tiberius (Jos. *AJ* 18. 103). Moreover, various phenomena that during the time of the republic were considered to be potentially dangerous *prodigia* by the early empire could be offered as wonderful public attractions—for example, a four-headed child born during the reign of Nero (Phlegon *FGrHist* II B F 36. 20). Indeed, even the previously feared hermaphrodite was considered, in Pliny's time, no longer a fearful *prodigium*, but rather a *delicia* (a delightful curiosity; see Plin. *Nat.* 7. 34; cf. Garland 1995: 45–58).

This interest in the abnormal was accompanied by a related trend. Wealthy persons now began to surround themselves with misformed slaves, a type of possession that eventually came to serve as a status symbol. Most popular were dwarves and hunchbacks. For instance, when a wealthy Roman matron once purchased an expensive candelabra, the hunchback slave Clesippus was generously thrown into the bargain by the seller; and so, this woman later displayed Clesippus, along with the new lighting fixture, to her guests (Plin. *Nat.* 7. 11–12; cf. Calabi Limentani

1957). But aside from their usefulness as objects of entertainment, it also came to be widely believed that such persons had an apotropaic effect against magical spells. This, too, will have led to their great popularity. And beyond all of this, these creatures (especially hunchbacks and hermaphrodites) possessed a great sexual allure for many; hence, Clesippus would rise to become his mistress' lover, and eventually, her heir.

As has just been noted, such deformed people were often exhibited, both privately and in public, as a form of entertainment. The enjoyment derived from such an appearance stemmed from different things. First, the extraordinary was highly attractive—on the one hand, simply because of the novelty involved, and on the other hand, because the presenter of such a curiosity could thereby gain prestige. Secondly, a pleasant alienation effect was achieved when persons had to engage in tasks to which they quite obviously were quite ill-suited—as, for example, when the emperor Domitian put on a gladiatorial show, pitting women and dwarves against each other (Dio 67. 8. 4, cf. Weiler 1995). The same kind of alienation effect occurred when deformed persons assumed a court-jester-like role, relativizing and rendering bearable their severe disfigurements through their now-accentuated ignoble status. Finally, another role was played by a motive more usual, or, let us say, more accepted in antiquity than it is today: schadenfreude.

Just how the persons, of whom such shows were made, evaluated their own situations, is impossible to say, for the voices of these lowly characters have not carried across the ages. In the case of deformed slaves, it would appear, in any case, that the disability was perhaps a double-edged sword. On the one hand, they were valuable, and therefore will probably have lived in more comfortable circumstances than those lowly slaves, who (say) worked the fields. Nonetheless, the deformed slave, kept as an entertainer, will have had to reckon with many encroachments and abasements from his master, and it is difficult to imagine that this will have been pleasant (D'Arms 1991: 178–81).

Reactions: Insult and Degradation

It was not only those who (willingly or unwillingly) performed for the amusement of others who had to deal with being derided—every disabled person was constantly subject to being mocked because of his or her physical condition. Jokes regarding the appearance of others were not at all taboo, but instead, were considered thoroughly appropriate (Cic. de Orat. 2. 239). The reasons for the popularity of insults regarding the disabled were multi-layered. Garland (1995: 74–75) rightly enumerates three different functions, which he describes as cohesive, cathartic, and pathological. Thus, by laughing at an outsider, the cohesion of the (insider) group is strengthened, and at the same time, social control is practiced. Fear of misformed persons—and the underlying angst that such a thing could happen to oneself—might be allayed by mockery, a cathartic experience. And finally, aggression and tension could simply be relieved at the expense of others.

Now, that disabled people might be insulted and debased without any apparent motivation beyond cruelty was not at all uncommon in Roman times. Nonetheless, when our sources mention the derision of these individuals, this behavior indeed tends to occur in particular contexts, and with particular goals. For example, this kind of insult surfaces with particular frequency in the context of legal and political contests during the Roman Republic. In both of these arenas, opponents, who in Roman terms were otherwise equally qualified, clashed with rhetorical weapons. Thus, in a campaign for political office, or in a court battle, one might use the bodily deficiencies of an opponent as ammunition. An impressive example of this phenomenon is furnished by the conflict of Cicero with Vatinius. In his attacks, Cicero repeatedly makes fun of Vatinius' *strumae*, the swollen adenoids on his neck. By constantly bringing these protrusions into play, and by comparing Vatinus to, among other things, a snake with a swollen neck (Cic. *Vat.* 4; cf. Corbeill 1996: 43–56), Cicero tries to depict his opponent as a man who is just as morally odious and degenerate as he is physically ugly. This confrontation was not, however, a one-sided affair. Vatinius tried as well to make fun of one of Cicero's physical weaknesses, and found an appropriate point of attack: Cicero had varicose veins (Macr. 2. 3. 5). This kind of insult, then, was primarily a matter of distinguishing oneself before the public at the cost of another, a contest in which the attacked always had the opportunity to turn the tables by means of a counter-attack—or sometimes even via self-irony, thus taking the wind out of the attacker's sails.

Things went differently, however, when it was a matter of an asymmetric insult, that is, when either someone of high social standing insulted someone of lower standing, or the inverse. The former was considered inappropriate, and was reported above all with regard to the 'bad' Roman emperors. Commodus, according to the *Historia Augusta*, was supposed to have had two hunchbacks smeared with mustard and served on a silver platter during a banquet; it may be remarked that he ordered them carried off right away, and richly compensated (*HA Comm.* 11. 2). Much crueler is the report, according to which he gave those whose leg he had broken or eye he had stabbed out the nicknames 'One-footed' and 'One-eyed' (*monopodios et luscinios*) (*HA Comm.* 10. 6). Similarly degrading and cruel escapades are told with regard to the emperor Elagabalus (*HA Heliog.* 29. 3; cf. Garland 1995: 85–86). One might suppose that the amusement of those who witnessed such acts was somewhat constrained, for whoever saw such things must have been reminded that he himself could also become the victim of an emperor's will and cruelty. Thus, any pleasure experienced in such a situation must have had a bitter aftertaste.

Insult could of course flow in the opposite direction, so that subjects mocked their rulers' physical characteristics. One can also assume that slaves made fun of their lords' ailments, above all if the master was dependent on the slaves' help, and could no longer adequately respond (e.g., [Quint.] *Decl.* 1. 6). A similar situation is depicted by the already mentioned attacks on the blind Messalinus, or by Seneca's parody of Claudius as limping and mute (Sen. *Apoc.* 5). In both cases, a formerly more powerful and more dangerous individual was ridiculed because of a bodily defect, though only after his death. Mocking the weaknesses of superiors reduced them to a more human level, and established an at least partial inversion of the otherwise thoroughly unequal social hierarchy. Such mockery of superiors also helped to assuage fear and aggression.

Making fun of the handicapped was thought to be particularly appropriate, though, when the objects of ridicule could somehow be made personally responsible for their condition. Needless to say, there are plenty of examples to be found in Roman literature where handicapped people, who certainly were not responsible for their flaws, found themselves nonetheless viciously mocked. In such cases, then, where there was no clear responsibility on the part of the disabled person for his or her malady, other reasons (should any at all be considered necessary) could be adduced for a decision to make sport of these people. The key here lies in behavior. For example, in Cicero's *De Oratore* (2. 237), it is pointed out that public ridicule of accidentally disabled persons was appropriate only when the afflicted individual did not carry himself with the requisite modesty. Thus, any handicapped person could conceivably, and regardless of his condition's origin, become the target of derision; behavior inappropriate (in the eyes of others) to his station and situation could entail precisely this result.

Reactions: Discrimination through Exclusion from Offices and Functions

On the whole, the idea that a priest should be physically a perfect specimen remained valid throughout Roman history. In any case, a fictive legal case presented by the elder Seneca sees things this way (*Con.* 4. 2). Bodily intactness was especially needed by candidates for election to the priesthood of Curia—so says a law ascribed to Romulus (D.H. 2. 21. 3). Particularly strict criteria were also the case for potential Vestal Virgins, who were not allowed to be afflicted by muteness, nor by hearing difficulties, or indeed otherwise with any kind of bodily defect (Gel. 1. 12. 3; Fro. *Ant.* 149. 5 N).

The underlying reason for these regulations had to do with the communication engaged in by such religious officials with the gods. In the case of handicapped priests, there existed the very real danger, that they would not be accepted by the gods. Thus, the regulations for priests are comparable to those for sacrificial animals, which had likewise to be without blemish (e.g., Plin. *Nat* 8. 183). Pre-conceived ideas regarding the nature of some handicaps may have also been occasion for concern. For example, the strictures against speech handicaps in the realm of cultic practices was ultimately intended to avert any possibility of unsuccessful communication with the gods.

But despite these rules, we are aware of a few instances in which the physical condition of a priest was open to some question (Graßl 1986: 119–20). According to the elder Pliny (*Nat.* 11. 174), a *pontifex* by the name of Metellus had a pronounced speech impediment. As a result, he once found it necessary to spend a month, and a great amount of effort, preparing a speech for the consecration of a temple. Thus, despite his handicap, Metellus was able to be named a priest. For his daily routine, Metellus had presumably developed strategies to deal with his disability, which in this situation he probably could not so easily fall back on. In any case, this and other examples show that regulations were not always so conscientiously adhered to in praxis. But in particular, the kind of strict rules laid down for the Vestal Virgins, including the bar on speech handicaps, must not have been entirely valid in the cases of other priestly positions, for otherwise, the case of Metellus would hardly be thinkable (cf. Morgan 1974).

There were also some secular offices to which the handicapped could not be admitted. In a number of cases, it would actually have been literally impossible for physically disabled persons to carry out the necessary tasks of the position; hence, the bans. The case of one Q. Pedius, born mute to a senatorial family (Plin. *Nat.* 35. 21; cf. Gourevitch 1998), represents one such instance; he simply could not, for example, have spoken in the senate, or commanded troops in the field. Pedius was finally trained to be a painter, a career choice that Augustus himself officially approved; there was, in short, no other possibility for the young man. Indeed, as has been indicated above, the occupation of higher state offices in Rome was from the beginning possible only for those candidates who were also deemed suitable for military service—even if this, as Mommsen long ago realized, is difficult to document in our extant source material (see Mommsen 1887: I 493–94). An obviously unsuitable candidate would from the start not have had a chance to be chosen, given that it lay in everyone's interest to name capable military leaders. Nor is it at all likely that a severely handicapped man would have offered himself for election, since his competitors would certainly have known no timidity in drawing lurid attention to the bodily flaws of such a candidate. For this reason, as it would appear, there were no legal rules created to deal with such situations; only later would the lawyers take up the topic, and then in a rather theoretical form (Ulp. *Dig.* 3. 1. 1. 5; Küster 1991: 152–54). Whoever was not in a position to meet the physical requirements of an office, then, was simply excluded (by customary practice) from its occupation.

Absolute physical perfection was, on the other hand, not required for most public offices. In the main, such impairments as would not hinder one's ability to command troops were not an obstacle to attaining office. The praetor Sergius Silus, for example, who had a prosthetic hand made of iron (Plin. *Nat.* 7. 104–5), demonstrates that a relatively light impairment might not represent an obstacle for the occupation of a civil post. Moreover, the criteria regarding what was allowed, and what not, was to a certain degree negotiable (Libero 2002: 188).

But let us return, for a moment, to the sphere of the military. It was not only advisable for purely pragmatic reasons (say, being able to ride a horse) that the holder of a command in the army should be physically well-suited: their esteem in the eyes of simple soldiers could be severely adversely affected if they were afflicted by a handicap. Thus, Hordeonius Flaccus, infirm from age and suffering from foot trouble, who under Galba was sent to command the legions in Upper Germany, was despised by his soldiers and not taken at all seriously by them (Tac. *Hist.* 1. 9). His assignment to this task, in other words, turned out to be unwise, given his disabilities.

Among the emperors there were also those who were afflicted by more or less serious handicaps; and like the disabled military commander, such an emperor faced the constant risk of losing his authority over the soldiers and the people. The emperor Vitellius, for example, was ridiculed by the masses on account of his size, his red face, and his slight limp—though it must be said that this misery befell him only when, in defeat, he was being dragged through town by Vespasian's victorious soldiers. Suetonius does not conceal the causes for the red face and limp of the deposed ruler, the former resulting from excessive consumption of wine, and the latter from an accident in the circus (Suet. *Vit.* 17—n.b., participation in the circus was, for a member of the elite, highly shameful). Thus, the wrong sort of physical appearance could easily damage a ruler's prestige, particularly since looks were widely taken to reveal signs of character flaws. In short, among the Romans, physical ugliness might easily have the same social results as did conditions that we would more easily categorize as disabilities. Indeed, in Roman terms, the ugly person was disabled.

A glimpse into the considerations of a ruling household, when it came to dealing with any of its members who happened to be disabled, is offered by the case of the young Claudius. In his youth, Claudius was regularly hindered by physical and mental infirmity, the results being that he was not held capable of assuming any official post whatsoever, and attempts were made to keep him generally out of the public eye (Suet. *Cl.* 2). The fear of the imperial family was plainly that he would make himself look ridiculous in front of everyone, would be treated accordingly, and that all of this would rub off very negatively on the rest of the family. For this reason, it was in the end decided not to entrust Claudius with any important post; instead, he was encouraged to dedicate himself to private scholarly activities (Suet. *Cl.* 4. 7, 5, 41–42). After he had come to the throne, however, Claudius proved himself physically perfectly able to wield the imperial position, despite a few curious behavioral quirks that are probably better attributed to his upbringing than to any illness.

Bodily defects and handicaps, therefore, did not absolutely preclude a man from becoming emperor—provided, of course, that his ability to carry out the functions of the position were not unduly compromised by his disability. Still, in such a situation, care was always necessary. Any physical impairment could conceivably contribute to undermining the ruler's authority, above all in crisis situations, or if the causes of the disability were themselves viewed as somehow reprehensible (and as we saw above, they could easily be).

Let us now move out of governmental circles and into the private realm. Here we encounter one occupation for which there existed clear regulations regarding physical constitution: undertakers were expected to be without blemish. According to an inscription from the Augustan period regulating the burial procedure for the city of Puteoli (*AE* 1971, 88 II 6–7; cf. Hinard and Dumont 2003: 17), "neither the bow-legged, nor the one-eyed, nor those impaired in the hand, nor the lame, nor the blind, nor those visibly marked" were allowed to perform this function. These demands are hardly to be accounted for by purely practical reasons alone (though it is understandable that a blind person, at least, would have a very difficult time carrying out the duties of an undertaker). Rather, this regulation has to do with the negative connotations of these physical traits that, especially in the context of such a delicate task as handling the dead, certainly counted as bad omens.

Reactions: Discrimination through Legal Disadvantages

The handicapped were excluded from using the legal system only if they could not meet the necessary formal requirements. Now, because many legal acts were based on oral communication and interaction, deaf and mute persons, above all, had to put up with significant disadvantages. Thus, individuals with these disabilities were prevented from drawing up a will (*Dig.* 28. 1. 6. 1). This was justified by the fact that a mute person could not speak the required words, and the deaf could not hear the words of the will's executor (Ulp. *Epit.* 20. 13). In addition, there was doubt about the ability of those without hearing to understand, and to conduct business altogether; hence, they were partly placed in the position of the mentally handicapped. It was only much later in Roman history that a more differentiated approach to such matters was adopted by the law (cf. *Inst.* 2. 12. 3).

As opposed to the mute and the deaf, the blind were, from a legal perspective, largely regarded as equal to those with sight, although here, too, there were some restrictions. Thus, the blind were allowed to plead in court only for themselves, not for others, which was justified by the fact that a blind person could not see the official regalia of the praetor and thus could not demonstrate the proper respect for the office (*Dig.* 3. 1. 1. 5; cf. Küster 1991: 157). This remained the only legal discrimination against the blind worthy of mention. Other bodily handicaps resulted in no legal discrimination, because they usually did not represent an obstacle to accomplishing the rituals necessary to most legal acts.

Reactions: Privileges and Special Care

In a few rare instances, we hear of certain privileges granted to a handicapped person by the state. For instance, Caecilius Metellus rescued the Palladium from the burning temple of Vesta, an act that resulted in his being blinded. It was thereupon decreed that he should henceforth always be carried in a wagon to the Curia (Plin. *Nat.* 7. 139–141). This privilege, however, had not really to do with Metellus' blindness, but was, rather, a legal equalizing of the honored person with the Vestal Virgins, to whom the use of a wagon was permitted, and whose responsibilities Metellus had assumed in saving Vesta's Palladium (Leuze 1905: 101–2). Metellus was thus not allowed to use the wagon because he was blind but instead because he had accomplished something great—and the reward for his deed was associated openly with those whom he had helped. Additionally, if soldiers who had suffered an impairment in war received an honorary gift, this was officially considered to be due to their military accomplishment and bravery, and was not thought of as a direct compensation for the injury, even if things could indeed sometimes be so perceived (e.g., Tac. *Ann.* 2. 9).

Now and again, an emperor might also bestow some concession upon a handicapped person. If Augustus permitted an old knight, who was no longer able to ride, to participate in a parade on foot, rather than on his horse, or if Claudius allowed a senator who was hard of hearing to sit on the praetor's bench so that he could hear more easily (Dio 60. 12. 3), these are small, understandable gestures that remain rare. The notion that handicapped persons should have a claim to some form of (more) favorable treatment from the general public remained a concept utterly foreign to the Romans. Sympathy and assistance were mostly of a spontaneous nature, though sometimes disabled beggars profited from kindly reactions to themselves. But generally speaking, the disabled person was entirely reliant on his or her family if he or she was to survive. Only the coming of Christianity brought about the notion that helping those in need was somehow a communal responsibility (see, for example, Bolkestein 1939; Hands 1968).

Now, if the discussion above has been concerned with the fact that handicapped persons could be discriminated against via the exclusion from military service, or because such persons were not allowed to hold political office, it should of course be said here that these exclusions could also be seen as privileges in some circumstances and, specifically, when military or civil duties were perceived not as an honor or benefit but as a burden. That this absolutely could be the case is shown in reports about conscripts who either made themselves or were made by their fathers unfit for service through mutilation, often by amputating a thumb (Wierschowski 1995: 221–27). Such offenders were punished severely by the senate, or in some cases even more harshly by the emperor. Unfortunately, the exact reasons for such decisions escape us, though it is likely enough that these were choices of a highly personal nature. In any case, it is remarkable that the individuals who took this course of action preferred to deal with the potentially disastrous everyday consequences of their impairment rather than to report for military service.

Beyond the sphere of the military, the population of the Roman Empire was frequently required to carry out various kinds of services (*munera*) for the state and the local authorities. These were widely considered to be onerous, and it was often considered advantageous when one could be freed from them by a legal excuse. Physical weakness (*corporis debilitas*—and note here the use of the word *debilitas*) was considered in general to be a legitimate excuse but was limited to those tasks that required physical action (*Dig.* 50. 5. 2. 7–7a). And while the blind could usually hope for release from most *munera* (*CJ* 10. 51. 1), the deaf and mute, who were not allowed to hold local political office on account of their disabilities, and who were usually barred from the law courts because of their physical flaws, were indeed expected to undertake *munera*, since they were considered able to carry out physical labor (*Dig.* 50. 2. 7. 1; cf. Küster 1991: 146–48). As can be seen, then, the Latin word that comes closest to our 'disabled,' namely, *debilis*, had a wide range of possible interpretations and, therefore, conceivable effects.

In a few rare cases, handicapped slaves could also profit from exceptional rules. According to a senate resolution of AD 10 (the *senatus consultum Silanianum*), in the case of the murder of their master, or his son, all those slaves found in his home were held responsible as accomplices. If those slaves had not demonstrably attempted to stop the act, or if they could not prove themselves to have been somehow unable to make such an attempt, they were to be executed (Mommsen 1899: 630–31). Later legal commentary on this statute reckoned those slaves, who were either very sick or who were disabled at the moment of the crime, to have been unable to offer help; such persons would be judged innocent of complicity (*Dig.* 29. 5. 3 pr). Slaves who were infirm, deaf, blind, or mute are explicitly listed in this context (*Dig.* 29. 5. 3. 7–10).

What all of these privileges have in common, though, is that they were not granted primarily out of sympathy for those concerned. In all of these cases, it was the functional criteria that were decisive. Note, however, that the same criteria in other situations would serve to exclude the disabled person from one kind of attractive possibility or another. Nonetheless, in the few instances just mentioned, disability might turn out to be a boon rather than a burden.

Conclusions

Roman society reacted to disabled people in a wide variety of ways. The most essential determining factors in the community's stance toward such individuals involved (a) the type of impairment in question and (b) the type of person who was saddled with that affliction. Moreover, the putative cause of the disability, as well as the burdened person's manner of handling his fate, ultimately played significant roles in his treatment by his peers. Strictly legal (viz., in some sense statutory) restrictions on these people were relatively uncommon, as were proper legal privileges. Nor does there seem to have been terribly much outright physical violence directed at these individuals; nor do they seem altogether often to have been in danger of losing their lives in violent attacks. Moreover, strong emotional reactions, such as fear and disgust, were perhaps, on the whole, the exceptions, and seem largely to have been associated with particular situations. Ultimately, then, what seems to have been the most frequent reaction to the disabled, aside from a certain level of patent apathy, was mockery (which was often enough quite harsh and brutal) and banishment from the Roman community's innermost circles.

This was especially ominous when the disabled individual was, for other reasons, already disliked; any physical blemish would then quickly be instrumentalized as a prop for attacking that individual. A handicap was likewise speedily employed as a means for assault if the unfortunate target was not well able to accept, and live in accord with, the fate heaped upon him. In short, a handicapped person was always significantly more vulnerable than someone of similar social level who was not thus plagued. And so, many a disabled person will have been tempted to hide, or reinvent as somehow positive, his stigma. The only other possibility was to try, insofar as this was possible, to live in accord with society's expectations. "The wretched are constantly vigilant, so as never to cease being pitiable. And so, he, who has lost his eyesight, must always strive mightily not to seem deservedly to have gone blind" ([Quint.] *Decl.* 1. 6). In short, disabled persons in the Roman world were in almost all situations pushed to the margins of society, or were integrated only by virtue of being made the butts of mockery and abuse. The only thing that might come to the rescue of such a person, again, generally speaking, was high social status.

SUGGESTED READING

Garland 1995 offers the most extensive analysis of this theme. Graßl 1986 and 1989, and Libero 2002 and 2003 also provide good overviews, as does Vlahogiannis 1998 regarding the social and connotative aspects. For the medical side, Michler 1961 and Bliquez 1996 are to be recommended, as are especially Esser 1961 on blindness and Küster 1991 regarding deafness. Although they concentrate predominantly on the Greek world, the studies in Dasen 1993 on 'dwarves' and Rose 2003 are well worth reading.

BIBLIOGRAPHY

Albrecht, G. L., K. D. Seelman, and M. Bury (eds.). 2001. *Handbook of Disability Studies.* Thousand Oaks, Calif.: Sage.

Allély, A. 2003. "Les enfants malformés et considerés comme prodiges à Rome et en Italie sous la république." *Revue des Etudes Anciennes* 105: 127–56.

Barasch, M. 2001. *Blindness: The History of a Mental Image in Western Thought.* London: Routledge.

Bien, C. G. 1997. *Erklärungen zur Entstehung von Mißbildungen im physiologischen und medizinischen Schrifttum der Antike.* Stuttgart: Franz Steiner Verlag.

Bliquez, L. J. 1996. "Prosthetics in Classical Antiquity. Greek, Etruscan, and Roman Prosthetics." In H. Temporini and W. Haase (eds.), *Aufstieg und Niedergang der Römischen Welt* II 37.3. Berlin: Walter de Gruyter. 2640–76.

Bodel, J. 2000. "Dealing with the Dead: Undertakers, Executioners and Potter's Fields in Ancient Rome." In V. M. Hope and E. Marshall (eds.), *Death and Disease in the Ancient City.* London: Routledge. 128–51.

Bolkestein, H. 1939. *Wohltätigkeit und Armenpflege im vorchristlichen Altertum: Ein Beitrag zum Problem "Moral und Gesellschaft."* Utrecht: Oosthoek.

Brisson, L. 2002. *Sexual Ambivalence. Androgyny and Hermaphroditism in Graeco-Roman Antiquity.* Berkeley: University of California Press.

Calabi Limentani, I. 1957. "Lo schiavo Clesippo, *accessio* di un candelabro." *Acme* 10: 17–20.

Corbeill, A. 1996. *Controlling Laughter: Political Humor in the Late Roman Republic.* Princeton: Princeton University Press.

Cloerkes, G. 2001. *Soziologie der Behinderten. Eine Einführung.* Heidelberg: Universitätsverlag Winter.

D'Arms, J. H. 1990. "The Roman *Convivium* and the Idea of Equality." In O. Murray (ed.), *Sympotica: A Symposium on the Symposion*. Oxford: Clarendon Press. 308–20.

———. 1991. "Slaves at Roman *convivia*." In W. J. Slater (ed.), *Dining in a Classical Context*. Ann Arbor: University of Michigan Press. 171–83.

Dasen, V. 1993. *Dwarfs in Ancient Egypt and Greece*. Oxford: Clarendon Press.

Delcourt, M. 1957. "Horatius Coclès et Mucius Scaevola." In *Hommages à Waldemar Deonna*. Brussels: Latomus. 169–80.

Esser, A. 1961. *Das Antlitz der Blindheit in der Antike: Die kulturellen und medizinhistorischen Ausstrahlungen des Blindenproblems in den antiken Quellen*. Leiden: E. J. Brill.

Ferreri, G. 1908. "Die Taubstummen in der lateinischen Literatur." *Eos* 4: 255–65.

Gager, J. G. (ed.). 1992. *Curse Tablets and Binding Spells from the Ancient World*. Oxford: Oxford University Press.

Garland, R. 1995. *The Eye of the Beholder: Deformity and Disability in the Graeco-Roman World*. Ithaca: Cornell University Press.

Gourevitch, D. 1998. "Au temps des lois Julia et Papia Poppaea, la naissance d'un enfant handicapé est-elle une affaire publique ou privée?" *Ktema* 23: 459–73.

Graßl, H. 1986. "Behinderte in der Antike: Bemerkungen zur sozialen Stellung und Integration." *Tyche* 1: 118–26.

———. 1989. "Behinderung und Arbeit." *Eirene* 25: 49–57.

Hands, A. R. 1968. *Charities and Social Aid in Greece and Rome*. Ithaca: Cornell University Press.

Hinard, F., and J. C. Dumont (eds.). 2003. *Libitina. Pompes funèbres et supplices en Campanie à l'époque d'Auguste: Edition, traduction et commentaire de la Lex Libitinae Puteolana*. Paris: de Boccard.

Küster, A. 1991. *Blinde und Taubstumme im römischen Recht*. Cologne: Böhlau.

Leuze, O. 1905. "Metellus caecatus." *Philologus* N.F. 18: 95–115.

Libero, L. de. 2002. "Mit eiserner Hand ins Amt? Kriegsversehrte römische Aristokraten zwischen Recht und Religion, Ausgrenzung und Integration." In J. Spielvogel (ed.), *Res publica reperta: Zur Verfassung und Gesellschaft der römischen Republik und des frühen Prinzipats*. Stuttgart: Franz Steiner Verlag. 172–91.

———. 2003. "Behinderung." *Der Neue Pauly* 12.2. Stuttgart: J. B. Metzler. 914–16.

Michler, M. 1961. "Die Krüppelleiden in De morbo sacro und De articulis." *Sudhoffs Archiv* 45: 303–28.

Mommsen, T. 1887. *Römisches Staatsrecht*. 3 vols. Leipzig: Akademische Druck- und Verlagsgesellschaft.

———. 1899. *Römisches Strafrecht*. Leipzig: Akademische Druck- und Verlagsgesellschaft.

Morgan, M. G. 1974. "Priests and Physical Fitness: A Note on Roman Religion." *Classical Quarterly* n.s. 24: 137–41.

Parkin, T. G. 2003. *Old Age in the Roman World: A Cultural and Social History*. Baltimore: Johns Hopkins University Press.

Rösger, A. 1996. "Der Umgang mit Behinderten im Römischen Reich." In M. Liedtke (ed.), *Behinderung als pädagogische und politische Herausforderung: Historische und systematische Aspekte*. Bad Heilbrunn: Verlag Julius Klinkhardt. 137–50.

Rose, M. L. 2003. *The Staff of Oedipus: Transforming Disability in Ancient Greece*. Ann Arbor: University of Michigan Press.

Rosenberger, V. 1998. *Gezähmte Götter: Das Prodigienwesen der römischen Republik*. Stuttgart: Franz Steiner Verlag.

Rosner, E. 1955. "Die Lahmheit des Hephaistos." *Forschungen und Fortschritte* 29: 362–63.

Schmidt, M. 1983–84. "Hephaistos lebt: Untersuchungen zur Frage der Behandlung behinderter Kinder in der Antike." *Hephaistos* 5–6: 133–61.

Sudhoff, K. 1916. "Die eiserne Hand des Marcus Sergius aus dem Ende des 3. Jahrhunderts vor Christo. Eine Prüfung." *Mitteilungen zur Geschichte der Medizin und der Naturwissenschaften* 15: 1–5.

Vlahogiannis, N. 1998. "Disabling Bodies." In D. Montserrat (ed.), *Changing Bodies, Changing Meanings*. London: Routledge. 13–36.

Weiler, I. (ed.). 1988. *Soziale Randgruppen und Aussenseiter im Altertum*. Graz: Leykam.

———. 1995. "Hic audax subit ordo pumilorum (Statius, silvae 1, 6, 57): Überlegungen zu Zwergen und Behinderten in der antiken Unterhaltungskultur." *Grazer Beiträge* 21: 121–45.

Wierschowski, L. 1995. "Kriegsdienstverweigerung im römischen Reich." *Ancient Society* 26: 205–39.

Wohlers, M. 1999. *Heilige Krankheit: Epilepsie in antiker Medizin, Astrologie und Religion*. Marburg: N. G. Elwert.

INDEX

....